Germany

Andrea Schulte-Peevers

Jeremy Gray, Anthony Haywood,
Sarah Johnstone, Daniel Robinson

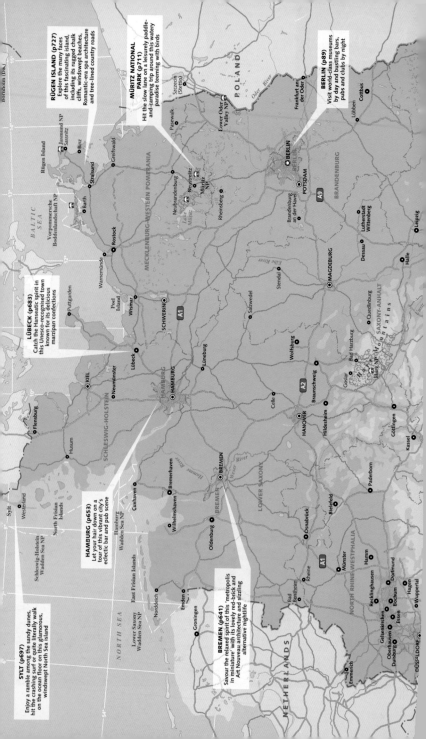

SYLT (p697)
Enjoy a ramble among the sandy dunes, hit the crashing surf or quite literally walk on the ocean floor on this glamorous, windswept North Sea island

LÜBECK (p683)
Catch the Hanseatic spirit in this Unesco-recognised town known for its delicious marzipan confections

RÜGEN ISLAND (p727)
Explore the many faces of this fascinating island, including its rugged chalk cliffs, windswept beaches, Romantic-era spa architecture and tree-lined country roads

MÜRITZ NATIONAL PARK (p711)
Hit the slow lane on a leisurely paddle-and-camping trip around this watery paradise teeming with birds

BERLIN (p89)
Visit world-class museums by day and bustling bars, pubs and clubs by night

HAMBURG (p653)
Let your hair down on a tour of this vibrant city's eclectic bar and pub scene

BREMEN (p641)
Savour the relaxed spirit of this 'metropolis in miniature' with its lovely red-brick and Art Nouveau architecture and sizzling alternative nightlife

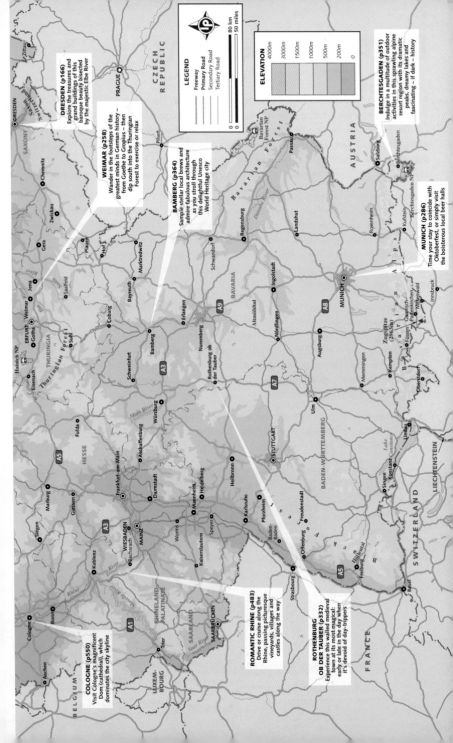

DRESDEN (p166)
Explore the treasures and grand buildings of this baroque beauty bisected by the majestic Elbe River

WEIMAR (p258)
Wander in the footsteps of the greatest minds in German history – from Goethe to Gropius – then dip south into the Thuringian Forest to exercise or relax

BAMBERG (p364)
Sample stellar local brews and admire fabulous architecture as you stroll through this delightful Unesco World Heritage city

BERCHTESGADEN (p351)
Indulge in a multitude of outdoor activities in this sprawling alpine resort region with its dramatic peaks, dreamy lakes and fascinating – if dark – history

MUNICH (p286)
Time your stay to coincide with Oktoberfest, or simply visit the boisterous local beer halls

COLOGNE (p550)
Visit Cologne's magnificent Dom (cathedral), which dominates the city skyline

ROMANTIC RHINE (p483)
Drive or cruise along the Rhine, passing picturesque vineyards, villages and castles along the way

ROTHENBURG OB DER TAUBER (p332)
Experience this walled medieval town at its most magical: early or late in the day when it's devoid of day-trippers

LEGEND
Freeway
Primary Road
Secondary Road
Tertiary Road

ELEVATION
4000m
3000m
1500m
1000m
500m
200m
0

80 km
50 miles

Destination Germany

Few countries have had as much impact on the world as Germany, a land of innovation that has given us the printing press, the automobile, aspirin and MP3 technology. This is the country where you can visit the birth places of Martin Luther, Albert Einstein and Karl Marx, of Goethe, Beethoven and the Brothers Grimm and other greats who, in some way, have forged the fate of humankind. The roots of modern architecture? Right here in Dessau where the Bauhaus movement began. For God's sake (so to speak), even the pope is German!

As you travel the country, you'll have plenty of such brushes with genius, but Germany's storybook scenery is perhaps even more memorable. There's something undeniably artistic in the way the landscape unfolds, from the serpentine, dune-fringed coasts of the north to the moody forests, romantic river valleys and vast vineyards of the middle regions to the off-the-charts splendor of the Alps, carved into rugged glory by glaciers and the elements. All are a part of the vast and magical natural quilt that'll undoubtedly have you burning up the pixels in your digicam.

You'll encounter history in towns where streets were laid out during the Middle Ages and in castles looming above prim, half-timbered villages where windows are bedecked with billowing geraniums. Berlin, Munich, Hamburg and other vibrant cities will wow you with progressive cuisine scenes and a cultural kaleidoscope bursting with a panoply of experiences – high-brow opera to underground dance parties. And wherever you go, Romanesque, Gothic and baroque classics rub rafters with architectural creations from modern masters such as IM Pei and Frank Gehry.

No matter whether you seek an adrenaline-fuelled foray on the autobahn or a leisurely ride on its latest-generation trains, Germany is a land that demands exploration. Just pack your curiosity and an open mind and we guarantee you'll have a ball.

NEIL SETCHFIELD

German Cities

South of Oranienburger Tor (p110), Berlin's vibrant entertainment district spills out onto the street
RICHARD NEBESKY

Spin out at Munich's Oktoberfest (p304)
CHERYL FORBES

Take a walk on the seedier side through Reeperbahn (p659), Hamburg's famous red-light district
MARTIN LLADO

Historic Towns

Get lost in the medieval laneways of Erfurt (p251)

JOHN BORTHWICK

The pristine Rothenburg ob der Tauber
(p332) is a must-see on the Romantic Road

ESBIN ANDERSON

DAVID PEEVERS

Discover Mark Twain in the university city
of Heidelberg (p403)

Great Outdoors

The Swiss Alps are a majestic backdrop to Lake Constance (p452)

Karl Friedrich Schinkel's famous lighthouse guards rugged Kap Arkona (p732), on romantic Rügen Island

Fashionable skiing spot Garmisch-Partenkirchen (p345) is also perfect for summer hiking

Castles & Palaces

DENNIS JOHNSON

Martin Luther's heretical hiding place, Wartburg (p270), is now a repository of significant art and artefacts

KRZYSZTOF DYDYNSKI

Schloss Charlottenburg (p114) contains a wealth of history and art

Let Schloss Neuschwanstein (p342) fulfil your fairy-tale fantasies along the Romantic Road

MANFRED GOTTSCHALK

Contents

Regional Map Contents

Schleswig-Holstein p679
Hamburg p654
Bremen p642
Mecklenburg-Western Pomerania p704
Lower Saxony p594-5
Berlin p91
Saxony-Anhalt p206
Brandenburg p146
North Rhine-Westphalia p540
Harz Mountains p230
Saxony p166
Hesse p511
Thuringia p251
Rhineland-Palatinate & Saarland p466
Bavaria p284-5
Baden-Württemberg p392

The Authors

ANDREA SCHULTE-PEEVERS
Coordinating Author, Getting Started, Itineraries, Berlin, Brandenburg, Saxony, North Rhine-Westphalia, Directory & Transport

Andrea has logged countless miles travelling in nearly 60 countries on five continents and carries her dog-eared passport like a badge of honour. Born and raised in Germany and educated in London and at UCLA, she's built a career on writing about her native country for almost two decades. She's authored or contributed to about 30 Lonely Planet titles, including all five editions of this book as well as the city guide to Berlin. For this trip she decided to trade her house in Los Angeles for a teensy rooftop apartment in Berlin for six months of research and writing – and didn't regret a day of it.

My Favourite Trip

In all my travels through Germany there remained one blank spot: Saxony. So naturally, I jumped at the chance of updating the chapter for this edition, and I wasn't going to be disappointed. Dresden (p166) was love at first sight, of course, but there were plenty of unexpected surprises too. Chemnitz (p194) charmed me with its can-do spirit, rejuvenated city centre and handsome Art Nouveau villas, while in Zwickau (p197) I spent hours exploring one of the best car museums anywhere. The medieval silhouette of Bautzen (p199) etched itself into my memory as much as the whimsical rock formations and unassailable Königstein fortress in Saxon Switzerland (p180). Leipzig struck me for its progressive art scene, intriguing GDR history museums and kicking nightlife. In Zittau (p203) I saw rare Lenten veils I'd never even heard of, while gorgeous Görlitz (p201), in its restored perfection, felt like the set of some period film. The wine in Meissen (p182) was so delicious, I took home a case. Come to think of it, I'm down to one bottle – time to go back.

LONELY PLANET AUTHORS

Why is our travel information the best in the world? It's simple: our authors are independent, dedicated travellers. They don't research using just the internet or phone, and they don't take freebies in exchange for positive coverage. They travel widely, to all the popular spots and off the beaten track. They personally visit thousands of hotels, restaurants, cafés, bars, galleries, palaces, museums and more – and they take pride in getting all the details right, and telling it how it is. For more, see the authors section on www.lonelyplanet.com.

JEREMY GRAY   Bavaria

Jeremy was born to English immigrants in the Bible-belt town of Shreveport, Louisiana, and went to university in Austin, Texas, where he tackled the devilish complexity of the German language. A scholarship landed him in Mainz, a perfect spot to deconstruct Brecht, cycle through vineyards and teach English grammar in nearby Rüsselsheim. Jeremy has a master's degree in International Relations (University of Canterbury) and is a former correspondent for news media in London, Amsterdam and Frankfurt am Main. He has travelled around North America and Europe for Lonely Planet, but Bavaria ranks high in the emotive landscapes department. Home is a renovated butter factory in Berlin.

ANTHONY HAYWOOD   Snapshot, History, The Culture, Thuringia, Hesse, Harz Mountains

Anthony is a journalist with a background in literature and Russian language. But it's travel he enjoys most of all. His first visit to Germany was in the late 1980s, when he spent time in a house with German students just before the Berlin Wall fell. Soon he was back again – to see friends while travelling to Moscow which had just collapsed into postcoup chaos. Since those heady days he has divided his time between Frankfurt am Main and Göttingen, working in writing professions and – among very many other things for this edition of Germany – watching *The Big Lebowski* in a down-at-heel pub in Goethe's Weimar.

SARAH JOHNSTONE   Environment, Food & Drink, Saxony-Anhalt, Lower Saxony, Bremen, Hamburg, Schleswig-Holstein, Mecklenburg-Western Pomerania

Sarah covered a large northern swathe of the country, including the hundreds of kilometres of sandy beaches of Mecklenburg-Western Pomerania and Schleswig-Holstein, the flat heathland of Lower Saxony and vibrant city of Hamburg that many people don't immediately identify with Germany. A freelance journalist based in London, she's previously worked at Reuters and several travel magazines. After some dozen or so Lonely Planet guidebooks (you think she'd learn) she still hates author bios.

DANIEL ROBINSON   Baden-Württemberg & Rhineland-Palatinate & Saarland

Daniel grew up in Northern California, Illinois and Israel. Based in Tel Aviv, he is active in groups promoting urban bike paths and Israeli-German dialogue. His travel writing, including Lonely Planet guides to France and Paris, has been published in nine languages. Daniel has an abiding interest in the minutiae of *Maultaschen* and is endlessly enchanted by the teeny-tiny trains – as seen from the heights of the Rheinhöhenweg trail – that slither along both banks of the Romantic Rhine. He prefers to indulge his weakness for apple strudel with vanilla ice cream on the shores of Lake Constance.

Getting Started

With centuries of practice, Germany has come quite close to perfecting its tourism infrastructure. Backpackers, families and jetsetters will all find their needs and expectations met. Room and travel reservations are a good idea during peak season (summer and around holidays), but otherwise you can keep your advance planning to a minimum.

WHEN TO GO

Any time is a good time to be somewhere in Germany, but when is the best time to visit pretty much depends on what type of holiday you envision. Most people arrive between May and September when roads are often clogged, lodging can be at a premium and you'll be jostling for space at major attractions. Still, summer is fabulous because skies are more likely to be sunny, much of life moves outdoors, beer gardens are in full swing, and festivals and outdoor events enliven cities and villages. Hiking, cycling, swimming and outdoor pursuits are popular during these months.

The shoulder seasons (from March to May and from October to early November) bring smaller crowds and often pleasant weather. In April and May, when wildflowers brighten meadows and fruit trees are in bloom, it can be mild and sunny. Indian summers that stretch well into autumn are not uncommon.

With the exception of winter sports, activities between November and early March are likely to focus more on culture and city life. In these months, skies are often gloomy and the mercury drops below freezing. On the plus side, there are fewer visitors and shorter queues (except in the winter resorts). Just pack the right clothes and keep in mind that there are only six to eight hours of daylight. In December the sun (if there is any) sets around 3.30pm.

See Climate Charts (p741) for more information.

The ski season usually starts in early to mid-December, moves into full swing after the New Year and closes down again with the onset of the snowmelt in March.

For related information, see p741 and p746.

COSTS & MONEY

Germany is fairly inexpensive, although what you spend depends largely on what kind of traveller you are, what experiences you wish to have and, to a lesser extent, the season in which you're visiting. Staying in midrange hotels, enjoying two sit-down meals a day, using public transportation, spending some money on sightseeing, activities and going to bars or clubs will costs

---

DON'T LEAVE HOME WITHOUT...

- Valid travel and health insurance (p746)
- Memorising at least a few basic words of German (p774)
- Hotel or camping reservations if travelling outside the cities in summer (p734)
- Nerves of steel for driving on the autobahns (p766)
- Towel and soap if staying in hostels, private rooms or cheap pensions
- A raincoat, rainproof shoes and/or umbrella for those days when the sun is a no-show
- A set of smart clothes and shoes for hitting big-city clubs, the opera or fancy restaurants
- This book and a curious mind

between €120 and €150 (per person, travelling as an adult couple). For mere survival, you'll need to budget from €40 to €70 per day, and this will have you sleeping in hostels or budget hotels, eating snack- and fast-food or preparing your own meals, and limiting your entertainment. You can stretch the euro further by taking advantage of various discounts; see p743 for some ideas. Of course, if you're a high roller, Germany has no shortage of luxury hotels, Michelin-starred restaurants and fancy bars to help you part with your money.

Comfortable midrange accommodation starts at about €80 for a double room with breakfast in the cities, and €60 in the countryside. Many hostels and hotels have special 'family' rooms with three or four beds, or they can supply sleeping cots for a small extra fee. In some places, children under a certain age pay nothing if staying in their parents' room without requiring extra bedding.

A two-course meal in an average restaurant costs between €20 and €30 per person, including a glass of beer or wine. Drinks prices (even nonalcoholic ones) can run surprisingly high, even in basic eateries. Eating out doesn't have to take a huge bite out of your budget, however, as long as you stick to cafés and casual restaurants where you'll get meals for under €10. If you're travelling with kids, ask about a special kids' menu or kids' dishes. Holiday flats with kitchens are ideal for trimming food costs. Generally, prices in supermarkets are a bit lower than in the UK, USA and Australia.

Museum admission ranges from €0.50 for small local history museums to €10 for international-calibre art museums, even more for blockbuster exhibits. Some sights and museums are free, or have admission-free days, and discounts are offered for children, teens, students and seniors. Tourist-geared discount cards (often called Welcome Cards, p743) offer free public transport and discounts on admissions, tours and the like and can be a good deal.

Car-hire costs vary; expect to pay around €45 a day for a medium-sized new car. Driving is the most comfortable and convenient mode of getting around the country, although in cities parking may be elusive and expensive. However, if there are three or more of you travelling together, it may be the most economical way of getting around. In cities, buying day or other passes for public transport is almost always cheaper than buying single tickets. If you're travelling by train, consider a rail pass (p770) or see if Deutsche Bahn is offering any special promotions.

HOW MUCH?

Cup of coffee €1.50-2

One hour of parking (in a garage) €1-2

Cinema ticket €6-11

Pack of 17 cigarettes €3.30-4

Internet access €1-5

TRAVEL LITERATURE

To get you in the mood for your trip, consider reading some of these titles written by travellers who have visited Germany before you:

A Tramp Abroad by Mark Twain is a literary classic that includes keen and witty observations about Germany garnered by the author during two visits in the 1880s. Twain's postscript 'The Awful German Language' is a hilarious read.

Three Men on the Bummel by Jerome K Jerome, the sequel to the even funnier *Three Men in a Boat,* is a classic comic tale that follows three English gentlemen on their cycling trip through the Black Forest in the 1890s.

Deutschland: A Winter's Tale by Heinrich Heine is a poetic travelogue about the author's journey from Paris to Hamburg. It also packs a satirical punch and strong criticism of Germany's mid-19th-century political landscape. It was censored immediately.

Mr Norris Changes Trains and *Goodbye to Berlin* are by Christopher Isherwood, who lived in Berlin during the Weimar years and whose stories inspired the movie *Cabaret*. The books brilliantly and often entertainingly

TOP 10S

Must-See German Movies

Planning and dreaming about your trip to Germany is best done in a comfy living room with a bowl of popcorn in one hand and a remote in the other. Go for a classic or pick from among the great crop of recent made-in-Germany flicks. Look for brief reviews on p63.

- *Metropolis* (1927) Director: Fritz Lang
- *Das Boot* (1981) Director: Wolfgang Petersen
- *Der Himmel über Berlin* (Wings of Desire, 1987) Director: Wim Wenders
- *Lola Rennt* (Run Lola Run, 1998) Director: Tom Tykwer
- *Good Bye, Lenin!* (2003) Director: Wolfgang Becker
- *Die Fetten Jahre Sind Vorbei* (The Edukators, 2004) Director: Hans Weingartner
- *Gegen die Wand* (Head-On, 2004) Director: Fatih Akin
- *Der Untergang* (Downfall, 2004) Director: Oliver Hirschbiegel
- *Sophie Scholl – Die Letzten Tage* (Sophie Scholl – The Final Days, 2005) Director: Marc Rothemund
- *Das Leben der Anderen* (The Life of Others, 2006) Director: Florian von Donnersmarck

Top Reads

One of the best ways to learn about a country's culture and grasp a sense of a people is to immerse yourself in a good book. The following Top 10 – from classics to contemporary works – have won kudos and critical acclaim in Germany and abroad. See p61 for more details.

- *Simplicissimus* (The Adventures of a Simpleton, 1668) Hans Jacob Christoffel von Grimmelshausen
- *Der Prozess* (The Trial, 1925) Franz Kafka
- *Berlin Alexanderplatz* (1929) Alfred Döblin
- *Im Westen Nichts Neues* (All Quiet on the Western Front, 1929) Erich Maria Remarque
- *Die Blechtrommel* (The Tin Drum, 1959) Günter Grass
- *Der Geteilte Himmel* (Divided Heaven, 1963) Christa Wolf
- *Die Ausgewanderten* (The Emigrants, 1997) WG Sebald
- *Russendisko* (Russian Disco, 2000) Wladimir Kaminer
- *Der Vorleser* (The Reader, 2002) Bernhard Schlink
- *Stasiland* (2004) Anna Funder

Our Favourite Festivals & Events

As was amply demonstrated during the 2006 FIFA World Cup, Germans really know how to let their hair down, and there's almost always something interesting happening around the country. The following list is our Top 10, but for additional festivals and events see the various destination chapters and p744.

- Internationale Filmfestspiele (Berlin Film Festival, Berlin) February (p124)
- Cannstatter Volkfest (Stuttgart) September/October (p398)
- Carnival/Fasching (various regions) Cologne, (p555); Munich, (p308) February
- Frankfurt Book Fair (Frankfurt-am-Main) September-October (p518)
- Hamburger Dom (Hamburg) March (p664)
- Kieler Woche (Kiel) June (p681)
- Bach Festival (Leipzig) Around Ascension Day (p190)
- Love Parade (Berlin) July (p124)
- Munich Oktoberfest (Munich) September-October (p308)
- Rhine in Flames (five locations in Rhineland-Palatinate) May-September (p484)

chronicle the era's decadence and despair. For a different take on the same era, also try *What I Saw: Reports from Berlin 1920–1933* by Joseph Roth, a dynamic and insightful chronicler. Finally there is *The Temple*, an auto-biographical novel by one of Britain's most celebrated 20th-century poets, Stephen Spender. It is based on his travels to Germany in the late 1920s and his encounters with, among others, Isherwood.

In a German Pension by Katherine Mansfield is a collection of satirical short stories written after Mansfield's stay in Bavaria as a young woman. Her ability to inject meaning into vignettes makes it an especially worthwhile read.

The Bells in Their Silence: Travels Through Germany (2004) was written by Michael Gurra, an American literature professor who spent a year living and travelling around Germany in the early 1990s. This travelogue combines a literary tour of the country with impressionistic observations about daily life.

From Berlin is by Armando, a Dutch writer, artist and (since 1979) Berlin resident, who has turned his observations about the city and the people who lived through WWII into a collection of snappy vignettes – from humorous to touching to heart-wrenching.

INTERNET RESOURCES

Hunt down bargain air fares, book hotels, check on weather conditions or chat with locals and other travellers about the best places to visit (or avoid!) by surfing the electronic waves. Start with **LonelyPlanet.com** (www.lonelyplanet .com), where you'll find travel news, links to useful resources and the Thorn Tree bulletin board.

CIA World Fact Book – Germany (www.cia.gov/cia/publications/factbook/geos/gm.html) Frequently updated data about geopolitical, demographic, economic and other aspects of Germany. You'll learn that Germans use 71 million mobile phones, that their median age is 42.6 years, that the country is slightly smaller than Montana and other fascinating nuggets.

Deutsche Welle (www.dw-world.de) The online version of the German international broadcasting service has news and background information about Germany, on-demand audio and video feeds and newsletter sign-ups.

Deutschland Online (www.magazine-deutschland.de) Online version of *Deutschland Magazine* with interesting features on culture, business and politics.

Deutschland Portal (www.deutschland.de) The ultimate gateway to online information about Germany.

Facts about Germany (www.tatsachen-ueber-deutschland.de) An excellent and comprehensive reference about all aspects of German society, including education, culture, media, foreign policy and the economy.

German National Tourist Office (www.germany-tourism.de) Official site packed with information on all aspects of travel to and within Germany.

Online German Course (www.deutsch-lernen.com) Free language lessons for absolute beginners and moderately advanced students.

Itineraries
CLASSIC ROUTES

CITY DELIGHTS
Two Weeks / Berlin to Hamburg

Book-ended by two great cities, this route offers some of the best in culture, character and architecture the country has to offer. Kick off in **Berlin** (p89) with its top-notch museums, old and bold architecture and nice-to-naughty nightlife. From here head south to **Dresden** (p166), sitting proud and pretty in its baroque splendour on the Elbe River. Next stop is **Munich** (p286), where an evening in a beer garden is the perfect finish to a day of palace- and museum-hopping. Next up is the Romantic Road where medieval **Rothenburg ob der Tauber** (p332) is a veritable symphony of half-timbered houses. Cut west to historic **Heidelberg** (p403), idyllically serenaded by its ancient fortress, then north to **Worms** (p472) and **Mainz** (p467) with their fantastic Romanesque cathedrals. Follow the Rhine through the fairy-tale scenery of the Middle Rhine to cosmopolitan **Cologne** (p550) for a spin around Germany's grandest Gothic cathedral. Wrap up your trip in lovable **Bremen** (p641) and open-minded **Hamburg** (p653), which welcome you with maritime charm.

Prepare for a roller coaster of urban treasures on this 1700km journey that takes in progressive big-city beauties, medieval metropolises mired in history and elegant residential towns shaped by royal visions.

THE GRAND CIRCLE   Four Weeks / Berlin to Berlin

Your epic Germany adventure launches with a few metro-intense days in **Berlin** (p89), followed by a spin around the royal splendours of Sanssouci Park and Palace in **Potsdam** (p147) before plunging south to **Dresden** (p166), a city that's literally risen from the ashes of WWII. Consider a quick detour to ruggedly romantic **Saxon Switzerland** (p180) with its fairy-tale rock formations, then hook west to **Weimar** (p258), the cradle of the German Enlightenment. Head south to picture-perfect **Bamberg** (p364), with its pristine Altstadt (old town) and excellent breweries, then compare its splendours to **Regensburg** (p378), one of Europe's best preserved medieval towns. After your big-city fix in **Munich** (p286) make the pilgrimage to the world's most famous palace, **Neuschwanstein** (p342), a sugary confection dreamed up by 'Mad' King Ludwig II of Bavaria. **Freiburg** (p439), your next stop, is a bustling university town and gateway to the southern **Black Forest** (p439).

Work your way north through cuckoo-clock country to historic **Heidelberg** (p403), idyllically snuggled into the steep Neckar Valley, and the castle-studded **Romantic Rhine** (p483) between Mainz and Koblenz. Then follow the sinewing **Moselle** (p495) to **Trier** (p496) to wander among the best-preserved Roman ruins north of the Alps. Heading east across the gentle Eifel mountain range, you'll arrive in **Cologne** (p550), whose glorious twin-towered cathedral can be spotted edging into the sky from afar. Swing by **Aachen** (p567), with its splendid Dom (cathedral) founded by Charlemagne, before heading up to **Hamburg** (p653), a bustling port city with a kicking nightlife and first-rate museums. Wind down your tour by catching the Hanseatic spirit in the cities of **Lübeck** (p683) and **Schwerin** (p704) before travelling back to Berlin.

Germany is a rich quilt of exciting cities, awe-inspiring scenery and spirit-lifting culture, as this grand, 1800km loop reveals. It can be 'done' in three weeks but more time lets you connect more deeply with this land and its feast of treats, treasures and temptations.

ROADS LESS TRAVELLED

MID-GERMAN MEANDERINGS

Two Weeks / Düsseldorf to Lutherstadt Wittenberg

Kick off your west–east corrida in bustling **Düsseldorf** (p540), a magnet for its art, shopping and rollicking earthy pubs. Those with a penchant for the offbeat will hit the mother lode on the Industrial Heritage Trail through the nearby **Ruhrgebiet** (p571). Quirky delights include former gas tanks filled with art (p579), blast furnaces turned into free-climbing zones (p579) and a colliery doubling as a concert venue (p573). East along the A44, stop in **Soest** (p585) and **Paderborn** (p587), both famous for their churches. Plunge into the world of fairy-tales in **Hamelin** (p603), the quaint, cobbled town of Pied Piper fame. Close by is restored **Hildesheim** (p614), celebrated for the huge bronze door gracing its cathedral. Continue on to charming **Goslar** (p231), which counts a 1000-year-old mine and an 11th-century palace among its considerable assets. It's also the gateway to the **Harz Mountains** (p229), whose natural splendours are perfect for a day or two in the slow lane. Don't leave without sampling the small-town beauty of **Wernigerode** (p238), famous for its colourfully painted medieval houses and as the terminus of the narrow-gauge Harzquerbahn railway to Nordhausen in Thuringia. Continue on to charming **Quedlinburg** (p243), a well-preserved symphony in half-timbered houses. Then make a beeline straight for **Dessau** (p211), a city that's synonymous with the Bauhaus school of architecture. Ramble around the lush gardens of **Wörlitz** (p215) before finishing up in the birthplace of the Reformation, **Lutherstadt Wittenberg** (p217).

This itinerary proves that 'lesser known' doesn't have to mean 'lesser'. Classic and quirky discoveries abound along this 600km-long belt cinched around Germany's surprising middle.

BEST OF THE BALTIC   Two Weeks / Flensburg to Greifswald

Though no stranger to domestic tourism, Germany's towns and resorts fringing the Baltic Sea rarely make it onto international travellers' itineraries – undeservedly so. The first stop, **Flensburg** (p693), easily reached by train or autobahn from Hamburg, is Germany's northernmost town and beckons with a handsome Altstadt. **Schleswig** (p690), a quick hop south, cradles a huge fjord and boasts the intriguing Viking Museum and art-filled Schloss Gottdorf. Next up is **Lübeck** (p683), a highlight on this route with its fairy-tale skyline, enchanting old town and delicious marzipan. East of here, Swedish-flavoured **Wismar** (p719) woos you with a postcard-pretty setting and a lovely step-gabled old town. En route to Rostock stop in **Bad Doberan** (p718), with its great red-brick minster, quirky Frank Zappa memorial and kid-friendly narrow-gauge train. Though aesthetically challenged, **Rostock** (p711) does have some interesting sights and serves as the region's nightlife hub. **Stralsund** (p722), by contrast, is more sedate but has a very attractive Altstadt and is also the gateway to **Rügen Island** (p727), which has tree-lined country roads, long sandy beaches and mysterious chalk cliffs. To truly traipse off the beaten path, head out to the remote **Darss-Zingst Peninsula** (p721), where nature puts on an especially handsome show. Conclude these meanderings in **Greifswald** (p725), an old university town close to beach-fringed **Usedom Island** (p726), a popular holiday island Germany shares with Poland.

A ride along Germany's magical Baltic coast reveals eye candy at every bend of the road. Take your sweet time as you travel along this 500km route from Germany's border with Denmark to where it rubs shoulders with Poland.

TAILORED TRIPS

CASTLES & PALACES

Until unification in 1871, Germany was a mosaic of fiefdoms whose overseers ruled from the comfort of their Schloss (palace) or *Burg* (castle). A sentimental favourite is **Wartburg** (p270) in Eisenach, where Martin Luther translated the Bible into German. Equally impressive is Saxony's **Festung Königstein** (p181) overlooking the Elbe and so big and formidable that nobody dared attack it. More refined are sublime **Schloss Sanssouci** (p148) and **Schloss Charlottenburg** (p114) in Berlin. Both are impressive residences of the Prussian Hohenzollern clan and are surrounded by their own park. The family's ancestral seat, **Burg Hohenzollern** (p426), is some 700km southwest near Tübingen. Looking medieval and mysterious, it's actually a 19th-century neo-Gothic confection, the original long ago destroyed. A similar fate befell **Schloss Heidelberg** (p403), although much of it survives as a romantic ruin. For more romance, visit the robber baron hang-outs along the Romantic Rhine, especially the rambling **Burg Rheinfels** (p490) and the pristine **Marksburg** (p488) which, like the fairy-tale **Burg Eltz** (p503) near the Moselle, has never been destroyed. Germany's most famous palace may be **Schloss Neuschwanstein** (p342), but the more playful **Schloss Linderhof** (p349) and **Schloss Herrenchiemsee** (p324) are even nicer. Another major Bavarian delight is the baroque **Würzburg Residenz** (p327), by star builder Balthasar Neumann.

CATHEDRALS & CHURCHES

Germany has a wealth of houses of worship, the most magnificent of which lift the spirit with their harmonious architecture and priceless treasures. Germany's best-known church is also its biggest, the Dom in **Cologne** (p551), whose twin spires dominate the city's distinctive skyline. Another exquisite Gothic cathedral is the *Münster* (minster) in **Freiburg** (p439), which has similarly awesome stained-glass windows. The title of 'world's tallest steeple' (reached by 786 steps!) belongs to the minster in **Ulm** (p427), while the Dom in **Berlin** (p108) claims to be Germany's largest Protestant cathedral. Older than all by several centuries is Charlemagne's octagonal palace chapel, now part of the Dom in **Aachen** (p568).

Fans of Romanesque architecture will hit the trifecta along the Rhine with the awe-inspiring cathedrals of **Mainz** (p467), **Worms** (p472) and **Speyer** (p474). In the deepest Black Forest, the Dom in **St Blasien** (p451) is a rare neoclassical gem lidded by the third-largest dome in Europe. Bavaria brims with baroque churches; the Asamkirche in **Munich** (p299) and the Wieskirche in **Steingaden** (p345) are both standouts. The landmark Frauenkirche in **Dresden** (p170), levelled during WWII, triumphantly reopened in 2005. Churches with amazing carved altars include the Jakobskirche in **Rothenburg ob der Tauber** (p332), the St Nikolaikirche in **Kalkar** (p549) and the Petrikirche in **Dortmund** (p577).

WINE

If you're a wine aficionado, why not build an entire itinerary around your favourite libation? Anywhere within Germany's 13 growing regions you can tour estates, explore musty cellars stocked with vintage barrels and chin-wag with vintners during wine tastings. Or you could hike along vineyard trails, drink a toast to Bacchus in cosy wine taverns, then retire to your room on a wine estate.

Germany's most famous grape is the noble riesling. The best vintages hail from the tiny Rheingau area, with tourist-ridden **Rüdesheim** (p494) at its heart, and from the Middle Rhine region (between Koblenz and Bingen), where **Bacharach** (p491) is the most appealing of the many wine towns. Fans of red wines should head to the **Ahr Valley** (p480), best explored on a hike

along the Rotweinwanderweg (Red Wine Hiking Trail). In southwestern Germany is the Baden region, whose **Kaiserstuhl** (p445) area produces exceptional late burgundies and pinot gris. In and around **Würzburg** (p327) is the Franken region, whose vintners make excellent dry and earthy wines bottled in curvy green flagons called *Bocksbeutel*. Germany's, and indeed Europe's, northernmost growing region is Saale-Unstrut, with **Freyburg** (p227) at its centre. Its famous Rotkäppchen (Little Red Riding Hood) sparkling wine was already popular in GDR times. Another eastern growing region – and the country's smallest – is the Sächsische Weinstrasse around **Meissen** (p182).

WORLD HERITAGE SITES

Germany has around 30 places recognised by Unesco for their historical and cultural importance. Wander the warren of lanes of well-preserved medieval towns such as **Quedlinburg** (p243), **Goslar** (p231), **Bamberg** (p364), **Lübeck** (p683) and **Regensburg** (p378). Take in the lifestyles of the rich and powerful at the baroque palaces of Sanssouci in **Potsdam** (p147) and Augustusburg in **Brühl** (p561), or the medieval castles along the **Romantic Rhine** (p483). The bulging coffers of the Church financed the cathedrals of **Aachen** (p568), **Cologne** (p551), **Hildesheim** (p615) and **Speyer** (p474), the monasteries in **Reichenau Island** (p458) and **Lorsch** (p527), the prince-bishops' residence in **Würzburg** (p327) and the Wieskirche in **Steingaden** (p345). Sites honouring Protestant reformer Martin Luther include Wartburg castle in **Eisenach** (p270) and memorials in **Eisleben** (p224) and **Lutherstadt Wittenberg** (p217). **Weimar** (p258) drew a who's who of German thinkers in the 18th century and is also the birthplace of the Bauhaus.

Bauhaus buildings in **Dessau** (p212) are also on Unesco's list. Recent additions include the Museumsinsel in **Berlin** (p107) and the Elbe valley around **Dresden** (p174), while the well-preserved Roman ruins in **Trier** (p496) were among the first five sites to make the cut. For a change of pace visit Zollverein colliery in **Essen** (p573) and the Völklinger Hütte near **Saarbrücken** (p508), both considered outstanding 'cathedrals of industry'.

Snapshot

'Who are we?' many Germans are asking themselves. 'Where to now?' Deep into the second decade of reunification, Germany has a pretty good idea. But its roads are strewn with challenges and contradictions. Germany is the world's third-largest economy, yet more than 4.5 million people languish on its dole queues. Germany, long considered an economic basket case with abysmally high wage and social welfare costs, was ranked Europe's most attractive business location in 2006 – and third in the world. At the same time, the top brass of a highly profitable local company threatens to pack its corporate bags for New Europe. The country is export champion of the world for the third successive year; its cities are bankrupt. Culturally, urban centres are exploding with creative energy as if reliving the wild 1920s. But ugly right-wing violence flared again on Germany's uneven social terrain, just as the football World Cup was about to begin under the motto *'Die Welt zu Gast bei Freunden'* (The World – A Guest Among Friends).

This is Germany today. Politically, Germans who lived through the Kohl and Schröder governments are hardened to political tedium. In late 2005 its voters saw no way out but to opt for arguably the highest form, a grand coalition between the two largest parties: the Sozialdemokratische Partei Deutschlands (SPD; Social Democratic Party) and the Christliche Demokratische Union Deutschlands (CDU; Christian Democratic Union) with its Bavarian offshoot, the Christliche Soziale Union (CSU; Christian Social Union). This tied the political knot on a de facto relationship existing for some years in an opposition-controlled upper house. But it also brought an unusual twist: Angela Merkel became Germany's first woman chancellor, and she also became the first eastern German to take on the job.

Unemployment, of course, remains high on the political agenda. Reforming the health and social security systems are tough hurdles, given Germany's ageing and declining population. The time is rapidly approaching for baby boomers to retire and devote themselves with gusto to patio barbecues, Toscana wine and French cheese. Someone has to pick up the bill, though, and new generations – those now entering the scorched earth left behind by the '68 generation after years of plenty – might just spit the dummy and stage a social revolution of their own one day.

For its fiscal problems, Germany is used to a flood of four-letter words from European partners. A hike in the consumption tax, if fully implemented in 2007, should allow Germany to meet EU obligations regarding its budget deficit for the first time in six years. But this might also throttle a domestic economy that steadfastly resists strong growth. In any case, it will lead to unpredictable price hikes.

On the environment front, laws to shut down the country's nuclear reactors by 2020 remain in force. And don't ditch those plastic bottles and tin cans – reforms to the refund system are now functioning, despite tooth-and-nail resistance by the retail industry. Ironically, it's the Green party's reforms from a seven-year taste of shared power that now look the most durable.

Germany is betting on continuity when it comes to proactively shaping its society. Laws passed in 2005 guaranteeing equal status for same-sex partnerships look rock solid these days, and the grand coalition enacted an antidiscrimination law that even went beyond EU obligations in areas of disability, age and sexual identity.

Can Germany be a 'normal' nation again? Yes, it would seem. During the football World Cup in 2006 Germans painted their faces in national colours,

FAST FACTS

Area: 357,045 sq km

Population: 82.41 million

GDP: €2.24 trillion (2005)

Inflation: 2% (Apr 2006)

Unemployment: 10.8% (May 2006)

Land use: 53% farming, 29.8% forest, 6.7% built-up areas

Life expectancy: women 81.3 years, men 75.6 years

Most famous civil criminal: Fritz Haarmann (allegedly killed 26 people and drank their blood, 1925)

Fat factor: 47% overweight, 11% obese

Museums: 6000 (101 million visits)

draped their cars with the German flag and celebrated their country in a cheerful show of national spirit. This reflected a new confidence in Germany as a nation. And why not? New generations today live in what is arguably one of the world's best-functioning democracies – one, in fact, where past national shame is being offset by various commitments to nation building abroad.

In 2006, under the aegis of the UN, the Bundeswehr (German National Army) led the enforcement of Congo's free elections. Also in 2006, Germany took over the leadership of efforts to rebuild Afghanistan, while reaffirming its active role in Kosovo. Meanwhile, its relations with the US have warmed from the deep freeze of 2003 – when Germany didn't join the coalition that invaded Iraq. An overwhelming majority of Germans still stand behind this decision to go an independent course.

It's the soft areas – the social topography – that are raising the tough issues. Germany has 82 million different views on what's wrong with its education system. Hardened to receiving miserable scores in the PISA (Programme for International Student Assessment) studies comparing standards worldwide, Germans saw salt rubbed into sensitive wounds in 2006 when a new PISA study showed their schools churned out second-generation migrant children without basic mathematics skills. The country of poets and thinkers was becoming a country of numerical illiterates.

Also concerning migrants, nothing sends the emotional temperature soaring in Germany like the integration issue. While riots like those engulfing French cities in 2005 were never likely to ignite Germany, this fact speaks more for the size and structure of German cities than for successful integration. In 2006 teachers at a school in Berlin's tough migrant district of Neukölln sent a plea to the city's senate requesting their school be closed down. The school was out of control. Overnight, the Rütli School, with its vast majority of Muslim pupils, unfairly became a symbol of twin horrors: poor integration and plummeting education standards.

With Muslims making up a high proportion of the country's migrant population, the Europe-wide debate on the so-called Muslim-Christian 'culture clash' issue is a lively one in Germany. The right of teachers to wear Muslim headdress in schools was confirmed by the constitutional court in 2004 in a test case, but many states have since amended laws to prevent this. A spate of so-called 'honour killings' of migrant women from forced marriages has also prompted heated discussion. Meanwhile, signs suggest that Germany still doesn't have a grip on right-wing Nazi violence in depressed rural regions, especially in parts of Brandenburg. A couple of high-profile assaults on migrant Germans in 2006 just before the football World Cup reopened this sensitive issue.

But right-wing – or any other winged – attempts to create conformity in Germany are doomed to glorious failure. The country is simply too diverse and culturally dynamic. In 2006 Unesco declared Berlin Europe's first City of Design. Berlin received this prestigious accolade for its fusion of design, architecture, art and culture, and it now joins Buenos Aires in the Unesco Creative Cities Network. But the cultural boom goes well beyond 'poor but sexy' Berlin – as its gay governing mayor likes to describe his city. German film is riding a new wave of popularity, while in eastern Germany the New Leipzig School of painting is showing the world that Germany, indeed, has not only caught up with its past, it is confidently breaking out into new and exciting directions.

History

The rollercoaster ride of Germany's fascinating history begins with the Celts and Germanic tribes who clashed with the invading Romans. By the 9th century all the regions east of the Rhine had developed an identity of their own. The Middle Ages, however, were a bleak, barbaric time of feudalism when more seemed to be lost than won, and squabbling feudal princes hindered the creation of a German state. Once a federal state did take shape in the 19th century, the scene was set for a tumultuous path from unification to war, from democracy to fascism and WWII, and from there to chilly Cold War division, peaceful reunification and the Germany that we know today.

For a comprehensive overview of German history, see the German Culture website www .germanculture.com.ua.

TRIBES & THE ROMANS

The early inhabitants of Germany were Celts and later the Germanic tribes. In the Iron Age (from around 800 BC) Germanic tribes on the North German Plain and in the Central Uplands lived on the fringes of Celtic regions and were influenced by the culture without ever melting into it. Evidence of this is still apparent today in Thale, in the Harz Mountains.

The Romans fought pitched battles with the Germanic tribes from about 100 BC. The Germanic tribes east of the Rhine and the Romans on the western side fought for control of territory across the river until AD 9, when the Roman general, Varus, lost three legions – about 20,000 men – in the bloody Battle of Teutoburg Forest and the Romans abandoned their plans to extend eastwards (see boxed text, p28). By AD 300, four main groups of tribes had formed: Alemans, Franks, Saxons and Goths.

The Roman presence is evoked today in the thermal baths and amphitheatre of Augusta Treverorum (Trier today), and in other Roman relics in Aachen, Xanten, Cologne, Bonn, Mainz (where 4th-century Roman shipwrecks can be viewed), Bingen (prized for its Roman surgical instruments), Koblenz, Augsburg and Regensburg. The Rhine and Moselle vineyards are a lasting tribute to the Romans' penchant for a tipple or two.

Did you know 9 November is Germany's 'destiny date'? It was the day of the uprising in 1848, the failed revolution in 1918, Hitler's Munich Putsch in 1923, the Night of Broken Glass in 1938, and the day the Wall fell in 1989.

THE FRANKISH REICH

Based on the Rhine's western bank, the Frankish Reich became Europe's most important political power in medieval times. This was due, in part, to the Merovingian king, Clovis (r 482–511), who united diverse populations. In its heyday the Reich included present-day France, Germany, the Low Countries and half the Italian peninsula. Missionaries such as St Boniface (675–754) – considered the father of German Christianity – crossed the Rhine to convert pagans.

When fighting broke out among aristocratic clans in the 7th century, the Merovingians were replaced by the Carolingians who introduced hierarchical Church structures. Kloster Lorsch in present-day Hesse is one fine relic of this era. From his grandiose residence in Aachen, Charlemagne (r 768–814), the Reich's most important king, conquered Lombardy, won territory in Bavaria, waged a 30-year war against the Saxons in the north and was crowned Kaiser by the pope in 800. The cards were reshuffled in the 9th century when attacks by Danes, Saracens and Magyars threw the eastern portion of Charlemagne's

The Roman Empire and Its Germanic Peoples by Herwig Wolfram and Thomas Dunlap (translator) is an authoritative history spanning five centuries of Germanic tribe migrations and the foundations of the Roman Empire.

TIMELINE	800 BC	100 BC–AD 9
	Germanic tribes and Celts inhabit the North German Plain and Central Uplands of the area called Germany today	Romans and Germanic tribes clash until defeat at the Battle of Teutoburg Forest halts Roman expansion eastwards

empire into turmoil and four dominant duchies emerged – Bavaria, Franconia, Swabia and Saxony.

Charlemagne's burial in Aachen Dom (Aachen Cathedral) turned a court chapel into a major pilgrimage site (and it remains so today). The Treaty of Verdun (843) saw a gradual carve-up of the Reich and when Louis the Child (r 900–11) – a grandson of Charlemagne's brother – died heirless, the East Frankish (ie German) dukes elected a king from their own ranks. Thus, the first German monarch was created.

The use of the title Kaiser was a direct legacy of Roman times (from 'Caesar').

EARLY MIDDLE AGES

Strong regionalism in Germany today has its roots in the early Middle Ages, when dynasties squabbled and intrigued over territorial spoils, watched on helplessly by a toothless, Roman-inspired central state.

The symbolic heart of power was Aachen Dom, which hosted the coronation and burial of dozens of German kings from 936. Otto I was first up in the cathedral. In 962 he renewed Charlemagne's pledge to protect the papacy and the pope reciprocated with a pledge of loyalty to the Kaiser. This made the Kaiser and pope strange and often acrimonious bedfellows for the next 800 years and created the Holy Roman Empire, a nebulous state that survived until 1806 (see boxed text, opposite).

Two Lives of Charlemagne edited by Betty Radice is a striking Charlemagne biography, beautifully composed by a monk and a courtier who spent 23 years in Charlemagne's court.

A power struggle between pope and Kaiser, who also had to contend with the local princes or clergy-cum-princes, was behind many of the upheavals in the early Middle Ages. In the Investiture Conflict under the reign of the Salian, Heinrich IV (r 1056–1106), the pope cracked down on the practice of simony (selling religious pardons and relics). Heinrich, excommunicated and contrite, stood barefoot in the snow for three days in Canossa in Italy begging forgiveness. He was absolved, but the Reich was convulsed by a 20-year civil war on the issue, which was finally resolved in a treaty signed in the Rhineland-Palatinate town of Worms in 1122. The graves of Heinrich and other Salian monarchs can today be found in the spectacular cathedral in nearby Speyer.

The first rulers to promote a strong German identity were Charlemagne's grandson, Louis the German (r 843–76) and Konrad I (r 911–18).

Under Friedrich I Barbarossa (r 1152–89), Aachen assumed the role of Reich capital and was granted its rights of liberty in 1165, the year Charlemagne

---

ROMAN LEGIONS

For many years, Mount Grotenburg near Detmold in North-Rhine Westphalia was thought to be the scene of the Battle of Teutoburg Forest, but no-one can really say for sure where it happened. Kalkriese, north of Osnabrück in Lower Saxony, has a museum and park (www.kalkriese -varusschlacht.de) where in the 1990s archaeologists found face helmets, breast shields, bone deposits and other grisly battle remains. The ill-named Battle of Teutoburg Forest might have been fought there.

In AD 1 the Romans started building what is today central Europe's largest archaeological site – a wall running 568km from Koblenz on the Rhine to Regensburg on the Danube. Some 900 watchtowers and 60 forts studded this frontier line, dubbed Der Limes (The Limes). The 800km-long Deutsche Limes-Strasse (German Limes Road) cycling route runs between Regensburg in the south and Bad Hönningen in the north (near Koblenz), largely tracing the tower- and fortress-studded fortification. See www.limesstrasse.de for more about the Limes and routes along the wall. Another 280km-long cycling route links Detmold with Xanten (where there's an archaeological park), taking cyclists past various Roman remains and monuments.

4th century	486
The arrival of Hun horsemen triggers the Great Migration and Germanic tribes flee or are displaced into southern Europe	The Western Empire collapses and Romans seek protection among resettled Germanic tribes

was canonised. Meanwhile, Heinrich der Löwe (Henry the Lion), a Welf with an eye for Saxony and Bavaria, extended influence eastwards in campaigns to Germanise and convert the Slavs who populated much of today's eastern Germany. A Slavic minority, the Sorbs, can still be found in the Spreewald region of eastern Germany today.

The Reich gained territory to the east and in Italy, but soon fell apart dramatically because of early deaths, squabbling between Welf and Hohenstaufen pretenders to the throne and the election of a king and pope-backed antiking. At this time kings were being elected by *Kurfürsten* (prince electors) but crowned Kaiser by the pope – a system that made an unwilling lackey out of a Kaiser. In 1245 the Reich plunged into an era called the Great Interregnum, or the Terrible Time, when Pope Innocent IV annulled his own Kaiser, the Reich was flush with kings and central authority collapsed into a political heap.

Although the central Reich was only a shadow of its former self, expansion eastwards continued unabated. Land east of the Oder River (now Germany's eastern border) had been settled by German peasants and city-dwellers in the mid-12th century. In the 13th century Teutonic knights pushed eastwards, establishing fortress towns such as Königsberg (present-day Kaliningrad). At its peak, the unified state of the knights stretched from the Oder to Estonia. (Later, in the 17th century, a large swathe of this land would become part of Brandenburg-Prussia.)

THE HOUSE OF HABSBURG

In 1273 a Habsburg dynasty emerged from the royal heap, mastered the knack of a politically expedient arranged marriage, and dominated European affairs until the 20th century. Rudolf's arrival (r 1273–91) ended the Terrible Time, but more importantly the Declaration of Rense (1338) dispensed with the pope's role in crowning a Kaiser. Now the king, elected by the *Kurfürsten*, was automatically Kaiser. In 1356 the Golden Bull set out precise rules for elections and defined the relationship between the Kaiser and the princes. It was an improvement but Kaisers were still dancing to the tune of the princes.

Hildesheim was a centre of power in the Ottonian Period (900–1050). Bishop Bernward raised young Otto III (r 983–1002) and graced the town with treasures to befit a new Rome, such as his famous Bernwardstüren in the Hildesheimer Dom.

Heinrich the Fowler: Father of the Ottonian Empire by Mirella Patzer brings 10th-century Germany to life in a heady blend of history and fiction.

Heinrich IV's *Gang nach Canossa* is now a German expression to describe doing penance – 'to go to Canossa'.

WHAT WAS THE HOLY ROMAN EMPIRE?

It was an idea, mostly, and not a very good one. It grew out of the Frankish Reich, which was seen as the successor to the defunct Roman Empire. When Charlemagne's father, Pippin, helped a beleaguered pope (Charlemagne would later do the same), he received the title *Patricius Romanorum* (Protector of Rome), virtually making him Caesar's successor. Having retaken the papal territories from the Lombards, he presented them to the Church (the last of these territories is the modern Vatican state). Charlemagne's reconstituted 'Roman Empire' then passed into German hands.

The empire was known by various names throughout its lifetime. It formally began (for historians, at least) in 962 with the crowning of Otto I as Holy Roman Emperor and finally collapsed in 1806, when Kaiser Franz II abdicated. From 1508, Maximilian I and his successors favoured 'Emperor-Elect', a title that evolved as 'King of the Romans' under the Habsburgs.

The empire sometimes included Italy as far south as Rome. Sometimes it didn't – the pope usually had a say in that. It variously encompassed present-day Netherlands, Belgium, Switzerland, Lorraine and Burgundy (in France), Sicily, Austria and an eastern swathe of land that lies in the Czech Republic, Poland and Hungary. It was also known as the 'First Reich' (not to be confused with Otto von Bismarck's Second Reich or Adolf Hitler's Third Reich).

<table>
<tr><td>800</td><td>911</td></tr>
<tr><td>The Frankish Reich reaches its zenith under the rule of Charlemagne who is crowned Kaiser by the pope</td><td>Louis the Child dies heirless, prompting Germany's first monarch to be elected</td></tr>
</table>

The name Habsburg
(Hapsburg) originates
from *Habichts Burg*
(literally 'Hawk Castle'),
the spot on the Rhine (in
present-day Switzerland,
immediately across the
border from Germany)
from where the great
Swabian family first
hailed.

Dancing, however, was the last thing on the minds of ordinary Germans. They battled with panic lynching, pogroms against Jews and labour shortages – all sparked off by the plague (1348–50) that wiped out 25% of Europe's population. While death gripped the (Ger)man on the street, universities were being established all over the country around this time. The first was in Heidelberg, making it Germany's oldest – and arguably its most spectacular – university city today.

A QUESTION OF FAITH

The religious fabric of Germany was cut from a pattern created in the 16th-century Reformation. In the university town of Wittenberg in 1517, German theology professor Martin Luther (1483–1546) made public his 95 theses that questioned the papal practice of selling indulgences to exonerate sins. Threatened with excommunication, Luther refused to recant, broke from the Catholic Church and was banned by the Reich, only to be hidden in Wartburg castle (outside Eisenach, in Thuringia) where he translated the New Testament into German. Today, the death mask of Luther can be viewed in the Marktkirche in Halle; another can be seen at Luthers Sterbehaus in Eisleben (p225).

The first Bible was printed
in Latin in 1456 using a
revolutionary technique –
hand-set type cast in
moveable moulds – by
the Mainz-born inventor
of moveable type,
Johannes Gutenberg
(1397–1468).

It was not until 1555 that the Catholic and Lutheran churches were ranked as equals, thanks to Karl V (r 1520–58) who signed the Peace of Augsburg (1555), allowing princes to decide the religion of their principality. The more secular northern principalities adopted Lutheran teachings, while the clerical lords in the south, southwest and Austria stuck with Catholicism.

But the religious issue refused to die. Rather, it degenerated into the bloody Thirty Years' War, which Sweden and France had joined by 1635. Calm was restored with the Peace of Westphalia (1648), signed in Münster and Osnabrück, but it left the Reich – embracing more than 300 states and about 1000 smaller territories – a nominal, impotent state. Switzerland and the Netherlands gained independence, France won chunks of Alsace and Lorraine, and Sweden helped itself to the mouths of the Elbe, Oder and Weser Rivers.

THE ENLIGHTENMENT TO THE INDUSTRIAL AGE

In the 18th century the Enlightenment breathed new life into Germany, inspiring a rabble of autocratic princes to build stunning grand palaces and gardens

---

THE HANSEATIC LEAGUE

The Hanseatic League, whose origins go back to guilds and associations established by out-of-town merchants, was founded in 1358 and was dominated by Lübeck (see boxed text, p683), which controlled a large slice of European shipping trade. At its zenith, the league had more than 150 member cities. It earned a say in the choice of Danish kings after the Danes inspired its wrath by sinking a flotilla of the league's ships off Gotland in 1361. The resulting Treaty of Stralsund turned the league into northern Europe's most powerful economic and political entity.

As well as Lübeck, the league included such cities as Riga and Danzig (now Gdansk) on the Baltic Sea, Hamburg and Bremen on the North Sea, and inland cities such as Cologne, Dortmund and Hildesheim. By the 15th century, however, competition from Dutch and English shipping companies, internal disputes and a shift in the centre of world trade from the North and Baltic Seas to the Atlantic had caused decline. Hamburg, Bremen, Rostock, Lübeck and Stralsund are still known as Hanse cities.

919–1125	1165
Saxon and Salian emperors rule Germany, creating the Holy Roman Empire in 962	Aachen becomes Reich capital under Friedrich I Barbarossa

across the German lands. Berlin's Schloss Charlottenburg, Potsdam's Sanssouci Park and Dresden's Zwinger are fine examples of the spirit of this new age. Meanwhile, Johann Sebastian Bach and Georg Friedrich Händel were ushered on stage and a wave of *Hochkultur* (high culture) swept through society's top sliver. For the time being, however, the masses remained illiterate.

Brandenburg-Prussia became an entity to be reckoned with, kick-started by the acquisition of former Teutonic Knights' territories and assisted by Hohenzollern king Friedrich Wilhelm I (the Soldier King) and his son, Friedrich II (r 1740–86). After the Seven Years' War (1756–63) with Austria, Brandenburg-Prussia annexed Silesia and sliced up Poland.

Between 1801 and 1803 an imperial deputation secularised and reconstituted German territory, usually at the behest of French emperor Napoleon Bonaparte during the Napoleonic Wars. In 1806 the Rhine Confederation eradicated about 100 principalities. Sniffing the end of the Holy Roman Empire, Kaiser Franz II (r 1792–1806) packed his bags for Austria, renamed himself Franz I of Austria and abdicated in 1806. That same year Brandenburg-Prussia fell to the French, but humiliating defeat prompted reforms that brought it closer to civil statehood: Jews were granted equality and bonded labour was abolished.

In 1813, with French troops driven back by the Russians, Leipzig witnessed one of Napoleon's most significant defeats. At the Congress of Vienna (1815), Germany was reorganised into a confederation of 35 states and an ineffective Reichstag (legislative assembly) was established in Frankfurt, an unsatisfactory solution that only minimally improved on the Holy Roman Empire. The Reichstag poorly represented the most populous states, however, and failed to rein in Austro-Prussian rivalry.

By the mid-19th century, the engines of the modern, industrial age were purring across the country. A newly created urban proletarian movement fuelled calls for central government, while the Young Germany movement of satirists lampooned the powerful of the day and called for a central state.

Berlin, along with much of the southwest, erupted in riots in 1848, prompting German leaders to bring together Germany's first ever freely elected parliamentary delegation in Frankfurt's Paulskirche. Austria, meanwhile, broke away from Germany, came up with its own constitution and promptly relapsed into monarchism. As revolution fizzled, Prussian king Friedrich Wilhelm IV drafted his own constitution in 1850, which would remain in force until 1918.

'HONEST OTTO' BISMARCK

The creation of a unified Germany with Prussia at the helm was the glorious ambition of Otto von Bismarck (1815–98), a former member of the Reichstag and Prussian prime minister. An old-guard militarist, he used intricate diplomacy and a series of wars with neighbours Denmark and France to achieve his aims. In 1871 – later than most other European countries – Germany was unified, with Berlin the proud capital of Western Europe's largest state. At that time, Germany extended from Memel (Klaipėda in present-day Lithuania) to the Dutch border, including Alsace-Lorraine (southwest) in present-day France and Silesia (southeast) in present-day Poland. The Prussian king was crowned Kaiser of the Reich – a bicameral, constitutional monarchy – at Versailles on 18 January 1871 and Bismarck became its 'Iron Chancellor'. Suffrage was limited to men in the new Reich and the national colours were black, white and red.

The first potato was planted in Germany in 1621, the Gregorian calendar was adopted in 1700 and Germany's first cuckoo clock started ticking in 1730.

In 1875 the Socialist Workers' Party was founded. This became the Sozialdemokratische Partei Deutschlands (SPD; German Social Democratic Party) in 1890, which by 1918 had renounced revolution and committed itself to parliamentary means.

A communist vision of a classless and stateless society is portrayed in *The Communist Manifesto*, written in exile by Trier-born Karl Marx and Friedrich Engels. Capitalism will be toppled by a new working class, the pair warns readers.

Bismarck to the Weimar Republic is the focus of Hans-Ulrich Wehler's *The German Empire 1871–1918*, a translation of an authoritative German work. For a revealing study of the Iron Chancellor himself, read *Bismarck, the Man and the Statesman* by Gordon Craig.

Bismarck's power was based on the support of merchants and Junker, a noble class of nonknighted landowners. An ever-skilful diplomat and power broker, Bismarck achieved much through a dubious 'honest Otto' policy, whereby he brokered deals between European powers and encouraged colonial vanities to distract others from his own deeds. He belatedly graced the Reich of Kaiser Wilhelm I with a few African jewels after 1880, acquiring colonies in central, southwest and east Africa as well as numerous Pacific paradises, such as Tonga, where a weary Prussian prince might one day lay down his steel helmet and relax in the sun.

When pressed, Bismarck made concessions to the growing and increasingly antagonistic socialist movement, enacting Germany's first modern social reforms, but this was not his true nature.

By 1888 Germany found itself burdened with a new Kaiser, Wilhelm II, who wanted to extend social reform, and an Iron Chancellor who wanted stricter antisocialist laws. Finally, in 1890, the Kaiser's scalpel excised Bismarck from the political scene. After that, the legacy of Bismarck's brilliant diplomacy unravelled and a wealthy, unified and industrially powerful Germany paddled into the new century with incompetent leaders at the helm.

THE GREAT WAR

Technological advances and the toughening of Europe into colonial power blocs made WWI far from 'great'. The conflict began with the assassination of the heir to the Austro-Hungarian throne, Archduke Franz-Ferdinand, in Sarajevo in 1914 and quickly escalated into a European and Middle Eastern affair: Germany, Austria-Hungary and Turkey against Britain, France, Italy and Russia. In 1915 a German submarine attack on a British passenger liner killed 120 US citizens. By 1917 the USA had also entered the war.

Marc Ferro's *The Great War 1914–18* is a compelling account of WWI.

The seeds of acrimony and humiliation that later led to WWII were sown in the peace conditions of the 'Great War'. Russia, in the grip of revolution, accepted humiliating peace terms from Germany. Germany, militarily broken, itself teetering on the verge of revolution and caught in a no-man's-land between monarchy and modern democracy, signed the Treaty of Versailles (1919), which made it responsible for all losses incurred by its enemies. Its borders were trimmed back and it was forced to pay high reparations. To allow negotiations, a chancellor was appointed who for the first time was responsible to parliament. A mutiny by sailors in the bustling port of Kiel in 1919 triggered a workers' revolt and a revolution in Berlin, spelling a bitter end for Germany's Kaiser, who abdicated and went to the Netherlands.

WEIMAR & THE RISE OF HITLER

After abdicating, Kaiser Wilhelm II could settle in Utrecht (Netherlands) on condition he didn't engage in political activity. One of his last acts was to send a telegram congratulating Hitler on the occupation of Paris.

The end of the war did not create stability – or peace – in Germany. Socialist and democratic socialist parties fought tooth and nail, while the radical Spartacus League (joined by other groups in 1919 to form the German Communist Party; KPD) sought to create a republic based on Marx' theories of proletarian revolution. Following the bloody quashing of an uprising in Berlin, Spartacus founders 'Red' Rosa Luxemburg (1871–1919) and Leipzig-born Karl Liebknecht (1871–1919) were arrested and murdered en route to prison by *Freikorps* soldiers (right-leaning war volunteers). Their bodies were dumped in Berlin's Landwehr canal, only to be recovered several months later and buried in Berlin.

1356	1414–18
Germany's first constitutional document, the Golden Bull, is adopted; the Hanseatic League is born two years later	The Great Schism in the Catholic Church is resolved at the Council of Constance in southern Germany

THE NIGHT OF THE LONG KNIVES

Conceived to police public meetings and enforce law, the brown-shirted Nazi state police, the Sturmabteilung (SA), had become a troublesome bunch by 1934 – for Germans and their dictator alike. So much so, that on the night of 30 June 1934, Hitler ordered Schutzstaffel (SS) troops to round up and kill high-ranking SA officers. Their leader, Ernst Röhm, was shot and 76 others were knifed to death.

Hitler hushed up the gruesome night (dubbed 'The Night of the Long Knives') until 13 July when he announced to the Reichstag that, henceforth, the SA (which numbered two million, easily outnumbering the army) would serve under the command of the army, which, in turn, would swear an oath of allegiance to Hitler. Justice would be executed by himself and the black-shirted SS under the leadership of former chicken-farmer Heinrich Himmler, effectively giving the SS unchallenged power and making it Nazi Germany's most powerful – and feared – force.

Meanwhile, in July 1919, in the Thuringian city of Weimar (where the constituent assembly briefly sought refuge during the Berlin chaos), the federalist constitution of a new democratic republic was adopted.

The so-called Weimar Republic (1919–33) was governed by a coalition of left and centre parties headed by President Friedrich Ebert of the Sozialdemokratische Partei Deutschlands (SPD; German Social Democratic Party) until 1925 and then by Field Marshal Paul von Hindenburg, a gritty 78-year-old monarchist. The republic, however, pleased neither communists nor monarchists.

The first blow to the new republic came in 1920, when right-wing militants forcibly occupied the government quarter in Berlin in the failed 'Kapp Putsch'. In 1923, hyperinflation rocked the republic. That same year Adolf Hitler (1889–1945), an Austrian-born volunteer in the German army during WWI, launched the Munich Putsch with members of his National Socialist German Workers' Party (NSDAP). Hitler wound up in jail for two years, where he wrote his nationalist, anti-Semitic tome, *Mein Kampf*. Once out, he began rebuilding the party.

Hitler's NSDAP gained 18% of the vote in the 1930 elections, prompting him to run against Hindenburg for the presidency in 1932, when he won 37% of a second-round vote. A year later, Hindenburg appointed Hitler chancellor, with a coalition cabinet of Nationalists (conservatives, old aristocrats and powerful industrialists) and National Socialists (Nazis). When Berlin's Reichstag mysteriously went up in flames in March 1933, Hitler had the excuse he needed to request emergency powers to arrest all communist and liberal opponents and push through his proposed Enabling Law, allowing him to decree laws and change the constitution without consulting parliament. The Nazi dictatorship had begun. When Hindenburg died a year later, Hitler fused the offices of president and chancellor to become *Führer* and chancellor of the Third Reich.

NAZIS IN POWER

The thumbscrews slowly tightened around Germany. In 12 short years of a 'Thousand Year Reich' proclaimed by Hitler, massive destruction would be inflicted upon German and other European cities; political opponents, intellectuals and artists would be murdered or forced to go underground or into exile; a culture of terror and denunciation would permeate almost all corners of society; and Europe's rich Jewish heritage would be decimated.

In 1923 a postage stamp cost 50 billion marks, a loaf of bread cost 140 billion marks and US$1 was worth 4.2 trillion marks. In November, the new Rentenmark was traded in for one trillion old marks.

'Laws are like sausages. It's better not to see them being made.'
BISMARCK

William Shirer's definitive 1000-page plus *The Rise & Fall of the Third Reich* remains a powerful reportage. His Berlin of those times is the literary equivalent of the brutal north face of the Eiger.

Martin Luther launches the Reformation with his 95 theses in the eastern German town of Wittenburg

The Peace of Augsburg allows princes to decide their principality's religion, equalising Catholicism and Protestantism

JEWS IN GERMANY

The first Jews arrived in present-day Germany with the conquering Romans, settling in important Roman cities on or near the Rhine, such as Cologne, Trier, Mainz, Speyer and Worms. As non-Christians, Jews had a separate political status. Highly valued for their trade connections, they were formally invited to settle in Speyer in 1084 and granted trading privileges and the right to build a wall around their quarter. A charter of rights granted to the Jews of Worms in 1090 by Henry IV allowed local Jews to be judged according to their own set of laws.

The First Crusade (1095–99) resulted in a wave of pogroms in 1096, usually against the will of local rulers and townspeople. Many Jews resisted the attacks before committing suicide once their situation became hopeless. This, the *Kiddush ha-shem* (martyr's death), established a precedent of martyrdom that became a tenet of European Judaism in the Middle Ages. But the attacks also set the tone for persecution by mobs during troubled times.

In the 13th century Jews were declared crown property by Frederick II, an act that afforded protection but exposed them to royal whim. Rabbi Meir of Rothenburg, whose grave lies in Europe's oldest Jewish cemetery in Worms, fell foul of King Rudolph of Habsburg in 1293 for leading a group of would-be emigrants to Palestine; he died in prison. The Church also prescribed distinctive clothing for Jews at this time, which later meant that in some towns Jews had to wear badges.

Things deteriorated with the arrival of the plague in the mid-14th century, when Jews were persecuted and libellous notions circulated throughout the Christian population. The 'blood libel' accused Jews of using the blood of Christians in rituals. The even more bizarre 'host-desecration libel' accused Jews of desecrating or torturing Christ by, among other dastardly deeds, sticking pins into communion wafers, which then wept tears or bled.

Money lending was the main source of income for Jews in the 15th century. Expulsions remained commonplace, with large numbers emigrating to Poland, where Yiddish developed. The Reformation (including a hostile Martin Luther) and the Thirty Years' War brought difficult times for Jewish populations, but by the 17th century they were valued again for their economic contacts.

Napoleon granted Germany's Jews equal rights, but reforms were repealed by the 1815 Congress of Vienna. Anti-Jewish feelings in the early 19th century coincided with German nationalism and a more vigorous Christianity. Pressure was applied on Jews to assimilate. Famous assimilated Jews, such as the Düsseldorf-born poet Heinrich Heine (1797–1856) – who claimed 'Christ rode on an ass, but now asses ride on Christ' – often exerted a liberal influence on society.

With unification in 1871, Jews enjoyed almost equal status in Germany, but they were still barred from government and could not become army officers. In the late 19th century Germany became a world centre of Jewish cultural and historical studies. There was a shift to large cities such as Leipzig, Cologne, Breslau (now Wroclaw in Poland), Hamburg, Frankfurt-am-Main and to the capital, Berlin, where one-third of German Jews lived.

Germany became an important centre for Hebrew literature after Russian writers and academics fled the revolution of 1917. The Weimar Republic brought emancipation for the 500,000-strong Jewish community, but also a backlash during the economic disasters in the 1920s. After Hitler came to power, the fate of German Jewry was sealed by new race laws. Increasing persecution led many to emigrate, and by 1939 less than half the 1933 population figure (530,000) remained in Germany. By 1943 Germany was declared *Judenrein*, or clean of Jews. This ignored the hundreds of thousands of Eastern European Jews incarcerated on 'German' soil. Around six million Jews died in Europe as a direct result of Nazism and its barbarity.

The number of Jews affiliated with the Jewish community in Germany is currently around 100,000 – the third largest in Europe – but the real number is probably twice that. Many Jews arrived from the former Soviet Union in the 1990s.

There are particularly informative Jewish museums in Berlin (p113) and Frankfurt (p517).

1618–48	1740–86
The Thirty Years' War sweeps through Germany and leaves the Reich a disempowered region of 300-plus states	Brandenburg-Prussia becomes a mighty European power under Frederick the Great

In April 1933 Joseph Goebbels, head of the well-oiled Ministry of Propaganda, announced a boycott of Jewish businesses. Soon after, Jews were expelled from public service and 'non-Aryans' were banned from many professions, trades and industries. The Nuremberg Laws (1935) deprived non-Aryans of German citizenship and forbade them to marry or have sexual relations with Aryans – anyone who broke these race laws faced the death penalty (and had to pay their own trial and execution costs to boot).

Hitler won much support among the middle and lower-middle classes by pumping large sums of money into employment programmes, many involving re-armament and heavy industry. In Wolfsburg, Lower Saxony, affordable cars started rolling out of the first Volkswagen factory, founded in 1938.

That same year, Hitler's troops were welcomed into Austria. Foreign powers, in an attempt to avoid another bloody war, accepted this *Anschluss* (annexation) of Austria. Following this same policy of appeasement, the Munich Agreement was signed in September 1938 by Hitler, Mussolini (Italy), Neville Chamberlain (UK) and Eduardo Daladier (France), and the largely ethnic-German Sudetenland of Czechoslovakia was relinquished to Hitler. By March 1939, he had also annexed Moravia and Bohemia.

WWII
Early Years
A nonaggression pact was signed between Hitler and Stalin's USSR in August 1939, whereby the Tokyo–Berlin–Rome axis (Hitler had already signed agreements with Italy and Japan) was expanded to include Moscow. Soviet neutrality was assured by a secret Soviet–German protocol that divided up Eastern Europe into spheres of interest.

In late August an SS-staged attack on a German radio station in Gleiwitz (Gliwice), Poland, gave Hitler the excuse to march into Poland. This proved the catalyst for WWII; three days later, on 3 September 1939, France and Britain declared war on Germany.

Poland, but soon also Belgium, the Netherlands and France, quickly fell to Germany. In June 1941 Germany broke its nonaggression pact with Stalin by attacking the USSR. Though successful at first, Operation Barbarossa soon ran into problems and Hitler's troops retreated. With the defeat of the German 6th army at Stalingrad (today Volgograd) the following winter, morale flagged at home and on the fronts.

The Final Solution
At Hitler's request, a conference in January 1942 on Berlin's Wannsee came up with a protocol clothed in bureaucratic jargon that laid the basis for the

A detailed history of WWII with Nazi leader biographies, a Holocaust timeline with more than 150 images, and a special focus on the pre-WWII years in Nazi Germany make this website stand out – www.historyplace .com.

Chester Wilmot presents an interesting account of WWII in his *The Struggle for Europe*, told from the perspective of an Australian journalist slap-bang in the thick of things.

The Colditz Story (1955), directed by Guy Hamilton, is a gripping if sobering watch. Based on the book *The Colditz Story* (1952) by prison escapee Pat Reid, it portrays the escapes of Allied prisoners of war during WWII from the Nazis' legendary high-security prison in Western Saxony.

THE NIGHT OF BROKEN GLASS

Nazi horror escalated on 9 November 1938 with the *Reichspogromnacht* (often called *Kristallnacht* or the 'Night of Broken Glass'). In retaliation for the assassination of a German consular official by a Polish Jew in Paris, synagogues and Jewish cemeteries, property and businesses across Germany were desecrated, burnt or demolished. About 90 Jews died that night. The next day another 30,000 were incarcerated, and Jewish businesses were transferred to non-Jews through forced sale at below-market prices.

1806	1815
Brandenburg-Prussia falls to the French and the Holy Roman Empire collapses	The Congress of Vienna redraws the map of Europe and divides Germany into 35 states

One of a clutch of fabulous films by Germany's best-known female director, Margarethe von Trotta, *Rosenstrasse* (2003) is a portrayal of a 1943 protest against the deportation of their Jewish husbands by a group of non-Jewish women.

murder of millions of Jews. The Holocaust was a systematic, bureaucratic and meticulously documented genocidal act carried out by about 100,000 Germans, but with the tacit agreement of a far greater number.

Jewish populations in occupied areas were systematically terrorised and executed by SS troops. Hitler sent Jews to concentration camps in Germany (including Sachsenhausen, Buchenwald and Mittelbau Dora) and Eastern Europe. Sinti and Roma (gypsies), political opponents, priests, homosexuals, resistance fighters and habitual criminals were also incarcerated in a network of 22 camps, mostly in Eastern Europe. Another 165 work camps (such as Auschwitz-Birkenau in Poland) provided labour for big industry, including IG Farbenindustrie AG, producer of the cyanide gas Zyklon B that was used in gas chambers to murder more than three million Jews. The former head-quarters of this conglomerate is now part of Frankfurt am Main's university campus (see p518). Of the estimated seven million people sent to camps, 500,000 survived.

Resistance to Hitler was quashed early by the powerful Nazi machinery of terror, but it never vanished entirely. On 20 July 1944, Claus Graf Schenk von Stauffenberg and other high-ranking army officers tried to assassinate Hitler and were executed. The mass extermination of Jews and other Nazi atrocities were outlined in the anti-Nazi leaflets distributed in Munich and other cities by the White Rose, a group of Munich university students whose resistance attempts cost most of them their lives (see boxed text, p302).

DEFEAT & OCCUPATION

Of the dozens of books covering Nazi concentration camps, *I Never Saw Another Butterfly: Children's Drawings and Poems from Terezin Concentration Camp 1942–1944* edited by Yana Volakova says it all. *This Way for the Gas, Ladies and Gentlemen* by Tadeusz Borowski is equally chilling.

Systematic air raids on German cities followed the invasion of Normandy in France in June 1944, and the return of the Allies to the European mainland. The brunt of the bombings was suffered by the civilian population; Dresden's Frauenkirche, Germany's greatest Protestant church, was destroyed during a British raid in February 1945 that killed 35,000 people, many of them refugees. (The church was painstakingly reconstructed for Dresden's 800th anniversary in 2006.)

With the Russians advancing on Berlin, a defeated and paranoid *Führer* and his new bride Eva Braun committed suicide on 30 April 1945 in Hitler's Berlin bunker, and on 7 May 1945, Germany capitulated and peace was signed at the US headquarters in Rheims and again in Berlin in what is now the Museum Berlin-Karlshorst (a German-Soviet history museum).

At the Yalta Conference (February 1945), Winston Churchill, Franklin D Roosevelt and Joseph Stalin had agreed to carve up Germany and Berlin into four zones of occupation controlled by Britain, the USA, the USSR and France. By July 1945, Stalin, Clement Attlee (who replaced Churchill after a surprise election win) and Roosevelt's successor Harry S Truman were at the table in Schloss Cecilienhof in Potsdam (Brandenburg) to hammer out the details. At Stalin's insistence, France received its chunk from the Allied regions. Regions east of the Oder and Neisse Rivers (where the border is today) went to Poland as compensation for earlier territorial losses to the USSR.

THE BIG CHILL

In 1948 the Allies put together an economic aid package, the Marshall Plan, and created the basis for West Germany's *Wirtschaftswunder* (economic miracle). Meanwhile, German cities were rising out of the rubble and first

steps were being taken to re-establish elected government. These advances
widened the rift between Allied and Soviet zones; in the latter inflation still
strained local economies, food shortages affected the population, and the
Communist and Social Democrat parties were forced to unite as the Sozialistische Einheitspartei Deutschlands (SED; Socialist Unity Party).

The showdown came in June 1948 when the Allies introduced the Deut-
schmark (DM) in their zones. The USSR saw this as a breach of the Potsdam
Agreement, whereby the powers had agreed to treat Germany as one economic zone. The USSR issued its own currency and promptly announced a
full-scale economic blockade of West Berlin. The Allies responded with the
remarkable Berlin Airlift, whereby American, British, Canadian and some
Australian air crews flew into Berlin's Tempelhof Airport (where there's a
monument today) the equivalent of 22 freight trains of 50 carriages daily, at
intervals of 90 seconds.

A NEW EAST & WEST GERMANY

In this frosty East–West climate, the Rhineland town of Bonn hosted West
German state representatives in September 1948 who met to hammer out a
draft constitution for a new Federal Republic of Germany (FRG, or BRD by
its German initials). A year later, 73-year-old Konrad Adenauer (1876–1967),
a Cologne mayor during the Weimar years, was elected West Germany's first
chancellor. Bonn – Adenauer's hometown – was the natural candidate for
the FRG's provisional capital.

East Germany reciprocated by adopting its own constitution for the German Democratic Republic (GDR; DDR by its German initials). On paper,
it guaranteed press and religious freedoms and the right to strike. In reality,
such freedoms were limited and no-one dared strike. In its chosen capital of
Berlin, a bicameral system was set up (one chamber was later abolished) and
Wilhelm Pieck became the country's first president. From the outset, however, the Socialist Unity Party led by party boss Walter Ulbricht dominated
economic, judicial and security policy.

In keeping with centralist policies, the East German states of Saxony,
Mecklenburg-Western Pomerania, Saxony-Anhalt and Thuringia were divided into 14 regional administrations and the notorious Ministry for State
Security (Ministerium für Staatssicherheit, also known as the Stasi) was created in 1950 to ensure SED loyalty (see boxed text, p39). Workers became
economically dependent on the state through the collectivisation of farms,
and nationalisation of production such as the Horch car factory in Zwickau
near Leipzig (which later produced Trabants as the GDR answer to the West
Germany's Volkswagen).

In Soviet zones the task of weeding out Nazis tended to be swift and harsh.
In the west the Allies held war-crimes trials in courtroom 600 of Nuremberg's
Court House (open to visitors today).

THE 1950S

The economic vision of Bavarian-born (from Fürth), cigar-puffing Ludwig
Erhard (1897–1977) unleashed West Germany's *Wirtschaftswunder*. Between
1951 and 1961 the economy averaged an annual growth rate of 8%.

Erhard was economic minister and later vice-chancellor in Konrad
Adenauer's government. His policies encouraged investment and boosted

German Boy: A Child In War by Wolfgang Samuel is the true tale of a German family, told through the eyes of the young Wolfgang, who fled Berlin as the Red Army approached.

A Train of Powder by Rebecca West ranks as one of the most informative books on the Nuremberg trials.

Interviews with former Stasi men in the mid-1990s forms the basis of Australian journalist Anna Funder's *Stasiland* – crammed with fresh and alternative insights into what the men of the Stasi did after it was disbanded.

1914–18	1919
WWI: Germany, Austria-Hungary and Turkey go to war against Britain, France, Italy and Russia; Germany is defeated	Monarchical rule ends; under the Weimar Republic, women are granted suffrage and basic human rights are embedded in law

GERMANY'S CHANGING BORDERS

HOLY ROMAN EMPIRE AT THE END OF THE THIRTY YEARS' WAR
(PEACE OF WESTPHALIA, 1648)

Swedish possession
Present borders

GERMAN EMPIRE 1871–1918

Present borders

GERMANY AFTER THE TREATY OF VERSAILLES (1919–38)

Present borders

GERMANY 1945–89

Present borders

economic activity to support West Germany's system of welfare-state capitalism. He helped create the European Coal and Steel Community to regulate
coal and steel production with France, Italy, West Germany and the Benelux
countries, and in 1958 West Germany joined the European Economic Community (the EU today). Adenauer's deep-rooted fear of the USSR saw him
pursue a ruthless policy of integration with the West.

In East Germany, Stalin's death in 1953 raised unfulfilled hopes of reform.
Extreme poverty and economic tensions merely persuaded the government
to set production goals higher. Smouldering discontent erupted in violence
on 17 June 1953 when 10% of GDR workers took to the streets. Soviet
troops quashed the uprising, with scores of deaths and the arrest of about
1200 people. Economic differences widened into military ones when West

1933	1939–45
Hitler becomes chancellor of Germany and creates a dictatorship	WWII: Hitler invades Poland, France and Britain declare war on Germany; Jews are murdered en masse during the Holocaust

Germany joined NATO in 1955 and East Germany moved into the fold of the Warsaw Pact, where it remained from 1956 to 1990.

THE WALL

The exodus of young, well-educated and employed East German refugees seeking a better fortune in West Germany strained the troubled GDR economy so much that the GDR government – with Soviet consent – built a wall to keep them in. The Berlin Wall, the Cold War's most potent symbol, went up between East and West Berlin on the night of 12 August 1961. The inner-German border was fenced off and mined.

Having walled in what was left of the struggling population (330,000 East Germans had fled to the west in 1953 alone, and in 1960 almost 200,000 voted with their feet), the East German government launched a new economic policy in a bid to make life better. And it did. The standard of living rose to the highest in the Eastern bloc and East Germany became its second-largest industrial power (behind the USSR).

The appointment of Erich Honecker (1912–94) in 1971 opened the way for *rapprochement* with the West and enhanced international acceptance of the GDR. Honecker fell in line with Soviet policies (replacing reunification clauses in the East German constitution with a declaration of irrevocable alliance to the USSR in 1974), but his economic policies did promote a powerful economy until stagnation took root in the late 1980s.

A Concrete Curtain: The Life & Death of the Berlin Wall is a stunning and informative online presentation of the Wall by the Deutsches Historisches Museum (German History Museum) in Berlin. See www.wall-berlin.org.

STASI SECRETS

The Ministry of State Security, commonly called the Stasi, was based on the Soviet KGB and served as the 'shield and sword' of the SED. Almost a state within the state, it boasted an astonishing spy network of about 90,000 full-time employees and 180,000 *inoffizielle Mitarbeiter* (unofficial co-workers) by 1989. Since 1990, only 250 Stasi agents have been prosecuted and since the 10-year limit ended in 2000, future trials are unlikely.

When it came to tracking down dissidents, there were no limits. One unusual collection of files found in its Berlin archive kept a record of dissidents' body odour. Some dissidents who had been hauled in for interrogation were made to deliver an odour sample, usually taken with a cotton wool pad from the unfortunate victim's crotch. The sample was then stored in an hermetic glass jar for later use if a dissident suddenly disappeared. To track down a missing dissident by odour, Stasi sniffer dogs were employed. These specially trained groin-sniffing curs were euphemistically known as 'smell differentiation dogs'.

What happened to the dogs after the Stasi was disbanded is unclear. What happened to the six million files the Stasi accumulated in its lifetime is a greater cause for concern. In January 1990, protestors stormed the Stasi headquarters in Berlin (today a museum, memorial and re-search centre – see p185 for details), demanding to see the files. Since then, the controversial records have been assessed and safeguarded by a Berlin-based public body. In mid-2000, 1000-odd information-packed CDs, removed by the US Central Intelligence Agency's (CIA's) Operation Rose-wood immediately after the fall of the Wall in 1989, were returned to Germany. A second batch of CIA files (apparently acquired by the CIA from a Russian KGB officer in 1992) were handed over in July 2003. The files, for the first time, matched code names with real names. Some of those with an *inoffizieller Mitarbeiter* file are fully fledged informants; others are 'contact' people who either knew they were giving information to someone from the Stasi or were unfortunate enough to be pumped of information without knowing it.

1945	1948
Hitler kills himself in a Berlin bunker while a defeated Germany surrenders; Germany is split into Allied- and Soviet-occupied zones	Allied-occupied West Germany becomes the FRG; Soviet-occupied East Germany becomes the GDR

ON THE WESTERN SIDE

View B&W photographs – including one of Walter Ulbricht announcing there 'would be no wall' and the subsequent graffiti-clad Wall – and map out your own Wall tour at www.the-berlin-wall.de.

Meanwhile, West Germany was still in the aged but firm hands of Konrad Adenauer, whose economics minister, Ludwig Erhard, once the Father of the Economic Miracle, was now importing foreign workers. By doing this he was making a post-hoc name for himself as the father of a multi-ethnic German society. About 2.3 million *Gastarbeiter* (guest workers) came to West Germany until the early 1970s, mainly from Italy, Spain, Turkey, Portugal, Morocco and former Yugoslavia, injecting new life into a host German culture that was slowly stirring after the mind-numbing strictures of the Nazi years. While Ludwig Erhard's guest workers arrived from one direction, young Germans who had been children under the Nazis now rode their imported Vespa motorcycles to Italy on holiday to bring home a piece of Europe for themselves.

In 1963 Adenauer was ousted by Ludwig Erhard, by then also his vice-chancellor, but in 1966 a fluctuating economy was biting deeply into Erhard's credibility, and Germany's first grand coalition government of Christian Democrats (CDU/CSU) and SPD took office, with Kurt Georg Kiesinger (CDU; 1904–88) as chancellor and Willi Brandt (SPD; 1913–92) as vice-chancellor. The absence of parliamentary opposition fuelled radical demands by the student movement for social reform.

Berlin and the Wall by Ann Tusa is a saga about the events, trials and triumphs of the Cold War, the building of the Wall and its effects on the people and the city of Berlin.

The turning point came in 1969 when the SPD formed a new government with the Free Democratic Party (FDP) under Willy Brandt. The Lübeck-born, 1971 Nobel Peace Prize winner spent the Hitler years working in exile as a journalist in Scandinavia, where he was stripped of his citizenship for anti-Nazi writings. Normalising relations with East Germany (his East-friendly policy was known as *Ostpolitik*) was his priority and in December 1972 the Basic Treaty was signed, paving the way for both to join the UN in 1973. The treaty guaranteed sovereignty in international and domestic affairs (but fudged formal recognition since it was precluded by the West German constitution).

Brandt was replaced by Helmut Schmidt (b 1918) in 1974 after a scandal (one of Brandt's close advisers turned out to be a Stasi spy). The 1970s saw antinuclear and green issues move onto the agenda, opposed by Schmidt and ultimately leading to the election of Greens party representatives to the Bonn parliament in 1979. In 1974 West Germany joined the G8 group of industrial nations. But the 1970s were also a time of terrorism in Germany, and several prominent business and political figures were assassinated by the anticapitalist Red Army Faction.

Brandt's vision of East–West cordiality was borne out by Chancellor Helmut Kohl (b 1930) who, with his conservative coalition government from 1982, groomed relations between East and West while dismantling parts of the welfare state at home. In the West German capital in 1987, Kohl received East German counterpart Erich Honecker with full state honours.

REUNIFICATION

Hearts and minds in Eastern Europe had long been restless for change, but German reunification came as a surprise to the world and ushered in a new and exciting era.

The so-called *Wende* ('change', ie the fall of communism) in Germany and reunification came about perhaps in the most German of ways: a gradual development that culminated in a big bang. Reminiscent of the situation in Berlin in the 1950s, East Germans began leaving their country in droves. They

1972

Social Democrat chancellor Willy Brandt's *Ostpolitik* normalises relations between the East and West; both countries join the UN

fled not across a no-man's-land of concrete, weeds and death strips between
East and West this time but through an open border between Hungary and
Austria. The SED was helpless to stop the flow of people wanting to leave,
some of whom sought refuge in the West German embassy in Prague. Around
the same time, East Germans took to the streets in Monday demonstrations
following services in Leipzig's Nikolaikirche and other churches in East Germany, safe in the knowledge that the Church supported their demands for
improved human rights.

Something had to give, and it did. With the demonstrations spreading and
escalating into violence, Erich Honecker accepted the inevitable, relinquishing
his position to Egon Krenz (b 1937). And then all hell broke loose: on the fateful
night of 9 November, 1989, party functionary Günter Schabowsky informed
GDR citizens they could travel directly to the West. Tens of thousands of East
Germans jubilantly rushed through border points in Berlin and elsewhere in
the country, bringing to an end the long, chilly phase of German division.

The unified Germany of today with 16 unified states (five of which are in
eastern Germany and called the 'new states') was hammered out after volatile
political debate at home and a series of treaties to end post-WWII occupation zones. The days of occupation by the four powers were now consigned
to the past. Berlin acquired the status it has today of a separate city-state, and
following reunification on 3 October, 1990 it was restored to the capital of
Germany.

The single-most dominant figure throughout reunification and the 1990s
was Helmut Kohl, whose CDU/CSU and FDP coalition was re-elected to office
in December 1990 in Germany's first postreunification election.

Under Kohl's leadership, East German assets were privatised; oversubsidised
state industries were radically trimmed back, sold or wound up completely;
and infrastructure was modernised (and in some cases over-invested in) to
create a unification boom that saw eastern Germany grow by up to 10% each
year until 1995. Growth slowed dramatically from the mid-1990s, however,
creating an eastern Germany that consisted of unification winners and losers.
Those who had jobs did well, but unemployment was high and the lack of opportunities in regions such as the eastern Harz Mountains or in cities such as
Magdeburg and Halle (both in Saxony-Anhalt) are still causing many young
eastern Germans to try their luck in western Germany or in boomtowns such
as Leipzig in Saxony. Berlin, although economically shaky – it has only one
company listed on the German Deutscher Aktien Index (DAX; German stock
index) – is the exception. Many public servants have since relocated there
from Bonn to staff the ministries, and young people from all over Germany
are attracted by its vibrant cultural scene.

Helmut Kohl also sought to bring former East German functionaries to
justice, notably Erich Honecker, who fled after he resigned and lived an ailing
and nomadic existence that culminated in his death in Chile in 1994. His court
case had by then been abandoned due to his ill health.

The unification legacy of Helmut Kohl is indisputable. His involvement
in a party slush fund scandal in the late 1990s, however, almost financially
ruined his own party and resulted in the CDU party stripping him of his
position as lifelong honorary chairman. In 1998, a coalition of the SPD and
Bündnis 90/Die Grünen (Alliance 90/Green parties) defeated the CDU/CSU
and FDP coalition.

After the Wall by Marc Fisher is an account of German society, with emphasis on life after the *Wende* (fall of communism). Fisher was bureau chief for the *Washington Post* in Bonn and presents some perceptive social insights.

Behind-the-scene footage, interviews, an account of the Wall's fall and shots of the 2500-brick wall rebuilt during the show is included on *The Wall: Live in Berlin*, the DVD of Pink Floyd's electrifying concert in Berlin in 1990.

1982	1989
A conservative coalition government is formed in West Germany under Christian Democrat Helmut Kohl	Hungary opens its border with Austria and East Germans are al-lowed to travel to the West – prompting the fall of the Berlin Wall

THE NEW MILLENNIUM

The election win in 1998 was a milestone for the SPD. For Germany's Greens, however, victory was historic: it was the first time an environmentalist party had governed nationally – in Germany or elsewhere in the world.

Two figures dominated German politics, and their own parties, during the 'red-green' era from 1998–2005: Chancellor Gerhard Schröder (b 1945) and the Greens party vice-chancellor and foreign minister Joschka Fischer. During this era, Germany faced the question of how much it could modernise, particularly in the areas of foreign policy, the social market economy, energy, immigration and gay rights. In foreign policy, it became more independent, deploying troops abroad (under a UN mandate) for the first time since 1945 when Kosovo erupted in violence. Germany also sent troops to Afghanistan in 2001 and currently plays a pivotal role in trying to rebuild that country. However, the government, backed by support from an overwhelming majority of Germans, didn't commit troops to the second Iraq war and had an abysmal relationship with the USA. Possibly because of this, Germany's efforts to become a permanent member of the UN Security Council had to be abandoned.

Not surprisingly, considering the Greens party participation in the government, progress was strong on environmental issues. An agreement was struck to switch off Germany's last nuclear reactor by about 2020. Work on modernising the economy and welfare structures, which also needed cross-party support to pass the upper house hurdle, was slow and often didn't go far enough. This included a series of labour market reforms which later formed part of an Agenda 2010 package, supported by all parties after much horse trading.

Keep on top of German politics with www .germany-info.org.

Germany is a constitutional democracy with a president and bicameral system based on the *Bundestag* (popularly elected lower house of 598 members) and the *Bundesrat* (upper house of delegates nominated by 16 states).

THE COLOUR MATCHING 'GREEN'

Love them or hate them, the Greens party has changed the face of German politics since the mid-1970s, when the party first emerged from the left-wing environmentalist and peace movements. Two figures that capture the spirit of the party best are Franco-German Daniel Cohn-Bendit (b 1945) and former German foreign minister, Joschka Fischer (b 1948).

Cohn-Bendit was a leader in France's student uprising in 1968 (the French government later tossed him out) and is co-president of the Greens party's European party faction. He's still very much a grass-roots type of Green, and you often see him on the street in Frankfurt's Bockenheim district – occasionally being hailed from across the street by a friendly newspaper seller, or being given an earful by a solid Hesse hausfrau at a newspaper stand. Joschka Fischer, one-time foreign minister, taxi driver and son of a butcher (German ancestry, but from Hungary) is notorious for his time as a member of a *Putzgruppe* (clean-up mob) which battled it out with police in squatter clashes in Frankfurt's Westend. Ironically, the elegant suburb of today owes its existence to the rebel squatters who fought tooth and nail to stop the bulldozers in the 1970s. Fischer is alleged to have punched a policeman (in an odd twist of fate, the policeman's surname name was Marx) in one violent clash. After a stint as Germany's highly popular foreign minister from 1998 to 2005, Fischer – five times married and, witty tongues might quip, the only Greens politician to practice his party's principle of leadership rotation – has now retired from parliament.

Given the politics of heavyweights such as Fischer and Cohn-Bendit, 'red' would seem the preferred colour of the Greens. Also, although it has yet to join forces with conservative parties at state or federal level, the Greens are no strangers to coalitions with 'black' (conservative) parties in city governments. It remains a hot issue, though.

1990	1998
Berlin becomes capital of the new Germany; Kohl's government charts a rigorous course towards East–West economic integration	A SPD and Bündnis 90/Die Grünen coalition government is formed; Lonely Planet publishes its first guide to Germany

During the early 2000s, Germany's economic motor, the (often family-owned) medium-sized companies, successfully trimmed and adapted to new times by replacing their ageing patriarchs with highly skilled young managers. Always one of the world's largest exporters, Germany has consistently been the largest since 2004, and overall it has the world's third-largest economy (after Japan and the US). But its domestic economy is hamstrung by low consumption and a high unemployment rate of about 11%, or about 4.5 million people.

GRAND COALITION

Economic wonders, woes and wobbles aside, by 2005 the country had ground to a political halt and people wanted change. In an act of political brinkmanship, Schröder engineered an early election and achieved what many believed was his aim: to force the creation of a grand coalition of the CDU/CSU and SPD. This turned out to be the political swansong of Germany's first SPD chancellor since the 1970s. After weeks of confusion, a deal was struck for a coalition led by Angela Merkel (b 1954), the first woman, eastern German, Russian speaker and quantum physicist in the job (see boxed text, below). The opposition is led by the FDP, which narrowly squeezed ahead of the Greens to become the third-largest party. Although a new grouping of the Partei des Demokratischen Sozialismus (PDS; Democratic Socialist Party), the successor of the East German SED, and the Arbeit und Soziale Gerechtigkeit – Die Wahlalternative (WASG; Work & Social Justice – The Election Alternative), won almost as many votes as the Greens, it remains a political pariah at federal level.

The use-by date of the grand coalition is formally five years, after which the parties are expected to go their own way. Nevertheless, the political glue holding this one together is very thin, especially when it comes to the stance on welfare and wage issues, and it would come as no surprise if Germany faces fresh elections earlier than the scheduled date of 2010.

Whatever happens, time is certain to bring new and exciting directions in the development of Germany, Western Europe's most powerful and populous country, situated at the heart of Europe.

Discover stat after stat on the Germany of a new Europe on the website of the *Statistisches Bundesamt Deutschland* (Federal Statistical Office) – www.destatis.de.

Keep abreast with current affairs at www .dw-world.de.

Two of the best websites for current reports and facts about Germany are *The Economist* magazine's country profile at www .economist.com /countries/Germany and the BBC News website (follow the Europe/ Country Profile links) at http://news.bbc.co.uk.

ANGELA MERKEL – THE ENIGMATIC CHANCELLOR

One remarkable aspect of Angela Merkel's rise to chancellor is that being a woman and an eastern German was scarcely an issue. Another is how she has managed to survive every attempt by feisty political stags in her own CDU party to depose her. There is more to Germany's chancellor than meets the eye.

Merkel was born in Hamburg in 1954 but grew up in the boondocks – in the Uckermark region (in Brandenburg, near the Polish border), where her father had a posting as a pastor in East Germany. She studied physics in Leipzig (quantum chemistry), entering politics as the GDR was falling apart. Soon she was honing her political skills in the ministries of a reunified Germany (Women and Youth was one, Environment, Natural Protection and Reactor Safety was another) under Helmut Kohl. Her breakthrough came in the late 1990s when the paws of several CDU alpha animals were suddenly found to be carrying the dirt of a party slush fund. Politically enigmatic, and not quite fitting any mould (probably how she is, rather than wants to be), Angela Merkel became chancellor in 2005 after an unusual election that saw no single party able to form a government and almost every party *except* the one with the most votes – hers – hailing itself on election night as the 'real winner'.

2005	2006
Angela Merkel becomes Germany's first woman chancellor, leading a grand coalition of major parties	Germany hosts the football World Cup amid national celebration

The Culture

THE NATIONAL PSYCHE

The German state of mind is always a favourite for speculation – two 20th-century wars and the memory of the Jewish Holocaust are reasons. Throw in the chilling razor's edge of Cold War division, a modern juggernaut economy that draws half of Europe in its wake and pumps more goods into the world economy than any other, and a crucial geographical location at the crossroads of Europe and this fascination becomes understandable.

Often, though, it pays to ignore the stereotypes, jingoism and those media military headlines at home – and maybe even forgive Germans for the systematic way they clog up a football field or conduct jagged discussion. Sometimes it helps to see the country in its regional nuances. Germany was very slow to become a nation, so if you look closely you will begin to notice many different local cultures within the one set of borders. You will also find it one of Europe's most multicultural countries (p49), with Turkish, Greek, Italian, Russian and Balkan influences.

Around 15 million people today live in a part of Germany where until 1989 travel was restricted, the state was almighty, and life was secure – but also strongly regulated – from the cradle to the grave. Not surprisingly, therefore, many eastern Germans are still coming to terms with a more competitive unified Germany.

The east is still losing people hand over fist. Take the eastern German state of Saxony-Anhalt, which is enduring especially rough times and currently sheds some 15,000 of its youngest, most talented people each year to western Germany. To dampen the impact, the University of Magdeburg-Stendhal began sending *Rückkehrpäckchen* (returnee packages) with knick-knacks like mouse pads, local internet resources and even local newspaper subscriptions to those who now work in cities like Munich and Stuttgart. The idea is to invest in the future by keeping the home fires burning. It's a winning battle, because eastern Germans like their region even if they have to leave it for a while. Although there's a thriving industry surrounding nostalgia for typical

The German embassy in Washington DC provides useful cultural insights online at www.germany-info.org.

Life after reunification (unemployment, racial violence etc) in the Thuringian small town of Altenburg is the contemporary focus of Ingo Schulze's *Simple Storys* (Simple Stories; 2001), a debut novel that instantly credited the author as one of Germany's best new writers.

OSTALGIE

Who would want to go back to East German times? Well, very few people, although there was more to the country than being a 'satellite of the Evil Empire', as 1980s Cold War warriors would portray it.

The opening lines of director Leander Haussmann's film *Sonnenallee* (1999) are revealing: 'Once upon a time there was a land, and I lived there, and if I am asked how it was, I say it was the best time of my life – because I was young and in love.' Another film, the smash hit *Goodbye Lenin!* (2003), looked at the GDR (German Democratic Republic, the former East Germany) with humour and pathos. It also gave the Ostalgie craze – from *Ost* (East) and *Nostalgie* (nostalgia) – the kick-start it needed to become a permanent cultural fixture in Germany.

Ostalgie is hip. These days dour, grinning Erich Honecker doubles in trademark specs bring parties to life; GDR Club Cola is 'cool'; an otherwise inconspicuous cucumber – *Spreewaldgurken* – is elevated to the status of heraldic symbol. Polished Trabants turn fashionable young heads on cobblestone streets; the cheesy East German *Ampelmännchen* – the little green man that helped East German pedestrians cross the road – is cherished like a rare species of desert lizard. It's all part of an Ostalgie movement that won't die. For a taste of it, tune into GDR music at www.musik-der-ddr.de, check out the online dictionary www.ddr-woerterbuch.de, or have a chuckle at the GDR jokes at www.ddr-witz.de.

GDR (German Democratic Republic, the former East Germany) products, few people long for a return to those days, and no-one regrets the loss of travel restrictions (see opposite).

Germans as a whole fall within the mental topography of northern Europe and are sometimes described as culturally 'low context'. That means, as opposed to the French or Italians, Germans like to pack what they mean right into the words they use rather than hint or suggest. Facing each other squarely in conversation, firm handshakes, and a hug or a kiss on the cheek among friends are also par for the course.

Most Germans look fondly upon the flourishing tradition of the apprentice carpenters who travel throughout Germany and Europe on *Wanderschaft* (wanderings) to acquire foreign skills, or the traditionally attired chimney sweeps in towns and villages dressed in pitch-black suits and top hats. Even an otherwise ordinary young Bavarian from, say, the financial controlling department of a Deutscher Aktien Index (DAX; German stock index) 30 company might don the Dirndl (traditional Bavarian skirt and blouse) around München Bierfest time and swill like a hearty, rollicking peasant. On Monday she'll be soberly back at the desk crunching the numbers like it was all just good fun – which it was, of course.

For all this popular tradition, Germans are not prudish. Nude bathing on beaches and mixed saunas (naked) are both commonplace, although many women prefer single-sex saunas (usually on a particular day). Wearing your swimming suit or covering yourself with a towel in the sauna is definitely not the done thing.

LIFESTYLE

The German household fits into the mould of households in other Western European countries. A close look, however, reveals some distinctly German quirks, whether that be a compulsion for sorting and recycling rubbish, a love of filter coffee and fizzy mineral water, or perhaps even an abhorrence of anything (but especially eggs) prepared in a frying pan before noon.

Tradition is valued, so in this household, Grandma's clock might grind and chime the morning hours somewhere in the room, although these

Flirting, fashion, fun, as well as everything else you need to gen up on culturally to study and live in Germany is on the Net at www.campus -germany.de.

Tune into current affairs in English with international German broadcaster Deutsche Welle at www.dw -world.de.

WHEN NAKED VEGETARIANS PUMP IRON

The idea of strapping young Germans frolicking unselfconsciously naked in the healthy outdoors is not new. A German *Körperkultur* (physical culture) first took shape in the late 19th century to remedy industrial society's so-called 'physical degeneration'. Out of this, Germany's modern *Freikörper* (naturist) movement was born.

The early movement was something of a right-wing, anti-Semitic animal, whose puritanical members were scorned by some outsiders as 'the lemonade bourgeoisie'. Achieving total beauty was the name of the game. Anathema to the movement, for example, was someone with a lascivious 'big-city lifestyle' that included smoking, fornicating, eating meat, drinking, and wearing clothes made of synthetic fibres, or anyone with predilections for artificial light. Early naturism also sprouted Germany's first vegetarian *Reform* restaurants and shops.

The most interesting characters to develop out of this odd era were bodybuilders – predominantly vegetarian and naturist but internationalist in spirit. Some achieved fame abroad under pseudonyms. Others were immortalised in Germany by sculptors, who employed them as models for their works.

Famous pioneers of the movement in Germany include Kaliningrad-born Eugene Sandow (1876–1925) who died trying to pull a car out of a ditch; Berlin-born Hans Ungar (1878–1970), who became famous under the pseudonym Lionel Strongfort; and Theodor Siebert (1866–1961), from Alsleben, near Halle, in eastern Germany.

days Grandma herself contemplatively sucks on her false teeth (which she might have had done cheaply in Poland) in an old-age home or discovers the benefits of having a voluble Romanian aged-carer in her own home. A TV will sit squarely in the living room and a computer somewhere else in the house (about 50% of households have one); maybe this is one of the 33% of households that have internet access. Eight in 10 Germans own a bike, and a car is also likely to be parked nearby, embodying the German belief that true freedom comes on four wheels and is best expressed tearing along a ribbon of autobahn at 200km/h or more while (illegally) talking on a mobile phone.

When it comes to hammering nails in coffins, about one-third of Germans are regular smokers.

With such high unemployment and many economically depressed regions in eastern Germany, there are large differences in the standard of living among Germans. A 50-something male working in manufacturing or insurance would earn on average about €3182 per month, but about 40% of that would disappear in tax and social security deductions; if the woman of the house also works – which could be difficult if the children are preschool or at half-day school – she might earn €2539. In eastern Germany, both might be on about €2300 per month.

The birth rate is low (1.34 children per woman), on par with Italy and Spain. On the face of it, though, the traditional nuclear family is still the most common ballistic model in Germany: 63% of children grow up with married parents and at least one sibling. But there's a big difference between eastern and western Germany. While 66% of children in western Germany have this upbringing, only 45% of eastern German kids do. People everywhere are marrying later, with men and women tying the knot at the average age of 32 and 29 respectively.

Abortion is illegal (except when a medical or criminal indication exists), but it is unpunishable if carried out within 12 weeks of conception and after compulsory counselling. Rape within marriage is punishable. Same-sex marriage (in the form of legally recognised same-sex partnerships) has been possible since 2001. Gays and lesbians walk with ease in most cities, especially Berlin, Hamburg, Cologne and Frankfurt-am-Main, although homosexuals do encounter discrimination in certain eastern German areas.

German school hours (from 8am to 1pm) and the under-funding of childcare make combining career and children difficult for German women. The plus side is that parents enjoy equal rights for maternity and paternity leave, and everyone has the right to work part-time.

On the whole, the number of women employed has increased – about 47% of the workforce is female. This is quite high for an EU country, but lower than in the USA and Scandinavia. In eastern Germany women tend to have be more of a presence on the managerial floors – one-third of upper management jobs – whereas the figure for western Germany is about one-fifth.

Most Germans have retired by the age of 63, but the government introduced changes in 2006 that increase the retirement age to 67 for those retiring in 2029. Changes are also in the pipeline to increase pension contributions among childless couples.

POPULATION

Germany is densely populated – 231 people for every square kilometre (compared with 118 per square kilometre in the expanded EU), although a far greater wedge is crammed into western Germany. The most densely populated areas are Greater Berlin, the Ruhr region, the Frankfurt-am-Main area, Wiesbaden and Mainz, and another region taking in Mannheim and

GERMAN HUMOUR

'According to a study by the Forsa-Institut one in 10 Germans has no problem with the idea that the Germans are dying out. Maybe after Germany loses the (football) match against the USA tonight it'll be one in five.'

FROM THE GERMAN CULTURE PROGRAMME *KULTURZEIT* (2006)

Women's issues are lobbied by the 52-member association Deutscher Frauenrat (German Women's Council) at www.deutscher-frau enrat.de.

The country's first gay publication, *Der Eigene*, went to press in 1906.

DOS & DON'TS

■ Germans draw a fat line between *Sie* and *du* (both meaning 'you'). Addressing an acquaintance with the formal *Sie* is a must, unless invited to do otherwise. Muttering a familiar *du* (reserved for close friends and family) to a shop assistant will only incite wrath and bad service, although *du* is often acceptable in young people–packed bars. If in doubt, use *Sie*.

■ Push firmly but politely with German bureaucracy; shouting will only slam down the shutters. Germans lower (rather than raise) their voices when mad.

■ Give your name at the start of a phone call, even when calling a hotel or restaurant to book a room or table.

Ludwigshafen. In eastern Germany, about 20% of the national population lives on 33% of the country's overall land.

Most people inhabit villages and small towns, and German cities are modest by world standards: Berlin aside (3.4 million), the biggest cities are Hamburg (1.7 million), Munich (1.3 million) and Cologne (one million).

The population in former East Germany fell below the 1906 level after reunification as easterners moved to the more lucrative west. Oddly, Berlin's postreunification population boom has been offset by the exodus of young families from the capital to the surrounding countryside. The total population figure is slipping downwards and will hit 74 million (compared with today's 82.41 million) by 2050 at its present rate.

For more on Germany's foreign population, see p49.

> After 14 days of bad weather your average German would be prepared to pay €33.45 for a sunny day, according to the weather site www .donnerwetter.de.

SPORT

Germany, always a keen sporting nation, has hosted the summer Olympics and football World Cup two times apiece; in 2006 the World Cup was very successfully hosted in 12 cities amid national fanfare and celebration.

Football

Football incites the passion of Germans everywhere and has contributed much to building Germany's self-confidence as a nation.

Germany has played in more World Cups than anyone else and has won the prestigious title three times, in 1954, 1974 and 1990. Its first victory against Hungary in Bern, Switzerland, was unexpected and miraculous for a country slumbering deeply in post-WWII depression. The 'miracle of Bern' – as the victory is called – sent national morale soaring.

West Germany won the 1974 World Cup in the home town of Munich's Franz Beckenbauer (b 1945) – dubbed 'Kaiser' and 'Emperor Franz' for his outstanding flair and elegance. Beckenbauer is the undisputed statesman of German football, a role that was strengthened during the World Cup in 2006, when he chaired the organising committee. The win in 1990 was remarkable because for the first time since 1945 Germany fielded a unified team from East and West.

> Berlin as it really is leaps off the pages of Vladimir Kaminer's highly readable and humorous short stories in *Russendisko* (Russian Disco; 2002).

> *Bundesliga* scoreboards, rankings and fixtures are online at www.german soccer.net (in English) and www.bundesliga.de (in German).

CAREFUL WITH THAT DU, DIETER!

It's definitely not a good idea to use the familiar *du* form with the police – this could land you in court. In one bizarre case, the German pop singer and music producer Dieter Bohlen was charged with offensive behaviour when he used the familiar form to a police officer after being approached about a parking offence. The judge let Bohlen off the hook because '*du*' is part of his style. Impolite, yes, offensive no, ruled the judge.

West Germany's 1954 World Cup victory provides the impetus for Sönke Wortmann's *Das Wunder von Bern* (Miracle of Bern; 2003), a family drama about a WWII prisoner of war returning to a football-crazy son he no longer recognises.

For a cracking read about football, the great football rivalry between England and Germany, and that famous match in 1966 with the controversial Wembley Goal, delve into Geoff Hurst's *1966 and all that*.

The Olympic torch was lit for the first time at the 1936 Olympics: 3000 athletes carried the flame from Olympia (Greece) to Berlin where medallists were later awarded a laurel crown and potted oak tree.

In 2005, Jürgen Klinsmann (b 1964) took over the reins as national trainer of the German team, only to relinquish the position to his assistant Joachim Löw (b 1960) after a good performance – and a sensational win against Argentina – in the World Cup. In 2006 the Dresden-born Matthias Sammer (b 1967) assumed responsibility for German football's junior talent as sport director. Sammer, whose father was a highly successful trainer of the GDR team Dynamo Dresden (for whom Matthias Sammer also played) is often traded as a candidate for national trainer. If he ever gets the post, this would be another unique achievement for the fiery Saxon, who was the last player to kick a goal for East Germany and the first East German to play in a unified German national team.

Friday-night, Saturday and Sunday games are televised live on pay-TV at sports bars all over Germany, and round-ups of the weekend matches are broadcast on the *Sportschau* on ARD (German National TV Consortium; see p50) around 6.30pm on Saturday and Sunday. Eurosport and Deutsches Sport Fernsehen (DSF; German Sports Television) also cover highlights. You can watch UEFA (Union of European Football Associations) Cup matches live on DSF, which has broadcast rights to the Cup until at least 2008.

Tennis

Tennis was a minor sport in Germany until 1985 when the unseeded 17-year-old Boris Becker (b 1967), from Leimen near Heidelberg, became Wimbledon's youngest-ever men's singles champion. Overnight every German kid aspired to be the next Boris Becker. The red-head mentor, known for his power play, went on to win five more Grand Slam titles in a career that ended in 1999.

The self-willed and erratic Becker was as entertaining off the court as he was on it. His 'affair' in a broom closet with a Russian model in a London hotel in the mid-1990s produced a daughter and newspaper headlines that claimed 'sperm theft', while his tragic – and not surprising given the broom-closet drama – marital breakdown culminated in a humiliating televised courtroom drama. Similarly, the marriage of his fiercest German opponent during the early 1990s and fellow Wimbledon champion, Michael Stich (b 1968), also sailed onto acrimonious rocks and sank in a public blaze. Becker and Stich were hard acts to follow, and potential men's singles successors to the German tennis crown have so far proved to have feet of clay.

Only the lingering, warm after-glow of Mannheim-born Steffi Graf (b 1969) currently lights the tennis darkness. Graf is among the few women to win all four Grand Slam events in one year, and in 1988 – after also winning gold in Seoul at the Olympic Games – she became the only player ever to win the Golden Slam. Germans had always secretly hoped for a Boris–Steffi marriage that might have produced a Teutonic tennis wunderkind. For better or worse, it didn't happen, but Steffi Graf did marry Becker's arch-rival from the USA, Andre Agassi, and unlike everyone else, seems to be living happily ever after.

Hamburg hosts the men's German Open tournament each May; women play in Berlin in June.

Other Sports

Though still a minor sport in Germany, basketball is gaining in popularity, boosted by the star US National Basketball Association (NBA) player – and captain of the Dallas Mavericks – Würzburg-born Dirk Nowitzki (b 1978), who is arguably Europe's finest player at the moment.

Cycling has boomed since Rostok-born Jan Ullrich (b 1973) became the first German to win the Tour de France in 1997. In 2006 a shadow was cast on Ullrich's career after he was allegedly implicated in a doping ring. Ullrich subsequently withdrew from the Tour de France and has since fought to salvage his reputation – and his undeniable achievements. Erik Zabel (b 1970), who comes from Berlin's Prenzberg district, achieved the remarkable by winning the green tricot six years in a row from 1996 to 2001 in the Tour de France.

With no less than seven World Champion titles and more than 50 Grand Prix wins, Michael Schumacher (b 1969) was the most successful Formula One racing driver ever to have taken to the circuit. After successive wins in 1994 and 1995 he also became the youngest double Formula One World Champion. Schumacher announced his retirement in 2006. Michael's younger brother Ralf (b 1975) made his Formula One debut in 1997 and has since notched up six big wins in his career. In Germany Formula One races are held at the Hockenheim circuit, which has been host to the German Grand Prix since 1977, and the European Grand Prix rips around Nürburgring.

The German team had good cause to celebrate at the Winter Olympics in Turin in 2006, winning 29 medals, including 11 gold. Five of these gold medals were in biathlon events, where Kati Wilhelm (b 1976) – like many of the winter sports stars, she comes from Oberhof in Thuringia – and Sven Fischer (b 1971) hobbled and shot their way through living rooms to the delight of millions of German fans.

MULTICULTURALISM

Germany would seem more a country of emigrants than immigrants. Not so: it has always attracted immigrants, be it French Huguenots escaping religious persecution (about 30% of Berlin's population in 1700 was Huguenot), 19th-century Polish miners who settled in the Ruhr region, post-WWII asylum seekers, or foreign *Gastarbeiter* (guest workers) imported during the 1950s and 1960s to resolve labour shortages. After reunification, the foreign population soared (from 4.5 million in the 1980s to 7.3 million in 2002) as emigrants from the collapsed USSR and then war-ravaged former Yugoslav republics sought shelter. Currently about 35,000 *Spätaussiedler* (people of German heritage, mainly from Eastern Europe and Kazakhstan) enter the country each year.

About 6.7 million foreigners (just under 9% of the population) live in Germany, almost one-third of these from EU countries and almost half from Europe. Ethnic Turks form the largest single group (1.8 million or 26%), followed by ethnic Italians and former Yugoslavians (both 8%), Greeks (5%) and Poles (4%). Ironically, over 20% of the 'foreign' population is actually German-born, reflecting poor progress on the integration of – mainly – ethnic Turks in the large cities.

Despite changes to Germany's antiquated 'blood-based' citizenship laws, patches of German society still inhabit the shadows on this question, with state political campaigns having been fought and won at the expense of foreigners, foreigners having to renounce previous citizenship before they can become German, and a recurring violence problem by extreme right-wing groups in eastern Germany directed (mainly) against foreigners – whose numbers rarely rise above a few percent of the population in towns there (see boxed text, p50).

Debate also regularly flares on the need to promote a German *Leitkultur* (lead culture), as opposed to multiculturalism; the trend to violence in schools with a high proportion of ethnic pupils (in some Berlin schools 80% of pupils are foreigners); and poor German skills among foreigners in the classroom.

Germany's most successful golfer, Bernhard Langer, is the son of a Russian prisoner of war who jumped off a Siberia-bound train and settled in Bavaria.

If you like a good 180, 360 or backside, check out the annual Monster Mastership Skateboarding World Championship and associated events at www.mastership.de.

Slavonic Sorbs live in pockets of Saxony and Brandenburg, and a small Danish minority can be found around Flensburg (Schleswig-Holstein) on the Danish border.

OF SKINHEADS & OTHER BONEHEADS

Recent media attention has focused on the rise in racially motivated incidents in Germany, which range from verbal taunts to severe physical assault. In 2005, the Federal Office for the Protection of the Constitution recorded 15,361 such episodes, including 958 violent crimes. This represents an increase of 27.5% over 2004 and a reversal of a trend that had lasted until that year. In April 2006, a German of Ethiopian descent was almost beaten to death in Potsdam and just a month later a Turkish-German politician was attacked in Berlin. In these, as in most, cases perpetrators belonged to right-wing skinhead or neo-Nazi organisations. Xenophobia seems to run especially deep in the former GDR states, whose people had little exposure to foreigners during the communist era and where chronic high unemployment fuels anger and frustration. In the most recent state elections, Brandenburg, Saxony and Mecklenburg-Western Pomerania all voted members of right-wing parties into their regional parliaments.

The spate of incidents even prompted a former government official, Uwe Karsten-Heye, to declare the eastern states a 'no-go' area for nonwhites just before the beginning of the World Cup. Heye now heads **Gesicht Zeigen!** (www.gesichtzeigen.de, in German), a nonprofit organisation striving to combat xenophobia, racism and right-wing violence. While his remarks were widely criticised as being too general and for stigmatising a large part of the country (there is some right-wing extremism in western Germany too, of course), many people welcomed his frankness and the debate it spurred. Politicians of all stripes agreed that measures need to be stepped up to reverse the trend through education, prevention and law enforcement. Stay tuned.

Die Ausgewanderten (Emigrants; 1997) by WG Sebald addresses the lost homeland of an exile in his vivid portrayal of four different journeys by Jewish emigrants – it's a good introduction to this weighty but wonderful novelist.

On the whole, Germany, whose citizens achieved the remarkable by coping with up to 500,000 former Yugoslavian refugees *each year* in the early 1990s, treats foreigners with respect, even if it still has some political catching-up to do.

MEDIA

Germany's former chancellor, Gerhard Schöder, once said that all he needed to govern the country were *Bild*, the Sunday edition of *Bild* (called *Bild am Sonntag*; BamS) and *die Glotze* (Idiot Box). If it were that easy, we'd all be doing it.

Licence fees subsidise the country's two public TV broadcasters ARD (known as the 1st channel) and ZDF (the so-called 2nd channel). Unlike Mainz-based ZDF, ARD groups together several regional public stations, which contribute to the nationwide programmes shown on the 1st channel as well as the wholly regional shows transmitted on the so-called 3rd channel. Due to the sheer choice of channels, private ownership is relatively diverse and pay TV low on impact; ProSiebenSat.1Media and the Bertelsmann AG groups have the largest stables.

The Bambi Awards – Germany's annual media awards – see national celebrities such as Düsseldorf-born supermodel Claudia Schiffer proffer statuettes of fawns to showbiz stars and celebrities.

About six million households are able to receive some form of digital TV (cable, satellite or terrestrial), but the vast majority of households are currently connected via cable, satellite receiver or terrestrial aerial.

For better or worse, it's still possible to fall asleep reading a German newspaper, which masters the art of dry, factual reporting. Print media has a strong regional bias, and overt backing for particular political parties by newspapers is rarely at the expense of the hard facts. The most influential newspaper is *Bild*, whose circulation exceeds four million. Axel Springer and Bertelsmann are the largest publishers. Both the press and broadcasters are independent and free of censorship.

For an overview of media ownership in Germany, go to the English pages of www.kek-online.de.

RELIGION

The constitution guarantees religious freedom, the main religions being Catholicism and Protestantism, each with about 26 million adherents (around one-third of the country's total population each). Religion has a stronger footing in western Germany, and especially Catholic Bavaria.

Unlike the Jewish community, which has grown since the early 1990s due to immigration from the former Soviet Union, the Catholic and Protestant churches are losing worshippers. This is attributed partly to the obligatory church tax (about 9% of income) paid by those belonging to a recognised denomination. Most German Protestants are Lutheran, headed by the Evangelische Kirche (Protestant Church), an official grouping of a couple of dozen Lutheran churches with Hanover headquarters. Lutherans don't deem Methodists, Jehovah's Witnesses or other non-Catholic Christians to be proper Protestants.

In 2005, for the first time in almost five centuries, a German became pope. German Catholics responded with mixed feelings to the election of Joseph Alois Ratzinger (b 1927), who took the name Benedict XVI; some had hoped for a more progressive successor to John Paul II.

The head of the Jewish community's Berlin-based umbrella organisation, the Zentralrat der Juden in Deutschland (Central Council of Jews in Germany), is Charlotte Knobloch (b 1932). The largest Jewish communities are in Berlin, Frankfurt-am-Main and Munich. Countrywide, 80 or more congregations are represented by the rather conservative council (see p34).

> The German Protestant Church is online at www .ekd.de; the Catholics are at www.catholic -hierarchy.org/country /de.html; and the Central Council of Jews at www .zentralratdjuden.de (in German).

ARTS
Visual Arts
FRESCOES TO EXPRESSIONISTS

Whether it be medieval fresco work, oil-on-canvas masterpieces, eclectic Bauhaus or exciting industrial design and fashion, Germany has visual arts for all tastes and interests.

Germany's earliest fresco work dates from Carolingian times (c 800) and is in Trier's St Maximin crypt and the Stiftskirche St Georg on Reichenau Island, whereas stained-glass enthusiasts will find colourful religious motifs lighting up Augsburg and Cologne cathedrals. By the 15th century, Cologne artists were putting landscapes on religious panels, some of which are on display in Hamburg's Kunsthalle.

The heavyweight of German Renaissance art is the Nuremberg-born Albrecht Dürer (1471–1528), who was the first to grapple seriously with the Italian masters; the Alte Pinakothek (Munich) has several famous works of Dürer, and his house is today a museum in Nuremberg. In Wittenberg, Dürer influenced Franconian-born court painter Lucas Cranach the Elder (1472–1553) whose Apollo und Diana in Waldiger Landschaft (Apollo and Diana in a Forest Landscape; 1530) hangs in Berlin's Gemäldegalerie (Picture Gallery).

Two centuries later, sculpture became integrated into Germany's buildings and gardens, creating the inspiration for Andreas Schlüter's (1660–1714) imposing Reiterdenkmal des Grossen Kurfürsten (Horseman's Monument of the Great Elector) in front of Berlin's Schloss Charlottenburg. The four-horse chariot with Victoria on Berlin's Brandenburg Gate is the work of Germany's leading neoclassical sculptor, Johann Gottfried Schadow (1764–1850).

During the baroque period (from the 17th to mid-18th century), palace walls were frescoed to create the illusion of generous space. Balthasar Neumann's (1687–1753) grand staircase in Würzburg Residenz is arguably the finest example.

In the mid-18th century, neoclassicism ushered back in the human figure and an emphasis on Roman and Greek mythology. Hesse-born Johann Heinrich Tischbein (1751–1829) painted Goethe at this time in a classical landscape surrounded by antique objects. View Goethe in der Campagna (1787) in Frankfurt-am-Main's Städelsches Kunstinstitut (Städel Art Institute).

> Old Catholics (www .alt-katholisch.de), of which there are 20,000 in Germany today, rejected papal infallibility to break away from the Catholic Church in 1871. Celibacy is not an issue and the first female priests were ordained in 1996.

> Frankfurt has hosted the world's largest literary marketplace, the international book fair (www.frankfurt-book -fair.com), since 1949 when centuries-old East German host, Leipzig, had its door slammed shut by Soviet occupiers.

Religious themes, occasionally mystic, dominated 19th-century Romanticism. Goethe hated the works of Caspar David Friedrich (1774–1840), indelicately suggesting they ought to be 'smashed against the table'. A room is dedicated to Friedrich's works in Hamburg's Kunsthalle.

Also in the exciting collection of Hamburg's Kunsthalle are works by the founder of the German Romantic movement, Philipp Otto Runge (1777–1810), as well as intensely religious works by the Nazarener (Nazareths). The museum also showcases some later realistic works of Cologne-born Wilhelm Leibl (1844–1900) who specialised in painting Bavarian folk.

German impressionists are well represented in the Moderne Galerie of Saarbrücken's Saarland Museum. Key exponents of the late-19th-century movement include Max Liebermann (1847–1935), often slammed as 'ugly' and 'socialist'; Fritz von Uhde (1848–1911); and Lovis Corinth (1858–1925) whose later work, *Die Kindheit des Zeus* (Childhood of Zeus; 1905) – a richly coloured frolic in nature with intoxicated, grotesque elements – is housed in Bremen's Kunsthalle.

The Dresden art scene spawned Die Brücke (The Bridge) in 1905. Its expressionist members Ernst Kirchner (1880–1936), Erich Heckel (1883–1971) and Karl Schmidt-Rottluff (1884–1976) employed primitivist and cubist elements, but Germany's best expressionist painter, the North Frisian Emil Nolde (1867–1956), was an artistic lone wolf who only fleetingly belonged to Die Brücke and was forbidden from working by the Nazis in 1941. His famous *Bauernhof* (1910) is housed in Museumsberg Flensburg.

Munich's Städtische Galerie im Lenbachhaus showcases a second group of expressionists, Munich-based Der Blaue Reiter (Blue Rider), centred on Wassily Kandinsky (1866–1944), Gabrielle Münter (1877–1962), Paul Klee (1879–1940) and Franz Marc (1880–1916).

BETWEEN THE WARS

One of Germany's most influential visual artists is Käthe Kollwitz (1867–1945), who travelled through naturalism and expressionism to arrive at agitprop and socialist realism. Complete series of her *Ein Weberaufstand* (A Weavers' Revolt; 1897) etchings and lithography based on a play by Gerhart Hauptmann (1862–1946), as well as other works, are showcased in Käthe Kollwitz museums in Berlin and Cologne.

Berlin's Bauhaus Archive/Museum of Design and Weimar's Bauhaus-Museum have fascinating exhibits on the Bauhaus movement, which continues to shape art and design. Works by Kandinsky, Hungarian László Moholy-Nagy (1895–1946), Klee and the sculptor Gerhard Marcks (1889–1981) are housed in the Berlin venue. See p212 for more on Bauhaus. Marcks' most visible work is *Die Bremer Stadtmusikanten* (Town Musicians of Bremen; see p644).

After a creative surge in the 1920s, the big chill of Nazi conformity sent Germany into artistic deep freeze in the 1930s and 1940s. In the capital, many artists were classified as 'degenerate' (opposite) and forced into exile – where a creative explosion abroad took place especially among the Bauhaus movement protagonists who settled in the USA. Other artists were murdered, retreated from public life or tossed in art altogether. In Quedlinburg a fine collection of works by Lyonel Feininger (1871–1956) survives thanks to a local citizen who hid them from the Nazis (see p245).

MODERN & CONTEMPORARY

Post-1945 revived the creative influence of expressionists such as Nolde, Schmidt-Rottluff and Kandinsky; and a new abstract expressionism took root in the work of Stuttgart's Willi Baumeister (1889–1955) and Ernst-Wilhelm Nay (1902–68) in Berlin.

Günter Grass' *tour de force, Die Blechtrommel* (Tin Drum; 1959), humorously traces recent German history – including Nazism – through the eyes of Oskar, a child who refuses to grow up. *Ein weites Feld* (Too Far Afield; 1992) addresses 'unification without unity' after the Wall falls.

In the 1950s and 1960s, Düsseldorf-based Gruppe Zero (Group Zero) plugged into Bauhaus, using light and space as a creative basis. The 'light ballets' of Otto Piene (b 1928), relying on projection techniques, were among the best known.

Arguably Germany's most exciting contemporary painter and sculptor is Anselm Kiefer (b 1945), some of whose works are in Berlin's (confusingly named) Hamburger Bahnhof – Museum für Gegenwart. His monumental *Census* (1967) consists of massive lead folios arranged on shelves as a protest against a 1967 census in Germany; another, the haunting *Mohn und Gedächtnis* (Poppy and Memory; 1989), is a large lead aircraft with three small glass windows in the side filled with poppy seeds.

The same Berlin museum displays works by Düsseldorf's Joseph Beuys (1921–86). Wherever Beuys laid his trademark hat, controversy erupted. *Strassenbahnhaltestelle* (Tram Stop; 1976) consists of rusty iron tram lines and a cannon with a head poking out of it. Beuys says it was inspired by a childhood experience, but bear in mind that he was a radio operator in a fighter plane shot down over Crimea during WWII. He claims to have been nursed back to health by local Tartars, who covered him in tallow and wrapped him in felt. The largest collections of his work are in Darmstadt's Hessisches Landesmuseum (p526; including his revealing *Stuhl mit Fett –* Chair with Fat; 1964) and in Schloss Moyland (p549), near Kalkar in North Rhine-Westphalia.

Anselm Kiefer is now working in stage design, while another contemporary, action-artist HA Schult (b 1939) has been busy travelling the world with his sculptures of people created from rubbish. His *Trash People* – 1000 life-sized figures – set out from Xanten in Germany more than a decade ago and has since visited about a dozen world locations. In April 2006 the famous 1000 arrived in Cologne and were complemented by Galaxy Man – made from Ford Galaxy car parts. Their final stations will be New York and Antarctica in 2007.

Bavarian Florian Thomas (b 1966) and Dresden-born Eberhard Havekost (b 1967) are two influential artists whose works are now in the Museum Frieder Burda in Baden Baden. Thomas' brand of photorealism owes much to the German contemporary icons Gerhard Richter (b 1932) and Sigmar Polke (b 1941). His *Lieber Onkel Dieter!* (Dear Uncle Dieter!) and *Arusha* are highlights. Eberhard Havekost uses computer reworked images as the basis for some of his photorealist works – often playing dramatically with light and shadow. Works by Sorb sculptor and painter Georg Baselitz (b 1938) are other indigenous highlights of the Museum Frieder Burda. Baselitz was tossed out of art school in the GDR for his artistic provocations, only

'Rubble in itself is the future. Because everything that is, passes.'
ANSELM KIEFER

'We produce rubbish, we're born of rubbish and return to rubbish'
HA SCHULT

DEGENERATE ART

Abstract expressionism, surrealism and Dadaism – 'Jewish subversion' and 'artistic bolshevism' in Nazi eyes – were definitely not Hitler's favourite movements. In fact by 1937, such forms of expression fell under the axe of *Entartung* (degeneracy), a German biological term borrowed by the Nazis to describe virtually all modern movements. The same year, paintings by Klee, Beckmann, Dix and others – all supposedly spawned by the madness of 'degenerates' – were exhibited in Munich and promptly defaced in protest. Ironically, the exhibition drew a daily scornful yet curious crowd of 20,000-odd.

A year later, a law was passed allowing for the forced removal of degenerate works from private collections. While many art collectors saved their prized works from Nazi hands, the fate of many other artists' works was less fortunate. Many works were sold abroad to rake in foreign currency and in 1939 about 4000 paintings were publicly burned in Berlin.

to have West German authorities confiscate works from his first exhibition there. Take a look at his *Die Grosse Nacht im Eimer* (Big Night Down the Drain), depicting a masturbating figure, and you can see – if not quite understand – why.

Thomas Bayrle (b 1937) is another name you will come across in German museums of contemporary art. Born in Berlin, he now lives in Frankfurt-am-Main and teaches at the Städel Art Institute. In 2006 the Museum fü Moderne Kunst in Frankfurt exhibited his installations entitled *40 Years of Chinese Rock 'n' Roll*. These are movable wood constructions depicting mass behaviour. One has an image of Mao Zedong with hundreds of gymnasts in the background, in others people are brushing their teeth or swilling beer.

The Neue Sammlung permanent collections of the double-banger Neues Museum in Nuremberg and Pinakothek der Moderne in Munich are not to be missed as stations on the contemporary art and design circuit; changing exhibitions have ranged from jewellery through GDR art-poster design to a retrospective of covers from the magazine *Der Spiegel*.

Contemporary photography is another area where Germany excels. Around the time Beuys waved adieu in the 1980s, photographers Andreas Gursky (b 1955) and Candida Höfer (b 1944) were honing their skills under Bernd Becher (b 1931) at Düsseldorf's Kunstakademie (Art Academy). Leipzig-born Gursky, whose work can be seen in Cologne's Museum Ludwig, encompasses superb images of architecture, landscapes and interiors, sometimes reworked digitally. Höfer's work, along with the works of other Becher students, can be found in Hamburg's Kunsthalle.

In 2003, another photographer from the Düsseldorf academy, Thomas Ruff (b 1958), provoked controversy with a series of nudes based on pornographic images he downloaded from the internet. More socially acceptable, London-based Bavarian Jürgen Teller (b 1964) is a darling of fashion photography and has shot Björk and a pregnant Kate Moss, among others.

In Leipzig, a Neue Leipziger Schule (New Leipzig School) of artists has emerged recently and achieved success at home and abroad, including painter Neo Rauch (b 1960).

For a comprehensive lowdown of Germany's contemporary art scene and events see www .art-in.de (in German).

Given Germany's rich collections, travelling the contours of visual arts might be an interesting way to organise a trip. In addition to excellent permanent collections in major museums, you'll find lots of smaller art spaces with changing exhibitions. Venues like Berlin's **Kunst-Werk** (www.kw-berlin.com) and **Galerie Eigen+Art** (www.eigen-art.com) offer a contemporary 'shock of the new'.

Berlin's **Art Forum Berlin** (www.art-forum-berlin.de) showcases video, photography, painting, sculpture, installations, graphics, and multimedia each year in September–October. For household design, the Bauhaus Museum in Weimar shows how it began and the Vitra Design Museums in Berlin (expected to open in 2007) and Weil am Rhein have other fascinating exhibits. Visual art of another variety, Berlin Fashion Week, takes place in late January and July each year, with some events usually open to the general public.

Berlin is not just the heart of a thriving art scene in Germany, in 2006 it became Europe's first City of Design as part of the Unesco Creative Cities Network – gaining recognition as a crossroads of design, architecture and the visual and performance arts.

Architecture
CAROLINGIAN TO ART NOUVEAU
Among the grand buildings of the Carolingian period, Aachen's Byzantine-inspired cathedral – built for Charlemagne from 805 – and Fulda's Michaelskirche are surviving masterpieces. A century on, Carolingian, Christian

GERMAN DESIGN TODAY

Mateo Kries heads the Vitra Design Museum in Berlin (scheduled for reopening in 2007): 'Designers leave their imprint on urban life as social actors. These are my personal favourites in German design.'

- Furniture – Konstantin Grcic, because he combines research in new technologies with original forms and smart minimalism.
- Textiles – Kostas Murkudis, because I like unpretentious clothing.
- Architecture – Realities United, because they try things out.
- Jewellery – everything that is not designed explicitly, because I want jewellery to be very personal and unique.
- Graphics – The illustrator LULU, because her illustrations look lovely and extremely cool at the same time.

(Roman) and Byzantine influences flowed together in a more proportional interior with integrated columns, reflected in the elegant Stiftskirche St Cyriakus in Gernrode (Harz Mountains) and the Romanesque cathedrals in Worms, Speyer and Mainz.

The Unesco-listed Kloster Maulbronn (1147) in Baden-Württemberg is considered the best preserved monastery of its ilk north of the Alps.

Early Gothic architecture, slow to reach Germany from its northern-French birthplace, kept many Romanesque elements, as the cathedral in Magdeburg (Saxony-Anhalt) illustrates. Later churches have purely Gothic traits – ribbed vaults, pointed arches and flying buttresses to allow greater height and larger windows, seen in Cologne's cathedral (Kölner Dom), Marburg (Elisabethkirche), Trier (Liebfrauenkirche), Freiburg (Münster) and Lübeck (Marienkirche). From the 15th century, elaborately patterned vaults and hall churches emerged. Munich's Frauenkirche and Michaelskirche are typical of this late Gothic period.

The Renaissance reached Germany around the mid-16th century, bestowing Heidelberg and other southern cities with buildings bearing ornate leaf work and columns, while in northern Germany the secular Weser Renaissance style produced the ducal palace (Schloss) in Celle (Lower Saxony).

From the early 17th century to the mid-18th century, feudal rulers ploughed their wealth into residences. In Baden-Württemberg, the residential retreat of Karlsruhe was dreamt up, while Italian architect Barelli started work on Munich's Schloss Nymphenburg. In northern Germany, buildings were less ornamental, as the work of baroque architect Johann Conrad Schlaun (1695–1773) in Münster or Dresden's treasure trove of baroque architecture demonstrates. One of the finest baroque churches, Dresden's Frauenkirche (1743), was destroyed in the 1945 fire-bombing of the city, reconstructed, and reopened in 2005. Late baroque ushered in Potsdam's rococo Schloss Sanssouci.

Berlin's Brandenburg Gate, based on a Greek design, is a brilliant showcase of neoclassicism. This late-18th-century period saw baroque folly and exuberance fly out the window – and strictly geometric columns, pediments and domes fly in. The colonnaded Altes Museum, Neue Wache and Schauspielhaus – all designed by leading architect Karl Friedrich Schinkel (1781–1841) – are other pure forms of neoclassicism still gracing the capital. In Bavaria, Leo von Klenze (1784–1864) chiselled his way through virtually every ancient civilisation, with eclectic creations such as the Glyptothek and Propyläen on Munich's Königsplatz.

For an informative and illustrated dip into Berlin architecture – past, present and future – visit the Senate Department of Urban Development at www.stadtentwicklung .berlin.de.

A wave of derivative architecture based on old styles swept through late-19th-century Germany. A German peculiarity was the so-called rainbow style, which blended Byzantine with Roman features. Renaissance revivalism found expression in Georg Adolph Demmler's (1804–86) Schloss in Schwerin, while sections of Ludwig II's fairy-tale concoction in Neuschwanstein (Bavaria) are neo-Romanesque.

Germany's iconic Reichstag building (1894) was designed by Paul Wallot (1841–1912) in the Wilhelmian (neobaroque) style; it was restored in the 1990s with a stunning glass-and-steel cupola (inspired by the original) by internationally acclaimed British architect Norman Foster. Wallots' use of steel to create a greater span and large glass surface was subsequently adopted by the early-20th-century Art Nouveau movement, which created some of the country's most impressive industrial architecture: look no further than Berlin's Wertheim bei Hertie department store.

Erich Mendelsohn and the Architecture of German Modernism by Kathleen James zooms in on Mendelsohn's expressionist buildings in Berlin and Frankfurt.

MODERN & CONTEMPORARY

No architectural movement has had greater influence on modern design than Bauhaus, which was spearheaded by the son of a Berlin architect, Walter Gropius (1883–1969). Through his founding in 1919 of the Staatliches Bauhaus – a modern architecture, art and design institute in Weimar – Bauhaus pushed the industrial forms of Art Nouveau to a functional limit and sought to unite architecture, painting, furniture design and sculpture. Critics claimed Bauhaus was too functional and impersonal, relying too heavily on cubist and constructivist forms. But any visit to the Bauhaus Building in Dessau (where the institute was based after 1925) or the nearby Meisterhäuser (Master Craftsmen's Houses), where teachers from the school (such as painters Kandinsky and Klee) lived, instantly reveals just how much the avant-garde movement pioneered modern architecture. In Berlin, the Bauhaus Archive/Museum of Design (Gropius designed the building himself in 1964) is a must-see. Also see Design for Life (p212).

The Nazis shut down the Bauhaus school in 1932 and rediscovered the pompous and monumental. One of the most successful attempts was Werner March's (1894–1976) Berlin Olympisches Stadion (Berlin Olympic Stadium; 1934) and surrounding features. Work on overhauling the ageing stadium was finished in 2004, with new roofing, restoration of original materials, and the lowering of the playing field to intensify the atmosphere.

COLLECTIVE MEMORY

Unesco's 'Memory of the World' programme safeguards the world's most precious documentary heritage. German contributions include the following:

- A unique collection of 145,000 pieces of worldwide music (excluding Western art and pop) in Berlin's Ethnologisches Museum (Museum of Ethnology), recorded between 1893 and 1952 (listed 1999; p117).

- Goethe's literary estate, stashed in the Goethe and Schiller Archives in Weimar's Stiftung Weimarer Klassik (2001).

- Beethoven's Ninth Symphony, the score of which is kept in the Alte Staatsbibliothek (Old National Library in Berlin; 2001; p106).

- The negative of the reconstructed version of Fritz Lang's silent film, *Metropolis* (1927), pieced together from a fragmented original (2001).

- The 1282-page *Gutenberg Bible* – Europe's first book to be printed with moveable type – is one of four of the original 30 to survive. Learn about the digital version at www.guten bergdigital.de (2001); the original cannot be viewed.

UNESCO WORLD HERITAGE SITES IN GERMANY

Following is a list of Germany's fabulous treasures and the years in which their Unesco status was declared:

- Aachen Dom (Cathedral; 1978; p568)
- Augustusburg and Falkenlust castles in Brühl (1984; p561)
- Bamberg (1993; p364)
- Bauhaus sites in Weimar and Dessau (1996; p262 and p212)
- Berlin's Museumsinsel (Museum Island; 1999; p107)
- Bremen Rathaus and Rolandstatue (2004; p642)
- Classical Weimar (1998; p261)
- Collegiate Church, Castle and Old Town of Quedlinburg (1994; p245)
- Cologne Dom (1996; p551)
- Dresden's Elbe Valley (2004; p174)
- Muskau Park in Bad Muskau (2004)
- Garden kingdom of Dessau-Wörlitz (2000; p215)
- Goslar Altstadt and mines of Rammelsberg (1992; p231 and p232)
- Hildesheim's Dom and St Michaeliskirche (1985; p615)
- Kloster Maulbronn (1993; p421)
- Lorsch Abbey and Altenmünster (1991; p527)
- Lübeck (1987; p683)
- Luther memorials in Eisleben and Lutherstadt Wittenberg (1996; p224 and p217)
- Messel Pit fossil site (1995; p527)
- Potsdam's parks and palaces (1990; p147)
- Regensburg (2006; p378)
- Reichenau Island (2000; p458)
- Speyer's Kaiserdom cathedral (1981; p474)
- Trier's Roman monuments, Dom and Liebfrauenkirche (1986; p497)
- Upper Germanic-Rhaetian Limes (2005; p28)
- Upper Middle Rhine Valley (2002; p483)
- Völklinger Hütte ironworks (1994; p508)
- Wartburg castle (1999; p270)
- Wieskirche, Wies' pilgrimage church (1983; p345)
- Wismar and Stralsund historic centres (2002; p719 and p722)
- Würzburg's Residence and Court Gardens (1981; p327)
- Zollverein colliery complex in Essen (2001; p573)

The monumental efforts of another political persuasion are captured attractively today in the buildings that line Berlin's (former East German) Frankfurter Allee. Yet another highlight that outlived the country that created it is the 361.5m-high TV tower (1969) on Alexanderplatz. One structure that was much less successful – and has survived history only in fragments – is that most potent symbol of the Cold War – the Berlin Wall.

Experimental design took off in the 1960s in Düsseldorf with Hubert Petschnigg's slender Thyssenhaus (1960), which inspired Tel Aviv's Eliyahu House. In the 1970s Munich was graced with its splendid tent-roofed Olympisches Stadion (1972), which today visitors can scale with a rope and snap hook or abseil down for an architectural kick of the hair-raising sort (see Visitor Service at www.olympiapark.de). In the meantime, Bayern-München football team has sailed over to the Allianz Arena, a remarkable rubber-dinghy-like translucent object that makes a fitting home for 'FC Hollywood'. A flurry of other building and roofing activity in stadiums took place in the lead up to the 2006 World Cup, including an interesting membrane roof supported by steel ropes over Frankfurt's Waldstadion in 2005.

Frank Gehry (b 1929) has left exciting imprints on German cities over the past two decades, first through the Vitra Design Museum in Weil am Rhein (1989), and later with his wacky Der Neue Zollhof (New Customs House; 1999) in Düsseldorf, the Gehry-Tower (2001) in Hanover, and the DZ Bank (1999) on Berlin's Pariser Platz.

Berlin, of course, is the locus of many of the most contemporary building projects in Germany today. On Potsdamer Platz Italian architect Renzo Piano (b 1937) designed DaimlerCity (1998) and Nuremberg-born Helmut Jahn (b 1940) turned a playful hand to the glass-and-steel Sony Center (2000). Another Jahn creation that raises eyebrows and interest in Berlin is the minimalist and edgy Neues Kranzler Eck (2000).

Two spectacular successes in Germany designed by American star-architect Daniel Libeskind (b 1946) are Osnabrück's Felix-Nussbaum-Haus (1998) and his more famous zinc-clad zigzag Jüdisches Museum (2001) in Berlin. His transparent wedged extension to the Militärhistorisches Museum in Dresden is scheduled for completion in 2008. Back in Berlin, New York contemporary Peter Eisenman achieved the remarkable by assembling 2700 concrete pillars – it also has a subterranean information centre – to create the haunting Holocaust Memorial (2005).

In 2006, Berlin christened its latest star attraction amid light shows – the vast Hauptbahnhof, a transparent-roofed, multiple-level *Turmbahnhof* (tower station; the lines cross at different levels) that takes glass-and-steel station architecture to new limits. The station was designed by Hamburg-based firm von Gerkan, Marg und Partner, who also designed Swissôtel-Kudamm-Eck (2001) with its eye-catching 70-sq-metre video screen.

The contrast (or collision, depending on your view) of old and new in the extension of Cologne's Wallraf-Richartz-Museum (2001), a design by Oswald Matthias Ungers (b 1926), is a worthy addition to a city with one of the world's most beautiful cathedrals. In 2003 Dresden-born Axel Schultes (b 1943) and Kiel's Charlotte Frank (b 1959), both Berlin-based, won the German Architecture Prize for their design of the Bundeskanzleramt (New Chancellery; 2001) dubbed 'the washing machine' by Berliners. Munich architect Stefan Braunfels (b 1950) masterminded Munich's modernist Pinakothek der Moderne (2002).

For an interaction of light and architecture, try to catch the Luminale festival in the Rhine-Main region (www.luminale.de), an event in April each year whereby light artists use sound and light to transform buildings, museums and parks into illuminated works of art or 'light laboratories'.

Music
LOVE BALLADS TO 20TH-CENTURY CLASSICAL
German music in the 12th century is closely associated with Walther von der Vogelweide (c 1170–1230), who achieved renown with love ballads. A

Jugendstil – an alternative name in German for Art Nouveau – takes its name from the arts magazine *Jugend* (the word *Jugend* means youth), first published in Munich in 1896.

Berlin Alexanderplatz: The Story of Franz Biberkopf by Alfred Döblin (translated by Eugene Jolas) is a masterful 600-odd-page epic set in the seedy Alexanderplatz district of 1920s Berlin (filmmaker Rainer Fassbinder made a 15-hour film version of it).

The Designpreis der Bundesrepublik Deutschland (German Design Prize) is Germany's prestige award for design. It is given annually in two categories – products and people (www.design preis.de).

more formalised troubadour tradition followed, but it was baroque organist Johann Sebastian Bach (1685–1750), born in Eisenach, who influenced early European music most. His legacy can be explored in Leipzig's Bach Museum in the house in which he died. Another museum in Eisenach is dedicated to his life and work.

Georg Friedrich Händel (1685–1759) was a contemporary of Bach who hailed from Halle in Saxony-Anhalt (his house is also now a museum), but lived and worked almost exclusively in London from 1714.

Händel's music found favour in the circle of Vienna Classic composers, and it was Joseph Haydn (1732–1809) who taught Bonn-born Ludwig van Beethoven (1770–1827), whose work reflects the Enlightenment. Beethoven is also the most important of the composers who paved the way for Romanticism.

Among the Romantic composers, Hamburg-born Felix Mendelssohn-Bartholdy (1809–47) is hailed as a sheer genius. He penned his first overture at the age of 17 and later dug up works by JS Bach to give the latter the fame he enjoys today.

Born in Leipzig, dying in Venice, Richard Wagner (1813–83) dominates 19th-century music like no other person. Other composers ignored him at their peril. Hitler, who picked up on an anti-Semitic essay and some late-life ramblings on German virtues, famously turned Wagner into a post-mortem Nazi icon. A summer music festival in Bayreuth celebrates Wagner's life and works (p369).

Hamburg brought forth Johannes Brahms (1833–97) and his influential symphonies, chamber and piano works. Two figures whose legacies can be explored today in cities such as Bonn, Leipzig and Zwickau are composer Robert Schumann (1810–56) and his gifted pianist-spouse Clara Wieck (1819–96). Schumann (born in Zwickau) and Wieck (born in Leipzig) are buried in Bonn's Alter Friedhof (p565). Pulsating 1920s Berlin ushered in Vienna-born Arnold Schönberg (1874–1951), inventor of a new tonal relationship that turned music on its head. One of his pupils, Hanns Eisler (1898–1962), went into exile in 1933 but returned to East Berlin to teach in 1950. Among his works was the East German national anthem, Auferstanden aus Ruinen (Resurrected from Ruins), lyric-less from 1961 when its pro-unification words fell out of favour with party honchos.

Hanau-born Paul Hindemith (1895–1963) was banned by the Nazis and composed his most important orchestral compositions outside his homeland. The **Hindemith Institute** (www.hindemith.org) in Frankfurt-am-Main promotes his music and safeguards his estate. Perhaps better-known is Dessau-born Kurt Weill (1900–50), another composer who fled the Nazi terror. He teamed up with Berthold Brecht (p66) in the 1920s and wrote the music for *Die Moritat von Mackie Messer* (Mack the Knife) in Brecht's *Dreigroschenoper* (Threepenny Opera). Weill ended up in New York where he wrote successful Broadway musicals.

Germany's most prestigious orchestra, the Berlin Philharmonic Orchestra (1882), was shaped by conductor Wilhelm Furtwängler (1886–1954) and, from 1954 until his death in 1989, the illustrious Herbert von Karajan (1908–89). Dresden Opera Orchestra and the Leipzig Orchestra are also important stops on the classical trail. The young Kammersymphonie Berlin (Berlin Chamber Symphony), established in 1991, recaptures the multifaceted music scene of 1920s Berlin through its focus on less common orchestral works. Acclaimed (and glamorous) German violinist, Anne-Sophie Mutter (b 1963), gave her first solo performance with the Berlin Symphony Orchestra (founded 1966) at the age of 14 and made her first recording with the Berlin Philharmonic a year later.

Fourteen informative essays bring the vibrant musical age of Luther et al alive in the 300-page-plus *Music in the German Renaissance*, edited by John Kmetz.

CONTEMPORARY

Jazz is popular in Germany, and most towns have a jazz club or two. The group Berlin Voices blends modern jazz, pop, Latin, soul and gospel in very strong performances, whether it be covering Billy Joel in new ways, exploring Manhattan Transfer rhythms, or performing their own stuff. Till Brönner (b 1971) – who studied at the Cologne Music School – has trumpeted, sung and composed his way to renown, recording his *Oceana* album (2006) in Los Angeles with contributions from Madeleine Peyroux (b 1974) and singing Italian model Carla Bruni (b 1968). The guitar-based (but backed with percussion and bass) M&M delivers a funky jazz sound mixed with Western and classical guitar. These contemporaries complement the soaring sounds of musicians such as Albert Mangelsdorff (b 1928), saxophonist Heinz Sauer (b 1932), and Klaus Doldinger (b 1936) who formed the legendary fusion band Passport. JazzFest Berlin brings the best of German and European jazz to the capital each November (p124).

One big question facing most German rock bands is whether to sing in German, English or both. Scorpions, probably the most successful band abroad, sang in English. Two other highly successful bands abroad that didn't really have this dilemma were the (mostly) instrumental Tangerine Dream and Kraftwerk. Tangerine Dream has the honour of being the first band to cut a chart success with Virgin Records in the 1970s. About three decades before its time, Düsseldorf-based Kraftwerk created the musical foundations for techno which in turn spawned Berlin's legendary techno-orientated Love Parade (p124) in 1989.

Remarkably, both bands are still active, but to witness what a new generation has done, visit Sven Väth's Cocoon Club in Frankfurt (p523), catch the Love Parade if it survives beyond 2006, or look for gigs by musician/DJs Ian Pooley, Paul van Dyk or Westbam.

Members of the Neue Deutsche Welle (NDW, German New Wave) always sang in German – although Nena, its tame international mothership, successfully recorded her hit single 99 Luftballons in English, too. The movement spawned the Hamburg School of Musicians, which later washed to the surface of Hamburg's lively music and arts scene. Recognised acts such as Blumfeld, Die Sterne and the Tocotronic are all still going strong since emerging in the 1990s. Die-hard legends gathering no moss are Germany's most enduring punk band, Düsseldorf-based Die Toten Hosen; punk queen Nina Hagen (whose transformations still seem ahead of their time); and Die Ärzte. Meanwhile, Herbert Grönemeyer, 'Germany's Springsteen' (also a decent actor) and leather legend Udo Lindenberg (who has resided in Hamburg's Hotel Atlantic longer than many of us have been alive) are still thriving. Grönemeyer's 2002 album *Mensch* was a monster hit, and he more recently composed and sang the anthem for the football World Cup in 2006.

German bands often move to Hamburg, or in many cases to Berlin, to plug into the music scene and break through. Giessen-bred Juli is one soft-rock band that works out of Hamburg, where the sound is often more melodic. Bautzen-born Silbermond is based in Berlin. Towering above these two newcomers is Wir Sind Helden, considered one of the best pop-rock bands around in Germany at the moment.

Element of Crime, led by multitalented Sven Regener (b 1961), has probably had more influence on the arts spectrum than anyone else, having composed and played scores for films including Leander Haussmann's *Sonnenallee* (Sun Alley) and *Herr Lehmann* (Regener wrote the book and script of the latter). All-girl feminist punk band, Chicks on Speed – a trio of gals from Munich, New York and rural Australia – are also good fun.

The tempestuous Schumanns inspired filmmakers worldwide: Katherine Hepburn played Clara in Clarence Brown's *Song of Love* (1947), and Berlin-born Nastassja Kinski starred alongside pop idol Herbert Grönemeyer in Peter Schamoni's *Fruehlingssinfonie* (Spring Symphony; 1999).

For more information, practical and historical, on the Berlin Philharmonic Orchestra tune into www.berlin-philharmonic.com.

Watch the videos and hear the music of Germany's most influential techno band at www.kraftwerk.com.

EXPLORING GERMAN MUSIC – IN 10 CDS

Stack your CD player with the following, sit back and take a whirlwind tour through German musical history:

- *Crusaders: In Nomine Domini & German Choral Song around 1600* by various composers (Christophorus label)
- *Brandenburg Concertos* by JS Bach
- 'Water Music' by Handel
- *Beethoven: Nine Symphonies* performed by the Berlin Philharmonic Orchestra
- *Tannhäuser und der Sägerkrieg auf dem Wartburg* (Tannhäuser and the Song Contest of the Wartburg) by Richard Wagner
- *Brahms: Violin Concerto, Double Concerto* performed by Anne-Sophie Mutter, Antonio Meneses and the Berlin Philharmonic Orchestra
- *Ataraxia* by Passport (sax and jazzy stuff; 2002)
- *Tour de France Soundtracks* by Kraftwerk (track No 9 is about a heart monitor)
- *In Between & The Remixes: 1997–2000* by Jazzanova (the second is the breakbeat–jazz lounge act's own debut album)
- *99 Cents* by Chicks on Speed (punk, funk and fashion fused)

The rap scene in Germany is never short of a protagonist and a tough plot – Germany has lots of rappers, some of dubious quality and politics. Heidelberg's Advanced Chemistry and Stuttgart-bred Die Fantastischen Vier are the mild-mannered godfathers of the form in Germany (some would say still the best), paving the way for a younger, more sinewy breed of Gangsta rappers like Bushido, the Berlin-based Sido, or Frankfurt-based Azad. Deichkind, a foursome from Hamburg, has some of the best lyrics. Mannheim has produced a raft of hard-nosed rappers; interestingly – and evident by his prose style – writer Feridun Zaimoglu (p63) emerged from a small, ethnic-Turk rap scene in Kiel.

Find reviews for the latest contemporary German titles to be translated into English at www.new-books-in-german.com.

Literature
EARLY LITERATURE

Oral literature during the reign of Charlemagne (c 800) and secular epics performed by 12th-century knights are the earliest surviving literary forms today, but the man who shook up the literary language was Martin Luther, whose 16th-century translation of the Bible set the stage for German writers.

In the 17th century, Christoph Martin Wieland (1733–1813) penned his *Geschichte des Agathon* (Agathon; 1766–67), a landmark in German literature because it was the first *Bildungsroman* (a novel showing the development of the hero); Wieland was also the first to translate Shakespeare into German.

Shortly after Wieland was summoned to Weimar in 1772, Johann Wolfgang von Goethe (1749–1832) rose to become Germany's most powerful literary figure, later joining forces with Friedrich Schiller (1759–1805) in a celebrated period known as Weimarer Klassik (Weimar classicism; p266).

Luther said, 'Look at their gobs to find out how they speak, then translate so they understand and see you're speaking to them in German.'

Writing in Goethe's lifetime, the lyricist and early Romantic poet, Friedrich Hölderlin (1770–1843), created delicate balance and rhythms. Interestingly, he was largely ignored from the mid-19th century, only to be rediscovered in the early 20th century and to be misused by Hitler for Nazi propaganda.

A 600km-long Fairy-Tale Road (p536) leads literary travellers around Germany in the footsteps of the Grimm brothers, Jakob (1785–1863) and

Wilhelm (1786–1859). Serious academics who wrote *German Grammar* and *History of the German Language*, they're best known for their collection of fairy tales, myths and legends.

The Complete Fairy Tales by Jacob and Wilhelm Grimm is a beautiful collection of 210 fairy tales, passed orally between generations and collected by German literature's most magical brothers.

The Düsseldorf-born Heinrich Heine (1797–1856) produced one of Germany's finest collections of poems when he published *Buch der Lieder* (Book of Songs) in 1827, but it was his politically scathing *Deutschland: Ein Wintermärchen* (Germany: A Winter's Tale) that contributed to his work being banned in 1835. By that time, Heine – one of Germany's most famous Jews – was in Paris, in love with an illiterate salesgirl, and was surrounded by pesky German spies.

MODERN & CONTEMPORARY

The Weimar years witnessed the flowering of Lübeck-born Thomas Mann (1875–1955), recipient of the Nobel Prize for Literature in 1929, whose greatest novels focus on social forms of the day. For Mann, 'Germany's first lady' was writer and poet Ricarda Huch (1864–1947), a courageous opponent of Nazism. Mann's older brother, Heinrich (1871–1950), adopted a stronger political stance than Thomas in his work; his *Professor Unrat* (1905) provided the raw material for the Marlene Dietrich film *Der Blaue Engel* (The Blue Angel; opposite).

A vivid picture of mid-19th-century German society is painted in Heinrich Heine's *Deutschland: Ein Wintermärchen* (Germany: A Winter's Tale), based on a trip the writer took from Aachen to Hamburg.

Berlin's underworld during the Weimar Republic served as a focus for Alfred Döblin's (1878–1957) novel *Berlin Alexanderplatz* (1929). Hermann Hesse (1877–1962), another Nobel prize winner, adopted the theme of the outsider in *Steppenwolf* (1927) and imbued New Romantic spirituality into his work after a journey to India in 1911. Osnabrück-born Erich Maria Remarque's (1898–1970) antiwar novel *Im Westen nichts Neues* (All Quiet on the Western Front; 1929) was banned in 1933 and remains one of the most widely read German books.

Of the generation writing today, Günter Grass (b 1927) is the most celebrated. Grass burst into the literary limelight with his first novel, *Die Blechtrommel* (Tin Drum; 1959) and is almost as much an icon as Social Democrat Willy Brandt, for whom he ghost-wrote in the 1970s.

Although East Germany no longer exists, fortunately most of its best writers still do. Christa Wolf (b 1929) is the best known and most controversial; she admitted to working as an informer for East Germany's secret police briefly in the late 1950s before the state got heavy on artists, and she later spoke out for dissidents. Like Wolf, Sarah Kirsch (b 1935) supported the cause of singer and songwriter Wolf Biermann (b 1936) during the furore that led to his loss of GDR citizenship.

Meaty Thomas Mann starters include *Buddenbrooks*, a look at declining bourgeois values; *Der Zauberberg* (Magic Mountain), which links personal and social illness around the time of WWI; and the menacing *Doktor Faustus* in which the central character exchanges health and love for creative fulfilment.

Thomas Brüssig (b 1965), a novelist and screenwriter from Berlin, rose to prominence in the mid-1990s with *Helden wie Wir* (Heros like Us; 1995). He also wrote the screenplay for the film *Sonnenallee* (p65) and is a member of the Lübeck-based Gruppe 05 – co-founded in 2005 by Günter Grass with other writers to get more young scribes involved in politics. Other members of the group whose works reward exploration include Burkhard Spinnen (b 1957), who has published more than a dozen novels and essays; and novelist, poet and essayist Matthias Politycki (b 1955).

Skipping back to a few relative old-timers for a moment, a trio of contemporary literary figures was born in 1944 – the strongly mystic Botho Strauss, crime novelist and Berlin professor Bernard Schlink (whose books have won prizes and much praise), and novelist WG Sebald (1944–2001) who assured his place as one of Germany's best writers with his powerful portrayal of four exiles in *Die Ausgewanderten* (Emigrants). Munich-based writer and playwright, Patrick Süskind (b 1949) achieved international acclaim with his *Das Parfum* (Perfume), his extraordinary tale of a psychotic 18th-century perfume-maker.

Russian-born Vladimir Kaminer (b 1967) is a popular and interesting author who hit Berlin in the early 1990s, started a regular disco with Russian beats in Berlin's Mitte district, and published his first collection of stories under the title *Russendisko* (Russian Disco; 2000). Today he tours regularly on readings and continues to spin vinyl at the disco and elsewhere. His collection of anecdotal travel stories, *Mein deutsches Dschungelbuch* (My German Junglebook; 2003), is a recent and highly enjoyable addition to his works.

Feridun Zaimoglu (b 1964) is Turkish-born, wrote an inaccessible first novel using the language of German rap (*Kanak Sprak;* 1995) and since then has become one of Germany's most important new generation of writers, producing a handful of eclectic novels and short stories. He is also one of its most vocal and incisive on social issues. His novel *Leyla* (2006) is about a girl growing up in Turkey in the 1950s and 1960s. Zaimoglu copped flak in 2006 for similarities to a novel by fellow Turkish-German author and playwright Emine Sevgi Özdamar (b 1946), whose *Das Leben ist eine Karawanserei* (Life is a Kervansaray; 1992) was *Times Literary Supplement* Novel of the Year in 1994.

So sind wir (That's the Way We Are; 2005) and earlier works by Gila Lustiger (b 1963), as well as *Berliner Verhältnisse* (Berlin Affairs; 2005) by Raul Zelik (b 1968) and *33 Augenblicke des Glücks* (33 Moments of Happiness; 1995) by Ingo Schulze (b 1962), will reward deeper exploration.

Pick up *Der geteilte Himmel* (Divided Heaven), by East German writer Christa Wolf, to discover the fate of a woman's love for a man who fled to West Germany.

Cinema

German film is happening again. After a couple of years in which it seemed to pause for breath and seek new directions, the industry is bringing out quality productions and film-goers are rediscovering German cinema, which nevertheless only accounts for about 20% of box office sales.

Local directors can draw upon a rich heritage out of the UFA (Universum Film AG; German film studios) studio in Babelsberg (Potsdam), founded in 1911 and now a large studio and multimedia complex on the fringe of Berlin. One early classic is Fritz Lang's silent proletarian classic *Metropolis* (1927), about a subterranean proletarian subclass – it's the first film to use back projection.

In the early 1930s film *Der Blaue Engel* (Blue Angel; 1930), directed by Josef von Sternberg, Marlene Dietrich (p64) wooed an audience with hypnotic sensuality and became a star overnight. The 1930s were productive but difficult years. The premier of Fritz Lang's talkie, *Das Testament des Dr Mabuse* (Testament of Dr Mabuse; 1933), about a psychiatric patient with plans to take over the world, had to be shifted to Austria because of some out-of-joint Nazi noses. Hitler would also drive acting greats like Peter Lorre (1904–64; an ethnic German Hungarian) and Billy Wilder (1906–2002; an ethnic Austro-German who wrote scripts in Berlin) to Hollywood exile.

In the 1960s film again entered a new age that brought forth the German New Wave movement (Der Junge Deutsche Film) and directors Rainer Werner Fassbinder (1946–82), Wim Wenders (b 1945), Volker Schlöndorff (b 1939), Werner Herzog (b 1942) and director-actor Margarethe von Trotta (b 1942). All except Fassbinder, Germany's *enfant terrible* of film who lived hard and left behind a cocaine-spiked wreck, are working today. The resonance of Fassbinder's *Die Sehnsucht der Veronika Voss* (Longing of Veronica Voss; 1981), Wenders' narrative classics *Paris Texas* (1984) and *Der Himmel über Berlin* (Wings of Desire; 1987), Herzog's *Aguirre, der Zorn Gottes* (Aguirre, the Wrath of God; 1972) and Schlöndorff's film rendition of the Günter Grass novel *Die Blechtrommel* (Tin Drum; 1979) can still be felt in local productions today.

A film from the 1990s that towered above all others was Tom Tykwer's electric-paced *Lola Rennt* (Run Lola Run; 1998), staring one of Germany's

Read *Simplicissimus* (Adventures of a Simpleton) by Hans Jacob Christoffel von Grimmelshausen as an appetiser to the German novel.

Fritz Lang's *Metropolis* (1927) stands out as an ambitious cinema classic. A silent science-fiction film, it depicts the revolt of a proletarian class that lives underground (see also p152).

MARLENE DIETRICH

Marlene Dietrich (1901–92), born Marie Magdalena von Losch into a good middle-class family in Berlin, was the daughter of a Prussian officer. After acting school, she worked in the silent film industry in the 1920s, stereotyped as a hard-living, libertine flapper. But she soon carved a niche in the film fantasies of lower-middle-class men as the dangerously seductive *femme fatale*, best typified by her appearance in the 1930 talkie *Der Blaue Engel* (Blue Angel), which turned her into a Hollywood star.

The film was the start of a five-year collaboration with director Josef von Sternberg, during which time she built on her image of erotic opulence – dominant and severe, but always with a touch of self-irony. Dressed in men's suits for *Marocco* in 1930, she lent her 'sexuality is power' attitude bisexual tones, winning a new audience overnight.

Dietrich stayed in Hollywood after the Nazi rise to power, though Hitler, no less immune to her charms, reportedly promised perks and the red-carpet treatment if she moved back to Germany. She responded with an empty offer to return if she could bring Sternberg – a Jew and no Nazi favourite. She took US citizenship in 1937 and sang on the front to Allied GIs.

After the war, Dietrich retreated slowly from the public eye, making occasional appearances in films, but mostly cutting records and performing live. Her final years were spent in Paris, bed-ridden and accepting few visitors, immortal in spirit as mortality caught up with her.

Der Blaue Engel (Blue Angel; 1930) tells the tragic tale of a pedantic professor who is hopelessly infatuated with a sexy cabaret singer. Watch this to see the vamp image that Marlene Dietrich enjoyed all her life.

finest actors today, Franka Potente (b 1974). Tykwer's film based on the Patrick Süskind novel *Das Parfum* (Perfume: The Story of a Murderer; 2006) is set to become another landmark for the director.

Die fetten Jahre sind Vorbei (Edukators; 2004) is arguably Germany's most underrated film. This Austro-German co-production by Austrian director Hans Weingartner, staring German actors Daniel Brühl and Julia Jentsch, brings together an anarchist new generation with an ex-hippy-cum-businessman in a kidnapping imbroglio with lots of telling twists. Marc Rothemund's (b 1968) highly acclaimed *Sophie Scholl – Die letzten Tage* (Sophie Scholl: The Final Days; 2005) portrays the interrogation, trial and judgement of Scholl's brave act of resistance against Nazism through her own eyes (see p302). Another highly esteemed production is director Fatih Akin's (b 1973) *Gegen die Wand* (Head-On; 2004), which brings the Turkish ethnic scene to the fore when a young ethnic-Turkish woman rebels against her upbringing by marrying a much older, down-at-heel German.

The most visible international face of contemporary German film is Wolfgang Becker's laconic and highly successful *Goodbye Lenin!* (2003), with its re-creation of GDR life for a bed-ridden mother. Oliver Hirschbiegel's (b 1957) *Der Untergang* (Downfall; 2004) is a chilling account of Hitler's last 12 days – from his final birthday to his suicide – mostly in his Berlin bunker. It caused a furore in Germany because some people thought it portrayed Hitler too harmlessly. The performance of Swiss Bruno Ganz (b 1941) as Hitler is undeniably brave and stunning.

Read what the critics say about 500-plus German films at www.german -cinema.de.

Other films that have gained kudos at recent Berlin International Film Festival screenings – Germany's premier film awards – are the disconcerting *Requiem* (2005) from director Hans-Christian Schmid (b 1965), about a true case of exorcism; Andreas Dresen's (b 1963) *Sommer vorm Balkon* (Summer in Berlin; 2004), a quirky relationship film set one summer in Berlin; and director Oskar Roehler's (b 1959) *Elementarteilchen* (Elementary Particles; 2005) based on the novel by French author Michel Houellebecq.

A film that scooped more awards than any other in 2006 was Florian von Donnersmarck's (b 1973) *Das Leben der Anderen* (Lives of Others; 2006), portraying the Stasi and its network of informants five years prior to the fall of the Berlin Wall.

Berlin's Babelsberg studio complex and film museums in Berlin and Frankfurt-am-Main are good starting points for anything to do with the German film tradition.

Television

For a general overview of media, see p50.

Social etiquette in Germany demands that you never telephone a friend at 8pm – this is when the state-funded ARD broadcasts its *Tagesschau* news programme. German TV itself is unlikely knock you off your lounge room chair, but it will give some interesting insights into the country. Big Brother achieved monumental heights of tedium in its heyday, and reality TV is still a force today, especially when it comes to raising difficult children or swapping your family.

At the high end, one area where Germany excels is in pan-European broadcasting, such as its Kulturzeit (Culture Age; 3Sat, various times) collaboration with Austria and Switzerland, and the ARTE channel collaboration with France.

The long-running *Tatort* (ARD, 8.15pm Sunday) police series is a top-rating show that rotates between a dozen or more German cities, plus Vienna. The opening music and graphic is original from the first show in 1970. The Cologne and Berlin productions are top-notch, often wry and up to the standard of a mini cinema production.

Although production stopped in 1998, the crime classic *Derrick* remains the most successful German TV production ever. However, with episodes like 'The Manure Fork Murder' and 'Death in Lingerie', *Der Bulle von Tölz* (Sat1, 8.15pm Wednesday) is an unlikely success, especially as it's set in bucolic Bad Tölz (p323); the main character, Kommissar Berghammer (played by Ottfried Fischer), lends his weight to the show's moniker as the 'corpulent crime series'.

Germany's most influential current affairs TV show is broadcast on ARD at 9.45pm each Sunday, and is usually studded with a half dozen prominent guests.

The Wonderful, Horrible Life of Leni Riefenstahl (1993), directed by Ray Muller, is a stunning three-hour biographical epic of Hitler's most famous filmmaker. Highlights include pieces to camera by a 90-year-old Riefenstahl.

Watch the news with ZDF at www.zdf.de or ARD at www.ard.de (in German).

TOP FIVE GDR RETRO FILMS

■ Leander Haussmann's *Sonnenallee* (Sun Alley; 1999) is set in a fantastical Wall-clad East Berlin in the 1970s, and evokes everything nostalgic for the former GDR.

■ *Helden wie wir* (Heroes like Us; 1999) directed by Sebastian Peterson, based on the novel by Thomas Brussig, sees the protagonist (who claims to have been Erich Honecker's personal blood donor) recount the story of his life, including how his penis allegedly leads to the collapse of the Berlin Wall.

■ Dull lives are led in dull Frankfurt an der Oder in dull East Germany – until Ellen and Chris are caught doing it. Laughs abound in *Halbe Trepe* (Grill Point; 2001), directed by East German–born Andreas Dresen.

■ The Wall falls the day the bartending lead actor hits 30 in West Berlin's bohemian Kreuzberg district. Haussmann's humorous *Herr Lehmann* (Berlin Blues; 2003) is based on a cult book by the Element of Crime lead singer Sven Regener.

■ *Goodbye Lenin!* (2003), the box-office smash hit by Wolfgang Becker, has cult status as a son tries to re-create the GDR for a bedridden ailing mother whose health can't stand the shock of a fallen Wall.

For more on Ostalgie, see p44.

Theatre

With more than 6000 stages across the country, Germany is a paradise for the theatre-goer. Most plays are staged in multipurpose theatres (opera and music will often be performed there too) and are subsidised by the state. The average theatre in the network of city, regional and national spaces will put on about 20 or more plays each year.

Past masters of the Enlightenment who frequently get a showing include Saxony's Gotthold Ephraim Lessing (1729–81); Württemberg-born Friedrich Schiller (1759–1805), who features especially strongly in Weimar's theatre landscape today; and of course Johann Wolfgang von Goethe, who tinkered with his two-part *Faust* for 60 years of his life and created one of Germany's most powerful and enduring dramas about the human condition.

Georg Büchner's (1813–37) *Woyzeck* is another popular piece and, having anticipated Theatre of the Absurd, lends itself to innovative staging. In 1894 the director of Berlin's Deutsches Theater hired a young actor, Max Reinhardt (1873–1943), who became German theatre's most influential expressionist director, working briefly with dramatist Bertolt Brecht (1898–1956). Both men went into exile under Nazism – Brecht to try his hand at a couple of Hollywood scripts and to answer for his vaguely Marxist politics before the House Committee on Un-American Activities during the McCarthy-era witch hunts. Brecht's *Leben des Galilei* (Life of Galileo; 1943/47) was rewritten with a new ending after atomic bombs fell on Hiroshima and Nagasaki. It was first performed in Beverly Hills.

The Augsburg-born dramatist (his birthplace is a pilgrimage site today) returned after WWII to East Berlin and in the 1950s he created the Berliner Ensemble (p140), a venue that produced his plays and became one of the capital's most vibrant theatres. See below for more details about Brecht.

Heiner Müller (1929–95), a Marxist who was critical of the reality of the GDR, became unpalatable in both Germanys in the 1950s. In the 1980s, existential works such as *Quartet* (1980) earned him an avant-garde label.

Read what's on the box this week with the online German TV programme guide at www.tvtv.de (in German).

The definitive read for anyone interested in a more detailed account of the rise of German theatre is Michael Patterson's hard-to-find but worth-the-search *The First German Theatre: Schiller, Goethe, Kleist and Büchner in Performance*.

BERTOLT BRECHT

Bertolt Brecht (1898–1956) is Germany's most controversial 20th-century playwright, poet and drama theorist. He wrote his first play, *Baal*, while studying medicine in Munich in 1918. His first opus to reach the stage, *Trommeln in der Nacht* (Drums in the Night; 1922), won the coveted Kleist Prize, and two years later he moved to the Deutsches Theater in Berlin to work with the Austrian actor and director Max Reinhardt.

Over the next decade, in plays such as *Die Dreigroschenoper* (Threepenny Opera; 1928), Brecht developed his theory of 'epic theatre', which, unlike 'dramatic theatre', forces its audience to detach itself emotionally from the play and its characters and to reason intellectually.

A staunch Marxist, Brecht went into exile during the Nazi years, surfaced in Hollywood as a scriptwriter, then left the USA after being called in to explain himself during the communist witch-hunts of the McCarthy era. The exile years produced many of his best plays: *Mutter Courage und ihre Kinder* (Mother Courage and Her Children; 1941), *Leben des Galilei* (Life of Galileo; 1943/47), *Der gute Mensch von Sezuan* (Good Woman of Setzuan; 1943) and *Der Kaukasische Kreidekreis* (Caucasian Chalk Circle; 1948).

Brecht returned to East Berlin in 1949 where he founded the Berliner Ensemble with his wife, the actress Helene Weigel, who directed it until her death in 1971. During his lifetime Brecht was suspected both in the East for his unorthodox aesthetic theories and scorned (and often boycotted) in much of the West for his communist principles. Others again saw him as a pragmatist and opportunist. His influence, however, is indisputable. Brecht's poetry, so little known in English, is also a fascinating string in the bow of German literature.

In the 1960s, Berlin director Rudolf Noelte (1921–2002) took centre stage as the master of German postwar theatre.

Directors like Peter Stein (b 1937) have earned contemporary German theatre its reputation for producing classic plays in an innovative and provocative manner. One of the Jungen Wilden (Young Wild Ones) in the 1970s and 1980s, Stein founded Berlin's Schaubühne (p140) theatre as a collective in 1970 (even the cleaner had a say as to what went on) and today it is one of Germany's best.

Also in the capital, Berlin-born Frank Castorf (b 1951) is arguably Germany's most dynamic contemporary director, heading up Berlin's Volksbühne (p140) and piecing together innovative productions in Germany and elsewhere in Europe. Christoph Schlingensief (b 1960) is the best-known of Germany's new breed, having staged productions at Berlin's Volksbühne and elsewhere; he's also active in film and action art. In 2004 he directed Wagner's *Parsifal* (Perceval) at the Bayreuth festival, raising Cain with critics and traditionalists alike – including his own Perceval actor, with whom a public brawl developed about Schlingensief's production style. His production was well-received, and he was back in Bayreuth in 2005 to great acclaim.

Read up-to-date reviews of the latest plays by German playwrights at www.goethe.de/enindex .htm.

Some of the contemporary playwrights to watch out for especially are Munich-born, Berlin-based Rainald Goetz (b 1954); Werner Fritsch (b 1960), whose dark plays portray a violent world, occasionally veering on the obscene; Simone Schneider (b 1962); and Moritz Rinke (b 1967).

Environment

THE LAND

Germany is not just about the Black Forest, the Alps and the Rhine River. Across its 356,866 sq km, Europe's fourth largest country boasts moor and heath, mud flats and chalk cliffs, glacial lakes and river wetlands. Hugged by Poland, the Czech Republic, Austria, Switzerland, France, Belgium, the Netherlands, Luxembourg and Denmark, the country is mountainous in the south, but flat in the north. Indeed, many visitors are surprised to learn Germany even possesses low-lying islands and sandy beaches.

True, the stereotypes have been forged in the south, where you'll find the 2962m Zugspitze, the highest peak, as well as the famous mountain resort of Berchtesgaden. However, only a small section of the Alps falls within Germany – compared to neighbouring Austria and Switzerland – and it's all in Bavaria. In the wooded mountain range of the Schwarzwald (Black Forest), in Baden Württemberg to the west, nothing rises above 1500m.

Bound to be controversial, the 2005 book *How Green Were the Nazis?: Nature, Environment, and Nation in the Third Reich* by Franz-Josef Bruggemeier, Mark Cioc and Thomas Zeller (eds) takes a look at the Nazis' love of the great outdoors and explores how fascist and conservationist practices overlap.

Starting its journey in Switzerland and travelling through Lake Constance, Germany's largest lake, the 1320km Rhine River winds its way around the Black Forest, before crawling up the west side of the map to drain into the North Sea. The Elbe, Oder and other German rivers likewise flow north, but the Danube flows east.

Moving towards the central belt, you'll find the most memorable vineyards and hiking areas in the warmer valleys around the Moselle River. Just north of here, the land was formed by volcanic activity. To the east, south of Berlin, you'll find the holiday area of the Spreewald, a picturesque wetland with narrow, navigable waterways.

Where Germany meets Holland in the northwest and Denmark in the north, the land is flat; the westerly North Sea coast consists partly of drained land and dykes. To the east, the Baltic Sea coast is first riddled with bays and fjords in Schleswig-Holstein, before it gives way to sandy inlets and beaches. On the country's northeastern tip, Rügen, its largest island, is renowned like England's Dover for its chalk cliffs.

WILDLIFE

Like most Western European countries, Germany has few large animals still living in the wild. Of the 76 German mammals studied for the 'Red List' of endangered or extinct species, 16% are in danger of dying out. However, wildlife watchers needn't despair, there are plenty of healthy smaller critters.

Animals

Snow hares, marmots and wild goats are easily found in the Alps (the marmot below the tree line, the goat and snow hare above it). The chamois is also fairly common in this neck of the woods, as well as in pockets of the Black Forest, the Swabian Alps and Elbsandsteingebirge (Sächsische Schweiz), south of Dresden.

Autobahns and animals are not a good mix, but luckily Germany is one of the leading countries for building wildlife overpasses or 'green bridges' across motorways. More than 40 are now complete.

A rare but wonderful Alpine treat for patient bird-watchers is the sighting of a golden eagle; Berchtesgaden National Park staff might be able to help you find one. The jay, with its darting flight patterns and calls imitating other species, is easy to spot in the Alpine foothills. Look for flashes of blue on its wings.

Pesky but sociable racoons, a common non-native species, scoot about eastern Germany, and soon let hikers know if they have been disturbed with a shrill whistle-like sound. Beavers can be found in wetlands near the Elbe River. Seals are common on the North Sea and Baltic Sea coasts.

The north coast also lures migratory birds. From March to May and August to October they particularly stop over in Schleswig-Holstein's Wattenmeer National Park and the Vorpommersche Boddenlandschaft National Park whilst going to and from southerly regions. Forests everywhere provide a habitat for a wide variety of songbirds, as well as woodpeckers.

Some animals are staging a comeback. Sea eagles, practically extinct in western Germany, are becoming more plentiful in the east, as are falcons, white storks and cranes. The east also sees wolves, which regularly cross the Oder River from Poland, and European moose, which occasionally appear on moors and in mixed forests.

The wild cat has returned to the Harz Mountains and other forested regions, but you shouldn't expect to see the related lynx. Having died out here in the 19th century, lynx were reintroduced in the 1980s, only to be illegally hunted to extinction again. Today, a few populate the Bavarian Forest National Park, although chances of seeing one in the wild are virtually zero.

Deer are still around, although with dwindling natural habitat and their shrinking gene pool, the **Deutsche Wildtier Stiftung** (German Wild Animal Foundation; www.deutschewildtierstiftung.de) has expressed concern for the animal's future.

Plants

Studded with beech, oak, birch, chestnut (mostly of the inedible horse-chestnut variety), lime, maple and ash trees, German forests are beautiful places to escape the madding crowds and relax. Mixed deciduous forest carpets river valleys at lower altitudes, and coniferous species grow thicker as you ascend. One-third of Germany's 3000 species of native ferns and flowering plants might be endangered, but you wouldn't realise it here.

Waldfrüchte (berries) are particularly colourful, but for the most part poisonous. The same applies to mushrooms, which are essential for the development of healthy root systems in trees, especially in deciduous forests. Chanterelle *(Pfifferlinge)* mushrooms are a seasonal culinary delight.

Alpine regions burst with wildflowers – orchids, cyclamen, gentians, pulsatilla, alpine roses, edelweiss and buttercups. Meadow species colour spring and summer, and great care is taken these days not to cut pastures until plants have seeded. Visitors should stick to paths, especially in alpine areas and coastal dunes where ecosystems are fragile. In late August, heather blossom is the particular lure of Lüneburg Heath, northeast of Hanover.

The highly unlikely title *Animals in the Third Reich: Pets, Scapegoats, and the Holocaust* by Klaus P Fischer and Boria Sax looks at the treatment of animals under Hitler's Third Reich and Nazism's symbolic use of nature for its own twisted means.

Owls of the World: Their Lives, Behaviour and Survival by James R Duncan makes the ideal companion for wildlife enthusiasts out to spot Germany's eagle-owls, Eurasian pygmy owls and other owl species.

Consisting mainly of firs and pines, the Black Forest derives its name from the dark appearance of these conifers, especially when seen from the hillsides.

SETTING FREE THE BEAR?

Although the bear is the symbol of the capital, Berlin, the wild animal hasn't lived on German soil since 1835. That changed briefly in 2006, when a brown bear wandered into Bavaria. However, the short life of 'Bruno', as he was christened by tabloid newspapers like *Bild,* was a rather sad footnote to history.

Bruno (officially codenamed JJ1) was part of a programme to reintroduce bears to the Italian Alps when he ambled into Germany and became the first wild bear there for more than 170 years. Spotted by local photographers, he became a media celebrity, sometimes vying with the football World Cup 2006 for headlines.

Animal rights activists began a strenuous campaign to protect the bear, hoping to capture him alive and move him. Farmers, however, started blaming Bruno for killing livestock, and because of a perceived risk to humans the Bavarian government gave the go-ahead to shoot him…which eventually hunters did.

Even after his death, the WWF (Worldwide Fund for Nature) hopes it can leverage the public affection Bruno engendered to establish a sensible bear repopulation programme in Germany. But for some Germans the story of Bruno is an unedifying episode they'd just rather forget.

Flora and Vegetation of the Wadden Sea Islands and Coastal Areas, by KS Diikema (ed) and WJ Wolff (ed), remains indispensable for anyone spending time in any of the three Wattenmeer (Wadden Sea) national parks.

For comprehensive national park details and hot links to park websites, surf www .germany-tourism.de.

NATIONAL PARKS

The country's vast and varied landscapes are protected to varying degrees by 90 nature parks, 13 biosphere reserves and 14 national parks (detailed in the table below), although only 0.04% of land is fully protected. In western Germany, the Upper Middle Rhine Valley is safeguarded as a Unesco World Heritage Area to prevent further damage.

ENVIRONMENTAL ISSUES

Germans are the original Greens. They cannot claim to have invented environmentalism, but they were there at the outset and it was they who coined the word to describe the movement. A few 'Values', or 'Ecology' parties were knocking around beforehand, but it was the group of politicians associated with Rudi Dutschke, Petra Kelly and artist Joseph Beuys who first hit on the name The Greens (Die Grünen) when contesting local and national elections in 1979 and 1980. They gained a strong foothold in Bremen, and other political groups across the world decided they quite liked the moniker. The rest, as they say, is history (see p42 for more on Die Grünen).

National Park & Website	Features	Activities	Best Time to Visit	Page
Bavarian Forest www.nationalpark-bayer ischer-wald.de	mountain forest & upland moors (243 sq km): deer, hazel grouse, foxes, otters, eagle-owls, Eurasian pygmy owls	walking, mountain biking, cross-country skiing, botany	spring & winter	p388
Berchtesgaden www.nationalpark -berchtesgaden.de	lakes, subalpine spruce, salt mines & ice caves (210 sq km): eagles, golden eagles, marmots, blue hares,	wildlife, walking, skiing	spring & winter	p351
Eifel www.nationalpark-eifel.de	beech forest (110 sq km): wild cats, beavers, kingfishers, wild yellow narcissus	wildlife, flora, hiking, hydrotherapy spa	spring & summer	p571
Hainich www.nationalpark-hainich.de	mixed deciduous forest (76 sq km): beech trees, black storks, wild cats, rare bats	walking	spring	p270
Hamburg Wadden Sea www.wattenmeer -nationalpark.de	mud flats with meadows & sand dunes (120 sq km): sea swallows, terns	mud-flat walking, bird-watching	spring & autumn	p677
Harz www.nationalpark-harz.de	amazing rock formations & caves (247 sq km): deer, black woodpeckers, wild cats	walking, climbing	spring, summer & autumn, not weekends (too busy)	p229
Jasmund www.nationalpark -jasmund.de	cretaceous landscape of chalk cliffs, forest, creeks & moors (30 sq km): white-tailed eagles	walking, cycling	not summer (paths like ant trails)	p732

The Greens' concern for the health of the planet and their strong opposition to nuclear power certainly struck a chord with the local populace. Contemporary Germans recycle regularly, often prefer to ride bicycles rather than catch buses, and carry their groceries in reusable cloth (rather than plastic) shopping bags; all this is simply second nature here.

Green ideology has also wielded an enormous influence on the political agenda. In the 1990s, Greenpeace Germany made international news trying to stop nuclear-waste transport in Lower Saxony and heavily populated North Rhine-Westphalia. German Greenpeace members also helped scuttle Shell's controversial plans to sink the Brent Spar oil platform in the North Sea.

For information on Germany's 90-odd nature parks, see www.natur parke.de (in German).

Even more tellingly, the Greens were in government between 1998 and 2005, as the junior partner in Gerhard Schröder's coalition. Under the leadership of Joschka Fischer, the party had a major say in decisions to cut carbon emissions and to wind down the nuclear industry. Although some of these policies are already being reversed under the new, more conservative 'grand coalition' government of CDU, CSU and SPD under chancellor Angela Merkel, individual Germans' commitment to green issues remains solid.

National Park & Website	Features	Activities	Best Time to Visit	Page
Kellerwald Edersee www.nationalpark kellerwald-edersee.de	beech & other deciduous trees, lake (57 sq km): black stork, wild cats, rare bats, stags	walking, wildlife	spring, summer & autumn	p533
Lower Oder Valley www.nationalpark -unteresches-odertal.de	riverplain (165 sq km): black storks, sea eagles, beavers, aquatic warblers, cranes	walking, cycling, bird-watching	winter (bird-watching), spring (other activities)	p162
Lower Saxony Wadden Sea www.nationalpark-watten meer-niedersachsen.de	salt-marsh & bog landscape (2780 sq km): seals, shell ducks	swimming, walking, bird-watching	late spring & early autumn	p637
Müritz www.nationalpark -mueritz.de	beech, bogs & lakes galore (318 sq km): sea eagles, fish hawks, cranes, white-tailed eagles, Gothland sheep	cycling, canoeing, bird-watching, hiking	spring, summer & autumn	p711
Saxon Switzerland www.nationalpark-saechsische-schweiz.de	spectacular sandstone & basalt rock formations (93 sq km): eagle-owls, otters, fat dormice	walking, climbing, rock climbing	not summer (throngs with Dresden day-trippers)	p180
Schleswig-Holstein Wadden Sea www.wattenmeer -nationalpark.de	dramatic seascape of dunes, salt marshes & mud flats (4410 sq km): sea life, migratory birds	bird-watching, tidewatching, mud-flat walking, swimming	spring & autumn	p696
Vorpommersche Boddenlandschaft www.nationalpark-vorpommer sche-boddenlandschaft.de	dramatic Baltic seascape (805 sq km): cranes, red deer, wild boar	bird-watching, water sports, walking	autumn (crane watching), summer (water sports)	p721

Energy

Travelling across Germany, one can't help but be struck by the number of giant wind turbines dotting the landscape, especially in the windswept north. You start to wonder just how many there are. Well, more than 16,000 at the last count, apparently.

While other countries debate its pros and cons, Germany has long embraced this technology. It's the world's leading producer of wind energy, accounting for between 32% and 40% of entire global capacity in 2005 (depending on whose figures you believe). This provides roughly 6% of German electricity, but by 2010 the country expects turbines to fuel 12.5% of its needs, and to help meet that target it's building huge wind farms far off the Schleswig Holstein coast. Up to 5000 turbines could be installed as far as 47km out to sea.

The federal government also backs research into other alternatives, with some €30 million invested in geothermal energy, solar power, hydroelectricity and biomass (animal waste, plants etc) projects. Near Regensburg, Bavaria boasts one of the world's largest solar plants, generating enough electricity for 4500 people (over 3.5 million kWh a year).

The current pre-eminence of renewable energies partly derives from the country's decision in 2001 to shut down its nuclear industry. That year, the so-called red-green government (with red representing Schröder's centre-left SPD party) developed a timetable to phase out all 19 of its nuclear energy plants by 2020. But these reactors provide a third of the country's energy needs, and the government was attempting simultaneously to reduce its carbon emission levels by 40% from 1990 levels, so it massively stepped up investment in alternative energies.

Each of the 19 nuclear reactors was to be shut down on its 32nd birthday, and the first to go was Stade (outside Hamburg) in November 2003. However, by 2005, with only one other reactor decommissioned, there was a change of government and seemingly a change of heart in Berlin. Critics were warning of an energy crisis and in 2006 the nuclear industry was lobbying environment minister Sigmar Gabriel (SPD) to postpone the closures by some five to eight years. Although a staunch nuclear opponent himself, Gabriel admitted to news magazine *Der Spiegel* that not everyone in the Grand Coalition government shared his views.

Pollution

When it comes to addressing pollution, Germany might recently have blotted an otherwise fairly enviable copybook. Until 2006, the country was seen as the European leader in reducing carbon-dioxide emissions and offsetting the effects of acid rain and river pollution. However, new carbon-emission quotas for industry announced in the middle of that year were criticised for being unambitious or even lax. Environmental groups accused Angela Merkel's government of not taking its commitments under the Kyoto Protocol seriously enough.

This controversy is a far cry from the period from 1987 to 2000, when Germany proudly achieved the environmental turnaround of the European century with the success of the Rhine Action Programme. Declared dead by 1970, the Upper Rhine was spawning salmon and sea trout again by 1997 – for the first time in 50 years. The transformation was all the more remarkable given that some 15% of the world's chemical industry plants are settled along the riverbanks.

A longer-term Action Plan High Water was put in place until 2020, working on restoring other riverbanks and important adjoining meadows, in a bid to stave off damaging floods.

Schleswig-Holstein is the German – and probably world – leader in wind power. The state generates 25% of its power from wind turbines, compared to 6% which is the national average.

Ting! Ting! Road rage in eco-friendly Germany often happens on the footpath (sidewalk), when inattentive pedestrians step into an oncoming cyclist's way. Watch out for the cycle lanes – and stay well out of them!

Green information galore, including daily ozone readings from 370 points, is posted on the website of the Federal Environment Agency (*Umweltbundesamt;* www .umweltbundesamt .de, in German).

HOW TO RECYCLE A TEABAG

It might be something of a national joke, but recycling a teabag really does require all but one of the five rubbish bins found in German homes.

Germans are Europe's biggest recyclers. Into the bio bin *(Biomüll)*, goes biodegradable waste – garden rubbish, potato peelings, food leftovers, coffee granules and used tea bags (minus metal clip, string and paper tag). The paper *(Papier)* bin takes recyclable paper, waxed cardboard, cardboard and teabag paper tags. There's a third *Grüne Punkt* bin for recyclable items – including packaging materials, margarine tubs, empty food tins, cans and teabag clips. Except for glass – which obviously a tea bag doesn't contain – everything left, including the synthetic string on a teabag, goes in the fourth bin for residuary waste *(Restmüll)*.

Bins found in train stations and airports are slightly different: *Glas* (glass), *Papier* (paper), *Verpackung* (packaging) and *Restmüll* (residuary waste).

Empty mineral water bottles (both plastic and glass) plus beer and other cans are another recycling story. When you buy these in the shop, many have a *Pfand* or returnable deposit, usually between €0.25 and €0.50 per bottle. This is to persuade even the laziest of consumers to return their empties to one of 100,000 specified shops and points of sale countrywide. Germans usually save these up until they have a bag full (or three) to return. Be prepared to wait if you find yourself behind such a customer in a supermarket queue!

Per capita, Germany produces 10kg of rubbish daily.

In 2002, the government was still polishing its green credentials when it stepped up an ecological tax on petrol, diesel, heating oil, natural gas and electricity. The same year it pledged to reduce Germany's 1990 level of greenhouse gas emissions by 21% between 2008 and 2012 – by 2004, its emissions were already 17.5% down on those notched up in 1990.

But in 2006 the German government throttled back on its greenhouse gas plans, asking that industry cut back just 0.6% on carbon emissions between 2008 and 2012. Even worse, it gave many business free carbon allowances and even totally exempted a number of major industrial plants from limits until 2022.

The German government insisted it would still meet its Kyoto targets, by teaching autobahn motorists to drive more slowly and hence economically. However, international critics were derisive – and concerned. They thought there could be ramifications for the rest of the EU now that such an important player has turned a slightly paler shade of green.

Charismatic Green Party co-founder Petra Kelly and partner Gerd Bastian were shot at their home in 1992 in mysterious circumstances. Joint suicide? Murder-suicide? Double murder? Secret service plot? *The Life and Death of Petra Kelly*, written by Sara Parkin, provides tantalising details.

Food & Drink

Unlike France or Italy, Germany has never been a culinary destination. In the international imagination, its food is often just something – usually a *Wurst* (sausage) – to accompany its superlative beer. Relying heavily on meat, cabbage and potato, the country's traditional cuisine has a not entirely undeserved reputation as hearty but dull. As one old saying cruelly has it, the problem with German food is that a week later you want some more!

However, Germany has been redeeming itself gastronomically in the past decade in much the same way as has happened in Britain. Top chefs have been experimenting with time-honoured dishes in a wave that's referred to as the *Neue Deutsche Küche* (New German Cuisine), and *multi-kulti* (multicultural) influences – ranging from Turkish to Mediterranean to Asian – have put baba ganoush, burritos and curries on menus and pesto, coconut milk and coriander on Aldi supermarket shelves.

You still won't find the love of excellent food – and the ability to produce it – permeating every corner of every neighbourhood restaurant as you will in, say, Italy. However, the *Imbiss* fast-food stall is a ubiquitous phenomenon, allowing you to eat on the run easily, and if you choose your restaurants with just a little care, it is possible to treat your palate here.

STAPLES & SPECIALITIES

The modern doner *(Döner)* kebab doesn't emanate from Turkey, but Germany. In 1971, Turkish immigrants running the Berlin restaurant Hasir introduced salad into an ancient Turkish dish; even outlets in Turkey have been making it this way ever since.

Wurst, *Brot*, *Kartoffeln* and *Sauerkraut* (sausage, bread, potatoes and cabbage): yes, sometimes all the national stereotypes ring true. In Germany you'll certainly find things like *Kalbshaxe* (knuckle of veal) and *Sauerbraten* (roast beef marinated in wine and vinegar), but were you aware that *Quark*, a yoghurt-like curd cheese, accounts for 50% of domestic cheese consumption? Or, did you realise that locals are equally devoted to asparagus, mushrooms, pumpkin and venison?

Sausage

In the Middle Ages, German peasants found a way to package and disguise animals' less appetising bits, and the *Wurst* (sausage) was born. Today, it's a noble and highly respected element of German cuisine, with strict rules determining the authenticity of *Wurst* varieties. In some cases, as with the finger-sized Nuremberg sausage, regulations even ensure offal no longer enters the equation.

There are more than 1500 sausage species, all commonly served with bread and a sweet *(süss)* or spicy *(scharf)* mustard *(Senf)*.

Bratwurst, served countrywide, is made from minced pork, veal and spices, and is cooked in different ways (boiled in beer, baked with apples and cabbage, stewed in a casserole or simply grilled or barbecued).

See how German chefs rank among Europe's best at the bang-up-to-date www.die-besten-koeche .com (also in English).

The availability of other sausages differs regionally. A *Thüringer* is long, thin and spiced, while a *Wiener* is what hot-dog fiends call a Frankfurter. *Blutwurst* is blood sausage (not to be confused with black pudding, which is *Rotwurst*), *Leberwurst* is liver sausage, and *Knackwurst* is lightly tickled with garlic.

Saxony has brain sausage *(Bregenwurst)*, Bavaria sells white rubbery *Weisswurst*, made from veal, and Berlin boasts the *Currywurst* (slices of sausage topped with curry powder and ketchup). For more on the latter, see the boxed text on p130.

Bread

In exile in California in 1941, German playwright Bertolt Brecht confessed that what he most missed about his homeland was the bread. That won't surprise anyone who has sampled the stuff. German bread is a world-beater, in a league of its own. It's tasty and textured, often mixing wheat and rye flour, and is available in 300 varieties.

'Black' rye bread *(Schwarzbrot)* is actually brown, but a much darker shade than the slightly sour *Bauernbrot*. *Pumpernickel* bread is steam-cooked instead of baked, making it extra moist, and actually is black. *Vollkorn* means wholemeal, while bread coated in sunflower seeds is *Sonnenblumenbrot*. If you insist on white bread *(Weissbrot)*, the Germans have that too.

Fresh bread rolls *(Brötchen* in the north, *Semmel* in Bavaria, *Wecken* in the rest of southern Germany) can be covered in poppy seeds *(Mohnbrötchen)*, cooked with sweet raisins *(Rosinenbrötchen)*, sprinkled with salt *(Salzstangel)* or treated in dozens of other different ways.

Brezeln are traditional pretzels, covered in rock salt.

Potato

Germans are almost as keen as Russians about the potato. The *Kartoffel* is not only Vegetable Nummer Eins in any meat-and-three-veg dish, it can also be incorporated into any course of a meal, from potato soup *(Kartoffelsuppe)* as a starter, to potato waffles *(Kartoffelwaffeln)* or potato pancakes *(Reibekuchen)* as a sweet treat.

In between, you can try *Himmel und Erde* (Heaven and Earth), a dish of mashed potatoes and stewed apples served with black pudding, or potato-based *Klösse* dumplings. *Pellkartoffeln* or *Ofenkartoffeln* are jacket potatoes, usually capped with a dollop of *Quark*.

Many 'potato festivals' are held throughout the country.

> Living in the USA? Shop for *Brot* und *Wurst* as if you're in Germany at www.germandeli.com.

Sauerkraut

Finally comes a quintessential German side dish that many outside the country find impossible to fathom: *Sauerkraut*. Before the 2006 FIFA World Cup, one football magazine suggested, with typical abrasiveness: 'It's pickled cabbage; don't try to make it sound interesting.' Okay, we won't. It's shredded cabbage, doused in white-wine vinegar and slowly simmered. But if you haven't at least tried *Rotkohl* (the red-cabbage version of the white-cabbage *Sauerkraut*) you don't know what you're missing. Braising the cabbage with sliced apples and wine turns it into *Bayrischkraut* or *Weinkraut*.

Regional Dishes

Although contemporary German restaurants offer as much of an international mix as anywhere in the world, the country's traditional cuisine has been much more resistant to outside influences than that of, say, Hungary or Italy. Consequently, traditional regional variations remain quite noticeable too.

The food in southern states features many pork and veal dishes, accompanied by noodles or dumplings. It's in the northern states that root vegetables such as potatoes predominate, and here there's a much greater focus on fish.

Towards the country's borders, its cuisine does take on French, Scandinavian and even Slavic flavours. But it's a subtle difference and the taste usually remains recognisably German.

> Indisputably *the* handbook of German cuisine since it was published in the 1960s, Dr Oetker's German *Cooking: The Original* was handily re-released in 2003, filling you in on all the basic techniques and classic dishes

BAVARIA

The Chinese say you can eat every part of the pig bar the 'oink', and Bavarian chefs seem to be in full agreement. No part of the animal is spared their attention as they cook up its knuckles *(Schweinshax'n)*, ribs *(Rippchen)*, tongue *(Züngerl)* and belly *(Wammerl)*. Pork also appears as *Schweinebraten* (a roast) and the misleadingly named *Leberkäse* (liver cheese), where it's combined with beef in a dish that contains no cheese – and in Bavaria at least – no liver. The Bavarians are also quite fond of veal *(Kalb)*.

Dumplings are another menu staple, from potato-based *Klösse* and *Leberknödel* (liver dumplings) to sweet *Senfknödel*, which is made from *Quark*, flour and eggs, then dunked in milk. Dumplings also make a major appearance in the Franconian favourite of *Hochszeitsuppe* (wedding soup) – a clear meat broth garnished with bread dumplings, liver dumplings and pancakes.

Discover 101 things to do with a pig in Olli Leeb's *Bavarian Cooking*, jam-packed with cultural and culinary insights into one of Germany's most distinctive regional cuisines.

BADEN-WÜRTTEMBERG

Neighbouring influences are evident in Baden-Württemberg. Snail soup *(Schneckensuppe)* crosses the border with Alsace, while locals also enjoy *Geschnetzeltes* (veal slices in a white wine and cream sauce) as much as the Swiss.

Pasta is another recurrent theme, with *Spätzle* (literally 'little sparrows') a type of egg-based noodle, served as a main meal or used to dress meat or fish. The ravioli-like *Maultaschen* are stuffed with ground meat, onion and spinach.

SAARLAND

Just as in Baden-Württemberg, the food here shows many French influences. Fried goose liver and *coq au vin* are common on menus, as is *Budeng mit Gellenewemutsch*, a *boudain* (hot black pudding) served with a German mash of carrots and potatoes.

When it comes to the crunch though, Saarlanders revert to true German form, and *Schwenkbraten* (marinated pork grilled on a spit) is probably their most popular dish.

RHINELAND-PALATINATE

Two former chancellors named dishes from this region as their favourite, selecting two meals as different as the men themselves. Helmut Kohl nominated *Saumagen*, a stuffed pork belly with pickled cabbage that's the German equivalent to Scottish haggis, while postwar chancellor Konrad Adenauer preferred *Reibekuchen*, small potato pancakes served with blueberry or apple sauce.

Despite all this, *Rheinischer Sauerbraten* (roast beef marinated in spiced vinegar and braised) is the region's signature dish.

HESSE & WESTPHALIA

Neighbouring Hesse and Westphalia produce outstanding cured and smoked hams (typically smoking them over juniper berries). In Hesse, they like pig in the form of *Sulperknochen*, a dish from trotters, ears and tails, served with mushy peas and pickled cabbage. Westphalians prefer *Pfefferpotthast*, a meat stew spiced with capers, lemon juice and beer.

HAMBURG & AROUND

No two dishes better sum up northern Germany's warming, seafaring fodder than *Labskaus* and *Grünkohl mit Pinkel*. There are variations, but traditional *Labskaus* from Hamburg is a minced dish of salt herring, corned beef, pig lard, potato and beetroot, topped with gherkins and a fried egg. It's a sailor's favourite and, some locals claim, brilliant hangover food – plenty of salt, plenty of fat and not too hard to chew.

Grünkohl mit Pinkel combines steamed kale with pork belly, bacon and *Pinkelwurst* (a spicy pork, beef, oat and onion sausage from Bremen).

Eel soup *(Aalsuppe)* is sweet-and-sour – it's garnished with bacon and vegetables, and spiced with apricots, pears or prunes.

FALSE FRIENDS

When ordering food in parts of the country, sometimes a little knowledge of German can be a dangerous thing. So, don't expect half a chicken when you order a *Halve Hahn* in Cologne. It's a rye-bread roll with gouda cheese, gherkin and mustard. *Kölscher Kaviar* is similarly confusing – it's not caviar, but black pudding. And *Nordseekrabben* in Hamburg and Lower Saxony? They're small prawns…of course.

As you move towards Scandinavia, the German diet begins to encompass Nordic staples such as rollmops and herring *(Hering)* in all its other guises (raw, smoked, pickled or rolled in sour cream).

MECKLENBURG WESTERN POMERANIA
This northeastern state shares Hamburg's obsession with herring, eel and other types of seafood, throwing in a propensity to smoke its fish and a penchant for Baltic cod. Otherwise, it has a quite distinctive cuisine, with locals famed for liking things sweet-and-sour.

Take *Mecklenburger Rippenbraten* for example, rolled pork stuffed with lemons, apples, plums, and raisins; or *Mecklenburgische Buttermilchsuppe*, which is a sweet buttermilk soup flavoured with spices and jam; or the Russian-style *Soljanka*, sour soup with sausage or fish, garnished with lemon and sour cream.

Other typical mixes include raisins with cabbage, honey with pork, and plums with duck. Even the typical *Eintopf* (stew, often a potato version) is served with sugar and vinegar on the side.

Bread pudding is a very popular dessert throughout the state, but visitors might prefer the more unusual and delicious *Sanddorn* (sallow thorn). Nicknamed the 'Mecklenburg lemon', this is a shrub berry with a subtle citrus flavour, and is used to great effect in teas, ice-creams and other dishes (as well as beauty products).

Germany's most famous TV chef, Tim Mälzer, updates some standards in his best-selling book, *Born To Cook*, such as making *Kalbshaxe* with star anise and *Labskaus* with poached salmon.

BERLIN
Alongside Hamburg, Berlin has one of the country's most cosmopolitan restaurant scenes, but it can still lay claim to a few local delicacies. First on the list comes *Eisbein*, or pigs' knuckles, then *Kohlsuppe* (cabbage soup) and *Erbensuppe* (pea soup).

Ironically, the *Berliner* doughnut, which President John F. Kennedy once claimed himself to be, does not emanate from the capital. For something sweet, locals are much more likely to tuck into the coffee cake known as *Kugelhupf* (also spelled *Gugelhupf*).

SAXONY & THURINGIA
These regions are slightly less meat-obsessed than some of their cousins. *Kartoffelsuppe* (potato soup) is a favourite, and *Leipziger Allerlei* (Leipzig hotpot) often comes in vegetarian versions. There are even lentils to be found in such dishes as *Linsensuppe mit Thüringer Rotwurst* (lentil soup with Thuringian sausages). For dessert, you can try *Quarkkeulchen*, made from curd, boiled potatoes, flour, sugar, and raisins – although these have spread to other parts of Germany, too.

Seasonal Specialities
In an era in which fruit jets around the globe clocking up frequent-flyer miles, and high-tech farming boosts year-round supplies, Germans remain touchingly devoted to their seasonal specialities.

No period ranks higher on the culinary calendar than *Spargelzeit* (asparagus season), when Germans devour great quantities of mostly white asparagus, which they generally consider tastier than the green variety.The season kicks off with the harvesting of the first crop in mid-April and lasts until 24 June – the feast-day of St John the Baptist – which is fitting, given the almost religious intensity with which this 'king of vegetables' is celebrated. You'll find restaurants with separate asparagus menus and whole books devoted to the subject, while many towns and cities even hold asparagus festivals in May and June.

Herring weeks are frequently held on the Baltic coast in spring. Other notable seasonal specialities include *Pfifferlinge* (chanterelles) and *Kürbis* (pumpkin), an autumn treat.

Sweets

> When Lübeck started producing marzipan in the Middle Ages, the almond paste was considered a medicine not a sweet. We want to know: can we get it on prescription?

Germans more often exercise their sweet tooth over *Kaffee und Kuchen* (coffee and cakes) than they do after a meal. Desserts (*Nachspeisen* or *Nachtische*) are usually light affairs, say custard and fruit, *Rote Grütze* (a tart fruit compote topped with vanilla sauce), ice cream or a fruit salad.

However, let's not forget that this is the country that brought the world the sugary, creamy, calorie-laden, over-the-top *Schwarzwälder Kirschtorte* (Black Forest Gateaux).

And if that isn't enough of a calling card for sugar fiends, Germany offers an enormous range of other delicious confections, from *Lebkuchen* (gingerbread) and *Nürnberger Lebkuchen* (soft cookies with nuts, fruit peel, honey and spices from Nuremberg) to *Leckerli* (honey-flavoured ginger biscuits) and *Lübecker Marzipan* (marzipan from Lübeck).

Christmas brings its own specialities. *Stollen* is a spiced cake loaded with sultanas, raisins and candied peel, sprinkled with icing sugar and occasionally spruced up inside with a ball of marzipan. It's rarely baked in German homes today (although when it is, it's exquisite), but you'll find it in abundance in Christmas markets – *Stollen* from Dresden is reputedly the best.

DRINKS

While coffee in Germany is not as strong as that served in France or Italy, you can expect a decent cup. All the usual varieties are on offer, including cappuccinos and lattes, although you still frequently see French-style bowls of milky coffee, or *Milchkaffee* (milk coffee).

Tea frequently comes in a glass or pot of hot water, with the teabag served to the side. East Frisians in Bremen and Lower Saxony are the country's biggest consumers of tea, and have dozens of their own varieties, which they traditionally drink with cream and *Kluntje* (rock sugar).

Germans once almost exclusively drank sparkling mineral water (*Mineralwasser*), with loads of bubbles (*mit Gas* or *mit Kohlensäure*). Truly still mineral water (*stilles* or *ohne Kohlensäure*) has become much more widespread, but it remains harder to find than in some other European countries.

Note that the price of many drinks in plastic bottles includes a *Pfand*, or deposit, which will be given back to you if you return the bottle to the shop or similar outlet. Soft drinks frequently come in cans (*Dosen*), too.

When not guzzling beer or wine (see opposite and p81), Germans like a shot of schnapps (any hard liquor). This comes in a variety of flavours, from apple (*Apfel*), pear (*Birne*), or plum (*Pflaume*) to wheat (*Korn*).

Digestive herbal drinks such as *Jägermeister* are also still popular, although mainly among the older population.

BETTER THAN GLÜHWEIN

Served in winter and designed to inure you to the sudden drop in temperatures, hot spiced *Glühwein* is a common commodity at Germany's popular Christmas markets. However, it's not the only mulled wine the country produces. Far more spectacular and intoxicating is *Feuerzangenbowle* – 'fire-tongs-punch' – which has become a cult tipple, thanks to a movie of the same name.

Contrary to the usual advice, *do* try this at home – providing you can get hold of the necessary equipment (try a German Christmas market). Fill a large saucepan with two or three bottles of red wine, cloves, a stick of cinnamon and slices of citrus fruit, and gently heat. Place a *Zuckerhut* (sugar cone) into a special silver cradle (the *Feuerzange* or 'tong'), and rest them both horizontally over the saucepan. Pour over-proof rum (between 50-60%) over the sugar cone with a ladle (for safety's sake, not straight from the bottle). Let it soak for a minute and then carefully put a lit match over the sugar, igniting it. As the flaming sugar falls into the spiced red wine below, it produces a delicious and heady drink.

The 1944 film *Feuerzangenbowle* has four men reminiscing about their school days over a bowl of the self-same punch; when it transpires that one of them was educated by a private tutor and has no idea what they're talking about, they disguise him and send him back to school as an adult. Long banned for its anti-authoritarian attitudes, it's now screened in cinemas before Christmas.

Beer

It's not as cheap as the Czech Republic's world-famous lagers, but German beer is patently up there with the best and is well worth the premium. Brewing here goes back to Germanic tribes, and later monks, so it follows in a hallowed tradition. Unsurprisingly, a trip to an atmospheric Bavarian beer garden or a Cologne beer hall is one of the first things on many foreign visitors' 'to-do' lists.

The 'secret' of the country's golden nectar dates back to the *Reinheitsgebot*, or purity law, demanding breweries use just four ingredients – malt, yeast, hops and water. Passed in Bavaria in 1516, the *Reinheitsgebot* stopped being a legal requirement in 1987, when the European Union struck it down as uncompetitive. However, many German brewers still conform to it anyway, seeing it as a good marketing tool against mass-market, chemical-happy competitors.

Horst Dornbusch's *Prost!: The Story of German Beer,* is exactly that.

Thanks to the tradition of the *Reinheitsgebot*, German beer is supposed to be unique in not giving you a *Katzenjammer* or *Kater* (hangover). However, partygoers downing 5 million litres of the stuff at Munich's Oktoberfest (see p304) must surely disagree!

VARIETIES

Despite frequently tying their own hands and giving themselves just four ingredients to play with, German brewers turn out 5000 distinctively different beers.

BREWERY TOURS

Most visitors to Germany are content just to quaff the country's excellent beer – whether from a huge Bavarian stein or one of Cologne's trademark skinny glasses. The more curious might be interested to see how it's mixed.

You can do this at any of the **Holsten breweries** (www.holsten.de), while Beck's (p645) and Friesisches Brauhaus zu Jever (p636) also run tours. Meanwhile, the art of 19th-century beer-making is unravelled at Maisel's Brauerei-und-Büttnerei-Museum in Bayreuth (p368), the world's most comprehensive beer museum (according to the *Guinness Book of Records*). There's also a new Brauerei-Museum in Dortmund (p577), once Germany's most important beer town. Tour details are included in the regional chapters.

They achieve this via subtle variations in the basic production process. At the simplest level, a brewer can choose a particular yeast for top or bottom fermenting (the terms indicating where the yeast lives while working – at the top or bottom of the brewing vessel).

The most popular form of brewing is bottom-fermentation, which accounts for about 85% of German beers, notably the Pils (Pilsener) popular throughout Germany, most Bock beers and the Helles type found in Bavaria.

Top-brewing is used for the Weizenbier/Weissbier (wheat or 'white' beer) popular in Berlin and Bavaria, Cologne's Kölsch and the very few stouts brewed in the country.

Many beers are regional, meaning a Saxon Rechenberger cannot be found in Düsseldorf, where the locally brewed Altbier is the taste of choice. The following list runs through some interesting varieties.

> What did Germany's first railway line carry when it opened between Nuremberg and Fürth in 1835? Beer.

BEER GLOSSARY

Alkoholfreies Bier Nonalcoholic beer.

Altbier A dark, full beer with malted barley from the Düsseldorf area.

Berliner Weisse With around 2.8% alcohol content, draught or Schankbier is mostly brewed in and around Berlin. It contains lactic acid, giving it a slightly sour taste, and a blend of malted wheat and barley. Top-fermented, it's often drunk *mit Grün* (with green or woodruff syrup), or with a dash *(mit Schuss)* of raspberry *(Himbeeren)* syrup.

Bockbier and Doppelbock These two strong beers are around 7% alcohol, but Doppelbock is slightly stronger. There's a 'Bock' for almost every occasion, such as Maibock (usually drunk in May/spring) and Weihnachtsbock (brewed for Christmas). Eisbock (ice Bock) is dark and more aromatic. Bock beers originate from Einbeck, near Hanover.

Dampfbier (steam beer) Originating from Bayreuth in Bavaria, this is top-fermented and has a fruity flavour.

Dunkles Lagerbier (dark lager) Dunkel (dark) is brewed throughout Germany, but especially in Bavaria. With a light use of hops, it's full-bodied with a strong malt aroma. Malt is dried at a high temperature, lending it a dark colour.

Export Traditionally with a higher alcohol content, to help it survive a long journey, this beer is closely associated today with Dortmund, and is often dry to slightly sweet.

Helles Lagerbier (pale lager) Helles (pale or light) refers to the colour, not the alcohol content, which is still around 4.6% to 5%. Brewing strongholds are in Bavaria, Baden-Württemberg and in the Ruhr region. It has strong malt aromas and is slightly sweet.

Hofbräu This is a brewery belonging to a royal court or *Hof* – for some time in Bavaria only a few nobles enjoyed the right to brew wheat beer.

Klosterbräu This type of brewery belongs to a monastery.

Kölsch By law, this top-fermented beer can only be brewed in or around Cologne. It is about 4.8% alcohol, has a solid hop flavour and pale colour, and is served in small glasses (0.2L) called *Stangen* (literally 'sticks').

Leichtbier (light beer) These low-alcohol beers are about 2% to 3.2% alcohol.

Leipziger Gose An unusual beer, flavoured with salt and coriander, this contrives to have a stingingly refreshing taste, with some plummy overtones. Tart like Berliner Weisse, it's also often served with sweeteners, such as cherry *(Kirsch)* liqueur or the almond-flavoured *Allasch*.

Malzbier (malt beer) A sweet, aromatic, full-bodied beer, this is brewed mainly in Bavaria and Baden-Württemberg.

Märzen (March) Full-bodied with strong malt aromas, this is traditionally brewed in March. Today, it's associated with the Oktoberfest.

Obergäriges Bier Top-fermented beer.

Pils (pilsener) This bottom-fermented full beer, with a pronounced hop flavour and a creamy head, has an alcohol content of around 4.8% and is served throughout Germany.

Rauchbier (smoke beer) This dark beer has a fresh, spicy or 'smoky' flavour.

Schwarzbier (black beer) Slightly stronger, this dark, full beer has an alcohol content of about 4.8% to 5%. Full-bodied, it's fermented using roasted malt.

Untergäriges Bier Bottom-fermented beer.

Weizenbier or Weissbier (wheat beer) Predominating in the south, especially in Bavaria, this is around 5.4% alcohol. A Hefeweizen has a stronger shot of yeast, whereas Kristallweizen is clearer with more fizz. These wheat beers are fruity and spicy, often recalling bananas and cloves. Decline offers of a slice of lemon, as it ruins the head and – beer purists say – also the flavour.

THE INDUSTRY

German beer is brewed by more than 1200 breweries, although many traditionally family-run concerns have been swallowed up by the big-boy brewers. Bremen-based Beck's, producer of one of Germany's best-known beers since 1873, was bought out by Belgian beer giant Interbrew in 2002, while Hamburg's Holsten (founded 1879) now has its roots firmly embedded in the USA.

Still, 11 German monasteries continue to produce beer. Kloster Weltenburg, near Kelheim on the Danube north of Munich, is the world's oldest monastery brewery, whose Weltenburg Barock Dunckel won a medal at the 2006 World Beer Cup in Seattle. This light, smooth beer has a malty, toasty finish.

Other connoisseurs believe the earthy Andechs Doppelbock Dunkel, produced by the Benedictines in Andechs near Munich, to be among the world's best.

Dortmund is the centre of the Export industry.

For more bare beer facts, statistics, tips on cooking with beer and more, surf with the German Federation of Brewers (in German) at www .brauer-bund.de.

Wine

Its name sullied for decades by the cloyingly sugary taste of *Liebfraumilch* white wine, German wine has been making a comeback in the 21st century. Following the 2002 marketing campaign – 'If you think you know German wine, drink again' – in the industry's biggest export market, the UK, sellers have been talking of a renaissance. And although the re-evaluation is still in its beginnings, it's not all public relations hype. Even discerning critics have been pouring praise on German winemakers, with *Decanter* magazine, for example, naming Ernst Loosen, of Weingut Dr Loosen in the Mosel region, its 'Man of the Year 2005'.

Germany is most commonly associated with white wines made from Riesling grapes. According to Tim Atkin, wine correspondent for the UK's *Observer* newspaper, wine producers in Australia, Austria and Alsace have recently done Germany a favour in using and promoting the grape. This, he says, 'has helped consumers realise that Germany makes the best Rieslings of all'. At the same time, the country itself has had 'a tremendous run of vintages since 2000', and its midrange wines have markedly improved, with brands like **Devil's Rock** (www.devils-rock.com), **Dr Loosen** (www.drloosen.com) and the **Vineyard Creatures series** (www.lingenfelder.com).

Having produced wines since Roman times, Germany now has more than 100,000 hectares of vineyards, mostly on the Rhine and Moselle riverbanks. Despite the common association with Riesling grapes, particularly in its best wine regions, the less acidic Müller-Thurgau or Rivaner grape is more widespread. Meanwhile, the Gewürztraminer grape produces spicy wines with an intense bouquet. What Germans call *Grauburgunder* is known to the rest of the world as Pinot Gris.

German reds are light and lesser known. *Spätburgunder*, or Pinot Noir, is the best of the bunch and goes into some velvety, full-bodied reds with an occasional almond taste.

Germany's wine market, from medieval times to present, is the fascinating focus of *The Wines of Germany* by Stephen Brook. Among other things he addresses the question of why German wine has long been mocked.

WINE REGIONS

There are 13 official wine-growing areas, the best being the Mosel-Saar-Ruwer region. It boasts some of the world's steepest vineyards, where the

TOP FIVE GERMAN WINE PRODUCERS

'Too many people still associate Germany with basic, sugary whites,' says Tim Atkin, wine correspondent for the UK's *Observer* newspaper. He points out there's much more to Germany, and suggests keeping a particular eye out for the following producers:

- **Fritz Haag** (☎ 06534-410; www.weingut-fritz-haag.de; Dusemonder Hof, Brauneberg, Mosel region)
- **Egon Müller Scharzhof** (www.scharzhof.de; Saar region)
- **Dönnhoff** (☎ 06755-263; www.doennhoff.com; Oberhausen, Nahe region)
- **JJ Prüm** (www.jjpruem.de; Uferallee 19, Bernkastel-Wehlen, Mosel region)
- **Wittmann** (☎ 06244-905036; www.weingutwittman.com; Mainzer Strasse 19, Westhofen bei Worms, Rheinhessen region)

predominantly Riesling grapes are still hand-picked. Slate soil on the hillsides gives the wines a flinty taste. Chalkier riverside soils are planted with the Elbing grape, an ancient Roman variety.

East of the Moselle, the Nahe region produces fragrant, fruity and full-bodied wines using Müller-Thurgau and Silvaner grapes as well as Riesling.

Riesling grapes are also the mainstay in Rheingau and Mittelrhein (Middle Rhine), two other highly respected wine-growing pockets. Rheinhessen, south of Rheingau, is responsible for *Liebfraumilch*, but also some top Rieslings.

Other wine regions include Ahr, Pfalz (both Rheinland-Palatinate), Hessische Bergstrasse (Hesse), Baden (Baden-Württemberg), Würzburg (Bavaria) and Elbtal (Saxony).

The Württemberg region, around Stuttgart, produces some of the country's best reds, while Saxony-Anhalt's Saale/Unstrut region is home to Rotkäppchen (Little Red Riding Hood) sparkling wine, a former GDR brand that's been a big hit in the new Germany.

For a comprehensive run-down of all German wine-growing regions, grape varieties, news of the hottest winemakers, and information on tours or courses, visit www.winesofgermany.co.uk (interested US citizens could also browse www.germanwineusa.org).

WINE GLOSSARY

Auslese A 'selected harvest', this is usually intense and sweet.

Beerenauslese (BA) Grapes are picked overripe, and it's usually a dessert wine.

Deutscher Landwein (country wine) Landwein is usually dry or semi-dry.

Deutscher Tafelwein (table wine) This is the lowest category of wine, and is of mostly poor to average quality.

Eiswein Grapes are picked and pressed while frozen and it's very sweet; a dessert wine.

QbA (Qualitätswein bestimmter Anbaugebiete) The lowest category of quality wine.

QmP (Qualitätswein mit Prädikat) 'Quality wine of distinction'.

Qualitätswein Wine from one of the 13 defined wine-growing regions, which has to pass a tasting test.

Sekt Sparkling wine.

Spätauslese Literally 'selected late-harvest', this type of wine has concentrated flavours, but is not necessarily sweet.

Trockenbeerenauslese (TBA) The grapes are so overripe they are shrivelled (intensely sweet) and resemble raisins.

WHERE TO EAT & DRINK

Dining out in Germany these days is little different from visiting a restaurant in the rest of the western world. Sure, you can try for a little authentic local cuisine in an atmospheric town-hall basement restaurant (*Ratskeller*), although you might often find that your fellow diners aren't locals, but other tourists looking for the same thing. It's much better to ask your hotel for a recommendation. German-only menus (*Speisekarte*) displayed outside an establishment are a good sign; the waiter will almost invariably be able to translate for you.

Diners seeking somewhere less formal can opt for a *Gaststätte*, a relaxed and often more 'local' place to eat with a large menu, daily specials and a beer garden out the back. Equally inviting are small bistros calling themselves *Weinkeller* or *Bierkeller* (cellars serving wine or beer), which cook up light meals as well as serving glasses of wine or beer. Most cafés and bars serve coffee and light snacks as well as alcohol.

For information on the customary business hours which restaurants and other eateries keep, see p740.

Quick Eats

A *Stehcafé* is a stand-up café where sweet cravers can indulge in coffee and cakes at speed and on the cheap. Stand-up food stalls (*Schnellimbiss*, or simply *Imbiss*) around town make handy speed-feed stops for savoury fodder. In Berlin and other cities, some stalls cook up quick Greek, Italian, Middle Eastern and Chinese bites.

Germany's Turkish population invented the modern doner *(Döner)* kebab, adding salad and sauces to slices of roasted beef, chicken or lamb sandwiched inside pitta bread. Most kebab joints also do veggie versions.

In the north, herring and other fish snacks abound. The Nordsee chain is found countrywide (as well as in Switzerland), while the similar – but slightly more upmarket – Gosch (see p701) is more of a quintessential German experience.

Bavarian beer gardens typically serve light snacks such as fresh warm pretzels *(Brez'n)*, Bavarian-style meatloaf *(Leberkäs)* and radishes *(Radi)* to their beer-swilling clientele.

VEGETARIANS & VEGANS

While vegetarians will have few tummy grumbles in Berlin and other major cities, the pickings in provincial Germany might be slimmer. Vegetables

You don't need your Michelin or Gault Millau guides to check out Germany's best restaurants, the country has its own ratings and guides, including *Der Feinschmecker* (www .feinschmecker.de), Aral's *Schlemmer Atlas* (www .schlemmer-atlas.de) and *Marcellino's Restaurant Report* (www.marcel linos.de)

GERMANY'S TOP EATS

Germany's 'best', in the conventional sense, they might not be, but we've followed our stomachs to nose out – several hundred meals later – the following tasty cross-section of tastebud ticklers:

- Auberge Moar-Alm (p324) – Franco-German cuisine in the crisp Alpine air north of Bad Tölz.
- Das Weisse Haus (p672) – Partake in prime-time dining in a fisherman's cottage in Hamburg.
- Die Quadriga (p132) – Toast your gourmet meal with one of Germany's 850 best wines at this Michelin-starred favourite.
- Hotel am Schloss restaurant (p426) – This Tübingen institution is renowned for making some of Baden-Württemberg's finest *Maultaschen* (German ravioli).
- Le Canard Nouveau (p672) – Exquisite innovation and one of Hamburg's best riverside seats.
- Margaux (p131) – First-class produce is deployed in skilful avant-garde spins on the classics at this Berlin dining shrine, honoured with a Michelin star.
- Strandhalle (p731) – Fine unfussy dining in a memorably decorated room with views of Binz's sandy shores.
- Don Camillo (p257) – Romantic atmosphere, bold culinary tones and some exciting wines in Erfurt's Andreasviertel.
- Tiger-Restaurant (p522) – Culinary guru Martin Göschel's stellar menus in the restaurant of Frankfurt's acclaimed Tigerpalast cabaret venue.

cooked with meat are often considered meat-free, while many so-called vegetarian places serve fish or chicken.

But all is not lost in this carnivorous land. Most city-based Thai, Vietnamese and other Asian eateries cook up dishes suitable for vegetarians. A couple of regional dishes also do not – miraculously – contain meat, including *Leipziger Allerlei*, a vegetarian option in Saxony. Vegetarians in Frankfurt can feast on *Grüne Sosse* – a tasty green sauce eaten as a main dish on top of boiled potatoes or hard-boiled eggs. Fresh basil, chives, cress, dill, sorrel, parsley and tarragon (estragon) are among the wealth of herbs to be found in this green, cream-based sauce – a seasonal dish available early spring to early autumn.

Vegetable- or cheese-stuffed strudel (*Gemüsestrudel* or *Topfenstrudel*), potato pancakes (*Kartoffelpuffer*) and potato and semolina dumplings (*Erdäpfelknödel*) are more widespread veg-inspired offerings.

Vegans should plan on sticking to vegetarian Asian cuisine. Most German vegetarian dishes come with cream or cheese; even salads sometimes come with mayonnaise- or yoghurt-based dressings.

EATING WITH KIDS

Dining with kids is by no means a whining affair in Germany. High chairs are a permanent fixture in restaurants – upmarket and budget alike – and, if you're lucky, the waiter will come clad with damp cloth at the end of your meal to wipe sticky little fingers clean. Most *Gaststätte* and less formal restaurants offer a small choice of *Kindermenü* (children's menu) and dishes for children (*Kinderteller* or *Für unsere kleinen Gäste*), and those that don't will almost certainly try to meet any special small-appetite requirements. Eating establishments are not equipped with nappy-changing facilities, but some fast-food and quick-eat places have a fold-down changing table in the women's loo.

Supermarkets sell a vast range of ready-made baby food and toddler meals – predominantly organic – as well as formula milk, organic fruit juices and teas.

HABITS & CUSTOMS

Germans eat three meals a day – breakfast (*Frühstück*), lunch (*Mittagessen*) and dinner (*Abendessen*).

Breakfast at home is served on a wooden board (rather than a plate). Great animal-shaped boards, complete with a hollowed-out eye to prop up a hard-boiled egg, can often be found at markets. Yoghurt, *Quark*, muesli, cereal, fruit salad and other typical breakfast staples feature in hotel buffets.

Traditionally, lunch would be the main meal of the day. In the domestic arena, modern working practices have changed this considerably, although many restaurants still tout lunchtime dishes or a fixed lunch menu (*Gedeck* or *Tagesmenü*).

Dinner is dished up at home around 7pm, and in restaurants between about 6pm and 11pm. Both meals are relaxed, and require few airs and graces beyond the obligatory '*Guten Appetit*' (meaning 'good appetite'), exchanged between diners before eating. German workers lunching at shared tables sometimes still exchange a courteous '*Mahlzeit*' (literally 'mealtime') before tucking in.

Tipping is quite an individual matter. Many locals, particularly older Germans, will tip absolutely nothing. Some round up the bill, while others tip between 10% and 15%. Do whatever you're comfortable with, given the service and setting – and remembering that Germans are still living through slightly testing economic times.

EAT YOUR WORDS

Pronunciation guidelines are included in the Language chapter (p774).

Useful Phrases

Can you recommend ...?
Können Sie ... empfehlen?   keu·nen zee ... emp·*fay*·len
a restaurant
ein Restaurant   ain res·to·*rang*
a bar/pub
eine Kneipe   ai·ne *knai*·pe

Where would you go for ...?
Wo kann man hingehen, um ...?   vaw kan man *hin*·gay·en um ...?
local specialities
örtliche Spezialitäten zu essen   eut·li·khe shpe·tsya·li·*tay*·ten tsoo e·sen
a cheap meal
günstig zu essen   *gewn*·stikh tsoo e·sen
a celebration
etwas zu feiern   et·vas tsoo fai·ern

I'd like to reserve a table for ...
Ich möchte einen Tisch für ... reservieren. ikh meukh·te ai·nen tish fewr ... re·zer·*vee*·ren
(two) people
(zwei) Personen   (tsvai) per·*zaw*·nen
(eight) o'clock
(acht) Uhr   (akt) oor

DOS & DON'TS

One early 20th-century German book of manners that we have seen exhorts dinner guests not to use their knives to carve their initials into the table of their hosts! Things have, fortunately, moved on somewhat since those days. With good manners now an automatic reflex, there's little need to panic at the dinner table, although the following tips might be helpful for first-time visitors to Germany.

■ Do bring a small gift – a bottle of wine or flowers – if you've been invited to a meal.

■ Do inform your hosts beforehand of any dietary needs.

■ Do say *'Guten Appetit'* (good appetite) before starting to eat, and *'Prost!'* when drinking a toast.

■ Do offer to help wash-up afterwards, particularly as locals tend to be quite punctilious about housework.

■ Do specify if you don't want your restaurant dishes slathered in mayonnaise, *Quark* or dressing. Germans are unbelievably generous in this department.

■ Do pay your bill at the table and give any tip directly to the server. Say either the amount you want to pay, or *'Stimmt so'* if you don't want change.

■ Don't expect to get a glass of tap water at a restaurant or café; it's an unusual request that probably won't be understood or honoured.

■ Don't get impatient or testy when waiting in a café, where many customers come to linger. If you're in a hurry, go to a *Stehcafé*.

■ Don't assume you can pay by credit card when eating out. Very few restaurants accept cards, and then only at the top end of the market. Take enough cash instead.

I'm starving!
 Ich bin am Verhungern!   ikh bin am fer·*hung*·ern
Are you still serving food?
 Gibt es noch etwas zu essen?   gipt es nokh *et*·vas tsoo e·sen?

Do you have ...?
 Haben Sie ...?   *ha*·ben zee ...?
 a menu in English
 eine englische Speisekarte   *ai*·ne *eng*·li·she *shpai*·ze·kar·te
 kosher food
 koscheres Essen   *kaw*·she·res e·sen
 vegetarian food
 vegetarisches Essen   ve·ge·*ta*·ri·shes e·sen

What would you recommend?
 Was empfehlen Sie?   vas emp·*fay*·len zee?
What's in that dish?
 Was ist in diesem Gericht?   vas ist in *dee*·zem ge·*rikht*
Is it cooked in meat stock?
 Ist es in Fleischbrühe?   ist es in flaish·*brew*·e?
Does it take long to prepare?
 Dauert das lange?   *dow*·ert das *lang*·e
I'd like a local speciality.
 Ich möchte etwas typisches aus der Region.   ikh *meukh*·te *et*·vas *tew*·pi·shes ows dair re·*gyawn*
That was delicious!
 Das hat hervorragend geschmeckt!/   das hat her·*fawr*·raa·gent ge·*shmekt*/
 Das war sehr lecker!   das var zair *le*·ker
My compliments to the chef!
 Mein Kompliment an den Koch!   main kom·pli·*ment* an dayn kokh

I'd like ..., please.
 Ich möchte ..., bitte.   ikh *meukh*·te ... *bi*·te
 a cup of tea/coffee
 eine Tasse Tee/Kaffee   *ai*·ne *ta*·se tay/*ka* fay
 with (milk)
 ... mit (Milch)   ... mit (milkh)

The bill, please.
 Die Rechnung, bitte/Zahlen, bitte.   dee *rekh*·nung *bi*·te/*tsaa*·len *bi*·te
 (less formal)

Food Glossary
STARTERS

Bauernsuppe	bow·ern·zu·pe	cabbage and sausage 'Farmer's soup'
Fleischbrühe	flaish·brew·e	bouillon
Frühlingssuppe/	frü·lingks·zu·pe/	vegetable soup
Gemüsesuppe	ge·*moo*·ze·zu·pe	
Graupensuppe	grow·pen·zu·pe	barley soup
Kieler Sprotten	kee·ler shpro·ten	small smoked herring
Kohlroulade	kawl·ru·laa·de	minced meat stuffed cabbage leaves
Vorspeisen	fawr·shpai·zen	starters

MAIN COURSES

Brathuhn	braat·hoon	roast chicken
Eintopf	ain·topf	one-pot meat and veg stew

Hackbraten	*hak*·braa·ten	meatloaf
Hauptgerichte	*howpt*·ge·rikh·te	main courses
Holsteiner Schnitzel	*hol*·shtai·ner *shni*·tsel	veal with fried egg, served with seafood
Rheinischer Sauerbraten	*rai*·ni·sher *zow*·er·braa·ten	marinated meat, slightly sour and roasted
Schweinshaxen	*shvains*·hak·sen	crispy Bavarian pork leg with potato dumplings

DESSERTS & CAKES

Aachener Printen	*aa*·khe·ner *prin*·ten	cakes with chocolate, nuts, fruit peel, honey and spices
Apfelstrudel	*ap*·fel·shtroo·del	apple strudel
Eis	ais	ice cream
Cremespeise	*kraym*·shpai·ze	mousse
Eierkuchen	*ai*·er·koo·khen	pancake
Frankfurter Kranz	*frank*·fur·ter krants	sponge cake with rum, butter cream and cherries
Gebäck	ge·*bek*	pastries
Kompott	kom·*pot*	stewed fruit
Kuchen	*koo*·khen	cake
Nachspeisen	*naakh*·shpai·zen	desserts
Obatzter	*aw*·bats·ter	Bavarian soft cheese mousse
Obstsalat	*awpst*·za·laat	fruit salad
Torte	*tor*·te	layer cake

BASICS

Brot	brawt	bread
Brötchen	*breut*·khen	bread roll
Butter	*bu*·ter	butter
Ei(er)	ai(·er)	egg(s)
Käse	*kay*·ze	cheese
Milch	milkh	milk
Nudeln	*noo*·deln	noodles
Pfeffer	*pfe*·fer	pepper
Reis	rais	rice
Salz	zalts	salt
Senf	zenf	mustard
Zucker	*tsu*·ker	sugar

FISH

Aal	aal	eel
Dorsch	dorsh	cod
Fisch	fish	fish
Forelle	fo·*re*·le	trout
Garnele	gar·*nay*·le	prawn
Hering	*hay*·ring	herring
Karpfen	*karp*·fen	carp
Lachs	laks	salmon

MEAT

Ente	*en*·te	duck
Fasan	fa·*zaan*	pheasant
Filet	fi·*lay*	fillet, tenderloin
Fleisch	flaish	meat
Gans	gans	goose
Geflügel	ge·*flew*·gel	poultry

Hackfleisch	*hak·flaish*	chopped or minced meat
Hähnchen or Huhn	*hayn·khen or hoon*	chicken
Kalbfleisch	*kalp·flaish*	veal
Lammfleisch	*lam·flaish*	lamb
Rindfleisch	*rint·flaish*	beef
Schinken	*shing·ken*	ham
Schweinefleisch	*shvai·ne·flaish*	pork
Wild	*vilt*	game

FRUIT & VEGETABLES

Apfel	*ap·fel*	apple
Apfelsine	*ap·fel·zee·ne*	orange
Artischocke	*ar·ti·sho·ke*	artichoke
Bohnen	*baw·nen*	beans
Gurke	*gur·ke*	cucumber, gherkins
Kartoffel	*kar·to·fel*	potato
Knoblauch	*knawp·lowkh*	garlic
Kohl	*kawl*	cabbage
Rotkohl	*rawt·kawl*	red cabbage

DRINKS

Apfelwein	*ap·fel·vaine*	apple cider
Bier	*beer*	beer
Glühwein	*glew vaine*	mulled wine
Kaffee	*ka·fay*	coffee
Saft	*zaft*	juice
Wasser	*va·ser*	water
Weisswein/Rotwein	*vais vaine/rawt·vaine*	white/red wine

Berlin

Brassy, bold and beautiful in its austerity, Berlin is a sexy temptress that ensnares with her infinite riches, a creative genius that amazes with unique ideas and trends, and a hotbed of hedonism, feasting passionately on the buffet of life. And above all, she's a clever chameleon, endlessly adaptable and thriving on change, almost pursuing it like a drug. Berlin is all that and then some to those who live here, and those ready for the journey to the depths of her past, present and future.

With a history that has disproportionately shaped Europe's destiny, Berlin is a galvanic force in German, European and world affairs, yet functions on a welcoming and exquisitely human scale. It's a city in which you can embrace and be embraced, relish and revel in its abundant charms and variety with total abandon, and feel energised in ways you'll feel in few other world-class cities.

If you've travelled around Germany, you'll know why Berlin feels like a most 'un-German' city, largely free of rigid social structure. A trendsetter by nature and necessity, Berlin feeds on fledgling moods, trends and appetites and processes them into the new *Zeitgeist*. The world has always looked to Berlin – in fascination, horror or sometimes in deep sympathy. At once repellent and seductive, light-hearted and brooding, Berlin continues to be a city of exhilarating extremes.

HIGHLIGHTS

- **Royal Encounters** Make a date with Nefertiti and her entourage at the Altes Museum (p108)
- **Chill-out Float** Let the sights drift by you while sipping a cool drink on the deck of a river cruiser (p123)
- **Life's a Beach** Sip mai tais while soaking up the rays at the Badeschiff (p120), a unique place for a refreshing dip
- **Views** Take in the panorama from the Reichstag cupola (p111) or the Fernsehturm (p109)
- **Party Animals** Make an in-depth exploration of the bars along Schlesische Strasse (p119), then party till breakfast at Watergate (p138)
- **Wall Art** Pick your favourite graffiti on a stroll along the longest remaining stretch of the Berlin Wall at the East Side Gallery (p115)
- **Offbeat** Descend into the dark and dank world of WWII bunkers on a tour of the Berliner Unterwelten (p124)

Berliner Unterwelten ★
Altes Museum, River Cruise & Fernsehturm
Reichstag ★★
Watergate & East Side Gallery
Badeschiff & Schlesische Strasse

| ■ TELEPHONE CODE: 030 | ■ POPULATION: 3.39 MILLION | ■ AREA: 889 SQ KM |

BERLIN

HISTORY

By German standards, Berlin entered onto the stage of history relatively late and puttered along in relative obscurity for centuries. Founded in the 13th century as a trading post, it merged with its sister settlement Cölln across the Spree River in 1307. The town achieved a modicum of prominence after the powerful Hohenzollern clan from southern Germany took charge in 1411, at least until the 17th century when it was ravaged during the Thirty Years' War (1618–48) with only 6000 people surviving the pillage, plunder and starvation.

Ironically, the war's aftermath gave Berlin its first taste of cosmopolitanism. Keen on quickly raising the number of his subjects, Elector Friedrich Wilhelm (called the Great Elector; r 1640–88) shrewdly invited foreigners to settle in Berlin. Some Jewish families arrived from Vienna, but the bulk of the new settlers were Huguenot refugees from France. By 1700, one in five locals was of French descent.

Elector Friedrich III, the Great Elector's son, presided over a lively and intellectual court, but was also a man of great political ambition. In 1701, he simply promoted himself to become King Friedrich I of Prussia, making Berlin a royal residence and capital of the new state of Brandenburg-Prussia.

His son, Friedrich Wilhelm I (r 1713–40), laid the groundwork for Prussian military might. Soldiers were this king's main obsession and he dedicated much of his life to building an army of 80,000, partly by instituting the draft (highly unpopular even then) and by persuading his fellow rulers to trade him men for treasure. History quite appropriately knows him as the *Soldatenkönig* (Soldier King).

Ironically, these soldiers didn't see action until his son Friedrich II (aka Frederick the Great; r 1740–86) came to power in 1740. Friedrich fought tooth and nail for two decades to wrest Silesia from Austria and Saxony. When not busy on the battlefield, 'Old Fritz', as he was also called, sought greatness through building (much of Unter den Linden dates back to his reign) and embracing the ideals of Enlightenment. With some of the day's leading thinkers in town (Gotthold Ephraim Lessing and Moses Mendelssohn among them), Berlin blossomed into a great cultural centre some even called 'Athens on the Spree'.

Old Fritz' death sent Prussia on a downward spiral, culminating in a serious trouncing of its army by Napoleon in 1806. The French marched triumphantly into Berlin on October 27 and left two years later, their coffers bursting with gold. The post-Napoleonic period saw Berlin caught up in the reform movement sweeping through Europe. Since all this ferment brought little change from the top, Berlin joined other German cities, in 1848, in a bourgeois democratic revolution. Alas, the time for democracy wasn't yet ripe and the status quo was quickly restored.

Meanwhile, the Age of Industrialisation had snuck up on Berliners, with companies like Siemens and Borsig vastly spurring the city's growth and spawning a new working class and political parties like the Social Democratic Party (SPD) to represent them. Berlin boomed politically, economically and culturally, especially after becoming capital of the German Reich in 1871. By 1900 the population had reached the two million mark.

Once again war, WWI in this case, stifled Berlin's momentum. In its aftermath, it found itself at the heart of a power struggle between monarchists, Spartacists and democrats. Though the democrats won out, the Weimar Republic (p33) only brought instability, corruption and inflation. Berliners responded like there was no tomorrow and made their city as much a den of decadence as a cauldron of creativity. Artists of all stripes flocked to this city of cabaret, Dada and jazz.

Hitler's rise to power put an instant halt to the fun. Berlin suffered heavy bombing in WWII and an invasion of 1.5 million Soviet soldiers during the final, decisive Battle of Berlin in April 1945. During the Cold War, it became ground zero for hostilities between the US and the USSR. The Berlin Blockade of 1948 and the construction of the Berlin Wall in 1961 were major milestones in the standoff. For 40 years, East and West Berlin developed as two completely separate cities.

With reunification, Berlin once again became the German capital in 1990 and the seat of government in 1999. Rejoining the two city halves, alas, has proved to be painful and costly. Mismanagement, excessive spending and corruption led to the collapse of the centre-right government and the election of Klaus Wowereit, an openly gay Social Democrat, as governing mayor. His agenda of severe spending cuts and attracting new business has done little so far to improve the balance sheet. Such lack of success, however, has done little to lessen Wowereit's popularity, as was confirmed by his re-election in September 2006.

Multiculturalism and the integration of immigrants have been other hot topics around dinner tables in recent years. In early 2005 a wave of 'honour killings' of young Muslim women wishing to live a western lifestyle shocked not only Berliners but the world as well. Schools in Kreuzberg and surrounds, where nearly every student is of non-German descent, have raised the spectre of *Parallelgesellschaften* (parallel societies) and challenged Berliners' legendary tolerance.

But the news isn't all bad. Berlin continues to be a hotbed of creativity. Fashion, design and tourism are all booming industries. And in 2006, the entire city was swept up in World Cup fever. Welcoming the global community with open arms and hearts, Berliners put aside their worries for a month and did what they do best: party!

ORIENTATION

Berlin is made up of 12 administrative districts of which the central ones hold the most interest to visitors. Mitte, formerly in East Berlin, is the city's historic core and packs such blockbuster sights as the Brandenburger Tor, the Holocaust Memorial, Unter den Linden boulevard, Museumsinsel and the Fernsehturm (TV Tower). The Scheunenviertel area, anchored by the Hackesche Höfe, is jammed with bars, restaurants, galleries and quirky boutiques. It segues into Prenzlauer Berg to the north, a gentrified and largely residential district with nightlife centred on Käthe-Kollwitz-Platz, Schönhauser Allee and Helmholtzplatz.

South of Mitte, Kreuzberg counts Checkpoint Charlie and the Jüdisches Museum (Jewish Museum) among its highlights. Eastern Kreuzberg, around Kottbusser Tor, has been nicknamed 'Little Istanbul' for its large Turkish population. Across the Spree River is Friedrichshain, where you'll find the East Side Gallery, the longest surviving section of the Wall.

West of Mitte, Tiergarten boasts most of Berlin's large-scale postreunification projects, including the government district, the spanking-new Hauptbahnhof and Potsdamer Platz. The vast Tiergarten park links Mitte with

Charlottenburg, the hub of western Berlin. Sights here cluster around Bahnhof Zoo (short for Zoologischer Garten), including the war-ruined Kaiser-Wilhelm Gedächtniskirche, the Kurfürstendamm (Ku'damm) shopping mile and the amazing Berliner Zoo. Further west is Schloss Charlottenburg (Charlottenburg Palace), one of the city's must-see sights, and still beyond, the newly renovated Olympiastadion. Much of Charlottenburg, though, is upmarket residential, as are adjoining Wilmersdorf and Schöneberg. The latter also has a throbbing gay and lesbian scene around Nollendorfplatz.

For details about Berlin's airports and train stations, see p142 and p144.

Maps

The maps in this book should suffice in most cases, although the foldout map available for €1 from the Berlin Infostores (p105) might be a useful supplement.

For detailed explorations of the outlying suburbs, you'll need a larger city map such as those published by ADAC, the RV Verlag Euro City or Falkplan. These are widely available at petrol stations, bookshops, newsagents and tourist offices and cost between €4.50 and €7.50.

INFORMATION
Bookshops

Another Country (Map pp100–1; ☎ 6940 1160; Riemannstrasse 7) Library-store run by an eccentric Brit.

Berlin Story (Map p98; ☎ 2045 3842; Unter den Linden 40) Berlin-related books, maps, videos, guides and magazines, many in English.

Dussmann – Das Kulturkaufhaus (Map p98; ☎ 2025 1111; Friedrichstrasse 90; ⏰ 10am-10pm Mon-Sat) The ultimate in books and music; lots of reading corners and occasional signings, concerts and other events.

East of Eden (Map pp96–7; ☎ 423 9362; Schreinerstrasse 10) Living room–type store perfect for browsing.

Hugendubel (☎ 01801-484 484) Charlottenburg (Map p102; Tauentzienstrasse 13); Mitte (Map p98; Friedrichstrasse 83); Potsdamer Platz (Map pp100–1; Potsdamer Platz Arkaden) Excellent chain shop with a café and sofas for lounging.

Schropp (Map pp96–7; ☎ 2355 7320; Potsdamer Strasse 129) Guidebooks and maps galore.

Cultural Centres

British Council (Map p98; ☎ 311 0990; Hackescher Markt 1) Well-stocked library with books, videos and periodicals, plus internet access and events.

BERLIN

BERLIN IN...

One Day

Get up early to beat the crowds to the dome of the **Reichstag** (p111), then snap a picture of the **Brandenburger Tor** (p106) before exploring the maze of the **Holocaust Memorial** (p106). From there you're off on a classic saunter along **Unter den Linden** (p106) with a detour to **Gendarmenmarkt** (p107) and the glamorous **Friedrichstadtpassagen** (p121). After lunch, take a peek inside the **Berliner Dom** (p108) before being awed by Nefertiti at the **Altes Museum** (p108) and the Pergamon Altar at the **Pergamon Museum** (p107). Finish up at the **Scheunenviertel** (p109) where you should have no trouble sourcing good spots for dinner, drinks and dancing.

Two Days

Follow the one-day itinerary, then revisit Cold War history at **Checkpoint Charlie** (p114) and the nearby **Haus am Checkpoint Charlie** (p114). Spend the rest of the morning at the amazing **Jüdisches Museum** (p113) before heading off to Berlin's showcase of urban renewal, the **Potsdamer Platz** (p111). Make a stop here at the **Filmmuseum Berlin** (p111) or walk a few steps west to the **Kulturforum** (p112) and the superb **Gemäldegalerie** (p113). At night, sample the cuisine and bar scene of **Prenzlauer Berg** (p129 and p134).

Three Days

Follow the two-day itinerary, then devote the morning of day three to **Schloss Charlottenburg** (p114) where you shouldn't miss the Neuer Flügel (New Wing) or a spin around the Schlossgarten park. Catch the U-Bahn to Bahnhof Zoo, then study the legacy of Helmut Newton at the **Museum für Fotografie** (p117). Pick up some last-minute souvenirs along the **Kurfürstendamm** (p140) and in the **KaDeWe** (p140), then have an early dinner before catching some live jazz at **Quasimodo** (p139) or the latest show at the **Bar Jeder Vernunft** (p135).

Goethe Institut (Map p98; ☎ 259 063; Neue Schönhauser Strasse 20)
Institut Français (Map p102; ☎ 885 9020; Kurfürstendamm 211)

Discount Cards

Berlin WelcomeCard (48/72hr €16/22) Entitles one adult and up to three children under 14 to unlimited public transport within the Berlin-Potsdam area and free or discounted admission to museums, shows, attractions and tours. It's available at the Berlin Infostores (p105), U- and S-Bahn ticket vending machines and many hotels.
Berlin WelcomeCard Culture+ (72hr €35) This excellent value card combines the Berlin WelcomeCard and the SchauLust Museen Berlin museum pass and is available at all Berlin Infostores.
CityTourCard (48/72hr €15/20) Includes transportation and small discounts for attractions and tours but only within Berlin. Available at some hotels and through U- and S-Bahn vending machines. The Premium version (€39.90) includes admission to 50 museums and a trip up the Fernsehturm (TV tower).
SchauLust Museen Berlin (adult/child €15/7.50) Unbeatable deal for culture vultures. Valid on three consecutive days, this pass gives unlimited admission to about 70 of Berlin's museums, including blockbusters like

the Pergamon and the Neue Nationalgalerie. Sold at the Berlin Infostores and participating museums.

Emergency

American Hotline (☎ 0177-814 1510) Crisis hotline and referral service, not only for Americans.
BVG Public Transport Lost & Found (Map p133; ☎ 194 49; Potsdamer Strasse 180/182)
Drug hotline (☎ 192 37)
Emergency numbers (☎ police 110, fire brigade & ambulance 112)
International Helpline (☎ 4401 0607; ☺ 6pm-midnight) Help in any crisis situation, in English.
Medical Emergencies for Berlin Visitors (☎ 01804-2255 2362)
Municipal Lost & Found (Map pp100-1; ☎ 7560 3101; Platz der Luftbrücke 6)
Rape Crisis Hotline (☎ 251 2828, 615 4243, 216 8888)
Wheelchair Breakdown Service (☎ 0180-111 4747)

Internet Access

Many hostels, hotels and cafés now offer wireless internet surfing, with the cafés sometimes providing it free with a purchase. The

(Continued on page 104)

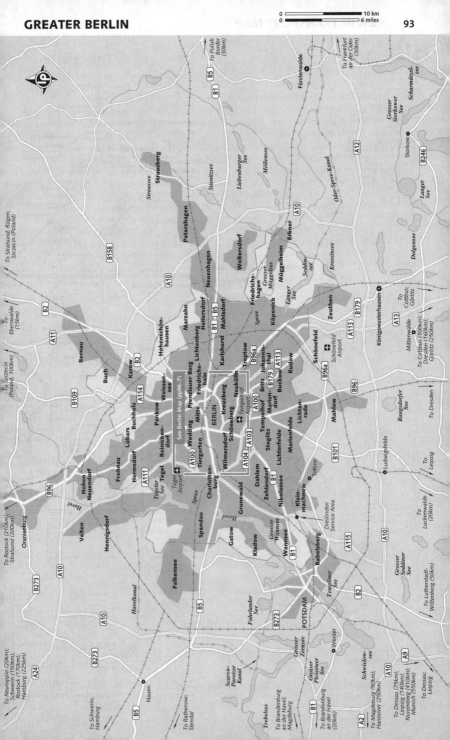

0 ___ 10 km
0 ___ 6 miles

To Stralsund; Rügen; Szczecin (Poland)

To Polish Border (30km)

To Frankfurt an der Oder (30km)

Fürstenwalde

B5

B1

B1

Scharmützel-see

Grosser Storkower See

Storkow

B246

Langer See

A12

A10

Strausee

Strausberg

Schmitzsee

Liebenburger See

Möllensee

Dolgensee

To Stralsund; Hamburg

To Eberswalde (15km)

To Szczecin (Poland; 100km)

B2

A11

B158

Petershagen

Neuenhagen

Hohenschön-hausen

Marzahn

Hellersdorf

Neuenhagen

Woltersdorf

Erkner

Friedrichs-hagen

Grosser Müggelsee

Müggelheim

Seddin-see

Krossinsee

A10

B109

Bernau

Buch

Karow

Weissen-see

Lichtenberg

B1 B5

Mahlsdorf

Karlshorst

Köpenick

Langer See

Zeuthen

To Cottbus; Görlitz

A113

A13

B179

A114

Buchholz

Pankow

Friedrichs-hain

Treptow

B96a

Königswusterhausen

To Cottbus (100km); Dresden (160km); Görlitz (250km)

B2

Reinicken-dorf

Lübars

See Berlin Map (pp96–7)

Prenzlauer Berg

Mitte

Neukölln

Johannis-thal

A113

Schönefeld Airport

Mittenwalde

Frohnau

Hermsdorf

BERLIN

Kreuzberg

Tempelhof Airport

Britz

Rudow

Schönefeld

B96a

Hohen Neuendorf

Tegel Airport

Tiergarten

Wedding

Schöneberg

Tempelhof

Marien-dorf

Buckow

B96

Tegeler See

A100

A103

Lichten-rade

To Dresden

B109

A111

Wilmersdorf

Steglitz

Marienfelde

Lichten-berg

Mahlow

Rangsdorfer See

To Leipzig

Charlotten-burg

A104

Lichterfelde

Havel

Spree

Velten

Hennigsdorf

Oranienburg

B96

Spandau

Dahlem

Zehlendorf

Teltow

B101

Ludwigsfelde

To Leipzig

Grunewald

Nikolassee

Klein-machnow

To Luckenwalde (20km)

A115

To Rostock (210km); Stralsund (200km)

To Neuruppin (20km); Schwerin (150km); Rostock (170km); Hamburg (225km)

A24

B273

A10

Havelkanal

Falkensee

B5

Gatow

Kladow

Wannsee

Grosser Wannsee

Dreilinden Service Area

Babelsberg

Belziger See

A115

A10

Grosser Seddiner See

To Lutherstadt; Wittenberg (50km)

B2

Fahrlander See

POTSDAM

Templiner See

B273

B1

Grosser Zernsee

Havel

Grosser Plessower See

Schwielow-see

A10

A9

To Schwerin; Hamburg

Scarow-Pareizer Kanal

Treblitz

Nauen

B5

To Rathenow; Stendal

To Brandenburg an der Havel; Magdeburg

To Brandenburg an der Havel (20km)

B1

Werder

To Magdeburg (90km); Leipzig (140km); Nuremberg (410km); Munich (550km)

A2

To Dessau (75km); Leipzig (120km)

To Dessau; Leipzig

A10

S U Netz M M

Tarifbereich Berlin A B C | A B Haltestellen in Berlin | C H

Legende

- S+U-Bahn-Linie
- MetroTram-MetroBus-Linie
- Bus-Anbindung zum Flughafen
- Umsteigemöglichkeit
- Halt nur in Pfeilrichtung
- Fernbahnhof
- Regionalbahnhof
- ZOB Zentraler Omnibusbahnhof

Barrierefrei durch Berlin
- Barrierefreier Zugang, S+U Aufzüge
- Barrierefreier Zugang/ Umsteigebahnhof, nur S Aufzug
- Barrierefreier Zugang/ Umsteigebahnhof, nur U Aufzug
- S+U Zugang über Rampe

Oranienburg
Lehnitz
Borgsdorf
Birkenwerder
Bergfelde — Schönfl

Hennigsdorf — Hohen Neuendorf
Heiligensee — Frohnau
Schulzendorf — Hermsdorf — Waidmannslust
Tegel — Rathaus Reinickendorf — Wittenau — Uhlands Wilhelmsr Damm
Alt-Tegel — Karl-Bonhoeffer-Nervenklinik — Wilhelmsruh
Borsigwerke — Eichborndamm — Alt-Reinickendorf — Schönholz
Holzhauser Str. — Lindauer Allee — Pa
Otisstr. — Paracelsus-Bad — Residenzstr.
Scharnweberstr. — Franz-Neumann-Platz Am Schäfersee
Kurt-Schumacher-Platz — Afrikanische Str. — Osloer Str.
Rehberge — Nauener Platz — Pankstr.
Seestr. — Leopoldplatz — Osloe Prin
Virchow-Klinikum — Amrumer Str. — Gesundbrunnen
Paulsternstr. — Rohrdamm — Siemens- damm — Halemweg — Beusselstr. — Westhafen — Wedding — Humboldthain
Haselhorst — Jakob-Kaiser-Platz — Jungfernheide — Reinickendorfer Str. — S42 S41
Zitadelle — Birkenstr. — Nordbahnhof — Schwartz- kopffstr.
Altstadt Spandau — Mierendorffplatz — Turmstr. — Zinnowitzer Str. — Oranien burge St
Rathaus Spandau — Hauptbahnhof — Oranien burger Tor
Stresow — Westend — Richard-Wagner-Platz — Bellevue — Bundestag — Fried rich
Ruhleben — Olympia-Stadion — Tiergarten — Hansaplatz — Unter den Lir Französisch
Pichelsberg — Neu-Westend — Th.-Heuss-Platz — Sophie- Charlotte-Platz — Deutsche Oper — Ernst-Reuter-Platz — Mohrenstr.
Olympiastadion — Kaiserdamm — Messe Nord/ ICC — Bismarckstr. — Mendelssohn-Bartholdy-Park — Potsdamer Platz — Anhalter Bhf
Heerstr. — Messe ZOB ICC — Wilmers- dorfer Str. — Zoologischer Garten
Messe Süd — Charlottenburg — Savignyplatz — Witten- bergplatz — Kurfürsten- str. — Gleis- dreieck — Möcker brücke
Westkreuz — Uhlandstr. — Kurfürsten- damm — Nollen- dorfplatz — Bülow- str. — Yorckstr.
Grunewald — Halensee — Adenauer- platz — Augsburger Str. — Yorckstr. — Platz der Luftb
Hohenzollerndamm — Spichernstr. — Hohenzollern- platz — Viktoria-Luise- Platz — Kleistpark — Para
Rosenneck — Konstanzer Str. — Güntzelstr. — Berliner Str. — Eisenacher Str. — Südkreuz — Temp
Fehrbelliner Platz — Blissestr. — Bayerischer Platz — Rathaus Schöneberg
Heidelberger Platz — Bundesplatz — Innsbrucker Platz — Schöneberg — Alt-Tem
Rüdesheimer Platz — Friedrich-Wilhelm-Platz — Friedenau
Breitenbachplatz — Walther-Schreiber-Platz — Feuerbachstr. — Priesterweg
Podbielskiallee — Schloßstr. — Friedenst. Grußbach
Dahlem-Dorf — Rathaus Steglitz — Südende — Attilastr.
Thielplatz — Oskar-Helene-Heim — Lankwitz — Marienfelde
Onkel Toms Hütte — Botanischer Garten — Lichterfelde Ost
Schlachtensee — Krumme Lanke — Goerzallee/ Drakestr. — Buckower Chaussee
Nikolassee — Mexikoplatz — Lichterfelde West — Waldsassener Str. — Schichauweg
Wannsee — Zehlendorf — Sundgauer Str. — Osdorfer Str. — Lichtenrade
Babelsberg — Lichterfelde Süd — Mahlow
Potsdam Hbf — Griebnitzsee — Teltow Stadt — Blankenfelde (Kr. Teltow-Fläming)

Tegel TXL X9 109 128

Johannesstift M45
Waldkrankenhaus M37
Freudstr./ Goldkäfer- weg — Falkenseer Ch./ Stadtrandstr. — Am Kiesteich — Moritzstr.
Heidebergplan — Staaken — Brunsbütteler D./ Stadtgrenze — Döberitzer Weg — Heerstr./Nennh.D. — Dallgow- Döberitz — Havelpark
Brunsbütteler Damm/ Ruhlebener Str. — Nennhauser Damm — Reimerweg — Heerstr./ Sandstr. — Hahneberg — Magis- tratsweg
Rathenauplatz
Grunewald

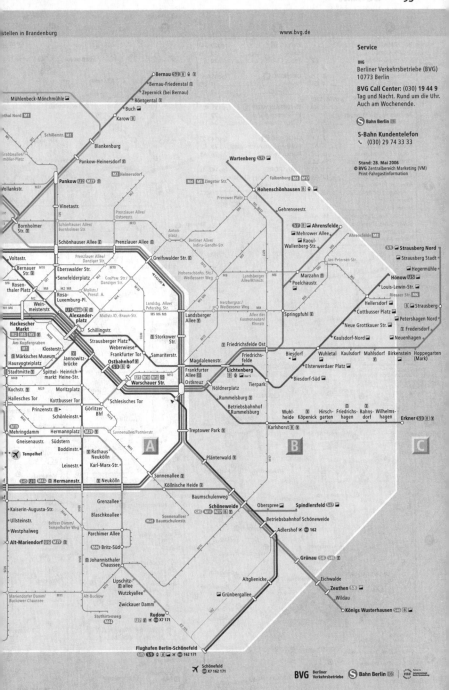

INFORMATION
Charité Campus
Virchow-Klinikum.....................1 C2
East of Eden.....................................2 H4
Schropp...3 D5
Spanish Embassy.............................4 C4

SIGHTS & ACTIVITIES (pp105-120)
Altes Schloss...........................(see 16)
Bauhaus Archiv/Museum für
  Design..5 C4
Belvedere...6 A3
Berliner Unterwelten.........................7 E1
Bröhan Museum................................8 A3
Erika-Hess-Eisstadion........................9 D2
Kindermuseum Labyrinth.................10 E1
Mausoleum......................................11 A3
Museum Berggruen...........................12 A3
Museum für Vor- und
  Frühgeschichte............................13 A3
Neuer Flügel...................................14 A3
Neuer Pavillon.................................15 A3
Schloss Charlottenburg...................16 A3
Sowjetisches Ehrenmal
  Treptow.......................................17 H5
Zucker Museum...............................18 C1

EATING (pp129-34)
Edd's..19 D4
Tapas Club.......................................20 C3

DRINKING (pp134-5)
Begine..21 D5
Sonntags Club.................................22 F1

ENTERTAINMENT (pp135-40)
Kino International............................23 G3
Wintergarten-Das Varieté................24 D5

SHOPPING (pp140-2)
Flohmarkt am Arkonaplatz..............25 F2
Platten Pedro...................................26 A3

TRANSPORT (pp142-4)
Classic Bike Harley-Davidson...........27 B3
Das Hässliche Entlein.......................28 C4

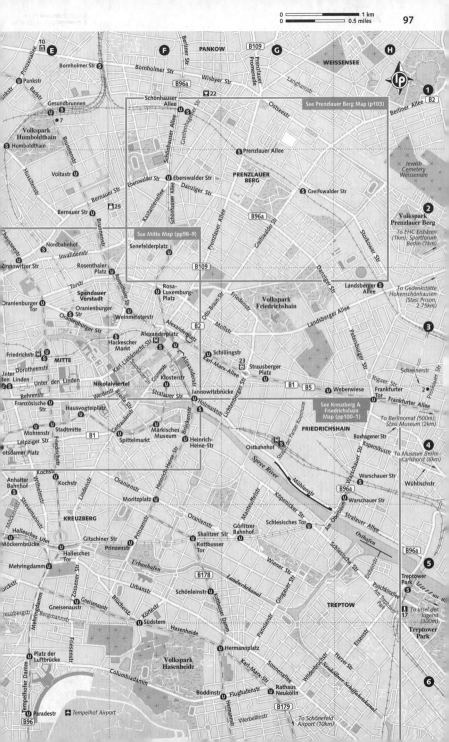

0 — 1 km
0 — 0.5 miles

PANKOW
B109
WEISSENSEE

10
E
Bornholmer Str S
Bornholmer Str
Wisbyer Str
B96a
Prenzlauer
Promenade
Langhansstr
Berliner Allee
B2

U Pankstr
Badstr
Schönhauser Allee
22
Ostseestr
Jewish
Cemetery
Weissensee

Gesundbrunnen S
7
See Prenzlauer Berg Map (p103)

**Volkspark
Humboldthain**
S Humboldthain
S Prenzlauer Allee

Voltastr U
**PRENZLAUER
BERG**
S Greifswalder Str
**Volkspark
Prenzlauer Berg**
To EHC Eisbären
(1km); Sportforum
Berlin (1km)

Eberswalder Str S Eberswalder Str
Danziger Str
B96a

Bernauer Str
Bernauer Str U
25
Kastanienallee
Schönhauser Allee
Prenzlauer Allee
Greifswalder Str
Stolkower Str

See Mitte Map (pp98–9)

Nordbahnhof S
Invalidenstr
Senefelderplatz U
B109
Landsberger
Allee S
To Gedenkstätte
Hohenschönhausen
(Stasi Prison,
2.75km)

Zinnowitzer Str
Rosenthaler
Platz U
Torstr
**Volkspark
Friedrichshain**
Landsberger Allee
Petersburger Str

Oranienburger
Tor U
**Spandauer
Vorstadt**
Oranienburger U
Oranienburger Str
Weinmeisterstr U
Rosa-
Luxemburg-
Platz U
Otto-Braun-Str
Friedenstr
Möllstr

Alexanderplatz U
B2
Schreinerstr

Friedrichstr U
Dorotheenstr
Unter
den Linden
MITTE
Hackescher
Markt S
Karl-Liebknecht-Str
Alexanderplatz
Schillingstr U
23
Strausberger
Platz U
Karl-Marx-Allee
Rigaer Str
Frankfurter
Tor
2
Frankfurter Allee

Unter den Linden
Nikolaiviertel
Klosterstr U
Stralauer Str
Jannowitzbrücke U
B1
B5
Weberwiese U

Behrenstr
Französische
Str U
Hausvogteiplatz U
Breite Str
Gertraudenstr
Brückenstr
Holzmarktstr
See Kreuzberg &
Friedrichshain
Map (pp100–1)
Boxhagener Str
Kopernikusstr
To Berlinomat (500m);
Stasi Museum (2km)

Mohrenstr U
Stadtmitte U
Leipziger Str
Spittelmarkt U
**Märkisches
Museum**
Heinrich-
Heine-Str U
FRIEDRICHSHAIN
Warschauer Str
Warschauer Str U
To Museum Berlin-
Karlshorst (8km)

Potsdamer Platz
B1
Friedrichstr
Heinrich-Heine-Str
Ostbahnhof
Spree River
Mühlenstr
Am Oberbaum
Stralauer Allee
Osthafen
Wühlischstr

Anhalter
Bahnhof S
Kochstr U
Kochstr
Oranienstr
Moritzplatz U
Oranienstr
Görlitzer
Bahnhof S
Schlesisches
Tor U
B96a
B96a

Hallesches Ufer
Möckernbrücke U
KREUZBERG
Gitschiner Str
Prinzenstr U
Skalitzer Str
Kottbusser
Tor U
Wiener Str
Treptower
Park S

Hallesches
Tor U
Prinzenstr
Urbanhafen
Landwehrkanal
B178
Schönleinstr U
Glogauer Str
Kottbusser Damm
Puschkinallee
Am Treptower
Park
To Insel der
Jugend
(300m)
17

Mehringdamm U
Urbanstr
Blücherstr
Körtestr
Hasenheide
TREPTOW
Eichenstr
**Treptower
Park**

Gneisenaustr U
Gneisenaustr
U Südstern
Hermannplatz U
Wildenbruchstr
Neuköllner Schifffahrtskanal

Platz der
Luftbrücke U
Friesenstr
**Volkspark
Hasenheide**
Karl-Marx-Str
Sonnenallee
Harzer Str
Eisenstr

Columbiadamm
Boddinstr U
Flughafenstr
Rathaus
Neukölln U
B179
Werbellinstr
Hermannstr

U Paradestr
Tempelhof Airport
B96
To Schönefeld
Airport (10km)

0 ____ 300 m
0 ____ 0.2 miles

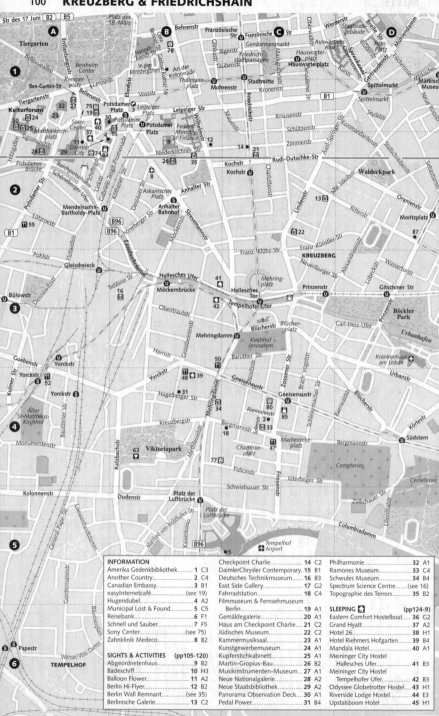

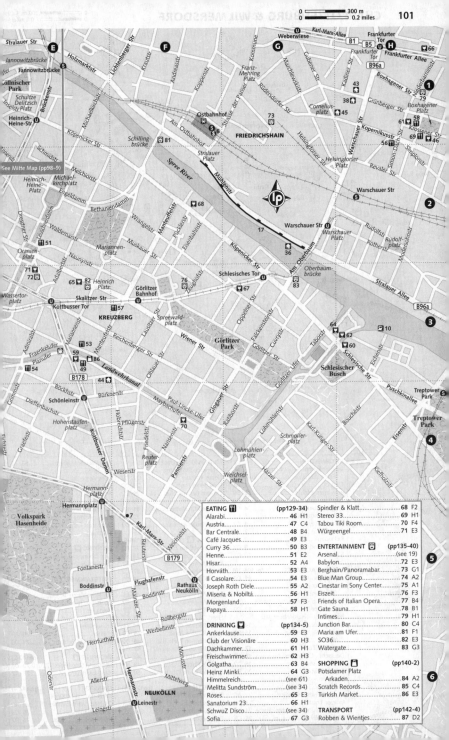

EATING 🍴 (pp129–34)
Alarabi.................................46 H1
Austria................................47 C4
Bar Centrale.......................48 B4
Café Jacques......................49 E3
Curry 36.............................50 B3
Henne.................................51 E2
Hisar..................................52 A4
Horváth..............................53 E3
Il Casolare..........................54 E3
Joseph Roth Diele...............55 A2
Miseria & Nobiltà...............56 H1
Morgenland........................57 F3
Papaya...............................58 H1

DRINKING 🍷 (pp134–5)
Ankerklause........................59 E3
Club der Visionäre..............60 H3
Dachkammer.......................61 H1
Freischwimmer....................62 H3
Golgatha............................63 B4
Heinz Minki........................64 G3
Himmelreich....................(see 61)
Melitta Sundström...........(see 34)
Roses.................................65 E3
Sanatorium 23....................66 H1
SchwuZ Disco..................(see 34)
Sofia..................................67 G3
Spindler & Klatt..................68 F2
Stereo 33............................69 H1
Tabou Tiki Room.................70 F4
Würgeengel........................71 E3

ENTERTAINMENT 🎭 (pp135–40)
Arsenal...........................(see 19)
Babylon..............................72 E3
Berghain/Panoramabar........73 G1
Blue Man Group..................74 A2
Cinestar im Sony Center......75 A1
Eiszeit...............................76 F3
Friends of Italian Opera.......77 B4
Gate Sauna........................78 H1
Intimes..............................79 H1
Junction Bar.......................80 C4
Maria am Ufer.....................81 F1
SO36..................................82 E3
Watergate...........................83 G3

SHOPPING 🛍 (pp140–2)
Potsdamer Platz
  Arkaden...........................84 A2
Scratch Records..................85 C4
Turkish Market...................86 E3

TRANSPORT (pp142–4)
Robben & Wientjes..............87 D2

0 ———— 300 m
0 ———— 0.2 miles

INFORMATION
Berlin Infostore Neues Kranzler
Eck......................................(see 27)
Darpol..1 A1
easyInternetcafé..........................2 D2
Euraide...3 D2
Hugendubel...................................4 D2
Institut Français............................5 D2
Post Office....................................6 D2
Post Office....................................7 D2
Reisebank.....................................8 D2
Schnell und Sauber.......................9 C3
STA Travel..................................10 C1

SIGHTS & ACTIVITIES   (pp105-20)
Aquarium.....................................11 D2
BBS Berliner Bären
Stadtrundfahrt............................12 D2
Berliner Zoo - Budapester Strasse
Entrance.....................................13 D2
Berliner Zoo - Hardenbergplatz
Entrance.....................................14 D2
Berolina Sightseeing...................15 C2
BVB...16 D2
BVG Top Tour.............................17 D2
Deutsches Currywurst Museum...18 C3
Erotik Museum............................19 D2
Fahrradstation............................20 B2
Herta Heuwer Memorial
Plaque..21 A2
Horst-Dohm-Eisstadion..............22 A5
Insider Tour.................................23 D2
Kaiser-Wilhelm-Gedächtniskirche..24 D2
Käthe-Kollwitz-Museum.............25 C3

Museum für Fotografie/Helmut
Newton Sammlung 26 D2
Neues Kranzler Eck....................27 D2
New Berlin Tours........................28 D2
Original Berlin Walks..................29 D2
Severin + Kühn...........................30 C2
Stadtbad Charlottenburg............31 A1
Story of Berlin............................32 C3
Tempelhofer Reisen....................33 D2

SLEEPING   (pp124-9)
A&O Hostel am Zoo...................34 D2
Brandenburger Hof.....................35 D3
Erste Mitwohnzentrale...............36 B2
Hecker's Hotel............................37 C2
HomeCompany...........................38 D3
Hotel Art Nouveau.....................39 B2
Hotel Askanischer Hof................40 B3
Hotel Bleibtreu...........................41 C2
Hotel Bogota..............................42 B3
Hotel QI.....................................43 C2
Hotel-Pension Dittberner.............44 B3
Hotel-Pension Funk.....................45 C3
Hotel-Pension Korfu II................46 B2
Hotel-Pension München..............47 D4
Ku'damm 101............................48 A3
Louisa's Place.............................49 A3
Propeller Island City Lodge........50 A3

EATING   (pp129-34)
Café Wintergarten im
Literaturhaus...............................51 C3
Die Quadriga...........................(see 35)
Engelbecken..............................52 A2

Franziskushof Laden....................53 B2
Gabriel's.....................................54 C2
Jules Verne.................................55 C2
Lon Men Noodle House...............56 B2
Mar y Sol...................................57 C2
Moon Thai..................................58 D2
Mr Hai & Friends.........................59 C2
Schleuskrug.................................60 D1
Schwarzes Café...........................61 C2
Tomasa.......................................62 D3

DRINKING   (pp134-5)
Gainsbourg.................................63 C3
Galerie Bremer............................64 C3

ENTERTAINMENT   (pp135-40)
A-Trane......................................65 C2
Bar Jeder Vernunft......................66 C3
Deutsche Oper Berlin...................67 B1
Hekticket....................................68 D2
Quasimodo..................................69 C2
Schaubühne am Lehniner
Platz..70 A3
Theaterkasse Centrum.................71 D3

SHOPPING   (pp140-2)
Flohmarkt Strasse des 17 Juni....72 D1
Harry Lehmann............................73 A2

TRANSPORT   (pp142-4)
BVG Information Kiosk.................74 D2
CityNetz Mitfahrzentrale..........(see 38)
Rent-a-Harley.............................75 D2
Shuttlenet...................................76 D2

0 ——— 300 m
0 ———— 0.2 miles

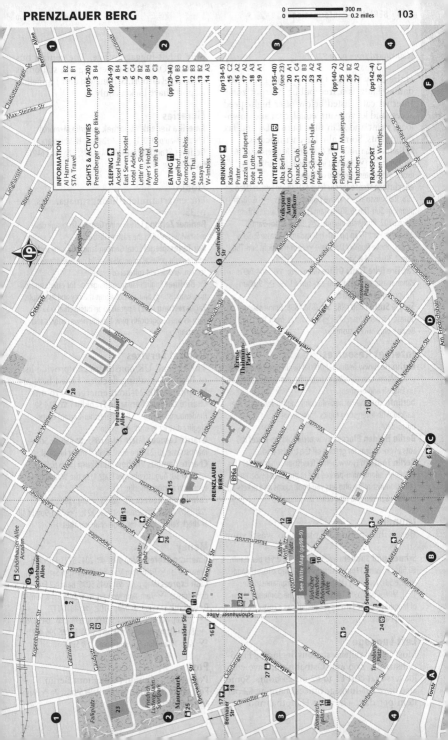

INFORMATION	
Al Hamra.....................................1	B2
STA Travel.................................2	B1

SIGHTS & ACTIVITIES	(pp105-20)
Prenzberger Orange Bikes....3	B4

SLEEPING	(pp124-9)
Acksel Haus................................4	B4
East Seven Hostel....................5	A4
Hotel Adele...............................6	C4
Lette'm Sleep...........................7	B2
Myer's Hotel..............................8	B4
Room with a Loo......................9	C3

EATING	(pp129-34)
Gugelhof..................................10	B3
Konnopke Imbiss....................11	B2
Mao Thai..................................12	B3
Sasaya......................................13	B2
W-Imbiss..................................14	A3

DRINKING	(pp134-5)
Kakao.......................................15	C2
Prater.......................................16	A2
Razzia in Budapest................17	A2
Rote Lotte...............................18	A3
Schall und Rauch...................19	A1

ENTERTAINMENT	(pp135-40)
Alba Berlin.................(see 23)	
ICON...20	A1
Knaack Club.............................21	C4
Kulturbrauerei.........................22	B3
Max-Schmeling-Halle.............23	A2
Pfefferberg..............................24	A4

SHOPPING	(pp140-2)
Flohmarkt am Mauerpark.....25	A2
Tausche...................................26	B2
Thatchers................................27	A3

TRANSPORT	(pp142-4)
Robben & Wientjes................28	C1

(Continued from page 92)

entire Sony Center (Map pp100–1) at Pots-damer Platz is a free public hotspot zone. Internet cafés listed below offer high-speed access and let you surf, email, chat and down-load, print and scan files, burn CDs and fax documents. Some also have wi-fi access.

Al Hamra (Map p103; ☎ 4285 0095; Raumerstrasse 16; per 15min €1; ☽ 10am-at least midnight) Surfing goes exotic with water pipes and cocktails.

easyInternetcafé (per hr from €2); Alexanderplatz (Map p98; Rathausstrasse 5, above Dunkin' Donuts; ☽ 6.30am-midnight Sun-Thu, 6.30am-1am Fri & Sat); Charlottenburg (Map p102; Kurfürstendamm 224; ☽ 6.30am-2am); Potsdamer Platz (Map pp100-1; Potsdamer Strasse 2, Sony Center, above Dunkin' Donuts; ☽ 6am-midnight Sun-Thu, 6am-1.30am Fri & Sat)

Fat Tire Bike Tours Office (Map p98; ☎ 2404 7991; Panoramastrasse 1a; all-you-can-surf €1.99; ☽ 9.30am-7.30pm) Below TV Tower.

Surf & Sushi (Map p98; ☎ 2838 4898; Oranienburger Strasse 17; per 30min €1; ☽ from noon, from 1pm Sun) Berlin's only 'wired' sushi bar.

Internet Resources

Berlin.de (www.berlin.de) Official Berlin government site with information on culture, transport, economy, politics etc (in English and German).

berlinfo.com (www.berlinfo.com) English-language site packed with interesting topics, though not all up-to-date.

Berlin Hidden Places (www.berlin-hidden-places.de) Lots of good ideas for getting off the tourist track.

Berlin Tourism (www.berlin-tourist-information.de) This excellent, information-packed site maintained by Berlin's official tourist office also lets you book rooms and tickets (in English, German and nine other languages).

Laundry

Berlin has plenty of places to wash your smalls.

Schnell und Sauber (washing €3-3.50, dryer per 10min €0.50; ☽ 6am-11pm) Charlottenburg (Map p102; Uhland-strasse 53); Kreuzberg (Map pp100-1; Bergmannstrasse 109); Mitte (Map p98; Torstrasse 115) The dominant chain of laundrettes. The latter even doubles as a cosy café with internet access.

Left Luggage

Most central railway stations, including Fried-richstrasse, Zoo and Ostbahnhof, have coin lockers that cost €1 to €2 for 24 hours. Some also have left-luggage offices charging €2 per item per day. The new Hauptbahnhof has only a left-luggage office. The central bus station ZOB also has a left-luggage station, as does Tegel airport. Schönefeld and Tempelhof airports have lockers only.

Libraries

Amerika Gedenkbibliothek (America Memorial Library; Map pp100-1; ☎ 9022 6401; Blücherplatz 1)

Berliner Stadtbibliothek (Map p98; ☎ 9022 6401; Breite Strasse 30-36)

Media

For entertainment listings magazines, see p135.

Berliner Zeitung Left-leaning German-language daily most widely read in the eastern districts.

Der Tagesspiegel Local German-language daily with centre-right political orientation, solid news and foreign section, and decent cultural coverage.

Ex-Berliner English-language magazine for expats and visi-tors, with listings and articles about the city and its people.

Tageszeitung (taz) Appeals to an intellectual crowd with its unapologetically pink-leaning news analysis and reporting.

Medical Services

The US and UK consulates can provide lists of English-speaking doctors. Listed here are hospitals with 24-hour emergency rooms.

Charité Campus Benjamin Franklin (☎ 844 50; Hindenburgdamm 30; ☒ Botanischer Garten) In the Steglitz district in southern Berlin.

Charité Campus Mitte (Map p98; ☎ 450 50; Schu-mannstrasse 20-21) The most central major hospital.

Charité Campus Virchow-Klinikum (Map pp96-7; ☎ 450 50; Augustenburger Platz 1) In the Wedding district in northern Berlin.

Zahnklinik Medeco (Dental Clinic; Map pp100-1; ☎ 2309 5960; Stresemannstrasse 121; ☽ 7am-9pm) Call or check Yellow Pages for additional branches.

Money

American Express (Map p98; ☎ 2045 5721; Friedrich-strasse 172; ☽ 9am-7pm Mon-Fri, 10am-1pm Sat)

Cash Express (Map p98; ☎ 2045 5096; Bahnhof Frie-drichstrasse; ☽ 7am-8pm Mon-Fri, 8am-8pm Sat & Sun)

Reisebank Bahnhof Zoo (Map p102; ☎ 881 7117; ☽ 7.30am-10pm); Hauptbahnhof (Map p98; ☎ 2045 3761; ☽ 8am-10pm); Ostbahnhof (Map pp100-1; ☎ 296 4393; ☽ 7am-10pm Mon-Fri, 8am-8pm Sat & Sun)

Post

Post offices abound throughout Berlin.

Post office (Map p102; Joachimstaler Strasse 7; ☽ 9am-8pm Mon-Sat)

ALL ABOARD! BERLIN FROM BUS 100 & 200

One of the best bargains in Berlin is a self-guided city tour aboard a public double-decker bus. Both bus 100 and 200 follow routes taking in nearly every major sight in the central city for the modest price of €2.10, the standard single BVG (Berlin's transport authority) ticket. You can even get off as often as you wish within the two hours of its validity. If you plan on exploring all day, the *Tageskarte* (Day Pass) for €5.80 is your best bet.

Bus 100 travels from Bahnhof Zoo to Alexanderplatz passing by such landmarks as the Gedächtniskirche, Tiergarten with the Siegessäule, the Reichstag, the Brandenburger Tor and Unter den Linden.

Bus 200 also starts at Bahnhof Zoo but takes a more southerly route via the Kulturforum and Potsdamer Platz before travelling on to Unter den Linden and as far east as the Jewish cemetery (Map pp96–7) in Weissensee.

Without interruptions the one-way journey takes about 30 minutes on bus 100 and 45 minutes on bus 200 in normal traffic. There's no commentary, so pick up a map and information leaflet from the BVG information kiosk (Map p102) outside Bahnhof Zoo. Note that both bus lines are targeted by pickpockets, so keep a close eye on your belongings.

Tourist Information

Berlin Tourismus Marketing (BTM; www.berlin-tourist-information.de) operates five tourist offices (Berlin Infostores) and a **call centre** (☎ 250 025; ✆ 8am-7pm Mon-Fri, 9am-6pm Sat & Sun) whose multilingual staff can book tickets and rooms. When they're closed, you can listen to recorded information or order brochures. From April to October extended hours are possible.

Berlin Infostore Brandenburger Tor (Map p98; south wing; ✆ 10am-6pm)

Berlin Infostore Fernsehturm (Map p98; ground level TV Tower; ✆ 10am-6pm)

Berlin Infostore Hauptbahnhof (Map p98; Invaliden-strasse exit; ✆ 8am-10pm)

Berlin Infostore Neues Kranzler Eck (Map p102; Kur-fürstendamm 23; ✆ 10am-8pm Mon-Sat, 10am-6pm Sun)

Berlin Infostore Pavillon am Reichstag (Map p98; Scheidemannstrasse, outside Reichstag; ✆ 8am-8pm Apr-Oct, 10am-6pm Nov-Mar)

Euraide (Map p102; www.euraide.de; Bahnhof Zoo; ✆ 8am-noon & 1-6pm daily Jun-Oct, 8am-noon & 1-4.45pm Mon-Fri Nov-May) Behind the Reisezentrum, this helpful office sells and validates rail passes and provides advice and information on trains, lodging, tours and other travel-related subjects, in English.

Travel Agencies

Darpol (Map p102; ☎ 342 0074; Kaiser-Friedrich-Strasse 19) Poland specialist.

Sputnik Travel (Map p98; ☎ 2030 2246; Friedrich-strasse 176) Russia specialist.

STA Travel Charlottenburg (Map p102; ☎ 310 0040; Hardenbergstrasse 9); Mitte (Map p98; ☎ 2016 5063; Dorotheenstrasse 30); Prenzlauer Berg (Map p103; ☎ 2859 8264; Gleimstrasse 28) Student and youth oriented; issues ISIC cards.

Ungarn Tours (Map p98; ☎ 247 8296; Karl-Liebknecht-Strasse 9) Hungary specialist.

DANGERS & ANNOYANCES

By all accounts, Berlin is among the safest and most tolerant of European capitals. Walking alone at night is not usually dangerous, although of course there's always safety in numbers as in any urban setting.

Despite some bad press, racially motivated attacks are actually quite infrequent in Berlin. Having said that, while people of any skin colour should be safe in the central districts, prejudice towards 'foreign-looking people', especially nonwhites, runs comparatively high in some of the economically depressed eastern districts (especially Lichtenberg, Marzahn-Hellerdorf and parts of Pankow). Since there's very little to see or do in these areas, there's really no reason to go there anyway, so our best advice is to avoid them altogether.

Most U- and S-Bahn stations are equipped with electronic information and emergency devices labelled 'SOS/Notruf/Information' and are indicated by a large red button. If you require emergency assistance simply push the 'SOS' button. The Information button allows you to speak directly with the stationmaster.

SIGHTS

Each of Berlin's districts has its own appeal, but must-see sights concentrate in Mitte and Tiergarten. The Jewish Museum and Check-point Charlie in Kreuzberg and Schloss

Charlottenburg also rank high on the list of major attractions. Of the outer districts, the prettiest is leafy Zehlendorf with fabulous museums, lush parks and lakes. For GDR-era relics, head to the eastern districts.

Mitte

Mitte is the glamorous heart of Berlin, a high-octane cocktail of culture, commerce and history. Packed with blockbuster sights, this is likely where you'll concentrate your time, where you come to play and learn, to admire and marvel, to be astounded and bewildered.

BRANDENBURGER TOR & PARISER PLATZ

A symbol of division during the Cold War, the recently restored landmark **Brandenburger Tor** (Brandenburg Gate; Map p98) now epitomises German reunification. The 1791 structure by Carl Gotthard Langhans is the only surviving one of 18 city gates. The Quadriga sculpture, a horse-drawn chariot piloted by the winged goddess of victory, perches triumphantly on top. In the south wing is a Berlin Infostore (p105).

The gate stands sentinel over **Pariser Platz** (Map p98), an elegant square once again framed by embassies and bank buildings as it was during its 19th-century heyday as the 'emperor's reception hall'. Pop inside the **DZ Bank** (Map p98) for a look at the outlandish conference room US-based architect Frank Gehry created in the atrium. Next door, the new US Embassy is taking shape and is expected to open in 2008.

Another landmark on Pariser Platz is the faithfully rebuilt **Hotel Adlon** (now called the Adlon Hotel Kempinski, p126). The *grande dame* of Berlin caravanserais, it has sheltered Charlie Chaplin, Greta Garbo, Bill Clinton and many other celebrity guests. Remember Michael Jackson dangling his baby out the window? It happened at the Adlon.

HOLOCAUST MEMORIAL

One of Berlin's newest landmarks, the **Memorial to the Murdered European Jews** (Map p98; colloquially known as the Holocaust Memorial) by American architect Peter Eisenmann consists of 2711 concrete stelae spread across a huge field like an abstract cemetery. You're free to access this maze at any point and make your individual journey through it. Also visit the excellent, if heart-wrenching, **Ort der**

Information (information centre; Map p98; ☎ 7407 2929; www.holocaust-mahnmal.de; admission free; ⊙ 10am-8pm) below the memorial. It presents a graphic timeline of Jewish persecution during the Third Reich and rooms documenting the fate of individuals and families.

HITLER'S BUNKER

In a strange twist, it wasn't far from the Holocaust Memorial where Hitler spent his final days ensconced in his bomb-proof bunker (Map p98). Here he married Eva Braun on 29 April 1945, then shot her, then himself, the following day. The site itself is now a parking lot, but since June 2006 a German-English explanatory panel provides a brief chronology of events at the bunker during the final days of WWII along with a diagram of the bunker network, technical data on how it was constructed and what happened to it after the war. It also addresses concerns about the place becoming a place of pilgrimage for neo-Nazis. Look for it in the area where In den Ministergärten meets Gertrud-Kolmar-Strasse.

UNTER DEN LINDEN

Berlin's most splendid boulevard (Map p98) extends for about 1.5km east of the Brandenburger Tor. First up on your right is the hulking **Russian embassy** (Map p98; Unter den Linden 63-65), a white marble behemoth built in pompous Stalin-era 'wedding cake' style. Further on, the **Deutsche Guggenheim** (Map p98; ☎ 202 0930; www .deutsche-guggenheim.de; Unter den Linden 13-15; adult/ concession/family €4/3/8, free Mon; ⊙ 11am-8pm Fri-Wed, 11am-10pm Thu) is a not terribly imposing gallery presenting international contemporary artists of some renown, such as Eduardo Chillida or Georg Baselitz.

Opposite, the **Alte Staatsbibliothek** (Old National Library; Map p98; Unter den Linden 8) has amassed an astonishing archive since its founding in 1661, including the original sheet music of Beethoven's 9th Symphony. Next up is the **Humboldt Universität** (Map p98), Berlin's oldest university where Marx and Engels studied and the Brothers Grimm and Albert Einstein taught. It occupies the palace of Prince Heinrich, brother of King Frederick the Great, whose pompous **equestrian statue** stands on Unter den Linden outside the university.

It was Frederick who created the ensemble of stately structures framing **Bebelplatz** (Map p98), the site of the first big official Nazi book-burning in May 1933. A simple but poignant memorial by Micha Ullmann consisting of an underground library with empty bookshelves commemorates this event. Surrounding the square are the baroque **Alte Königliche Bibliothek** (Old Royal Library; Map p98; 1780), now part of the university; the **Staatsoper Unter den Linden** (State Opera; 1743, p139); and the domed **St Hedwigskirche** (Map p98; 1783), partly modelled on Rome's Pantheon and Berlin's only Catholic church until 1854.

Just east of here, the perkily turreted **Friedrichswerdersche Kirche** (☎ 2090 5577; Werderscher Markt; admission free; ☽ 10am-6pm) shelters 19th-century sculptures and an exhibit on the life and accomplishments of Karl Friedrich Schinkel.

For more Schinkel, return to Unter den Linden and the neoclassical **Neue Wache** (Map p98; admission free; ☽ 10am-6pm). Originally a Prussian guardhouse, it is now a memorial to the 'victims of war and tyranny'. Käthe Kollwitz's emotional sculpture *Mother and her Dead Son* dominates the austere room.

The pink building next door is the baroque **Zeughaus** (Map p98), a former armoury whose glass-covered central courtyard features 22 baroque mask sculptures of dying warriors by Andreas Schlüter. Since June 2006, the building has again been home of the **Deutsches Historisches Museum** (German Historical Museum; Map p98; ☎ 2030 4444; www.dhm.de; Unter den Linden 2; adult/under 18yr €4/free; ☽ 10am-6pm), which chronicles 2000 years of German history. Intriguing objects include a full medieval body armour for horse and rider and a big globe that originally stood in Hitler's chancellery with bullet holes where Germany should be. All panelling is in German and English and audio-guides are available for €3.

Temporary exhibits occupy the museum's modern extension, the so-called **IM Pei Bau** (Map p98) named after its architect. It's a truly striking space, starkly geometric, yet imbued with a sense of lightness achieved through an airy atrium and generous use of glass.

GENDARMENMARKT

Once a thriving marketplace, Gendarmenmarkt (Map p98) is Berlin's most graceful square. The twin churches of Deutscher Dom and Französischer Dom frame Schinkel's **Konzerthaus** (p139) to form a superbly harmonious architectural trio. Plenty of luxury hotels and fancy restaurants are nearby.

Inside the **Deutscher Dom** (Map p98) is a free but hopelessly academic exhibit on German parliamentarianism that has bored thousands of school children to tears. The **Französischer Dom** (Map p98) was built for the French Huguenots who fled to Berlin following their expulsion from France in 1685. Their story is chronicled in the **Hugenottenmuseum** (Map p98; ☎ 229 1760; adult/concession/family €2/1/3.50; ☽ noon-5pm Tue-Sat, 11am-5pm Sun), located in the tower, which unfortunately is currently closed for restoration.

MUSEUMSINSEL

East of the Zeughaus, the sculpture-studded **Schlossbrücke** (Palace Bridge; Map p98) leads to the little Spree island where Berlin's settlement began in the 13th century. On its northern half, Museumsinsel (Museum Island) is a treasure-trove of art, sculptures and objects spread across four grand old museums with a fifth one, the Neues Museum (New Museum), under reconstruction. Collectively they became a Unesco World Heritage Site in 1999.

Separate tickets are available for each museum or you can buy a day pass valid at all four for €12/6. Admission is free if you're under 16 and for everyone during the last four hours on Thursday.

Alte Nationalgalerie

A sensitively restored Greek-temple building by August Stüler, the **Alte Nationalgalerie** (Old National Gallery; Map p98; ☎ 2090 5577; Bodestrasse 1-3; adult/concession €8/4; ☽ 10am-6pm Tue, Wed & Fri-Sun, 10am-10pm Thu) is an elegant setting for an exquisite collection of 19th-century European art. Highlights include the mystical landscapes of Caspar David Friedrich and works by Monet and Renoir. The elegant rotunda presents the emotionally charged sculptures of Reinhold Begas, while the marble stairwell is decorated with Otto Geyers' patriotic frieze of German greats.

Pergamon Museum

If you only have time for one museum while in Berlin, make it the **Pergamon Museum** (Map p98; ☎ 2090 5555; Am Kupfergraben; adult/concession incl audio-guide €8/4; ☽ 10am-6pm Tue, Wed & Fri-Sun, 10am-10pm Thu). A feast of classical Greek, Babylonian, Roman, Islamic and Middle Eastern art and architecture, it will amaze and enlighten you. The three sections (Collection of Classical Antiquities, Museum of Near Eastern Antiquities and Museum of Islamic Art) are all worth seeing at leisure, but if you're pressed for time, make a beeline to the following key exhibits.

The museum's namesake and crowd magnet is the **Pergamon Altar** (165 BC) from today's Turkey. It's a gargantuan raised marble shrine surrounded by a vivid frieze of the gods doing battle with the giants. The next room features the immense **Market Gate of Miletus** from the 2nd century, a masterpiece of Roman architecture. Passing through it leads you straight into another culture and century: Babylon during the reign of King Nebuchadnezzar II (604–562 BC). Top billing here goes to the brilliant **Ishtar Gate**, sheathed in glazed bricks glistening in a luminous cobalt blue and ochre. The striding lions, horses, dragons and unicorns are so striking that you can almost hear the roaring and fanfare.

Upstairs in the Islamic collection, top billing goes to the fortresslike 8th-century **Caliph's palace** from Mshatta in today's Jordan and the **Aleppo Room** from 17th-century Syria with its richly wood-panelled walls.

Altes Museum

For more art and sculpture from ancient Rome and Greece head to the **Altes Museum** (Map p98; ☎ 2090 5577; Am Lustgarten; adult/concession €8/4; ☺ 10am-6pm Tue, Wed & Fri-Sun, 10am-10pm Thu). To meet the museum's current 'star', however, venture upstairs where the famous bust of Nefertiti, she of the long graceful neck and stunning good looks, is the undisputed highlight of the **Egyptian Museum**. Selections from this famous collection are housed here until the completion of the Neues Museum, possibly in 2009.

Bodemuseum

This **museum** (Map p98; ☎ 2090 5555; Monbijoubrücke; adult/concession €8/4; ☺ 10am-6pm Fri-Wed, 10am-10pm Thu), in a neobaroque edifice by Ernst von Ihne, reopened in October 2006 after an ambitious €153 million renovation. The magnificently restored rooms shelter one of Germany's largest collections of sculptures from the Middle Ages onward, fine examples of Christian and Byzantine art from the 3rd to the 19th centuries and a precious collection of ancient coins. Kids can enjoy the children's museum.

Berliner Dom

Serenading Museumsinsel is the great 1905 neo-Renaissance **Berliner Dom** (Berlin Cathedral; Map p98; ☎ 202 690; Am Lustgarten; adult/concession/

under 14yr €5/3/free; ☺ church & crypt 9am-8pm Mon-Sat, noon-8pm Sun Apr-Sep, to 7pm Oct-Mar, viewing gallery 9am-8pm Apr-Sep, 9am-5pm Oct-Mar), the former court church of the royal Hohenzollern family, members of whom are buried in its crypt. There are some pretty good views from the upper viewing gallery and concerts, guided tours and readings year-round.

SCHLOSSPLATZ

Nothing of today's Schlossplatz (Map p98) evokes memory of the magnificent edifice that stood here from 1451 to 1951: the Berliner Stadtschloss, for centuries the primary residence of the Hohenzollern kings. Despite international protests, the GDR government razed the barely war-damaged palace in 1951 and, 25 years later, replaced it with the **Palast der Republik** (Palace of the Republic; Map p98), a functional, multipurpose structure used for meetings of the GDR parliament as well as for cultural events. Alas, the GDR 'palace' will soon be relegated to the history books as well.

After more than a decade of heated debate, demolition of this concrete, steel and orange glass monstrosity finally began in January 2006. The current plan foresees a rebuilding of the historic palace shell with a modern interior that might house a museum, a hotel, a library or some other institution. Given Berlin's empty coffers, it's anyone's guess when reconstruction might actually take place. Meanwhile, have a look at the scale model in the **Berliner Schloss Infocenter** (Map p98; ☎ 2067 3093; Hausvogteiplatz 3; admission free; ☺ 9.30am-6pm).

ALEXANDERPLATZ & AROUND

Eastern Berlin's main commercial hub, Alexanderplatz (Map p98) – 'Alex' for short – was named in honour of Tsar Alexander I on his 1805 visit to Berlin. Today it's light years away from the low-life district Alfred Döblin called 'the quivering heart of a cosmopolitan city' in his 1929 novel *Berlin Alexanderplatz*.

Major construction in recent years has tempered the socialist look the square received after WWII. The **Galeria Kaufhof** (Map p98) department store got a total makeover and now sports a sleek travertine-and-glass skin and a glass-domed light court. Nearby, the protected 1929 **Berolinahaus** (Map p98) by Peter Behrens has been restored as a clothing store. And not far away, in an area bounded by Alexanderstrasse, Dircksenstrasse and Grunerstrasse, the new **Alexa** (Map p98) megamall is taking shape with an opening date set for early 2007.

The main sight around Alexanderplatz is the **Fernsehturm** (TV Tower; Map p98; ☎ 242 3333; adult/child €7.50/3.50; ☯ 9am-midnight Mar-Oct, 10am-midnight Nov-Feb), at 368m Berlin's tallest structure. If it's a clear day and the queue isn't too long, it's worth paying for the elevator ride to the top. In sunlight, the steel sphere below the antenna produces the reflection of a giant cross – a source of embarrassment for the secular-minded GDR honchos who built the tower in 1969. West Berliners gleefully dubbed the phenomenon 'the Pope's revenge'.

Dwarfed by the TV Tower is the nearby brick **Marienkirche** (Map p98; ☎ 242 4467; Karl-Liebknecht-Strasse 8; admission free; ☯ 10am-6pm Apr-Oct, 10am-4pm Nov-Mar), Berlin's second-oldest church, built in 1270. Inside, turn your attention to the alabaster pulpit by Andreas Schlüter and the Dance of Death fresco, still an amazing work of art despite being badly faded. Outside is the epic **Neptunbrunnen** (Neptune Fountain; 1891; Map p98) by Reinhold Begas; the female figures symbolise the rivers Rhine, Elbe, Oder and Weichsel.

North of here, across Karl-Liebknecht-Strasse, **Sealife Berlin** (Map p98; ☎ 992 800; Spandauer Strasse 3; adult/child/student €13.50/10/12.60; ☯ 10am-7pm Apr-Aug, 10am-6pm Sep-Mar) is an entertaining if pricey aquarium that takes you on a virtual journey along the Spree, Havel and Elbe Rivers into the frigid waters of the North Atlantic. Visits conclude with an ultra-slow lift ride through the **AquaDom**, a 16m-tall cylindrical aquarium teeming with tropical fish. It's in the lobby of the Radisson SAS Hotel (p126) from where you could sneak a free preview.

In the same complex, the Dom Aquaree, the new **DDR Museum Berlin** (Map p98; ☎ 030-847 123 731; Karl-Liebknecht-Strasse 1; adult/concession €5/3; ☯ 10am-8pm Sun-Fri, 10am-10pm Sat), offers a nostalgic journey through daily life in the GDR. On display are mostly now-extinct brands and products, such as Narva light bulbs, Jamboree bubble gum and hilarious old radios. You can even get behind the wheel of a Trabi, the GDR-era automobile.

Back south across the street looms the 1860 **Rotes Rathaus** (Red Town Hall; Map p98; ☎ 902 60;

Rathausstrasse 15; admission free; ☯ 9am-6pm Mon-Fri), the office of Berlin's mayor. The moniker 'red', by the way, was inspired by the colour of the brick façade and not the political leanings of its occupants.

Just behind the town hall is the twee **Nikolaiviertel** (Nicholas Quarter; Map p98), a fairly successful attempt by GDR architects to re-create Berlin's medieval birthplace. The result is a maze of narrow cobbled lanes lined with historic buildings, some original, most reconstructed. Lording it over the quarter are the twin spires of the 1230 **Nikolaikirche** (Map p98; ☎ 2472 4529; admission by donation; ☯ 10am-6pm Tue & Thu-Sun, noon-8pm Wed), Berlin's oldest church. Inside are lavish baroque epitaphs and an exhibition on the church's role in local history.

To get a grasp on how the tiny trading village of Berlin-Cölln evolved into today's metropolis, visit the **Märkisches Museum** (March of Brandenburg Museum; Map p98; ☎ 3086 6215; Am Köllnischen Park 5; adult/concession €4/2; ☯ 10am-6pm Tue & Thu-Sun, noon-8pm Wed). Rooms are organised by theme rather than chronology. An armoury, a magnificent Guild Hall and a collection of religious sculptures are among the items representing medieval times.

The three **brown bears** in the Köllnischer Park (Map p98) just south of the museum are the city's official mascots. They're named Thilo, Maxi and Schnute and can usually be seen from 8am to 5pm April to September and 9am to 3pm October to March.

SCHEUNENVIERTEL

North of Alexanderplatz, the Scheunenviertel (Map p98) is one of Berlin's liveliest areas, teeming with bars, restaurants and nightclubs, especially around Hackescher Markt and along Oranienburger Strasse and its side streets. Alte Schönhauser Strasse and Neue Schönhauser Strasse are hip shopping streets, while Auguststrasse has become a gallery mile.

Since reunification the quarter has also reprised its historical role as the centre of Jewish life, with the gleaming gold dome of the **Neue Synagoge** (Map p98) on Oranienburger Strasse as its most visible symbol. Built in Moorish-Byzantine style, the 1866 original seated 3200 and was Germany's largest synagogue. During the 1938 Kristallnacht pogroms, a local police chief prevented Nazi thugs from setting it on fire, an act of courage commemorated by a plaque. It was eventually desecrated anyway but not destroyed until hit by bombs in 1943.

The rebuilt version is primarily a museum and information centre called **Centrum Judaicum** (Map p98; ☎ 8802 8477; Oranienburger Strasse 28-30; adult/concession €3/2; 🕑 10am-8pm Sun & Mon, 10am-6pm Tue-Thu, 10am-5pm Fri Apr-Sep, reduced hours Oct-Mar) with displays on the building's history and architecture and the lives of the people who worshipped here. The dome is accessible from April to September (€1.50).

The crumbling ruin just up the street is the **Kunsthaus Tacheles** (Map p98; ☎ 282 6185; Oranienburger Strasse 54-56), a one-time department store that became an artists' squat after reunification and has since evolved into an alternative art and cultural centre. Some of the anarchic edge is gone, but it's still a chaotic, graffiti-covered warren of artists' studios, galleries, a cinema, café and beer garden.

The Scheunenviertel is famous for its interlinked courtyard complexes that have been beautifully restored and filled with cafés, boutiques and entertainment venues. The best known is the **Hackesche Höfe** (Map p98); the nicest of its eight courtyards is Hof 1 (court 1) whose façades are emblazoned with colourful Art Nouveau tiles. Next door, the **Rosenhöfe** (Map p98) is really just a single courtyard that owes its whimsical quality to a sunken rose garden and tendril-like metal balustrades.

Nearby, between Sophienstrasse and Gipsstrasse, is the quiet and dignified **Sophie-Gips-Höfe** (Map p98) with artistic light installations. The nicest complex for our money, though, is the breezy **Heckmannhöfe** (Map p98) between Oranienburger Strasse and Auguststrasse, where a fountain and small playground invite lingering.

Back next to the Hackesche Höfe is the **Museum Blindenwerkstatt Otto Weidt** (Map p98; ☎ 2859 9407; Rosenthaler Strasse 39; admission €1.50; 🕑 noon-8pm Mon-Fri, 11am-8pm Sat & Sun), a small exhibit about a broom and brush maker who saved many of his blind and deaf Jewish workers from the Nazi death camps. The same building also houses the **Anne Frank Zentrum** (Map p98; ☎ 3087 2988; Rosenthaler Strasse 39; adult/concession/family €3.50/2/6; 🕑 10am-6pm Tue-Sun), which tells the story of the German-Jewish girl famous for her diary written while hiding from the Nazis in Amsterdam.

ORANIENBURGER TOR AREA

Oranienburger Strasse eventually merges with Friedrichstrasse at Oranienburger Tor (Map p98). The area south of here has traditionally been Berlin's premier theatre district. Major venues include the flashy Friedrichstadtpalast (p136), the well-respected Deutsches Theater (p140) and the Berliner Ensemble (p140), founded by Bertolt Brecht in the 1950s.

Brecht, in fact, lived just a short walk north of Oranienburger Tor in what is now the **Brecht-Weigel Gedenkstätte** (Brecht-Weigel Memorial House; Map p98; ☎ 283 057 044; Chausseestrasse 125; tours adult/concession €3/1.50; 🕑 tours half-hourly 10-11.30am Tue, Wed & Fri, 10am-noon & 5-6.30pm Thu, 9.30am-1.30pm Sat & hourly 11am-6pm Sun). A half-hour tour takes in Brecht's relatively modest office, large library and tiny bedroom where he died in 1956. Downstairs are the cluttered quarters of his actress wife Helene Weigel who lived here until her death in 1971. Call ahead about English-language tours. The basement restaurant serves Austrian food based on Weigel's recipes (mains €7 to €15).

The couple is buried in the adjacent **Dorotheenstädtischer Friedhof** (Map p98; 🕑 8am-sunset), the cemetery with the greatest concentration of celebrity corpses in Berlin. German greats buried here include the architect Schinkel, the philosopher Hegel and the writer Heinrich Mann.

North of here is the Humboldt University's **Museum für Naturkunde** (Natural History Museum; Map p98; ☎ 2093 8591; Invalidenstrasse 43; adult/concession/family €3.50/2/7; 🕑 9.30am-5pm Tue-Fri, 10am-6pm Sat & Sun), a vast repository where star exhibits include a gigantic brachiosaurus skeleton, meteorites from Mars and the largest piece of amber ever found. Note that some sections may be closed due to a renovation expected to be completed some time in 2007.

Andy Warhol's smiling Mao, Anselm Kiefer's expressionist sculpture *Mohn und Gedächtnis*, Joseph Beuys' provocative installations – they're all part of the collection of the **Hamburger Bahnhof** (Map p98; ☎ 3978 3439; Invalidenstrasse 50-51; adult/under 16yr/concession €8/free/4, last 4hr Thu free; 🕑 10am-6pm Tue-Fri, 11am-8pm Sat, 11am-6pm Sun), Berlin's premier contemporary art museum. It's housed in a late-neoclassical train station centred on a vaulted hall with the loftiness of a Gothic cathedral. In 2004, the museum expanded into the adjacent Rieckhallen, a series of austere warehouses.

Tiergarten

Named after the sprawling urban park, the Tiergarten district received the lion's share of new construction and harbours two of Berlin's most headline-grabbing megadevelopments: the Regierungsviertel (Government Quarter) and Potsdamer Platz, both tourist magnets of the first rank. In May of 2006, Berlin's first-ever central train station, the sparkling Hauptbahnhof, opened in northern Tiergarten.

POTSDAMER PLATZ

A showcase of urban renewal, Potsdamer Platz (Map pp100–1) is perhaps the most visible symbol of the 'New Berlin'. The historical Potsdamer Platz was a busy traffic hub that became synonymous with metropolitan life and entertainment in the early 20th century. In 1924, Europe's first (hand-operated) traffic light was installed here, a replica of which was recently hoisted in the same spot. WWII sucked all life out of the area, which soon plunged into a coma, bisected by the Wall until reunification.

In the 1990s, the city tapped an international cast of star architects, including Renzo Piano, Arata Isozaki, Rafael Moneo, Richard Rogers and Helmut Jahn, to design 'Potsdamer Platz – The Sequel'. Hamstrung by city-imposed building guidelines, the result is hardly avant-garde, but it's nevertheless a pleasant and above all human-scale cityscape.

Potsdamer Platz is divided into three sections: **DaimlerCity**, home to a large mall and lots of public art, including Jeff Koons' Balloon Flower on Marlene-Dietrich-Platz; the flashy **Sony Center** with its central plaza canopied by a glass roof whose supporting beams emanate like bicycle spokes; and the **Beisheim Center**, which was inspired by classic American skyscraper design.

Berliners and visitors have by and large embraced the development with its mix of cinemas, restaurants, bars, public spaces and shops. For a look at it all from above, take what is billed as the world's fastest elevator to the **Panorama Observation Deck** (Map pp100–1; ☎ 2529 4372; www.panoramapunkt.de; Potsdamer Platz 1; adult/concession €3.50/2.50; ☒ 11am-8pm, last admission 7.30pm, closed Mon Nov-Mar).

A multimedia journey through German film history and a behind-the-scenes look at special effects are what await visitors to the **Filmmuseum Berlin** (Map pp100–1; ☎ 300 9030; Potsdamer Strasse 2; adult/concession/family €6/4.50/12; ☒ 10am-6pm Tue, Wed & Fri-Sun, 10am-8pm Thu). Themed galleries zero in on pioneers and early divas, Fritz Lang's silent epic *Metropolis*, Leni Riefenstahl's *Olympia*, and Marlene Dietrich. Tickets also include admission to the new **Fernsehmuseum** (Museum of TV; Map pp100–1) upstairs, which presents a romp through German TV back to the earliest image experiments in the 1920s.

Fans of 20th-century abstract, conceptual and minimalist art should pop into the **DaimlerChrysler Contemporary** (Map pp100–1; ☎ 2594 1420; Weinhaus Huth, Alte Potsdamer Strasse 5; admission free; ☒ 11am-6pm), a quiet and minimalist gallery space in the only surviving historic structure on Potsdamer Platz. Ring the bell to be buzzed in.

GOVERNMENT QUARTER

Berlin's government quarter snuggles into the Spreebogen, a horseshoe-shaped bend of the Spree River. Its historic anchor is the 1894 **Reichstag** (Map p98; Platz der Republik 1), since 1999 home to the German parliament, the Bundestag, following a total makeover by Lord Norman Foster. Its most striking contemporary feature is the glistening glass dome. A trip on the **lift** (admission free; ☒ 8am-midnight, last entry 10pm) and up a spiralling ramp to the top is a highlight of any Berlin visit, as much for the 360-degree panorama as for the close-ups of the dome and the mirror-clad funnel at its centre. Come early or expect to queue.

The Reichstag has been the setting of numerous milestones in German history. After WWI, Philipp Scheidemann proclaimed the German Republic from one of its windows. The Reichstag fire on the night of 27 February 1933 allowed Hitler to blame the communists and seize power. A dozen years later, the victorious Soviets nearly obliterated the building. Restoration – without the dome – wasn't finished until 1972. At midnight on 2 October 1990 the reunification of Germany was enacted here. In summer 1995, the artist Christo and his wife, Jeanne-Claude, wrapped the edifice in fabric for two weeks. Lord Norman set to work shortly thereafter.

Opposite the Reichstag, the **Bundeskanzleramt** (Federal Chancellery; Map p98; Willy-Brandt-Strasse 1) is a sparkling, modern design by Axel Schultes. A central white cube containing the chancellor's office and residence is flanked by two long office blocks, giving the compound an 'H' shape if viewed from above. For the best perspective, take a stroll along the paved **river promenade** paralleling the Spree.

TIERGARTEN PARK

Berlin's 'green lung' (Map p98) bristles with huge shady trees, groomed paths, woodsy groves, lakes and meadows and is great for a jog, picnic or simply drifting around. At 167 hectares, it is one of the world's largest city parks, sweeping westward from Brandenburger Tor all the way to Bahnhof Zoo in Charlottenburg.

On the park's northern edge, the **Haus der Kulturen der Welt** (House of World Cultures; Map p98; ☎ 397 870; John-Foster-Dulles-Allee 10; admission varies; ☺ 10am-9pm Tue-Sun) was the American contribution to a 1957 architectural exhibition. Thanks to its gravity-defying parabolic roof, Berliners have nicknamed it 'pregnant oyster'. A congress hall by design, it's now a cultural centre with lectures, exhibits and concerts from around the world. Under renovation, it will reopen in September 2007. Meanwhile, chime concerts still ring out at noon and 6pm daily from the 68-bell **carillon** just east of the hall.

Strasse des 17 Juni, named after the date of the 1953 workers' uprising in East Berlin, cuts east–west through the park. Along here, near the Brandenburger Tor, the **Sowjetisches Ehrenmal** (Soviet War Memorial; Map p98) commemorates the Red Army soldiers who died in the Battle of Berlin. The reddish-brown marble was allegedly scavenged from Hitler's chancellery.

Further west looms the landmark **Siegessäule** (Victory Column; Map p98; ☎ 391 2961; adult/concession €2.20/1.50; ☺ 9.30am-6.30pm Mon-Fri, 9.30am-7pm Sat & Sun Apr-Oct, 10am-5pm Mon-Fri, 10am-5.30pm Sat & Sun Nov-Mar), which commemorates successful 19th-century Prussian military exploits. The gilded lady on top stands 8.3m tall and predictably represents the goddess of victory, although locals irreverently call her 'Gold-Else'. And yes, you can climb to the top, but the views are only so-so. The column has become a symbol of Berlin's gay community (the largest of Berlin's gay publications is named after it). The park around here is a cruising zone, especially around the Löwenbrücke.

North of the column, **Schloss Bellevue** (Map p98), a white neoclassical palace from 1785, is the official residence of the German president.

SOUTH OF TIERGARTEN PARK

The Diplomatic Quarter south of the Tiergarten is home to several spectacular new embassy buildings. Stand-outs include the **Nordic embassies** (Map p98; Rauchstrasse 1), a joint complex of the Scandinavian countries distinguished by a shimmering turquoise façade, and the **Mexican embassy** (Map p98; Klingelhöferstrasse 27), a boldly modern concrete and glass edifice.

Just south of here is the striking silhouette of the **Bauhaus Archiv/Museum für Gestaltung** (Map pp96-7; ☎ 254 0020; Klingelhöferstrasse 14; adult/concession €6/3; ☺ 10am-5pm Wed-Mon), which documents the enormous influence the Bauhaus School (1919–33; p212) exerted on all aspects of modern architecture and design. The collection includes everything from study notes to workshop pieces to photographs, models and blueprints by such important Bauhaus members as Klee, Kandinsky, Schlemmer and Feininger.

Further east is the **Gedenkstätte Deutscher Widerstand** (Map p98; ☎ 2699 5000; Stauffenbergstrasse 13-14; admission free; ☺ 9am-6pm Mon-Wed & Fri, 9am-8pm Thu, 10am-6pm Sat & Sun) with an exhibit detailing German resistance efforts against the Nazis. It's in the very rooms where high-ranking officers led by Graf von Stauffenberg plotted the ill-fated assassination attempt on Hitler on 20 July 1944. He and his co-conspirators were shot in the courtyard right after the failed coup.

KULTURFORUM

This cluster of museums and concert venues (Map pp100–1) off the southeastern edge of Tiergarten park was master-planned in the 1950s by Hans Scharoun, one of the era's premier architects. A day pass to all museums mentioned in this section is €12/6 (adult/concession). Admission is free if you're under 16 and for all during the last four hours on Thursday.

The first of the Kulturforum museums to be completed was the **Neue Nationalgalerie** (New National Gallery; Map pp100-1; ☎ 266 2651; Potsdamer Strasse 50; adult/concession €8/4; ☺ 10am-6pm Tue & Wed, 10am-10pm Thu-Sun), a major repository of visual art by 20th-century European artists until 1960. All major genres are represented: cubism (Picasso, Gris Leger), surrealism (Dalí, Miró, Max Ernst), new objectivity (Otto Dix, George Grosz), Bauhaus (Klee, Kandinsky) and, above all, German expressionism (Kirchner, Nolde, Schmitt-Rottluff). The gallery is housed in a 1968 glass-and-steel 'temple' by Mies van der Rohe.

If you only have time for one art museum, make it the **Gemäldegalerie** (Picture Gallery; Map pp100-1; ☎ 266 2951; Matthäikirchplatz; adult/concession incl audio-guide €8/4; ☼ 10am-6pm Tue, Wed & Fri-Sun, 10am-10pm Thu). Set in a glorious building, it has a star-studded collection of European paintings from the 13th to the 18th centuries. The roll-call of artists includes Cranach, Dürer, Rubens, Holbein, Botticelli, Raphael, Titian, Watteau, Gainsborough, Reynolds, Goya and Velázquez. The world's largest Rembrandt collection is also here.

Nearby, the cavernous **Kunstgewerbe Museum** (Map pp100-1; ☎ 266 2951; adult/concession €8/4; ☼ 10am-6pm Tue-Fri, 11am-6pm Sat & Sun) brims with decorative objects from the Middle Ages to the present, from gem-encrusted reliquaries to modern appliances. Don't miss the Chinese Room from the Graneri Palace in Turin, Italy and Carlo Bugatti's crazy suite of furniture.

Across the plaza, the **Kupferstichkabinett** (Museum of Prints & Drawings; Map pp100-1; ☎ 266 2951; Matthäikirchplatz; adult/concession €8/4; ☼ 10am-6pm Tue-Fri, 11am-6pm Sat & Sun) has one of the world's largest and finest collections of art on paper, including exceptional works by Dürer, Rembrandt, Picasso and other top practitioners.

The honey-coloured building east of here is Berlin's premier classical concert venue, the Hans Scharoun-designed **Philharmonie** (p139; 1961) with otherworldly acoustics achieved through a complicated layout of three pentagonal levels twisting and angling upward around a central orchestra pit. It's the home of the world-class Berliner Philharmoniker orchestra. Scharoun also designed the adjacent **Kammermusiksaal** (Chamber Music Hall; 1987; Map pp100-1), the 1978 **Neue Staatsbibliothek** (New National Library; Map pp100-1; ☎ 2660; Potsdamer Strasse 33; ☼ 9am-9pm Mon-Fri, 9am-7pm Sat) across Potsdamer Strasse, and the **Musikinstrumenten-Museum** (Musical Instruments Museum; Map pp100-1; ☎ 2548 1178; Tiergartenstrasse 1; adult/concession €8/4; ☼ 9am-5pm Tue, Wed & Fri, 9am-10pm Thu, 10am-5pm Sat & Sun). The latter counts some fun items among its vast collection, including a glass harmonica invented by Ben Franklin, a flute played by Frederick the Great, Johann Sebastian Bach's cembalo and a Mighty Wurlitzer, an organ with more buttons and keys than a troop of Beefeater guards. It is cranked up at noon on Saturday.

Kreuzberg

South of Mitte, Kreuzberg (Map pp100-1) has a split personality. Its eastern end, bordering the Spree River, has preserved some of the counter-cultural vibe that drew scores of students, punks, hippies and others in search of an alternative lifestyle here long before reunification. Some of the edginess has since worn off, but the area still teems with no-nonsense bars, clubs and alternative cinemas. This is also the hub of Berlin's Turkish community with a colourful market held along the Maybachufer on Tuesday and Friday afternoons.

Kreuzberg's western half around Viktoriapark has tended toward the upmarket in recent years. Its main strip, Bergmannstrasse, has excellent cafés, boutiques and bars. Northern Kreuzberg feels more like an extension of Mitte and harbours the district's heavy-weight sights: the Jewish Museum and Checkpoint Charlie.

For a cool view over the city, you can sway 150m above ground in a hot-air balloon (that's tethered safely to the ground) with **Berlin Hi-Flyer** (Map pp100-1; ☎ 01805-708 708; www .air-service-berlin.de; cnr Wilhelmstrasse & Zimmerstrasse; adult/concession €19/10; ☼ 10am-10pm Sun-Thu, 10am-12.30am Fri & Sat Mar-Nov, 11am-6pm Sun-Thu, 11am-7pm Fri & Sat Dec-Feb, weather permitting).

JÜDISCHES MUSEUM

The history of German Jews and their contributions to culture, art, science and other fields are creatively chronicled at the sprawling **Jüdisches Museum** (Jewish Museum; Map pp100-1; ☎ 2599 3300; www.jmberlin.de; Lindenstrasse 9-14; adult/ concession/family €5/2.50/10; ☼ 10am-10pm Mon, 10am-8pm Tue-Sun), one of Berlin's must-do sights. It's an engaging presentation with listening stations, videos, documents 'hidden' in drawers and other multimedia devices.

Only one section directly deals with the Holocaust, but its horrors are poignantly reflected by the museum's architecture. Designed by Daniel Libeskind, the building serves as a metaphor for the tortured history of the Jewish people. Zinc-clad walls rise skyward in a sharply angled zigzag ground plan that's an abstract interpretation of a star. Instead of windows, irregular gashes pierce the gleaming facade.

Tickets include same- or next-day admission to the Museum Blindenwerkstatt Otto Weidt (p110).

BERLIN

BERLINISCHE GALERIE

Artworks created in Berlin since the late 19th century are the focus of the **Berlinische Galerie** (Map pp100-1; ☎ 7890 2600; Alte Jakobstrasse 124-128; adult/concession €5/4; ⊙ 10am-6pm) in a spectacularly converted glass warehouse near the Jewish Museum. Two floors linked by two intersecting floating stairways cover all major artistic movements from Berlin Secessionism (Lesser Ury, Max Liebermann) to New Objectivity (Otto Dix, George Grosz) and contemporary art by Salomé and Rainer Fetting.

CHECKPOINT CHARLIE

A potent symbol of the Cold War, Checkpoint Charlie (Map pp100-1) was the main gateway for Allies, other non-Germans and diplomats between the two Berlins from 1961 to 1990. The crossing has been partly reconstructed with a US Army guardhouse and a copy of the famous sign warning 'You are now leaving the American sector'.

The original is now next door at the private **Haus am Checkpoint Charlie** (Map pp100-1; ☎ 253 7250; www.mauermuseum.de; Friedrichstrasse 43-45; adult/concession €9.50/5.50; ⊙ 9am-10pm), a popular if cluttered museum reporting mostly on the history and horror of the Berlin Wall. The exhibit is strongest when documenting the courage and ingenuity displayed by some GDR citizens in escaping to the West using hot-air balloons, tunnels, concealed compartments in cars and even a one-man submarine.

TOPOGRAPHIE DES TERRORS & AROUND

In the wasteland along Niederkirchner Strasse once stood some of the most feared institutions of the Third Reich: the Gestapo headquarters, the SS central command, the SS Security Service and, after 1939, the Reich Security Main Office. In place of the buildings there is now a harrowing open-air exhibit called **Topographie des Terrors** (Topography of Terror; Map pp100-1; ☎ 2548 6703; Niederkirchnerstrasse 8; admission free; ⊙ 10am-8pm May-Sep, 10am-dusk Oct-Apr). It's an excellent primer on the Third Reich with particular focus on the brutal institutions that wielded power from this site. A free English-language audio-guide is available from the information kiosk. Some images may be too graphic for children.

The palatial building overlooking the grounds is the **Martin-Gropius-Bau** (Map pp100-1; ☎ 254 860; Niederkirchner Strasse 7; admission varies; ⊙ hours vary), now used for travelling shows

of international stature. Designed by the great-uncle of Bauhaus founder Walter Gropius, it's an Italian Renaissance-style cube adorned with mosaics and terracotta reliefs. Across the street is the **Abgeordnetenhaus** (Map pp100-1), the seat of Berlin's state parliament.

DEUTSCHES TECHNIKMUSEUM

Fantastic for kids, the giant **Deutsches Technikmuseum** (German Museum of Technology; Map pp100-1; ☎ 902 540; www.dtmb.de; Trebbiner Strasse 9; adult/concession €4.50/2.50; ⊙ 9am-5.30pm Tue-Fri, 10am-6pm Sat & Sun) is a vast treasure trove that counts the world's first computer, an entire hall of vintage locomotives and new exhibits on aviation and navigation among its top attractions. At the adjacent **Spectrum science centre** (Map pp100-1; enter from Möckernstrasse 26; admission included) you can participate in some 250 experiments and get the low-down on such things as why the sky is blue or how a battery works.

Charlottenburg

Until reunification, this upmarket district was the glittering centre of West Berlin, an intense cauldron of restaurants, bars, boutiques and snazzy hotels. Things have definitely quieted down since the *Wende* (change) when the wave of attention swapped over to Mitte. Theatres are closing, Nefertiti and her entourage from the Egyptian museum have moved to the Altes Museum and even Bahnhof Zoo has been demoted (for now) to a regional train station since the opening of the sleek new Hauptbahnhof.

But Charlottenburg's main draws are in no danger of disappearing. Shopaholics can still get their fix on Kurfürstendamm, 'royal' groupies continue to delight in Schloss Charlottenburg and there's some bold new architecture (most notably Helmut Jahn's **Neues Kranzler Eck** (an office and shopping complex; Map p102) and museums to keep things dynamic and interesting.

SCHLOSS CHARLOTTENBURG

Schloss Charlottenburg (Map pp96–7) is an exquisite baroque palace and one of the few remaining sites in Berlin reflecting the one-time grandeur of the royal Hohenzollern clan. It was commissioned by Elector Friedrich III (later King Friedrich I) as a summer residence for his wife, Sophie-Charlotte. Reconstruction became a priority after WWII and when it was finished Andreas Schlüter's epic **Reiterdenkmal des Grossen Kurfürsten** (1699), which shows the Great Elector on horseback, also returned to the front courtyard.

Schloss Charlottenburg is on Spandauer Damm, about 3km northwest of Bahnhof Zoo. Each of the palace buildings charges separate admission, but the combination ticket (adult/ concession €7/5) is good for one-time admission on a single day to all sections except the lower floor of the Altes Schloss. Seeing the entire complex takes a full day. Arrive early on weekends and in summer to avoid the worst crowds.

The palace's central – and oldest – section is the **Altes Schloss** (Map pp96-7; ☎ 3209 1440; www .spsg.de; guided tour & upper fl adult/concession €8/5, upper fl only €2/1.50; 🕙 10am-5pm Tue-Sun Apr-Oct, 11am-5pm Nov-Mar). On the lower floor are the baroque living quarters of Friedrich I, which must be visited on a 50-minute tour (in German only, but free English pamphlets are available). Each room is an extravaganza in stucco, brocade and overall opulence. Highlights include the Oak Gallery, a wood-panelled festival hall draped in family portraits; the lovely Oval Hall with views of the gardens; the Belgian-tapestry-filled Audience Chamber; Friedrich I's bedchamber, with the first-ever bathroom

THE BERLIN WALL

Shortly after midnight of 13 August 1961 construction began on a barrier that would divide Berlin for 28 years. The Berlin Wall was a desperate measure by a GDR government on the verge of economic and political collapse to stem the exodus of its own people: 2.6 million of them had left for the West since 1949.

Euphemistically called 'Anti-Fascist Protection Barrier', this grim symbol of oppression stretched for 160km, turning West Berlin into an island of democracy within a sea of socialism. Continually reinforced and refined over time, its cold concrete slabs backed up against a 'death zone' of barbed wire, mines, attack dogs and watchtowers staffed by trigger-happy border guards.

More than 5000 people attempted an escape, but only about 1600 made it across; most were captured and 191 were killed. The full extent of the system's cruelty became blatantly clear on 17 August 1962 when 18-year-old Peter Fechtner was shot during his attempt to flee and was then left to bleed to death while the East German guards looked on.

At the end of the Cold War this potent symbol was eagerly dismantled. Memento seekers chiselled away much of it and entire sections ended up in museums around the world. Most of it, though, was unceremoniously recycled for use in road construction. Today little more than 1.5km of the Wall is left, but throughout Berlin segments, memorial sites, museums and signs commemorate this horrifying but important chapter in German history. Besides the places mentioned below, the **Haus am Checkpoint Charlie** (opposite) also chronicles this period.

East Side Gallery

This is the longest, best-preserved and most interesting stretch of Wall and the one to see if you're pressed for time. Paralleling the Spree (Map pp100–1), the 1300m-section was turned into an open-air gallery by international artists in 1990. The better works are located near the Ostbahnhof end.

Gedenkstätte Berliner Mauer

The fascinating if horrifying history of the Berlin Wall is the theme of the **Gedenkstätte Berliner Mauer** (Map p98; ☎ 464 1030; Bernauer Strasse 111; admission free; 🕙 10am-6pm Apr-Oct, 10am-5pm Nov-Mar), a memorial site that combines a documentation centre, a bizarre art installation and a chapel. Plans to expand the centre were approved in 2006.

Wall Victims Memorial

Just south of the Reichstag, on the eastern end of Scheidemannstrasse, is this sad memorial (Map p98) to the 191 people who died trying to scale the Wall – the last only nine months before it crumbled.

in a baroque palace; and the fabulous Porcelain Chamber, smothered top to bottom in Chinese and Japanese blueware.

Before or after the tour, you're free to head upstairs to the apartment of Friedrich Wilhelm IV. It's filled with paintings, vases, tapestries, weapons, Meissen porcelain and other items essential to a royal lifestyle.

The reign of Friedrich the Great saw the addition, in 1746, of a new wing, the **Neuer Flügel** (Map pp96-7; ☎ 3209 1440; adult/concession incl audio-guide €5/4; ☯ 10am-5pm Tue-Sun Apr-Oct, 11am-5pm Nov-Mar) by Knobelsdorff. Here you'll find the palace's most beautiful rooms, including the confection-like White Hall, the Golden Gallery (a rococo fantasy of mirrors and gilding) and the Concert Room. To the right of the staircase are the comparatively austere Winterkammern (Winter Chambers) of Friedrich Wilhelm II. You're free to explore on your own, but it's worth following the two audiotours included in the admission price.

In the former palace theatre, the **Museum für Vor- und Frühgeschichte** (Museum of Pre- & Early History; Map pp96-7; ☎ 3267 4840; adult/under 16yr/concession €3/free/1.50, last 4hr Thu free; ☯ 9am-5pm Tue-Fri, 10am-5pm Sat & Sun) sheds light on the cultural evolution of Europe and parts of Asia from the Stone Age to the Middle Ages. Pride of place goes to the Trojan antiquities (some originals, some replicas) unearthed by Heinrich Schliemann in 1870. A combined ticket for same-day admission to Museum Berggruen and Museum für Fotografie/Helmut Newton Sammlung costs €6/3 (adult/concession).

A stroll through the sprawling **Schlossgarten Charlottenburg** (palace garden; Map pp96-7; admission free) makes for a nice respite from all that sightseeing, although there's still more of it right in the park. The 1824 **Neuer Pavillon** (Map pp96-7; ☎ 3209 1443; adult/concession €2/1.50; ☯ 10am-5pm Tue-Sun), a small summer palace designed by Schinkel, houses paintings by early-19th-century Berlin artists alongside furnishings, porcelain and sculpture from the same period. The pintsize rococo **Belvedere** (Map pp96-7; ☎ 3209 1445; adult/concession €2/1.50; ☯ 10am-5pm Tue-Sun Apr-Oct, noon-4pm Tue-Fri, noon-5pm Sat & Sun Nov-Mar) is an elegant backdrop for the porcelain masterpieces by the royal manufacturer KPM. The beloved Queen Luise, her husband King Friedrich Wilhelm III and Emperor Wilhelm I and his wife are among those resting in the neoclassical **Mausoleum** (Map pp96-7; ☎ 3209 1446; admission €1; ☯ 10am-5pm Tue-Sun Apr-Oct).

SCHLOSS AREA MUSEUMS

Across from the Schloss, the **Museum Berggruen** (Map pp96-7; ☎ 326 9580; Schlossstrasse 1; adult/concession €6/free/3, last 4hr Thu free; ☯ 10am-6pm Tue-Sun) is a delicacy for fans of classical modern art. Picasso is particularly well presented with more than a hundred paintings, drawings and sculptures from all his major creative phases, but there are also some nice pieces by Klee, Matisse and Giacometti. The ticket for this museum is also valid for same-day admission to Museum für Vor- und Frühgeschichte and Museum für Fotografie/Helmut Newton Sammlung.

Art Nouveau, Art Deco and Functionalism take centre stage at the adjacent **Bröhan Museum** (Map pp96-7; ☎ 3269 0600; Schlossstrasse 1a; adult/concession €4/2; ☯ 10am-6pm Tue-Sun). Downstairs, you can wander past outstanding period rooms by such famous designers as Hector Guimard, Émile Ruhlmann and Peter Behrens, while upstairs the emphasis is on works by Berlin Secession painters.

KURFÜRSTENDAMM & AROUND

The 3.5km-long Kurfürstendamm (Ku'damm for short) is a ribbon of commerce that started as a bridle path to the royal hunting palace in the Grunewald forest. In the 1880s, Bismarck had it widened, paved and lined with fancy residential buildings.

On Breitscheidplatz, its eastern terminus, the landmark **Kaiser-Wilhelm-Gedächtniskirche** (Kaiser Wilhelm Memorial Church; 1895; Map p102) stands quiet and dignified amid the roar. Allied bombs left only the husk of the west tower intact; it now contains the **Gedenkhalle** (Memorial Hall; Map p102; ☯ 10am-4pm Mon-Sat) whose original ceiling mosaics and marble reliefs hint at the church's prewar opulence. The adjacent octagonal **hall of worship** (☯ 9am-7pm), added in 1961, has intensely midnight-blue windows and a giant golden Jesus floating above the altar.

Northeast of the church, an exotic Elephant Gate marks the entrance to the **Berliner Zoo** (Map p102; ☎ 254 010; Budapester Strasse; ☯ 9am-6.30pm mid-Mar–mid-Oct, 9am-5pm mid-Oct–mid-Mar), Germany's oldest and most visited animal park. Some 14,000 furry, feathered and flippered creatures from all continents, 1500 species total, make their home here. Perennial crowd pleasers include cheeky orang-utans, endangered rhinos, playful penguins and the giant panda Bao Bao. The adjacent **Aquarium** (Map p102; Budapester

Strasse 32; adult/student/child €11/5.50/8, zoo & aquarium €16.50/8.50/13; ✆ 9am-6pm) has three floors of fish, amphibians, reptiles and insects, including the famous crocodile hall. There's a second entrance to the zoo on Hardenbergplatz.

At the nearby **Erotik Museum** (Map p102; ✆ 8862 0666; Joachimstaler Strasse 4; adult/concession €5/4, over 18yr only; ✆ 9am-midnight) displays from wacky to sophisticated, raunchy to romantic tell the story of physical pleasure through the ages and around the world. It's the brainchild of Beate Uhse, Germany's late sex-toy marketing queen.

For another dose of eroticism, head to the newish **Museum für Fotografie/Helmut Newton Sammlung** (Map p102; ✆ 3186 4825; Jebensstrasse 2; adult/under 16yr/concession €6/free/3, last 4hr Thu free; ✆ 10am-6pm Tue, Wed & Fri-Sun, 10am-10pm Thu), a repository for the photographs of Berlin-born Helmut Newton, the late *enfant terrible* of fashion photography. Besides presenting a selection of his works, including his famous female nudes, the exhibit is also a bit of a shrine to the man, displaying his cameras, his partially recreated Monte Carlo office and his library. Your ticket is also valid for same-day admission to Museum Berggruen and Museum für Vor- und Frühgeschichte.

Appealing to a different kind of sensibility is the exquisite **Käthe-Kollwitz-Museum** (Map p102; ✆ 882 5210; www.kaethe-kollwitz.de; Fasanenstrasse 24; adult/concession €5/2.50; ✆ 11am-6pm Wed-Mon), which presents the graphics, sculptures, lithographs, woodcuts and drawings of one of Germany's greatest woman artists. Highlights include the haunting *Ein Weberaufstand* (A Weavers' Revolt, 1897) and the woodcut series *Krieg* (War; 1922–23). English-language audio-guides cost an additional €3.

Further west on Ku'damm, the **Story of Berlin** (Map p102; ✆ 8872 0100; www.story-of-berlin.de; Kurfürstendamm 207-208; adult/concession/family €9.30/7.50/21; ✆ 10am-8pm, last admission 6pm) presents city history with a high-tech twist. You'll be outfitted with space-age headsets whose narration (in English or German) magically activates as you enter each of the 20 exhibition rooms. The Cold War period comes creepily to life during a tour of a still fully functional atomic bunker beneath the building.

OLYMPIASTADION
Built for the 1936 Olympic Games, the **Olympiastadion** (Olympic Stadium; ✆ 2500 2322; www .olympiastadion-berlin.de; adult/concession €3/2, tours €6/5;

✆ 10am-7pm Apr-Oct, 10am-4pm Nov-Mar on nonevent days; ✆ ♿ Olympiastadion) recently underwent a four-year, €290 million revamp that created a high-tech facility with snazzy VIP boxes and new-millennium-worthy sound, lighting and projection systems. The most dazzling improvement, though, is the new oval roof sheltering nearly all 74,400 seats. A spidery web of glass, steel and fibre-glass membrane, it beautifully softens the monumental bulk of Werner March's original coliseum-like structure. The stadium is used for soccer, track and other sporting events; in July 2006 Italy beat France in the FIFA World Cup final here.

The **Maifeld**, a vast field west of the stadium, was used for Nazi mass rallies. Soaring above the grounds is the 77m-high **Glockenturm** (Clock Tower; ✆ 305 8123; adult/concession €3.50/1.50; ✆ 9am-6pm; ♿ Pichelsberg), which offers views over the stadium, the city and the Havel River. Admission includes entry to a new exhibit about the history of the grounds and the 1936 Olympic Games in particular. Northwest of here, the **Waldbühne** (✆ 2308 8230; ♿ Pichelsberg) is a lovely outdoor amphitheatre used for summer concerts, film screenings and other cultural events.

Southwestern Berlin
Much of Berlin's southwest is covered by forest, rivers and lakes. Besides the **Freie Universität** and the **Botanischer Garden** (✆ 8385 0027; Königin-Luise-Strasse 6-8; adult/concession €4/2; ✆ 9am-dusk; ♿ Botanischer Garten), you'll find several excellent museums here.

MUSEEN DAHLEM
This enormous **museum complex** (✆ 830 1438; Lansstrasse 8; adult/under 16yr concession/ €6/free/3, last 4hr Thu free; ✆ 10am-6pm Tue-Fri, 11am-6pm Sat & Sun; ♿ Dahlem Dorf) combines four extraordinary collections under one roof. The **Ethnologisches Museum** (Museum of Ethnology) has one of the world's largest, most prestigious collections of pre-industrial, non-European art and objects. Budget at least two hours to explore its labyrinth of halls – it's an eye-opening journey of discovery that'll fly by in no time. The Africa exhibit is particularly impressive with its wealth of masks, ornaments, vases, musical instruments and other objects of ceremonial and everyday life. The South Seas hall, meanwhile, impresses with its cult objects, outriggers and other vessels from New Guinea, Tonga and other islands.

Also here is the **Museum für Indische Kunst** (Museum of Indian Art), which presents two millennia of art from India, Southeast Asia and Central Asia. The most prized items are exquisite terracottas, stone sculptures and bronzes as well as wall paintings and sculptures scavenged from Buddhist cave temples along the Silk Route.

The **Museum für Ostasiatische Kunst** (Museum of East Asian Art) has a similar array of objects, including great lacquerware and jade objects, from China, Japan and Korea. Highlights include a Japanese tearoom and a 16th-century Chinese Imperial throne.

In April 2005, the **Museum Europäischer Kulturen** (Museum of European Cultures) also moved into the complex. It collects objects from daily life from throughout Europe starting with the 18th century.

Admission also includes the **JuniorMuseum** (enter at Arnimallee 23; ⌚ 1-6pm Mon-Fri, 11am-6pm Sat & Sun), where touch-intensive and interactive changing exhibits help broaden kids' horizons.

ALLIIERTENMUSEUM

Housed in a former cinema for US troops, the **AlliiertenMuseum** (Allied Museum; ☎ 818 1990; Clayallee 135; admission free; ⌚ 10am-6pm Thu-Tue; Ⓞ Oskar-Helene-Heim, then any bus north on Clayallee) is an engaging multimedia exhibit that documents the history and challenges faced by the Western Allies during the Cold War. The original guard cabin from Checkpoint Charlie stands in the courtyard, as does a small section of the Wall and a GDR guard tower. Inside, highlights include exhibits on the Berlin Airlift and the partly reconstructed Berlin Spy Tunnel, built by US and British intelligence agents to tap into the central Soviet phone system.

BRÜCKE MUSEUM

In 1905 Karl Schmidt-Rottluff, Erich Heckel and Ernst Ludwig Kirchner founded the artist group Die Brücke in Dresden. Its members rejected the traditional art that was taught in academies and instead experimented with bright, emotional colours and warped perspectives. A small but fine collection of the group's experimental art works can be viewed at the **Brücke Museum** (☎ 831 2029; Bussardsteig 9; adult/concession €4/2; ⌚ 11am-5pm Wed-Mon; Ⓞ Oskar-Helene-Heim, then bus 115 to Pücklerstrasse).

HAUS DER WANNSEEKONFERENZ GEDENKSTÄTTE

In January 1942, a group of elite Nazi officials met in a stately villa on Wannsee lake to discuss the so-called 'Final Solution' – the systematic deportation and annihilation of European Jews. The same building now houses the memorial **Haus der Wannseekonferenz Gedenkstätte** (☎ 805 0010; www.ghwk.de; Am Grossen Wannsee 56-58; admission free; ⌚ 10am-6pm; Ⓡ Wannsee, then bus 114 to Jugenderholungsheim). You can stand in the fateful room where discussions took place, study the minutes of the meeting and look at photographs of the Nazi thugs. English-language pamphlets are available.

Eastern Berlin

The outlying eastern districts are a prime destination for East German history buffs, but otherwise they're a Petri dish of discontent that has spawned large numbers of both neo-Nazis and neo-communists.

In Lichtenberg, the one-time Stasi headquarters now houses the so-called **Stasi Museum** (☎ 553 6854; Ruschestrasse 103, House 1; adult/concession €3.50/3; ⌚ 11am-6pm Mon-Fri, 2-6pm Sat & Sun; Ⓞ Magdalenenstrasse). You can walk around the surprisingly bland and functional office of longtime Stasi chief Erich Mielke, once the most feared man in the GDR. Marvel at primitive yet cunning surveillance devices and snicker at kitschy communist trinkets (Lenin paperweight, anyone?). Explanation panelling is in German only, but an English-language booklet is available for €3.

Victims of Stasi persecution often ended up at a fearsome prison, now a memorial site called **Gedenkstätte Hohenschönhausen** (☎ 9860 8230; Genslerstrasse 66; tour adult/concession €3/1, free on Mon; ⌚ tours 11am & 1pm Mon, Wed & Fri, 11am, 1pm & 3pm Tue & Thu, hourly 10am-4pm Sat & Sun), now a memorial site. Tours of the complex, sometimes led by former prisoners, reveal the full extent of the terror and cruelty perpetrated here upon thousands of people, many of them utterly innocent. Call ahead for tours in English. To get here, take tram M5 to Freienwalder Strasse, followed by a 10-minute walk along Freienwalder Strasse.

Southeast of here, the **Museum Berlin-Karlshorst** (☎ 5015 0810; Zwieseler Strasse 4; admission free; ⌚ 10am-6pm Tue-Sun; Ⓡ Karlshorst) served as the Soviet army headquarters in the waning days of WWII. German commanders signed the unconditional surrender of the Wehrmacht on 8 May 1945. A joint Russian-German exhibit commemorates this fateful day and the events leading up to it with documents, photographs, uniforms and various knick-knacks. The museum is about a 10- to 15-minute walk from the Karlshorst S-Bahn station; take the Treskowallee exit, then turn right onto Rheinsteinstrasse.

At the heart of Treptower Park, the gargantuan **Sowjetisches Ehrenmal Treptow** (Soviet War Memorial; Map pp96-7; ☺ 24hr) stands on the graves of 5000 Soviet soldiers killed in the Battle of Berlin. It attests both to the immensity of the wartime losses and to the overblown self-importance of the Stalinist state. Enter the park from Pushkinallee.

ACTIVITIES
Cycling
The German bicycle club **ADFC** (Map p98; ☎ 448 4724; Brunnenstrasse 28; ☺ noon-8pm Mon-Fri, 10am-4pm Sat) publishes an excellent guide showing all the bike routes throughout Berlin. It's available at their office/shop and also in bookshops and bike stores.

Bike-hire outfits charge €10 to €25 per day or €35 to €85 per week, depending on the model. A minimum cash deposit (around €30) and/or ID is required.

Fahrradstation (☎ information & reservations 0180-510 8000) Charlottenburg (Map p102; ☎ 9395 2757; Goethestrasse 46; ☺ 10am-7pm Mon-Fri, 10am-4pm Sat); Friedrichstrasse (Map p98; ☎ 2045 4500; Dorotheenstrasse 30; ☺ 10am-7pm daily Mar-Oct, 10am-7pm Mon-Fri, 10am-3pm Sat Nov-Feb); Kreuzberg (Map pp100-1; ☺ 215 1566; Bergmannstrasse 9; ☺ 10am-7pm Mon-Fri, 10am-4pm Sat); Scheunenviertel (Map p98; ☎ 2859 9661; Auguststrasse 29a; ☺ 10am-7pm Mon-Fri, 10am-3pm Sat)

Fat Tire Bike Tours (Map p98; ☎ 2404 7991; Panoramastrasse 1a, below TV Tower; ☺ 9.30am-7.30pm)

Pedal Power (Map pp100-1; ☎ 7899 1339; Grossbeerenstrasse 53; ☺ 10am-6.30pm Mon-Fri, 11am-2pm Sat)

Prenzlberger Orange Bikes (Map p103; ☎ 442 8122; Kollwitzstrasse 35; per day €5; ☺ 2.30-7pm Mon-Fri, 10am-7pm Sat) Run by a youth group.

Ice Skating
Berlin's municipal indoor ice rinks are usually open from October to March. The cost is €3.30/1.60 for an adult/child per two-hour session, plus €2.50 to €5 to hire skates. Call for specific hours, although 9am to 9pm is a good general guideline.

MY FAVOURITE HIDDEN BERLIN PLACES

Henrik Tidefjärd, creator of the Gastro-Rallye (p123) and owner of **Berlinagenten** (www.berlinagenten.de), which specialises in customised urban insider tours, reveals his favourite spots in his adopted home town:

Berlin is a truly electric city full of creative people, crazy parties and historical spots. It's magnetic, interesting and filled with unique discoveries. I'm a true traveller and I think no other city has such a diversity of lifestyles, cultural life and environments. It's hard to believe it all exists in one single city. Ah Berlin, I love you!

■ I love to eat in either hidden private dining locations or in stylish trendy restaurants. The **Tapas Club** (Map pp96-7; ☎ 0177-302 8412; Waldenser Strasse 4) and its delicacies are a bit of both and fulfil most of my expectations.

■ If I feel in the mood for a thrilling and crazy night out, I head for legendary hot spot **Panoramabar** (p138). The doorman will tell you if you fit in…

■ **Schlesische Strasse** (Map pp100–1) is another tip for rather new experiences. Different kinds of alternative bars, lounges, clubs, shops à la Berliner Style attract a laid-back scene. I'm especially fond of the Club der Visionäre (p134) in the summer, because I can chill out on the river pontoons outdoors and soak up the real living culture.

■ The medieval town of **Werder** (Map p93), 45 minutes away from Berlin by train, is my absolute favourite place for relaxing off the beaten track. Situated on an island (!) in the river delta, this place is a true treasure for romantic walks along picturesque streets and for dining on fish in one of the restaurants along the quay.

Erika-Hess-Eisstadion (Map pp96-7; ☎ 200 945 551; Müllerstrasse 185)

Horst-Dohm-Eisstadion (Map p102; ☎ 823 4060; Fritz-Wildung-Strasse 9)

Running

There are great running terrains in Berlin's many parks. By far the most popular jogging ground is the Tiergarten (Map p98), although the Grunewald in Wilmersdorf/Zehlendorf is even prettier. The trip around the scenic Schlachtensee (in Grunewald) is 5km. The park of Schloss Charlottenburg (Map pp96-7) is also good for a nice, easy trot.

Swimming

Berlin has lots of indoor and outdoor public pools. Opening hours vary widely by day, time and pool, so call ahead before setting out. Many facilities also have saunas, which generally cost between €10 and €15.

Badeschiff (Map pp100-1; ☎ 533 2030; Eichenstrasse 4; admission €3; ⏰ 8am-midnight) This 'only-in-Berlin' lifestyle pool, converted from an old container boat, actually floats on the Spree itself, offering fab views across to the Oberbaumbrücke and eastern bank. A sandy area and wooden decks invite lounging and there's a bar as well. In summer it often fills to capacity by early afternoon. In winter it's covered and heated and a sauna is added.

Sommerbad Olympiastadion (☎ 3006 3440; Osttor, Olympischer Platz; adult/concession €4/2.50; ⏰ 8am-8pm May-Sep; ⏰ ⏰ Olympiastadion) Do your laps in the 50m pool built for the 1936 Olympic athletes.

Stadtbad Charlottenburg (Map p102; ☎ Alte Halle 3438 3860, Neue Halle 3438 3865; Krumme Strasse 10; adult/concession €4/2.50; ⏰ 8am-8pm) Alte Halle is a beautiful Art Nouveau pool with colourful tiles and popular with gay men on nude bathing nights; Neue Halle is modern with a 50m lap pool and sauna.

Strandbad Wannsee (☎ 803 5612; Wannseebadweg 25, Zehlendorf; adult/concession €4/2.50; ⏰ 8am-8pm May-Sep; ⏰ Nikolassee, then bus 513) Possibly Europe's largest lakeside lido with 1km of sandy beach and plenty of infrastructure.

WALKING TOUR

This meander takes in all of central Berlin's blockbuster sights, plus some fabulous hidden corners. From Potsdamer Platz it winds through the Government Quarter to Unter den Linden into historic Berlin, ending in the Scheunenviertel. Along the way, you'll be treated to great views, tremendous architecture, interesting nosh spots and plenty of places you might recognise from the history books.

WALK FACTS
Start Potsdamer Platz (⏰ ⏰ Unter den Linden)
Finish Hackesche Höfe (⏰ Hackescher Markt)
Distance 9km
Duration From three to four hours without museums, all day with some museums

Kick off your tour at **Potsdamer Platz (1)** (p111), Berlin's newest quarter and a showcase of contemporary architecture. Check out the short section of the **Berlin Wall (2)** at the top of Stresemannstrasse, the public art in **DaimlerCity (3**; p111) and the tented plaza at the **Sony Center (4**; p111). Continue north on Ebertstrasse to the gargantuan **Holocaust Memorial (5**; p106) where you should wander among the concrete blocks for the full visual and emotional impact and also check out the underground exhibit. Next, get your camera ready for the majestic **Brandenburger Tor (6**; Brandenburg Gate; p106), the ultimate symbol of German reunification. It anchors **Pariser Platz (7**; p106), a harmoniously proportioned square where you should pop into the **DZ Bank (8)** and gawk at Frank Gehry's outrageous atrium. Continue north on Ebertstrasse past the moving **Wall Victims Memorial (9**; p115), which honours those who died trying to escape the clutches of the GDR. The hulking **Reichstag (10**; p111), where the German parliament meets, looms nearby.

Walk north to the **Paul-Löbe-Haus (11)**, where members of parliament keep their offices, then west on Paul-Löbe-Allee to the **Bundeskanzleramt (12; p111)**, the office and residence of the German chancellor. Head north across Otto-von-Bismarck-Allee to the **Spreebogenpark (13)** from where you can easily spot the sweeping glass roof of the shiny new **Hauptbahnhof (14)** across the Spree River.

Heading back from the station, follow the promenade along the Spree River east past the **Marie-Elisabeth-Lüders-Haus (15)**, home of the parliamentary library, to Luisenstrasse. Cross the bridge, which offers good views back to the Reichstag. Continuing south on Luisenstrasse soon takes you to **Unter den Linden (16**; p106), Berlin's grand historic boulevard. Turn left and on your right you'll spy the **Russische Botschaft (17**; Russian Embassy; p106), a monumental confection in white marble.

Hook a right onto Friedrichstrasse to get to the **Friedrichstadtpassagen**, a trio of spectacularly designed – on the inside, anyway – shopping complexes called 'quartiers', which are linked by a subterranean walkway. Inside the **Galeries Lafayette** (18; p140), check out architect Jean Nouvel's glass funnel that reflects light like some mutated hologram. Next door, **Quartier 206 (19)** is a stunning Art Deco–inspired symphony in glass and marble beneath a tented glass roof. **Quartier 205 (20)** offers upscale fast-food options for fighting off hunger pangs.

For a dose of Cold War history, carry on along Friedrichstrasse for another 500m to the site of **Checkpoint Charlie** (21; p114), the most famous ex-border crossing between East and West Berlin. The nearby **Haus am Checkpoint Charlie (22**; p114) has good exhibits about the history of the Berlin Wall and the people who escaped across it.

Otherwise proceed from Quartier 205 by turning left on Mohrenstrasse to get to **Gendarmenmarkt** (p107), Berlin's most beautiful square, which is anchored by Schinkel's **Konzerthaus (23**; p139) and the sumptuous towers of the **Deutscher Dom (24**; p107) and the **Französischer Dom (25**; p107).

Walk north on Markgrafenstrasse, then east on Behrenstrasse to **Bebelplatz** (p106), site of the infamous Nazi book burnings in 1933. A trio of stately 18th-century buildings orbits this handsome square: the **Alte Königliche Bibliothek (26**; p107), the **St-Hedwigskirche (27**; p107) and the **Staatsoper Unter den Linden (28**; p139). Nearby is the epic **Reiterdenkmal Friedrich des Grossen (29)**, an equestrian monument of the king who financed this lovely ensemble.

On the north side of Unter den Linden are the **Humboldt Universität (30**; p106) and, a bit further east, Schinkel's **Neue Wache (31**; p107). Across the street is the **Kronprinzenpalais (32)**, a one-time royal palace, while the pink building opposite is the Zeughaus, an armoury converted into the **Deutsches Historisches Museum (33**; p107). Also check out the **IM Pei Bau (34**; p107), the new wing designed by, duh, IM Pei.

Continue on to Bodestrasse, then head east and cross the bridge to the **Museumsinsel** (p107), a cluster of world-class repositories

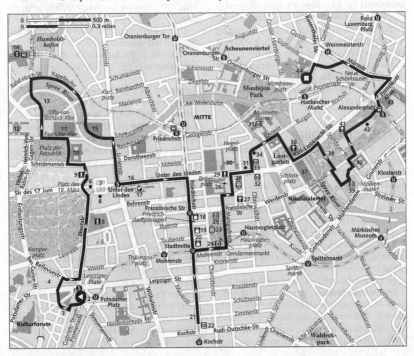

of art and sculpture. If you have only time for one, make it the **Pergamon Museum** (**35**; p107).

Looming before you is the city's magnificent cathedral, the **Berliner Dom** (**36**; p108), the burial place of many Hohenzollern royals. Across from the cathedral once stood the hideous GDR-era **Palast der Republik** (**37**; p108).

Behind the ex-'palace', turn right for the **Marx-Engels-Forum** (**38**), walking past the statue of Karl Marx and Friedrich Engels to the **Nikolaiviertel** (Nikolai Quarter; p109), where Berlin was founded in the 13th century. Wander among the cutesy, cobbled lanes, perhaps popping into the Gothic **Nikolaikirche** (**39**; p109) for its free historical exhibit and ornate epitaphs.

Make your way towards the **Rotes Rathaus** (**40**; p109), home of the city government, to the **Marienkirche** (**41**; p109), Berlin's oldest still operating church filled with artistic treasures. Continue east, perhaps catching a ride up the **Fernsehturm** (**42**; p109), to **Alexanderplatz** (**43**; p108), once the commercial heart of communist Berlin.

From here follow Münzstrasse to the **Scheunenviertel** (p109), Berlin's historic Jewish quarter and now among the most vibrant parts of town, with great eating, shopping and nightlife. Turn left on Neue Schönhauser Strasse, which is lined with fun boutiques, and left again on Rosenthaler Strasse to get to the **Hackesche Höfe** (**44**; p110), a beautifully restored series of courtyards filled with cafés, shops and entertainment venues. Our tour concludes here.

BERLIN FOR CHILDREN

Believe it or not, Berlin is tailor-made for tots. Kids love animals, of course, making the huge **Berliner Zoo & Aquarium** (p116), with its giant pandas, cuddly koalas and fearsome crocodiles, a sure winner. Dinosaur fans should stop in at the **Museum für Naturkunde** (p110) for close-ups of the largest dino skeleton on display anywhere. The **Spectrum science centre** (p114) has hundreds of interactive stations where kids can find answers to the mysteries of the universe.

In the southwestern suburb of Zehlendorf is the **Domäne Dahlem** (☎ 666 3000; Königin-Luise-Strasse 49; adult/concession €2/1, Wed free; ☉ 10am-6pm Wed-Mon; ◉ Dahlem-Dorf), an outdoor museum that illustrates the daily working life on a 17th-century farm. You'll be transported back

even further in time at the **Museumsdorf Düppel** (☎ 802 6671; Clauertstrasse 11; adult/concession €2/1; ☉ 3-7pm Thu, 10am-5pm Sun Apr-Oct; ☒ Zehlendorf, then bus 115), a re-created medieval village with Sunday demonstrations of old-time crafts.

Younger kids especially enjoy the **Kindermuseum Labyrinth** (Map pp96-7; ☎ 4930 8901; Osloer Strasse 12; adult/child/family €4/3.50/10; ☉ 1-6pm Tue-Sat, 11am-6pm Sun; ◉ Osloer Strasse, Pankstrasse), a sort of educational playground where tots can fancy themselves a pirate, princess or boat captain.

Another fun diversion is the antics of **Cabuwazi** (☎ 530 0040; www.cabuwazi.de in German), a nonprofit circus troupe of children aged 10 to 17 performing at various venues around town. Traditional puppetry and marionettes play to crowds of all ages at **Puppentheater Firlefanz** (Map p98; ☎ 283 3560; Sophienstrasse 10), next to the Hackesche Höfe.

Parks and imaginative playgrounds abound in all neighbourhoods, but especially in Prenzlauer Berg (Map p103), the district most popular with young families. On hot summer days, a few hours spent at a public outdoor pool (p120) or on a lakeside beach will go a long away towards keeping toddlers' tempers cool.

It's fine to bring your kids along to all but the fanciest restaurants, but if you're up for a romantic night for two, try the following babysitter services or ask at your hotel for a referral:

Aufgepasst (☎ 851 3723; www.aufgepasst.de) English-speaking babysitters, nannies and day care.

Asterix (☎ 8459 1604) For 24-hour babysitting.

Kinder-Hotel (Map p98; ☎ 4171 6928; www.kinder insel.de; Eichendorffstrasse 17) For 24-hour day care in 12 languages. Fees are €10 per hour, €60 overnight (14 hours) and €100 for 24 hours.

TOURS
Bus Tours

Most sightseeing tours operate on the 'hop on, hop off' principle, taking in the major sights on two-hour loops (without getting off) with commentary – sometimes taped, sometimes live – in several languages. Buses depart every 15 minutes (less frequently from November to March) between 10am and 5pm or 6pm daily. Besides the main departure points mentioned here, you can start your tour at any of the other stops around town. Tickets cost about €20 for adults and €10 or €15 for children and are sold on the bus. For full details, call, check the websites or look for flyers in hotel lobbies and at the tourist offices.

BBS Berliner Bären Stadtrundfahrt (☎ 3519 5270; www.bbsberlin.de) Tours start at the corner of Kurfürstendamm and Rankestrasse (Map p102) and on Alexanderplatz (p98), opposite the Park Inn Hotel.

Berolina Sightseeing (Map p102; ☎ 8856 8030; www.berolina-berlin.com) Starts at Kurfürstendamm 220.

BVB (Map p102; ☎ 683 8910) Tours originate at Kurfürstendamm 225.

BVG Top Tour (Map p102; ☎ 2562 6570; adult/child 6-14yr €20/15) Open-top double-decker buses with live German and English commentary. Route starts at Kurfürstendamm 19.

Severin + Kühn (Map p102; ☎ 880 4190; www .severin-kuehn-berlin.de) Board at Kurfürstendamm 216.

Tempelhofer Reisen (☎ 752 4057; www.tempelhofer .de) Starts at Kurfürstendamm 231 (Map p102) and Unter den Linden 14 (Map p98).

Cruises

A lovely way to tour Berlin, especially on a sunny day, is from the deck of a boat cruising the city's rivers, canals and lakes. Tours range from one-hour spins around Museumsinsel taking in the historic sights (from €5) to longer trips into the green suburbs (from €12) and dinner cruises. Narration is usually in English and German. Food and drinks are sold on board, or bring along a picnic. Small children travel for free, while those under 14 and seniors can expect a 50% discount. The season runs roughly from April to October. Our maps indicate embarkation points which are served by one of the following companies.

Berliner Wassertaxi (☎ 6588 0203; www.berliner -wassertaxi.de)

Reederei Bruno Winkler (☎ 349 0011; www.reederei winkler.de)

Reederei Riedel (☎ 693 4646; www.reederei-riedel.de)

Stern und Kreis Schifffahrt (☎ 536 3600; www .sternundkreis.de)

Walking Tours

Several companies offer scheduled guided English-language tours of Berlin led by well-informed and sharp-witted guides eager to answer your questions. Look for their flyers in hostels, hotels and the tourist offices.

Brewer's Berlin Tours (☎ 2248 7435, 0177-388 1537; www.brewersberlin.de; tours €10-12) Founded by Terry Brewer, an ex-intelligence officer and official guide to the Allied Forces, this is the tour company offering the legendary

All Day Berlin marathon which runs eight hours or more. Nightlife tours are available also. If you want to meet the man himself, book a 'Tuesdays with Terry' tour. Tours meet outside the Australian Ice Cream Shop at the corner of Friedrichstrasse and Georgenstrasse (Map p98).

Insider Tour (☎ 692 3149; www.insidertour.com; tours €10-12, bike tour incl bike €22, discounts for students, under 26yr, seniors & WelcomeCard holders) For an excellent introduction to the city's major sights, join the Famous Insider Tour. In summer, this well-established company also runs the always intriguing Third Reich and Iron Curtain tours, a pub crawl and the Berlin by Bike tour. Tours meet outside McDonalds on Hardenbergplatz (Map p102) and outside CoffeeMamas below the S-Bahn station Hackescher Markt (Map p98).

New Berlin Tours (☎ 0179-973 0397; www.newberlin tours.com; general tour free, speciality tours adult/student €10/8) This outfit offers free city tours, but the guides work for tips, so don't be stingy. Bike tours are free also; bikes rent for €7. Fee-based speciality tours cover Berlin's Nazi and Communist past and the Mitte pub scene. Pick up is at Dunkin' Donuts on Hardenbergplatz (Map p102) and Starbucks on Pariser Platz (Map p98).

Original Berlin Walks (☎ 301 9194; www.berlinwalks .com; tours €12-15, discounts if under 26yr or with WelcomeCard, free if under 14yr) This long-standing company offers a thorough general introduction to the city daily or twice daily on its Discover Berlin Walk. The Infamous Third Reich Sites, Jewish Life in Berlin, Potsdam, and Sachsenhausen concentration camp tours run on a more limited schedule. Meet your guide by the taxi rank on Hardenbergplatz (Map p102) or at Häagen-Dazs opposite S-Bahn station Hackescher Markt (Map p98).

Other

For information about tours of the underbelly of Berlin and the Trabi Safari, see the boxed text, p124.

Foodies wanting an instant inside scoop on the city's culinary and lifestyle scenes should book a **Gastro-Rallye** (☎ 4372 0701; www .berlinagenten.com; tours from €59, incl food & drink). During this entertaining evening of hopping around some of Berlin's hippest restaurants, you'll enjoy one course at each stop while being peppered with insider tips, history and insights. Book at least one day in advance.

QUIRKY BERLIN

Sure, Berlin wouldn't be the same without the Pergamon, Reichstag and Unter den Linden, but the city also has plenty in store for those tired of the lemming routine. Catch that authentic GDR vibe while venturing into the city's 'wild east' behind the wheel of your own Trabi on a **Trabi Safari** (☎ 2759 2273) or explore Berlin's dark and dank underbelly with **Berliner Unterwelten** (Map pp96-7; ☎ 4991 0518; www.berliner-unterwelten.de; adult/concession €9/7) on a tour of two WWII-era underground bunkers built around U-Bahn station Gesundbrunnen.

Even Berlin's museum scene gets into the bizarro business with such entries as the **Zucker Museum** (Sugar Museum; Map pp96-7; ☎ 3142 7574; Amrumer Strasse 32), dedicated to the sweeter things in life. Punk fans might like to head to the private **Ramones Museum** (Map pp100-1; www.ramonesmuseum.com; Solmsstrasse 30; admission free; ☺ noon-6pm Sat & Sun), where you can admire Marky Ramone's drumsticks, Johnny Ramone's jeans and other flotsam and jetsam. Across town, you'll need a strong stomach to deal with the grizzly pathology collection of the **Berliner Medizinhistorisches Museum** (Medical History Museum; Map p98; ☎ 450 536 122; Schumannstrasse 20-21; adult/concession/family €4/2/8; ☺ 10am-5pm Tue-Sun, 10am-7pm Wed), which includes two-headed babies and cancer-stricken lungs.

FESTIVALS & EVENTS

Berlin is very much a party town, and almost every weekend sees some form of event, anniversary or celebration. Check www.berlin .de/eventkalender/btm for complete listings or contact the tourist offices. The following is just a small sampling:

Internationale Filmfestspiele (☎ 259 200; www .berlinale.de) Better known as Berlinale, this film festival is Germany's answer to Cannes and no less prestigious; held in February.

Internationale Tourismusbörse (☎ 303 80; www .itb-berlin.com) The world's largest travel show with up to 10,000 global exhibitors; held in March and open to the public at the weekend.

Festtage in der Staatsoper (☎ 203 540; www .staatsoper-berlin.org) Ten days of gala concerts and operas drawing renowned conductors, soloists and orchestras; held in April.

Theatertreffen Berlin (☎ 2548 9269; www .theatertreffen-berlin.de) Three weeks of new productions by emerging and established German-language ensembles from Germany, Austria and Switzerland; held in May.

Karneval der Kulturen (☎ 622 2024; www.karneval -berlin.de) Lively street festival with a parade of flamboyantly costumed people dancing and playing music, sometimes on floats; in late May/early June.

Christopher Street Day (☎ 0177-277 3176; www .csd-berlin.de) Berlin's biggest gay parade with outrageous costumes, techno music and naked torsos guaranteed; held in late June.

Love Parade (☎ 284 620; www.loveparade.net) This on-off-and-on-again techno event may have peaked long ago, attracting only 250,000 (down from one million) ravers in 2006; held in mid-July.

Berlin Marathon (www.berlin-marathon.com) The best street race in the country, with a route that takes it past a lot of people's front doors; held in September.

Jazzfest Berlin (☎ 2548 9279; www.jazzfest-berlin .de) Top-rated jazz festival with performances held at venues throughout the city in November.

Christmas Markets Held daily from late November to around Christmas Eve at locations around Berlin, including Breitscheidplatz (Map p102), Alexanderplatz (Map p98) and outside the Opernpalais (Map p98) on Unter den Linden.

SLEEPING

Berlin is usually busiest between May and September when room reservations are a good idea. Rooms can be booked through the Berlin Infostores (p105), although only at partner hotels (which includes many of the properties listed here). This is a free service and they even have a best-price guarantee.

Berlin's hospitality scene continues to expand. Every international chain from Best Western to Ritz-Carlton has opened flagship houses in the German capital, while the new hostels keep upping the ante in terms of comfort levels and facilities on offer. Privately-run midrange places, meanwhile, have been forced to modernise or risk falling by the wayside. There's also a new crop of designer and boutique hotels with such *Zeitgeist*-capturing features as in-room bathtubs, lobby-lounges and custom furniture. A subgroup typical of Berlin are the so-called *Kunsthotels* (art hotels), which are designed by artists and/or liberally sprinkled with original art.

Berlin's excellent public transportation system puts you within easy reach of everything, no matter where you unpack your suitcase. However, if you enjoy being within walking distance of the trophy sights, find a place in Mitte or Tiergarten, although you'll pay a premium for the privilege. Charlottenburg and Wilmersdorf generally offer better value and the greatest concentration of midrange abodes. This is where traditional Old Berlin *pensions* rub shoulders with urbanhipster temples. Lodging options are thinner on the ground in Kreuzberg, Friedrichshain (where your euro will stretch furthest) and, inexplicably, also in lovely and fairly central Prenzlauer Berg.

Unless mentioned otherwise, rates listed here include breakfast.

Mitte & Prenzlauer Berg
BUDGET

Baxpax Downtown (Map p98; ☎ 2787 4880; www .baxpax-downtown.de; Ziegelstrasse 28; dm €15-22, s €25-45, d €43-88, apt €75-120; ✕ 🖳) This hostel takes budget hospitality to a whole new level with modern rooms as well as such party zones as a rooftop terrace with wading pool, a leafy courtyard and an in-house club. Most rooms have en suite bathrooms as well as TV, telephone and internet access.

Circus Hostel Weinbergsweg (Map p98; ☎ 2839 1433; www.circus-berlin.de; Weinbergsweg 1a; dm €15-20, s/d/tr without bathroom €32/48/60, s/d with bathroom €45/60, linen €2, 2-/4-person apt with 2-night minimum €75/130; ✕ 🖳) This hostel consistently fires on all cylinders. Clean, cheerfully painted rooms, plenty of showers and helpful staff are just a few factors that give this place an edge. Stay in dorms, private rooms or a penthouse apartment with kitchen and terrace. The downstairs café with free wi-fi serves breakfast, drinks and small meals, and the basement bar has different activities nightly. It's fully wheelchair accessible.

Citystay Hostel (Map p98; ☎ 2362 4031; www .citystay.de; Rosenstrasse 16; dm €15-18, s/d €34/48, linen €2.50; ✕ 🖳) This newcomer quickly made its mark with travellers, and for three good reasons: location, service and design. Modern and sophisticated, it's loaded with mod-cons, including top security, quality mattresses, a lift and restaurant-bar with courtyard tables. Bus About (p142) stops outside.

Lette'm Sleep (Map p103; ☎ 4473 3623; www.back packers.de; Lettestrasse 7; dm €15-19, d without bathroom €48, apt €66; ✕ 🖳) This hostel is as hostels used to be: low-key, low-tech, welcoming and equipped with a kitchen-lounge for meeting fellow travellers. It's right on hip Helmholtzplatz, perfect for plunging into Berlin's swirling nightlife vortex.

Acksel Haus (Map p103; ☎ 4433 7633; www.acksel haus.de; Belforter Strasse 21; apt €66-160) This charismatic place has 10 apartments (most sleeping two, some up to four people, with full kitchen) decked out in unique décor ranging from romantic (with four-poster bed) to exotic (with African sculptures) and nautical (lots of blue). The nicest ones overlook the flowery garden. Nice café and wi-fi throughout.

Also recommended:

East Seven Hostel (Map p103; ☎ 9362 2240; www .eastseven.de; Schwedter Strasse 7; dm €12-19, s €28-30, d €40-44; ✕ 🖳) Friendly, familial and fun hostel with great kitchen and idyllic back garden.

Circus Hostel Rosa-Luxemburg-Strasse (Map p98; ☎ 2839 1433; www.circus-berlin.de; Rosa-Luxemburg-Strasse 39; dm €15-20, s/d/tr without bathroom €32/48/60, s/d with bathroom €45/60, 2-/4-person apt €75/130, linen €2; ✕ 🖳) The sister location of the Circus Hostel Weinbergsweg offers many of the same comfort factors and a fine street-level café-bar reception area.

Heart of Gold Hostel (Map p98; ☎ 2900 3300; www .heartofgold-hostel.de; Johannisstrasse 11; dm €17-19, s/d €40/56; ✕ 🖳) Spacey, central hostel with *Hitchhiker's Guide to the Galaxy* theme.

MIDRANGE

Hotel Adele (Map p103; ☎ 4432 4350; www.adele -hotel.de; Greifswalder Strasse 227; s/d €80/120; 🖳) Tucked between a chic coffee shop and a bistrolounge, this is a designer hotel with street cred. Retire to rooms brimming with exquisite detail: diaphanous curtains, leather headboards, sensuous faux fur blankets, lacquered furniture. Even the sleekly Italian bathrooms are oh-so-stylish.

Myer's Hotel (Map p103; ☎ 440 140; www.myers hotel.de; Metzer Strasse 26; s €85-140, d €110-155; ✕ 🏊) This 41-room boutique hotel combines the elegance of your rich uncle's mansion, the cheerful warmth of your parents' home and the casual comforts of your best friend's pad. Unwinding spots include the 24-hour lobby bar, a ruby-walled tearoom, the gallery lounge and a bucolic garden.

Honigmond Garden Hotel (Map p98; ☎ 2844 5577; www.honigmond-berlin.de; Invalidenstrasse 122; s €90-115, d €110-165; 🅿 ✕) Never mind the busy thoroughfare: this 20-room guesthouse is an enchanting retreat where antique-filled rooms overlook an idyllic garden with koi pond. The clubby lounge with internet access, an honour bar and magazines is tailor-made for gathering with other guests.

Künstlerheim Luise (Map p98; ☎ 284 480; www .kuenstlerheim-luise.de; Luisenstrasse 19; s €80-95, d €120-140, breakfast €8; P ✗) At this 'gallery with rooms' you can sleep in a bed built for giants (room 107), in the company of astronaut suits (room 310) or many other fantasy environments designed by artists who receive royalties for each overnight stay. Art fans on a budget should ask about the smaller rooms without bathroom. The website has pictures.

Arcotel Velvet (Map p98; ☎ 278 7530; www.arco tel.at; Oranienburger Strasse 52; r €110-220, ste €150-450, breakfast €15; P ✗ ✗ ☐) This sassy new kid in town wows you with edgy custom design, from the chill street-level lounge to the swank penthouse suites. Rooms feature a plethora of mould-breaking perks, including high-tech window vents and blackout blinds perfect for sleeping off that hangover.

Radisson SAS Hotel (Map p98; ☎ 238 280; www .radissonsas.com; Karl-Liebknecht-Strasse 3; r €140-380, ste €230-380, breakfast €21; P ✗ ✗ ☐ ☒) At this swish contender you will quite literally 'sleep with the fishes', thanks to the AquaDom (p109), a 25m-high aquarium in the lobby. Overall, the streamlined design scheme radiates urban poshness rarely found in chain hotels. This also extends to the two restaurants and the hipper-than-thou Aqua Lounge. Free wi-fi.

TOP END

Wallstreet Park Plaza (Map p98; ☎ 847 1170; Wallstrasse 23-24; r €190-220, ste €250-300, breakfast €15; P ✗ ✗) Coins embedded in the floor, clever dollarbill carpets and a gold-and-silver-hued bar: this stylish newcomer takes the stockexchange theme seriously. To help you ink that deal, you'll find all the latest communication devices, including free DSL, at your fingertips. Special promotional rates dip as low as €84: be sure to ask.

Dorint Sofitel Am Gendarmenmarkt (Map p98; ☎ 203 750; www.dorint.de/berlin-gendarmenmarkt; Charlottenstrasse 50-52; s €230-250, d €260-280, breakfast €23; P ✗ ✗ ☐) This cocoon of quiet sophistication couples the flair of a small boutique hotel with the amenities of a 'hotel de luxe'. After a day of turf pounding, relax in the stress-melting spa before retiring to your stylish room, which, like the rest of the place, is a sensory interplay of marble, glass and light.

Adlon Hotel Kempinski (Map p98; ☎ 226 10; www .hotel-adlon.de; Unter den Linden 77; s €320-440, d €370-490, breakfast €32; P ✗ ✗ ☐ ☒) Berlin's most high-profile defender of the grand tradition has been a celebrity magnet since first opening its portals in 1907. With front-row vistas of the Brandenburger Tor, top-notch rooms and off-the-charts service, it leaves no desire unfulfilled.

Tiergarten

Mandala Hotel (Map pp100-1; ☎ 590 050 000; www .themandala.de; Potsdamer Strasse 3; ste €140-450, breakfast €21; P ✗ ✗ ☐) How 'suite' it is to be staying at this discrete retreat, a place of casual sophistication and unfussy ambience. Six sizes of suites are available, each outfitted for maximum comfort and ideal working conditions in case you're all business. Bonuses: a Michelinstar restaurant and snazzy hotel bar.

Grand Hyatt (Map pp100-1; ☎ 2553 1234; www .berlin.grand.hyatt.com; Marlene-Dietrich-Platz 2; s €230-305, d €260-345, breakfast €24; P ✗ ✗ ☐ ☒) Madonna, Gwyneth Paltrow and Marilyn Manson are among the celebs who've slept, dined and partied at this stomping ground of the rich and famous. And no wonder: the moment you step into the lavish, cedar-clad lobby, you sense that it's luxury all the way from here to the breathtaking rooftop pool.

Kreuzberg & Friedrichshain

BUDGET

Odyssee Globetrotter Hostel (Map pp100-1; ☎ 2900 0081; www.globetrotterhostel.de; Grünberger Strasse 23; dm €13-19, s/d without bathroom €35/45, d with shower €52, incl linen, breakfast €3; ✗ ☐) This hostel puts the 'fun' in funky and is a great base for making an indepth study of Friedrichshain's nightlife. Its young and energetic owners constantly dream up new ways to keep their guests happy and entertained. The artily decorated rooms are clean and have lockers.

Meininger City Hostels (Map pp100-1; ☎ 6663 6100, toll-free 0800-634-6464; www.meininger-hostels.de; Hallesches Ufer 30 & Tempelhofer Ufer 10; dm €13.50-25, s/d/tr €49/66/87, all incl linen & breakfast; P ✗ ☐) Occupying two buildings separated by a busy road, the canal and the U-Bahn tracks (which run above-ground here), Meininger offers modern rooms with private bathrooms and a comfort level rivalling basic hotels. Freebies include linen, towels, lockers and breakfast, but party types are probably better off elsewhere. Check-in is at the Hallesches Ufer building.

Eastern Comfort Hostelboat (Map pp100-1; ☎ 6676 3806; www.eastern-comfort.com; Mühlenstrasse 73-77; dm €17-19, s €32-58, d €50-72, breakfast €3; ✗) Berlin's first floating hostel is moored in the Spree River right by the East Side Gallery (p115), close to the entertainment districts of Friedrichshain and Kreuzberg. Cabins are carpeted and trimmed in wood but pretty snug. The '70s-inspired top deck lounge is great for chilling with a beer at sunset.

Riverside Lodge Hostel (Map pp100-1; ☎ 6951 5510; www.riverside-lodge.de; Hobrechtstrasse 43; dm €17-22, d €52, linen €2.50, breakfast €3.50; ✗ 🖳) This sweet little 12-bed hostel is as warm and welcoming as an old friend's hug, thanks to its wonderful owners, Jutta and Liane. Both avid travellers, they have created a cosy retreat where you can enjoy free coffee, tea and fruit, surf the web and burn CDs and rent bikes or canoes. In the large dorm, beds can be curtained off for extra privacy.

Hotel 26 (Map pp100-1; ☎ 297 7780; www.hotel26-berlin.de; Grünberger Strasse 26; s €50-80, d €70-100; 🅿 ✗ 🖳) This modern hotel decked out in cheery citrus colours may seem sparse and no-nonsense, but it has a lot going on that doesn't immediately meet the eye, including an eco-friendly approach to hospitality. Rooms are nonsmoking and the breakfast is entirely organic.

MIDRANGE

Upstalsboom Hotel (Map pp100-1; ☎ 293 750; www.upstalsboom-berlin.de; Gubener Strasse 42; s €85-150, d €100-165; 🅿 ✗) If this modern and well-kept hotel feels like a breath of fresh air, it may be because it's the Berlin branch of a small chain of German seaside resorts. Rooms have a clean, uncluttered look and come in four sizes. An unexpected spot is the lavender-scented rooftop garden. Rates include bicycle rentals and access to sauna, solarium and fitness area.

Hotel Riehmers Hofgarten (Map pp100-1; ☎ 7809 8800; www.riehmers-hofgarten.de; Yorckstrasse 83; s €98-108, d €125-140; ✗ 🖳) Near Viktoriapark, this intimate 20-room hotel is part of a protected 1891 building complex with a lush inner courtyard certain to delight romantics. Large double French doors lead to mostly spacious, high-ceilinged rooms that are modern but not stark. Gourmet restaurant.

Charlottenburg & Wilmersdorf

BUDGET

A&O Hostel Am Zoo (Map p102; ☎ 297 7810; www.aohostel.com; Joachimstaler Strasse 1-3; dm €10-17, linen €3, s/tw incl linen from €30/34, breakfast €5; ✗ 🖳) Opposite Zoo station, this is a convivial, international place with a big communal room and a fun bar right next to the train tracks. Dorms and rooms are bright with neat laminate flooring, metal-frame beds and large lockable cabinets.

Hotel-Pension Korfu II (Map p102; ☎ 212 4790; www.hp-korfu.de; Rankestrasse 35; s €53-80, d €67-100, breakfast €6; 🖳) Opposite the Gedächtniskirche, this is a great bargain base for exploring Berlin. The pleasantly bright, carpeted rooms sport high ceilings, Scandinavian-style furniture and more amenities than one would expect for the price, including cable TV, telephone, hairdryer and in-room safe.

Hotel-Pension München (Map p102; ☎ 857 9120; www.hotel-pension-muenchen-in-berlin.de; Güntzelstrasse 62; s €55-60, d €70-80, apt €75-105; ✗) This *pension* is filled with works by Berlin-based artists and your gracious hostess, Renate Prasse. Furnishings, though, are mostly of the Ikea persuasion, the chrome-and-leather Marcel Breuer chairs in the lobby notwithstanding. For extra legroom and pretty Mediterranean style, book the studio apartment with kitchen.

Hotel Bogota (Map p102; ☎ 881 5001; www.hotel-bogota.de; Schlüterstrasse 45; s with/without bathroom €72/44, d €98/69; 🅿 ✗) This rambling, slightly eccentric place feels like a cross between a friendly *pension* and a fading grand hotel, all at prices even the cash-strapped can afford. Room sizes and amenities vary greatly, so inspect before deciding.

MIDRANGE

Hotel-Pension Funk (Map p102; ☎ 882 7193; www.hotel-pensionfunk.de; Fasanenstrasse 69; s €52-82, d €82-112) Once the home of Danish silent-movie siren Asta Nielsen, this charismatic *pension* transports you back to the glamour and decadence of the 1920s. Filled with antiques and old-time accoutrements, it's also incredibly good value and often booked to bulging.

Hotel Art Nouveau (Map p102; ☎ 327 7440; www.hotelartnouveau.de; Leibnizstrasse 59; s/d/ste €95/120/175; 🅿 ✗ 🖳) A rickety *belle époque* lift drops you off at one of Berlin's finest boutique *pensions*. Its rooms (all nonsmoking) neither skimp on space nor on charisma and offer a unique blend of youthful flair and tradition. The

BERLIN

honour bar is handy for feeding late-night cravings. Great freebies, too: wi-fi, tea and coffee.

Hotel-Pension Dittberner (Map p102; ☎ 884 6950; www.hotel-dittberner.de; Wielandstrasse 26; s €67-87, d €95-120) It's hard not to be charmed by this traditional 3rd-floor *pension* and its friendly owner, Frau Lange. The soaring ceilings, plush oriental rugs and armloads of paintings and lithographs ooze genuine Old Berlin flair. Direct-dial phones and free wi-fi and DSL make keeping in touch with home a snap.

Hotel Askanischer Hof (Map p102; ☎ 881 8033; www.askanischer-hof.de; Kurfürstendamm 53; s €95-120, d €107-165; ✗ 💻) In a city that likes to teeter on the cutting edge, this charismatic 17-room hotel catapults you back to the Roaring Twenties. It's a quiet oasis of antiques, lacy curtains, frilly chandeliers and fading oriental rugs. Its quaint charms have long been a magnet for celebs, including David Bowie and Helmut Newton.

Ku'damm 101 (Map p102; ☎ 520 0550; www .kudamm101.com; Kurfürstendamm 101; s €100-138, d €120-145, breakfast €13; 🅿 ✗ 💻) This sassy lifestyle hotel gets minimalism right. Pillars punctuate the lobby and rooms, which are dressed in cool colours and edgy furniture by young German designers. Breakfast is a liberal buffet spread above the rooftops of Berlin. Only downside: the less than central location.

Louisa's Place (Map p102; ☎ 631 030; www.louisas place.de; Kurfürstendamm 160; ste €120-250, breakfast €18; 🅿 ✗ 💻 🐾) Louisa's is a discrete deluxe hideaway perfect for people tired of anonymous big-city hotels. Few properties put more emphasis on customising guest services. They'll even send you a pre-arrival questionnaire asking for your likes and dislikes. Suites here are huge, the spa heavenly and the library regal.

Hecker's Hotel (Map p102; ☎ 889 00; www.heck ers-hotel.de; Grolmannstrasse 35; s €125-250, d €140-280; 🅿 ✗ 😵 💻) Flaunting a subdued urban feel,

this private boutique hotel has a neat ice-blue backlit bar; over-sized, elegant rooms, some with walk-in closets and thoughtful touches such as complimentary mineral water. The hotel's ultimate trump card, though, is its three themed suites: cool Bauhaus, cosy Tuscany and exotic Colonial.

Hotel Bleibtreu (Map p102; ☎ 884 740; www.bleibtreu .de; Bleibtreustrasse 31; s €120-220, d €130-230, breakfast €15; ✗ 💻) The Bleibtreu flaunts an edgy, urban feel tempered by the warmth of Italian design and the ample use of natural, eco-friendly materials. Subtlety is king here. In fact, from the street it doesn't even look like a hotel, tucked away as it is behind a flower shop, a bar and a deli.

TOP END

Hotel Q! (Map p102; ☎ 810 0660; www.loock-hotels .com; Knesebeckstrasse 67; s €150-170, d €170-190, studios & penthouse €190-290; 🅿 ✗ 😵 💻) With its sleek, boundary-pushing look, Hotel Q! pulls in style-conscious hipsters and even such gossip mag royalty as Brad Pitt and Drew Barrymore. Corners are eschewed, from the tunnel-like crimson lobby to the risqué rooms where you could literally slide from tub to bed.

Brandenburger Hof (Map p102; ☎ 214 050; www .brandenburger-hof.com; Eislebener Strasse 14; s €170-260, d €245-295, ste €345-515; 🅿 ✗ 😵 💻) In an amazing feat of stylistic alchemy, this intimate grand hotel blends Prussian elegance with Italian dolce vita, Zen influences and edgy Bauhaus. Every detail speaks of refinement here, from the glass-tented indoor piazza wrapped around a petite garden to the Michelin-starred restaurant and the airy and spacious rooms.

Long-Term Rentals

If you're planning to stay in Berlin for a month or longer, consider renting a room or an apartment through a *Mitwohnzentrale*

THE AUTHOR'S CHOICE

Propeller Island City Lodge (Map p102; ☎ 8am-noon 891 9016, noon-8pm 0163-256-5909; www.propeller -island.de; Albrecht-Achilles-Strasse 58; r €65-180, breakfast €7; ✗) It is only fitting that Berlin's most original hotel takes its name from a novel by the master of imagination, Jules Verne. Each of its 32 rooms is a journey to a unique, surreal and slightly wicked world spawned by the vision of artist-composer-owner Lars Stroschen who designed and crafted every accessory and piece of furniture. To be stranded on Propeller Island means waking up on the ceiling (in the Upside-Down Room), in a prison cell (Freedom Room) or inside a kaleidoscope (Mirror Room). This is no conventional hotel, so don't expect pillow treats or other trappings.

(flat-sharing agency), which matches people willing to let their digs to those needing a temporary home. Accommodation can be anything from rooms in shared student flats to furnished apartments. Agencies to try:

Erste Mitwohnzentrale (Map p102; ☎ 324 3031; www.mitwohn.com; Sybelstrasse 53)

HomeCompany (Map p102; ☎ 194 45; www.home company.de; Joachimstaler Strasse 17)

Room with a Loo (Map p103; ☎ 4737 2964; www .roomwithaloo.com; Jablonskistrasse 3) English-speaking.

EATING

Foodies find lots to like about Berlin these days. Once considered a culinary wasteland, getting good grub in the city is no longer a challenge. Wherever you look, clever young chefs, many brimming with ideas collected abroad, give the cuisine scene an adventurous edge. Quality is up, waaay up.

These days, Berlin is absorbing international food trends faster than a sponge on Benzedrine. One of the latest waves is 'wellness' food, which translates into any dish that's light, healthy and uses fresh ingredients. Vietnamese restaurants are all the rage, while pan-Asian restaurants have become so ubiquitous that one almost wishes someone would invent a vaccine. Meanwhile, vegetarians will be happy to discover that asking for tofu, tempeh and seitan no longer earns blank stares from clueless servers.

One of life's little luxuries is a leisurely breakfast and Berliners have just about perfected the art, especially on Sundays when many cafés dish out lavish buffets. Another favourite guilty pleasure – and Berlin tradition – is the Currywurst (see boxed text, p130). If there ever was a fast food with cult status, this humble sausage is it. The Döner (doner kebab), invented here some 20-odd years ago by a Turkish immigrant, comes a close second, though.

Thankfully, eating out is not a budget-buster in Berlin. It's easy to fill up remarkably well for just a few euros, and even the gourmet restaurants dole out great value. Many places now offer a weekday 'business lunch', which usually includes an appetiser, main course and drink for a fixed price.

Mitte & Prenzlauer Berg
BUDGET

Schlemmerbuffet Zach (Map p98; ☎ 283 2153; Torstrasse 125; dishes €1.50-7; ☼ 24hr) If there was an award

for best doner, this clean and friendly *Imbiss* (food stall) would be a serious contender. Portions are huge, the veal or chicken perfectly slivered, the bread toasted to perfection, the salads fresh and the yoghurt sauce garlicky.

Dada Falafel (Map p98; ☎ 2759 6927; Linienstrasse 132; meals €3-4; ☼ 10am-2am) This tiny takeaway makes scrumptious falafel and shwarma sandwiches. One bite and you're hooked, we swear.

W-Imbiss (Map p103; ☎ 4849 2657; Kastanienallee 49; dishes €4-10) Culinary performance artist Gordon W makes progressive fusion nosh, including his famous 'naan pizzas'. To truly understand his genius, though, order the daily special, usually some fish marinated in 'top-secret' spices. For a vitamin high, slug down a fresh apple–wheat grass cocktail.

Monsieur Vuong (Map p98; ☎ 3087 2643; Alte Schönhauser Strasse 46; mains €6.50) Despite its pepper-red walls and beautiful dishware, this bustling noshery only looks expensive. The Vietnamese fare – soups and two or three main courses daily – is uniformly delicious, as are the fresh fruit cocktails and the exotic teas. No reservations, so come in the afternoon or be prepared to queue.

Other recommendations:

Konnopke Imbiss (Map p103; ☎ 442 7765; Schön-hauser Allee 44a; sausages €1.50; ☼ 5.30am-8pm Mon-Fri, noon-6.30pm Sat) Legendary *Currywurst* kitchen.

Piccola Italia (Map p98; ☎ 283 5843; Oranienburger Strasse 6; dishes €1.50-7; ☼ 11am-1am Sun-Thu, to 3am Fri & Sat) Tasty and generously topped take-away pizza.

MIDRANGE

Sasaya (Map p103; ☎ 4471 7721; Lychener Strasse 50; mains €5-25; ☼ noon-3pm & 6-10.30pm Thu-Tue) The space is minimalist, the Japanese food is not. Everything we tried had perfect pitch – sushi to salads, tempura to fish. Tables fill quickly with Japanese expats and plugged-in locals, so make reservations.

Good Time (Map p98; ☎ 2804 6015; Chausseestrasse 1; mains €6-17) Take a trip to Thailand without packing your bags at this warm and friendly restaurant. Some dishes have Indonesian inflections (satay chicken and the like) but it's the fragrant coconut-based curries that steal the show.

Ishin Mitte (Map p98; ☎ 2067 4829; Mittelstrasse 24; meals €6.50-16.50; ☼ 11am-8pm Mon-Fri, 11am-6pm Sat) This big sushi parlour has cafeteria charm but never mind: you're here for the high quality and the generous portions. The free hot green tea is a welcome bonus.

Vino e Libri (Map p98; ☎ 4405 8471; Torstrasse 99; mains €8-16; ☾ dinner) Two of civilization's greatest assets – wine and books – form the name, décor and soul of this family-run *ristorante*. The pizza is excellent but chef Bruno truly shines when it comes to experimental flavour combinations. Strawberry salmon and tagliatelle with wild boar in a chocolate-based sauce are surprisingly delicious.

Gugelhof (Map p103; ☎ 442 9229; Knaackstrasse 37; mains €8-14; ☾ dinner Mon-Fri, 10am-midnight Sat & Sun) This unpretentious place is a favourite among Berlin politicos, and not just since Bill Clinton popped by a few years ago. The menu features classic Alsatian soul food, including hearty *choucroute* (a sauerkraut-based stew), cheese fondue and *flammekuche* (a pizza-like dish).

Zoe (Map p98; ☎ 2404 5635; Rochstrasse 1; mains €8.50-16; ☾ noon-midnight Mon-Fri, 6pm-midnight Sat & Sun) Dressed in virginal white, Zoe seems to be

a study in minimalism, but fortunately plenty of creativity flows out of the kitchen with its duelling chefs. One's in charge of Mediterranean, the other of Asian dishes; the results are exquisite in both cases.

Mao Thai (Map p103; ☎ 441 9261; Wörther Strasse 30; mains €8.50-20; ☒) If you love Thai food, your tastebuds will do cartwheels at this sophisticated Siam outpost. The duck is a signature dish, but even simple pad thai noodles demonstrate great complexity.

TOP END
Mandala Suites (Map p98; ☎ 202 920; Friedrichstrasse 185-190; breakfast buffet incl drinks €20; ☾ 6.30am-11am Mon-Fri, 7am-noon Sat & Sun) Like froth on a cappuccino, this breakfast sky-lounge floats above the rooftops of Berlin. Atop the stylish sister property of the Mandala Hotel (p126), it's a discrete retreat for lovers of aesthetics and gourmets. Views are memorable, reservations essential.

GETTING VERSED IN WURST

Its aroma catches your nose like a crisp left hook. It's been ravenously gobbled up by chancellors, Madonna and George W and even been celebrated in popular song. 'It', of course, is the humble *Currywurst*, the iconic treat that's as much a part of Berlin's cultural tapestry as the Brandenburg Tor.

To the uncouth or uninitiated, we're talking about a smallish fried or grilled wiener sliced into bite-sized ringlets, swimming in a spicy tomato sauce, dusted with curry powder and served on a flimsy paper plate with a plastic toothpick for stabbing. The wurst itself is subtly spiced and served with or without its crunchy epidermis.

The people of Hamburg might disagree, but Berliners know that their city is the true birthplace of this beloved calorie bomb. The first sausage started its triumphal course to snack stands across the nation from the steaming *Imbiss* (food stall) of Herta Heuwer on 4 September, 1949. These days, *Currywursts* are so ubiquitous in the German capital that they're even sold by roving street vendors with steaming minikitchens strapped around their bellies.

What exactly went into Herta's sauce will never be known; in 1999 she took the secret to her grave. Her contribution to culinary history has garnered her a plaque at Kantstrasse 101 (Map p102) where her *Imbiss* once stood. And as if to cement Berlin's claim to being the German *Currywurst* capital, the **Deutsches Currywurst Museum** (Map p102; ☎ 8871 8630; www.currywurstmuseum .de; Kurfürstendamm 46) should have opened by the time you're reading this. Call for opening hours and admission prices.

There's always a healthy debate about where to find the best dog in town, but we're going to stick our necks out and share our very own top-three list:

■ Konnopke Imbiss (p129)

■ Witty's (p133)

■ Curry 36 (opposite)

PS: Check out *Best of the Wurst* (2004), a hilarious short film made by a Korean-American woman about her quest to get to know Berlin and its people one sausage at a time. See it for free on **iFilm** (www.ifilm.com).

Borchardt (Map p98; ☎ 8188 6262; Französische Strasse 47; mains €15-30, 3-course menu €46) This Mitte institution is on the speed dial of politicians, actors and other power-crowd types. This generally makes for top-notch people-watching in the dining hall, which has ceilings as lofty as the chef's ambitions. The Wiener schnitzel – thin, juicy and huge – is reputedly among the best in town.

Margaux (Map p98; ☎ 2265 2611; Unter den Linden 78; mains €28-45; ❤ noon-2.30pm & 7-10.30pm Tue-Sat) It took culinary wunderkind Michael Hoffman only one year to wow the Michelin testers with his 'cuisine avantgarde classique'. Expect first-rate ingredients, refined flavours and artistic presentation, all set against lush back-lit onyx walls.

Tiergarten

Joseph Roth Diele (Map pp100-1; ☎ 2636 9884; Potsdamer Strasse 75; dishes €4-7; ❤ 10am-midnight Mon-Fri) Named after an Austrian Jewish writer forced into exile by the Nazis, this quirky retreat time-warps you back to the 1920s when Roth used to live next door. Come here for coffee, cakes or home-cooked meals.

Schleusenkrug (Map p102; ☎ 313 9909; Müller-Breslau-Strasse at Tiergarten locks; breakfasts & mains €4.50-10; ❤ 10am-11pm) This classic beer garden by a Landwehrkanal lock gets punters from morn' to midnight. People from all walks of life share pints of Pils, grilled meats and exotic treats.

Edd's (Map pp96-7; ☎ 215 5294; Lützowstrasse 81; mains €8-22; ❤ 11.30am-3pm & 6pm-midnight Tue-Fri, 5pm-midnight Sat, 2pm-midnight Sun) Edd's grandma used to cook for Thai royals and the man himself has regaled Berlin foodies for over three decades with such palate-pleasers as twice-roasted duck, chicken steamed in banana leaves and curries that are like culinary poetry. Reservations are essential.

Kreuzberg & Friedrichshain
BUDGET

Curry 36 (Map pp100-1; ☎ 251 7368; Mehringdamm 36; snacks €1.50-5; ❤ 9am-3am) Don't let the prosaic name deter you: this *Imbiss* makes some of the best *Currywurst* in town.

Henne (Map pp100-1; ☎ 614 7730; Leuschnerdamm 25; ½ chicken €6; ❤ dinner Tue-Sun) At this Berlin institution the name is the menu: roast chicken it is, take it or leave it. It's a concept that's been cult since 1907, so who are we to argue? Garden seating in summer. Reservations recommended.

Alarabi (Map p100-1; ☎ 2977 1995; Krossener Strasse 19; mains €4-8; ❤ 10am-midnight) Candlelight, exotic décor and *shishas* (water pipes) characterise this welcoming refuge. You can sample the free sesame-seed dip while perusing the menu. The €9 appetiser platter easily feeds two. During crunch times, the youthful service can be a bit challenged.

Il Casolare (Map pp100-1; ☎ 6950 6610; Grimmstrasse 30; pizzas €4.50-7.50) The staff often has a serious case of attitude but here's why it's worth putting up with: the canal-side setting and the pizza – thin, crispy, cheap and wagon-wheel-sized.

MIDRANGE

Morgenland (Map pp100-1; ☎ 611 3191; Skalitzer Strasse 35; mains €5-12; ❤ 10am-1am) This café is a breakfast institution, especially on Sunday when they dish out a smorgasbord of a buffet (€9; reservations advised). Otherwise the food's pan-European – pasta to lamb to fried fish.

Papaya (Map pp100-1; ☎ 2977 1231; Krossener Strasse 11; mains €6.50-14.50) At this bustling eatery, you can watch the chefs stirring up delicious hangover preventions in the open kitchen. Perkily spiced *tom ka* soups, tangy pad thai noodles, toothsome Thai basil chicken and other classics are all freshly prepared for loyal fans.

Café Jacques (Map pp100-1; ☎ 694 1048; Maybach ufer 8; mains €7.50-15; ❤ dinner) Flattering candle-light, good wine, world music and delicious Mediterranean supper choices – listed on a blackboard – make this easy-going café a fine choice. The couscous is excellent.

Miseria & Nobiltá (Map pp100-1; ☎ 2904 9249; Kopernikusstrasse 16; mains €10-20; ❤ dinner) When

Eduardo Scarpetti penned the comedy *Poverty and Nobility* in 1888, he didn't know that, over a century later, it would inspire the name of this popular family-run trattoria. You'll definitely feel more king than pauper here when digging into the deftly prepared southern Italian compositions.

Austria (Map p100-1; ☎ 694 4440; Bergmannstrasse 30; mains €13-18; ☼ dinner) This place looks like a hunting lodge designed in Hollywood, and the Wiener schnitzel (€16.50) – thin, tender, huge – are indeed worthy of an Oscar. Thursday's traditional suckling pig special brings out the devotees in droves.

TOP END

Bar Centrale (Map pp100-1; ☎ 786 2989; Yorckstrasse 82; appetisers & pastas €7-14, mains €15-20) Creative Italian (not a pizza in sight) is the name of the game here. Most of the imagination goes into the antipasto menu, which may feature grilled calamari, truffled fois gras or tuna carpaccio. Hungry yet?

Horváth (Map pp100-1; ☎ 6128 9992; Paul-Lincke-Ufer 44a; three-course menu €30, mains €18-24; ☼ 6pm-midnight Tue-Sun) Eastern Kreuzberg may feel more grunge than gourmet, but this food temple is all about culinary flights of fancy: caramelised potato soup with frogs legs, or Barbary duck with shitake mushrooms are typical entries. For the whole enchilada order the 10-course small-plate menu (€60).

Charlottenburg & Wilmersdorf
BUDGET

Lon Men Noodle House (Map p102; ☎ 3151 9678; Kantstrasse 33; soups €2.50-6.50) This tiny and unassuming Taiwanese kitchen churns out authentic broths paired with thin or wide rice noodles and vegetables, meats or wontons. Most are pretty spicy but you could ask the cooks to lay off the heat.

Franziskushof Laden (Map p102; ☎ 8867 5176; Mommsenstrasse 63; mains €3-5; ☼ 11am-3pm Mon-Fri) This lunch hotspot *cum* butcher shop is the fundraising outpost of a Franciscan-run farming monastery in Brandenburg. All home-style German meals are made with organic meats and produce grown right on the farm.

Schwarzes Café (Map p102; ☎ 313 8038; Kantstrasse 148; dishes €4.50-9; ☼ 24hr) Not many cafés have shown as much staying power as this rambling multifloor icon, founded in 1978 by 15 women. It's great for a bite, a beer or breakfast no matter where the hands of the

clock are. The toilets are a hoot, the little garden idyllic

MIDRANGE

Moon Thai (Map p102; ☎ 3180 9743; Kantstrasse 32; mains €6.50-14) Orange walls accented with Thai art create feel-good ambience at this family affair serving a huge repertory of classic dishes. Anything with duck is excellent and even the seitan dishes strut their stuff when paired with fresh vegetables and bold spices.

Engelbecken (Map p102; ☎ 615 2810; Witzlebenstrasse 31; mains €8-16; ☼ 4pm-midnight Mon-Sat, noon-midnight Sun) It's no Munich beer hall, but this corner restaurant still lays on the Bavarian charisma with a trowel. The menu features all the usual suspects: *Weisswurst* (veal sausage) with chewy pretzels, roast pork with dumplings and red cabbage, apple strudel with custard... All meats are hormone-free.

Café Wintergarten im Literaturhaus (Map p102; ☎ 882 5414; Fasanenstrasse 23; mains €8-16; ☼ 9.30am-midnight) Bookworms, artists and shoppers gather at this lovely Art Nouveau villa with graceful stucco-ornamented ceilings. When the weather plays along, the idyllic garden is ideal for breakfast, a light lunch or afternoon coffee.

Jules Verne (Map p102; ☎ 3180 9410; Schlüterstrasse 61; breakfasts €4-10, 2-course lunches €5.50-8, dinner mains €8.50-17; ☼ 8am-1am) Jules Verne was a well-travelled man, so it's only fitting that a restaurant bearing his name would feature a global menu. French *flammekuche*, Austrian schnitzel and North African couscous are all perennial bestsellers. Breakfast is served until 3pm.

Mar y Sol (Map p102; ☎ 313 2593; Savignyplatz 5; tapas €2-4, mains €10-18; ☼ dinner) Grab a table on the fountain-studded patio and feel yourself transported to Seville while munching on *manchego* (cheese), bacon-wrapped dates, Serrano ham, garlic prawns and other taste-bud-tickling tapas.

Other recommendations:

Mr Hai & Friends (Map p102; ☎ 3759 1200; Savignyplatz 1; mains €8-16; ☼ 11am-1am) Stylish Vietnamese restaurant where dishes are veritable flavour bombs.

Gabriel's (Map p102; ☎ 882 6138; Fasanenstrasse 79; mains €10-17, buffet €18) Berlin's only glatt kosher restaurant, inside the Jewish Community House.

TOP END

Die Quadriga (Map p102; ☎ 2140 5650; Eislebener Strasse 14, inside Brandenburger Hof Hotel; menus €55-115; ☼ dinner Mon-Fri) This intimate dining shrine is a

highlight on any gourmet quest. Michelin-starred chef Bobby Bräuer turns only the finest ingredients into gimmick-free meals. The wine list features the 850 best German wines. Reservations required.

Schöneberg
BUDGET

Dolce Pizza (Map p133; ☎ 2005 1585; Maassenstrasse 6; pizza €1.50-10) Lines can be long for what many believe is the best take-away pizza in town. The affiliated ice-cream parlour next door ain't bad either.

Witty's (Map p133; ☎ 853 7055; Wittenbergplatz; snacks €2-4; ⏲ 11am-1am) If there is such a thing as healthy fast food, you'll probably find it at this 'doggeria' serving only certified organic sausages.

Hisar (Map pp100-1; street level S-Bahnhof Yorkstrasse; dishes €2.50-5; ⏲ 9am-midnight) It's off-the-beaten track, but tried-and-true Hisar is, hands-down, one of the best doner kebab stands in town. You'll be glad you made the pilgrimage.

Habibi (Map p133; Winterfeldtplatz 24 & Akazienstrasse 9; snacks €2.50-5; ⏲ 10am-3am) This small

chain is the granddaddy of Berlin's falafel and shwarma circuit. Its late hours make it handy for restoring balance to the brain after an extended bar-hop. Fresh carrot juice provides an extra energy jolt.

MIDRANGE

Tim's Canadian Deli (Map p133; ☎ 2175 6960; Maassenstrasse 14; mains €5-13; ⏲ 9am-1am) When the sun's out, there are few better places than this corner café's outdoor tables facing Winterfeldtplatz. Burgers, bagels, baked goods and other feel-good food keep the cash register ringing as do the good-value lunches (€5).

Trattoria á Muntagnola (Map p133; ☎ 211 6642; Fuggerstrasse 27; pizza & pasta €5.50-11.50, mains €15-20; ⏲ dinner) The owners hail from the deep Italian south whose sun-baked hills have spawned a rustic cuisine with feisty flavours. Olive oil, wine, prosciutto, even sorrel and fennel are imported straight from the Boot and turned into pizzas, pastas and mouth-watering meat dishes.

Other recommendations:

Ousies (Map p133; ☎ 216 7957; Grunewaldstrasse 16; dishes €3.50-14; ⏲ dinner) Bubbly and kitsch-free ouzeria, the Greek spin on the tapas bar. Reservations advised.

Tomasa (Map p102; ☎ 213 2345; Motzstrasse 60; breakfast €5-15) Original branch of a small breakfast/brunch emporium with unusual selections, big portions and pleasantly unobtrusive service.

BERLIN

TOP END

Storch (Map p133; ☎ 784 2059; Wartburgstrasse 54; mains €14-20; ☽ dinner) The wooden floors are worn smooth from legions of patrons hungry for crusty *flammekuche*, stuffed goose, wild-boar ragout or other robust mains. Owner Volker Hauptvogel – whose mellow demeanour belies his punk-rocker past – is often around to greet patrons with disarming charm.

DRINKING

As you'd expect from the capital of beer-obsessed Germany, Berlin elevates drinking culture to a fine art, offering everything from spit-and-sawdust *Kneipen* (pubs) to shiny cocktail lounges. The emphasis is on style, atmosphere and inspiration, and some proprietors have gone to extraordinary lengths to come up with unique concepts. That said, you'll quickly be struck by the overwhelming prevalence of the colour red!

Mitte & Prenzlauer Berg

Prater (Map p103; ☎ 448 5688; Kastanienallee 7-9; ☽ from 4pm Mon-Fri, from noon Sat, from 10am Sun) Berlin's oldest beer garden is also one of the prettiest and is great for quaffing away beneath the chestnut trees. The complex includes a small *Volksbühne* stage, a cocktail bar, an old-fashioned restaurant and the popular Bastard club.

Razzia in Budapest (Map p103; ☎ 4862 3620; Oderberger Strasse 38) Prenzlauer Berg meets Kreuzberg: this hip joint fuses retro sophistication with more than a touch of kitsch, tasselled lamp shades, electro DJs, all without the pretense. A true Mitte gem.

Rote Lotte (Map p103; ☎ 0172-318 6868; Oderberger Strasse 38) Grandma's living room has gone hip at Lotte, right next to Razzia. The plush retro velvet sofas orbiting little wooden tables make great conversation pits.

Kakao (Map p103; ☎ 4862 3423; Dunckerstrasse 10; ☽ from noon) If chocolate is the elixir of the gods (according to the Aztecs), then this laid-back lounge must be heaven. Soothing browns create a suitable backdrop for all sorts of libations, from hot chocolate to chocolate-infused rum to chocolate-flavoured cocktails.

Windhorst (Map p98; ☎ 2045 0070; Dorotheenstrasse 65) This is a small, smart bar of the classic American model helmed by a man who knows how to shake those cocktails. The range of house specials is impressive.

Reingold (Map p98; ☎ 2838 7676; Novalisstrasse 11) Inside the metal cocoon flutters the butterfly heart of a beautifully opulent 1930s glamour lounge where deep house and Latin sounds dominate the decks.

Kreuzberg & Friedrichshain

Freischwimmer (Map pp100-1; ☎ 6107 4309; Vor dem Schlesischen Tor 2; ☽ from noon in summer, from 6pm in winter) In fine weather, there are few more idyllic places for a beer or a bite than this rustic former boathouse right on a canal.

Club der Visionäre (Map pp100-1; ☎ 6951 8944; Am Flutgraben 1; ☽ from 4pm Mon-Fri, from noon Sat & Sun) Across from Freischwimmer, this place is also good for quaffing and catching some rays at the same time. On Sunday it hosts one of the best after-parties in town.

Würgeengel (Map pp100-1; ☎ 615 5560; Dresdner Strasse 122) The 'Exterminating Angel' pays homage to the 1962 Luis Buñuel movie, its dramatic blood-red velvet décor reminiscent of a *belle époque* brothel. The place is crammed the second the adjacent Babylon cinema closes.

Sanatorium 23 (Map pp100-1; ☎ 4202 1193; Frankfurter Allee 23; ☽ from 2pm) The look is Oriental-meets-pop-art-in-hospital, the vibe is relaxed and friendly, the DJs know their dubplates and the long, low seating is quite literally made for lounging. Very, very cool.

Ankerklause (Map pp100-1; ☎ 693 5649; Kottbusser Damm 104) Ahoy there: this nautical Neukölln favourite occupies an old glass-panelled harbour-master's house above the Landwehr-kanal, and still packs 'em in at all hours.

Golgatha (Map pp100-1; ☎ 785 2453; Dudenstrasse 48-64; ☽ Apr-Oct) The pilgrimage to this beer garden in Viktoriapark is a beloved summer ritual. Relax with beers and grilled snacks, then make a night of it on the dance floor.

Spindler & Klatt (Map pp100-1; ☎ 6956 6775; Köpenicker Strasse 16-17) This stunning club-restaurant takes the age-old concept of the converted warehouse and adds the unthinkable: discreet sophistication. Wispy drapes, riverside terrace, Asian fusion food and a dash of Oriental style – late nights have never been so chic.

Heinz Minki (Map pp100-1; ☎ 6953 3766; Vor dem Schlesischen Tor 3; ☽ from noon Tue-Sun) Colourful lights and old trees give this riverside beer garden a romantic vibe. On colder days, retire inside to the bar (open nights only) or the upstairs restaurants (Friday to Sunday).

Tabou Tiki Room (Map pp100-1; Maybachufer 39; Tue-Sun) This silly bar-club has enough Polynesian props to restage *South Pacific*, exotic music (sci-fi jazz, Hawaiian swing, rock'n'roll, country…) and drinks with little umbrellas.

Stereo 33 (Map pp100-1; ☎ 9599 9433; Krossener Strasse 24; Mon-Sat) Modern, minimalist design, well-schooled DJs and bargain sushi all add to the appeal of this sleek bar in Friedrichshain.

Dachkammer (Map pp100-1; ☎ 296 1673; Simon-Dach-Strasse 39) This split personality place pairs a casual downstairs pub with a fantastically convincing 1950s flashback in the multiroom cocktail bar.

Charlottenburg & Schöneberg

Galerie Bremer (Map p102; ☎ 881 4908; Fasanenstrasse 37) Former proprietor Rudolf van der Lak sadly passed away in 2006, but the living-room-sized, very grown-up bar he presided over for 50 years is still worth a visit. It's behind a prestigious gallery.

Gainsbourg (Map p102; ☎ 313 7464; Savignyplatz 5) This cramped, American-style bar speaks to a 30-something intellectual crowd, and might well have appealed to Serge himself. Relax in the warmly lit interior while sipping one of the award-winning (and copyrighted) cocktails.

Green Door (Map p133; ☎ 215 2515; Winterfeldtstrasse 50) Only the door is green at this shoebox-sized bar tended by capable mixologists. Inside, you'll sip your drinks surrounded by vanilla walls and chocolate leather sofas. Ring the bell.

ENTERTAINMENT

Being entertained is what Berliners do best – even the most steadfast workaholic will have a life outside the office. The party scene is one of the most diverse in Europe, constantly spawning new trends and providing platforms for infinite experimentation in music, fashion and design. The most cutting-edge clubs tend to be in bizarre locations – old breweries, vaults, swimming pools, postal offices and warehouses. Electronica still dominates, but the sound spectrum now ranges from drum 'n' bass, house and trance to punk, Latin and African.

Berlin also has plenty in store for fans of highbrow pursuits. Despite serious budget shortfalls, the city sustains three (!) world-class opera houses. Mainstream, offbeat and fringe theatre are all thriving, as are cabaret and variety shows. And in a city that hosts its own international film festival, there are cinemas aplenty, from slick multiplexes to scruffy art houses.

Listings
Zitty (www.zitty.de) and the more mainstream **Tip** (www.tip-berlin.de) are the best of the biweekly German-language listings magazines. Of the freebie mags, *Uncle Sally's*, *030* and *Fresh* are recommended.

Tickets
Credit-card bookings by telephone or online through a venue's box office are still not commonplace in Berlin. Most will take reservations over the phone but make you show up in person to pay for and pick up your tickets. If this is too much hassle, an alternative is to buy tickets through an agency, although this will add a service charge of up to 15% to the ticket price.

Berlin Infostores (p105) All Berlin Infostores sell tickets to events in person, by phone and online. Discounts of up to 50% are available for select same-day performances.

Hekticket (www.hekticket.de) Alexanderplatz (Map p98; ☎ 2431 2431; Karl-Liebknecht-Strasse 12; noon-7pm Tue-Fri, 10am-8pm Sat); Bahnhof Zoo (Map p102; ☎ 230 9930; Hardenbergstrasse 29a; 10am-8pm Mon-Sat, 2-6pm Sun)

Hekticket Last Minute (☎ 230 9930) Discounted tickets after 4pm for select performances that night.

Theaterkasse Centrum (Map p102; ☎ 882 7611; Meinekestrasse 25)

Cabaret & Varieté
The light, lively and lavish variety shows of the Golden Twenties have been undergoing a sweeping revival in Berlin. Get ready for an evening of dancing and singing, jugglers, acrobats and other entertainers. These 'cabarets' should not be confused with 'Kabarett', which are political and satirical shows with monologues and short skits.

Bar Jeder Vernunft (Map p102; ☎ 883 1582; www .bar-jeder-vernunft.de; Schaperstrasse 24) The elegant Art Nouveau tent makes a perfectly nostalgic setting for the sophisticated cabaret, comedy and chanson acts for which this place is famous. There's a free piano bar after the main show and a lovely beer garden in summer. It's at the back of the parking lot.

GAY & LESBIAN BERLIN

Berlin's legendary liberalism has spawned one of the world's biggest gay and lesbian scenes. Anything goes in 'Homopolis' – and we mean anything – from the high-brow to the hands-on, the bourgeois to the bizarre, the mainstream to the flamboyant.

Berlin's emergence as a gay mecca was kick-started by sexual scientist Magnus Hirschfeld who, in 1897, founded the Scientific Humanitarian Committee in the city, which paved the way for gay liberation. The 1920s were especially wild and wacky, a demimonde that drew and inspired writers like Christopher Isherwood until the Nazis put an end to the fun in 1933. Postwar recovery came slowly, but by the 1970s the scene was firmly re-established, at least in the western city. Since 2001, Berlin has been governed by an openly gay mayor, Klaus Wowereit, who outed himself by saying 'I'm gay, and that's a good thing', which has since become a popular slogan in the community. To learn more about Berlin's queer history, visit the nonprofit **Schwules Museum** (Gay Museum; Map pp100-1; ☎ 693 1172; Mehringdamm 61; adult/concession €5/3; ◷ 2-6pm Wed-Mon), which is exhibition space, research centre and community hub all rolled into one.

Berlin doesn't have a dedicated 'gay ghetto', although established bar and club scenes are along Motzstrasse and Fuggerstrasse in Schöneberg (Map p133), Schönhauser Allee and Gleimstrasse in Prenzlauer Berg (Map p103) and Mehringdamm in Kreuzberg (Map pp100-1). In early June, huge crowds turn out for the **Schwul-Lesbisches Strassenfest** (Gay-Lesbian Street Fair) in Schöneberg, which basically serves as a warm-up for **Christopher Street Day** (p124) later that month.

The freebie **Siegessäule** (www.siegessaeule.de) is the Berlin bible for all things gay and lesbian. *Sergej* magazine is strictly for men.

For advice and information, gay men can turn to **Mann-O-Meter** (Map p133; ☎ 216 8008; Bülowstrasse 106) or the **Schwulenberatung** (Gay Advice Hotline; ☎ 194 46). For lesbians, there's the **Lesbenberatung** (☎ 215 2000). Brochures and other information are also available at the Berlin Infostores (p105) and at www.berlin-tourist-information.de.

Mitte & Prenzlauer Berg

Kino International (Map pp96-7; ☎ 2475 6011; Karl-Marx-Allee 33) With its camp cavalcade of glass chandeliers, glitter curtains and parquet floor, this GDR-era cinema is a show in itself. Monday is 'MonGay' with homo-themed classics, imports and previews. The Chicks De Luxe (www.chicks united.de) lesbian party also packs the place.

Schall und Rauch (Map p103; ☎ 443 3970; Gleimstrasse 23) A bistro by day, this trendy gay place morphs into a chic cocktail bar when the moon gets high. The Sunday brunch (€7) has cult status.

Sonntags Club (Map pp96-7; ☎ 449 7590; Greifenhagener Strasse 28) This friendly, relaxed, lesbigay café-bar project is open to all and holds frequent events. There is also a piano just begging to have its ivories tickled.

Gate Sauna (Map pp100-1; ☎ 229 9430; Wilhelmstrasse 81; admission €14; ◷ 11am-7am Mon-Thu, 24hr Fri-Sun) This is one of the biggest and most active gay saunas with a bar, restaurant and video room, cabins and a swing (no, not the kind for the kiddies).

Chamäleon Varieté (Map p98; ☎ 282 7118; www .chamaeleon-variete.de; Hackesche Höfe) This intimate club presents variety shows (think comedy, juggling acts and singing) often in a sassy and unconventional fashion.

Wintergarten-Das Varieté (Map pp96-7; ☎ 2500 8888; www.wintergarten-berlin.de; Potsdamer Strasse 96) Come here for vaudeville shows that have been updated for the 21st century, all performed in a glitzy theatre with a starry-sky ceiling. The crowd's tourist-heavy, but the shows can be quite fun.

Friedrichstadtpalast (Map p98; ☎ 2326 2326; www .friedrichstadtpalast.de; Friedrichstrasse 107) With 2000 seats, this is the largest revue theatre in Europe with Vegas-style productions featuring leggy showgirls and an excellent in-house orchestra.

Blue Man Group (Map pp100-1; ☎ 01805-4444) This group's whimsical show, which has been performing to capacity crowds in the Theater am Potsdamer Platz, should have moved to its own permanent home in the former Imax theatre across Marlene-Dietrich-Platz by spring 2007.

Kreuzberg & Friedrichshain

Melitta Sundström (Map pp100-1; ☎ 692 4414; Mehringdamm 61; ☺ from 10am) A great place for breakfast or a coffee and chat while the sun's up, this place turns cruisy after dark, especially at weekends when drag queens and party lions invade to liquor up before moving on to the SchwuZ disco at the back.

Himmelreich (Map pp100-1; ☎ 7072 8306; Simon-Dach-Strasse 36) Proving all those stereotypes about gays having good taste, this smart red-hued cocktail bar makes most of the competition look like a straight guy's bedsit.

Sofia (Map pp100-1; ☎ 0163-283 2519; Wrangelstrasse 93) Sofia apparently started life as a kebab shop, but its new incarnation is rather more pleasing, offering comfy seats, moulded waterfall-effect décor and posters of one Ms Loren. Thanks to the chirpy owners it's become a favoured, though by no means exclusive, lesbigay hangout.

SO36 (Map pp100-1; ☎ 6140 1306; Oranienstrasse 190) The 'Esso' is Kreuzberg's punk heart and also hosts Gayhane, a monthly 'homoriental' party with Turkish and German pop, transvestites and belly dancing.

Roses (Map pp100-1; ☎ 615 7570; Oranienstrasse 187; ☺ from 9pm) Kitschy yet pretty, Roses has been a Kreuzberg fixture for over 10 years and still draws patrons in party mode with its strong drinks and seductively plush setting.

Schöneberg

Connection (Map p133; ☎ 218 1432; Fuggerstrasse 33; ☺ Fri & Sat) This well-established gay disco is one of the most popular boozing and cruising spots in town with three floors of men-only action, a mirrored dance floor and blaring techno.

Tom's Bar (Map p133; ☎ 213 4570; Motzstrasse 19) Tom's is another main stop on the party circuit. Its dark cavernous bar is a serious pick-up joint, and there's an active cellar as well. If you're OFB – out for business – don't get here before midnight. Men only.

Hafen (Map p133; ☎ 211 4118; Motzstrasse 19) A permanent fixture on the good-time gay circuit, the 'Harbour' pulls in all kinds of guys and gals with its friendly free-for-all vibe. It's also a popular warm-up venue for those heading to hardcore cruising dens such as Tom's Bar and Mutschmanns.

So & So (Map p133; ☎ 2145 9766; Fuggerstrasse 35) Drinking here is the next-best thing to drinking inside a lava lamp: expect trippy projections, cool DJs and strong cocktails. Less try-hard butch than the raucous places opposite, and so low-key you'll barely notice it's at least nominally a gay bar.

Xenon (Map p133; ☎ 782 8850; Kolonnenstrasse 5-6) Built in 1909, the city's second-oldest movie theatre is dedicated entirely to lesbigay cinema, with lots of juicy imports and themed seasons.

Begine (Map pp96-7; ☎ 215 1414; Potsdamer Strasse 139) This men-free zone has a radical 'herstory': it started out as a militant feminist squat in the 1980s, and now puts on concerts, readings, films and events with an intellectual bent.

Cinemas

Going to the movies is pretty pricey, with Saturday-night tickets at the multiplexes fetching up to €11. Almost all cinemas also add a sneaky *Überlängezuschlag* (overrun supplement) of €0.50 to €1 for films longer than 90 minutes. Seeing a show on a *Kinotag* (film day, usually Monday to Wednesday) or before 5pm can save up to 50%. Indie neighbourhood theatres are usually cheaper. In summer, watching movies al fresco in a *Freiluftkino* (outdoor cinema) is a venerable tradition.

Movies that are screened in their original language are denoted in listings by the acronym 'OF' (*Originalfassung*) or 'OV' (*Originalversion*); those with German subtitles are marked 'OmU' (*Original mit Untertiteln*).

The venues in the following list all screen English-language films, but do also check the recommended listings magazines for additional options.

Arsenal (Map pp100-1; ☎ 2695 5100; Filmhaus, Potsdamer Strasse 2, Sony Center) Nonmainstream fare from around the world.

BERLIN

Babylon (Map pp100-1; ☎ 6160 9693; Dresdener Strasse 126) Broad-appeal art house.

Cinestar im Sony Center (Map pp100-1; ☎ 2606 6260; www.cinestar.de; Potsdamer Strasse 4) Hollywood blockbusters, all in English, all the time.

Eiszeit (Map pp100-1; ☎ 611 6016; Zeughofstrasse 20) Obscure, alternative and experimental films.

Intimes (Map pp100-1; ☎ 2966 4633; Niederbarnim-strasse 15) Off-beat releases and cult classics.

Clubs

Doors open at 10pm or 11pm, but nothing really happens until midnight.

Berghain/Panoramabar (Map pp100-1; Am Wriezener Bahnhof; ☒ Fri & Sat) When this hugely successful postindustrial techno-electro outpost is fully open on Saturday night it really is a sight and a half: there are three levels of concrete, speakers and partitions, full of hidden corners (including some dark rooms) and packed out with the most mixed crowd you'll find in all of Berlin. Panoramabar, which is up-stairs, became an instant fixture within days of opening.

Watergate (Map pp100-1; ☎ 6128 0394; Falckenstein-strasse 49a; ☒ Fri & Sat) Watergate has a fantastic location with a lounge overlooking the Spree and a floating terrace actually on it, opposite the colour-changing logo of the Universal Music building.

Kaffee Burger (Map p98; ☎ 2804 6495; Torstrasse 60; ☒ daily) Indie, rock and punk parties and gigs are often preceded by literature and po-etry readings at this place famous for writer Wladimir Kaminer's legendary *Russendisko* (Russian Disco).

Maria am Ufer (Map pp100-1; ☎ 2123 8190; Stral-auer Platz 33-34; ☒ Fri & Sat) The DJs playing here are invariably among the best in their field, whether it's breakbeat, down-tempo or some other strand of electronica. Occasional live concerts on weekdays.

Sage Club (Map p98; ☎ 278 9830; Köpenicker Strasse 76; ☒ Thu-Sun) The door policy is pretty tight here, but it's worth braving the goons just to see the amazing garden area (with pool) and four dance floors (with fire-breathing dragons). Different sounds nightly, rock to R&B to house.

Knaack Club (Map p103; ☎ 442 7060; Greifswalder Strasse 224; ☒ Mon, Wed, Fri & Sat) Part venue, part club, this 1953-vintage warren is known for its popular rock, punk and indie concerts, but the regular five-floor dance parties are pretty good too.

Delicious Doughnuts (Map p98; ☎ 2809 9279; Rosenthaler Strasse 9; ☒ Thu-Sat) A tasty slice of Mitte nightlife, Doughnuts has perfected the cosy velvet lounge look and is a friendly place with a small but lively dance floor, table football and a tendency to stay open well into daylight hours.

Also recommended:

ICON (Map p103; ☎ 4849 2878; Cantianstrasse 15; ☒ Tue, Fri & Sat) Top location for seriously heavy-duty drum 'n' bass.

SO36 (Map pp100-1; ☎ 6140 1306; Oranienstrasse 190; ☒ daily) Punk palace with relentlessly offbeat live concerts and theme nights (p137).

KitKat Club (Map pp96-7; ☎ 7889 9704; Bessemer-strasse 2-14; ☒ Thu-Sun) Be brave, be bold, be naked at Berlin's original den of decadence. Most parties are open to all comers, subject to the erotic dress code (check the website for details).

Culture Centres

Cultural centres are an integral part of Berlin's entertainment scene. These multi-use venues impose few limits on their stages – on any given night you might find cinema, dance, live music, theatre, art, literature or even cir-cus acts.

Kunsthaus Tacheles (Map p98; ☎ 282 6185; www .tacheles.de; Oranienburger Strasse 54-56) Behind the postatomic shell is an active offbeat venue with dance, jazz, movies, cabaret, readings, workshops, artist studios and galleries, and a cinema.

Kulturbrauerei (Map p103; ☎ 443 150; www.kultur brauerei.de; Schönhauser Allee 36-39) The red-brick buildings of this 19th-century brewery are now a cultural powerhouse with a small vil-lage worth of venues, from concert and theatre halls to restaurants, nightclubs, galleries and a multiscreen cinema.

Insel der Jugend (☎ 5360 8020; www.insel-berlin.net; Alt-Treptow 6; bus 265 to Rathaus Treptow) The Island of Youth is a former GDR youth club housed in a mock medieval castle on an island in the Spree. There's something for everybody, from workshops to live rock concerts, open-air cinema (June to September) and dance parties of all musical stripes.

Pfefferberg (Map p103; ☎ 4438 3342; www.pfefferberg .de; Schönhauser Allee 176) Also converted from a brewery, Pfefferberg is rougher and more alter-native than the Kulturbrauerei, promoting a lot of cross-cultural and antifascist projects. Nice beer garden. In 2007 the Vitra Design Museum was expected to open on its grounds.

Tesla (Map p98; ☎ 2474 9777; www.tesla-berlin.de; Klosterstrasse 68-70) Renamed from Podewil, this self-styled 'laboratory' for multimedia art devotes itself to highly experimental projects. As well as concerts, exhibitions and workshops, regular radiotesla productions explore the mysteries of the airwaves.

Live Music

CLASSICAL & OPERA

Philharmonie (Map pp100-1; ☎ 2548 8132; www .berliner-philharmoniker.de; Herbert-Von-Karajan-Strasse 1; tickets €7-120) This justly famous concert hall has supreme acoustics and not a bad seat in the house.

Konzerthaus (Map p98; ☎ 203 090; www.konzerthaus .de; Gendarmenmarkt; tickets €13-43) Another of Berlin's top classical venues, the Schinkel-designed Konzerthaus counts the Berliner Sinfonie-Orchester as its 'house band' but others, such as the Rundfunk-Sinfonieorchester Berlin, perform here as well.

Staatsoper Unter den Linden (Map p98; ☎ 2035 4555; www.staatsoper-berlin.org; Unter den Linden 7; tickets €8-120) Led by Daniel Barenboim, Berlin's oldest and most gorgeous opera house presents opera from four centuries along with classical and modern ballet, including high-calibre visiting troupes.

Deutsche Oper Berlin (Map p102; ☎ 343 8401; www .deutscheoperberlin.de; Bismarckstrasse 35; tickets €12-112) Berlin's largest opera house may look unsightly but its musical supremacy is seldom questioned, and the arrival of first-ever female boss Kirsten Harms looks set to shake off a slightly stuffy image.

Komische Oper (Map p98; ☎ 4799 7400; www .komische-oper-berlin.de; Behrenstrasse 55-57; tickets €8-93) Musical theatre, light opera, operetta and dance are the domain of this high-profile venue with its plush interior. All productions are sung in German. The box office is on Unter den Linden 41.

JAZZ

A-Trane (Map p102; ☎ 313 2550; www.a-trane.de; Bleib-treustrasse 1) There's not a bad seat in this intimate place with round cocktail tables and a small stage. The talent is invariably top-class and everyone's usually standing by the end of the show.

Quasimodo (Map p102; ☎ 312 8086; www.quasimodo .de; Kantstrasse 12a) Underneath the Delphi cinema, Berlin's oldest jazz club consistently attracts high-calibre national and interna-

tional acts. Its petite size puts you close to the stage but the low ceiling, black walls and smoky air can be just a tad claustrophobic.

B-flat (Map p98; ☎ 283 3123; www.b-flat-berlin.de; Rosenthaler Strasse 13) Modern jazz in all its variants dominates the programme here, with increasing doses of world, Latin and other beats. Wednesday is acoustic night (free entry) and Sunday is tango, while the film lounge takes over one Thursday a month.

Junction Bar (Map pp100-1; ☎ 694 6602; www.junction -bar.de; Gneisenaustrasse 18) Check your lungs at the door when entering this groovy, smoke-filled cellar where you'll be showered by everything from traditional jazz to jazz-rap, along with blues, soul and funk. After the show, DJs keep the sounds coming. The upstairs bar serves snacks.

Sport

Hertha BSC (☎ 01805-189 200, 300 9280; www.herthabsc .de; Olympiastadion; 🚇 🖉 Olympiastadion) Berlin's long-standing Bundesliga (National League) football (soccer) team plays home games at the Olympic Stadium. Tickets are usually available on game-day and start at €10.

Alba Berlin (Map p103; Am Falkplatz; ☎ 01805-300 777; www.albaberlin.de; tickets €7.50-32) Berlin's top basketball team competes hard on a European level and has a solid winning record. Home games take place at the Max-Schmeling-Halle.

Berlin Thunder (☎ 3006 4400; www.berlin-thunder .de; Olympiastadion; tickets €8-31.50; 🚇 🖉 Olympiastadion) American football is gaining popularity, largely thanks to Thunder's storming record – the team consistently tops the league and has two World Bowls to its name.

EHC Eisbären (☎ 9718 4040; www.eisbaeren.de; Sportforum Berlin, Steffenstrasse, Hohenschönhausen; tickets €15-30; 🚇 Hohenschönhausen) Fervent ice-hockey fans ensure that every home game of the Polar Bears practically explodes with atmosphere, especially since the team became national champion in 2005 and 2006.

Theatre

Berlin has more than 100 theatres. The main drama drags are Friedrichstrasse and the Kurfürstendamm, but every district has its own set of smaller stages. Many theatres are dark on Monday and from mid-July to late August. Tickets are often available on the day of performance and best purchased directly from the theatre's box office.

Discounts of up to 50% for students and seniors are common.

Admiralspalast (Map p98; ☎ 4799 7499; www .admiralspalast.de; Friedrichstrasse 101-102) A major party palace during the Roaring Twenties, the Admiralspalast reopened in August 2006 with a production of Brecht's *Threepenny Opera* led by Campino of German band Die Toten Hosen as Mack the Knife. In keeping with the original venue, the restored complex harbours not only a theatre but also galleries, a night club, a café and even a mineral-water-fed swimming pool.

Deutsches Theater (Map p98; ☎ 2844 1225; www .deutschestheater.de; Schumannstrasse 13a) This historic theatre achieved its greatest acclaim under Max Reinhardt who directed it from 1905 to 1933. From classic plays to experimental works by contemporary authors, it makes for a stimulating repertoire.

Berliner Ensemble (Map p98; ☎ 2840 8155; www .berliner-ensemble.de; Bertolt-Brecht-Platz 1) Brecht's former theatre was a lavish interior and presents works by him and other European 20th-century playwrights, with the occasional Shakespeare thrown into the mix.

Volksbühne am Rosa-Luxemburg-Platz (Map p98; ☎ 2406 5777; www.volksbuehne-berlin.de; Rosa-Luxemburg-Platz) Nonconformist, radical and provocative: performances here are not for those squeamish about blood and nudity.

Schaubühne am Lehniner Platz (Map p102; ☎ 890 020; www.schaubuehne.de; Kurfürstendamm 153) West Berlin owes any cutting-edge theatrical credentials to this former 1920s cinema, rescued from bland obscurity under the forceful leadership of choreographer Sasha Waltz and director Thomas Ostermeier.

Friends of Italian Opera (Map pp100-1; ☎ 691 1211; Fidicinstrasse 40) Despite the name, this is actually Berlin's most established English-language theatre. Visiting troupes from the US, UK, Canada and other countries supplement the in-house productions.

SHOPPING

Berlin may not traditionally rank among the world's great shopping cities but, frankly, that's quite an outdated perception. Fact is, Berlin is a great place to shop and prices tend to be lower than in many other European capitals.

The closest the German capital comes to having an Oxford Street–type retail spine is Kurfürstendamm and its extension, Tau-

entzienstrasse. Both are lined with many of the chain stores you already know from the high street back home (H&M, Mango, Esprit), with a few German shops thrown into the mix.

But mostly, shopping in Berlin means venturing into the neighbourhoods, each with its own flair, identity and mix of stores calibrated to the needs, tastes and pockets of locals. Go to posh Charlottenburg for international couture and to Kreuzberg for second-hand fashions. In Mitte, ritzy Friedrichstrasse has cosmopolitan flair, while the Scheunenviertel and Prenzlauer Berg are hotbeds of hip local designers. Schöneberg has the big KaDeWe department store and side streets lined with speciality boutiques. Note that many stores, especially smaller ones, do not accept credit cards.

Department Stores & Malls

KaDeWe (Kaufhaus des Westens; Map p133; ☎ 212 10; Tauentzienstrasse 21) Shopaholics will get their fix at this amazing eight-floor department store, the largest in Europe after London's Harrods. It sells just about everything from yarn to washing machines, but if you're pushed for time, make sure you at least hurry up to the gourmet food hall on the 6th floor – it's legendary.

Galeries Lafayette (Map p98; ☎ 209 480; Friedrich-strasse 76) The Berlin branch of the exquisite French emporium is centred on a glass cone shimmering with kaleidoscopic intensity. Head upstairs for designer wear, downstairs to the gourmet food hall.

Potsdamer Platz Arkaden (Map pp100-1; ☎ 255 9270; Alte Potsdamer Strasse) This is a good all-purpose indoor mall filled with mainstream chains, supermarkets, fast-food eateries and one of Berlin's best ice cream parlours upstairs.

Farmers' Markets

Winterfeldtmarkt (Map p133; Winterfeldtplatz; ☉ 8am-2pm Wed, 8am-4pm Sat) Spending Saturdays at this upscale farmers' market is a ritual for many Berliners. Do as they do and cap off your fruit-and-veggie shopping spree with coffee or breakfast in a local café.

Turkish Market (Map pp100-1; Maybachufer; ☉ noon-6.30pm Tue & Fri) Olives, feta spreads, loaves of fresh bread and fruit and vegetables galore, all at bargain prices, are what you'll find at this colourful canal-side market.

A PLATFORM FOR DESIGN

Creativity is king in Berlin, a city where individualism trumps conformity. Jörg Wichmann and Theresa Meirer have tapped into this dynamism and created a showcase for about 140 home-grown designers with **Berlinomat** (☎ 4208 1445; Frankfurter Allee 89; ☺ 11am-8pm Mon-Fri, 10am-6pm Sat; ☺ ☺ Frankfurter Allee), a mini-department store tucked in among the Stalinist behemoths of Frankfurter Allee. In halogen-flooded, snowy-white rooms, they present the latest visions from a pool of about 140 creatives working in fashion, accessories, furniture and jewellery. Don't expect stodgy couture: Berlin fashion, accessories, furniture and jewellery are down-to-earth, slightly irreverent, with a fresh edge you won't find in Paris or Milan. A selection from the Berlinomat designers is also available on the top floor of Galeries Lafayette (opposite). To bone up on who's who in the Berlin fashion scene, get a copy of the English/German 'trend shopping guide' called *Designpole Berlin*. It's available at bookstores, Berlinomat and at Berlin Infostores.

Flea Markets

Flohmarkt am Mauerpark (Map p103; Bernauer Strasse 63, Mauerpark; ☺ 10am-5pm Sun) It's getting more commercial, but for now most of the vendors are simply locals cleaning out their closets, which keeps prices low, often ridiculously so. The outdoor café and 'beach' bar are welcome refuelling pits.

Flohmarkt am Arkonaplatz (Map pp96–7; Arkonaplatz; ☺ 10am-5pm Sun) A short walk from Mauerpark, this smallish flea market feeds the retro frenzy with groovy furniture, accessories, clothing, vinyl and books from the 1960s and '70s.

Flohmarkt Strasse des 17 Juni (Map p102; ☺ 10am-5pm Sat & Sun) West of the Tiergarten S-Bahn station, this big market is a tourist favourite, making bargains as rare as tulips in Tonga. Still, good Berlin memorabilia, plus grandma's furniture and jewellery make it a fun browse.

Galleries

Berlin has about 300 commercial galleries located in courtyards, patrician villas, old warehouses or factories, or in spacious, elegant collections of rooms on major boulevards. You'll find concentrations of them along Ku'damm and Fasanenstrasse in Charlottenburg (Map p102), as well as on August-strasse in Mitte (Map p98).

For a comprehensive and up-to-date overview, pick up a copy of *Berlin Artery – Der Kunstführer* (€2.50; in both German and English) available at newsstands, bookshops and some museums.

Made in Berlin

Bonbonmacherei (Map p98; ☎ 4405 5243; Oranienburger Strasse 32, Heckmann-Höfe) The lost art of handmade sweets has been lovingly revived in this little basement store cum kitchen where candy-makers Katja and Hjalmar produce everything from tangy sour drops to green leaf-shaped *Maiblätter* (May leaves).

Harry Lehmann (Map p102; ☎ 324 3582; Kantstrasse 106) Time seems frozen at this endearingly old-fashioned perfume maker. Scents are kept in big-bellied jars and then syphoned into smaller flasks and sold by weight with prices starting at just €3 for 10g.

Tausche (Map p103; ☎ 4020 1770; www.tausche-berlin .de; Raumerstrasse 8) Tausche makes messenger-style bags that are practical, durable, stylish and kitted out with exchangeable logo flaps that zip on and off in seconds.

Thatchers (Map p98; ☎ 2462 7751; Hof IV, Hackesche Höfe) These local design veterans specialise in making professional women look good in clothing that's feminine but not fussy, sexy but not vulgar, and always well tailored. Also at Kastanienallee 21 (Map p103).

Yoshiharu Ito (Map p98; ☎ 4404 4490; Rosa-Luxemburg-Strasse 5) This Tokyo-trained couture designer puts a personal spin on classic cuts. Men's clothing is his main strength, but his women's line is turning heads as well.

Music

Mr Dead & Mrs Free (Map p133; ☎ 215 1449; Bülowstrasse 5) This Berlin institution has an eclectic assortment of rock, pop, country, indie, alternative, even jazz, soul and blues, much of it UK and US imports. Vinyl rules, but there are also a few CDs.

Platten Pedro (Map pp96–7; ☎ 344 1875; Tegeler Weg 102) Vinyl purists happily make the trip out to this cu ltish store packed to the rafters with vintage albums, from pop to punk to polka – and not a CD in sight!

Scratch Records (Map pp100-1; ☎ 6981 7591; Zossener Strasse 31) Come here to flick through a small but choice selection of soul, funk, electro, R&B, soundtracks and jazz on vinyl (in back) and CD (in front), much of it hard-to-find imports.

GETTING THERE & AWAY
Air
Berlin has two main airports; the general information number for both is ☎ 0180-500 0186 (www.berlin-airport.de). Tegel (TXL; Map pp96–7) is about 8km northwest of the city centre and primarily serves destinations within Germany and Western Europe. Direct flights on Delta and Continental from New York also land here. Schönefeld (SXF; Map p93), some 22km southeast of the centre, handles mostly flights to/from Eastern Europe, Africa and Asia.

Many major international airlines serve one or both of Berlin's airports as do discount carriers Ryan Air, easyJet, Air Berlin and German Wings. For airline contact information, see p755.

A third airport, Tempelhof (THF; Map pp96–7), was expected to cease operation in 2007. However, it has received prior reprieves, so it's anyone's guess what will actually happen.

Bus
Berlin's central bus station, **ZOB** (Masurenallee 4-6), is actually not particularly central but about 4km west of Bahnhof Zoo, right by the Funkturm radio tower in western Charlottenburg. To get there, take the U2 to Kaiserdamm or the S41, S42, S45, S46 or S47 to Messe Nord/ICC.

Tickets are available from the **ZOB Reisebüro** (☎ 301 0380; Masurenallee 4-6; ☼ 6am-9pm Mon-Fri, 6am-3pm Sat & Sun), although many in-town travel agencies also sell them. The main operator is **BerlinLinienBus** (☎ 861 9331; www.berlinlinienbus.de) with departures for destinations throughout Germany and Europe. **Gulliver's** (☎ 311 0211; www.gullivers.de) also has an extensive route system.

Backpacker-oriented hop-on, hop-off service **Bus About** (☎ in UK 020 7950 1661; www.busabout.com) stops at the Citystay Hostel (p125) in Mitte.

Car & Motorcycle
The A10 ring road links Berlin with other German and foreign cities, including the A11 to Szczecin (Stettin) in Poland; the A12 to

Frankfurt an der Oder; the A13 to Dresden; the A9 to Leipzig, Nuremberg and Munich; the A2 to Hanover and the Ruhrgebiet cities; and the A24 to Hamburg.

RIDE-SHARE SERVICES
Berlin has several *Mitfahrzentralen* (ride-share agencies; p759), which typically charge €15 for shared rides to Hamburg, €31 to Frankfurt and €29 to Munich. The people answering the phone in these offices usually speak English well.

CityNetz Mitfahrzentrale (Map p102; ☎ 194 44; www.mfz-citynetz.de; Joachimstaler Strasse 17; ☼ 9am-8pm Mon-Fri, 10am-6pm Sat & Sun)

Shuttlenet (Map p102; ☎ 194 20; www.shuttlenet.de /berlin; Hardenbergplatz 14; ☼ 8am-8pm)

Train
Berlin is well connected by train to other German cities, as well as to popular European destinations, including Prague, Warsaw and Amsterdam.

In May 2006, Berlin's spectacular new Hauptbahnhof (main train station; Map p98) opened just north of the government quarter. The futuristic glass hall hemmed in by two office buildings is among Europe's largest and most modern railway hubs. National and international long-distance trains departing in all directions are joined by S-Bahn trains.

The U-Bahn and north- and southbound trains depart below-ground, while east- and westbound trains, as well as the S-Bahn, run from the upper platforms. There are plenty of shops, which stay open until 10pm.

While all long-distance trains converge at the Hauptbahnhof, some may also stop at other Berlin stations such as Spandau, Ostbahnhof and Lichtenberg. Bahnhof Zoo, meanwhile, has been demoted to a regional train station (although this may change again).

Hauptbahnhof predictably has the best infrastructure with left-luggage offices, coin lockers, car rental agencies, currency exchange offices and plenty of shops and fast-food restaurants. The other stations, though smaller, have many of the same facilities.

GETTING AROUND
To/From the Airport
SCHÖNEFELD
Schönefeld airport (Map p93) is served twice hourly by the AirportExpress train, with departures from Bahnhof Zoo (30 minutes),

Friedrichstrasse (23 minutes), Alexanderplatz (20 minutes) and Ostbahnhof (15 minutes). Note that these are regular regional Regionalexpress (RE) or Regionalbahn (RB) trains, although they are also designated as Airport-Express train in the timetable.

The S9 makes the trip from Alexanderplatz in 40 minutes and from Bahnhof Zoo in 50 minutes. The S45 is another alternative if you're headed somewhere outside the central city.

The Schönefeld train station is about 300m from the terminal; they're linked by a free shuttle bus every 10 minutes. Walking takes about five to 10 minutes.

Bus 171 and express bus X7 link the terminal directly with the U-Bahn station Rudow (U7) with connections to central Berlin.

The fare for any of these trips is €2.10.

A taxi from Schönefeld to central Berlin costs between €25 and €35.

TEGEL

Tegel airport (Map pp96–7) is connected to Mitte by the JetExpressBus TXL, which makes the trip to/from Alexanderplatz via Unter den Linden and Hauptbahnhof in about 30 minutes. If you're heading to the western city centre, you're better off hopping aboard JetExpressBus X9, which takes you to Bahnhof Zoo in just under 20 minutes. Bus 109 is slower but handier if you need to go somewhere along the Kurfürstendamm.

Tegel is not directly served by U-Bahn. The nearest station is Jakob-Kaiser-Platz (U7), which is connected to the airport by bus 109.

The fare for any of these rides is a standard AB zone ticket for €2.10 (see p144).

The average taxi fare from Tegel is €15 to Bahnhof Zoo and €20 to Alexanderplatz.

TEMPELHOF

Tempelhof airport (Map pp96–7) is served by the U6 (get off at Platz der Luftbrücke) for €2.10. A taxi to Bahnhof Zoo or Alexanderplatz costs between €10 and €15.

Car & Motorcycle

Berlin is less congested than other capitals, making getting around by car comparatively easy.

Parking in garages is expensive (about €1 to €2 per hour), but often it'll be your only choice. Parking meters are rare but the 'pay and display' system is quite widespread. Free street parking, while difficult to find in central areas, is usually available in the outer districts.

CAR HIRE

All the major international chains maintain branches at the airports, major train stations and throughout town. Check the Yellow Pages (under *Autovermietung*) for local branches or call the central reservation numbers (see above).

Local independent outfits may have better prices and fewer restrictions on age or driving records, although you won't be driving the latest models.

Das Hässliche Entlein (Map pp96-7; ☎ 0180-343 3683; www.die-ente.de; Budapester Strasse 6) Daily rentals from €14, including full insurance, VAT and unlimited kilometres.

Robben & Wientjes (www.robben-wientjes.de) Kreuzberg (Map pp100-1; ☎ 616 770; Prinzenstrasse 90-91); Prenzlauer Berg (Map p103; ☎ 421 036; Prenzlauer Allee 96)

MOTORCYCLE HIRE

If you get 'Harley Hunger', you can hire bikes from the following outfits. Daily rates are about €55 for the Sportster 883 and €115 for the Fat Boy.

Classic Bike Harley-Davidson (Map pp96-7; ☎ 616 7930; Salzufer 6)

Rent-a-Harley (Map p102; ☎ 882 4915; Lietzenburger Strasse 90)

Public Transport

Berlin's public transport system is composed of buses, trams, the U-Bahn (subway trains), the S-Bahn (suburban trains), Regionalbahn (RB) and Regionalexpress (RE) trains and ferries.

The main operator, BVG, operates an **information kiosk** (Map p102; Hardenbergplatz; ☯ 6am-10pm) outside Zoo station. The staff hand out free route network maps and also sell tickets. For general and trip-planning information, call the 24-hour hotline on ☎ 194 49 or use the online function at www.bvg.de.

For information on S-Bahn, RE and RB connections, you can also visit the Reisezentrum (Travel Centre) at train stations, call ☎ 11861 or ☎ 0800-150 7090 or check www.bahn.de.

BUYING & USING TICKETS

Bus drivers sell single tickets and day passes, but tickets for U- and S-Bahn trains and other multiple, weekly or monthly tickets must be purchased before boarding. They're available from orange vending machines (with instructions in English) at any U- or S-Bahn station or from any kiosk or shop bearing the BVG logo.

Tickets must be stamped (validated) at station platform entrances. The on-the-spot fine for getting caught without a valid ticket is €40.

FARES & TICKETS

Berlin's metropolitan area is divided into three tariff zones – A, B and C. Tickets are available for zones AB, BC or ABC. Unless you're venturing to Potsdam or the very outer suburbs, you'll only need the AB ticket. For short trips, buy the *Kurzstreckenticket* or €1.20. It's good for three stops on the U- and S-Bahn or six on any bus or tram. The group day pass is valid for up to five people travelling together. Kids below age six travel for free. Children aged six to 14 qualify for reduced (*ermässigt*) rates.

Ticket type	AB	BC	ABC
single	€2.10	€2.30	€2.60
reduced single	€1.40	€1.60	€1.90
day pass	€5.80	€5.70	€6
group day pass	€14.80	€14.30	€15
7-day pass	€25.40	€26.20	€31.30

BUSES & TRAMS

Berlin's buses are rather slow, but being ensconced on the upper level of a double-decker makes for some inexpensive sight-seeing – see the boxed text, p105.

Bus stops are marked with a large 'H' (for *Haltestelle*) and the name of the stop. The next stop is usually announced via a loudspeaker or digitally displayed. Push the button on the handrails if you want to get off. Night buses take over from about 12.30am to 4.30am, running at roughly 30-minute intervals. Normal fares apply.

Trams only operate in the eastern districts. The M10, N54, N55, N92 and N93 offer continuous service nightly.

S-BAHN & REGIONAL TRAINS

S-Bahn trains make fewer stops than U-Bahns and are therefore handy for longer distances, but they don't run as frequently. They operate from around 4am to 12.30am and throughout the night on Friday, Saturday and public holidays.

Destinations further afield are served by Regionalbahn (RB) and Regionalexpress (RE) trains. You'll need an ABC or Deutsche Bahn ticket to use these trains.

U-BAHN

The most efficient way to travel around Berlin is by U-Bahn, which operates from 4am until just after midnight, except at weekends and public holidays when service continues through the night on all lines but the U4. The next station is usually announced and also digitally displayed in newer carriages. Starting in 2007 a new U-Bahn line, the U55, is scheduled to begin service between the new Hauptbahnhof and Brandenburger Tor.

Taxi

You'll find taxi ranks at the airports, major train stations and throughout the city. Flag fall is €2.50, then it's €1.50 per kilometre up to 7km and €1 for each kilometre after that. Taxis can be ordered on ☎ 194 10, ☎ 0800-8001 1554 and ☎ 0800-222 2255.

For short trips, you can use the €3 flat rate, which entitles you to ride for up to 2km, but it's only available if you flag down a moving taxi and request this special rate (called *Kurzstreckentarif* – short trip rate – or *€3 Tarif*) before the driver has activated the meter. If you continue past 2km, regular rates apply.

Brandenburg

Although it surrounds bustling Berlin, the Brandenburg state of mind is as far from the German capital as Shangri-La. It's a quiet, gentle state with vast expanses of unspoilt scenery, much of it in protected nature reserves. Its landscape is quilted in myriad shades, from emerald beech forest to golden fields of rapeseed and sunflowers, but it's also rather flat, windswept and perhaps even a bit melancholic.

This is a region shaped by water – not only by the rippling Oder, Havel and Spree Rivers that sinuously wend through it, but also by the thousands of ponds and lakes and the labyrinthine waterways connecting them. Water also characterises the Spreewald, where indigenous Sorbs keep alive their customs in island hamlets, and the Lower Oder Valley National Park, whose idyllic wetlands provide shelter for rare and endangered bird species. Like a fine wine, Brandenburg is best appreciated in sips, not gulps. It invites slowing down and exploring by bike, boat or on foot.

As the germ cell of Prussia, and thus modern Germany, Brandenburg is a land of great culture. Nowhere is this more apparent than in off-the-charts Potsdam, the 'German Versailles', with its wealth of parks, museums, stately palaces and the famous UFA film studios. Fine architecture awaits in the Rheinsberg palace and the Chorin monastery, while the Niederfinow ship-lift ranks squarely as one of the great technological monuments of the early 20th century.

HIGHLIGHTS

- **Parks & Palaces** Tackle all of Potsdam's treasures and be sure not to miss the exotic Chinese Teahouse (p147)

- **Watery Ramblings** Take a float in the slow lane while kayaking around the idyllic waterways of the Spreewald Biosphere Reserve (p156)

- **Techno Wonders** Rub your eyes in disbelief while watching entire barges being hoisted 60m in the air at the massive ship-lift (p164) in Niederfinow

- **Music** Feast your ears on classical music during a summer concert at the romantically ruined medieval Chorin monastery (p163)

- **History of Terror** Try to grasp the horrors of Nazi Germany while touring what's left of the Sachsenhausen concentration camp (p160) at Oranienburg

- POPULATION: 2.58 MILLION
- AREA: 24,479 SQ KM

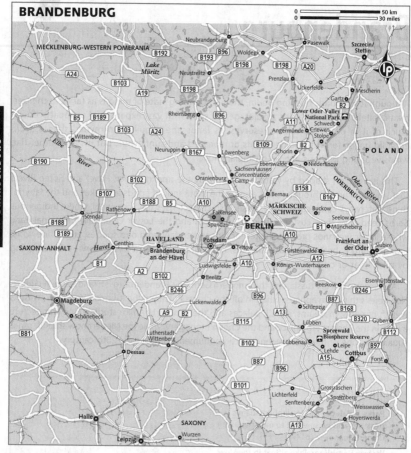

BRANDENBURG

Information

The excellent website maintained by **Tourismus Marketing Brandenburg** (☎ 0331-200 4747; www .brandenburg-tourism.com) should satisfy all your pre-trip planning needs and also has a room-booking function.

Getting Around

The Brandenburg-Berlin Ticket entitles you and up to four accompanying passengers (or one or both parents or grandparents plus all their children or grandchildren up to 14 years) to one day of travel anywhere within Berlin and Brandenburg on local and regional public transport from 9am to 3am the following day (midnight to 3am on weekends). It is valid on RE, IRE, RB and S-Bahn trains as well as

buses, U-Bahn and trams. The ticket costs €24 if bought online at www.bahn.de or at station vending machines, and €26 if bought from a Reisezentrum ticket agent. For timetable information, see www.vbb-online.de.

POTSDAM & HAVELLAND

The prime attraction of Brandenburg state and the most popular day trip from Berlin, Potsdam is a mere 24km southwest of the capital's city centre and easily accessible by S-Bahn. If time allows, venture another 36km west to the historic city of Brandenburg an der Havel, the centre of the watery Havelland region. Picturesque and less tourist-saturated than Potsdam, it's a perfect introduction to the state for which it's named.

POTSDAM

☎ 0331 / pop 131,000

Potsdam, on the Havel River just southwest of Greater Berlin, is the capital and crown jewel of the state of Brandenburg. The captivating architecture of this former Prussian royal seat and the elegant air of history that still hangs over its parks and gardens prove an intoxicating cocktail to the millions of visitors who descend upon the town each year. A visit here is essential if you're spending any time in the region at all. All this splendour didn't go unnoticed by Unesco, which gave World Heritage site status to the entire city in 1990.

No single individual shaped Potsdam more than King Friedrich II (Frederick the Great), the visionary behind many of Sanssouci's fabulous palaces and parks. Although WWII bombing squadrons largely reduced the historic town centre to rubble, the palaces escaped with nary a shrapnel wound.

To emphasise their victory over the German military machine, the Allies chose Schloss Cecilienhof for the Potsdam Conference of August 1945, which set the stage for the division of Berlin and Germany into occupation zones.

The suburb of Babelsberg is the site of a historic – and now once again functioning – film studio (with a less than historic theme park).

Orientation

Potsdam Hauptbahnhof (central train station) is just southeast of the Altstadt, across the Havel River. Park Sanssouci is west of the historic centre, while the Neuer Garten with Schloss Cecilienhof is north. Babelsberg is quite a bit east of here.

Information

BOOKSHOPS

Alexander-von-Humboldt Buchhandlung (☎ 200 460; Am Kanal 47) Good general bookstore.

Das Internationale Buch (☎ 291 496; cnr Friedrich-Ebert-Strasse & Brandenburger Strasse) Great selection of maps and travel books.

DISCOUNT CARDS

Potsdam Card (€11.50) Three consecutive days of unlimited public transport plus one year of discounts to sights,

restaurants and events. It is sold at the tourist office, hotels and all participating venues.

EMERGENCY

Emergency medical service (☎ 01805-304 505)
Fire & ambulance (☎ 112)
Police (☎ 110)

INTERNET ACCESS

Staudenhof (☎ 0176-5215 8276; Am Alten Markt 10; per hr €1.50; ☼ 9am-midnight or later) Enter from the pedestrian zone behind the building.

MEDICAL SERVICES

Klinikum Ernst-von-Bergmann (☎ 2410; Charlottenstrasse 72)

MONEY

Commerzbank (☎ 281 90; Lindenstrasse 45)
Dresdner Bank (☎ 287 8200; Yorckstrasse 28)
Eurochange (☎ 280 4033; Brandenburger Strasse 29)

POST

Main post office (cnr Am Kanal & Platz der Einheit)

TOURIST INFORMATION

Potsdam tourist office (☎ 275 580; www.potsdam tourismus.de; Brandenburger Strasse 3; ☼ 9.30am-6pm Mon-Fri, to 4pm Sat & Sun Apr-Oct, 10am-6pm Mon-Fri, 9.30am-2pm Sat & Sun Nov-Mar)

Sanssouci Besucherzentrum (☎ 969 4202; www .spsg.de; Zur Historischen Windmühle; ☼ 8.30am-5pm Mar-Oct, 9am-4pm Nov-Feb)

Sights

PARK SANSSOUCI

Park Sanssouci is the oldest and most splendid of Potsdam's many gardens, a vast landscaped expanse of mature trees, rare plants and magnificent palaces. Its trump card is Schloss Sanssouci, Frederick the Great's favourite retreat, a place where he could be 'sans souci' (without cares). In the 19th century, Friedrich Wilhelm IV also left his mark on the park.

The park is open from dawn till dusk year-round. Admission is free, but there are machines by the entrance where you can make a voluntary donation of €2. The palaces and outbuildings all have different hours and admission prices. Most are closed on Monday and some of the lesser sights open only at weekends and holidays outside the main season. A two-day pass including all sights in the park costs €15/10 adult/concession.

BRANDENBURG

The palaces are fairly well spaced – it's almost 2km between the Neues Palais (New Palace) and Schloss Sanssouci. Take your sweet time wandering along the park's meandering paths, away from the tourist hubs, to discover your personal favourite spot. Free maps are available at the tourist office. Cycling is officially permitted along Ökonomieweg and Maulbeerallee, which is also the route followed by bus 695 (see p153).

Schloss Sanssouci & Around

The biggest stunner, and what everyone comes to see, is **Schloss Sanssouci** (☎ 969 4190; mandatory tour adult/concession €8/5; ☼ 9am-5pm Tue-Sun Apr-Oct, to 4pm Nov-Mar), the celebrated rococo palace designed by Georg Wenzeslaus von Knobelsdorff in 1747. Only 2000 visitors a day are allowed entry (a rule laid down by Unesco), and the timed tickets sometimes sell out by noon – arrive early, preferably at opening, and avoid weekends and holidays. You can only take the tour leaving at the time printed on your ticket. The only way to guarantee entry is by joining the guided tours operated by the tourist office (see Tours, p152).

The 40-minute tour (in German, but excellent English-language pamphlets are available) takes in all 12 rooms of this intimate palace. The exquisite circular **Bibliothek** (library), with its cedar panelling and gilded sunburst ceiling, is undoubtedly a highlight, but unfortunately you're only allowed to peak through the glass door. Other favourites include the **Konzertsaal** (Concert Room), playfully decorated with vines, grapes, seashells and even a cobweb where three spiders frolic. The most elegant room is the domed **Marmorhalle** (Marble Hall), a symphony in white Carrara marble.

An expansion instigated by Friedrich Wilhelm IV added the **Damenflügel** (Ladies' Wing; adult/concession €2/1.50; ☼ 10am-5pm Tue-Sun mid-May–mid-Oct), where the ladies-in-waiting had their apartments. In the eastern wing is the **Schlossküche** (palace kitchen; adult/concession €2/1.50; ☼ 10am-5pm Tue-Sun Apr-Oct), whose *pièce de résistance* is a giant, wood-fired 'cooking machine'.

As you exit the palace, don't be fooled by the **Ruinenberg**, a pile of classical 'ruins' looming in the distance: they're merely a folly conceived by Frederick the Great.

East of the Schloss, the **Bildergalerie** (Picture Gallery; ☎ 969 4181; adult/concession €2/1.50; ☼ 10am-5pm Tue-Sun mid-May–mid-Oct), completed in 1763, is considered Germany's first purpose-built art museum. Inside is a feast of baroque paintings, including works by Rubens, Caravaggio and van Dyck.

West of the Schloss, the **Neue Kammern** (New Chambers; ☎ 969 4206; adult/concession without tour €2.50/1.50, with tour €3/2.50; ☼ 10am-5pm Tue-Sun mid-May–mid-Oct, Sat & Sun Apr–mid-May & mid-Oct–end Oct) is a former orangery and guesthouse, whose fancy interior includes the festive *Ovidsaal*, a grand ballroom with a patterned marble floor surrounded by gilded reliefs.

There are subtropical plants thriving west of here in the **Sizilianischer Garten** (Sicilian Garden).

Orangerieschloss & Around

Maulbeerallee is the only road cutting straight through Park Sanssouci. Along its northern side are a number of buildings, starting in the east with the **Historische Mühle** (☎ 550 6851; adult/concession €2/1; ☼ 10am-6pm daily Apr-Oct, 10am-4pm Sat & Sun Nov & Jan-Mar), a functioning replica of an 18th-century windmill that actually predated Schloss Sanssouci by six years. Admission buys you close-ups of the enormous grinding mechanism and a look at still-evolving exhibits.

The dominant building in this corner of the park is the elegantly ageing **Orangerieschloss** (Orangery Palace; ☎ 969 4280; mandatory tour adult/concession €3/2.50; ☼ 10am-5pm Tue-Sun mid-May–mid-Oct),a Renaissance-style palace conceived by Italophile Friedrich Wilhelm IV in 1864. At 300m long, it is grandiose in dimension but hardly the most interesting park structure. In the central section is the **Raphaelsaal**, with 19th-century copies of the painter's masterpieces, and a tower that can be climbed (€2) in summer for views over the Neues Palais and the park. The west wing is used to store sensitive plants in winter.

From the Orangery, a tree-lined path forms a visual axis to the rococo **Belvedere auf dem Klausberg** (☎ 969 4282; admission €2; ☼ 10am-5pm Sat & Sun Apr-Oct), a temple-like pavilion whose sumptuous interior was beautifully restored following war damage. There are nice views from the top.

Along the way, you'll meander past the fantastical **Drachenhaus** (Dragon House, 1770), a teensy Chinese palace inspired by the Ta-Ho pagoda in Canton and decorated with 16 dragons. It now houses a pleasant café-restaurant (p153).

POTSDAM

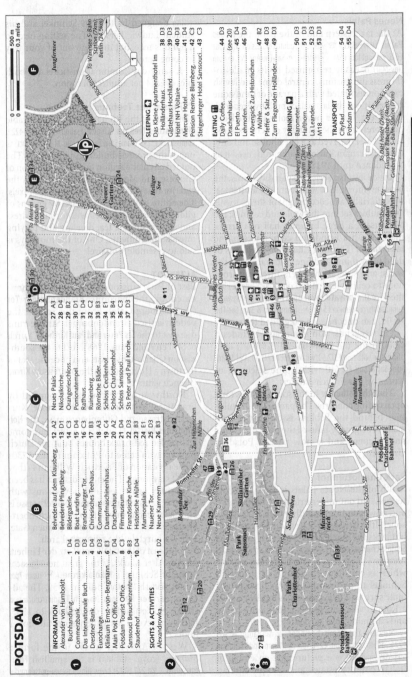

INFORMATION

Alexander von Humboldt	
Buchhandlung	1 D4
Commerzbank	2 D3
Das Internationale Buch	3 D3
Dresdner Bank	4 D4
Eurochange	5 D3
Klinikum Ernst-von-Bergmann	6 E3
Main Post Office	7 D4
Potsdam Tourist Office	8 C3
Sanssouci Besucherzentrum	9 B3
Staudenhof	10 D4

SIGHTS & ACTIVITIES

Alexandrowka	11 D2
Belvedere auf dem Klausberg	12 A2
Belvedere Pfingstberg	13 D1
Bildergalerie	14 C2
Boat Landing	15 D4
Brandenburger Tor	16 C3
Chinesisches Teehaus	17 B3
Communs	18 A3
Dampfmaschinenhaus	19 C4
Drachenhaus	20 A2
Filmmuseum	21 D4
Französische Kirche	22 D3
Historische Mühle	23 B3
Marmorpalais	24 E1
Nauener Tor	25 D3
Neue Kammern	26 B3
Neues Palais	27 A3
Nikolaikirche	28 D4
Orangerieschloss	29 B2
Pomonatempel	30 D1
Rathaus	31 D4
Ruinenberg	32 C2
Römische Bäder	33 B3
Schloss Cecilienhof	34 E1
Schloss Charlottenhof	35 B4
Schloss Sanssouci	36 C3
Sts Peter und Paul Kirche	37 D3

BRANDENBURG

Neues Palais

At the far western end of the park, the **Neues Palais** (New Palace; ☎ 969 4361; adult/concession with tour €6/5, without tour €5/4; ☒ 9am-5pm Sat-Thu Apr-Oct, to 4pm Nov-Mar) is easily recognised by its made-to-impress dimensions, central dome and lavish exterior decorated with a parade of sandstone figures. It was the last palace built by Frederick the Great, but he never really camped out here, preferring the intimacy of Schloss Sanssouci. Later it served as a guesthouse and only the last German Kaiser, Wilhelm II, used it as a residence until 1918.

Inside awaits a series of splendid rooms, the most memorable of which are the **Grottensaal** (Grotto Hall), a rococo delight of shells, fossils and baubles set into the walls and ceilings; the **Marmorsaal**, a large banquet hall of Carrara marble with a wonderful ceiling fresco; the **Jagdkammer** (Hunting Chamber), with lots of dead furry things and fine gold tracery on the walls; and several chambers fitted out from floor to ceiling in rich red damask. Frederick the Great's **private royal apartments** (Königswohnung; adult/concession €5/4; ☒ 11am, 1pm & 3pm Sat-Thu Apr-Oct) can only be seen on guided tours.

On weekends, admission also includes a peak inside the **Pesne-Galerie** (gallery only adult/concession with tour €3/2.50, without tour €2/1.50; ☒ 10am-5pm Sat & Sun Apr-Oct) with a fine selection of works by this French painter.

The **Schlosstheater** in the south wing is only open during concerts. The pair of lavish buildings behind the Schloss is called the **Communs**. It originally housed the palace servants and kitchens and is now part of Potsdam University.

Park Charlottenhof

South of the Neues Palais is Park Charlottenhof, laid out under Friedrich Wilhelm IV and now blending smoothly with Park Sanssouci. It's considerably less tourist-saturated but lacks the blockbuster sights. Its anchor is **Schloss Charlottenhof** (☎ 969 4228; mandatory tour adult/concession €4/3; ☒ 10am-5pm Tue-Sun mid-May–mid-Oct), which is considered one of Karl Friedrich Schinkel's finest works, although we're not quite sure why. The palace was modelled after a Roman villa and sports a fountain terrace and charming rose garden.

Nearby, the **Römische Bäder** (Roman Baths; ☎ 969 4224; adult/concession €2/1.50; ☒ 10am-5pm Tue-Sun mid-May–mid-Oct) is a picturesque ensemble of Italian country estates and antique Roman villas designed in 1840 by Schinkel and his student Ludwig Persius. The setting next to a pond is nice, but don't go out of your way to come here.

A same-day combination ticket for both sites is €5/4 per adult/concession.

Chinesisches Teehaus

Northeast of the Roman Baths, the adorable **Chinesisches Teehaus** (Chinese Teahouse; ☎ 969 4222; admission €1; ☒ 10am-5pm Tue-Sun mid-May–mid-Oct) is one of the prettiest buildings in the park. The domed circular pavilion houses a collection of Chinese and Meissen porcelain, but it's the exterior that'll have you burning up the pixels. The entire building is encircled by groups of gilded sandstone figures with oriental dress and shown sipping tea, dancing and playing musical instruments. One of the monkeys is said to resemble Voltaire!

ALTSTADT

East of Park Sanssouci, Luisenplatz is dominated by the baroque **Brandenburger Tor** (Brandenburg Gate). From this square, the pedestrianised Brandenburger Strasse runs due east to the **Sts Peter und Paul Kirche** (Church of Sts Peter and Paul, 1868). Just to the southeast on Charlottenstrasse, and once the seat of the town's Huguenots, is the **Französische Kirche** (French Church, 1753).

Northwest of the churches, bounded by Friedrich-Ebert-Strasse, Hebbelstrasse, Kurfürstenstrasse and Gutenbergstrasse, the **Holländisches Viertel** (Dutch Quarter) has some 134 gabled red-brick houses built for Dutch workers who came to Potsdam in the 1730s at the invitation of Friedrich Wilhelm I (they didn't stay long). The entire district has been beautifully gentrified and now brims with galleries, cafés and restaurants; Mittelstrasse is especially scenic. Further up Friedrich-Ebert-Strasse is the fanciful **Nauener Tor** (Nauen Gate, 1755), a fairytale-like triumphal arch.

Southeast of the GDR-era Platz der Einheit, on Am Alter Markt, is the great neoclassical dome of Schinkel's **Nikolaikirche** (☒ 10am-7pm May-Oct, shorter hr Nov-Apr), built in 1850. The adjacent former **Rathaus** (town hall; adult/concession €3/1.50; ☒ 2-6pm Tue-Sun), dating back to 1753, harbours several art galleries on the upper floors.

West of Am Alter Markt in the former *Marstall* (royal stables) is the smallish **Filmmuseum** (☎ 271 8112; www.filmmuseum-potsdam.de;

Breite Strasse; adult/concession €3.50/2.50, film €4.50/3.50; ✆ 10am-6pm) with a permanent exhibit on the history of the UFA and DEFA (the GDR film company) studios in Babelsberg. The cinema shows historic flicks.

Further west is the curious **Dampfmaschinenhaus** (Pump House; ☎ 969 4248; cnr Breite Strasse & Zeppelinstrasse; mandatory tour adult/concession €2/1.50; ✆ 10am-5pm Sat & Sun mid-May–mid-Oct), looking very much like a mosque, but in reality housing the former palace waterworks.

NEUER GARTEN

The winding lakeside Neuer Garten (New Garden), laid out in natural English style on the western shore of the Heiliger See, is another fine park in which to relax. Right on the lake, the neoclassical **Marmorpalais** (Marble Palace; ☎ 969 4246; adult/concession with tour €5/4, without tour €4/3; ✆ 10am-5pm Tue-Sun Apr-Oct, 10am-4pm Sat & Sun Nov-Mar), built in 1792 by Carl Gotthard Langhans (he of Berlin's Brandenburg Gate fame) for Friedrich Wilhelm II, has recently been carefully restored. Though not quite as fancy as Schloss Sanssouci, the interior is still stunning with its grand central staircase, marble fireplaces, stucco ceilings and collection of Wedgwood porcelain. The most fanciful room is the upstairs **Orientalisches Kabinett**, which looks like a Turkish tent.

In the northern park, **Schloss Cecilienhof** (☎ 969 4244; adult/concession with tour €5/4, without tour €4/3; ✆ 9am-5pm Tue-Sun Apr-Oct, to 4pm Nov-Mar) was completed in 1917 as the last Hohenzollern palace ever built. Looking very much like an English country manor, it was the residence of crown prince Wilhelm and his wife Cecilie. The couple's **royal apartments** (adult/concession €3/2.50; ✆ 11am, 1pm & 3pm Tue-Sun) can only be seen on a guided tour, but the palace is really more famous for being the site of the 1945 Potsdam Conference where Stalin, Truman and Churchill hammered out the post-war fate of Germany. The conference room with its giant round table looks as though the delegates have just left. You're free to explore on your own, but the 30-minute tours, offered in several languages, are excellent. Bus 692 makes it up here.

A same-day combination ticket for Cecilienhof and the Marmorpalais costs €6/5.

ALEXANDROWKA & PFINGSTBERG

A short walk north of the Altstadt is Potsdam's most unusual neighbourhood, the Russian colony **Alexandrowka** (www.alexandrowka .de; Am Schragen). Its 13 wooden houses were built in 1826–27 by Friedrich Wilhelm III for the Russian singers of a military choir that performed for the king. Four of the families living in the colony are descendants of the original settlers. Take tram 92 or 95 to Reiterweg/ Alleestrasse or Am Schragen.

For the best view over Potsdam and surrounds, head uphill to the beautifully restored **Belvedere Pfingstberg** (☎ 270 1972; adult/child/student €3.50/1.50/2.50; ✆ 10am-8pm Jun-Aug, 10am-6pm Apr, May & Sep, 10am-4pm Oct, 10am-4pm Sat & Sun Mar & Nov). This elegant Renaissance-style summer palace was commissioned by Friedrich Wilhelm IV but not completed until 1863, two years after the king's death. A series of spiralling wrought-iron staircases lead up to the towers for spectacular 360-degree views. On the ground floor is a small exhibit chronicling the amazing restoration process this nearly dilapidated building recently went through. Also up here is the 1801 **Pomonatempel** (☎ 270 1972; admission free; ✆ 3-6pm Sat & Sun mid-Apr–Oct), the first of Schinkel's many buildings ever to be completed.

BABELSBERG

The eastern suburb of Babelsberg is best known as the home of UFA, Germany's one-time response to Hollywood. Shooting began in 1912 but the studio had its heyday in the 1920s, when such silent-movie epics as Fritz Lang's *Metropolis* (see boxed text, p152) were shot, along with some early Greta Garbo films.

Cameras are rolling again in Babelsberg, but mostly it's restyled itself as the **Filmpark Babelsberg** (☎ 721 2750; www.filmpark.de; enter on Grossbeerenstrasse; adult/child 4-14/concession €17/12.50/15.50; ✆ 10am-6pm mid-Apr–Oct). It's a movie theme park complete with live shows, including a rather impressive stunt show, and a few poky rides. During the studio tour, you'll be whisked around the back lot for a peek at film sets and the prop and costume departments. To get there, take the S1 to Babelsberg station and then bus 690 to 'Filmpark'.

Park Babelsberg, yet another great Potsdam garden, is where you'll find the Schinkel-designed neo-Gothic **Schloss Babelsberg** (☎ 969 4250; adult/concession with tour €4/3.50, without tour €3/2.50; ✆ 10am-5pm Tue-Sun late Jun-Oct) and the **Flatowturm** (☎ 969 4249; admission €2; ✆ 10am-5pm Tue-Sun Apr-late Jun, Sat & Sun late Jun-Oct), modelled after a medieval town gate in Frankfurt am Main.

BRANDENBURG

METROPOLIS

Potsdam isn't readily associated with class warfare, but it was here, at the UFA studios, that Fritz Lang shot much of his allegorical melodrama *Metropolis* (1927), which deals with exactly that. The film depicts a society literally split in two, with the Thinkers living in idle luxury above ground and the Workers toiling in subterranean caverns to serve the terrible Moloch machine. Threatened by nonviolent protest advocated by the saintly Maria, the Thinkers dispatch a robot clone of her to provoke riots. The sheer scale of the film was unprecedented (Lang hired 10,000 extras), and its relevance has endured, not just in its message of class cooperation but also in its themes of revolution, technology and voyeurism. Some elements were far ahead of their time – the robot Futura is a clear predecessor of the Terminator!

Tours

The Potsdam tourist office (see Information, p147) runs the 3½-hour **Potsdam Sanssouci Tour** (€26; 🕑 11am Tue-Sun Apr-Oct, Fri-Sun Nov-Mar), which guarantees admission to Schloss Sanssouci, and the two-hour **Altstadt Tour** (adult/concession €8/6; 🕑 3pm daily Jan-Sep). Tours are in English and German and tickets are available at the tourist office.

Weisse Flotte Potsdam (☎ 275 9210; www.schiffahrt-in-potsdam.de; Lange Brücke 6; 🕑 Apr-Oct) operates dozens of boat tours on the Havel and the lakes around Potsdam, including a lovely trip out to Wannsee and Pfaueninsel (€9 return). Its sister company **Havel Dampfschifffahrt** (☎ 275 9210; Lange Brücke 6; 🕑 Apr-Oct) runs nostalgic steamboat tours around the same areas. Boats depart from Lange Brücke (bridge), right below the Mercure Hotel.

Festivals & Events

Potsdam's biggest annual events include the **Tulip Festival** in the Dutch Quarter around 20 April, the **Musikfestspiele Potsdam Sanssouci** (www.musikfestspiele-potsdam.de) in early June and the **Bachtage** (www.bachtage-potsdam.de) in August/September (see boxed text, p154).

Sleeping

Most people visit Potsdam on a day trip from Berlin, but only by spending the night can you savour the town's quiet majesty without the tour bus crowds. The tourist office books private rooms and hotels in person, by phone (☎ 275 580) or online (www.postdam-tourismus.de).

DJH hostel (☎ 581 3100; www.jh-potsdam.de; Schulstrasse 9; dm under/over 26yr €21/24; P ✗ 🖳) Potsdam's new hostel is a snazzy 152-bed property with a 12-bed dorm for people under 26 and smaller rooms, all with shower and toilet. It's around the corner from S-Bahn station Babelsberg.

Gästehaus Hochlland (☎ 270 0835; www.hochlland.de; Gutenbergstrasse 78; per person €19.50, linen €5) This is a smaller and more central budget alternative to the hostel, with dorm-style accommodation and guest kitchens in two buildings on the edge of the Dutch Quarter.

Pension Remise Blumberg (☎ 280 3231; www.pension-blumberg.de; Weinbergstrasse 26; s/d €55/86; P ✗) Close to Park Sanssouci, this backyard pension may be petite but the rooms, all with kitchenette, are not. Bike hire is available, and the leafy courtyard is perfect for sipping your morning coffee.

Mercure Hotel (☎ 2722; www.mercure.com; Lange Brücke; s €62-120, d €77-127; P ✗ ✗ 🖳) From the outside it's undeniably an ugly GDR-era skyscraper, but all style concerns will likely evaporate the moment you enter this fully renovated property near the Hauptbahnhof and right by the little harbour.

Das Kleine Apartmenthotel im Holländerhaus (☎ 279 110; www.hollaenderhaus.potsdam.de; Kurfürstenstrasse 15; apt €80-120, ste €90-180; P) This gem combines the charm of a historic Dutch Quarter building with an edgy, creative design scheme. Wood, steel and lots of colour give the good-sized apartments with kitchens a contemporary look. A small gym, sauna and leafy courtyard are good unwinding spots.

Steigenberger Hotel Sanssouci (☎ 909 10; www.potsdam.steigenberger.de; Allee nach Sanssouci 1; s €94-137, d €108-160; P ✗ ✗) Between the Brandenburger Tor and the Park Sanssouci gate, this high-class property seeks to evoke the glamour of 1940s Hollywood. The 133 rooms are decked out in soothing greens and earth tones and sprinkled with rattan. The spa offers some exotic treatments: hot chocolate massage, anyone?

Eating

El Puerto (☎ 275 9225; Lange Brücke; tapas from €3.20; 🕑 11am-midnight Apr-Oct, 11am-5pm Tue-Sat Nov-Mar)

THE AUTHOR'S CHOICE

Hotel NH Voltaire (☎ 231 70; www.nh
-hoteles.com; Friedrich-Ebert-Strasse 88; s/d from
€80/110; P ✗) Modern, quiet and run
with panache, this delightful hotel opposite the Dutch Quarter gets you first-class
treatment at surprisingly moderate prices.
The 143 rooms spread out across a historic
Palais (preferable) and a modern annex.
Local students collaborated with such
famous German artists as Elvira Bach
to create the cheerful canvasses sprinkled throughout. The wellness area with
rooftop terrace makes for a lovely unwinding oasis.

It's fiesta time at this restaurant right in the
newly revamped Potsdam harbour. Sit amid
soaring palm trees, sangria in hand, tapas
on the table, and watch the boats bopping
in the breeze.

Daily Coffee (☎ 201 1979; Friedrich-Ebert-Strasse 31;
mains €4-10; ☷ 9am-10.30pm or later) Right by the
frilly Nauener Tor, this friendly café presents
you with a global menu ranging from Thai
soups to wholesome wraps, crispy nachos to
Chinese stir-fry. Snag an outdoor table for
primo people-watching.

Pfeffer & Salz (☎ 200 2777; Brandenburger Strasse
46; pizza & pasta €5-11) In this street of tourist
traps, this little Italian eatery stands out for
its authenticity. All noodles are homemade
daily, the antipasto counter is mouthwater-
ing and the pizza comes crispy hot from the
wood oven.

Meierei Potsdam (☎ 704 3211; Im Neuer Garten 10;
mains €5-12; ☷ 10am-10pm) Just north of Schloss
Cecilienhof, this brewpub is especially lovely
in summer when you can count the boats sailing on the Jungfernsee from your beer-garden
table. The hearty dishes are a perfect match for
the delicious suds brewed on the premises.

Zum Fliegenden Holländer (☎ 275 030; Benkertstrasse 5; mains €8-16, 2-course weekday lunch €8.50;
☷ 10am-10pm) The name is apropos for this
Dutch Quarter restaurant, with its traditional
blue-and-white Delft tiles, wood-burning
fireplace and historic etchings. The kitchen
prefers no-nonsense German fare to culinary
flights of fancy.

Lehmofen (☎ 280 1712; Dortusstrasse 62; mains €10-
17) In a new location, this smart Turkish place
is a world away from your average doner shop,

serving dishes from its eponymous clay oven.
Service can be slow, though. Enter through
the Stadtpalais or the Karstadt department
store.

Recommended eateries in Park Sanssouci:
Mövenpick Zur Historischen Mühle (☎ 281 493;
Zur Historischen Mühle 2; mains €8-15; ☷ 8am-midnight)
International cuisine from breakfast to dinner with huge
beer garden and children's playground.
Drachenhaus (☎ 505 3808; Maulbeerallee; mains
€8.50-14; ☷ 11am-7pm Mar-Oct, 11am-6pm Tue-Sun
Nov-Feb) Coffee, cake and regional cuisine.

Drinking

Hafthorn (☎ 280 0820; Friedrich-Ebert-Strasse 90) This
low-key pub is great for quaffing a cold one
in the funky beer garden or amid masklike
sconces wrought from sheet metal. The giant
burgers (€4) are a great hangover antidote.

M18 (☎ 280 5111; Mittelstrasse 18) This is a serious booze parlour with a bewildering menu of
brain erasers – beer to whiskey, burgundy to
tequila. In summer, the leafy backyard is the
place to be. Salads and grilled meats provide
sustenance.

Barometer (☎ 270 2880; Gutenbergstrasse 103) This
vaulted cellar lounge is one for grown-ups
willing to peel off the bills for serious cocktails. Access is via the back courtyard.

La Leander (☎ 270 6576; Benkertstrasse 1) The rainbow flags fly proudly over this low-key pub
in the Dutch Quarter that's a good place for
plugging into the local lesbigay scene.

Getting There & Away

S-Bahn line S7 links central Berlin with
Potsdam Hauptbahnhof about every 10
minutes. Regional (RB/RE) trains leaving
from Berlin-Hauptbahnhof, Berlin-Zoo and
Berlin-Charlottenburg are faster; some also
stop at Potsdam-Charlottenhof and Potsdam-
Sanssouci, which are closer to Park Sanssouci
than Hauptbahnhof. There's also an hourly
RB train to Berlin-Schönefeld airport. Berlin
transit passes must cover Zones A, B and C
(€2.60) to be valid for the trip to Potsdam.

Drivers coming from Berlin should take the
A100 to the A115.

Getting Around

Buses and trams operate throughout Potsdam.
The most useful line is bus 695, which connects the Hauptbahnhof with the Altstadt
and Park Sanssouci. Tickets costs €1.60 and
a day pass €3.70.

For bike hire, try **CityRad** (☎ 0177-825 4746; per day €11; ☻ 9am-7pm Mon-Fri, to 8pm Sat & Sun mid-Apr–mid-Oct) outside the Bahnhofspassagen at Potsdam Hauptbahnhof (exit Babelsberger Strasse). A larger outfit is **Potsdam per Pedales** (☎ 748 0057; per day €8-12), which is headquartered at the Griebnitzsee S-Bahn station (open 9am to 6.30pm, Easter to October) and also has offices at Potsdam Hauptbahnhof and Wannsee stations (both open 9.30am to 7pm, May to September).

For a taxi, ring ☎ 292 929 or ☎ 0800-292 9298.

BRANDENBURG AN DER HAVEL
☎ 03381 / pop 75,000

About 50km west of Berlin, Brandenburg may not be Venice but it's still a city shaped by water. Set amid a pastoral landscape of lakes, rivers and canals perfect for boating, it has a historic centre with some fine examples of northern German red-brick architecture. First settled by Slavs in the 6th century, Brandenburg was a bishopric in the early Middle Ages and a margravial capital until the 15th century. Darker times arrived when the Nazis picked the town to carry out their forced euthanasia programme for the mentally disabled, killing tens of thousands. Wartime bombing and GDR neglect left their scars, but these are gradually healing, making Brandenburg once again an attractive day trip from Berlin or Potsdam.

Orientation

Brandenburg is split into three sections by the Havel River, the Beetzsee and their various canals. The Neustadt occupies an island in the centre and is connected to the Altstadt by the Jahrtausendbrücke (Millennium Bridge), while the Dominsel is north of the Neustadt.

The train station is about 1km south of the central Neustädtischer Markt.

Information

Dresdner Bank (Neustädtischer Markt 10) Has an ATM.
Post office (St Annenstrasse 30-36)
Tourist information (☎ 585 858; www.stadt -brandenburg.de; Steinstrasse 66/67; ☻ 9am-7pm Mon-Fri year-round, 10am-3pm Sat & Sun May-Sep, 10am-2pm Sat & Sun Oct-Apr)

Sights & Activities

An exploration of Brandenburg might start at the mostly Gothic **Dom St Peter und Paul** (Cathedral of Sts Peter & Paul; ☎ 211 2221; Burghof 9; ☻ 10am-4pm Mon-Fri, to 5pm Sat, 11am-5pm Sun) on Dominsel. Treasures include a carved 14th-century Bohemian altar in the south transept, the vaulted and painted Bunte Kapelle (Colourful Chapel), and a fantastic baroque organ (1723). The **Dommuseum** (☎ 200 325; adult/concession €3/2; ☻ 10am-4pm Mon-Fri, to 5pm Sat, 11am-5pm Sun) has outstanding medieval vestments and a so-called *Hungertuch* (hunger blanket), with embroidered medallions depicting the life of Jesus.

South of here, across Mühlendamm, the octagonal **Mühlentorturm** (Mill Gate Tower) marked the border between Dominsel and Neustadt in the days when they were separate towns. A former prison, it is one of four surviving towers that were once part of the medieval fortifications. Just beyond are the Neustädtischer Markt and the **Katharinenkirche** (☻ 10am-5pm Mon-Sat), a vast Gothic brick church with a lavishly detailed and decorated façade. See if you can spot your favourite biblical characters on the 'Meadow of Heaven' painted ceiling. South of here, a new archaeological museum is taking shape in the once-ruined **Paulikloster** (Monastery of St Paul; ask

---

BACH-ING MAD

The state of Brandenburg has links with many influential German composers, but few can compete with Johann Sebastian Bach – even the most blinkered techno-head has probably heard of the *Brandenburg Concertos*! These six *concerti grossi* were composed in 1721 for Margrave Christian Ludwig of Brandenburg, who was then based (a tad ironically) at Köthen in Saxony-Anhalt.

Some years later, in 1747, Frederick the Great managed to lure Bach to Potsdam, where the great composer wrote *The Musical Offering* on a theme proposed by the king himself. Since then Bach's place in Brandenburg history has been assured, but it's only in recent times that his legacy has been fully celebrated. In 2000 the first Potsdamer Bachtage (Bach Days) was inaugurated, comprising a two-week festival of concerts, workshops and readings dedicated to making the master's work accessible to modern audiences.

at tourist office for more details), while the **Steintorturm** (cnr Steinstrasse & Neustädtische Heidestrasse; adult/concession €3/1; ☺ 9am-5pm Tue-Fri, 10am-5pm Sat & Sun) has a small exhibit on Havel shipping and can be climbed for nice city views.

To reach the Altstadt, follow the pedestrianised Hauptstrasse to the Jahrtausendbrücke. A little further on, the **Stadtmuseum im Frey-Haus** (☎ 522 048; Ritterstrasse 96; adult/concession €3/1; ☺ 9am-5pm Tue-Fri, 10am-5pm Sat & Sun) is a local history museum with much emphasis on the Ernst Paul Lehmann factory, makers of cute mechanical toys and pottery. Bearing right, you'll come to the **Altstädtisches Rathaus**, a red-brick gem-box fronted by a lanky statue of the mythological figure Roland, a symbol of justice and integrity.

Outside the city centre, the **Landesklinik Brandenburg** (☎ 782 202; Haus 23, Anton-Saefkow-Allee 2; admission free; ☺ 10am-5pm Tue & Thu) harbours a fascinating if sickening exhibit on Nazi psychiatric practices and the cruel experiments performed on mentally disabled patients.

In warm weather, Brandenburg's charms are best appreciated from the water. A number of outfitters rent canoes and kayaks, including Cafébar (right) and **Wasserwanderrastplatz Am Slawendorf** (☎ 0175-215 7774), both near the Jahrtausendbrücke. There's good **lake swimming** in the Freibad Grillendamm on the Kleiner Beetzsee off the northern Dominsel.

Tours

The tourist office rents out free audioguides (deposit required) for a self-guided English-language tour of the city's medieval churches.

Boat tours around the Havel lakes are operated by **Nordstern** (☎ 226 960; www.nordstern-reederei.de in German) and **Reederei Röding** (☎ 522 331; www.fgs-havelfee.de) and leave from Am Salzhof, just south of the Jahrtausendbrücke.

Sleeping

Backpacker Hostel Caasi (☎ 3290; www.caasi.de; Caasmannstrasse 7; dm €15-18, linen €5, s/d €30/50; P X ⌨) On the edge of town, this is a good option for shoestringers, even though many of the 250 rooms are filled with long-term guests. Facilities include a kitchen for self-caterers and a pub.

Pension Zum Birnbaum (☎ 527 500; www.pension-zum-birnbaum.de; Mittelstrasse 1; s/d from €31/48; P) A singing host, breakfast under a pear tree and handsomely furnished, if snug, rooms

recommend this little inn that places you close to the train station and the Neustadt.

Sorat Hotel Brandenburg (☎ 5970; www.sorat-hotels.com; Altstädtischer Markt 1; s €94-186, d €110-202; P X X) The top-notch Sorat has 88 bright, modern rooms in pretty surroundings right by the Rathaus. Rates include a champagne breakfast and sauna use; weekend rates are significantly lower.

Eating

Cafébar (☎ 229 048; Ritterstrasse 76; breakfast €3.60) The best place for coffee and homemade nut cake, this is a teensy kiosk right by the Jahrtausendbrücke with canalside beach chairs in summer.

Herzschlag (☎ 410 414; Grosse Münzenstrasse 17; tapas €4-7, mains €7-13; ☺ from 11.30am) Urban sophistication in sleepy Brandenburg? Look no further than this place, complete with artsy décor, lounge music, tasty cocktails and a broad menu featuring everything from tapas to fajitas to crocodile steaks.

An der Dominsel (☎ 224 535; Neustädtische Fischerstrasse 14; mains €8-14; ☺ 9.30am-10pm May-Sep, 11am-10pm Oct-Apr) The regional food – especially the fish dishes – is dependable here, but what you'll probably remember most are the fabulous Dom views across the canal. It's right by the Mühlentorturm.

Bismarck Terrassen (☎ 300 939; Bergstrasse 20; mains €8-16, two-course menus from €7.80) Discover your inner Prussian at this traditional restaurant whose proprietor may greet you in Bismarck costume and seat you in a room brimming with Iron Chancellor memorabilia. The kitsch quotient is undeniably there, but the Brandenburg food is authentic, delicious and plentiful.

For a quick fish snack (from €1.50), pop into one of the little **fishing shacks** (☺ usually to 6pm Mon-Fri, to noon Sat) operated by professional fisherfolk along Mühlendamm. In summer, they set up tables on floating pontoons.

Getting There & Around

Regional trains link Brandenburg twice hourly with all major stations in central Berlin, including Hauptbahnhof (€6, 50 minutes), and with Potsdam (€4.80, 30 minutes).

From the station, it's about a 10-minute walk via Geschwister-Scholl-Strasse and St-Annenstrasse-Strasse to the Neustädtischer Markt. Trams 6 and 9 will get you there as well. Free parking is available at the corner of Grillendamm and Krakauer Strasse, just north of the Dom.

SPREEWALD

With its lush meadows, idyllic forest and vast web of gently meandering waterways, the Spreewald is great for slowing down and communing with nature. About 80km southeast of Berlin, the region has been a Unesco Biosphere Reserve since 1991 and is famous for its pickled gherkins – over 40,000 tons are produced here every year! Lübben and Lübbenau, the main tourist towns, often drown beneath the weight of visitors vying for rides aboard a *Kahn* (shallow punt boat), once the only way of getting around in these parts. To truly appreciate the Spreewald's unique charms, hire your own canoe or kayak or get yourself onto a trail.

The Spreewald is also home base to large numbers of Germany's Sorbian minority (see boxed text, p158).

Getting There & Around

Frequent regional trains depart central Berlin (eg Hauptbahnhof) for Lübben (€8.40, 1¼ hours) and Lübbenau (€9.60, 1½ hours) en route to Cottbus. The towns are also linked by an easy 13km trail along the Spree. Bikes can be hired at the Lübben tourist office or from **Fahrradverleih Enrico Arndt** (☎ 872 910; Dammstrasse 10-12) in Lübbenau.

LÜBBEN

☎ 03546 / pop 15,000
Compared to Lübbenau, about 13km southeast, tidy Lübben is considerably less cutesy and feels more like a 'real' town. Activity centres on the Schloss and the adjacent harbour area, both about 1.5km east of the train station. Follow Bahnhofstrasse southeast, turn left on Logenstrasse and continue to Ernst-von-Houwald-Damm, where you'll also find the **tourist office** (☎ 3090; www.luebben.de; Hafen 1, Ernst-von-Houwald-Damm 15; ♥ 10am-6pm Apr-Oct, to 4pm Mon-Fri Nov-Mar). The Markt and Hauptstrasse are two blocks north.

Sights & Activities

The prettiest building in town is the compact **Schloss** (☎ 187 478; Ernst-von-Houwald-Damm 14; adult/concession €4/2; ♥ 10am-5pm Tue-Sun Apr-Oct, 10am-4pm Wed-Fri, 1-5pm Sat & Sun Nov-Mar), which contains a

progressively presented regional history museum. Behind it is the **Schlossinsel** (admission free), an artificial archipelago with gardens, a leafy maze, playgrounds, cafés and the harbour area where you can board punts for leisurely tours (from €7/4 adult/child). If you'd rather go at your own speed, rent a canoe or kayak from **Bootsverleih Gebauer** (☎ 7194; Lindenstrasse 18; per hr €7).

Sleeping

The tourist office can help you find private rooms from €13 per person.

DJH hostel (☎ 3046; www.jh-luebben.de; Zum Wendenfürsten 8; dm €14-19; P ✗) This 127-bed hostel is right on the Spree, about 3km south of the train station, and also has camp sites (€9.50, including breakfast).

Hotel Spreeufer (☎ 272 60; www.spreewaldhotel.de; Hinter der Mauer 4; d €50-90; P ✗) This friendly hotel has simple but adequate rooms and a central location by the bridge just south of Hauptstrasse.

Spreewaldhotel Stephanshof (☎ 272 10; www.spreewaldreisen.de; Lehnigksberger Weg 1; s €45-60, d €68-84; P ✗) About a 10-minute walk north of the centre, this modern riverside hotel has its own boat landing, a regional restaurant and bike rentals.

Eating

Ladencafé im alten Gärtchen (☎ 186 956; Ernst-von-Houwald-Strasse 6; mains €4-9) Lovingly decorated, this little cottage with a small beer garden out the back serves tasty Mediterranean fare and also has local crafts and handmade products for sale.

Bubak (☎ 186 144; Ernst-von-Houwald-Damm 9; mains €4-15; ♥ 11.30am-2.30pm & 5.30-10pm Mon-Fri, 11.30am-10pm Sat & Sun) Close to the Schloss, this characterful roadside restaurant was named for a local bogeyman and has weekly concerts starring its singing proprietor. The menu is a mix of typical Spreewald dishes and classic German food, all prepared creatively and using local products whenever possible.

Goldener Löwe (☎ 7309; Hauptstrasse 15; mains €6.50-11.50) For traditional Spreewald dishes, visit this suitably old-fashioned restaurant with its nice beer garden.

LÜBBENAU

☎ 03542 / pop 15,700
Lübbenau is more picturesque than Lübben but feels more like a tourist town, especially

in the harbour areas. The entire Altstadt is a forest of signs pointing to hotels, restaurants and other businesses, making navigating a snap. Near the church you'll find the **tourist office** (☎ 3668; www.spreewald-online.de; Ehm-Welk-Strasse 15; ☼ 9am-6pm Mon-Fri, to 4pm Sat Apr-Oct, 9am-4pm Mon-Fri Nov-Mar). The train and bus stations are on Poststrasse, about 600m south of the Altstadt.

Sights & Activities

Behind the tourist office, the **Haus für Mensch und Natur** (☎ 892 10; Schulstrasse 9; admission free; ☼ 10am-5pm Apr-Oct, 10am-4pm Mon-Fri Nov-Mar) has exhibits and information about the Spreewald Biosphere Reserve. If you're interested in the region's cultural history, visit the **Spreewald-Museum** (☎ 2472; Am Topfmarkt; adult/child/concession €3/1/2; ☼ 10am-6pm Tue-Sun Apr-mid-Oct, to 5pm mid-Oct-Mar) inside a historic brick building that's gone through stints as a courthouse, jail and town hall.

Several operators offer pretty much the same **punt boating** tours, including the popular two-hour trip to Lehde (€7), a completely protected village known as the 'Venice of the Spreewald'. Here you'll find the wonderful **Freilandmuseum** (☎ 2472; adult/child/concession €3/1/2; ☼ 10am-6pm Apr–mid-Sep, to 5pm mid-Sep–Oct), an open-air museum of traditional Sorbian houses and farm buildings. Lehde is also reached via an easy 30-minute trail.

The main embarkation points are the **Kleiner Hafen** (☎ 403 710; www.spreewald-web.de; Spreestrasse 10a), about 100m northeast of the tourist office, and the more workmanlike **Grosser Hafen** (☎ 2225; www.grosser-spreewaldhafen.de; Dammstrasse 77a), 300m southeast. Buy tickets at the embarkation points or from the captain. Active types can hire canoes and kayaks from several outfitters, including **Bootsverleih Francke** (☎ 2722; Dammstrasse 72), for about €4 per hour.

Sleeping & Eating

Check with the tourist office about the availability of private rooms (from €14) or simply walk about town and look for signs saying *Gästezimmer*.

Naturcamping Am Schlosspark (☎ 3533; www.spreewaldcamping.de; Schlossbezirk; adult/child/tent €5/2.50/5, two-person cabins €19) This four-star camp site, just east of the Schloss, has lots of amenities, including bike and canoe rentals.

Pension Am Alten Bauernhafen (☎ 2930; www.am-alten-bauernhafen.de; Stottoff 5; s €20-35, d €35-50;

P) Charmingly decorated, large rooms and a fantastic riverside location make this big, family-run house a bargain.

Hotel Schloss Lübbenau (☎ 8730; www.schloss-luebbenau.de; Schlossbezirk 6; s €76-96, d €108-158; P ⊠) Check in at this handsome palace for a surprisingly reasonable splurge with all the class you can handle and lovely park surroundings. The restaurant here is your only fine-dining option in Lübbenau (dinner only; mains €13 to €26). The three-course Spreewaldmenü is great value at €24.

Otherwise, the town has a surprising dearth of decent eateries. One low-key option is **Strubel's** (☎ 2798; Dammstrasse 3; mains €4-11), which serves typical Spreewald dishes, including a fish platter featuring eel, pike and perch.

COTTBUS

☎ 0355 / pop 105,000

The southern gateway to the Spreewald, Cottbus has a pretty historic centre anchored by the **Altmarkt**, a handsomely restored square hemmed in by baroque and neoclassical town houses. East of here is the late-Gothic **Oberkirche** (☼ 10am-5pm) with its climbable tower (€1). The **tourist office** (☎ 754 20; www.cottbus.de; Berliner Platz 6; ☼ 9am-6pm Mon-Fri, to 1pm Sat) is a short walk west of the Altmarkt, behind the Spree-Galerie shopping centre.

Cottbus, or Chosébuz, is also the unofficial capital of the Sorbian Blota region. To learn about this Slavic group's history, language and culture, visit the **Wendisches Museum** (☎ 794 930; Mühlenstrasse 12; adult/concession €2.50/1.50; ☼ 8.30am-6pm Tue-Fri, 2-6pm Sat & Sun) or the cultural centre called **Lodka** (☎ 4857 6468; August-Bebel-Strasse 82; ☼ 10am-4.30pm Mon-Fri). Its café serves authentic Sorbian dishes (eg boiled beef with horseradish).

Not far from Lodka is the **Staatstheater Cottbus** (☎ 01803-440 344; Karl-Liebknecht-Strasse 23), an Art Nouveau marvel of a theatre. Southeast of the centre, **Branitzer Park** contains a lovely 18th-century baroque Schloss, the Fürst-Pückler-Museum and the *Wasserpyramide*, a curious grass-covered pyramid 'floating' in a little lake.

Frequent regional trains link Berlin-Hauptbahnhof and other central Berlin stations to Cottbus (€12, 1¾ hours), also stopping in Lübben and Lübbenau.

Trams 1 and 3 run to the centre from the train station.

BRANDENBURG

THE SORBS

The Spreewald region is part of the area inhabited by the Sorbs, Germany's only indigenous minority. This intriguing group, numbering just 60,000, descended from the Slavic Wends, who settled between the Elbe and Oder Rivers in the 5th century in an area called Lusatia (Luzia in Sorbian).

Lusatia was conquered by the Germans in the 10th century, subjected to brutal Germanisation throughout the Middle Ages and partitioned in 1815. Lower Sorbia, centred around the Spreewald and Cottbus (Chośebuz), went to Prussia, while Upper Sorbia, around Bautzen (Budyšin), went to Saxony. The Upper Sorbian dialect, closely related to Czech, enjoyed a certain prestige in Saxony, but the Kingdom of Prussia tried to suppress Lower Sorbian, which is similar to Polish. The Nazis, of course, tried to eradicate both.

The Sorbs were protected under the GDR, but their proud folk traditions didn't suit the bland 'proletarian' regime. Since reunification, interest in the culture has been revived through the media and colourful Sorbian festivals such as the *Vogelhochzeit* (Birds' Wedding) on 25 January and a symbolic 'witch-burning' on 30 April.

For further details, visit www.sorben-wenden.de or contact the **Sorbian Institute** (☎ 03591-497 20; www.serbski-institut.de) in Bautzen or the **Institute of Sorbian Studies** (☎ 0341-973 7650; www .uni-leipzig.de/~sorb) in Leipzig.

AROUND COTTBUS

South of Cottbus, in an area called Fürst Pückler Land, a giant project is taking shape as part of IBA, an international building exhibition. A vast opencast lignite mining area is being turned into Germany's largest artificial lake district. By 2010 the **Lausitzer Seenland** will be a recreational haven offering boating, swimming, golfing and other activities. You can observe and learn more at the **IBA Terraces** (☎ 035753-2610; www.iba-see.de; Seestrasse 100) viewing area and take a free tour (in German, Friday to Sunday) around what still resembles a lunar landscape. It's in Grossräschen, about 30km south of Cottbus, on the B96 just east off the A13.

For another perspective on the project, drive 20km west on B96 to Lichterfeld, where you'll spot a huge steel construction looking a bit like a reclining Eiffel Tower. This is the **F60** (☎ 03531-608 00; www.f60.de/index_e.htm; Bergheider Strasse 4; admission €8; ☯ 10am-7pm Tue-Sun Mar-Oct, to 4pm Nov-Feb), a 500m-long conveyor bridge used in lignite mining. You can take a tour of the behemoth and peruse the exhibits in the visitors centre.

EASTERN BRANDENBURG

BUCKOW

☎ 033433 / pop 1800

Buckow is the hub of the 205-sq-km Naturpark Märkische Schweiz, a land of clear streams,

romantic lakes and gently undulating hills that has long been a popular getaway for Berliners. Its bucolic charms have provided creative fodder for numerous artists, most prominently the poet Theodor Fontane, who praised its 'friendly landscape' in *Das Oderland* (1863), the second book in his four-volume travelogue (see boxed text, p163). In the 1950s, the GDR's 'first couple of the arts', Bertolt Brecht and Helene Weigel, spent their summers here, away from Berlin's stifling heat. Buckow has long been famous for its clean and fresh air; in fact, in 1854 Friedrich Wilhelm IV's physician advised His Majesty to visit the village, where 'the lungs go as on velvet'. No surprise, then, that Buckow has of late reclaimed its position as one of Brandenburg's most popular spa resort towns.

Orientation & Information

Buckow is surrounded by five lakes, the largest being the Schermützelsee. Berliner Strasse, the main street, parallels the lake before becoming Wriezener Strasse, where you'll find the **tourist office** (☎ 575 00; www.kurstadt-buckow.de; Wriezener Strasse 1a; ☯ 9am-noon & 1-5pm Mon-Fri year-round, 10am-5pm Sat & Sun Apr-Oct, 10am-2pm Sat & Sun Nov-Mar). Beyond here it becomes Hauptstrasse.

For nature park information, visit the **Besucherzentrum Schweizer Haus** (☎ 158 41; Lindenstrasse 33; ☯ 10am-4pm Mon-Fri, 11am-6pm Sat & Sun).

Sights & Activities

The **Brecht-Weigel-Haus** (☎ 467; Bertolt-Brecht-Strasse 30; adult/concession €2/1; ☯ 1-5pm Wed-Fri, 1-6pm Sat & Sun

Apr-Oct, 10am-noon & 1-4pm Wed-Fri, 11am-4pm Sat & Sun Nov-Mar) is where the couple summered from 1952 to 1955. Exhibits include photographs, documents and original furnishings as well as the covered wagon first used in the 1949 premiere of *Mother Courage*. In the fine gardens are copper tablets engraved with Brecht poems. The easiest way to reach the place is west along Werderstrasse, but it's more fun strolling along Ringstrasse and Bertolt-Brecht-Strasse admiring the posh prewar villas.

Buckow is a paradise for hikers and walkers. Staff at the tourist office can help find routes matching your fitness level and also sell a variety of useful maps. In summer you can hire rowing boats or go on a cruise with **Seetours** (☎ 232; Bertolt-Brecht-Strasse 11; tours adult/child €6/3; ☺ 10am-5pm Tue-Sun Apr-Oct). Tours leave from Strandbad Buckow at the northwestern end of the Schermützelsee.

Sleeping & Eating

Buckow has several high-end hotels that offer amazing value. The tourist office can organise private rooms from €15 per person. A *Kurtaxe* (resort tax) of €1 per person per night is added to most hotel bills.

DJH hostel (☎ 286; www.jh-buckow.de; Berliner Strasse 36; dm €14-19; Ⓟ ✗) The local hostel is on the town outskirts, close to the Weisser See, and can accommodate up to 106 people in rooms sleeping two to eight.

Bellevue Beauty & Wellness Hotel (☎ 6480; www.bellevue-buckow.de; Hauptstrasse 16/17; s/d €40/70; Ⓟ ✗ ⓦ) This swish option in a neoclassical building has 10 elegant rooms, great views, a restaurant serving updated regional cuisine (mains €8 to €18) and a good-sized fitness and spa area with pool.

Bergschlösschen Hotel & Restaurant (☎ 573 12; www.bergschloesschen.com; Königstrasse 38; s €55, d €65-75; Ⓟ ✗) It may resemble the house from *Psycho*, but you'd be mad (ha ha!) to complain about the upstairs views from this excellent hillside hotel.

Stobbermühle (☎ 668 33; www.stobbermuehle.de; Wriezener Strasse 2; s €54, d €78-88, apt €88-200; ✗) Fancier than Louis XIV's undies, this romantic hotel has a superb and inventive restaurant (mains €7 to €15) with a separate lobster menu. Rooms are plush and fantastically over-equipped, boasting fax machine, VCR and the odd Jacuzzi.

Fischerkehle (☎ 374; Fischerberg 7; mains €9-18) This popular historic restaurant on the southwest shore of the Schermützelsee specialises in locally caught fish and game.

Getting There & Away

Buckow is not directly served by train but there are handy hourly train/bus connections from Berlin-Lichtenberg train station. Take the RB26 to Müncheberg and change either to bus 928 or 930 (€6, one hour) or to the Buckower Kleinbahn (weekends from Easter to October). Drivers should follow the B1/B5 to Müncheberg, then steer north towards Buckow via Waldsieversdorf.

FRANKFURT AN DER ODER

☎ 0335 / pop 68,000

Germany's 'other' Frankfurt, 90km east of Berlin, was practically wiped off the map in the final days of WWII and never recovered its one-time grandeur as a medieval trading centre and university town. It didn't help that the city was split in two after the war, with the eastern suburb across the Oder River becoming the Polish town of Słubice. The GDR era imposed a decidedly unflattering Stalinist look, but still, the scenic river setting, a few architectural gems and the proximity to Poland (cheap vodka and cigarettes, for all you hedonists) are all good reasons for a stopover.

Orientation

The Hauptbahnhof is on the southwestern edge of the city centre. Walking north on Bahnhofstrasse and east on Heilbronner Strasse delivers you to the landmark Oderturm, a GDR-era high-rise. It borders the giant Brunnenplatz, where the tourist office is ensconced in a glass pavilion. The Marktplatz is just northeast of the square, a short walk from the Oder River and the bridge to Słubice.

Information

California (☎ 685 1316; Rosa-Luxemburg-Strasse 10; per hr €2; ☺ 8am-midnight) Internet access.

Tourist office (☎ 325 216; www.frankfurt-oder-tourist.de; Karl-Marx-Strasse 1; ☺ 10am-6pm Mon-Fri, to 2pm Sat)

Sights

Much of Frankfurt might be called 'aesthetically challenged', but you wouldn't know it standing on Marktplatz. To the south looms the crenellated tower of the **Marienkirche** (☺ 10am-5pm Apr-Oct, to 4pm Nov-Mar), one of Germany's largest brick Gothic hall churches.

Ruined by wartime and GDR disregard, it now boasts a proud new roof and fantastic medieval stained-glass windows. These were recently returned by the Russians, who had kept them as war booty in St Petersburg for the past 60 years. Otherwise the church is bare, its treasures, including a seven-armed candelabrum and the Gothic high altar, now on display in the **Gertraudkirche** (Gertraudenplatz 6; ☺ 10am-noon & 2-5pm Mon-Fri), south of here.

Back on Marktplatz, standing almost as tall as the Marienkirche, is the equally impressive **Rathaus** with its ornate south gable. Besides the mayor's office, it houses the **Museum Junge Kunst** (☎ 552 4150; www.museum-junge-kunst.de; Marktplatz 1; adult/concession €2/1.40; ☺ 11am-5pm Tue-Sun), which presents art by GDR and contemporary eastern German artists. It also has a second location in the riverside **PackHof** (CPE-Bach-Strasse 11; admission free; ☺ 11am-5pm Tue-Sun), a short walk east. Adjacent to the PackHof, in a restored baroque mansion, the **Museum Viadrina** (☎ 401 560; www.museum-viadrina.de; CPE-Bach-Strasse 11; adult/concession €2/1.40; ☺ 11am-5pm Tue-Sun) presents regional history in a comprehensive but rather turgid fashion.

If you're a fan of German dramatist Heinrich von Kleist (1711–1811), you might want to follow the new Oderpromenade river walk south to the **Kleist-Museum** (☎ 531 155; www.kleist -museum.de; Faberstrasse 7; adult/concession €3/2; ☺ 11am-5pm Tue-Sun), which chronicles the life, works and importance of Frankfurt's famous son. At the northern end of the Oderpromenade, past the bridge to Słubice, is the **Konzerthalle CPE Bach** (☎ 663 880; Lebuser Mauerstrasse 4; admission €1; ☺ 10am-6pm), a Gothic monastery church (1270) that's been turned into a concert hall. It also houses an exhibit on the life of the quirky composer Carl Philipp Emmanuel Bach, who was the son of the great Johann Sebastian Bach.

Sleeping & Eating

Pension Am Kleistpark (☎ 238 90; Humboldtstrasse 14; s €32-36, d €50-60; ✕) If you put a premium on value and can do without most mod-cons, you'll be happy in the large and light rooms at this property opposite Kleistpark.

Hotel Gallus (☎ 561 50; www.hotel-gallus.com; Fürstenwalder Strasse 47; s €50-80, d €63-83; P ✕) Also near the Kleistpark, behind a lovely Art Nouveau façade, Gallus has 25 bright and modern rooms decked out in friendly and inoffensive colours and patterns.

Oderspeicher (☎ 401 3963; Hanewald 9; mains €6-12; ☺ 5pm-midnight Wed-Fri, 11am-1am Sat, 11am-10pm Sun Oct-May, from 11am daily Jun-Sep) This storehouse turned beer hall has a great riverside setting (with summer terrace), occasional live music and a no-nonsense menu of German classics.

Turm 24 (☎ 504 517; Logenstrasse 8; mains €9-16) The chef's ambitions are as lofty as the 24th-floor setting of this smart restaurant. The spectacular views definitely compete with such dishes as boar with walnut-herb sauce or homemade tagliatelle with salmon and lobster.

Getting There & Around

Frankfurt is served twice hourly by regional trains from central Berlin (eg Hauptbahnhof; €8.40, 70 minutes) and Cottbus (€9.60, 1¼ hours).

Trams 1 and 3 run from the Hauptbahnhof to the centre; get off at Schmalzgasse. The tourist office rents bicycles.

NORTHERN BRANDENBURG

SACHSENHAUSEN CONCENTRATION CAMP

In 1936 the Nazis opened a 'model' *Konzentrationslager* (concentration camp) in Sachsenhausen, near the town of Oranienburg (pop 30,000), about 35km north of Berlin. By 1945 about 220,000 men from 22 countries had passed through the gates, which had signage reading, as at Auschwitz, *Arbeit Macht Frei* (Work Sets You Free). About 100,000 were murdered here, their remains consumed by the relentless fires of the ovens.

After the war, the Soviets set up Speziallager No 7 (Special Camp No 7) for ex-Nazis, regime opponents and anyone else who didn't fit into their mould. An estimated 60,000 people were interned at the camp between 1945 and 1950, and up to 12,000 are believed to have died here. There's a mass grave of victims at the camp and another one 1.5km to the north.

Sights

The **Gedenkstätte und Museum Sachsenhausen** (☎ 03301-200 200; www.gedenkstaette-sachsenhausen .de; Strasse der Nationen 22; admission free; ☺ 8.30am-6pm mid-Mar–mid-Oct, to 4.30pm mid-Oct–mid-Mar, most exhibits closed Mon) consists of several parts. Even before you enter you'll see a memorial to the 6000 prisoners who died on the *Todesmarsch* (Death March) of April 1945, when the Nazis tried to drive the camp's 33,000 inmates to the Baltic in advance of the Red Army.

About 100m inside the camp is a mass grave of 300 prisoners who died in the infirmary after liberation in April 1945. Further on is the camp commander's house and the so-called Green Monster, where SS troops were trained in the finer arts of camp maintenance. At the end of the road, the **Neues Museum** (New Museum) has a permanent exhibit about the camp's precursor, the KZ Oranienburg, which was set up in a disused brewery right in town shortly after Hitler's rise to power in 1933.

Northeast of here are **Barracks 38** and **39**, reconstructions of typical huts housing most of the 6000 Jewish prisoners brought to Sachsenhausen after Kristallnacht in November 1938. North of here is the **Zellenbau** (prison), where particularly brutal punishment was meted out.

At the centre of the grounds is the former **Häftlingsküche** (prison kitchen), which houses a new exhibit about the history of the camp. In the former laundry room opposite, you can see a variety of films, including a particularly gruesome one showing the camp after liberation.

Left of the tall, ugly monument (1961) erected by the GDR in memory of political prisoners interned here stood the various killing stations, including a **gallows**, where four prisoners could be hanged simultaneously, and **Station Z extermination site**, a pit for shooting prisoners in the neck with a wooden 'catch' where bullets could be retrieved and recycled. An exhibit documents these horrifying mass killings.

Getting There & Away

Oranienburg is frequently served by the S1 from Berlin-Friedrichstrasse (€2.60, 50 minutes) and regional trains from Berlin-Hauptbahnhof (€2.60, 25 minutes). From Oranienburg station it's a signposted 20-minute walk to the camp, or catch buses 804 or 821.

RHEINSBERG

☎ 033931 / pop 5300

Rheinsberg, a delightful town on Grienericksee about 50km northwest of Berlin, has a strong cultural pedigree. It all started with Frederick the Great who, when still a crown prince, enjoyed giving flute concerts at the Schloss. The tradition continued with his brother Heinrich who turned the palace into a 'court of the muses'. The town also inspired Theodor Fontane's gushy travelogue called *Wanderungen durch die Mark Brandenburg* (Walks through the March of Brandenburg) and Kurt Tucholsky's 1912 breakthrough novel *Rheinsberg – ein Bilderbuch für Verliebte* (Rheinsberg – A Picture Book for Lovers). Cultural events, along with the palace, its park, plenty of boating and some top-notch restaurants, still make Rheinsberg a pleasant getaway.

Information

Infoladen (☎ 395 10; www.rheinsberg-tourismus.de; Rhinpassage, Rhinstrasse 19; 🕑 10am-6pm Mon-Sat, to 4pm Sun) Private tourist office with internet access (€0.50 per 15 minutes).

Post office (Paulshorster Strasse 18b)

Tourist office (☎ 2059; www.tourismus-rheinsberg.de; Kavalierhaus, Markt; 🕑 10am-5pm Mon-Sat, to 4pm Sun)

Volksbank (Rhinstrasse 10)

Sights

The town's star attraction is the eponymous **Schloss Rheinsberg** (☎ 7260; adult/concession incl audio-guide Apr-Oct €6/5, Nov-Mar €4/3; 🕑 10am-5pm Tue-Sun Apr-Oct, to 4pm Nov-Mar), prettily set right on Grienericksee and surrounded by a sprawling park. Friedrich Wilhelm I purchased it in 1734 for his 22-year-old son, Crown Prince Friedrich, the future Frederick the Great. The prince, who spent four years here studying and preparing for the throne, later said this period was the happiest of his life. In 1744 he gave the palace to his brother Heinrich, a closet homosexual whom Frederick forced into marriage with Wihelmine of Hessen-Kassel. You'll learn this and other juicy titbits on a self-guided audio tour (available in English).

Unfortunately, the interior, though filled with art, isn't quite on a par with what you might have seen in Schloss Sanssouci or Schloss Charlottenburg. This is not surprising, really, given that the palace was used as a sanatorium in GDR times. Still, there are a few highlights, especially the **Spiegelsaal** (Hall of Mirrors), decorated with a ceiling fresco by Antoine Pesne. The **Muschelsaal** (Shell Room) also doesn't fail to impress.

Tickets are also good for the **Tucholsky Lit-eraturmuseum** (☎ 390 07; adult/concession/family if purchased separately €3/2/5) on the ground floor of the north wing. It is dedicated to the life of journalist, satirist, poet and social critic Kurt Tucholsky (1890–1935), who went into exile in Sweden when the Nazis came to power.

Activities

Reederei Halbeck (☎ 386 19; www.schiffahrt-rheinsberg .de, in German; Markt 11; 1hr trip from €6.50), next to the tourist office, offers a range of lake and river cruises and hires out canoes, paddle-boats and kayaks. **Rheinsberger Adventure Tours** (☎ 392 47; www.rhintour.de, in German; Schlossstrasse 42) also hires out canoes, boats and bikes, and can arrange all kinds of excursions in the area.

Festivals & Events

Rheinsberger Musiktage (Rheinsberg Music Days; ☎ 7210) Three-day festival of music round the clock – from jazz and chamber music to children's cabaret. Held around Whitsun/Pentecost in May/June.

Kammeroper Schloss Rheinsberg (Chamber Opera; 392 96; www.kammeroper-rheinsberg.de) A prestigious international opera festival promoting young talent, held from late June to mid-August.

Sleeping & Eating

Private rooms (from €15 per person) are plentiful in Rheinsberg – just look for the 'Zimmer Frei' signs.

Pension Holländermühle (☎ 2332; http://rheinsberg .de/hollaender-muehle; Schwanower Strasse; s €45, d €60-70; P ⓧ) It's about a 10-minute walk from the Schloss, but the setting of this windmill-turned-pension is nice and quiet and there's a good restaurant. Rooms range from fresh to frilly.

Zum Jungen Fritz (☎ 4090; www.junger-fritz.de; Schlossstrasse 8; s €46-48, d €66-72; P) This sweet little inn has big-hearted owners but only nine cute rooms. The old-time German restaurant is a fine place to send your cholesterol count through the roof.

Der Seehof (☎ 4030; www.seehof-rheinsberg.com; Seestrasse 18; s €65-75, d €100-110; P ⓧ) This top-flight option in a 1750 farmhouse has lovely rooms furnished in a modern, uncluttered country style with wooden floors and plenty of natural light. The restaurant (mains €6 to €19) serves exceptional fish dishes, including a mean bouillabaisse.

Café Tucholsky (☎ 343 70; Kurt-Tucholsky-Strasse 30a; mains €5-10) This smart lakeside café is a good one-size-fits-all option with grill parties, live music on Fridays and fresh fish, meat and vegetarian dishes. In summer only, they also serve late breakfast starting at 10am.

Zum Alten Fritz (☎ 2086; Schlossstrasse 11; mains €6-13.50) The beautiful old porcelain, books, lamps and other old-timey décor here almost transport you back to the 18th century. Some of the dishes were even inspired by recipes from that era.

Eisfabrik (☎ 7240; Kurt-Tucholsky-Strasse 36) To feed your sweet-tooth cravings, swing by Eisfabrik, which makes its own ice cream, including some from herbs, vegetables and other unusual ingredients.

Entertainment

Musikakademie Rheinsberg (☎ 7210; www.musik akademie-rheinsberg.de; Kavalierhaus, Schloss) The academy presents year-round concerts, ballet, musical theatre and other cultural events at the palace theatre, inside the Hall of Mirrors and at other venues. Tickets are available online and from the tourist office.

Shopping

Rheinsberg is a traditional centre of faïence and ceramics; check out the local firms **Rheinsbergischer Keramikhandel** (☎ 349 510; www .rkh-rheinsberg.de; Damascheweg 3) and **Carstens Keramik** (☎ 2003; www.carstens-keramik.de; Rhinstrasse 1).

Getting There & Around

Getting to Rheinsberg by public transport is not easy. From Berlin, the least complicated train route leaves from Berlin-Charlottenburg and requires only one change in Spandau (€8.40, 2¼ hours). Drivers should head north via the B96 and consult a map or www.map24 .de for precise directions.

You can hire bikes from **Fahrradhaus Thäns** (☎ 2622; Schlossstrasse 16; per day €6-8; ⏰ 9am-9pm Mon-Sat).

LOWER ODER VALLEY NATIONAL PARK

In the far northeastern corner of Brandenburg, the **Lower Oder Valley National Park** (National park Unteres Odertal; www.unteres-odertal-nationalpark.de, in German) is guaranteed to get you away from the tourist crowds. It protects one of the last relatively unspoiled delta regions in Europe and boasts an enormous range of flora and fauna. Meadows, marshland and deciduous forest make up much of the park, which hugs the Polish border for 60km but is just 2km to 3km wide in most spots. It also serves

---

BRANDENBURG'S FONTANE OF KNOWLEDGE

As you move around Brandenburg, you'll often find yourself following in the footsteps of Theodor Fontane (1819–98), a Huguenot writer from Neuruppin who made a series of walking tours of the March in 1859 and set down his experiences in the four-volume *Wanderungen durch die Mark Brandenburg* (Walks through the March of Brandenburg), with no shortage of appreciative comments.

Looking at all the plaques, book displays and name-dropping brochures you might get the impression that Fontane was just an old travel hack who 'did' Brandenburg, but in fact he is better known to literature students as one of the first proponents of the social novel in Germany, comparable to Flaubert or Balzac in France. His most famous work is probably *Effi Briest;* the well-known 1974 film version was directed by none other than Rainer Werner Fassbinder.

Fittingly, with all the French comparisons flying around, Fontane is buried in the Französischer Friedhof (French Cemetery), which is integrated into the Dorotheenstädtischer Friedhof in Berlin's Mitte district. But prepare for company; he still enjoys a wide following, and there are always devotees milling about his modest tombstone.

---

as a breeding ground for such endangered bird species as sea eagles and black storks. More than 100,000 geese and ducks make the park their winter home. In October, the sky darkens with up to 13,000 migratory cranes stopping off on their way south.

Orientation & Information

The gateway town to the park is Schwedt, about 100km northeast of Berlin. Here you'll find most commercial activity as well as the regional **tourist office** (☎ 03332-255 90; www .unteres-odertal.de; Berliner Strasse 47; ☺ 9am-12.30pm & 2-6pm Mon-Fri, 10am-12.30pm Sat May-Sep, 9am-12.30pm & 2-5pm Mon-Fri Oct-Apr).

Another good place to get oriented is the **Nationalparkhaus** (☎ 03332-267 7244; adult/child €1/0.50) in Criewen. This is the park's main visitor centre and the knowledgeable (though not always English-speaking) folks here are happy to suggest activities and hand out maps. While here, you can admire 20-odd local fish species flitting around the giant aquarium.

Activities

Boats and bikes can be hired from **Fahrrad- und Touristikcenter Butzke** (☎ 03332-839 500; www .kanufahrradverleihbutzke.de; Kietz 11, Schwedt; per day bikes €4.50-6, canoes €25-35). The company also organises customised guided and self-guided tours, including canoe-bike combinations.

Sleeping

The tourist office in Schwedt can help you find private or hotel rooms in the entire region.

Campingplatz Mescherin (☎ 033332-807 07; www .campingplatz-mescherin.de; Dorfstrasse 6; per person/car

€3/€2, per tent €3-5) To really commune with nature, try this, the only camping ground in the park. It's fairly basic, but in a lovely setting on the Oder near the northern end of Mescherin.

Getting There & Around

Regional trains to Schwedt leave almost hourly from Berlin-Hauptbahnhof (€9.60, 1¼ hours). From Schwedt, bus 468 goes to Criewen in 20 minutes (€1.30). Alternatively, take the regional train to Angermünde and switch to bus 468 there for Criewen (€9.60, 1¾ hours, every two hours).

Drivers should follow the A11 to the Joachimsthal exit, then continue on the B2 towards Angermünde.

CHORIN

☎ 033366 / pop 520

About 60km northeast of Berlin, **Kloster Chorin** (Chorin Monastery; ☎ 703 77; www.kloster-chorin.de; Amt Chorin 11a; adult/concession €3/2, parking €2.50; ☺ 9am-6pm Apr-Oct, to 4pm Nov-Mar) is a romantically ruined monastery near a little lake and surrounded by a lush park. Chorin was founded by Cistercian monks in 1273, and 500 of them laboured over six decades to erect what is widely considered to be among the finest red-brick Gothic structures in northern Germany. The monastery was secularised in 1542 and fell into disrepair after the Thirty Years' War. Renovation has gone on in a somewhat haphazard fashion since the early 19th century.

You enter the complex from the south and first arrive at the former cloister, with the monastic quarters off to the sides and the church, with its sleekly carved portals and elongated lancet windows, to the north. For more beautiful architecture, walk around to the western façade, with its beautifully detailed step gable.

The church, which is said to have near-perfect acoustics, and the cloister are an enchanting setting for classical concerts held throughout the summer. On weekends from June to August, expect to hear some top talent during the celebrated **Choriner Musiksommer** (☎ 03334-657 310; www.musiksommer-chorin.de; tickets €6-22). In Berlin, tickets are sold at **Berliner Theater-und Konzertkasse** (☎ 030-241 4635; Am Spreeufer 6).

Chorin is served hourly by regional trains from Berlin-Hauptbahnhof (€7.20, 45 minutes). Trains are often met by bus 912, which takes you within a five-minute walk of the monastery. Alternatively, it's a 2.5km walk through the woods. If you're stopping off in Chorin en route to somewhere else, note that there is no left luggage (or indeed anything else) at the station.

NIEDERFINOW
☎ 033362 / pop 700

Tiny Niederfinow, about 20km southeast of Chorin, would be a mere blip on the map were it not for the spectacular **Schiffshebewerk** (ship-lift; ☎ 033362-215; www.schiffshebewerk-niederfinow .info, in German; Hebewerkstrasse; adult/child €1/0.50, parking €2.50; ☼ 9am-6pm Apr-Oct, to 4pm Nov-Mar), one of the most remarkable feats of engineering

from the early 20th century. Looking a bit like the exoskeleton of an aircraft carrier, it was completed in 1934 and measures 60m high, 27m wide and 94m long. Huge barges sail into a sort of giant bathtub, which is then raised or lowered 36m, water and all, between the Oder River and the Oder-Havel Canal. It's great fun, especially for kids.

The lift can be viewed from the street (free), but for better views climb to the upper canal platform and view the 20-minute operation from above. Even more memorable is a trip on the lift itself aboard a little boat operated by **Fahrgastschifffahrt Neumann** (☎ 03334-244 05; www.finowkanalschifffahrt.de in German; adult/child €6/3; ☼ times vary). Tickets are sold at the information kiosk, which is in the car park alongside a few snack stands.

If you think this ship-lift is impressive, come back in 2012 when a second, much bigger one is scheduled to begin operation adjacent to the existing one. The new behemoth will be 130m long and able to accommodate larger barges capable of transporting 1500 tonnes of goods (the equivalent of 50 trucks). Construction was supposed to commence in 2006.

Niederfinow is served by regional train from Berlin-Hauptbahnhof (€6, 1¼ hours) with a change in Bernau or Eberswalde, or directly from Berlin-Lichtenberg (€6, one hour). The Schiffshebewerk is a scenic 2km walk north of the station; turn left and follow the road.

Saxony

Saxony has everything you could want in a German state: storybook castles peering down from craggy mountaintops, cobbled marketplaces serenaded by Gothic churches, exuberantly baroque palaces, nostalgic steam trains, indigenous Sorb folk traditions, great wine and food, and friendly locals who are justifiably proud of their riches. And through it all zigzags the broad-shouldered Elbe River, in a steady eternal flow, its banks lined by a gently dramatic landscape of neatly arrayed vineyards, sun-dappled parks, villa-studded hillsides, precipitous sandstone cliffs sculpted by time and the elements, and shaggy meadows where sheep graze amid sprouting wildflowers.

It's a natural mosaic that for centuries has tugged mightily at the hearts of visionaries, artists and wanderers. Canaletto and Caspar David Friedrich captured the baroque brilliance of Dresden and the mystical beauty of Saxon Switzerland on canvas; JS Bach penned some of his most famous works in Leipzig; and the 19th-century 'musical poet' Robert Schumann grew up in Zwickau. Saxony's musical legacy is kept alive everywhere, but nowhere more so than at Dresden's Semperoper and the Gewandhaus in Leipzig, two of the world's most famous halls.

Dresden and Leipzig are the most high-profile cities, and each has its own personality. While the capital is playful, pretty and historic, bustling Leipzig has a more progressive, contemporary spirit. The latter sparked the 'peaceful revolution' of 1989, bringing down the Berlin Wall.

Reunification has brought enormous change to Saxony, which was heavily industrialised. Cities that once crouched under the weight of neglect and pollution are again sparkling and proud, their centres alive with cafés and shops, and people walking with a spring in their step. Now is a good time to immerse yourself in this multifaceted and endlessly fascinating state.

HIGHLIGHTS

- ■ **Time-Warp** Gain an insight into the bizarre world of the GDR at museums in Leipzig (p185) and Radebeul (p179)

- ■ **Fine Wining** Savour sparkling wine at Radebeul's Schloss Wackerbarth winery (p179)

- ■ **Views** Stand atop the Bastei (p180) for breathtaking panoramas of Saxon Switzerland and the Elbe

- ■ **Castles** Ramble around the massive Festung Königstein (p181) with its glorious views

- ■ **Treasure Trove** Be dazzled by the artistry of objects at Dresden's Grünes Gewölbe (p170)

■ POPULATION: 4.35 MILLION   ■ AREA: 18,413 SQ KM

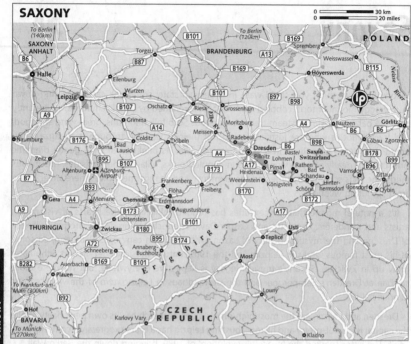

Information

If you need to book a room, or just want more information about Saxony, turn to www.visit saxony.com.

Getting Around

A serious enticement to use public transport is the good-value **Saxony-Ticket** (€24), giving you and up to four accompanying passengers (or one or both parents or grandparents, plus all their children or grandchildren up to 14 years) unlimited train travel during the period of its validity (9am to 3am the next day). Tickets are good for 2nd-class travel throughout Saxony, as well as in Thuringia and Saxony-Anhalt. As well as any regional Deutsche Bahn trains (IRE, RE, RB and S-Bahn), you can also use some private trains, including the LausitzBahn.

CENTRAL SAXONY

DRESDEN

☎ 0351 / pop 478,000

There are few city silhouettes more striking than Dresden's. The classic view from the

Elbe's northern bank takes in a playful phalanx of delicate spires, soaring towers and dominant domes belonging to palaces, churches and stately buildings. Numerous artists, most notably the Italian Canaletto, have set up their easels to capture this breathtaking panorama.

'Florence of the north', the Saxon capital was called in the 18th century, when it was a centre of artistic activity presided over by the cosmopolitan Augustus the Strong (August der Starke) and his son Augustus III. Their vision produced many of Dresden's iconic buildings, including the Zwinger, the Frauenkirche and the Hofkirche.

But the fact that these monumental edifices are even here today is really a bit of a miracle. On the night of 13 February 1945, in the waning days of WWII, an Allied firebombing campaign reduced the baroque city to a heap of flaming, toxic rubble. Exact numbers are blurred by politics and the presence of thousands of untraceable refugees, but somewhere between 25,000 and 100,000 civilians were killed as a direct result of these attacks, the strategic justification of which remains extremely debatable.

But Dresden is a survivor and there is no more potent symbol of its people's determination than the resurrected Frauenkirche. Although the city celebrated its 800th anniversary in 2006, it is also forward-looking and solidly rooted in the here and now. There's some great new architecture, a constantly evolving arts and cultural scene, and zinging pub and nightlife quarters.

Take a few days and allow yourself to be caught up in this visual and cultural feast. We promise that Dresden's world-class museums will mesmerise you, its riverside beer gardens relax you and its light-hearted, almost Mediterranean, disposition, charm you.

Orientation

The meandering Elbe River separates the Altstadt (Old Town) to the south from the Neustadt (New Town) to the north. From the Hauptbahnhof (central train station) it's just a 10-minute walk north on pedestrianised Prager Strasse, the main shopping street, to the Frauenkirche and other blockbuster sights.

The main walking bridge to the Neustadt is the Augustusbrücke, just west of the famous riverside promenade called Brühlsche Terrasse, with the Terrassenufer boat landing docks below.

Augustusbrücke segues into pedestrianised Hauptstrasse, the main commercial strip in the so-called Innere Neustadt (Inner New Town), which culminates at Albertplatz. Beyond this lies the Äussere Neustadt (Outer New Town), Dresden's main pub and bar quarter.

About half a kilometre west of Albertplatz is Dresden-Neustadt, the city's second train station (most trains stop at both). A third station, Dresden-Mitte, is little more than a forlorn platform between the two main ones. Dresden's central bus station is next to the Hauptbahnhof.

Dresden airport is 9km north of the city centre.

Information

BOOKSHOPS

Das Internationale Buch (☎ 656 460; Altmarkt 24) Excellent selection of English books.
Der Reisebuchladen (☎ 899 6560; Louisenstrasse 70b) Travel books and maps galore.
Haus Des Buches (☎ 497 360; Dr-Külz-Ring 12; 🖳) Lots of Lonely Planet titles, plus internet access.

DISCOUNT CARDS

Dresden City-Card (per 48/72hr €19/29) Provides admission to 12 museums, discounted city tours and boats, and free public transport. Buy it at the tourist office.
State Museums Day Card (adult/concession/family €10/6/20) Good at all museums administered by the Staatliche Kunstsammlungen Dresden, including the Zwinger museum and Neues Grünes Gewölbe. All State Museums sell this card.

EMERGENCY

Ambulance (☎ 112/19222)
Police (☎ 110)

INTERNET ACCESS

Joker Spielothek (☎ 288 0034; Wallstrasse 11; per hr €3; ☉ 6am-2am Mon-Sat, 8am-2am Sun)
K&E Callshop (Wiener Passage; per hr €2; ☉ 10am-10pm) In the subterranean passageway outside the Hauptbahnhof.
Spiel-In (Königsbrücker Strasse 54; per hr €2; ☉ 7am-midnight Mon-Fri, 10am-midnight Sat & Sun).

SAXON SPEAK

The Saxons speak a dialect as incomprehensible to non-Saxons as Bavarian is to outsiders. Many visitors find themselves saying 'Huh?' more often than usual. It's as if the Saxons learned German from the Scots, with their very soft pronunciation of consonants. For example, when a Saxon says '*lahip*-tsch', he means Leipzig, and they pronounce 'ü' like an English short 'i' – '*bit*-nershtrazze' for Büttnerstrasse.

But Saxon-speak is far from an odd off-shoot of German; on the contrary, it was from Saxony that the German language developed. Martin Luther's translation of the Bible into the Saxon language laid the foundation for a standard German language, and Saxons can also hark back to a 1717 Dutch reference to the Saxon dialect as 'the purest, most comprehensible, charming and delightful to the ear of all German dialects'.

In general, though, no outside praise is needed to reinforce Saxon pride in their dialect; '*sächseln*' is the norm, and the worst thing a native can do here is '*berlinern*' – start talking with a Berlin accent!

DRESDEN

SAXONY

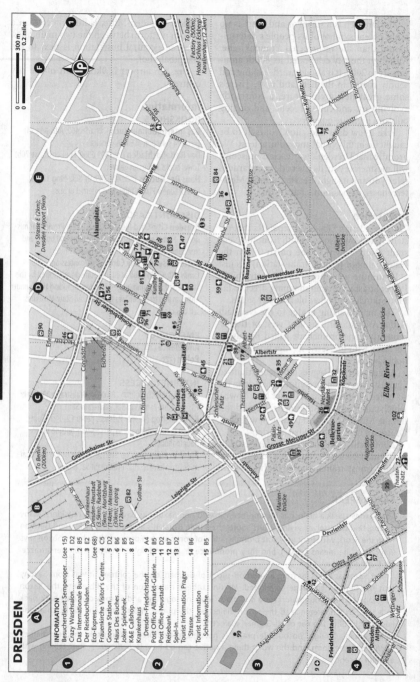

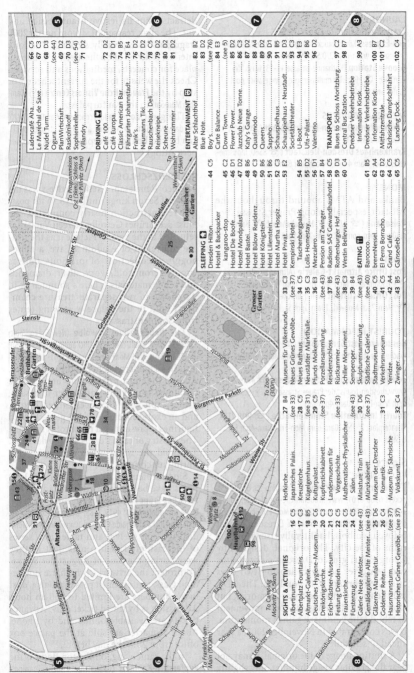

SAXONY

SIGHTS & ACTIVITIES
Albertinum.........................16 C5
Albertplatz Fountains............17 C3
Altmarkt-Galerie..................18 B5
Deutsches Hygiene-Museum...19 C6
Dreikönigskirche..................20 C3
Erich-Kästner-Museum...........21 C3
Festung Dresden..................22 C5
Frauenkirche.......................23 C5
Fürstenzug.........................24 C5
Galerie Neue Meister......... (see 43)
Gemäldegalerie Alte Meister..(see 43)
Gläserne Manufaktur............25 D6
Goldener Reiter...................26 C3
Hausmannsturm................(see 37)
Historisches Grünes Gewölbe.(see 37)

Hofkirche............................27 B4
Japanisches Palais............(see 33)
Kreuzkirche.........................28 C5
Kügelgenhaus......................29 C5
Kulturpalast.....................(see 31)
Kupferstichkabinett...........(see 37)
Landesmuseum für
  Vorgeschichte...............(see 33)
Mathematisch-Physikalischer
  Salon...........................(see 43)
Miniature Train Terminus........30 D6
Münzkabinett...................(see 43)
Museum der Dresdner
  Romantik..........................31 C3
Museum für Sächsische
  Volkskunst......................32 C4

Museum für Völkerkunde........33 B4
Neues Grünes Gewölbe.......(see 37)
Neues Rathaus.....................34 C5
Neustädter Markthalle...........35 C3
Pfunds Molkerei...................36 E3
Porzellansammlung...........(see 43)
Residenzschloss....................37 B5
Rüstkammer....................(see 43)
Schiller Monument.................38 C3
Semperoper.........................39 B4
Skulpturensammlung.........(see 43)
Städtische Galerie.............(see 37)
Stadtmuseum.......................40 C5
Verkehrsmuseum..................41 C4
Yenidze...............................42 A4
Zwinger..............................43 B5

SLEEPING ☐
Dresden Hilton.....................44 C5
Hostel & Backpacker
  kangaroo-stop....................45 C2
Hostel Die Boofe...................46 D1
Hostel Mondpalast................47 D2
Hotel Bastei........................48 B6
Hotel Bülow Residenz............49 C3
Hotel Königstein...................50 B6
Hotel Lilienstein...................51 B6
Hotel Martha Hospiz..............52 C3
Hotel Privat.........................53 E2
Kempinski Hotel
  Taschenbergpalais...............54 B5
Lollis Homestay....................55 D2
Mezcalero...........................56 D1
Pension am Zwinger...............57 B4
Radisson SAS Gewandhaushotel..58 C5
Rothenburger Hof..................59 D3
Westin Bellevue....................60 C4

EATING ☐
Barococo............................61 B5
brennNessel........................62 A4
El Perro Borracho..................63 D2
Grand Café..........................64 C5
Gänsedieb...........................65 C4

Ladencafé Aha.....................66 C5
Le Maréchal de Saxe..............67 C3
Nudel Turm.........................68 D3
Ogura............................(see 44)
PlanWirtschaft.....................69 D2
Raskolnikoff........................70 D3
Sophienkeller...................(see 54)
Villandry............................71 D2

DRINKING ☐
Café 100.............................72 D2
Café Europa.........................73 D1
Classic American Bar..............74 B5
Fährgarten Johannstadt..........75 E4
Frank's...............................76 D2
Neumanns Tiki......................77 D2
Rauschenbach Deli.................78 C5
Reisekneipe.........................79 D2
Scheune.............................80 D2
Wohnzimmer........................81 D2

ENTERTAINMENT ☐
Alter Schlachthof..................82 B2
Blue Note........................(see 76)
Boy's.................................83 D2
Carte Balance......................84 E3
Down Town......................(see 5)
Flower Power........................85 D2
Jazzclub Neue Tonne..............86 C5
Katy's Garage......................87 D2
Quasimodo..........................88 A4
Queens...............................89 D1
Sappho...............................90 D1
Schauspielhaus - Neustadt......91 B5
Schauspielhaus.....................92 D3
Societätstheater...................93 C3
U-Boot...............................94 E3
Ufa-Palast...........................95 B6
Valentino............................96 D2

TRANSPORT
Buses to Schloss Moritzburg...97 C2
Central Bus Station................98 B7
Dresdner Verkehrsbetriebe
  Information Kiosk.................99 A3
Dresdner Verkehrsbetriebe
  Information Kiosk...............100 B7
Mitfahrzentrale...................101 C2
Sächsische Dampfschiffahrt
  Landing Dock.....................102 C4

LAUNDRY

Crazy Waschsalon (Louisenstrasse 6)

Eco-Express (Königsbrücker Strasse 2 & Rudolf-Leonard-Strasse 16; wash/dry €2/0.50; ⏰ 6am-11pm)

Groove Station (Katharinenstrasse 11-13; wash/dry €2/0.50; 💻) Popular multipurpose lounge, with pool tables and music.

MEDICAL SERVICES

Krankenhaus Dresden-Friedrichstadt (☎ 4800; Friedrichstrasse 41)

Krankenhaus Dresden-Neustadt (☎ 8560; Industriestrasse 40) Tram 4 to Am Trachauer Bahnhof.

MONEY

Banks and ATMs abound throughout the Altstadt, especially along Prager Strasse.

Reisebank (☎ 471 2177; Hauptbahnhof; ⏰ 8am-7.30pm, 9am-4pm Sat, 9am-1pm Sun)

POST

Post Office Altmarkt-Galerie (Altmarkt-Galerie; ⏰ 9.30am-8pm Mon-Sat) Enter from Wallstrasse.

Post Office Neustadt (Königsbrücker Strasse 21; ⏰ 9am-7pm Mon-Fri, 10am-1pm Sat)

TOURIST INFORMATION

Besucherdienst Semperoper (☎ 491 1705; Schinkelwache, Theaterplatz 2; ⏰ 10am-6pm Mon-Fri, 10am-1pm Sat) Opera tickets and tours.

Tourist Information Prager Strasse (☎ 4919 2104; www.dresden-tourist.de; Prager Strasse 21; ⏰ 9.30am-6pm Mon-Fri, 9.30am-4pm Sat)

Tourist Information Schinkelwache (☎ 4919 2104; Theaterplatz 2; ⏰ 10am-6pm Mon-Fri, 10am-4pm Sat & Sun)

Sights

FRAUENKIRCHE

The domed **Frauenkirche** (information ☎ 6560 6100, tickets 6560 6701; www.frauenkirche-dresden.de; admission free; ⏰ 10am-noon & 1-6pm Mon-Fri, limited hours on weekends), which is one of Dresden's most beloved symbols, has literally risen from the ruins of the city. The original, designed by Georg Bähr, graced Dresden's skyline for two centuries before collapsing two days after the February 1945 bombing. The GDR left the rubble there as a war memorial, but after reunification a grass-roots movement to rebuild the landmark gained momentum. It was consecrated in November 2005, a year ahead of schedule.

A spitting image of the original, it may not bear the gravitas of age but that only slightly detracts from its festive beauty inside and out. The altar, reassembled from nearly 2000 fragments, is especially striking. The lofty interior, galleried like a theatre, is a wonderful place for concerts, meditations and services. Check the website for the current schedule or stop by the **Frauenkirche Visitors Centre** (⏰ 10am-6pm Mon-Sat) in the Kulturpalast.

The great **dome** (adult/concession/family €8/6/20; ⏰ daily Mar-Oct), known as the 'stone bell', can be climbed for sweeping views (weather permitting).

RESIDENZSCHLOSS

The neo-Renaissance **Residenzschloss** was the home of Saxon kings until 1918. With postwar reconstruction nearly completed, the must-see Grünes Gewölbe (Green Vault) has returned to the palace. Picture it as the real-life equivalent of Aladdin's Cave, a mind-boggling collection of precious objects wrought from gold, ivory, silver, diamonds and other materials. There's so much of it, it's shown in two separate 'treasure chambers', both in the palace west wing (enter from Sophienstrasse).

The **Neues Grünes Gewölbe** (New Green Vault; ☎ 4914 2000; adult/concession incl audio-guide €8/5.50; ⏰ 10am-6pm Wed-Mon) presents some 1000 objects in 10 modern rooms on the upper floor. Among the most prized items are a frigate fashioned from ivory with wafer-thin sails, a cherry pit with 185 faces carved into it, and an exotic ensemble of 132 gem-studded figurines representing a royal court in India. The artistry of each item is simply dazzling. To avoid the worst crush of people, visit during lunchtime.

Since September 2006, an additional 3000 items have been exhibited below in the **Historisches Grünes Gewölbe** (Historical Green Vault; tickets & information ☎ 4919 2285; www.skd-dresden.de; admission incl audio-guide €10; ⏰ 10am-7pm Wed-Mon), displayed on shelves and tables in a series of increasingly lavish rooms, just as they were during the time of August der Starke. To protect the artworks, which are not behind glass, visitors must pass through a 'dust lock'; numbers are limited to 100 an hour. Admission is by timed ticket only. Advance tickets are available online and by phone. About a quarter are sold at the palace box office from 2pm the day before.

In the same wing, on the top floor, is the **Kupferstich-Kabinett** (Collection of Prints & Drawings;

☎ 4914 2000; adult/concession €3/2; ☉ 10am-6pm Wed-Mon).

For fine views, head up the **Hausmannsturm** (palace tower; adult/concession €2.50/1.50; ☉ 10am-6pm Wed-Mon Mar-Nov). Numismatists might like to pop into the **Münzkabinett** (Coin Collection; ☎ 4914 2000; adult/concession/family incl tower access €3/2/7; ☉ 10am-6pm Wed-Mon), also in the tower.

SEMPEROPER

The original Semperoper (Opera House; ☎ 491 1496; www.semperoper.de; tours adult/concession €6/3) burned down a mere three decades after its 1841 inauguration. When it reopened in 1878, the neo-Renaissance jewel entered its most dazzling period, which saw the premieres of works by Richard Strauss, Carl Maria von Weber and Richard Wagner. Alas, WWII put an end to the fun, and it wasn't until 1985 before music again filled the grand hall.

ZWINGER

Next to the opera house is the sprawling **Zwinger** (☎ 4914 2000; ☉ 10am-6pm Tue-Sun), which is among the most ravishing baroque buildings in all of Germany. A collaboration between the architect Matthäus Pöppelmann and the sculptor Balthasar Permoser, it was primarily a party palace for royals, despite the odd name (which means dungeon). Several charming portals lead into the vast fountain-studded courtyard, which is framed by buildings lavishly festooned with baroque sculpture. Atop the western pavilion stands a tense-looking Atlas with the world on his shoulders; opposite him is a cutesy carillon of 40 Meissen porcelain bells, which chime on the hour.

The Zwinger houses six museums. The most important one is the **Gemäldegalerie Alte Meister** (Old Masters Gallery; combined ticket with Rüstkammer adult/concession/family €6/3.50/10), which features masterpieces including Raphael's Sistine Madonna. The ticket also includes admission to selections from the **Galerie Neue Meister**, where works by leading Impressionists and other modern masters are in exile while the collection's usual home, the Albertinum, is undergoing renovation until at least 2009.

Another Albertinum collection, the **Skulpturensammlung** (adult/concession/family €2.50/1.50/6), has also found a temporary home in the Zwinger. All epochs are represented, from ancient Egypt, Rome and Greece to the Renaissance, the baroque period and the 20th century. Medieval sculpture, meanwhile, is shown in the Albrechtsburg (p183) in Meissen.

The following are the other three Zwinger museums:

Rüstkammer (Armory; adult/concession/family €3/2/5) A grand collection of ceremonial weapons.

Porzellansammlung (Porcelain Collection; adult/concession/family €5/3/10) A dazzling assortment of Meissen classics and East Asian treasures in the new Ostasien-Galerie.

Mathematisch-Physikalischer Salon (adult/concession/family €3/2/5) Old scientific instruments, globes and timepieces, including a 13th-century Arabian celestial globe and a calculator from 1650.

NEUSTADT

Despite its name, Neustadt is actually an older part of Dresden that was considerably less smashed up in WWII than the Altstadt. After reunification it was taken over by the alternative scene, which today still dominates the so-called Äussere (Outer) Neustadt north of Albertplatz. South of here, the Innere (Inner) Neustadt, with Hauptstrasse as its main artery, is now solidly gentrified – especially along Königstrasse, which again sparkles in baroque splendour.

The first thing you see when crossing Augustusbrücke is the blindingly gleaming **Goldener Reiter** (1736) statue of Augustus the Strong. East of here, the **Museum für Sächsische Volkskunst** (Museum of Saxon Folk Art; ☎ 4914 2000; Köpckestrasse 1; adult/concession/family €3/2/5; ☉ 10am-6pm Tue-Sun) has such quaint things as antique furniture, traditional garments and puppet theatres.

North of the statue, Hauptstrasse is a pleasant pedestrian mall where the **Museum der Dresdner Romantik** (Museum of Dresden Romanticism; ☎ 804 4760; Hauptstrasse 13; adult/concession €2/1; ☉ 10am-6pm Wed-Sun) documents the city's artistic and intellectual movements during the early 19th century.

Beyond is the renovated **Dreikönigskirche** (☎ 812 4102; tower adult/concession €1.50/1; ☉ 10am-6pm Mon-Sat, 11am-6pm Sun May-Oct, to 4pm Nov-Mar, to 5pm Apr) designed by Zwinger-architect Pöppelmann. Eye-catching features include a baroque altar ruined in 1945 and left as a memorial, and the Dance of Death frieze, a rare Renaissance artwork. The tower can be climbed.

SAXONY

A great spot to satisfy your shopping cravings is the **Neustädter Markthalle**, a gorgeously restored old market hall (enter on Metzer Strasse).

Hauptstrasse culminates at **Albertplatz** with its two striking fountains representing turbulent and still waters. Also found here are an evocative marble **Schiller monument** and the interactive **Erich-Kästner-Museum** (☎ 804 5086; Antonstrasse 1; adult/concession €3/2; ⏰ 10am-6pm Sun-Tue, 10am-8pm Wed), dedicated to the beloved children's book author and outspoken Nazi critic.

Königstrasse runs southwest of Albertplatz, all the way to the not-very-Japanese **Japanisches Palais** (1737). Inside is Dresden's famous **Museum für Völkerkunde** (Museum of Ethnology; ☎ 814 4814; Palaisplatz 11; adult/concession €4/2; ⏰ 10am-6pm Tue-Sun), which boasts well over 70,000 anthropological items from far-flung corners of the world, as well as the **Landesmuseum für Vorgeschichte** (State Museum of Prehistory; ☎ 892 6603; adult/concession €3/2; ⏰ 10am-6pm).

North of Albertplatz, the Äussere Neustadt is a spidery web of narrow streets, late-19th-century patrician houses and hidden courtyards, all chock full of pubs, clubs, galleries and one-of-a-kind shops. A highlight here is the **Kunsthofpassage** (enter from Alaunstrasse 70 or Görlitzer Strasse 21), a series of five whimsically designed courtyards each reflecting the vision of a different Dresden artist. Our favourites are the Hof der Tiere (Court of Animals), presided over by a giant giraffe, and the Hof der Elemente (Court of Elements) with its neat sculpture of steel pipes and funnels.

Also not to be missed is **Pfunds Molkerei** (☎ 816 20; Bautzner Strasse 79; admission free; ⏰ 10am-6pm Mon-Sat, 10am-3pm Sun) in the eastern Äussere Neustadt. Billed as 'the world's most beautiful dairy shop', it's a riot of hand-painted tiles and enamelled sculpture, all handmade by Villeroy & Boch. The shop sells replica tiles, wines, cheeses and milk. Not surprisingly, the upstairs café-restaurant has a strong lactose theme. To avoid the steady stream of coach tourists, visit the shop around lunchtime.

GROSSER GARTEN & AROUND

Southeast of the Altstadt, occupying the former royal hunting grounds, is the aptly named Grosser Garten (Large Garden), an enchanting refuge during the warmer months. A visitor magnet here is the excellent **zoo** (☎ 478 060; Tiergartenstrasse 1; adult/child/concession €7/4/5; ⏰ 8.30am-6.30pm Apr-Oct, 8.30am-4.30pm Nov-Mar), where crowds gravitate towards the Africa Hall and the new Tundra exhibit with arctic foxes and snowy owls. At the garden's northwestern corner is the **Botanischer Garten** (botanical garden; admission free). From April to October, a fun way to get around the park is aboard a **miniature train** (adult/concession €3.10/1.55).

Nearby, the striking Volkswagen **Gläserne Manufaktur** (Transparent Factory; ☎ 0180-589 6268; www .glaesernemanufaktur.de; cnr Grunaerstrasse & Lennéstrasse; admission €4; ⏰ 8am-8pm) is a working factory producing Bentleys and the prestige Phaeton line, with much of the process visible through the glass windows. Tours in German are offered by prior appointment only.

The name may be odd, but don't let that deter you from visiting the unique **Deutsches Hygiene-Museum** (German Hygiene Museum; ☎ 484 6670; www.dhmd.de; Lingnerplatz 1; adult/concession €6/3; ⏰ 10am-6pm Tue-Sun), which is really all about you, the human being. The revamped permanent exhibit is a virtual journey through the body, drawing from anatomy, cultural studies, social science, history and scientific research. You'll learn about various aspects of the human experience – from eating, drinking and thinking to remembering, moving, grooming and dying. Oddly, people seem to linger just a tad longer in the room dealing with sexuality…must be all those nude pictures. A highlight is the *Gläserne Mensch* in room 1, the first transparent human model complete with bones, muscles and arteries.

If you've got tots in tow, they're likely to have more fun in the Hygiene Museum's integrated Children's Museum. Located in the basement, it's a highly interactive romp through the mysteries of the five senses.

YENIDZE

West of the Altstadt, you can't miss what looks like a gaudy mosque with a great stained-glass onion dome. The **Yenidze** (☎ 486 5300, 490 5990; Weisseritzstrasse 3), the world's first reinforced concrete-framed building, actually started out life as a tobacco factory in 1907, manufacturing an unsuccessful pseudo-exotic cigarette named Salaam Alakhem. Today it houses a restaurant with a beer garden, and hosts concerts and other cultural events in its dome.

Walking Tour

Our Altstadt circuit begins at Altmarkt and makes an arc northwest along the Elbe, taking in the main churches, the Semperoper, the Residenzschloss and the Zwinger palace. It's a 1½-hour stroll, but with stops you could easily stretch the tour to a day.

The **Altmarkt (1)** was once the historic heart of Dresden. Postwar reconstruction here was heavily influenced by a socialist aesthetic, which meant lots of stark granite, an impractically wide square and the obnoxiously squat **Kulturpalast (2;** ☎ 486 60; www.kulturpalast-dresden .de; Schlossstrasse 2), home to the Dresden Philharmonic Orchestra. The starkness is tempered by street-side cafés, the spanking new **Altmarkt-Galerie (3)** shopping mall and the late baroque **Kreuzkirche (4**; tower €1.50/1; ☿ 10am-6pm Mon-Sat Apr-Oct, to 4pm Nov-Mar). Rebuilt after the war, the church's interior was left deliberately plain and is best enjoyed during a concert, or at 6pm evening prayers (5pm December to March), which are accompanied by the church's world-famous boys' choir, the 700-year-old Kreuzchor.

Following Kreuzstrasse east, you'll soon spot the neo-Renaissance **Neues Rathaus (5**; New Town Hall; ☎ 1905-10; tower adult/concession/family €2.50/1.24/6; ☿ 10am-6pm Apr-Oct) with its 100m-high climbable tower. Cut north through pedestrianised Weisse Gasse, the Altstadt's most delightful eat street, to Wilsdruffer Strasse, where the **Stadtmuseum (6**; ☎ 6564 8613; www.museen-dresden.de; Wilsdruffer Strasse 2; adult/ concession €3/2; ☿ 10am-6pm Tue-Thu, Sat & Sun, noon-8pm Fri) presents exhibits on general city history as well as on the reconstruction of the Frauenkirche. Also here is the **Städtische Galerie (7**; ☎ 6564 8638; adult/concession €3/2; ☿ 10am-6pm Tue-Thu, Sat & Sun, noon-8pm Fr), where the baroque city presents its modern side with a respectable collection of 20th-century art. Enter from Landhausstrasse.

Follow Landhausstrasse northwest to Neumarkt, which is again dominated by the landmark **Frauenkirche (8**, p170), whose reconstruction was completed in 2005. On Neumarkt, all around the church, construction is progressing at a steady clip, with new hotels and shopping complexes called 'quartiers' springing up. For a preview, check www .neumarkt-dresden.de.

From the north side of Neumarkt, narrow Münzgasse leads straight to the **Brühlsche Terrasse (9)**, a spectacular promenade that's

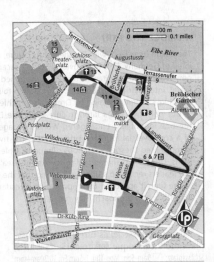

WALK FACTS

Start Altmarkt
Finish Zwinger
Distance 3.5km
Duration 1½ hours

been called the 'balcony of Europe', with a pavement nearly 15m above the southern embankment of the Elbe. It's a must for strolling, with expansive views of the river and the Neustadt on the opposite bank.

Beneath the promenade is the Renaissance brick bastion known as the **Festung Dresden (10**; Dresden Fortress; ☎ 491 4786; adult/child incl audio-guide €3.10/2; ☿ 10am-5pm Apr-Oct, 10am-4pm Nov-Mar), now a museum. The free audio-guide helps bring the place to life. Enter from Georg-Treu-Platz.

Otherwise, take the staircase down to Brühlsche Gasse, which leads back to the Neumarkt. From here, turn right onto Augustusstrasse, with its 102m-long **Fürstenzug (11**; Procession of Princes) mural depicted on the façade of the former Stallhof (royal stables). The scene, a long row of royalty on horses, was first painted in 1876 by Wullhelm Walther and then transferred to some 24,000 Meissen porcelain tiles in 1904.

Also on Augustusstrasse, you'll find a superb collection of vehicles, including penny-farthings, trams, dirigibles and carriages, at the **Verkehrsmuseum (12**; Transport Museum; ☎ 864 40; www.verkehrsmuseum.sachsen.de; Augustusstrasse 1; adult/ concession €3/1.50; ☿ 10am-5pm Tue-Sun).

SAXONY

A BRIDGE TOO FAR?

The Saxon heartland, with Dresden at its centre, represents one of the richest cultural tapestries in all of Germany. This fact obviously didn't escape the Unesco officers in charge of designating new World Heritage sites, who in 2004 welcomed a 20km section of the river valley, the Dresdner Elbtal, into their prestigious club. This stretch follows the Elbe downstream from Schloss Pillnitz to Schloss Übigau, passing by Dresden's matchless baroque magnificence along the way.

But only two years later, in July 2006, the Elbtal ended up on a far less honourable list: the one identifying endangered World Heritage sites. The reason? The planned construction of a controversial four-lane bridge across the river near the scenic spot where Canaletto once immortalised Dresden's fabulous silhouette. Unless the city gives up – or seriously modifies – its plans, Unesco has threatened to revoke the area's World Heritage status. At the time of writing, city leaders remained stubborn, insisting that the organisation had known about the bridge plans at the time it approved their application. Dresden was given until the summer of 2007 to come up with a new approach. Stay tuned.

Augustusstrasse leads directly to Schlossplatz and the baroque **Hofkirche** (13; ☎ 484 4712; Schlossplatz; 🕑 9am-5pm Mon-Thu, 1-5pm Fri, 10.30am-4pm Sat, noon-4pm Sun May-Oct; 10.30am-5pm Sat Nov-Apr). Completed in 1755, its crypt contains the heart of Augustus the Strong; his body is in Cracow. Note the parade of fabulous sculptures peering down from the church's exterior balustrade.

Just south of the church is the neo-Renaissance **Residenzschloss** (14, p170), which now houses several museums. These include the must-see Historisches Grünes Gewölbe and Neues Grünes Gewölbe. On the western side of the Hofkirche is Theaterplatz, with Dresden's dramatic and long-suffering **Semperoper** (15, p171). Next to the opera house is the sprawling **Zwinger** (16, p171), a former palace recycled into a major museum complex that includes Dresden's foremost collection of painting, the Gemäldegalerie Alte Meister.

Tours

The tourist offices can help you book the following tours:

Barokkoko (☎ 479 8184; www.erlebnisrundgang .de; adult/concession €14/9) The Dresden of the 18th century comes alive during these interactive 1½-hour tongue-in-cheek tours, led by costumed actor-guides who'll even teach you the proper way to curtsey and bow. Ask about English-language tours, usually held at 6pm Fridays from April to October.

NightWalk Dresden (☎ 801 3361; www.nightwalk -dresden.de; tours incl three drinks €12; 🕑 9pm) Learn all about the intriguing culture and history of the happening Neustadt, one pub at a time,

during this fun walk led by clued-in locals. It's organised by Hostel Die Boofe (opposite); just show up at Albertplatz.

Sächsische Dampfschiffahrt (☎ 866 090; www .saechsische-dampfschiffahrt.de; adult/child €11/5.50; 🕑 Apr-Oct) Ninety-minute river tours on rebuilt paddle-wheel steam boats leave from the Terrassenufer dock at 11am, 1pm, 3pm and 5pm daily. There's also regular service up the Elbe to Schloss and Park Pillnitz (p178) and the Sächsische Schweiz (p180) and down-river to Meissen (p182).

Stadtrundfahrt Dresden (☎ 899 5650; www .stadtrundfahrt.com; tour €18) This narrated hop-on, hop-off tour has 22 stops in the centre and the elegant outer villa districts along the Elbe. It includes short tours of the Zwinger, Fürstenzug, Frauenkirche and Pfunds Molkerei.

Trabi Safari (☎ 899 0060; www.trabi-safari.de; per person from €20) Get behind the wheel of the ultimate GDR-mobile for this 1½-hour guided drive.

Festivals & Events

Major annual events include the following:
Internationales Dixieland Festival (www.dixieland .de) Early each May, with bands from around the world.
Dresdener Musikfestspiele (Music Festival; www .musikfestspiele.de) Held mid-May to June, with mostly classical music.
Bunte Republik Neustadt (www.bunte-republik -neustadt.net) In mid-June, with lots of free alternative concerts.
Dresdener Stadtfest (City Festival) Mid-July, with something for everyone.
Striezelmarkt (www.striezel-markt.de) In December, one of Germany's oldest Christmas markets and a great place to sample the famous Dresdener Stollen (a fruitcake).

Sleeping

Dresden accommodation can be horrendously expensive, with rates among the highest in the Germany. The **tourist offices** (☎ 4919 2222) can find private rooms from €20 per person.

BUDGET

A crop of excellent indie hostels has sprung up in the hip Neustadt.

Hostel Die Boofe (☎ 801 3361; www.boofe.de; Hechtstrasse 10; q per person €17, s €31, d €46, studio €69, breakfast €5; ✗ ☐) A big thumbs up for this friendly place with above-average rooms, a leafy courtyard and – drum roll please! – a sauna. Gregarious types gravitate to the lively bar and communal kitchen, while privacy-seekers can retire to spacious studios with individual kitchens in the garden house.

Mezcalero (☎ 810770; www.mezcalero.de; Königsbrücker Strasse 64; dm €17-23, linen €2.30, s/d €50/64, breakfast €6; P ✗) Definitely one for the 'oddities' basket: how often do you get to stay in a Mexican-Aztec B&B, complete with sombreros, festive colours, tiles and tequila bar? Very random, very cool.

Hostel Mondpalast (☎ 563 4050; www.mondpalast .de; Louisenstrasse 77; dm €13.50-16, s €39, d €50, linen €2, breakfast €5; ✗ ☐) Check in at the outta-this-world bar-café (with cheap drinks) before being 'beamed up' to your room in the Moon Palace – each one dedicated to a sign of the zodiac or some other spacey theme. Bike rentals and large kitchen are also available.

Also recommended:

Lollis Homestay (☎ 810 8458; www.lollishome.de; Görlitzer Strasse 34; dm €13-19, s €27-38, d €36-42; ✗ ☐) Small, chirpy, artsy.

Hostel & Backpacker kangaroo-stop (☎ 314 3455; www.kangaroo-stop.de; Erna-Berger-Strasse 8-10; dm €12.50-14.50, s/d/tr/q €27/34/48/60, apt €70-80; breakfast €4.50; P ✗ ☐) Welcoming and low-key, with rooms spread over two buildings; one for backies, the other for families.

MIDRANGE

Pension am Zwinger (☎ 8990 0100; www.pension -zwinger.de; Ostra-Allee 27; s €60, each extra person €20; P ✗) Self-caterers, families and space-cravers will appreciate these modern, subtly stylish studios with full kitchens. Ring the bell and wait for someone to check you in (check-in times are 9am to 8pm).

Hotel Privat (☎ 811770; www.das-nichtraucher-hotel .de; Forststrasse 22; s €51-66, d €67-91; P ✗) This small, family-run hotel has Saxon charm galore and 30 good-sized rooms, some with alcoves and balconies. It's entirely nonsmoking, and that includes the garden.

Hotel Martha Hospiz (☎ 817 60; www.vch.de/martha hospiz.dresden; Nieritzstrasse 11; s €77-84, d €107-118; P) Hospitality is taken very seriously at this lovely, quiet inn, with a quirky cellar restaurant. Newer rooms are decked out in Biedermeier-style and seven are wheelchair-accessible.

Hotel Schloss Eckberg/Kavaliershaus (☎ 809 90; www.schloss-eckberg.de; Bautzner Strasse 134; s €85-97, d €118-135; P ✗ ☐) You'll feel like royalty when arriving at this romantic estate set in its own riverside park east of the Neustadt. Rooms in the historic Schloss are pricier and have more flair, but staying in the modern Kavaliershaus lets you enjoy almost as many amenities and the same dreamy setting.

Rothenburger Hof (☎ 812 60; www.rothenburger -hof.de; Rothenburger Strasse 15-17; s €105-115, d €135-145, apt €125-165; P ✗ ☒ ☒) This quiet launch pad for Neustadt explorations counts among its assets apartments with kitchenette and balcony, a Moorish-style steam room and an extra-lavish breakfast.

The three Ibis hotels – in identical GDR-era concrete beehives along Prager Strasse – are not pretty, but they do offer good value for money. They all have snug, functional rooms (singles €53 to €66, doubles €68 to €91, breakfast is €9):

Hotel Bastei (☎ 4856 6661; ✗ ☒)
Hotel Königstein (☎ 4856 6662; ✗ ☒)
Hotel Lilienstein (☎ 4856 6663; ✗ ☒)

TOP END

Dresden Hilton (☎ 864 20; www.hilton.com; An der Frauenkirche 5; s/d from €122/142, breakfast €19; P ✗ ☒ ☐ ☒) Big, busy and very central, the Hilton is a small village with 333 handsome rooms, over a dozen bars and restaurants, a full-service spa and fitness club, and security worthy of a president. Kids stay free in their parents' room.

Radisson SAS Gewandhaushotel (☎ 494 90; www .radissonsas.com; Ringstrasse 1; r €125-290, ste €450-550, breakfast €19; P ✗ ☒ ☐ ☒) Another top choice for class and personal service. Housed in a former fabric factory, the public areas are stunning and most Biedermeier-style rooms have whirlpool baths in their marble-fitted bathrooms.

Hotel Bülow Residenz (☎ 800 30; www.buelow -residenz.de; Rähnitzstrasse 19; s/d €190/240, breakfast €19; P ✗ ☒) This place is a class act all-round, from the welcome drink to the cute bears delivered at turndown, the free minibar to free DSL. Even the standard rooms are spacious and the restaurant has a fine reputation as well.

Westin Bellevue (☎ 8050; www.westin.com/dresden; Grosse Meissner Strasse 15; s €160-230, d €180-260, breakfast €19; Ⓟ ✕ ⬚ ⬚ ⬚) Baroque and modern elements blend smoothly in this sprawling and elegant property, where the nicest rooms give you unparalleled views of Dresden's famous silhouette.

Kempinski Hotel Taschenbergpalais (☎ 491 20; www.kempinski-dresden.de; Taschenberg 3; s €270-355, d €300-385, ste €480-900, breakfast €24; Ⓟ ✕ ⬚ ⬚ ⬚) This restored 18th-century mansion is Dresden's heavyweight, with views over the Zwinger, incredibly quiet corridors and Bulgari toiletries. In winter, the courtyard turns into an ice rink.

Eating
ALTSTADT

The Altstadt brims with restaurants, most of them targeting the tourist hordes. For a bit more local flavour, try some of the places on pedestrianised Weisse Gasse (or head to the Neustadt).

brennNessel (☎ 494 3319; Schützengasse 18; mains €4.50-10) The city's best vegetarian cuisine is prepared in the kitchen of this cute half-timbered house with a woodsy interior and leafy cobbled courtyard. It's a favourite hangout for off-duty Semperoper musicians.

Ladencafé Aha (☎ 496 0673; Kreuzstrasse 7; mains €5-12; ⏲ 10am-midnight) At this warm and cheerful smoke- and stress-free zone above a one-world store, you can sip delicious coffee, pick from the international menu, leaf through the many magazines or watch your kiddies play with the provided toys.

Sophienkeller (☎ 497 260; Taschenberg 3; mains €7-16) The tourist-oriented 1730's theme may be a bit overdone, but the costumed wenches do actually serve up good local specialities and wines. Try the famous Dresden *Trichter* (drinking funnel).

Barococo (☎ 862 3040; Altmarkt 10; snacks from €4.50, mains €8-20) Often packed to the gills, this fish restaurant has nice Altstadt views from the upstairs dining room and amazing Piscean wall sculptures made from silver cutlery.

Gänsedieb (☎ 485 0905; Weisse Gasse 1; mains €8-15) One of nearly a dozen choices on Weisse Gasse, the 'Goose Thief' serves hearty schnitzels, goulash and steaks alongside a full range

of Bavarian Paulaner beers. The name, by the way, was inspired by the fountain outside.

Also recommended:

Grand Cafe (☎ 496 2444; An der Frauenkirche 12; mains €10-20; ⏲ 10-1am) Yummy cakes and more in the gold-trimmed Coselpalais.

Ogura (☎ 864 2975; An der Frauenkirche 5; meals from €25; ⏲ noon-2pm, 5.30-10.30pm) Dresden's best sushi restaurant, inside the Hilton.

NEUSTADT

Raskolnikoff (☎ 804 5706; www.raskolnikoff.de; Böhmische Strasse 34; mains €4-12) This bohemian café in a former artists' squat was one of the Neustadt's first post-Wende pubs. The menu is sorted by compass direction (borscht to quiche Lorraine to smoked fish) and there's a sweet little beer garden out the back, and a gallery and pension (single/double room €30 to €45) upstairs.

Nudely Turm (☎ 804 3094; Bautzner Strasse 1; mains €5-13) A lifesaver for families, this pasta place has cartoony menus and great views. Children under four eat free.

PlanWirtschaft (☎ 801 3187; Louisenstrasse 20; mains €6-15; ⏲ 9-1am) Only fresh, organic ingredients sourced from local butchers and farmers make it into the international potpourri of dishes at this long-time favourite. There's a romantic courtyard for balmy days and a small hostel (☎ 889 4894; www.louise20.de) upstairs.

El Perro Borracho (☎ 803 6723; Alaunstrasse 70, Kunsthof; tapas €2.90) A glass of Rioja, a platter of tapas, a cobblestoned courtyard, a balmy summer night – close your eyes and you'll feel (almost) transported to Seville at this buzzy place in the cheerful Kunsthofpassage.

Villandry (☎ 899 6724; Jordanstrasse 8; mains €8-16; ⏲ 6.30-11.30pm Mon-Sat) The folks in the kitchen here sure know how to coax maximum flavour out of even the simplest ingredients, and to turn them into super-tasty Mediterranean treats for eyes and palate. Meals are best enjoyed in the lovely courtyard.

Le Maréchal de Saxe (☎ 810 5880; Königstrasse 5; mains €9-14) One of several upmarket restaurants in this smart area, offering proper 18th-century Saxon court cuisine.

Drinking
ALTSTADT

Fährgarten Johannstadt (☎ 459 6262; Käthe-Kollwitz-Ufer 23b; ⏲ 10-1am Apr-Oct) East of the Altstadt, right on the Elbe, is this idyllic beer garden with great ales, grilled meats, memorable views and a children's playground.

Rauschenbach Deli (☎ 821 2760; Weisse Gasse 2; mains €7-15; ☼ 9-1am) A café by day, this contempo spot morphs into a chic bar with an endless cocktail menu when the moon gets high. Nice terrace, too.

Classic American Bar (☎ 491 2720; Kleine Brüdergasse) This one's for the grown-ups – all clubby with dark wood, red leather banquettes, a piano and some neat Wild West murals inspired by the books of Karl May.

NEUSTADT

If you're up for a night on the razzle, head to the Äussere Neustadt, which is chock-a-block with café-bars. Alaunstrasse, Louisenstrasse and Görlitzer Strasse are the main drags.

Scheune (☎ 802 6619; Alaunstrasse 36-40) A GDR-era youth club has been reborn as an artsy pub and alternative rock venue here, with a beer garden and Indian food on the menu (mains €5 to €10).

Neumanns Tiki (☎ 810 3837; Görlitzer Strasse 21) This Polynesian cocktail bar and (homemade) ice-cream parlour in the Kunsthofpassage has shown that it's not just 'flavour of the month'. Caipirinha happy hour runs until 9pm.

Café 100 (☎ 801 7729; Alaunstrasse 100) Wine lovers should make a beeline for this candle-lit pub, with its romantic cavernous cellar and 250 wines on the menu. It's a great place for first dates.

Frank's (☎ 802 6727; Alaunstrasse 80) Famed for its huge cocktail menu, this is a long-running Neustadt stalwart.

Wohnzimmer (☎ 563 5956; Alaunstrasse 27) Take grandma's sofas, combine with flowery wallpaper and candlelight, add some smooth sounds and you've got yourself one stylish and conversation-friendly watering hole.

Café Europa (☎ 804 4810; Königsbrücker Strasse 68; ☼ 24hr; ▯) Newspapers, intimate lighting and free internet facilities feature at this smart, relaxed café that's open around the clock.

Reisekneipe (☎ 267 1930; Görlitzer Strasse 15; ▯) Dream of faraway places at this exotic pub while quaffing a beer in a thatched hut, an oriental lounge or a Sherpa lodge. Hardened globetrotters give mid-week slide-show talks.

Entertainment

The finest all-round listings guide to Dresden is *SAX* (€1.30), sold at newsstands. Regular freebies include *Blitz* and *Frizz*, and the

Kneipensurfer and *Nachtfalter* maps. They can be found at the tourist offices, and in cafés and pubs.

CLASSICAL MUSIC

Dresdner Philharmonie (☎ 486 6306; www.dresdner philharmonie.de) The city's renowned orchestra performs mostly at the Kulturpalast on Altmarkt. Also check the listings magazines for concerts at the Hofkirche, Dreikönigskirche, Kreuzkirche and Frauenkirche.

Sächsische Staatsoper (☎ 491 1705; www.semper oper.de) Dresden is synonymous with opera, and performances at the spectacular Semperoper (p171) are brilliant. Tickets are hard to come by, though, so plan well ahead or hope for returns.

CLUBS

Strasse E (www.strasse-e.de; Werner-Hartmann-Strasse 2) Dresden's most high-octane party zone is in an industrial area between Neustadt and the airport. Half a dozen venues cover the entire sound spectrum, from disco to dark wave, electro to pop. Take tram 7 or 8 to Industriegelände. Some of the clubs below are closer to town.

Dance Factory (☎ 802 0066; Bautzner Strasse 118; ☼ Thu-Sat) This very popular spot, east of the Neustadt, has the usual mix of R&B, cheese and trance/techno in four rooms. The bouncers can be choosy.

Down Town (☎ 811 5592; Katharinenstrasse 11-13; ☼ Fri, Sat & Mon) This iconic old factory gives you early *Saturday Night Fever* with its 1970s and '80s nights on Fridays. On Mondays latex lovers invade for the legendary Nasty Love Club.

Flower Power (☎ 804 9814; www.nubeatz.de/fpd; Eschenstrasse 11) The spirit of the '60s is kept alive at this staple of the Dresden student scene, with DJs every night.

U-Boot (Bautzner Strasse 75; ☼ Wed, Fri & Sat) Anything from reggae to nu-punk, catering for the skater crowd.

LIVE MUSIC

Alter Schlachthof (☎ 858 8529; Gothaer Strasse 11) The industrial charm of an old slaughterhouse draws a party-happy crowd for mostly alternative concerts, from bands like Calexico to Fury in the Slaughterhouse…how appropriate.

Blue Note (☎ 801 4275; www.jazzdepartment.com; Görlitzer Strasse 2b; ☼ to 5am or later) Small, smoky and smooth, this converted smithy has live

SAXONY

jazz almost nightly until 11pm, then turns into a night-owl magnet until the wee hours. The talent is mostly regional.

Katy's Garage (☎ 656 7701; Alaunstrasse 48) This place, a key venue for indie gigs and club nights throughout the week, is in a former tyre shop.

Jazzclub Neue Tonne (☎ 8026017;www.jazzclub-tonne .de; Königstrasse 15) Bigger names hit the stage here, and it's a bit more polished than Blue Note.

GAY & LESBIAN VENUES

Dresden's gay scene is concentrated in the Neustadt. For listings, turn to **GegenPol** (www .gegenpol.net, in German).

Boy's (☎ 796 8824; www.boysdresden.de; Alaunstrasse 30; ☯ Tue-Sun) A lively bar-club with parties on Friday and Saturday. A top venue for S&M (standing and modelling, not what you were thinking…).

Queens (☎ 803 1650; Görlitzer Strasse 3) The kitsch décor is the perfect backdrop for this pulsating hot spot, famous for its *Schlager* (schmaltzy German pop songs) parties.

Sappho (☎ 404 5136; Hechtstrasse 23) This new women's café is an excellent addition to Dresden's thriving lesbigay map.

Valentino (☎ 889 4996; Jordanstrasse 2; ☐) A low-key café with great cakes, ice cream and internet access.

CINEMAS

Check www.kinokalender.com for monthly listings. Undubbed English films are shown at the following:

Programmkino Ost (☎ 310 3782; Schandauer Strasse 73) South of the Altstadt.

Quasimodo (☎ 866 0224; Adlergasse 14)

Ufa-Palast (☎ 482 5825; St-Petersburger-Strasse 24a)

THEATRE

There's an active theatre scene in Dresden. Many small companies perform throughout the city; *SAX* has the scoop. Buy theatre tickets at tourist offices or the theatre's box office an hour before the performance. Many theatres close from mid-July to the end of August.

Schauspielhaus (☎ 491 3555; www.staatsschauspiel dresden.de; Altstadt Ostra-Allee 3; Neustadt Glacisstrasse 28) The renowned Staatsschauspiel ensemble plays mostly crowd-pleasers by German playwrights in two venues.

Carte Blanche (☎ 204 720; www.carte-blanche -dresden.de; Priessnitzstrasse 10) Drag queen shows at their finest.

Societätstheater (☎ 803 6810; www.societaets theater.de; An der Dreikönigskirche 1a) A modern and experimental theatre.

Getting There & Away

Dresden airport (☎ 881 3360; www.dresden-airport .de) has mostly domestic and holiday charter flights.

Dresden is 2¼ hours south of Berlin-Hauptbahnhof (€32). For Leipzig choose from hourly ICE trains (€26, one hour) or RE trains (€18.30, 1¾ hours). The S-Bahn runs half-hourly to Meissen (€4.80, 40 minutes). There are connections to Frankfurt (€76, 4¾ hours) and Prague (€26, 2½ hours).

Dresden is connected to Leipzig via the A14/A4, to Berlin via the A13/A113, and to the Czech Republic via the B170 south.

For ride shares contact **Mitfahrzentrale** (☎ 194 40; Dr-Friedrich-Wolf-Strasse 2).

Getting Around

Public transport is operated by **Dresdner Verkehrsbetriebe** (☎ 857 1011), which has several information kiosks, including one outside the Hauptbahnhof.

The S2 train serves the airport from the Hauptbahnhof and Dresden-Neustadt (€1.70, 23 and 14 minutes respectively). Budget about €10 for a taxi to the Hauptbahnhof.

Single bus and tram tickets cost €1.70, a day pass is €4.50. The family day pass, for two adults and up to four kids, is a steal at €5.50. Tickets are available aboard and from vending machines at stops.

The starting rate for taxis is €2.10. Taxis line up at the Hauptbahnhof and Neustadt station, or ring ☎ 211 211. For short hops within the Altstadt, consider a Velotaxi pedicab (rickshaw), which charge €2.50 per person for the first kilometre, then €1 for each additional kilometre.

Bicycle hire is available at the Hauptbahnhof (☎ 461 3262) and Neustadt (☎ 461 5601) stations for €7 per day.

AROUND DRESDEN
Schloss & Park Pillnitz

Baroque has gone exotic at this **pleasure palace** (☎ 261 3260; park admission free; ☯ park 5am-dusk, visitors centre 9am-6pm May-Oct, 10am-4pm Nov-Apr), festooned with fanciful Chinese flourishes. This is where the Saxon rulers once lived it up during long hot Dresden summers. A mere 10km southeast of Dresden, Pillnitz is dreamily wedged in between vineyards and the Elbe, and is best reached aboard a steamer operated by **Sächsische Dampfschiffahrt** (☎ 0351-866 090; one-way/return €9.20/14.30; ⏱ 1½ hr); boats leave from the Terrassenufer in Dresden (Map pp168–9). Otherwise, bus 83 goes pretty close to the palace.

You can explore the wonderful gardens on your own or join a **guided park tour** (adult/concession/family €3/2/8; ⏱ 11am & 1pm May-Oct). To learn more about the history of the palace and life at court, visit the new **Schlossmuseum** (adult/concession €3/2; ⏱ 10am-6pm Apr-Oct, guided tours 11am & 1pm Sat & Sun Nov-Mar) in the Neues Palais.

Two other buildings, the Wasserpalais and the Bergpalais, house the **Kunstgewerbemuseum** (Arts & Crafts Museum; ☎ 4914 2000; adult/concession/family €3/2/5, more during special exhibits; ⏱ Bergpalais 10am-6pm Tue-Sun May-Oct, Wasserpalais 10am-6pm Wed-Mon), which is filled with fancy furniture and objects from the Saxon court, including Augustus the Strong's throne.

Schloss Moritzburg

Rising impressively from a lake 14km northwest of Dresden, **Schloss Moritzburg** (☎ 035207-8730; adult/concession/family €6/4/10; ⏱ 10am-5.30pm daily Apr-Oct, 10am-4pm Tue-Sun Nov, Dec & Mar, 10am-4pm Sat & Sun Jan & Feb) is yet another baroque playground of August der Starke. The rich interior boasts ornate leather wall coverings, paintings, furniture and the recently restored Federzimmer (Feather Room), featuring August's fanciful bed. Guided tours in German (€2) are conducted hourly. The palace parkland is ideal for drifting around.

Buses 326 and 458 run to Moritzburg from behind Dresden's Neustadt train station (€3.40, 25 minutes). For a more atmospheric approach, first take the S1 train to Radebeul-Ost (€1.70, 13 minutes), then catch the 1884 narrow-gauge **Lössnitzgrundbahn** (€5.30, 30 minutes) to Moritzburg, from where it's a short walk to the Schloss.

Radebeul

Although a separate town, Radebeul serves as an upmarket bedroom community of Dresden, and has a couple of quirky museums. First up is the **Karl-May-Museum** (☎ 0351-837 300; Karl-May-Strasse 5; adult/concession/child €6/4/2; ⏱ Tue-Sun 9am-6pm Mar-Oct, 10am-4pm Nov-Feb), essentially a tribute to Germany's greatest adventure writer. May's rousing tales have sold over 100 million copies worldwide and for generations shaped the image of the American Wild West

and the Near East in German minds. Villa Shatterhand charts his life and work, while Villa Bärenfett has a highly-rated exhibition on Native Americans.

Further west along Meissener Strasse, the oddly intriguing **Zeitreise Lebensart DDR 1949–1989** (☎ 0351-811 3860; Wasastrasse 50; adult/concession €6/4.50; ⏱ 10am-6pm Tue-Sun) provides a fascinating glimpse into daily life in the GDR. There are three floors crammed with memorabilia, including a great collection of Trabis, ingenious self-contained camping units, plus tons of toys, toasters, televisions and other trinkets.

The sun-kissed slopes around here produce some fairly good wine, with some of the finest hailing from **Schloss Wackerbarth** (☎ 0351-895 5200; www.schloss-wackerbarth.de; Wackerbarthstrasse 1; ⏱ 9.30am-8pm), another 4km further west. You can taste wine (€1 per mini-serving) whenever the store is open, but it's more fun to combine a tasting with a tour (most tour guides have English skills). Wine tours run daily at 2pm, with sparkling wine tours going at 5pm. The cost for either is €9 and includes three tastes.

From Dresden, take the S1 train to Radebeul-Ost (€1.70, 13 minutes).

Schloss Weesenstein

A magnificent sight, high above the Müglitz River, **Schloss Weesenstein** (☎ 035027-6260; www.schloss-weesenstein.de; adult/child/concession €4.50/2/3; ⏱ 9am-6pm Apr-Oct, 10am-5pm Nov-Mar) is one of the most undervisited and untouched palaces in Germany. In an amazing alchemy of styles, it blends its medieval roots with later Renaissance and baroque embellishments. This results in an architectural curiosity where the horse stables somehow ended up above a much younger residential tract.

Weesenstein owes much of its distinctive looks to the noble Bünau family, who were granted the palace by the Margrave of Meissen in 1406, and continued to live there for 12 generations until 1772. In the 19th century, it became the home of philosopher-king Johann of Saxony, who also took time off from his royal duties to translate Dante into German. Lavishly furnished and decorated rooms on the ground floor contain an exhibit about the man and life at court. This is completed by two or three annually changing exhibits.

There are several restaurants, including a café in the former palace prison, a traditional brewpub and the upmarket Königliche Schlossküche. After filling your belly, you can take a digestive saunter in the lovely baroque park.

During the Whitsun (Pentecost) weekend, the town holds its **Mittelalterfest** (adult/concession €7/5), a medieval festival featuring jousting, crafts, food and freshly brewed beer.

Schloss Weesenstein is about 16km southeast of Dresden. Coming by train from Dresden requires a change in Heidenau (€5.10, 30 minutes). Weesenstein train station is about 500m south of the castle – follow the road up the hill. By car, take the A17 to Pirna, then head towards Glashütte and follow the signs to the Schloss.

SAXON SWITZERLAND

Also known as Elbsandsteingebirge (the Elbe Sandstone Mountains), Saxon Switzerland (Sächsische Schweiz) embraces one of Germany's most unique and evocative landscapes within its 275-sq-km boundaries. This is wonderfully rugged country where Nature has chiselled porous rock into bizarre columns, battered cliffs, tabletop mountains and deep valleys and gorges. The Elbe courses through thick forest, past villages and mighty hilltop castles. No wonder such fabled beauty was a big hit with artists of the Romantic Age, including the painter Caspar David Friedrich and fairytale writer Hans Christian Andersen. In 1990, about a third of the area became Saxony's first and only national park.

You could check off the area's highlights on a long day trip from Dresden, but to truly 'get' the magic of Saxon Switzerland, consider spending at least a couple of days here. Hitting the trail will quickly get you away from the tourist hordes and there are plenty of intriguing pockets tucked away in the valleys. The area is also among the country's premier rock climbing meccas, offering over 15,000 routes, and cyclists can follow the lovely Elberadweg.

Getting There & Around

There are only three bridges across the Elbe: two in Pirna and one in Bad Schandau. Passenger ferries (bicycles allowed) cross the Elbe in several other villages.

BOAT

From April to October, steam boats operated by **Sächsische Dampfschiffahrt** (☎ 0351-866 090) plough up the Elbe several times daily between Dresden and Schöna, stopping in Rathen, Königstein, Bad Schandau and other towns. You can make the entire trip from Dresden or travel between towns.

BUS

From mid-April to October, a bus service operated by **Frank Nuhn Freizeit und Tourismus** (☎ 035021-676 14; www.frank-nuhn-freizeit-und-tourismus.de) shuttles between Königstein, Bad Schandau and the Bastei four times daily. The same company also operates the so-called Bastei-Kraxler, which makes hourly runs between 9.30am and 5pm from the town of Wehlen up to the Bastei. Buy tickets from the bus driver.

CAR & MOTORCYCLE

Towns are linked to Dresden and each other by the B172; coming from Dresden, it's faster to take the new A17 and pick up the B172 in Pirna.

TRAIN

The handy S1 connects Bad Schandau, Königstein, Rathen and other Saxon Switzerland towns with Dresden, Radebeul and Meissen every 30 minutes. Bad Schandau is also a stop on some long-distance trains travelling between Hamburg, Berlin and Vienna.

Bastei

The open fields and rolling hills surrounding the Bastei region, on the Elbe, give little clue as to the drama that lies beyond. One of the most breathtaking spots in Germany, this is a wonderland of fluted pinnacles (up to 305m high) and panoramic views of the surrounding forests, cliffs and mountains – not to mention a magnificent sightline along the river itself. This is the single most popular spot in the national park, so crowds are pretty much guaranteed unless you get here very early or late in the day.

Bastei is an old-fashioned word meaning 'bastion' or 'fortress', in this case the **Felsenburg** (☎ 03501-581 00; adult/concession €1.50/0.50; ✆ 9am-6pm), a wooden castle occupying this strategic spot from the early 13th century until 1469. These days, a series of footbridges links the crags on which the castle was built, but its remnants are so few that it requires archaeological training, or at least a lot of imagination, to picture the place. A highlight is the replica of a catapult once used by castle residents to

WHAT'S IN A NAME?

Its highest peak rises to 723m, meaning Saxon Switzerland ain't exactly the Alps, so how did the region get its name? Credit belongs to the Swiss, actually. During the 18th century, the area's romantic scenery, with its needle-nose pinnacles and craggy cliffs, lured countless artists from around the world. Among them was the Swiss landscape artist Adrian Zingg and his friend, the portraitist Anton Graff, who had been hired to teach at Dresden's prestigious art academy. Both felt that the landscape very much resembled their homeland (the Swiss Jura) and *voilà*, the phrase 'Saxon Switzerland' was born. Travel writers picked it up and so it remains to this day.

pelt attackers with ball-shaped rocks. During sieges they would simply destroy the wooden bridges, sending their enemies plummeting to their deaths. Fortunately, these days the much-photographed **Basteibrücke** leading to the castle grounds is made of stone. For the classic view, follow the little unpaved trail veering left off the main track just before reaching the bridge.

SLEEPING & EATING

The only hotel option up here is **Berghotel Bastei** (☎ 035024-7790; www.bastei-berghotel.de; s €44-48, d €72-116; **P**), a nicely spruced-up GDR-era hotel with comfy rooms, a decent restaurant with superb views, plus extras like bowling and sauna.

Otherwise, you can find rooms from about €15 per person in the convenient but nondescript village of **Lohmen** (tourist office ☎ 03501-581 024; Schloss Lohmen 1), a couple of kilometres due northeast, or in nearby **Rathen** (☎ 035024-704 22; Füllhölzelweg 1), a tiny but postcard-pretty resort town right on the Elbe. A characterful, good-value option here is **Burg Altrathen** (☎ 035024-7600; www.burg-altrathen.de; Am Grünbach 10-11; dm €13, d €44-76, tower ste €100; ✗) in a medieval castle above town.

GETTING THERE & AWAY

The nearest train station is in Rathen, where you need to catch the ferry across the Elbe, then follow a sweat-inducing 30-minute trail to the top of the Bastei. En route you'll pass the lovely **Felsenbühne** (☎ 035024-7770), an open-

air summer theatre that stages light-hearted fare beneath a spectacular rocky backdrop.

To get there by bus, see opposite. Public bus 237 also makes the trip to the Bastei from Pirna or Lohmen.

Drivers should arrive before 10am to snag a spot in the inner Bastei car park (€3 for three hours, €5.50 all day), from where it's only a 10-minute walk to the viewpoints. Otherwise, you need to park in the outer lot (€2.50 all day) and catch the frequent shuttle bus (€1 each way) or walk for at least half an hour.

Königstein

South of Rathen, the Elbe has carved an S-curve ending at Königstein 6km away. The town would be unremarkable were it not for the massive citadel built right on a tabletop mountain some 260m above the river. **Festung Königstein** (☎ 035021-646 07; adult/concession/family €5/3/12, audio-guide €2.50; ⊙ 9am-8pm Apr-Sep, 9am-6pm Oct, 9am-5pm Nov-Mar) is the largest intact fortress in the country, and so imposing and formidable that it was never even attacked. Begun in the 13th century, it was repeatedly enlarged and is now a veritable textbook in military architecture, with 30 buildings spread across 9.5 hectares. Highlights include the **Brunnenhaus**, with its seemingly bottomless well, Germany's oldest extant barracks, and the **Georgenburg**, once Saxony's most feared prison, whose famous inmates included Meissen porcelain inventor Johann Friedrich Böttger. During WWII, it served as a POW camp and a refuge for art treasures from Dresden.

More than anything, however, it is the spectacular views deep into the national park and across to the Lilienstein tabletop mountain that give this place its special appeal.

There are several eateries up at the fortress and more in the town below. The **tourist office** (☎ 035021-682 61; www.koenigstein-sachsen.de; Schreiberberg 2) can help with finding lodging. A great budget pick is **Ferdinands Homestay** (☎ 035022-547 75; www.ferdinandshomestay.de; Halbestrasse 51; dm €7.50-15, s/d/tw €26.50/33/33, tent/adult €2.50/4; **P** ✗), a small and friendly riverside hostel and campsite combo in a secluded, remote spot on the northern bank. Call for directions.

Daily, from April to October, a tourist train makes the steep climb half-hourly, starting at 9am from Reissiger Platz in Königstein (€1.70). Both drop you at the bottom of the fortress, from where you can get a lift or walk.

Alternatively it's a strenuous 30- to 45-minute climb from the bottom. The nearest car park is down below, off the B172.

Bad Schandau

☎ 035022 / pop 3300

Bad Schandau, a poky little spa town on the Elbe just 5km north of the Czech border, is the most central of Saxon Switzerland's towns and a great base for hikes.

The **tourist office** (☎ 900 30; www.bad-schandau .de; Markt 12; ◷ 9am-9pm daily May-Oct, 9am-6pm Mon-Fri, 9am-1pm Sat & Sun Nov-Apr) and the **Nationalparkhaus** (☎ 502 40; www.lanu.de; Dresdner Strasse 2b; adult/concession/family €4/3/7.50; ◷ 9am-6pm daily Apr-Oct, 9am-5pm Tue-Sun Nov-Mar) are in the centre of town. At the latter's interactive exhibit you'll learn how the sandstone formations were shaped and get an easy general introduction to the park's flora and fauna. A free English-language audio-guide is available.

At the southern end of town, the century-old **Personenaufzug** (passenger lift; adult/child return €2.50/1.50; ◷ 9am-6pm Apr & Oct, 9am-7pm May-Sep, 9am-5pm Nov-Mar) whisks you up a 50m-high tower for a commanding view. A footbridge links the structure to a pretty forest path that runs partially along the ridge. A good destination to head for is the **Schrammsteinaussicht**, a viewpoint about an hour's moderately strenuous walk away. It overlooks the rugged Schrammsteine, the densest rock labyrinth in the national park and hugely popular with rock hounds.

The **Kirnitzschtalbahn** (one-way/return €3/4) is a museum-piece tram that runs 7km northeast along the Kirnitzsch River to the **Lichtenhainer Wasserfall**, a good spot to begin a hike among the sandstone cliffs. Trams run every 30 minutes from April to October.

Another fun excursion is to the hamlet of **Hinterhermsdorf**, in a remote cul-de-sac about 14km east of Bad Schandau. Here you can hire flat-bottomed boats for floats on the Kirnitzsch River through an idyllic canyon – you can't feel much more secluded than this. Bus 241 (€1.70, 35 minutes) leaves from Bad Schandau several times (daily).

SLEEPING & EATING

Lindenhof (☎ 4890; www.lindenhof-bad-schandau.de; Rudolf-Sendig-Strasse 11; s €36-50, d €46-84; **P**) Smart hotel with a good traditional restaurant.

Parkhotel (☎ 520; www.parkhotel-bad-schandau.de; Rudolf-Sendig-Strasse 12; s €50-70, d €76-96; **P** ✕) An excellent spot to feed your craving for luxury, the

Parkhotel has cheerful rooms in three buildings in a parklike riverside setting. Stress-melting spots include the elegant spa, a good-sized fitness area and a popular restaurant.

MEISSEN

☎ 03521 / pop 29,000

Some 27km northwest of Dresden, at the heart of a rich wine-growing region, Meissen is a compact, perfectly preserved old town. Crowning a rocky ridge above it is the Albrechtsburg palace, which in 1710 became the cradle of European porcelain manufacturing. The world-famous Meissen china, easily recognised by its trademark insignia of blue crossed swords, is still the main reason the town is such a favourite with coach tourists. Fortunately, the Altstadt's cobbled lanes, dreamy nooks and idyllic courtyards make getting away from the shuffling crowds a snap.

Orientation

Meissen straddles the Elbe, with the old town on the western bank and the train station on the eastern. The pedestrian-only Altstadt-brücke (bridge) near the station is the quickest way across, and it presents you with a picture-postcard view of the town. Follow Elbstrasse west to the central square, Markt, and the tourist office. Drivers need to take the Elbtalbrücke further north.

Information

Commerzbank (Hauptbahnhof)

Café Domizil (☎ 407 852; Burgstrasse 9; per 30min €1.70) Internet access.

Tourist office (☎ 419 40; www.touristinfo-meissen.de; Markt 3; ◷ 10am-6pm Mon-Fri, 10am-4pm Sat & Sun Apr-Oct, 10am-5pm Mon-Fri, 10am-3pm Sat Nov, Dec, Feb & Mar)

FUMMEL VISION

While you're in Meissen, it's virtually compulsory to try the peculiar local patisserie known as the *Meissner Fummel*. Resembling an ostrich egg made of very delicate pastry, legend has it the Fummel was invented in 1710 as a test to stop the royal courier from drinking between deliveries – great care is required if you want to get it home in one piece! Test your skills at the 150-year-old **Café Zieger** (Burgstrasse), by the foot of the Rote Stufen.

Sights

The Markt is framed by the **Rathaus** (1472) and the Gothic **Frauenkirche** (☎ 453 832; tower adult/concession €2/1; ☼ 10am-noon & 1-5pm Apr-Oct) whose carillon is the world's oldest made from porcelain; it chimes a different ditty six times daily. Climb the tower for fine views of the Altstadt.

Even grander vistas will be your reward after schlepping up the Burgberg via a series of steep, stepped lanes. On top, the 15th-century **Albrechtsburg** (☎ 470 70; Domplatz 1; adult/concession/family €3.50/2.50/9; ☼ 10am-6pm Mar-Oct, 10am-5pm Nov-Feb, closed 10-31 Jan) is considered to be Germany's first residential palace, and it housed the original Meissen porcelain factory from 1710 to 1864. Exhibits currently include a selection of medieval sculpture normally on view at the Albertinum in Dresden, which at the time of writing was being renovated. Mostly, though, it's the intriguing architecture that's likely to impress, most notably the Grosser Wendelstein staircase and the eye-popping room vaulting.

Next to the palace is the towering **Dom** (cathedral; ☎ 452 490; Domplatz 7; adult/concession/family €2.50/1.50/6; ☼ 10am-6pm Mar-Oct, 10am-4pm Nov-Feb), a Gothic masterpiece with medieval stained-glass windows and delicately carved statues in the choir. Combination tickets for both buildings are €5.50/3.50/14.50.

Queues may be long, but we recommend you brave them anyway to witness the stunning artistry and craftsmanship that makes Meissen porcelain so unique at the recently expanded **Porzellan-Museum** (☎ 468 700; Talstrasse 9; adult/concession/family €8/4/18; ☼ 9am-6pm May-Oct, 9am-5pm Nov-Apr). It's right next to the actual porcelain factory, about 1km south of the Altstadt. Start with a 30-minute tour (with English audio-guide) of the Schauwerkstätten, a series of four studios where you can observe the creative process during live demonstrations. It'll help you gain a better appreciation for the finished product on display at the Schauhalle inside an integrated Art Nouveau villa. Highlights include a 12-person table setting and a 3.6m-high table-top 'temple'.

Sleeping

Herberge Orange (☎ 454 334; www.herberge-orange .de; Siebeneichener Strasse 34; s/d/tr with shared bathroom €20/32/45) This former home of porcelain-factory apprentices has been converted into

friendly and unpretentious accommodation, which is most popular with wallet-watching nomads.

Mercure Grand Hotel Meissen (☎ 722 50; www .dresden-hotel-meissen.de; Hafenstrasse 27-31; s/d/ste from €75/87/127; P ✗ ✗) If you usually associate Mercure properties with cookie-cutter flair, you'll be pleasantly surprised by this contender. Inside a park-framed Art Nouveau villa on the east bank, it has stylish rooms and a good restaurant.

Hotel Burgkeller (☎ 414 00; www.meissen-hotel .com; Domplatz 11; s/d €69/115, with balcony €85/125; P) This luxury hill-top option has everything you could want – commanding views, glorious beer garden and its location adjacent to the cathedral.

Hotel Goldener Löwe (☎ 411 10; www.meissenhotel .com; Heinrichsplatz 6; s €70-90, d €115-135; P ✗) Everything works like a well-oiled machine at this warm and welcoming hotel in a handsome 17th-century building near the Markt. The 36 rooms have imaginative furnishings and all major amenities.

Eating

Zollhof (☎ 402 614; Elbstrasse 7; mains €4-12) The flower-festooned beer garden with its eccentric fountain is the best place to sample the typical German dishes here, or to try lighter ones officially 'stolen' from Jamie Oliver.

Domkeller (☎ 457 676; Domplatz 9; mains €5-10) Meissen's oldest restaurant offers breathtaking city views from the leafy terrace and good-value local dishes; the menu's even 'translated' into Saxon.

Grüner Humpen (☎ 453 382; Burgstrasse 15; mains €5.40-9) Fill your belly with home-style German cooking amid old radios, vinyl albums and other eclectic flea-market décor.

Weinschänke Vincenz Richter (☎ 453 285; An der Frauenkirche 12; mains €11-17; ✗) The romance factor is high at this top-flight restaurant, despite the rather martial décor (historic guns and armour) and the decidedly unromantic torture chamber (unless you're into S&M, that is). Expect attentive service, expertly prepared regional cuisine and wines from their own estate.

Getting There & Around

From Dresden, take the half-hourly S1 train (€5.10, 35 minutes) to Meissen. For the porcelain factory, get off at Meissen-Triebischtal.

SAXONY

A slower but more fun way to get there is by steam boat operated by Sächsische Dampfschiffahrt. These leave the Terrassenufer in Dresden (Map pp168–9) daily between May and September at 9.45am (one-way €11, two hours). Boats return to Dresden at 2:45pm. Many people opt to go up by boat and back by train, or vice versa.

The hop-on, hop-off **City-Bus Meissen** (adult/concession/family €3.60/2.50/9) links all important sights between 10am and 6pm daily from April to October.

WESTERN SAXONY

LEIPZIG

☎ 0341 / pop 500,000

In Goethe's *Faust*, a character named Frosch calls Leipzig 'a little Paris'. He was wrong – Leipzig is more fun and infinitely less self-important than the Gallic capital. It's an important business and transport centre, a trade-fair mecca, and arguably the most dynamic city in eastern Germany.

Leipzig became known as the *Stadt der Helden* (City of Heroes) for its leading role in the 1989 democratic revolution. Its residents organised protests against the communist regime in May of that year; by October, hundreds of thousands were taking to the streets, placing candles on the steps of Stasi headquarters and attending peace services at the Nikolaikirche.

By the time the secret police got round to pulping their files, Leipzigers were partying in the streets, and they still haven't stopped – from late winter street-side cafés open their terraces, and countless bars and nightclubs keep the beat going through the night.

Leipzig also stages some of the finest classical music and opera in the country, and its art and literary scenes are flourishing. It was once home to Bach, Schumann, Wagner and Mendelssohn, and to Goethe, who set a key scene of *Faust* in the cellar of his favourite watering hole. And the university still attracts students from all over the world. It's the kind of city you just can't help liking.

Orientation

Leipzig's city centre – and most of the key sights – lie within a ring road tracing the former medieval fortifications. From the Hauptbahnhof on the ring's northeastern edge, simply follow Nikolaistrasse south for a couple of minutes to Grimmaische Strasse, the main east–west artery connecting ex-socialist Augustusplatz with the historic Markt.

The impressive 26-platform Hauptbahnhof (1915, renovated 1998) isn't just one of the largest passenger terminals in Europe, but it also houses a fabulous two-storey shopping mall with more than 150 shops (open until 10pm, with many open on Sunday). It's probably the only station on the planet where it's genuinely fun to shop, despite the hideously expensive toilets (€1.10!).

Leipzig's dazzling Neue Messe (trade fairgrounds) are 5km north of the Hauptbahnhof (take tram 16). The central tram station is outside the station.

The Leipzig-Halle airport is 18km to the north of the city (see p193).

Information

BOOKSHOPS

Hugendubel (☎ 01801-484 484; Petersstrasse 12) Three floors of books, including foreign-language novels.
Lehmanns Buchhandlung (☎ 3397 5000; Grimmaische Strasse 10) Great selection and free coffee upstairs.
Reisefibel (☎ 215 870; Salzgässchen 24) Travel books, maps and a travel agency.

DISCOUNT CARDS

Leipzig Card (for one day €7.90, for 3 days €16.50) Free or discounted admission to attractions, plus free travel on public transport. It's sold at the tourist office and most hotels.

EMERGENCY

Police (☎ emergency 110)
Police headquarters (☎ 9660; Dimitroffstrasse 5)

INTERNET ACCESS

Copytel.de (☎ 993 8999; Grimmaische Strasse 23; per hr €1.50; ◉ 9am-10pm Mon-Sat, noon-10pm Sun)
Internet Cafe (☎ 462 5879; Brühl 66; per hr €2; ◉ 10am-10pm)
Le Bit Café (☎ 0163-298 2092; Rosa-Luxemburg-Strasse 32; per hr €2.50; ◉ 10-3am)
Webcafé (Reichsstrasse 16-18; per hr €2; ◉ 10am-10pm)

LAUNDRY

Maga Pon (☎ 993 8798; Gottschedstrasse 11; wash/dry €3.50/0.50) Combination laundry and hip café.
Schnell und Sauber (Dresdner Strasse 19; €3)

LIBRARIES
Deutsche Bücherei (German National Library; ☎ 227 10; Deutscher Platz 1; 🖳) The largest library in Germany, with 13.5 million volumes in a fabulously restored building.
Bibliotheka Albertina (☎ 973 0577; Beethovenstrasse 6; 🖳) Beautifully restored university library, good for periodicals and foreign-language books.

MEDICAL SERVICES
After-hours emergencies (☎ 192 92; 🕑 7pm-7am)
Klinikum St Georg (☎ 9090; Delitzscher Strasse 141) Take tram 16 to this hospital.
Universitätsklinikum Leipzig (☎ 971 7300; Liebigstrasse 20) Hospital and clinic.

MONEY
Reisebank (☎ 980 4588; Lower Level, west hall, Hauptbahnhof; 🕑 9am-8pm Mon-Sat, 1-6pm Sun)

POST
Post Office Augustusplatz (🕑 9am-8pm Mon-Fri, 9am-3pm Sat)
Post Office Hauptbahnhof (🕑 6am-10pm) Inside Presse & Buch bookshop on train level, western end.

TOURIST INFORMATION
Leipzig Tourist Service (☎ 710 4260; www.lts-leipzig .de; Richard-Wagner-Strasse 1; 🕑 9am-7pm Mon-Fri, 9am-4pm Sat & Sun)

Dangers & Annoyances
Don't leave any valuables in your car, as there is plenty of smash-and-grab theft.

Sights
MUSEUM DER BILDENDEN KÜNSTE
An edgy glass cube is the new home of the **Museum der Bildenden Künste** (Museum of Fine Arts; ☎ 216 990; Katharinenstrasse 10; adult/concession permanent exhibit €5/3.50, temporary exhibit €6/4, combination ticket €8/5; 🕑 10am-6pm Tue & Thu-Sun, noon-8pm Wed), which has a well-respected collection of paintings from the 15th century to today, including works by Caspar David Friedrich, Lucas Cranach the Younger and Claude Monet. Highlights include rooms dedicated to native sons Max Beckmann, Max Klinger, whose striking Beethoven monument is a veritable symphony of marble and bronze, and Neo Rauch, a chief representative of the New Leipzig School.

STADTGESCHICHTLICHES MUSEUM
This **museum** (City History Museum; ☎ 965 130; Markt 1; adult/child €4/3; 🕑 10am-6pm Tue-Sun), found in the Altes Rathaus, chronicles the ups and downs of Leipzig's history. Some temporary themed exhibits are on display nearby in a **new building** (Böttchergässchen 3; adult/concession; 🕑 10am-6pm Tue-Sun).

ZEITGESCHICHTLICHES FORUM
Opened in 1999, the engaging **Zeitgeschichtliches Forum** (Forum of Contemporary History; ☎ 222 20; Grimmaische Strasse 6; admission free; 🕑 9am-6pm Tue-Fri, 10am-6pm Sat & Sun) depicts the history of the GDR from division and dictatorship to resistance and demise. You can see legendarily harsh GDR cleaning products, watch video clips of stunned and despairing people as the Berlin Wall was built between them, and be moved by the events of the peaceful revolution of 1989 that started right here in Leipzig. Ask for the English-language pamphlet translating the main captions.

STASI MUSEUM
In the GDR the walls had ears, as is vividly documented in this **museum** (☎ 961 2443; Dittrichring 24; admission free; 🕑 9am-6pm Mon-Fri, 10am-6pm Sat & Sun) on the all-pervasive power of the Ministry for State Security (Stasi for short), the country's secret police. It's housed in the former Leipzig Stasi headquarters, in a building known as the Runde Ecke (Round Corner). Displays on propaganda, preposterous disguises, cunning surveillance devices, Stasi recruitment among children, scent storage and other chilling machinations reveal the GDR's all-out zeal when it came to controlling, manipulating and repressing its own people.

NIKOLAIKIRCHE
Originally Romanesque and Gothic, **Nikolaikirche** (St Nicholas Church; ☎ 960 5270; 🕑 10am-6pm) now sports an amazing classical-style interior with palm-like pillars and cream-coloured pews. More recently, the church was a key player in the nonviolent movement that eventually brought down the GDR regime. In 1982 it began hosting 'peace prayers' every Monday at 5pm (which are still ongoing) and in 1989 it became the chief meeting point for peaceful demonstrators. A pamphlet recounts the 'miracle' of 9 October 1989, when 600 SED party faithful, who had been sent to the church to break up the services, ended up listening to the sermon and joining the protesters.

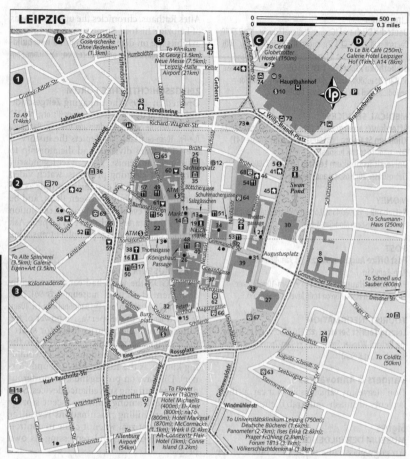

THOMASKIRCHE

The composer Johann Sebastian Bach worked in the **Thomaskirche** (St Thomas Church; ☎ 212 4676; www.thomaskirche.org; Thomaskirchhof 18; ☺ 9am-6pm) as a cantor from 1723 until his death in 1750, and his remains lie buried beneath a bronze epitaph near the altar. The Thomaner-chor (p193), once led by Bach, is still going strong and now includes 100 boys aged eight to 18. The church tower can be climbed on weekends (€2).

BACH-MUSEUM

Opposite the Thomaskirche, in a baroque house, is the **Bach-Museum** (☎ 964 110; www.bach -leipzig.de; Thomaskirchhof 16; adult/concession/family €4/2/6; ☺ 10am-5pm), which focusses on the composer's

life in Leipzig. After all, this is where he wrote the *Matthäus Passion*, the *Johannes Passion* and the *Weihnachtsoratorium*. There are portraits, manuscripts and other Bach memorabilia. Admission to the Bach-Museum includes an English-language audio-guide.

MENDELSSOHN-HAUS & SCHUMANN-HAUS

Two other important composers have mu-seums dedicated to them in Leipzig: Felix Mendelssohn-Bartholdy, who lived (and died) in the **Mendelssohn-Haus** (☎ 127 0294; www .mendelssohn-stiftung.de; Goldschmidtstrasse 12; admission €3; ☺ 10am-6pm); and Robert Schumann, who spent the first four years of his marriage to Leipzig pianist Clara Wieck in the **Schumann-Haus** (☎ 393 9620; www.schumann-verein.de; Inselstrasse

18; admission €3; 2-5pm Wed-Fri, 10am-5pm Sat & Sun). Combined admission to these two and the Bach-Museum is €6.

GRASSIMUSEUM

Recently renovated, the university-run **Grassimuseum** (www.grassimuseum.de; Johannisplatz 5-11; 10am-6pm Tue-Sun) unites several collections. At the fabulous **Musikinstrumenten-Museum** (973 0750; http://mfm.uni-leipzig.de; adult/concession/family €3/2/7) you can discover music from five centuries in the prestigious and rarity-filled exhibits, in an interactive sound laboratory, and during concerts. At the **Museum für Völkerkunde** (Ethnological Museum; 973 1900; www.mvl-grassimuseum.de; adult/concession €3/2) you can plunge into an eye-opening journey through the cultures of the world. Still to return to its permanent base in 2007 is the **Museum für Angewandte Kunst** (Museum for Applied Arts; 213 3719). Call for times and admission.

GALERIE FÜR ZEITGENÖSSISCHE KUNST

Edgy contemporary art in all media is the platform of the **Galerie für Zeitgenössische Kunst** (140 810; Karl-Tauchnitz-Strasse 9/11; adult/concession per space €4/2, both spaces €7/3, free admission Wed; 2-7pm Tue-Sat, noon-7pm Sun), which has changing exhibits housed in a minimalist container-like space and a late-19th-century villa. The latter is the future home of the gallery's permanent collection of 1950s and '60s German informal art.

VÖLKERSCHLACHTDENKMAL

Some 100,000 soldiers lost their lives in the epic 1813 battle that led to the decisive victory of Prussian, Austrian and Russian forces over Napoleon's army. Built a century later, the **Völkerschlachtdenkmal** (878 0471; Battle of Nations Monument; Prager Strasse; adult/concession €5/3; 10am-6pm Apr-Oct, 10am-4pm Nov-Mar) is a sombre and imposing 91m colossus, which towers above southeastern Leipzig, not too far from the actual killing fields. The **Forum 1813** (adult/concession €3/2, combination ticket €7/4.50) chronicles the events, or else you can rent an audio-guide with English-language commentary. In June/July, the naTo culture club (see p192) hosts its annual 'bath tub race' in the large reflecting pool that sits below the monument. The best way to get out to the monument is to take tram 15 to Völkerschlachtdenkmal.

SAXONY

PANOMETER

The happy marriage of a *pan*orama (a giant painting) and a gas*ometer* (a giant gas tank) is a **panometer** (☎ 121 3396; www.asisi-factory.de; Richard-Lehmann-Strasse 114; admission €8/6; ☽ 9am-7pm Tue-Fri, 10am-8pm Sat & Sun). The unusual concept is the brainchild of artist Yadegar Asisi, who creates a new image every 15 months or so. Past examples have included scenes from the Himalayan mountains and ancient Rome. Take tram 16 to Richard-Lehmann-Strasse/ Zwickauer Strasse.

ALTE SPINNEREI

'Cotton to culture' is the motto of the **Alte Spinnerei** (☎ 498 0270; Spinnereistrasse 7; ☽ 11am-6pm Tue-Sat), a 19th-century cotton spinning factory turned artist colony. Around 80 New Leipzig School artists, including Neo Rauch, have their studios in this huge pile of red-brick buildings, alongside designers, architects, goldsmiths and other creative types. Their work is displayed in about 10 galleries, including **Galerie Eigen + Art** (☎ 960 7886; www.eigen-art .com), internationally famous for championing young artists. It's in the southwestern district of Plagwitz; take tram 14 to S-Bahnhof Plagwitz.

ZOO

Not your run-of-the-mill **zoo** (☎ 593 3385; www .zoo-leipzig.de; Pfaffendorfer Strasse 29; adult/child/concession €11.50/7.50/10; ☽ 9am-7pm May-Sep, 9am-6pm Apr & Oct, 9am-5pm Nov-Mar), the Leipzig version has lots of rare species, plus perennial crowd-pleasers such as tigers, lions and gorillas. The new elephant habitat, built to look like a Cambodian temple, has been a highlight since 2006. Take tram 12.

Walking Tour

This 4km Historic Centre circuit starts at the Markt and moves clockwise to Augustusplatz, before exploring the attractive south of the old quarter. It's a 1½-hour walk, but will take the best part of a day if you make all the stops.

On the Markt, the arcaded Renaissance **Altes Rathaus (1**; 1556), one of Germany's most stunning town halls, houses the Stadtgeschichtliches Museum (p185). On the opposite side of the Markt, the **Marktgalerie (2)** is one of the shiny new shopping complexes that have been popping up throughout central Leipzig in recent years.

These modern malls continue the tradition spawned by the historic **Mädlerpassage (3)**, easily among the world's most beautiful shopping arcades. Enter it from Grimmaische Strasse, south of the Markt. A mix of neo-Renaissance and Art Nouveau, it opened as a trade hall in 1914 and was renovated at great expense in the early 1990s. Today it's home to shops, bars and restaurants, most notably, Auerbachs Keller (see Eating, p191). There are statues of Faust, Mephistopheles and some students near the Grimmaische Strasse exit; according to tradition you should touch Faust's foot for good luck.

Next door, the **Zeitgeschichtliches Forum** (**4**; p185) is a must for anyone interested in GDR history. Immediately opposite is the Naschmarkt (snack market) which is dominated by the **Alte Börse (5**; ☎ 961 0368; ☽ Mon-Fri by appointment), an ornate former trading house (1687). In front is a **statue of Goethe (6**; 1903), showing him as a young law student at Leipzig University. Today the Alte Börse is a cultural centre hosting concerts, plays and readings throughout the year.

Continue north on Naschmarkt, turn right on Salzgässchen and go to the corner of Reichsstrasse and Schuhmachergässchen, which is dominated by the beautiful Art Nouveau façade of the **Cafe Riquet (7**; p191). Continue a bit south on Reichsstrasse, then turn left into **Specks Hof (8)**, another shopping arcade, where you'll pass a water basin that functions as an upside-down bell; ring it by wetting your hands with the water and running them back and forth over two pommels. If you hit it right, the water starts to fizz. Specks Hof itself contains a beautiful series of tile and stained-glass reliefs by Halle artist Moritz Götze. The eastern portal of Specks Hof takes you straight to the **Nikolaikirche (9**, p185).

Carry on east through the Theaterpassage to reach Augustusplatz, Leipzig's cultural nerve centre. The glass structures (which conceal lifts to the underground car park) glow at night, lending the concrete slabs some much-needed warmth. The Theaterpassage itself runs through the 11-storey **Kroch-Haus (10)**, which was Leipzig's first 'skyscraper' and now houses part of the university's art collection. Topped by a clock and two muscular bronze sentries who bash the bell at regular intervals, the motto (in Latin) reads: 'Work conquers all'.

The behemoth ahead is the functional **Opernhaus (11**; opera house; 1956–60), backed by a little park with a pond and a **statue of**

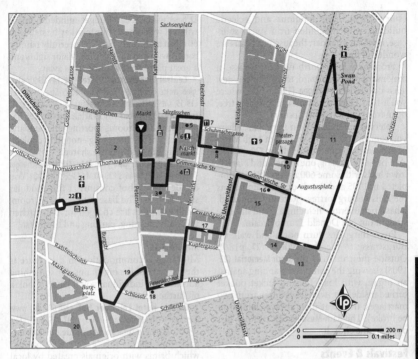

WALK FACTS

Start Markt
Finish Bach-Museum
Distance 4km
Duration 1½ hours

Richard Wagner (12). At the opposite end of Augustusplatz is the boxy **Neues Gewandhaus (13**; 1981), home to the world-famous Gewandhaus Orchestra, which was founded in 1743 and is one of Europe's oldest civic orchestras. Just next door, and sticking out like the tall kid in your third-grade picture, is the landmark **MDR Hochhaus (14**; lift €2; ☺ 11am-11pm), a rather attractive skyscraper from 1970, with a viewing platform and restaurant on top.

On the west side of Augustusplatz, the run-down GDR-era **Universität Leipzig (15**; university building), with its bronze relief depicting Karl Marx, is expected to soon have a date with the wrecking ball. Not too many Leipzigers will likely shed a tear, for many still

remember the medieval Paulinerkirche which stood here until being demolished in 1968 by GDR authorities. A handful of beautiful **epitaphs (16)** salvaged from the church are on display in a glass case on Grimmaische Strasse.

From Grimmaische Strasse, hook a left on Universitätsstrasse and look for the entrance to the **Städtisches Kaufhaus (17**; Universitätsstrasse 16), the site of the city's first cloth exchange (Gewandhaus) and later the inaugural concert hall of the Gewandhaus Orchestra. Composer Felix Mendelssohn-Bartholdy once led a music school here, and there are now free concerts in the summer. Since August 2005, the central courtyard has featured the Strasse der Stars, Leipzig's version of the Walk of Fame. Michael Schumacher, Joe Cocker and Mariah Carey are among the celebrities whose plaster-cast hands are displayed in a series of cube-shaped cases.

Exit the Städtisches Kaufhaus, head south on Neumarkt, then turn right on Peterskirchhof and you'll come to **arko (18**; ex-Café Richter; ☎ 960 5235; Petersstrasse 43; ☺ 9.30am-8pm Mon-Fri, 10am-1pm Sat), the oldest coffee retailer in town (since 1879). This fabulous and eclectic building, with its golden iron spiral staircase, is worth a gander; the luscious beans are wonderful too.

From here head north on Petersstrasse, a major shopping boulevard, to the glorious new glass-covered **Petersbogen (19)** arcade, where you'll find Leipzig's Casino (admission free, open from 2pm to 2am) upstairs.

Petersbogen spills out on Burgplatz, where you confront the impressive 114m-high tower of the neo-baroque **Neues Rathaus (20**; ☎ 1230; 🕑 6.45am-4.30pm Mon-Fri), one of the world's largest town halls with some 600 rooms. It was completed in 1905 and stands on the foundations the Pleissenburg fortress. Recently renovated, it has a rich interior, including a grand staircase straight out of a Donald Trump dream.

From Burgplatz, turn north and walk up Burgstrasse to the **Thomaskirche (21**, p186). Outside the church is the **Bach Memorial (22**; 1908) showing the composer standing against an organ, with his left-hand jacket pocket turned inside-out (with 20 children from two marriages, the great man always claimed to be broke). The **Bach-Museum (23**; p186) is just opposite the church.

Festivals & Events

Highlights of Leipzig's annual events calendar include the **Leipziger Buchmesse** (Book Fair; www .leipziger-buchmesse.de) in late March, the second biggest in the country after Frankfurt. The **Honky Tonk** (www.honky-tonk.de) pub festival in May features dozens of bands and a shuttle bus between drinking holes. On Whitsuntide, goths from around the world descend for the **Wave-Gotik-Treffen** (www.wave-gotik-treffen .de), the world's largest goth festival, with a pagan village, a medieval market and lots of dark music and merriment. The 10-day **Bach Festival** (www.bach-leipzig.de) takes place in late May or early June.

Sleeping

The Leipzig tourist office runs a free **accommodation service** (☎ 710 4255), with singles/doubles from around €22.50/40.

Mitwohnzentrale (☎ 194 30; Goethestrasse 7-10; 🕑 9am-8pm) arranges flat rental (from €20 per person per night).

BUDGET

Hostel Sleepy Lion (☎ 993 9480; www.hostel-leipzig .de; Käthe-Kollwitz-Strasse 3; dm €13-16, s/d €28/40, linen €2, breakfast €3; ✗ 🖳) Budget-minded nomads will feel welcome at this low-key hostel, with 60 clean and comfy beds in cheerfully painted rooms with private facilities. Major sights and a great party zone are just steps away.

Central Globetrotter Hostel (☎ 149 8960; www .globetrotter-leipzig.de; Kurt-Schumacher-Strasse 41; dm €13-15, s/d €24/36, linen €2, breakfast €4; ✗ 🖳) This friendly Hauptbahnhof-adjacent hostel has 80 beds in artsy rooms sporting pine beds and lockers. The kitchen is big enough to cook up a storm, but facilities are shared.

Pension Schlaf Gut (☎ 211 0902; www.schlafgut -leipzig.de; Brühl 64-66; s €30-40, d €43-53; Ⓟ ✗) You decide the level of comfort at this modular sleep station. The base rate buys the room; small extra fees are charged for TV, kitchen use, daily cleaning, parking and breakfast.

MIDRANGE

Midrange accommodation in the centre is the preserve of the big chains; for something a little more individual you'll have to look a bit further afield.

Galerie Hotel Leipziger Hof (☎ 697 40; www .leipziger-hof.de; Hedwigstrasse 1-3; s €47-115, d €57-135; Ⓟ ✗ 🖳) Leipzig's most unique place to unpack your bags is this 'gallery with rooms', which brims with originals created by local artists since 1989. It's a first-rate stay, yet surprisingly affordable, as is the restaurant.

Alt-Connewitz Flair Hotel (☎ 3013770; www.flairhotel .com/connewitz; Meusdorfer Strasse 47a; s €45-60, d €70-90; Ⓟ ✗ 🖳) Saxon hospitality is alive and well at this traditional mum-and-son operation in the southern suburb of Connewitz. Rooms are older but in great shape, and the restaurant serves delicious home-cooked meals.

Hotel Markgraf (☎ 303 030; www.markgraf-leipzig.de; Körnerstrasse 36; s €40-55, d €55-75, apt €65-100; Ⓟ ✗) This smartly run hotel puts you within staggering distance of the Karl-Liebknecht-Strasse nightlife. Many rooms overlook a pretty little park and there's a sauna for relaxing.

Hotel Michaelis (☎ 267 80; www.hotel-michaelis.de; Paul-Gruner-Strasse 44; s €75-150, d €90-180; Ⓟ ✗ ❧ 🖳) Close to the Karl-Liebknecht-Strasse hipster mile and the city centre, this well-run place gets our thumbs up for its 59 handsome rooms, well-respected restaurant (with a leafy terrace) and original art collection.

Also recommended:

Hotel Vier Jahreszeiten (☎ 985 10; Kurt-Schmacher-Strasse 23-29; s €73-114, d €92-150; Ⓟ ✗) Spotless, well-maintained and near the Hauptbahnhof.

Dorint Novotel (☎ 995 80; Goethestrasse 11; s/d €64/89, breakfast €14; P ☒ ☒ ☒) Good value, central and great for families.

TOP END

Hotel Fürstenhof (☎ 1400; www.luxurycollection .com/fuerstenhof; Tröndlinring 8; r €230-300, breakfast €19; P ☒ ☒ ☒ ☒) This intimate but grand hotel, with a 200-year pedigree, finds umpteen ways to spoil its guests. It has updated old-world flair, impeccable service, a gourmet restaurant and an oh-so-soothing grotto-style pool and spa.

Westin Leipzig (☎ 9880; Gerberstrasse 15; r €100-400; P ☒ ☒ ☒) Never mind the bland façade, because it merely conceals Leipzig's most design-conscious hotel, whose mega-cool lobby leads to 436 luxurious rooms. Don't miss having a drink at the Falco bar on the 17th floor with the entire city panorama unfolding below.

Eating

RESTAURANTS

Sol y Mar (☎ 961 5721; Gottschedstrasse 4; mains €4-12; ☕ 9am-open end) This is a sensuous place, with soft lighting, ambient sounds and a lush interior (including padded pods for noshing in recline). Despite the concept, the pretence factor is surprisingly low, and so are the prices.

Koslik (☎ 998 5993; Zentralstrasse 1; mains €8-13; ☕ 9am-3am) A stylish wood interior complements the tasty world cuisine offered here, with great breakfasts and meals from pizza to Thai soup to Swiss potato *rösti*.

Auerbachs Keller (☎ 216 100; Grimmaische Strasse 2-4, Mädlerpassage; mains €7-20) Founded in 1525, Auerbachs Keller is one of Germany's best-known restaurants. It's cosy and touristy, but the food's actually quite good and the setting memorable. In Goethe's *Faust – Part I*, Mephistopheles and Faust carouse here with some students before they ride off on a barrel. The scene is depicted on a carved tree trunk in what is now the Goethe Room (where the great writer allegedly came for 'inspiration').

Barthel's Hof (☎ 141 310; Hainstrasse 1; mains €7-20; ☕ 7am-midnight) This is a sprawling place with outdoor seating in a courtyard, occasional buffet specials and quirky Saxon dishes such as *Heubraten* (marinated lamb roasted on hay).

Retschenka (☎ 149 2235; Steibs Hof, Nikolaistrasse 28-32; mains €7-16; ☕ 11am-midnight Tue-Sun) Gorbachev ate at this kitschy-blue but endearing traditional Russian restaurant tucked away in

a courtyard. On weekends, enjoy your borscht to the sound of live folk music.

Zill's Tunnel (☎ 960 2078; Barfussgässchen 9; mains €7-15; ☕ 11.30am-midnight) Empty tables are a rare sight at this outstanding restaurant offering a classic menu of robust Saxon dishes. Sit on the outside terrace, in the rustic cellar, or in the covered 'tunnel' courtyard.

Medici (☎ 211 3878; Nikolaikirchhof 5; mains €19-35; ☕ noon-2.30pm & 6-11pm Mon-Sat) The interior may resemble a suspension bridge, but this classy Italian spot is widely mentioned as a Leipzig favourite. Mains come in small or large, but serious gourmets go for the three- to five-course set menus (€46 to €62).

Gosenschenke 'Ohne Bedenken' (☎ 566 2360; Menckestrasse 5; mains €4-12; ☕ noon-1am) This historic tavern, backed by the city's prettiest beer garden, is the perfect place to sample *Gose*, a local top-fermented beer often served with a shot of liqueur. The menu has a distinctly carnivorous bent.

El-Amir (☎ 308 2568; Karl-Liebknecht-Strasse 59; mains €2.50-5) For the best (and biggest) doner in Leipzig, bar none, come to this little hole-in-the-wall place, across from naTo (p192).

CAFÉS

Café Riquet (☎ 961 0000; Schuhmachergässchen 1; mains €6-12; ☕ 9am-10pm Sun-Thu, 9am-midnight Fri & Sat) Two bronze elephants guard the entrance to this Viennese-style coffeehouse in a superb Art Nouveau building.

Café Kandler (☎ 213 2181; Thomaskirchhof 11; mains €6-12; ☕ 10am-8pm) This café's antiquated ambience is a fine place to enjoy the delicious local sweets called Bachtaler (essentially a giant chocolate truffle) and Leipziger Lerchen (cake filled with marzipan and jam). It has an excellent tea selection.

Zum Arabischen Coffe Baum (☎ 961 0061; Kleine Fleischergasse 4; mains €7.50-15; ☕ 11am-midnight) Despite the exotic name, Leipzig's oldest café is as stuffy as your grandma's attic, but the cakes and meals are excellent and there's a free coffee museum to boot. Composer Robert Schumann used to be a regular.

Drinking

Leipzig has several party zones. In the centre, the so-called Drallewatsch, which centres on Barfussgässchen and Kleine Fleischergasse, is the place for the see-and-be-seen scene, with plenty of outdoor tables for showing off that tan. Locals tend to prefer the more low-key watering holes west of here, especially along Gottschedstrasse. A more alternative vibe rules south, along student-flavoured Karl-Liebknecht-Strasse, sometimes known as Karli or Südmeile. Nearby, Münzgasse is another up-and-coming party strip. Also see below and right for more drinking ideas.

Milchbar (☎ 980 9594; Gottschedstrasse 1) Colourful lighting makes everyone look good in this youthful bar where live DJs spin house music nightly after 9pm. They've got cocktails and great milk shakes in case you feel like laying off the booze.

Sixtina (☎ 0177-476 4855; Katharinenstrasse 11) At some point in the last few years the word 'absinthe' has ceased to mean 'bad idea', and the result is places like Sixtina, wholly dedicated to the deadly green fairy. We blame the parents.

Spizz (☎ 960 8043; Markt 9) Classic brass instruments dangle above the stage at this city slicker, where you might catch some cool jazz. It has three levels, a good range of wine and beer and slow service (due to sheer numbers).

Cafe Barbakane (☎ 702 5590; Universitätsstrasse 9) Part of the cavernous Moritz-Bastei, this is an always lively café-bar with courtyard seating and dirt-cheap yet delicious fare (€2 to €4) to vanquish that hangover.

McCormacks (☎ 301 9796; Karl-Liebknecht-Strasse 75) The high-octane vibe, foamy pints of Guinness and lovely flower-filled beer garden make this one of the best Irish pubs in town.

Luise (☎ 961 1488; Bosestrasse 4; ☺ 9am-open end) Empty tables are a rare sight at this perennial favourite, where a mostly not-so-very-young crowd has a good time from morning till the wee hours.

Entertainment

The best listings magazine is *Kreuzer* (€1.80), although the free monthlies *Frizz* and *Blitz* might do just fine.

LIVE MUSIC

Moritz-Bastei (☎ 702 590; Universitätsstrasse 9) This classic student club occupies a warren of historic cellars below the old city fortifications. It has live bands or DJs most nights, and the neat Cafe Barbakane (see Drinking, above), and runs films outside in summer.

naTo (☎ 391 5539; www.nato-leipzig.de; Karl-Liebknecht-Strasse 46) The mother of Leipzig's alternative music pub-clubs, with jazz, experimental and indie sounds alongside films and theatre. Take trams 10 or 11.

Conne Island (☎ 301 3038; Koburger Strasse 3) This former squatter's haunt has morphed into the city's top venue for punk, indie, ska, rock and hip-hop concerts. It's in the southern suburb of Connewitz; take tram 9 to Koburger Brücke.

Werk II (☎ 308 010; www.werk-2.de; Kochstrasse 132) This large cultural centre in an old factory is great for catching up-and-coming bands or alternative film and theatre. It's also in Connewitz; take tram 9 to Connewitzer Kreuz.

CLUBS

Flower Power (☎ 961 3441; Riemannstrasse 42) It's party time any time at this wackily decorated haunt (check out the old pinball machines). The action doesn't reach a crescendo until 4am and the music tends to be older than the crowd.

Dark Flower (☎ 0163-633 0011; Hainstrasse 12-14) This sweaty and cavernous cellar is the darling of the Goth crowd, although electro, rock and '80s also make it onto the turntable.

Ilses Erika (☎ 306 5111; Bernhard-Göring-Strasse 152) The living-room look makes this small but legendary club feel warm and welcoming. Music-wise, expect indie, electronic and whatever the mostly student-age crowd has on their iPod.

Bounce 87 (☎ 149 6687; Nikolaistrasse 12-14) This is a key venue for black music: mellow R&B and soul in the Red Lounge, cool rap classics in the Blue Basement.

GAY & LESBIAN VENUES

GegenPol magazine (www.gegenpol.net, in German) and several free publications keep track of the ever-changing gay scene. Also check www.gayleipzig.de (in German) for ideas.

Rosa Linde (☎ 149 9360; www.rosalinde.de; Steibs Hof, Brühl 64-66) Nice, intimate bar, café and information centre for men and women.

Blaue Trude (☎ 212 6679; Sternwartenstrasse 16) This lesbi-gay-bi-transgender club is a scene stalwart, but it recently moved to new digs outside the city centre.

New Orleans (☎ 960 7989; Brühl 56) A low-key mixed place with a modern interior, some Cajun flavour and flirt-friendly table telephones.

CINEMAS

Prager Frühling (☎ 306 5333; www.kinobar-leipzig.de; Bernhard-Göring-Strasse 152) 'Prague Spring' might sound a bit militant, but this is actually an excellent arthouse cinema, which sometimes shows offbeat foreign films in the original. It's above Ilses Erika (see Clubs, above).

CLASSICAL MUSIC

Gewandhausorchester (☎ 127 00; www.gewandhaus .de; Augustusplatz 8) Led by Ricardo Chailly since 2005, this is one of Europe's finest and oldest orchestras, with a tradition harking back to 1743 – Mendelssohn was one of its conductors. It performs primarily at the Neues Gewandhaus as well as in the Thomaskirche.

Thomanerchor (☎ 984 420; www.thomaskirche .org; Thomaskirchhof 18) This famous boys' choir performs Bach motets and cantatas at 6pm on Friday and 3pm on Saturday, and also sings during Sunday services at 9.30am and 6pm at the Thomaskirche (p186). Special concerts take place throughout the year.

Oper Leipzig (☎ 126 1261; www.oper-leipzig.de; August-usplatz 12) Leipzig's Opernhaus (opera house) has a 300-year tradition, and has had Henri Maier at the helm since 2002. The programme is an eclectic mix of classics, contemporary works like *Angels in America* and newly commissioned operas such as *The Black Monk,* based on a Chekhov novel. Best of all, the Gewandhausorchester provides the music.

Also check the listings magazines for concerts at the Bach-Museum (p186), the Schumann-Haus (p186), the Mendelssohn-Haus (p186) and the Nikolaikirche (p185).

THEATRE & CABARET

Schauspielhaus (☎ 126 80; www.schauspiel-leipzig.de; Bosestrasse 1) The repertory at Leipzig's largest theatre ranges from classics infused with modern elements to new plays by up-and-coming writers.

Theater Neue Szene (☎ 980 9393; Gottschedstrasse 16) The Schauspielhaus also operates this intimate stage where works by contemporary playwrights, often with a critical bent, are the bread and butter.

Krystallpalast (☎ 140 660; www.krystallpalastvariete .de; Magazingasse 4) This company puts on the finest variety shows in town, with snake women, flamenco, trapeze acts and more.

Academixer (☎ 2178 7878; Kupfergasse 3) For a dose of satirical cabaret, head to this place near the university.

Getting There & Away
AIR

Leipzig-Halle airport (☎ 224 1155; www.leipzig-halle -airport.de) is served by domestic and international flights from two dozen airlines, including Lufthansa, German Wings, Air

Berlin, Condor and Cirrus. RyanAir flies into **Altenburg airport** (www.flughafen-altenburg.de) from London-Stansted.

CAR & MOTORCYCLE

Leipzig lies just south of the A14 Halle–Dresden autobahn and 15km east of the A9, which links Berlin to Nuremberg. It's best to leave your vehicle in a car park or garage. The one at the Leipzig Hauptbahnhof charges a maximum of €3 for 24 hours (except on Saturday, when the rate goes up to €15). Between 8am and 6pm, parking at the zoo costs a reasonable €2.50 for four hours.

RIDE SERVICES

The **Mitfahrzentrale** (☎ 194 40; Goethestrasse 7-10; 9am-8pm) can organise shared rides.

TRAIN

Leipzig is an important link between eastern and western Germany, with connections to all major cities. There are frequent services to Frankfurt (€61, 3½ hours), Munich (€74, five hours), Dresden (€18, 1¾ hours), Berlin (€36, 1¼ hours) and Hamburg (€79, three hours).

Getting Around
TO/FROM THE AIRPORTS

Leipzig-Halle airport is served by RE trains twice hourly (€3.40, 15 minutes), leaving from the Hauptbahnhof. A taxi to or from the city centre costs around €30.

Altenburg airport is located about 50km south of Leipzig and is connected to the city centre by a bus shuttle (€12, 1¼ hours). It goes to/from the central bus station on the eastern side of the Hauptbahnhof. For further information, contact ☎ 03447-850 613 or www.thuesac.de.

BICYCLE

Zweirad Eckhardt (☎ 961 7274; Güterstrasse; 6am-8pm Mon-Fri, 9am-4pm Sat), right by the Hauptbahnhof, hires out bikes for €8 per 24 hours.

PUBLIC TRANSPORT

Public transport is operated by **LVB** (☎ 194 49; www.lvb.de), which runs an **information kiosk** (8am-8pm Mon-Fri, 8am-4pm Sat) on Willy-Brandt-Platz outside the Hauptbahnhof. The central tram station is here as well. The S-Bahn circles the city's outer suburbs. Single tickets cost €1.30 for up to four stops and €1.70 for longer trips; day passes are €4.90.

SAXONY

TAXI

Funktaxi (☎ 4884) and **Löwen Taxi** (☎ 710 00) are the main local firms. There is a €2.10 hire charge and then it's €1 per kilometre.

AROUND LEIPZIG
Colditz Escape Museum

Built high on a crag above the sleepy town of Colditz, some 46km southeast of Leipzig, is the impressive **Schloss Colditz** (☎ 034381-437 77; www.schlosscolditz.com; Schlossgasse 1; adult/concession/family €5/3/12; ✆ 8.30am-5pm Mon-Fri, 9am-5pm Sat, 10am-5pm Sun Apr-Oct, 10am-4pm daily Nov-Mar), a Renaissance palace that's seen stints as a hunting lodge, a poorhouse and a mental hospital. Mostly, though, it's famous as Oflag IVC, a WWII-era high-security prison for Allied officers, including a nephew of Winston Churchill. Most had already escaped from less secure camps and been recaptured. Some 300 made further attempts, and 31 actually managed to flee. The would-be escapees were often aided by ingenious self-made gadgetry, including a glider fashioned from wood and bed sheets, and a homemade sewing machine for making bogus German uniforms. Most astounding, perhaps, is a 44m-long tunnel below the chapel that French officers dug in 1941–42, before the Germans caught them. You can see some of these contraptions, along with lots of photographs, in the small but fascinating Fluchtmuseum (Escape Museum) within the palace. Several inmates wrote down their experiences later, of which Pat Reid's *The Colditz Story* is the best known account.

At the time of writing, sections of the palace were being remodelled into a new DJH hostel.

Bus 931 runs to Colditz from Leipzig. You can also take a train to Bad Lausick and catch bus 613 from there. The one-way trip takes between 90 minutes and two hours. The town is at the junction of the B107 and B176 roads between Leipzig and Chemnitz.

CHEMNITZ
☎ 0371 / pop 250,000

Like most eastern German cities, Chemnitz (pronounced *kem*-nits) has had to completely reinvent itself since reunification, and it has done so with remarkable success. Its smokestack industries once earned it the nickname of 'Saxon Manchester', and the GDR dubbed it Karl-Marx-Stadt, and gave it a Stalinist

makeover. Such scars don't heal easily, but Chemnitz has done its best. Nowhere is this more noticeable than in the revitalised city centre, now an attractive, pedestrianised shopping and entertainment district. New architecture by Helmut Jahn and Hans Kollhof mixes nicely with a few surviving Renaissance buildings. Add to that a lively cultural scene, one of Europe's largest intact Art Nouveau quarters and an unpretentious air, and you've got more than a few good reasons for a stopover.

Orientation

Chemnitz is 80km southwest of Dresden and is a gateway to the Erzgebirge (Iron Ore Mountains). The city centre, anchored by the Markt and encircled by a ring road, is about a 10-minute walk south of the train station via Bahnhofstrasse or the Stalinist-flavoured Strasse der Nationen. Trams 1, 2, 4 and 6 also link the two; get off at Zentralhaltestelle. The tallest building in town, the Hotel Mercure, is great for keeping your bearings. The little Chemnitz River, west of the city centre, flows north–south.

Information

There are several banks with ATMS in the Markt area.

Main post office (cnr Posthof & Strasse der Nationen)

Tourist office (☎ 690 680; www.chemnitz-tourismus .de; Markt 1; ✆ 10am-8pm Mon-Fri, 10am-3pm Sat)

Vobis (☎ 533 6515; basement, Galerie Roter Turm; per hr €2) Internet access.

Sights
KUNSTSAMMLUNGEN CHEMNITZ

A palatial 1909 building, just off the GDR-era Strasse der Nationen, shelters the **Kunstsammlungen Chemnitz** (Chemnitz Art Museum; ☎ 488 4424; adult/concession €3/2; ✆ noon-7pm Tue-Sun), a high-calibre collection of 19th- and 20th-century German artists. The list of heavy hitters includes Caspar David Friedrich and Lovis Corinth and, most famously, the Chemnitz-born Expressionist painter Karl Schmidt-Rottluff, a co-founder of the artist group Die Brücke.

In late 2007 the museum will expand into a second building, the Museum Gunzenhauser at Stollberger Strasse 2. The focus will be on New Objectivity artists, including Otto Dix, and will also include works by Max Beckmann, Ernst Ludwig Kirchner and others.

KARL-MARX-DENKMAL & AROUND

A rare vestige from the GDR era awaits near the corner of Strasse der Nationen and Brücken-strasse, where a humongous 7.1m-high **bronze head of Karl Marx** occupies a spot in front of a wall-size frieze. It exhorts: 'Workers of all countries, unite!' in several languages.

Across the street, past the Stadthalle/Hotel Mercure complex, is the **Roter Turm**, a medieval defence tower.

DASTIETZ

Chemnitz's new pride and joy, **DAStietz** (Mo-ritzstrasse 20) is a former department store reborn as a cultural centre. Besides the public library and a few shops, it now harbours the **Neue Sächsische Galerie** (☎ 367 6680; adult & concession €2, under 14yr free; ☷ 10am-6pm Thu-Mon, 10am-8pm Tue), which presents postwar works by Saxon art-ists. It's a small but growing collection, begun only in 1990 when its founders set up shop locally in the former Stasi headquarters. Also here is the **Museum für Naturkunde** (Natural History Museum; ☎ 488 4551; adult/concession/family €4/2.50/8; ☷ 10am-8pm Mon-Fri, 10am-6pm Sat, closed Wed), where the most interesting display, the Versteinerter Wald (petrified forest), can be admired for free in the atrium; some of the stony trunks are 290 million years old.

MARKT

Chemnitz's compact centre has been given a complete facelift since reunification, and it has evolved into an attractive commercial hub. Now, historic buildings rub shoulders with such notable newcomers as the glass-and-steel Galeria Kaufhof department store (designed by Helmut Jahn), and the Galerie Roter Turm, a shopping mall ensconced by a sandstone façade.

Both form part of the ensemble encircling the bustling Markt, which is dominated by the **Altes Rathaus** (Old Town Hall), an impos-ing white 15th-century building with a Ren-aissance portal, and the **Neues Rathaus** (New Town Hall), which looks older but only dates to 1911. Completing this impressive silhouette is the **Hoher Turm** (High Tower) behind the Altes Rathaus. The adjacent **Jakobikirche** is a Gothic church topped by a neat roof turret and updated with an Art Deco façade.

SCHLOSS AREA

Across the river, the **Schlossteich** is a large park-ringed pond, with a music pavilion for summer concerts. Towering over it is the **Schlosskirche** (☷ 10am-5pm Tue-Sat, 2.30-5.30pm Sun Apr-Oct, 11am-4pm Tue-Sat Nov-Mar), a 12th-century Benedictine monastery later recast into a weighty Gothic hall church. Its treasures include Hans Witten's intriguing sculpture *Christ at the Column* (1515). Just south of the church stands the reconstructed **Schloss** itself, which houses the **Schlossbergmuseum** (☎ 488 4501; Schlossberg 12; adult/concession €3/1.80; ☷ 1-7pm Tue-Fri, noon-9pm Sat, 10am-6pm Sun). The vaulted interior is actually better than the historical displays and paintings.

HENRY VAN DE VELDE-MUSEUM

Fans of multitalented Belgian artist Henry Van de Velde will enjoy this small **museum** (☎ 533 1088; Parkstrasse 58; admission free; ☷ 10am-6pm Wed, Fri, Sat & Sun) inside the 1903 Villa Esche, his first commission in Germany. The downstairs din-ing room and music salon have been restored as period rooms, while upstairs you'll find a small collection of the artist's crafts and furniture. It's about 2.5km south of the centre (tram 4 to Haydnstrasse).

If you enjoy Art Nouveau architecture, you might also find a stroll through the **Kassberg** neighbourhood rewarding; it's about 1km west of the centre (bus 26 to Barbarossa-strasse). The building at the corner of Bar-barossastrasse and Weststrasse is especially stunning.

Sleeping

Hotel Sächsischer Hof (☎ 461 480; www.saechsischer -hof.de; Brühl 26; s/d €55/75; P ☒) This family-run hotel is on a quiet street not far from the Hauptbahnhof and the Schlossberg, and is a good bet if you're simply looking for a decent, solid place to stay.

Hotel Mercure (☎ 6830; www.mercure.com; Brücken-strasse 19; r €50-125, breakfast €14; P ☒ ☒ ☐) This hotel stands out from the pack, and not only because of its lofty 26-floor tower. Modern, efficient and with full service, it has some neat features, including an old-timer vehicle exhibit in the lobby, a free sauna and a lavish breakfast buffet served in the restaurant on the 26th floor. Rooms are snug but great views are guaranteed.

Hotel Chemnitzer Hof (☎ 6840; www.guennewig .de; Theaterplatz 4; s €82-92, d €108-126; P ☒ ☐) Behind the stolid façade awaits this classy establishment, with Bauhaus-style décor, ec-centric artworks and 98 comfortable rooms sheathed in warm colours; some overlook Theaterplatz.

Eating & Drinking

An der Schlossmühle (☎ 335 2533; Schlossberg 3; mains €4-20) One of several options at the foot of the castle, this 1704 half-timbered gem serves German food and has a woodsy interior and gardenlike terrace.

Turmbrauhaus (☎ 909 5095; Neumarkt 2; mains €3-10) The hearty food at this upbeat brewpub is pitched to mainstream tastes, but the service is swift, the prices are low, the ale is tasty and the outdoor tables are great for people-watching.

Ratskeller (☎ 694 9875; Markt 1; mains €8-18) This atmospheric place is wildly popular for huge portions of local cuisine, and it has over 120 dishes on the menu! You can choose between rustic or sophisticated sections, and the painted and vaulted ceilings are so gorgeous you may want to eat them too.

Getting There & Around

Chemnitz is linked by direct train to Dresden (€11.70, 1½ hours), Leipzig (€13.40, one hour) and Zwickau (€3.90, 55 minutes). The east–west A4 skirts Chemnitz, while the A72 heading south for Munich originates here.

Buses and trams make up the local public transport system. Single tickets start at €1 for short rides; individual day passes are €2.90 per person, or €5 for families.

AROUND CHEMNITZ
Augustusburg

About 13km east of Chemnitz, draped across a craggy mountain top above forests and fields, Augustusburg (population 5100) is one of those relatively undiscovered gems people rave about, with friendly locals to boot. The big draw here is the oversized **Schloss** (☎ 037291-380 18; www.die-sehenswerten-drei.de; ⏰ 9.30am-6pm Apr-Oct, 10am-5pm Nov-Mar), built in 1572 as the summer residence of Elector August, the great-great-great grandfather of Saxon ruler Augustus the Strong. Combined admission to the complex's five museums is €6.60 for adults, €5 with a concession and €18 for a family, but individual tickets can be purchased as well.

The Schloss is nicknamed the 'Palace of the Bikers' for good reason. This is where you'll find the **Motorradmuseum** (adult/concession €3.20/2.40), one of the largest and most prestigious collections of motorcycles in Europe. Treasures include classic Horch, DKW (later MZ) and BMW roadsters, and some very rare Harley models. In the former stables, the focus is on a somewhat earlier mode of transportation in the **Kutschenmuseum** (adult/concession €1.60/1.20), which brims with Cinderella-worthy horse-drawn carriages.

Another wing contains the **Jagdtier- und Vogelkundemuseum** (adult/concession €2.80/2.10), which has adorable dioramas featuring local feathered and furry creatures – a likely winner with the kiddies. Admission is also good for several antler-filled rooms dealing with the palace's hunting history. The main reason for coming up here, though, is to see the Venussaal, a vast hall decorated with original 16th-century murals depicting a spooky, mythical mountainscape. Finally, there's the **Kerker** (adult/concession €1.60/1.20), a dark, damp and cold underground prison that is now filled with medieval torture instruments.

Other palace sections can only be seen on **guided tours** (adult/concession €3/2) in German. These include the **residential wing**, the **palace church,** which has an altar painting by Lucas Cranach the Younger, and the **Brunnenhaus**, which still contains the wooden mechanism that once brought water up from a 130m-deep well.

You also have to pay separately to climb the **Aussichtsturm** (viewing tower; €1), for clear views across the region.

Outside the north entrance is the **Adler- und Falkenhof** (falconry; demonstrations adult/concession €5/3; ⏰ 11am & 3pm Tue-Sun Apr-Oct), with owls, buzzards, eagles, and other trained hunting birds performing in-flight demonstrations.

The complex also contains a **DJH hostel** (☎ 202 56; dm under 26yr €15.30-17.30, over 26yr €18.30-20.30; ✗) and several restaurants. For more lodging and eating options, head down into the village, where you'll also find the **tourist office** (☎ 395 50; www.augustusburg.de; Marienberger Strasse 24; ⏰ 9am-noon & 1-5pm Mon-Fri).

GETTING THERE & AWAY

Trains run from Chemnitz to Erdmannsdorf (€2.80, 20 minutes), from where you take the *Drahtseilbahn* (funicular) to Augustusburg (one-way/return €4/3).

On weekends and holidays between Easter and October, an excursion bus called *Der Augustusburger* travels directly from the Zentralhaltestelle in Chemnitz (see p194) to the palace (return €6, 30 minutes). This service is operated by **CVAG** (☎ 237 0333; www.cvag.de, in German).

Coming from Chemnitz, motorists should follow the L236 country road east to the Schloss. From the A4, get off at Frankenberg, take the B169 to Flöha, then switch to the B180 to Augustusburg.

ZWICKAU
☎ 0375 / pop 101,000

A gateway to the Erzgebirge (Iron Ore Mountains), Zwickau has written an especially important chapter in German automobile history. It is the birthplace of both the Audi brand (in 1910) and the GDR-era Trabant, which began rolling, very slowly, off assembly lines in 1957 (also see boxed text, p198). The city's newly revamped car museum is a must for anyone even remotely interested in the subject. Production continues today courtesy of Volkswagen, which brought much-needed jobs to the area. As a result, Zwickau feels less depressed than other former GDR industrial cities, and also has a fairly lively centre teeming with pubs and restaurants. This, plus an impressive cathedral, the birth house of composer Robert Schumann and some of Germany's oldest homes, make Zwickau worth a stop.

Orientation

The compact and largely pedestrianised Altstadt is encircled by Dr-Friedrichs-Ring. The Hauptbahnhof (central train station) is about 800m west of the ring road; simply follow Bahnhofstrasse, then Schumannstrasse.

Vogtlandbahn regional trains to the Czech spa town of Karlovy Vary stop right in the heart of town, just south of the Markt and Rathaus.

Information

Main post office (Hauptstrasse 18-20)
Deutsche Bank (☾ 271 90; cnr Innere Plauensche Strasse & Dr-Friedrichs-Ring)
Tourist office (☎ 271 3240; www.zwickau-tourist.de; Hauptstrasse 6; ☾ 9am-6.30pm Mon-Fri, 10am-4pm Sat)

Sights

AUGUST HORCH MUSEUM

A century of automobile history comes alive in this amazing **car museum** (☎ 2717 3812; www .horch-museum.de; Audistrasse 7; adult/concession €5/3.50; ☾ 9.30am-5pm Tue-Sun) that will enlighten and entertain even non-car-buffs. Exhibits sprawl within the original early-20th-century Audi factory, and are presented with great imagination. Old-timer gems include a 1911 Horch Phaeton, Silberpfeil racing cars from the 1930s, and – yes – plenty of Trabants (produced here until 1989). You can walk inside an early gas station, inspect Audi founder August Horch's original office, stroll down a GDR streetscape and even learn how Trabants were made. English-language audio-guides are available for €2. The museum is about 2.5km north of the Altstadt; take tram 7 to Kurt-Eisner-Strasse.

PRIESTERHÄUSER ZWICKAU

Next to the Dom, the **Priesterhäuser Zwickau** (Priests' Houses; ☎ 834 551; Domhof 5-8; adult/concession/ family €4/2/9; ☾ 1-6pm Tue-Sun) give you a close-up look at medieval living conditions. This ensemble of pint-sized cottages were built between the 13th and 15th centuries, and they rank among the country's oldest surviving residential buildings. Church employees lived here as late as the 19th century. Imagine the people who've come before you as you climb up the creaky stairs, duck into small chambers or inspect the soot-stained kitchen. A modern annex has changing exhibits about the town history.

DOM ST MARIEN

West of the Schumann-Haus, **Dom St Marien** (Domhof; admission €1, tower €1; ☾ 10am-6pm Mon-Sat) is a late-Gothic hall church that will quicken the pulse of art fans. Foremost among its treasures is the 1479 altar painting by Michael Wohlgemuth (a teacher of Albrecht Dürer) plus an emotionally charged pietà (1502) by famous local sculptor Peter Breuer, and some ultra-rare Protestant confessionals. For details, ask to borrow the English pamphlet.

ROBERT SCHUMANN-HAUS

Behind Hauptmarkt is the **Robert-Schumann-Haus** (☎ 215 269; Hauptmarkt 5; adult/concession/family €4/2/9; ☾ 10am-5pm Tue-Sat), where this renowned composer of the Romantic Age was born and spent the first seven years of his life. Exhibits trace the various life stations of the man who sadly went seriously bipolar in his 30s, and died young in Bonn (p565). A highlight is the piano once played by Schumann's wife, Clara Wieck, herself a noted pianist. There's a monument to the man in the northeast corner of the Hauptmarkt.

JOHANNISBAD

A 10-minute walk north of the Altstadt, the **Johannisbad** (☎ 272 560; Johannisstrasse 16; adult/concession per hr €3/2.50, per 2hr €4.50/3.50; ☺ 10am-10pm Mon & Wed, 8am-10pm Tue & Thu, 10am-11pm Fri, 9am-10pm Sat & Sun) is a beautiful old Art Nouveau swimming pool and sauna complex, which is worth a look even without taking a dip. Walk north on Max-Pechstein-Strasse, then right on Johannisstrasse.

Sleeping & Eating

Brauereigasthof Zwickau (☎ 303 2032; www.brauhaus -zwickau.de; Peter-Breuer-Strasse 12-20; s/d €45/60; P) This is an excellent bargain base. It has five simple but cosy rooms, with ancient exposed beams, above a sprawling resto-pub that makes its own beer and schnapps and serves hearty meals in belt-loosening portions (€6 to €13).

Zum Uhu (☎ 295 044; www.zum-uhu.de; Bahnhofstrasse 51; s/d/tr €33/62/75) This little family-run place is an excellent place for soaking up some local colour, especially in the congenial restaurant – specialists in Saxon cuisine. Rooms range from rustic to modern and are pretty spacious.

Achat Hotel (☎ 8720; www.achat-hotel.de; Leipziger Strasse 180; s/d Mon-Thu €106/118, Fri-Sun €63/75; P ✕ ▣) This modern and spotless hotel feels all business all the time, but it has plenty of comfort factors to satisfy the leisure brigade. These include a 24-hour sauna, supersized rooms and a restaurant that even draws locals (mains €7 to €14). Take tram 4 to 'Neue Welt'.

Zur Grünhainer Kapelle (☎ 204 8255; Peter-Breuer-Strasse 3; mains €8-14.50) Feast on Saxon dishes in this old chapel with its cross-vaulted ceilings, fabulous carved furniture and uneven art exhibits. The house speciality is the charmingly named *besoffne Wildsau* (drunken boar)!

El Greco (☎ 273 7002; Alter Steinweg 2; mains €8-16) Huge menus are not usually a sign of quality, but that rule doesn't apply at this rock-solid Greek eatery where we haven't had a bad meal yet. Expect authentic dishes, quality ingredients and smiling service.

Sky Lounge (☎ 390 9969; Peter-Breuer-Strasse 19; dinner mains €12-27; ☺ from 9am) This hipster place is a surprising island of sophistication. An elevator whisks you to the top floor, where you'll find a lounge, a restaurant and two terraces to catch the morning and afternoon sun. Breakfast is served any time.

Drei Schwäne (☎ 204 7650; www.drei-schwaene.de; Gartenstrasse 1; mains €18-22) Food fanciers will want to make the trip out to this tiptop place, where the cuisine is inspired by the robust flavours of Provence, Tuscany and the Alsace. Excellent wines and welcoming hosts ensure a memorable evening.

THE LORD OF THE RINGS

More than anything else, Zwickau has been shaped by the automobile industry and by one man in particular: August Horch (1868–1951). The first Horch cars rolled into the streets in 1904 and quickly became the queen among luxury vehicles, besting even Mercedes Benz. Horch, alas, was a better engineer than a businessman and in 1909 he was fired by his investors. Not missing a step, he simply opened another factory across town, calling it Audi (Latin for Horch, which means 'listen' in German).

Ever wondered why the Audi symbol is four interlinking rings? They stand for Audi, Horch, DKW and Wanderer, the four Saxon car makers who merged into a single company called Auto-Union during the Great Depression. After the war, Audi moved to Ingolstadt in Bavaria. As for Zwickau, it became the birthplace of the Trabant – the GDR's answer to the Volkswagen Beetle. The name means 'satellite' in German, and was inspired by the launch of the world's first satellite – the Soviet Sputnik – in 1957, a year before production started.

By the time it ceased in 1991, more than three million Trabis had rolled off the assembly lines here, most of them for export to other socialist countries – which is why regular GDR folks had to wait up to 13 years (!) to get one.

Because of the country's chronic steel shortage, the Trabi's body was made from reinforced plastic called Duroplast. Powered by a two-stroke engine similar to that of a large lawnmower, this rolling environmental disaster pumped out five times the amount of fumes as the average Western vehicle. Berlin residents still talk of waking up the day the Wall opened to see a vast queue of Trabants stretching down the road, with a dull brown cloud gathering overhead…

Drinking

Berlin it ain't, but you can still have a rollicking good time along Zwickau's **Kneipenstrasse** (pub row), aka Peter-Breuer-Strasse. Choices include **egghead** (☎ 303 3386; Peter-Breuer-Strasse 34), a sleek but unpretentious cocktail bar with all kinds of mixed drinks, shakes and tasty crêpes for sustenance.

Kick back with a cocktail amid the gilded baroque mirrors, huge aquarium and red leather lounges in buzzy **La Bodeguita del Medio** (☎ 440 6741; Innere Schneeberger Strasse 2a; ☷ Tue-Sat).

Getting There & Around

Zwickau has direct train links to Leipzig (€13.40, 1¼ hours), Chemnitz (€3.90, 55 minutes), Dresden (€19.10, 1¾ hours) and other cities. Drivers should take the A4 rather than the A72, which will have construction delays for years to come.

Single tickets on trams and buses are €1.60, day passes are €2.90.

AROUND ZWICKAU

In an old palace in Lichtenstein, about 14km east of Zwickau, the mind-boggling **Daetz-Centrum** (☎ 037204-585858; www.daetz-centrum.com; Schlossallee 2; admission incl audio-guide €8/6; ☷ 10am-6pm) is a private collection of wood sculpture from five continents. Its owner promises to 'take you around the world in 80 minutes', past Native American kachina dolls, intricate masks from Micronesia, delicate figurines from China and other treasures – some 600 in all. You can also watch a changing crew of international artists carving away in the workshop. Take the Hohenstein-Ernsthal exit off the A4 or the Hartenstein exit off the A72.

EASTERN SAXONY

BAUTZEN

☎ 03591 / pop 42,200

The deep valley of the Spree River and the medieval towers that rise from cliffs above it create a fine metaphor for the dual nature of Bautzen, which celebrated its 1000th anniversary in 2002. While the town is undeniably German, its heritage is also influenced by the Sorbs, Germany's sole indigenous minority (see boxed text, p158). Several Sorb cultural institutions are based here, and public signage

is bilingual, though you'd be lucky to hear the language spoken.

Though badly damaged many times over its history, the Altstadt's labyrinth of cobbled lanes has hardly changed for centuries, and many beautifully restored historic buildings remain, including no fewer than 17 towers and much of the town fortification.

Orientation

The Spree River ribbons along the western side of Bautzen's Altstadt, which is centred on the Hauptmarkt. The Hauptbahnhof is a 15-minute walk south of the old quarter, and is reached via Bahnhofstrasse, Karl-Marx-Strasse and Lauengraben. For the classic view of the town silhouette, follow Lauenstrasse west to the Friedensbrücke.

Information

Internetcafé Bautzen (☎ 277 110; Steinstrasse 13; per 30min €1.50; ☷ 9am-11pm Mon-Sat, 2-11pm Sun)
Post office (Postplatz)
Sparkasse (Kornmarkt) A bank.
Tourist office (☎ 420 16; www.bautzen.de; Hauptmarkt 1; ☷ 9am-6pm Mon-Fri year-round, 10am-4pm Sat & Sun Mar-Oct, 10am-2pm Sat & Sun Nov-Feb)

Sights
REICHENTURM

An exploration of Bautzen might start with a climb up the **Reichenturm** (☎ 460 431; Kornmarkt; adult/child €1.20/0.60; ☷ 10am-5pm Apr-Oct), on the eastern edge of the Altstadt. The addition of the baroque cupola in 1718 caused the 53m-high structure to start tilting. Today it deviates 1.4m from the centre, making it one of the steepest leaning towers north of the Alps. Nearby, the **Stadtmuseum** (city museum; ☎ 498 50; Kornmarkt 1) is scheduled to reopen with a new, modern concept in 2008.

HAUPTMARKT

Reichenstrasse leads west from the tower, past fancy baroque houses to the **Hauptmarkt**, site of the tourist office and thrice-weekly farmers markets. The square is dominated by the impressive **Rathaus**, with an 18th-century baroque exterior that masks a Gothic origin. The intriguing **sundial** measures time, as well as the lengths of the days and nights for each date.

DOM ST PETRI

North of the Hauptmarkt is the **Fleischmarkt**, the old meat market, dominated by the **Dom St**

Petri. This is the only *Simultankirche* in eastern Germany, meaning it serves both Catholics and Protestants. When the Reformation reached Bautzen in 1524, both congregations agreed to share the church, with the Protestants holding services in the nave and the Catholics in the choir. There's a waist-high iron grating separating the two – although it was 4m high until 1952!

Just behind the Dom is the **Domstift**, a U-shaped bishop's palace entered via a richly decorated baroque portal. Loads of objects gleam inside the **Domschatzkammer** (treasury; ☎ 351 950; ☼ 10am-noon & 1-4pm Mon-Fri), the oldest being a portable 13th-century enamel altar.

Behind the palace, a lane leads down to the **Nicolaiturm** tower and a cemetery cradled by the romantically ruined **Nicolaikirche**, which was destroyed in the Thirty Years' War.

SCHLOSS ORTENBURG

Further west is Schloss Ortenburg, on a strategic cliff-top spot that's been occupied by a series of castles since the 7th century. You enter the complex through its most interesting structure, the late-Gothic **Matthiasturm** (Matthias Tower), named for the Hungarian king Matthias Corvinus who ruled over the region in the late 15th century – you can see him depicted on horseback as a monumental relief on the tower.

The main palace houses a regional courthouse and is not open to the public. A smaller one, off the courtyard, contains the **Sorbisches Museum** (☎ 424 03; adult/concession €2.50/1.50; ☼ 10am-5pm Mon-Fri, 10am-6pm Sat & Sun Apr-Oct, 10am-4pm Mon-Fri, 10am-5pm Sat & Sun Nov-Mar), which displays Sorb folk art, musical instruments, costumes and other items in the old salt storehouse.

Across the square is Bautzen's new theatre, noteworthy mostly for the amazingly detailed **neoclassical sandstone frieze** that's been incorporated into the façade. Sculpted by Ernst Rietschel in 1804, it depicts the tragedy of Orest from ancient Greek mythology and originally decorated the now-destroyed Hoftheater in Dresden.

ALTE WASSERKUNST

South of the Schloss, and along the old town wall, is the **Alte Wasserkunst** (☎ 415 88; adult/concession €1.50/1; ☼ 10am-5pm Apr-Oct, 10am-4pm Nov-Mar), a tower containing an ingenious late-medieval pump station, which is once again operational.

BAUTZEN PRISONS

It seems incongruous that this pretty, historic town has been known as *Gefängnisstadt* (prison town) for over a century. The first facility, **Bautzen I**, a yellow brick structure from 1904, gained such notoriety under the Nazis and later the Soviets that it earned the moniker *Gelbes Elend* (Yellow Misery). Completely modernised, it's still used as a correctional facility today.

South of town is **Bautzen II**, which became a Stasi prison in GDR times. Many famous regime opponents – including Rudolf Bahro, who later co-founded the Green Party in West Germany – served their sentences here. Today, it's a **Gedenkstätte** (memorial site; ☎ 404 74; www.gedenkstaette-bautzen.de; Weigangstrasse 8a; admission free; ☼ 10am-4pm Tue-Sun) for the victims of political oppression.

Sleeping

DJH hostel (☎ 403 47; jhbautzen@djh.de; Am Zwinger 1; dm under/over 26yr €16.40/19.40, s €20.40/26.40, d €53/60; ☒) The local hostel has a fairytale location in the old ramparts behind the Domstift.

Alte Gerberei (☎ 301 011; www.hotel-alte-gerberei-de; Uferweg 1; s/d €45/65; ☒) You'll find Old European charm galore in this historic eight-room pension right by the river. The flower-filled courtyard, the river-facing rooms and the wine restaurant are great for unwinding.

Dom-Eck Hotel Garni (☎ 501 330; www.wjelbik.de; Breitengasse 2; s/d €55/70; ☒) Right by the Dom, this family pension was designed by Sorbian and German artists, and has good-sized modern rooms. Breakfasts start with a big buffet served in a bright wintergarden.

Schloss-Schänke (☎ 304 990; www.schloss-schaenke .net; Burgplatz 5; s/d €46/66; meals €10-18; ☒) This was once a Franciscan residence, but the 11 renovated rooms are hardly monastic. The restaurant has good-value set menus for around €20.

Hotel Goldener Adler (☎ 486 60; www.goldeneradler .de; Hauptmarkt 4; s/d €67/97; ☒ ☒) History spills from every nook and cranny of this spiffy four-star hotel with its doesn't-get-more-central location. Cap off a day about town with dinner or a drink in the romantic vaulted cellar.

Eating & Drinking

Sam's Bar (☎ 490 964; Fleischmarkt 4; dishes €3-12) For salads, sandwiches and other café-style fare, come to this relaxed hangout that stays open longer than any other place in town.

Mönchshof (☎ 490 141; Burglehn 1; mains €4-10) With servers dressed like monks and dishes served in rustic earthenware, this place may go a bit overboard with the medieval theme, but the creative food is worth the drama. It also has a pretty terrace.

Wjelbik (☎ 420 60; Kornstrasse 7; mains €8-13) You can't help but be charmed by your host here, Veronika Mahling, who will greet you, Sorbian style, with a little bread and salt and a hearty *Witajæe k nam!* (Welcome!). It's the best place to try specialities such as the Sorbian Wedding (braised beef with horseradish sauce) under wonderful beamed ceilings. There's no service here on weekday afternoons.

If Bautzen had something like a 'restaurant row', it would be Schlossstrasse, where you'll find about half a dozen eateries, including **Zur Apotheke** (☎ 480 035; Schlossstrasse 21; mains €8-11) inside an olde-worlde pharmacy. It has a progressive menu of German food, including some calorie-reduced chicken dishes.

Getting There & Away

Regional trains service Bautzen from Görlitz (€6.40, 40 minutes) and Dresden (€9.10, one hour). The A4 to Dresden or Görlitz runs just south of town. You can park fairly cheaply at Parkplatz Centrum on Äussere Lauenstrasse.

GÖRLITZ

☎ 03581 / pop 59,000

Some 100km east of Dresden, on the Neisse River, Görlitz is Germany's easternmost city, and is also one of its prettiest. It miraculously came through WWII with nary a shrapnel wound and today is a veritable encyclopaedia of architecture, with stunning examples from the Gothic, Renaissance, baroque and Art Nouveau periods. GDR honchos declared the entire city a protected monument, but then invested little in its upkeep. Only after reunification did huge federal cash infusions restore beauty to this ageing grande dame. Largely unmarred by the trappings of commercialisation (no 'golden arches' here), the nearly 4200 heritage buildings make the place feel almost like a film set. No surprise, then, that Görlitz stood in for 19th-century Paris and New York in the 2004 remake of *Around the World in 80 Days*, starring Jackie Chan.

The Berlin Wall may have tumbled long ago, but Görlitz is still a divided city. After WWII it was split in two when the Allies made the Neisse River the boundary between Germany and Poland. Görlitz' former eastern suburbs are now known as Zgorzelec (zgo-*zhe*-lets).

Orientation

The Altstadt spreads to the north of the Hauptbahnhof. From here, Berliner Strasse and Jakobstrasse, the main shopping streets, run south to Postplatz. Beyond, the city is organised around a trio of squares starting with Demianiplatz in the west, followed by Obermarkt and then Untermarkt. From the latter, Neissstrasse leads down to the Neisse River and the new Altstadtbrücke, the footbridge to Zgorzelec. Bring your passport if crossing.

Information

There's a Deutsche Bank on Demianiplatz, and a Sparkasse and Dresdner Bank on Postplatz.

Görlitz tourist office (☎ 475 70; www.g-tm.de, www .goerlitz.de; Brüderstrasse 1; ☉ 9am-6.30pm Mon-Fri, 10am-4pm Sat, 10am-2pm Sun)
I-Vent tourist office (☎ 421 362; www.goerlitz -tourismus.de; Obermarkt 33; ☉ 9am-7pm Mon-Fri, 9.30am-5pm Sat, 9.30am-3pm Sun Apr-Oct, 9am-6pm Mon-Fri, 9am-3pm Sat Nov-Mar) Private tourist office.
Post office (Postplatz)

Sights

OBERMARKT & SOUTHERN ALTSTADT

Obermarkt, Görlitz' largest square, is flanked by some great baroque buildings on its north side. At the eastern end is the 16th-century **Dreifaltigkeitskirche** (☉ 10am-6pm Mon-Sat, 11am-6pm Sun), which has an odd floor plan and nifty late-Gothic altar.

Punctuating the square's west end like the dot in an exclamation point is the 49m-high **Reichenbacher Turm** (☎ 671 355; adult/concession €1.50/1; ☉ 10am-5pm Tue-Sun, to 8pm Fri May-Oct), part of the old fortification, which was still inhabited until 1904. Inside are exhibits, but most people just want to climb to the top for the views.

Just behind the tower is the 1490 **Kaisertrutz**, a squat structure also formerly part of the city's defence system. It normally houses an art collection, but has been under restoration for years. Meanwhile, restoration has been completed on the **Theater Görlitz** (☎ 474 747; Demianiplatz 2), which many consider Dresden's Semperoper in miniature; it's behind the Kaisertrutz.

East of here, on Marienplatz, is the **Dicker Turm** (Fat Tower), with walls almost 6m thick in some places. Walking south on Steinstrasse, past the **Frauenkirche**, soon gets you to the **Karstadt department store** (An der Frauenkirche 5-7), which would be unremarkable were it not for its most amazing Art Nouveau interior, canopied by a kaleidoscopic glass ceiling. Another architectural delicacy from the same period is the sparkling **Strassburg Passage**, a light-flooded shopping arcade connecting Berliner Strasse and Jacobstrasse.

UNTERMARKT & EASTERN ALTSTADT

The most beautiful patrician houses flank the Untermarkt, linked to Obermarkt by Brüderstrasse. The building at the square's centre is the **Alte Börse** (old stock exchange), now a hotel.

First up on your right, on the south side of Untermarkt, is the magnificent 1526 Schönhof, Germany's oldest residential Renaissance structure. It now houses the brand-new **Schlesisches Museum zu Görlitz** (☎ 879 10; Untermarkt 4; adult/concession €3/1.50; ☺ 10am-5pm Tue-Sun), which offers a creatively presented romp through the rich cultural history of Silesia in 17 themed rooms (start at the top). A free English-language guide is available and audio-guides are planned.

Immediately opposite, taking up the square's entire western side, is the **Rathaus** (town hall), begun in 1537 and built in three sections and styles. If you take a moment to observe the lower of the two clocks on the tower, you'll notice that the helmeted soldier in the middle briefly drops his chin every minute.

As you continue clockwise, other buildings of note are the peculiar late-Gothic **Flüsterbogen** at No 22, where you can whisper sweet nothings to your sweetie via the reverberating stone arch in the entranceway, and the Renaissance **Ratsapotheke** (pharmacy) at No 24, easily recognised by its spidery sun dial.

Circling the square eventually takes you to Neissstrasse. At No 30 stands the town's only pure baroque house, the **Barockhaus** (☎ 671 410; adult/concession €2/1; ☺ 10am-5pm Tue-Sun, to 8pm Fri), now a museum filled with fancy furniture and art. Also note the **Biblisches Haus** next door, whose façade is like a Bible carved in sandstone. The river and the Altstadtbrücke crossing to Poland are a few more steps downhill.

Turn left on Kränzelstrasse for the Gothic **Peterskirche** (☺ 10am-6pm Mon-Sat, 1-6pm Sun), where the star attraction is the fascinating 'Sun Organ' fashioned by Silesian-Italian Eugenio Casparini, with tiny pipes shooting off like rays.

HEILIGES GRAB

A 10-minute walk along Grüner Graben, north of the Reichenbacher Turm, drops you at the **Heiliges Grab** (admission €1.50; ☺ 10am-6pm Mon-Sat, 11am-6pm Sun), an exact replica of the original Holy Sepulchre in Jerusalem (which has since been altered repeatedly). It was commissioned some 500 years ago, by a local mayor in atonement for getting the neighbour's girl knocked up when he was a youngster.

Sleeping

DJH hostel (☎ 406 510; Goethestrasse 17; dm under/over 26yr €15/18, s/d €19/25; ✗) For this, rather sober hostel, take the Hauptbahnhof south exit, turn left and walk for 15 minutes (or take tram 1 to Goethestrasse).

Picobello Pension (☎ 420 010; www.picobello-pension.de; Uferstrasse 32; s €19-25, d €32-44, breakfast €5; P ✗ ▢) Near the river, these bargain apartments are simple but surprisingly good. Amenities include a sauna and bike rentals.

Hotel Börse (☎ 764 20; www.boerse-goerlitz.de; Untermarkt 16; s €60-75, d €95-115; P ✗ ▢) Four-poster beds, huge glass chandeliers, patterned parquet floors and elegant antiques are the hallmarks of this stylish yet spirited hotel. Mineral water and DSL are welcome freebies.

Herberge Zum Sechsten Gebot (☎ 764 20; www .boerse-goerlitz.de; s/d €50/70; P ✗) Hotel Börse's owner also runs this excellent place across the square. The name pays homage to the sixth commandment (Thou shalt not commit adultery), but hilariously the spacious, modern rooms are named for famous sinners, such as Henry VIII and the Marquis de Sade.

Gästehaus im Flüsterbogen (☎ 764 20; www .boerse-goerlitz.de; s €58-70, d €75-85, tr/q €110/125; P ✗) Check in here (another good option from the owners of Hotel Börse) if you need plenty of elbow room. Wonderful sleigh beds and other antique furnishings add character by the armload.

Sorat Hotel Görlitz (☎ 406 577; www.sorat-hotels .com; Struvestrasse 1; s €66-90, d €86-110; P ✗) Days kick off with a champagne breakfast at this central hotel with tasteful, modern rooms (some with wheelchair access). Ask about weekend rates.

Romantik Hotel Tuchmacher (☎ 473 10; www.tuchmacher.de; Petersstrasse 8; s €95-110, d €120-143; ℗ ✕) The most unusual rooms at this posh oasis of charm near the Peterskirche (bell alert!) sport richly painted baroque ceilings, but others are just as nice with warm hues and classical furnishings. There's a lovely wellness area for relaxing, and a popular restaurant for refuelling.

Eating

Acanthus (☎ 661 810; Neissstrasse 20; mains €6-12) Among the many eating options on Neissstrasse is this superb and versatile noshery, with a varied menu, a secluded riverside beer garden and a confusing but atmospheric network of internal passages.

St Jonathan (☎ 421 082; Peterstrasse 16; mains €7-12) Despite its sleek furniture and stunning historic setting, this place only looks expensive. Enjoy delicious German food below the painted vaulted ceiling or, for a romantic tête-à-tête, book the single table inside (!) the fireplace. Also explore the back of the building with its atrium staircase, where textile merchants used to display their wares.

Vierradenmühle (☎ 406 661; Hotherstrasse 20; mains €8-14) Service is slow but the Saxon and Silesian food is excellent at this place. Sticking out into the Neisse next to the new Altstadtbrücke, it is Germany's easternmost restaurant.

Restaurant Lucie Schulte (☎ 410 260; Untermarkt 22; mains €12-26; ⏰ 6pm Mon-Sat) Your tastebuds are likely to do cartwheels when you try the creative flavour pairings at this refreshingly progressive venue. It's set in historic barrel-vaulted rooms off the romantic courtyard of the Flüsterbogen building, and has great wines, too.

Getting There & Away

Frequent trains run between Görlitz and Dresden (€16.10, 1½ hours) via Bautzen (€6.40, 40 minutes). For Berlin (€33, three hours), a change in Cottbus is likely. Buses and private Lausitzbahn trains also serve Zittau (€5.60, 40 minutes). There are also four trains daily to Wroclaw (Breslau; €15.70, three hours) with one crawling on to Warsaw (10 hours).

Görlitz is just off the A4 autobahn from Dresden; turn off after the Königshainer Berge tunnel, which at 3.3km is currently Germany's second-longest – the longest is the Rennsteig tunnel in Thuringia, an astonishing 7.9km in length! The B6, B99 and B115 converge just north of town.

ZITTAU

☎ 03583 / pop 25,000

About 35km south of Görlitz, Zittau is an intriguing outpost in a far-flung corner of Germany, hemmed in by Poland and the Czech Republic. Basically untouched during WWII, it preserves a largely intact baroque Altstadt. Post-reunification restoration, however, hasn't progressed quite as far here as in other Saxon cities, and the many dilapidated buildings still provide a glimpse of Zittau's appearance in GDR times. Since 1999, the town's star attraction has been the *Grosse Zittauer Fastentuch*, an ultra-rare Lenten veil that was joined by a second, smaller one in 2005. These treasures make Zittau the hub of the newly founded Via Sacra, a cross-border holiday route linking sites of religious importance.

Orientation & Information

The Altstadt is a 10-minute walk south of the Hauptbahnhof, via Bahnhofstrasse and Bautzener Strasse.

Post office (Haberkornplatz 1)

Sparkasse (cnr Neustadt & Frauenstrasse)

Tourist office (☎ 752 200; www.zittau.de; Markt 1; ⏰ 9am-6pm Mon-Fri, 9am-1pm Sat, 1-4pm Sun May-Oct)

Sights & Activities

Zittau's central square, the **Markt**, exudes almost Mediterranean flair thanks to its baroque fountain, patrician townhouses and imposing Italian-palazzo-style **Rathaus** (town hall), drafted by none other than Prussian building master Karl Friedrich Schinkel.

Schinkel also designed the **Johanniskirche** (☎ 510 933; tower adult/concession €1.50/1; ⏰ 10am-6pm Mon-Fri, 10am-4pm Sat & Sun Apr-Oct, 10am-4.30pm Mon-Fri, 10am-4pm Sat & Sun Nov-Mar) north of the Markt. It's a neoclassical church with two towers that don't match, one of which can be climbed for sweeping views of the mountains. If you're here at noon or 6pm, you might run into the city trumpeter who plays little tunes daily at those times.

East of the Markt, via Frauenstrasse, is the **Neustadt** square, with several fountains and the weighty **Salzhaus**. Originally a 16th-century salt storage house, this now houses shops, restaurants and the public library.

Continuing on Frauenstrasse soon takes you to the **Museum Kirche zum Heiligen Kreuz** (☎ 500 8920; adult/concession €4/2; ⏰ 10am-6pm Tue-Sun Apr-Oct, 10am-5pm Nov-Mar). This former church now shelters Zittau's most famous attraction, the

1472 **Grosses Zittauer Fastentuch** (large Lenten veil). This house-sized painted linen cloth shows a complete illustrated Bible in 90-odd scenes – Genesis to the Last Judgement. Its original purpose was to conceal the altar from the congregation during Lent. Also note the morbidly charming tombstones in the little church cemetery.

Smaller in size, but no less precious or rare, is the 1573 **Kleines Zittauer Fastentuch**, which is the new star exhibit at the **Kulturhistorisches Museum Franziskanerkloster** (☎ 554790; Klosterstrasse 3; adult/concession €2/1.50; ☑ 10am-noon & 1-5pm Tue-Sun), a short walk west of here. This depicts the crucifixion scene framed by 40 symbols of the Passion of Christ and is one of only six such veils that have survived. Combination tickets for both veils are €5 per adult (€3 concession), which includes an English-language audio-guide. The rest of the museum has exhibits chronicling regional history.

Sleeping & Eating

Hotel Dreiländereck (☎ 5550; www.hotel-dle.de; Bautzener Strasse 9; s €60-65, d €75-85; P ✗) This one-time brewery right in the Altstadt is a top choice, with warmly furnished rooms dressed in green-and-gold hues, and a contemporary brasserie with vaulted ceilings. The only downside is the proximity of the Johanniskirche bells!

Hotel Dresdener Hof (☎ 573 00; www.hotel-dresdener-hof.de; Äussere Oybiner Strasse 9/12; s/d €46/64; P ✗) Set in its own small park with a sparkling pond, this is an old-fashioned affair, but the rooms are large, the staff are friendly and accommodating, and the Altstadt is only a five-minute walk away.

Savi (☎ 708 297; Bautzener Strasse 10; meals €2-8; ☐) This in-crowd café-bar-gallery is great for a snack, light meal, drink or checking email (€0.60 per 15 minutes).

Dornspachhaus (☎ 795 883; Bautzener Strasse 2; mains €5-11) Dripping with history, this upmarket option next to the Johanniskirche serves delicious regional cuisine and also has a lovely courtyard. It's named after the mayor who commissioned the building.

Klosterstübl (☎ 517 486; Johannisstrasse 4; mains €5-12) This updated inn has an uncluttered look – all the better to show off the rich oak wainscoting, huge tile oven and hilarious murals featuring frolicking monks. The menu features several regional dishes, including *Wickelklösse* (vegetable-stuffed dumplings).

Getting There & Away

There are direct trains to Dresden (€15.90, two hours) and Görlitz (€5.60, 40 minutes). Going to Bautzen usually requires a change in Görlitz or Löbau (€6.40, 1½ hours). For Berlin, change in Cottbus (€37.60, four hours).

The B96 (to Bautzen), B178 (to Löbau) and B99 (to Görlitz) all converge in the town centre.

AROUND ZITTAU
Zittauer Gebirge

South of Zittau, hugging the Czech and Polish borders, the Zittauer Gebirge is the smallest low-mountain range in Europe. With its idyllic gorges, thick forests and whimsical rock formations, it's great for hiking and relaxing.

You can drive or take the bus, but getting there is more fun aboard the 110-year-old narrow-gauge **Bimmelbahn**. This was originally designed for brown-coal mining work, but now puffs up to the sleepy resort villages of Oybin and Jonsdorf, splitting at Bernsdorf. The service to Oybin (€5.90, 40 minutes) stops at the **Teufelsmühle** (Devil's Mill), built for silver miners in the 17th century; here you can glimpse the **Töpfer peak** (582m) to the east.

Alternatively, you can hike to Oybin on a clearly marked trail, taking you south along the Neisse River before veering off into the hills (11km). Oybin and Jonsdorf both make good bases for extended hikes, though Oybin is more picturesque.

Burg und Kloster Oybin (☎ 7340; www.burgundkloster-oybin.de; adult/concession/family €3.50/2.50/9; ☑ 9am-6pm Apr-Sep, 10am-4pm Oct-Mar), a romantically ruined castle and monastery on a beehive-shaped hill north of the town, was commissioned by German emperor Charles IV in the 14th century. The dramatic ensemble is an ideal setting for summer concerts, or just for poking around on your own.

Saxony-Anhalt

Saxony-Anhalt (Sachsen-Anhalt) is the German underdog, the economic runt of the litter. With the highest unemployment, the lowest birth rate and the biggest outward flow of people, this former GDR region often makes headlines for all the wrong reasons.

History hasn't always been so unkind. There's plenty of time-honoured appeal here, and the state is slowly showing signs of responding to treatment (including an injection of billions under the 'Aufbau Ost' federal regeneration project). More than 80 years after some of the world's most famous architects took up residence, Dessau has refurbished its iconic Bauhaus buildings. The capital, Magdeburg, has gone in another direction, adding a wonderful Austrian folly to its enclave of early 1900s terrace houses and ancient cathedral.

Immerse yourself in nature and pagan mythology in the Harz Mountains (p229). Though, in the era of a controversial, Prada-wearing German pope, it's interesting to reflect on how one of his countrymen launched the Reformation, and Protestantism, in 16th-century Wittenberg.

Biotech and other businesses still haven't filled the employment gap left when the East German districts of Magdeburg and Halle were merged to create Saxony-Anhalt in 1990, and their heavy industry was dismantled. However, with the air much sweeter these days, interest in the great outdoors has been revived – Germans now cycle enthusiastically along the Elbe River. And, on a wave of Ostalgie, sparkling wine from Saale-Unstrut has become fashionable.

It might have gone from the GDR's powerhouse to the new Germany's poorhouse, but Saxony-Anhalt is rich in under-appreciated treasures and its fortunes should only improve.

SAXONY-ANHALT

HIGHLIGHTS

- **Grand Designs** Marvel at the sleek lines of Dessau's refurbished Bauhaus gems (p212)
- **Sweet Dreams** Book a night inside cult architect Hundertwasser's wacky Magdeburg building (p208)
- **Green Haven** Cycle through garden realms around Dessau and Wörlitz (p215)
- **Bar-Hopping** Sip cocktails in the historic enclave of Magdeburg's Hasselbachplatz (p209)
- **Pilgrimage** Retrace Martin Luther's footsteps around Lutherstadt Wittenberg (p217)
- **Offbeat experience** Sail high above the Elbe River outside Magdeburg (p208)

★ Magdeburg

Dessau ★ ★ ★ Lutherstadt
Wörlitz Wittenberg

- POPULATION: 2.72 MILLION
- AREA: 20,455 SQ KM

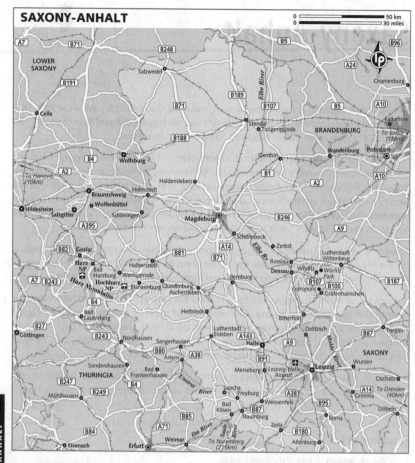

SAXONY-ANHALT

SAXONY-ANHALT

MAGDEBURG

☎ 0391 / pop 228,775

Something old, something new: Magdeburg is constantly characterised by the juxtaposition of those two. Home to Germany's most ancient cathedral, the city now also boasts the newest – and last – of Austrian architect Friedensreich Hundertwasser's bonkers buildings.

And that's not the only marriage of anachronisms you'll find in Saxony-Anhalt's capital. While 90% of the city was destroyed by WWII bombing and rebuilt in the GDR style of wide boulevards and enormous concrete *Plattenbauten* apartments, a small enclave of early-20th-century terraces and cobbled streets survived around Hassel-

bachplatz; today, entering and leaving this historic district is like being transported in a time machine.

Chosen as the state capital over Halle at the time of reunification, Magdeburg has been the recipient of generous federal funding over the past decade. This doesn't completely disguise the underlying economic malaise downtown, but the plentiful bars around Hasselbachplatz and the city's series of leafy parks are more than enough to brighten the mood.

Orientation

The huge GDR-era street grid makes navigation easy. The best place to get your bearings is at the intersection of east–west-running Ernst-Reuter-Allee and the major north–south artery of Breiter Weg. From here, Breiter Weg leads south to the cathedral and Hasselbachplatz, and north to the nearby Alter Markt (old market square) and eventually the university.

Ernst-Reuter Allee continues east across the Elbe River to the parks. The Hauptbahnhof (train station) lies west along the same street.

Information

INTERNET

Internet & Game Café (Kepler Passage, Keplerstrasse 9; per hr €2; ☺ 2pm-midnight)

Mocc@ (☎ 734 6350; www.mymocca.de; Olvenstedter Strasse 45a; per hr €3; ☺ 10am to last customer Mon-Fri, from 6pm Sat)

LAUNDRY

Anne's Waschparadies (☎ 541 2593; Walther-Rathenau-Strasse 60; ☺ 9am-9pm Mon-Fri, 9am-3pm Sat)

MEDICAL SERVICES

Krankenhaus Altstadt (☎ 591 90; Max-Otten-Strasse 11-15) Hospital with emergency services.

POST

Post office (☎ 01802-3333; Breiter Weg 203-206; ☺ 9am-7pm Mon-Fri, 9am-noon Sat)

TOURIST INFORMATION

Tourist Information Magdeburg (☎ 194 33; www .magdeburg-tourist.de; Ernst-Reuter-Allee 12; ☺ 10am-7pm Mon-Fri, to 4pm Sat May-Sep, 10am-6.30pm Mon-Fri, to 3pm Sat Oct-Apr)

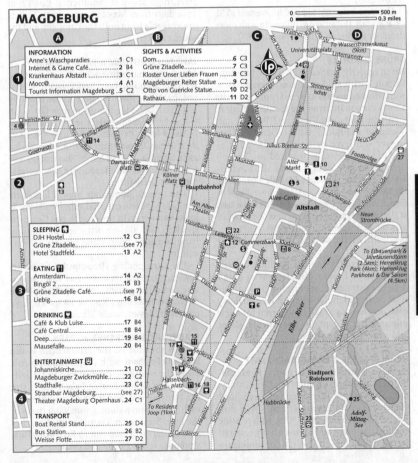

MAGDEBURG

INFORMATION	
Anne's Waschparadies	1 C1
Internet & Game Café	2 B4
Krankenhaus Altstadt	3 C1
Mocc@	4 A1
Tourist Information Magdeburg	5 C2

SIGHTS & ACTIVITIES	
Dom	6 C3
Grüne Zitadelle	7 C3
Kloster Unser Lieben Frauen	8 C3
Magdeburger Reiter Statue	9 C2
Otto von Guericke Statue	10 D2
Rathaus	11 D2

SLEEPING	
DJH Hostel	12 C3
Grüne Zitadelle	(see 7)
Hotel Stadtfeld	13 A2

EATING	
Amsterdam	14 A2
Bingöl 2	15 B3
Grüne Zitadelle Café	(see 7)
Liebig	16 B4

DRINKING	
Café & Klub Luise	17 B4
Café Central	18 B4
Deep	19 B4
Mausefalle	20 B4

ENTERTAINMENT	
Johanniskirche	21 D2
Magdeburger Zwickmühle	22 C2
Stadthalle	23 C4
Strandbar Magdeburg	(see 27)
Theater Magdeburg Opernhaus	24 C1

TRANSPORT	
Boat Rental Stand	25 D4
Bus Station	26 B2
Weisse Flotte	27 D2

SAXONY-ANHALT

Sights & Activities

DOM

Magdeburg was established as a trading post by Charlemagne in 805, but the city was made great by King Otto I, whose **tomb** is found in its weather-beaten Gothic **cathedral** (☎ 543 2414; ☺ 10am-4pm Mon-Sat, 11.30am-4pm Sun). Apparently the first of its kind on German soil when it was erected between 1209 and 1363, the twin-towered Dom features an impressive high-ceilinged interior and art spanning eight centuries.

Highlights include a pensive **WWI memorial** by Ernst Barlach and, through the doors beside it – push hard, the latch jams – the sculpture of the **Magdeburger Virgins** (dating from the 13th century and undergoing renovation).

German-language **tours** (adult/concession €3/1.50; ☺ at 2pm daily, 11.30am Sunday) fill you in with more detail, or ask for an English booklet (€3).

GRÜNE ZITADELLE

An irregularly shaped pink-and-white confection – with golden domes, asymmetrical windows and a grass-covered roof – now sits across the square from the iconic cathedral. Can you guess what it is yet? Fans of cult Viennese architect Friedensreich Hundertwasser will have by now recognised it as one of his organically inspired (or 'green') designs. In fact, design it was all Hundertwasser did, for the **Grüne Zitadelle** (Green Citadel; ☎ 400 9650; www.gruene-zitadelle.de; Breiter Weg 8-10; German tours €5; ☺ information office 10am-6pm, tours at 11am, 3pm & 5pm Mon-Fri, hourly 10am-5pm Sat & Sun) was only completed in 2005, five years after his death. All the same, it's officially his last building.

In stark contrast to the Bauhaus designers in nearby Dessau, Hundertwasser didn't believe in straight lines or minimalism. His final design might look like an iced birthday cake accidentally stuck in the oven for a few minutes, but it contains apartments, shops and a hotel – and you can tour it.

HEGELSTRASSE & HASSELBACHPLATZ

Sometimes just turning the corner in Magdeburg can transport you into another century, metaphorically at least. Step onto tree-lined Hegelstrasse, for example, and you'll find yourself back in the early 1900s, with pristine cobbled footpaths and immaculately restored terraced buildings. It's worth continuing on to Hasselbachplatz, where more pretty-as-a-picture historic streets radiate off the square. The whole area feels like a film set plonked down in the middle of a GDR town – as patrons in the cluster of trendy cafés and bars here would probably agree.

WASSERSTRASSENKREUZ

Local boat firm **Weisse Flotte** (☎ 532 8891; www .weisseflotte-magdeburg.de, in German; Petriförder 1) has long run 1½-hour scenic cruises on the Elbe (adult/child €9/4.50). Now, with Magdeburg's new Wassenstrassenkreuz (water intersection), it offers something even more unusual. The world's longest aqueduct – a 'trough' bridge, 918m long and full of water – has been built over the Elbe River, so you can sail across the river, high above it (adult/child €20/12; at 1pm daily from May to September). Tickets are available from both the company and the tourist office.

JAHRTAUSENDTURM & ELBAUENPARK

Magdeburg has a fine scientific reputation, with the air pump (and hence vacuum technology) being invented here in the 1650s by physicist and Magdeburg mayor Otto von Guericke. Consequently, the **Jahrtausendturm** (Millennial Tower; ☎ 01805-251 999; www.elbauenpark .de, in German; Tessenowstrasse 5a; adult/child/family incl park & butterfly house €2.50/2/6; ☺ 10am-6pm, last entry 5.30pm Tue-Sun Apr-Oct) museum of science history is entirely fitting.

The tower's immediate appeal lies in its conical shape and external spiral walkway. It looks wonderful lit up a night, but German-speakers will also be attracted by the fun, hands-on experiments and physics exhibits within.

The surrounding **Elbauenpark** (☺ 9am-8pm May-Sep, reduced hours in winter) has rose, sculpture and other gardens, plus a **butterfly house** (☺ 10am-6pm, last entry 5.30pm Tue-Sun Apr-Oct). Take tram 6 to Messegelände/Elbauenpark.

STADTPARK & HERRENKRUG PARK

Just to the east of the Hubbrücke is the **Stadtpark Rotehorn**, with playgrounds, picnic areas, the Stadthalle concert hall and Adolf-Mittag-See (Adolf-Mittag Lake), where you can hire rowboats and there's a major festival each May. Tram 6 stops about 300m north of the lake. Staying on Tram 6 until it reaches its terminus will take you to **Herrenkrug Park**, a popular spot to stroll and cycle.

OTHER ATTRACTIONS

Kloster Unser Lieben Frauen (Cloister of Our Beloved Lady; ☎ 565 020; cloister admission free, museum adult/concession €2/1; ☒ 10am-5pm Tue-Sun) is Magdeburg's oldest building. Truthfully, there's not much to it, but the front door, designed by popular local artist Heinrich Apel (b 1935), is fun: you knock with the woman's necklace and push down on the man's hat to enter.

At the southeastern end of the so-called old market, or Alter Markt (mostly rebuilt after WWII), is a gold-plated copy of the iconic **Magdeburger Reiter statue** (1240), which is variously said to be city champion King Otto and his two wives, or the king of Hungary and companions, or perhaps just any old king.

The bronze door to the **Rathaus** (town hall; 1698), depicting the city's history to 1969, is by Heinrich Apel. Above the door is an image of the **Magdeburger Jungfrau** (Magdeburg Maiden), the city's symbol. North of the Alter Markt, the **Otto von Guericke statue** commemorates the father of the vacuum (1602–86).

Sleeping

DJH hostel (☎ 532 1010; www.jugendherberge.de/jh /magdeburg; Leiterstrasse 10; dm under/over 26yr €18/20.70; ℗ ☐ ☒) This large modern hostel is the total package – it's close to the train station, is in the middle of town, and yet is on a quiet street. The friendly staff are on duty until the wee hours and, although the place is within easy reach of Berlin, it usually has good availability.

Hotel Stadtfeld (☎ 506 660; www.hotelstadtfeld.de; Maxim-Gorki-Strasse 31/37; s/d €55/70; ℗) You're in your own little business-world bubble in this hotel atop an apartment building. The no-nonsense, masculine furnishings (dark wood and shades of blue) cater to a largely corporate clientele who enjoy the privacy and quiet.

Residenz Joop (☎ 626 60; www.residenzjoop.de; Jean Burgerstrasse 16; s €84-124, d €102-124; ℗) Although the owners are in no way related to German clothing designer Wolfgang Joop, their small place (not far from Hasselbachplatz) offers the same kind of discreet elegance and luxury. Stay in their small villa, and you'll discover nothing is too much trouble for your hosts.

Grüne Zitadelle (☎ 620 780; www.hotel-zitadelle .de; Breiter Weg 9; r from €105; ℗ ☒) One of just two Hundertwasser hotels in the world and the only one within a city, this allows you to get inside the architect's whirring mind and study at close quarters his penchant for

uneven, organic forms. Rooms, drawn up by the architect's assistants, are reasonably restrained, so your sleep won't be disturbed. However, the bathrooms erupt into wild tile mosaics that look like they've come down from the man himself.

Herrenkrug Parkhotel (☎ 850 80; www.herrenk rug.de; Herrenkrug 3; s €85-165, d €115-200; ℗ ☒ ☒) The four-star rooms are spacious and stylish – think black-and-white striped furnishing, or tartan features – plus you get the use of the spa included in the price. However, it's the parkland setting and jaw-dropping Art Deco restaurant (Die Saison, below) that's really appealing.

Eating

Grüne Zitadelle Café (☎ 620 780; Breiter Weg 9; €3.20-4.20; ☒ 7am-7pm) Don't come here with a big appetite, or you'll be left hungry. However, if it's a light snack of pasta, a sandwich or a slice of cake you're after, this informal place towards the back of the Hundertwasser building hits the spot.

Bingöl 2 (☎ 744 8640; Breiter Weg 226; most mains €2-8.50; ☒ 10am-midnight, to 6am Fri & Sat) Night owls rely on this superior doner kebab shop for enormous portions of falafel, Turkish pizza, börek and grilled dishes. There's a large sit-down section and frequently clumsy, if apologetic, staff.

Amsterdam (☎ 662 8680; Olvenstedter Strasse 9; dishes €4.60-14; ☒ 10am-midnight Sun-Fri, 3pm-1am Sat) There's a slight Italian influence detectable in the bruschetta and paninis served in this fashionable modern bistro, but the cuisine also has its Californian touches, with the likes of tuna steaks, a dedicated vegetarian selection and smoothies.

Liebig (☎ 555 6754; Liebigstrasse 1-3; snacks €2.80-8.90, meals €4.90-15.90; ☒ 10-1am) Private alcoves and pleated curtains lining the walls create a feeling of warmth and privacy amid this trendy bar-café-restaurant. Mediterranean fare, curries and steaks are all served.

Die Saison (☎ 850 80; Herrenkrug 3; mains €18-30) Treat yourself to a marvellous meal within the ornately detailed dark-green walls of the Herrenkrug Parkhotel's Art Deco dining room. They serve German cuisine with a modern international twist.

Drinking

Although within Germany's poorest state, Magdeburg has a large student population and therefore a vibrant nightlife. Listings magazine *DATEs* has further details (in German). Alternatively, simply head to the nightlife hub of Hasselbachplatz.

Café Central (☎ 544 2791; Leibnitzstrasse 34; ☺ from 8pm) Echoing the historic street on which it stands, this hip bar-cum-literary salon recreates the early 1900s, with velvet sofas, flock wallpaper and Persian carpets – all genuinely antique. There's comedy, public readings, films or lectures on many evenings, but the décor means it's always worth a visit.

Deep (☎ 544 2791; Breiter Weg 231, entrance Einsteinstrasse) This dimly lit basement bar is hip but extremely friendly, with DJs spinning discs on weekends.

Café & Klub Luise (☎ 597 5961, 544 6812; cnr Keplerstrasse & Otto-von-Guericke strasse; ☺ club from 9pm Fri & Sat) There's a young and relaxed vibe at this ever-so-slightly retro café where, despite the menu, most guests come to drink. The club below it has a wide-ranging programme, with everything from house, indie and 1960s flower power to karaoke and table-tennis competitions.

Mausefalle (☎ 543 0135; Breiter Weg 224) The crowds spilling out of here on weekends prove that Mausefalle's relaxed mix of drinks, music and the occasional bit of communal TV hits the spot.

Entertainment

Stadthalle (☎ 593 450; Stadtpark Rotehorn) From Mozart to Motorhead – as Magdeburg's premier venue, this 2000-seat venue in the leafy central park has pretty well heard it all.

Johanniskirche (St John's Church; ☎ 593 4650; Jacobstrasse 1) Popular for classical music concerts, the atmospheric Johanniskirche dates back, in parts, to 1131.

Theater Magdeburg Opernhaus (☎ 540 6444; Universitätsplatz 9) The Magdeburg Philharmonic plays here, and it's also a venue for opera and ballet.

Magdeburger Zwickmühle (☎ 541 4426; www .magdeburger-zwickmuehle.com; Leiterstrasse 2a) This acclaimed cabaret will be appreciated by German-speakers.

Strandbar Magdeburg (☎ 0175-594 0059; Petri-förder 1; ☺ 11am-midnight daily May-Sep) Magdeburg's small answer to Paris Plage, this city beach run by the local boat company has fast become a hot summer destination, with imported sand, deck chairs, food stalls, cocktails, film evenings and parties.

Getting There & Away

Magdeburg is directly connected to Berlin-Hauptbahnhof (€22, 1½ hours) and Leipzig (€23, 1¼ hours). Trains to Dessau go regularly (€9.10, one hour).

The city is located just south of the A2 Berlin–Hanover autobahn, while the A14 runs to Leipzig.

Getting Around

Bus and tram tickets can be bought from the machines at all stops. They cost €0.80 to go a few stops in the city, €1.50 for a normal single and €4 for a day ticket.

Free street parking is plentiful north and south of the centre. Parking near the Hauptbahnhof and bus station is by permit only.

Taxis wait outside the Hauptbahnhof (Kölner Platz exit), or call **Taxi Ruf** (☎ 737 373).

THE ALTMARK

The Altmark is one of Germany's most idyllic and least populated regions, where flat fields stretch out in all directions and horses probably outnumber humans. Sleepy and out of the way, it's hard to imagine the place attracting many non-Germans visitors. However, if business or personal ties bring you this way, the place revolves around two towns.

STENDAL

☎ 03931 / pop 39,000

In this 'town of red-brick Gothic', as it calls itself, the architecture is pretty, but also overwhelmingly provincial. A former Hanseatic trading post with a cluster of splendid medieval buildings, its contemporary landmarks are its remaining two **town gates**.

Built more for prestige than defence, these fancy brick portals look a bit lonely now that most of the town has gone, but they're still striking. The **Tangermünder Tor** is at the south of the old town and closest to the train station. The **Uenglinger Tor** (adult/concession €2/1; ☺ 10am-noon & 12.30-4pm Sat & Sun May-Sep) can be climbed for good views.

The old market square is dominated by the late-Renaissance **Rathaus** and an 8m-high statue of the legendary knight **Roland**, clutching a 4m-long sword. In early June, there's a town festival in Roland's honour.

However, Stendal's most fun attraction is the 16m-tall, 45-tonne **Trojan Horse** in the grounds of the **Winckelmann-Museum** (☎ 215 226; www.winckelmangesellschaft.de; Winckelmannstrasse 36-38; entry without/with horse €2.50/5; ☺ 10am-6pm, to 8pm Wed, closes an hour earlier Nov-Mar), an exhibition otherwise devoted to the father of modern archaeology, Johann Joachim Winckelmann. Kids and adults will love climbing into the belly of the horse (the world's largest replica, according to the *Guinness Book of Records*), just as ancient Greek warriors did. There's also a children's section to the museum.

The town is compact and easily seen on foot; town maps are available at the train station. The beginning of the Altstadt (Old Town) is a ten-minute walk northeast of the Hauptbahnhof along Bahnhofstrasse.

You'll find **Stendal Information** (☎ 651 190; www.stendal.de; Kornmarkt 8; ☺ 9am-5pm Mon-Fri, 10am-1pm Sat, plus 10am-1pm Sun Apr-Oct), which can help with accommodation, diagonally opposite the Roland statue, near the Hotel Schwarzer Adler.

Other sleeping options include **Pension am Mönchskirchhof** (☎ 715 599; www.pensionstendal.de; Mönchskirchhof 2b; s/d €35/50), inside an attractive Art Deco building, and the classical and central **Alstadt Hotel** (☎ 698 90; fax 698 939; Breite Strasse 60; s €45-60, d €70-110; P), which is renowned locally for its traditional German restaurant.

Hotel am Bahnhof (☎ 715 548; Bahnhofstrasse 30; s/d €50/65; P) has much better, more modern rooms than you might expect for an establishment just across from the station.

The slightly motel-like **Hotel am Uenglinger Tor** (☎ 684 80; www.hotelstendal.de, in German; Moltkestrasse 17; s/d €45/60; P) is a good 15- or 20-minute walk from the train station, but its modern rooms (with balconies or attic windows) are roomy and extremely congenial.

Stendal is an important rail junction connecting north–south lines to east–west lines. There are IC services to Berlin (€25, 45 minutes) and Leipzig (€53, 2¼ hours), as well as cheaper regional trains. Regional services also run to Magdeburg (€9.10, 50 minutes). The B188 and B189 intersect in the south of town.

TANGERMÜNDE

☎ 039322 / pop 10,000

Its location at the confluence of the Elbe and Tanger Rivers makes Tangermünde even prettier than Stendal – although it's even quieter still. The second home of Charles

IV, king of Bohemia during the 14th century, it is most notable for its surviving town walls, ostentatious towers (similar to those in Stendal) and a ruined castle, which now has a hotel inside.

The Altstadt is a five-minute walk south of the Hauptbahnhof, along Albrechtstrasse. The **tourist office** (☎ 223 93; www.tourismus-tangermuende.de; Kirchstrasse 59; ☺ 10am-6pm Apr-Oct, 10am-6pm Mon-Fri, 1-4pm Sat & Sun Nov-Mar) can help with accommodation.

Trains run hourly from Stendal (€1.80, 17 minutes), some 10km northwest. **Reederei Kaiser** (☎ 3654, 0171-421 8162) runs two-hour scenic trips up the Elbe (€8), and also sails to Magdeburg (one-way/return €16/25).

EASTERN SAXONY-ANHALT

DESSAU

☎ 0340 / pop 78,950

The 'built manifesto of Bauhaus ideas', Dessau was the epicentre of the Modernist movement. Crucially, it wasn't just home to the 20th century's most influential design school, the Bauhaus, it was also the first place Walter Gropius and his cronies were actually allowed to practise their architectural principles. As a result, it still boasts some of their earliest buildings.

After being hounded out of Weimar in 1925 by right-wing conservatives, Gropius and colleagues – including the painters Paul Klee and Wassily Kandinsky – shifted reluctantly to industrial Dessau. However, after erecting their radical, purpose-built school in 1926, they went on to enjoy their most creative period here, and the block-faced logo 'Bauhaus Dessau' soon won them a place in history.

In 1932, the Bauhaus spent its last year in Berlin (see Bauhaus Archiv/Museum für Design, p112), but having refurbished buildings left to rot during the GDR period, Dessau is the true keeper of the flame.

Orientation

The town is south of the confluence of the Elbe and Mulde Rivers. The leading Bauhaus sights are west of the Hauptbahnhof, all within easy walking distance. The town centre lies east, reachable on foot or by tram.

DESIGN FOR LIFE

'Less is more,' asserted the third and final Bauhaus director, Ludwig Mies van der Rohe. Given that this school survived fewer than 15 years yet exerted more influence on modern design than any other, one has to bow to his logic. As Frank Whitford put it in *Bauhaus: World of Art* (1984): 'Everyone sitting on a chair with a tubular steel frame, using an adjustable reading lamp or living in a house partly or entirely constructed from prefabricated elements is benefiting from a revolution…largely brought about by the Bauhaus.'

Founded in Weimar in 1919 by Berlin architect Walter Gropius, this multidisciplinary school aimed to abolish the distinction between 'fine' and 'applied' arts, and unite the artistic with the everyday. Gropius reiterated that form follows function, and exhorted his students to craft items with an eye to mass production. Consequently, Bauhaus products stripped away decoration and ornamentation and returned to the fundamentals of design, with strong, clean lines.

Already, in Weimar, the movement had attracted a roll call of the era's greatest talents, including Lyonel Feininger, Wassily Kandinsky, Paul Klee, László Moholy-Nagy, Piet Mondrian and Oskar Schlemmer, plus now legendary product designers Marianne Brandt, Marcel Breuer and Wilhelm Wagenfield. After conservative politicians closed the Weimar school in 1925, these artists all moved to Dessau.

Right-wing political pressure continued, however, against what was seen as the Bauhaus' undermining of traditional values, and Gropius resigned as director in 1928. He was succeeded by Swiss-born Hannes Meyer, whose Marxist sympathies meant that he, in turn, was soon replaced by Ludwig Mies van der Rohe. The latter was at the helm when the school moved to Berlin in 1932 to escape Nazi oppression.

Mies ran the school as a private institution until it was dissolved by the Third Reich in 1933 and the Bauhaus' leading lights fled the country. But the movement never quite died. After WWII, Gropius took over as director of Harvard's architecture school, while Mies van der Rohe (the architect of New York's Seagram Building) held the same post at the Illinois Institute of Technology in Chicago. Both men found long-lasting global fame as purveyors of Bauhaus' successor, the so-called International Style.

Information

Bauhaus Foundation (☎ 650 8251; www.bauhaus -dessau.de; Gropiusallee 38; ☯ 10am-6pm Mon-Fri) For info on, and tours of, Bauhaus buildings (including in English).

Internet café (1st fl, Hauptbahnhof; per hr €2; ☯ 10am-10pm daily) Up the spiral stairs of the train station, to the right of the exit doors.

Post office (Kavalierstrasse 30-32)

Tourist office (☎ 204 1442; accommodation 220 3003; www.dessau-tourismus.de; Zerbster Strasse 2c; ☯ 9am-6pm Mon-Fri, 9am-1pm Sat Apr-Oct, 9am-5pm Mon-Fri, 10am-1pm Sat Nov-Mar) Offers tours in German at 10am Saturday (April to October; adult/ concession €5.10/4.10).

Sights

BAUHAUSGEBÄUDE

Across the world, many Modernist masterpieces have fallen into ruin. Although it too once looked like it might go that way, the seminal **Bauhausgebäude** (Bauhaus Bldg; ☎ 650 8251; Gropiusallee 38; exhibition adult/concession €5/4, combination ticket with Meisterhäuser €8/6; ☯ 10am-6pm) has

now been definitively rescued. Extensive refurbishment was finished in time to celebrate the 80th anniversary of its October 1926 opening.

If you consider its history, it's almost impossible to overstate the significance of this school building. Two of the three men said to have fathered modern architecture (Walter Gropius and Ludwig Mies van der Rohe) worked here. (Switzerland's Le Corbusier completes the trio.) Gropius claimed that the ultimate of all artistic endeavours was architecture, and this was the first real example of his handiwork. It was revolutionary, bringing industrial construction techniques, such as curtain walling and wide spans, into the public domain and presaging untold buildings worldwide.

Furthermore, as the Bauhaus' Hochschule für Gestaltung (Institute for Design), it disseminated the movement's ideals of functionality and minimalism. The tubular steel-frame chair and other enduring industrial designs were born here.

Yet, perhaps more impressive than all these arguments is how fresh and modern the building looks after more than 80 years. Cubist, concrete and mostly white, it has three interconnecting rectangular wings boasting enormous plate-glass windows. The grey southern façade boasts the Bauhaus logo; the eastern side has quirky 'swimming pool' balconies.

A postgraduate **Bauhaus Kolleg** (☎ 650 8403; www.bauhaus-dessau.de) now uses many of the rooms, but sections are still open to the public, including an exhibition hall in the former workshop wing, which stages rotating shows. There's also a great gift shop here, selling books, posters, postcards and trinkets – from toys and egg cookers to ashtrays, wine glasses, crockery and lamps.

One-hour **tours** (adult/concession €4/3, in German) start at 11am and 2pm daily (and 4pm on Saturday, Sunday and during holidays). Even if you don't speak the language, they're instructive as you're allowed into some otherwise locked rooms. Alternatively, you can hire an audio-guide in English (€4).

The complex is a five-minute walk west of the Hauptbahnhof, via Schwabestrasse and Bauhausstrasse.

MEISTERHÄUSER

On a picturesque leafy street in Dessau's north stand the **Meisterhäuser** (master craftsmen's houses; Ebertallee 63-71; admission to all three houses adult/concession €5/4; ☺ 10am-6pm Tue-Sun summer, to 5pm winter) where several 20th-century geniuses once lived together as neighbours. In the febrile environment of the 1920s, you could sit at home here with the Kandinskys, on furniture donated by Marcel Breuer, and with the possibility that Paul Klee or László Moholy-Nagy might drop over for tea.

Designed by Gropius for the school's senior staff, these white cubist structures exemplify the Bauhaus aim of 'design for living' in the modern, industrial world.

They expose some of the movement's contradictions, too. Locals sometimes describe these them as 'villas', emphasising that while it focused on providing decent housing for all, Bauhaus still had its own elite. Another irony is that the interiors are largely bereft of original Bauhaus furniture, which is too expensive to replace today.

All this said, a visit here is an intensely satisfying aesthetic experience, with photos helping to conjure up past interiors.

Originally there was a stand-alone home for the Bauhaus director, plus three duplexes, each half of which provided a living/working space for a senior staff member and family. Sadly, the director's home was destroyed in WWII, along with one half of the neighbouring duplex (originally the Moholy-Nagy/Feininghaus).

The remaining **Feininghaus**, where artist Lyonel Feininger once lived, now pays homage to another German icon with the **Kurt-Weill-Zentrum** (☎ 619 595). There's a room devoted to Dessau-born Weill, who later became playwright Bertolt Brecht's musical collaborator in Berlin, and composed *The Threepenny Opera* and its hit 'Mack the Knife'.

In the **Muche/Schlemmer Haus** it becomes apparent that the room proportions and some of the experiments, such as low balcony rails, don't really cut it in the modern world. At the same time, you also realise how startlingly innovative other features are. The partially black bedroom here is also intriguing; look out for the leaflet explaining the amusing story behind it – Marcel Breuer apparently burst in to paint it when reluctant owner Georg Muche was away on business.

The **Kandinsky/Klee Haus** (☎ 661 0934) is most notable for the varying pastel shades in which Wassily Kandinsky and Paul Klee painted their walls (re-created today). There's also biographical information about the two artists and special exhibitions of their work.

To get to the Meisterhäuser, turn right (north) onto Gropiusallee from the Bauhausgebäude, and continue for a few minutes before turning left (west) into Ebertallee. Alternatively, buses 10 and 11 from the train station will drop you close by (they both stop at Gropiusallee).

A further 20-minute walk north on Elballee, on the Elbe, stands the **Kornhaus**, a beer-and-dance hall designed by Carl Flieger, a Gropius assistant. It is now a terraced restaurant with river views (see p215). From the Hauptbahnhof, take bus 10 or 11 to Kornhausstrasse and then walk.

TÖRTEN

If the term 'housing estate' conjures up an image of grim concrete tower blocks, rubbish-blown courtyards and shutters flapping on the abandoned communal shop, leafy Törten, in Dessau's south, might prompt a slight rethink. Built in the 1920s, it is *the* prototype of the modern working-class estate. However, it's refreshingly low-rise, and you can just about see what the architects were trying to achieve. Although many of the 300-plus homes have been altered in ways that would have outraged their purist creator Walter Gropius (patios and rustic German doors added to a minimalist façade?), others retain their initial symmetry.

The **Stahlhaus** (Steel House; ☎ 858 1420; Südstrasse 5; admission free; ⏰ 10am-5pm Tue-Sun, 10am-6pm Feb-Oct) is home to a Bauhaus information centre and the starting point for German-language **tours** (adult/concession €4/3; ⏰ at 2pm Tue-Fri, 3pm Sat & Sun) of the Törten estate. These look inside one of the red-brick, balcony-access apartments by the second Bauhaus director, Hannes Meyer.

Other highlights include the **Konsumgebäude** (co-op building, still the site of a communal shop) and the **Moses Mendelssohn Zentrum** (☎ 850 1199; Mittelring 38; adult/child €2/1; ⏰ 10am-7pm Mar-Oct, 1-4pm Sat & Sun Jan-Feb). Here you can learn about Dessau-born humanist philosopher Moses Mendelssohn, who was the grandfather of composer Felix Mendelssohn-Bartholdy. It's also the only Walter Gropius building on the estate where you can look inside. Sure, it's small, but think of the tenements it replaced. Printed English-language descriptions of the architecture are available; just ask.

To reach Törten, take tram 1 towards Dessau Süd (€1.20). Alight at Damaschkestrasse, where there are signposts to the 'Bauhaus Architektur'.

SAXONY-ANHALT

OTHER ATTRACTIONS

Dessau has recently reinforced its architectural reputation with the eye-catching new headquarters for the **Umweltbundesamt** (Federal Environment Agency; Wörlitzer Platz 1). Its two separate sections of green-coloured and flesh-coloured windows make a striking sight as your train pulls into town, but this energy-efficient building also boasts a wonderful, light-infused atrium, which can be visited on tourist office city tours.

Aviation fans will be wowed by the vintage aircraft at the **Technikmuseum Hugo Junkers** (☎ 661 1982; www.technikmuseum-dessau.de, in German; Kühnauer Strasse 161a; adult/concession €2.50/1.25; ⏰ 10am-5pm). Take tram 3 or bus 16 to Junkerspark.

Dessau's centre is rather Eastern Bloc – uninspiring and a mere footnote to the town's Bauhaus attractions. The **Rathaus**, rebuilt in simplified form after the war, has a Bauhaus-style clock. The **Anhaltisches Theater** (☎ 251 110; www.anhaltisches-theater.de; Friedensplatz 1a) is a rather pompous neo-Roman structure that was commissioned by the Nazis and is at odds with most of the town's architecture, whether it be Bauhaus or GDR.

Dessau also boasts some quite impressive parks and gardens, such as Georgium park; for more information on these see the Garden Realm (opposite).

Festivals & Events

Although more closely associated with Berlin, and later New York, the composer Kurt Weill was born in Dessau. Every March, in his honour, the city hosts a **Kurt Weill Festival** (www.kurt-weill.de, in German), reprising and updating his collaborations with Bertolt Brecht such as *The Threepenny Opera*. Performances take place in Dessau and surrounds.

Sleeping

DJH hostel (☎ 619 452; www.jugendherberge.de/jh/dessau; Waldkaterweg 11; dm under/over 26yr €15.50/17.20; P) Dessau's DJH hostel is pretty basic, and it also closes its doors early and is slightly tricky to reach without a car, so it's probably more convenient for most budget travellers to book a room at the Bauhaus dorms.

Bauhaus dorms (☎ 650 8318; oede@bauhaus-dessau.de; Gropiusallee 38; r per person from €28; P ⊠) Since the Bauhaus school was renovated in 2006, you can really live the Modernist dream, by hiring the former students' dorms inside. If the main building's booked out, opt for a taste of the GDR instead, by reserving a cheaper bed (€15) in the 1970s *Plattenbau* apartment complex at Heidestrasse 33.

An den 7 Säulen (☎ 619 620; www.pension7saeulen.de, in German; Ebertallee 66; s €50-55, d €65-75; P) Not the most luxurious option in town, but one of the most memorable, this pleasant *pension* has a garden and glass-fronted breakfast room overlooking the Meisterhäuser across the leafy street. Popular with cyclists and families, it now boasts a sauna, too.

NH Hotel (☎ 251 40, 0800 0115 0116; www.nh-hotels.com; Zerbster Strasse 29; r €65-105; P ⊠) Neutral white and grey tones somehow feel more stylish than clinical here, although the friendly service might have a helping hand in creating that impression. Set in one of the pedestrianised areas leading to the Rathaus and tourist office, the hotel is also reasonably well located.

Hotel Fürst Leopold (☎ 251 50, 00800 7846 8357; www.dessau.steigenberger.de; Friedensplatz; s/d from €100/130; Ⓟ ✲) Form certainly follows function in Dessau's most comfortable hotel. Stylish and spacious rooms are each decorated with chunky armchairs and a Kandinsky print, while there's a bar, excellent restaurant and pampering spa. Ask about the hotel's 'Roaring Twenties' packages, should you really want to get into the Kurt Weill–Bauhaus mood.

Eating
In Dessau, you really can eat, drink and sleep Bauhaus. For a different diet, investigate the main thoroughfare of Zerbster Strasse. Restaurants are all much of a muchness, although we do suggest avoiding the cheap but unappetising canteen of the Umweltbundesamt.

Bauhaus Mensa (☎ 650 8421; Gropiusallee 38; mains €2.50-5.50; ⓒ 8am-2pm Mon-Fri) Join students at the postgrad college for a cheap canteen meal, on the iconic but somewhat uncomfortable long benches and low stools.

Bauhaus Klub (☎ 650 8444; Gropiusallee 38; €3-7) Starting to see a pattern here? The occasional cool dude in black polo-neck jumper and horn-rimmed glasses can be seen among the broad mix of people in this basement bar of the Bauhaus school.

Kornhaus (☎ 640 4141; Kornhausstrasse 146; mains €7-13) Treat yourself to traditional local specialities and a refined evening in the curved Bauhaus dining room, with its striking 1930s patterned carpet. Alternatively, enjoy a light meal on the balcony overlooking the Elbe River.

Getting There & Around
RE trains serve Dessau from Berlin-Hauptbahnhof (€22, 1½ hours). Regional trains come from Lutherstadt Wittenberg (€66, 40 minutes). Dessau is almost equidistant from Leipzig, Halle and Magdeburg (all €9.10, one hour). The Berlin–Munich autobahn (A9) runs east of town.

Single bus and tram tickets cost €1.20 (valid for 60 minutes). **Fahrradverleih Dieter Becker** (☎ 216 0113; Coswiger Strasse 47; per day €5-7.50) hires out bicycles.

THE 'GARDEN REALM'
Bauhaus and Garden – as well as boasting iconic modern architecture, Dessau is surrounded by a verdant belt of landscaped parkland. Throughout this greenery is dotted a series of palaces in varying styles, from English neo-classical to rococo.

This so-called **Gartenreich** (garden realm) owes its existence to the educated and well-travelled Prince Leopold III (Fürst Friedrich Franz von Anhalt-Dessau), who oversaw its creation between 1764 and 1800, in a quest to enrich the local cultural heritage. The Park Georgium is the easiest section to reach, being in Dessau itself, while Wörlitz is the most impressive and elaborate.

The whole landscape lies within the Unesco-protected **Biosphärenreservat Flusslandschaft Mittlere Elbe** (Riverland Biosphere of the Central Elbe; www.biosphaerenreservatmittlereelbe.de, in German). For nature lovers, there's an **information centre** (☎ 034904-4060; Am Kapenschlössen 3, Oranienbaum) on the way to Schloss Oranienbaum, and a nearby **beaver compound** (adult/child €1/0.50; ⓒ 11am-5pm Sat & Sun May-Oct, by arrangement at other times), where you can watch the animals through a screen. Ask the Dessau Tourist Office for a free map of the entire region.

Wörlitz Park & Schloss
With peacocks feeding on the lawn before a Gothic house, a tree-lined stream flowing towards a Grecian-style temple and a gap in a hedge framing a distant villa, the 112-hectare English-style **Wörlitz Park** (admission free) is a surprising find in eastern Germany. This is the tour de force of Prince Leopold's garden region, and its mosaic of paths, hedges and follies continues to woo numerous visitors.

Between May and early November, hand-cranked **ferries** (adult/concession €0.60/0.30) cross the Wörlitzer See, which lies between garden sections. During these months, 45-minute **gondola tours** (adult/concession €6/4) ply the lake, departing when eight people or more gather at the dock – this doesn't take long in summer; indeed the problem is more often too many customers for gondolas. Weekend concerts are another summer highlight.

On the edge of the park nearest the town lies Prince Leopold's former country house, **Schloss Wörlitz** (☎ 034905-409 20; admission by tour only adult/concession €4.50/2.50; ⓒ 10am-6pm Tue-Sun May-Sep, to 5pm Apr & Oct, closed Nov-Mar, last tours 1hr before closing), which displays neoclassical English touches. Like the garden, it could almost be in England.

Wörlitz-Information (☎ 034905-202 16, room reservations 034905-194 33; www.woerlitz.de; Förstergasse 26; ⓒ 9am-6pm Mar-Oct, 9am-4pm Mon-Fri Nov-Jan, 9am-4pm

---

ON YER BIKE

You won't spend long in Saxony-Anhalt without noticing the large number of cycle tourists. After 1990's unification, many Germans wanted to rediscover the mighty Elbe River, large tracts of which had been off-limits to Westerners previously. The **Elberadweg** (Elbe River cycle path; www.elberadweg.de) is now among Germany's top three cycling routes, and wends its way some 860km west alongside the river, from the Czech border to Cuxhaven. The scenic 360km stretch in Saxony-Anhalt is particularly popular, helped along by low accommodation costs and a generally laidback pace of life. Tourist offices in the region have very specific guides of individual stretches; they're in German but mainly contain hotel and restaurant listings, plus route maps, so can be quite useful.

However, you don't have to set off on such an epic journey to enjoy wheeling around Saxony-Anhalt, as there are many shorter trails. One easy and immensely enjoyable route is the **Fürst Franz Garden Realm Tour** (60km), which travels between all the palaces around Dessau and Wörlitz, and passes along the Elbe River and the biosphere reserve information office. The Dessau Tourist Office (see p212) has a free pamphlet, while bike rental (p215) is available in the train station.

The grape-growing Saale-Unstrut region (see p225) also boasts a cycle-friendly **Weinstrasse** (Vineyard Rd; ☎ 034464-261 10; www.natuerlich-saale-unstrut.de) between some 750 of its vineyards. Local tourist offices sell copies of *Weinstrasse-Land der Burgen* (€5), a regional map showing the main route, as well as associated bicycle paths.

Mon-Fri 11am-3pm Sat & Sun Feb) can provide more details, plus a free map of the garden.

GETTING THERE & AWAY

The train from Dessau to Wörlitz only operates Wednesday, Saturday and Sunday, from March to November, and then only makes five return trips a day, so check the train station timetable carefully. Bus 333 operates every two hours daily from around 7am to 6pm (€3.80, 30 minutes). However, you can sometimes travel in between times by using bus 12; ask at the information stand in front of the train station.

By road from Dessau, take the B185 east to the B107 north, which brings you right into town.

Wörlitz is only 23km from Lutherstadt Wittenberg; by car take the B187 west and head south on the B107.

The large lakeside car park charges more than the two other car parks in town.

Other Parks & Palaces

None of Dessau's other parks is quite as stunning as Wörlitz, but visiting it does tend to give you a taste for more of the same, so head first to the **Georgium**. This sprawling 18th-century park is northwest of the Hauptbahnhof, within walking distance. At its heart stands the neoclassical **Schloss Georgium**, housing the **Anhalt Art Gallery** (☎ 0340-613 874; Puschkinallee 100; adult/concession €3/2; ⏰ 10am-5pm

Tue-Sun), with paintings by the old masters, including Rubens and Cranach the Elder. The leafy grounds are also dotted with ponds and fake ruins. At the Georgium's eastern edge is the **Lehrpark**, an educational garden and zoo, with the huge domed **mausoleum** you can see from the train station.

Otherwise, the rococo **Schloss Mosigkau** (☎ 0340-521 139; Knobelsdorffallee 3, Dessau; admission €4.50; ⏰ 10am-6pm Tue-Sun May-Sep, to 5pm Oct-Apr, closed Nov-Mar) lies southwest of central Dessau; take bus 16 to stop Schloss. The baroque Dutch **Schloss Oranienbaum** (☎ 034904-202 59; admission €4.50; ⏰ 10am-6pm Tue-Sun May-Sep, 10am-5pm Sat & Sun Apr & Oct, closed Nov-Mar) is towards Wörlitz; take bus 331 or 333. **Schloss Luisium** (☎ 0340-218 3711; Dessau; admission €4.50; 10am-6pm Tue-Sun May-Sep, 10am-5pm Sat & Sun Apr & Oct, closed Nov-Mar) evinces a combination of neo-Gothic and classical styles; it's reached via bus 13 to Vogelherd.

You can even stay overnight in the elegant **Elbpavilion** (3-4 people €150-200) in parkland north of the Georgium. The Dessau tourist office (p212) is responsible for reservations.

FERROPOLIS

Some 15km south of Wörlitz, Ferropolis answers that nagging question: 'What do you do with an abandoned open-pit GDR coal mine and leftover mining equipment that look like they were dispatched from some postapocalyptic nightmare?'

In 1991, some Bauhaus-inspired designers came up with a solution – a 25,000-seat concert venue and museum…of course! An amphitheatre was built, the mine pit was filled with water diverted from the Mulde River, and the monstrous machines (with charming names like Mad Max, Big Wheel and Medusa) were placed just so.

The **museum** (☎ 034953-351 20; www.ferropolis .com; adult/concession €3.50/2.50; ☺ 10am-6pm Mon-Fri, 10am-7pm Sat & Sun summer, 10am-dusk winter) is an interesting monument to mining, and the changes wrought by industrial society. Most people go to Ferropolis, however, to watch old rock bands like Deep Purple play, or to attend musicals like *Jesus Christ Superstar*. Fortunately, the highlight of the calendar, the annual **Melt Festival** (www.meltfestival.de) is a great deal more hip. Check the website for more event details.

From Dessau, take bus 331 (in the direction of Gräfenhainichen) to the stop Jüdenberg B107/Ferropolis (€2.80 one way, 42 minutes); note that this is the third stop with Jüdenberg in its name. From here, it's a dusty 2km walk into the grounds. By car, take the B185 east to the B107 and turn south towards Gräfenhainichen (20 minutes in all); the entrance to Ferropolis is on your left, just past Jüdenberg.

From Lutherstadt Wittenberg, you can take a train to Gräfenhainichen (20 minutes) and then catch a bus heading towards Dessau or Oranienbaum to the Ferropolis gate. Driving from Lutherstadt Wittenberg, take the B100 to its junction with the B107 and turn north; the entrance is on the right.

LUTHERSTADT WITTENBERG
☎ 03491 / pop 53,000

Wittenberg is the very crucible of the Reformation that led to the division of the Christian Church into Catholics and Protestants in the 16th century. A hotbed of progressive ideas then, it saw long-term resident Martin Luther write his famous 95 theses (see the boxed text, p219), priests get married, and educators like Philipp Melanchthon argue for schools to accept female pupils.

Not a lot has happened since, but then with such a legacy it hasn't been needed. The town retains its significance for the world's 340 million Protestants, including 66 million Lutherans, as well as for those who simply admire Luther for his principled stand against authority.

As a result, Wittenberg's popularity has steadily grown since reunification in 1990 and – like it or not – even a nascent Luther industry has developed.

'*Hier stehe ich. Ich kann nicht anders*' (Here I stand. I can do no other), Luther once declared during a determined anticorruption campaign that changed the face of Europe and the course of history. Today, you can buy souvenir socks bearing the same credo.

Orientation

Hauptbahnhof Lutherstadt-Wittenberg is the stop for trains to and from outlying regions, but smaller stations, such as Wittenberg-Elbtor, exist for local trains. Bus 304 (every 15 minutes) goes from the Hauptbahnhof to the city centre; otherwise it's a signposted 15- to 20-minute walk.

Most major sights can be found within the Altstadt ring. The main street, Collegienstrasse, runs east–west through the Markt and becomes Schlossstrasse at its western end.

Information

Internetcafé Dot.Komm (☎ 437 927; Fleischerstrasse 6; per hr €3; ☺ from 3pm)

Paul-Gerhardt-Stiftung (☎ 500; Paul-Gerhardt-Strasse 42) Hospital.

Post office (Wilhelm-Weber-Strasse 1)

Wittenberg-Information (☎ information 498 610/11, room reservations 414 848; www.wittenberg.de; Schlossplatz 2; ☺ 9am-6pm Mon-Fri, 10am-3pm Sat, 11am-4pm Sun May-Oct, 9am-4pm Mon-Fri, 10am-2pm Sat, 11am-3pm Sun Nov-Mar) Offers a portable audio-guide to the town in several languages (€6, and your passport as deposit), two-hour city tours (€7; tours at 2pm May-Oct, in German) plus night tours, English tours and more.

Sights & Activities
LUTHERHAUS

Extensively revamped a few years ago – to the tune of €17.5 million – the **Lutherhaus** (☎ 420 30; www.martinluther.de; Collegienstrasse 54; adult/concession €5/3; ☺ 9am-6pm Apr-Oct, 10am-5pm Tue-Sun Nov-Mar) uses a combination of antiquities and modern displays; even those with no previous interest in the subject will be drawn in by its combination of accessible narrative (in German and English), personal artefacts (ie Bibles, cloak), oil paintings by Cranach the Elder and interactive multimedia displays. There's also an original room furnished by Luther in 1535, and decorated with a bit of royal graffiti from Russian Tsar Peter the Great in 1702.

An excellent addition to the museum is **Café Bora**, in the courtyard, overlooking archaeological finds.

The **Luthereiche** (Luther's oak), marking the spot where the preacher burned the 1520 papal bull threatening his excommunication, is on the corner of Lutherstrasse and Am Bahnhof, though the oak tree itself was planted around 1830.

SCHLOSSKIRCHE

Legend has it that it was to the door of the **Castle Church** (☎ 402 585; admission free; ☼ 10am-5pm Mon-Sat, 11.30am-5pm Sun, to 4pm Nov-Mar) that Luther nailed his 95 theses on 31 October 1517 (see the boxed text Luther Lore, opposite). There's no hard evidence that this happened, especially as the door in question was destroyed by fire in 1760. In its place, however, stands an impressive bronze memorial (1858) inscribed with the theses in Latin.

Inside is Luther's tombstone; it lies below the pulpit, opposite that of his friend and fellow reformer Philipp Melanchthon. Information sheets are available in several languages.

Next door, you can climb the city's landmark **Schlossturm** (castle tower; adult/concession €2/1; ☼ noon-4pm Mon-Fri, 10am-4pm Sat & Sun), but be warned that the floor feels a little shaky in parts, and the view is expansive rather than breathtaking.

STADTKIRCHE ST MARIEN

If the Schlosskirche was the billboard used to advertise the forthcoming Reformation, its sister **Stadtkirche St Marien** (City Church of St Marien; ☎ 403 201; admission free; ☼ 10am-5pm Mon-Sat, 11.30am-5pm Sun, to 4pm Nov-Mar) was where the ecumenical revolution began, with the world's first Protestant worship services in 1521. It was also here that Luther preached his famous Lectern sermons in 1522, and where, three years later, he married ex-nun Katharina von Bora.

The centrepiece is the large altar, designed jointly by Lucas Cranach the Elder and his son. The side facing the nave shows Luther, Melanchthon and other Reformation figures, as well as Cranach himself, in biblical contexts. Unusually, though, the altar is painted on its reverse side. Behind it, on the lower

LUTHERSTADT WITTENBERG

INFORMATION	
Internetcafé Dot.Komm..............1	C3
Paul-Gerhardt-Stiftung..............2	D2
Wittenberg-Information..........3	A2

SIGHTS & ACTIVITIES	
Event & Touring........................4	C3
Fronleichnamskapelle..............(see 14)	
Galerie im Cranachhaus............5	B3
Haus der Geschichte.................6	B3
Historiche Druckerstube..........(see 5)	
Luthereiche (Luther's Oak)........7	D3
Lutherhaus...............................8	C3
Melanchthon Haus.....................9	C3
MS Lutherstadt Wittenberg (Booking Office)..................10	A3

Rathaus...............................11	B2
Schlosskirche........................12	A3
Schlossturm..........................13	A3
Stadtkirche St Marien..............14	B3
Wittenberg English Ministry.....(see 3)	

SLEEPING 🏠	
Alte Canzley..........................15	A2
Best Western Stadtpalais Wittenberg.....................16	C3

DJH Hostel...........................17	A3
Luther-Hotel........................18	C3
Pension am Schwanenteich......19	B2
Stadthotel Wittenberg Schwarzer Baer........................20	B3

EATING 🍴	
Café Hundertwasserschule........21	B2
Tante Emmas Bier- & Caféhaus .22	B3
Zur Schlossfreiheit 23	B2

DRINKING 🍷	
Barrik..................................24	B3
Brauhaus Wittenberg 25	B3
Café Bora..............................(see 8)	
In Vino Veritas 26	B3
Independent.........................27	C3
Marc de Café 28	A2
Sweet Apple..........................29	C3

TRANSPORT	
Bus Station...........................30	C2
Fahrradhaus Kralisch.............31	C2

LUTHER LORE

'When the legend becomes fact, print the legend,' a journalist famously tells Jimmy Stewart in the classic Western movie *The Man Who Shot Liberty Valance,* and that is exactly what has happened with Martin Luther and his 95 theses. It's been so often repeated that Luther nailed a copy of his revolutionary theses to the door of Wittenberg's Schlosskirche on 31 October 1517, that only serious scholars continue to argue to the contrary.

Certainly, Luther did write 95 theses challenging some of the Catholic practices of the time, especially the selling of 'indulgences' to forgive sins and reduce the buyer's time in purgatory. However, it's another question entirely as to whether he publicised them in the way popular legend suggests.

Believers point to the fact that the Schlosskirche's door was used as a bulletin board of sorts by the university, that the alleged posting took place the day before the affluent congregation poured into the church on All Saints' Day (1 November), and the fact that at Luther's funeral, his influential friend Philipp Melanchthon said he witnessed Luther's deed.

But Melanchthon didn't arrive in town until 1518 – the year *after* the supposed event. It's also odd that Luther's writings never once mentioned such a highly radical act.

While it's known that he sent his theses to the local archbishop to provoke discussion, some locals think it would have been out of character for a devout monk, interested mainly in an honest debate, to challenge the system so publicly and flagrantly without first exhausting all his options.

In any event, nailed to the church door or not, the net effect of Luther's theses was the same. They prompted the onset of the Reformation and Protestantism, altering the way that large sections of the world's Christian population worship to this day.

---

rung, you'll see a seemingly defaced painting of heaven and hell; medieval students etched their initials into the painting's divine half if they passed their final exams – and into purgatory if they failed.

CHURCH SERVICES

From April to October, the **Wittenberg English Ministry** (☎ 498 610; www.wittenberg-english-ministry .com; Schlossplatz 2) holds services in English from 6.30pm to 7.30pm on Saturday evening in either the Schlosskirche or Stadtkirche. Watch for notices, or ask at the tourist office. Services in English are also held at 4pm Wednesday and 11.30am Friday in the tiny Fronleichnamskapelle (Corpus Christi Chapel) attached to the Stadtkirche.

HAUS DER GESCHICHTE

Another side to Luther-obsessed Wittenberg is shown at the **Haus der Geschichte** (House of History; ☎ 409 004; Schlossstrasse 6; adult/senior & student €4/2.50; ⏱ 10am-5pm Tue-Fri, 11am-6pm Sat & Sun), a heartwarming museum of everyday life in the GDR. The ground floor is devoted to temporary exhibitions, while living rooms, kitchens, bedrooms and bathrooms on the next two levels have been reconstructed in various styles from the 1940s to the 1980s. There's something

comforting about the homely lounge suites, clunky early consumer items, and the tins and jars that would have been gold-dust for the son recreating the good ol' East in the movie *Good Bye, Lenin!*

HUNDERTWASSERSCHULE

Eastern Germans seem to be staunch fans of Friedensreich Hundertwasser's curvy organic architecture, the polar opposite of the boxy *Plattenbauten* tower blocks they grew up in. Magdeburg boasts the architect's last building (see p208), while Wittenberg's **Hundertwasserschule** (Hundertwasser School; ☎ 881 131; Strasse der Völkerfreundschaft 130; ⏱ 1.30-5pm Tue-Fri, to 4pm Nov-Mar, 10am-4pm Sat & Sun) was his penultimate. Shortly before his death in 2000, Hundertwasser helped remodel a series of staid GDR concrete blocks into one of his signature buildings, with brightly coloured baubles, touches of gold, mosque-like cupolas and rooftop vegetation.

The school is a 20-minute walk northeast of the centre. From the Markt, follow Judenstrasse, turn left into Neustrasse and continue into Geschwister-Scholl-Strasse. Turn left into Sternstrasse, right into Schillerstrasse, and the school is at the next intersection on the left. Of course, it's possible to view the exterior anytime, but tours of the interior (€2) wait for at least four participants before they start. Ring ahead for tours in English.

OTHER ATTRACTIONS

Alongside the Lutherhaus, the former homes of two other Reformation stalwarts are now museums. The **Galerie im Cranachhaus** (☎ 420 1911; Schlossstrasse 1; adult/concession €4/3; ⌚ 10am-5pm Mon-Sat, 1-5pm Sun, closed Mon Nov-Mar) is devoted to artist Lucas Cranach the Elder, who lived in Wittenberg during the Reformation and captured the action in fine detail. Meanwhile, the rather text-heavy **Melanchthon Haus** (☎ 403 279; Collegienstrasse 60; adult/concession €2.50/1.50; ⌚ 10am-6pm Tue-Sun Apr-Oct, to 5pm Nov-Mar) discusses the life of university lecturer and humanist Philipp Melanchthon. An expert in ancient languages, Melanchthon helped Luther translate the Bible into German from Greek and Hebrew, becoming the preacher's friend and his most eloquent advocate.

The **Historische Druckerstube** (☎ 432 817; Cranach-Hof, Schlossstrasse 1) is a basement gallery selling ancient-looking black-and-white sketches of Martin Luther, both typeset and printed by hand.

Tours

The **MS Lutherstadt Wittenberg** (☎ 769 0433; Schlossstrasse 16; €7.50) runs 1½-hour panoramic river cruises on the Elbe in summer. The booking office will fill you in about times and how to find the pier in Dessauerstrasse.

Meanwhile, ask at the tourist office about canoeing, which is offered in nearby villages.

To savour more of the same *Ostalgie* (nostalgia for the old East Germany) pedalled by the Haus der Geschichte, hire a Trabant East German car from **Event & Touring** (☎ 660 195; www.event-touring.com; Collegienstrasse 59a; per 3hr from €35-40). They also arrange Trabi 'safaris' or 'slaloms' for groups.

Festivals & Events

Wittenberg is busiest during **Luther's Wedding festival** (Luthers Hochzeit) in early June, and on **Reformation Day** (Reformation Tag) on 31 October, the publication date of the 95 theses.

Sleeping

BUDGET

Brückenkopf Marina-Camp Elbe (☎ 4540; www.marina-camp-elbe.de; Brückenkopf 1; adult & tent €7, car €2.50, hotel s/d/tr €40/60/90; 🖳) How many camp-

ing grounds boast their own wine cellar? This well-equipped one does. But then it also offers a yacht harbour, a restaurant, simple huts, a hotel, holiday apartments, beach volleyball, table tennis, a sauna, a small grocery selection, modern wash facilities and more. On the banks of the Elbe, near the Wittenberg-Elbtor train station, the location is scenic, too.

DJH hostel (☎ 403 255; www.jugendherberge.de /jh/wittenberg; Schloss; dm under/over 26yr €16.80/19.50; 🅿 🖳) Don't get carried away when you hear that this is in the town's castle building. The dimly lit interior is quite kitschy, with old linoleum floors, low ceilings, wood-laminate walls and plastic chairs. Still, once you've navigated the winding stairs, it's central and cheap.

Pension am Schwanenteich (☎ 402 807; Töpferstrasse 1; www.wittenberg-schwanenteich.de; s €32-38, d €54; 🅿) Small and humble, but friendly and familiar, this pension has equipped its rooms with TV, hairdryer and internet connections, which is excellent for the price. With a restaurant and convenient location, it traditionally hasn't taken credit cards but is hoping to soon.

MIDRANGE & TOP END

Stadthotel Wittenberg Schwarzer Baer (☎ 420 4344; www.stadthotel-wittenberg.de; Schlossstrasse 2; s/d/q from €56/70/106; 🅿 ✗) The modern rooms in this 500-year-old heritage-listed building (no lift) are light, airy and clean-smelling, with wooden floors and cork headboards. Staff are on the ball, too.

Luther-Hotel (☎ 3491 4580; www.luther-hotel-wittenberg.de; Neustrasse 7-10; s €65-100, d €80-115; 🅿 ✗) Brand-new rooms here boast bathtubs, and there are two rooms for guests with disabilities. The huge reception space is impressive, as is the restaurant, but the place does welcome a lot of conference groups.

Alte Canzley (☎ 429 190; www.alte-canzley.de; Schlossstrasse 3; s €75-120, d €80-135; 🅿) Even if you're not in need of the super-healthy non-smoking environment with non-allergic pillows, bedclothes and floors, the eight stylish apartments here will make you swoon. Six of them overlook the Schlosskirche and are generously sized, particularly the huge Linus Pauling apartment. In the town provost's former home, the hotel also has an organic restaurant with vaulted arches.

Best Western Stadtpalais Wittenberg (☎ 4250; www.stadtpalais.bestwestern.de; Collegienstrasse 56/57; s €95-115, d €105-115, breakfast €11; 🅿 ✗ 🐾) The dark orange bedspreads and studded wooden headboards hark back to Luther's area, as do the lithographs on the wall, but this hotel is essentially about contemporary luxury. There's a sauna, a restaurant with touches of Asian décor and very helpful staff.

Eating

Try some *Lutherbrot* – a gingerbread-like concoction with chocolate and sugar icing.

Café Hundertwasserschule (☎ 410 685; Markt 15; mains €5.50-14; ✗) There's a health-conscious streak at this café – from the no-smoking policy to the vegetarian options and fresh juices – but you're still free to indulge yourself with lamb, venison, home-made cakes or beer should you choose. Hundertwasser touches are dotted around the room.

Tante Emmas Bier- & Caféhaus (☎ 419 757; Markt 9; mains €8.50-16; ✗ closed Mon evening) Take a step back in to 'the good old times' in this German country kitchen, where the serving staff wear frilly white aprons and the room is chockfull of bric-a-brac – from dolls and books to irons and a gramophone. The homey German cuisine has also received the seal of approval from cookery magazine *Kochlöffel*.

Zur Schlossfreiheit (☎ 402 980; Coswigerstrasse 24; mains €9-14; ✗ closed Sun) Traditional local dishes are all given historical themes in this cosy, wood-lined restaurant. Treats include *Lutherschmaus* (duck breast in orange and chocolate sauce, with sultanas) and the *Cranachteller* (grilled pork fillets with a gratin of *spirellini*, mushrooms, broccoli and hollandaise sauce).

Drinking

Brauhaus Wittenberg (☎ 433 130; Im Beyerhof, Markt 6) This place – with a cobbled courtyard, indoor brewery and shiny copper vats – thrums with the noise of people having a good time on both summer and winter evenings.

Barrik (☎ 403 260; Collegienstrasse 81) Built more than 500 years ago, during Luther's lifetime, this wine bar really does feel like an upscale New York club,

Marc de Café (☎ 459 114; Pfaffengasse 5) Hidden away behind the tourist office, this trendy French café is a delight, with everything from cake and coffee to whiskey. It also has nice pictures on the wall and a quiet courtyard.

In Vino Veritas (☎ 7690 565; Mittelstrasse 3; ✗ from 6pm) Order a plate of antipasti (€9–14) as you sample the Italian, Spanish, French and Chilean wines at this upmarket *vinothek*.

A series of pubs at the eastern end of Collegienstrasse include **Sweet Apple** (No 38), where you can suck on a hookah pipe, and **Independent** (☎ 413 257; No 44).

See the listings magazine *Ingo* for further details.

Entertainment

The Stadtkirche has organ concerts at 6pm Friday from May to October, while the Schlosskirche has choir and organ music at 2.30pm every Tuesday during the same period.

Getting There & Away

Wittenberg is on the main train line to Halle and Leipzig (both €10, one hour). Both ICE (€25, 50 minutes) and RE (€17.60, 1¼ hours) go to various Berlin stations. Coming from Berlin, be sure to board for 'Lutherstadt-Wittenberg', as there's also a Wittenberge west of the capital.

Getting Around

The main bus station is along Mauerstrasse just west of Neustrasse; single tickets are €1.30.

Parking enforcement is quite stringent, so use the car parks on the fringes of the Altstadt (such as near Elbtour and along Fleischerstrasse).

You'll find some rickshaw operators around town who are willing to take you to far-flung attractions such as the Hundertwasserschule. For bike rental, head to **Fahrradhaus Kralisch** (☎ 403 703; www.fahrradhaus-kralisch.de, in German; Jüdenstrasse 11).

SOUTHERN SAXONY-ANHALT

HALLE

☎ 0345 / pop 238,500

You can still feel the dread hand of the communist era on Halle more than in many other Eastern cities. As an important GDR bastion – the centre of its chemical industry – some locals feel it has since been punished for its 'complicity'. It lost out on becoming the capital of Saxony-Anhalt in 1990, to the slightly smaller Magdeburg, and subsequently missed the government funding that accompanied that decision. Consequently, plenty of hideous tower blocks remain planted between the frequently grimy medieval buildings of composer Georg Friedrich Händel's hometown.

Yet most people who've visited over the past decade agree that Halle has pulled itself up by its bootstraps, and is definitely improving. Indeed, its central shopping precinct is more lively than Magdeburg's, and it is famous for its cultural festivals. While local tram 1 travels to Frohe Zukunft (Happy Future), that's a destination all of Halle is still trying to reach.

Orientation

The Altstadt lies northwest of the Hauptbahnhof and is circled by a road known as the Stadt Ring. To walk to the central Markt from the train station takes about 15 to 20 minutes; head left from the main entrance and turn left. Continue along pedestrianised Leipziger Strasse.

Information

Halle Tourist Information (☎ 122 9984; www.halle -tourist.de; Leipziger Strasse 105; ☿ 10am-7pm Mon-Fri, 10am-4pm Sat, 10am-2pm Sun) On the Markt.

Halle Welcome Card (1/3 days €7.50/15) Gives you free public transport and discounted museums entry.

Speed/Eiscafé (☎ 694 2727; Grosse Brauhausstrasse; per hr €3.50; ☿ 10am-midnight Mon-Sat, noon-midnight Sun) Internet access.

Sights

HÄNDELHAUS

As a paean to Halle's most famous son, the **Händelhaus** (☎ 500 900; www.haendelhaus.de; Grosse Nikolai Strasse 5-6; admission free; ☿ 9.30am-5.30pm Tue-Sun, to 7pm Thu) is a pretty static affair. It's the house in which Händel was born in 1685, and it charts the composer's life through his moves to Hamburg, Hanover, Italy and eventually London, where he achieved great fame before dying in 1759. The exhibition boards are in German, but call ahead and the museum will arrange a tour in your own language for no extra charge. There's also a collection of antique musical instruments, including an interesting 'glass harmonica' designed by the father of hypnotism, Franz Anton Mesmer.

If you're interested in the composer, it's best to come in the second week of June, when Halle hosts its **Händel Festival**.

BEATLES MUSEUM

Imagine! The Continent's only full-time **Beatles Museum** (☎ 290 3900, www.beatlesmuseum.halle.de; Alter Markt 12; adult/child €3/1.50; ☿ 10am-8pm Wed-Sun, last entry 7pm, closed Sep) is in the unlikely location of Halle (as a result of prohibitive rents in its first home, Cologne). Even in this roomy three-storey building, only a fraction of owner Rainer Moers's 10,000 items are displayed – from legendary photos, record covers and film posters to merchandise like wigs, jigsaws and even talcum powder. The gift shop sells many Beatles souvenirs.

SCHLOSS MORITZBURG

In one tower of the atmospheric 15th-century Moritzburg Palace is the **Stadtmuseum** (Town Museum; ☎ 212 590; www.moritzburg.halle.de; Friedemann-Bach-Platz 5; adult/concession €5/3; ☿ 11am-8.30pm Tue, 10am-6pm Wed-Sun). Here you'll find a small but well-presented collection of German Expressionism and other contemporary art. Works include several by Franz Marc, Ernst Ludwig Kirchner and influential Bauhaus devotee Lyonel Feininger. There are also single pieces by Edvard Munch and Emil Nolde, while temporary exhibitions occupy other halls. Do not confuse this Schloss Moritzburg with the much grander baroque palace in Saxony (see p179).

HALLE-NEUSTADT

Reconstruction around the train station (as well as the Marktplatz and the Alter Markt) has given the city a new sheen, but it has taken away some of its quirkier *Ostalgic* attractions, such as a huge concrete fist and Der Tunnel, an approach to the train station where every inch was covered in graffiti.

Halle-Neustadt, the communist satellite town built between 1964 and 1979 to house workers in the chemical industries, is unlikely to disappear any time soon. However, as home to 60,000 people, it's now only at half-capacity. More curious visitors might appreciate a visit to the 4 sq km of concrete *Plattenbauten* towers that compromises 'Hanoi' (as it's known, from Ha-Neu, the abbreviation of Halle-Neustadt) before it changes any more.

Take tram 2 to Soltauer Strasse, or trams 9, 10 or 11 to Göttinger Bogen. In fact, you needn't even alight from the tram to see the place, but it's more fun if you do.

BURG GIEBICHENSTEIN

If it's a nice day, wander around the ruins of this **castle** (☎ 523 3857; Seebener Strasse 1; adult/child €2.10/1.30; ☿ 9am-6pm Tue-Fri, to 6.30pm Sat & Sun Apr-Oct). Tram 7 will get you here.

Reederei Riedel (☎ 283 2070; www.reederei-riedel
-halle.de; Giebichensteinbrücke, office on the ship Rheinpfalz;
adult/child €4.50/2.50) runs a series of 45-minute
river tours from the nearby bank, leaving on
the hour between 10am and 6pm daily, May
to September.

Sleeping

DJH hostel (☎ 202 4716; www.jugendherberge.de/jh/halle;
August-Bebel-Strasse 48a; dm under/over 26yr €17.50/21.20;
🖳) Much of this hostel evinces 1970s kinder-
garten style, with old lino and plastic chairs.
Not so the lovely dining room, where the carved
wood harks back to the 1930s. The hostel's a
15-minute walk north of the centre but is close
to the nightlife of Kleine Ulrichstrasse.

Marthahaus (☎ 510 80; www.stiftung-marthahaus
.de, in German ; Adam-Kuckhoff-Strasse 5; s €45-60, d €65-85;
✖) Run by the Christian mission that man-
ages the retirement home next door, this hotel
can seem quite hushed at times. Yet, as far
as its furnishings go, it's the best three-star
hotel in town, with soft carpet underfoot and
cosy, well-furnished rooms. The stained-glass
windows in the lounge, stairwell and beautiful dining hall only confirm this impression,
as does the unusually pleasant neighbourhood. **Apart-Hotel Halle** (☎ 525 90; www.apart-halle
.de; Kohlschütter Strasse 5-6; s/d from €70/85, ste from €100;
P) Have a bit of fun in this theatrical hotel.
Inside the red Art Deco building, with its
amusing statue out the front, you'll find stylish standard rooms and suites themed around
German cultural colossi. Although it's a little
north of the centre, it sets the perfect tone if
you're coming for the Händel Festival.

Dorint Novotel Halle Charlottenhof (☎ 292 30;
www.accorhotels.com; Dorotheenstrasse 12; s/d from €80/100;
P ✖ 🐕) Rooms blend Art Deco and con-
temporary features in this leading hotel. The
dark colour scheme gives it a no-nonsense
business feel.

Kempinski Rotes Ross (☎ 233 430; www.kempinski
-halle.de; Leipziger Strasse 76; s €150-170, d €170-190, breakfast
€17; P ✖ 🐕) Halle's only five-star hotel is
decorated in a wedding-cake style, with lots
of red, white and ornate detailing.

Also recommended:

Apartementhaus am Dom (☎ 500 980; Robert-Franz-
Ring 4; s/d from €45/75; P) Simple but business-like
apartments with kitchenettes. There's a sauna, too.

City Hotel am Wasserturm (☎ 298 20; www.cityhotel
-halle.de; Lessingstrasse 8; s €55-70, d €75-80; P ✖)
Very pleasant modern hotel set over two buildings; rooms
have kitchenettes.

Eating

Many of the bars listed in this section can
be relied on for a reasonably priced snack
or meal.

Lesecafé NT (☎ 202 1770; Grosse Ulrichstrasse 51; dishes
€2.10-8.50; ☽ closed Mon evening) This café is not
just a good place to hit before an evening at
the edgy Neues Theater (think Ibsen, Brecht
and contemporary playwrights). Behind its
eye-catching glass, imprinted with the names
of literary greats, and its window display of
teacups and tea sets, you can fuel up on breakfast, lunch and, most evenings, dinner.

Wok Bar (☎ 470 4588; Grosse Ulrichstrasse 41; mains
€7.50-15) This upbeat noodle bar does a good
job of keeping things ticking, with a regular
programme of 'After Wok' parties, DJ events,
cocktail and tempura evenings. It's also excellent for lunch or dinner, when you can
design your own stir-fry meal by choosing
your ingredients from a list of 30.

Palais S (☎ 977 2651; Ankerstrasse 3c; mains €4.50-14;
☽ from 6pm Mon-Sat, from 10am Sun) From paella
to pelmeni, by way of pasta, schnitzels and
Argentine steaks – this rustic restaurant, in a
large half-timbered house on the river, really
does offer the 'jungle' of choices it promises. Although it's a local haunt, the chirpy
owner loves to practise his English and has
translated the menu. There's a waterside
terrace in summer. Follow the signs through
the business park.

Ackerbürgerhof (☎ 2798 0432; Grosse Klaussstrasse 15;
mains €4-11) As much a sightseeing attraction
as a restaurant, this one-time stables building was converted into a house in the 13th
century. Goethe and Händel are alleged to
have supped within its six rooms, although
probably not on the same modern international cuisine you'll be served.

Also recommended:

Ökoase (☎ 290 1604; Kleine Ulrichstrasse 2; mains €3.50-
6.50; ☽ Mon-Fri 10am-7pm) Cheap, healthy vegie bistro.

Café Nöö (☎ 202 1651; Grosse Klaussstrasse 11; mains
€4-6.50) Grungy, alternative caff with surprisingly tasty
food and a rose-covered summer terrace. The sign says
Reformhaus.

Sushi am Opernhaus (☎ 681 6627; August-Bebel-
Strasse 3; dishes €1.70-15) Run by the same crew as the
Wok Bar.

Drinking

Kleine Ulrichstrasse is the first place to head,
being lined with bars. These include the relaxed **Emilie** (☎ 202 5333; Kleine Ulrichstrasse 26) and

Russian-themed vodka specialist Йотемкинъ (Potemkin; ☎ 960 6491; Kleine Ulrichstrasse 27). Lujah (☎ 478 9900; Kleine Ulrichstrasse 36) is a hip and happening place – the name comes from Hallelujah!

Sternstrasse is another good place to drink, and is where you'll find the bar **Don Camillo** (☎ 290 1056; Sternstrasse 3) and others.

Entertainment
For further listings, consult the free magazines *Aha!, Blitz* or *Frizz*.

CLUBS
Mainstream discos include **Flower Power** (☎ 688 8888; Moritzburgring 1) and **Easy Schorre** (☎ 212 240; www.easyschorre.de; Philipp-Müller-Strasse 77-78). **Objekt 5** (☎ 522 0016; Seebener Strasse 5) and **Turm** (☎ 202 3737; Friedemann-Bach-Platz 5) are where to head for music events including jazz and tango.

CLASSICAL MUSIC
Two of the most important venues during June's Händel Festival are the modern 1900-seat **Händel-Halle** (☎ 292 90; Salzgrafenplatz 1) and the more venerable, highly respected **Opernhaus** (Opera House; ☎ 511 00; Universitätsring 24).

For tickets, contact **Ticket-Galerie** (☎ 6888 6888; Stadtcenter Rolltreppe, Grosse Ulrichstrasse 50).

Getting There & Away
AIR
Leipzig-Halle airport lies between both cities, which are about 25km apart. It's a major link with Frankfurt, Munich and other major German and European cities. ICE trains head from the airport train station to Leipzig and Dresden in one direction and Halle, Magdeburg and Hanover in the other. RE and ICE trains run directly between **Leipzig-Halle airport** (www.leipzig-halle-airport.de) and Halle Hauptbahnhof (from €6, 13 minutes).

CAR & MOTORCYCLE
From Leipzig, take the A14 west to the B100. A new extension of the A14 connects Halle and Magdeburg in about one hour. The B91 runs south from Halle and links up with the A9 autobahn, which connects Munich and Berlin.

TRAIN
Leipzig and Halle are linked by frequent trains (€5.70, 35 minutes). To Magdeburg there are IC trains (€17, 50 minutes) and RE trains (€13.40, one hour, 20 minutes) and direct IC

trains go to Berlin (various stations, €34, two hours). Local trains serve Eisleben (€6.20, 40 minutes) and Wittenberg (€10, one hour).

Getting Around
Trams 2 and 5 (at one stop) and 7 and 9 (at another) will all take you from the train station to the Marktplatz. Fares are usually €1.50 for singles (€1.10 for rides of up to four stops) and €4.10 for day cards. However, if you have an EC/Maestro debit card, buy tickets on the trams – they're cheaper.

For drivers, the one-way street system in Halle is fiendishly complex, and the streets busy. Your best bet is to park near the Hauptbahnhof, or at one of the municipal garages, and take trams.

EISLEBEN
☎ 03475 / pop 24,500
It seems odd for a well-travelled man whose ideas revolutionised Europe to have died in the town where he was born. However, as native son Martin Luther himself put it before expiring here, *'Mein Vaterland war Eisleben'* (Eisleben was my fatherland). Whereas Lutherstadt Wittenberg has other distractions, this former mining town focuses on the devout follower these days. Every where you turn, it's Luther, Luther, Luther, in this town, which also answers to the double-barrelled Lutherstadt Eisleben.

Orientation
Most sights are knotted together around the Markt, just southwest of Hallesche Strasse-Freistrasse (B80), the main thoroughfare. From the train station (turn left out of the main exit), it's a 10-minute walk north along Bahnhofsring and Bahnhofstrasse.

Information
Kreisinformationzentrum Mansfelder Land (☎ 667 790; www.mansfelderland.de; Markt 58; 9am-5.30pm Mon-Fri, to 4.30pm Nov-Mar) Tourist information. Has a tendency to put a price on brochures.
Tourist Office Lutherstadt Eisleben (☎ 602 124; www.eisleben-tourist.de, in German; Bahnhofstrasse 36; 10am-5pm Mon-Fri, 10am-6pm Tue, 9am-noon Sat)

Sights
LUTHER MUSEUMS
Chock-full of Luther souvenirs from down through the ages, the annexe at the back is the most visually appealing feature of **Luthers Ge-**

burtshaus (Luther's birth house; ☎ 602 775; Seminarstrasse 16; adult/concession €2/1; ☼ 10am-6pm Apr-Oct, 10am-5pm Tue-Sun Nov-Mar). The main house, where the reformer was born, is now sparsely furnished.

In the centre of town, just past the Markt, lies **Luthers Sterbehaus** (Luther's death house; ☎ 602 285; Andreaskirchplatz; adult/concession €2/1), an altogether more reverential affair. There's lots of information (in German) about the Reformation downstairs, and upstairs Luther's reconstructed living quarters and death chamber include copies of his death mask and last testimony.

Luther returned to Eisleben to help settle a legal dispute over the family copperworks, but he was already ill and died a day after finalising an agreement, on 18 February 1546.

Although it was long believed that this was where the great man departed this world, new research has revealed that Luther died in the building now occupied by the Graf von Mansfeld hotel. With such a long tradition of people paying respects to him here, however, there are no plans to move the exhibition.

MARKT & CHURCHES

See where Luther delivered his last sermons in 1546! That's the **St Andreaskirche** (☼ 10am-noon & 2-4pm Mon-Sat, 11am-1pm & 2-4pm Sun May-Oct), a late-Gothic hall church on the hill behind the central Markt. See where Luther stayed while district vicar! That would be the apartments of the **St Annenkirche** (☼ 1-3pm Mon-Fri May-Oct), 10 minutes west of the Markt. This church also features a stunning Steinbilder-Bibel (stone-picture Bible; 1585), the only one of its kind in Europe, and a wittily decorated pulpit. Finally, see where Luther was baptised – the **St Petri Pauli Kirche** (Church of Sts Peter & Paul; ☼ 1-3pm Mon-Fri May-Oct) near the Fremdverkehrsein.

By now, we think you get the picture of what Eisleben is about. The historic **Kloster Helfta** (Helfta Cloister; ☎ 711 400; www.kloster-helfta.de; Lindenstrasse 34) is undergoing further renovation, but the nuns still offer group tours by arrangement and organise religious workshops; there's also a hotel attached (see right).

Sleeping & Eating

Parkhotel (☎ 540; fax 253 19; Bahnhofstrasse 12; s/d €40/55) The green metallic bathroom blinds and purple cushions seem to have been here since the '70s, but this pleasant enough family-run hotel is clean and has a pretty hill-top setting, across from a leafy park.

Mansfelder Hof (☎ 6690; www.mansfelderhof .de; Hallesche Strasse 33; s/d €50/80; ℗) Behind its vine-covered, faded green stucco façade, the Mansfelder Hof turns out to have modern but entirely forgettable rooms. The real draw is the restaurant serving local specialities, often with Luther-related names.

Hotel an der Klosterpforte (☎ 714 40; www.klosterp forte.com; Lindenstrasse 34; s/d €60/80; ℗ ✖ ♨) Eisleben's youngest hotel, built in 2002, features uncluttered modern rooms, a buffet restaurant and a brewery adjacent to the historic Kloster Helfta. It's a little out of the centre, though, and it's helpful to have your own transport.

Graf von Mansfeld (☎ 250 722; www.hotel-eisleben .de; Markt 56; s/d from €50/80; ✖) In a completely different class from anything else in this slightly depressed town, the Graf von Mansfeld has real style, with parquet flooring, rugs and four-poster beds – all with just a hint of rococo. The restaurant serves modern international cuisine (mains €8.50 to €17).

Getting There & Away

There are trains to Halle (€6.20, 35 minutes), Leipzig (€11.70, 70 minutes), Erfurt (€14.70, 1¾ hours) and Weimar (from €17.20, two hours).

Eisleben is a half-hour drive west of Halle on the B80.

SAALE-UNSTRUT REGION

It will never rival the likes of Bordeaux as a connoisseur's paradise, but the wine-growing region along the rivers Saale and Unstrut (pronounced *zah*-leh and *oon*-shtroot) nevertheless provides a wonderfully rural summer retreat. Europe's most northerly wine district, it produces crisp whites and fairly sharp reds, which you can enjoy at regular vineyard tastings. Bicycle and hiking paths meander through rolling, castle-topped hills and past small family-owned farms (see the boxed text, p216 for more details).

NAUMBURG
☎ 03445 / pop 31,500
Like Cologne, Naumburg is famous for its huge cathedral. It's just that here the architecture is late Romanesque rather than Gothic

and the local accompaniment is wine, not beer. Famously, philosopher Friedrich Nietzsche spent some of his final years in this town. Aside from this, Naumburg's a quiet place featuring several ornate medieval buildings: the Rathaus, and the Portal von 1680 at the eastern end are examples of what's called 'Naumburg Renaissance' style.

Orientation

The Hauptbahnhof is 1.5km northwest of the old town, which is encircled by a ring road. You can take bus 2 from the Hauptbahnhof to the Markt (€1.20) or walk along Rossbacher Strasse (keep bearing left and uphill). Doing the latter takes you past the cathedral. The bus station is at the northeastern edge of town on Hallesische Strasse.

Information

Post office (Heinrich von Stephan Platz 6) Just north of Marientor.

Tourist office (☎ 273 112; www.naumburg-tourismus .de; Markt 12; ☯ 9am-6pm Mon-Fri, 9am-4pm Sat, 10am-1pm Sun Apr-Oct, ☯ 9am-6pm Mon-Fri, 9am-2pm Sat Nov-Mar)

Sights

DOM

In the western quarter of town, on a road in from the train station, stands the enormous medieval **Cathedral of Sts Peter & Paul** (☎ 201 675; Domplatz 16-17; adult/concession/child €4/3/2). Its size is impressive enough, but the cathedral is also rather unusual in having two choirs. The western choir, built from 1250 to 1260 in late Romanesque style, is the more interesting. Considered the magnum opus of the anonymous Master of Naumburg, it not only contains some of Germany's oldest and most valuable stained-glass windows, but also houses the celebrated 13th-century **statues of Uta and Ekkehard**, who were among the dome's many benefactors. Uta of Naumberg is a German icon and her serene face decorates souvenirs all over town.

The elevated eastern choir was built around 1330 in Gothic style. The staircase up to it is interesting, too, although it's a contemporary touch. Magdeburg artist Heinrich Apel has decorated the banisters with all sorts of farmyard animals, hobgoblins and fairy-tale characters.

An informative tour (in German) is included in the admission price, but you can pick up a leaflet, or buy a brochure in English (€5.50), and walk around on your own.

NIETZSCHE HAUS

The home of Friedrich Nietzsche's mother, who brought the philosopher here to nurse him when he was dying from syphilis, this requires a lot of concentration – just like the man's work itself. That's to say there's not much to the **Nietzsche Haus** (☎ 201 638; Weingarten 18; adult/concession €2/1.25; ☯ 2-5pm Tue-Fri, 10am-4pm Sat & Sun) apart from photos and reams of biographical text (all in German). The exhibition pointedly stays *stumm* (silent) on the controversy surrounding the man who wrote *Also Sprach Zarathustra* (Thus Spoke Zarathustra) and became a Nazi favourite.

Festivals & Events

The normally sedate town goes wild on the last weekend of June with the **Kirschfest** (Cherry Festival; www.kirschfest.de), held at the Vogelwiese field at the southeastern end of town. It celebrates the unlikely medieval tale of the lifting of a blockade by Czech soldiers, when their leader, Prokop, gave in to requests by the town's children (dressed in their Sunday finest) to please leave and let the townsfolk eat again.

Tent stalls offer regional food, wine and beer, and there is live music. An enormous fireworks display and a parade, with actors dressed as Uta and Ekkehard, are held on the Sunday.

Sleeping & Eating

Camping Blütengrund (☎ 202 711; www.camping naumburg.de; Blütengrund Park; adult/tent/car €4.50/4/2) This large leafy camp site, 1.5km northeast of Naumburg at the confluence of the Saale and Unstrut Rivers, is very sports-orientated, with equipment hire and even canoe rental (from €25 a day) nearby.

DJH hostel (☎ 703 422; www.jugendherberge .de/jh/naumburg; Am Tennisplatz 9; dm under/over 26yr €14/16.70, breakfast €4) Naumburg's large and well-equipped hostel is 1.5km south of the town centre.

Hotel Garni St Marien (☎ 235 40; fax 235 422; Marienstrasse 12; s/d €45/85; Ⓟ) You're guaranteed a good night's rest here, in rooms set well back from a not particularly noisy street. The generic décor won't keep you awake either. Nice touches in the public areas include a magazine rack and honour bar. Service is friendly, too.

Hotel Stadt Aachen (☎ 2470; www.hotel-stadt-aachen.de, Markt 11; s €50-70, d €80-100) With its country-style floral curtains, its patterned duvet covers and its heavy wooden wardrobes, the Stadt Aachen is the place for rustic German charm. The vine-covered façade is located right on the Markt, and the hotel's Carolus Magnus restaurant is also popular.

Zur Alten Schmiede (☎ 243 60; www.hotel-zur-alten-schmiede.de; Lindenring 36-37; s €45-60, d €60-85) Combining the friendly (very) and smiley service of a family-run business, with effortless unstuffy elegance, this is the most chic place to stay in Naumburg. Hearty fare is served in the ground-floor restaurant.

Alt Naumburg (☎ 205 294; Marienplatz 13; mains €3.60-12) Although many come here just for the local wines or fine beer, Alt Naumburg also serves a range of casual fare, from jacket potatoes and salads to fish and schnitzels. The outside tables on the cobblestones are packed in summer.

Getting There & Around

There are regional trains to Naumburg from Halle (€6.80, 40 minutes), Leipzig (€8, 1¼ hours), Jena (€6.20, 35 minutes) and Weimar (€7.60, 30 minutes). A local line runs to Freyburg (€2.30, nine minutes) and Bad Kösen (€2.30, five minutes).

ICE trains serve Berlin (€41, two hours), Frankfurt (€55, three hours) and Munich (€71, 4½ hours).

By road from Halle or Leipzig, take the A9 to either the B87 or the B180 and head west; the B87 is less direct and more scenic, though it's the first exit from the A9.

FREYBURG

☎ 034464 / pop 5000

With its cobblestone streets and medieval castle above vine-covered slopes, sleepy wine-growing Freyburg has a vaguely French atmosphere. It's the sort of village that puts the 'r' in rustic – or would if it could stay awake to do so. Although it boasts Germany's most famous sparkling wine brand, and a rare example of ex-GDR commercial success, you wouldn't realise it from the exterior. The town only really comes alive for its **wine festival** in the second week of September.

Orientation

To reach the town centre from the train station, turn right at the Fiedelak shop, left into the park and cross the bridge over the river. For the castle, take the second road to the right (Schlossstrasse). Keep bearing left for the Markt and tourist office.

Information

Freyburg tourist office (☎ 272 60; www.freyburg-info.de; Markt 2; ⌚ 8am-6pm Mon-Fri, 8am-noon Sat)

Sights

Established in 1856, and one of the best-known sparkling wine producers in the former GDR, the **Rotkäppchen sparkling wine factory** (☎ 340; www.rotkaeppchen.de, German only; Sektkellereistrasse 5; tours €4; ⌚ tours at 2pm daily & 11am Sat & Sun) has enjoyed something of a (slightly *Ostalgie*-fuelled) comeback in the united Germany. Its *Sekt* (sparkling wine) is perhaps a little sweet for some tastes, but increased sales mean 'Little Red Riding Hood' has acquired enough muscle to buy several Western brands, including Mumm, in recent years. Before she was promoted to the top job, they proudly point out, German Chancellor Angela Merkel also made a VIP visit to this factory.

The usual (non-VIP) one-hour tours include the two-storey 120,000L Sekt barrel decorated with ornate carvings (no longer in use), a tasting, and the Lichthof – a glorious gymnasium-sized hall with 100-year-old skylights, where concerts are held year round. Telephone for details.

Between 10am and 5pm, you can also taste and buy a whole range of *Sekt* at the shop out the front.

Reached via winding woodland steps, the large medieval **Schloss Neuenburg** (☎ 355 30; www.schloss-neuenburg.de, in German; Schloss 25; adult/concession €3.50/2.50; ⌚ 10am-6pm Tue-Sun Apr-Oct, to 5pm Nov-Mar), on the hill above town, houses an excellent museum. There's an unusual two-storey (or 'double') chapel, fascinating explanations of medieval life and a free-standing tower behind the castle, the **Dicker Wilhelm** (adult/concession €1.50/0.75; ⌚ 10am-6pm Tue-Sun Apr-Oct), which offers further historical exhibitions and splendid views. There's a fun Knight's Tournament in June, too.

Getting There & Around

Trains run every hour (€2.30, eight minutes), as do buses (€2.30, 15 minutes), between Naumburg's Hauptbahnhof/ZOB and Freyburg's Markt; the services are drastically curtailed on weekends. The well-marked bicycle route (Radwandern) between the two cities makes for a wonderful ride. Bikes can be hired from **Fiedelak** (☎ 7080; Bahnhofstrasse 4; per day €6).

Perhaps the most scenic way to get to Freyburg is by boat from Blütengrund, at the confluence of the Saale and Unstrut Rivers, just outside Naumburg. The historic, 19th-century **MS Fröhliche Dörte** (☎ 03445-202 830) tootles its way up the Unstrut at 11am, 1.30pm and 4pm daily between May and September. The 70-minute journey costs €6 per adult and €3.80 per child one way, and €10 and €6 return. It runs back from Freyburg at 12.15pm, 2.45pm and 5.15pm.

Harz Mountains

The Harz Mountains rise picturesquely from the North German Plain, covering an area 100km long and 30km wide at the junction of Saxony-Anhalt, Thuringia and Lower Saxony. Although the scenery here is a far cry from the dramatic peaks and valleys of the Alps, the Harz region is a great year-round sports getaway, with plenty of opportunities for hiking, cycling and skiing (downhill and nordic) in and around the pretty Harz National Park.

The regular influx of visitors in all seasons is testament to the enduring appeal of the Harz; historically, too, its status as a prime national holiday destination has never been questioned. From 1952 until reunification, the region was divided between West and East Germany, effectively becoming an uneasy political holiday camp straddling the Iron Curtain.

The Brocken (1142m) is the focal point, and has had more than its fair share of illustrious visitors: the great Goethe was frequently seen striding the local trails and set 'Walpurgisnacht', an early chapter of *Faust*, on the mountain, while satirical poet Heinrich Heine spent a well-oiled night here, as described in *Harzreise* (Harz Journey; 1824). Elsewhere the charming medieval towns of Wernigerode and Quedlinburg pull the crowds, while equally venerable steam trains pull them along between the mountain villages, spas and sports resorts that litter the region. Get out your knee socks or your ski mask and treat yourself to a taste of the active life.

HIGHLIGHTS

- **Pagan Rituals** Trek to the Brocken or party on Hexentanzplatz, Thale, for Walpurgisnacht festival (p249)
- **Venues** Sleep in a Renaissance mansion, eat in a Gothic cellar and walk among 1400 half-timbered houses from over six centuries in Quedlinburg (p243)
- **Free Wheeling** Get on a mountain bike and pedal the forest trails (p240) behind Wernigerode in the Harz National Park
- **Mother Lode** Descend rocky shafts into the mining past in Clausthal-Zellerfeld (p238) and explore 1000 years of mining history in Goslar (p231)
- **Night Walks** Explore the Wernigerode Altstadt (p239) at night and marvel at the floodlit ducal castle
- **Mountain Steaming** Wind through the spectacular wilds of the Selketal from Quedlinburg or Gernrode on a steam train (p241)

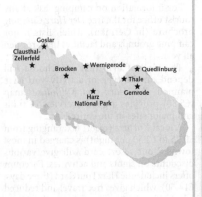

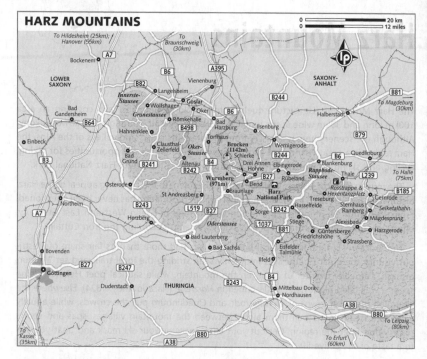

HARZ MOUNTAINS

Information

The main information centre for the Harz Mountains is the **Harzer Verkehrsverband** (☎ 05321-340 40) in Goslar, but information on the eastern Harz is best picked up in towns there, particularly in Wernigerode.

For information on camping, ask at any tourist office for the free *Der Harz Camping* brochure (in German), which lists major camping grounds and facilities that are open all year.

The kind of map that you choose will depend on the type of activity you have planned. *Der Harz und Kyffhäuser* map (€5.80) provides a good overview of trails and major sites in the entire Harz.

A local *Kurtaxe* (resort tax; ranging from €0.75 to €2.50 per night) is charged in most towns. Your resort card will give various discounts on sights and activities. Discount offers include the HarzTourCard (three days, €14.50), which gives free travel and reduced admission to attractions, and the Harz-MobilCard (one month, €13), which entitles the user to concession-priced tickets on all public transport.

Activities

CYCLING

Anyone seeking a challenge will enjoy cycling or mountain biking in the Harz, especially in quieter eastern areas. Buses will transport your bike when space allows.

HIKING

The main attraction in summer is hiking the integrated trail network in the Harz National Park. Trail symbols are colour-coded in red, green, blue and yellow on a square or triangular plate. **Harzklub** (www.harzklub.de) hiking association maps also show trail numbers; the 1:50,000 editions are the best for hikers. Harzklub offices in mountain towns are also good sources of information, including hiking tips, itineraries and the availability of partners and guides. Tourist offices also stock the club's leaflets. Weather conditions can change quickly throughout the year; be prepared.

SKIING

The main centres for downhill skiing are Braunlage, Hahnenklee and St Andreasberg, with many other smaller runs dotted throughout the mountains. The quality of the slopes might disappoint real enthusiasts; conditions for cross-country skiing, however, can be excellent, with lots of well-marked trails and equipment-hire shops. For weather reports and snow conditions, ring the **Harzer Verkehrsverband** (☎ 05321-340 40). There's also a German-language **information service** (☎ 05321-200 24).

SPAS
Often mocked by young Germans as a pensioners' paradise, the Harz is sprinkled with thermal spas and baths where the weary and/or infirm can take a cure. Most spa towns have a *Kurzentrum* (spa centre) or *Kurverwaltung* (spa administration), which often doubles as a tourist office.

Getting There & Away
The area's main towns of Goslar, Wernigerode and Quedlinburg are serviced by daily trains, with Hanover the nearest major hub for onward travel; contact **Deutsche Bahn** (☎ reservations 118 61, automated timetable information 0800-150 7090; www.bahn.de).

    BerlinLinienBus (www.berlinlinienbus.de) runs to Goslar, and some smaller towns, from Berlin (€40), and there are plenty of regional bus services to take you further into the mountains.

    If you're driving, the area's main arteries are the east–west B6 and the north–south B4, which are accessed via the A7 (skirting the western edge of the Harz on its way south from Hanover) and the A2 (running north of the Harz between Hanover and Berlin).

Getting Around
The Harz is one part of Germany where you'll rely on buses as much as trains, and the various local networks are fast and reliable. Narrow-gauge steam trains run to the Brocken and link major towns in the eastern Harz.

WESTERN HARZ

GOSLAR
☎ 05321 / pop 46,000
The hub of tourism in the Western Harz, Goslar has a charming medieval Altstadt, which, together with its historic Rammelsberg mine, is a Unesco World Heritage site.

Founded by Heinrich I in 922, the town's early importance centred on silver and the Kaiserpfalz, the seat of the Saxon kings from 1005 to 1219. It fell into decline after a second period of prosperity in the 14th and 15th centuries, reflecting the fortunes of the Harz as a whole, and relinquished its mine to Braunschweig in 1552 and then its soul to Prussia in 1802. The Altstadt, Rammelsberg mine and Kaiserpfalz attract visitors by the busload in summer, when it's always best to reserve ahead.

Orientation
Rosentorstrasse leads to the Markt, a 10-minute walk from the train and bus stations. The small Gose River flows through the centre south of the Markt. Streets in the old town are numbered up one side and down the other.

Information
Asklepios Harzkliniken (☎ 440; Kösliner Strasse 12) Medical services, about 6km north of town.
City-Textilpflege (☎ 242 77; Petersilienstrasse 9) Laundry.
Deutsche Bank (☎ 757 20; Fischemäkerstrasse 13) Bank services and ATM.
Harzer Verkehrsverband (☎ 340 40; www.harzinfo .de; Bäckergildehaus, Marktstrasse 45; ⊙ 8am-5pm Mon-Fri) Tourist information.
MuseumSpass (adult/child €9/4.50) This card gives admission to Goslar's major attractions (except the Rathaus).
Police (☎ 3390; Heinrich-Pieper-Strasse 1)
Post office (Klubgartenstrasse 10)
Spielzentrum (Breite Strasse; per hr €2.50) Internet access.
Tourist-Information (☎ 780 60; www.goslar.de; Markt 7; ⊙ 9.15am-6pm Mon-Fri, 9.30am-4pm Sat, 9.30am-2pm Sun Apr-Oct, 9.15am-5pm Mon-Fri, 9.30am-2pm Sat Nov-Mar)

Sights
AROUND THE MARKT
One of the nicest things to do in Goslar is to wander through the historic streets around the Markt. **Hotel Kaiserworth** (p233) was erected in 1494 to house the textile guild, and sports almost life-size figures on its orange façade. The impressive late-Gothic **Rathaus** comes into its own at night, when light shining through stained-glass windows illuminates the stone-patterned town square. The highlight inside is a beautiful cycle of 16th-century religious

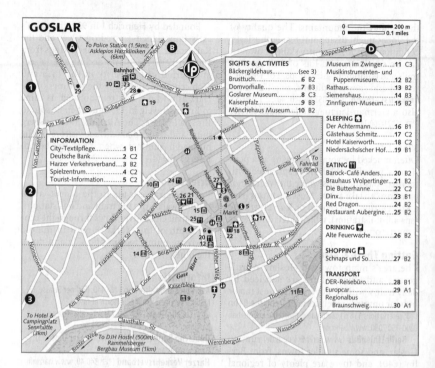

GOSLAR

0 ————— 200 m
0 ————— 0.1 miles

SIGHTS & ACTIVITIES
Bäckergildehaus..............(see 3)
Brusttuch.........................6 B2
Domvorhalle......................7 B3
Goslar Museum..................8 C3
Kaiserpfalz........................9 B3
Mönchehaus Museum....10 B2
Museum im Zwinger.......11 C3
Musikinstrumenten- und
  Puppenmuseum............12 B2
Rathaus............................13 B2
Siemenshaus....................14 B3
Zinnfiguren-Museum.......15 B2

SLEEPING
Der Achtermann.............16 B1
Gästehaus Schmitz.........17 C2
Hotel Kaiserworth...........18 C2
Niedersächsischer Hof.....19 B1

EATING
Barock-Café Anders........20 B2
Brauhaus Wolpertinger....21 B2
Die Butterhanne..............22 C2
Dinx.................................23 B1
Red Dragon.....................24 B2
Restaurant Aubergine.....25 B2

DRINKING
Alte Feuerwache.............26 B2

SHOPPING
Schnaps und So..............27 B2

TRANSPORT
DER-Reisebüro.................28 B1
Europcar..........................29 A1
Regionalbus
  Braunschweig.............30 A1

INFORMATION
City-Textilpflege..............1 B1
Deutsche Bank..................2 C2
Harzer Verkehrsverband....3 B2
Spielzentrum.....................4 C2
Tourist-Information...........5 C2

paintings in the **Huldigungssaal** (Hall of Homage; adult/child €3.50/1.50; 11am-3pm Apr-Oct).

The **market fountain**, crowned by an ungainly eagle symbolising Goslar's status as a free imperial city, dates from the 13th century; the eagle itself is a copy – the original is on show in the Goslarer Museum (opposite). Opposite the Rathaus is the **Glockenspiel**, a chiming clock depicting four scenes of mining in the area. It plays at 9am, noon, 3pm and 6pm.

The baroque **Siemenshaus** (780 620; Schreiberstrasse 12) is the 17th-century ancestral home of the Siemens industrial family, but the interior can only be viewed on tourist office tours or with advance notice. The **Brusttuch** (opposite), at Hoher Weg 1, and the **Bäckergildehaus**, on the corner of Marktstrasse and Bergstrasse, are two fine early 16th-century houses.

KAISERPFALZ

Goslar's pride and joy is the reconstructed 11th-century Romanesque palace, **Kaiserpfalz** (311 9693; Kaiserbleek 6; adult/concession €4.50/2.50; 10am-5pm). After centuries of decline and neglect, the palace was resurrected in the 19th century and adorned with interior frescoes of

idealised historical scenes. On the southern side is **St Ulrich Chapel**, housing a sarcophagus containing the heart of Heinrich III. Below the Kaiserpfalz is the recently restored **Domvorhalle**, displaying the 11th-century Kaiserstuhl, the throne used by Salian and Hohenstaufen emperors. Behind the palace, in pleasant gardens, is an excellent sculpture by Henry Moore called the *Goslarer Krieger* (Goslar Warrior).

RAMMELSBERGER BERGBAU MUSEUM

About 1km south of the town centre, the shafts and buildings of this 1000-year-old **mine** (7500; www.rammelsberg.de; Bergtal 19; adult/concession €10/8; 9am-6pm, last admission 4.30pm) are now a museum and Unesco World Heritage site. Admission to the mine includes a German-language tour and a pamphlet with English explanations of the 18th- and 19th-century Roeder Shafts, the mine railway and the ore processing section. Bus 808 stops here.

OTHER MUSEUMS

The five-floor private **Musikinstrumenten- und Puppenmuseum** (269 45; Hoher Weg 5; adult/child €3/1.50; 11am-5pm) will delight both kids and

HARZ MOUNTAINS

fans of musical instruments and/or dolls. The owner began collecting instruments about 50 years ago; the doll collection is his daughter's addition.

The **Zinnfiguren-Museum** (☎ 258 89; Münzstrasse 11; adult/concession €3.50/1.50; ☼ 10am-5pm) exhibits a colourful collection of painted pewter figures in a courtyard.

For a good overview of the natural and cultural history of Goslar and the Harz, visit the **Goslarer Museum** (☎ 433 94; Königstrasse 1; adult/concession €3/1.50; ☼ 10am-5pm Tue-Sun Apr-Oct, to 4pm Nov-Mar). One room contains the treasures from the former Goslar Dom (cathedral), and there's also a cabinet with coins dating from the 10th century. The original golden eagle from the fountain is also here.

The **Mönchehaus Museum** (☎ 295 70; Mönchestrasse 3; adult/child €3/1.50; ☼ 10am-5pm Tue-Sat, to 1pm Sun), in a 16th-century half-timbered house, has changing exhibits of modern art, including works by the most recent winner of the prestigious Kaiserring art prize – past winners include Henry Moore, Joseph Beuys and Rebecca Horn. Look for the interesting sculptures in the peaceful garden.

For a real 'scream', take a look inside the **Museum im Zwinger** (☎ 431 40; www.zwinger.de; Thomasstrasse 2; adult/child €2/1.20; ☼ 10am-5pm, closed mid-Nov–Feb), a 16th-century tower that was once part of the ramparts, which has a collection of such late-medieval delights as torture implements, coats of armour and weapons used during the Peasant Wars.

Sleeping

DJH hostel (☎ 222 40; jh-goslar@djh-hannover.de; Rammelsberger Strasse 25; under/over 26yr €16.50/19.50; ☒) Take bus 808 to Theresienhof to reach this pretty hostel out near the mining museum. Facilities are excellent, with conference rooms, two- to eight-bed dorms, and barbecue and sports areas.

Hotel & Campingplatz Sennhütte (☎ 225 02; Clausthaler Strasse 28; s €21, d €42, adult/child €3.50/2, car/tent €2/2.50) This camping ground is 3km south of Goslar via the B241 (bus 830 to Sennhütte). The rooms are simple but clean, and it's advisable to reserve through the tourist office before setting out.

Gästehaus Schmitz (☎ 234 45; Kornstrasse 1; s/d €35/45) This slightly eccentric guesthouse is an excellent choice in the heart of town for those on low budgets or wanting an apartment. Book ahead.

Das Brusttuch (☎ 346 00; brusttuch.goslar@treff-hotels.de; Hoher Weg 1; s €63-71, d €81-112; P ☒ ☒) The soft colours and smart rooms in this historic hotel make it a comfortable snooze-zone. It's very central and some rooms have double doors to the hallway.

Hotel Kaiserworth (☎ 7090; www.kaiserworth.de; Markt 3; s €66-96, d €117-177; P ☒) This magnificent 500-year-old former merchant guild building has tasteful rooms and a good restaurant open daily from 6am to 11pm. For insomniacs and barflies there's the dungeon-like Dukaten Bar, which is open till 6am.

Niedersächsischer Hof (☎ 3160; www.niedersaechsischer-hof-goslar.de; Rosentorstrasse 20; s €91, d €124; P ☒) Opposite the train station, the 'Hof' toys with the idea of being an art hotel (the kids will love the piece near the foyer with the cindered toy cars) and has light rooms well insulated against the bustle outside. When you look closely, the art is thin on the ground, but there's still flair to be found in the rooms.

Der Achtermann (☎ 700 00; www.der-achtermann.de; Rosentorstrasse 20; s €99-119, d €145-165; P ☒ ☒) The only drawbacks with this otherwise very good hotel are its sprawling size and the number of business conference guests buzzing in swarms between its ample amenities.

Eating & Drinking

Barock-Café Anders (☎ 238 14; Hoher Weg 4; cake from €2.30; ☼ 10am-6pm) The first thing that strikes you here is the wonderful smell of cakes and confectionery, the delicious specialities.

Dinx (☎ 383 488; Bahnhof; mains €5.50-12.50; ☼ 8am-midnight Mon-Thu, 8am-3am Fri & Sat, 10am-midnight Sun) Food ranges from the finger variety through to potatoes, vegetarian food and hearty steaks in this large restaurant and bar.

Red Dragon (☎ 709 659; Bäckerstrasse 18; mains €6.50-15; ☼ 10.30am-10.30pm Mon-Sat) The name and fittings at this restaurant point to China, it's Vietnamese-run, and the menu promises a *scharf* (hot) Thai-style beef stir-fry with chilli. It tastes great, even if it's not always clear where you stand on the culinary map.

Die Butterhanne (☎ 228 86; Marktkirchhof 3; mains €7-14; ☼ from 11am) The fare is traditional and regular here, the outdoor seating is nice and each Saturday the whole place becomes a throbbing nightspot from 10pm. The name refers to a famous local frieze showing a milk-maid churning butter while clutching her buttock to insult her employer – don't try it on disco night.

HARZ MOUNTAINS

Brauhaus Wolpertinger (☎ 221 55; Marstallstrasse 1; mains €8.50-15; ☻ noon-2pm & 5pm-midnight Mon-Fri, noon-1am Sat, 10am-midnight Sun) This pub is a popular former brewery with lots of wood fittings inside. There's also outdoor seating in the forecourt and next door is the Alte Feuerwache (open 9pm till late Friday and Saturday), an affiliated bar for late-night drinking.

Restaurant Aubergine (☎ 421 36; www.aubergine -goslar.de; Marktstrasse 4; mains €13-19.50; ☻ noon-3pm & 5.30-11.30pm) The classiest act on the non-traditional side of town, this Mediterranean restaurant has earned a lot of kudos in the region and beyond.

Shopping

Hoher Weg has shops selling souvenirs, especially puppets and marionettes, many of them portraying witches.

Schnaps und So (☎ 396 636; Hokenstrasse 3) This is a great local booze store, but approach the Harz fruit wines and herbal schnapps with caution – some of them may leave you the worse for wear.

Getting There & Away

BUS

The office of **Regionalbus Braunschweig** (RBB; ☎ 194 49; www.rbb-bus.de; Bahnhof), from where buses depart, has free timetables for services throughout the Harz region. Buses 861 and 831 run between Goslar and Altenau in the south; 861 continues to St Andreasberg. Bus 830 runs to Clausthal-Zellerfeld via Hahnenklee. Trains are easier to get to Bad Harzburg, where you can take bus 810 to Torfhaus. The BEX BerlinLinienBus runs daily to Berlin (€40) via Magdeburg. For timetables and bookings, refer to **DER-Reisebüro** (☎ 757 90; Bahnhof).

CAR & MOTORCYCLE

The B6 runs north to Hildesheim and east to Bad Harzburg, Wernigerode and Quedlinburg. The north–south A7 is reached via the B82. For Hahnenklee, take the B241. Car rental is available at **Europcar** (☎ 251 38; Lindenplan 3).

TRAIN

Bad Harzburg–Hanover trains stop here often, as do trains on the Braunschweig–Göttingen line. There are direct trains to Wernigerode (€7.60, 50 minutes, every two hours); for more frequent services change at Vienenburg.

Getting Around

Local bus tickets cost €1.90. To book a taxi, ring ☎ 1313. **Fahrrad Hans** (☎ 685 734; hans -speed@freenet.de; Breite Strasse 30-31) rents mountain and city bikes for €13 per day.

OKER VALLEY

The Oker Valley, which begins at Oker, a small industrial town now part of Goslar, is one of the prettiest in the western Harz. An 11km hike (marked with a red triangle) follows the course of the Oker River and leads to a 47-million-cu-metre **dam**, constructed in the 1950s to regulate water levels and generate power. Along the way you'll pass the 60m-high **Römkerhalle** waterfall, created in 1863. The B498 leads to the dam. If travelling by bus, take bus 806 or 810 to the Okertalsperre stop. **Okersee-Schiffahrt** (☎ 05329-811; www.okersee.de; ☻ Apr-Oct) runs boat trips and tours on the Oker lake.

HAHNENKLEE

☎ 05325 / pop 1300

Surrounded by forest some 12km southwest of Goslar, this small spa town is one of the more tasteful ski resorts in the Harz Mountains and makes a good base for summer hikes in the western Harz.

The **tourist office** (☎ 510 40; www.hahnenklee .de; Kurhausweg 7; ☻ 9am-5pm Mon-Fri, 10am-noon Sat & Sun May-Oct, 9am-4pm Mon-Fri, 10am-noon Sat Nov-Apr) is in the Kurverwaltung building off Rathausstrasse.

Sights & Activities

Apart from hiking and skiing, the main attraction in Hahnenklee is the unusual **Gustav-Adolf-Kirche** (Gustav-Adolf Church; 1907), a Norwegian-style wooden stave church with an interior of Byzantine and Scandinavian features.

In winter, most visitors come for the downhill and cross-country skiing on the Bocksberg. Day tickets for the *Seilbahn* (cable car) and lifts cost €17. **Snow-Fun** (☎ 2172) is the main equipment-hire place in town – head to Hindenburgstrasse 4 for nordic skis, and Rathausstrasse 6 for snowboards and alpine skis. The **Berghotel** (☎ 2505; An der Buchwiese 1) is another ski-hire option. **Hahnenkleer Skischule** (☎ 0175-507 9138; Rathausstrasse 6), alongside the cable-car station, runs various ski courses.

Hahnenklee is also popular for its hiking, with trails leading to the Bocksberg from the car park near the stave church, and longer trails to Goslar (trail 2G, blue dot, 11km) via Windsattel and Glockenberg. Remember to take the Harzclub 1:50,000 walking map and be prepared for changing weather conditions.

Sleeping & Eating

The tourist office has a free reservation service and can book apartments for longer stays.

DJH hostel (☎ 2256; jh-hahnenklee@djh-hannover.de; Hahnenkleer Strasse 13; under/over 26yr €14.80/17.50; ✕) The 120-bed DJH hostel is about 2.5km south of town in Bockswiese. The rural flavour and outdoor summer seating area make it attractive.

Hotel Hahnenkleer Hof (☎ 511 10; www.hahnenkleerhof.de; Parkstrasse 24a; s €57-77, d €114-124; P ✕ ⏦) This large hotel built in Swiss-chalet style caters for conference guests and tourists. It's a good option for those in wheelchairs, and it has one of the best eating options in town, with an informal café lounge and a panorama restaurant where German and international dishes can be enjoyed with a view over woodland.

Getting There & Away

Hahnenklee is just west of the B241, between Goslar and Clausthal-Zellerfeld. Bus 830 serves Hahnenklee from Goslar on the way to Clausthal-Zellerfeld. The BEX BerlinLinienBus stops here daily.

BAD HARZBURG

☎ 05322 / pop 258,000

This pretty spa town just 9km from Goslar is a magnet for visitors seeking health and curative spas. Unless you're one of the many cure-seekers, the main attraction will be the nearby Harz National Park and trails, which offer excellent access to some typically gorgeous Harz landscapes.

Information

Haus der Natur (☎ 784 337; Berliner Platz; adult/concession €2/1; ⏰ 10am-5pm Tue-Sun) Harz National Park information centre, with a small interactive exhibition that kids will enjoy most.

Spielpunkt (Herzog-Wilhelm-Strasse 42; per hr €2.50) Internet access.

Tourist-Information (☎ 753 30; www.bad-harzburg.de; Kurzentrum, Herzog-Wilhelm-Strasse 86; ⏰ 8am-8pm Mon-Fri, 9am-4pm Sat, 10am-1pm Sun May-Oct, 8am-8pm Mon-Fri, 9am-4pm Sat Nov-Apr)

Activities

A pleasant thing to do is to hike or ride to **Grosser Burgberg**, a hill that sits above Bad Harzburg and has the ruins of an 11th-century fortress built by Heinrich IV. There's a 481m-long **cable car** (☎ 753 71; adult/child return €3/1.60; ⏰ 9am-5pm May-Oct, to 4pm Nov-Apr) that goes up to the fortress, and it can be reached by walking up Bummelallee to the Kurpark.

Marked hiking trails lead into the national park from Berliner Platz and Grosser Burgberg, the latter just over 3km from Berliner Platz on foot. Among the many walks are those from Berliner Platz to Sennhütte (1.3km), Molkenhaus (3km) and scenic Rabenklippe (7km), overlooking the Ecker Valley. All destinations have restaurants; a board inside the cable-car station indicates which ones are open.

From Grosser Burgberg you can take the Kaiserweg trail, which leads to Torfhaus and connects to the Brocken. A marked trail also leads to the 23m-high **Radau Waterfall**, some 7km from Grosser Burgberg. If snow conditions are good, it's possible to ski cross-country to/from Torfhaus (p243), which has equipment-hire facilities.

Sleeping & Eating

Several good hotels are situated west of the tourist office on Am Stadtpark.

Villa Märchen (☎ 2672; www.villa-maerchen.de; Am Stadtpark 43; s €33.50-37, d €52-58; ✕) Rooms in this *pension* with friendly young management are spotless and have furnishings in light tones; some have a balcony.

Villa Feise (☎ 967 00; www.villa-feise.de; Rudolf-Huch-Strasse 20; s €40, d €65-70; P ✕) Given its proximity to the promenade, this place is great value, offering much more comfort and style than some places that charge double the rate. If you don't have a room with a balcony, there's a nice garden down below.

Ringhotel Braunschweiger Hof (☎ 7880; www.hotel-braunschweiger-hof.de; Herzog-Wilhelm-Strasse 54; s €86-116, d €132-168; P ✕ ⏦) You can relax in the lap of luxury here, where you'll find fine rooms, lots of wellness deals, a lovely garden and a top-class restaurant downstairs (mains €11.50-48).

Hexenklause (☎ 2982; Berliner Platz 3; mains €8-16; ⏰ 11am-10pm) This longtime local favourite serves traditional fare that's a notch above the pack along the promenade.

Getting There & Around

The Hauptbahnhof and bus station are on the northern side of town, a 10-minute walk from the pedestrian mall. Bus 810 leaves regularly for Goslar, and bus 877 heads for Wernigerode (€3.40, 50 minutes). Bus 820 shuttles almost hourly to Braunlage via Radau Waterfall and Torfhaus. Frequent train services link Bad Harzburg with Goslar, Hanover, Braunschweig and Wernigerode.

Bad Harzburg is on the A395 to Braunschweig; the B4 and B6 lead to Torfhaus and Wernigerode, respectively.

BRAUNLAGE

☎ 05520 / pop 6000

Braunlage, though not the prettiest of Harz towns, is the area's largest winter-sports centre and is very popular with hikers in summer. The skiing here is the best in the region, although it can get crowded on the slopes when the snow is good.

Orientation

Braunlage's heart is the junction of Elbingeröder Strasse and the main thoroughfare, Herzog-Wilhelm-Strasse. The latter changes names several times.

Information

Post office (Herzog-Wilhelm-Strasse 14) Post agency inside the souvenir shop.
Spielhalle (Elbingeröder Strasse 5; per 30 min €1.50; ⊙ 9am-11pm Mon-Sat, 11am-11pm Sun) Internet access.
Tourist-Info (☎ 930 70; www.braunlage.de; Kurverwaltung, Elbingeröder Strasse 17; ⊙ 9am-12.30pm & 2-5pm Mon-Fri, 9.30am-12.30pm Sat)
Volksbank (☎ 8030; Herzog-Wilhelm-Strasse 19) ATM.

Activities

HIKING

The tourist office has two good free leaflets: *Wandervorschläge Rund Um Braunlage* (Hiking Suggestions Around Braunlage), covering trails in the area and restaurant stops; and *Wanderwege Braunlage* (Braunlage Hiking Trails). If you are heading east, a trail follows the B27 to Elend (red triangle, 7km), where you can pick up the narrow-gauge railway to Wernigerode.

SKIING

A cable car will take you up the 971m **Wurmberg**, from where you can ski down or use the three lifts on the mountain itself. Return

tickets cost €10.50. Downhill ski equipment can be rented at **Café-Restaurant Zur Seilbahn** (☎ 600) from €21 a day, or at one of the many ski shops dotted around town. Braunlage has several smaller pistes, groomed cross-country trails and a ski jump where high fliers can land on the former East German border (see boxed text, p242). Plenty of places in town offer cross-country skis for hire.

Sleeping & Eating

DJH hostel (☎ 2238; jh-braunlage@djh-hannover.de; Von-Langen-Strasse 28; under/over 26yr €15.30/18.30; ⊠) This DJH *Jugendherberge* is central to town and located on the edge of spruce forest about 300m south of Elbingeröder Strasse, near hiking and skiing trails. Facilities are good for those travelling with babies.

Pension Parkblick (☎ 1237; Elbingeröder Strasse 13; s/d €25/50; Ⓟ) The interior of this *pension* is dowdy and furnished like grandma's living room, but it's good value and very central.

Romantik Hotel Zur Tanne (☎ 931 20; www.tanne-braunlage.de; Herzog-Wilhelm-Strasse 8; s €52-149, d €80-199; Ⓟ ⊠) The three categories of rooms in this hotel make it a crossover from the midrange to the high end. It begins with the rustic stuff and climbs to the giddy heights of luxury.

relaxa Hotel Harz-Wald Braunlage (☎ 8070; braunlage@relaxa-hotel.de; Karl-Röhrig-Strasse 5a; s €75, d €80-199; Ⓟ ⊠ 🛒) Located on the northern edge of town, this modern hotel has lots of wellness extras and free use of city bikes. Nonguests can hire mountain and city bikes here (€8 to €15 per day). Rooms come with balcony.

Omas Kaffeestube und Weinstube (☎ 2390; Elbingeröder Strasse 2; fortified coffee €4.50; ⊙ 11am-6pm) Coffee with shots of firewater or liqueur is the speciality in this café, which serves cakes and some light meals in a very olde-worlde atmosphere.

Puppe Brotzeitstube (☎ 487; Am Brunnen 2; gourmet snacks €5-11.90; ⊙ 9am-8pm Mon-Sat, 11am-8pm Sun) This unusual gourmet sandwich shop does German-style open sandwiches with local cuts of ham, sausage and other products for eat-in, takeaway or picnic.

Getting There & Away

Bus 850 runs to St Andreasberg from the Von-Langen-Strasse or Eissporthalle stops. For Torfhaus and Bad Harzburg, take bus 820 from the Eissporthalle stop, which is near Elbingeröder Strasse. The B4 runs north to Torfhaus and Bad Harzburg. The B27 leads southwest to the St Andreasberg turn-off and northeast to the eastern Harz.

ST ANDREASBERG
☎ 05582 / pop 2500

Known for its mining museums, clean air and hiking and skiing options, this resort sits on a broad ridge surrounded by wistful mountains, 10km west of Braunlage. St Andreasberg is a pleasant town that offers a quiet base for trips into the national park; it's wonderful to visit during a warm snowless spring or a 'golden October'.

The **tourist office** (☎ 803 36; www.sankt-andreasberg.de; Am Kurpark 9; ♥ 9am-12.30pm & 2-5pm Mon, Tue, Thu & Fri, 9am-12.30pm Wed, 10am-noon Sat, 11am-noon Sun Jan-Oct, 10am-noon Mon-Fri & 2-4pm Mon, Tue, Thu & Fri Nov-Dec) is in the split-level, wheelchair-friendly Kurverwaltung building.

Most shops close for several hours around noon.

Sights & Activities

German-language tours of the interesting **Grube Samson Mining Museum** (☎ 1249; tours €4.50; ♥ 8.30am-4.30pm, tours at 11am & 2.30pm) take you 20m down to view early forms of mine transportation. Follow the signs from Dr-Willi-Bergmann-Strasse.

The nearby Catharina Neufang **tunnel** (admission €2.75; ♥ 1.45pm Mon-Sat) includes a mining demonstration, and the **Harzer Roller Kanarien-Museum** (Canary Museum; admission adult/child €2.75/2; ♥ 8.30am-4pm Mon-Sat, 10.30am-4pm Sun) is probably worthy of its claim of being the world's only museum dedicated to canaries (used in the mines). The display takes you back to the 15th century, and the first miners' 'friends' came to St Andreasberg in 1730 with workers from Tyrol.

The skiing in St Andreasberg can be excellent. The closest piste is on **Mathias-Schmidt-Berg** (☎ 265); day passes cost €16 or you pay €1.50 per ride. You'll also find pistes that have lifts out of town on **Sonnenberg** (☎ 513). A company that rents out ski and snowboard equipment is **Sport Pläschke** (☎ 260; www.skischule-harz.de; Dr-Willi-Bergmann-Strasse 10).

Cross-country skiers should pick up the *Wintersportkarte* map (€1) from the tourist office, because it shows both groomed and ungroomed trails as well as some good ski hikes.

The Rehberger Grabenweg is a unique hiking trail that leads into the Harz National Park and to the **Rehberger Grabenhaus** (☎ 789; ♥ closed Mon), a forest café 3km from St Andreasberg and only accessible on foot. In the evening from late December to early March you can sit in the darkened café and watch wild deer feeding outside. To avoid disturbing the animals, visitors have to arrive by 5pm and aren't let out until 7pm. Bring a torch (flashlight) to find your way back.

There are exhibits on the area's cultural history, plus park information and a multimedia show in the **Nationalparkhaus** (☎ 923 074; www.nationalpark-harz.de; Erzwäsche 1; ♥ 9am-5pm Apr-Oct, 10am-5pm Nov-Mar).

Sleeping & Eating

Hostel (☎ 809 948; www.harz-herbergen.de; Am Gesehr 37; under/over 26yr €25/28) This independent hostel is popular with school and other groups. Prices include full board.

Pension Haus am Kurpark (☎ 1010; www.haus.am.kurpark.harz.de; Am Kurpark 1; s €23-31, d €40-56) Bears on scooters and skis on walls adorn this quiet, friendly and very well-run *pension* just outside the park. There's a choice of shared and private bathrooms.

Pension Holloch (☎ 1005; www.pension-holloch.harz.de; Glückauf-Weg 21; s €25-32, d €50-64) Most rooms have a balcony overlooking the valley and ski piste, so you can see who's breaking a leg – or someone else's – from this very comfortable, well-managed and friendly *pension*. Best to book ahead.

La Piazza (☎ 999 987; Schützenstrasse 35; pizza & pasta €5-7, mains €8.50-14; ♥ noon-3pm & 5.30-11pm) On the main street, this restaurant will give you the carbohydrate boost you need to tackle or recover from the pistes. The outdoor seating is popular in summer. For delivery the minimum order is €9.

Getting There & Away

Bus 850 runs between St Andreasberg and Braunlage. Bus 861 is a direct service that runs several times daily to Goslar. The frequent bus 840 runs to Clausthal-Zellerfeld.

St Andreasberg can be reached via the B27, which winds along the scenic Oder Valley from Bad Lauterberg to Braunlage. The L519 (Sonnenberg) leads north to the B242 and Clausthal-Zellerfeld, to the B4 and Bad Harzburg, and to Goslar (B241 or the B498 along the Oker Valley).

HARZ MOUNTAINS

CLAUSTHAL-ZELLERFELD

☎ 05323 / pop 15,300

Formerly two settlements, this small university town was once the region's most important mining centre. Its main attractions are mineral and spiritual: an excellent mining museum and a spectacular wooden church. There are over 60 lakes in the vicinity, mostly created for the mines, and almost all are now suitable for swimming.

Orientation & Information

As in many similar linear towns in the Harz, Clausthal-Zellerfeld's main street changes names several times, with Kronenplatz as the hub. Clausthal lies to the south, while Zellerfeld begins just beyond Bahnhofstrasse, roughly 1km to the north.

The **tourist office** (☎ 810 24; www.harztourismus.com; Bergstrasse 31; ☙ 9am-1pm & 2-5pm Mon-Fri, 10am-noon Sat) is near the Oberharzer Bergwerksmuseum, and **Harzklub HQ** (☎ 817 58; www.harzklub.de; ☙ 9am-noon Mon-Fri) is in the former train station, 10 and 15 minutes on foot respectively north of Kronenplatz.

Sights

The **Oberharzer Bergwerksmuseum** (☎ 989 50; www.oberharzerbergwerksmuseum.de; Bornhardtstrasse 16; adult/concession €4/2; ☙ 9am-5pm) has an interesting open-air exhibition of mine buildings and mining methods, including a horse-driven carousel that was used to power a lift into the mine. The museum has a good English-language brochure with background information and explanations on the different buildings, and there are tours in German (translators are available) that take you into the depths. A 26km underground viaduct used to drain one of the other mines in the region, and part of this was used to transport ore below ground in vessels to the Ottiliae-Schacht shaft in Clausthal. Today an original miniature **train** (adult/child €4.50/2.25; ☙ at 11am Sat, 11am & 2pm Sun May-Oct), which was used to transport miners overland to the Ottiliae-Schacht shaft, leaves from the former train station.

South of Kronenplatz and in the technical university is the **Geosammlung** (☎ 722 737; Adolph-Roemer-Strasse 2a; adult/concession €1.50/1; ☙ 9.30am-12.30pm Tue, Wed & Fri, 9.30am-12.30pm & 2-5pm Thu, 10am-1pm Sun), Germany's largest collection of mineral samples. It also has a section on evolution and fossils.

Very close by is the baroque **Marktkirche Zum Heiligen Geist** (☎ 7005; Hindenburgplatz 1; ☙ 10am-12.30pm & 2-5pm Mon-Sat, 1-5pm Sun), which was consecrated in 1642 and – another local record – is the country's largest wooden church. It is situated just off Adolph-Roemer-Strasse, opposite the imposing yellow Oberbergamt.

Sleeping & Eating

Hotel Zellerfelder Hof (☎ 3745; Marktstrasse 13; s/d €35/50; P) The singles are small, but otherwise this hotel in Zellerfeld, near the Oberharzer Bergwerksmuseum and tourist office, offers very good value and all the essential comforts. Steaks in the steakhouse downstairs start from €9.80.

Goldene Krone (☎ 9300; goldene.krone@t-online.de; Am Kronenplatz 3; s €50-65, d €75-120; P) Though moderately priced, this hotel is not only the best address in town, it's right in the middle of it. Rooms are bright, a very decent size and decorated in tasteful shades of blue. The Italian restaurant downstairs is one of the best around, too, with pasta, pizza and meat dishes (pasta €5.50, mains €9 to €14).

Restaurant Glück Auf (☎ 1616; An der Marktkirche 7; mains €9-15; ☙ 11.30am-2.30pm & 5.30-9.30pm Thu-Tue) This outstanding traditional restaurant established in 1720 is almost an attraction in itself: the historic banquet hall holds about 280 people and has galleries and even a stage at one end. The menu has a good choice of game. Downstairs is a surprise for the kids on the theme of Harz folk tales.

Getting There & Around

Regular bus services leave 'Bahnhof', the former train station, and Kronenplatz for Goslar (bus 830). Catch bus 840 for St Andreasberg and bus 831 for Altenau. The B241 leads north to Goslar and south to Osterode, while the B242 goes east to Braunlage and St Andreasberg. To reach the A7, take the B242 west.

EASTERN HARZ

WERNIGERODE

☎ 03943 / pop 35,000

A bustling, attractive town on the northern edge of the Harz, Wernigerode is a good starting point for exploring the eastern regions of the Harz National Park. The winding streets of the Altstadt are flanked by pretty half-timbered houses, and high above the Altstadt hovers a romantic ducal castle from the 12th century.

History is carved deeply into the features of this town. During the early Middle Ages it was hampered by centuries of royal squabbles. Fires followed in the 15th and 16th centuries, changing the face of Wernigerode forever, and later the Thirty Years' War took its population to the brink and back.

Today it is the northern terminus of the steam-powered narrow-gauge Harzquerbahn (see boxed text, p241), which has chugged along the breadth of the Harz for almost a century; the line to the summit of the Brocken (1142m), northern Germany's highest mountain, also starts here.

Orientation

The bus and train stations are on the northern side of town at the end of Rudolf-Breitscheid-Strasse. The ducal castle is southeast of Markt.

Information

Harz-Klinikum Wernigerode (☎ 610; Ilsenburger Strasse 15) Medical services.

Police (☎ 6530; Nicolaiplatz 4)

Post office (cnr Marktstrasse & Kanzleistrasse)

Spielcenter Jackpot (Johann-Sebastian-Bach-Strasse 5; per hr €3; ☉ 8am-10pm Mon-Sat, 10am-10pm Sun) Internet access.

Volksbank (Breite Strasse 4) Banking services and ATM.

Wernigerode Tourismus (☎ 633 035; www.werni gerode-tourismus.de; Nicolaiplatz 1; ☉ 9am-7pm Mon-Fri, 10am-4pm Sat, 10am-3pm Sun May-Oct, 9am-6pm Mon-Fri, 10am-4pm Sat, 10am-3pm Sun Nov-Apr) Tourist information and room-booking service.

Zimmervermittlung und Information am Krummelschen Haus (☎ 606 000; Krummelsches Haus, Breite Strasse 72; ☉ 10am-6pm May-Oct, to 4pm Nov-Apr) Private tourist information and room-booking service.

Sights

ALTSTADT

The colourful and spectacular towered **Rathaus** on Markt began life as a theatre around 1277, but what you see today is mostly late-Gothic from the 16th century. The artisan who carved the town hall's 33 wooden figures was said to have fallen foul of the authorities and added a few mocking touches. The neo-Gothic **fountain** (1848) was

dedicated to charitable nobles, whose names and coats of arms are immortalised on it.

One of the prettiest half-timbered houses in town is in the cosy Oberpfarrkirchhof, which surrounds the **Sylvestrikirche**; here you'll find **Gadenstedtsches Haus** (1582), with its Renaissance oriel. The **Harz Museum** (☎ 654 454; Klint 10; adult/concession €2/1.30; ☉ 10am-5pm Mon-Sat), a short walk away, has some interesting exhibits on local geology, history and half-timbered houses.

Crossing Markt to Breite Strasse, the pretty **Café Wien** building (1583) at No 4 is a worthwhile stopover for both architectural and gastronomical reasons. The carved façade of the **Krummelsches Haus** depicts various countries symbolically; America is portrayed, reasonably enough, as a naked woman riding an armadillo.

Nearby is the **Krell'sche Schmiede** (☎ 601 772; www.schmiedemuseum-wernigerode.de; Breite Strasse 95; adult/concession €2.50/1.50; ☉ 10am-2pm Sat), a historic smithy built in 1678 in the south German baroque style.

Just off Breite Strasse you'll find the **Feuerwehrmuseum** (Fire Brigade Museum; ☎ 654 450; Steingrube 3; ☉ 2.30-4.30pm Thu, 2.30-5pm Sat), a collection of fire-fighting machines from 1890 onwards staffed by volunteers of almost the same vintage!

SCHLOSS

Originally built in the 12th century to protect German Kaisers on hunting expeditions in the Harz, **Schloss Wernigerode** (☎ 553 030; www .schloss-wernigerode.de; adult/concession/child €4.50/4/2.50; ☉ 10am-6pm May-Oct, 10am-4pm Tue-Fri, to 6pm Sat & Sun Nov-Apr) was enlarged over the years to reflect late-Gothic and Renaissance tastes. Its fairy-tale façade came courtesy of Count Otto of Stolberg-Wernigerode in the 19th century. The museum inside includes portraits of Kaisers, beautiful panelled rooms with original furnishings and the opulent **Festsaal** (Banquet Hall).

The stunning **Schlosskirche** (1880) has an altar and pulpit made of French marble. You can climb the castle **tower** (admission €1), but the views from the castle or restaurant terrace (best appreciated late in the day) are free and just as spectacular.

You can walk (1.5km) or take a Bimmelbahn wagon ride (adult/child €4.50/2 return) from Marktstrasse. In summer, horse-drawn carts make the trek from Markt.

HARZ MOUNTAINS

Activities

The beautiful deciduous **forest** behind the castle is crisscrossed with lovely trails and *Forstwege* (forestry tracks). Wernigerode is also a good starting point for hikes and bike rides into the Harz National Park. **Bad-Bikes** (☎ 626 868; www.badbikes-online.de; Grosse Bergstrasse 3) rents mountain and city bikes for €7.50 per day.

Festivals & Events

The **Harz-Gebirgslauf** (☎ 633 329; www.harz -gebirgslauf.de) is an annual charity hiking and running event held on the second Saturday in October, including a Brocken marathon. An annual festival of music and theatre is held in the castle from early July to mid-August.

Sleeping

DJH hostel (☎ 606 176; jh-wernigerode@djh-sachsen -anhalt.de; Am Eichberg 5; dm under/over 26yr €15.50/18.20, s €28.50; ✗) On the edge of the forest about 2.5km west of town in Hasserode, the renovated DJH hostel has three- and four-bed dorms with bathrooms. Take bus 1 or 4 towards Hasserode.

Hotel und Restaurant zur Post (☎ 690 40; www .hotelzurpost.de; Marktstrasse 17; s/d €49/86; Ⓟ) This is a very decent choice and great value, with bright rooms, a tiled floor and elegant furnishings in a half-timbered house.

Altwernigeroder Apparthotel (☎ 949 260; www .appart-hotel.de; Marktstrasse 14; s/d €51/75; Ⓟ ✗) This large hotel has bright and modern rooms in a former postal administrative building. There's a good sauna area and a potato restaurant downstairs.

Hotel am Anger (☎ 923 20; www.hotel-am-anger .de; Breite Strasse 92; s €50, d €90-112; Ⓟ ✗) Labyrinthine it may be, and there's an awful lot of pine forest in the 40 rooms, but this place is pleasant and some rooms have views of the castle.

Parkhotel Fischer (☎ 691 350; Mauergasse 1; s €55-65, d €90-105; Ⓟ ✗) The rooms are good, but it's the deliciously tranquil indoor swimming pool (plus sauna) with Roman-style pillars and a worrying rubber crocodile that are the magnet here.

Hotel Gothisches Haus (☎ 6750; gothisches -haus@travelcharme.com; Am Markt 1; s €94-114, d €136-196, ste €250-270; Ⓟ ✗) The warm Tuscan colours and thoughtful design of this luxury hotel make it very attractive. There's a log fire downstairs in the Kaminbar, and evening restaurants and a wine cellar to explore. Note that suites have waterbeds.

Eating

Brauhaus (☎ 695 727; www.brauhaus-wernigerode.de; Breite Strasse 24; mains €7-14; ⏰ 11.30am-late) This is an enormous, multilevel pub and bistro with meat and vegetarian dishes, and – on Saturday from 9pm – a dance floor upstairs. It's probably the best all-round option for a meal and drink, or to get down into Sunday morning.

Café am Markt & Lounge (☎ 604 030; Marktplatz 6-8; mains €7.50-12; ⏰ 8am-late Mon-Sat, from 9am Sun) This interesting all-rounder started life as a café, but seems to have bred with an Italian restaurant next door (Baldinis; similar menu) to beget a small lounge area and occasional late-night venue (upstairs).

Altes Amtshaus (☎ 501 200; Burgberg 15; mains €7-18; ⏰ 5-11pm Mon, 11.30am-11pm Tue-Sun) Game and traditional dishes for everyman are served in this former ducal courthouse with a lovely ambience.

Krummelsches Haus (☎ 602 626; Breite Strasse 72; mains €8-13; ⏰ 11am-11pm) Game, if you're game, beef and other meats, and Bohemian favourites are served at this traditional bistro in a building with a spectacular façade.

Weisser Hirsch (☎ 602 020; www.hotel-weisser-hirsch .de; Marktplatz 5; mains €10-27) The crisp white tablecloths and glistening cutlery offer a foretaste of what's to follow at this restaurant, which is the finest eating establishment in town. Expect tradition with a creative edge. Three- to five-course menus are also available (€23.50 to €43).

Drinking

Tommi's Pub (☎ 632 162; www.tommis-pub.de; Marktstrasse 5) You can enjoy a Guinness and watch a football match, or even catch a spot of Irish folk music, in this rustic pub about the size of a large living-room.

Humphrey (☎ 905 445; Grosse Bergstrasse 2a) Bogart is the theme here: he does Cajun/Tex-Mex food, popular drinks and even has a personable dance space upstairs on Friday and Saturday nights where Sam spins it again.

Ars Vivendi (☎ 626 606; Bahnhofstrasse 33; ⏰ from 8pm Fri & Sat) Beyond the muscle-clad bouncers you'll find a cocktail bar where the hopeful young, the restless old and the wistful inbetweens tug on straws while hanging onto the bar in décor that might jar.

NARROW-GAUGE RAILWAYS

Fans of old-time trains or unusual journeys will be in their element on any of the three narrow-gauge railways crossing the Harz. This 140km integrated network – the largest in Europe – is served by 25 steam and 10 diesel locomotives, which tackle gradients of up to 1:25 (40%) and curves as tight as 60m in radius. Most locomotives date from the 1950s, but eight historic models, some from as early as 1897, are proudly rolled out for special occasions.

The network, a legacy of the GDR, consists of three lines. The *Harzquerbahn* runs 60km on a north–south route between Wernigerode and Nordhausen. The serpentine 14km between Wernigerode and Drei Annen Hohne includes 72 bends; you'll get dropped off on the edge of Harz National Park.

From the junction at Drei Annen Hohne, the *Brockenbahn* begins the steep climb to Schierke and the Brocken. Direct services to the Brocken can also be picked up from Wernigerode and Nordhausen, or at stations en route; tickets cost €16/24 single/return from all stations.

The third service is the *Selketalbahn*, which begins in Quedlinburg and runs to Eisfelder Talmühle or Hasselfelde. At Eisfelder Tal, you can change trains for other lines. The picturesque *Selketalbahn* crosses the plain to Gernrode and follows Wellbach, a creek with a couple of good swimming holes, through deciduous forest to Mägdesprung, before joining the Selke Valley and climbing past Alexisbad to high plains around Friedrichshöhe, Stiege and beyond.

Passes for three/five days cost €40/45 for adults (children half-price). Timetables and information can be picked up from **Harzer Schmalspurbahnen** (☎ 03943-5580; www.hsb-wr.de; Friedrichstrasse 151, Wernigerode).

Brauhaus (opposite) is an all-purpose bar and dance club.

Getting There & Away

Direct buses run to most major towns in this region; the timetable (€2) available from the **WVB bus office** (☎ 5640; www.wvb-gmbh.de; Hauptbahnhof) includes a train schedule. Bus 253 runs to Blankenburg and Thale, while bus 257 serves Drei Annen Hohne and Schierke.

There are frequent trains to Goslar (€7.60, 50 minutes) and Halle (€17, 1½ hours). Change at Halberstadt for Quedlinburg (€7.60, 50 minutes) and Thale (€9.10, one hour).

Getting Around

Buses 1 and 2 run from the bus station to the Rendezvous bus stop just north of the Markt, connecting with bus 3. Tickets cost €0.90. For a taxi, call ☎ 633 053.

RÜBELAND CAVES

Rübeland, a small town just 13km south of Wernigerode, has a couple of interesting **caves** (☎ 039454-491 32; www.harzer-hoehlen.de; adult/child €5/3.50; ☼ 9am-5.30pm Jul & Aug, 9am-4.30pm Feb-Jun & Sep-Oct, 9am-3.30pm Nov-Jan). Admission gets you a guided tour, in German, of either cave (note that only one is open from November to April).

Baumannshöhle was formed about 500,000 years ago, and the first tourists visited in 1646, just over a century after its 'rediscovery'. Human presence in the caves dates back 40,000 years. The Goethesaal, which has a pond, is sometimes used for concerts and plays.

Hermannshöhle was formed 350,000 years ago and was rediscovered in the 19th century. Its stalactites and stalagmites are spectacular, especially in the transparent Kristallkammer. Salamanders, introduced from southern Europe by researchers, inhabit one pond.

WVB bus 265 leaves Wernigerode for Rübeland hourly. You can join the magnificent Bodetal trail (blue triangle, 16km) to Thale at Rübeland, crossing the Rappbodetalsperre, a 106m-high dam wall across the Harz's largest reservoir, on foot.

If driving from Wernigerode, take the B244 south to Elbingerode, then the B27 east.

SCHIERKE

☎ 039455 / pop 1000

Situated at 650m in the hills at the foot of the Brocken and just 16km west of Wernigerode, Schierke is a lovely village and the last stop for the *Brockenbahn* before it climbs the summit. Schierke has an upper town on the main road to the Brocken and a lower town

BREAKFAST WITH A VIEW

Uncomfortably close to the Iron Curtain during the Cold War, Schierke was once sealed off from the outside world by a 5km restricted zone. Its inhabitants had to pass through strict control points to enter and leave. How strange it was, therefore, that Schierke was also a vantage point to watch ski jumpers zipping through capitalist air space from the ski jump in Braunlage. Jumpers used to land right on the border in those days. One or two tables in the breakfast room at the Waldschlösschen hotel (right) offer a distant view of the jump today.

down in the valley of the Kalte Bode River. It is also a popular starting point for exploring the Harz National Park and the home of the ubiquitous 'Schierker Feuerstein' *digestif*.

Information

DAV Basislager Brocken (☎ 515 46; www.dav -basislager-brocken.de; Mühlenweg 1; ☺ 9am-1pm) Local HQ of the German Alpine Club; offers outdoor sports and equipment hire.

Kurverwaltung (☎ 8680; Brockenstrasse 10; ☺ 9am-noon & 1-4pm Mon-Fri, 10am-noon & 2-4pm Sat, 10am-noon Sun) Tourist information.

Nationalparkhaus Schierke (☎ 814 44; Brocken-strasse 10; ☺ 8.30am-4.30pm) Hiking brochures and national park information.

Activities

Schierke is a popular place for climbing, offering all levels of difficulty on nearby cliffs. **DAV Basislager Brocken** (☎ 515 46; www .dav-basislager-brocken.de; Mühlenweg 1; ☺ 9am-1pm) hires out climbing gear, mountain bikes and snow shoes, as well as ski equipment for the 70km of groomed trails. Courses are also offered, and there's a climbing wall and abseiling area.

You can hike to the Brocken via the bitumen Brockenstrasse (12km), closed to private cars and motorcycles. More interesting is the 7km hike via Eckerloch. Pick up the free *Wanderführer 2* hiking guide from the Nationalparkhaus. Marked trails also lead to the rugged rock formations of Feuersteinklippen (30 minutes from the tourist office) and Schnarcherklippen (1½ hours).

Horse-drawn wagons travel from Schierke to the Brocken and cost adult/child €20/10

return. **Dirk Klaus** (☎ 512 12) also operates horse-drawn sleigh services in winter.

On the night of 30 April, Walpurgisnacht (see boxed text, p249), Schierke attracts about 25,000 visitors, most of whom set off on walking tracks to the Brocken.

Sleeping & Eating

There is plenty of accommodation in town, particularly along Borckenstrasse, but you may need to book ahead.

Hotel König (☎ 383; www.harz-hotel-koenig.de; Kirchberg 15; s €33-50, d €50-70) This hotel has a remarkable carved foyer and offers clean and comfortable rooms, with or without bathrooms (some have a veranda), and a decent restaurant.

Waldschlösschen (☎ 8670; www.waldschloesschen -schierke.de; Hermann-Löns-Weg 1; s €59, d €85-115; P ☒) The best in town for service, comfort and facilities, this excellent hotel tacked onto a *Jugendstil* (Art Nouveau) villa has an Italian panorama-style restaurant and ultra-modern rooms. See the boxed text, left.

Getting There & Around

WVB bus 876 runs six times daily to Braunlage via Elend. Bus 257 between Wernigerode and Braunlage is also quite frequent and connects with the 876. Narrow-gauge railway services between Wernigerode and Schierke cost €5/9 single/return. Driving from the west, take the B27 from Braunlage and turn off at Elend. From Wernigerode, take Friedrichstrasse.

MITTELBAU DORA

From late in 1943, thousands of slave labourers (mostly Russian, French and Polish prisoners of war) toiled under horrific conditions digging tunnels in the chalk hills north of Nordhausen. From a 20km labyrinth of tunnels, they produced the V1 and V2 rockets that rained destruction on London, Antwerp and other cities during the final stages of WWII, when Hitler's grand plan became to conduct war from production plants below the ground.

The camp, called Mittelbau Dora, was created as a satellite of the Buchenwald concentration camp after British bombers destroyed the missile plants in Peenemünde in far northeastern Germany. During the last two years of the war, at least 20,000 prisoners died at Dora, many having survived Auschwitz only to be worked to death here.

HARZ MOUNTAINS

The US army reached the gates in April 1945, cared for survivors and removed all missile equipment before turning the area over to the Russians two months later. Much of the technology was later employed in the US space programme.

After years of mouldering away in the GDR period, the memorial has gradually been improved over the years to give a deeper insight into the horror of Hitler's undertaking. In late 2006 a new exhibition building was opened with a multilanguage library, a café and various new exhibits.

The horrible truth of the place permeates the memorial, and a visit may be among the most unforgettable experiences you have in Germany.

Orientation & Information

Mittelbau Dora is 5km north of Nordhausen, a dull town of interest only as regards changing trains.

Visitors have independent access to the grounds, crematorium and **museum** (☎ 03631-495 820; www.dora.de; admission free; ⏱ 10am-6pm Tue-Sun Apr-Sep, to 4pm Oct-Mar). The tunnels, which are the diameter of an aircraft hangar, are accessible by guided tour. Within the dank walls you can see partially assembled rockets that have lain untouched for over 50 years.

Free 90-minute tours operate at 11am and 2pm from Tuesday to Friday, and at 11am, 1pm and 3pm on weekends (also 4pm April to September).

Getting There & Away

The *Harzquerbahn* links Nordhausen with Wernigerode (€9, 2¾ hours). The nearest stop to Dora is Nordhausen–Krimderode, which is served by almost hourly trains from Nordhausen-Nord (11 minutes), next to the main station.

From the Krimderode stop, cross the tracks and walk south along Goetheweg, which curves and becomes Kohnsteinweg. Follow this for 1km towards the unassuming hill and you are at the camp.

Trains run to Halle (€15, 1¾ hours) and to Göttingen (€18, 1½ hours) from Nordhausen.

BROCKEN & TORFHAUS

There are prettier landscapes and hikes in the Harz, but the 1142m Brocken is what draws the crowds: about 50,000 on a summer's day.

When he wasn't exploring mines, Goethe also scaled the mountain – in stockings.

Goetheweg from Torfhaus

The 8km Goetheweg trail to the Brocken from the western Harz starts at Torfhaus. Easier than other approaches, it initially takes you through bog, follows an historic aqueduct once used to regulate water levels for the mines, then crosses the Kaiserweg, a sweaty 11km trail from Bad Harzburg. Unfortunately, your next stop will be a dead forest, though the trail becomes steep and more interesting as you walk along the former border. From 1945 to 1989 the Harz region was a frontline in the Cold War, and the Brocken was used by the Soviets as a military base. For 28 years the summit was off limits and was virtually the only mountain in the world that couldn't be climbed. Hike along the train line above soggy moorland to reach the open, windy summit, where you can enjoy the view, eat pea soup and *Bockwurst*, and think of Goethe and Heine.

On top is the **Brockenhaus** (☎ 039455-500 05; www.nationalpark-brockenhaus.de; adult €4, concession €3-3.50, child €2; ⏱ 9.30am-5pm), with café, interactive displays and a viewing platform, plus an **alpine garden** and a 2.5km trail following what was once a wall around the summit.

Torfhaus itself is a good starting point for **cross-country skiing** or winter ski treks, with plenty of equipment available for hire. Downhill skiing is limited to 1200m (on two pistes); one recommended route is the Kaiserweg. Make sure you pack a good map and take all precautions. The **Nationalparkhaus** (☎ 05320-263; www.torfhaus .info; Torfhaus 21; ⏱ 9am-5pm Apr-Oct, 10am-4pm Nov-Mar) has information on the park.

Getting There & Away

Bus 820 stops at Torfhaus on the well-served Bad Harzburg–Braunlage route.

QUEDLINBURG

☎ 03946 / pop 23,600

With its intact Altstadt and over 1400 half-timbered houses dating from six centuries ago, Quedlinburg is a highlight of any trip to the Harz. In 1994 the city became a Unesco World Heritage site; since then, work to save the crumbling treasures lining its romantic cobblestone streets has gradually progressed.

In the 10th century the Reich was briefly ruled from here by two women, Theophano and Adelheid, successive guardians of the 10th-century child-king Otto III, and Quedlinburg itself is closely associated with the *Frauenstift*, a medieval foundation for widows and daughters of the nobility that enjoyed the direct protection of the Kaiser.

Although the Altstadt can get crowded in summer and on weekends, any time of year is nice for a visit.

Orientation

The circular medieval centre of the old town is a 10-minute walk from the Hauptbahnhof (central train station) along Bahnhofstrasse. To reach the Markt, follow the road around and turn left into Heiligegeiststrasse after the post office. Hohe Strasse, off the Markt, leads south to the castle.

Information

Dorothea Christiane Erxleben Clinic (☎ 9090; Ditfurter Weg 24) Medical services.

Harzerschmalspurbahnen (☎ 527 191; www.hsb-wr.de; Marktstrasse 1; ☼ 9am-6pm Mon-Fri, to 5pm Sat & Sun) Narrow-gauge railway information.

Play-Fun (☎ 4401; Breite Strasse 39; per hr €2; ☼ 9am-10pm Mon-Sat, 2-10pm Sun) Internet access.

Police (☎ 9770; Schillerstrasse 3)

Post office (Bahnhofstrasse)

Quedlinburg-Tourismus (☎ 905 625; www.quedlinburg.de; Markt 2; ☼ 9am-6.30pm Mon-Fri, 9.30am-4pm Sat, 9.30am-3pm Sun May-Oct, 9.30am-6pm

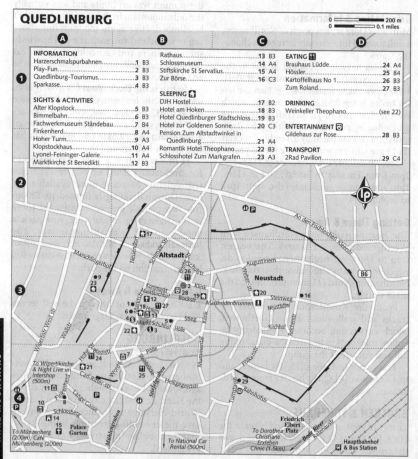

QUEDLINBURG

0 _____ 200 m
0 _____ 0.1 miles

INFORMATION	
Harzerschmalspurbahnen	1 B3
Play-Fun	2 B3
Quedlinburg-Tourismus	3 B3
Sparkasse	4 B3

SIGHTS & ACTIVITIES	
Alter Klopstock	5 B3
Bimmelbahn	6 B3
Fachwerkmuseum Ständebau	7 B4
Finkenherd	8 A4
Hoher Turm	9 A3
Klopstockhaus	10 A4
Lyonel-Feininger-Galerie	11 A4
Marktkirche St Benedikti	12 B3

Rathaus	13 B3
Schlossmuseum	14 A4
Stiftskirche St Servatius	15 A4
Zur Börse	16 C3

SLEEPING	
DJH Hostel	17 B2
Hotel am Hoken	18 B3
Hotel Quedlinburger Stadtschloss	19 B3
Hotel zur Goldenen Sonne	20 C3
Pension Zum Altstadtwinkel in Quedlinburg	21 A4
Romantik Hotel Theophano	22 B3
Schlosshotel Zum Markgrafen	23 A3

EATING	
Brauhaus Lüdde	24 A4
Hössler	25 B4
Kartoffelhaus No 1	26 B3
Zum Roland	27 B3

DRINKING	
Weinkeller Theophano	(see 22)

ENTERTAINMENT	
Gildehaus zur Rose	28 B3

TRANSPORT	
2Rad Pavillon	29 C4

Mon-Fri, 9.30am-2pm Sat Nov-Apr) Visit here for tourist information.

Sparkasse (☎ 9050; Markt 15) ATM and banking services.

Sights

AROUND THE MARKT

Built in 1320, the **Rathaus** has been expanded over the years and was adorned with a Renaissance façade in 1616. Inside, the beautiful Festsaal is decorated with a cycle of frescoes focusing on Quedlinburg's colourful history. The **Roland statue** (1426) in front of the Rathaus dates from the year Quedlinburg joined the Hanseatic League.

Behind the Rathaus is the late-Gothic **Marktkirche St Benedikti**. On the tower you'll see a small house used by town watchmen until 1901. The **mausoleum** nearby survived the relocation of the church graveyard during the 19th century.

There are some fine half-timbered buildings near Marktkirche; arguably the most spectacular is the **Gildehaus zur Rose** (1612) at Breite Strasse 39, with a richly carved and panelled interior (see p247).

Return to the Markt and walk through Schuhhof, a shoemakers' courtyard which is on the east side, and has shutters and stable-like 'gossip doors'. **Alter Klopstock** (1580), which is found at Stieg 28, has scrolled beams typical of Quedlinburg's 16th-century half-timbered houses.

From Stieg it's a short walk north along Pölle to Zwischen den Städten, a historic bridge connecting the old town and **Neustadt**, which developed alongside the town wall around 1200 when peasants fled a feudal power struggle on the land. Behind the Renaissance façade, tower and stone gables of the **Hagensches Freihaus** (1558) is now the Hotel Quedlinburger Stadtschloss (p246). Many houses in this part of town have high archways and courtyards dotted with pigeon towers. Of special note are the **Hotel zur Goldenen Sonne** building (1671; see p246) at Steinweg 11 and **Zur Börse** (1683) at No 23.

For a spectacular view of town, climb the 119 steps of **Hoher Turm** (€1) in the grounds of the Schlosshotel Zum Markgrafen (see p246).

Forty-five-minute rides through the Altstadt and Neustadt on the **Bimmelbahn** (☎ 918 888; per person €5; ☺ 10am-4pm Apr-Oct) leave hourly from Marktstrasse.

FACHWERKMUSEUM STÄNDEBAU

Germany's earliest half-timbered houses were built using high perpendicular struts. The building from 1310 that now houses the **Fachwerkmuseum Ständebau** (☎ 3828; Wordgasse 3; adult/concession €2.50/1.50; ☺ 11am-4pm Fri-Wed) is one of the oldest, and inside there are exhibits on the style and construction technique. Nearby is **Finkenherd** and a cluster of more recent half-timbered houses, built where Heinrich der Vogler (Henry the Fowler, also Heinrich I; 919–36) was said to be trapping finches when told he had been elected king.

KLOPSTOCKHAUS

The early classicist poet Friedrich Gottlieb Klopstock (1724–1803) is one of Quedlinburg's most celebrated sons. He was born in this 16th-century house, which is now a **museum** (☎ 2610; Schlossberg 12; adult/concession €3/2; ☺ 10am-4pm Wed-Sun) containing some interesting exhibits on Klopstock himself and Dorothea Erxleben (1715–62), Germany's first female doctor.

LYONEL-FEININGER-GALERIE

The **Lyonel-Feininger-Galerie** (☎ 2238; Finkenherd 5a; adult/concession €6/3; ☺ 10am-6pm Tue-Sun Apr-Oct, to 5pm Nov-Mar) houses the work of influential Bauhaus artist Lyonel Feininger (1871–1956). Feininger was born in Germany and became an American citizen. The original graphics, drawings, watercolours and sketches on display are from the period 1906 to 1936 and were hidden from the Nazis by a Quedlinburg citizen.

SCHLOSSBERG

The **Schlossberg** (☺ 6am-10pm), on a 25m-high plateau above Quedlinburg, was first graced with a church and residence under Henry the Fowler. The present-day Renaissance Schloss contains a revamped **Schlossmuseum** (☎ 2730; adult/concession €2.50/1.50; ☺ 10am-4pm Sat-Thu), with some fascinating Ottonian period exhibits dating from 919 to 1056. A multimedia display explains how the Nazis used the site for propaganda by staging a series of events to celebrate Heinrich – whose life they reinterpreted to justify their own ideology and crimes.

The 12th-century **Stiftskirche St Servatius** (☎ 709 900; adult/concession €4/3; ☺ 10am-3.30pm Tue-Sat, noon-3.30pm Sun) is one of Germany's most significant of the Romanesque period. Its treasury contains valuable reliquaries and early Bibles. The crypt has some early religious frescoes and contains the graves of Heinrich and his widow, Mathilde, along with those of the abbesses.

MÜNZENBERG & WIPERTIKIRCHE

Across Wipertistrasse, on the hill west of the castle, are the ruins of **Münzenberg**, a Romanesque convent. It was plundered during the Peasant Wars in 1525, and small houses were later built among the ruins. This fascinating hilltop settlement then became home to wandering minstrels, knife grinders and other itinerant tradespeople. At the time of research, a small museum was being created here behind the café (see right).

The **Wipertikirche** crypt was built around 1000, and the **church** (☎ 915 084; 🕙 10am-noon & 2-5pm Mon-Sat, 2-5pm Sun May-Oct) itself was used as a barn from 1812 until its restoration in the 1950s. The church is surrounded by a tranquil cemetery and grounds. The only way to see the crypt is by taking the tourist office's **Auf den Spuren der Ottonen tour** (per person €7; 🕙 10am Sat year-round, 10am Tue Apr-Oct).

Festivals & Events

A programme of classical music is held in the Stiftskirche every year from June to September. For tickets and information, contact the tourist office.

Sleeping

DJH hostel (☎ 811 703; jh-quedlinburg@djh-sachsen-anhalt .de; Neuendorf 28; under/over 26yr €14/16.70; 🗷) This excellent DJH hostel has a quiet and very central location. It's relatively small and fills quickly in summer.

Pension Zum Altstadtwinkel in Quedlinburg (☎ 919 975; www.altstadtwinkel.de; Hohe Strasse 15; s/d €35/60; 🅿 🗷) The 10 rooms in this renovated *pension* are simple but comfortable; some have exposed wooden floors.

Hotel zur Goldenen Sonne (☎ 962 50; www.hotel zurgoldenensonne.de; Steinweg 11; s €49-53, d €69-88; 🅿 🗷) Both the old and new buildings of this hotel have very decent rooms, but those in the old building are better furnished, have better windows and are mostly away from the restaurant's interior yard.

Hotel am Hoken (☎ 525 40; www.hotel-am-hoken .de; Hoken 3; s €54, d €69-84; 🗷) This highly recommended hotel off Markt has elegance, lots of traditional style and some light decorative touches. Floors and furnishings are in attractive timber.

Hotel Quedlinburger Stadtschloss (☎ 526 00; www .hotelstadtschloss.de; Bockstrasse 6/Klink 11; s €65-75, d €90-120; 🅿 🗷) The modern rooms and tasteful features and design of this hotel in a recently restored Renaissance residence make it a great midrange choice in the town centre. Enter from Bockstrasse.

Romantik Hotel Theophano (☎ 963 00; www .hoteltheophano.de; Markt 13-14; s €67, d €98-135; 🅿 🗷 💻) Each room is decorated in an individual style at this rambling, rustic hotel. Most are spacious and very comfortable, but the many staircases (no lift) and low thresholds might be a problem for some. There's internet access for nonguests as well.

Schlosshotel Zum Markgrafen (☎ 811 40; www .schlosshotel-zum-markgrafen.de; Weingarten 30; s €105, d €140-165; 🅿 🗷) Some rooms have a whirlpool, most have leadlight windows, and all are comfortable in this neo-Gothic mansion from 1904. You can chill out on the café terrace or eat and drink in the hotel restaurant/cocktail bar. Its park is locked after dark and reserved for guests.

Eating & Drinking

Hössler (☎ 915 255; Steinbrücke 21; meals €2.50-10; 🕙 9am-6pm Mon-Thu, to 10pm Fri & Sat) This is an excellent fish cafeteria with a restaurant through the passage.

Kartoffelhaus No 1 (☎ 708 334; Breite Strasse 37; mains €2.50-12; 🕙 11am-midnight) Tasty potato and grill dishes – nothing more, nothing less – are served here in large quantities. Enter from Klink.

Café Münzenberg (☎ 907 134; Münzenberg 1/17; snacks €3-10; 🕙 11am-6pm Fri-Wed) Perched upon the cliff of Münzenberg, this sleek little café has outdoor seating, a few snacks and a wonderful view of town.

Zum Roland (☎ 4532; Breite Strasse 2-6; mains €6-15; 🕙 10am-10pm) Sprawling through seven houses and seating over 700 people, this café does quite good international nosh and a delicious apple strudel.

Brauhaus Lüdde (☎ 705 206; Blasiistrasse 14; mains €10-14; 🕙 11am-midnight Mon-Sat, to 10pm Sun; 🅿) After the arrival of a coach group, the average age can soar to 70 years, decreasing slowly as the night grinds on in this lively microbrewery. Decent food and good boutique beer (despite some rather unappetizing names for the local drop) are the order of the day in Lüdde.

Weinkeller Theophano (☎ 963 00; Markt 13-14; mains €10-20, menu €28; ⏰ 6pm-midnight Mon-Sat) Everything is seasonal in this wonderful otherworldly Gothic wine cellar with some of the best food in town.

Entertainment

Unfortunately, Quedlinburg is pretty close to being an entertainment-free zone.

Gildehaus zur Rose (Breite Strasse 39; ⏰ from 9pm Fri & Sat) This is an occasional venue, but the panelled interior alone justifies a visit.

Night Live im Intershop (www.intershop-qlb.de; Wipertistrasse 9; ⏰ Fri & Sat) This club in the wasteland along Wipertistrasse has DJs, local bands and various parties for a (mostly) young crowd. It occasionally opens on Wednesday.

Getting There & Away

For trains to Wernigerode (€7.60, 25 minutes), change at Halberstadt. The narrow-gauge *Selketalbahn* runs to Gernrode (€3, 15 minutes) and beyond; other frequent trains go to Thale (€1.80, 11 minutes). The station hall closes at 6pm; you can buy tickets on the train, but use the luggage lockers wisely, as there's no access after closing.

The **QBus** (☎ 2236; www.qbus-ballenstedt.de; Hauptbahnhof) office has timetables and information on its frequent regional services. Buses to Thale alternate half-hourly with trains and leave from the bridge in front of the train station (stop 9).

The **Strasse der Romanik** (Romanesque Road; not to be confused with the Romantic Road in Bavaria) leads south to Gernrode. This theme road follows the L239 south to Gernrode and connects towns that have significant Romanesque architecture. The B6 runs west to Wernigerode, Goslar, the A395 (for Braunschweig) and the A7 between Kassel and Hanover. For Halle take the B6 east, and for Halberstadt the B79 north.

Getting Around

Cars can be hired from **National Car Rental** (☎ 770 70; Gernröder Weg 5b). There's a **taxi service** (☎ 707 070) in town. **2Rad Pavillon** (☎ 709 507; Bahnhofstrasse 16) hires out bicycles from €6 per day.

GERNRODE

☎ 039485 / pop 4000

Only 8km south of Quedlinburg, Gernrode makes an ideal day trip. Its Stiftskirche St Cyriakus is one of Germany's finest churches, while hikers, picnickers and steam-train enthusiasts will also enjoy this pretty town, which boasts the largest thermometer and *Skat* (a card game) table in the world.

The **tourist office** (☎ 354; www.gernrode.de; Suderode Strasse; ⏰ 9am-3.30pm Mon-Fri) is a 10-minute walk from the Hauptbahnhof and another 10 minutes from the town centre.

Sights & Activities

Stiftskirche St Cyriakus (☎ 275; guided tour €3; ⏰ 9am-5pm Mon-Sat, noon-5pm Sun Apr-Oct, tours 3pm daily year-round) is one of the purest examples of Romanesque architecture from the Ottonian period. Construction of the basilica, which is based on the form of a cross, was begun in 959. Especially noteworthy is the early use of alternating columns and pillars, later a common Romanesque feature. The octagonal **Taufstein** (Christening stone), whose religious motifs culminate in the Ascension, dates from 1150. In the south aisle you will find **Das Heilige Grab**, an 11th-century replica of Christ's tomb in Jerusalem. The tourist office has information on summer organ concerts and tours.

The **narrow-gauge railway** (€3, 30 minutes) from Gernrode to Mägdesprung is especially picturesque; you can break the trip at Sternhaus Ramberg, where a short trail leads through the forest to **Bremer Teich**, a pretty swimming hole with a camp site and hostel. You can also walk to Mägdesprung and beyond from Gernrode along paths beside the train track.

From the corner of Bahnhofstrasse and Marktstrasse, marked hiking trails lead east to **Burg Falkenstein** (11km), the historic castle in the Selke Valley, and west to Thale (about 13km).

Getting There & Away

Regular QBus services for Thale and Quedlinburg stop at the Hauptbahnhof and in front of the tourist office. Night buses also stop here, including the Nacht3 between Quedlinburg and Thale. The recently extended *Selketalbahn* passes through Gernrode from Quedlinburg (see boxed text, p241); buy tickets at the Hauptbahnhof.

THALE

☎ 03947 / pop 15,000

Situated below the northern slopes of the Harz Mountains, Thale is a small industrial and tourist centre. The first steelworks was established here in 1686. During the GDR era 8000 employees worked at the town's steelworks, the Eisen-und Hüttenwerk Thale. Although only 500 people work in the successor companies today, Thale retains its identity as a workers' town.

The main focus for visitors, however, is the sensational landscape of rugged cliffs and a lush river valley that makes for ideal hiking. On the two cliffs at the head of the valley are Hexentanzplatz and Rosstrappe, both magnets for postmodern pagans, who gather in grand style and numbers each year on 30 April to celebrate Walpurgisnacht (see boxed text, opposite).

Orientation & Information

Thale's two main streets are Poststrasse, which runs diagonally off Bahnhofstrasse (left from the Hauptbahnhof), and Karl-Marx-Strasse, which runs northeast to the Bode River.

The **tourist office** (☎ 2597; www.thale.de; Bahnhofstrasse 3; ☼ 7am-5pm Mon-Fri, 9am-3pm Sat & Sun) is in Friedenspark opposite the Hauptbahnhof. Pick up the English-language brochure *Thale Fabulous* or book a themed tour with a witch (€4).

There's a Sparkasse bank at the top of Karl-Marx-Strasse; the post office is in the Kaufhaus department store at No 16.

Sights

Hexentanzplatz and **Rosstrappe** are two rugged outcrops flanking the Bode Valley that once had Celtic fortresses and were used by Germanic tribes for occult rituals and sacrifices (see boxed text, opposite). The landscape also inspired the myth of Brunhilde, who escaped a loveless marriage to Bohemian prince Bodo by leaping the gorge on horseback; her pursuing fiancé couldn't make the jump and plunged into the valley that now bears his name, turning into a hell-hound on the way. The impact of Brunhilde's landing supposedly left the famous hoof imprint in the stone on Rosstrappe. It is worth climbing up here for the magnificent views alone.

A **cable car** (return €4.50; ☼ 9.30am-6pm May-Sep, 10am-4.30pm Oct-Apr) runs to Hexentanzplatz, or you can take a **chairlift** (return €3.50; ☼ 9.30am-6pm May-Sep, 10am-4.30pm Oct-Apr) to Rosstrappe. Go early or late in the day to avoid crowds. Signs direct you from the Hauptbahnhof.

The wooden museum **Walpurgishalle** (Hexentanzplatz; adult/child €1.50/1; ☼ 10am-6pm May-Oct) has

exhibitions and paintings on matters heathen (German only), including the *Opferstein,* a stone once used in Germanic sacrificial rituals. Nearby is a 10-hectare **Tierpark** (☎ 2880; www.tierpark-thale.de; adult/concession/child €4/3.50/2; ☼ 10am-7pm Jun-Aug, 9am-6pm May, Sep & Oct, 9am-5pm Feb-Apr, 10am-4pm Nov-Jan) with lynxes, wild cats and other furry friends. The Hexentanzplatz itself is now basically a coach park full of souvenir shops.

Activities

The **hiking** brochures *Wanderführer* (€1) and *Führer durch das Bodetal* (€1.50) are excellent if your German is up to it. Highly recommended is the Bode Valley 'Hexenstieg' walk between Thale and Treseburg (blue triangle, 10km). If you take the bus from Thale to Treseburg, you can walk downstream and enjoy the most spectacular scenery at the end. WVB bus 264 does the trip from April to early November, and QBus 18 does it all year via Hexentanzplatz. Another 10km trail (red dot) goes from Hexentanzplatz to Treseburg; combine with the valley walk to make a round trip.

Festivals & Events

The open-air **Harzer Bergtheater** (☎ 2324; www.harzer-bergtheater.de; Hexentanzplatz) has a summer programme of music and plays, plus a performance on Walpurgisnacht. Tickets are sold at the venue and the tourist office.

Sleeping & Eating

Book extremely early for Walpurgisnacht. The number of cheap private rooms is limited, but the tourist office can help, especially in finding holiday flats.

DJH hostel (☎ 2881; jh-thale@djh-sachsen-anhalt.de; Bodetal-Waldkater; under/over 26yr €14.50/17.20; ℗ ✗) This DJH hostel is central to the train and bus stations and nestled in lush surroundings where the trail begins for the Bode Valley.

Kleiner Waldkater (☎ 2826; www.kleiner-waldkater.de; Bodetal-Waldkater; s/d €35/54; ℗) Pine panelling and a cat theme dominate this cute half-timbered *pension* alongside the hostel. You can also get a filling goulash with dumplings and other elementary cuisine in the hotel restaurant.

Hotel Haus Sonneneck (☎ 496 10; www.haus-sonneneck-thale.de; Heimburgstrasse 1a; s €35-49, d €55-80; ℗ ✗) Situated between Friedenspark and the forest, this recently renovated hotel is an

WITCHES & WARLOCKS

The Bodetal once contained Celtic fortresses built to fend off northern tribes; by 500 BC Germanic tribes had driven out the Celts and appropriated the sites for meetings and ritual sacrifices. These played an important role in the 8th-century Saxon Wars, when Charlemagne embarked upon campaigns to subjugate and Christianise the local population. Harz mythology blends these pagan and Christian elements.

One popular – but misleading – explanation for the Walpurgisnacht festival is that it was an invention of the tribes who, pursued by Christian missionaries, held secret gatherings to carry out their rituals. They are said to have darkened their faces one night and, armed with broomsticks and pitchforks, scared off Charlemagne's guards, who mistook them for witches and devils. In fact the name 'Walpurgisnacht' itself probably derives from St Walpurga, but the festival tradition may also refer to the wedding of the gods Wodan and Freya.

According to local mythology, witches and warlocks gather on Walpurgisnacht at locations throughout the Harz before flying off to the Brocken on broomsticks or goats. There they recount the year's evil deeds and top off the stories with a bacchanalian frenzy, said to represent copulation with the devil. Frightened peasants used to hang crosses and herbs on stable doors to protect their livestock; ringing church bells or cracking whips were other ways to prevent stray witches from dropping by.

One of the best places to celebrate Walpurgisnacht is Thale, where not-so-pagan hordes of 35,000 or more arrive for colourful variety events and the Walpurgishalle tells you all you need to know about sacrifices, rituals and local myths. Schierke, also popular, is a starting point for Walpurgisnacht treks to the Brocken. Wherever you are, expect to see the dawn in with some very strange characters!

excellent choice – central, quiet and close to the walks and lifts.

Ferienpark Bodetal Thale (☎ 776 60; www.ferienpark -bodetal.de; Hubertusstrasse 9-11; s €65-90, d €80-110; P ✗ ☒) Directly across Friedenspark, this new hotel and holiday apartment complex has very smart rooms with balconies, a children's playground, a restaurant and various health and fitness extras. It also rents mountain bikes for €10 per day.

La Romantica (☎ 630 99; Musestieg 28; pizza €5-8, pasta €7.50-10, mains €11-15) Though it's a 20-minute hike northeast from the station along Bahnhofstrasse and Sputnikweg, this Italian restaurant gets good recommendations from locals. It also has a delivery service.

Both Hexentanzplatz and Rosstrappe have restaurants. The **Berghotel Hexentanzplatz**

(☎ 4730; Hexentanzplatz; mains €9-14) is the best option for a sit-down meal.

Getting There & Around

Frequent trains travel to Halberstadt (€4.60, 45 minutes), Quedlinburg (€1.80, 11 minutes), Wernigerode (€9.10, 1¼ hours) and Magdeburg (€12.40, 1½ hours). Karl-Marx-Strasse leads to the main junction for roads to Quedlinburg and Wernigerode.

The bus station is located alongside the train station. For Wernigerode, take bus WVB 253; to get to Treseburg, take QBus 18. Bus WVB 264 goes to Treseburg and Blankenburg via Rosstrappe. The night buses N3 and N4 go to Harzgerode and Quedlinburg respectively, via Hexentanzplatz. For a taxi, call ☎ 2505 or ☎ 2244.

THURINGIA

Thuringia

Few German regions can match the rolling green hills and bucolic forest trails found in Thuringia (Thüringen), once part of the GDR. This picturesque state is quite aptly called the 'green heart' of Germany, but Thuringia's moniker does not account for its fascinating and exciting cities – places like the capital, Erfurt; Weimar, a cultural icon in itself; and Eisenach, remarkable for being both a centre of historic German Lutheranism, and of car manufacturing. Beyond these cities are hundreds of smaller towns that invite exploration.

But Thuringia has also felt the cold double-edge of German history. In 1930 it became the first German state to be governed by the Nazis, and it quickly stocked its police and other public services with obedient followers of the NDSAP. The former Buchenwald concentration camp is a grim reminder of the period, standing in bleak contrast to the cultural legacy left by Goethe and Schiller 150 years earlier, and the radical Bauhaus movement which was born in the city in 1919.

Today Thuringia is one of the most popular tourist destinations for hiking and cultural tourism; it also offers many opportunities to combine both. Although its roads and trails are well-trodden, and its cities were long ago sketched on the world cultural map, Thuringia brings many unexpected rewards for visitors who put aside the map for a moment and immerse themselves in the gentle momentum of slow travel.

HIGHLIGHTS

- **Culture** Experience the finest of both classic and cutting-edge culture in Weimar (p258)

- **Escapism** Tour Wartburg Castle, Martin Luther's hideout in Eisenach (p270)

- **Bizarre Beds** Sleep in a former police lock-up, or a 13th-century monastery, in Erfurt (p256)

- **Views** Take in the Kyffhäuser Monument and Panorama Museum in Bad Frankenhausen (p269)

- **Hiking & Cycling** Tackle a leg or two of the Rennsteig (p273), Germany's oldest and most famous trail, by foot or on your bike from Eisenach

- **Slow Travel** Roll across meadows and through forest on a country tram (p268) from Gotha to beautiful Friedrichroda and beyond

- POPULATION: 2.34 MILLION
- AREA: 16,172 SQ KM

THURINGIA

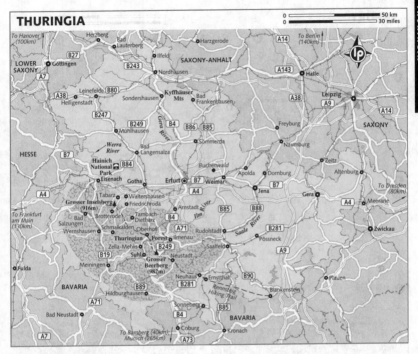

Getting There & Away

Thuringia's main cities, Erfurt and Weimar, are serviced by daily trains from Berlin, Frankfurt, Dresden and Hanover; contact **Deutsche Bahn** (☎ 118 61 for reservations, ☎ 0800-150 7090 for automated timetable information; www.bahn.de) for full details.

If you're driving, the area's main arteries are the east–west A4, which runs just south of Erfurt and Weimar (linking Frankfurt and Dresden), and the north–south B4, which skirts Erfurt before heading into the heart of the Thuringian Forest on its way south to Munich. The Berlin–Munich A9 cuts through the eastern part of Thuringia.

Getting Around

Trains are supplemented by comprehensive local bus networks and an efficient road system. There are two good-value DB discount tickets available in Thuringia. The Thüringen-Ticket (€26) gives up to five people (or a family) unlimited travel on regional trains for a day; the Hopper-Ticket (€4.50) is valid for a day return to any town within 50km of your starting point, including places in Saxony-Anhalt.

A weekly pass for the 'Verbundsgebiet' is also available for all transport covering city zones and the regions between Erfurt, Weimar and Jena (€50).

CENTRAL THURINGIA

ERFURT

☎ 0361 / pop 199,000

The capital of Thuringia is a charming and lively town that lies just 45km south of the geographical centre of reunified Germany. Although WWII bombing took its toll on this university town, its numerous architectural gems include a spectacular cathedral and monastery, some lovely winding streets in the restored Altstadt (Old Town) and one of Europe's most interesting bridges.

Erfurt was founded by St Boniface as a bishopric in 742, and was catapulted to prominence and prosperity in the Middle Ages when it began producing a precious blue pigment from the woad plant. However, due to a fire that raged through the city in 1472, none of its surviving buildings date from before the 15th

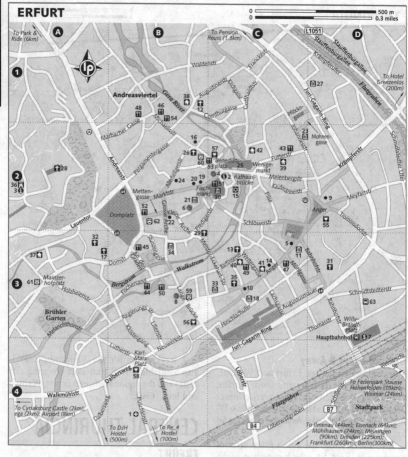

century. In 1392, rich merchants founded the university, allowing students to study common law, not religious law. Its most famous graduate was Martin Luther, who studied philosophy here between 1501 and 1505.

Despite being Germany's geographical heartland, an international atmosphere pervades the capital; it has a lively student and cultural scene and is a good springboard for exploring other parts of Thuringia.

Orientation

The Hauptbahnhof (central train station) and bus stations are just beyond the southeastern edge of the town centre, outside the ring roads. It's a five-minute walk north from Hauptbahnhof along Bahnhofstrasse to Anger, the

main shopping and business artery. The little Gera River bisects the Altstadt, spilling off into numerous creeks.

Information
BOOKSHOPS

Hugendubel (☎ 484 484; Am Anger 62) Large, multi-level bookshop with English language books.

DISCOUNT CARDS

ErfurtCard (per 48hr €9.90) Available from the tourist office; covers admission to museums, public transport, guided city tours and entertainment discounts.

EMERGENCY

Ambulance (☎ 112)
Police (☎ 110; Andreasstrasse 38)

INTERNET ACCESS

FAM (☎ 601 2733; Fischmarkt 18-20; 10am-1am Tue-Sat)
Free wireless internet points for laptops.
Internettreff (☎ 262 3834; Ratskellerpassage, Fischmarkt
5; per hr €2.40; ☯ 10am-8pm Mon-Fri, 11am-7pm Sat)
Spielothek Oase (Lange Brücke; per 30min €1; ☯ 8am-
1am Mon-Sat, 10am-1am Sun) One of several in a chain.

MEDICAL SERVICES

Emergency Clinic (☎ 224 990; Puschkinstrasse 23;
☯ 24hr)

MONEY

Reisebank (☎ 643 8361; Hauptbahnhof; ☯ 8am-8pm
Mon-Fri, 9am-2pm Sat, 9am-1pm Sun) Has an ATM inside
the station.

POST

Main post office (☎ 5990 321; Anger 66-73)

TOURIST INFORMATION

Erfurt Tourismus Benediktsplatz (☎ 664 00; www.erfurt
-tourismus.de; Benediktsplatz 1; ☯ 10am-7pm Mon-Fri,
10am-6pm Sat, 10am-4pm Sun Apr-Dec, to 6pm Mon-Sat
Jan-Mar) Petersberg (☎ 6015 384; ☯ 10am-6.30pm
Apr-Dec)

Sights
DOM & SEVERIKIRCHE

Situated on top of an artificial hill on the site
of a small 8th-century church, **Dom St Marien**

(St Mary's Cathedral; ☎ 646 1265; Domplatz; ☯ 9am-5pm
Mon-Fri, 9am-4.30pm Sat, 1-5pm Sun May-Oct, 10-11.30am
& 12.30-4pm Mon-Sat, 2-4pm Sun Nov-Apr) was rebuilt
in the 14th century after the collapse of early
predecessors. The steps of this Gothic cathedral are the venue for the **Domstufenfestspiele**
in August each year, when operas are performed against the dramatic background.

Highlights inside are the superb **stained-
glass windows** (1370–1420) featuring Biblical
scenes; the **Wolfram** (1160), a bronze candelabrum in the shape of a man; the **Gloriosa bell**
(1497); a Romanesque stucco **Madonna**; and
the 14th-century **choir stalls**.

Adjacent to the cathedral is the **Severikirche**
(☎ 576 960; Domplatz; ☯ 9am-12.30pm & 1.30-5pm Mon-
Fri May-Oct, 10am-12.30pm & 1.30-4pm Mon-Fri Nov-Apr),
a five-aisled hall church (1280) with a stone
Madonna (1345) and a 15m-high baptismal
font (1467), as well as the sarcophagus of
St Severus, whose remains were brought to
Erfurt in 836.

ZITADELLE PETERSBERG

One reason why Erfurt today has so many
towers without churches attached, is that
parts were demolished to erect the **Zitadelle
Petersberg** (☎ 211 5270), situated on a natural
hill north of the Dom complex. The fortress
has a fascinating series of subterranean tunnels within the walls, which can be viewed on

a **guided tour** (adult/concession €6/3; ☼ 11.30am-5.30pm hourly Apr-Dec) from the tourist office. The nearby Romanesque **Peterskirche** (☼ 10am-6pm Wed-Sun) can be visited separately without a tour.

AUGUSTINERKLOSTER

Nestled in the heart of the Andreasviertel, the **Augustinerkloster** (☎ 576 600; adult/concession €5/3; ☼ tours hourly 10am-noon & 2-5pm Mon-Sat, 11am & 2pm Sun Apr-Oct, 10am-noon & 2-4pm Mon-Sat, from 11am Sun Nov-Mar) is where Luther was a monk from 1505 to 1511, and where he read his first mass after being ordained as a priest. There are exhibits on the Reformation and Luther's cell, and the tour includes the magnificent cloister. The grounds and church are free of charge throughout the day; enter from Kirchgasse or Comthurgasse. An order of Protestant nuns resides in the monastery; public prayer services are held four times daily.

KRÄMERBRÜCKE

The 18m-wide and 120m-long medieval **Krämerbrücke** (merchant bridge) is Europe's longest bridge with houses. It was originally constructed from wood but rebuilt in stone in 1325 and adorned with churches at each end. Today the only church building remaining is the deconsecrated Aegideuskirche remains, now part of the Sorat Hotel (see p257).

CHURCHES

Erfurt's churches give an interesting insight into the city's history. The most haunting is the partially destroyed **Barfüsserkirche** (☎ 554 560; Barfüsserstrasse 20; adult/concession €1/0.50; ☼ 10am-1pm & 2-6pm Apr-Oct), now part of the Angermuseum, with a small collection of medieval religious art. Bombed in WWII, the west wall is still connected by an exposed aisle with Gothic arches. The **Predigerkirche** (☎ 5504 8484; Predigerstrasse 4; ☼ 10am-5pm Tue-Sat, noon-4pm Sun) was completed in 1400, and has regular organ recitals in summer on its reconstructed baroque organ. The **Michaeliskirche** (☎ 346 7212; cnr Michaelisstrasse & Allerheiligenstrasse; ☼ 10am-5pm) was where Martin Luther preached in 1522; it boasts a magnificent **organ** (1652) by Erfurt master Ludwig Compenius.

MUSEUMS

Inside the Haus zum Stockfisch, the **Stadtmuseum** (☎ 655 5650; www.stadtmuseum-erfurt.de; Johannesstrasse 169; adult/concession €1.50/0.75; ☼ 10am-6pm Tue-Sun) has among its exhibits a medieval

bone-carver's workshop and displays on Erfurt in the 20th century, including the GDR era. The **Angermuseum** (☎ 562 3311; www.angermuseum.de; Anger 18) has been undergoing restoration and is expected to reopen in late 2007. Visitors will once again find collections of medieval art and crafts, 19th- and 20th-century landscape paintings and 18th-century Thuringian *faïence* (glazed earthenware).

For an insight into Thuringian folk art, visit the **Museum für Thüringer Volkskunde** (☎ 655 5607; www.volkskundemuseum-erfurt.de; Juri-Gagarin-Ring 140a; adult/concession €1.50/0.75; ☼ 10am-6pm Tue-Sun). West of the city centre is the **ega** (Erfurter Gartenausstellung; ☎ 564 3700; www.ega-erfurt.com; adult/concession €5/4; ☼ 9am-8pm), a huge garden showground centred on **Cyriaksburg castle** (Gothaer Strasse 38). Take tram 2 from Anger.

GALLERIES

The **Kunsthalle Erfurt** (☎ 655 5660; www.kunsthalle-erfurt.de; Fischmarkt 7; adult/concession €3/1.50; ☼ 11am-6pm Tue, Wed & Fri-Sun, 11am-10pm Thu) is located in Haus Zum Roten Ochsen on Fischmarkt, and is Erfurt's largest gallery; others with changing exhibitions of contemporary art are **Galerie Haus Dacheröden** (☎ 654 8420; Anger 37-38; ☼ 10am-6pm Tue-Sun) and **Galerie Waidspeicher** (☎ 655 1960; www.kroenbacken.de; Michaelisstrasse 10; ☼ noon-6pm Wed-Sun), inside the Kulturhof Krönbacken cultural centre (see p258).

Walking Tour

This walking tour takes you to all the major attractions starting from the heart of the city. You'll find so much to entrance that you may spend hours completing it.

From the Hauptbahnhof head north on Bahnhofstrasse. Just after crossing Juri-Gagarin-Ring, you'll come upon the 14th-century **Reglerkirche (1)**. The portal and the southern tower of this former monastery church are Romanesque, and the large carved altar dates back to 1460.

Bahnhofstrasse intersects with Anger, which is flanked by houses from seemingly different historical periods (most of them are actually only 100 years old). Off to your right you'll see the enormous **Anger 1 shopping complex (2)**, while immediately to your left is the yellow, stuccoed **Angermuseum (3**; see opposite). As you head west on Anger, look for the pretty façades at No 23 and No 37–38. You'll also pass the **Bartholomäusturm (4)**, a tower with a 60-bell *Glockenspiel* (there are

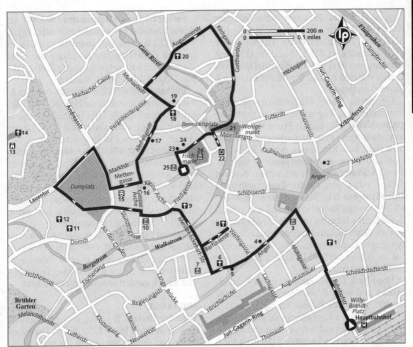

WALK FACTS

Start Hauptbahnhof
Finish Fischmarkt
Distance 3.2km
Duration Two hours

live concerts at 11am on Saturday, and automatic melodies several times daily).

When you get to the **Angerbrunnen (5)** fountain, keep to the right and follow Regierungsstrasse past **Wigbertikirche (6)** to the Renaissance and baroque **Stadthalterpalais (7)**, now the office of Thuringia's chancellor. Turn north on Meister-Eckehart-Strasse, then right on Barfüsserstrasse, where haunting **Barfüsserkirche (8**; opposite) awaits. Backtrack to Meister-Eckehart-Strasse and turn right to get to the 13th-century **Predigerkirche (9**; see opposite). From here head west on Paulstrasse and Kettenstrasse, past the GDR-themed **Thüringer Produkte Museum (10**; Paulstrasse 26) to the giant Domplatz, presided over by the **Dom St Marien (11**; p253) and stunning **Severikirche (12**; p253).

North of the Dom complex, on another hill, are the **Zitadelle Petersberg (13**; p253) and Romanesque **Peterskirche (14**; opposite).

Back on the Domplatz, explore the ornate façades of the houses on its eastern side, then duck into the tiny Mettengasse, an alley. Immediately to your right is the **Waidspeicher (15**; p258), now a puppet theatre and cabaret but formerly a storage house for *Waid* (woad) crops. A few metres further is the **Haus zum Sonneborn (16)**, built in 1536 with a spectacular portal; it's now the city's marriage office.

At the end of Mettengasse, turn north into Grosse Arche, cross Marktstrasse and head northeast on Allerheiligenstrasse to the Andreasviertel, the former university quarter. At Allerheiligenstrasse 20 is the **Haus zur Engelsburg (17)**, where a group of humanists met between 1510 and 1515 to compose at least two of the contentious *Dunkelmännerbriefe* (Obscurantists' Letters), satirical letters mocking contemporary theology, science and teaching practices.

Further along, on the corner of Michaelisstrasse and Allerheiligenstrasse, you'll find the Gothic **Michaeliskirche (18**; opposite), and diagonally across the street is the **Collegium Majus (19)**, the site of the main building of Erfurt's venerable university. The university itself (founded in 1392, closed in 1816 and reopened in 1994) was so influential that even Luther referred to it as: 'my mother to which I owe everything'.

Go north along Michaelisstrasse, then turn right onto Augustinerstrasse to the **Augustinerkloster (20**; p254). From the monastery, continue along Augustinerstrasse and turn right into Kirchgasse, which leads into Gotthardstrasse and runs south to the medieval **Krämerbrücke (21**; see p254). A short detour takes you to the **Begegnungsstätte Kleine Synagoge (22**; ☎ 655 1660; An der Stadtmünze 4/5; ☉ 11am-6pm Tue-Sun) a cultural and educational facility focusing on Jewish tradition and history. This classical building was Erfurt's synagogue from 1840 to 1884. The basement has an exhibit on Jews in Erfurt, as well as a small *mikve* (ritual bath).

Head back to the western end of Krämerbrücke and walk down Marktstrasse to **Fischmarkt**, the medieval market square with a gilded statue of a Roman warrior at its centre. It's flanked by several noteworthy buildings, including the **Haus zum Breiten Herd (23)** from 1584, with a rich Renaissance façade and a frieze depicting the five human senses; this theme continues with the four virtues on the adjacent **Gildehaus (24)** built in 1892. Look for the **Haus zum Roten Ochsen (25)**, a Renaissance gem from 1562, which now houses the art museum **Kunsthalle Erfurt** (see p254). The neo-Gothic **Rathaus (26**; ☉ 8am-6pm Mon, Tue & Thu, to 4pm Wed, to 2pm Fri, 10am-5pm Sat & Sun), built 1870-75, has a series of interior murals depicting scenes from Luther's life, as well as the Tannhäuser and Faust legends. On the 3rd floor is an extravagant festival hall. The walking tour ends here.

Tours

The tourist office offers two-hour **walking tours** (adult/concession €5.50/3; ☉ 1pm Mon-Fri Apr-Dec, 11am & 1pm Sat & Sun year-round) of the Altstadt and Petersberg, as well as other tours on themes such as architecture or Martin Luther in Erfurt.

Sleeping

BUDGET

The tourist office can book **private rooms** (☎ 664 0110) from about €20 per person; there's lots of choice and some surprisingly central options.

Ferienpark Stausee Hohenfelden (☎ 036450-420 81; www.hohenfelden.de; Hohenfelden; adult/child €5.50/3.50, car/tent €2/2.50) You can swim in the lake in summer at this large, modern camp site about 15km south of Erfurt in the pretty Ilmtal. Take bus 155 to Hohenfelden Stausee.

DJH hostel (☎ 562 6705; jh-erfurt@djh-thueringen.de; Hochheimer Strasse 12; under 26/over 26 €17/20; P X ⌨) Erfurt's comfortable DJH Jugendherberge is nestled among villas about 2km from the city centre (take tram 5 to Steigerstrasse).

Re_4Hostel (☎ 6000 110; www.re4hostel.de; Pushkinstrasse 21; dm €12-15, d €50; P X ⌨) If you've ever spent a night in a police lock-up, maybe this isn't your thing; rooms in this former police station range from hotel-like twins to hostel-like dorms. Bedding and towels cost extra. Room 13 has a chilling surprise.

Pension Reuss (☎ 731 0344; www.pension-reuss.de; Spittelgartenstrasse 15; s €27, d €42-50; P) This *pension* north of the centre is good value, with comfy rooms – some with cooking facilities – and a back garden to sooth eyes and soul.

MIDRANGE

Augustinerkloster (☎ 576 600; www.augustinerkloster.de; Augustinerstrasse 10; s/d €45/76; P X) The nicest twins and singles here are in the main monastery building (there's also a Renaissance-Hof section), with views over the wonderful cloister. All guests have access to this tranquil sanctuary.

Hotel Grenzenlos (☎ 6013 2600; www.behindertenverband-erfurt.de; Jonny-Schehr-Strasse 12; s €45, d €70; P X) Close to the centre and catering especially for physically disabled (it's also deaf- and blind-friendly), this small hotel is comfortable and has easy wheelchair access.

Hotel Ibis (☎ 664 10; www.ibis.com; Barfüsserstrasse 9; r €59; P X) This chain hotel opposite the Barfüsserkirche offers rooms that are small and no-frills, but they serve their purpose admirably.

Hotel & Gasthof Nikolai (☎ 5981 7119; www.hotel-nikolai-erfurt.com; Augustinerstrasse 30; s €69-75, d €84-110; P X) The location alongside the river, the overall high standard of rooms, and the friendly owners make this a prime choice, even if some rooms are small.

Hotel am Kaisersaal (☎ 658 560; info@hotel-am-kaisersaal.de; Futterstrasse 8; s €74-98, d €101-117; P X) Rooms are tip-top and appointed with all the necessaries in this highly-rated hotel. Request a room to the yard, though, if street noise disturbs.

Sorat Hotel (☎ 674 00; erfurt@sorat-hotels.com; Gotthardtstrasse 27; s €60-142, d €80-162; P ☒ ☒) Sorat has two buildings, one an annex on the historic Krämerbrücke with cheaper rooms. All rooms have a designer edge, and it's a wonderful location on the willow-fringed arm of the Gera River.

Hotel Zumnorde (☎ 568 00; www.hotel-zumnorde .de; Anger 50/51; s €100-130, d €120-150, ste €180-250; P ☒ ☒) The rooms and suites are modern, quite large and avoid decoration-overload in this fine hotel in the centre. There's a pretty garden, with a view to the neighbouring shoe shop, and a good restaurant here. Enter from Weitergasse.

TOP END

Grand Hotel am Dom (☎ 644 50; www.grand-hotel -am-dom.de; Theaterplatz 2; s €125-140, d €135-150, ste €230-560; P ☒ ☒) Slick, central and sparkling with five stars, 'the Grand' is designed so rooms either have windows facing the foyers, or windows looking to the world, so it's best to state your preference when booking. All are tastefully appointed in subdued light-browns, and there's a whirlpool in the Zen-inspired wellness area.

Eating

TRADITIONAL

Zum Goldenen Schwann (☎ 2623 742; Michaelisstrasse 9; mains €5-12.50; ☯ 10am-midnight) It's not so much the unpretentious traditional food that makes this place popular locally, rather the highly-rated unfiltered boutique beer.

Zwiesel (☎ 7897 207; Michaelisstrasse 31; mains €5.50; ☯ 11am-1am Sun-Thu, 11am-2am Fri & Sat) If you've just been cut out of the family will, take heart, you can still afford to fill up here – virtually everything costs the same in this relaxed student classic.

Erfurter Brauhaus (☎ 562 5827; Anger 21; mains €7-12; 11.30am-midnight Mon-Sat, noon-10pm Sun) As well as tasty square meals, we found the ubiquitous Three Wise Men of German boutique brewing here: one pilsner, one wheat beer and one dark beer. The fourth, the Märzbier (a blended pilsner and dark beer), must be popular because it had run out on the day.

Haus Zur Pfauen (☎ 211 5244; Marbacher Gasse 12-13; mains €7-10; ☯ 10am-1am) This jack-of-all-trades wears tradition on its sleeve – it's a restaurant, has its own microbrewery (a dark beer and a pilsner), its own *pension* (upstairs), and its own beer garden; it even does city tours.

INTERNATIONAL

Il Mulino (☎ 561 7069; Lange Brücke 37a; mains €7-17; ☯ 11am-midnight) On a warm day or night the riverside setting and garden seating are a treat in this Italian restaurant – the menu could do with an abridged edition, though.

Alboth's Restaurant (☎ 568 8207; Futterstrasse 15-16; 4- to 7-course set menus €33-79; ☯ from 6pm Tue-Sat) This restaurant is a French-inspired port of call for those seeking a serious gourmet plunge in the region. The **Lutherkeller** (☎ 568 8205; mains €7-15; ☯ from 6pm Tue-Sat) theme-eatery downstairs is a different kettle of fish – straw on the floor, chirpy personnel and prices in German Thaler (one-to-one exchange rate, they say). Each to their own, both are excellent.

Si Ju (☎ 6552 295; www.si-ju-erfurt.de; Fischmarkt 1; mains €7.50-20; ☯ 9am-late Mon-Sat, 10am-late Sun) The name is a shocking word play on 'see you', but this restaurant, café and lounge behind the Rathaus (actually part of the building) is a fashionable choice for diners and drinkers of all ages. The mood swings according to the time of day.

Vamos (☎ 654 6765; Domstrasse 15; tapas & mains €3-9.50; ☯ 10am-1am Sun-Thu, 10am-3am Fri & Sat) Vegetarians will find more than enough to fire the palate in this lively Spanish restaurant and bar.

Bombay (☎ 5400 535; Domplatz 35; mains €9-17; ☯ 11.30am-midnight) Although the curries aren't hot and it sets its sights resolutely on the tourist trade, this Indian eating house is very decent, with lots of vegetarian dishes.

Don Camillo (☎ 219 2366; Michaelisstrasse 29; €8-17; ☯ 11am-2pm & 6pm-midnight Tue-Sat, 11am-2pm Sun) Highly recommended for its creative Mediterranean cuisine, Don Camillo has many surprises up its sleeve – not least its interesting wine list.

CAFÉS

Altstadt Café (☎ 5626 473; www.erfurt-altstadtcafé .de; Fischersand 1; snacks €2.50-6; ☯ 11am-11pm Mon-Fri, noon-11pm Sat, 2-7pm Sun) Enjoy a coffee, tea, alcoholic drink or snack here, on an idyllic terrace alongside a canal.

Henner (☎ 654 6691; www.henner-sandwiches.de; Weitergasse 8; sandwiches from €2.50; ☯ 9am-8pm Mon-Fri, 9am-5pm Sat) This stylish sandwich bar has sleek orange colours and delicious food.

Drinking

Erfurt's former university quarter, the Andreasviertel, is a hub of nightspots, pubs and bars, especially along Michaelisstrasse and Futterstrasse.

Dubliner (☎ 644 2072; Neuwerkstrasse 47a) Though not in the Andreasviertel, this is the main Irish pub in town and a highly convivial place for a drink or two. Whiskey is all the go here, especially downstairs.

Hemingway (☎ 551 9944; www.hemingwaybar-erfurt .de; Michaelisstrasse 26) Everything the macho scribe loved is here in abundance: cigar humidors with personal drawers, 148 types of rum, and 30 different Daiquiri cocktails. The Africa Lounge has a local Bambi, though, not an elephant bagged from under Kilimanjaro.

Studentenzentrum Engelsburg (☎ 244 770; www .eburg.de; Allerheiligenstrasse 20-21) Lots of venues rolled into one, this student haunt has a pub in the Steinhaus, a positively labyrinthine cellar for music (most nights), and the Café DuckDich cultural forum upstairs.

Presseklub (☎ 262 3369; www.presseklub.net; Dalbersweg 1) Set right on Karl-Marx-Platz, in a monolith, this club has lots of live music and DJs, usually from Tuesday till Saturday.

Centrum (☎ 789 7388; www.centrum-club.de; Anger 7) This club gets a young crowd for dance music, live bands and occasional film screenings.

Entertainment

Free magazines such as *Erfurt magazin*, *t.akt*, *Partysan* and the local editions of *Blitz* and *Frizz* provide nightlife and event listings for Erfurt and other major towns.

Studentenzentrum Engelburg, Presseklub and Centrum (above) are all good clubs and live music places.

JAZZ

Jazzkeller (☎ 6422 600; www.jazzclub-erfurt.de; Gildehaus, Fischmarkt 13/16) This is the best address in town for quality jazz.

Kulturhof Krönbacken (☎ 655 1960; Michaelisstrasse 10) In summer, music events, including occasional jazz, are held now and again in this courtyard near former woad warehouses.

THEATRE & CLASSICAL MUSIC

Theater Erfurt (☎ 223 30; tickets ☎ 223 3155; Theaterplatz) This new theatre building beyond the cathedral is a state-of-the-art venue for theatre, opera, ballet and concerts.

Theater Waidspeicher (☎ 598 2924; www .waidspeicher.de; Domplatz 18) This puppet theatre is on the ground floor of an attractive woad warehouse (reached via Mettengasse). Above

is the Die Arche cabaret, Erfurt's premier address for political cabaret.

DasDie (☎ 551 166; www.dasdielive.de; Marstallstrasse 12) Stages here host everything from cabaret through to operettas, transvestite shows and Simon and Garfunkel revival bands.

Throughout summer, from the end of May, classical concerts take place beneath linden trees in the romantic courtyard of Michaeliskirche (Friday). Organ concerts are held at the Predigerkirche and Michaeliskirche (Wednesday), and at the Dom (Saturday).

Getting There & Away

Erfurt has direct IC train links to Berlin-Hauptbahnhof (€47, 3¼ hours) and ICE connections with Dresden (€42, 2¼ hours) and Frankfurt-am-Main (€46, 2¼ hours). There are also direct services to Meiningen (€15, 1½ hours) and Mühlhausen (€10, 45 minutes). Trains to Weimar (€4.40, 15 minutes) and Eisenach (€9, 50 minutes) run several times hourly.

Erfurt is just north of the A4, and is crossed by the B4 (Hamburg to Bamberg) and the B7 (Kassel to Gera). The new A71 autobahn runs south to Ilmenau. Most major car rental agencies have offices at the airport. There's a Park & Ride on Europaplatz (B4), 6km north of town.

Getting Around

Tickets in the central (yellow) zone for trams and buses cost €1.50, or €5 for a day pass. For information, call ☎ 194 49. Tram 4 runs direct to the airport from Anger (€1.50, 20 minutes). A taxi should cost around €14. To order a taxi, ring ☎ 511 11 or ☎ 666 666.

WEIMAR
☎ 03643 / pop 64,000

Neither a monumental town nor a medieval one, Weimar draws visitors whose tastes run to cultural or intellectual pleasures. It is the epicentre of the German Enlightenment, having grown into a symbol for all that is good and great in German culture. Its parks and gardens bring tranquil colour to the city in summer and lend themselves to contemplation, whereas its many museums take the visitor into the epoch of the Enlightenment (and its characters) and beyond.

The pantheon of intellectual and creative giants who lived and worked here amounts to a virtual Germanic hall of fame: Cranach the Elder, Johann Sebastian Bach, Wieland,

Schiller, Herder, Goethe, Liszt, Nietzsche, Gropius, Feininger, Kandinsky, Klee...the list goes on (and on, and on).

The town is best known as the place where Germany's first republican constitution was drafted after WWI (see below), though there are few reminders of this historical moment. The ghostly ruins of the Buchenwald concentration camp, on the other hand, still provide haunting evidence of the terrors of the Nazi regime. The Bauhaus and classical Weimar sites are protected as Unesco World Heritage sites.

While the city can sometimes feel like a giant tourist-filled museum, it is one of Germany's most fascinating places and belongs on every itinerary.

Orientation

The town centre is a 20-minute walk south of the Hauptbahnhof (central train station). Several buses serve Goetheplatz, on the northwestern edge of the Altstadt.

Information

Many of Weimar's museums and parks are administered by Stiftung Weimarer Klassik (right).

BOOKSHOPS
Thalia (☎ 828 10; Schillerstrasse 5a)

DISCOUNT CARDS
WeimarCard (per 72hr €10) Available from the tourist office; covers admission or gives discounts for museums, travel on city buses and other benefits.

INTERNET ACCESS
Die Eule (☎ 850 388; www.die-eule-buchhandlung.de; Frauentorstrasse 9-11; per 20min €1; ☺ 10am-6pm Mon-Fri, 10am-1pm Sat)

roxanne (☎ 800 194; Markt 21; per 30min €1; ☺ 10am-late Mon-Sat, 1pm-late Sun)

EMERGENCY
Police station (☎ 908 106; Markt 13-4)

MONEY
Reisebank ATM Located at Hauptbahnhof.
Sparkasse (Graben 4) Bank services and ATM.

POST
Main post office (☎ 2310; Goetheplatz 7-8)

TOURIST INFORMATION
Buchenwald Information (☎ 430 200; Markt 10; ☺ 9.30am-6pm Mon-Fri, 9.30am-3pm Sat & Sun Apr-Oct, 9.30am-6pm Mon-Fri, 9.30am-2pm Sat & Sun Nov-Mar)
DJH Service Centre (☎ 850 000; www.djh-thueringen .de; Carl-August-Allee 13; ☺ 1-4pm Mon, 9am-noon & 1-5pm Tue & Thu, 9am-noon Fri) Reservations and information for DJH hostels.
Stiftung Weimarer Klassik main office (Weimar Classics Foundation; ☎ 545 401; www.swkk.de; Frauentorstrasse 4; ☺ 9am-4pm Mon-Fri) Information stand (☎ 545 407; Markt 10; ☺ 9.30am-6pm Mon-Fri, 9.30am-3pm Sat & Sun Apr-Oct, 9.30am-6pm Mon-Fri, 9.30am-2pm Sat & Sun Nov-Mar) Museum tickets, literature and information.
Tourist Information (☎ 7450; www.weimar.de; Markt 10; ☺ 9.30am-6pm Mon-Fri, 9.30am-3pm Sat & Sun Apr-Oct, 9.30am-6pm Mon-Fri, 9.30am-2pm Sat & Sun Nov-Mar)

Sights
GOETHE HAUS
No other individual is as closely associated with Weimar as Johann Wolfgang von Goethe, who lived here from 1775 until his death in 1832. In 1792, his sponsor and employer, Duke Carl August, gave him a house as a gift. **Goethe Haus** (☎ 545 401; Frauenplan 1;

HOW THE WEIMAR REPUBLIC GOT ITS NAME

Despite its name, the Weimar Republic (1919–33), Germany's first dalliance with democracy, was never actually governed from Weimar. The town on the river Ilm was merely the place where, in 1919, the National Assembly drafted and passed the country's first constitution.

Assembly delegates felt that the volatile and explosive political climate rocking post-WWI Berlin would threaten the democratic process if it took place there, and looked for an alternative location. Weimar had several factors in its favour: a central location, a suitable venue (the Deutsches Nationaltheater), and a humanist tradition entirely antithetical to the militaristic Prussian spirit that had led to war.

Weimar's spot in the democratic limelight lasted only briefly. With the situation in Berlin calming down, the delegates returned to the capital just one week after passing the constitution on 31 July.

THURINGIA

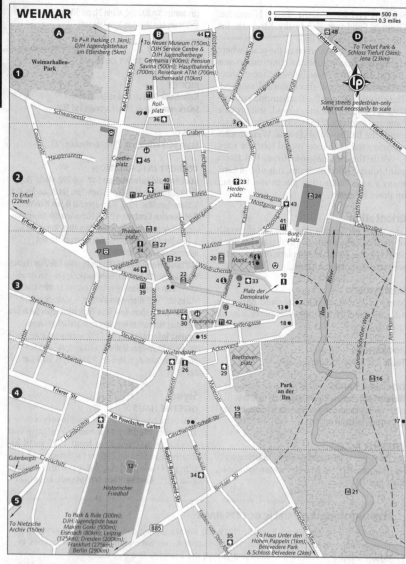

adult/concession €6.50/5; 9am-6pm Tue-Fri, 9am-7pm Sat, 9am-6pm Sun Apr-Sep, 9am-6pm Tue-Sun Oct, 9am-4pm Tue-Sun Nov-Mar) is where he worked, studied, researched and wrote such immortal works as *Faust*. Each of the rooms is painted in a different shade, according to Goethe's own theories about the correlation of mood and colour. After entering through a broad stair-case inspired by his Italian travels, you'll see his dining room, study and the bedroom with his deathbed.

Because the demand to visit Goethe Haus often exceeds its capacity, you'll be given a time slot to enter the museum. Once inside, however, you can stay there for as long as you want.

INFORMATION			
Buchenwald Information	(see 6)	Haus am Horn	17 D4
Die Eule	1 C3	Haus der Frau von Stein	18 C3
roxanne	2 C3	Liszt Haus	19 C4
Sparkasse	3 C1	Rathaus	20 C3
Stiftung Weimarer Klassik	4 C3	Römisches Haus	21 D5
Stiftung Weimarer Klassik		Schiller Haus	22 B3
Information Stand	(see 6)	Schlossmuseum	(see 24)
Thalia	5 B3	Stadtkirche St Peter und Paul	
Tourist Information	6 C3	(Herderkirche)	23 C2
		Stadtschloss	24 D2
SIGHTS & ACTIVITIES		Weimar Haus	25 B3
Anna Amalia Library	7 C3	Wieland Statue	26 B4
Bauhaus Museum	8 B2	Wittumspalais	27 B3
Bauhaus Universität	9 B4		
Carl August Statue	10 C3	SLEEPING	
Cranachhaus	11 C3	DJH am Posecschen Garten	28 A4
Fürstengruft	12 B5	Dorint Sofitel am Goethepark	29 C4
Fürstenhaus	13 C3	Hotel Am Frauenplan	30 B3
Goethe & Schiller Statue	14 B3	Hotel Amalienhof	31 B4
Goethe Haus	15 B3	Hotel Anna Amalia	32 B2
Goethe Nationalmuseum	(see 15)	Hotel Elephant	33 C3
Goethes Gartenhaus	16 D4	Villa Hentzel	34 B5
		Wolff's Art Hotel	35 C5

Zur Sonne	36 B1		
EATING			
Anno 1900	37 B2		
Brasserie Central	38 B1		
Da Cono	39 B3		
Jo Hanns	40 B2		
Residenz-Café	41 C2		
Zum Weissen Schwan	42 C3		
DRINKING			
ACC	43 C2		
Planbar	44 B1		
Studentenclub Kasseturm	45 B2		
Studentenclub Schützengasse	46 B3		
ENTERTAINMENT			
Deutsches Nationaltheater	47 A3		
E-Werk	48 D1		
Theater im Gewölbe	(see 11)		
TRANSPORT			
Grüne Liga	49 B1		

GOETHE NATIONALMUSEUM

Less about the great man of letters himself than his epoch, the **Goethe Nationalmuseum** (☎ 545 401; Frauenplan 1; adult/concession €2.50/2; 9am-6pm Tue-Fri, 9am-7pm Sat, 9am-6pm Sun Apr-Sep, 9am-6pm Tue-Sun Oct, 9am-4pm Tue-Sun Nov-Mar) focuses on the late 17th- and early 18th-century, a period referred to as Weimar Classicism. Goethe, Schiller, his ducal patrons (Anna Amalia and Carl August), his muse (Charlotte von Stein) and various cultural spear-carriers feature in this loose collection of paintings, books, busts, letters and other objets d'art.

Part of the museum complex, the **Faustina café** has a controversial Christoph Hodgson mural depicting Weimar's glorious Who's Who; lurking among the famous faces – with a couple of amusing touches – is one Adolf Hitler.

SCHILLER HAUS

The dramatist Friedrich von Schiller lived in Weimar from 1799 until his early death in 1805. Unlike Goethe, however, he had to buy his own house: **Schiller Haus** (☎ 545 401; Schillerstrasse 12; adult/concession €4/3; same as Goethe Haus, closed Tue). The study at the end of the 2nd floor contains his deathbed, as well as the desk where he penned *Wilhelm Tell* and other works.

Both Goethe and Schiller were interred at the **Historischer Friedhof** (Historic Cemetery) in the neoclassical **Fürstengruft** (adult/concession €2.50/2; 10am-6pm Apr-Oct, 10am-4pm Nov-Mar), along with Duke Carl August.

PARK AN DER ILM

The sprawling Ilm Park, the eastern flank of the Altstadt, is an inspiring and romantic spot, named after the little river that runs through it. Its most famous feature is **Goethes Gartenhaus** (☎ 545 401; adult/concession €3.50/2.50; same as Fürstengruft). This simple cottage (1776) was an early present from Duke Carl August and was intended to induce Goethe to stay in Weimar. It worked: he lived in this building until 1782, and also helped landscape the park. In 1999, an exact replica of the house was built in Bad Sulza to protect the original from the tourist invasions.

Within view of the Gartenhaus is the **Römisches Haus** (☎ 545 401; adult/concession €2.50/2; 10am-6pm Tue-Sun Apr-Oct), Carl August's summer retreat, built between 1792 and 1797 under Goethe's supervision. Perched on top of an artificial bluff, Weimar's first neoclassical house now contains restored period rooms and an exhibit on Ilm Park.

Nearby, on the western edge of the park, is the **Liszt Haus** (☎ 545 401; Marienstrasse 17; adult/concession €2/1.50; 10am-6pm Wed-Mon Apr-Oct). The composer and pianist Franz Liszt resided in Weimar in 1848 and again from 1869 to 1886 in this house, when he wrote *Hungarian Rhapsody* and *Faust Symphony*.

ART NOUVEAU IN WEIMAR

Architecture fans may want to see the home of Belgian Art Nouveau architect, designer and painter, Henry van de Velde, the **Haus Unter den Hohen Pappeln**. Visible only from the outside, it looks a bit like a ship on its side and features natural stone, stylised chimneys, loggias and oversized windows. To reach it, take bus 1 or 12 to Papiergraben.

Van de Velde also designed the ground floor of the **Nietzsche Archiv** (☎ 545 401; Humboldtstrasse 36; adult/concession €2.50/2; ☉ 1-6pm Tue-Sun Apr-Oct), where the philosopher spent his final years in illness, and the building that now houses the **Bauhaus Universität** (Geschwister-Scholl-Strasse).

Other splendidly restored Art Nouveau buildings cluster on Cranachstrasse, Gutenbergstrasse and Humboldtstrasse, just west of the Historischer Friedhof.

BAUHAUS IN WEIMAR

The **Bauhaus Museum** (☎ 545 401; Theaterplatz; adult/ concession €4.50/3.50; ☉ 10am-6pm) gives a fascinating insight into this group of artists and artisans, who shaped our understanding of modern design (particularly in the city of Chicago) like no other. The Bauhaus School and movement was founded in Weimar in 1919 by Walter Gropius, who drew top artists including Kandinsky, Klee, Feininger and Schlemmer as teachers. In 1925 the Bauhaus moved to Dessau, and in 1932 to Berlin, where it was dissolved by the Nazis, scattering the key figures throughout the world. They of course took their ideas with them, laying the foundations for the success of the school worldwide.

In addition to its modest permanent collection, the museum chronicles the group and its protagonists, has excellent changing exhibitions, and shows documentary footage (in German) explaining their methods. Students were as much artisans as artists, making the products they designed.

Only one Bauhaus building was ever constructed in Weimar. Called the **Haus am Horn** (☎ 904 056; Am Horn 61; ☉ 11am-5pm Wed, Sat & Sun), today it's used for exhibitions and events.

For more on the movement, see Modern Design (p56), our coverage of Dessau (p212) and the Bauhaus Archiv/Museum für Design in Berlin (p112).

NEUES MUSEUM

The **Neues Museum** (New Museum; ☎ 545 963; Carl-August-Allee; adult/concession €3.50/2.50; ☉ 11am-6pm Tue-Sun Apr-Oct, 10am-4pm Tue-Sun Nov-Mar) houses works of contemporary art in Weimar. The complex was built in 1863, as a gallery exclusively for works relating to Homer's *Odyssey*,

but another odyssey occurred after it was used as a *Halle der Volksgemeinschaft* (literally 'people's solidarity hall') by the Nazis, and was then renamed Karl-Marx-Platz under the GDR.

BELVEDERE & TIEFURT PARKS

Outside Weimar, the lovely **Belvedere Park** harbours Carl August's former hunting palace. **Schloss Belvedere** (☎ 545 401; adult/concession €4/3; ☉ 10am-6pm Tue-Sun Apr-Sep), displays glass, porcelain, faïence and weapons from the late 17th and 18th centuries. Bus 12 runs hourly from Goetheplatz.

A few kilometres east of the Hauptbahnhof, **Tiefurt Park** is an English-style garden that envelops Anna Amalia's **Schloss Tiefurt** (☎ 545 401; Hauptstrasse 14, Weimar-Tiefurt; adult/concession €3.50/2.50; ☉ closed Mon), her own 'temple of the muses'. The rooms are furnished to give visitors an impression of the age and her round-table gatherings, which often included Goethe; take bus 3.

WEIMAR HAUS

Near Schiller House, **Weimar Haus** (☎ 901 890; www.weimarhaus.de; Schillerstrasse 16-18; adult/concession €6.50/5.50; ☉ 10am-7pm Apr-Oct, 10am-6pm Nov-Mar) offers a half-hour Disneyland-style multimedia history of Weimar, from prehistory to classicism. The guide – purists hold your breath – has an animatronic Goethe (it's also available in English).

Walking Tour

Our tour begins on Herderplatz, dominated by the **Stadtkirche St Peter und Paul (1**; ☎ 851 518; Herderplatz; ☉ 10am-noon & 2-4pm Mon-Sat, 11am-noon & 2-3pm Sun Apr-Oct, 11am-noon & 2-4pm daily Nov-Mar). Built in 1500, this is popularly known as the Herderkirche after Johann Gottfried Herder, whom Goethe brought to Weimar as court preacher in 1776. His statue stands on the church square, and he's buried inside. The church itself has a famous altarpiece (1555), begun by Lucas Cranach the Elder and completed by his son. In the left aisle is an interesting triptych showing Martin Luther as a knight, professor and monk.

Walk east on Vorwerksgasse to Burgplatz, anchored by the **Stadtschloss (2)**, former residence of the ducal family of Saxe-Weimar. Inside is the **Schlossmuseum** (☎ 545 960; Burgplatz; adult/concession €5.50/3.50; ☉ 10am-6pm Tue-Sun Apr-Oct, 10am-4pm Tue-Sun Nov-Mar), with a good collection

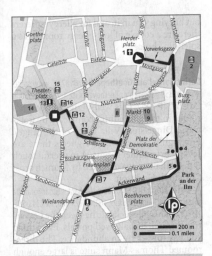

WALK FACTS

Start Herderplatz
Finish Theaterplatz
Distance 2km
Duration 1½ hours

of painting and sculpture; the Cranach Gallery has several portraits by Albrecht Dürer, and collections of Dutch masters and German romanticists. Several restored palace residence rooms can also be viewed.

To the south of here, on Platz der Demokratie, is the **Fürstenhaus (3)**, a former palace that is now home of a renowned music academy founded by Franz Liszt in 1872. The statue in front represents Duke Carl August. On the eastern side of the square is the **Anna Amalia Library (4)**, once managed by Goethe. In 2004 a fire raged through the library, home to some 900,000 books, and badly damaged the top two floors of the building, including parts of the magnificent **Rokokosaal** (Rococo Room; ☎ 545 401; Platz der Demokratie 1). The damaged works and the room are being restored, and visitors are expected to be able to visit from 2008.

The pink building behind the Fürstenhaus is the **Haus der Frau von Stein (5)**. She was a married woman who was Goethe's long-time muse and, if author Ettore Ghibellino is to be believed, a decoy to cover up the great author's socially unacceptable affair with Duchess Anna Amalia. The house is now

home to the Goethe Institut, a language school and culture centre.

Head west on Ackerwand to Wielandplatz, with the **Wieland statue (6)**. It was Wieland (1733–1813) who first translated Shakespeare's works into German. Then turn north onto Frauenplan, where you'll find the **Goethe Haus** and **Goethe Nationalmuseum (7**; see p259).

A short walk further north leads to the Markt, with its neo-Gothic **Rathaus (8**; 1841) facing two Renaissance jewels: the **Cranachhaus (9)**, where painter Lucas Cranach the Elder lived for two years before his death in 1553, and the **Stadthaus (10)**, which now houses the tourist information office.

Backtrack a few steps, then turn right onto the pedestrianised Schillerstrasse, which leads past the **Schiller Haus (11**; see p261) and the new **Weimar Haus (12**; see opposite) to Theaterplatz. Here, the famous statue of **Goethe and Schiller (13**; 1857) fronts the **Deutsches Nationaltheater (14**; German National Theatre), best known as the place where the National Assembly drafted the constitution of the Weimar Republic in 1919. The theatre has several artistic claims to fame: Goethe was director here from 1791 to 1817, and Liszt and Strauss were its music directors in the late 19th century.

Across from here is the **Bauhaus Museum (15**; see opposite), adjacent to the baroque **Wittumspalais (16**; ☎ 545 401; adult/concession €4/3; ⏰ 10am-6pm Tue-Sun Apr-Nov, 10am-4pm Tue-Sun Nov-Mar), once a residence of Anna Amalia, the premier patron of the arts in late-18th-century Weimar. The walking tour ends here.

Festivals & Events

The **Weimar Kunstfest** (☎ 81140; www.kunstfest-weimar .de) is an innovative festival of classical music supplemented by theatre, dance, literature and performance, held in late August each year.

Sleeping

Visitors to Weimar pay a supplement of between €0.50 and €2 per room per stay for the upkeep of cultural sites.

BUDGET

The tourist office can arrange private rooms starting from €22 per person.

Hostels

Weimar has four DJH hostels. The **DJH Service Centre** (☎ 850 000; Carl-August-Allee 13) can book accommodation.

THURINGIA

DJH Am Poseckschen Garten (☎ 850 792; www
.jh-posgarten.de; Humboldtstrasse 17; under 26/over 26
€17/20; ✗ 🖵) Near the Historischer Friedhof.

DJH Jugendherberge Germania (☎ 850 490; jh
-germania@djh-thueringen.de; Carl-August-Allee 13;
under 26/over 26 €17/20; ✗) Just south of the centre.

DJH Jugendgästehaus Maxim Gorki (☎ 850
750; Zum Wilden Graben 12; under 26/over 26 €18/21;
P ✗ 🖵) On the hilly southern side of town.

DJH Jugendgästehaus am Ettersberg (☎ 421
111; Ettersbergsiedlung; under 26/over 26 €18/21;
P ✗ 🖵 🐾) In a nature reserve north of town.

Hotels

Pension Savina (☎ 866 90; www.pension-savina.de;
Meyerstrasse 60; s/d €38/60; ✗) This *pension*, near
Hauptbahnhof, is difficult to beat for value
and extras – which include a small sauna,
a solarium, and a pick-up service if you call
ahead.

Zur Sonne (☎ 862 90; hotelzursonne@web.de; Rollplatz
2; s/d €51/77; P) Although rooms are small and
nondescript in this traditional hotel, it's clean,
reliable and right in town.

MIDRANGE

Villa Hentzel (☎ 865 80; info@hotel-villa-hentzel.de; Bauhausstrasse 12; s €54-67, d €75-95; P) This hotel in a
classical villa has comfortable modern rooms
just out of the centre, in a residential wedge
between the Ilmpark and the Historischer
Friedhof.

Hotel Anna Amalia (☎ 495 60; www.hotel-anna
-amalia.de; Geleitstrasse 8-12; s €55-70, d €75-140; P ✗)
Rooms are very spacious and quiet in this
hotel near Goetheplatz. The feel-good factor
is high here – even the breakfast room is fine
at peak hour.

Hotel Am Frauenplan (☎ 494 40; www.hotel
-am-frauenplan.de; Brauhausgasse 10; s/d €51/77; P ✗)
A sister-hotel of Zur Sonne, rooms here have
a tad more style and are a cat's whisker larger.
Somehow they still seem plain, but the rustic
staircase and location offset this.

Wolff's Art Hotel (☎ 540 60; www.art-hotel-weimar
.net; Freiherr-vom-Stein-Allee 3a/b; s €75, d €95; P ✗)
An art-hotel favoured by tourists and business visitors alike, Wolff's is a very classy and
contemporary place with a spa/fitness area
and gourmet restaurant.

Hotel Amalienhof (☎ 5490; amalienhofweimar@
t-online.de; Amalienstrasse 2; s €65-80, d €80-100; P ✗)
The charms of this Church-affiliated hotel
are manifold: lots of neoclassical furnishings,
richly styled rooms that point to history with-

out burying you in it, and for allergy sufferers
there are a couple of low-allergy rooms. It's a
splendid choice.

TOP END

Dorint Sofitel am Goethepark (☎ 8720; www.sofitel
.com; h5359@accor.com; Beethovenplatz 1-2; s €95-150, d
€121-177; P ✗) This well-designed hotel has
rooms in three buildings connected by walkways (Dingelstedt Villa is top of the range).
For highly noise-sensitive guests there are
several extra-quiet rooms. A masterful touch
is the Italianate spa designed by Munich artist
Christoph Hodgson.

Hotel Elephant (☎ 8020; elephant.weimar@arabella
sheraton.com; Markt 19; s €99-162, d €125-186, ste €343-585;
P ✗) This plush classic has seen the best arrive through its hallowed portals. Everything
you pay for is here in abundance. The three-
roomed Thomas Mann suite is large enough
for a decent game of hide and seek with your
bodyguards; after that, visit the highly-rated
Elephantenkeller restaurant.

Eating

Although much of the fare is traditional in
Weimar, vegetarians will find choices in most
places.

Residenz-Café (☎ 594 08; www.residenz-café.de;
Grüner Markt 4; mains €5-15) The 'Resi' is one of
Weimar's enduring favourites, and for good
reason: everyone finds something for their
taste here. The Lovers' Breakfast is €18 for
two, but for the un-in-love – or the less well-
off – the regular meat and vegetarian dishes
will do the trick.

Brasserie Central (☎ 852 724; Rollplatz 8a; breakfast
€2-10, mains €8.50-10.50; 🕙 10am-1am) This popular
bistro-bar starts the day with breakfast and
becomes a relaxed eatery, or a place to indulge
in coffee and a wine or beer, as the clock loops
the hours.

Zum Weissen Schwan (☎ 908 751; Frauentorstrasse
23; mains €10-18; 🕙 noon-midnight Wed-Sun) Goethe's
favourite dish is served here (broiled beef
with Frankfurt green sauce, red beet salad
and potatoes). Schiller and lots of others have
apparently graced the tables of this traditional
classic, too.

Anno 1900 (☎ 903 571; www.anno1900-weimar
.de; Geleitstrasse 12a; mains €8-14; 🕙 11am-1am Mon-Fri,
10am-1am Sat & Sun) On the scene since 1920,
this attractive café in an Art Nouveau-style
conservatory is a lovely stopover; it has some
vegetarian offerings and killer desserts.

Jo Hanns (☎ 493 617; Scherfgasse 1; mains €5-14; 11am-1am) The food is satisfying but it's the 130 wines from the Saale-Unstrut region that make Jo Hanns different. Keeping 130 local bottles open and fresh is of course impossible, so Jo also sells them to quaff in your room, or wherever, for half the listed restaurant price – 'Jo-to-go', so to speak.

Da Cono (☎ 514 285; Hummelstrasse 5; mains €8-19; 11.30am-2.30pm & 5.30-11.30pm Mon-Thu, 11.30am-11.30pm Fri & Sat) Not just the decor is from another age here, the food is too – it's unpretentious, Italian and full of ingredients. Even the simple *penne Arabiatta* gets complex when you think about it. Like the rest of Da Cono, the service has character.

Drinking

Though not renowned for high-kicking nightlife, Weimar nevertheless has a few nice ports of call for the visitor.

Planbar (☎ 502 785; Jakobsplan 6) Students and the young-at-heart flock to this trendy bar that's hooked right into club events locally.

Studentenclub Kasseturm (☎ 851 670; www.kasseturm.de; Goetheplatz 10) This clunky stone tower has DJs, an assorted bag of live music and other events over three floors, for young and old.

ACC (☎ 851 161; www.acc-weimar.de; Burgplatz 1) Eat here from 11am, just hang out and take drinks, or wander upstairs to visit the art space (changing exhibitions). It's a doorway to the contemporary arts scene.

Studentenclub Schützengasse (☎ 904 323; www.schuetzengasse.de; Schützengasse 2) We watched *The Big Lebowski* here – on one of its Monday night film screenings (9pm start). Other antidotes to highbrow burn-out are beer from €1 and lots of club and live music – be warned, the grunge factor is high.

Entertainment

Deutsches Nationaltheater (German National Theatre; ☎ 755 334; www.nationaltheater-weimar.de; Theaterplatz; closed Jul-Aug). Expect a grab-bag of classic and contemporary theatre, opera and concerts here.

Theater im Gewölbe (☎ 777 377; Markt 11/12) Anything goes here – from Goethe to cult barfly Charles Bukowski.

E-Werk (www.strassenbahndepot.info; Am Kirschberg 4) This former tram depot is the sharp edge of contemporary culture in Weimar. The people at ACC were involved in bringing it to life, the National Theatre has a stage here now, and there's cinema, live music and cultural events at various times (try to visit the Rebecca Horn exhibit). Check the website for events.

Getting There & Away

Regular ICE services go to Frankfurt (€59, 2½ hours), Leipzig (€22, 50 minutes), Dresden (€39, two hours) and Berlin-Hauptbahnhof (€47, 2¾ hours). Erfurt (€4.40, 15 minutes) and Eisenach (€12, 1¼ hours) are served several times hourly, plus there's frequent services to Jena West (€4.60, 15 minutes).

Getting Around

For trips outside the centre, there's a good bus system (single €1.60, day pass €3.80). For a taxi, call ☎ 903 600.

Grüne Liga (☎ 492 796; Goetheplatz 9b) rents city bikes from €6 per day (enter from Rollplatz). Unless staying in an Altstadt hotel, drivers must leave their car in one of the paid parking lots outside the centre. Look for the signs saying 'P+R'.

BUCHENWALD

The Buchenwald concentration camp **museum and memorial** (☎ 03643-4300; Ettersberg Hill; www.buchenwald.de; admission free; 10am-6pm Tue-Sun Apr-Oct, 10am-4pm Tue-Sun Nov-Mar) are 10km northwest of Weimar. You first pass the memorial erected above the mass graves of some of the 56,500 victims from 18 nations that died here – including German antifascists, Soviet and Polish prisoners of war, and Jews. The concentration camp and museum are 1km beyond the memorial. Many prominent German communists and social democrats, Ernst Thälmann and Rudolf Breitscheid among them, were murdered here. After 1943, prisoners were exploited in the production of weapons. Many died during medical experimentation. Shortly before the end of the war, some 28,000 prisoners were sent on death marches. Between 1937 and 1945, more than one-fifth of the 250,000 people incarcerated here died. On 11 April 1945, as US troops approached and the SS guards fled, the prisoners rebelled (at 3.15pm – the clock tower above the entrance still shows that time), overwhelmed the remaining guards and liberated themselves.

After the war, the Soviet victors turned the tables by establishing Special Camp No 2, in which 7000 so-called anticommunists and ex-Nazis were literally worked to death.

Their bodies were found after the Wende in mass graves north of the camp and near the Hauptbahnhof.

Pamphlets and books in English are sold at the bookshop. Last admission is 30 minutes before closing.

To get here take bus 6 from Weimer; by car, head north on Ettersburger Strasse from Weimar station and turn left onto Blutstrasse.

GOTHA

☎ 03621 / pop 47,000

Situated between Eisenach and Erfurt, Gotha was once described in historic documents as Thuringia's wealthiest and most beautiful city. This century it can no longer lay claim to either, but it remains a pleasant town with a handful of interesting attractions.

Gotha grew and rose to prominence in the 17th century, when Duke Ernst I made it his residence and built the enormous yet gracious Schloss Friedenstein and gardens. Duke Ernst I was founder of the House of Saxe-Coburg-Gotha, the dynasty that reinvented itself after WWI as Windsor and now occupies the British royal throne. The royal court warmly embraced the Enlightenment of the 18th century. In fact, Gräfin Louise Dorothea regularly corresponded with Voltaire, who passed through Gotha in his years of wandering Europe and fanning the embers of the Enlightenment.

Although the Schloss is Gotha's main attraction, highly enjoyable is a ride on the Thüringerwaldbahn, a small city tram that rattles, squeaks and winds through the countryside to Tabarz in the Thuringian Forest.

Orientation

Perched up a hill, Schloss Friedenstein and its gardens take up about half of Gotha's city centre, with the Altstadt to the north, and to the south, the Hauptbahnhof (central train station). It's only a brisk 15-minute walk from the Hauptbahnhof to the central squares – the long Hauptmarkt and the busier Neumarkt. The central bus station is on Mühlgrabenweg, northeast of the centre.

Information

Gothaer Netcafé (☎ 211 411; Gutenbergstrasse 11; per 30min €1.30; ☼ 10am-11pm) Internet and phone access.

Gotha-Information (☎ 222 138; www.gotha.de; Hauptmarkt 2; ☼ 9am-6pm Mon-Fri, 10am-3pm Sat year-round, 10am-2pm Sun May-Sep) Tourist information.

Main post office & bank (Ekhofplatz 1) With an ATM; a Reisebank ATM is also at the train station.

Tourist information (☎ 363 111; Margarethenstrasse 2-4; ☼ 10am-5pm Mon-Fri)

GOETHE – THE LITERARY COLOSSUS

Johann Wolfgang von Goethe bestrides German culture like a colossus. He's often called the 'German Shakespeare', but not even Shakespeare lived to be 82, having written novels, fairy tales, essays, literary criticism, philosophical treatises, scientific articles and travelogues, as well as plays and poetry. Goethe also dabbled in politics, town planning, architecture, landscaping and social reform, and collaborated with the likes of Christopher Marlowe. In short, he was the last Renaissance man – the last man to be able to do everything.

Born in Frankfurt-am-Main and trained as a lawyer, Goethe quickly overcame the disadvantages of a wealthy background and a happy childhood to become the driving force of the Gothic-influenced 1770's *Sturm und Drang* (Storm and Stress) literary movement. Though he worked and experimented in various styles throughout his life, his work with Friedrich Schiller fostered the theatrical style known as Weimar classicism. Goethe himself once described his work as 'fragments of a great confession'. Small fragments they were not – the Weimar Edition of his complete works numbers 133 volumes!

Goethe was revered across Europe even in his own lifetime. Napoleon invited him to France to be the Imperial Laureate. Though fascinated by Napoleon, Goethe was no blind admirer; he didn't go to Paris. Goethe was probably the first author ever to have a celebrity stalker – the talented but tormented JMR Lenz (1751–92), part of the Sturm und Drang circle, was so obsessed with his mentor that he imitated his writing, followed him around and even slept with his old lovers!

Goethe's defining work was *Faust*, a lyrical but highly charged retelling of the classic legend of a man selling his soul for knowledge. It took Goethe almost his entire life to complete it to his own satisfaction, and it's still probably the most-performed piece of theatre in Germany today; a fitting legacy for a genuine giant.

Sights

SCHLOSS FRIEDENSTEIN

Built between 1643 and 1654, this horseshoe-shaped palace is the largest surviving early baroque palace in Germany. It was never bombed – supposedly because of the link with the British royal family – and survived WWII thanks to one Josef Ritter von Gadolla, who surrendered the town to the Allies in 1945, and was executed by his own side. The exterior remains largely unchanged, with two distinctive towers – one round and the other square. Among the museums it contains, the **Schlossmuseum** (☎ 823 414; adult/concession €4/2; ☉ 10am-5pm Tue-Sun) has top billing, with lavish baroque and neoclassical royal apartments and eclectic collections. Expect to spend at least two hours here.

In addition to works by Rubens, Tischbein, Lucas Cranach the Younger and his father Lucas Cranach the Elder, don't miss the (pre-Dürer period) medieval delight, *Gothaer Liebespaar*, painted by an unknown artist around 1480. This depicts two lovers and is believed to be the first German double portrait.

On the 2nd floor you'll find the **Festsaal**, an exuberant hall of stuccoed ceilings, walls and doors. The less flashy neoclassical wing contains a collection of sculptures, of which the Renaissance work by Conrad Meit called *Adam und Eva* deserves special mention. The **Kunstkammer** is jammed with miniature curiosities and treasures, including exotica like engraved ostrich eggs and a cherry pit sporting a carved portrait of Ernst the Pious. The palace also houses one of Europe's oldest Egyptian collections.

In the west tower is the **Museum für Regionalgeschichte und Volkskunde** (☎ 823 451; adult/concession €5/2; ☉ 10am-5pm Tue-Sun); the real gem, though, is the refurbished **Ekhof-Theater**, one of the oldest baroque theatres in Europe. The stage tradition at Schloss Friedenstein goes back to 1683, and a mechanised set-changing device survives from that period in working order.

The **Schlosskirche** occupies the northeastern corner, while the east wing contains a **research library** with more than half a million books spanning 12 centuries. You can also take a tour of the atmospheric **Kasematten** (underground passages; €3.50; ☉ 1pm & 2pm Tue-Sun).

HAUPTMARKT

The **Rathaus**, with its colourful Renaissance façade and 40m-tall **tower** (€0.50; ☉ 11am-6pm Apr-Oct, 11am-4pm Nov-Mar) commands Hauptmarkt. It was built as a store in 1567, was later inhabited by Duke Ernst I until Schloss Friedenstein was completed, and was then turned into the town hall in 1665. The **Wasserkunst** (cascading fountain) was created in the 14th century, as a canal to supply the city with water; it's now purely decorative, and the pump is deep inside the baroque Lucas-Cranach-Haus at No 17. Other houses on Hauptmarkt also reward exploration, or if the legs are tired, a picnic lunch in the 18th-century **Orangerie** of the Schloss is a nice way to enjoy these luscious surroundings.

Festivals & Events

The cultural highlight each year in Gotha is the **Ekhof-Festival** (☎ 222 138; www.ekhof-festival.de) in July and August, when there are theatre and concert performances on a baroque note in this famous theatre. Various other smaller events are held throughout the year, which should be listed in *Kulturkalender*, a booklet available from the tourist office.

Sleeping

The tourist office makes free reservations for hotels and has a good brochure listing private rooms from around €17 per person.

Pension am Schloss (☎ 853 206; Bergallee 3; s/d €21.50/48; **P**) Most rooms have showers and toilets, and some have antiques, in this comfortable *pension* situated near the palace in a 1920s building.

Café Suzette (☎ 856 755; www.cafe-suzette.com; Bebelstrasse 8; s €31.50-36, d €54; **P**) This is a small but well-equipped *pension* with no-frills rooms above a cake shop, five minutes from Hauptbahnhof. Bike hire is available here.

Pension Regina (☎ 408 020; www.pension-regina.de; Schwabhäuser Strasse 4; s €29-36, d €50-60; **P**) Rooms are plain but functional in this *pension* in the town centre.

Toscana (☎ 295 93; www.toscana-gotha.de; Pfortenwallstrasse 1; s/d €45/65; **P**) An excellent Italian-run hotel and restaurant (see p268). Although opposite a few architectural nightmares on the ring road, it has lovely and well-appointed rooms.

Hotel Am Schlosspark (☎ 4420; www.hotel-am-schlosspark.de; Lindenauallee 20; s €90-110, d €115-136; **P** ✗) Rooms in the only central top-end choice in Gotha are modern and fully equipped. It is the best option for wheelchair users, and kids will like the adjacent playground.

Eating & Drinking

Most eating options are centred on the area around the Hauptmarkt and Neumarkt.

Café Loesche (☎ 240 25; Buttermarkt 6; cakes €0.80-1.50; ⏲ 9.30am-6pm Mon-Fri, 10.30am-6pm Sat, 10am-6pm Sun) Watch the world go by from this charming café near Hauptmarkt.

Toscana (☎ 295 93; www.toscana-gotha.de; Pfortenwallstrasse 1; mains €6-20; ⏲ 11.30am-2.30pm & 6-10.30pm) For a delicious taste of Italy, this is the place to be. There's a small cocktail bar at the entrance for Toscana barflies, and it's part of the hotel of the same name.

König Sahl (☎ 852 506; Brühl 7; mains €7-14, ⏲ 11.30am-2pm & 5pm-midnight, 11.30am-midnight Sun) The good king is worthy for two reasons: he does monster Tex-Mex lava grills and some vegetarian dishes, and he brews his own beer. The astounding 'metre of beer' consists of 13 glasses lined up on a wooden rack exactly one metre long. Service is earthy and charming.

Carnaby (☎ 706 834; 18.-März-Strasse 24) This long-standing Gotha favourite does a few snacks, attracts a crowd of all ages and sizes, and sometimes has live music. It's still open after the good König Sahl has put away his rack.

Getting There & Away

Gotha is easily reached by regional train from Eisenach (€4, 25 minutes), Erfurt (€5, 20 minutes) and Weimar (€8, 35 minutes). It's also a regular stop for IC trains going to Berlin-Hauptbahnhof (€44.60, 3½ hours) and for ICE ones going to Frankfurt-am-Main (€43, 2¼ hours). Gotha is just north of the A4 and is crossed by the B247 and B7.

For the Thüringerwaldbahn see the boxed text (right).

NORTHERN THURINGIA

MÜHLHAUSEN

☎ 03601 / pop 37,000

Mühlhausen, situated in the pretty Unstrut River valley about 40km north of Gotha, has picture-book architecture from the Middle Ages. Cobbled alleyways wind through a historic centre that is surrounded by one of Germany's most attractive and intact city walls. The city is also famous for being a centre of revolt during the 16th-century Peasants' War, and the place where Thomas Münzer preached (against Luther) in favour of rebellion. The reminders of this and other historical events are never far from the surface of this interesting city today.

The **tourist office** (☎ 404 770; www.muehlhausen.de; Ratsstrasse 20; ⏲ 9am-5pm Mon-Fri, 10am-1pm Sat & Sun) is about 1km west of Hauptbahnhof, between Obermarkt in the north and Untermarkt in the south. Steinweg (near Obermarkt) is the main shopping street.

Sights

The most important sights are located in the centre, which is best taken in with a leisurely stroll. The **Divi-Blasii-Kirche** (☎ 887 9950; Johann-Sebastian-Bach-Platz 4; ⏲ 10am-12.30pm & 1-5pm Mon-Sat, 1-5pm Sun) on **Untermarkt** is a good starting point if you've entered town on the continuation of Karl-Marx-Strasse from the Hauptbahnhof. The church was built by the Teutonic Knights in the 13th century, and Johann Sebastian Bach worked as organist here, inaugurating a new organ in 1709.

From here, walk north along Linsenstrasse to **Kornmarkt** and the **Kornmarktkirche** (☎ 404 684; Ratsstrasse; adult/concession €3/2; ⏲ 11am-5pm Tue-Sun), where a museum is dedicated to the history of the Peasants' War and the Reformation. The building itself was deconsecrated in 1802, and was later used as a grain warehouse. The tourist office is just north of here on Ratsstrasse, in the **Rathaus** (☎ 4520; Ratsstrasse 19; adult/concession €1/0.50). This building is a sprawling concoction of Gothic, Renaissance and baroque influences, put together over several centuries from 1300.

Continuing north you reach **Obermarkt** and the **Marienkirche**, another of the 13 churches in

---

A WEIRD RIDE

Thuringia has some nice rides on the rails. Much of the regional network off the main Eisenach–Erfurt line is regularly serviced by single carriage drive cars. When you see one, hop on, buy a ticket from the machine and explore the countryside at will. It's slow travel at its finest.

The **Thüringerwaldbahn** (☎ 4310; www.waldbahn-gotha.de), however, is a weird one. This ordinary city tram (the No 4) starts at Gotha's Hauptbahnhof, curves around the city ring road, crawls through some unlovely suburbs and then just keeps going, right into the beautiful forest to Tabarz (€3.60, 22km, one hour).

Mühlhausen. With five naves, it is the second-largest church in Thuringia – after the Dom in Erfurt. In 1525, the priest and reformer Thomas Müntzer preached here to his rebel followers before the disastrous final battle of the Peasants' War on the Schlachtberg. There is a **memorial** (☎ 870 023; adult/concession €3/2; ⊙ 11am-5pm Tue-Sun) to him, along with exhibitions on his life and work.

Go west along Herrenstrasse to the **Inneres Frauentor**, the entrance for a 200m stretch of the 12th-century **town wall** (☎ 816 020; adult/concession €3/2; ⊙ 11am-5pm Apr-Oct). The wall is just under 3km long, and has two gates and three towers still standing. You can walk as far as the lookout platform on **Rabenturm**.

Finally, pocket your guidebook, let the town wall and spires be your landmarks, and explore Mühlhausen's fascinating back streets.

Sleeping & Eating

DJH hostel (☎ 813 318; jh-muehlhausen@djh-thueringen.de; Auf dem Tonberg 1; under 26/over 26 €13/16; ☒ ☐) This hostel is about 2km northwest of town (bus 5 or 6 to Blobach).

An der Stadtmauer (☎ 465 00; www.hotel-an-der-stadtmauer.de; Britenstrasse 15; s €49-55, d €69-75; ℗ ☒) The tasteful fittings, comfort and old-town location make this a very good choice. Some rooms open onto a courtyard, and there's a small bar and beer garden.

Brauhaus zum Löwen (☎ 4710; www.brauhaus-zum-loewen.de; Kornmarkt 3; s €55-63, d €80-95; ℗) This hotel-restaurant has three different buildings that cater for any taste. It also brews its own beer and even has an impressive pub for kicking up your heels – don't try this after eating the restaurant's 1m Bratwurst, though. Mains are €7 to €13.

Zum Nachbarn (☎ 812 513; Steinweg 65; mains €10-17; ⊙ 11.30am-10pm) One of the top restaurants in town, in an old red house with beamed ceilings and windows galore, this place has Thuringian and international cuisine on the menu.

Postkeller (☎ 440 091; Steinweg 6; mains €7-17; ⊙ 11am-2.30pm Tue-Sun & 6pm-1am Thu-Sat) In a town short on entertainment options, this might be your place: local food from the kitchen is served in a lovely room with Art Nouveau tiles, and there's a pub-club upstairs for getting down and dancing.

Getting There & Away

Hourly trains run from Erfurt (€10, 45 minutes). Coming from Eisenach (€10, 50 minutes) requires a change in Gotha. Mühlhausen is at the crossroads of the B249 from Sondershausen, and the B247 from Gotha.

THE KYFFHÄUSER

This low forested mountain range, wedged between the Harz Mountains to the north and the Thuringian Forest to the south, harbours several unique and intriguing sights. It is best explored from **Bad Frankenhausen**, a quiet spa town at the forest's southern edge. The **Tourismusverband Kyffhäuser** (☎ 034671-717 16; www.kyffhaeuser-tourismus.de; Anger 14; ⊙ 9.30am-6pm Mon-Fri, 9am-noon Sat) sells the **Kyffhäuser Card** (card €14) for admission to the main attractions here.

Kyffhäuser Monument

Above the dense forests and steep ravines of the 457m-high Kyffhäuser mountain, looms the bombastic **Kyffhäuser Monument** (☎ 034651-2780; adult/concession €5/4; ⊙ 9am-7pm) to Emperor Wilhelm I, built in 1896. A statue showing Wilhelm on horseback stands below a 60m-high tower, and above the stone throne of Emperor Friedrich I (1125–90; better known as Barbarossa) whom he considered his spiritual predecessor.

The monument stands on the foundations of the Oberburg (Upper Castle) of the medieval Burg Kyffhäusen, Germany's largest castle complex (608m long, 60m wide) before its destruction in 1118. Today, the only ruins remaining are those of the Unterburg (Lower Castle), as well as a gate and a 172m-deep well.

The remote monument is best reached by car, but there's also a sporadic bus service from Bad Frankenhausen.

Panorama Museum

On the Schlachtberg, 3km north of Bad Frankenhausen's centre, stands a giant concrete cylinder that harbours a painting which is truly epic – in both proportion and content. **Frühbürgerliche Revolution in Deutschland** (Early Civil Revolution in Germany; ☎ 034671-6190; www.panorama-museum.de; adult/concession/child €5/4/1; ⊙ 10am-6pm Tue-Sun Apr-Oct, 10am-5pm Tue-Sun Nov-Mar) is an oil painting measuring 14m by 123m (!) and representing a style called 'fantastical realism', reminiscent of such classical artists as Bruegel and Hieronymus Bosch. More than 3000 figures, assembled in numerous scenes, metaphorically depict the tumultuous transition from the Middle Ages in 15th- and 16th-century Europe to the modern era.

It took artist Werner Tübke and his assistants five years to complete this complex allegorical work, which was opened in 1989 as one of the last official acts of the GDR government. Its artistic merit and political context have been questioned, but its size and ambitious themes impress.

Barbarossahöhle

A highlight of the impressive plaster caves at **Barbarossahöhle** (☎ 034671-5450; www.hoehle.de; Mühlen 6, Rottleben; adult/child €6/4; ☿ 10am-5pm Apr-Oct, to 4pm Nov-Mar, hourly tours), some 5km from Bad Frankenhausen, are the slabs described by legend as Barbarossa's table and chair.

Sleeping & Eating

Alte Hämmelei (☎ 034671-5120; www.alte-haemmelei .de; Bornstrasse 33; dm €24, s €40, d €60-80; P) Tradition is worn on the sleeve of this historic half-timbered house with wooden interiors. The restaurant has a nice beer garden and a good wine list.

Hotel Residenz (☎ 034671-750; www.residenz -frankenhausen.de; Am Schlachtberg 3; s €69, d €99-119, ste €150; P ✗ ☑) This large hotel close to the Panorama Museum is a good midrange choice for overnight stays, and even better for last minute deals and wellness packages that include use of a huge spa section. The restaurant is one the best options in town (mains €8 to €20).

Weinlokal Zum Schwan (☎ 034671-624 32; Erfurter Strasse 9; mains €8.50-13) This restaurant, in one of the oldest half-timbered buildings in town, serves local Sauerbraten and various steaks, and has about 30 bottled wines on its list.

Getting There & Around

Train connections to Bad Frankenhausen usually require a change in Bretleben or Sömmerda. Erfurt has the best connections (€9, 1½ hours). By car or motorcycle, take the B4, B86 and then the B85.

To get to outlying sights, it's best to go under your own steam. **FAU Radwanderzentrum** (☎ 034671-777 71; Hauptbahnhof) rents bikes (€3 to €5 per day).

THURINGIAN FOREST

The Thuringian Forest (Thüringer Wald), a mountainous region about 35km wide and 160km long, stretches between Eisenach in the northwest and Saalfeld in the southeast. This central upland, which is studded with crags and peaks rising to about 1000m, is crossed by Germany's most popular trail, the Rennsteig, which runs for 168km along spectacular ridges. The Thuringian Forest also incorporates the 76-sq-km **Hainich National Park** (☎ 3603- 390728; www.nationalpark-hainich.de).

Despite the impact of acid rain and thoughtless development in patches (especially near Suhl), the climate, dense woodlands and rural paths make the region a wonderful place to explore by foot, bike or in modern single-carriage railcars on the regional railway network.

EISENACH

☎ 03691 / pop 44,000

Situated on the western edge of the Thuringian Forest, the modest and pretty town of Eisenach is famous for being the birthplace of Johann Sebastian Bach, and as the place where Martin Luther went into hiding on the eve of the Reformation. Luther's refuge, the Wartburg, is now a Unesco World Heritage site. Beyond the castle itself, Eisenach offers the visitor plenty of culture and is a convenient gateway to the picturesque Rennsteig, Germany's most popular hiking trail.

Orientation

Except for the Wartburg, which is 2km southwest of town, most sights are concentrated around the Markt, a 15-minute walk from the Hauptbahnhof. Local buses stop right outside the Hauptbahnhof, while overland buses go to Müllerstrasse one block northwest.

Information

Eisenach Classic Card (per 72hr €16) Covers public transport and gives you free or reduced admission to important sights.
Main post office (Markt 6)
Sparkasse (☎ 685 854; Markt 2) Bank with ATM.
Surf Planet (Alexanderstrasse 63; per 30min €1.50; ☿ 6am-3am) Internet café.
Tourist-Information (☎ 792 30; www.eisenach.de; Markt 9; ☿ 10am-6pm Mon-Fri, 10am-4pm Sat year-round, 11am-1pm Sun Apr-Oct)
Wartburg Information (☎ 2500; Auf der Wartburg; ☿ 8.30am-8pm Mar-Oct, 9am-5pm Nov-Apr) In the Wartburg.

Sights

WARTBURG

Caught in turbulence like no other, the medieval **Wartburg** (☎ 2500; www.wartburg-eisenach

.de; tour adult/concession €6.50/5.50, museum & Luther room only €3.50/2; ⏱ tours 8.30am-5pm) is thought to have been created in 1067 by Count Ludwig der Springer (the Jumper; see p273). Sections of the castle are monuments to the late-Romanesque style, while other rooms are more recent and date from restoration work at Goethe's behest to save Wartburg from becoming historic rubble. The result is a delightful blend of Romanesque, Gothic, Renaissance and Revivalism.

Richard Wagner based his opera *Tannhäuser* on a famous minstrels' contest that took place at the castle between 1206 and 1207. It was also notably the residence of the much-revered Elisabeth, wife of the Landgrave of Thuringia. She was canonised shortly after

her death in 1235 for abandoning a pompous court lifestyle in favour of helping the poor.

From 1521 to 1522, Martin Luther went into hiding here under the assumed name of Junker Jörg, after being excommunicated and put under papal ban. During this time he translated the entire New Testament from Greek into German, contributing enormously to the development of the written German language. His modest wood-panelled **study** is part of the guided tour (available in English), which is the only way to view the interior. Many of the rooms you'll see contain extravagant 19th-century impressions of medieval life rather than the original fittings. The Romanesque **Great Hall** is one highlight.

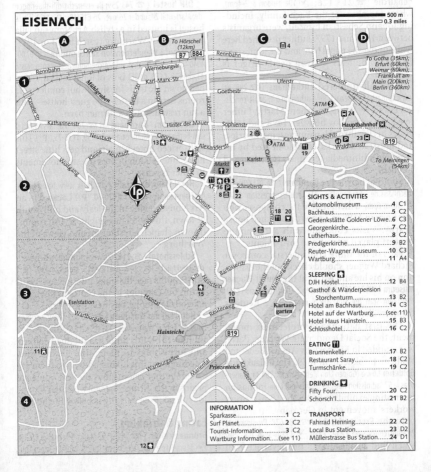

The **museum** houses famous paintings of Luther by Lucas Cranach the Elder, and important Christian artefacts from all over Germany. Between Easter and October, crowds can be horrendous, so arrive before 11am.

To get to the Wartburg from the Markt, walk one block west to Wydenbrugkstrasse, then head southwest along Schlossberg through the forest via Eselstation (this takes about 40 minutes, and parts are rather steep). A more scenic return route is via the Haintal (50 minutes). From April to October, buses 10 and 13 run roughly hourly to the Eselstation, just below the castle (€1.10).

CITY CENTRE

The Markt is dominated by the galleried **Georgenkirche** (☎ 213 126; ⏰ 10am-noon & 2-4pm), where members of the Bach family, including Johann Sebastian himself, were organists between 1665 and 1797. Luther preached here while under the papal ban, and the tombstone of the ubiquitous Ludwig der Springer is also here.

The half-timbered **Lutherhaus** (☎ 298 30; www.lutherhaus-eisenach.de; Lutherplatz 8; adult/concession €3/1.50; ⏰ 10am-5pm), where Martin Luther lived as a schoolboy between 1498 and 1501, traces his life through paintings, manuscripts and illustrated works, complemented by interactive multimedia terminals (German and English).

South of here is the **Bachhaus** (☎ 793 40; www.bachhaus.de; Frauenplan 21; adult/concession €4/3; ⏰ 10am-6pm), a memorial to the composer who was born in 1685 in a now-demolished house nearby. Visits conclude with a 25-minute concert played on antique instruments.

Fans of the more controversial composer Richard Wagner should check out the exhibition on his life and works at the **Reuter-Wagner Museum** (☎ 743 293; Reuterweg 2; adult/concession €3/2; ⏰ 11am-5pm Tue-Sun) in writer Fritz Reuter's former villa.

The first nationwide proletarian movement, the Social Democratic Workers Party, was founded in Eisenach by August Bebel and Wilhelm Liebknecht in 1869. The **Gedenkstätte Goldener Löwe** (Golden Lion Memorial; ☎ 754 34; Marienstrasse 57; admission free; ⏰ 9am-4pm Mon-Fri) has an interesting exhibit covering the 19th-century workers' movement in Germany.

In the **Predigerkirche** (☎ 784 678; Predigerplatz 2; adult/concession €2.60/1.60; ⏰ 11am-5pm Tue-Sun) you'll find a collection of medieval art from Thuringia, including sculpture, paintings and liturgical objects.

Though now a shadow of its former self, car manufacturing revved up in Eisenach in 1896 when a factory was built to manufacture Wartburgs, which were based on a French car called the Decauville. The **Automobilmuseum** (☎ 772 12; Friedrich-Naumann-Strasse 10; adult/concession €3/2; ⏰ 11am-5pm Tue-Sun), with its Wartburg Dixi dating from 1899, a legendary BMW 328 sports car and other exhibits, celebrates this history.

Sleeping

The tourist office has a free room-finding service – private rooms start at €15 a single and €25 for a double.

DJH hostel (☎ 743 259; jh-eisenach@djh-thueringen.de; Mariental 24; under 26/over 26 €15/18; P ✗) This hostel is housed in a stylish Art Nouveau villa at the foot of Wartburg (catch bus 3 or 10).

Gasthof & Wanderpension Storchenturm (☎ 07 00-4040 4050; www.gasthof-am-storchenturm.de; Georgenstrasse 43; dm €18, s €23, d €36) Lots of long-socked hikers pad down the trails for simple but comfortable rooms here in a hostel-type guest house – with a fun restaurant in a former barn.

Hotel am Bachhaus (☎ 204 70; www.hotel-am-bachhaus.de; Marienstrasse 7; s €50, d €70-75; P) This well-designed hotel is plain and gets little street noise, but you might hear guests' movements in other rooms.

Hotel Haus Hainstein (☎ 2420; www.hainstein.de; Am Hainstein 16; s €45-60, d €70-80; P) Located in an Art Nouveau villa in the leafy and hilly south of town, this hotel has bright, stylish rooms, its own chapel, a restaurant and views of the Wartburg.

Schlosshotel (☎ 214 260; www.schlosshotel-eisenach.de; Marktplatz 10; s €78, d €105-115, ste €124-180; P) Most rooms face the quiet interior courtyard in this big complex in the centre of town. It's a favourite among business travellers.

Hotel auf der Wartburg (☎ 797 223; www.wartburghotel.de; Auf der Wartburg; s €135-155, d €200-320; P ✗) Built in 1914, this hotel has subdued colours and furnishings to match the historic site. The singles at this luxury address in town are called 'Luther' rooms, but the real opulence begins in the 'Prince' category (similar to junior suites). Free parking is below the hotel.

Eating & Drinking

Brunnenkeller (☎ 212 358; Markt 10; mains €8-12; ⏰ 11am-11pm Apr-Oct, 11am-3pm & 5.30-11.30pm Thu-

Mon, 5.30-11pm Tue & Wed Nov-Mar) Here you might hear James Blunt's voice echoing as if from a distant sewer, followed by a low-volume Jackson Five – the waiter's favourites on a quiet night, it seems. But all is well in this former monastery cellar, which serves local culinary favourites.

Turmschänke (☎ 213 533; Wartburgallee 2; mains €22-25; ☷ 6pm-midnight Mon-Sat) A Jackson Five free zone – just class and good food in a thoroughly atmospheric wine restaurant that is part of the Hotel Kaiserhof.

Restaurant Saray (☎ 720 851; Frauenberg 13; mains €8-13; ☷ 5.30pm-midnight Mon-Fri, 11.30am-2.30pm & 5.30pm-midnight Sat & Sun) Dishes in this tasty Turkish restaurant will delight vegetarians especially.

Schorsch'l (☎ 213 049; www.schorschl.de; Georgenstrasse 19) This relaxed pub draws an upbeat alternative crowd for drinks, light eats and live music.

Fifty Four (☎ 888 830; Wartburgallee 54; ☐) Chill out in this café-bar that offers snacks, good cocktails and lots more (like internet access) till late.

Getting There & Around

Direct regional trains run frequently to Erfurt (€9, 50 minutes), Gotha (€5, 25 minutes) and Weimar (€12, 1¼ hours) from Eisenach. ICE trains are faster and also run to Frankfurt-am-Main (€39, 1¾ hours) from here; direct IC trains to Berlin-Hauptbahnhof (€54, 3¾ hours) stop in Eisenach. Bus services are sporadic at best; two useful connections include the 280b to Friedrichroda, and the 30 to Mühlhausen (all from the Müllerstrasse bus station).

If you're driving, Eisenach is right on the A4 (exits Eisenach Ost or Eisenach West) and is crossed by the B7, B19 and B84.

Fahrrad Henning (☎ 784 738; Schmelzerstrasse 4-6) rents bikes for €8 per day. Pick up a cycling map from the tourist office.

RENNSTEIG

Famous, perhaps even notorious, as Germany's most popular long-distance trail, the 168km Rennsteig wends and winds southeast from Hörschel (just outside Eisenach) along forested mountain ridges to Blankenstein on the Saale River. The trail is marked by signposts reading 'R', and is best hiked in May/June and September/October. You should be moderately fit, but otherwise no special skills or equipment are needed – just good shoes and a set of strong thighs to carry you for five days. Day hikes, such as between Hörschel and Oberhof, offer a taste of the trail, and if you do want to stay overnight, villages and towns below the trail have plenty of *pensions* and hotels.

A Rennsteig bike trail also begins in Hörschel, but it is mostly parallel to the hiking trail. The tourist office in Eisenach has cycling and hiking brochures and maps. You can also pick up information and professional maps – Kompass Wanderkarte No 118 (€7) is a good one – from the **Rennsteigwanderhaus** (☎ 036928-911 94; Rennsteigstrasse 9, Hörschel; ☷ 8.30-10.30am & 2-4pm Mon-Fri, 9-11am & 2-4pm Sat, 9-11am Sun).

There's a local tradition of dipping your walking stick into the Werra and picking up a pebble from its waters before starting out. Upon leaving the Rennsteig, the pebble is given back to the forest.

Hörschel is regularly serviced by regional trains and buses from Eisenach's Hauptbahnhof and Müllerstrasse bus station respectively (in the direction of Oberellen). Blankenstein has good connections with Saalfeld, Jena and beyond.

LUDWIG DER SPRINGER – TAKING THE JUMP

German gentry is rife with monikers. Henry the Fowler was supposedly out catching birds one day when someone told him he'd just become king. The unfortunate 13th-century Thuringian landgrave, Henry the Illustrious, squabbled for years over Thuringia and other territories, and had a son called Albert the Degenerate. Karl the Bald got his by-name for obvious reasons. Ludwig the Rich probably didn't even earn his. But what about Ludwig der Springer (Ludwig the Jumper)? Ludwig supposedly got his jumping-Jack-moniker when he sprang out of a window into the Saale River in Halle. The great leap occurred after he was jailed for fatally stabbing the margrave Friedrich III in a squabble over Saxony. To make good his foul deed against Friedrich, he founded the Benedictine monastery that lies under the foundations of Schloss Reinhardsbrunn in what is now – you guessed it – Friedrichroda (see p274).

THURINGIA

FRIEDRICHRODA

☎ 03623 / pop 5500

Dangling down into a valley from wooded slopes about 20km south of Gotha, Friedrichroda was the second-busiest resort town in GDR days. When the freshly liberated proletariat collectively set its sights on Majorca and other beach destinations in the 1990s, even picturesque resorts like this couldn't compete. However, its popularity has since grown again, especially with improved infrastructure and the development of health and spa tourism. The town now has a state-of-the-art therapeutic bath centre and it is also establishing itself as a location for winter sports.

Orientation & Information

Friedrichroda has two train stations: Bahnhof Friedrichroda in the east and Bahnhof Reinhardsbrunn north of the centre – both stops for the Thüringerwaldbahn (which is actually a tram, see the boxed text p268). The **tourist office** (☎ 332 00; www.friedrichroda.de; Marktstrasse 13-15; ⏱ 9am-5pm Mon-Thu, 9am-6pm Fri, 9am-noon Sat) is in the centre of town. A bank with an international ATM is in the centre, at Hauptstrasse 35–37.

Sights & Activities

Friedrichroda's prime attraction is the **Marienglashöhle** (☎ 304 953; tour adult/concession €4/2; ⏱ tours 9am-5pm, 9am-4pm Nov-Mar), a large gypsum cave featuring an underwater lake and a crystal grotto. You enter the latter in the dark, then – just to give you that otherworldly feel – the theme from *Close Encounters of the Third Kind* plays in the background as the light gradually brightens, unveiling a sparkling universe. Most of the crystallised gypsum here has been harvested and used to decorate statues of the Virgin Mary and altars in the region and beyond.

The cave is about a 40-minute walk through the woods from the city centre, and is also a stop on the Thüringerwaldbahn (see box, p268).

In the northern part of town, in the midst of a lavish English park with ancient trees, stands the neo-Gothic **Schloss Reinhardsbrunn** (1828), built on the foundations of a medieval Benedictine monastery founded by Wartburg builder Ludwig the Springer; see the box p273. Queen Victoria of England first met her cousin, Duke Albert of Saxe-Coburg-Gotha, here; they married in 1840.

An English buyer has since bought it and plans to reopen its hotel.

Just south of the Schloss is the lovely landscaped **Kurpark**, home to the Ludowinger spring, where excellent mineral water bubbles up from a depth of 58m. Much of it is bottled, but you can also go to one of the glass pavilions in the park and fill up from the taps.

For an easy day excursion into the forest, you can take the Thüringer Wald-Express bus (€4.50) to the **Heuberghaus** on the mountain ridge, hike along the ridge to the **Inselsberg** peak (90 minutes), then take the Inselsberg Express bus (€4.50) down to Tabarz and catch the Thüringerwaldbahn back to Friedrichroda (€1.20).

Sleeping & Eating

Friedrichroda has no shortage of hotels and *pensions*, but nor is there a shortage of visitors in mid-summer. **Private rooms** (from €14) are one option. There's a compulsory *Kurtaxe* of €1.20 on all accommodation giving discounts for many sights.

Pension Feierabend (☎ 304 386; Büchig 1; s/d €25/40; P) This remarkable three-storey timbered house is surely impossible to beat for value, comfort and character. It's opposite the Kurpark and set back from the main road leading from Friedrichroda Bahnhof to the information office. Rooms 8 and 9 are especially spacious.

Pension Villa Phönix (☎ 200 880; www.villa-phoenix.de; Tabarzer Strasse 3; s €30, d €45) Although this Phönix rises up right alongside the road (with weird little balconies), double glazing or double doors keep out the street noise. It's bright and friendly, and a cut above the rest. The midrange restaurant serves meat and vegetarian dishes.

Berghotel (☎ 354 4440; reservierung.berghotel@t-online.de; Bergstrasse 1; s €50-57, d €77-91; P ☺) This 1000-bed GDR block is an absolute beast. The rooms are variable; some still have GDR furnishings, while others have been completely overhauled. But the hilltop location is great and you can't beat the views from the terrace restaurant (mains €8 to €20).

In addition to the eating options mentioned here, Hauptstrasse has many places to satisfy a country hunger – walk along, sniff and take your pick. Virtually all have a traditional ambience.

Getting There & Around

The Thüringerwaldbahn (No 4), a historic tram, serves Gotha (€3.60) and Tabarz (€0.90) several times hourly. The most scenic stretch begins right after Friedrichroda, running through the forest to Tabarz. Bus 451 runs to Schmalkalden twice on weekdays.

If you're driving, take the Waltershausen/ Friedrichroda exit off the A4. The town is also on the B88 to Ilmenau.

Berghotel rents out mountain bikes for €8 per day.

ILMENAU

☎ 03677 / pop 27,000

Goethe visited Ilmenau, a sleepy little town on the northern slopes of the Thuringian Forest, no fewer than 28 times in his lifetime. It's therefore little wonder that it is also the gateway to the famous Goethewanderweg hiking trail (see p276). Even Goethe, however, could not halt the decline of Ilmenau's once prosperous mining industry, which was active in the Middle Ages. Today, as well as Goethe's free and wandering spirit (look out for a statue of him reposing on a bench at the Markt), visitors will find a small student population from the technical university.

The **tourist office** (☎ 202 358; www.ilmenau.de; Lindenstrasse 12; ☼ 9am-6pm Mon-Fri, 9am-1pm Sat) reserves hotels and private rooms from €25.

The **DJH hostel** (☎ 884 681; jh-ilmenau@djh -thueringen.de; Am Stollen 49; under 26/over 26 €15/18; ☒ ☐) is 2km east of the train station off Langewiesener Strasse.

Hotel Tanne (☎ 6590; www.hotel-tanne-thueringen .de; Lindenstrasse 38; s €55-60, d €75-85, ste €100; ☐ ☒) has comforts such as sauna, solarium and massage facilities to rejuvenate the body after a tough day on the Goetheweg.

Direct trains to Erfurt leave about once an hour (€9.10, 1 hour); change in Neudietendorf for Eisenach (€13.40, 1½ hours). Ilmenau is easily reached via the B88 from Eisenach, the B4 from Erfurt and the B87 from Weimar.

SCHMALKALDEN

☎ 03683 / pop 18,000

Stretching along a broad river valley and up the southwestern slopes of the Thuringian Forest, Schmalkalden is at first sight not as picture-book pretty as some of its neighbours. It's only once you explore the centre that you discover the real charms of this medieval town, located some 17km south of Friedrich-roda. Schmalkalden will forever be tied to the Reformation, for it was here that the Protestant princes met in 1530 and formed the Schmalkaldic League, to counter the central powers of Catholic Emperor Charles V, paving the way for the Peace of Augsburg and freedom of religion for the German states in 1546.

The Altstadt sighs under the sheer weight of its half-timbered houses, which are said to make up about 90% of buildings in the historic heart. All this is crowned by a handsome hilltop castle, Schloss Wilhelmsburg.

Orientation & Information

It's about a 10-minute walk from the train and bus stations to the Altmarkt, the town's central square, and another seven minutes to Schloss Wilhelmsburg. There's an ATM booth on Weidebrunner Gasse, near Lutherplatz, and the post office is at the southern end of Altmarkt.

The **tourist office** (☎ 403 182; www.schmalkalden .de; Mohrengasse 1a; ☼ 9am-6pm Mon-Fri, 10am-3pm Sat Apr-Oct, 9am-5pm Sat Nov-Mar) is just off Altmarkt.

Sights & Activities

Towering above the city centre is the well-preserved late-Renaissance-style **Schloss Wilhelmsburg** (☎ 403 186; Schlossberg 9; adult/concession €3.50/2; ☼ 10am-6pm Apr-Oct, 10am-4pm Tue-Sun Nov-Mar). It was built between 1585 and 1590 by Landgrave Wilhelm IV of Hessen, as a hunting lodge and summer residence. The Schloss has kept its original design from the Renaissance period, with lavish murals and stucco decorating most rooms, of which the **Riesensaal**, with its coffered and painted ceiling, is the most impressive. The playfully decorated **Schlosskirche**, the palace chapel, has a rare wood organ that is thought to be the oldest working organ of its type in Europe. Concerts are held from May to September on this Renaissance gem (contact the tourist office).

The **Rathaus** (1419) on Altmarkt functioned as the meeting place of the Schmalkaldic League; nearby the incongruous towers of the late-Gothic **St Georgenkirche**, another place where Luther once preached, also look out over the square.

Schmalkalden is the western terminus of the **Martin-Luther-Weg**, a 17km easy-to-moderate hiking trail that ends at Tambach-Dietharz,

THURINGIA

GOETHEWANDERWEG

This lovely, and at times challenging, 18.5km day hike follows in the footsteps of Johann Wolfgang von Goethe, who spent much time around Ilmenau in the employ of Carl August, Duke of Saxe-Weimar. The hike encompasses level forest terrain, steep climbs and everything in between; it's marked with the letter 'G' in Goethe's own handwriting. An excellent 1:30,000 hiking map by Grünes Herz is available at the tourist office (€4).

The starting point is the Amtshaus, a subdued baroque structure on the Markt that was Goethe's Ilmenau home, where five rooms have been turned into a **memorial exhibit** (☎ 03677-202 667; adult/concession €1/0.50; ☒ 9am-noon, 1-4.30pm).

From here the trail heads west via the Schwalbenstein and Emmasteinfelsen peaks to the village of Manebach, where the steep climb up the Kickelhahn (861m) begins. Near the top, you'll pass the replica of the little forest cabin, Goethehäuschen, where Goethe wrote the famous poem *Wayfarer's Night Song*. At the top is a restaurant, **Berggasthaus Kickelhahn** (☎ 03677-202 034; Kickelhahn 1), and a lookout tower with views over the great green blanket of the Thuringian Forest.

The trail descends to **Jagdhaus Gabelbach** (☎ 202 626; adult/concession €2/1.50; ☒ 10am-5pm Sat & sun Apr-Oct, 11am-3pm Nov-Mar), a hunting lodge and former guesthouse with exhibits on Goethe's scientific research. From here, it meanders south to the village of Stützerbach, where the **Goethe-Museum Stützerbach** (☎ 036784-502 77) features the rooms (still originally furnished) where Goethe used to stay and work.

Check with the tourist office (or online at www.rennsteig-bus.de) about the No 300 bus service back to Ilmenau. You can also walk directly to the Kickelhahn from Ilmenau, bypassing Manebach, in about 1½ hours. Or you can drive up Waldstrasse to the parking lot at Herzogröder Wiesen, from where it's a 25-minute uphill walk to the Kickelhahn peak.

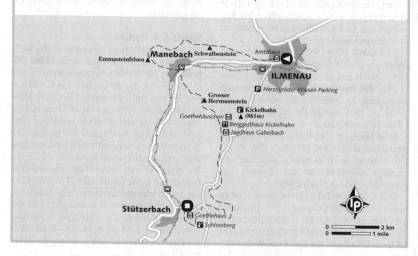

from where there are bus services back to town (weekdays only; the tourist office can help with times).

About 6km north of town, **Neue Hütte** (☎ 403 018; Gothaer Strasse; adult/concession €2/1; ☒ 10am-5pm Apr-Oct only) will thrill both kids and the technically minded. One of the few surviving 19th-century smelting plants in Europe, it has a waterwheel, turbines and other industrial knick-knacks.

Sleeping & Eating

Stadthotel Patrizier (☎ 604 514; www.stadthotel -patrizier.de; Weidebrunner Gasse 9; s €41-52, d €72-98) This hotel is very comfortable and well run, and provides a nice place to stay. The restaurant, one of the best options around, is in a vaulted cellar and opens for dinner on weekdays, and lunch and dinner on weekends (mains €9 to €32).

Teichhotel (☎ 402 661; teichhotel@t-online.de; Teichstrasse 21; s/d €42/70; P ✗) Just outside the Altstadt, this hotel has plain but comfortable rooms. The restaurant serves well-priced hearty fare to keep the hikers and bikers happy.

Maykel's (☎ 608 970; Lutherplatz 1; mains €6-10; ☷ 10am-midnight Sun-Thu, 10am-1am Fri & Sat) This relaxed café-bar and restaurant does tasty dishes, including some for vegetarians.

Drinking & Entertainment

The Castle (☎ 466 703; www.thecastle-schmalkalden.de; Schlossberg 1b; ☷ 7pm-midnight Mon-Thu, 7pm-2am Fri & Sat, also Sun May-Oct) This is the scene of most night-time happenings in town. A young-ish crowd gathers indoors in winter, and in summer spills outdoors into the yard.

Getting There & Around

Trains to Erfurt (€25, 1¾ hours) require changes in Wernshausen and Eisenach. Schmalkalden is about 5km east of the B19, which connects Eisenach and Meiningen.

Fahrrad Anschütz ☎ 403 909; Stiller Gasse 17; bikes per day €5-10) rents city, touring and mountain bikes. The 23km Mommelstein bike trail follows a former railway line and some forest trails through a tunnel and viaduct, and past the big sights (the tourist office can help).

MEININGEN

☎ 03693 / pop 22,000

Tranquil, idyllic and blessed with vast expanses of parkland, Meiningen is one the nicest towns in a region glistening with rural gems. It is situated on the Werra River about 30km south of Schmalkalden, between the Thuringian Forest and the Rhön mountain range, and is the former residence of the dukes of Saxe-Meiningen. It owes its reputation as a regional cultural centre to the vision of Duke Georg II (1826–1914), who in 1866 founded a resident theatre troupe that staged productions in far-flung Moscow and London, and is said to be the forerunner of the Royal Shakespeare Company. Georg II also catapulted the court orchestra (the Meininger Hofkapelle) to international fame by appointing pianist-conductor Hans von Bülow as musical director; the baton later passed to Richard Strauss and Max Reger. The annual theatre festival in spring has an excellent reputation at home and abroad.

Orientation & Information

The Schlosspark to the west and the English Garden to the north fringe Meiningen's town centre. The train and bus stations are on the eastern side of the English Garden, which also contains the Meiningen Theatre. Signs near the train station point across the English Garden towards the tourist office on Markt, with a post office and banks.

The **tourist office** (☎ 446 50; www.meiningen.de; Markt 14; ☷ 10am-6pm Mon-Fri, 10am-3pm Sat) is behind the Stadtkirche. **Das Waschcafé** (☎ 885 571; www.das-waschcafé.de; Anton-Ulrich-Strasse 49; ☷ 9am-noon & 2-10pm Mon-Fri, 2-10pm Sat) has a finger in many pies – being both a café and a travel agency, and with internet access.

Sights

The lavish late-17th-century **Schloss Elisabethenburg** (☎ 503 641; www.meiningermuseen.de; adult/concession €3/2; ☷ 10am-6pm Tue-Sun) served as the ducal residence until 1918, and in addition to the pure-baroque central floors of the main wing it has neo-Renaissance and other revivalist features. Inside is a medieval and Renaissance **art collection**, a **Music Museum** (a series of rooms that are dedicated to the musical directors of the Meininger Hofkapelle), and just down the road is the **Baumbachhaus** (☎ 502 848; Burggasse 2), a small literature museum (included in admission to the Schloss).

The nearby **Theatermuseum** (☎ 471 290; tour adult/concession €2.50/1.50; ☷ 10am, noon, 2pm & 4pm Tue-Sun) displays some of the 275 original stage backdrops from the early days of the Meininger Theater, sketches of set designs and costumes drawn by Georg II, and historic photographs of well-known actors.

A combined ticket for the Schloss and the museums costs €5/3.

Sleeping & Eating

Gasthof Schlundhaus (☎ 813 838; www.meininger-hotels-mit-flair.de; Schlundgasse 4; s €55, d €80, ste €100; P) Rustic-style rooms with new furnishings in a historic hotel make this a comfortable place to repose. The restaurant is worthy, well-priced and is apparently where someone had the brainwave of inventing Thuringian potato dumplings.

Schloss Landsberg (☎ 440 90; Landsberger Strasse 150; s €95, d €120-150; P)The same people run this place. It is a genuine castle converted into a fabulous luxury hotel on the northern edge of town.

THURINGIA

Sächsischer Hof (☎ 4570; www.saechsischerhof
.com; Georgstrasse 1; s €78-102, d €110-140; **P** **X**) This
200-year-old full-service inn is a destination
in itself. The standard rooms are spacious,
others are palatial (most have ante-rooms),
even if the bathrooms are a trifle small.
The hotel has two dynamite restaurants:
the Kutscherstube (mains €8 to €15, open
11am to 2pm and 5pm-midnight) serves
local specialities and a couple of vegetarian
dishes, whereas the Posthalterei (mains €15
to €21, 3- to 6-course menus €29 to €51,
open 5pm to midnight Tuesday to Saturday,
11am to 2pm Sunday), housed in what was
once the building for keeping postal coaches,
is upmarket and Mediterranean in flavour.
Dip into one or more of the 280 different
wines in the cellar – they're served in both
restaurants.

Turmcafé (☎ 881 036; Schloss Elisabethenburg; food
€2-5) Over-the-top in all ways, this baroque
café in the Hesse Room high in the Schloss has
lovely coffee and cake, or soup and salad.

Entertainment

Apart from reaching too deeply into the Sächsischer Hof's wine cellar, low-life options are
not all that forthcoming in Meiningen.

Clubs worth the short trot on the right
night include **Studio2** (☎ 470 444; www.studio2.de;
Steinweg 28; ☺ from 10pm Wed, Fri & Sat) and the more
serious **Elanclub** (www.elanclub.de; Bernhardstrasse 1);
see their websites for events.

The **Das Meininger Theater** (☎ 4510; www
.das-meininger-theater.de; Bernhardsstrasse 5), with a very
strong classical focus on Goethe, Schiller and
European names, is always worth a trot among
the greenery of the English Garden.

Getting There & Away

Direct trains travel to Erfurt every two hours
(€15, 1¾ hours). Regular buses and trains link
Meiningen with Schmalkalden, Zella-Mehlis
and other towns in the Thuringian Forest.
Meiningen is on the B19 from Eisenach to
Schweinfurt in Bavaria, and is also on the B89
to Sonneberg in southern Thuringia.

THE SAALE VALLEY

JENA

☎ 03641 / pop 100,000

Located about 23km east of Weimar, the university town of Jena is a landmark of culture

and science in the region. The architecture
here can be patchy, but work is continuing
on the restoration of its historic buildings,
and even the large and once-ugly Intershop
tower rising up from the Altstadt has been
transformed from an eye-sore into something
of an attraction.

Culturally, Jena can be a beguiling town,
with the students (some 20,000 of them)
creating a lively atmosphere. Science buffs
will know Jena in connection with the development of optical precision technology and
names like Carl Zeiss, Ernst Abbe and Otto
Schott. There are several interesting museums
relating to this tradition, which continues
today through corporations like Carl Zeiss
Jena, Schott Jenaer Glaswerk and Jenoptik.

Orientation

Jena's main attractions are all within walking
distance of each other. There are two main
train stations: Jena West (Westbahnhof), in
the southwest, and Jena Paradies next to the
Saale River, near the centre and the main bus
station. The Saalbahnhof station north
of town is rarely used.

Information

C-Net (☎ 357 352; www.café-c.net; Teutonengasse 2;
per 30min €2; ☺ 1pm-midnight Mon-Thu, 1pm-1am
Fri, 11am-1am Sat, 11am-midnight Sun) Internet access.
Entrance on Grietgasse.
JeNah Service Centre (☎ 414 330; www.jenah.de;
Holzmarktpassage) Transport information and local
information.
Main post office (Engelplatz 8)
Police (☎ 810; Anger 30)
Sparkasse Jena (☎ 01801-679 679; Ludwig-
Weimar-Gasse) Bank with ATM.
Tourist information (☎ 806 400; www.jena.de;
Johannisstrasse 23; ☺ 9.30am-7pm Mon-Fri, 9.30am-
4pm Sat, 11am-3pm Sun Apr-Oct, 9.30am-7pm Mon-Fri,
9.30am-3pm Sat Nov-Mar)

Sights

AROUND THE MARKT

Despite the forces of time and developers'
bulldozers, Jena's **Markt** still reflects a measure
of the city's medieval heritage. At its southern
end stands the **Rathaus** (1380), with an astronomical clock in its baroque tower. Every
hour, on the hour, a little door opens and a
devil/fool called Schnapphans appears, trying
to catch a golden ball (representing the human
soul) that dangles in front of him.

The square is anchored by a **statue** of Prince-Elector Johann Friedrich I, founder of Jena's university and popularly known as 'Hanfried'. The handsome building with the half-timbered upper section at the western end contains the **Stadtmuseum & Kunstsammlung der Stadt Jena** (☎ 359 80; www.stadtmuseum.jena.de; adult/concession €4/2; ☽ 10am-5pm Tue, Wed & Fri, 2-10pm Thu, 11am-6pm Sat & Sun). Here you will find an interesting regional history collection on themes as diverse as wine-making, the Reformation and student fraternities.

A walkway beneath the museum leads to the Gothic **Stadtkirche St Michael** (10am-1pm & 2-5pm Mon-Fri, also 10am-1pm Sat May-Sep) which contains the original engraved tombstone of Martin Luther and has a subterranean passage right under the altar.

Visible from almost everywhere in Jena, the 128m-tall cylindrical **Intershop tower** (€3; ☽ 11am-midnight) is the city's most conspicuous building. In the early 1970s, the medieval Eichplatz was razed to make room for this concrete behemoth, built as a Zeiss research facility. It proved unsuitable, and the building languished for some time before receiving a complete facelift and reopening with an observation platform and a good restaurant (see p280).

UNIVERSITÄT JENA

Jena's university was founded as Collegium Jenense in 1558, in a former monastery in Kollegiengasse. Still part of the campus today, it features a nice courtyard festooned with the coat of arms of Johann Friedrich I. North of here, in an excellent example of urban re-engineering, is the former **Zeiss optics factory**, now part of the university. Several buildings wrap around Ernst-Abbe-Platz, dotted with abstract sculptures by Frank Stella; the copies of antique sculptures in the lobby of the main building are a little more aesthetically pleasing. The campus borders the **Goethe Galerie**, a high-tech split-level glass shopping mall.

The university **headquarters** (Füstengraben 1) are in a century-old complex on the northeastern edge of the Altstadt. Inside are a Minerva bust by Rodin and a wall-sized painting showing Jena students going off to fight against Napoleon.

GOETHE & SCHILLER

As minister for the elector of Saxe-Weimar, Goethe spent five years in Jena. When not busy regulating the flow of the Saale, building streets, designing the botanical garden or cataloguing the university library, he crafted *Faust* and *Wilhelm Meister*. He also discovered the obscure central jawbone while researching anatomy in the **Anatomieturm** (cnr Teichgraben & Leutragraben), a former fortification tower. Most of the time he lived in what is now the **Goethe Gedenkstätte** (☎ 949 009; Fürstengraben 26; adult/concession €1/0.50; ☽ 11am-3pm Wed-Sun Apr-Oct), which focuses on his accomplishments as a natural scientist, poet and politician. Goethe himself planted the ginkgo tree just east of here, which is part of the **Botanical Garden** (☎ 949 274; adult/concession €2/1; ☽ 9am-6pm).

Goethe is also credited with bringing Schiller to Jena University. A plaque near the headquarters marks where Schiller gave his inaugural lecture. He liked Jena and stayed for 10 years – longer than anywhere else – mostly in the **Gartenhaus** (☎ 931 188; Schillergässchen 2; adult/concession €2.50/1.30; ☽ 11am-5pm Tue-Sun Apr-Oct). Schiller wrote *Wallenstein* in the little wooden shack in the garden, where he also liked to wax philosophical with Goethe.

CARL ZEISS & ERNST ABBE

These scientists are two more notables who helped put Jena on the map. Zeiss opened his mechanical workshop here in 1846 and began building rudimentary microscopes. With Abbe's help from 1866, he developed the first scientific microscope. In cooperation with Otto Schott, the founder of Jenaer Glasswerke, they pioneered the production of optical precision instruments, propelling Jena to global prominence in the early 20th century.

Their life stories and the evolution of optical technology are the themes of the **Optisches Museum** (☎ 443 165; Carl-Zeiss-Platz 12; adult/concession €5/4; ☽ 10am-4.30pm Tue-Fri, 11am-5pm Sat). There's an interesting collection of microscopes, cameras (including a chunky Polaroid from 1948), spectacles and various other optical instruments. Don't miss the peep shows (originally magnified painted landscapes and the like) and the magic lantern images painted on glass as a forerunner to film projection. An English-language pamphlet is available, and there are tours of the reconstructed Zeiss workshop (1866) next door. The octagonal **pavilion** outside the museum, designed by Belgian Art Nouveau artist Henry van de Velde, dates from 1911 and contains a marble bust of Abbe.

THURINGIA

The **Zeiss Planetarium** (☎ 885 488; www
.planetarium-jena.de; Am Planetarium 5; adult/concession
€6/5) houses the world's oldest public planetarium (1926). Today it boasts a huge state-
of-the-art telescope and does cosmic shows,
such as one based on Pink Floyd's album *Wish
You Were Here*. Its opening hours follow a
varying event schedule. A combined ticket
for the Optical Museum and planetarium is
€9 for adults or €7 with concession.

Festivals & Events

Not to be missed is the **Kulturarena Jena** (☎ 498
060; www.jenaonline.de/kulturarena) music festival
from July to August each year; it's jam-packed
with all kinds of music from blues and rock
to classic and jazz.

Sleeping

The tourist office runs a free reservation service
for hotels and **private rooms** (from €20).

Campingplatz Unter dem Jenzig (☎ 666 688; www
.jenacamping.de; Am Erlkönig 3; adult/child €4/2, car €3, tent
€2-3) This convenient and pretty camp site is
3km north of town.

IB Jugendgästehaus (☎ 687 230; jugendgaestehaus
.jena@internationaler-bund.de; Am Herrenberge 9; s/d €26/38;
P) The mortal shell is the original GDR
1970s exterior, and is not the most aesthetic,
but this hostel is outside the centre and near
forest. Take bus 10, 11, 33 or 40 to Mühlenstrasse.

Hotel Thüringer Hof (☎ 292 90; www.thueringerhof
-jena.de; Westbahnhofstrasse 8; s/d €45/62; P) The main
advantage of this hotel – where the rooms are
otherwise fairly standard for the price – is that
it's just a short crawl for the weary from Jena
West station.

Gasthof Zur Schweiz (☎ 520 50; www.zur-schweiz
.de; Quergasse 15; s/d €48/68; P X) This hotel is
unassuming but well managed and comfortable. Room furnishings vary from period to
more modern. It's situated just off the main
nightlife mile.

Ibis Hotel City am Holzmarkt (☎ 8130; www.ibishotel
.com; Teichgraben 1; s/d €62/71; P) Purpose-built and
still relatively new, this chain hotel is right
among the major sights. The bathrooms are
interesting works of functional art – moulded
plastic with pseudo-decking.

Gasthaus zur Noll (☎ 597 710; www.zur-noll.de; Oberlauengasse 19; s €60-70, d €70-90; P) In a historic
building, but thoroughly modern inside, this
hotel has elegant furnishings and fine character. It's a good choice (see right).

Steigenberger Hotel Esplanade (☎ 8000; www
.jena.steigenberger.de; Carl-Zeiss-Platz 4; s €88-112, d €101-
162, ste €127-600; P X X) Psychologists have
been known to bring vertigo sufferers up to
the 7th floor here for exposure therapy (it has
a glass lift and – parents of toddlers note – low
walkway railings). It's got lots of class, especially as rooms have a light and breezy feel.

Eating

Literaten-Café (☎ 443 154; Unterm Markt 3; cakes €3-
4; ☯ 8am-6pm) If you can find the book you
want, it will cost €1 in this remarkable café-
cum-bookstore with upstairs seating.

Roter Hirsch (☎ 443 221; www.jembo.de; Holzmarkt
10; mains €5-14; ☯ 9am-10pm Mon-Sat) With wooden
panelling, a warren of rooms with secluded
corners, and the heady atmosphere of another
age (like 500 years ago) the interior here is an
attraction in itself. The menu will satisfy, with
hearty local culinary delights.

Rotonda (☎ 8000; Goethe Galerie; mains €5-22;
☯ 10am-10pm Mon-Fri, 10am-7pm Sat & Sun) Vegetarians will love the lunchtime salad or evening
antipasto buffet in this stylish place, part of
the Hotel Esplanade. There's a €22 three-
course menu in the evening and other lunch
dishes to make it a highly worthwhile stopover. A brunch is served every Sunday, with
piano backing.

Zur Noll (☎ 441 566; Oberlauengasse 19; mains €9-
17; ☯ from 10.30am) This historic restaurant-
pub serves some of the best and most varied
German food in town. Its garlic soup is a delicious culinary interlude and offerings such
as a suckling-pig buffet soar to unexpected
heights. The patio out the back is another
reason to come here.

Scala (☎ 356 666; www.scala-jena.de; Intershop-Tower;
mains €15-25; ☯ 11am-midnight) Gaze over the pan-
optic landscape around Jena, while sipping
wine and downing very decent international
cuisine in this tower restaurant. Other tower
restaurants may be higher, maybe others are
even better, but this has character – you can
even drink coffee outside if the weather's fine.
Book ahead.

Drinking & Entertainment

Jena's 'pub mile' is along Wagnergasse, on the
northwestern edge of the city centre. Stroll
along and take your pick.

Café Stilbruch (☎ 827 171; Wagnergasse 2; 8.30am-1am
Mon-Fri, 9am-late Sat & Sun) This is the best address for
a tipple or for delicious bistro fare and salads.

There's even a table-for-four up among the plants at the top of the iron spiral staircase.

Rosenkeller (☎ 931 190; Johannisstrasse 13) Steps away, this historic student club with a network of cellars offers live concerts and party nights.

F-Haus (☎ 558 10; www.f-haus.de; Johannisplatz 14) Linked to the university, serious student clubbers get a full programme of events (and bowling) here. Enter from Krautgasse.

Getting There & Away

ICE trains go to Berlin-Hauptbahnhof from Jena-Paradies (€47, 2½ hours) and Hamburg-Altona either from Jena-Paradies or Jena-West (€87, 1½ hours). Half-hourly regional services from Jena-Paradies go to Rudolstadt (€6.20, 45 minutes) and Saalfeld (€7.60, 50 minutes). To get to Weimar (€4.60, 15 minutes) and Erfurt (€7.50, 30 minutes), you must go to Jena West. The Hopper-Ticket (see p251) can work out cheaper.

Jena is just north of the A4 from Dresden to Frankfurt, and just west of the A9 from Berlin to Munich. It's also crossed by the B7 (east–west) and B88 (north–south).

Getting Around

Individual tickets on buses and trams cost €1.50 and are valid for one hour. Day passes cost €3.80. For a taxi, call ☎ 458 888. **Fahrrad Kirscht** (☎ 441 539; Löbdegraben 8) rents bikes for €15 for the first day and €5 thereafter.

AROUND JENA
Dornburger Schlösser

Perched on a plateau above the Saale River about 15km north of Jena, these palaces make a pleasant excursion in summer. The southernmost is the **Renaissance Palace** (☎ 036427-222 91; adult/concession €2/1.50; ☼ 10am-6pm Tue-Sun Apr-Oct only), where Goethe sought solitude after the death of his patron, Duke Carl August. The rooms he stayed in have been restored more or less to their 1828 state.

After restoration, the attractive **Rococo Palace** is scheduled to open its doors to visitors in late 2006. The third in this triumvirate, the **Altes Schloss**, blends Romanesque, late-Gothic, Renaissance and baroque elements, and can only be viewed from the outside. The **gardens** (☼ 8am-dusk) are open year-round.

Trains go hourly from Jena Paradies to Dornburg (€2.80, 15 minutes), from where it's a steep 20- to 30-minute climb uphill.

RUDOLSTADT
☎ 03672 / pop 26,000

With its crumbling station, Rudolstadt at first glance looks like it is still catching up with its own history. No less endearing for this, until 1918 it was the main residence of the princes of Schwarzburg-Rudolstadt, and had its heyday during the 18th-century Enlightenment. In 1788 Goethe and Schiller met here for the first time. The Rudolstadt theatre, founded in 1793 and where Liszt, Wagner and Paganini all worked, is still putting on performances today. The prime attraction, however, is a baroque castle high above town.

Rudolstadt's **tourist office** (☎ 414 743; www .rudolstadt.de; Marktstrasse 57; ☼ 9am-6pm Mon-Fri, 9am-1pm Sat) is just west of the Markt.

The baroque **Schloss Heidecksburg** (☎ 429 00; www.heidecksburg.de; adult/concession €4.50/2.50; ☼ 10am-6pm Tue-Sun Apr-Oct, 10am-5pm Nov-Mar) is a hulking edifice on a lofty bluff. Besides lavishly decorated and furnished rooms, the complex also harbours regional history exhibits and collections of paintings, weapons and minerals. Perhaps the palace's best features, though, are free: a terrific view over the valley, the local decorative porcelain (usually with figurines) in the ticket office hall and, especially, the fantastic wooden sleighs by the entrance. It's a 10-minute uphill walk from the central Markt.

The tourist office publishes *Rudolstadt und seine Ecken*, a small German-language brochure map with 16 sights to help visitors explore the town on their own. The second port of call is the **Stadtkirche St Andreas** on Kirchgasse, a Gothic hall-church rich in treasure. The final one (which kids will obviously want to do first!) is the **Spielhaus Richtersche Villa** (☎ 411 451; Schwarzburger Chaussee 74; adult/child €2.50/1.50; ☼ 1-6pm Wed-Sat), where you can fashion miniature buildings in turn-of-the-19th-century style using stone bricks called *Anker* (meaning 'Anchor'), a classic German plaything.

Sleeping & Eating

Rudolstadt has only a couple of hotels located in or near the centre. The tourist office books hotel and private rooms (from about €18).

Jugendgästehaus Rudolstadt (☎ 313 610; www .froebelhaus.org; Schillerstrasse 50; dm under 26/over 26 €15.50/19.50; ☒ ▣) This DJH-affiliated guest house is located in the Altstadt and rents bikes for €5 per day to guests.

THURINGIA

Hotel Adler (☎ 4403; www.hotel-adler-rudolstadt.de; Markt 17; s €50, d €80-90) Situated right on Markt, this hotel has light rooms in a stone building dating from 1512. The restaurant (mains €6.50 to €11, open 11am to 10pm Tuesday to Saturday, to 4pm Sunday) serves good traditional dishes, as well as a couple of vegetarian choices.

Getting There & Away

There is an hourly train service to Jena (€6.20, 30 minutes). Long-distance trains require a change in Saalfeld, which is served twice hourly (€1.80, eight minutes). Rudolstadt is on the B88 between Ilmenau and Jena, and the B85 to Weimar.

SAALFELD

☎ 03671 / pop 28,000

Saalfeld has nestled quietly alongside the Saale River, about 15km south of Rudolstadt, for over a millennium. It has an attractive historic centre and is home to one of Thuringia's most popular natural attractions, the Feengrotten (Fairy Grottoes).

The Hauptbahnhof is east of the Saale River, about a 10-minute walk from the Markt and the **tourist office** (☎ 522 181; www.saalfeld-info.de; Markt 6; ⏰ 9am-6pm Mon-Fri, 10am-2pm Sat).

Sights

The Altstadt can easily be covered on a brief stroll. If you enter town from the Hauptbahnhof, you pass through (and can climb) the 15th-century **Saaltor** (town gate). Just west of here on Markt, is the striking Renaissance **Rathaus**, with its spiked turrets and ornate gables. Opposite is the partly Romanesque **Marktapotheke**, the former town hall and a pharmacy since 1681.

Behind Markt, the twin towers of the Gothic **Johanniskirche** (☎ 2784; Kirchplatz 2; ⏰ 11am-4pm Mon-Fri, 1-5pm Sat & Sun) rise into view. This enormous hall-church features dramatic cross-and-net vaulting, plus a life-size carved figure of John the Baptist.

Brudergasse, west of the Markt, leads uphill to the former Franciscan monastery, now home to the **Stadtmuseum** (☎ 598 471; www.museumimkloster.de; Münzplatz 5; adult/concession €4/2.50; ⏰ 10am-5pm Tue-Sun). Its major allure is the celestial building itself, and the collection of local late-Gothic carved altarpieces.

Feengrotten

These underground **grottoes** (☎ 550 40; www.feengrotten.de; tour adult/concession €6.50/4; ⏰ 9am-

5pm Mar-Oct, 10am-3.30pm Dec-Feb, 10am-3.30pm Sat & Sun Nov only) are Saalfeld's prime attraction. Formerly alum slate mines (from 1530 to 1850) these were opened for tours in 1914. In 1993 they entered the Guinness Book of Records as the world's most colourful grottoes, but 'colour' here refers mostly to different shades of brown, ochre and sienna, with an occasional sprinkling of green and blue. Small stalactite and stalagmite formations add to a bizarre and subtly impressive series of grottoes, with names like Butter Cellar and Blue-Green Grotto. The highlight is the Fairy-tale Cathedral and its Holy Grail Castle.

The cave air is said to help people overcome allergies – some people sit around on deck chairs (in a sleeping bag) in stints here over 10 days at 10°C and 98% humidity.

Sleeping & Eating

Accommodation is comparatively inexpensive, and the **tourist office** (☎ 339 50) can book rooms of all kinds.

Jugendwanderheim (☎ 517 320; wanderheim@drk-saalfeld.de; Am Schieferhof 4; dm €15) This hostel is operated by the German Red Cross. Guests without reservations should report between 6pm and 8pm.

Hotel Anker (☎ 5990; www.hotel-anker-saalfeld.de; Am Markt 25/26; s €47-60, d €74-90; Ⓟ) This gracious hotel-restaurant has almost everything you need. It has some very pleasant rooms (especially in the older building, where each room has a small table) and two restaurants that serve traditional dishes, including game (€8 to €16).

Sächsische Kaffeestube (☎ 2944; Saalstrasse 62; ⏰ 10am-7pm) This is the place for delicious ice cream and coffee on a back terrace overlooking the leafy Saale River.

Zum Pappenheimer (☎ 330 89; www.zum-pappenheimer.de; Fleischgasse 5; mains €6.80-11; ⏰ 8am-midnight Mon-Fri, 9am-2.30pm & 6pm-midnight Sat, 9am-2.30pm Sun) Explore the centre for a couple of other options too, but this cosy, ceramic-tiled bistro-pub is a good place to start or end an evening.

Getting There & Away

Regional trains run twice hourly to Rudolstadt (€1.80, eight minutes) and hourly to Jena (€7.60, 50 minutes). There's also an ICE connection to Berlin-Hauptbahnhof (€54, three hours). Saalfeld lies at the intersection of routes B281 and B85 from Weimar or Jena.

Bavaria

The largest state in Germany, Bavaria (Bayern) is well endowed with natural riches: snowy Alpine peaks, rushing streams and velvety forests that stir the romantic soul. Bolstering Bavarian pride yet more is a wealth of historic buildings, arguably Germany's best art museums, and an economy bigger than Sweden's.

Staunchly conservative, but with a flair for innovation, Bavarians see themselves as separate from the rest of Germany. They still pine for an odd 19th-century monarch, Ludwig II, whose opulent palaces draw millions of visitors each year. Traditions are relished and earthy, and lederhosen-clad men still exist, quaffing frothy steins of beer to the strains of an oompah band. But Bavaria actually embraces three peoples – the Bavarians, Franconians and Swabians.

The old banking powerhouse, Augsburg, lies in Swabia. To the north the fabulous bishops' cities of Nuremberg, Bamberg and Würzburg are part of Franconia, where locals don't regard themselves as Bavarian. In the east, the Danube flows past the medieval stronghold of Regensburg towards the Italianate Passau, close to the rugged wilderness of the Bavarian Forest.

The most popular route through Bavaria is the Romantic Road, a trail of walled towns and ancient watchtowers culminating in the world's most famous castle, the sugary Neuschwanstein in the Bavarian Alps. The mountains have first-class resorts for hiking and skiing, incredible scenery and a wealth of beautiful frescoed villages.

But Munich is Bavaria's real heart and soul. It's a stylish metropolis, a vortex of art and culture, yet a relaxed place that manages to combine Alpine air with Mediterranean joie de vivre. Wherever you go, be prepared for oceans of beer served with legendary, thigh-slapping hospitality.

HIGHLIGHTS

- **Green Escape** Explore the wonders of Altmühltal Nature Park (p371)
- **Legal Speed** Stoke your adrenaline on the Zugspitze (p346)
- **Karl's Place** Revel in the Carolingian charm of Regensburg (p378)
- **Bishop's Bastion** Wander the Venetian-style canals of Bamberg (p364)
- **Out of Thin Air** Soar to the Eagle's Nest (p351) in Berchtesgaden
- **Experience Delusions of Grandeur** Go castle-mad at Schloss Linderhof (p349)

- POPULATION: 12.4 MILLION
- AREA: 70,548 SQ KM

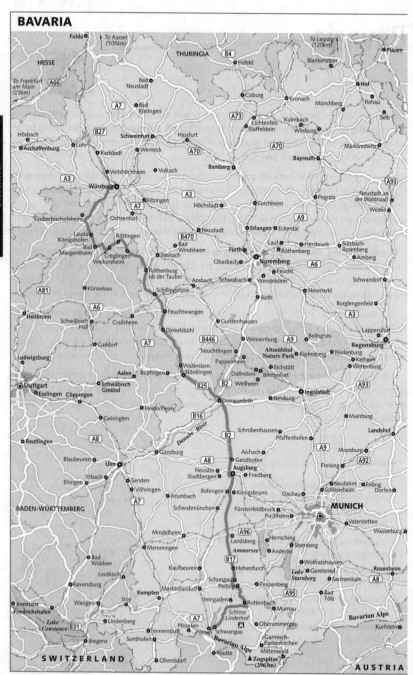

BAVARIA

History

For centuries Bavaria was ruled as a duchy in the Holy Roman Empire, a patchwork of nations that extended from Italy to the North Sea. In the early 19th century, a conquering Napoleon annexed Bavaria, elevated it to the rank of kingdom and doubled its size. The fledgling nation became the object of power struggles between Prussia and Austria and, in 1871, was brought into the German Reich by Bismarck.

Bavaria was the only German state that refused to ratify the Basic Law (Germany's near-constitution) following WWII. Instead, Bavaria's leaders opted to return to its prewar status as a 'free state', and drafted their own constitution. Almost ever since, the *Land* (state) has been ruled by the Christlich-Soziale Union (CSU), the arch-conservative party that is peculiar to Bavaria. Its dominance of a single *Land*'s politics is unique in postwar Germany. Its sister party, the CDU, operates in the rest of the country by mutual agreement.

Getting There & Around

Munich is Bavaria's main transport hub, second only to Frankfurt in flight and rail connections. Rail service in Munich is exemplary, as it is in all major German cities, and this is also true throughout much of Bavaria. Air links are much less extensive (see p754 for more information).

In deepest Bavaria, a car will allow you more flexibility in your travel plans, otherwise you may have to rely on buses. Trips along the Romantic Road are done by tour bus, although again a car is a better idea.

If you're travelling in a group, or can assemble one, you can make enormous savings with the **Bayern-Ticket** (€25). This allows up to five adults unlimited travel on one weekday from 9am to 3am. It's good for 2nd-class rail travel across Bavaria (regional trains only, no ICs or ICEs) as well as all public transport.

Accommodation

DJH youth hostels in Bavaria will now accept guests aged over 26 (who will pay a €4 surcharge), although priority is still given to younger travellers. In some areas a new breed of independent, all-age hostels offer a nice alternative.

Bavaria's parks are generally open to free camping. Parks such as the Altmühltal Nature

Park restrict camping to designated areas, for a small fee. Be sure to follow the local code of ethics and common decency, and pack up everything you brought along – litter, bottles, cans – and bury human waste before you leave.

Bavaria for Children

Kinderland Bavaria is a classification system for family-friendly sights, hotels, leisure facilities, museums and camp sites. For more information, go to www.kinderland.by.

MUNICH

☎ 089 / pop 1.28 million

Pulsing with prosperity and *Gemütlichkeit* (cosiness), Munich (München) revels in its own contradictions. Folklore and age-old traditions exist side by side with sleek BMWs, designer boutiques and high-powered industry. Its museums include world-class collections of artistic masterpieces, and its music and cultural scenes give Berlin a run for its money.

Despite all its sophistication, Munich retains a touch of provincialism that visitors find charming. The people's attitude is one of live-and-let-live – and Müncheners will be the first to admit that their 'metropolis' is little more than a *Weltdorf*, a world village. During Oktoberfest representatives of the entire planet turn out to toast the town.

HISTORY

It was Benedictine monks, drawn by fertile farmland and the closeness to Catholic Italy, who settled in what is now Munich. The city derives its name from the medieval *Munichen*, or monks. In 1158, the Imperial Diet in Augsburg sanctioned the rule of Heinrich der Löwe, and Munich the city was born.

In 1240, the city passed to the House of Wittelsbach, who would govern Munich (as well as Bavaria) until the 20th century. Munich prospered as a salt-trading centre but was hit hard by the plague in 1349. The epidemic subsided only after 150 years, whereupon the relieved *Schäffler* (coopers) initiated a ritualistic dance to remind burghers of their good fortune. The *Schäfflertanz* is performed every seven years but it is re-enacted daily by the little figures on the city's *Glockenspiel* (carillon) on Marienplatz.

By the 19th century an explosion of monument-building gave Munich its spectacular architecture and wide Italianate avenues. Things got out of hand after King Ludwig II ascended the throne in 1864, as spending for his grandiose projects (such as Neuschwanstein Palace) bankrupted the royal house and threatened the government's coffers. Ironically, today they are the biggest money-spinners of Bavaria's tourism industry.

Munich has seen many turbulent times but last century was particularly rough. WWI practically starved the city to death, the Nazis first rose to prominence here and next world war nearly wiped the city off the map. The 1972 Olympic Games began as a celebration of a new democratic Germany, but ended in tragedy when 17 people were killed in a terrorist hostage-taking incident. In 2006 the city won a brighter place in sporting history, when it hosted the opening game of the FIFA World Cup.

Today, Munich's claim to being the 'secret capital' of Germany is alive and well. The city is recognised for its high living standards, with the most millionaires per capita after Hamburg, and for a haute couture that rivals Paris and Milan.

ORIENTATION

The Hauptbahnhof (central train station) is less than 1km west of Marienplatz, the heart of the historic Altstadt (old town). To get there, walk east on Bayerstrasse to Karlsplatz, then take Neuhauser Strasse – Munich's main shopping street – to Marienplatz.

North of Marienplatz is the Residenz (the former royal palace), packed with museums and theatres, and Odeonsplatz with the landmark Theatinerkirche St Kajetan. To the east of Marienplatz is the Platzl quarter, with its traditional pubs and restaurants such as the Hofbräuhaus. Hipper bars and venues are south of the square in the Gärtnerplatzviertel quarter, which, along with the Glockenbachviertel west of here, is the centre of Munich's gay and lesbian scene. The Isar River flows through the eastern part of the city from south to north.

Munich is divided into various districts, each with their own distinct character. Schwabing, north of the Altstadt, is home to Munich's university and a host of cafés and restaurants. East of Schwabing is the Englischer Garten (English Garden), one of

Europe's largest city parks. North of Schwabing, the main attraction is the Olympiapark, site of the 1972 Olympic Games, and further north again the BMW Museum.

East of the Altstadt is the district of Haidhausen, a trendy neighbourhood packed with pubs. South and west of the Altstadt, and near the Hauptbahnhof, is Ludwigsvorstadt – a half-seedy, half-lively area packed with shops, restaurants and hotels. The Westend, further west, bristles with renovated houses, hip cafés and wine bars, all near the Theresienwiese, the meadow where Oktoberfest is held.

North of here is cosmopolitan Neuhausen, a more residential area that's home to **Schloss Nymphenburg** (Nymphenburg Palace) with its lovely gardens a little further northwest. Munich's airport is almost 36km northeast of the city.

INFORMATION
Bookshops
Geobuch (Map p292; ☎ 265 030; Rosental 6) Best travel bookshop in town.
Hugendubel (☎ 01803-484 484); Marienplatz (Map p292); Karlsplatz (Map p292) National chain with tons of English-language books.
Max&Milian (Map p292; ☎ 260 3320; Ickstattstrasse 2) The city's best gay bookshop.
Words' Worth Books (Map p295; ☎ 280 9141; Schellingstrasse 21a) Great selection of English-language books.

Cultural Centres
Amerika Haus (Map p296; ☎ 552 5370; Karolinenplatz 3)
British Council (Map p292; ☎ 2060 3310; Herzog-Heine-Strasse 7) Recorded telephone message listing cultural events and activities.
Goethe-Institut (Map p292; ☎ 551 9030; Sonnenstrasse 25)
Institut Français (Map p295; ☎ 286 6280; Kaulbachstrasse 13)

Discount Cards
Munich Welcome Card (1/3 days €7.50/17.50; 3-day card for up to 5 adults €25.50) Unlimited public transport and up to 50% discount on 30 museums and attractions.

Emergency
Ambulance (☎ 192 22)
Fire (☎ 112)
Police (Map p292; ☎ 110; Arnulfstrasse 1) Police station right beside the Hauptbahnhof.

Internet Access
The city libraries (*Stadtbibliotheken*, below) have cheap access, but there may be queues.
Cyberice-C@fe (Map p295; ☎ 3407 6955; Feilitzschstrasse 15; per 30min €2.50; ☺ 11am-1am) In an ice-cream parlour near the Englischer Garten.
easyInternetCafe (Map p292; Bahnhofplatz 1; per hr €1.50-3.50; ☺ 7.30am-11.45pm) Over 400 terminals and demand-driven rates.
Munich Internet Service Center (Map p292; ☎ 2070 2737; Tal 31; per 30min €1; ☺ 24hr) 60 terminals plus services like printing and CD burning.
Times Square Online Bistro (Map p292; ☎ 5126 2600; Bayerstrasse 10a; per 5min €0.50; ☺ 7am-1am) In the Hauptbahnhof, south side.

Internet Resources
Munich Tourist Office (www.munich-tourist.de) Munich's official website.
Munichfound (www.munichfound.de) Munich's expat magazine.

Laundry
Laundries can be difficult to find. Typical costs are €2.50 to €4 per load, plus about €0.50 for 10 to 15 minutes' dryer time.
City-SB Waschcenter (Map p292; Paul-Heyse Strasse 21; ☺ 7am-11pm)
Der Wunderbare Waschsalon (Map p296; Theresienstrasse 134; ☺ 6am-midnight) The best laundry close to the centre.
Schnell und Sauber (Map p296; Landshuterallee 77; ☺ 24hr) In Neuhausen.

Left Luggage
Gepäckaufbewahrung (Map p292; ☎ 1308 3468; Hauptbahnhof; per piece €4; ☺ 8am-8pm Mon-Sat, 8am-6pm Sun) A staffed storage room, located in the north part of the station's main hall.
Lockers (Map p292; Hauptbahnhof; per 24hr €2-4; ☺ 4am-12.30am) In the main hall of the station and opposite tracks 16, 24 and 28–36.

Libraries
Bayerische Staatsbibliothek (Bavarian State Library, Map p295; ☎ 286 380; Ludwigstrasse 16; ☺ 10am-7pm Mon-Fri Sep-Jul, 10am-5pm Aug, reading hall 8am-midnight Mon-Sat)
Stadtbücherei (City library; ☺ 10:30am-7pm Mon-Fri) Haidhausen (Map p294; ☎ 4809 8316; Rosenheimer Strasse 5); Schwabing (Map p295; ☎ 336 013; Hohenzollernstrasse 16); Westend (Map p292; ☎ 507 109; Schrenkstrasse 8)
Universitätsbibliothek (Map p295; ☎ 2180 2428; Geschwister-Scholl-Platz 1; ☺ 9am-7pm Mon-Thu, 9am-5pm Fri)

BAVARIA

Media

Abendzeitung Light broadsheet that, despite the name, has a morning delivery.

Münchner Merkur The city's arch-conservative daily.

Süddeutsche Zeitung Widely read regional paper with a liberal streak. Monday's edition has a *New York Times* supplement in English.

tz Local tabloid similar to the saucy Bild-Zeitung, Germany's biggest-selling paper.

Medical Services

The US and UK consulates can provide lists of English-speaking doctors on request. Most pharmacies have employees who speak passable English, but there are several designated as 'international', with staff fluent in English.

Ärztlicher Bereitschaftsdienst (☎ 01805 191 212; ☻ 24hr) Emergency medical service.

Bahnhofs-Apotheke (Map p292; ☎ 555 830; Bahnhofsplatz 7)

Ludwigs-Apotheke (Map p292; ☎ 260 3021; Neuhauser Strasse 11) English-speaking pharmacy.

Money

ATMs are available throughout the city; a few key ones are listed below.

American Express (Map p292; ☎ 2289 1387; Neuhauser Strasse 47)

Citibank (Map p292; ☎ 236 6310; Rosental 10)

Deutsche Bank (Map p292; Marienplatz)

Reisebank (Map p292; Hauptbahnhof; ☻ 7am-10pm) EurAide's newsletter the *Inside Track* gets you a 50% reduction on commissions at this branch.

Sparkasse (Map p292; Sparkassenstrasse 2)

Post

Post office Hauptbahnhof (Map p292; Bahnhofsplatz 1; ☻ 7.30am-8pm Mon-Fri, 9am-4pm Sat, closed Sun)

Post office Altstadt (Map p292; Residenzstrasse 2; ☻ 8am-6.30pm Mon-Fri, 9am-12.30pm Sat, closed Sun)

Tourist Information

EurAide (Map p292; ☎ 593 889; www.euraide.de; Room 3, platform 11, Hauptbahnhof; ☻ 7.45am-noon & 1-6pm Jun-Oct, 7.45am-12.45pm & 2-6pm Jun-Oct; 8am-noon & 1-4pm Mon-Fri Nov-May) The office makes reservations, sells tickets for DB trains and a variety of tours, and finds rooms (€3 per booking). EurAide's free newsletter, the *Inside Track,* is packed with practical info about the city and surroundings, and gives discounts on money changing (see above).

Jugendinformationszentrum (Youth Information Centre; Map p292; ☎ 5141 0660; Paul-Heyse-Strasse 22; ☻ noon-6pm Mon-Fri, to 8pm Thu) A wide range of information for young visitors.

Tourist Office Hauptbahnhof (Map p292; ☎ 2339 6500; Bahnhofsplatz 2; ☻ 9am-8pm Mon-Sat, 10am-6pm Sun); Marienplatz (Map p292; ☎ 2339 6500; Neues Rathaus; ☻ 10am-8pm Mon-Fri, 10am-4pm Sat) The room-finding service is free, or you can book in person by calling ☎ 2333 0236/37.

Travel Agencies

EurAide is the best place to go with complicated rail pass inquiries, or to book train travel in Germany and elsewhere in Europe.

Atlas Reisen (Map p292; ☎ 269 072; www.atlas-reisen .de; Kaufingerstrasse 1-5) In the Kaufhof department store.

Travel Overland (Map p295; ☎ 01805-276 370; www .travel-overland.de; Barer Strasse 73)

Universities

Munich is home to about 87,000 students. The biggest universities are listed below.

Ludwig-Maximilians-Universität München (Map p295; ☎ 218 00; www.uni-muenchen.de; Geschwister-Scholl-Platz 1) Runs German-language courses for foreigners throughout the year.

Technische Universität München (Map p296; ☎ 289 01; Arcisstrasse 21) Renowned faculties of science, engineering and medicine.

DANGERS & ANNOYANCES

During Oktoberfest crime and staggering drunks are major problems, especially at the southern end of the Hauptbahnhof. It's no joke: drunk people in a crowd trying to get home can get violent, and there are dozens of assault cases every year. Leave early or stay very cautious, if not sober, yourself.

The *Föhn* (pronounced 'foon') is a weather-related annoyance peculiar to southern Germany. Static-charged wind from the south brings exquisite views clear to the Alps and an area of dense pressure that sits on the city. Visiting filmmaker Ingmar Bergman wrote that the *Föhn* makes 'nice dogs bite, and cats spew lightning'. Müncheners claim that it simply makes them cranky.

SIGHTS

Munich's major sights are clustered around the Altstadt, with the main museum district near the Residenz. However, it will take another day or two to discover the delights of Bohemian Schwabing, the sprawling Englischer Garten, and trendy Haidhausen to the east. Northwest of the Altstadt you'll find cosmopolitan

(Continued on page 297)

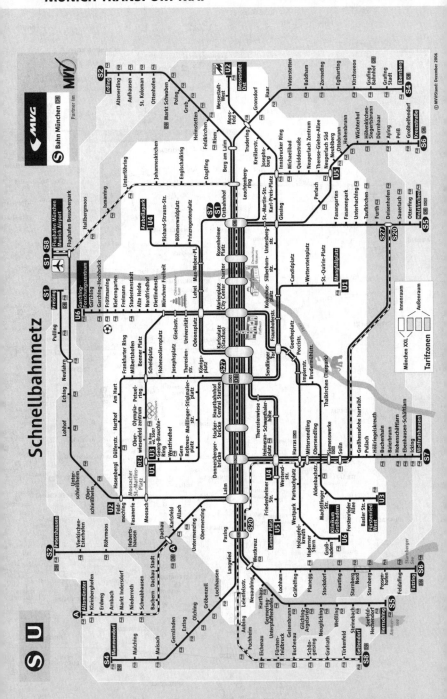

Schnellbahnnetz

© MVV/Stand: December 2006

MUNICH TRANSPORT MAP

ANGER

Otto-Warburg-Str

To Dachau
(10km)

Allacher
Tunnel

Allacher
Forst

FASANERIE NORD

BIRKENRIED

LUDWIGSFELD

Am Blütenanger

SIEDLUNG
AM LERCHENAUER
SEE

ALLACH

Campingplatz
Nord-West

KOLONIE
EGGARTEN

To Augsburg (31km);
Ulm (125km);
Stuttgart (205km)

A99

Allach

Moosacher-Str

Olympiapark

See Nymphenburg, Neuhausen & Olympiapark Map (p296)

Georg-Brauchie-Ring

LANGWIED

A8

MOOSACH

BORSTEI

Olympiase

Campingplatz
Obermenzing

Westfriedhof

Olympiaben

NEULANGWIED

NEULUSTHEIM

GERN

AUBING

Langwied

Bergson Str

Schlosspark

NEUHAUSEN

Schloss
Nymphenburg

Westkreuz

NYMPHENBURG
Nymphenburg

Rotkreuzplatz

Mailingstr

Nymphenburger

Donnersberger-
brücke

Laim

Hackerbrück

Landsberger Str

Landsberger Str

Theresie
wiese

Agnes-Bernauer-Str

WESTEND

Friedenheimer
Str

Heimeran
platz

Messe-
gelände

Klein
Gärten

Gotthardstr

Laimer
Platz

LAIM

Westend-
str

SCHWANTHALE
HÖHE

Theresien-
wiese

To Lindau
(170km)

LOCHHAM

A96

Ammerseestr

KLEINHADERN

Ammerseestr

Westpark
(Ost)

Poccis

Südbahn-
hof

Lochham

Haderner
Stern

UNTERSENDLING

Implers

Gräfelfing

Großhaderner Str

NEUHADERN

Westpark
(West)

Partnach-
platz

Westpark

Harras

GRÄFELFING

Grosshadern

Holzapfel-
kreuth

MITTERSENDLING

Brudermühls

Brudermühl

Klinikum
Grosshadern

GROSSHADERN

Waldfriedhof

Heckenstaller Str

Mitter-
sendling

PLANEGG

PLANEGG

Olympiastr

Südpark

Thalkircher

DJH
Hostel

Münchner
Tierpark

KREUZHOF

Aidenbach-
str

Oberendling

Hellabrun

FÜRSTENRIEDOST

Boschetsrieder Str

Siemens-
werke

MARIA
EINSIEDEL

FÜRSTENRIED-
WEST

Machtlfinger
Str

OBERSENDLING

Fürstenried
West

Basler
Straße

Forstenrieder
Allee

Siemensallee

Campingplatz
Thalkirchen

MAXHOF

FORSTENRIED

HINTERBRÜHL

NEU-
FORSTENRIED

A95

STADT
SOLLN

SOLLN

PRINZ-
LUDWIGS-
HÖHE

Forstenrieder Park

Soll

UNTERDILL

To Bavaria
Filmstadt (1km)

To Starnberg (18km); Andechs
(31km); Garmisch-Partenkirchen
(76km); Füssen (95km);
Oberammergau (80km)

0   500 m
0   0.3 miles

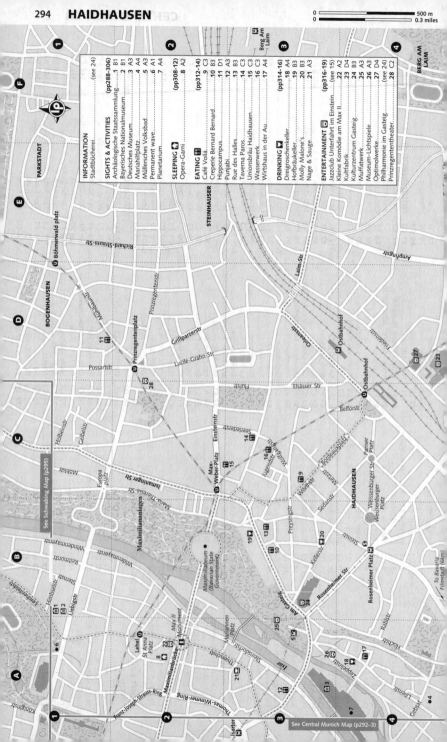

See Schwabing Map (p295)

See Central Munich Map (p292-3)

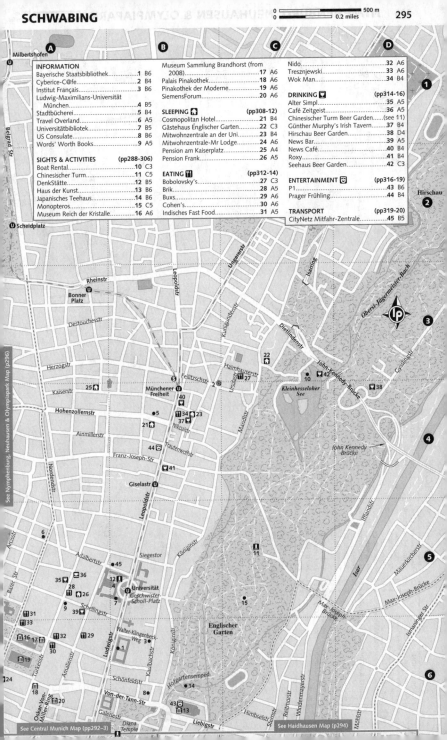

SCHWABING

500 m
0 0.2 miles

INFORMATION
Bayerische Staatsbibliothek.....................1 B6
Cyberice-C@fe..2 B4
Institut Français...3 B6
Ludwig-Maximilians-Universität
München...4 B5
Stadtbücherei..5 B4
Travel Overland...6 A5
Universitätbibliotek...................................7 B5
US Consulate...8 B6
Words' Worth Books...................................9 A5

SIGHTS & ACTIVITIES   (pp288–306)
Boat Rental..10 C3
Chinesischer Turm...................................11 C5
DenkStätte...12 C5
Haus der Kunst...13 B6
Japanisches Teehaus................................14 B6
Monopteros..15 C5
Museum Reich der Kristalle......................16 A6

Museum Sammlung Brandhorst (from
2008)..17 A6
Palais Pinakothek......................................18 A6
Pinakothek der Moderne...........................19 A6
SiemensForum..20 A6

SLEEPING   (pp308–12)
Cosmopolitan Hotel...................................21 B4
Gästehaus Englischer Garten.....................22 C3
Mitwohnzentrale an der Uni.....................23 B4
Mitwohnzentrale-Mr Lodge.......................24 A6
Pension am Kaiserplatz.............................25 A4
Pension Frank...26 A5

EATING   (pp312–14)
Bobolovsky's...27 C3
Brik...28 A5
Buxs..29 A5
Cohen's...30 A6
Indisches Fast Food..................................31 A5

Nido..32 A6
Tresznjewski...33 A6
Wok Man...34 B4

DRINKING   (pp314–16)
Alter Simpl..35 A5
Café Zeitgeist..36 A5
Chinesischer Turm Beer Garden........(see 11)
Günther Murphy's Irish Tavern..................37 B4
Hirschau Beer Garden...............................38 D4
News Bar...39 A5
News Café...40 B4
Roxy...41 B4
Seehaus Beer Garden...............................42 C3

ENTERTAINMENT   (pp316–19)
P1...43 B6
Prager Frühling...44 B4

TRANSPORT   (pp319–20)
CityNetz Mitfahr-Zentrale..........................45 B5

See Schwabing Map (p295)

See Central Munich Map (p292-3)

INFORMATION

Amerika Haus	1	F4
Der Wunderbare Waschsalon	2	F4
Info Pavilion	3	E1
Schnell und Sauber	4	D3
Technische Universität München	5	F4

SIGHTS & ACTIVITIES (pp288-306)

Alte Pinakothek	6	F4
Amalienburg	7	B3
Antikensammlungen	8	F4
Badenburg	9	B3
BMW Museum (from summer 2007)	10	F1
BMW Museum (till summer 2007)	11	E1
BMW Welt	12	E1
Glyptothek	13	F4

EATING (pp312-14)

| Il Mulino | 14 | F4 |

DRINKING (pp314-16)

Hirschgarten	15	E1
Löwenbräukeller	16	E2
	17	E1
Olympiaturm	18	A3
Pagodenburg	19	A3
Propyläen	20	F4
Schloss Nymphenburg	21	B3
Sealife	22	E1
Städtische Galerie im Lenbachhaus	23	F4
Swimming Centre	24	E2

SLEEPING (pp308-12)

DJH Hostel	25	D4
Hotel Flora	26	F4
Hotel Laimer Hof	27	B4

ENTERTAINMENT (pp316-19)

Cinema	31	E4
Circus Krone	32	E4
Münchner Theater für Kinder	33	F4

SHOPPING (p319)

Porzellan Manufaktur		
Nymphenburg	(see 21)	
Weissblauer Gay Shop	34	F4

Neue Pinakothek 28 F3

29 C4

30 F4

(Continued from page 288)

Neuhausen, the Olympiapark, and one of Munich's jewels – Schloss Nymphenburg.

Marienplatz & Around

The heart and soul of the Altstadt is **Marienplatz** (Map p292), the old town square. At the northwest corner stands the **Mariensäule** (Mary Column), erected in 1638 to celebrate the removal of Swedish forces at the end of the Thirty Years' War. From its pinnacle the golden figure of the Virgin Mary, carved in 1590, reaches skyward.

NEUES RATHAUS

The coal-blackened façade of the neo-Gothic **Neues Rathaus** (New Town Hall; Map p292) is festooned with gargoyles and statues, including a dragon scaling the turrets. Inside, six grand courtyards host festivals and concerts throughout the year. For a good view of the city, ascend the 85m **tower** (adult/concession €2/1; 9am-4pm Mon-Thu, 9am-1pm Fri).

The highlight of the building is the **Glockenspiel** (carillon). Note the three levels: two portraying the Schäfflertanz (see p286) and another the Ritterturnier, a knights' tournament held in 1568 to celebrate a royal marriage. The characters spring into action at 11am and noon (also 5pm November to April). The night scene featuring the Münchener Kindl (a girl in a monk's robe) and Nachtwächter (night watchman) runs at 9pm.

ST PETERSKIRCHE

Opposite the Neues Rathaus stands the **St Peterskirche** (Church of St Peter; Map p292). Severely Gothic in inspiration, the interior is now a flamboyant baroque with a magnificent high altar and eye-catching statues of the four church fathers (1732), by Egid Quirin Asam. For spectacular views of the city, you can climb the rectangular 92m **tower** (adult/concession €1.50/1; 9am-6pm Mon-Sat, 10am-7pm Sun), also known as 'Alter Peter', via 297 steps.

FISCHBRUNNEN

Local legend suggests that dipping an empty purse into the **Fischbrunnen** (Map p292) on Ash Wednesday guarantees that it will always be full. The Fish Fountain was used to keep river fish alive during medieval markets, and later as the ceremonial dunking spot for butchers' apprentices.

ALTES RATHAUS

The Gothic **Altes Rathaus** (1474) was destroyed by lightning and bombs, and then rebuilt in a plainer style after WWII. In its south tower is the city's **Spielzeugmuseum** (Toy Museum; Map p292; 294 001; Alter Rathausturm; adult/concession €3/1; 10am-5.30pm) with its huge collection of toys, Barbie dolls and teddy bears.

Behind the Altes Rathaus, the **Heiliggeistkirche** (Map p292; Church of the Holy Spirit; Tal 77) was built in 1392. It appears spartan in design until you look up to see the amazing frescoes by Cosmas Damian Asam, completed in an 18th-century sprucing-up of the church.

Viktualienmarkt & Around

The bustling **Viktualienmarkt** (Map p292) is one of Europe's great food markets. In summer the entire place is transformed into one of the finest and most expensive beer gardens around, while in winter people huddle for warmth and schnapps in the small pubs around the square. The merchandise and food are of the finest quality, and prices tend to be high. The enormous **maypole** bears artisans' symbols and the traditional blue-and-white Bavarian stripes. On the south side of the square you'll see a statue of Karl Valentin, Germany's most celebrated comedian.

The **Schrannenhalle**, a reconstructed 19th-century grain hall, stands just off the southwest corner of the market. It is home to a classy food court selling dim-sum, Tandoori curries and legs of Bavarian pork, and has a stage for live bands.

STADTMUSEUM

A rambling collection of collections, the **Stadtmuseum** (City Museum; Map p292; 2332 2370; St-Jakobs-Platz; adult/concession €4/2; 10am-6pm, closed Mon) is a fascinating attic of a museum that can keep you going for hours. The themed rooms range from brewing and photography to musical instruments, puppetry and the city's own tangled history. One hall spotlights the exquisitely carved and spritelike Morris Dancers, the medieval entertainers who once performed in the Altes Rathaus. The film museum restores and shows vintage films nightly from its enormous archive.

A separate Stadtmuseum exhibit, **Nationalsozialismus in München** (National Socialism in Munich) explores the darker corners of the city's role in Nazism after 1918. Set in a windowless hall among riveted steel plates,

BAVARIA

this powerful display taps a vast pool of photographs, propaganda posters, Gestapo uniforms, underground resistance papers and letters from concentration camp victims.

MÜNCHNER JÜDISCHES MUSEUM

Slated to open in early 2007, the **Münchner Jüdisches Museum** (Munich Jewish Museum; Map p292; ☎ 2332 8198; St Jakobsplatz1; admission free; ☺ 10am-6pm, closed Mon) is a major effort to come to terms with one of the city's most sinister chapters. Housed in a modernist glass cube that integrates a new synagogue and community centre, the exhibit aims to show – in a balanced, sensitive fashion – the Jewish place in Munich's cultural landscape over the ages, from medieval times through to the horrors of the Third Reich and today's slow regeneration. The site is near that of the Romanesque synagogue that was razed by the Nazis in 1938.

HOFBRÄUHAUS

No visit to Munich would be complete without a visit to the **Hofbräuhaus** (see p314), Bavaria's most celebrated beer hall. The writhing hordes of tourists tend to overshadow the fabulous interior, where dainty twirled flowers adorn the medieval vaults. The ballroom upstairs was the site of the first large meeting of the National Socialist Party on 20 February 1920.

BIER & OKTOBERFESTMUSEUM

Located in a 14th-century timber-framed house, the cute little **Bier & Oktoberfestmuseum** (Map p292; ☎ 2423 1607; Sterneckerstrasse 2; adult/concession €4/2.50; ☺ 1-5pm Tue-Sat) provides a potted history of Germany's national drink and favourite drink-up. Pore over old brewing vats, historic photos and some of the earliest Oktoberfest regalia. The earthy pub is open 5pm to midnight (closed Monday).

Max-Joseph-Platz

Munich's most glamorous shopping street, Maximilianstrasse, begins at **Max-Joseph-Platz** (Map p292), home to some of the city's most beloved edifices. Among them is the grandiose **Nationaltheater**, home to the Bavarian State Opera and the granddaddy of them all – the Residenz. The square centres on a statue of **Max I Joseph**, the Bavarian king who proclaimed Germany's first constitution in 1818.

At the southern end of the square is the **old central post office** with a frescoed Italianate arcade.

RESIDENZ

On the north side of Max-Joseph-Platz looms the oldest section of the **Residenz** (Map p292), the huge palace that housed Bavarian rulers from 1385 to 1918. Statues of **two lions** guard the gates to the palace on Residenzstrasse; rubbing one of their shields is said to bring you wealth. The northern wings open into several interior courtyards – the Emperor, the Apothecary and the Fountain – as well as two smaller ones, Chapel and King's Tract.

Residenzmuseum

The Wittelsbachs' amazing treasures, as well as the trappings of their lifestyles, are on display at the **Residenzmuseum** (Map p292; ☎ 290 671; enter from Max-Josephs-Platz 3; adult/under 18yr with parents/concession €6/free/5, combiticket with Schatzkammer €9/8/free; ☺ 9am-6pm Apr–mid-Oct, 9am-8pm Thu, 10am-4pm mid-Oct–Mar). The museum has roughly 130 rooms, and is so large that it's divided into two sections – one open in the morning, one in the afternoon. You can see it all with a free audio-guide.

The enclosed Grotto Court, one of the first places you'll see when you enter, features the wonderful **Perseusbrunnen** (Perseus Fountain). Next door is the famous **Antiquarium**, a lavishly ornamented barrel vault, smothered in frescoes and built to house the Wittelsbachs' huge antique collection. Other highlights include the **Ancestral Gallery**, with portraits of the rulers of Bavaria including the great conqueror Charlemagne; the **Schlachtensäle** (Battle Halls); the **Porcelain Chambers**, containing 19th-century porcelain from Berlin, Meissen and Nymphenburg; and the **Asian Collections**, with precious Chinese and Japanese porcelain, tapestries and jewellery.

One of Europe's finest rococo stages, the **Cuvilliés-Theater**, hosted the opening performance of Mozart's opera *Idomeneo*. Designed by Belgian architect François Cuvilliés, the sumptuous interior is closed for renovations until late 2008.

Schatzkammer der Residenz

The Residenzmuseum entrance also leads to the **Schatzkammer der Residenz** (Residence Treasury; Map p292; ☎ 290 671; enter from Max-Joseph-Platz 3; adult/concession/under 18 with parents €6/5/free; ☺ 9am-6pm, 9am-8pm Thu). It exhibits an Aladdin's cave of baubles and precious objects. Included among the mind-boggling treasures are portable altars, the pearl-studded golden cross of Queen

Gisela of Hungary, a cup from Mannhaim carved out of bloodstone, and 'exotic handicrafts' from Turkey, Iran, Mexico and India. It's well worth the entry price.

Staatliches Museum Ägyptischer Kunst

German explorers of the Near East brought back treasures that made their way into **Staatliches Museum Ägyptischer Kunst** (Egyptian Art Museum; Map p292; ☎ 298 546, enter from Hofgartenstrasse 1; adult/ concession €5/4; 🕑 9am-5pm Tue-Fri, also 7-9pm Tue, 10am-5pm Sat & Sun). The excellent collection dates from the Old, Middle and New Kingdoms (2670–1075 BC).

Odeonsplatz to Karlsplatz

The elongated square called Odeonsplatz (Map p292) was the site of the so-called Beer Hall Putsch (revolt) by the Nazis in 1923, which landed Hitler in jail. At its southern end looms the **Feldherrnhalle** (Field Marshals' Hall). The statues under its Italian-style arches are of pre-20th-century military heroes Johann von Tilly and Carl Philipp von Wrede, both cast from the copper of melted-down cannon.

The imposing baroque church swelling up on the west side is the **Theatinerkirche St Kajetan** (Map p292; Theatinerstrasse 22), built in the 17th century to commemorate the birth of Prince Max Emanuel. Its massive twin towers flanking a giant cupola are a landmark of Munich's skyline. Inside, the intensely ornate high dome stands above the **Fürstengruft** (royal crypt), containing the remains of Wittelsbach family members. Opposite and a bit to the north, a neoclassical gate leads the way to the former **Hofgarten** (Royal Gardens).

On Theatinerstrasse you'll find the entrance to the **Fünf Höfe** (Map p292), a chic shopping complex that embraces five courtyards. The sleek glass-and-steel passages are lined with upscale designers, cafés and gift shops (see p319). The building also houses the **Kunsthalle der Hypo-Kulturstiftung** (☎ 224 412; Theatinerstrasse 8; adult/child €6/3, Mon half price; 🕑 10am-8pm), a modern gallery renowned for quality cross-genre exhibits.

Munich's main shopping drag is Kaufinger Strasse, which becomes Neuhauser Strasse in the west. Along it, the **Michaelskirche** (St Michael's Church; Map p292) is worth visiting for its ceiling alone, a 20m-wide barrel-vaulted expanse that's remarkable for the absence of supports. The crypt contains the tombs of some members of the Wittelsbach

family, including the humble final resting place of castle-mad King Ludwig II. The façade shows the triumph of Catholicism over Protestantism: up above is Christ holding a golden Earth, while a bronze archangel Michael is shown in combat with the devil.

Neuhauser Strasse culminates in Karlsplatz, punctuated by the medieval **Karlstor** (Map p292), the western gate and perimeter of the Altstadt, and an enormous modern fountain, a favourite meeting point. About 250m north of Karlsplatz stands another fountain, the bombastic **Wittelsbacher Brunnen** (Map p292) that displays the power of water with some powerful mythical figures.

FRAUENKIRCHE

Visible from just about anywhere in the Altstadt, the twin copper onion domes of the **Frauenkirche** (Church of Our Lady; Map p292) can also be found on Munich's official emblem. In contrast to its red-brick Gothic exterior, the interior is a soaring passage of light. The tomb of Ludwig the Bavarian, guarded by knights and noblemen, can be found in the choir. Near the door, look for the footprint cast in the pavement; according to legend, the devil lost a bet with the architect and stamped out in a huff. The 98m-tall south **tower** (adult/concession €3/1.50; 🕑 10am-5pm Mon-Sat Apr-Oct) affords excellent views – on clear days as far as the Alps.

ASAMKIRCHE

Near the **Sendlinger Tor**, a 14th-century gate, you'll come upon the pint-sized St Johann Nepomuk church, better known as the **Asamkirche** (Map p292; Sendlinger Strasse 62). It was designed and built in the 18th century as a private chapel by the Asam brothers, who lived next door. The jaw-dropping interior shows a harmonious unity of architecture, painting and sculpture, with scarcely a single unembellished surface. As you enter note the golden skeleton of Death trying to cut the string of Life.

More of the younger Asam's masterful frescoes can be viewed in the ornate **Damenstiftskirche** (Map p292; Damenstiftstrasse 1) just north of Sendlinger Strasse.

Königsplatz & Around

Northwest of the Altstadt is **Königsplatz** (Map p296), a Greek Revivalist square created under King Ludwig I. It is anchored by the

BAVARIA

Doric-columned **Propyläen** gateway and orbited by three museums. A short walk to the north you'll find the Kunstareal (literally 'Art Area'), home to Munich's three major art museums, the **Pinakotheks** (www.pinakothek.de). To get there, take the U2 or tram 27.

ALTE PINAKOTHEK

A treasure-trove full of the works of Old European Masters awaits visitors in the **Alte Pinakothek** (Map p296; ☎ 2380 5216; Barer Strasse 27, enter from Theresienstrasse; adult/child €5/3.50, Sun €1; ☉ 10am-5pm, to 8pm Tue, closed Mon). Housed in a neoclassical temple built by King Ludwig I, it is one of the most important collections in the world.

Nearly all the paintings were collected or commissioned by Wittelsbach rulers over the centuries. The strongest section is **Old German Masters**: the four church fathers by Michael Pacher stands out, as does Lucas Cranach the Elder's *Crucifixion* (1503), an emotional rendition of the suffering Jesus.

Another key room is the so-called **Dürersaal** upstairs. Here hangs Albrecht Dürer's famous Christ-like *Self-Portrait* (about 1500), showing the gaze of an artist brimming with self-confidence. His final major work, *The Four Apostles*, depicts John, Peter, Paul and Mark as rather humble men, in keeping with ideas post-Reformation.

There is a choice bunch of **Old Dutch Masters**, including an altarpiece by Rogier van der Weyden called *The Adoration of the Magi*, plus *The Seven Joys of Mary* by Hans Memling, *Danae* by Jan Gossaert and *The Land of Cockayne* by Pieter Bruegel the Elder.

Rubens fans have reason to rejoice. At 6m in height, his *Large Last Judgement* (1617) was so big that court architect Leo van Klenze had to design the hall around the canvas. One of his most memorable portraits is *Hélène Fourment* (1631), a youthful beauty who was the ageing Rubens' second wife. Other Flemish 17th-century artists represented include Anthonis van Dyck and Rembrandt, with his intensely emotional *Passion Cycle*.

Free audio-guides with taped commentary about 90 works in four languages, including English, are available in the lobby.

NEUE PINAKOTHEK

Picking up where the Alte Pinakothek leaves off, the **Neue Pinakothek** (Map p296; ☎ 2380 5195; Barer Strasse 29; adult/child €5/3.50, Sun €1; ☉ 10am-5pm, to 8pm Wed, closed Tue) contains an extensive collection of 18th- to early-20th-century paintings and sculpture, from rococo to *Jugendstil* (Art Nouveau).

The core of the exhibit is 19th-century German art from the private stock of King Ludwig I, who had nearly 400 paintings when he died in 1868. An entire room is dedicated to Hans Marées (1837–87), whose country scenes are infused with a touch of sentimentality.

BEST OF THE ALTE PINAKOTHEK

We asked Reinhold Baumstark, director of the Bayerische Staatsgemäldesammlungen (Bavarian State Painting Collections), to name his five favourite paintings in the Alte Pinakothek. His answers are below:

- *The Battle of Issus* by Alexander Altdorfer (1529): 'Altdorfer showed what no human could see and what only the artist's vision could make possible: a view halfway across the world, over a huge battlefield and the entire Mediterranean to Egypt.'

- *Christ Crowned with Thorns* by Titian (c 1570): 'Titian shows us the picture of God's tortured son: artistically exaggerated but immediately moving. The influence of his use of light and colour extends to the modern era.'

- *Rubens and Isabella Brant in a Honeysuckle Bower* by Rubens (c 1609): 'Rubens' twin portrait is a personal dedication to his wife; more than just a portrait, it displays warmth, trust and optimism.'

- *The Deposition* by Rembrandt (1633): 'Rembrandt portrays a highly dramatic event but also – the first time by any artist – the body of Christ in almost painful realism. Rembrandt's likeness under the cross gives us the consolation that man is capable of mercy.'

- *Portrait of Madame de Pompadour* by Francois Boucher (1756): 'Madame Pompadour demonstrates the splendour and sophisticated lifestyle of rococo.'

Munich society painters Wilhelm von Kaulbach and Karl von Piloty are given due time, reflecting a renewed interest in German history in the late 19th century. The king had a special affinity for the 'Roman Germans', a group of neo-Classicists centred around Johann Koch who favoured Italian landscapes.

The most memorable canvases include those by Romantic painter Caspar David Friedrich, such as his *Riesengebirge Landscape with Rising Mist*. Like these landscapes, the works of English portraitist Thomas Gainsborough display a high emotionalism and ominous mood.

Other masters on display with a high recognition value include Edgar Degas, Gauguin, Manet and Van Gogh, one of whose *Sunflowers* (1888) is on display.

Fans of off-beat classics will enjoy Walter Crane's *The Seeds of Neptune*, with watery steeds galloping on incoming waves, and Goya's chilling kitchen still-life, *Plucked Turkey*.

PINAKOTHEK DER MODERNE

Opened in 2002 after six years of construction, **Pinakothek der Moderne** (Map p295; ☎ 2380 5360; Barer Strasse 40; adult/child €9/5, Sun €1; 10am-5pm Tue-Wed, Sat & Sun, to 8pm Thu & Fri, closed Mon) is Germany's biggest collection of modern art. The spectacular interior is dominated by a huge eye-like dome, spreading natural light throughout the soft white galleries over four floors.

The museum pools several collections under a single roof: a survey of 20th-century art, plus design, sculpture, photography and video. A variety of sources were tapped, including the Bavarian royal family and the State Graphics Collection of 400,000 drawings, prints and engravings.

There are oils and prints by household names such as Picasso, Dali, Klee, Kandinsky and Warhol, mostly lesser-known works that will be fresh to many visitors. A piece likely to become a signature work is Joseph Beuys' *End of the 20th Century*, comprising 21 columns of basalt strewn about an otherwise blank chamber.

The basement covers the evolution of design from the industrial revolution to today. VW Beetles, Eames chairs and early Apple Macs stand alongside more obscure items such as AEG's latest electric kettles in 1909.

In early 2008 a new collection of 'modern classics', the **Museum Sammlung Brandhorst** (Map p296; ☎ 2380 5118), will open its doors in a sleek new building next door.

PALAIS PINAKOTHEK

The latest addition to the Pinakothek family is the **Palais Pinakothek** (Map p295; ☎ 2380 5284; Türkenstrasse 4), which organises art-related events such as thematic walks and workshops for both kids and adults. The schedule and admission fees vary, but there's usually something going on Sunday afternoons.

SIEMENSFORUM

Southeast of the Pinakotheks is the **Siemens-Forum** (Map p295; ☎ 6363 2660; Oskar-von-Miller-Ring 20; admission free; 9am-5pm, closed Sat). It's a fun, hands-on kind of place, with five floors of promotional exhibits on electronics and microelectronics, ranging from the telegraph to the PC.

LENBACHHAUS

Leading late-19th-century painter Franz von Lenbach used his considerable fortune to construct a residence in Munich in the 1880s. His widow sold it to the city and threw in a bunch of his works as part of the deal. Today this villa houses the **Städtische Galerie im Lenbachhaus** (Map p296; ☎ 2333 2000; Luisenstrasse 33; adult/concession €6/3; 10am-6pm, closed Mon). It features a staggering range of 19th-century masterpieces by German masters such as Franz Marc and Wassily Kandinsky, leading members of *Der Blaue Reiter* (Blue Rider) movement.

OTHER MUSEUMS

Munich's oldest museum is the **Glyptothek** (Map p296; ☎ 286 100; Königsplatz 3; adult/concession €3.50/2.50, Sun €1, combined with Antikensammlungen €5.50/3.50; 10am-5pm, 10am-8pm Tue & Thu). Like all the buildings on Königsplatz, Glyptothek is a piece of Greek fantasy. Classical busts, portraits of Roman kings and sculptures from a Greek temple in Aegina are among its prize exhibits.

One of Germany's best antiquities collections is housed in the **Antikensammlungen** (Map p296; ☎ 598 359; Königsplatz 1; adult/concession €3.50/2.50, €1 Sun; 10am-5pm, 10am-8pm Tue & Thu). It features vases, gold and silver jewellery and ornaments, bronze work, and Greek and Roman sculptures and statues.

The **Museum Reich der Kristalle** (Map p295; ☎ 2394 4312; Theresienstrasse 41; adult/concession €3/1.50; 1-5pm Tue-Sat, 10am-5pm Sun) has a truly

---

THE WHITE ROSE

Open resistance to the Nazis was rare during the Third Reich; after 1933, intimidation and the instant 'justice' of the Gestapo and SS served as powerful disincentives. One of the few groups to rebel was the ill-fated Weisse Rose (White Rose), led by Munich University students Hans and Sophie Scholl.

The White Rose began operating in 1942, its members stealing around at night to smear slogans like 'Freedom!' and 'Down With Hitler!'. Soon they printed anti-Nazi leaflets reporting on the mass extermination of the Jews and other Nazi atrocities. One read: 'We shall not be silent – we are your guilty conscience. The White Rose will not leave you in peace.'

In February 1943, Hans and Sophie were caught distributing leaflets at the university. Together with their best friend, Christian Probst, the Scholls were arrested and charged with treason. After a summary trial, all three were found guilty and beheaded the same afternoon. Their extraordinary courage inspired the award-winning film *Sophie Scholl – Die Letzten Tage* (Sophie Scholl – The Final Days, 2005).

A memorial exhibit to the White Rose, **DenkStätte** (Map p295; ☎ 2180 3053; Geschwister-Scholl-Platz 1; admission free; ☉ 10am-4pm Mon-Fri, 10am-9pm Thu), located within Ludwig-Maximilians-Universität. .

---

dazzling collection of crystals. A large Russian emerald, meteorite fragments from Kansas and diamonds are also among the museum's most prized possessions.

Englischer Garten & Around

The **Englischer Garten** (English Garden; Map p295) is one of Europe's most monumental city parks – bigger even than London's Hyde Park or New York's Central Park. It was laid out in the late 18th century by an American-born physicist, Benjamin Thompson, an advisor to the Bavarian government and at one time its war minister. There are no English flower beds, but it's a great place for strolling, drinking, paddle-boating and even surfing (see p306), conveniently located between the Isar River and the Schwabing district. In balmy weather you'll see hundreds of naked sunbathers in the park, with their jackets, ties and dresses stacked neatly beside them.

Several follies lend the park a playful charm. The **Chinesischer Turm** (Chinese Tower), now in the centre of the city's best-known beer garden, dates back to 1789. Just south of here is the heavily photographed **Monopteros**, a faux Greek temple with pearly white columns. The **Japanisches Teehaus** (Japanese Teahouse) was built during the 1972 Olympics, and holds authentic tea ceremonies every second and fourth weekend in summer at 3pm, 4pm and 5pm. You can also rent a paddle-boat and navigate the **Kleinhesseloher See**, a picturesque little lake.

On the southern edge of the garden, the monolithic **Haus der Kunst** (House of Art; Map p295;

☎ 2112 7113; Prinzregentenstrasse 1; ☉ 10am-8pm Mon-Sun, to 10pm Thu) was once a Nazi gallery that ridiculed so-called 'degenerate' art. Today it holds high-calibre shows of paintings, photography and modern art exhibitions.

BAYERISCHES NATIONALMUSEUM

Off the southeastern corner of the Englischer Garten is a highlight of Munich's museum scene, the **Bayerisches Nationalmuseum** (Bavarian National Museum; Map p294; ☎ 211 2401; Prinzregentenstrasse 3; adult/concession €3/2, Sun €1; ☉ 10am-5pm Tue-Sun, 10am-8pm Thu). It's chock-full of exhibits illustrating the art, folklore and cultural history of southern Germany, and Bavaria in particular.

The ground floor has treasures from the early Middle Ages to the rococo period, including evocative sculptures by Erasmus Grasser and Tilman Riemenschneider, two of the greatest artists of the era. Upstairs are 19th-century highlights including Nymphenburg porcelain, precious glass and an exquisite collection of *Jugendstil* (Art Deco) items. Also here is a celebrated collection of cots from the 17th to the 19th centuries.

To get there take U4 to Lehel, tram 17 or bus 100.

ARCHÄOLOGISCHE STAATSSAMMLUNG

You can trace the settlement of Bavaria from the Stone Age to the early Middle Ages at the **Archäologische Staatssammlung** (Map p294; ☎ 211 2402; Lerchenfeldstrasse 2; adult/concession €4.50/2.50, Sun free; ☉ 9am-4.30pm, closed Mon), which is behind the Bayerisches Nationalmuseum. The exhibit features objects from Celtic, Roman and Germanic civilisations, including the well-preserved body of a ritually sacrificed young girl.

Olympiapark & Around

More than three decades after the Olympic Games for which it was built, the **Olympiapark** (Map p296) is still an integral part of life in the city. The centrepieces are the 290m Olympiaturm and the massive undulating 'tented' roof covering the west side of the Olympic Stadium, hall and swimming centre.

Today the complex is open as a collection of public facilities. The grounds are the site of celebrations, concerts, fireworks displays and professional sporting events throughout the year. Both the swimming hall and ice-skating rink are open to the public. There's an **Info Pavilion** (☎ 3067 2414; www.olympiapark-muenchen.de; ☺ 10am-6pm Mon-Fri, 10am-3pm Sat) at the **Olympia-Eissportzentrum** (ice-skating rink; ☺ open skating sessions 10am-noon & 1.30-4pm Mon-Fri, 8-10.30pm Wed-Sun).

Wandering around the grounds is free but you'll have to pay to see inside the **Olympia-Stadion** (Olympic Stadium; adult/children €2/1; ☺ 9am-4.30pm Oct–mid-Apr, 8.30am-6pm mid-Apr–Sep, closed event days). You can take the one-hour **Soccer Tour** (adult/concession €5/3.50; ☺ Apr-Oct), which visits the Olympic Stadium, VIP area and locker rooms, or the 90-minute **Adventure Tour** (adult/concession €7/5), which covers the entire Olympiapark both on foot and in a little train. When the weather's good you can enjoy stunning views of the city from the top of the **Olympiaturm** (Olympic Tower; adult/concession €4/2.50; ☺ 9am-midnight, last trip 11.30pm), which houses a restaurant and an unexpected display of rock-music memorabilia (free with tower ticket).

Kids will particularly enjoy the park's latest attraction, **SeaLife** (☎ 450 000; adult/child 3-14 yr €12.50/9.50; ☺ 10am-7pm). Reef sharks, moray eels and magical sea horses are among the 10,000 creatures on display, all presented in realistic aquaria with recessed glass viewing ports. Tunnel walkways lead you right through some tanks – the next best thing to scuba diving.

BMW MUSEUM

Near the Olympiaturm stands the temporary **BMW Museum** (Map p296; ☎ 3822 5625; www.bmw-welt .de; Petuelring 130; adult/concession €2/1.50; ☺ 10am-10pm, last entry 9.15pm). You can see highlights from its splendid car and motorcycle collection parked in a globe-like tent. Free tours of the assembly line (in German and English) are run at the **BMW factory** (Map p296; ☎ 3822 3306).

From summer 2007, exhibits will move into a sleek, newly revamped museum at the company headquarters to the east, underneath the famous towers shaped like automobile pistons. Visitors will also be able to take tours of the firm's architectural showpiece, the cloud-shaped **BMW Welt**, a car delivery and events centre just north of the Olympiapark.

MUNICH'S OLYMPIC TRAGEDY

The 1972 Summer Olympics presented Munich with a historic chance. It was the first time the country would host the prestigious sporting event since 1936, when the Games were held in Berlin under Hitler. The motto was the 'Happy Games', and the emblem was a blue solar 'Bright Sun'. The city built a shiny Olympic Park, which included the tent-like plexiglass canopies that, at the time, were revolutionary in design. It was the perfect opportunity to present a new, democratic Germany full of pride and optimism.

In the final week of the Olympics, however, members of the Palestinian terrorist group 'Black September' killed two Israeli athletes and took nine others hostage at the Olympic Village, demanding the release of political prisoners and escape aircraft. During a failed rescue attempt by German security forces at Fürstenfeldbrück, a military base west of Munich, all of the hostages and most of the terrorists were killed. The competition was suspended briefly before Avery Brundage, the International Olympic Committee president, famously declared 'the Games must go on'. The bloody incident cast a pall over the entire Olympics and sporting events in Germany for years to follow.

The events are chronicled in an Oscar-winning documentary, *One Day in September* (2000) by Kevin McDonald, as well as in Steven Spielberg's historical fictional account, *Munich* (2005). The killings prompted German security to rethink its methods and create the elite counter-terrorist unit, GSG 9.

South of the Altstadt

DEUTSCHES MUSEUM

You can spend days wandering the **Deutsches Museum** (Map p294; ☎ 217 91; www.deutsches-museum .de; Museumsinsel 1; adult/concession/family €8.50/7/17, children under 6yr free; ✆ 9am-5pm), said to be the world's largest science and technology museum. This vast museum is on an island southeast of Isartor (Isar Gate) and features just about anything ever invented. There are loads of interactive displays (including glass blowing and paper making), model coal and salt mines, and wonderful sections on musical instruments, caves, geodesy, microelectronics and astronomy. Demonstrations take place throughout the day; a popular one is in the power hall where a staff member is raised in the insulated Faraday Cage and zapped with a 220,000V bolt of lightning.

West of the Altstadt

THERESIENWIESE

About 1.5km west of the old town, the Theresienwiese (Theresa Meadow) is the site of the annual Oktoberfest (below). At the far western end of the meadow looms the classical **Ruhmeshalle** (Hall of Fame; admission free), an open gallery of famous Bavarians whose busts adorn the wall like hunting trophies. The hall curls horseshoe-like around the green-tinged **Bavaria statue** (Map p292; adult/ under 18yr with parents/concession €2.50/free/1.50; ✆ 10am-noon & 2-4pm Tue-Sun). Climb up to the head cavity to get a great view of the 'Wies'n', as the locals call the festival grounds. Generations of visitors have perched on the inside of Bavaria's cast-iron lips to peer out of her hollow eyes at the crowds below.

VERKEHRSZENTRUM

Sheltered in a historic trade fair hall, the **Verkehrszentrum** (Transport & Mobility Centre; Map p292; ☎ 217 9529; Thersienhöhe 14a; adult/child €2.50/1.50; ✆ 9am-5pm Fri-Wed, 9am-8pm Thu) features some fascinating exhibits, with hands-on displays about pioneering research and famous inventions, plus cars, boats and trains, and the history of car racing. In 2006, the museum opened a new section showing the Deutsche Museum's entire vehicle collection, ranging from the first motorcars to high-speed ICE trains.

OKTOBERFEST

It all started as an elaborate wedding toast – and turned into the world's biggest collective drink-up. In October 1810 the future king, Bavarian Crown Prince Ludwig I, married Princess Therese, and the newlyweds threw an enormous party at the city gates, complete with a horse race. The next year Ludwig's fun-loving subjects came back for more. The festival was extended and, to fend off autumn, was moved forward to September. As the years drew on the racehorses were dropped and sometimes the party had to be cancelled, but the institution called Oktoberfest was here to stay.

Nearly two centuries later, this 16-day extravaganza draws over six million visitors a year to celebrate a marriage of good cheer and outright debauchery. A special beer is brewed for the occasion (Wies'nbier), which is dark and strong. Munichers spend the day at the office in Lederhosen and Dirndl in order to hit the festival right after work. It is Bavaria's largest tourist draw, generating about €1 billion in business. No admission is charged, but most of the fun costs something.

On the meadow called Theresienwiese (Wies'n for short), a little city is erected, consisting of beer tents, amusements and rides – just what drinkers need after several frothy ones! The action kicks off with the Brewer's Parade at 11am on the first day of the festival. The parade begins at Sonnenstrasse and winds its way to the fairgrounds via Schwanthalerstrasse. At noon, the lord mayor stands before the thirsty crowds at Theresienwiese and, with due pomp, slams a wooden tap into a cask of beer. As the beer gushes out, the mayor exclaims, *O'zapft ist's!* (It's tapped!). The next day resembles the opening of the Olympics, as a young woman on horseback leads a parade of costumed participants from all over the world.

Hotels book out very quickly and prices skyrocket, so reserve accommodation as early as you can (like a year in advance). The festival is a 15-minute walk southwest of the Hauptbahnhof, and is served by its own U-Bahn station 'Theresienwiese'. Trams and buses have signs reading 'Zur Festwiese' (literally 'to the Festival Meadow').

Schloss Nymphenburg

The amazing **Schloss Nymphenburg** (Map p296; ☎ 179 080; combined ticket to everything except Marstall-museum adult/concession €10/8) and its lavish gardens sprawl about 5km northwest of the Altstadt. Begun in 1664 as a villa for Electress Adelaide of Savoy, the palace and gardens were expanded over the next century to create the royal family's summer residence. To get there take tram 17 or bus 51 from Karlsplatz.

SCHLOSS

The primary palace building (adult/concession €5/4; ☼ 9am-6pm, 9am-8pm Thu) consists of a main villa and two wings. The rooms are all sumptuous, but one of the most majestic is the **Schönheitengalerie** (Gallery of Beauties), in the southern wing, formerly the apartments of Queen Caroline. It's now the home of 38 portraits of beautiful women chosen by an admiring King Ludwig I. The most famous is of Helene Sedlmayr, the daughter of a shoemaker, wearing a lavish frock the king gave her for the sitting. Here you'll also find Ludwig's beautiful but notorious lover, Lola Montez, whose antics spelled the king's downfall.

Also in the south wing are the coaches and riding gear of the royal families, suitably displayed in the **Marstallmuseum** (adult/concession €2.50/2; ☼ 9am-6pm Fri-Wed, 9am-8pm Thu). Ludwig II's over-the-top sleigh, fitted with oil lamps for his nocturnal outings, is not to be missed. The 1st floor features a collection of porcelain made by the legendary Nymphenburger Manufaktur and a shop.

The north wing is occupied by the **Museum Mensch und Natur** (Museum of Humankind and Nature; adult/under 15yr with parents/concession €2.50/free/1.50; ☼ 9am-5pm Tue-Sun). This is a fun place to bring children for its interactive (if aged) displays on the animal kingdom, planet earth and the mysteries of the human body (German only).

GARDENS & OUTBUILDINGS

The royal gardens take the form of a magnificently sculpted English-style park. They contain a number of intriguing buildings, including the **Amalienburg** (adult/concession €2/1; ☼ 9am-6pm Fri-Wed, 9am-8pm Thu), a small hunting lodge with a large domed central room; the **Pagodenburg** Chinese teahouse; and the **Badenburg** (adult/concession €2/1; ☼ 9am-6pm, 9am-8pm Thu) sauna and bathing house.

Other Sights

MÜNCHENER TIERPARK HELLABRUNN

About 5000 animals are housed in Munich's 'geo-zoo' (one with distinct sections dividing animals by continents). The **Münchener Tierpark Hellabrunn** (Map pp290-1; ☎ 625 080; Tierparkstrasse 30; adult/concession €9/6; ☼ 8am-6pm Apr-Sep, 9am-5pm Oct-Mar), to the south of the city, was one of the first of its kind. The sprawling, well-maintained grounds boast some impressive rhinos, elephants, deer and gazelles. It's absolutely worth the admission if only to gain access to the petting zoo, full of cuddly sheep, deer and lambs. To get there take the U3 to Thalkirchen or bus 52 from Marienplatz.

ALLIANZ ARENA

Sporting and architecture fans alike should take a side trip to the northern Munich suburb of Fröttmaning to see Munich's sparkling new football stadium – already a historic site after hosting the opening game of the World Cup 2006. Nicknamed the 'life belt' and 'rubber boat' *(Schlauchboot)*, the state-of-the-art, €340 million **Allianz Arena** has walls made of inflatable cushions that can be individually lit to match the jerseys of the host team – be it local sides FC Bayern München and TSV 1860 München (who share the stadium) or the national team. Take a **tour** (☎ 01805 555 101; adult/child 7-12yr €8/4; ☼ at 11am, 1pm, 3pm & 5pm) of the stadium but expect to queue in summer. To get there take U6 to Fröttmaning.

BAVARIA FILMSTADT

One of Germany's most important movie studios is the **Bavaria Filmstadt** (Map pp290-1; ☎ 6499 2304; Bavariafilmplatz 7; adult/concession €10/7; ☼ tours 9am-4pm, 1pm in English) in the southern suburb of Geiselgasteig. The top-grossing German film of all-time, *Das Boot*, was among the classics shot here, but today's German audience is more interested in sets of the family soap, *Marienhof*. Crash-and-burn stunt shows (€8) take place at noon, 1.30pm and 3pm in summer (noon only in other periods). To get there take the S2 to Silberhornstrasse, then tram 25 to Bavariafilmplatz.

ACTIVITIES

Munich makes a perfect base for outdoor exploits. For information about hiking and climbing, contact the Munich chapter of the **Deutscher Alpenverein** (German Alpine Club; Map p292; ☎ 551 7000; Bayerstrasse 21) near the Hauptbahnhof.

BAVARIA

BAVARIA

Boating

Take your sweetie out for a leisurely spin at the Kleinhesseloher (Kleinhesseloher Lake; Map p295) in the Englischer Garten (p302), where rowing and pedal boats can be rented for around €7 per half-hour for up to four people. You can also hire boats at the Olympiapark (p303).

Cycling

Munich is an excellent place for cycling. Pumped full of bracing Alpine air and a network of leafy paths, the Englischer Garten is a good place to start a day's tour.

Radius Tours & Bikes (Map p292; ☎ 596 113; www .radiusmunich.com; at the end of track 32 in the Haupt-bahnhof; ☒ 10am to 6pm mid-Apr–mid-Oct) hires out bikes for €3 per hour or €14 per day, with a €50 deposit. Staff speak English and are happy to provide tips and advice on touring around Munich.

Mike's Bike Tours (Map p292; ☎ 2554 3988; www .mikesbiketours.com; tour €24; ☒ Mar–mid-Nov) offers guided bike tours of the city. Their point of contact is **Discover Bavaria** (Map p292; cnr Brau-hausstrasse & Hochbrückenstrasse). The standard four-hour tour is an easy ride with a 45-minute break at a beer garden.

Tours leave from the archway of the Altes Rathaus on Marienplatz (in front of the Toy Museum).

Surfing

At the southern tip of the Englischer Garten (Map p294) is an artificial 'permanent wave' in a frigid arm of the Isar, where crowds gather to watch surfers in thermal suits practise their moves.

Swimming

The authorities warn grimly against bathing in the crystalline Isar River, but plenty of Müncheners can't resist. On warm days the pebbly islets in the riverbed are lined with natives seeking a healthy glow; tanlines are optional.

Munich also has many swimming pools to cool your desires. The **Olympia-Schwimmhalle** (Map p296; ☎ 3067 2290; Olympiapark; adult/child €3/2.50; ☒ 7am-11pm) has long laps, while the spectacular **Müllersches Volksbad** (Map p294; ☎ 2361 3434; Rosenheimer Strasse 1; adult/child €2.90/2.30; ☒ 7.30am-11pm) harks back to the turn of the 20th century. To get there take tram 18 from Karlsplatz.

WALKING TOUR

WALK FACTS

Start Michaelskirche
Finish Chinesischer Turm
Distance 5km
Duration 2½ hours

This 5km Altstadt circuit (Map p307) takes in the key sights in Munich's historic centre and the Englischer Garten. If you include visits to all the museums and churches mentioned here, you've got a two-day itinerary on your hands.

Commence at the **Michaelskirche (1)**, a richly ornamented church with barrel vaults, and the final resting place of King Ludwig II. Proceed east along Sendlinger Strasse, the main shopping drag, passing by the Frauenkirche, Munich's landmark church. The way opens into Marienplatz, the old town square, punctuated by the **Mariensäule (2**; Mary Column) in front of the neo-Gothic **Neues Rathaus (3**; New Town Hall). The blue-bottomed **Fischbrunnen (4**; Fish Fountain) gushes peacefully near the entrance. The steeple of **St Peterskirche (5**; Church of St Peter) affords a great vista of the old town, including the **Altes Rathaus (6**; Old Town Hall), now home to a toy museum. To see amazing Asam frescoes, peek inside **Heiliggeistkirche (7**; Church of the Holy Spirit).

Head east on Im Tal, taking a left into Maderbräustrasse to Orlandostrasse, site of the **Hofbräuhaus (8)**, the celebrated beer hall. Then zigzag through the backstreets – west on Münzstrasse, left into Sparkassenstrasse and then into the alley Ledererstrasse. At Burgstrasse, turn right into the courtyard of the **Alter Hof (9)**, the Wittelsbach's early residence in Munich. Exit north and proceed along Hofgraben, past the former **Münzhof (10**; mint). The street opens into the grand Maximilianstrasse and Max-Joseph-Platz, address of the grand **Nationaltheater (11)** and fine opera. A treasure-filled palace and museum, the **Residenz (12)** was the seat of the Wittelsbach rulers for over four centuries.

Stroll north on Residenzstrasse to reach Odeonsplatz, site of the Nazis' first lunge at power. Here looms the **Feldherrnhalle (13**; Field Marshals' Hall), a hulking shrine to war heroes. The bombastic, mustard-yellow **Theatinerkirche St Kajetan (14)**, contains the Wittelsbachs' family

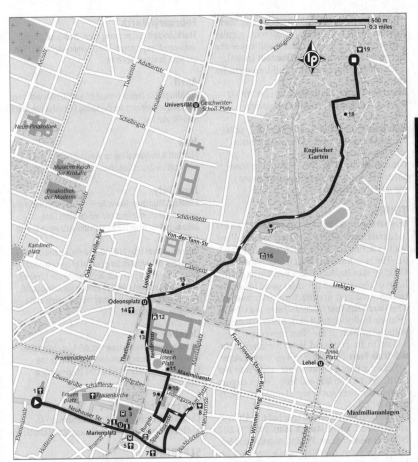

crypt. The tour heads into green territory from here, starting with the neoclassical **Hofgarten** (**15**; Royal Gardens). Cross it diagonally and go through the underpass to enter the Englischer Garten. Proceed north past the sinister-looking **Haus der Kunst (16)**, a gallery and onetime forum for Nazi art propaganda. The leafy route winds past the ceremonial **Japanisches Teehaus (17**; Japanese Teahouse) and into a vast meadow popular with frisbee experts and nude sunbathers. A little hill with a classical folly, the **Monopteros (18)** completes the leisurely scene. At the end of the tour you can plop down in the beer garden alongside the curious, multitiered **Chinesischer Turm (19**; Chinese Tower) where an oompah band belts out traditional tunes.

MUNICH FOR CHILDREN

Munich is a great city for children. Many of the museums have hands-on exhibits to play with, the zoo is stunning, and there are plenty of parks and children's theatre events.

You can safely leave the little ones at **Münchner Kindl** (Map p292; ☎ 2423 1600; www.muenchner kindlgruppe.de; Burgstrasse 6; per hr €7, 1st hr free; ☼ 9am-6pm Mon-Fri, 10am-4pm Sat). Kids aged 18 months to 10 years old are welcome in this toy-filled childcare centre near Marienplatz.

Sure-fire hits include the **Hellabrunn Zoo** (p305), which has a huge petting section and an aviary, and **SeaLife** (p303), an entertaining aquarium in the Olympiapark. The **Deutsches Museum** (p304) has lots of interactive science exhibits and a reconstructed coal mine.

The darling puppet collection in the **Stadtmuseum** (p297) includes a stage with regular performances. Older children will enjoy the fiery stunt show at **Bavaria Filmstadt** (p305).

Other entertainment for children includes the following:

Münchner Theater für Kinder (Map p296; ☎ 593 858; Dachauer Strasse 46) Children's performances year-round.

Münchner Marionettentheater (Map p292; ☎ 265 712; Blumenstrasse 32) Munich's main puppet theatre often shows Mozart's musical plays.

Circus Krone (Map p296; ☎ 545 8000; Zirkus-Krone-Strasse 1-6; ☷ Dec-Apr) An enduring favourite and venerable Munich tradition.

TOURS

Original Munich Walks (Map p292; ☎ 5502 9374; www.radiusmunich.com) offers a variety of excellent walks starting from the Hauptbahnhof, track 32. The two-hour **City Walk** (adults/child under 14yr €10/5; ☷ 10am May-Aug) takes you through the heart of the city and provides good historical background and architectural information. The **Third Reich Tour** (adults/child under 14yr €10/9.50; ☷ at 3pm Apr-Oct) visits all major sites associated with the growth of the Nazi movement.

Not to be confused with the above, **Munich Walk Tours** (☎ 2070 2736; www.munichwalktours.de) offer a **Beer & Brewery Tour** (adults/under 26yr €17/15; ☷ at 6.15pm May–mid-Sep). Tours depart from under the Glockenspiel on Marienplatz (Map p292).

Free three-hour guided tours of the Altstadt are offered by **New Munich Tours** (☎ 0176-2330 2959; www.newmunich.com; ☷ at 10.45am May–mid-Sep) and leave from the Siegessäule column on Marienplatz.

Münchener Stadtrundfahrten (☎ 5490 7560; www.msr-muc.de; A&O Touristik, Arnulfstrasse 8; adult/child €11/6) bus tours (one hour, eight tours daily) around Munich leave from the Hertie department store opposite the Hauptbahnhof (Map p292).

FESTIVALS & EVENTS

Munich always has something to celebrate. The list below gives just a few of the highlights; for more details check www.muenchen-tourist.de.

January/February

Fasching A six-week carnival beginning on 7 January with all kinds of merriment, including costume parades and fancy-dress balls.

February/March

Starkbierzeit Potent spring beers, traditional dancing and stone-lifting contests. The Löwenbräukeller (p315) is the place to experience it all.

April

Frühlingsfest Theresienwiese (Map p292) fills with beer tents and amusements for the Spring Festival, a two-week mini-Oktoberfest.

May

Maidult A traditional fair on Mariahilfplatz (Map p294), with crafts, antiques and amusement rides.

June/July

Filmfest München (www.filmfest-muenchen.de) World premieres of international and independent films.

Jakobidult Summer fair on Mariahilfplatz much like the Maidult.

Opera Festival (☎ 2185 1021; www.bayerische.staatsoper.de) A month-long festival of opera concluding on 31 July with Wagner's *Die Meistersinger von Nürnberg*.

Tollwood Festival (☎ 383 8500; www.tollwood.de) A world culture gala with nightly music concerts at the Olympiapark (Map p296).

October

Oktoberfest (www.oktoberfest.de) A legendary beer-swilling party running from mid-September to the first Sunday in October. Held on the Theresienwiese (Map p292).

November/December

Christkindlmarkt (www.christkindlmarkt.de) A traditional Christmas market on Marienplatz (Map p292).

SLEEPING

Room rates in Munich tend to be high, and skyrocket during Oktoberfest. Book well ahead to avoid disappointment.

Traditional hostels exist, but overall the new hotel-hostels offer a more attractive deal for budget travellers, especially those around the Hauptbahnhof. This area has many *pensions* and hotels of varying quality; some are grotty but the standard is improving in leaps and bounds. The Altstadt has the most top-end hotels.

Around the Hauptbahnhof
BUDGET

A&O City Hotel (Map p292; ☎ 4523 5760; www.aohostels.com.de; Bayerstrasse 75; dm €12, d €32-80; 🖵) On a busy street near the main train station, the A&O teeters between simple hotel and fancy hostel. Settle into a bunk in the 14-person 'Easy Dorm', or there are plenty of singles and doubles. Rooms are smallish but clean, and all have en suite shower and toilet, satellite TV and a hairdryer.

Euro Palace Station Hostel (Map p292; ☎ 5525 210; www.easypalace.de; Schützenstrasse 7; dm €19.90, s €29-49, d €44-69; 🖳) For quarters with a vintage flair try this hostel, based in an aging hotel. Styles run the gamut, from a '50s brass bed to a rustic oak from the disco era. Only seven of the 55 rooms are dorms (sleeping four to six); the rest are singles and doubles available in three categories of comfort – most being spacious, quiet and facing an inner courtyard.

Wombat's (Map p292; ☎ 5998 9180; www.wombats -hostels.de; Senefelderstrasse 1; dm €12-22, d €29-31; 🅿 🖳). This stylish little hostel-hotel has a great location right by the train station. All rooms (dorms and doubles only) have Ikea-style furniture, pleasing colours and en suite showers and toilets. Most of the 14 doubles are sunny and have a large balcony facing an inner courtyard.

Euro Youth Hotel (Map p292; ☎ 5990 8811; www .euro-youth-hotel.de; Senefelderstrasse 5; dm/s/d €17.50/38/48; 🆇) A large, well-run hostel in a great old building that oozes history with every dangling chandelier and creaky staircase. It has two 20-bed dorms with tightly placed bunk beds as well as snug private rooms.

Hotel Jedermann (☎ 543 240; www.hotel-jedermann .de; Bayerstrasse 95; s €49-99, d €67-149; 🅿 🆇 🄴 🖳) This renovated hotel with English-speaking staff is excellent value, with small but quite comfortable rooms. There's a wide range of prices and room options; ones with showers but shared toilet cost from €57 to €86.

Meininger's (Map p292; ☎ 6663 6100; www.meininger -hostels.de; Landsbergerstrasse 20; dm/s/d €19/49/78; 🅿 🆇 🖳) About 800m west of the Hauptbahnhof, this energetic hostel-hotel on the doorstep of the Augustiner brewery has interiors and facilities similar to Wombat's, but also a rooftop terrace and underground parking. Take tram 18 or 19 to Holzapfelstrasse.

MIDRANGE

Hotel Belle Blue (Map p292; ☎ 550 6260; www.hotel -belleblue.com; Schillerstrasse 21; s from €75, d from €89; 🅿 🆇 🄴 🖳) This chic little hotel employs subtle, attractive colour schemes and tasteful furnishings to great effect. The bathrooms are a hit, with their glass cubicle showers, underfloor heating and designer fixtures. All

this lets you overlook the fact that the rooms are a little snug.

Creatif Hotel Elephant (Map p292; ☎ 555 785; www .creatifelephanthotel.com; Lämmerstrasse 6; s €65-149, d €85-189; 🅿 🆇) This sparkling new hotel offers a range of simple rooms with bright, trendy décor and good room facilities, like hairdryers and even faxes. It is family run and the service is extremely friendly, with a big welcome for children.

Alpen Hotel (Map p292; ☎ 559 300; www.alpenhotel -muenchen.de; Adolf-Kolping-Strasse 14; s €75-135, d €95-195; 🆇 🖳) This place manages to merge seamlessly the atmosphere of an Alpine inn with a boutique hotel. The newer rooms are as sleek as a catwalk, but many have a countrified loo (No 35 has a big four-poster bed). The salon features a cosy fireplace with a portrait of Sisi over the mantle.

Hotel Hotelissimo (Map p292; ☎ 557 855; Schillerstrasse 4; www.hotelissimo.com; s €69-119, d €98-149; 🆇 🖳) An extreme makeover has catapulted this family-run hotel from shabby to chic, while keeping it a stone's thrown from the main train station. The cheery décor reflects a real appreciation for design, colour and fabrics.

Also recommended:

Hotel Schweitz (Map p292; ☎ 543 6960; www .hotel-schweitz.de; Goethestrasse 26; s €70-90, d €90-165; 🅿 🆇 🖳) Bright but cosy hotel with maple-wood furniture, a small wellness area and an open-air terrace.

Hotel Bristol (Map p292; ☎ 5951 5154; www.bristol -muc.com; Pettenkofer Strasse 2; s €59-199, d €79-249; 🅿 🆇 🖳) Comfy, well-furnished rooms with friendly service and generous breakfast.

TOP END

Anna Hotel (Map p292; ☎ 599 940; www.annahotel.de; Schützenstrasse 1; s from €145, d from €165; 🅿 🆇 🄴 🖳) Take a top location, add a generous dose of style and trendiness and you've got one killer designer hotel. The classy Donghia furniture is dressed in gold, black and burgundy fabrics so rich you want to run your hands over them, while the sensuous bathrooms feature a gushing 'rainforest' shower.

Dorint Sofitel (Map p292; ☎ 599 480; www.dorint.com; Bayernstrasse 12; r €155-425; 🅿 🆇 🄴 🖳 🄿) The brilliantly restored Renaissance façade of the former Royal Bavarian Post Office contains a jewel that satisfies all cravings for luxury. The 396 rooms and suites are a cocktail of style, surprise lighting effects and supreme comfort.

Altstadt & Around
MIDRANGE
Hotel Blauer Bock (Map p292; ☎ 231 780; www
.hotelblauerbock.de; Sebastiansplatz 9; s €41-60, d €71-
109; P ⊠) This hotel once provided beds
for Benedictine monks and coachmen for
the grain market nearby. It's comfy, familiar and spacious, and front rooms overlook
the Schrannenhalle, a blink away from the
Viktualienmarkt.

Hotel Alcron (Map p292; ☎ 228 3511; Ledererstrasse
13; www.hotel-alcron.de; s €60-70, d €80-95; ⊠ ▣) This
quaint hotel is ideally located just stumbling
distance from the Hofbräuhaus. A wonderful spiral wooden staircase leads up to the
small simple rooms, with traditional furnishings and comfortable beds to sleep off any
excesses.

TOP END
Bayerischer Hof (Map p292; ☎ 212 00; www.bayer
ischerhof.de; Promenadeplatz 2-6; s €223-254, d €302-442;
P ⊠ ⊠ ▣ ⊠) Room doors fold away into
the stucco mouldings at the Hof, one of the
grande dames of the Munich hotel trade. It
boasts a supercentral location, a pool and a
jazz club. Marble, antiques and oil paintings
abound, and you can dine till you drop at
any one of the three fabulous restaurants.
Rates include a champagne breakfast. There's
wheelchair access.

Kempinski Vier Jahreszeiten München (Map p292;
☎ 212 50; www.kempinski-vierjahreszeiten.de; Maximilianstrasse 17; s from €205, d €230-390; P ⊠ ⊠ ▣ ⊠)
This illustrious hotel has a grand façade
featuring statues of the managers, the four
seasons and four continents. The rooms don't
have as many amenities as you'd think, but the
suites are palatial and the rooftop pool is an
incredible blue-sky swim.

Schwabing
BUDGET
Pension Frank (Map p295; ☎ 281 451; www.pension-frank
.de; Schellingstrasse 24; s €40-45, d €50-60) Large rooms
and a convivial atmosphere make this small
pension a popular choice with young backpackers and school groups. Rooms (all with
shared bathroom) have lovely wrought-iron
beds; there is a small collection of English
novels and a communal kitchen.

Pension am Kaiserplatz (Map p295; ☎ 349 190;
fax 339 316; Kaiserplatz 12; s €31-47, d €49-59) The
façade of this Jugendstil villa is a throwback
to more romantic times, when Schwabing
was a vortex of art and culture. The rooms
(just 10, all with hall bathrooms) are lovingly
decorated with a family touch, and breakfast
is delivered to your door by the congenial
host herself.

MIDRANGE
Gästehaus Englischer Garten (Map p295; ☎ 383 9410;
www.hotelenglischergarten.de; Liebergesellstrasse 8; s €68-
180, d €68-180; P) Just steps away from the
Englischer Garten, this cosy *pension* occupies
a graceful old mill with a private garden for
breakfast (€9 extra) on warm summer mornings. Most of the antique-filled rooms have
en suite bath and TV.

TOP END
Cosmopolitan Hotel (Map p295; ☎ 383 810; www
.cosmopolitan-hotel.de; Hohenzollern Strasse 5; s €110-170,
d €120-200; P ⊠) The Cosmopolitan is a mod-
ern hotel that has comfortable and tastefully
furnished rooms, plenty of dark wood and
subtle lighting. It's ideally located for access to Schwabing's nightlife, and is recommended as a good place for party animals to
get their beauty sleep.

THE AUTHOR'S CHOICE

Two fabulous and distinctly individual hotels in Munich just cry out to be visited.

Cortiina (Map p292; ☎ 242 2490; www.cortiina.com; Ledererstrasse 8; s/d/ste €146/186/286 P ⊠ ⊠ ▣)
This stunning, modern hotel is a great place for anyone looking for stylish elegance without the
antiques. The design is chic and minimalist without losing any comfort. Dark wood and low lighting
run throughout the hotel, while the bedrooms are lined with oak panelling, have parquet floors
and individual furnishings, as well as glass-encased bathrooms lined with Jura stone.

Opera-Garni (Map p294; ☎ 5210 4940; www.hotel-opera.de; Annastrasse 10; r €185-265, ste €275-355;
⊠ ▣) Step inside the Opera and you'll step back in time. This charming hotel is pure old-world
elegance and refinement. Breakfast is served in the garden between graceful statues, and the
sumptuous rooms are stunningly decorated with individual combinations of rich colours and
fabrics, antiques, chandeliers and Persian carpets.

Nymphenburg, Neuhausen & Around
BUDGET
DJH hostel (Map p296; ☎ 131 156; www.djh.de; Wendl
-Dietrich-Strasse 20; dm under/over 26yr €23.40/27.40;
☒ closed Dec; ✕) The Jugendherberge München
is the most central DJH hostel, in Neuhausen
northwest of the Altstadt. Relatively loud and
busy, it's also popular and friendly. There's a
restaurant, a garden, bikes for hire, and no
curfew. Take the U1 to Rotkreuzplatz.

Hotel Flora (Map p296; ☎ 597 067; www.hotel
-flora.de; Karlstrasse 49; s €45-60, d €65-80; ☐) This
is a quiet, simple hotel in a venerable complex with good-value rooms, including quads
(€88), that are an ideal setup for families.
Rates include breakfast. It's just a 5-minute
walk north of the Hauptbahnhof.

Other recommendations:
Campingplatz Nord-West (Map pp290-1; ☎ 150
6936; www.campingplatz-nord-west.de; Auf den Schreder-
wiesen 3; tent €3.80-7.50, car/person €3.20/4.70) Pleasant
camp site about 2km from Olympiapark and within
walking distance of three swimming lakes.
Campingplatz Obermenzing (Map pp290-1; ☎ 811
2235; www.campingplatz-muenchen.de; Lochhausener
Strasse 59; car & tent/person €6.50/4.50; ☒ mid-Mar–
Oct) Parklike camp site in western Munich with
coin laundry and small store.

MIDRANGE
Hotel Laimer Hof (Map p296; ☎ 1780 380; www
.laimerhof.de; Laimer Strasse 40; s/d from €69/89; ☐) Run
by possibly the nicest couple on the planet,
this cute little villa – a listed monument incidentally – has a relaxed country feel, despite
being just five minutes' walk from Schloss
Nymphenburg. Of the 23 rooms, those on
the upper floors have the most character and
best views.

Westend & Ludwigsvorstadt
BUDGET
Easy Palace (Map p292; ☎ 558 7970; www.easypalace
.de; Mozartstrasse 4; dm/s/d €16.90/29/50; ☐☐) Converted from a hotel, this hostel has a good
range of facilities, from pool tables to bike
hire and luggage storage. The rooms are fairly
simple, but comfy, and the management is
friendly.

Pension Westfalia (Map p292; ☎ 530 377; www
.pension-westfalia.de; Mozartstrasse 23; s €35-55, d €50-78;
☒) This stately four-storey villa stands just
off the Oktoberfest meadow with a bull's-
eye view of the Bavaria statue. Outside the
beer festival this cosy, family-run *pension* is

a peaceful base for sightseeing. The comfy,
modern rooms are all reached by lift, and
most have private bathrooms.

MIDRANGE
Hotel-Pension Mariandl (Map p292; ☎ 534 108; www
.mariandl.com; Goethestrasse 51; s €60-75, d €70-110) Old-
world charm, huge rooms with high ceilings
and oriel windows make this neo-Gothic
mansion a real treat. The downstairs restaurant (Café am Beethovenplatz; p312 and
p317) has live jazz or classical music nightly
at 8pm. Children are welcome.

Hotel Uhland (Map p292; ☎ 543 350; www.hotel
-uhland.de; Uhlandstrasse 1; s €64-135, d €77-180; ℗ ☒ ☐)
Just east of the Theresienwiese you'll find this
lovely Art Nouveau villa with a relaxed atmosphere and English-speaking staff. The large,
comfy rooms (some with a tiny balcony),
quaint garden and good service make it an
enduring favourite with visitors. The waterbed
room is popular.

Southwest of the City
BUDGET
DJH hostel (Map pp290-1; ☎ 723 6550/60; www.djh
.de; Miesingstrasse 4; dm under/over 26yr €23.40/27.40;
℗ ☒) Still fairly accessible to the centre,
the modern Jugendgästehaus München is
southwest of the Altstadt in the suburb of
Thalkirchen. There's no curfew. Take the
U-Bahn to Thalkirchen and then follow the
signs.

Campingplatz Thalkirchen (Map pp290-1; ☎ 7243
0808; www.camping.muenchen.de; Zentralländstrasse 49; tent
€3-4, car €4.30, person €4.50-8.10; ☒ mid-Mar–Oct) This
is the closest camp site to the city centre but
can get very crowded. It's scenically located
on the Isar River, 5km southwest of the city
centre. Take the U3 to Thalkirchen and then
bus 57, or it's a 15-minute walk.

Long-Term Rentals
If you're planning to stay in Munich for
a month or longer, you might consider
renting through a Mitwohnzentrale (flat-
sharing agency, p737). Accommodation can
be anything from rooms in shared student
flats to furnished apartments.

Generally speaking, a room in a flat costs
about €330 to €500 per month, while a one-
bedroom apartment ranges from €450 to
€750. Commission (up to one month's rent),
VAT (19%) and, in some cases, a deposit must
be added to the rent.

Agencies to try include the following:

City Mitwohnzentrale (Map p292; ☎ 194 30; www .mitwohnzentrale.de; Lämmerstrasse 4)

Mitwohnzentrale an der Uni (Map p295; ☎ 286 6060; www.mwz-munich.de; Fendstrasse 6)

Mitwohnzentrale – Mr. Lodge (Map p295; ☎ 340 8230; www.mrlodge.de; Barer Strasse 32)

EATING
Cafés & Bistros
Trachtenvogl (Map p292; ☎ 201 5160; Reichenbachstrasse 47; snacks €3-6) A send-up of the Black Forest, complete with cuckoo clock and braying elk, this warped little café-lounge has good sandwiches, cakes and 30 different kinds of hot chocolate (cold if you like). It takes reservations for chocolate fondue, served Sundays after 8pm.

Woerners (Map p292; ☎ 265 231; Marienplatz 1; dishes €3-15) Two cafés merge into one here: the outdoor Café am Dom on the ground floor, giving some of the best seating on the square, and Café Reber upstairs – a Munich institution, with parquet floors, crystal chandeliers and a long, long history.

Creperie Bernard Bernard (Map p294; ☎ 480 1173; Innere-Wiener-Strasse 32; crepes €5-9; ☺ dinner Mon-Sat) The best crepes in town can be found at this small place that serves up delicious savouries oozing goat's cheese or shrimp, and lavish desserts dripping with the finest French chocolate.

Café Voilà (Map p294; ☎ 489 1654; Wörthstrasse 5; mains €5-10) High stucco ceilings, giant mirrors and large windows make this café a great place for watching the world go by. It's buzzing for breakfast and later in the day for fairly priced baguettes, burgers and interesting vegetarian dishes.

Brik (Map p295; ☎ 2899 6630; Schellingstrasse 24; sushi €5-10) This slick Japanese-style café, bar and lounge is a temple of minimalism with delicious sushi snacks. The crowd is as discerning as the sophisticated cocktail list.

Café am Beethovenplatz (Map p292; ☎ 5440 4348; Goethestrasse 51; mains €5-11) This relaxed café with a musical theme has high ceilings, chandeliers and a cultivated atmosphere. The breakfast selections are named after famous composers; the divine evening meals are accompanied by live jazz or classical music.

Dukatz im Literaturhaus (Map p292; ☎ 291 9600; Salvatorplatz 1; mains €5-22) A stomping ground for the chic and the intellectual, the Dukatz serves up designer sandwiches and latte macchiato in its café section, and stratospherically priced but impressive mains in its restaurant.

Nido (Map p295; ☎ 2880 6103; Theresienstrasse 40; mains €6-8) This popular place is a trendy spot with lots of brushed aluminium and big picture windows. They serve a small menu of simple Italian-influenced dishes and a large dose of unpretentious cool.

Wasserwerk (Map p294; ☎ 4890 0020; Wolfgangstrasse 19; mains €6-15; ☺ dinner only) This quirky bistro – strewn with ducts, pipes and wheels – plays up the waterworks theme to marvellous effect. Expect a consistently delicious range of quality international cuisine.

Bobolovsky's (Map p295; ☎ 297 363; Ursulastrasse 10; mains €7-10) The varied menu at this bustling bistro includes all the old favourites, such as fajitas, *quesadillas* and chilli. Portions are very generous and on weekdays this place takes the happy-hour concept to new lengths, with incredibly cheap deals on breakfast, lunch and cocktails.

Tresznjewski (Map p295; ☎ 282 349; www.tresznjewski.de; Theresienstrasse 72; mains €8-12) This classy brasserie has daring artworks and waiters in full-length aprons. Its hip clientele come for breakfast and, later, a flexible menu ranging from delectable pastas and sandwiches to burgers and *Bratwurst*.

Nage & Sauge (Map p294; ☎ 298 803; Mariannenstrasse 2) This hip little Italo-café is packed every night with young, creative souls who snuggle up to the candlelit tables for the 'Ente Elvis' pasta, *saltimbocca* or a sublime cocktail. It's tucked away in a side street in Lehel, so quiet you wonder if it's still within the city limits.

Café Zeitgeist (Map p295; ☎ 2865 9873; Türkenstrasse 74) Simply a perfect spot to pore over coffee and cake to watch, from a shady courtyard, the steady flow of students and trendoids pulsing along Türkenstrasse.

Quick Eats
Throughout the city, branches of **Vinzenzmurr** (Map p292; Sendlinger Str 38 & Sonnenstr 8; ☺ 8.15am-6pm) offer the quintessential fast-food experience, with hot buffets and prepared meals. Favourites like *Weisswurst* (white veal sausage), *Leberkäse im Semmel* (a spicy meatloaf sandwich) or *Schweinebraten mit Knödel* (roast pork with dumplings) are among the best lunch deals in town. Salad bars provide some lightweight relief.

South of the Hauptbahnhof, hone in on the street window of **Ristorante Ca'doro** (Map p292; Bayerstrasse; pizza slices from €2). To the north of the train station, **Stop & Soup** (Map p292; Dachauer Strasse 25; snacks €1.50-4; ✆ Mon-Fri) has soups, casseroles and salads. Opposite Karlsplatz, on the ground floor of the Kaufhof department store (Karlsplatz 21), are three good options: a **Müller bakery**, **Nordsee** seafood and **Grillpfanne** for sausages (Map p292). All three are open from 9.30am to 8pm, Monday to Saturday, and snacks cost around €2 to €5.

Another good spot, just north of the Frauenkirche, is **Münchner Suppenküche** (Map p292; Schäfferstrasse 7; dishes €3-6; ✆ closed Sun), a self-service soupery serving chicken casseroles, chilli con carne and other filling snacks.

Schwabing has lots of cheap places to eat, including **Wok Man** (Map p295; Leopoldstrasse 68; mains €4.50-6), which dishes up a good selection of decent Chinese food.

For cheap Indian food try **Indisches Fast Food** (Map p295; Barer Strasse 46; mains €5-8) near the Neue Pinakothek, where fragrant Basmati rice accompanies the tasty Indian standards.

Restaurants
ASIAN
Sushi & Soul (Map p292; ✆ 201 0992; Klenzestrasse 21; mains €8-18) This stylish joint charms with soft lighting and a long central table that points dramatically towards the backlit open kitchen. But one thing's for sure – the sushi is fabulous. During the long-standing and popular happy hour (6pm to 8pm) a multicourse Bento palette of sushi, not to mention all the cocktails, is half-price. Reservations are a must.

Shida (Map p292; ✆ 269 336; Klenzestrasse 32; mains €9-16) Shida's excellent Thai food and intimate atmosphere are justly famous and perennially popular. It's about the size of a shoe box but packs a mean punch in the food stakes. Reservations are essential.

Punjabi (Map p294; ✆ 2554 2424; Zweibrückenstrasse 15; mains €5.50-7.50) Excellent, tasty Indian specialities, from veggie samosas to fiery curries and tandooris cooked in a traditional clay oven. Top it off with a baked banana served with honey and grated coconut, and waddle home.

BAVARIAN & GERMAN
Weisses Bräuhaus (Map p292; ✆ 2299 875; Im Tal 10; mains €7-15) The *Weisswurst* (veal sausage) served here sets the city's standard. The upstairs dining hall and the locals who frequent

it are as authentic as they come. People come for the excellent Bavarian fare, the house's own Schneider Weissbier, and for the creative treatment of innards.

Fraunhofer (Map p292; ✆ 266 460; Fraunhoferstrasse 9; mains €6-12) This bustling restaurant is a homely place where the olde-worlde atmosphere and décor (featuring mounted animal heads and a portrait of Ludwig II) contrasts with the menu. Its fresh takes on classical fare draw a hip, intergenerational crowd.

Unionsbräu Haidhausen (Map p294; ✆ 477 677; Einsteinstrasse 42; mains €6-14) Dried hops dangle from the ceiling of this sophisticated brewpub that caters to business types at lunchtime and a more rollicking crew after dark. There's a jazz club in the basement (Jazzclub Unterfahrt im Einstein, p317).

Other recommendations:
Wirtshaus in der Au (Map p294; ✆ 448 1400; Lilienstrasse 51; mains €8-16) Creative Bavarian cuisine in an unpretentious setting.
Hundskugel (Map p292; ✆ 264 272; Hotterstrasse 18; mains €10-18) Munich's oldest restaurant, founded in 1440, feels a bit like an old-fashioned doll's house.

FRENCH & INTERNATIONAL
Rue des Halles (Map p294; ✆ 485 675; Steinstrasse 18; mains €19-28) The gourmet French cuisine draws a high-octane crowd to this designer restaurant near the Kulturzentrum Gasteig. Count on about €80 for a three-course meal, including a glass of wine.

Königsquelle (Map p292; ✆ 220 071; Baaderplatz 2; mains €11-20) This local restaurant has long been a Munich institution for its attentive service, consistently excellent food and dark, well-stocked hardwood bar. The dishes are straightforward but expertly prepared, from Wiener schnitzel to boiled beef tips to spinach ravioli, proving you can do wonders with a few good ingredients.

GREEK
Taverna Paros (Map p294; ✆ 470 2995; Kirchenstrasse 21; mains €8-18) The simple wooden tables and photos of earthy Greek islanders belie the sophistication of this splendid little eatery. You can cut the lamb roast stuffed with feta cheese with your fork.

ITALIAN
Café Osteria La Vecchia Masseria (Map p292; ✆ 550 9090; Mathildenstrasse 3; mains €5-15) This is one of the best Italian places in Munich, loud but

BAVARIA

unquestionably romantic. Earthy wood tables, antique tin buckets, baskets and clothing irons conjure up the ambience of an Italian farmhouse. The chef comes out to greet customers in his trademark straw hat.

Hippocampus (Map p294; ☎ 475 855; Mühlbaurstrasse 5; mains €15-28) One of Munich's top restaurants, this trendy, upmarket Italian temple right near the Prinzregententheater serves a great range of Italian specials. It has a stylish interior, romantic ambience and celebrity clientele.

Also recommended:

Il Mulino (Map p296; ☎ 523 3335; Görresstrasse 1; pizzas €5-17) Classy neighbourhood eatery in Neuhausen, with a leafy beer garden.

La Fiorentina (Map p292; ☎ 534 185; Goethestrasse 41; mains €7.50-12) Cosy hang-out with Tuscan country cooking and mouth-watering pizzas.

JEWISH
Cohen's (Map p295; ☎ 280 9545; Theresienstrasse 31; mains €9-15; ⏲ dinner Sun-Fri) Tucked away in a quiet courtyard, this brightly lit, refined eatery serves up big portions of German–Eastern European dishes that change with the seasons. Specials include *Königsberger Klopse* (veal dumplings in caper sauce), Hungarian lamb goulash and gefilte fish. Every Friday evening there's live *klezmer* music.

LATIN AMERICAN
Joe Peña's (Map p292; ☎ 226 463; Buttermelcherstrasse 17; mains €10-17) This festive cantina-style restaurant is regarded as Munich's best Tex-Mex place and can get very crowded, especially during happy hour (5pm to 8pm). The food's tasty but calibrated to Germanic tastes.

VEGETARIAN
Buxs (Map p292; ☎ 291 9550; Frauenstrasse 9; dishes €2 per 100g; ⏲ closed Sat evening & Sun) One of Munich's few outposts of veggie culture, this bright self-service place serves 40-plus varieties of soups, salads and antipasti – not to mention the glorious smoothies and desserts.

Zerwirk (Map p292; ☎ 2323 9191; Ledererstrasse 3; mains €5-12; ⏲ closed Sun) Through a twist of fate the Zerwirk, once a purveyor of wild game, now houses one of Munich's few vegan restaurants. Dishes like pasta carbonara, tofu fennel or *rucola* chili are served in elegant minimalist surrounds in the 2nd-floor dining rooms. Downstairs, the vaulted chambers are thrown open every weekend for club nights.

Prinz Myschkin (Map p292; ☎ 265 596; www .prinzmyshkin.com; Hackenstrasse 2; mains €8-16.50; ⏲ closed Sun) Considered by many to be Munich's best vegetarian restaurant, this spacious, trendy haunt has an impressive Italian- and Asian-influenced menu, including some macrobiotic choices. If you just want a light snack, half-portions are available.

Self-Catering
At Viktualienmarkt (Map p292), south of Marienplatz, deep-pocketed travellers can put together a gourmet picnic of breads, cheeses and salad to take off to a beer garden or the Englischer Garten. The basement of the Kaufhof (Map p292) department store on Karlsplatz has a more upmarket selection, plus goodies like fresh cheeses, superb sliced meats and a good bakery.

For a world-class selection of deli goods try the legendary **Alois Dallmayr** (Map p292; ☎ 01805 006 522; Dienerstrasse 14), with a raft of exotic foods from every corner of the earth.

DRINKING
Not surprisingly, beer drinking is an integral part of Munich's nightlife. Germans in general each drink an average of 114L of the amber liquid per year, but Bavarians average some 170L!

Beer Halls & Gardens
One of the finer ways to sample Bavaria's best brews is in the local beer halls and gardens. People come here primarily to drink, and although food may be served it is generally an afterthought – for food options at beer halls, see the boxed text, p316. A few places still allow you to bring along a picnic lunch and just buy the beer, but in most cases outside food is forbidden.

Most places listed here are either gardens or gardens-cum-restaurants; almost all open from 10am to at least 10pm. Even in the touristy places, be careful not to sit at the *Stammtisch*, a table reserved for regulars (there will be a brass plaque).

You sometimes have to pay a *Pfand* (deposit) for the glasses (usually €2.50). Beer costs €5 to €6.50 per litre.

ALTSTADT
Hofbräuhaus (Map p292; ☎ 221 676; Am Platzl 9) This is certainly the best-known and most celebrated beer hall in Bavaria, but apart from a few local

yokels you'll be in the company of tourists. A live band is condemned to play Bavarian folk music most of the day.

Augustiner-Grossgaststätte (Map p292; ☎ 5519 9257; Neuhauser Strasse 27) This sprawling place has a less raucous atmosphere and better food. Altogether it's a much more authentic example of an old-style Munich beer hall, complete with secluded courtyards and hunting trophies.

Braunauer Hof (Map p292; ☎ 223 613; Frauenstrasse 42) This pleasantly warped beer garden has a hedge maze, a bizarre wall mural and a golden bull that's illuminated at night.

ENGLISCHER GARTEN

There are three beer gardens in the park (Map p295).

The **Chinesischer Turm** (☎ 383 8730; Englischer Garten 3) is an institution known to every Münchener from an early age. This popular watering hole derives extra atmosphere from a classic Chinese pagoda and entertainment by a good-time oompah band (in an upper floor of the tower, fenced in like the Blues Brothers).

The other two beer gardens are better suited for families and sweethearts: **Hirschau** (☎ 369 942; Gysslingstrasse 15) and **Seehaus** (☎ 381 6130, Kleinhesselohe 3) are both on the shores of the park's glistening ponds.

NEUHAUSEN

Augustiner Keller (☎ 594 393; Arnulfstrasse 52) Every year this enormous leafy beer garden, about 500m west of the Hauptbahnhof, buzzes with activity from the first hint of springtime. It's a beautiful spot with a laid-back atmosphere ideal for leisurely drinking.

Löwenbräukeller (Map p296; ☎ 526 021; Nymphenburger Strasse 2) This enormous beer hall is a local fixture for its regular Bavarian music and heel-slapping dances. During the Starkbierzeit (the springtime 'strong beer season'), the famous stone-lifting contests are held here. There's a beer garden that rambles round the entire complex. Interestingly, the house brew, Löwenbräu, has a larger following abroad than in Germany.

Hirschgarten (Map p296; ☎ 172 591; Hirschgartenallee 1) Locals and savvy visitors flock to the Hirschgarten, just south of Schloss Nymphenburg. This quaint country beer garden has deer wandering just the other side of the fence. To get there take the S-Bahn to Laim.

HAIDHAUSEN

Hofbräukeller (Map p294; ☎ 448 7376; Innere Wiener Strasse 19) Not to be confused with its better-known cousin in the city centre, this sprawling, very atmospheric restaurant-cum-beer garden retains an early 20th century air. Locals in *Tracht* (traditional costume) come here to guzzle big mugs of foaming beer alongside the regular specials of roast pork (€5).

Bars & Pubs
ALTSTADT & AROUND

Alter Simpl (Map p295; ☎ 272 3083; Türkenstrasse 57; mains €5 to €13) This watering hole has good jazz, a reasonable menu and an art-house vibe. Thomas Mann and Hermann Hesse were among the writers and artists that used to meet here in the early 20th century.

Dreigroschenkeller (Map p294; ☎ 489 0290; Lilienstrasse 2) Cosy and labyrinthine, this cellar pub has rooms based upon Bertolt Brecht's *Die Dreigroschenoper* (The Threepenny Opera), ranging from a prison cell to a red satiny salon. There's great beer and wine, and an extensive menu (mostly hearty German stuff).

Jodlerwirt (Map p292; ☎ 8922 1249; Altenhofstrasse 4; ☺ from 6pm Tue-Sat) One of Munich's earthiest pubs has an accordion-playing host and stand-up comic who spread good cheer in yodelling sessions at the upstairs bar. By the end of the evening you'll find yourself locked arm-in-arm with complete strangers.

Other recommendations:

Baader Café (Map p292; ☎ 201 0638; Baaderstrasse 47) A literary think-and-drink place with a high celebrity quotient and possibly the best Sunday brunch in town.

Pacific Times (Map p292; ☎ 2023 9470; Baaderstrasse 28) Trendy joint decked out in dark wood and wicker chairs to attract the beautiful people.

SCHWABING

If you want a variety of hip bars within spitting distance of each other, then Leopoldstrasse is for you.

Roxy (Map p295; ☎ 349 292; Leopoldstrasse 48) *The* place to talent spot and people watch, this slick bar attracts a designer crowd keen to hang out, look good and sip cocktails. By day it offers surprisingly good food at decent prices.

News Bar (Map p295; ☎ 281 787; Amalienstrasse 55; mains €5-10). This trendy café has a great selection of magazines and newspapers (including English ones) for sale. It's an ideal spot for brunch or a lazy morning poring over a paper.

News Café (Map p295; ☎ 3838 0600; Leopoldstrasse 74) Not just another news-bar clone, the plush leather seating, rows of glowing red lamps and African-inspired art make this hip joint a great place to hang out. It serves light food and a multitude of cocktails.

Irish Pubs

Munich has a huge Irish expat population; if you're out looking for friendly, English-speaking people, you're in luck. Most of the pubs have live music at least once a week and cluster in Schwabing.

Günther Murphy's Irish Tavern (Map p295; ☎ 398 911; Nikolaistrasse 9a) One of the most popular Irish pubs in Munich, this cellar bar is usually packed to the gills with a good mix of locals, expats and tourists.

Molly Malone's (Map p294; ☎ 688 7510; Kellerstrasse 21) This award-winning Irish pub is a better bet if you'd like a quiet drink or a decent conversation. It's famous for its authentic fish and chips and has over 100 types of whiskey on hand.

ENTERTAINMENT

Munich's entertainment scene will keep you busy. Apart from discos, pubs and beer halls, try not to miss the city's excellent classical, jazz and opera venues.

Listings

Go Muenchen (www.gomuenchen.com; €3) What's-on guide to the city including exhibitions, concerts etc.

In München (www.in-muenchen.de; free) The best source of information; available free at bars, restaurants and ticket outlets.

München im… (free) Excellent A-to-Z pocket-sized booklet of almost everything the city has to offer.

Münchner Stadtmagazin (€2.50) Complete guide to the city's bars, discos, clubs, concerts and nightlife in general.

Munich Found (www.munichfound.de; €2.50) English-language city magazine with somewhat useful listings.

Tickets

Tickets to entertainment venues and sports events are available at official ticket outlets (*Kartenvorverkauf*).

Kartenvorverkauf Karlsplatz (Map p292; ☎ 5450 6060); Marienplatz (Map p292; ☎ 264 640) Branches all over the city and kiosks in these U-Bahn stations.

München Ticket (Map p292; www.muenchenticket.de; Neues Rathaus; ☎ 5481 8181)

Cinemas

For information about screenings check any of the Munich listings publications. Admission usually ranges from €6.50 to €8.50, though one day, usually Monday or Tuesday, is 'Kinotag' with reduced prices. Non-German films in mainstream cinemas are almost always dubbed. Films showing in the original language with subtitles are labelled 'OmU' (Original mit Untertiteln); those without subtitles are 'OV' or 'OF' (Originalversion or Originalfassung). **Amerika Haus** (p287) shows undubbed films, as do the following movie theatres:

AND THERE'S FOOD, TOO

In beer gardens, tables laid with a cloth and utensils are reserved for people ordering food. If you're only planning a serious drinking session, or if you have brought along a picnic, don't sit there.

If you do decide to order food, you'll find very similar menus at all beer gardens. Typical dishes include roast chicken (about €9 for a half), spare ribs (about €11.50, and probably not worth it), huge pretzels (about €3) and Bavarian specialities such as *Schweinebraten* and schnitzel (€9 to €12).

Radi is a huge, mild radish that's eaten with beer; you can buy prepared radish for about €4.50. Or, buy a radish at the market and a *Radimesser* at any department store, stick it down in the centre and twist the handle round and round, creating a radish spiral. If you do it yourself, smother the cut end of the radish with salt until it weeps to reduce the bitterness – and increases your thirst!

Obatzda (oh-batsdah) is Bavarian for 'mixed up'. This cream cheese–like speciality is made of butter, ripe Camembert, onion and caraway (about €4 to €6). Spread it on *Brez'n* (a pretzel) or bread.

Another speciality is *Leberkäs* (liver cheese), which is nothing to do with liver or cheese but is instead a type of meatloaf that gets its name from its shape. It's usually eaten with sweet mustard and soft pretzels.

Atlantis (Map p292; ☎ 555 152; Schwanthalerstrasse 2)
Cinema (Map p296; ☎ 555 255; Nymphenburger Strasse 31) The pick of the bunch: comfy and modern, with great balcony seats, ice cream and salty popcorn (not a given).
City & Atelier (Map p292; ☎ 591 918; Sonnenstrasse 12)
Filmmuseum (Map p292; ☎ 2332 4150; St-Jakobs-Platz 1) In the Stadtmuseum.
Museum-Lichtspiele (Map p294; ☎ 482 403; Lilienstrasse 2)

Clubs

Munich has a thriving club scene with something to suit most tastes. Bouncers are notoriously rude and 'discerning', so dress to kill (or look, as locals say, *schiki-micki*) and keep your cool. The cover prices for discos vary but average between €4 and €10.

Kultfabrik (Map p294; www.kultfabrik.de; Grafingerstrasse, Haidhausen) and **Optimolwerke** (Map p294; www .optimolwerke.de; Grafingerstrasse, Haidhausen) are back-to-back villages of pubs, bars and clubs – nearly 40 in total. They're a party animal's mecca, where you can roam from an '80s disco to hip-hop, trance and heavy metal venues. The latest 'in' spot is **Drei Türme** (☎ 4502 8817; ☺ 9pm-4am Tue, 10pm-6am Wed, Fri & Sat), a chic living-room club disguised as a Hollywood castle and lit by a forest of glass-fibre tubes. If you're an aficionado of Russian pop try **Kalinka** (☎ 4090 7260; ☺ 10pm-5am Fri, 10pm-9am Sat), a trendy place decked out with lots of red velvet, dancing girls and a giant bust of Lenin. Other options include **Milch & Bar** (☎ 4502 8818; ☺ 10pm-6am Sun-Thu, 10pm-9am Fri-Sat), a more mainstream choice catering to disco divas; and the padded crimson **Living4** (☎ 4900 1260; ☺ 10pm-4am Tue-Thu, 10pm-6am Fri-Sat), playing a good mix of hip hop, Latin and house. To get there take U5 to the Ostbahnhof.

Muffatwerk (Map p294; ☎ 4587 5075; www.muffat werk.de; Zellstrasse 4) This is another big complex that holds large concerts and, in summer, an open-air disco on Friday with drum 'n' bass, acid jazz and hip-hop (it's always crowded, so expect queues). Its new club, **Ampere** (☺ 10pm-5am Fri or Sat) is a bastion of retro-flavoured cool.

P1 (Map p295; ☎ 294 252; Prinzregentenstrasse 1) P1 is a bit of a Munich institution and is still the see-and-be-seen place for the city's wannabes, with extremely choosy and effective bouncers, snooty staff and the occasional celebrity.

Registratur (Map p292; ☎ 2388 7758; Blumenstrasse 4) No mistake, the dusty halls and '60s panelling

of this old city building have the charm of an off-location. The humour isn't lost on the (mostly 20s) crowd, who come for a diet of African beats, shock rock and indie pop.

Live Music
CLASSICAL

Philharmonie im Gasteig (Map p294; ☎ 480 980; www .gasteig.de; Rosenheimer Strasse 5) As home to the city's Philharmonic Orchestra, Munich's premier high-brow cultural venue has a packed schedule. The Symphonieorchester des Bayerischen Rundfunks (Bavarian Radio Symphony Orchestra) is also based here, and performs on Sundays throughout the year.

Nationaltheater (Map p292; ☎ box office 2185 1920; www.staatstheater.bayern.de; Max-Joseph-Platz 2) The Bayerische Staatsoper (Bavarian State Opera) performs here. Its prestigious opera festival takes place in July. You can buy tickets at regular outlets or at the box office.

Staatstheater am Gärtnerplatz (Map p292; ☎ 2185 1960; www.staatstheater-am-gaetnerplatz.de; Gärtnerplatz 3) This venue has occasional classical concerts, but opera, operetta, jazz, ballet and musicals also feature.

JAZZ

Munich has a very hot jazz scene.

Jazzclub Unterfahrt im Einstein (Map p294; ☎ 448 2794; Einsteinstrasse 42) This is perhaps the best-known place in town, with live music from 9pm and regular international acts. Sunday nights feature an open jam session.

Jazzbar Vogler (Map p292; ☎ 294 662; Rumfordstrasse 17; ☺ Tue-Sun) Conceived as a 'cultural living room' by ex-journalist Vogler, this intimate little club has grown into one of the city's top jazz venues. The musicians are some of Munich's baddest cats.

Prager Frühling (Map p295; ☎ 260 3021; Leopoldstrasse 27; ☺ Wed-Sun) The programme at this indie club with the orange '70s décor is always turbo-charged. Wednesdays are a climax of funky, unfettered jazz for the dance-mad. Concerts begin at 9pm and then, around midnight, DJs take over with soulful grooves.

Also recommended:
Night Club Bar (Map p292; ☎ 212 0994; Promenadeplatz 2-6) Intimate club in the Hotel Bayerischer Hof where you can catch top talent almost nightly.
Café am Beethovenplatz (Map p292; ☎ 5440 4348; Goethestrasse 51) Atmospheric café with live music most weekdays and a piano brunch every Sunday.

BAVARIA

BAVARIA

GAY & LESBIAN MUNICH

Munich has a strong gay and lesbian community and the best listings can be found in the German-language **Rosa Seiten** (Pink Pages, €3.50) or **Our Munich** (free), a monthly guide to gay and lesbian life in the city. You can pick up both at the **Weissblauer Gay Shop** (Map p296; ☎ 522 352; Theresienstrasse 130). Another good bet for information is the website www.munich-cruising.de.

Information and support for gay men and lesbians is available through the following places:

Schwules Kommunikations und Kulturzentrum ('the Sub'; Map p292; ☎ 260 3056; ☎ counselling 194 46; Müllerstrasse 43; ⊙ 7-11pm, counselling 7-10pm Mon-Fri)

LeTra/Lesbentelefon (Map p292; ☎ 725 4272; Angertorstrasse 3; ⊙ 2.30-5pm Mon & Wed, 10.30am-1pm Tue)

Bars & Cafés

Nightlife is centred in the so-called 'Bermuda Triangle' formed by Sendlinger Tor, Gärtnerplatz and Fraunhoferstrasse. Hans-Sachs-Strasse is the latest hotspot.

Morizz (Map p292; ☎ 201 6776; Klenzestrasse 43) *The* premiere hang-out for pretty faces, Morizz resembles an Art Deco Paris bar with red leather armchairs and plenty of mirrors. The service is impeccable, the food's good and the wine and whisky list will keep everyone happy. It's quiet early in the evening but livens up as the night wears on.

Deutsche Eiche (Map p292; ☎ 231 1660; Reichenbachstrasse 13) A Munich institution, this was once film maker Rainer Werner Fassbinder's favourite hang-out. It's still a popular spot and packs in a mixed crowd for its comfort food, fast service and classy hotel rooms (see below).

Peter & Paul (Map p292; ☎ 5454 0780; Sonnenstrasse 19) Tucked away in a rear courtyard, this groovy café-lounge with the comic-book colours is a welcome change from the baroque angels of its predecessor. Its liberal clientele comes as much for the fresh sushi as the latest prospects on the courtyard patio.

Also recommended are **Cabaret Mrs Henderson** (Map p292; ☎ 263 469; Müllerstrasse 2), a transvestite and cabaret club where Freddie Mercury made his last video, and **Nil** (Map p292; ☎ 265 545; Hans-Sach-Strasse 2), whose octagonal bar attracts a young fun-loving crowd and a handful of faded German stars.

Accommodation

See www.munich-cruising.de for additional listings.

Deutsche Eiche (Map p292; ☎ 231 1660; www.deutsche-eiche.com; Reichenbachstrasse 13; s €70-85, d €95-100; Ⓟ) This 150-year-old Munich institution was once saved from the wrecker's ball by German film director Rainer Fassbinder. Its modern rooms are fully equipped and there's a big sauna and roof terrace.

Pension Eulenspiegel (Map p292; ☎ 266 678; www.pensioneulenspiegel.de; Müllerstrasse 43a; s €49-69, d €79-99; ☒ ▢) Recently done over with a designer's touch, this small, cosy guesthouse lies in a quiet courtyard of Munich's gay district. There are only eight rooms, all with showers but they share a toilet.

ROCK

Large rock concerts are staged at the Olympiapark, or at venues listed under Clubs (p317). The **Brunnenhof der Residenz** (Map p292; ☎ 936 093; Residenzstrasse 1) hosts open-air performances ranging from rock, jazz and swing to classical and opera in stunning surroundings.

Theatre

Munich has a lively theatre scene. The two biggest companies are the Bayerisches Staatschauspiel and the Münchener Kammerspiele.

The **Bayerisches Staatschauspiel** (☎ tickets 2185 1940) performs at the **Residenztheater** (Map p292; Max-Joseph-Platz 1) and at the **Theater im Marstall** (Map p292; Marstallplatz) behind the Nationaltheater.

Münchener Kammerspiele (Map p292; ☎ 2333 7000; Maximilianstrasse 26-28) This theatre stages large-scale productions of serious drama by German writers or foreign playwrights whose works are translated into German.

Deutsches Theater (Map p292; ☎ 5523 4444; Schwanthalerstrasse 13) Munich's answer to London's

West End has touring road shows (usually popular musicals like *Grease*) perform here.

Kulturzentrum Gasteig (Map p294; ☎ 480 980; Rosenheimer Strasse 5) This is a major cultural centre with theatre, classical music and other special events held in its several halls, with their excellent acoustics.

Other venues include the **Prinzregententheater** (Map p294; ☎ 2185 2959; Prinzregentenplatz 12) and the **Kleine Komödie am Max II** (Map p294; ☎ 221 859; Maximilianstrasse 47), which shows lightweight comedy.

SHOPPING

Fashionistas with flexible credit should head for Maximilianstrasse, Theatinerstrasse, Residenzstrasse and Brienner Strasse. For high street shops and department stores try the pedestrian area around Marienplatz, Neuhauser Strasse and Kaufingerstrasse. For streetwear, head for the indie boutiques around Gärtnerplatz, Glockenplatz, Schwabing and Haidhausen. Beer steins and *Mass* (1L tankard) glasses are available at all the department stores and the beer halls themselves.

Ludwig Beck (Map p292; ☎ 2423 1575; Marienplatz 11) Munich's most venerable department store has some chic but reasonably priced clothes, a large CD shop, a trendy coffee bar and restaurant.

Christkindlmarkt (Christmas market; Map p294; Mariahilfplatz) Held in December, this is a well-stocked fulfiller of traditional dreams. Crèche scenes, 'smoking figures' carved in the Erzgebirge and spicy-sweet Lebkuchen are some of the favourites.

Foto-Video Sauter (Map p292; ☎ 551 5040; Sonnenstrasse 26) A good stock of all the top names fills the shelves at this photo emporium. Good deals can be had on Leica cameras and binoculars.

Loden-Frey (Map p292; ☎ 210 390; Maffeistrasse 5-7) Loden-Frey stocks a wide range of traditional Bavarian wear. Expect to pay at least €200 for a good leather jacket, lederhosen or a women's dirndl.

Manufactum (Map p292; ☎ 2424 3669; Kardinal-Faulhaber-Strasse 5) In the exclusive Fünf Höfe mall, Manufactum specialises in hits of ageless German design. Look out for Bauhaus lamps, Porsche pepper mills and 4711 Kölnisch Wasser.

Porzellan Manufaktur Nymphenburg (Map p296; ☎ 1791 9710; Schloss Nymphenburg; ☼ 10am-5pm Mon-Fri) It has made fine porcelain for Bavarian

royals and quite a few commoners since being founded in 1747. They also have an outlet in the Fünf Höfe shopping passage (Map p292).

Schuh Seibel (Map p292; ☎ 2601 7237; Reichenbachstrasse 8) Yes, Birkenstocks really *are* cheaper here. A major stocker of the brand, this place also offers the convenience of home shipment.

GETTING THERE & AWAY
Air

Munich's **international airport** (MUC; ☎ 089-975 00; www.munich-airport.de) is second in importance only to Frankfurt for international and domestic flights. There's direct service to/from many key destinations including London, Paris, Rome, New York, Sydney and all major German cities.

Airlines flying to Munich are Air France, British Airways, Delta Airlines, easyJet, Germanwings, Lufthansa and Scandinavian Airlines. For contact details, see p754.

Bus

Munich is a stop for **Busabout** (www.busabout .com) on circular routes that take in Amsterdam, Berlin, Paris, Prague, Rome and Vienna, among other cities (also see p758).

Europabus (see p763) links Munich to the Romantic Road. For details of fares and timetables inquire at EurAide (see p288) or **DTG** (Map p292; ☎ 8898 9513; www.deutsche-touring.de; Hirtenstrasse 14) near the Hauptbahnhof; it's the vendor for Deutsche Touring and Eurolines buses.

BEX BerlinLinienBus (☎ 01801-546 436; www.berlin linienbus.de) runs daily buses between Berlin and Munich (one-way/return €44/81, 9½ hours), via Ingolstadt, Nuremberg, Bayreuth and Leipzig. It picks up from the north side of the Hauptbahnhof. There are big reductions on one-way fares for passengers aged under 26 or over 60.

A&O Touristik (Map p292; ☎ 591 504; Arnulfstrasse 8) is a vendor for Graylines touring buses and Gulliver's cross-country coaches.

Car & Motorcycle

Munich has autobahns radiating on all sides. Take the A9 to Nuremberg, the A92/A3 to Passau, the A8 to Salzburg, the A95 to Garmisch-Partenkirchen and the A8 to Ulm or Stuttgart.

For roads information, try **ADAC** (German Auto Association; Map p292; ☎ 5491 7234; www.adac.de; Sendlinger-Tor-Platz 9).

All major car-hire companies have offices at the airport and/or the 2nd level of Munich's Hauptbahnhof, including **Hertz** (☎ 01805-333 535; ☯ 24hr booking; office 7am-9pm Mon-Fri, 9am-5pm Sat-Sun), **Avis** (☎ 550 2251; ☯ 7am-9pm) and **Europcar** (☎ 549 0240; ☯ 8am-6pm).

For shared rides, consider using one of Germany's *Mitfahrzentralen* (ride-share agencies), whose fares are considerably cheaper than by rail or coach. The **ADM-Mitfahrzentrale** (Map p292; ☎ 194 40; www.mitfahrzentralen.de; Lämmerstrasse 6; ☯ 8am-8pm Mon-Sat) is conveniently near the Hauptbahnhof. **CityNetz Mitfahrzentrale** (Map p295; ☎ 194 44; www.citynetz-mitfahrzentrale.de; Adalbertstrasse 6) in Schwabing has a good online booking function.

Train

Train services to and from Munich are excellent. There are swift connections every one to two hours to all major German cities as well as frequent services (often nondirect) to European destinations such as Vienna (five hours, €68), Prague (six to eight hours, €79) and Zürich (four hours, €59). Prices vary according to demand and the class of train.

There are direct links to Berlin (€96, six hours) and Hamburg (€115, six hours). Trains to Frankfurt often require a change in Mannheim or Nuremberg (€61, 3¾ hours).

Prague extension passes (add-on tickets to Eurail and German rail passes) are sold at the rail-pass counters in the Reisezentrum at the Hauptbahnhof, or through EurAide (p288).

GETTING AROUND

Central Munich is compact enough for exploring on foot. In order to get to the outlying suburbs, make use of the efficient public transport system.

To/From the Airport

Munich's **Flughafen Franz-Josef Strauss** (www.munich -airport.de) is connected by the S1 and S8 to the Hauptbahnhof – €9 with a single ticket or €8 if using eight strips of a *Streifenkarte* (see right). The trip takes about 40 minutes and runs every 20 minutes from around 3.30am until midnight.

The Lufthansa Airport Bus travels at 20-minute intervals from Arnulfstrasse near the Hauptbahnhof (one-way/return €9.50/15, 40 minutes) between 5.10am and 8.08pm. A taxi from the airport to the Altstadt costs about €55.

Car & Motorcycle

It's not worth driving in the city centre; many streets are pedestrian-only, ticket enforcement is Orwellian and parking is a nightmare. The tourist office map shows city car parks, which generally cost about €1.50 to €2.50 per hour.

Public Transport

Getting around is easy on Munich's excellent public transport network (MVV). The system is zone-based, and most places of interest to visitors (except Dachau and the airport) are within the 'blue' inner-zone (Innenraum).

Tickets are valid for the S-Bahn, U-Bahn, trams and buses, but must be time-stamped in the machines at station entrances and aboard buses and trams before use. Failure to validate a ticket puts you at the mercy of ticket inspectors (usually plain-clothed) who possess admirable efficiency when it comes to handing out fines.

Short rides (four bus or tram stops; two U-Bahn or S-Bahn stops) cost €1.10, while longer trips cost €2.20. It's cheaper to buy a strip-card of 10 tickets called a *Streifenkarte* for €10.50, and stamp one strip per adult on rides of two or less tram or U-Bahn stops, two strips for longer journeys.

Some of the other deals on offer are the following:
Tageskarten (day passes) One day (individual/up to 5 people €4.80/8.50); Three day (individual/up to 5 people €11.80/20) Valid for the inner zone only.
IsarCard Wochenkarte (€15.10) Weekly pass covering all four zones, valid Monday till noon the following Monday; if you buy later, it's still only good until next Monday.

Rail passes are also valid on S-Bahn trains. A bicycle pass costs €2.50 and is valid all day except during rush hour (6am to 9am and 4pm to 6pm Monday to Friday), when bikes are banned.

The U-Bahn ceases operation around 12.30am on weekdays and 1.30am at weekends, but a network of night buses (Nachtbusse) still operates. Pick up the latest route and time schedule from any tourist office.

Taxi

Taxis cost €2.90 at flagfall, plus a per-kilometre price of €1.25 to €1.60. For a radio-dispatched taxi, ring ☎ 216 10 or ☎ 194 10. Taxi ranks are indicated on the city's tourist map.

AROUND MUNICH

DACHAU CONCENTRATION CAMP MEMORIAL

The way to freedom is to follow one's orders; exhibit honesty, orderliness, cleanliness, sobriety, truthfulness, the ability to sacrifice and love of the Fatherland.

Inscription from the roof of the concentration camp at Dachau

Dachau was the Nazis' first concentration camp, built by Heinrich Himmler in March 1933 to house political prisoners. All in all it 'processed' more than 200,000 inmates, killing at least 32,000, and is now a haunting memorial. Expect to spend two to three hours here to fully absorb the exhibits.

The **memorial** (☎ 669 970; www.kz-gedenkstaette -dachau.de; Alte Römerstrasse 75; admission free; ☑ 9am-5pm Tue-Sun) is in the northeastern corner of Dachau. A 22-minute English-language documentary runs at 11.30am and 3.30pm. Note that children under 12 may find the experience too disturbing.

You enter the compound through the **Jourhaus**, originally the only entrance. Set in wrought iron, the chilling slogan 'Arbeit Macht Frei' (Work Sets You Free) hits you at the gate.

First stop is the **Documentary Exhibit,** with photographs and models of the camp, its officers and prisoners, and of horrifying 'scientific experiments' carried out by Nazi doctors. Other exhibits include a whipping block, a chart showing the system of prisoner categories (Jews, homosexuals, Jehovah's Witnesses, Poles, Roma and other 'asocial' types) and documents on the persecution of 'degenerate' authors banned by the party.

Outside, in the former roll call square, is the **International Memorial** (1968), inscribed in English, French, Yiddish, German and Russian, which reads 'Never Again'. Behind the exhibit building, the **bunker** was the notorious camp prison where inmates were tortured. Executions took place in the prison yard.

Inmates were housed in large barracks, now demolished, which used to line the main road north of the roll-call square. In the camp's northwestern corner is the **crematorium** and gas chamber, disguised as a shower room but never used. Several religious shrines are nearby.

Tours

Dachauer Forum (☎ 996 880; €3; ☑ 2pm Tue-Sun May-Sep; 1pm Thu, Sat & Sun Oct-Apr) Tours (2½ hours) by dedicated volunteers in English, departing from the main hall. There are also half-hour introductions (€1.50) at 1pm Tuesday to Sunday May to October, and Thursday, Saturday and Sunday November to April.

Radius Tours & Bikes (Map p292; ☎ 089-5502 9374; www.radiusmunich.com; adult/concession €19/7.50; ☑ 9.15am & 12.30pm Tue-Sun Apr-Oct, also 11.30 Jun-Sep; 12.40pm Nov-Mar; 5hr) Five-hour English-language tours leave from opposite track 32 in the Hauptbahnhof. They include public transport from Munich. Book ahead.

Self-guided Audio Tour (adult/child €3/2) Covers the history, key buildings and the exhibits (up to 2 hours). Available from the ticket desk.

Getting There & Away

The S2 makes the journey from Munich Hauptbahnhof to Dachau Hauptbahnhof in 22 minutes. You'll need a two-zone ticket (€6.60, or four strips of a *Streifenkarte*), including the bus connection. From here change to local bus 726. By car, follow Dachauer Strasse straight out to Dachau and follow the KZ-Gedenkstätte signs.

SCHLEISSHEIM

☎ 089 / pop 5700

The northern Munich suburb of Schleissheim is worth a visit for its three palaces and the aviation museum.

The crown jewel of the palatial trio is the **Neues Schloss Schleissheim** (☎ 315 8720; Max-Emanuel-Platz 1; adult/under 15 yr/concession €4/free/3; ☑ 9am-6pm Apr-Sep, 10am-4pm Oct-Mar, closed Mon). Modelled after Versailles, this pompous pile was dreamed up by prince-elector Max Emanuel in 1701. Inside, you'll be treated to stylish period furniture and a vaulted ceiling smothered in frescoes by the prolific Cosmas Damian Asam. The palace is surrounded by an impressive manicured park that's ideal for picnics.

Nearby, the **Altes Schloss Schleissheim** (☎ 315 5272; Maximilianshof 1; adult/concession €3/2; ☑ 9am-6pm Apr-Sep, 10am-4pm Oct-Mar, closed Mon) is only a shadow of its former Renaissance self. It houses exhibits on religious festivals and Prussian culture. On a little island at the eastern end of the Schlosspark stands **Schloss Lustheim** (☎ 315 8720; adult/concession €3/2; ☑ 9am-6pm Apr-Sep, 10am-4pm Oct-Mar, closed Mon), featuring the finest collection of Meissen porcelain after Dresden's Zwinger museum.

BAVARIA

Near the palaces you'll find **Flugwerft Schleissheim** (☎ 315 7140; Effnerstrasse 18; adult/concession €3.50/2.50; ☺ 9am-5pm), the aviation branch of the Deutsches Museum (p304). Displays are housed in three historical buildings – the command, the tower and the construction hall – as well as a new hall, and include about 60 planes and helicopters, plus hang-gliders, engines and flight simulators.

To get to Schleissheim take the S1 (in the direction of Freising) to Oberschleissheim. It's about a 15-minute walk from the station along Mittenheimer Strasse towards the palaces. By car, take Leopoldstrasse north until it becomes Ingolstadter Strasse. Then take the A99 to the Neuherberg exit, at the south end of the airstrip.

STARNBERG
☎ 08151 / pop 22,000

Once a royal retreat, and still popular with politicians, celebrities and the merely moneyed, Starnberger See is a fast and easy option to get out onto the water and away from the urban bustle of Munich.

The town of Starnberg, at the northern end of the lake, is the heart of the Fünf-Seen-Land (Five-Lakes-District). Besides Lake Starnberg the district comprises the Ammersee and the much smaller Pilsensee, Wörthsee and Wesslinger See. Swimming, yachting and windsurfing are popular activities on all lakes.

The district **tourist office** (☎ 906 00; www .sta5.de; Wittelsbacherstrasse 2c, Starnberg; ☺ 8am-6pm Mon-Fri & 9am-1pm Sat May–mid-Oct) has a room-finding service.

Lake Starnberg is best known as the place where King Ludwig II drowned (see the boxed text, p344). The spot where his body was found, in the town of Berg on the eastern shore, is now marked with a memorial cross in the shallows, near the Votivkapelle. To get there, take bus 961 from Starnberg.

From Easter Sunday to mid-October, **Bayerische-Seen-Schifffahrt** (☎ 8061) runs boat services from Starnberg to the other lake towns, as well as 60-, 90- and 180-minute tours (€7.50/9.60/14.50 respectively). Its docks are behind the S-Bahn station. Boats pass by five palaces as well as the Ludwig II cross.

You can also take the ferry south to the **Buchheim Museum** (☎ 08158 997 060; Bernried; adult/child €8.50/3.50; combined boat & museum ticket €16;

☺ 10am-6pm Tue-Fri Apr-Oct, 10am-5pm Tue-Fri Nov-Mar). The museum has a fascinating collection of expressionist art and German modern art, as well as folklore and ethnological exhibits from around the world.

If you'd rather get around the lake yourself, you can hire bikes at **Bike It** (☎ 746 430; Maximilianstrasse 4, Starnberg; per day €15-20). **Paul Dechant** (☎ 08151-121 06; Bootshaus 2), near the train station, has rowing, pedal and electric-powered boats for €11 per hour.

Starnberg is 30 minutes by S-Bahn (S6) from Munich (two zones or four strips of a *Streifenkarte*). To get to Starnberg by car from Munich, take the autobahn A95 and drive about 20km southwest.

ANDECHS

Founded in the 10th century, the lovely hill-top monastery of **Andechs** (☎ 08152-3760; admission free; ☺ 8am-7pm Apr-Sep, 8am-5pm Oct-Mar) has long been a place of pilgrimage, although more visitors come to slurp the Benedictines' fabled beers.

The church owns two relics of enormous importance: branches that are thought to come from Christ's crown of thorns, and a victory cross of Charlemagne, whose army overran much of Western Europe in the 9th century. In the Holy Chapel the votive candles, some of them over 1m tall, are among Germany's oldest. The remains of Carl Orff, the composer of *Carmina Burana*, are interred here as well.

The nearby **Braustüberl** is the monks' beer hall and garden. There are six varieties of beer on offer, from the rich and velvety Doppelbock dark to the fresh unfiltered Weissbier. The place is often so overrun by tourists that it's easy to forget you're in a religious institution, pious as your love for the brew may well be. Summer weekends can get insanely busy.

Andechs is served three times daily (but only twice on Sunday) by bus from the S-Bahn station in Starnberg Nord (S6; €8.80, 35 minutes) and the one in Herrsching (S5; €2.20, 10 minutes). The last bus going from Andechs to Herrsching leaves at 6.40pm; the last bus to Starnberg leaves at 4.43pm.

If you're travelling by car from Starnberg, it's best to take Andechser Strasse west and drive 15km (it's well signposted). Herrsching lies another 5km further to the west, via Seefelder Strasse.

Bad Tölz

☎ 08041 / pop 17,500

Bad Tölz is a spa town in a stunningly beautiful location. The gentle inclines provide a delightful spot for its attractive, frescoed houses and the quaint shops of the old town. Munich residents flock here to enjoy the ultramodern swimming complex, Alpine slide and rafting trips down the Isar River. Bad Tölz is also the gateway to the Tölzer Land region and its emerald-green lakes, the Walchensee and the Kochelsee.

Every year on 6 November, its residents pay homage to the patron saint of horses, Leonhard. The famous **Leonhardifahrt** is a pilgrimage up to the Leonhardi chapel on Kalvarienberg, where townsfolk dress up in traditional costume and ride dozens of garlanded horsecarts to the strains of brass bands.

Bad Tölz' **tourist office** (☎ 786 70; www.bad-toelz .de; Max-Höfler-Platz 1; ☽ 9am-noon Mon-Sat & 2-5.30pm Mon-Fri) can book accommodation and organise tours.

Altstadt

Cobble-stoned and car-free, the **Marktstrasse** is flanked by statuesque townhouses with overhanging eaves that look twice as high on the sloping street. The **Heimatmuseum** (☎ 504 688; Marktstrasse 48; adult/concession €2/1; ☽ 10am-noon & 2-4pm, closed Mon) touches on practically all aspects of local culture and history, with a good collection of painted armoires (the so-called Tölzer Kisten), beer steins, folkloric garments and some pretty odd religious items.

In a side alley a few steps south of Marktstrasse, through Kirchgasse, is the **Pfarrkirche Maria Himmelfahrt** (Church of the Assumption; ☎ 761 260; Frauenfreithof), a late Gothic three-nave hall church with brilliantly painted glass and an expressive floating Madonna. Wandering down Marktstrasse, you'll soon spot the baroque **Franziskanerkirche** (Franciscan Church; ☎ 769 60; Franziskanergasse 1) across the Isar. Surrounded by lovely gardens, its blanched interior is enlivened by several beautiful altars.

Above the town, on Kalvarienberg, looms Bad Tölz' landmark, the twin-towered **Kalvarienbergkirche** (Cavalry Church). This enormous baroque church stands side-by-side with the petite **Leonhardikapelle** (Leonhardi Chapel; 1718), the destination of the Leonhardi pilgrimage.

Alpamare

In the spa section of town, west of the Isar River, you'll find the fantastic water complex **Alpamare** (☎ 509 991; www.alpamare.de; Ludwigstrasse 14; 4hr pass adult/child €25/19, day pass €31/21; ☽ 9am-10pm). This huge centre has heated indoor and outdoor mineral pools, a wave and surfing pool, a series of wicked waterslides (including Germany's longest, the 330m-long Alpabob-Wildwasser), saunas, solariums and its own hotel. There's a bus stop on Wilhelmstrasse nearby, served almost hourly from the Hauptbahnhof, which is 3km away.

Blomberg

Southwest of Bad Tölz, the **Blomberg** (1248m) is a family-friendly mountain that has a natural toboggan track in winter, plus easy hiking and a fun Alpine slide in summer.

Unless you're walking, getting up the hill involves a chairlift ride aboard the **Blombergbahn** (☎ 3726; top station return adult/child €7/3, midway one-way €2; ☽ 9am-5pm May-Oct, 9am-4pm Nov-Apr weather permitting). Over 1km long, the fibreglass **Alpine slide** snakes down the mountain from the middle station. You zip down through the 17 hairpin bends on little wheeled bobsleds with a joystick to control braking. You can achieve speeds of up to 50km/h but if you do, chances are you'll ram the rider ahead of you or fly clean off the track. A long-sleeved shirt and jeans provide a little protection.

Riding up to the midway station and sliding down costs €3.50 per adult (€3 concession), with discounts for multiple trips. In winter, a day pass good for skiing or the toboggan track costs €14 per adult (€12 concession), and sleds can be hired for €8 per day.

Getting There & Away

Bad Tölz has hourly train connections with Munich (€8.10, one hour) on the private **Bayerische Oberlandbahn** (BOB; ☽ 08024-997 171; www.bayerischeoberlandbahn.de). The trains depart from the Munich Hauptbahnhof. Alternatively, take the S2 from central Munich to Holzkirchen, then change to the BOB.

CHIEMSEE

☎ 08051 / elev 518m

The Bavarian Sea, as Chiemsee is affectionately known, is a haven for stressed-out city dwellers and anyone on the grand palace tour. Most visitors come to see King Ludwig II's homage to Versailles – Schloss

Herrenchiemsee – but the lake's natural beauty and water sports are as much reasons for its popularity.

The towns of Prien am Chiemsee and, about 5km south, Bernau am Chiemsee (both on the Munich–Salzburg rail line) are perfect bases for exploring the lake. Of the two twons, Prien is the larger and more commercial.

Information

All tourist offices have free web terminals for brief walk-in use.

Bernau tourist office (☎ 986 80; www.bernau-am -chiemsee.de; Aschauer Strasse 10)

Chiemsee Info-Center (☎ 965 550; www.chiemsee .de; ☯ 9am-7pm Mon-Fri, 10am-4pm Sat & Sun) On the southern lakeshore, near the Bernau-Felden autobahn exit. Information for the whole area.

Prien tourist office (☎ 690 50; www.tourismus.prien .de; Alte Rathausstrasse 11)

Sights

SCHLOSS HERRENCHIEMSEE

The island Herreninsel in the Chiemsee is home to a fantastical palace spawned by Ludwig II's warped imagination: **Schloss Her-renchiemsee** (☎ 688 70; www.herren-chiemsee.de; adult/ under 18yr/concession €7/free/6; ☯ tours continuously 9am-5pm Apr–mid-Oct, 9.40am-4.14pm mid-Oct–Mar). Begun in 1878, it was never intended as a residence but as a homage to absolutist monarchy, as epitomised by Ludwig's hero, the French Sun King, Louis XIV. Ludwig spent only 10 days here and even then was rarely seen, preferring to read at night and sleep all day.

The palace is both a knock-off and an attempt to upstage Versailles, with larger

and more lavishly decorated rooms. Ludwig managed to spend more money on this palace than on Neuschwanstein (p342) and Linderhof (p349) combined. When cash ran out in 1885, one year before his death, 50 rooms remained unfinished.

The rooms that were completed outdo each other in opulence. The vast **Gesandtentreppe** (Ambassador Staircase), a double staircase leading to a frescoed gallery and topped by a glass roof, is the first visual knock-out on the guided tour, but that fades in comparison to the stunning **Grosse Spiegelgalerie** (Great Hall of Mirrors). This tunnel of light runs the length of the garden (98m, or 10m longer than that in Versailles). It sports 52 candelabra and 33 great glass chandeliers with 7000 candles, which took 70 servants half an hour to light. In late July it becomes a superb venue for classical concerts.

The **Paradeschlafzimmer** (State Bedroom) features a canopied bed perching altarlike on a pedestal behind a golden balustrade. This was the heart of the palace, where morning and evening audiences were held. It is the king's bedroom, the **Kleines Blaues Schlafzim-mer** (Little Blue Bedroom), that really takes the cake. The decoration is sickly sweet, encrusted with gilded stucco and wildly extravagant carvings. The room is bathed in a soft blue light emanating from a glass globe at the foot of the bed. It supposedly took 18 months for a technician to perfect the lamp to the king's satisfaction.

Admission to the palace also entitles you to a spin around the **König-Ludwig II-Museum**, where you can see the king's christening and coronation robes, more blueprints of megalomaniac buildings and his death mask.

WORTH THE TRIP

While he was annexing Bavaria, Napoleon is said to have introduced a recipe for a tender, red-wine marinated beef fillet called *boeuf à la mode* – known in Germany as *Sauerbraten*. The Bavarians ejected the little emperor but kept their love of French cuisine. A great place to savour it and the crisp Alpine surrounds is **Auberge Moar-Alm** (☎ 08021-5520; www.moar-alm.de; Holzkirchner Strasse 14, Sachsenkam; mains €18-24, 3-course meals €25-38; ☯ Wed-Mon). This handsome chalet about 10km north of Bad Tölz, just off the main B13, occupies a magnificent spot – a grassy moraine girded by velvety pastures with a panorama of the snow-capped Karwendel mountains. The cuisine is just as breathtaking. Managed by Christine Roberts, a lifelong Francophone and one of Germany's top chefs, the kitchen swings between a Mediterranean brio (excellent fish and seafood dishes) and hearty, cockle-warming dishes from the north of France in winter. Local farmers provide most of the classy ingredients, but the fresh goat's cheese and snails come from *la belle France*, as do most of the fine wines. The warm, congenial hosts also offer cooking courses and baby-sitting for guests. Reservations are advised.

To get to the palace take the ferry from Prien-Stock (€5.90 return, 15 to 20 minutes) or from Bernau-Felden (€7.50, 25 minutes, May to October). From the boat landing on Herreninsel, it's about a 20-minute walk through lovely gardens to the palace. The palace tour, offered in German or English, takes 30 minutes.

FRAUENINSEL

This island is home to the **Frauenwörth Abbey**, founded in the late 8th century and one of the oldest nunneries in Bavaria. The 10th-century abbey church, whose freestanding campanile sports a distinctive onion-dome top (11th century), is worth a visit. Opposite the church is the AD 860 Carolingian **Torhalle** (☎ 08054-72 56; admission €1.50; ☼ 10am-6pm May-Oct). It houses medieval objets d'art, sculpture and changing exhibits of regional paintings from the 18th to the 20th centuries.

Return ferry fare, including a stop at Herreninsel, is €7 from Prien-Stock and €7.50 from Bernau-Felden.

Activities

The swimming beaches at Chieming and Gstadt (both free) are the easiest to reach, on the lake's eastern and northern shores respectively. A variety of boats are available for hire at many beaches, for €5 to €20 per hour. In Prien, **Bootsverleih Stöffl** (☎ 2000; Seestrasse 64) has two-seater paddleboats for €5 per hour and electric boats for €9 to €19.

The futuristic-looking glass roof by the harbour in Prien-Stock shelters **Prienavera** (☎ 609 570; Seestrasse 120; 4hr pass adult/concession €7.90/3.50, day pass €9.90/5.50; ☼ seasonal, usually 10am-9pm). This popular pool complex has an enormous wellness area, water slides and a restaurant.

Sleeping

The tourist offices can set up **private rooms** (per person from €18) in town and in farmhouses.

Panorama Camping Harras (☎ 904 60; www .camping-harras.de; per person/tent/car €5.40/3/1.60) This camp site is scenically located on a peninsula with its own private beach, catamaran and surfboard hire. The restaurant has a delightful lakeside terrace.

DJH hostel (☎ 687 70; www.djh.de; Carl-Braun-Strasse 66; dm under/over 26yr €17.80/21.80; ☼ closed Dec-Jan) Prien's hostel organises lots of activities and has an environmental study centre for young people. It's in a bucolic spot, a 15-minute walk from the Hauptbahnhof.

Hotel Garni Möwe (☎ 5004; www.hotel-garni -moewe.de; Seepromenade 111, Prien; s €45-60, d €64-86; ℗) This traditional Bavarian hotel right on the lakefront is excellent value, especially the loft rooms. It has its own bike and boat hire, plus a fitness centre, and the large garden is perfect for travellers with children.

Hotel Bonnschlössl (☎ 890 11; www.alter-wirt -bernau.de; Kirchplatz 9, Bernau; s €44-72, d €72-104; ℗) Built in 1477, this pocket-sized palace hotel with the faux-turrets once belonged to the Bavarian royal court. Rooms are stylish and packed with amenities, and there's a wonderful terrace with rambling garden.

Eating

Badehaus (☎ 970 300; Rasthausstrasse 11, Bernau; mains €6-16) Near the Chiemsee Info-Center and the lakeshore, this contemporary beer hall and garden has quirky décor and gourmet fare enjoyed by a mix of locals and visitors. A special attraction is the 'beer bath', a glass tub filled (sometimes) with a mix of beer and water.

Der Alte Wirt (☎ 890 11; Kirchplatz 9, Bernau; mains €7-16, brotzeit €4-9; ☼ closed Mon) For great Bavarian cuisine with swift service, drop by this listed monument, a massive half-timbered inn with five centuries of history. The Leberkäs is clearly the star of the menu, but the meat and fish dishes are uniformly excellent.

Westernacher am See (☎ 4722; Seestrasse 115, Prien; mains €8-16) This lakeside dining haven has a multiple personality, with a cosy restaurant, cocktail bar, café, beer garden and glassed-in winter terrace. Its speciality is modern twists on old Bavarian favourites. They also have spacious double rooms (€88) with a splendid view of the Chiemsee.

Getting There & Around

Prien and Bernau are served by hourly trains from Munich (€13.40, one hour). Hourly bus 9505 connects the two lake towns.

Local buses run from Prien Bahnhof to the harbour in Stock. You can also take the historic Chiemseebahn (1887), the world's oldest narrow-gauge **steam train** (one-way/return €2/3; ☼ May-Sep).

Ferries operated by **Chiemsee Schifffahrt** (☎ 6090; www.chiemsee-schifffahrt.de; Seestrasse 108) ply the lake every hour with stops at Herreninsel, Fraueninsel, Seebruck and Chieming

BAVARIA

on a schedule that changes seasonally. You can circumnavigate the entire lake and make all these stops (getting off and catching the next ferry that comes your way) for €9.80. Children aged six to 15 get a 50% discount.

Radsport Reischenböck (☎ 4631; Bahnhofsplatz 6, Prien) hires out city/mountain bikes for €8/15 per day.

THE ROMANTIC ROAD

Two million people ply the **Romantische Strasse** (Romantic Road) every year, making it by far the most popular of Germany's holiday routes. That means lots of signs in English and Japanese, tourist coaches and kitsch galore. For the most part the trail rolls through pleasant, if not spectacular, landscape that links some of the most picturesque towns in Bavaria and the eastern fringes of Baden-Württemberg.

Despite the hordes of visitors, it's worth falling for the sales pitch – you won't be alone, but you certainly won't be disappointed. For the best trip, pick and choose your destinations carefully, or risk an overdose of the incredible medieval architecture.

Orientation & Information

The Romantic Road runs north–south through western Bavaria, covering 420km between Würzburg and Füssen near the Austrian border. It goes through more than two dozen cities and towns, including Rothenburg ob der Tauber, Dinkelsbühl and Augsburg.

Each town en route has its own local tourist office, in addition to the central **Romantic Road tourist office** (☎ 09851-902 71; www.romantischestrasse .de; Marktplatz) in Dinkelsbühl.

Getting There & Away

Though Frankfurt is the most popular gateway for the Romantic Road, Munich is a good choice as well, especially if you decide to take the bus (see also right).

BICYCLE

With its gentle gradients and bucolic flavour between towns, the Romantic Road is ideal for the holidaying cyclist. Bikes can be hired at many train stations; tourist offices keep lists of bicycle-friendly hotels that permit storage. Ask for a copy of *Radwandern*, a German-language booklet of maps and route suggestions.

BUS

Half a dozen daily buses connect Füssen and Garmisch-Partenkirchen (€8.70, all via Neuschwanstein and most also via Schloss Linderhof). There are also several connections between Füssen and Oberstdorf (via Pfronten or the Tirolean town of Reutte).

BerlinLinienBus (☎ 030-861 9331; www.berlin linienbus.de) runs buses between Berlin and Rothenburg (one-way/return €46/73, seven hours).

Deutsche Touring's Europabus (☎ 01805-790 303; www.deutsche-touring.com) operates a daily Castle Road coach service between Heidelberg and Rothenburg (one-way/return, 3½ hours €34.90/48.80).

TRAIN

To start at the southern end, take the hourly train link from Munich to Füssen (€19.80, two hours). Rothenburg is linked by train to Würzburg (€10, one hour), Munich (from €37, three hours), Nördlingen (€23, 2½ hours) and Augsburg (€24, 2½ hours), with several changes needed to reach some destinations.

There are regional trains from Nuremberg Hauptbahnhof to Rothenburg (€8.30; 1½ to two hours) several times a day.

Getting Around

BUS

It *is* possible to do this route using train connections or local buses, but it's complicated, tedious and slow. The ideal way to travel is by car, though many foreign travellers prefer to take the Deutsche Touring's Europabus, seven hours), which can get incredibly crowded in summer. From April to October, Europabus runs one coach daily in each direction between Frankfurt and Füssen (for Neuschwanstein); the entire journey takes about 12 hours. There's no charge for breaking the journey and continuing the next day. Also see p763.

Reservations & Fares

Tickets are available for short segments of the trip, and reservations are only necessary during peak-season weekends. Reservations can be made through travel agents, **Deutsche Touring** (☎ 01805-790 303; www.deutsche-touring .com), **EurAide** (☎ 089-59 38 89; www.euraide.de) in Munich, and Deutsche Bahn's Reisezentrum offices in the train stations.

The most heavily travelled circuits – along with the one-way and return fares from Frankfurt – are listed below.

Destination	Cost (one-way/return)
Augsburg	€59.80/83.70
Füssen	€79.40/111.20
Munich	€98.80/138.40
Nördlingen	€47.70/66.70
Rothenburg ob der Tauber	€34.70/48.60
Würzburg	€21.90/30.70

The following are the fares from Munich.

Destination	Cost (one-way/return)
Augsburg	€40/56.10
Nördlingen	€52.20/73.10
Rothenburg ob der Tauber	€65.20/91.20
Würzburg	€78/109.10

Luggage (per piece €2) and bicycles (per 12/30 stops €9/15) cost extra. Students, children, pensioners and rail-pass holders qualify for discounts of between 10% and 60%.

WÜRZBURG
☎ 0931 / pop 131,000

'If I could choose my place of birth I would consider Würzburg,' wrote author Hermann Hesse, and it's not difficult to see why. This scenic town straddles the Main River and is renowned for its art, architecture and delicate wines. Its historic buildings shine again today, having been carefully reconstructed from wartime damage after 1945.

Würzburg was a Franconia duchy when, in 686, three Irish missionaries tried to persuade Duke Gosbert to convert, and ditch his wife. Gosbert was mulling it over when his wife had the three bumped off. When the murders were discovered decades later, the martyrs became saints and Würzburg was made a pilgrimage city, and, in 742, a bishopric.

For centuries the resident prince-bishops wielded enormous power and wealth, and the city grew in opulence under their rule. Their crowning glory is the Residenz, one of the finest baroque structures in Germany and a Unesco World Heritage Site.

Orientation
Würzburg's centre is compact and, perhaps by more than accident, shaped like a bishop's

mitre. The Hauptbahnhof and bus station are at the northern end of the Altstadt. The main shopping street, Kaiserstrasse, runs south from here into the town centre. The Main River forms the western boundary of the Altstadt; the fortress is located on the west bank, with other key sights to the east.

Information

BOOKSHOPS
Hugendubel (☎ 354 040; Schmalzmarkt 12) Good stock of English-language titles.

DISCOUNT CARDS
Welcome Card (per 7 days €2) Available from tourist offices; gives reduced admission prices to main sights and tours.

EMERGENCY
Ambulance (☎ 192 22)
Ärztliche Notfallpraxis (Medical Emergency Practice; ☎ 322 833; Domerschulstrasse 1)

INTERNET ACCESS
N@tcity (☎ 3041 9494; Sanderstrasse 27, per 10min €0.60; ☼ 10am-midnight) Big state-of-the-art internet café.
Stadtbücherei (City Library; ☎ 373 294; Falkenhaus am Markt; per 20min €1) In the same building as the tourist office.

LAUNDRY
SB Waschsalon (☎ 416 773; Frankfurter Strasse 13a; per load €4)

MONEY
Deutsche Bank (Juliuspromenade 66)

POST
Post office (Bahnhofsplatz 2 & Paradeplatz)

TOURIST INFORMATION
Tourist office Marktplatz (☎ 372 335; Falkenhaus; www .wuerzburg.de; ☼ 10am-6pm Mon-Sat, 10am-2pm Sun Apr-Dec, 10am-4pm Mon-Fri, 10am-1pm Sat Jan-Mar); Am Congress Centrum (☎ 372 335; Am Congress Centrum; ☼ 8am-5pm Mon-Thu, 8am-1pm Fri)

TRAVEL AGENCIES
STA Travel (☎ 521 76; Zwinger 6)

Sights

RESIDENZ
A symbol of wealth and prestige for the Würzburg bishops, the **Residenz** (☎ 355 170; Balthasar-Neumann-Promenade; adult/concession €5/4; ☼ 9am-6pm

WÜRZBURG

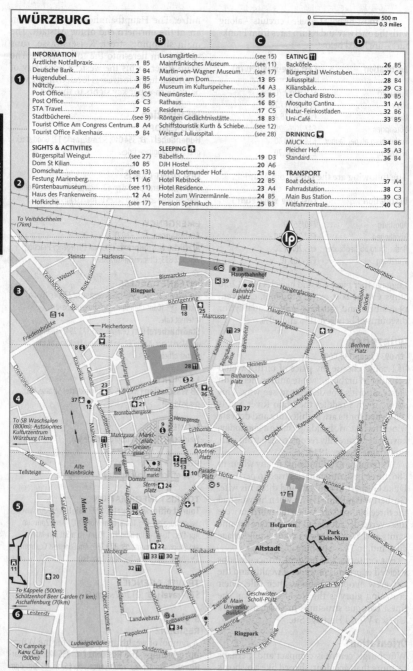

INFORMATION	
Ärztliche Notfallpraxis	1 B5
Deutsche Bank	2 B4
Hugendubel	3 B5
N@tcity	4 B6
Post Office	5 C5
Post Office	6 C3
STA Travel	7 B6
Stadtbücherei	(see 9)
Tourist Office Am Congress Centrum	8 A4
Tourist Office Falkenhaus	9 B4

SIGHTS & ACTIVITIES	
Bürgerspital Weingut	(see 27)
Dom St Kilian	10 B5
Domschatz	(see 13)
Festung Marienberg	11 A6
Fürstenbaumuseum	(see 11)
Haus des Frankenweins	12 A4
Hofkirche	(see 17)

Lusamgärtlein	(see 15)
Mainfränkisches Museum	(see 11)
Martin-von-Wagner Museum	(see 17)
Museum am Dom	13 B5
Museum im Kulturspeicher	14 A3
Neumünster	15 B5
Rathaus	16 B5
Residenz	17 C5
Röntgen Gedächtnisstätte	18 B3
Schiffstouristik Kurth & Schiebe	(see 12)
Weingut Juliusspital	(see 28)

SLEEPING	
Babelfish	19 D3
DJH Hostel	20 A6
Hotel Dortmunder Hof	21 B4
Hotel Rebstock	22 B5
Hotel Residence	23 A4
Hotel zum Winzermännle	24 B5
Pension Spehnkuch	25 B3

EATING	
Backöfele	26 B5
Bürgerspital Weinstuben	27 C4
Juliusspital	28 B4
Kiliansbäck	29 C3
Le Clochard Bistro	30 B5
Mosquito Cantina	31 A4
Natur-Feinkostladen	32 B6
Uni-Café	33 B5

DRINKING	
MUCK	34 B6
Pleicher Hof	35 A3
Standard	36 B4

TRANSPORT	
Boat docks	37 A4
Fahrradstation	38 C3
Main Bus Station	39 C3
Mitfahrzentrale	40 C3

Apr-Oct, 10am-4pm Nov-Mar; English-language tours 11am & 3pm), is one of the most important and beautiful palaces in southern Germany.

Almost immediately upon entering you'll see the brilliant **grand staircase** come into view on the left. Miraculously, the vaulted ceiling survived the war intact and Tiepolo's magnificent fresco *The Four Continents* (1750–53) – said to be the world's largest above a staircase – dazzles in all its glory. Look closely to see Balthasar Neumann, architect of the Residenz, perched smugly on a cannon.

For opulence, the bishops' imperial apartments rivalled those of kings. The **Kaisersaal** (Imperial Hall) is a combination of marble, gold stucco and more incredible frescoes. The **Spiegelsaal** (Hall of Mirrors) is the most memorable, with gilded stucco dripping from the ceiling and walls lined with glass-like panels. In the building's southern wing is the magnificent **Hofkirche** (Court Church; admission free), an early example of Neumann's penchant for spatial illusions. The side wings of the altar are decorated with paintings by Tiepolo.

Next to the church, the **Martin-von-Wagner Museum** (☎ 312 288; admission free; ☾ closed Mon) shows the whimsical works of court sculptor Peter Wagner. The museum backs onto the spectacular French- and English-style gardens of the **Hofgarten** (☾ dawn-dusk).

FESTUNG MARIENBERG
On the Main's left bank, the **Festung Marienberg** (Marienberg fortress) has presided over Würzburg since the city's prince-bishops commissioned a 'new' castle in 1201. It was only ever taken once, by Swedish troops in the Thirty Years' War. The lovely walk up from the river via the vine-covered hill takes 20 minutes, or bus 9 will take you there from the central bus station.

The fortress' residential wing now holds the **Fürstenbaumuseum** (☎ 438 38; adult/concession €2.50/2; ☾ 9am-6pm Tue-Sun Apr–mid-Oct; 10am-4pm Tue-Sun mid-Oct–Mar), the city's history museum. A highlight is a huge tapestry showing the entire family of Julius Echter von Mespelbrunn, a wealthy duke-bishop who refashioned the inner fortress as a Renaissance at the end of the 17th century. The baroque Zeughaus (armoury) houses the **Mainfränkisches Museum** (☎ 205 940; adult/concession €3/1.50, combined ticket for both museums €4/2.50; ☾ 10am-7pm Tue-Sun Apr-Oct; 10am-4pm Tue-Sun Nov-Mar). It has a world-famous collection of works by master sculptor Tilman Rie-

menschneider, and in the Kelterhalle, where grapes once fermented, there's an exhibit on winemaking.

CHURCHES
In the Altstadt, the perfectly symmetrical **Neumünster** (☾ 7am-6pm) stands on the site where the ill-fated missionaries met their maker. The baroque interior has busts of the three martyrs (the three Irish missionaries – Kilian, Colonan and Totnan) on the high altar and the tomb of St Kilian in the crypt. The north exit leads to the lovely **Lusamgärtlein** with the grave of Walther von der Vogelweide, one of Germany's most famous minstrels. Even today wreaths of flowers are regularly laid on his tomb.

On the same square is **Dom St Kilian** (St Kilian Cathedral), rebuilt in a hotchpotch of modern, baroque and Romanesque styles after significant damage during WWII. Of note are the prince-bishops' tombstones on the pillars; the two in red marble in the left aisle are by Riemenschneider.

MUSEUM AM DOM & DOMSCHATZ
Würzburg's newest museum is in a beautiful building by the cathedral. The **Museum am Dom** (☎ 386 261; Domerschulstrasse 2; adult/concession €3.50/2.50 combined ticket with Domschatz €4.50; ☾ 10am-6pm Apr-Oct; 10am-5pm Nov-Mar, closed Mon) houses a collection of modern art on Christian themes. Works of international renown by Joseph Beuys, Otto Dix and Käthe Kollwitz are on display, as well as masterpieces of the Romantic, Gothic and baroque periods.

At the Würzburger **Domschatz** (Cathedral Treasury; ☎ 3856 5600; Plattnerstrasse; adult/student €2/1.50; ☾ 2-5pm Tue-Sun) you can wander through a rich display of church artefacts from the 11th century to the present.

MUSEUM IM KULTURSPEICHER
In a born-again historic granary right on the Main River you'll find the **Museum im Kulturspeicher** (☎ 322 250; Veitshöchheimer Strasse 5; adult/concession €3.50/2; ☾ 1-6pm Tue, 11am-6pm Wed, 11am-7pm Thu, 11am-6pm Sat & Sun). This fascinating museum has choice artworks from the 19th to the 21st centuries, with an emphasis on German impressionism, neorealism and contemporary art. It also houses the post-1945 constructivist art of the Peter C Ruppert Collection, a challenging assembly of computer art, sculpture, paintings and photographs.

BAVARIA

RÖNTGEN GEDÄCHTNISSTÄTTE

Würzburg's most famous modern scion is Wilhelm Conrad Röntgen, discoverer of the X-ray. The **Röntgen Gedächtnisstätte** (Röntgen Museum; ☎ 351 1103; Röntgenring 8; admission free; ☑ 9am-4pm Mon-Thu, 9am-3pm Fri) is a tribute to his life and work.

Tours

Schiffstouristik Kurth & Schiebe (☎ 585 73; Alter Kranen; €9) offers quickie river cruises (40 minutes) to the wine-growing town of Veitshöchheim.

The tourist office runs 1½-hour English-language **guided tours** (adult/child €5/3; ☑ 11am & 3pm, May-Oct) departing from Falkenhaus. You can also borrow an audio-guide with a recorded tour (€5) of all the major sights.

Würzburg is the centre of the Franconian wine industry, and you can sample some of the area's finest vintages on any of the following tours of the historic wine cellars. (reservations are advised).

Bürgerspital Weingut (☎ 350 3403; Theaterstrasse 19; tours €5; ☑ tours 2pm Sat Mar-Oct) At the Bürgerspital Weinstuben; includes a small bottle of wine.

Haus des Frankenweins (☎ 390 1111; Kranenkai 1) Wine sampling and sales.

Weingut Juliusspital (☎ 393 1400; Juliuspromenade 19; tours €5; ☑ tours 3pm Fri Apr-Nov, in German) In the splendid complex with the Juliusspital wine-bar.

Festivals & Events

For full details check www.wuerzburg.de.

Africa-Festival Europe's largest festival of black music (tickets from the tourist office), held in late May and early June.

Mozart Festival (☎ tickets 373 336) The Residenz is the ultimate backdrop for this series of classical concerts, held in late May/early June.

Sleeping

The toll-free 24-hour room reservation hotline is ☎ 0800-194 1408.

BUDGET

Camping Kanu Club (☎ 725 36; Mergentheimer Strasse 13b; per person/tent €2.50) The closest camp site to the town centre. Take tram 3 or 5 to the Judenbühlweg stop, which is on its doorstep.

DJH hostel (☎ 425 90; www.djh.de; Burkarder Strasse 44; dm under/over 26yr €20.30/24.30) At the foot of the fortress, this well-equipped hostel has room for 254 warm bodies in three- to eight-bed dorms. Take tram 3 or 5 to Ludwigsbrücke, then it's a five-minute walk north along the river. Has wheel-chair access.

Babelfish (☎ 304 0430; www.babelfish-hostel.de; Prymstrasse 3; dm €16-24, d €45-60; ⓟ 🖳) Operated by two fun-loving locals, this cute all-ages hostel, with wheelchair access, offers a good deal for independent travellers. Rooms are spacious and have Ikea-style bunk beds and cheery colours. Free internet access, kitchen and washing facilities are some of the perks. The name comes from a creature in Douglas Adams' novel *Hitchhiker's Guide to the Galaxy*.

Pension Spehnkuch (☎ 547 52; www.pension-spehnkuch.de; Röntgenring 7; s €29-33, d €52-60) Rooms are no-frills and snug, but they're clean. There's also English-speaking staff and a sunny breakfast room.

MIDRANGE & TOP END

Hotel zum Winzermännlle (☎ 541 56; www.winzermaennle.de; Domstrasse 32; s €56-70, d €86-100) This former winery was rebuilt in its original style after the war by the same charming family. Rooms in the front are cavernous and equipped with TVs and telephones. It's right in the pedestrian zone with parking nearby.

Hotel Dortmunder Hof (☎ 561 63; www.dortmunder-hof.de; Innerer Graben 22; s €40-65, d €70-100) In a handy position two blocks from the Markt, this cycling-friendly hotel is in a pretty lemon-coloured building with clean, comfy rooms including cable TV. Parking can be arranged close by.

Hotel Residence (☎ 535 46; www.wuerzburg-hotel.de; Juliuspromenade 1; s €63-74, d €83-105; ⓟ) With comely dormer windows and royal-hued interiors, this charming hotel, replete with all the trimmings, is a short walk from the river, congress centre and the city's main sights.

Hotel Rebstock (☎ 309 30; www.rebstock.com; Neubaustrasse 7; s €96-139, d €163-220; ⓟ) Class, hospitality and a touch of nostalgia are the characteristics of this family-run hotel, one of Würzburg's best snooze temples. Meticulously restored, this rococo mansion has superbly furnished rooms and amenities galore. The warm ambience recalls the south of France.

Eating

For a town of its size, Würzburg has a bewildering array of enticing pubs, beer gardens, cafés and restaurants, with plenty of student hang-outs among them.

Backöfele (☎ 590 59; Ursulinergasse 2; mains €7-18) For romantic atmosphere, it's hard to beat this rustic restaurant set around a pretty courtyard. The menu features innovative twists on traditional game, steak and fish dishes. Marbled slabs of meat are grilled over the wood oven.

Bürgerspital Weinstuben (☎ 352 880; Theaterstrasse 19; mains €7-10; ☼ closed Aug) The cosy nooks of this labyrinthine medieval place are among Würzburg's most popular eating and drinking spots. Choose from a broad selection of Franconian wines and wonderful regional dishes, including *Mostsuppe*, a tasty wine soup.

Juliusspital (☎ 352 880; Juliuspromenade 19; mains €7-10; ☼ closed Aug) This attractive *Weinstube* (traditional wine bar) features fabulous Franconian delicacies. The Juliusspital was first founded as a hospital in 1576 by Julius Echter von Mespelbrunn, whose name pops up everywhere in Würzburg. The basement has a cave-like bakery with a clutch of tables.

Le Clochard Bistro (☎ 129 07; Neubaustrasse 20; dishes €4-8) This trendy hang-out for bright young things has a French-influenced menu and a host of divine sweet and savoury crepes to choose from.

Mosquito Cantina (☎ 510 22; Karmelitenstrasse 31; mains €8-14; ☼ dinner only) This popular Mexican restaurant does a booming biz in stuffed tacos, grilled fajitas and some good vegetarian dishes. Relaxed in the early evening, the meal crowd is gradually replaced by the pre-club set later on.

Uni-Café (☎ 156 72; Neubaustrasse 2; snacks €3-7) This is a hugely popular student hang-out on the lively Neubaustrasse strip. It has two floors of chilled-out clientele who come for the cheap snacks, cool music and – most of all – some fun.

Natur-Feinkostladen (Sanderstrasse 2a; dishes from €2.50) Come here for wholesome snacks and healthy fare, such as grain burgers; this place also runs the specialist grocery right next door.

Kiliansbäck (Kaiserstrasse 20) South of the Hauptbahnhof this bakery is a good bet for cheap snack specials and tasty goodies.

Drinking & Entertainment

The town's monthly listing magazine is *Fritz* (in German).

MUCK (☎ 465 1144; Sanderstrasse 29) This fun place has loads of board games to while away the hours. One of the earliest openers in town, and serving a mean breakfast from 7am, the café morphs into something of an informal party after nightfall.

Schützenhof beer garden (☎ 724 22; Mainleitenweg 48) For a drink with sun and a bucolic view, head for this delightful beer garden about 500m south of the Käppele chapel on the east bank of the Main. The main ingredients are ultra-fresh – listen for the farmyard animals protesting to the rear – and the beer (try the Balthasar Neumann) is served with a donkey-shaped *Brezel*.

Standard (☎ 465 1144, 511 40; Oberthuerstr 11a) Beneath a corrugated-iron ceiling and stainless-steel fans are newspaper racks, art and soulful jazz, with focaccias and pasta on the menu. Downstairs there's a second, dimly lit bar where bands and DJs perform a couple of times a week.

Pleicher Hof (☎ 970 70; Pleichertorstrasse 30; ☼ café 5.30pm-1am Tue-Sat, bar 9.30pm-4am Wed, Fri & Sat) This cool café spreads Med-style vibes during the evening, with light meals and coffees being the favoured fare. In the cellar music bar the agenda goes for the jugular, with heavy garage, funk and amped-up student parties.

Autonomes Kulturzentrum Würzburg (AKW; ☎ 417 800; Frankfurter Strasse 87; ☼ Thu-Sat, pub only Sun) There's little this 1880s brewery complex doesn't do. Inside you'll find artists' studios, a small indie theatre, a disco and a split-level bar with squashy sofas to sink into. Alternative bands play regularly, and in summer there's a bustling beer garden. Take tram 2 to the Siebold-Museum stop.

Getting There & Away

There are frequent train connections to Frankfurt (€24, 1½ hours), Bamberg (from €15.50, 1½ hours) and Nuremberg (€20, one hour) as well as Rothenburg ob der Tauber (€10, one hour).

The Romantic Road Europabus stops at the main bus station next to the Hauptbahnhof.

Getting Around

Würzburg is best seen on foot, but you can also take buses and trams for €1.10 (for short journeys) or €2 (for regular journeys); the cheaper ticket will do for trips in town. Day passes are €4; passes bought on a Saturday can also be used on Sunday. For a taxi call ☎ 194 10.

Bicycle-hire shops include the **Fahrrad-station** (☎ 574 45; Hauptbahnhof; bikes per day €8; ☼ closed Sun & Mon).

ASCHAFFENBURG

☎ 06021 / pop 68,500

The cobbled lanes and half-timbered houses of this charming town make a good day trip from Würzburg or Frankfurt. In style terms it's more Hessian than Bavarian, but King Ludwig II was so chuffed with the mild climate he dubbed Aschaffenburg the 'Bavarian Nice'.

The **tourist office** (☎ 395 800; www.aschaffenburg.de; Schlossplatz 1; 9am-5pm Mon-Fri, 10am-1pm Sat) runs 90-minute guided walks (€3.50) on Saturdays at 2pm from April to October.

Aschaffenburg's most spectacular draw is the magnificent Renaissance **Schloss Johannisburg**, the summer residence of the Mainz archbishops. Today it is home to the **Schlossmuseum** (☎ 386 570; Schlossplatz 4; adult/concession €4/3, combined ticket with Pompejanum €6/5; 9am-6pm Tue-Sun Apr-Sep, 10am-4pm Tue-Sun Nov-Mar). The modest interior has the usual oil paintings and period furniture, but the true highlight is the collection of architectural cork models depicting landmarks from ancient Rome.

Behind the beautiful palace garden is the **Pompejanum** (☎ 386 570; adult/child €4/free; 9am-6pm Tue-Sun Apr-Sep). Built for King Ludwig I, this replica of a Pompeian villa comes complete with frescoes, mosaics and Roman antiquities.

From there, follow Schlossgasse into the Altstadt. On Stiftsplatz you'll come upon the **Stiftskirche**. This has its origins in the 10th century, but is now an oddly skewed but impressive mix of Romanesque, Gothic and baroque styles. The attached **Stiftsmuseum** (☎ 330 463; adult/concession €2.50/1.50; 11am-5pm Tue-Sun) is home to some intriguing relics and paintings.

Three kilometres west of town lies the **Park Schönbusch**, a shady 18th-century expanse dotted with ornamental ponds and follies, and the **Schlösschen** (☎ 386 570; Kleine Schönbuschallee 1; tours adult/concession €3/2; 9am-6pm Tue-Sun Apr-Sep), a country retreat of the archbishops. The hourly tours are in German.

Hearty Franconian fare can be found at the tiny **Schlossgass' 16** (☎ 123 13; Schlossgasse 16; mains €7-14) wine tavern, and **Wirtshaus Zum Fegerer** (☎ 156 46; Schlossgasse 14; mains €8-15), a charming inn with courtyard dining.

Trains to and from Würzburg (€17, one hour) and Frankfurt (€11, 30 minutes) operate at least hourly. The A3 autobahn runs right past town.

ROTHENBURG OB DER TAUBER

☎ 09861 / pop 12,000

A well-polished gem from the Middle Ages, Rothenburg ob der Tauber (meaning 'above the Tauber River') is the main tourist stop along the Romantic Road. With its web of cobbled lanes, higgledy-piggledy houses and towered walls, the town is impossibly charming. Preservation orders here are the strictest in Germany – and at times it feels like a medieval theme park – but all's forgiven in the evenings, when the yellow lamplight casts its spell long after the last tour buses have left.

Orientation

The Hauptbahnhof is a 10-minute walk east of the Altstadt along Ansbacher Strasse. The main shopping drag is Schmiedgasse, which runs south to Plönlein, a scenic fork in the road anchored by a half-timbered ochre cottage and gurgling fountain that's become Rothenburg's unofficial emblem.

Information

Dresdner Bank (Galgengasse 23)
Post office Altstadt (Milchmarkt 5); Bahnhof (Zentro mall, Bahnhofstrasse 15)
Rothenburger Reisebüro (☎ 4611; Hauptbahnhof) Travel agency.
Tourist office (☎ 404 800; www.rothenburg.de; Marktplatz 2; 9am-noon & 1-6pm Mon-Fri, 10am-3pm Sat & Sun May-Oct, 9am-noon & 1-5pm Mon-Fri, 10am-1pm Sat Nov-Mar) There is an electronic room-booking board in the foyer, which is always open, plus internet.
Volksbank (Marktplatz) To the right of the tourist office.
Wäscherei Then (☎ 2775; Johannitergasse 9; per load €3.50) Laundry.

Sights

The **Rathaus** (town hall) on the Markt was begun in Gothic style in the 14th century, and completed during the Renaissance. The 220-step viewing platform of the **Rathausturm** (adult/concession €1/0.50; 9.30am-12.30pm & 1.30-5pm Apr-Oct, noon-3pm Dec) provides majestic views of the Tauber.

North of the Marktplatz, the glorious Gothic **Jakobskirche** (☎ 700 60; Klingengasse 1; adult/concession €1.50/0.50, during services free; 9am-5.30pm Apr-Oct, 10am-noon & 2-4pm Nov-Mar) is Rothenburg's major place of pilgrimage. The main draw is the carved **Heilig Blut Altar** (Holy Blood Altar), set on a raised platform at the western end of the nave. It depicts the Last Supper with Judas, unusually, at the centre, receiving bread

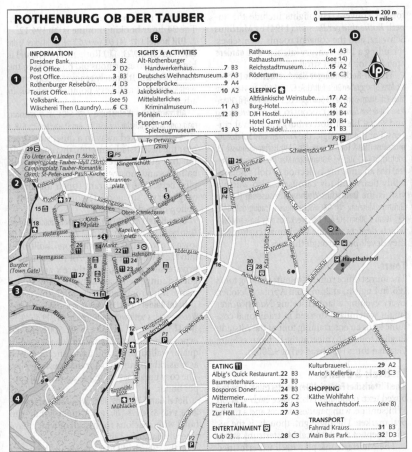

ROTHENBURG OB DER TAUBER

INFORMATION		
Dresdner Bank	1	B2
Post Office	2	D2
Post Office	3	B3
Rothenburger Reisebüro	4	D3
Tourist Office	5	A3
Volksbank	(see 5)	
Wäscherei Then (Laundry)	6	C3

SIGHTS & ACTIVITIES		
Alt-Rothenburger		
Handwerkerhaus	7	B3
Deutsches Weihnachtsmuseum	8	A3
Doppelbrücke	9	A4
Jakobskirche	10	A2
Mittelalterliches		
Kriminalmuseum	11	B3
Plönlein	12	B3
Puppen-und		
Spielzeugmuseum	13	A3

Rathaus	14	A3
Rathausturm	(see 14)	
Reichsstadtmuseum	15	A2
Röderturm	16	C3

SLEEPING		
Altfränkische Weinstube	17	A2
Burg-Hotel	18	A2
DJH Hostel	19	B4
Hotel Garni Uhl	20	B4
Hotel Raidel	21	B3

EATING		
Albig's Quick Restaurant	22	B3
Baumeisterhaus	23	B3
Bosporos Doner	24	B3
Mittermeier	25	C2
Pizzeria Italia	26	A3
Zur Höll	27	A3

ENTERTAINMENT		
Club 23	28	C3

Kulturbrauerei	29	A2
Mario's Kellerbar	30	C3

SHOPPING		
Käthe Wohlfahrt		
Weihnachtsdorf	(see 8)	

TRANSPORT		
Fahrrad Krauss	31	B3
Main Bus Park	32	D3

BAVARIA

from Christ. The rock crystal inside is said to contain a drop of Christ's blood.

Brutal implements of torture and punishment from medieval times are on display at the fascinating **Mittelalterliches Kriminalmuseum** (Medieval Crime Museum; ☎ 5359; Burggasse 3; adult/concession €3.50/2.30; ☺ 9.30am-6pm Apr-Oct, 2-4pm Nov & Jan-Feb, 10am-4pm Mar & Dec). Displays include chastity belts, masks of disgrace for gossips, a cage for errant bakers, a neck brace for quarrelsome women and a beer-barrel pen for drunks. The exhibits (also explained in English) are so popular that the museum was recently expanded.

The intact city walls form a ring around the city. You can walk 2.5km of the wall and get good city views from the eastern tower,

Röderturm (Rödergasse; adult/child €1.50/1; ☺ 9am-5pm). It's staffed by volunteers and often closed. For the most impressive views, though, go to the west side of town, where a sweeping view of the Tauber Valley includes the **Doppelbrücke**, a double-decker bridge. Also visible is the head of a trail that leads down the valley and over to the lovely Romanesque **St-Peter-und-Pauls-Kirche** (☎ 5524; Detwang; adult/child €1/0.50; ☺ 8.30am-noon & 1.30-5pm Apr-Oct; 10am-noon & 2-4pm Nov-Mar, closed Mon) which contains another stunning Riemenschneider altar. There's a beer garden (Unter den Linden) about halfway along the trail.

The city's showcase of local art, culture and history is the **Reichsstadtmuseum** (Imperial City Museum; ☎ 939 043; Klosterhof 5; adult/child €3/2; ☺ 10am-5pm Apr-Oct, 1-4pm Nov-Mar), which is housed in a former convent. Highlights include the superb *Rothenburger Passion* (1494) by Martinus Schwarz, and the convent rooms themselves, including a 14th-century kitchen. The **gardens** are ideal for a quiet stroll.

The **Alt-Rothenburger Handwerkerhaus** (☎ 942 80; Alter Stadtgraben 26; adult/child €2.20/1.60; ☒ 11am-5pm Mon-Fri, 10am-5pm Sat & Sun Apr-Oct, 2-4pm Mon-Fri, 10am-4pm Sat & Sun Nov & Dec) reconstructs the working and social life of Rothenburg's medieval citizens. For the nostalgic, the **Puppen-und Spielzeugmuseum** (Doll & Toy Museum; ☎ 7330; Hofbronnengasse 13; adult/child €4/1.50; ☒ 9.30am-6pm Mar-Dec, 11am-5pm Jan-Feb) has an amazing collection of doll's houses, teddy bears and toy carousels. Also worth a visit is the **Deutsches Weihnachtsmuseum** (German Christmas Museum; ☎ 409 365; Herrngasse 1; adult/child €4/2; ☒ 10am-5.30pm late Apr-Dec, weekends only Jan-early Apr), which depicts various Christmas customs as they developed through the ages.

Tours

The tourist office runs 90-minute walking tours (€6, in English) at 2pm from April to October. Every evening a lantern-toting *Nachtwächter* (night watchman) dressed in traditional costume leads an entertaining tour of the Altstadt; English tours (€6) meet at the Rathaus at 8pm, German tours (€5) head off at 9.30pm.

Festivals & Events

The **Historisches Festspiel 'Der Meistertrunk'** (see the boxed text, opposite) takes place each year on Whitsuntide, with parades, dances and a medieval market. The highlight, though, is the re-enactment of the mythical Meistertrunk story.

The Meistertrunk play itself is performed three more times: once during the **Reichsstadt-Festtage** in early September, when the entire city's history is re-enacted in the streets, and twice during the Rothenburger Herbst, an autumn celebration in October.

The **Historischer Schäfertanz** (Historical Shepherds' Dance), featuring colourfully dressed couples, takes places on Marktplatz several times between April and October.

The **Weihnacht-Reiterlersmarkt** (Christmas Market, opposite) in Rothenburg is one of the most romantic in Germany. It takes place each year around the central Marktplatz from late November until 22 December.

Sleeping

Accommodation in Rothenburg is surprisingly good value. The tourist office has an electronic room reservation board in the foyer. The 24-hour booking hotline is ☎ 194 12.

DJH hostel (☎ 941 60; www.djh.de; Mühlacker 1; dm under/over 26yr €19/23; ☐) Rothenburg's hostel is housed in two enormous old buildings in the south of town. It's nicely renovated, extremely well equipped and very popular, so book in advance.

Altfränkische Weinstube (☎ 6404; www.romantic road.com/altfraenkische-weinstube; Am Klosterhof 7; s €48, d €55-65; ☐) Tucked away in a quiet side street near the Reichsstadtmuseum, this enchanting inn has atmosphere-laden rooms, all with bathtubs and most with four-poster or canopied beds. The restaurant (open for dinner only) serves up good regional fare with a dollop of medieval cheer.

Burg-Hotel (☎ 948 90; www.burghotel.rothenburg.de; Klostergasse 1-3; r €90-170; ℗ ☐) The best views in town are from this charming hotel, built right into the town fortifications. All 15 rooms have private sitting areas, and there's an elegant guest lounge with an antique baby grand piano. If it's romance you're after, this is it.

Hotel Raidel (☎ 3115; www.romanticroad.com/raidel; Wenggasse 3; s with/without bathroom €39/19 d €49/39; ℗ ☐) An utter delight, with 500-year-old exposed beams studded with wooden nails, quaint wallpapering and pastel sheets, as well as musical instruments for the guests to play. The cosy breakfast room has an original copper boiler.

Hotel Garni Uhl (☎ 4895; www.hotel-uhl.de; Plönlein 8; s €65-85, d €98-120; ℗) A quiet family-run hotel with spacious rooms, all of which have recently had a face lift.

In the suburb of Detwang, about 2km north of the Altstadt by car (or a pleasant 3km walk along the Tauber River), you'll find two caming grounds situated in an idyllic natural setting. **Campingplatz Tauber-Idyll** (☎ 3177; Camping-Tauber-Idyll@t-online.de; Detwang 28a) and **Campingplatz Tauber-Romantik** (☎ 6191; info@camping-tauberromantik.de; Detwang 39) both charge around €4.50 per person and €4 for a tent, and open Easter to late October.

Eating

Rothenburg's most obvious speciality is *Schneeballen,* balls of sweet dough dipped in cinnamon or sugar, which is available all over town.

Zur Höll (☎ 4229; Burggasse 8; dishes €5-15) This medieval wine tavern, with an appreciation for slow food, is in the town's oldest original

---

DRINK AND YE SHALL BE FREE

In 1631 the Thirty Years' War – pitching Catholics against Protestants – reached the gates of Rothenburg ob der Tauber. Catholic General Tilly and 60,000 of his troops besieged the Protestant market town and demanded its surrender. The town resisted but couldn't stave off the onslaught of marauding soldiers, and the mayor and other town dignitaries were captured and sentenced to death.

And that's pretty much where the story ends and the legend begins. As the tale goes, Rothenburg's town council tried to sate Tilly's bloodthirstiness by presenting him with a mug of wine fit for a giant. Tilly, after taking a sip or two, presented the men with an unusual challenge, saying: 'If one of you has the courage to step forward and down this mug of wine in one gulp, then I shall spare the town and the lives of the councilmen!' Mayor Georg Nusch accepted – and succeeded! And that's why you can still wander though Rothenburg's wonderful medieval lanes today.

It's pretty much accepted that Tilly was really placated with hard cash. Nevertheless, local poet Adam Hörber couldn't resist turning the tale of the *Meistertrunk* into a play, which since 1881 has been performed every Whitsuntide (Pentecost), the seventh Sunday after Easter. It's also re-enacted several times daily by the clock figures on the tourist office building.

---

building that dates back to the year 900. The menu of regional specialities is limited but refined, though it's the wine that people really come for.

Baumeisterhaus (☎ 947 00; Obere Schmiedgasse 3; mains €8-20) This traditional German inn is one of the town's most atmospheric, and that's saying something. The woody dining area is set around a beautiful vine-clad courtyard and bristles with old hunting relics. The daily menu has a wealth of fine traditional fare.

Mittermeier (☎ 945 40; Vorm Würzburger Tor; mains €18-26) The kitchen dynamos at this classy establishment serve top-notch Michelin-starred cuisine in five settings, including a black-and-white tiled 'Temple', an alfresco terrace and a barrel-shaped wine cellar. The artistic chefs rely on locally harvested produce, and the wine list (400-plus varieties) is among Franconia's best.

Pizzeria Italia (☎ 2225; Herrngasse 8; mains €4-14) This is a better-than-average pizza joint, run by friendly people. It's a great place to sit out on the street in summer and just people watch.

Also recommended:

Bosporos Doner (☎ 934 716; Hafengasse 2; dishes €3-6) For delicious kebabs and Middle Eastern goodies.

Albig's Quick Restaurant (Hafengasse 3; dishes €1.50-7) For schnitzels, burgers and hospitality like at your grandparents'.

Entertainment

Based in a historic old brewery with faux turrets, **Kulturbrauerei** (☎ 919 26; Mergentheimer Strasse 1; ☽ Fri-Sun 2-8pm) stages any and every-thing from cutting-edge art exhibits to jazz and indie pop concerts.

Rothenburg isn't exactly a party town but **Club 23** (☎ 3686; Ansbacher Strasse 1; ☽ Wed-Sat) has been throwing dance parties since the disco era. In a little passage of bars and dives nearby, **Mario's Kellerbar** (☎ 0173-167 0415; Ansbacherstrasse 15) has amped up R&B and hip-hop.

Shopping

Christmas reigns eternal at **Käthe Wohlfahrt Weihnachtsdorf** (☎ 4090; Herrngasse 1), with its mind-boggling assortment of Yuletide decorations and ornaments. Many of the items are handcrafted with amazing skill and imagination, and prices are accordingly high.

Getting There & Away

There are frequent trains to Würzburg (€10, one hour) but travel to and from Munich (from €40, three hours) may require several changes. The Europabus stops in the main bus park at the Hauptbahnhof. The A7 autobahn runs right past town.

Getting Around

The city has five car parks right outside the walls; P5 and the lower part of P4, both in the northeast, are free. The town centre is closed to nonresident vehicles from 11am to 4pm and 7pm to 5am weekdays, and all day at weekends; hotel guests are exempt.

Some hotels have bicycle hire, or try **Fahrrad Krauss** (☎ 3495; Wenggasse 42; per half-day/day €4/8). Horse-drawn carriage rides of 25 to 30 minutes cost about €6 per person, but you can haggle for a better price. You can catch these carriages from the Markt, or hail them down throughout town. Call ☎ 4405 for taxis.

DINKELSBÜHL
☎ 09851 / pop 12,000

Dinkelsbühl, another colourful medieval town, proudly traces its roots to a royal residence founded by Carolingian kings in the 8th century. The whole town is immaculately preserved, having been spared destruction in the Thirty Years' War and WWII, and has a far less contrived feel than its more famous neighbour Rothenburg. For a good overall impression of the town, walk along the fortified walls with their 18 towers and four gates.

Orientation & Information

The Altstadt is five minutes' walk west of the Busbahnhof (bus station), via the town gate called Wörnitzer Tor. The **tourist office** (☎ 902 40; www.dinkelsbuehl.de; Marktplatz; ☼ 9am–6pm Mon-Fri, 10am–4pm Sat, 10am–1pm Sun Apr–Oct, 9am–5pm Mon-Fri & 10am–1pm Sat Nov–Mar) is located on Marktplatz. Here you'll also find the central **Romantic Road tourist office** (☎ 902 71; ☼ 9am–6pm Mon-Fri, 9am–1pm & 2–4pm Sat, 9am–noon Sun Apr–Oct). The post office and police station are located next to the bus station.

Sights

Weinmarkt, the main square, is lined by a row of splendid Renaissance mansions. The corner building is the step-gabled **Ratsherrntrinkstube**, which hosted Emperor Karl V and King Gustav Adolf of Sweden long before it became today's tourist office.

Standing sentry over Weinmarkt is **Münster St Georg** (Marktplatz; ☼ 9am–noon & 2-6pm), one of southern Germany's purest late Gothic hall churches. Rather austere from the outside, the interior stuns with an incredible fan-vaulted ceiling. A curiosity is the **Pretzl Window** donated by the bakers' guild, in the upper section of the last window in the right aisle.

If you follow Martin Luther King Strasse north past the Schranne, you'll reach the **Spitalanlage**. Founded in 1280 as a hospital, this is now a seniors' residence and home to the Historisches Museum.

Just outside the western town gate, the **Museum of the 3rd Dimension** (☎ 6336; Nördlinger Tor; adult/concession €5.50/4.50; ☼ 10am–6pm Apr–Oct, 11am–4pm Sat & Sun Nov–Mar) has three floors of holographic images, stereoscopes and 3D imagery.

Opened just a few years ago, the displays already conjure up a feeling of nostalgia.

Tours

Altstadt walking tours (€2.50, one hour) leave from Münster St Georg at 2.30pm and 8.30pm from mid-April to October (2.30pm Saturday November to March). There's also a free tour (in German) with the lamp-toting night watchman at 9pm mid-April to October (Saturday only in winter).

Festivals & Events

In the third week of July, Dinkelsbühl celebrates the 10-day **Kinderzeche** (Children's Festival; www.kinderzeche.de), commemorating how, in the Thirty Years' War, the town's children persuaded the invading Swedish troops to spare the town from ransacking. The festivities include a pageant, re-enactments in the festival hall, lots of music and other entertainment.

Sleeping & Eating

The tourist office can help find private rooms from €30.

DJH hostel (☎ 9509; www.djh.de; Koppengasse 10; dm €14.20; ☼ closed Nov–Feb) Dinkelsbühl's hostel in the western Altstadt occupies a beautifully restored 15th-century granary with doll's house qualities.

DCC-Campingplatz Romantische Strasse (☎ 7817; www.campingpark-dinkelsbuehl.de; Kobeltsmühle 2; per tent/person €8.50/4) This camping ground is set on the shores of a swimmable lake just 300m northeast of Wörnitzer Tor.

Gasthof Goldenes Lamm (☎ 2267; www.goldenes .de; s €35-41, d €57-67) This relaxed family-run inn has pleasant rooms at the top of a creaky staircase, and a funky rooftop garden deck with plump sofas. The attached restaurant serves up Franconian-Swabian specialities, including some vegetarian choices.

Dinkelsbühler Kunststuben (☎ 6750; www.kunst -stuben.de; Segringer Strasse 52; s €50, d €55-80) No room is the same in this snug bohemian B&B where guests receive personal attention. The whole place drips with charm and character, and the lovely inner courtyard is perfect for relaxing in warm weather.

Deutsches Haus (☎ 6058; www.deutsches-haus-dkb .de; Weinmarkt 3; s €90-115, d €110-130) This historic building plays games with visitors, thanks to an illusion created by its 13th-century architects: it looks straight but is actually off-kilter. Inside, rooms are superbly equipped with a baroque flourish, and the formal restaurant serves game and fish prepared according to age-old recipes.

Weib's Brauhaus (☎ 579 490; Untere Schmiedgasse 13; dishes €3-11) A female brewmaster presides over the copper vats at this lively restaurant-pub. The menu is traditional and features the house brew, including the popular *Weib's Töpfle* (woman's pot) of pork and deep-fried mashed potatoes.

Café Extrablatt (☎ 2297; Weinmarkt 10; dishes €4-12) This trendy bistro with a beautiful garden serves big breakfasts, invigorating salads and reams of regional specialities. Menus are designed like newspapers, and Hollywood posters and knick-knacks provide added charm.

Getting There & Around

Dinkelsbühl is not served by trains. Regional buses to and from Rothenburg (€8.60, one hour) and to Nördlingen (€6.30, 40 minutes) stop at the Busbahnhof. The Europabus stops right in the Altstadt at Schweinemarkt.

The tourist office hires out bicycles for €3.60 per day. The Altstadt is closed to vehicles from noon to 6pm on Sunday, Easter to October.

NÖRDLINGEN
☎ 09081 / pop 20,000

About 70km northwest of Augsburg, the charming medieval town of Nördlingen lies within the Ries Basin, a huge crater created by a meteorite more than 15 million years ago. The crater – some 25km in diameter – is one of the best preserved on earth, and was used by US astronauts to train for the first moon landing. The 14th-century walls, all original, follow the crater's rim and are almost perfectly circular. The city sees relatively few tourists and manages to retain an air of authenticity, a relief after some of the Romantic Road's worst excesses.

Orientation & Information

St Georgskirche is the heart of circular Nördlingen. From here, five main roads radiate towards the 12 town gates, which are completely intact. The Hauptbahnhof, which embraces the main post office, is outside the walls and just southeast of the centre. You can circumnavigate the entire town in about an hour by taking the sentry walk (free) on top of its covered old walls.

Stadtbibliothek (☎ 843 00; Marktplatz 2a; ☼ 10am-6pm Mon-Wed, 2-6.30pm Thu, 10am-1pm Sat) Internet access for €0.50 per 15 minutes.

Tourist office (☎ 841 16; www.noerdlingen.de; Marktplatz 2; ☼ 9am-6pm Mon-Thu, 9am-4.30pm Fri, 9.30am-1pm Sat Easter-early Nov, Mon-Fri only mid-Nov–Easter) Sells the Museumscard (€5.80) for free admission to three historical museums and the Daniel tower.

Sights
ST GEORGSKIRCHE

The massive late Gothic **St Georgskirche** is one of the largest in southern Germany. Its high altar and the intricate pulpit (1499) are worth a look, but the real draw is the 90m **Daniel Tower** (adult/concession €1.75/1; ☼ 9am-7pm Apr-Oct, 9am-5pm Nov-Mar). Only from the tower can you appreciate Nördlingen's shape and the gentle landscape of the Ries crater. The watchman, who actually lives up here, sounds out the watch every half-hour from 10pm to midnight.

RIESKRATER MUSEUM

Situated in an ancient barn, the **Rieskrater Museum** (☎ 273 8220; Eugene-Shoemaker-Platz 1; adult/concession €3/1.80; ☼ 10am-noon & 1.30-4.30pm Tue-Sun) explores the formation of meteorite craters and the consequences of such violent collisions with Earth. Rocks, including a genuine moon rock (on permanent loan from NASA), fossils and other geological displays shed light on the mystery of meteors.

BAYERISCHES EISENBAHNMUSEUM

One of Germany's largest collections of classic steam trains can be found at the **Bayerisches Eisenbahnmuseum** (Bavarian Railway Museum; ☎ 09083-340; www.bayerisches-eisenbahnmuseum.de; Am Hohen Weg; adult/child €4/2; ☼ noon-4pm Tue-Sat, 10am-5pm Sun). Its 100 nostalgic vehicles range from sleek high-speed engines for transporting passengers to cute little railyard shunters. An old-time locomotive puffs its way to Dinkelsbühl (adult/child €18/12, two hours return) every Sunday from June to August. The museum is located right behind the Hauptbahnhof.

OTHER MUSEUMS

The **Stadtmuseum** (☎ 273 8230; Vordere Gerbergasse 1; adult/concession €3/1.50; ☼ 10.30am-4.30pm Tue-Sun Mar-early Nov) features costumes and displays on local history. More enlightening is the exhibit on the history of the old town walls and fortifications at the **Stadtmauermuseum** (☎ 9180; Löpsinger Torturm; admission €1; ☼ 10am-4.30pm Apr-Oct).

BAVARIA

Tours

The tourist office runs hour-long German-language walking tours (€3, under 12 free) at 2pm from Easter to October, and at 8.30pm from mid-May to mid-September.

Festivals & Events

The largest annual celebration is the 14-day **Nördlinger Pfingstmesse** at Whitsuntide/Pentecost. It's an exhibition of regional traders, with a huge market featuring beer tents, food stalls and entertainment.

Sleeping & Eating

Jugend & Familengästehaus (☎ 842 984; www.culture lounge.at; Bleichgraben 3a; s/d €26/52; 🖳) Located in the heart of town, this shiny, new 170-bed hostel is spacious and modern. There are two- to four-bed rooms, ideal for couples or families. Facilities include sauna, café with web terminals and even a small cinema. You'll need to show an official youth hostel card.

Hotel Altreuter (☎ 4319; hotel-café-altreuter@ nordschwaben.de; Marktplatz 11; s €33-45, d €48-64) The air is delectably sweet at this pert hotel above a café and *Konditorei* (baked goods shop). Its attractive, renovated rooms have TVs, and there's a public parking area in front of the hotel.

Kaiserhof Hotel Sonne (☎ 5067; www .kaiserhof-hotel-sonne.de; Marktplatz 3; s €55-65, d €75-120; 🅿 ⊠) Nördlingen's top hotel has hosted a procession of emperors and their entourages since 1405. Rooms tastefully mix traditional charm with modern comforts, and there's an atmospheric regional restaurant and cellar wine bar.

Café Radlos (☎ 5040; Löpsinger Strasse 8; mains €5-11; ⊙ closed Tue) This, the hippest and most entertaining café in town, serves a good range of international cuisine and some creative veggie options. Slinky jazz sets a mellow tone for surfing the net (€2 per 30 minutes) or just enjoying a drink in the beer garden.

La Fontana (☎ 211 021; Bei den Kornschrannen 2; mains €4.30-11.50; ⊙ closed Mon) This stylish Italian eatery occupies a vast 1602 barn house, the Kornschrannen. You'll find tasty pasta and pizza as well as Mediterranean dishes, and a market hall selling farm-fresh meats, cheeses and produce sits under the same blood-red roof.

Getting There & Around

There are hourly trains to Munich (€20.20, two hours) and regular services to Augsburg (€11.70, one hour) and Stuttgart (€17.60,

two hours). The Europabus stops at the Rathaus. The regional VGN bus 501 goes to Dinkelsbühl and Feuchtwangen.

There are free car parks at all five city gates. You can hire bicycles at **Radsport Böckle** (☎ 801 040; Reimlinger Strasse 19) from €8 per day.

AUGSBURG
☎ 0821 / pop 270,000

One of the oldest cities in Germany, Augsburg has been shaped by Romans, bankers, traders and medieval artisans. It was founded by the stepchildren of Roman emperor Augustus over 2000 years ago, and during the Middle Ages it became an economic powerhouse. Europe's most influential merchant families, the Fuggers and the Welsers, lent money to kings and countries from Augsburg.

Reminders of this golden era can be seen in the Renaissance and baroque façades of the palaces and patrician houses dotted around town. Bavaria's third-largest city has a relaxed attitude and strolling the leafy streets is a real pleasure. An easy day trip from Munich, it's a good accommodation option during Oktoberfest and an ideal base for exploring the Romantic Road.

Orientation

The Hauptbahnhof is at the western end of Bahnhofstrasse, which runs into Fuggerstrasse at Königsplatz, the city's main bus transfer point. The heart of the Altstadt is Rathausplatz, reached on foot from Königsplatz up Annastrasse.

Information

Banks with ATMs are clustered around the main train station and along Bahnhofstrasse.

Buchhandlung Rieger & Kranzfelder (☎ 517 880; Maximilianstrasse 36, Fugger Stadtpalast) Bookshop with lots of English-language titles.

Easy Internet Café (☎ 508 1878; Bahnhofstrasse 29; per hr €1; ⊙ 7am-midnight Mon-Fri, 8am-midnight Sat, 10am-midnight Sun) Cheapest surfing option in town.

Fernweh (☎ 155 035; Dominikanergasse 10) STA Travel representative.

Post office (Hauptbahnhof)

Rotes Kreuz (Red Cross; ☎ 192 22) For a doctor or ambulance.

Tourist office (☎ 502 2070; www.augsburg-tourismus .de; Rathausplatz; ⊙ 9am-6pm Mon-Fri, to 5pm Nov-Mar, 10am-4pm Sat, 10am-2pm Sun) A €2 booking fee applies for room reservations.

Sights

RATHAUSPLATZ

This square at the city's heart is dominated by the twin onion-dome spires of the Renaissance **Rathaus** (Town Hall; 1615–20). Its roof is crowned by a 4m pine cone, Augsburg's emblem and an ancient fertility symbol. Inside, the star attraction is the meticulously restored

Goldener Saal (Golden Hall; ☎ 324 9196; Rathausplatz; admission €1; ⏲ 10am-6pm), the main meeting hall. It is a dazzling space canopied by a gilded and coffered ceiling, interspersed with frescoes.

For a city panorama, climb the **Perlachturm** (Perlach Tower; ☎ 502 070; Rathausplatz; adult/concession €1/0.50; ⏲ 10am-6pm May-Oct, 2-7pm Sat & Sun Dec) next to the *platz*.

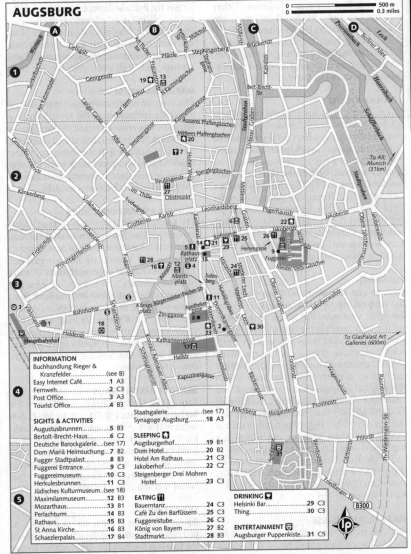

AUGSBURG

0 ————— 500 m
0 ————— 0.3 miles

BAVARIA

B300

DOM MARIÄ HEIMSUCHUNG

North of Rathausplatz you'll find the cathedral, **Dom Mariä Heimsuchung** (Hoher Weg;
☽ 10.15am-6pm Mon-Sat) which dates back to the
10th century. Over the years many alterations
have been made here, including the addition
of the 14th-century bronze doors with their
Old Testament scenes. The oldest section is
the crypt underneath the west choir, which
features a Romanesque Madonna. Other
treasures include medieval frescoes, the
Weingartner Altar by Hans Holbein the Elder,
and – dating from the 12th century – the
Prophets' Windows (depicting Daniel, Jonah,
Hosea and Moses), some of the oldest stained-
glass windows in Germany.

ST ANNA KIRCHE

The rather plain-looking **St Anna Kirche** (Church
of St Anna; Im Annahof 2; ☽ 10am-noon & 3-5pm Tue-Sat,
noon-6pm Sun) contains a bevy of treasures as well
as the sumptuous **Fuggerkapelle**, where Jacob
Fugger and his brothers lie buried, and the
lavishly frescoed **Goldschmiedekapelle** (Goldsmiths' Chapel; 1420). The church played an
important role during the Reformation. In
1518 Martin Luther, in town to defend his
beliefs before the papal legate, stayed at what
was then a Carmelite monastery. His rooms
have been turned into the **Lutherstiege**, a small
museum about the Reformation.

FUGGEREI

Built to provide homes for poor Catholics,
the **Fuggerei** (☎ 319 8810; adult/child €2/1; ☽ 8am-
8pm Apr-Oct, 9am-6pm Nov-Mar) is one of the oldest
welfare settlements in the world. Jacob Fugger
financed the project in the 16th century and it
is still home to several hundred people. Many
of the 52 apartments have been modernised but
the exterior is pretty much unchanged, with
the original bellpulls beside each door. For
centuries the rent has remained at one Rhenish
Gilder (€0.88) per year, plus utilities and three
daily prayers. The Fugger Foundation isn't as
flush as it once was, however, and in 2006 first
began to charge admission to the complex.

To see how Fuggerei residents lived in
the past, visit the **Fuggereimuseum** (☎ 450 3770;
Mittlere Gasse 13; free with Fuggerei admission; ☽ 9am-8pm
Mar-Oct, 9am-6pm Nov-Apr).

MAXIMILIANSTRASSE

Only the richest merchant families could afford to live on this grand boulevard, which
is so wide you might mistake it in parts for a
square. The former residence of Jakob Fugger,
the **Fugger Stadtpalast**, is at 36–38. It embraces
the Damenhof (Ladies' Court), a gorgeous
Italian Renaissance–style inner courtyard.
A nearby rococo palace, the **Schaetzlerpalais**
(☎ 324 4117; Maximilianstrasse 56; adult/concession €3/1.50;
☽ 10am-5pm Tue-Sun) was built for a wealthy
banker between 1765 and 1770, and today
houses the **Deutsche Barockgalerie** (German Baroque Gallery) and the **Staatsgalerie** (Bavarian
State Gallery). The pièce de résistance is the
23m-long ballroom – a riot of carved decorations, stucco and mirrors, all topped off with
a kinetic ceiling fresco.

MAXIMILIANMUSEUM

This restored patrician's house (1546) is home
to the **Maximilianmuseum** (☎ 324 4125; Philippine-
Welser Strasse 24; adult/child €3/1.50; ☽ 10am-5pm Tue-
Sun), which traces the cultural and municipal
history of Augsburg. It also has a large exhibition of gold and silver work from baroque
and rococo masters. A second floor displays
sculptures and architectural models.

GLASPALAST ART GALLERIES

The **GlasPalast** (☎ 324 4155; Beim Glaspalast 1; admission varies; ☽ 10am-9pm Tue, 10am-5pm Wed-Sun) is an
industrial monument made of iron, concrete
and glass that houses two new art galleries.
The **H2 Zentrum für Gegenwartskunst** (Center
of Contemporary Art) is a cutting-edge gallery, while the **Staatsgalerie Moderne Kunst** (State
Gallery of Modern Art), which shows American highlights of the genre from after 1950,
is an offshoot of Munich's Pinakothek der
Moderne. Its public art library is open during
visiting hours. Also look out for guided tours,
concerts and films.

BERTOLT BRECHT HAUS

Fans of the *Threepenny Opera* will enjoy the
Bertolt-Brecht-Haus (☎ 324 2779; Am Rain 7; adult/
concession €1.50/1; ☽ 10am-4pm Wed-Sun), the birthplace of the famous playwright and poet.
Brecht's work was banned by the Nazis for his
communist leanings and he was later shunned
by West Germans for the same reason (see
boxed text about Brecht, p66).

SYNAGOGUE

About 300m east of the main train station, as
you head towards the Altstadt you'll come to
the **Synagoge Augsburg**, an Art Nouveau temple

built between 1914 and 1917. Inside is the excellent **Jüdisches Kulturmuseum** (Jewish Cultural Museum; ☎ 513 658; Halderstrasse 8; adult/concession €2/1.50; ☻ 9am-4pm Tue-Fri, 10am-5pm Sun), with exhibitions on Jewish life in the region, Germany and Central Europe.

Tours

Guided **walking tours** (adult/child €7/5; ☻ Apr-Oct, Sat only Nov-Mar) in English and German leave from the Rathaus at 2pm.

Sleeping

Jakoberhof (☎ 510 030; www.jakoberhof.de; Jakoberstrasse 41; s €39-49, d €54-64; **P**) One of the best-value options in town is this simple place near the Fuggerei. Rooms have few frills, but are bright and airy with modern bathrooms, and your hosts are congenial sorts.

Dom Hotel (☎ 343 930; www.domhotel-augsburg.de; Frauentorstrasse 8; s €64-105, d €74-125; **P** ⊠ ⊛) This charming hotel with spacious, tastefully decorated rooms is excellent value. The smaller attic rooms have beamed ceilings and great views. Guests have free use of the garden, pool and sauna, and children are welcome.

Augsburger Hof (☎ 343 050; www.augsburger-hof .de; Auf dem Kreuz 2; s €78-105, d €88-130; **P** ⊠ ▣) The high-priced rooms open into the courtyard at this pretty window-boxed hotel. All are thoughtfully furnished with high-class linens, and have cable TV and phones. It's near the Mozarthaus, an easy walk north of the Dom.

Hotel am Rathaus (☎ 346 490; www.hotel-am -rathaus-augsburg.de; Am Hinteren Perlachberg 1; s €90, d €90-110; **P** ⊠ ▣) As central as it gets, and moments away from Rathausplatz, this boutique hotel has fresh neutral décor and a sunny little breakfast room. The trendy Italian restaurant is surprisingly good.

Steigenberger Drei Mohren Hotel (☎ 503 60; www.augsburg.steigenberger.de; Maximilianstrasse 40; s/d €115/150; **P** ⊛ ⊠ ▣) This landmark hotel, with luxurious décor, is a stunning place where both Mozart and Goethe have stayed. Marble bathrooms, original art and a beautiful garden terrace are among the elegant touches.

Eating

In the evening, Maximilianstrasse is the place to hang out, with cafés overflowing onto the pavements and plenty of young things watching the world go by.

RESTAURANTS

Café zu den Barfüssern (☎ 450 4966; Barfüsserstrasse 10; dishes €2-6) A few steps down from the street through a covered passageway bring you out into the sun at this pretty canalside café. It serves homemade cakes and pastries, as well as a limited daily lunch menu.

König von Bayern (☎ 349 7990; Johannisgasse 4; mains €5-9) This beautiful, secluded restaurant and beer garden are great places to sit and relax. The food is traditional, but lighter than usual. Try the *Brauerfladen*, a kind of thin-crust pizza covered with anything from smoked salmon to broccoli and melted cheese.

Also recommended:

Bauerntanz (☎ 153 644; Bauerntanzgässchen 1; mains €8-16) A local favourite serving big portions of creative Swabian and Bavarian food.

Fuggereistube (☎ 308 70; Jakoberstrasse 26; mains €10-20) Vintage 1970s hunting-lodge décor, with Bavarian food and good service.

QUICK EATS

There are lots of cheap places to eat or buy snacks on Bahnhofstrasse. The local **Stadtmarkt** (btwn Fuggerstrasse & Annastrasse; ☻ 7am-6pm Mon-Fri, 7am-2pm Sat) is a snacker's fantasy. Besides fresh produce, bread and meat, you'll find dozens of stand-up eateries serving everything from Thai and Bavarian to Greek.

Drinking

Helsinki Bar (☎ 372 90; Barfüsserstrasse 4; dishes €3-7) A café by day and a bar by night, this place attracts the beautiful people, intent on hanging out in an alternative venue with cool Nordic fare and slick furnishings.

Thing (☎ 395 05; Vorderer Lech 45) Augsburg's coolest beer garden is an institution that often gets crowded in the evenings.

Entertainment

The celebrated **Augsburger Puppenkiste** (☎ 434 440; www.augsburger-puppenkiste.de; Spitalgasse 15; afternoon shows €7.50-9.50, evening shows €13-18; ☻ 3pm & 7.30pm Wed, Fri-Sun) holds performances of modern and classic fairy tales that are so endearing, and the sets and costumes so fantastically elaborate, that even non-German speakers will enjoy a show. Advance reservations are advised.

Getting There & Away

Nonstop regional trains run hourly between Augsburg and Munich (€10, 45 minutes) and every other hour to Nuremberg (€20.80, 1¾ hours). ICE (InterCity Express) trains travel to Würzburg (€41, two hours) and Regensburg (€21.20, 2¼ hours).

The Romantic Road Europabus stops at the Hauptbahnhof. Augsburg is just off the A8 autobahn northwest of Munich.

Getting Around

Most journeys within town on the bus and tram network cost €1.10; longer trips to the outlying suburbs are €2. A 24-hour ticket costs €5 and is good for up to three adults.

FÜSSEN & SCHWANGAU

☎ 08362 / pop 17,700

The last stops on the Romantic Road are Füssen, a small town nestled between towering Alpine peaks, and Schwangau, a village about 4km further east. Together they form the Königswinkel (Royal Corner), home to Germany's biggest tourist attractions: Ludwig II's fantasy castles Neuschwanstein and Hohenschwangau. If you still haven't learned enough about his highness after those, book a seat at the extravagant musical *Ludwig 2*, performed in a custom-built theatre on the Forggensee.

Orientation & Information

Schwangau and the castles are about 4km east of Füssen via the B17 (Münchener Strasse).
Füssen tourist office (☎ 938 50; www.fuessen.de; Kaiser-Maximilian-Platz 1; ⏰ 8am-12.30pm & 1.30-5pm Mon-Fri, 10am-1pm Sat May-Oct, 9am-5pm Mon-Sat Nov-Apr) A three-minute walk west from the train and bus station.
Schwangau tourist office (☎ 819 80; www.schwangau .de; Münchener Strasse 2; ⏰ 8am-12.30pm & 1.30-5pm)

Sights
CASTLES
Schloss Neuschwanstein

Appearing through the mountain-tops like a misty mirage is the world's most famous castle, and the model for Disney's citadel, **Schloss Neuschwanstein** (☎ 930 830; adult/concession €9/8, with Hohenschwangau €17/15; ⏰ 9am-6pm Apr-Sep, 10am-4pm Oct-Mar).

Ludwig planned this castle himself, with the help of a stage designer rather than an architect, and it provides a fascinating glimpse into the king's state of mind. Built as a romantic medieval castle, it was started in 1869 and, like so many of Ludwig's grand schemes, was never finished. For all the money spent on it, the king spent just over 170 days in residence.

Ludwig imagined his palace as a giant stage to recreate the world of Germanic mythology in the operatic works of Richard Wagner. Its centrepiece is the lavish **Sängersaal** (Minstrels' Hall), created to feed the king's obsession with Wagner and medieval knights. Wall frescoes in the hall depict scenes from the opera *Tannhäuser*. Concerts are held here every September.

Other completed sections include **Ludwig's bedroom**, dominated by a huge Gothic-style bed crowned with intricately carved spires; a gaudy artificial grotto (another nod to *Tannhäuser*); and the Byzantine **Thronsaal** (Throne Room) with a great mosaic floor and a chandelier shaped like a giant crown.

The wooded hills framing the castle make for some wonderful walks. For the postcard view of Neuschwanstein and the plains beyond, walk 10 minutes up to **Marienbrücke** (Mary's Bridge), which spans the spectacular Pöllat Gorge over a waterfall just above the castle.

Schloss Hohenschwangau

Ludwig spent his formative years at the sunyellow **Schloss Hohenschwangau** (☎ 930 830; adult/concession €9/, with Neuschwanstein €17/15 ; ⏰ 9am-6pm Apr-Sep, 10am-4pm Oct-Mar). His father, Maximilian II, rebuilt this palace in a neo-Gothic style from 12th-century ruins left by Schwangau knights. It's much less ostentatious than Neuschwanstein, however, and today has a distinct lived-in feeling. After his father died, Ludwig's main alteration was having stars, illuminated with hidden oil-lamps, painted on the ceiling of his bedroom.

Here Ludwig first met Wagner, and the **Hohenstaufensaal** room features a square piano where the hard-up composer would entertain Ludwig with excerpts from his latest oeuvre. Some rooms have frescoes from German history and legend (including the story of the Swan Knight, Lohengrin).

Tickets & Tours

Both castles must be seen on guided tours (in German or English), which last about 35 minutes. Tickets are available only from the **Ticket Centre** (☎ 930 830; www.ticket-center-hohenschwangau .de; Alpseestrasse 12) at the foot of the castles. In summer it's advisable to come as early as 8.30am to ensure you get a ticket.

It's a steep 30- to 40-minute walk between the castles, though you can shell out €5 for a horse-drawn carriage ride, which is only slightly faster.

If you're pressed for time, consider going on an organised tour. **EurAide** (p288; www.euraide .de) runs tours to Neuschwanstein and Linderhof with a brief stop in Oberammergau (adult/child €47/24, plus castle admission).

ALTSTADT FÜSSEN

Füssen's compact historical centre is a tangle of lanes lorded over by the **Hohe Schloss**, a late Gothic confection and one-time retreat of the bishops of Augsburg. The inner courtyard is a masterpiece of illusionary architecture dating back to 1499; you'll do a double take before realising that the gables, oriels and windows are not quite as they seem. The north wing of the palace contains the **Staatsgalerie im Hohen Schloss** (☎ 903 164; Magnusplatz 10; adult/concession €2.50/2, with Städtische Gemäldegalerie €3) with regional paintings and sculpture from the 15th and 16th centuries. The **Städtische Gemäldegalerie** (City Paintings Gallery) below is a showcase of 19th-century artists.

Below the Hohen Schloss, integrated into the former Abbey of St Mang, is the **Museum Füssen** (☎ 903 146; Lechhalde 3; adult/child under 14 €2.50/free; ⏰ 10am-4pm Apr-Oct, 1-4pm Nov-Mar, closed Mon). Füssen's heyday as a 16th-century violin-making centre is recalled here, and you can view the abbey's festive baroque rooms, Romanesque cloister and the St Anna Kapelle (AD 830).

TEGELBERGBAHN

For fabulous views of the Alps and the Forggensee, take this **cable car** (☎ 983 60; one-way/return €9.50/16; ⏰ 8.30am-5pm Jul-Oct, 9am-5pm Nov-Jun) to the top of the Tegelberg (1707m), a prime launch point for hang-gliders and parasailers. From here it's a wonderful hike down to the castles (two to three hours; follow the signs to Königsschlösser). To get to the valley station, take RVO bus 73 or 78 from the Bahnhof in Füssen, or from the Schwangau village centre.

Sleeping

Accommodation in the area is surprisingly good value and the tourist offices can find private rooms from €18 per person.

House LA (☎ 7607 366; www.geocities.com/houselafuessen; Welfenstrasse 39, Füssen; dm €17) A 15-minute

walk west of the train station, this newly opened 13-bed hostel has rooms that are spacious, renovated and comfy, and some come with balconies. Breakfast is served on the rear patio with mountain views. The owner will pick you up from the station if you call.

Pension Kössler (☎ 4069; www.pension-koessler.de; Zalinger Strasse 1, Füssen; s €30-33, d €60-66; P) This small *pension* with a friendly atmosphere offers outstanding value. Rooms are simple but comfortable and have private bathroom, TV, phone and balcony – some overlook the attractive garden.

Hotel zum Hechten (☎ 916 00; www.hotel-hechten .com; Ritterstrasse 6, Füssen; s €45-55, d €74-84; P X) This is one of Füssen's oldest hotels and a barrel of fun. Public areas are traditional in style but the bedrooms (such as No 44) are bright and modern. The owner has decorated the restaurant in campy Ludwig II colours. Children are welcome.

Hotel Weinbauer (☎ 9860; www.hotel-weinbauer.de; Füssener Strasse 3, Schwangau; s/d €40/80) Large, bright rooms, decorated in contemporary styles and with a decent range of amenities, make this friendly hotel a winner. The frescoed restaurant downstairs (mains €8 to €16) opens onto a pretty garden.

Hotel Sonne (☎ 9080; www.hotel-sonne.de; Reichenstrasse 37, Füssen; r €99-129; P X ▢) Traditional-looking from outside, this Alstadt hotel has undergone a designer facelift within. Rooms have quality leather chairs, red-gold royal carpets and fancy flat-screen TVs, not to mention some kickin' bathroom fittings.

Campers should head for the following modern lakeside camp sites:

Campingplatz Bannwaldsee (☎ 930 00; www .camping-bannwaldsee.de; Münchner Strasse 151, Schwangau; per site/person €7/6.80)

Campingplatz Brunnen am Forggensee (☎ 8273; www.camping-brunnen.de; Seestrasse 81, Schwangau; per site/person €8/9.50)

Eating

Kulturcafé (☎ 924 924; Lechhalde 1, Füssen; mains €5-13) This sophisticated little eatery at the rear of the Rathaus is perfect for a wholesome snack, an art exhibition or a jazz concert…sometimes all at once. The tables in the old monastery gardens afford beautiful views high above the river.

Franziskaner Stüberl (☎ 371 24; Kemptener Strasse 1, Füssen; mains €7.50-12.50; ⏰ closed Thu) This quaint restaurant specialises in *Schweinshaxe* (pork

BAVARIA

LUDWIG II, THE FAIRY-TALE KING

Every year on 13 June, a stirring ceremony takes place in Berg, on the eastern shore of Lake Starnberg. A small boat quietly glides towards a cross just offshore and a plain wreath is fastened to its front. The sound of a single trumpet cuts the silence as the boat returns from this solemn ritual in honour of the most beloved king ever to rule Bavaria – Ludwig II.

The cross marks the spot where Ludwig died under mysterious circumstances in 1886. His early death capped the life of a man at odds with the harsh realities of a modern world no longer in need of a romantic and idealistic monarch.

Prinz Otto Ludwig Friedrich Wilhelm was a sensitive soul, fascinated by romantic epics, architecture and music, but his parents, Maximilian II and Marie, took little interest in his musings and he suffered a lonely and joyless childhood. In 1864, at 18 years old, the prince became king. He was briefly engaged to the sister of Elisabeth (Sisi), the Austrian empress, but as a rule he preferred the company of men. He also worshipped composer Richard Wagner, whose Bayreuth opera house was built with Ludwig's funds.

Ludwig was an enthusiastic leader initially, but Bavaria's days as a sovereign state were numbered, and he became a puppet king after the creation of the German Reich in 1871 (which had its advantages, as Bismarck gave Ludwig a hefty allowance). Ludwig now withdrew completely to drink, draw castle plans and view concerts and operas in private. His obsession with French culture and the Sun King, Louis XIV, inspired the fantastical palaces of Neuschwanstein, Linderhof and Herrenchiemsee – lavish projects that spelt his undoing.

Contrary to popular belief, though, it was only Ludwig's purse – and not the state treasury – that was being bankrupted. However, by 1886 his ever-growing mountain of debt and erratic behaviour was perceived as a threat to the natural order of things. The king, it seemed, needed to be 'managed'.

In January 1886, several ministers and relatives arranged a hasty psychiatric test that diagnosed Ludwig as mentally unfit to rule. That June he was removed to Schloss Berg on Lake Starnberg. One evening the dejected bachelor and his doctor took a lakeside walk and were found several hours later, drowned in just a few feet of water.

No-one knows with certainty what happened that night. There was no eyewitness or any proper criminal investigation. The circumstantial evidence was conflicting and incomplete. Reports and documents were tampered with, destroyed or lost. Conspiracy theories abound. That summer the authorities opened Neuschwanstein to the public to help pay off Ludwig's huge debts. King Ludwig II was dead, but the myth was just being born.

knuckle) and schnitzel, prepared in more varieties than you can shake a leg at. Non-carnivores go for the excellent *Kässpätzle* (rolled cheese noodles) and the huge salads.

Pizzeria San Marco (☎ 813 39; Füssener Strasse 6, Schwangau; mains €5-16) This cosy place decorated in a rustic Italian style serves up a good range of interesting pizzas and pastas as well as healthy salads and other Mediterranean fare.

Snack options include the local **Nordsee** (Reichenstrasse 40) and **Vinzenzmurr** (Reichenstrasse 35), both in Füssen.

Entertainment

He's back! After a brief hiatus, the tragic story of King Ludwig II's life again unfolds in music, sound and special effects on the western shore of the Forggensee. **Ludwig 2** (☎ 01805-131 132; www.ludwig2musical.com; tickets

€15-100) is part fantasy, part history and all monumental spectacle. Sung in German with English supertitles, it takes place nightly and on weekend afternoons on the largest revolving stage in Germany. The name is a poke at the first production, which couldn't meet costs. You can take a one-hour **backstage tour** (€7/3.50; ☿ 3pm & 4pm Tue-Fri, 11am & noon Sat & Sun), which shows the secrets behind the spectacle.

Getting There & Away

If you want to 'do' the royal castles on a day trip from Munich (€19.80, two hours) you'll need to start early. The first train leaves Munich at 4.57am, getting to Füssen at 7.24am. Later trains depart at roughly 10 minutes to the hour, but always check schedules before you go.

Getting Around

RVO bus 78 goes to the castles from Füssen Bahnhof and Schwangau village centre (€3.30 return), stopping also at the Tegelbergbahn valley station. Taxis to the castles are about €10.

With the Alps on one side and the lake-filled plains on the other, the area around Füssen is a cyclist's paradise. You can hire two-wheelers at the **Radsport Zacherl** (3292; Kemp-tenerstrasse 19, Füssen; per day €8).

AROUND FÜSSEN

Known as 'Wies' for short, the **Wieskirche** (☎ 8862-932 930; www.wieskirche.de; Steingaden) is one of Bavaria's best-known baroque churches and a Unesco-listed heritage site. About a million visitors a year flock to see its pride and joy, the monumental work of the legendary artist-brothers, Dominikus and Johann Baptist Zimmermann.

In 1730, a farmer in Steingaden, about 30km northeast of Füssen, witnessed the miracle of his Christ statue crying. So many pilgrims poured into the town that the local abbot commissioned a new church to house the weepy work. Inside, gleaming white pillars are topped by gold capital stones and swirling decorations; the pastel ceiling fresco celebrates Christ's resurrection. Not even the constant deluge of visitors can detract from these charms.

From Füssen regional RVO bus 72 or 73 makes the journey up to six times daily (one-way/return €4.80/8). The Europabus also makes a brief stop at the Wieskirche. By car, take the B17 northeast and turn right (east) at Steingaden.

BAVARIAN ALPS

Stretching west from Germany's remote southeastern corner to the Allgäu region near Lake Constance, the Bavarian Alps (Bayerische Alpen) form a stunningly beautiful natural divide along the Austrian border. The ranges further south are higher, but these mountains shoot up from the foothills so abruptly that the impact is all the more dramatic.

The region is dotted with quaint frescoed villages, spas and health retreats and has a wealth of outdoor possibilities for skiing, snowboarding, hiking, canoeing and para-

gliding – much of it year-round. The ski season lasts from about late December until April, while summer activities stretch from late May to November.

One of the largest resorts in the area is Garmisch-Partenkirchen, one of Munich's favourite getaway spots. Other noteworthy bases are Berchtesgaden, Füssen and Oberstdorf.

Most of the resorts have plenty of reasonably priced accommodation, though some places levy a surcharge (usually about €3) for stays of less than two or three days in peak seasons. Most resorts also charge a *Kurtaxe* (less than €2) for overnight stays, but this entitles you to certain perks, like free tours, a city bus service and entry to special events.

Getting Around

Buses are the most efficient method of public transport in the alpine area; there are few direct train routes between main centres. If you're driving, sometimes a short cut via Austria works out to be quicker (such as between Garmisch-Partenkirchen and Füssen or Oberstdorf).

Regional passes on RVO buses (www.rvo-bus.de) give unlimited travel on the upper-Bavarian bus network (a weekly pass is between €9.60 and €50, depending on distance covered). Buy them directly from the bus driver.

GARMISCH-PARTENKIRCHEN

☎ 08821 / pop 27,000

A favourite haunt for outdoor enthusiasts and moneyed socialites, the resort of Garmisch-Partenkirchen is blessed with a fabled setting a stone's throw from the Alps. To say you were 'skiing in Garmisch' has a fashionable ring. The area offers some of the best skiing in the land, including runs on Germany's highest peak, the Zugspitze (2964m). The towns of Garmisch and Partenkirchen were merged for the 1936 Winter Olympics, and to this day host international skiing events. In 2011 the Alpine World Skiing Championships will be held here for the first time since 1978, with cameras trained on the breakneck pistes and dizzying ski ramp at the town's impressive Olympia Skistadion (wintersports stadium).

Garmisch-Partenkirchen also makes a handy base for excursions to Ludwig II's palaces, including nearby Schloss Linderhof and the lesser-known Jagdschloss Schachen.

Orientation

The train tracks that divide the two towns culminate at the Hauptbahnhof. From here, turn west on St-Martin-Strasse to get to Garmisch, or east on Bahnhofstrasse to reach Partenkirchen. From the Hauptbahnhof the centre of Garmisch is about 500m away, the centre of Partenkirchen about 1km.

Information

Hypo-Vereinsbank (Am Kurpark 13) There's another branch in the train station.

Hobis Cyber Café (☎ 2727; Zugspitzstrasse 2; per 15min €1; ☺ 6am-6pm Mon-Fri, 6am-noon Sat, 8-11am Sun) Internet access in the garden atrium of a bustling bakery.

Klinikum (☎ 770; Auenstrasse 6) Full-service hospital.

Post office (Bahnhofplatz)

Presse + Buch (☎ 4400; Hauptbahnhof) International papers and mags.

Tourist office (☎ 180 700; www.garmisch-parten kirchen.de; Richard-Strauss-Platz 1, Garmisch; ☺ 8am-6pm Mon-Sat, 10am-noon Sun)

Sights & Activities

ZUGSPITZE

Views from the top of Germany are literally breathtaking, especially during *Föhn* weather when they extend into four countries. Skiing and hiking are the main activities here. To get to the top, you can walk (right), or take a cogwheel train or a cable car.

The **Zugspitzbahn** (the cogwheel train) has its own station right behind the Hauptbahnhof. From here it chugs along the mountain base to the Eibsee, a forest lake, then winds its way through a mountain tunnel up to the Schneeferner Glacier (2600m). From there a cable car makes the final ascent to the summit.

Alternatively, the **Eibsee-Seilbahn**, a steep cable car, sways and swings its way straight up to the summit from the Eibsee lake in about 10 minutes – it's not for the faint-hearted! Most people go up on the train and take the cable car back down, but it works just as well the other way around.

Whichever route you take, the entire trip costs €37/23 per adult/child in winter and €45/31.50 in summer. Winter rates include a day ski-pass.

Expect serious crowds at peak times in winter and through much of the summer. Skiers may find it easier, but slower, to schlep their gear up on the train, which offers exterior ski-holders.

SKIING

Garmisch has three ski fields: the Zugspitze plateau (2964m), the Classic Ski Area (Alpspitze, 2050m; Hausberg, 1340m; Kreuzeck, 1651m; day pass adult/child €29.50/19) and the Eckbauer (1236m; day pass €18/15). A Happy Ski Card (three-day minimum, adult/child €85.50/51.50) covers all three ski areas, plus three other ski areas around the Zugspitze, including Mittenwald. Local buses serve all the valley stations.

Cross-country ski trails run along the main valleys, including a long section from Garmisch to Mittenwald; call ☎ 797 979 for a weather or snow report.

For ski hire and courses try the following:

Flori Wörndle (☎ 583 00; www.skischule-woerndle.de; Alpspitze & Hausberg)

Sport Total (☎ 1425; www.agentursporttotal.de; Marienplatz 18) Also organises paragliding, mountain biking, rafting and ballooning.

HIKING

Garmisch-Partenkirchen is prime hiking territory. Mountain guides are at the tourist office on Monday and Thursday between 4pm and 6pm to give help and information to hikers. Brochures and maps are also available with route suggestions for all levels.

Hiking to the **Zugspitze summit** is only possible in summer and is recommended only for those with experience of mountaineering. Another popular route is to King Ludwig II's hunting lodge, **Jagdschloss Schachen** (☎ 2996; admission €2.50, child under 14yr free; ☺ Jun-Oct), which can be reached via the Partnachklamm (below) in about a four-hour hike. A plain wooden hut from the outside, the interior is surprisingly magnificent; the **Moorish Room** is something straight out of the *Arabian Nights*.

For guided hikes and courses contact the following:

Bergsteigerschule Zugspitze (☎ 589 99; www .bergsteigerschule-zugspitze.de; Am Gudiberg 7)

Deutscher Alpenverein (☎ 2701; www.alpenverein -ga-pa.de; Hindenburgstrasse 38)

PARTNACHKLAMM

One of the area's main tourist attractions is the beautiful **Partnachklamm** (☎ 3167; adult/child €2/1), a narrow 700m-long gorge with walls rising up to 80m. A circular walk hewn from the rock takes you through the gorge, which is really spectacular in winter when you can walk beneath curtains of icicles and frozen waterfalls.

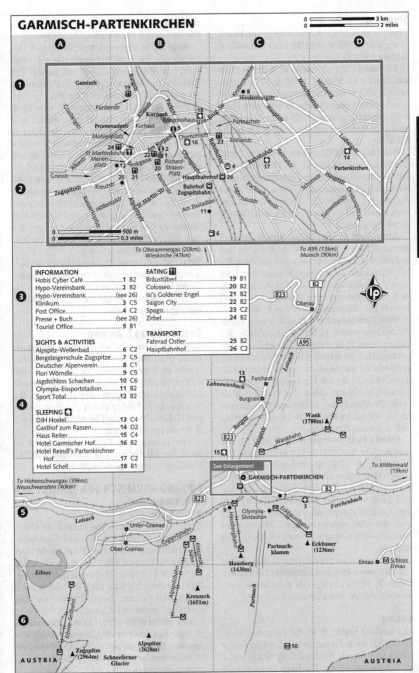

GARMISCH-PARTENKIRCHEN

BAVARIA

INFORMATION	
Hobis Cyber Café	1 B2
Hypo-Vereinsbank	2 B2
Hypo-Vereinsbank	(see 26)
Klinikum	3 C5
Post Office	4 C2
Presse + Buch	(see 26)
Tourist Office	5 B1

SIGHTS & ACTIVITIES	
Alpspitz-Wellenbad	6 C2
Bergsteigerschule Zugspitze	7 C5
Deutscher Alpenverein	8 C1
Flori Wörndle	9 C5
Jagdschloss Schachen	10 C6
Olympia-Eissportstadion	11 B2
Sport Total	12 B2

SLEEPING	
DJH Hostel	13 C4
Gasthof zum Rassen	14 D2
Haus Reiter	15 C4
Hotel Garmischer Hof	16 B2
Hotel Reindl's Partenkirchner Hof	17 C2
Hotel Schell	18 B1

EATING	
Bräustüberl	19 B1
Colosseo	20 B2
Isi's Goldener Engel	21 B2
Saigon City	22 B2
Spago	23 C2
Zirbel	24 B2

TRANSPORT	
Fahrrad Ostler	25 B2
Hauptbahnhof	26 C2

To Oberammergau (20km); Wieskirche (47km)

To A95 (13km); Munich (90km)

To Hohenschwangau (39km); Neuschwanstein (40km)

To Mittenwald (19km)

AUSTRIA

AUSTRIA

Sleeping

There is an outdoor room-reservation board at the tourist office and a 24-hour reservation hotline (☎ 194 12).

DJH hostel (☎ 2980; www.djh.de; Jochstrasse 10; dm under/over 26yr €21.50/25.50; P ⊠ ⌐) The standards at this smartly revamped hostel are as good at some chain hotels. Rooms have Ikea-style furnishings and fruity colour schemes, and an Alpine stream gurgles right past the building.

Hotel Schell (☎ 9575; www.hotel-schell.de; Partnachauenstrasse 3; s €35-50, d €65-90; P) This traditional Alpine home has built up a returning clientele with friendly service and spotless, good-value rooms. It's close to the Hauptbahnhof but very quiet, and children and adults alike will enjoy the garden.

Gasthof Zum Rassen (☎ 2089; www.gasthof-rassen .de; Ludwigstrasse 45; s €32-53, d €52-90; P ⊠) In this beautifully frescoed 14th-century building, the bright, modern rooms provide quite a contrast with the traditional décor of the public areas. A former brewery, the massive event hall houses the oldest folk theatre in Bavaria.

Hotel Garmischer Hof (☎ 9110; www.garmischer -hof.de; Chamonixstrasse 10; s €58-80, d €90-132; P ☎) Generations of athletes, artists and outdoor enthusiasts have stayed at this refined chateau, property of the Seiwald family since 1928. Tasteful and cosy are the rooms, many with incredible Alpine views. All of them have cable TV, direct-dial phones and safes. Breakfast is served in the vaulted café-restaurant with a garden terrace.

Reindl's Partenkirchner Hof (☎ 08821-943 870; www.reindls.de; Bahnhofstrasse 15; s €73-95, d €106-150, ste €132-294; P ⊠ ⌐ ☎) It doesn't get much better than this: an elegant, three-winged luxury hotel stacked with perks, a wine bar and a top-notch gourmet restaurant. Its very comfortable rooms have touches of royalty and splendid mountain views. Most celebrities visiting Garmisch-Partenkirchen end up here.

Another recommendation is **Haus Reiter** (☎ 2223; www.reiter-gap.com; Burgstrasse 55; s €20-30, d €40-60; P ⊠), a chalet-style guesthouse with modern rooms and a garden.

Eating

Isi's Goldener Engel (☎ 948 757; Bankgasse 5; mains €9-17) This local favourite has hunting-lodge décor that blends frescoes, stag heads and a gilded stucco ceiling. The huge menu ranges from simple schnitzel to game dishes, though the best deal is the generous lunch special.

Spago (☎ 966 555; Partnachstrasse 50; mains €6-8) This trendy café-bistro off the main drag serves up light fare like salads, crepes and pastas. The slick design, outdoor seating and international menu tend to draw a local clientele.

Colosseo (☎ 528 09; Klammstrasse 7; mains €6-18) The Roman sculptures, chirpy waiters and mountain views make this upstairs pizzeria a sure winner. The menu includes excellent pastas and pizzas as well as delicious fish and meat dishes, all for takeaway if you like.

Bräustüberl (☎ 2312; Fürstenstrasse 23; mains €6-16) This place, a bit outside the centre, is quintessentially Bavarian, complete with enormous enamel coal-burning stove and dirndl-clad waitresses. The dining room is to the right, the beer hall (with more ambience) is to the left.

Other recommendations:

Zirbel (☎ 7671; Promenadestrasse 2; meals €7-17) Relaxed, tunnel-shaped pub serving snacks and small meals.
Saigon City (☎ 969 315; Am Kurpark 17a; mains €5-11; ☾ closed Sun) Simple Vietnamese diner serving crispy duck, egg noodles and seafood.

Getting There & Around

Garmisch-Partenkirchen is serviced by hourly trains from Munich (€15.50, 1½ hours), and special packages combine the return trip with a Zugspitze day ski pass. RVO bus 9606 travels to Füssen, with stops at Oberammergau, the Wieskirche and the castles at Neuschwanstein and Hohenschwangau. The A95 from Munich is the direct road route.

Bus tickets cost €1.30 for journeys in town. For bike hire try **Fahrrad Ostler** (☎ 3362; Kreuzstrasse 1; per day/week from €10/40).

AROUND GARMISCH-PARTENKIRCHEN
Oberammergau
☎ 08822 / pop 5400

A study in piety, kitsch and bucolic art, Oberammergau, some 20km north of Garmisch-Partenkirchen, is renowned the world over for its epic Passion Play. Set in a wide valley surrounded by forest and mountains, the village is undeniably beautiful. It's packed with traditional painted houses, wood-carving shops and awestruck tourists.

The **tourist office** (☎ 923 10; www.oberammergau .de; Eugen-Papst-Strasse 9a; ☾ 8.30am-6pm Mon-Fri, 9am-5pm Sat, 1-5pm Sun mid-Jun–mid-Oct, 8.30am-6pm Mon-Fri, 8.30am-noon Sat mid-Oct–mid-Jun) can help find accommodation.

A blend of opera, ritual and Hollywood epic, the **Passion Play** has been performed every decade since the 17th century as a collective thank-you for being spared the plague. Townspeople sew costumes and grow beards for their roles, and half the village takes part. The next performances are in 2010. Tours of the **Passionstheater** (☎ 923 10; Passionswiese 1; tours adult/concession €2.50/1.50; ☻ tours 9.30am-5pm May-Oct, 10am-4pm Nov-Apr) include a peek at the costumes and sets. In the years between Passion Plays, spectacular opera events are held monthly from July to September; ask at the tourist office for details.

The town's other claim to fame is **Lüftmalerei**, the eye-popping house façades painted in an illusionist style. Images usually have a religious flavour, but some also show hilarious beer-hall scenes or fairy-tale motifs, like *Hansel & Gretl* at Ettaler Strasse No 41, or *Little Red Riding Hood* down the road at No 48. The pick of the crop is the amazing **Pilatushaus** (☎ 923 10; Ludwig-Thoma-Strasse 10; admission free; ☻ 1-6pm Mon-Fri May-Oct), whose painted columns snap into 3D as you approach. It contains a gallery and several workshops.

Oberammergau is also known for its intricate **woodcarvings**. Workshops abound around town, churning out everything from corkscrews to life-sized saints and nativity scenes. Some amazing examples can be seen in the little parish cemetery on Pfarrplatz and in the **Oberammergau Museum** (☎ 941 36; Dorfstrasse 8; adult/child €3/1; ☻ 10am-5pm Tue-Sun).

You can stay at the **DJH hostel** (☎ 4114; www .djh.de; Malensteinweg 10; dm under/over 26yr €16/20) or the **Hotel Böld** (☎ 9120; www.hotel-boeld.de; König-Ludwig-Strasse 10; s €60-68, d €78-105; P 🗶), a towering chalet of a hotel that neatly pairs traditional touches with a fine wellness area.

Hourly trains connect Munich with Oberammergau (change at Murnau, €14.70, 1¾ hours). RVO bus 9606 goes to Garmisch-Partenkirchen and Füssen almost hourly.

Schloss Linderhof

A pocket-sized trove of weird treasures, **Schloss Linderhof** (☎ 08822-920 30; adult/concession Apr-Sep €7/6, Oct-Mar €6/5; ☻ 9am-6pm Apr-Sep, 10am-4pm Oct-Mar) was Ludwig II's smallest but most sumptuous palace. Finished in 1878, the palace hugs a steep hillside in a fantasy landscape of French gardens, fountains and follies. The reclusive king used the palace as a retreat and

hardly ever received visitors here. Like Herrenchiemsee (p324), Linderhof was inspired by Versailles and dedicated to Louis XIV, the French 'sun king'.

Linderhof's myth-laden, jewel-encrusted rooms are a monument to the king's excesses that so unsettled the governors in Munich. The **private bedroom** is the largest room, heavily ornamented and anchored by an enormous 108-candle crystal chandelier weighing 500kg. An artificial waterfall, built to cool the room in summer, cascades just outside the window. The **dining room** reflects the king's fetish for privacy and inventions. The king ate from a mechanised dining board, whimsically labelled 'Table, Lay Yourself', that sank through the floor so that his servants could replenish it without being seen.

The gardens and outbuildings, open April to October, are as fascinating as the castle itself. The highlight is the oriental-style **Moorish Kiosk**, where Ludwig, dressed in oriental garb, would preside over nightly entertainment from a peacock throne. Underwater light dances on the stalactites at the **Venus Grotto**, an artificial cave inspired by a stage set for Wagner's *Tannhäuser*. Now sadly empty, Ludwig's fantastic conch-shaped boat is moored by the shore.

Linderhof is about 13km west of Oberammergau and 26km northwest of Garmisch-Partenkirchen. Bus 9622 travels to Linderhof from Oberammergau several times a day, while RVO 9606 comes from Garmisch-Partenkirchen (€7, 1½ hours). If you're driving, parking costs €2.

Mittenwald

☎ 08823 / pop 8300

Nestled in a cul-de-sac under snow-capped peaks, the valley town of **Mittenwald**, 20km southeast of Garmisch-Partenkirchen, is the most natural spot imaginable for a resort. Known far and wide for its master violinmakers, the citizens of this dozy little place seem almost bemused by its popularity. The air is ridiculously clean, and on the main street the loudest noise is a babbling brook.

The **tourist office** (☎ 339 81; www.mittenwald.de; Dammkarstrasse 3; ☻ 8am-5pm Mon-Fri, 9am-noon Sat, 10am-noon Sun May-Sep) has details of excellent hiking and cycling routes. Popular hikes with cable-car access will take you up the granddaddy Alpspitze (2628m), as well as the Wank, Mt Karwendel and the Wettersteinspitze. Return tickets to Karwendel, which boasts

Germany's second-highest cable-car route, cost €21 per adult and €12 per child.

The Karwendel ski field has one of the longest runs (7km) in Germany, but it is primarily for hotdoggers and freestyle pros. Day ski passes to the nearby Kranzberg ski fields, the best all-round option, cost €21 per adult and €14 per child. For equipment hire and ski/snowboard instruction contact the **Erste Skischule Mittenwald** (☎ 3582; www.skischule -mittenwald.de; Bahnhofsplatz).

Other special events include **Fasnacht** (carnival) held in late February or early March, where locals in traditional masks handed down through families over centuries mix old rituals with new in an attempt to drive out winter.

The town gem, **Hotel-Gasthof Alpenrose** (☎ 927 00; www.alpenrose-mittenwald.de; Obermarkt 1; s €21-44, d €46-85; P) has cosy, old-style rooms, a cute, backwoodsy restaurant and live Bavarian music almost nightly. For gourmet fare, subtle sauces and flaming desserts, head to **Restaurant Arnspitze** (☎ 2425; Innsbrucker Strasse 68; mains €16-23; closed Tue).

Mittenwald is served by hourly trains from Garmisch-Partenkirchen (€3.40, 20 minutes), Munich (€18, 1¾ hours) and Innsbruck, across the border in Austria, (€8.90, one hour).

RVO bus 9605 connects Mittenwald with Garmisch-Partenkirchen (30 minutes) several times a day.

OBERSTDORF

☎ 08322 / pop 11,000

Spectacularly situated in the western Alps, the Allgäu region feels like a long, long way from the rest of Bavaria, both in its cuisine (more *Spätzle* noodles than dumplings) and the dialect, which is closer to the Swabian of Baden-Württemberg. Allgäu's chief draw is the car-free resort of Oberstdorf, a major skiing centre a short hop from Austria.

The **tourist office** (☎ 7000; www.oberstdorf .de; Marktplatz 7; 8.30am-noon & 2-6pm Mon- Fri, 9.30am-noon Sat) and its **branch office** (☎ 700 217; Bahnhof; 9am-8pm Mon-Sat, 9am-6pm Sun May-Oct, 9am-noon & 2-6pm Nov-Apr) can help with finding accommodation.

Like Garmisch, Oberstdorf is surrounded by towering peaks and offers superb hiking. For an exhilarating day walk, ride the Nebelhorn **cable car** (adult/child €18.50/8.50) to the upper station, then hike down via the **Gaisalpseen**, two lovely alpine lakes (six hours).

In-the-know skiers value the resort for its friendliness, lower prices and less-crowded pistes. The village is surrounded by 70km of groomed cross-country trails and three ski fields: the **Nebelhorn** (day/half-day passes €30/25.50), **Fellhorn/Kanzelwand** (day/half-day passes €32/27) and **Söllereck** (day/half-day passes €24/19.50). Ski passes good at all areas for one/two/three days cost €33/64/81.

For ski hire and tuition, try **Neue Skischule** (☎ 2737; www.neue-skischule-oberstdorf.de; Oststrasse 39), with outlets at the valley stations of the Nebelhorn and Söllereck lifts.

The **Eislaufzentrum Oberstdorf** (☎ 915 130), behind the Nebelhorn cable-car station, is the biggest ice-skating complex in Germany, with three separate rinks.

Sleeping & Eating

Oberstdorf is chock-full of private guesthouses, but some owners may be reluctant to rent rooms for just one night, especially during high season.

DJH hostel (☎ 2225; www.djh.de; Kornau 8; dm under/ over 26yr €17.30/21.20; Jan–mid-Nov) A relaxed chalet-type hostel with commanding views of the Allgäu Alps and very cool staff. Take the Kleinwalsertal bus to the Reute stop; it's in the suburb Kornau, near the Söllereck chairlift.

Hotel Sonnenheim (☎ 809 980; www.sonnenheim .oberstdorf.com; Waltenbergstrasse 6; s €24-35, d €48-90; P) This spacious and traditional hotel, a few minutes' walk east of the centre, has an intimate, hospitable feel. The nicer rooms have terraces with big sun shades, and facilities include a solarium.

Filser Kur-und Ferienhotel (☎ 7080; www.filserhotel .de; Freibergstrasse 15; s €81-104, d €81-112; P) This is one of many luxurious – but good-value – health resorts in the area, with sparkling facilities, including fitness rooms, pool and sauna. Rooms are stylishly decorated with modern simplicity and some elegant traditional touches. There's wheelchair access.

Mohren (☎ 9120; Marktplatz 6; mains €7-19; closed Mon) Right in the heart of town, this upscale restaurant has elegant striped chairs beneath a mirrored ceiling. The house speciality is mountain hay, employed in dishes from cream of hay soup to hay-flower sorbet with lemon balm.

Bella Italia (☎ 606 425; Sonthofener Strasse 19; mains €5-9; closed Mon) This earthy Italian eatery just outside the centre does some of the best pizzas in town, with incredibly tasty chewy crusts and generous toppings. Big-band tunes are piped into the dining area, which has a fine Alpine view.

Getting There & Away

There are some direct trains from Munich (€24.60, 2½ hours) and more with a change in Immenstadt. RVO buses 81 and 9718 go several times daily between Oberstdorf and Füssen (one-way/return €9/15.70, two hours).

BERCHTESGADEN & BERCHTESGADENER LAND

☎ 08652 / pop 7700

Steeped in myth and legend, Berchtesgadener Land enjoys a natural beauty so abundant that it's almost preternatural. A tale has it that angels, charged with handing out the Earth's wonders, were startled by God's order to hurry up and dropped them all here. Framed by six formidable mountain ranges and home to Germany's second-highest mountain, the Watzmann (2713m), the dreamy fir-lined valleys are filled with gurgling streams and peaceful Alpine villages.

Much of the terrain is protected by law within the Berchtesgaden National Park, home to the pristine Königssee, perhaps Germany's most photogenic lake. Outdoor activities, notably hiking, are plentiful. The mountain-top Eagle's Nest, a lodge built for Hitler, is a major drawcard, as is the Dokumentation Obersalzberg, a museum that chronicles the region's dark Nazi past. The area's wartime legacy is never far below the surface, as demonstrated by the prolonged debate over the propriety of building the Hotel Intercontinental on the nearby site of the Platterhof, once a Nazi 'people's hotel'. The prospect of drawing more luxury cash to the area outweighed the local council's qualms about erasing part of a key historical site, and the new hotel complex was finally unveiled in 2004.

Information

The Hauptbahnhof is also the bus station.

Hypovereinsbank (Weihnachtsschützenplatz 2½)

Internet Stadl (☎ 690 556; Königsseer Strasse 2; per 15min €1.50; 9am-7pm Mon-Sat, closed Wed morning & Sun) Coin-operated, high-speed internet access.

Nationalpark office (☎ 643 43; www.nationalpark -berchtesgaden.de; Franziskanerplatz 7, Berchtesgaden; 9am-5pm Mon-Sat) For hiking information.

Post Office (cnr Angergasse & Ludwig-Ganghofer-Strasse)

Tourist office (☎ 9670; www.berchtesgadener.de; Königsseer Strasse 2; 9am-6pm Mon-Sat, 10am-1pm & 2-6pm Sun May–mid-Oct, 9am-5pm Mon-Fri, 9am-noon Sat mid-Oct–Apr) Has a free room-booking service and an electronic room-reservation board outside.

Sights

DOKUMENTATION OBERSALZBERG

This should be the first stop on any tour of Berchtesgadener Land. A quiet mountain retreat 3km east of Berchtesgaden, Obersalzberg became the southern headquarters of Hitler's government. The fascinating **Dokumentation Obersalzberg** (☎ 947 960; Salzbergstrasse 41; adult/child under 16 €2.50/free; 9am-5pm Apr-Oct, 10am-3pm Tue-Sun Nov-Apr) leaves few stones unturned. The forced takeover of the area, the construction of the compound and the daily life of the Nazi elite are documented, and all facets of the Nazi terror regime – Hitler's near-mythical appeal, his racial politics, the resistance movement and the death camps – are covered in extraordinary depth. A section of the underground bunker network is open for touring. To get there take bus 838 from the Hauptbahnhof.

EAGLE'S NEST

Berchtesgaden's most sinister draw is Mt Kehlstein, a sheer-sided peak at Obersalzberg where Martin Bormann, a key henchman of Hitler's, engaged 3000 workers to build a diplomatic meeting-house for the Führer's 50th birthday. Perched at 1834m, the innocent-looking lodge (called Kehlsteinhaus in German) occupies one of the world's most breathtaking spots. Ironically, Hitler is said to have suffered from vertigo and rarely enjoyed the spectacular views himself.

From mid-May to October, the **Eagle's Nest** is open to visitors. To get there, drive or take bus 849 (€3.50 return) from the Hauptbahnhof to the Kehlstein bus departure area. From here the road is closed to private traffic and you must take a special **bus** (www.kehlsteinhaus.de; adult/child €13/12; 7.20am-4pm) up the mountain (35 minutes). The final 124m stretch to the summit is in a luxurious, brass-clad lift (elevator). The Eagle's Nest now houses a restaurant that donates profits to charity.

SALZBERGWERK

Once a major producer of 'white gold', Berchtesgaden has thrown open its **salt mines** (☎ 600 20; adult/concession €12.90/7.50; 9am-5pm May–mid-Oct, 12.30-3.30pm Mon-Sat mid-Oct–Apr) for fun-filled tours (90 minutes). Visitors don traditional miners' gear and slip down a wooden slide into the depths of the mine. Down below, the highlights include mysteriously glowing salt grottoes and the crossing of a 100m-long subterranean salt lake on a wooden raft.

KÖNIGSSEE

Crossing the beautiful, emerald-green **Königssee** is an unforgettable experience. Framed by steep mountain walls just 5km south of Bercht esgaden, it's the country's highest lake (603m) with clear waters shimmering into fjord-like depths. Electric boat tours (adult/child €11/5, two hours) operate year-round to **St Bartholomä**, a quaint onion-domed chapel on the western shore. At some point, the boat will stop while

the captain plays a Flügelhorn towards the amazing **Echo Wall** – the melody will bounce seven times. About an hour's hike from the dock at St Bartholomä is the **Eiskapelle** (Ice Chapel), where an ice dome grows every winter to heights of over 200m. In late summer the ice melts and the water tunnels a huge opening in the solid ice.

Activities
HIKING

The wilds of the 210-sq-km Berchtesgaden National Park offer some of the best hiking in Germany. A good introduction is a 2km path up from St Bartholomä beside the Königssee to the notorious Watzmann-Ostwand, where scores of mountaineers have met their deaths.

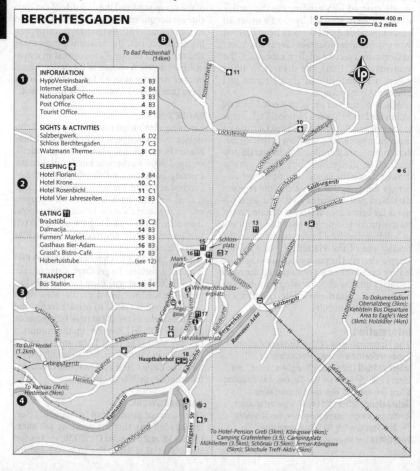

BERCHTESGADEN

Another popular hike goes from the southern end of the Königssee to the Obersee. For details of hiking routes visit the Nationalpark office (p351).

SKIING

The **Jenner-Königssee area** (☎ 958 10; daily passes adult/child €24/13.50) at Königssee is the biggest, most varied of five local ski fields. For equipment hire and courses, try **Skischule Treff-Aktiv** (☎ 667 10; www.treffaktiv.de; Jennerbahnstrasse 19, Schönau).

WATZMANN THERME

Berchtesgaden's thermal wellness and fun **pool complex** (☎ 946 40; Bergwerkstrasse 54; tickets per 2/4/10hr €8.30/10.80/€15.30; ☺ 10am-10pm) has several indoor and outdoor pools with various hydrotherapeutic treatment stations, a sauna and fabulous Alpine views.

Tours

An excellent way to experience the creepy legacy of the Obersalzberg area, including the Eagle's Nest and the underground bunker system, is a four-hour guided tour with **Eagle's Nest Tours** (☎ 649 71; www.eagles-nest-tours .com; adult/child €40/30; ☺ 1.30pm mid-May–Oct). Buses depart from the tourist office and reservations are advised, although a second service runs at 8.30am on request.

Sleeping

Berchtesgaden has plenty of private rooms from €25 per person; check with the tourist office about availability.

DJH hostel (☎ 943 70; www.djh.de; Gebirgsjägerstrasse 52; dm under/over 26yr €6.10/21.10; ☺ closed Nov-late Dec)

This 360-bed hostel is situated in the suburb of Strub, and has great views of Mt Watzmann, but has a 10pm curfew. It's a 25-minute walk from the Hauptbahnhof or a short journey on bus 9539.

Hotel Floriani (☎ 660 11; www.hotel-floriani.de; Königsseer Strasse 37; s €35-43, d €46-66; P) This incredibly friendly and English-speaking *pension* is just past the tourist office and within walking distance of the station. The comfortable, modern rooms are great value and some have spacious balconies. There are also a couple of reasonably priced apartments.

Hotel-Pension Greti (☎ 946 50; www.pension-greti .de; Waldhauserstrasse 20, Schönau; s €34-37, d €58-68; P) Warm and welcoming, and just a 15-minute walk from the Königssee, all of Greti's rooms are in a well-appointed country style with balconies. The cellar bar is perfect for winding down post-piste.

Hotel Krone (☎ 946 00; Am Rad 5; www.hotel-krone -berchtesgaden.de; s €35-48, d €70-96; P) This family-run English-speaking gem, a short walk from the town centre, has fine views of the valley and the Alps beyond. Lodge-style rooms are generously sized, with carved wooden ceilings, niches and bedsteads. The sunny terrace is perfect for breakfast.

Hotel Vier Jahreszeiten (☎ 9520; www.berchtes gaden.com/vier-jahreszeiten; Maximilianstrasse 20; s €49-72, d €79-138; P ☎) For a glimpse of Berchtesgaden's storied past, stay at this traditional Alpine lodge where Bavarian royalty once entertained. Rooms have panoramic views of the mountains and the in-house restaurant couldn't be more atmospheric.

Hotel Rosenbichl (☎ 944 00; www.hotel-rosen bichl.de; Rosenhofweg 24; d €88-148; P ✗) This

---

HITLER'S MOUNTAIN RETREAT

Of all the German towns tainted by the Third Reich, Berchtesgaden has a burden heavier than most. Hitler fell in love with nearby Obersalzberg in the 1920s, and bought a small country home, later enlarged into the imposing Berghof.

After seizing power in 1933, Hitler established a part-time headquarters here and brought much of the party brass with him. They bought, or often confiscated, large tracts of land and tore down farmhouses to erect a 7ft-high barbed-wire fence. Obersalzberg was sealed off as the fortified southern headquarters of the NSDAP (National Socialist German Workers' Party). In 1938, British prime minister Neville Chamberlain visited for negotiations (later continued in Munich) which led to the infamous promise of 'peace in our time' at the expense of the invasion of Czechoslovakia.

Little is left of Hitler's Alpine fortress today. In the final days of WWII, the Royal Air Force levelled much of Obersalzberg, though the Eagle's Nest, Hitler's mountain-top eyrie, was left strangely unscathed. The historical twist and turns are dissected at an impressive exhibit called Dokumentation Obersalzberg (p351).

comfortable wellness hotel in the middle of the protected nature zone offers exceptional value. The rooms are spacious, modern and packed with perks, while guests enjoy a sauna, whirlpool, solarium and fitness area.

The nicest camping grounds are near the Königssee in Schönau. **Campingplatz Mühlleiten** (☎ 4584; www.camping-muehlleiten.de; Königsseer Strasse 70; site/person €6/5.20) and **Camping Grafenlehen** (☎ 4140; www.camping-grafenlehen.de; Königsseerfussweg 71; site/person €6/5.20) are the best bets.

Eating

Weekly farmer's markets that sell meats, cheese and produce are held at Marktplatz every Friday morning between April and October.

Bräustübl (☎ 1423; Bräuhausstrasse 13; mains €5-16, Brotzeit €3.50-9) Come to this 19th-century brewery for organic schnitzel and classy salads, served in a pretty inner courtyard tucked away in a quiet spot. In summer, the beer-hall stage is witness to a heel-whacking Bavarian stage show every Saturday night.

Hubertusstube (☎ 9520; Maximilianstrasse 20; mains €10-22) Part of the Hotel Vier Jahreszeiten, this restaurant offers rich pickings such as roasted brook trout or sauté of venison, plus there's a choice vegetarian menu. The dining areas have excellent views of the mountains.

Holzkäfer (☎ 621 07; Buchenhöhe 40; dishes €4-9; ☽ dinner only, closed Tue) This funky log-cabin restaurant in the hills around Obersalzberg is a great spot for a night out with fun-loving locals. Crammed with antlers, carvings and backwood oddities, it's known for its tender pork roasts, dark beers and list of Franconian wines. There's wheelchair access.

Other possibilities:

Gasthaus Bier-Adam (☎ 2390; Markt 22; mains €5-18) Cheerful place with a good range of traditional fare and nonsmoking room.

Dalmacija (☎ 976 027; Marktplatz 5; dishes €5-7) Pizzas, pastas and a whiff of the Balkans in a bistro-café teeming with young patrons.

Getting There & Away

From Munich, the quickest train link involves a change at Freilassing (€25.20, three hours). There are direct trains from Salzburg (€7.60, one hour), although RVO bus 840 (one-way/return €6.40/4.80) makes the trip in about 45 minutes and has more departures. Berchtesgaden is south of the Munich–Salzburg A8 autobahn.

Getting Around

The various communities of Berchtesgadener Land are well connected by **RVO bus** (www.rvo -bus.de). To get to the Königssee, take bus 9541 or 9542 from the Hauptbahnhof. Bus 9538 goes up the Obersalzberg. For a taxi call ☎ 4041.

FRANCONIA

In the northern part of Bavaria, the lovely rolling hills of Franconia are home to delicate wines, stunning parks and the meanders of the slow-moving Main River. Franconians see themselves as a breed apart from the brash extroverts of Upper Bavaria further south, and offer refreshingly low-key hospitality.

In the northwest, the region's wine-growers produce some exceptional wines sold in a distinctive teardrop-shaped bottle, the *Bocksbeutel*. For outdoor enthusiasts, the Altmühltal Nature Park offers wonderful hiking, biking and canoeing. But it is Franconia's old royalty and incredible cities – Nuremberg, Bamberg and Würzburg – that draw the most interest.

NUREMBERG

☎ 0911 / pop 493,000

Nuremberg (Nürnberg), Bavaria's second-largest city, is a vibrant place where the nightlife is intense and the beer is as dark as coffee. The city is one of Bavaria's biggest draws and is alive with visitors during summer and the spectacular Christmas market.

For centuries Nuremberg was the unofficial capital of the Holy Roman Empire and the preferred residence of German kings, who kept their crown jewels here. Rich and stuffed with comely architecture, it was also a magnet for famous artists like Albrecht Dürer, a native son. 'Nuremberg shines throughout Germany like a sun among the moon and stars,' gushed Martin Luther. In the 19th century the city was at the heart of the industrial revolution in Germany.

The Nazis saw in Nuremberg a perfect stage for their activities. It was here that the fanatical party rallies were held, the boycott of Jewish businesses began and the infamous Nuremberg Laws outlawing Jewish citizenship were enacted. On 2 January 1945, Allied bombers reduced the city to rubble and 6000 people were killed.

After WWII the city was chosen as the site of the War Crimes Tribunal, now known as the Nuremberg Trials. Later, the painstaking reconstruction – using the original stone – of almost all the city's main buildings, including the castle and old churches in the Altstadt, have returned the city to some of its former glory.

Orientation

Most major sights are within the Altstadt. The Hauptbahnhof is just outside the old city walls to the southeast. From here, pedestrian Königstrasse runs to the city centre, where the shallow Pegnitz River flows from east to west.

About 4km southeast of the centre is the enormous Reichsparteitagsgelände, the Nazi rally grounds also known as Luitpoldhain. The courthouse where the Nuremberg Trials were held is just off the Altstadt.

Information

BOOKSHOPS

Buchhandlung Edelmann (☎ 992 060; Kornmarkt 8) Travel section upstairs and some English-language novels downstairs.

Schmitt & Hahn (☎ 2146 711; Hauptbahnhof; ✆ 5.30am-11pm) Full selection of international press and a decent section of current paperbacks for those travelling light.

CULTURAL CENTRES

Amerika Haus (☎ 230 690; Gleissbühlstrasse 13) Impressive range of cultural and artistic programmes each month.

EMERGENCY

Ambulance (☎ 192 22)

INTERNET ACCESS

Netzkultur (☎ 211 0782; Färberstrasse 11, 3rd fl; per hr €3; ✆ 10am-1am Mon-Sat)

LAUNDRY

Schnell und Sauber (☎ 180 9400; per load €4; ✆ 6am-midnight) East (Sulzbacher Strasse 86; tram 8 to Deichslerstrasse); South (Allersberger Strasse 89; tram 4, 7 or 9 to Schweiggerstrasse); West (Schwabacher Strasse 86; U2 to St Leonhard)

MEDICAL SERVICES

Full-service hospitals close to the Altstadt:

Poliklinik (☎ 192 92; Kesslerplatz 5)
Unfallklinik Dr Erler (☎ 272 80; Kontumazgarten 4-18)

MONEY

Commerzbank (Königstrasse 21)
Hypovereinsbank (Königstrasse 3)
Reisebank (Hauptbahnhof)

POST

Main post office (Bahnhofplatz 1)

TOURIST INFORMATION

Tourist offices (☎ 233 60; www.tourismus.nuernberg .de) Königstrasse (Königstrasse 93; ✆ 9am-7pm Mon-Sat); Hauptmarkt (Hauptmarkt 18; ✆ 9am-6pm Mon-Fri, 10am-4pm Sun May-Sep, 9am-7pm Mon-Sat & 10am-7pm during Christkindlesmarkt) Staff sell the Nürnberg + Fürth Card (€18), good for two days of unlimited public transport and admission to most museums and attractions in both cities.

TRAVEL AGENCIES

Plärrer Reisen (☎ 929 760; Gostenhofer Hauptstrasse 27) Good all-round travel agency with a last-minute ticket desk at the airport.

Sights

HAUPTMARKT

This bustling square in the heart of the Altstadt is the site of markets and in particular the famous Chriskindlesmarkt (Chrismas Market). The ornate Gothic **Pfarrkirche Unsere Liebe Frau** (1350–58), better known as the Frauenkirche, was built as a repository for the crown jewels of Charles IV who, fearing theft, sent them instead to Prague for safekeeping. Beneath the clock the seven electoral princes march around Charles IV every day at noon.

Standing like a space probe on the north-west corner of the square is the 19m **Schöner Brunnen** (Beautiful Fountain). A replica of the late 14th-century original, it is a stunning golden vision of 40 electors, prophets, Jewish and Christian heroes and other allegorical figures. The first version, made of badly eroded sandstone, stands in the Germanisches Nationalmuseum. On the market side hangs a seamless **golden ring**, polished bright by millions of hands. A local superstition has it that if you turn it three times, your wish will come true.

ALTES RATHAUS & ST SEBALDUSKIRCHE

Beneath the Altes Rathaus (1616–22), a hulk of a building with lovely Renaissance-style interiors, you'll find the gory **Lochgefängnisse** (Medieval Dungeons; ☎ 231 2690; Rathausplatz; tours adult/

BAVARIA

concession €2/1; 10am-4.30pm Tue-Sun Apr-Oct; 10am-4.30pm Tue-Fri Nov-Mar, daily during Christkindlesmarkt). The 12 small cells and torture chamber must seen on a guided tour (held every half-hour) and might easily put you off lunch.

Opposite the Altes Rathaus stands the 13th-century **St Sebalduskirche**, which is Nuremberg's oldest church. Check out the ornate carvings that are over the **Bridal Doorway** to the north, and depict the Wise and Foolish Virgins. Inside the church, the highlight is the bronze shrine of **St Sebald**, which is a Gothic and Renaissance masterpiece that took its maker, Peter Vischer the Elder, as well as his two sons, more than 11 years to complete. Vischer is in it too, sporting a skullcap.

STADTMUSEUM FEMBOHAUS

Set in an ornate 16th-century merchant house, the **Fembo House Municipal Museum** (231 2595; Burgstrasse 15; adult/concession €4/2 for Noricama or general exhibit, both €6/3; 10am-5pm Tue-Fri, 10am-6pm Sat & Sun). Highlights of this entertaining overview include the restored historic rooms of this 16th-century merchant house and a flashy multimedia show, Noricama, which journeys through 950 years of Nuremberg's history.

FELSENGÄNGE

Under the **Albrecht Dürer Monument** on Albrecht-Dürer-Platz are four storeys of chilly corridors through the **Felsengänge** (227 066; adult/concession €4/3; tours at 11am, 1pm, 3pm & 5pm, 3-person minimum). Bur-

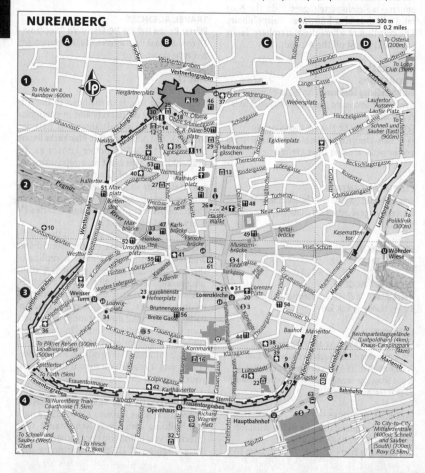

rowed into the sandstone in the 14th century to house a brewery and beer cellar, it also served as an air-raid shelter during WWII. The tunnels, which can only be seen on a tour, can get pretty chilly so take a jacket.

TIERGÄRTNERPLATZ

Framed by charming half-timbered houses, the **Tiergärtnertor** is a square tower from the 16th century. The long, dark passage underneath gives a suitable impression of the city's walls, in places up to 6m thick. On the square stands the beautiful late Gothic half-timbered **Pilatushaus**, owned by a wealthy maker of armour for kings and nobles. In front is Jürgen Goetz' bronze sculpture *Der Hase – Hommage à Dürer* (The Hare – A Tribute to Dürer, 1984). This nod to Dürer's watercolour original, called *Junger Feldhase* (1502), shows the dire results of tampering with nature.

A few steps further east is the **Historischer Kunstbunker** (☎ 227 066; Obere Schmiedgasse 52; tours adult/concession €4.50/3.50; ☼ tours 3pm Apr–Oct & Dec, Sat & Sun only Jan–Mar & Nov), a climate-controlled bomb shelter used to protect key artworks during WWII. Works were kept here by Albrecht Dürer, sculptor Veit Stoss and Martin Behaim, the maker of a bafflingly accurate 15th century globe. Tickets are available only from brewpub **Hausbrauerei Altstadthof** (Burgstrasse 19).

KAISERBURG

A must-see is the humungous **Kaiserburg** (Imperial Castle; ☎ 244 6590; Burg; adult/concession incl museum €6/5, well & tower only €3/2; ☼ 9am–6pm Apr–Sep, 10am–4pm Oct–Mar). Construction began here during the Hohenstaufen reign in the 12th century, and dragged on 400 years. The complex embraces the Kaiser's living quarters, a Romanesque chapel, the Imperial and Knights' Halls and the **Sinwellturm** (Sinwell Tower; 113 steps). There's also the amazing **Tiefer Brunnen** (Deep Well; 48m-deep), which still yields drinking water.

The **Kaiserburg Museum** (☎ 200 9540; Burg; adult/concession €5/4) chronicles the history of the castle and sheds light on medieval defence techniques. The grassy knoll in the southeast corner of the castle gardens is **Am Ölberg**, a great spot to sit and gaze out over the city's rooftops.

ALBRECHT-DÜRER-HAUS

Germany's most famous Renaissance draughtsman, Dürer lived and worked at the **Albrecht-Dürer-Haus** (☎ 231 2568; Albrecht-Dürer-Strasse 39; adult/concession €5/2.50; ☼ 10am–5pm Tue–Sun, 10am–8pm Thu) from 1509 till his death in 1528. Several of his graphic works are on display, and a multimedia version of Agnes, his wife, takes visitors through the master's recreated workshop.

BAVARIA

BAVARIA

SPIELZEUGMUSEUM

The **Spielzeugmuseum** (Toy Museum; ☎ 231 3164; Karlstrasse 13-15; adult/concession €5/2.50; ☼ 10am-5pm Tue-Fri, 10am-6pm Sat & Sun) exhibits playthings from many periods – from wooden ships and paper figures to electric trains and computer games. Kids and parents will love the play area.

WEINSTADL & HENKERSTEG

On the north side of the Pegnitz, near the Karlsbrücke, is the impressive half-timbered **Weinstadel**, an old wine depot with two half-timbered stories jutting out over the Pegnitz. It has had a storied life, ranging from lepers' refuge to student dorm. Crossing the river is the covered wooden **Henkersteg** (Hangman's Bridge), built to keep the hangman's exposure to disease at a minimum.

EHEKARUSSELL BRUNNEN

At the foot of the fortified **Weisser Turm** (White Tower) stands the amazing **Ehekarussell Brunnen** (Marriage Roundabout), a metallic fountain with six interpretations of marriage (from first love to quarrel to death-do-us-part) all based on a verse by Hans Sachs, the medieval cobbler-poet. The artist, Jürgen Weber, faced a storm of criticism when the fountain was unveiled in 1984. On Hefnersplatz, the townsfolk had fewer quibbles with another modern fountain, the **Peter-Henlein-Brunnen** dedicated to the 16th-century tinkerer who is credited with making the first pocket watch.

LORENZKIRCHE

Lorenzer Platz is dedicated to one of the church's first archivists, St Lawrence, a revered Catholic saint. Nuremberg's Catholics were once split into competing factions, one north and the other south of the river; the latter made a statement with **Lorenzkirche** (Church of St Lawrence), a massive 15th-century church crammed with artistic treasures. Highlights include the stained-glass windows (including a Rosetta window 9m in diameter) and Veit Stoss' *Engelsgruss* (Annunciation), a wooden carving with life-size figures suspended above the high altar.

The **Tugendbrunnen** (Fountain of Virtues), on the north side of the church, shows the seven ladies proudly spouting water from their breasts in the shadow of a figure of Justice.

REICHSPARTEITAGSGELÄNDE

The black-and-white images of ecstatic Nazi supporters hailing their Führer were filmed in Nuremberg. This orchestrated propaganda began as early as 1927, but after 1933 Hitler opted for a purpose-built venue, the **Reichsparteitagsgelände** (Nazi Party Rally Grounds). Much of the outsized grounds was destroyed during Allied bombing raids, but enough is left to get a sense of the megalomania behind it.

At the northwestern edge was the **Luitpoldarena**, designed for mass SS and SA parades. The area is now a park. South of here, the half-built **Kongresshalle** (Congress Hall) was meant to outdo Rome's Colosseum in both scale and style.

To put the grounds into a historical context, visit the **Dokumentationszentrum** (Documentation Centre; ☎ 231 7538; Bayernstrasse 110; adult/student €5/2.50; ☼ 9am-6pm Mon-Fri, 10am-6pm Sat & Sun) in the north wing of the Kongresshalle. A stunning walkway of glass cuts diagonally through the complex, ending with an interior view of the congress hall. Inside, the exhibit *Fascination and Terror* examines the rise of the NSDAP, the Hitler cult, the party rallies and the Nuremberg Trials. Don't miss it.

East of the Kongresshalle, across the artificial Dutzendteich (Dozen Ponds), is the **Zeppelinfeld**, fronted by a 350m-long grandstand, the **Zeppelintribüne**, where most of the big Nazi parades, rallies and events took place. Sporting events and rock concerts take place here now, although this rehabilitation is still hotly disputed.

The grounds are bisected by the 60m-wide **Grosse Strasse** (Great Road), which culminates, 2km south, at the **Märzfeld** (March Field), which was planned as military exercise grounds. West of the Grosse Strasse was to have been the **Deutsches Stadion** with a seating capacity of 400,000. Things never got beyond the first excavation, and the hole filled with groundwater – today's Silbersee.

To get to the grounds, take tram 4 to Dutzendteich or tram 9 to Luitpoldhain. Both trams pass the Hauptbahnhof.

NUREMBERG TRIALS COURTHOUSE

Nazi war criminals were tried for crimes against peace and humanity in the **Schwurgerichtssaal 600** (Courtroom 600; ☎ 231 5421; Fürther Strasse 110; adult/concession €2.50/1.25; ☼ tours 1-4pm hourly Sat & Sun). The Allies chose Nuremberg for obvious symbolic reasons. In addition, the building was easily accessible and one of few such complexes to survive the war intact.

Held in 1945–46, the trials resulted in the conviction and sentencing of 22 Nazi leaders and 150 underlings, and the execution of dozens. Among those condemned to death were Joachim von Ribbentrop, Alfred Rosenberg, Wilhelm Frick and Julius Streicher. Hermann Göring, the Reich's field marshal, cheated the hangman by taking cyanide in his cell hours before his scheduled execution.

To get there take the U1 to Bärenschanze.

GERMANISCHES NATIONALMUSEUM

One of the most important museums of German culture, the **Germanisches Nationalmuseum** (☎ 133 10; Kartäusergasse 1; adult/concession €5/4; ☺ 10am-6pm Tue-Sun, 10am-9pm Wed) is strangely underrated. It features an archaeological collection, arms and armour, musical and scientific instruments and toys – but the jewel in its crown is the **art section**. This varied exhibit not only boasts exquisite paintings, but also sculpture, historical garments, porcelain and glass objects. The display is due to expand in 2007, when the original hall is reopened after a lengthy revamp.

Dürer's work is featured prominently. It affords insight into the artist's enormous prestige at the Holy Roman court; his commissions included portraits for emperors Charlemagne and Sigrimund, whose faces appeared on the doors of the imperial chambers. The artist's celebrated *Hercules Slaying the Stymphalian Birds* confirms his superb grasp of anatomical detail and a flash of mischief (Dürer put his own facial features on the Greek hero). The many other gems include Albrecht Altdorfer's *Victory of Charlemagne over the Avars near Regensburg*, whose impossible detail tests the human eye. Large, lavishly coloured parchments abound, such as Valchenborch's *Crossing of the Red Sea*.

Pick up an audio-guide (€1.50) as few labels are in English. Free guided tours in English take place at 2pm on the first and third Sunday of each month (normal admission is still charged).

At the street leading to the museum, the **Way of Human Rights** is a row of symbolic white concrete pillars (and one oak tree) bearing the 30 articles of the Universal Declaration of Human Rights. Each pillar is inscribed in German and, in succession, the language of a people whose rights have been violated. The oak represents the languages not explicitly mentioned.

VERKEHRSMUSEUM

Nuremberg's impressive **Verkehrsmuseum** (☎ 0180-444 22 33; Lessingstrasse 6; adult/concession €3/2; ☺ 9am-5pm Tue-Sun) combines two exhibits under one roof: one about the **Deutsche Bahn** (German Railways) and one about **Kommunikation**. The former is an entertaining display that explores the history of Germany's legendary rail system. You'll see the country's first engine, the *Adler*, which ran from Nuremberg to nearby Fürth in 1852. Other fine specimens include Ludwig II's gilded carriage (dubbed the 'rolling Neuschwanstein' for its starry ceiling fresco and lavish decoration) and Bismarck's sober quarters for official visits. A highlight is the hourly demonstration of one of Germany's largest model railways, run by a controller at a huge console of blinking lights and switches. The upstairs section covers the evolution of the postal system, but apart from some elaborate delivery coaches, isn't terribly riveting.

NEUES MUSEUM

Housed in a spectacular building with an all-glass façade, the **Neues Museum** (☎ 240 2010; Luitpoldstrasse 5; adult/concession €3.50/2.50; ☺ 10am-8pm Tue-Fri, 10am-6pm Sat & Sun) has the suitable panache of a museum devoted to art and design. The upper floor displays contemporary art (mostly abstracts) while the lower showcases the major developments in design since 1945. For a free peek at the exhibits, just stand in the courtyard outside.

HANDWERKERHOF

A re-creation of a crafts quarter of old Nuremberg, the Handwerkerhof is a self-contained tourist trap by the Königstor. It's about as quaint as a hammer on your thumbnail, but if you're cashed up you may find some decent merchandise.

JÜDISCHES MUSEUM FRANKEN IN FÜRTH

A quick U-Bahn ride away in the neighbouring town of Fürth is the **Jüdisches Museum Franken in Fürth** (Frankish Jewish Museum; ☎ 770 577; Königstrasse 89; adult/concession €3/2; ☺ 10am-5pm Wed-Sun, 10am-8pm Tue). Fürth once had the largest Jewish congregation of any city in southern Germany, and this museum, housed in a handsomely

BAVARIA

restored building, chronicles the history of Jewish life in the region from the Middle Ages to today. To reach the museum, you take the U1 to the Rathaus stop in Fürth.

Walking Tour

> **WALK FACTS**
> **Start** Hauptmarkt
> **Finish** Hauptmarkt
> **Distance** 2.5km
> **Duration** 2 hours

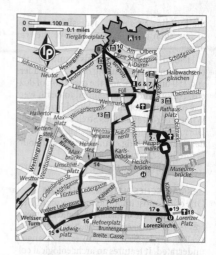

This circuit covers the main sights of the historic city over a leisurely 2.5km walk. With visits to all the museums and attractions listed, it could take the best part of two days.

The tour starts on **Hauptmarkt**, the main square. At the eastern end is the ornate Gothic **Pfarrkirche Unsere Liebe Frau (1)**, or Frauenkirche. The clock's figures spring into action every day at noon. The **Schöner Brunnen (2**; Beautiful Fountain) rises up from the cobblestones like a misplaced spire. Walk north to the Altes Rathaus, the old town hall with its **Lochgefängnisse (3)**, the medieval dungeons. Opposite stands the 13th-century **Sebalduskirche (4)**, with an exterior smothered in religious sculptures and a bronze shrine of St Sebald inside. Just up Burgstrasse, the **Fembo House Municipal Museum (5)** covers the highs and lows of Nuremberg's past with a multimedia show. Backtrack south to Halbwachsengässchen and turn right into Albrecht-Dürer-Platz and a dignified statue of the great painter, the **Albrecht Dürer Monument (6)**. Directly beneath are the **Felsengänge (7)**, tunnels once used as an old beer cellar and an air-raid shelter.

Moving up Bergstrasse, you'll reach the massive **Tiergärtnertor (8)**, a 16th century tower. Nearby is the comely, half-timbered **Pilatushaus (9)** and a strange, glassy-eyed hare dedicated to master Dürer. A few steps east is the **Historischer Kunstbunker (10)** where precious art was stored in WWII. Looming over the scene is the **Kaiserburg (11)**, the castle of medieval knights with imperial chambers. Go south to the **Albrecht-Dürer-Haus (12)** where the Renaissance genius lived and worked. Continue south along Albrecht-Dürer-Strasse, turn left on Füll and skirt the back of Sebalduskirche to Karlsstrasse, where you'll reach the **Spielzeugmuseum (13)**, with masses of amusing toys.

Cross the Karlsbrücke to enjoy a view of the **Weinstadel (14)**, an old wine depot overlooking the river. Continue across the Henkersteg (Hangman's Bridge) and wend your way south to Vordere Ledergasse, which leads west to the amazing **Ehekarussell Brunnen (15)**, with its outrageous views on marriage. Head east on Ludwigsplatz past the **Peter-Henlein-Brunnen (16)**, with a statue of the first watch-maker, and proceed along Karolinenstrasse to reach the city's oldest house, **Nassauer Haus (17)** at No 2, and the massive **Lorenzkirche (18)**, a 15th-century tabernacle with a suspended carving of the Annunciation. The **Tugendbrunnen (19)**, a fountain of the seven Virtues, is on the north side of the church.

Continuing north up Königstrasse will return you to the Hauptmarkt, your starting point.

Tours

The tourist office runs English-language **Old Town walking tours** (adult/child under 14yr €8/free; ☼ 1pm May-Oct & Dec), which include admission to Kaiserburg. Tours leave from the Hauptmarkt branch and take 2½ hours.

Other organised tours include the following:
History for Everyone (☎ 307 360; adult/concession €5/3.50; ☼ 2pm Sat & Sun, Sun only Dec-Mar; 2hr) Intriguing two-hour tours of the Nazi rally grounds by a nonprofit association, in English. Meet at Luitpoldhain, the terminus of tram 9, 4km to the east.
Nachtwächterin (☎ 997 207; tours €6; ☼ 9pm Mar-Sep, 7pm Oct-Dec) Night watchman tours, in German; meets at Hauptmarkt.

Festivals & Events

From late November to Christmas Eve, the Hauptmarkt is taken over by the most famous **Christkindlesmarkt** (Christmas Market) in Germany. Scores of colourful stalls selling mulled wine, spirits, roast sausages and trinkets fill the square as the smell of *Lebkuchen* (large, soft, spicy biscuits) wafts overhead.

Sleeping

Accommodation gets tight and rates rocket during the Christmas market and toy fair (trade only) in late January to early February. At other times, cheap rooms can be found, especially if you book ahead.

BUDGET

Knaus-Campingpark 'Am Dutzendteich' (☎ 981 2717; knaus.camp.nbg@freenet.de; Hans-Kalb-Strasse 56; per tent/person €2/5) A camping ground near the lakes in the Volkspark, southeast of the city centre. Take the U1 to Messezentrum, then walk about a kilometre.

Lette 'm sleep (☎ 992 8128; www.backpackers.de; Frauentormauer 42; dm €16-20, d €44-52, linen €3; 🖳) A backpacker favourite, this independent hostel is conveniently located within the old town wall, just five minutes from the Hauptbahnhof. It's a great place to meet fellow travellers, with a cosy common room, kitchen, bar and free web access, and the hosts are a mine of local information. The many options include dorms, doubles and apartments.

DJH hostel (☎ 230 9360; www.djh.de; Burg 2; dm under/over 26yr €20.70/24.70) In the former castle stables, this excellent, spotless hostel has 317 beds in bright airy dorms, as well as a piano and table tennis. It's about a 20-minute walk north of the Hauptbahnhof.

Probst-Garni Hotel (☎ 203 433; fax 205 93 36; Luitpoldstrasse 9; s €42-51, d €57-67) A pleasant, family-run outfit in the old centre, with spacious modern quarters, as clean as a new pin. All 34 rooms are on the third floor and are nicely removed from the bustle at street level. Rooms with bathrooms have TVs, and there are a couple of smaller, cheaper rooms with shared bath.

MIDRANGE

Hotel Lucas (☎ 227 845; www.hotel-lucas.de; Kaiserstrasse 22; s €65-105, d €90-125; ✗ 🖳) This boutique hotel in the heart of the city offers excellent value and service. There are refined touches throughout, like exposed beams and moveable bed frames that instantly convert two singles

into a double bed. The nicer rooms jut out over the rushing waters of the Regnitz, just upstairs from the pleasant café.

Hotel Drei Raben (☎ 274 380; www.hotel-drei-raben.de; Königstrasse 63; s €50-170, d €80-170; ✗) This designer hotel builds upon the legend of three ravens perched on the building's chimney stack, who tell each other stories from Nuremberg lore. Each of the 21 rooms uses its style and humour and to tell a particular tale – from the life of Dürer to the history of the locomotive. The FC Nürnberg room features a foosball table-cum-writing desk. Staff are delightful.

Hotel Deutscher Kaiser (☎ 242 660; www.deutscher-kaiser-hotel.de; Königstrasse 55; s €70-138, d €98-178; 🅿 ✗ 🖳) A grand sandstone staircase leads to ornately decorated rooms in this 1880s-built hotel in the Altstadt. The 'Kaiser' rooms are slightly dearer but superior to the standard doubles, with bidets in the bathrooms, brocaded curtains and carved bedsteads. The elegant reading room is a gem.

Hotel Elch (☎ 249 2980; www.hotel-elch.de; Irrerstrasse 9; s €65, d €85; 🖳 ⚅) This friendly hotel, based in a 14th-century half-timbered house near the Kaiserburg, has small but comfy rooms up a narrow medieval staircase. Breakfast is served in the quaint woody restaurant, the Schnitzelria, which does a good line in Franconian beers and, yes, schnitzel.

Am Jakobsmarkt (☎ 200 70; www.hotel-am-jakobsmarkt.de; Schottengasse 5; s €79-125, d €103-179; 🅿 ✗ 🖳) Choose from contemporary or traditional rooms at this well-run hotel, reached via a tiny courtyard near the Spittlertor. Unexpected extras include a sauna, solarium and fitness room.

TOP END

Agneshof (☎ 214 440; www.agneshof-nuernberg.de; Agnesgasse 10; s €90-175, d €112-225; 🅿 ✗ 🖳) The Agneshof is a real pleasure – an oasis of calm with an upbeat artsy air, top-notch facilities and elegant modern rooms. If you feel like some pampering, try the whirlpool and in-house health treatments. The comfy Kaiser suites offer unparalleled views of the castle. There's also wheelchair access.

Eating

RESTAURANTS

Barfüsser Kleines Brauhaus (☎ 204 242; Königstrasse 60; mains €6-13) Munch on hearty Franconian specialities among the copper vats, enamel advertising plaques and oodles of knick-knacks in this atmospheric old grain warehouse, where you can practically lose yourself in the cavernous vaulted cellar. Serious quaffers go for the *Eichenholzfässchen*, a 5L oak-wood keg of beer.

Café am Trödelmarkt (☎ 208 877; Trödelmarkt; dishes €3.50-11) A gorgeous spot on a sunny day, this café is an excellent choice for breakfast or lunch. It overlooks the covered Henkersteg bridge and offers creative salads, filled baguettes and a bevy of seasonal dishes, such as pike-perch grilled fresh off the hook.

Hütt'n (☎ 201 9881; Burgstrasse 19; mains €8-12) This local haunt is perpetually overflowing with admirers of *Krustenschäufele* (roast pork with crackling, dumplings and sauerkraut salad) so be prepared to queue. There's also a near-endless supply of schnapps.

Burgwächter (☎ 222 126; Am Ölberg 10; mains €5.50-12) In the shadow of the castle, this is a great place, with a terraced beer garden and terrific city views. The prime steaks and grilled cuts will please carnivores but there are also homemade filled pastas and salads.

Kettensteg (☎ 221 081; Maxplatz 35; mains €6.50-15) This leafy restaurant is Nuremberg's best open-air option away from the crowds. It offers a modern twist on Franconian fare, serving traditional dishes with a waistline-friendly approach.

Enchilada (☎ 244 8498; Obstmarkt 5; mains €8-12) This Mexican haunt with faux adobe walls does generous taco platters, burritos and nachos in a candlelit setting. Later on, the cocktail lists come out for the patrons flowing in from the Hauptmarkt nearby.

Prison St Michel (☎ 221 191; Irrerstrasse 2-4; mains €7-20; ☽ dinner) This is one of Nuremberg's elegant gourmet restaurants, with the evening's fresh cuts displayed in the window. It's noted for its excellent sole and dorade, as well as choice cuts of prime beef; try the Chateaubriand and lamb filets. It's great for an intimate, romantic night out in a quiet street near the castle.

Also recommended:

Heilig-Geist-Spital (☎ 221 761; Spitalgasse 12; mains €7.50-19) Classic Nuremberg restaurant with an extensive wine list.

Landbierparadies (☎ 287 86 73; Rothenburger Strasse 26; mains €4.50-6.50; ☽ evenings) Pork roast and a wellspring of beers from deepest Franconia.

Osteria (☎ 558 283; Pirckheimer Strasse 116; mains €6-12) Boisterous hole-in-the-wall serving big tasty pizzas that dwarf your plate.

QUICK EATS

Naturkostladen Lotos (☎ 266 180; Untere Kreuzgasse; dishes €2-7) The organic fare at this health-food shop will go some way towards unclogging those arteries – try the lentil crème, spinach soup or veggie pizza. The fresh bread and cheese counter is a treasure chest of picnic supplies.

Souptopia (☎ 240 6697; Lorenzer Strasse 27; soups €2.50-5; ☽ closed Sun) These homemade soups, made fresh daily and backed up by a good choice of sandwiches, salads and other veggie options, are a real winner.

Sushi to Go (☎ 242 5143; Hintere Ledergasse 2; mains €6-15; ☽ noon-2pm & 6-8pm) This Californian-style sushi bar in a former Bavarian pub has great deals, such as a 'Bento' – miso soup, three pieces of sushi, a spring roll and chicken teriyaki for €9.45. They do great business with takeaway customers.

Wok Man (☎ 240 6697; Lorenzer Strasse 27; soups €2.50-5; ☽ closed Sun) This is a decent, self-service Chinese fast-food place in the pedestrian zone, with spring rolls and large platters of chow mein.

NUREMBERG SAUSAGES

There's hot competition between Regensburg and Nuremberg over whose sausages are the best; the latter's are certainly more famous. Sample them for yourself at the following places.

Bratwursthäusle (☎ 227 695; Rathausplatz 1; dishes €5.80-12; ☽ closed Sun) Cooked over a flaming beechwood grill, the little links sold at this rustic inn arguably set the standards for *Rostbratwürste* across the land. You can dine in the timbered restaurant or on the terrace with views of the Hauptmarkt.

Bratwurstglöcklein im Handwerkerhof (☎ 227 625; Handwerkerhof; dishes €3-7) Despite its location in the kitsch Handwerkerhof, the sausages here are good. *Drie in a Weckla* (three links in a roll) will cost you loose change.

Drinking

Saigon Bar (☎ 244 8657; Lammsgasse 8; ☽ from 9pm Thu-Sun) A worthy last gasp to any night out, the Saigon is the quintessential late-night bar for steel-livered Nurembergers. The poison of choice is a *caipirinha*, prepared with smashed limes, brown sugar, crushed ice and white Pitú rum, just like they do it in Rio.

Treibhaus (☎ 223 041; Karl-Grillenberger-Strasse 28) Well off the path of most visitors, this bustling, smoky café is a Nuremberg institution. It serves breakfast till evening and drinks into the wee hours to students and weary shoppers.

Meisengeige (☎ 208 283; Am Laufer Schlagturm 3) This comfortable hole-in-the-wall bar draws an intense crowd of film intellectuals thanks to the tiny indie cinema next door.

Entertainment

The excellent **Plärrer** (www.plaerrer.de; €2), available at newsstands throughout the city, is the best source of information for events around town. Otherwise try the free **Doppelpunkt** (www.doppelpunkt.de), a monthly listings magazine found in bars, restaurants and the tourist office.

CLUBS

BA Hotel (☎ 237 30 51; Bahnhofstrasse 5; ☺ Wed-Sat) A play on its predecessor, the opulent Bavarian American Hotel, this smart new club-lounge features house music spun by top-flight DJs in retro surrounds. The spacious layout includes a cool lounge area, two bars and a ballroom, with plenty of corners for couples to edge into.

Loop Club (☎ 686 767; Klingenhofstrasse 52; ☺ Thu-Sat) With three dance areas and a languid chill-out zone with lounge music, this place attracts a more mature crowd. Every Thursday is 50-Cent night, a collective send-up with cheap mixed drinks flowing to the sound of '80s hits and karaoke. Take the U2 to Herrnhütte, turn right and it's a five-minute walk.

Hirsch (☎ 429 414; Vogelweiherstrasse 66) This converted factory south of the centre has live alternative music almost daily, as well as theme nights and a summer beer garden. Take the U1 to Frankenstrasse.

Mach1 (☎ 203 030; Kaiserstrasse 1-9; cover €4-8; ☺ Thu-Sat) This legendary dance temple has been around for decades but still holds a spell over fashion victims. Line up and be mustered.

CINEMA

Roxy (☎ 488 40; Julius-Lossmann-Strasse 116) This cinema shows first-run films in the original English version, a rarity in Nuremberg. Take tram 8 to the Südfriedhof stop.

THEATRE & CLASSICAL MUSIC

Nuremberg's magnificent **Städtische Bühnen** (Municipal Theatres; Richard-Wagner-Platz 2; www.staats

theater-nuernberg.de) serves up an impressive mix of dramatic arts. The renovated Art Nouveau opera house presents opera, ballet and readings, while the Kammerspiele offers a varied programme of classical and contemporary plays. Tickets are available at the box office or by calling ☎ 231 3808. The Nürnberger Philharmoniker also performs here.

Getting There & Away

Nuremberg airport (☎ 937 00), 7km north of the centre, is served by regional and international carriers, including Lufthansa, Air Berlin and Air France.

Trains run hourly to/from Frankfurt (€39, 2½ hours) and Munich (€41, 1½ to two hours). There are direct connections several times daily to Berlin (€77, five to 6½ hours) and Vienna (€96, 5½ hours), while a few slow trains also go to Prague (€42, six hours).

BerlinLinien buses leave for Berlin daily at 12.10pm (standard one-way €39, four hours). They leave from the Hauptbahnhof.

There's a ride-share service **CityToCity Mitfahrzentrale** (☎ 194 40; www.citytocity.de; Hummelsteiner Weg 12; ☺ 9am-6pm Mon-Fri, 9am-1.30pm Sat) right behind the south exit of the Hauptbahnhof.

Getting Around

TO/FROM THE AIRPORT

U-Bahn 2 runs every few minutes from Hauptbahnhof to the airport (€1.80, 12 minutes). A taxi to/from the airport will cost you about €15.

BICYCLE

The tourist office sells the ADFC's *Fahrrad Stadtplan* (€4.50), a detailed map of the city and surrounding area. It also hands out a list of bicycle-friendly hotels in town that will store bicycles for travellers. For bike hire try **Ride on a Rainbow** (☎ 397 337; Adam-Kraft-Strasse 55; per day €10-18).

PUBLIC TRANSPORT

The best transport around the Altstadt is at the end of your legs. Tickets on the VGN bus, tram and U-Bahn/S-Bahn networks cost €1.40/1.80 per short/long ride. A day pass costs €3.60. Saturday passes are valid all weekend.

TAXI

The starting rate for a **taxi ride** (☎ 194 10) is €2.50.

BAVARIA

ERLANGEN

☎ 09131 / pop 103,000

Erlangen, about 24km north Nuremberg, gained the vaunted status of a religious haven when Huguenots expelled from France settled here in the late 17th century. The town has quaint streets, a lovely palace garden and – unbeknownst to most visitors – a first-class botanical garden. Siemens, the electronics giant, is a major employer. Around Pentecost the **Erlanger Bergkirchweih**, a popular folk and beer festival, takes over the Burgberg for 12 days.

Orientation & Information

Hugenottenplatz is a short walk east of Bahnhofplatz, from where the pedestrianised Hauptstrasse leads north to Schlossplatz and the prettiest parts of the Altstadt. The **tourist office** (☎ 895 10; www.ekm-erlangen.de; Carreé am Rathausplatz; ⏰ 8.30am-5pm Mon-Thu, 8.30am-3pm Fri) is 1km south of the train station.

Sights & Activities

The pretty **Schloss** (a city palace, now home to the university administration) has a manicured Schlossgarten leading off to the rear. The striking, weathered sandstone fountain, the **Hugenottenbrunnen**, depicts the refugees at the bottom and a leading city elder at the top – surprise.

The adjacent **Botanischer Garten** (Botanical Garden; ☎ 852 2669; admission free; ⏰ 8am-5.30pm Mon-Fri Apr-Oct, 8am-3pm Mon-Fri Nov-Mar) is a hidden delight, with an exquisite set of dim, moss-lined greenhouses. Expect to find dense, fragrant rainforests, mini-biotopes with birds and fish, and paths with vines from Brazilian guava trees hanging in your face. Open-air concerts take place on the grounds.

Eating

Alter Simpl (☎ 256 26; Bohlenplatz 2; mains €6-12; ⏰ closed Sat eve & Sun) On a square just off Friedrichstrasse, this congenial, labyrinthine place is decorated in a rustic style with a great outdoor seating area. Try one of the hearty meat specials grilled over beechwood.

Tio (☎ 817 191; Südliche Stadtmauerstrasse 1a; mains €6-14) Over two striking levels of polished concrete, glass and steel, this trendy blue-lit bistro has smart, contemporary cuisine and good-value pizzas and salads.

A bustling **farmers market** (Marktplatz) is held daily. It overflows with produce and crackling-fresh snack options.

Getting There & Away

Regional trains to Nuremberg leave several times hourly (€3.40, 20 minutes).

BAMBERG

☎ 0951 / pop 71,000

It's difficult not to be impressed by Bamberg, clearly one of Germany's most beautiful cities. With a majestic centre, wonderful cathedral and superb palaces, this Unesco-listed place was built by archbishops on seven hills, earning it the sobriquet of 'Franconian Rome'.

Miraculously, Bamberg emerged from WWII with hardly a scratch, and most of the city's finest buildings are originals. Pristine examples of architecture from the Romanesque era onwards have survived, and a genuine charm and romance pervade the city. Bamberg is also justly famous for its beer; there are 10 breweries in town and another 80 or so in the vicinity.

Orientation

Two waterways bisect the city: the Main-Danube Canal, just south of the Hauptbahnhof, and the Regnitz River, which flows through the town centre. The city's bus hub, the Zentral-Omnibus Bahnhof (ZOB) is on Promenadestrasse, just off Schönleinsplatz.

Information

Bamberg Card (per 48hr €8) Provides admission to city attractions, use of city buses and a walking tour. It's available from the tourist office.

Citibank (Schönleinsplatz)

Hübscher (☎ 982 250; Grüner Markt 16; internet per 15min €1; ⏰ 9am-7pm Mon-Fri, 9am-5pm Sat) Large bookshop with English-language titles and web access upstairs.

Post office (Promenadestrasse & Ludwigstrasse 25)

Tourist office (☎ 871 161; www.bamberg.info; Geyerswörthstrasse 3; ⏰ 9.30am-6pm Mon-Fri, 9.30am-2.30pm Sat, 9.30am-2.30pm Sun Apr-Dec)

Sights

ALTSTADT

Bamberg's main appeal lies in its sheer number of fine historic buildings, their jumble of styles and the paucity of modern eyesores. Most attractions are sprinkled along the Regnitz River, but the town's incredibly statuesque **Altes Rathaus** is actually on it, perched on twin bridges like a ship in dry dock (note the cherub's leg sticking out from the fresco on the east side). To the northwest are the charming half-timbered homes of **Klein Venedig**

(Little Venice), complete with punts, canals and river docks.

DOM

Bamberg's princely and ecclesiastical roots are felt strongest around Domplatz on the southern bank of the Regnitz. The dominant structure is the soaring **cathedral** (Dom), which is the outcome of a Romanesque-Gothic duel fought by church architects after the original edifice burnt down (twice) in the 12th century. Politics dictated the final floor plan, which was altered each winter during 20 years of building. The interior is renowned for its fine acoustics, and from May to October free 30-minute organ concerts take place at noon on Saturday.

The pillars have the original light hues of Franconian sandstone thanks to Ludwig I, who in the 19th century ordered the removal of all postmedieval decoration. Traces of the bright 13th-century reliefs can still be seen in the choir. Look out for the **Lächelnde Engel** (Smiling Angel) in the north aisle, who smirkingly hands the martyr's crown to the headless St Denis. In the west choir is the marble tomb of **Pope Clemens II**, the only papal burial spot north of the Alps.

The star turn, however, and Bamberg's enduring mystery, is the statue of the **Bamberger Reiter**, a chivalric king-knight on a steed. Nobody knows for sure who he is, but one leading theory points towards Konrad III, the Hohenstaufen king buried in the cathedral. The Nazis seized on the heroic medieval image as a symbol of Aryan perfection.

Outside, an intriguing feature is the **Prince's Portal**, which shows Christ in an ornate sculpture of the Last Judgment. On the south side of the Dom, in a separate building off the cloisters, is the **Diözesan Museum** (☎ 502 316; Domplatz 5; adult/concession €3/2; 10am-5pm Tue-Sun). Top ranking among its ecclesiastical treasures goes to Heinrich II's Blue Coat of Stars, kept not far from the pontifical knee-socks of Clemens II.

AROUND DOMPLATZ

Northwest of the Dom is the **Alte Hofhaltung** (old court hall), a former prince-bishops' palace that contains the **Historisches Museum** (☎ 871 142; Domplatz 7; adult/concession €2.10/1.50; 9am-5pm Tue-Sun May-Oct). Its highlights include a model of the fantastic pilgrimage church Vierzehnheiligen (p371) and the Bamberger

Götzen, ancient stone sculptures found in the region.

Across the square, you'll spot the stately **Neue Residenz** (☎ 519 390; Domplatz 8; adult/concession €4/3; 9am-6pm Apr-Sep, 10am-4pm Oct-Mar), a huge episcopal palace. You can shuffle through 40-odd rooms, such as the elaborately decorated Kaisersaal (Imperial Hall), where the ceiling is smothered in a complex allegorical fresco. The **Rosengarten** (Rose Garden) behind the palace has fabulous views over the red-tiled roofs of the Altstadt.

MICHAELSBERG

Above Domplatz, at the top of Michaelsberg, is the Benedictine **Kloster St Michael**, a former monastery and now an aged person's home. The monastery church is a must-see, both for its baroque art and the meticulous depictions of nearly 600 medicinal plants and flowers on the vaulted ceiling. The manicured garden terrace boasts a splendid city panorama.

Also up here is the **Fränkisches Brauerei museum** (Franconian Brewery Museum; ☎ 530 16; Michaelsberg 10f; adult/concession €2/1.50; 1-5pm Wed-Sun Apr-Oct). Exhibits show plaster(ed) dummies of monks, who began brewing their Benediktiner Dunkel beer as early as 1122.

Tours

German-language guided **walking tours** (adult/child €5/3.50; 10.30am & 2pm Mon-Sat, 2pm Sun Apr-Oct; 2pm Mon-Sat, 11am Sun Nov-Mar) depart from the tourist office. You can also borrow an audioguide (€5) from the tourist office.

Sleeping

To book a room (from about €40/60 for singles/doubles) through the room reservations hotline, call ☎ 297 6310.

DJH hostel (☎ 339 09; www.djh.de; Oberer Leinritt 70; dm under/over 26yr €17.20/21.20, d €36.50; closed mid-Dec–Jan) About 2km from the Altstadt, this hostel has a terrific location on a slow-moving part of the Regnitz, in a former boathouse that's more like a hunting lodge. Take bus 18 to Rodelbahn.

Campingplatz Insel (☎ 563 20; www.campinginsel .de; Am Campingplatz 1; tents €3.50-7, adult/car €3.90/3.50) This well-equipped place, in a tranquil spot right on the river, is the sole camping option. Take bus 18 to Campingplatz.

Ambiente Klein Venedig (☎ 221 14; www .unterkunft-ferienwohnung-bamberg.de; Fischerei 31; s/d €37/55; P) If you want quiet upstairs rooms with an apartment quality, overlooking the Regnitz River, congenial English-speaking hosts and a big dollop of atmosphere…look no further.

Brauereigasthof Fässla (☎ 265 16; www.faessla .de; Obere Königstrasse 19-21; s/d €37/55; P) Those with more than a passing interest in the local brews should try this atmospheric guesthouse, where snug but modern rooms are just up the stairs from the pub and covered courtyard. Chairs in the popular restaurant are embossed with the Fässla logo, a gnome rolling a beer barrel.

Barockhotel am Dom (☎ 954031; www.barockhotel .de; Vorderer Bach 4; s/d €65/91; P X ▣) The sugary façade, a sceptre's swipe from the Dom, gives a hint of the baroque heritage and original details within. Rooms have sweeping views of the cathedral or over the roofs of the Altstadt, and breakfast is served in a 14th-century vault.

Hotel Sankt Nepomuk (☎ 6984 20; www.hotel -nepomuk.de; Obere Mühlbrücke 9; s/d €80/120; P) This classy but family-friendly place is located in an A-framed former mill right on the Regnitz. It has rustic rooms, a superb gourmet restaurant on the premises and bicycles for hire.

Hotel Residenzschloss (☎ 609 10; www.residenz schloss.com; Untere Sandstrasse 32; s/d €130/165; P X) Opposite the concert hall, one of Bamberg's best hotels occupies a historic former hospital. Its swanky furnishings, from the Roman-style steam bath to the flashy piano bar, have little in common with institutional care.

BAMBERG

0   300 m
0   0.2 miles

INFORMATION
Citibank..............................1 C3
Hübscher............................2 C2
Post Office..........................3 D1
Post Office..........................4 C2
Tourist Office......................5 C3

SIGHTS & ACTIVITIES
Alte Hofhaltung...................6 A3
Altes Rathaus......................7 B3
Diözesan Museum................8 B3
Dom...................................9 B3
Fränkisches Brauereimuseum....10 A2
Historisches Museum.........(see 6)
Klein Venedig (Little Venice)....11 B2

Kloster St Michael................12 A2
Michaelsberg...................(see 12)
Neue Residenz....................13 B3
Rosengarten.......................14 A3

SLEEPING
Ambiente Klein Venedig.......15 B2
Barockhotel am Dom...........16 B3
Brauereigasthof Fässla.........17 C2
Hotel Residenzschloss..........18 A3
Hotel Sankt Nepomuk..........19 C3

EATING
Ambräusianum....................20 B3
Bolero...............................21 B3
Josch.................................22 D3
Klosterbräu.........................23 B4
Messerschmitt....................24 C3
Salino................................25 C3
Spezial-Keller......................26 C4
Wirtshaus zum Schlenkerla....27 B3

DRINKING
Bassanese...........................28 B3
Café Esspress......................29 B3
Pelikan..............................30 A2

ENTERTAINMENT
Blues Bar & Jazz Keller.........31 B3
Downstairs.........................32 C3
Live Club............................33 B3

TRANSPORT
Fahrradhaus Griesmann.......34 C2
ZOB (Central Bus Station)....35 C2

Hauptbahnhof

To DJH Hostel (1.5km);
Campingplatz Insel (2.5km)

Eating

Grüner Markt, the main shopping drag, has a daily produce market and a number of fast-food options.

Bolero (☎ 509 0290; Judenstrasse 7-9; tapas €2.80, mains €5-16; ☺ dinner) This sprawling and atmospheric place has tapas galore, served at wooden tables illuminated by candlelight. It's a popular spot and often full of happy diners.

Messerschmidt (☎ 297 800; Lange Strasse 41; mains €10-22) In the house where plane engineer Willy Messerschmidt was born, this stylish gourmet eatery oozes old-world tradition, with dark woods, white linens and formal service. Above the ornate exterior is a charming alfresco terrace overlooking a pretty park, and there's an attached wine tavern with a more relaxed atmosphere.

Klosterbräu (☎ 522 65; Obere Mühlbrücke 3; mains €5-11; ☺ closed Mon) This beautiful half-timbered brewery is Bamberg's oldest. It draws a youthful clientele who wash down the filling slabs of meat and dumplings with its excellent range of beers.

Wirtshaus zum Schlenkerla (☎ 560 60; Dominikanerstrasse 6; dishes €3.50-9.50; ☺ closed Tue) A local legend that's known nationwide, this dark, rustic 16th-century restaurant with long wooden tables serves tasty Franconian specialities and its own superb *Rauchbier*, poured straight from the oak barrel.

Spezial-Keller (☎ 548 87; Sternwartstrasse; dishes €4-10) The smoky *Rauchbier* served here is superb. Coupled with great views of the Dom and the Altstadt from the beer garden, this place is a comfortable distance from the crowds in the Altstadt. Crowds do gather in November though, to ring in the *Bockbier* (malty beer) season.

Ambräusianum (☎ 509 0262; Dominikanerstrasse 10; dishes €5-9) The newest brewpub on the scene does a killer Weisswurst breakfast – parsley-speckled veal sausage served with a big fresh-baked pretzel and a Weissbier. You can sit next to the copper vat and listen to the beer ferment.

Also recommended:

Josch (☎ 208 3095; Herzog-Max-Strasse 21) Creative French and Bavarian-inspired dishes by a Dutch chef.

Salino (☎ 579 80; Schillerplatz 11) The best stone-oven-cum-beer-garden in town is also one of Germany's earliest pizza-bakers.

Drinking & Entertainment

Consult the free listings magazines *Franky* or *Treff* for the latest 'in' spots and events. For chilled-out entertainment the best place to head for is Austrasse, where the hip hang out by day and night.

Café Esspress (☎ 208 2634; Austrasse 33) A studenty place that hovers somewhere between coffee house and cocktail bar.

Bassanese (☎ 509 568; Karolinenstrasse 2) Serves authentic Italian *gelato*, strudels and handmade chocolates to fans in wicker chairs on the cobblestones near the old town hall.

Other possible options include **Pelikan** (☎ 603 410; Untere Sandstrasse 45), a candle-lit pub with occasional live music, and **Downstairs** (☎ 208 3786; Generalsgasse 3), a cool alternative dance club with an underground vibe.

Live Club (☎ 603 410; Oberer Sandstrasse 7) is a premier venue for live music. Down the road, **Blues Bar & Jazz Keller** (☎ 603 410; Oberer Sandstrasse 18) is a fixture on the scene for intimate, high-quality acts.

Getting There & Around

There are at least hourly RE and RB trains from Nuremberg (€10, 45 to 60 minutes) or from Würzburg (€15.50, one hour), as well as ICE trains every hour to/from Munich (€48, 2½ hours) and Berlin (€69 to €105, 4½ hours). The A73 runs direct to Nuremberg.

Several buses, including 1, 2 and 14, connect the train station with the central bus station, ZOB. Bus 10 goes from the ZOB to Domplatz.

Once you're in town walking is the best option, but you can also hire bicycles at **Fahrradhaus Griesmann** (☎ 229 67; Kleberstrasse 25; per day €5-8). Cars are a colossal pain in town, so park on the outskirts or take a bus (€1.10, or €6.60 for a Tourist Ticket good for 48 hours of unlimited travel). For a taxi, call ☎ 150 15.

BAYREUTH

☎ 0921 / pop 75,000

But for Richard Wagner, the city of Bayreuth would probably just be a sleepy petit bourgeois town. For 11 months of the year it still is, but over a few weeks every summer, the town's Wagner Festival becomes the world's top operatic venue, drawing musical talent from around the globe.

Bayreuth's glory days began in 1735 when Wilhelmine, sister of King Frederick the Great of Prussia, was forced to marry stuffy Margrave Friedrich. Bored with the local scene, the cultured Anglo-oriented Wilhelmine invited the finest artists, poets, composers and architects in Europe to court. Apart from its musical pedigree the city gained some superb rococo and baroque architecture, still on display for all to see.

Orientation

The Hauptbahnhof is five to 10 minutes' walk north of the historic cobblestone centre. Head south on Bahnhofstrasse to Luitpoldplatz and on to the pedestrianised Maximilianstrasse, the main drag also known as Markt. The Eremitage, a baroque palace with manicured gardens, is about 6km to the east, while the Festspielhaus, the theatre for the Wagner Festival performances, is 1.5km north of the town centre.

Information

Bayreuth Card (72hr €9) Good for unlimited trips on city buses, museum entry and a two-hour guided city walk (in German).

Commerzbank (Luitpoldplatz 8) Opposite the tourist office.

Internet Telecafé (☎ 507 2224; Maximilianstrasse 85; per hr €0.75; ☻ 9.30am-10pm) Internet access at a friendly chicken-run of a café.

Post office (Hauptbahnhof & Kanzleistrasse 3)

Tourist office (☎ 885 88; www.bayreuth-tourismus.de; Luitpoldplatz 9; ☻ 9am-6pm Mon-Fri, 9.30am-1pm Sat)

Sights

TOWN CENTRE

Outside of the Wagner Festival from late July to the end of August the streets of Bayreuth slip into a kind of provincial slumber, although the town's strong musical traditions ensure there are good dramatic and orchestral performances all year.

Designed by Giuseppe Galli Bibiena, a famous 18th-century architect from Bologna, the **Markgräfliches Opernhaus** (Margravial Opera House; ☎ 759 6922; Opernstrasse; tours adult/under 18yr/concession €5/free/4; ☻ tours 9am-6pm Apr-Sep, 10am-4pm Oct-Mar) is a stunning baroque masterpiece. Germany's largest opera house until 1871, it has a lavish interior smothered in carved, gilded and marbled wood. Yet Richard Wagner deemed the place too modest for his serious work and conducted here just once. German speakers especially will enjoy the 45-minute sound-and-light multimedia show, which is a glorification vehicle for the Duchess Wilhemine more than the great composer.

Just south of here is Wilhelmine's **Neues Schloss** (New Palace; ☎ 759 690; Ludwigstrasse 21; adult/

concession €4/3; ☻ 9am-6pm Apr-Sep, 10am-4pm Oct-Mar), which opens into the vast **Hofgarten** (admission free; ☻ 24hr). A riot of rococo style, the margravial residence after 1753 features a collection of 18th-century porcelain made in Bayreuth. The annual VIP opening gala of the Wagner Festival is held in the Cedar Room. Also worth a look is the **Spiegelscherbenkabinett** (Broken Mirror Cabinet), which is lined with irregular shards of broken mirror – supposedly Wilhelmina's response to the vanity of her era.

To learn more about the man behind the myth, visit Haus Wahnfried, Wagner's former home on the northern edge of the Hofgarten. It now houses the **Richard Wagner Museum** (☎ 757 2816; Richard-Wagner-Strasse 48; adult/concession €4/2; ☻ 9am-5pm, 9am-8pm Tue & Thu Apr-Oct). Wagner had this lovely home built with cash sent by King Ludwig II. Inside is a thorough, if unexciting, exhibit on Wagner's life, with glass cases crammed with documents, photographs, clothing and private effects. The composer is buried in the garden with his wife Cosima and his loving companion, the dog Russ.

OUTSIDE THE TOWN CENTRE

North of the Hauptbahnhof, the **Festspielhaus** (☎ 787 80; Festspielhügel 1-2; adult/concession €3/2.50; ☻ tours 10.45am & 2.15pm, closed Mon & Nov) was constructed in 1872 with Ludwig's II's backing. The structure was specially designed to accommodate Wagner's massive theatrical sets, with three storeys of mechanical works hidden below stage (see p370). Take bus 5 to Am Festspielhaus.

About 6km east of the centre lies the **Eremitage**, a lush park girding the **Altes Schloss** (☎ 759 6937; Eremitage; adult/concession €3/2; ☻ tours half-hourly 9am-6pm Apr-Sep, 10am-4pm Oct, closed mid-Oct–Mar). This was Friedrich and Wilhelmine's summer residence. Its rooms are an odd mix of rococo indulgence and monastic abstention. Also in the park is horseshoe-shaped **Neues Schloss** (not to be confused with the one in town), which centres on a mosaic Sun Temple with gilded Apollo sculpture. Around both palaces you'll find grottoes and gushing fountains. To get there take bus 2 from Markt.

For a fascinating look at the brewing process, head to the enormous **Maisel's Brauerei-und-Büttnerei-Museum** (Maisel's Brewery & Coopers Museum; ☎ 401 234; Kulmbacher Strasse 40; tours adult/concession €4/2) next door to the brewery of one of Germany's finest wheat-beer makers. The 90-minute guided tour (2pm daily, in German) takes you into the bowels of the 19th-century plant, with atmospheric rooms filled with 4500 beer mugs and amusing artefacts. A foaming glass of Weissbier is served in the bottling room, now a saloon with old-timey slot machines.

Tours

Altstadt **walking tours** (adult/child €4.50/2.50; 10.30am May-Oct, Sat 10.30am Nov-Apr, in German) leave from the tourist office.

Festivals & Events

The **Wagner Festival** has been a summer fixture for over 130 years. The event lasts 30 days, with each performance attended by an audience of 1900. Demand is insane, with an estimated 500,000 fans vying for less than 60,000 tickets. You have to stick with it, as the waiting period is five to 10 years. Tickets are allocated by lottery but preference is given to patrons and Wagner enthusiasts. To apply, send a letter (no phone, fax or email) by mid-September for the next year's festival to the Bayreuther Festspiele, Kartenbüro, Postfach 10 02 62, 95402 Bayreuth, or one of the authorised ticket vendors (see www .bayreuther-festspiele.de for details). You must write in every year until you 'win'. Lucky concert-goers then face another endurance test – the seats are hard wood, ventilation is poor and there's no air-conditioning.

Sleeping

Be warned that sleeping options – like the tickets themselves – are rare as hen's teeth during the Wagner Festival, with most places booked out months in advance.

DJH hostel (☎ 764 380; www.djh.de; Universitätsstrasse 28; dm under/over 26yr €17.20/21.40; closed mid-Dec–Jan) The excellent 150-bed hostel near the university has lovely modern rooms.

Camp Site (☎ 511 239; tent/person €2/3; Jul-Aug) In peak season the city council operates this simple camp site behind the DJH building. Walk about 15 minutes south of the centre or take bus 6 to Kreuzsteinbad.

Hotel Goldener Hirsch (☎ 230 46; www.bayreuth -goldener-hirsch.de; Bahnofstrasse 13; s €55-75, d €65-89; P) This landmark site has had the same name since 1753, and has been a hotel since 1900. Behind its forest-green exterior there's more than a whiff of the '70s, but rooms are spacious and welcoming. It's nicely positioned not far from the train station.

Jagdschloss Thiergarten (☎ 09209-984 050; www .schlosshotel-thiergarten.de; Oberthiergärtner Strasse 36; r €80-170; P) A former hunting castle, this gorgeous place has its own white deer wandering in the gardens and luxurious rooms with canopied beds. The gourmet, traditional restaurant has a domed 13m ceiling, and there's a library and bar with open fireplace. The hotel is about 6km south of Bayreuth.

Hotel Goldener Anker (☎ 650 51; www.anker -bayreuth.de; Opernstrasse 6; s €68-118, d €98-178; P) The refined elegance of this hotel, owned by the same family since the 16th century, is hard to beat. It's just a few metres from the opera house, in the pedestrian zone. The rooms are decorated in heavy traditional style with swag curtains and dark woods.

Eating

Bayreuth's dining options, apart from the many restaurants attached to hotels, hail from all round the globe.

Oskar (☎ 516 0553; Maximilianstrasse 33; dishes €6-12) This updated version of a Bavarian beer hall bustles from morning to night, with patrons often spilling into the street. The menu includes salads and baked potato dishes, but the speciality is anything involving dumplings.

Sinnopoli (☎ 620 17; Badstrasse 13; mains €4-8) Eccentric lamps and artwork set the scene in this contemporary café, which serves up creative pastas, baguettes, vegetarian dishes and, at the weekends, an all-you-can-eat breakfast buffet (€11). There's a lovely garden and terrace area, and children are welcome.

Hansl's Wood Oven Pizzeria (☎ 543 44; Friedrich-strasse 15; pizzas €5-9) The best pizza in town is found at this hole-in-the-wall. A check-list menu lets you choose your own gourmet toppings, and *voilà*, you can name your creation. In summer, the long outdoor tables ease the indoor crush.

Kraftraum (☎ 800 2515; Sophienstrasse 16; mains €4-7) This vegetarian eatery has plenty to tempt the most committed meat-eater. Pastas and jacket potatoes hold the fort, alongside some amazing salads and antipasti platters. Sunday brunch has a devoted following.

Other restaurant recommendations:
Miamiam Glouglou (☎ 656 66; Von-Römer-Strasse 28; mains €6-13) Delightful Parisian-style restaurant with respectable prices.
Hua Hin (☎ 644 97; Ludwigstrasse 30; mains €8-16; 11.30am-2.30pm & 5.30-11.30pm) A temple of tasty Thai food.

BAVARIA

BAVARIA

RICHARD WAGNER

With the backing of King Ludwig II, Richard Wagner (1813–83), the gifted, Leipzig-born composer and notoriously poor manager of money, turned Bayreuth into a mecca of opera and high-minded excess. Bayreuth profited from its luck and, it seems, is ever grateful.

For Wagner, opera-listening was meant to be work, and he tested his listeners wherever possible. The *Götterdämmerung*, *Parsifal*, *Tannhäuser* and *Tristan and Isolde* are grandiose pieces that will jolt any audience geared for light entertainment. Four days of *The Ring of the Nibelungen* are good for limbering up.

After poring over Passau and a few other German cities, Wagner designed his own festival hall in Bayreuth. The unique acoustics are bounced up from a below-stage orchestra via reflecting boards onto the stage and into the house. The design took the body density of a packed house into account, still a remarkable achievement today.

Wagner was also a notorious womaniser, an infamous anti-Semite and a hardliner towards 'non-Europeans'. So extreme were these views that even fun-loving Friedrich Nietzsche called Wagner's works 'inherently reactionary, and inhumane'. Wagner's works, and by extension Wagner himself, were embraced as a symbol of Aryan might by the Nazis, and even today there is great debate among music lovers about the 'correctness' of supporting Wagnerian music and the Wagner Festival in Bayreuth.

Getting There & Away

Bayreuth is well served by rail from Nuremberg (€14.70, one hour). Trains from Munich (€53, three hours) and Regensburg (€25, 2½ hours) require a change in Nuremberg.

COBURG

☎ 09561 / pop 43,000

If marriage is diplomacy by another means, Coburg's rulers were surely masters of the art. Over four centuries, the princes and princesses of the house of Saxe-Coburg intrigued, romanced and ultimately wed themselves into the dynasties of Belgium, Bulgaria, Denmark, Portugal, Russia, Sweden and, most prominently, Great Britain. The crowning achievement came in 1857, when Albert of Saxe-Coburg-Gotha took the vows with his first cousin, Queen Victoria, founding the present British royal family. They quietly adopted the less-Germanic name of Windsor during WWI.

Coburg languished in the shadow of the Iron Curtain during the Cold War, all but closed in by East Germany on three sides, but since reunification the town has undergone a revival. Its proud Veste is one of Germany's finest medieval fortresses. What's more, some sources contend that the original hot dog was invented here.

Orientation

Markt is the old town's central square. The Hauptbahnhof lies to the northwest, Veste Coburg to the northeast.

Information

Postbank (Hindenburgstrasse 6)

Stadtbücherei Coburg (☎ 891 421; Herengasse 17; noon-6pm Mon, Tue & Thu, 9am-1pm Wed, 11am-5pm Fri, 9am-noon Sat) Free internet access.

Tourist office (☎ 741 80; www.coburg-tourist.de; Herrengasse 4; 9am-6.30pm Mon-Fri, 9am-1pm Sat Apr-Oct, 9am-5.30pm Mon-Fri Nov-Mar) Just off Markt.

Sights & Activities

Markt, the town's magnificent square, oozes a colourful, aristocratic charm. The fabulous Renaissance façades and ornate oriels of the **Stadthaus** (Town House) and the **Rathaus** compete for attention, and lord over the imposing statue of Prince Albert.

The lavish **Schloss Ehrenburg** (☎ 808 832; Schlossplatz; tours in German adult//under 18yr/concession €4/free/3; tours hourly, 9am-5pm Tue-Sun Apr-Sep, 10am-3pm Tue-Sun Oct-Mar) was once the town residence of the Coburg dukes. Albert spent his childhood in this sumptuous, tapestry-lined palace, and Queen Victoria stayed in a room with Germany's first flushing toilet (1860). The splendid **Riesensaal** (Hall of Giants) has a baroque ceiling supported by 28 statues of Atlas.

Towering above everything is a storybook medieval fortress, the **Veste Coburg** (courtyard dawn-dusk). With its triple ring of fortified walls, it's one of most impressive fortresses in Germany, but curiously it has a dearth of foreign visitors. It houses the vast collection of the **Kunstsammlungen** (☎ 8790; adult/concession €3.30/1.80; 10am-5pm daily Apr-Oct, 1-4pm Tue-Sun Nov-Mar), with works by star painters such as Rembrandt, Dürer and Cranach the Elder. The elaborate Jagdintarsien-Zimmer (Hunting Marquetry Room) is a superlative example of carved woodwork.

Protestant reformer Martin Luther, hoping to escape an imperial ban, sought refuge at the fortress in 1530. His former quarters has a writing desk and, in keeping with the Reformation, a rather plain bed.

The **Veste-Express** (one-way/return €2/3; Apr-Oct), a tourist train, makes the trip to the fortress every 30 minutes. Bus 8 goes uphill year-round from Herrengasse near the Markt (€1.25 each way). Otherwise it's a steep 3km climb up the path on foot.

Festivals & Events
In mid-July, the streets of Coburg explode during the annual **Samba Festival**, an orgy of song and dance that draws around 90 bands and up to 200,000 visitors.

Sleeping & Eating
DJH hostel (☎ 153 30; www.djh.de; dm under/over 26yr €17.10/21.10) Coburg's spick-and-span hostel is housed in a mock redbrick castle, Schloss Ketschendorf, some 2km from town. Take bus 1 or 11 from the Hauptbahnhof.

Gasthof Fink (☎ 249 40; www.gasthof-fink.de; Lützelbucher Strasse 12; s €29-43 d €47-64) This smart English-speaking inn, 4km south of town, consists of a traditional *Gasthof* (inn), with timber-lined rooms and a light-strewn contemporary hotel with balconies.

Coburger Tor (☎ 250 74; fax 288 74; Ketschendorfer Strasse 22; s €59-80, d €80-130; P X) A refined ambience, impeccable service, nicely equipped rooms with thoughtful décor, and one of the best restaurants in town (mains €18 to €26) make this place a winner. It's about a 15-minute walk from the centre.

Tie (☎ 334 48; Leopoldstrasse 14; mains €8-14; from 5pm Tue-Sun) Heavenly food is made with fresh organic ingredients at this bright vegetarian restaurant. Dishes range from vegetarian classics to Asian inspirations, with the odd fish or meat dish for the unconverted.

Café Prinz Albert (☎ 945 20; Ketschengasse 27; dishes €3-5; to 6.30pm) Coburg's links with the British royals are reflected here in both the décor and menu. This is a fine place for a Prince Albert breakfast – a cross-cultural marriage of sausage, egg and Bamberger croissants.

Getting There & Away
Direct trains to Bamberg (€9.10, 45 minutes) and Nuremberg (€17.60, 1½ hours) leave every other hour. The trip to Bayreuth (€13.40, 1½ hours) requires a change in Lichtenfels. Berlin LinienBus links Coburg to Berlin (€40, 5½ hours) twice a week.

AROUND COBURG
About 25km south of Coburg is the ornate gilded 18th-century pilgrimage church, **Basilika Vierzehnheiligen** (☎ 09571-950 80; admission free; 6.30am-7pm Apr-Oct, 7.30am-dusk Nov-Mar). It stands on the spot where a local shepherd reported having recurring visions of the infant Jesus flanked by the 14 *Nothelfer* (Holy Helpers), a group of saints invoked in times of adversity since the 14th-century Black Plague.

The church is one of the masterpieces of Balthasar Neumann, the renowned architect. The intersecting oval rotundas, play of light and trompe l'oeil ceiling create an optical illusion, making the interior appear much larger than it is and creating a sense of constant motion. Statues of the saints line the freestanding central altar, the focal point of the sumptuous interior.

Alte Klosterbrauerei (☎ 09571-3488; snacks €3.50-5; 10am-8pm) is a wonderful brewery attached to the adjacent convent at the back of Vierzehnheiligen (up past the wooden stands peddling kitsch). Grab a table in the leafy beer garden, order a half-litre of bracing *Nothelfertrunk* beer and drink in the stunning view. Snacks include hearty bread-and-sausage platters, but you can also bring your own. Stay long enough and you may glimpse the nun in her habit who lugs in cases for refill.

Getting There & Away
Regional trains connect Coburg with Lichtenfels (€4.60, 20 minutes), from where there are two buses a day to Vierzehnheiligen. A taxi from Lichtenfels is about €6. The basilica is near the town of Staffelstein, just off the B173, about a 30-minute drive from Coburg.

ALTMÜHLTAL NATURE PARK
The Altmühltal Nature Park is one of Germany's largest nature parks and covers some of Bavaria's most gorgeous terrain. The Altmühl River gently meanders through a region of little valleys and hills before joining the Rhine-Main Canal and eventually emptying into the Danube. You can explore the park on your

BAVARIA

well-marked hiking and biking trails, or by canoe. There's basic camping in designated spots along the river, and plenty of accommodation in the local area.

The park main information centre is in the city of Eichstätt (opposite), a charming place at the southern end of the park that makes an excellent base for exploring.

For information on the park and for help with planning an itinerary, contact the **Informationszentrum Naturpark Altmühltal** (☎ 08421-987 60; www.naturpark-altmuehltal.de; Notre Dame 1, Eichstätt; ⏰ 9am-5pm Mon-Sat, 10am-5pm Sun Apr-Oct, 9am-noon & 2-4pm Mon-Thu, 9am-noon Fri Nov-Mar). Upstairs in the centre is a museum of the park's wildlife and habitats, complete with a re-creation of landscapes in the garden.

Orientation

The park takes in 2900 sq km of land southwest of Regensburg, south of Nuremberg, east of Treuchtlingen and north of Eichstätt. The eastern boundaries of the park include the town of Kelheim.

There are bus and train connections between Eichstätt and all the major milestones along the river including, from west to east, Gunzenhausen, Treuchtlingen and Pappenheim. North of the river, activities focus around the towns of Kipfenberg, Beilngries and Riedenburg.

Activities

CANOEING & KAYAKING

The most beautiful section of the river is from Treuchtlingen or Pappenheim to Eichstätt or Kipfenberg, about a 60km stretch that you can do lazily in a kayak or canoe in two to three days. There are lots of little dams along the way, as well as some small rapids about 10km northwest of Dollnstein. Signs warn of impending doom, but locals say that if you heed the warning to stay to the right, you'll be pretty safe.

San-Aktiv Tours (☎ 09831-4936; www.san-aktiv-tours .de; Bühringer Strasse 11, 91710 Gunzenhausen) and **Natour** (☎ 09141-922 929; www.natour.de; Gänswirtshaus 12, 91781 Weissenburg) are the largest and best-organised canoe-hire companies in the park, with a network of vehicles to shuttle canoes, bicycles and people around the area.

Canoe trips through the park run from April to October and cost around €21 for a half-day trip and €160 for a three-day tour. You can canoe alone or join a group. Packages generally include the canoe, swim vests, maps,

instructions, transfer back to the embarkation point and, for overnight tours, luggage transfer and accommodation. Most trips start in Dietfurt near Treuchtlingen.

You can hire canoes and kayaks in just about every town along the river. Expect to pay about €15/€25 per day for a one-/two-person boat, more for bigger ones. Staff will haul you and the boats to or from your embarkation point for a small fee.

You can get a full list of boat-hire outlets from the Informationszentrum Naturpark Altmühltal. Some recommendations include the following:

Bootsverleih Otto Rehm (☎ 08422-987 654; www .rehm-r.de; Dollnstein)

Fahrradgarage (☎ 08421-21 10; www.fahrradgarage .de; Eichstätt)

Franken-Boot (☎ 09142-4645; www.frankenboot.de; Treuchtlingen)

Lemming Tours (☎ 09145-235; www.lemmingtours .de; Solnhofen)

CYCLING & HIKING

Around 800km of bicycle trails and 3000km of hiking trails crisscross the nature park. The most popular route is the Altmühltal Radweg, which runs parallel to the river for 160km. Cycling trails are clearly labelled and have long rectangular brown signs bearing a bike symbol. Hiking-trail markers are yellow.

You can hire bikes in almost every town within the park, and prices are more or less uniform. Most bike-hire agencies will also store bicycles. Ask for a list of bike-hire outlets at the Informationszentrum Naturpark Altmühltal.

In Eichstätt, Fahrradgarage (above) hires out bicycles for €8 per day. Staff will bring the bikes to you or take you and the bikes to anywhere in the park for an extra fee.

ROCK CLIMBING

The worn cliffs along the Altmühl River offer some appealing terrain for climbers of all skill levels. The medium-grade 45m-high rock face of Burgsteinfelsen, located between the towns of Dollnstein and Breitenfurt, has routes from the fourth to eighth climbing level with stunning views of the valley. The Dohlenfelsen face near the town of Wellheim has a simpler expanse that's more suitable for children. For more details of the area's climbing options, contact the Informationszentrum Naturpark Altmühltal (left).

Getting There & Away

BUS

From mid-April to October the FreizeitBus Altmühltal-Donautal takes passengers and their bikes around the park. Buses run three to five times a day from mid-April to early October (see www.naturpark-altmuehltal .de for a timetable, listed in German under 'Freizeit/Tipp'. Route FzB1 runs from Regensburg and Kelheim to Riedenburg on weekends and holidays only. Route FzB2 travels between Dollnstein, Eichstätt, Beilngries, Dietfurt and Riedenburg with all-day service on weekends and holidays and restricted service on weekdays. All-day tickets cost €9/€6 for passengers with/without bicycles, or €20.50/€15 per family with/without bikes.

TRAIN

Trains run between Eichstätt Bahnhof and Treuchtlingen at least hourly (€4.60, 25 minutes), and between Treuchtlingen and Gunzenhausen (€3.40, 15 minutes, at least hourly). RE trains from Munich that run through Eichstätt Bahnhof also stop in Dollnstein, Solnhofen and Pappenheim.

EICHSTÄTT

☎ 08421 / pop 13,000

The wide, cobbled streets of Eichstätt have a distinct Mediterranean flair. They meander past elegant buildings and leafy squares, giving this sleepy town a general sense of refinement. Italian architects, notably Gabriel de Gabrieli and Maurizio Pedetti, rebuilt the town after Swedes razed the place during the Thirty Years' War (1618–48) and it has remained undamaged ever since. In 1980 it became home to Germany's sole Catholic university.

Orientation

Eichstätt has two train stations. Mainline trains stop at the Bahnhof, 5km from the centre, from where diesel trains shuttle to the Stadtbahnhof. From here walk north across the Spitalbrücke and you'll end up in Domplatz, the heart of town. Willibaldsburg castle is about 1km southwest of the Stadtbahnhof.

Information

Kreiskrankenhaus (☎ 6010; Ostenstrasse 31) Hospital.
Post office (Domplatz 7)
Raiffeisenbank (Domplatz 5)
Tourist office (☎ 6001 400; www.eichstaett.de; Dom-

platz 8; ○ 9am-6pm Mon-Sat & 10am-1pm Sun Apr-Oct; 10am-noon & 2-4pm Mon-Thu, 10am-noon Fri Nov-Mar)

Sights

TOWN CENTRE

Eichstätt's centre is dominated by the richly adorned **Dom** (cathedral). Standout features include an enormous stained-glass window by Hans Holbein the Elder, and the carved sandstone **Pappenheimer Altar** (1489–97), depicting a pilgrimage from Pappenheim to Jerusalem. The seated statue is of St Willibald, the town's first bishop.

The **Domschatzmuseum** (Cathedral Treasury; ☎ 507 42; Residenzplatz 7; adult/children €2/1; ○ 10.30am-5pm Wed-Fri & 10am-5pm Sat & Sun Apr-Oct) includes the robes of St Willibald and baroque Gobelin tapestries.

The **Residenz** (Residenzplatz; admission €1; ○ tours 11am & 3pm Mon-Thu, 11am Fri, 10.15am & 3.30pm Sat) is the former prince-bishops' palace, completed in 1736. It has a stunning main staircase and Spiegelsaal (Hall of Mirrors) and a fresco from Greek mythology. In the square is a golden statue of Mary on a 19m-high column.

North of the Dom is another baroque square, the **Markt**, where markets are held on Wednesday and Saturday mornings. About 300m northwest of here, on Westenstrasse, is the **Kloster St Walburga**, the burial site of St Willibald's sister and a pilgrimage site: every year between mid-October and late February, water oozes from Walburga's relics and drips down into a catchment. The nuns bottle diluted versions of the so-called *Walburgaöl* (Walburga oil) and give it away to the faithful. The walls in the upper chapel are covered with beautiful *ex voto* tablets as a thank you to the saint.

WILLIBALDSBURG

The hill-top castle of Willibaldsburg (1355) houses two museums. The **Jura-Museum** (☎ 2956; Burgstrasse 19; adult/under 18 €4/free; ○ 9am-6pm Apr-Sep, 10am-4pm Nov-Mar, closed Mon) is great, even if fossils usually don't quicken your pulse. Highlights are a locally found archaeopteryx (the oldest-known fossil bird) and the aquariums with living specimens of the fossilised animals. Also up here is the **Museum of Pre-History & Early History** (☎ 894 50) with a 6000-year-old mammoth skeleton. Descend to the cellar to find the 76.5m-deep well – toss in a coin and listen for about 10 seconds for the

BAVARIA

plop. The **Bastiongarten**, built on the ramparts, affords a fantastic view of Eichstätt.

Looking across the valley, you can make out the **limestone quarry** (adult/child €2/1; ⏱ 9am-5pm) where you can dig for fossils. At the base of the quarry is the **Museum Berger** (☎ 4663; Harthof; adult/child €2/0.50; ⏱ 1.30-5pm Mon-Sat, 10am-noon Sun Apr-Oct, or by request), which displays geological samples.

Tours

The tourist office runs walking tours of the town centre (€3, 1½ hours) at 1.30pm on Saturday from April to October (also Wednesday at 1.30pm in July and August).

Sleeping & Eating

Camping Daum (☎ 90847; fax 90846; Westenstrasse 47; site €6; ⏱ Apr-Oct) This pretty camping ground is on the northern bank of the Altmühl River, about 1km east of the town centre. It closes for 10 days during the Volksfest (a mini-Oktoberfest) in late August or early September. Towed caravans are not allowed.

DJH hostel (☎ 980 410; www.djh.de; Reichenaustrasse 15; dm under/over 26yr €18.40/23.40; ⏱ closed Dec-Jan) This comfy, modern place has 122 beds and a commanding view of the Altstadt. The double rooms, if available, have their own shower and toilet.

Fuchs (☎ 6789; Ostenstrasse 8; www.hotel-fuchs.de; s €38-48, d €60-80; Ⓟ ⓧ) A super-central, family-run hotel with underfloor heating in the bathrooms, which adjoins a cake shop with a sunny dining area. It's convenient to a launch ramp on the river, and you can lock your boat in the garage.

Hotel Adler (☎ 6767; www.adler-eichstaett.de; Markplatz 22; s €59-67, d €89-95; Ⓟ ⓧ) A superb ambience reigns at this ornate 300-year-old building right on Markt. The rooms are bright, airy and modern, and it offers all the trappings, including bike and boat hire and a generous breakfast buffet. There's wheelchair access.

Café im Paradeis (☎ 3313; Markt 9; mains €6-14) This sophisticated spot on Markt is prime for people-watching. Recharge with a snack or full meal, either in the antique-lined interior or out on the Mediterranean-style terrace.

Zum Ammonit (☎ 2929; Luitpoldstrasse 19; mains €5-15) Within this royal baker's home you can enjoy gourmet salads and seasonal Bavarian fare with lots to please the eye – vaulted ceilings, hunting trophies and oil paintings, even

an indoor well. The Bierstube to the rear has cosy raised nooks perfect for a tête-à-tête.

For fast food, try **Metzgerei Schneider** (Markt).

Getting There & Away

Trains run hourly or more between Ingolstadt and Eichstätt (€4.60, 25 minutes).

INGOLSTADT

☎ 0841 / pop 122,000

Even by Germany's high standards Ingolstadt is awfully prosperous. Audi, the auto manufacturer, has its headquarters here, flanked by a clutch of oil refineries in the outskirts. But industry has left few marks on the charming medieval centre, with its cobblestoned streets and historic buildings. Ingolstadt's museum church has the largest flat fresco ever made. And few people know that its old medical school figured in the literary birth of Frankenstein, the monster by which all others are judged.

Orientation

The Hauptbahnhof is 2.5km southeast of the Altstadt; buses 10, 11, 15 and 16 run between them every few minutes (€1.80). The Danube (Donau) is south of the Altstadt; the Audi factory is about 2km north of the centre.

Information

City Internet Café (☎ 142 865; Münzberger Strasse 6; internet access per hr €3; ⏱ 10am-11pm)
Dresdner Bank (Rathausplatz)
Post office (Am Stein) Also in Hauptbahnhof.
Stadtbücherei (☎ 305 1831; Hallstrasse 2-4) Free internet access.
Tourist office (☎ 305 3030; www.ingolstadt-tourismus.de; Rathausplatz 4; ⏱ 8am-5.30pm Mon-Fri, 9am-2pm Sat, 10am-3pm Sun)

Sights

ASAMKIRCHE MARIA DE VICTORIA

The crown jewel among Ingolstadt's sights, the **Asamkirche** (☎ 175 18; Neubaustrasse 11/2; adult/concession €2/1.50; ⏱ 9am-noon & 1-5pm Tue-Sun Mar-Oct, 10am-noon & 1-4pm Nov-Mar) is a baroque masterpiece designed by brothers Cosmas Damian and Egid Quirin Asam between 1732 and 1736.

Its shining glory is the trompe l'oeil ceiling (painted in just six weeks in 1735). This mesmerising piece of work, the world's largest fresco on a flat surface, is full of stunning optical illusions. Stand on the little circle in the diamond tile near the door and everything snaps into 3D; look over your left shoulder here at the archer with the flaming red turban, and his arrow will follow you around the room. Focus on anything – the Horn of Plenty, Moses' staff, the treasure chest – and it will alter dramatically when you move around the room. The Asams took the secrets they used to the grave.

The side chamber features the Lepanto Monstrance, a gold and silver depiction of a Christian sea victory over the Ottoman Turks in 1571. Note the beaten sultan departing in a lifeboat on the bottom right.

Across the street is the **Tilly House** (Neubaustrasse 2), where General Tilly, a famous Field Marshal in the Thirty Years' War, died in 1652 from tetanus (the result of a war wound). There's a commemorative plaque around the corner on Johannesstrasse.

DEUTSCHES MEDIZINHISTORISCHES MUSEUM

Located in the stately Alte Anatomie (Old Anatomy) at the city's university, the **Deutsches Medizinhistorisches Museum** (German Museum of Medical History; ☎ 305 1860; Anatomiestrasse 18/20; adult/child €3/free; ✆ 10am-noon & 2-5pm Tue-Sun) chronicles the evolution of medical science as well as the many instruments and techniques used. Pack a strong stomach for the visit.

The ground floor eases you into the exhibition with birthing chairs, enema syringes and lancets for blood-letting. Upstairs things get closer to the bone in displays of human skeletons with preserved musculature and organs, foetuses of conjoined twins, a pregnant uterus and a cyclops.

Although presented in a completely scientific, almost clinical, fashion, there's a ghoulishness to the place. After your visit, you can recover in the bucolic medicinal plant garden, which includes a garden of smells and touch designed for the blind.

NEUES SCHLOSS, BAYERISCHES ARMEE MUSEUM & REDUIT TILLY

The ostentatious Neues Schloss (New Palace) was built for Duke Ludwig the Bearded in 1418. Fresh from a trip to wealth-laden France, Ludwig borrowed heavily from Gallic design and created an ostentatious new home with 3m-thick walls, Gothic net vaulting and individually carved doorways. Today the building houses the **Bayerisches Armee Museum** (Bavarian Military Museum; ☎ 937 70; Paradeplatz 4; adult/concession

€3.50/3, on Sun €1, combined ticket with Reduit Tilly €4.50/3.50; ✆ 8.45am-4.30pm Tue-Sun). Expect details of long-forgotten battles, armaments dating back to the 14th century and thousands of tin soldiers.

The second part of the museum is in the **Reduit Tilly** (adult/concession €3.50/3, on Sun €1, combined ticket with Neues Schloss €4.50/3.50; ✆ 8.45am-4.30pm Tue-Sun) across the river. This 19th-century fortress has an undeniable aesthetic, having been designed by Ludwig I's chief architect. It was named after Johann Tilly – a field marshall of the Thirty Years' War who was known as the 'butcher of Magdeburg' – and features exhibits covering the history of WWI and post-WWI Germany.

MUSEUM MOBILE

This high-tech car museum is part of the **Audi Forum** (☎ 283 4444; Ettinger Strasse 40; admission adult/concession €2/1.50, tours €4/3; ✆ 10am-8pm). Exhibits on three fancy floors chart Audi's humble beginnings in 1899, to its latest high-octane roadsters. Some 50 cars and 20 motorbikes are on display, including prototypes that glide past visitors on an open lift. One-hour tours (some in English) run twice hourly. Take bus 11 to the terminus from the Hauptbahnhof or Paradeplatz.

The two-hour tours of the **Audi factory** (☎ 0800-282 4444; tours free; ✆ 9am-2pm production days only) entail a heavy dose of PR.

LIEBFRAUENMÜNSTER

The city's largest church was founded by Duke Ludwig the Bearded in 1425 but was enlarged over the next 100 years. A classic Gothic hall church, the **Liebfrauenmünster** (Minster of Our Dear Lady; ✆ 8am-6pm) has a pair of strangely oblique square towers that flank the main entrance. Inside, subtle colours and a nave flooded with light intensify the magnificence of the soaring ceiling vaults, with strands of delicate stonework. Worth a closer look are the brilliant stained-glass windows and the high altar by Hans Mielich (1560). On the rear altar panel is an odd scene of St Katharina debating with a gathering of professors at Ingolstadt's new university, ostensibly in a bid to convert the Protestant faculty to Catholicism. The painting was a poke at Luther's Reformation.

KREUZTOR

The red-brick **Kreuztor** (1385), with its Gothic outline of pixie-capped turrets, was just one of four main city gates until the 19th century.

BAVARIA

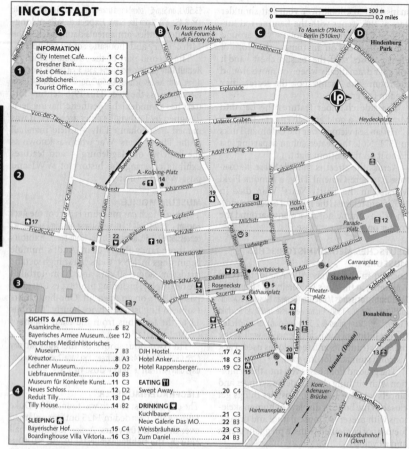

INGOLSTADT

INFORMATION
City Internet Café...............1 C4
Dresdner Bank..................2 C3
Post Office.......................3 C3
Stadtbücherei...................4 D3
Tourist Office...................5 C3

SIGHTS & ACTIVITIES
Asamkirche......................6 B2
Bayerisches Armee Museum...(see 12)
Deutsches Medizinhistorisches
  Museum.........................7 B3
Kreuztor..........................8 A3
Lechner Museum.................9 D2
Liebfrauenmünster..............10 B3
Museum für Konkrete Kunst...11 C3
Neues Schloss...................12 D2
Reduit Tilly.......................13 D4
Tilly House........................14 B2

SLEEPING
Bayerischer Hof..................15 C4
Boardinghouse Villa Viktoria...16 C3

DJH Hostel........................17 A2
Hotel Anker.......................18 C3
Hotel Rappensberger.............19 C2

EATING
Swept Away.......................20 C4

DRINKING
Kuchlbauer........................21 C3
Neue Galerie Das MO............22 B3
Weissbräuhaus...................23 C3
Zum Daniel.......................24 B3

The former **fortifications**, which are now flats, still encircle the city.

OTHER ATTRACTIONS

Ingolstadt has two of Germany's leading art galleries for experimental materials. The **Museum für Konkrete Kunst** (Museum of Concrete Art; ☎ 305 1871; Tränktorstrasse 6-8; adult/concession €2/1; ☉ 11am-6pm Tue-Sun) features creative abstracts and fascinating three-dimensional works in concrete, with artists of international renown.

The **Lechner Museum** (☎ 305 2250; Esplanade 9; adult/concession €3/1.50; ☉ 11am-6pm Tue-Sun) highlights works cast in steel, a medium that's more expressive than you might think. Exhibits are displayed in a striking glass-covered factory hall from 1953.

Sleeping

DJH hostel (☎ 341 77; www.djh.de; Friedhofstrasse 41/2; dm under/over 26yr €16.15/20.15; ☉ closed mid-Dec–Jan;) This beautiful hostel is in a renovated city fortress (1828), about 150m west of the Kreuztor. It's a well-equipped place with wheelchair access, near the swimming pool and skating rink.

Bayerischer Hof (☎ 934 060; Münzbergstrasse 5; www.bayerischer-hof-ingolstadt.de; s/d €56/82; P) The corridors here won't win any ambience prizes, but the rooms themselves, located around a Bavarian eatery, are furnished with hardwood furniture, TVs and modern (albeit brown) bathrooms. And there are little 'we care' touches like biscuits laid out on the pillows.

THE BIRTH OF FRANKENSTEIN

Mary Shelley's *Frankenstein,* published in 1818, set a creepy precedent in the world of monster fantasies. The story is well known: young scientist Viktor Frankenstein travels to Ingolstadt to study medicine. He becomes obsessed with the idea of creating a human being and goes shopping for parts at the local cemetery. Unfortunately his creature is a problem child and sets out to destroy its maker.

Shelley picked Ingolstadt because it was home to a prominent university and medical faculty. In the 19th century, a laboratory for scientists and medical doctors was housed in the Alte Anatomie (now the Deutsches Medizinhistorisches Museum, p375). In the operating theatre, professors and their students carried out experiments on corpses and dead tissue.

Hotel Anker (☎ 300 05; www.hotel-restaurant-anker .de; Tränktorstrasse 1; s €52, d €80-84) Bright rooms, a touch of surrealist art and a great location make this family-run hotel a good central choice. Rooms have direct-dial phone and cable TV, and a traditional German restaurant attracts a loyal local following.

Boardinghouse Villa Viktoria (☎ 620 55; www.villa -viktoria.com; Tränktorstrasse 13; r €95-115; P) These stylish designer apartments are a perfect solution for families seeking quality without breaking the bank. They boast full-service kitchens, split-level living and bedrooms and smart Mediterranean-hued bathrooms. Rates drop sharply for longer stays.

Hotel Rappensberger (☎ 3140; www.rappensberger .de; Harderstrasse 3; s €80-135, d €97-175; P) This small, stylish hotel specialises in minimalist rooms with designer lighting and traditional German touches. The standard rooms are snug, but accommodation becomes quite roomy a step up. The attached café-restaurant is a byword for chic.

Eating & Drinking

Local drinkers are proud that Germany's Beer Purity Law of 1516 was issued in Ingolstadt. To find out why, try a mug of smooth Herrnbräu, Nordbräu or Ingobräu.

Zum Daniel (☎ 352 72; Roseneckstrasse 1; mains €5-12; ⓨ closed Mon) This is the oldest pub in town and just drips with character and tradition.

The owner, a Frankenstein fan, has a monster kit-car that he parks in the garden. Locals say Daniel has the town's best pork roast.

Weissbräuhaus (☎ 328 90; Dollstrasse 3; mains €9-15) This modern beer hall serves standard Bavarian dishes, including the delicious Weissbräupfändl (pork filet with homemade Spätzle noodles). There's a beer garden with a charming fountain in the back.

Neue Galerie Das MO (☎ 339 60; Bergbräustrasse 7) Right opposite the Liebfrauenmünster, this trendy café-bar holds art exhibits and has probably the nicest beer garden in town, in a dense copse of chestnut trees.

Also recommended:

Swept Away (☎ 931 1679; Donaustrasse 14; mains €7-15; ⓨ dinner) Quirky bamboo-clad décor with a purely veggie menu, cocktails and live bands.

Kuchlbauer (☎ 335 512; Schäffbräustrasse 11a) A brewpub almost painful in its quaintness but with oodles of neat brewing gear.

Getting There & Around

Trains to Regensburg (€11.70, one hour) and Munich (€13.40, one hour) leave hourly. BEX BerlinLinien buses leave for Berlin daily at 10.55am (one-way/return €44/81, five hours).

Single journeys on local buses cost €1.80.

EASTERN BAVARIA

Few foreigners know that Eastern Bavaria was a seat of power in the Dark Ages, ruled by rich bishops at a time when Munich was but a modest trading post. A conquering Napoleon lumped Eastern Bavaria into river districts, and King Ludwig I sought to roll back these changes by re-creating the boundaries of a glorified duchy from 1255. Though it brought a sense of renewed Bavarian-ness, the area remained very much on the margins of things, the odd and appealing mixture of ancient Roman cities, undulating farmland and rugged wilderness that it is today.

Regensburg, a former capital, is one of Germany's prettiest and liveliest cities. From here the Danube gently winds its way to the Italianate city of Passau. Thanks to its relative remoteness, the Bavarian Forest is a well-kept secret with an enviable array of hiking and skiing facilities that exist alongside the ancient tradition of glass-blowing. What's more, it's all easy on the wallet.

REGENSBURG

☎ 0941 / pop 149,000

Regensburg is one of the best-preserved medieval towns in Europe, with a wealth of landmarks in the centre going back over 2000 years. The city's brand-new Unesco heritage listing hasn't gone to its head and the old centre remains an unpretentious, very livable whole. A Roman settlement completed under Emperor Marcus Aurelius, Regensburg became the first and foremost capital of Bavaria, the residence of dukes, kings and bishops, and for 600 years an imperial free city. Outstanding features such as the Old Stone Bridge and the cathedral date from this period in the Middle Ages. Since then the Altstadt seems hardly to have changed – there are still towering patrician's houses, friendly locals and lots of flourishing businesses.

Oskar Schindler lived in Regensburg for years, and now one of his houses bears a **plaque** (Am Watmarkt 5) to his achievements commemorated in the Spielberg epic *Schindler's List*.

Orientation

The city is divided by the east-flowing Danube, which separates the Altstadt from the northern banks. Islands in the middle of the river, mainly Oberer and Unterer Wöhrd, are populated as well. The Hauptbahnhof is at the southern end of the Altstadt. From there, Maximilianstrasse leads north to Kornmarkt, the centre of the historic district.

Information

BOOKSHOPS

Bücher Pustet (☎ 585 320; Gesandtenstrasse 6-8) Good collection of English-language novels and travel books.

Presse + Buch (Hauptbahnhof) Stocks English books and magazines.

EMERGENCY

Ambulance (☎ 192 22)

Police (☎ 110; Minoritenweg 1)

INTERNET ACCESS

C@fe Netzblick (☎ 599 9700; Am Römling 9; per 30min €1.50; ⊗ 6pm-1am)

INTERNET RESOURCES

City of Regensburg (www.regensburg.de) Regensburg's useful website.

LAUNDRY

Münz Wasch Center (Winklergasse 14; per 6kg load €3; ⊗ 6am-10pm Mon-Sat)

LIBRARIES

Stadtbücherei (☎ 507 1477; Haidplatz 8, Thon Dittmer Palais)

MEDICAL SERVICES

Evangelisches Krankenhaus (☎ 504 00; Emmeramsplatz)

MONEY

More banks are located along Maximilianstrasse.

Sparkasse City Center (Neupfarrplatz)

POST

Post office (Domplatz) Also in the Hauptbahnhof.

TOURIST INFORMATION

Tourist office (☎ 507 4410; Altes Rathaus; ⊗ 9.15am-6pm Mon-Fri, 9.15am-4pm Sat, 9.30am-4pm Sun)

Sights

DOM ST PETER

Regensburg's soaring landmark, the **Dom St Peter** (☎ 597 1002; Domplatz; admission free, tours in German adult/concession €3/1.50; ⊗ tours at 10am, 11am & 2pm Mon-Sat, 1pm & 2pm Sun May-Oct) ranks among Bavaria's grandest Gothic cathedrals. Construction dates from the late 13th century, but the distinctive filigree spires weren't added until the 19th; the extravagant western façade from this period is festooned with sculptures. Inside are kaleidoscopic stained-glass windows above the choir and in the south transept. Another highlight is a pair of charming sculptures (1280), attached to pillars just west of the altar, which features the Angel Gabriel beaming at the Virgin on the opposite pillar as he delivers the news that she's pregnant.

The **Domschatzmuseum** (Cathedral Treasury; ☎ 576 45; adult/concession €2/1; ⊗ 10am-5pm Tue-Sat, noon-5pm Sun Apr-Nov) brims with monstrances, tapestries and other church treasures.

SCHLOSS THURN UND TAXIS & MUSEUM

In the 15th century, Franz von Taxis (1459–1517) assured his place in history by setting up the first European postal system, which remained a monopoly until the 19th century. To compensate for the loss the family was given a new palace, the former Benedictine monastery St Emmeram, henceforth known as **Schloss Thurn und Taxis** (☎ 504 8133; www.thurnund taxis.de; Emmeramsplatz 6; combined ticket adult/concession €11.50/9; ☿ tours at 11am, 2pm, 3pm & 4pm Mon-Fri, also 10am Sat & Sun). It was soon one of the most modern palaces in Europe, and featured such luxuries as flushing toilets, central heating and electricity. Tours include a look into the Basilika St Emmeram (p380).

The palace complex also contains the **Thurn und Taxis-Museum** (☎ 504 8133; adult/concession €3.50/2.50; ☿ Tue-Fri 10am-5pm, Sat & Sun 11am-5pm). The jewellery, porcelain and precious furnishings on display here belonged, for many years, to the wealthiest dynasty in Germany. The fortune, administered by Prince Albert II, is still estimated at well over €1 billion.

BAVARIA

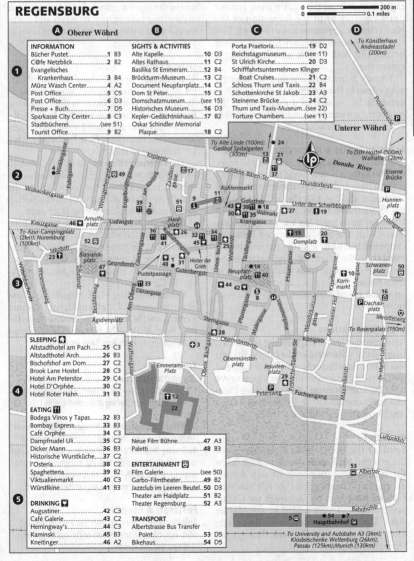

JEWISH MEMORIALS

Regensburg once had a thriving medieval Jewish community centred around Neupfarrplatz. When the city fell on hard economic times in the early 16th century, the townspeople expelled all Jews and burned their quarter to the ground. A multimedia exhibit, the **Document Neupfarrplatz** (☎ 507 1452; tours adult/concession €5/2.50; ☽ 2.30pm Thu-Sat) explains events on the square from ancient times right up until the formation of the Nazi resistance movement in 1942–43. You can visit a Roman legionary fortress, Jewish houses and both Gothic and Romanesque synagogues.

There's a memorial plaque to Regensburg's Jews in the pavement west of the Neupfarrkirche, as well as a memorial to the concentration-camp victims on the north side of the Steinerne Brücke.

ALTES RATHAUS & REICHSTAGSMUSEUM

The seat of the Reichstag for almost 150 years, the **Altes Rathaus** is now home to Regensburg's three mayors and the **Reichstagsmuseum** (Imperial Diet Museum; ☎ 507 4411; Altes Rathaus; adult/concession €6/3; ☽ tours 9.30am, 10.30am, 2pm & 3pm Mon-Sat, 10am & 11am Sun; tours in English 3pm Mon-Sat). Tours take in not only the richly decorated **Reichssaal** (Imperial Hall) but also the original **torture chambers** in the basement. The interrogation room bristles with tools such as the rack, the Spanish Donkey (a tall wooden wedge on which naked men were made to sit) and spiked chairs.

STEINERNE BRÜCKE

An incredible feat of engineering for its day, Regensburg's **Steinerne Brücke** (Stone Bridge) was at one time the only fortified crossing of the Danube. Ensconced in its southern tower is the **Brückturm-Museum** (☎ 567 6015; Weisse-Lamm-Gasse 1; adult/concession €2/1.50; ☽ 10am-5pm Apr-Oct), a small historical exhibit about the bridge.

CHURCHES

South of the Dom, the humble exterior of the graceful **Alte Kapelle** (Alter Kornmarkt 8) belies the stunning interior with its rich rococo decorations. The core of the church, however, is about 1000 years old, although the Gothic vaulted ceilings were added in the Middle Ages. The church is open only during services but you can always peek through the wrought-iron gate.

Near the Schloss is a masterpiece by the Asam brothers, the **Basilika St Emmeram** (☎ 510 30; Emmeramsplatz 3; ☽ closed Fri & Sun morning). There are two giant ceiling frescoes and, sheltered in its crypt, the remains of Sts Emmeram, Wolfgang and Ramwold, all Regensburg bishops in the early days of Christianity.

The 12th-century main portal of the **Schottenkirche St Jakob** (Jakobstrasse 3) is considered one of the supreme examples of Romanesque architecture in Germany. Its reliefs and sculptures form an iconography that continues to baffle the experts.

OTHER SIGHTS

The most tangible reminder of the ancient Castra Regina (Roman fortress), where the name 'Regensburg' comes from, is the remaining **Roman wall**, which follows Unter den Schwibbögen and veers south onto Dr-Martin-Luther-Strasse. The impressive **Porta Praetoria** arch is a key reminder of the city's heritage.

The **Historisches Museum** (☎ 507 2448; Dachauplatz 2-4; adult/concession €2.20/1.10; ☽ 10am-4pm Tue-Sun) has exhibits ranging from the Stone Age to the Middle Ages, with an emphasis on the Roman period and the city's medieval glory days.

In the former bishop's residence, the **Domschatzmuseum** (Cathedral Treasury; ☎ 516 68; adult/concession €2/1; ☽ 10am-5pm Tue-Sun Apr-Oct) brims with vestments, monstrances, tapestries and other riches. It's housed in the painted medieval St Ulrich Kirche.

Other interesting visits include the house of astronomer and mathematician Johannes Kepler, now the **Kepler-Gedächtnishaus** (Kepler Memorial House; ☎ 507 3442; Keplerstrasse 5; adult/concession €2.20/1.10; ☽ 10.30am-4pm, Sat & Sun Apr-Oct).

Tours

City walking tours (adult/child €6/4; ☽ in English 1.30pm Wed & Sat May-Sep, in German 2.45pm Mon-Sat, 10.45am & 2pm Sun) Starting at the tourist office (1½ hours).

Schifffahrtsunternehmen Klinger (☎ 521 04; www .schifffahrtklinger.de) Offers short cruises (50 minutes) on the Danube (adult/child €7/3; hourly from 9am to 4pm, April to mid-October) and to the Walhalla monument (adult/child single €7/3, return €10/4.50; at 10.30am and 2pm, two hours each way plus a one-hour stop at the monument).

Festivals & Events

Dult Oktoberfest-style party with beer tents, carousel rides, entertainment and vendors on the Dultplatz, during Pentecost and late August.

Weihnachtsmarkt Christmas Market, with stalls selling roasted almonds, spiced biscuits and traditional wooden toys. At Neupfarrplatz and Schloss Thurn und Taxis, during December.

Sleeping

BUDGET
DJH hostel (☎ 574 02; www.djh.de; Wöhrdstrasse 60; dm under/over 26yr €19.20/23.20) Regensburg's modernised hostel occupies a beautiful old building on a large island about a 10-minute walk north of the Altstadt. Take bus 3 from Albertstrasse to Eisstadion.

Hotel Am Peterstor (☎ 545 45; www.hotel-am -peterstor.de; Fröhliche-Türken-Strasse 12; s €35-50, d €45-60; P) A convenient location, bright modern rooms and affordable rates make this hotel a good choice. It's a no-frills place with simple taste, but the quarters are bright, clean and in great shape.

Also recommended:
Azur-Campingplatz (☎ 270 025; www.azur-camping .de/regensburg; Weinweg 40; per person €5.50-7.50, per tent €6-9). A pretty site about 2km from the Altstadt on the southern bank of the Danube. Take bus 6.
Brook Lane Hostel (☎ 690 0966; www.hostel -regensburg.de; Obere Bachgasse 21; dm €17, d €30) Indie backpacker hostel with bunks for 10 and one double room, plus kitchen.

MIDRANGE
Hotel Roter Hahn (☎ 595 090; www.roter-hahn.com; Rote-Hahnen-Gasse 10; s/d €85/105; P) Old on the outside but modern within, this swish family-run hotel is a winner for its quirky rooms (some with trompe l'oeil murals, others very modern) and its good restaurant.

Altstadthotel Arch (☎ 586 60; www.altstadthotel -arch.de; Haidplatz 4; s €71-97, d €96-130; X) This landmark hotel located in a medieval patrician mansion, puts you right into charismatic Haidplatz, which is a hub of activity on balmy summer nights. Rooms here have an air of understated elegance. The beamed *Ratsherrenzimmer* (councilmen's room) is the ticket for romance.

Altstadthotel am Pach (☎ 298 610; www.ampach .de; Untere Bachgasse 9; s €80-100, d €100-180; X) Those who have shaped Regensburg history, from Marcus Aurelius to Emporor Karl V, are commemorated in the 21 rooms of this sleek new hotel. Rooms vary in size but all are warmly furnished with thick carpets, comfy mattresses and a minifridge with complimentary beer and water.

Künstlerhaus Andreasstadel (☎ 5960 2300; www .kuenstlerhaus-andreasstadel.de; Andreasstrasse 26; r €95-135; P X) Now this is savvy: a historic salt store where huge, carefully restored guestrooms reveal a tasteful mix of Sri Lankan chests, marble-topped French tables and sleek German bathrooms – with wi-fi throughout. Add polished-wood floors, kitchens, a river-facing garden terrace and beautiful hosts, and no-one will blink when you wheel your bicycle inside for safekeeping.

TOP END
Bischofshof am Dom (☎ 584 60; www.hotel-bischofshof .de; Krauterermarkt 3; s €67-97, d €149-175; P) The sprawling residence of the former bishops is now a romantic upmarket hotel, with stylish rooms set around a beautiful leafy courtyard. The beer garden is a popular spot on summer evenings, and there's wheelchair access.

Eating
'In Regensburg we ate a magnificent lunch, had a divine musical entertainment, an English hostess and a wonderful Moselle wine,' Mozart wrote to his wife Constance in 1790. Available in Mozart's day, but better washed down with a local Kneitinger Pils, is a delectable *Bratwurstl* (grilled sausage) and *Händlmaier's Süsser Hausmachersenf*, a distinctive sweet mustard.

RESTAURANTS
Spaghetteria (☎ 0130-785 700; Am Römling 12; dishes €6-8) For heavenly pastas and a spirited crowd, step into this former 17th-century chapel. You can pick fresh noodles, sauces and side dishes from the buffet and get out the door for the cost of a cocktail in Munich. The entrance fresco has a pasta-sucking character from *Commedia dell' Arte*.

Café Orphée (☎ 529 77; Untere Bachgasse 8; mains €11-16; ☺ 9am-1am) This delightful brasserie, decked out in red velvet, dark wood and plenty of mirrors, is straight off a Parisian street. Patés, snacks, coffee or a light lunch all stem from a menu of delectable French cuisine.

Dicker Mann (☎ 573 70; Krebsgasse 6; mains €8-14) One of the oldest restaurants in town, this stylish, very traditional restaurant has dependable Bavarian food, swift service and a lively flair thanks to its young and upbeat staff. On a balmy evening, grab a table in the lovely beer garden out back.

THE AUTHOR'S CHOICE

Behind a humble door right in the heart of the city lies a world of genuine charm, unexpected extras and real attention to detail. The striped floors, wrought-iron beds, original sinks and common rooms with soft cushions and well-read books give **Hotel D'Orphée** (☎ 596 020; www .hotel-orphee.de; Wahlenstrasse 1; s €65-98, d €79-115) the feel of a home lovingly attended rather than a hotel. Each room is unique: number seven is stunningly romantic, while number five has a bathroom accessed through a hidden door. For single travellers on a budget there's one attic room with a taste of luxury at an affordable rate. A mouth-watering breakfast is served at the connected Café Orphée (p381), where a new branch of the hotel has opened.

Rosenpalais (☎ 599 7579; Minoritenweg 20; bistro mains €11-18, restaurant mains €22.50-29; ☺ closed Sun) This two-tone establishment caters for a well-heeled clientele at the graceful silver-service restaurant upstairs, and for gourmets on a more restrictive budget downstairs. Either way the food is superb. For the best possible deal try the weekday two-course lunch special (€9.50).

Other recommendations:

Bodega Vinos y Tapas (☎ 584 0486; Von der Grieb 1a; tapas €4-7) Delectable Spanish snacks served in the elegant, torch-lit surrounds of a former horse butcher's.

l'Osteria (☎ 599 9181; Watmarkt 1; mains €7-11) The big steaming plates of pasta and thick toppings inspire its patrons to loud, spirited conversation.

QUICK EATS

Historische Wurstküche (Thundorfer Strasse 3; dishes €2.70-7.60) Justifiably famous for its little sausages grilled over beechwood and served with *Kraut* (cabbage). There's also wheelchair access.

Würstlkine (Rotehahnengasse 2) If Historische Wurstküche is closed, head for this sausage stand with cult status among night owls.

Dampfnudel Uli (☎ 532 97; Watmarkt 4; dishes under €5; ☺ closed Sun & Mon) For a speciality you're unlikely to find anywhere else, try the steamed doughnuts with custard (€4).

Bombay Express (☎ 584 0954; Am Ölberg 3; mains €5-8; ☺ 11am-7pm Mon-Sun) Has fragrant Indian curries made with choice ingredients for takeaway or eating at stand-up tables.

Viktualienmarkt (☺ daily) There is a fresh produce market at Neupfarrplatz.

Drinking
BEER GARDENS

Augustiner (☎ 584 0455; Neufarrplatz 15) This popular beer garden and restaurant (meals €5 to €16) is ideally located in the heart of the city. The sprawling garden and cavernous interior swell with happy locals enjoying the good food and local brews.

Kneitinger (☎ 524 55; Arnulfplatz 3; ☺ 9am-11pm) Everyone from students to actors to regular burghers flock to this quintessential Bavarian brewpub for its hearty home cooking (meals €5 to €13) and delicious house suds. It's been in business since 1530. Tours of its brewery are given Wednesday afternoons at 3pm.

Alte Linde (☎ 880 80; Müllerstrasse 1) A lovely place at any time of year, but especially worth a visit on summer evenings, the Alte Linde is a large and leafy beer garden with a panoramic view of the Altstadt. They also do food (meals €6 to €11). It's accessed via the romantic Steinerne Brücke.

PUBS & BARS

Café Galerie (☎ 561 0408; Kohlenmarkt 6) This multi-level fun spot on Kohlenmarkt, an old coal-seller's square, affords partiers untold options. Buy a scoop at the ice-cream bar, bypass the sports TV to meet your mate on the dance floor, or just slip behind a mellow sidewalk table for a cocktail.

Kaminski (☎ 5999 9033; Hinter der Grieb 6) Whether for afternoon coffee, a champagne breakfast or red wine with mussels, this self-assured café with pin-striped décor has something for everyone. Breakfast always has a classical soundtrack.

Paletti (☎ 515 93; Pustetpassage; ☺ 8am-1am Mon-Sat, 3pm-1am Sun) Tucked into a covered passageway off Gesandtenstrasse, this buzzy Italian café-bar is a hip hang-out with seen-and-be-seen windows and art-clad walls. Patrons come for thimble-sized espressos, hearty pastas or chilli Pinot Grigio.

Hemingway's (☎ 561 506; Obere Bachgasse 5) Black wood, big mirrors and lots of photos of Papa himself add to the cool atmosphere of this Art Deco–style bar. It fills up with the trendy set in the late evening.

Neue Film Bühne (☎ 570 37; Bismarckplatz 9) Theatrical décor and the odd disco ball characterise this funky café-bar frequented by an eclectic crowd of students, yuppies and young families. In summer, the terrace overlooking Bismarckplatz is great for lounging.

Entertainment

Ask for a free copy of *Logo*, the local listings mag, in cafés and bars around town.

CINEMAS

Film Galerie (☎ 560 901; Bertoldstrasse 9) Part of the Leerer Beutel cultural centre, this cinema concentrates on arthouse films, often shown in the original language (including English).

Garbo-Filmtheater (☎ 575 86; Weissgerbergraben) This theatre shows classic Hollywood and modern films in English.

JAZZ & FINE ARTS

Jazzclub im Leeren Beutel (☎ 563 375; Bertoldstrasse 9) This moody jazz club is a vortex of talent, putting on two to three concerts a week. The host art centre also has an art gallery, cinema and stylish restaurant.

Theater Regensburg (☎ 507 2424; Bismarckplatz) runs a packed and varied programme of opera, ballet, classical concerts and drama. The **Theater am Haidplatz** (Haidplatz 8) also has open-air performances in summer.

The cathedral's famous boys' choir, the Regensburger Domspatzen, sings at the 10am Sunday service in the Dom.

Getting There & Away

Regensburg has direct train links to Frankfurt-am-Main (€56, three hours), Munich (€21, 1½ hours), Nuremberg (€15.50, 1½ hours) and Passau (€22, one hour).

Regensburg is about an hour's drive southeast of Nuremberg and northwest of Passau via the A3 autobahn. The A9 runs south to Munich.

Getting Around

BICYCLE

Bikehaus (☎ 599 8808; Hauptbahnhof; bikes per day €9/6; ☯ 10am-7pm Mon-Sat) Staff here can help plan bike trips along the Danube and in other regions. It also has bike storage.

BUS

The Altstadtbus runs between the Hauptbahnhof and the Altstadt every six minutes for just €0.70, except Sunday. The bus transfer point is one block north of the Hauptbahnhof,

on Albertstrasse. Tickets cost €1.70/2.30 for short/long journeys in the centre; strip tickets cost €5.60 for five rides (two strips per ride in town). An all-day ticket (€3.50 at ticket machines, more on the bus) is a better deal.

CAR & MOTORCYCLE

The Steinerne Brücke and much of the Altstadt is closed to private vehicles. Car parks in the centre charge from €1.20 per hour and are well signposted.

TAXI

For a taxi, call ☎ 194 10 or ☎ 520 52.

AROUND REGENSBURG

Klosterschenke Weltenburg

When you're this close to the world's oldest monastic brewery, there's just no excuse to miss out. **Klosterschenke Weltenburg** (☎ 09441-3682; www.klosterschenke-weltenburg.de; Asamstrasse 32; ☯ 8am-7pm mid-Mar–mid-Nov, closed Mon-Tue Mar & Nov) has been brewing its delicious dark beer since 1050. Now a state-of-the-art brewery, it is a favourite spot for an excursion, and the comely beer garden can get quite crowded on warm weekends and holidays.

Not everyone comes for the brew alone, as the complex is also home to a most magnificent church, **Klosterkirche Sts Georg und Martin**, designed by Cosmas Damian and Egid Quirin Asam. Its eye-popping high altar shows St George triumphant on horseback, with the dead dragon and rescued princess at his feet. Also worth noting is the oval ceiling fresco, with a sculpture of CD Asam leaning over the railing.

The nicest approach to Weltenburg is by boat from the Danube river town of Kelheim (about 30km southwest of Regensburg on the B16) via the **Danube Gorge**, a particularly dramatic stretch of the river as it carves through craggy cliffs and past bizarre rock formations. From mid-March to October, you can take a trip up the gorge for €4/7 one-way/return; bicycles are an extra €1.80/3.60.

Walhalla

Modelled on the Parthenon in Athens, the **Walhalla** (adult/children €3/2.50; ☯ 9am-5.45pm Apr-Sep, 10am-noon & 1-3.45pm Oct-Mar) is a breathtaking Ludwig I monument dedicated to the giants of Germanic thought and deed. Marble steps seem to lead up forever from the banks of the Danube to this stunning marble hall, with a gallery of 127 heroes in marble. It includes a few dubious cases, such as astronomer Copernicus, born in a territory belonging to present-day Poland. The latest addition (2003) was Sophie Scholl, a member of *Die Weisse Rose* resistance group (see p302).

To get there take the Danube Valley country road (unnumbered) 10km east from Regensburg to the village of Donaustauf, then follow the signs. Alternatively, you can take a two-hour boat cruise with **Schifffahrtsunternehmen Klinger** (☎ 0941-521 04; €7/10 one-way/return; ☼ 10.30am & 2pm Apr–mid-Oct), which includes a one-hour stop at Walhalla.

Befreiungshalle

Perched on a hill above the Danube, this mustard-coloured tankard of a building is the **Befreiungshalle** (Hall of Liberation; ☎ 09441-15 84; Befreiungshallestrasse 3; adult/concession €3/2; ☼ 9am-6pm Apr-Sep, 9am-4pm Oct-Mar). Erected in 1863, it's an outrageous piece of Bavarian nationalism ordered by King Ludwig I to commemorate the victories over Napoleon (1813–15). Inside you'll find a veritable shrine lorded over by white marble angels modelled on the Roman goddess Victoria.

STRAUBING
☎ 09421 / pop 45,000

Some 30km southeast of Regensburg, Straubing enjoyed a brief heyday as part of a wonky alliance that formed the short-lived Duchy of Straubing-Holland. As a result, the centre is chock-a-block with historical buildings that opened new horizons in a small town. In August, the demand for folding benches soars during the **Gäubodenfest**, a 10-day blow-out that once brought together grain farmers in 1812, but now draws over 20,000 drinkers.

Orientation & Information

Compact and quite walkable, the historical centre is squeezed between the Danube and the Hauptbahnhof. The central square is shaped more like a street and consists of Theresienplatz and Ludwigsplatz. The **tourist office** (☎ 944 307; www.straubing.de; Theresienplatz 20; ☼ 9am-5pm Mon-Fri, 9am-noon Sat) makes free room referrals.

Sights & Activities

Lined with pastel-coloured houses from a variety of periods, the pedestrian square is lorded over by the Gothic **Stadtturm** (1316).

It stands next to the richly gabled **Rathaus**, originally two merchants' homes but repackaged in neo-Gothic style in the 19th century. Just east of the tower is the gleaming golden **Dreifaltigkeitssäule** (Trinity Column), erected in 1709 as a nod to Catholic upheavals during the Spanish War of Succession.

Straubing has about half a dozen historic churches. The most impressive is **St Jakobskirche** (Pfarrplatz), a late Gothic hall church with original stained-glass windows but also a recipient of a baroque makeover, courtesy of the amazing Asam brothers. The pair also designed the interior of the **Ursulinenkirche** on Burggasse, their final collaboration. Its ceiling fresco depicts the martyrdom of St Ursula surrounded by allegorical representations of the four known continents. Also worth a look is the nearby **Karmelitenkirche** on Hofstatt.

North of here is the former ducal residence **Herzogsschloss** (Schlossplatz), which overlooks the river. This rather austere 14th-century building was a tax office and home to a small collection of **religious art** (☎ 211 14; adult/child €2.50/1.50; ☼ 10am-4pm Thu-Sun Apr-Jan).

One of Germany's most important vaults of Roman treasure is the intimate **Gäubodenmuseum** (☎ 974 10; Frauenhoferstrasse 9; adult/concession €2.50/1.50; ☼ 10am-4pm Tue-Sun). Displays include imposing armour and masks for both soldiers and horses, probably plundered from a Roman store.

Getting There & Away

Straubing is on a regional train line from Regensburg (€7.60, 30 minutes) and Passau (€11.70, one hour). Trains to and from Munich (€20.60, two hours) require a change. Drivers should take the Kirchhof exit off the A3 (the Nuremberg–Passau autobahn). There's free parking at Unter den Hagen, a five-minute walk south of Stadtplatz.

PASSAU
☎ 0851 / pop 50,000

Straddling the confluence of three rivers, the Danube, Inn and Ilz, Passau was predestined to become a powerful trading post. The waterways brought wealth, especially from 'white gold' (salt), and Christianity brought prestige as the city evolved into the largest bishopric in the Holy Roman Empire. The beautiful old centre has a distinct Italian look, with winding medieval lanes, tunnels and archways. The *Niebelungenlied*, the epic poem about a dragon-slayer, is believed to originate from here, at the bishop's 13th-century court.

Passau is a major river-cruise stop and is often deluged with day visitors. It is also the hub of many long-distance cycling routes, eight of which converge here, and a good springboard for explorations into upper Austria.

Orientation

Passau's Altstadt is a narrow peninsula with the confluence of the three rivers at its eastern tip. From the north the little Ilz brings soily water from the Bavarian forest, which meets the murkier Danube as it flows from the west and the greenish Alpine water of the Inn from the south. The Hauptbahnhof is about a 10-minute walk west of the Altstadt. The Veste Oberhaus is on the north side of the Danube.

Information

Citibank (Theresienstrasse 1)
Coffee Fellows (Schrottgasse 10; per 30min €1.30) One of the trendier coffee and internet bars in town.
Commerzbank (Ludwigstrasse 13)
Post office (Bahnhofstrasse 27)
Tourist office Altstadt (☎ 955 980; www.passau.de; Rathausplatz 3; ☼ 8.30am-6pm Mon-Fri, 9.30am-3pm Sat & Sun, closed lunch & weekends mid-Oct–Easter); Hauptbahnhof (☎ 955 980; Bahnhofstrasse 36; ☼ 9am-5pm Mon-Thu, 9am-4pm Fri year-round, 9am-1pm Sat & Sun Easter–mid-October)

Sights

VESTE OBERHAUS

This 13th-century fortress, built by the prince-bishops, towers over the city with patriarchal pomp. Views are superb, either from the castle tower (€1) or from the **Battalion Linde**, a lookout that gives the only bird's-eye view of the confluence of all three rivers.

Inside the bastion is the **Oberhausmuseum** (☎ 493 350; Oberhaus 125; adult/concession €5/4; ☼ 9am-5pm Mon-Fri, 10am-6pm Sat & Sun, closed mid-Dec–mid-Mar). Some of the best exhibits here uncover the mysteries of medieval castle-building and a knight's rites of passage.

DOM ST STEPHAN

The characteristic green onion domes of Passau's cathedral, the **Dom**, float serenely above the town silhouette. There has been a church on this spot since the 5th century, but the current baroque look emerged after the Great Fire

of 1662. The interior was designed by a crew of Italian artists, notably the architect Carlo Lurago and the stucco master Giovanni Carlone. The frescoes show fascinating scenes of heaven, but the true masterpiece is the church organ – it's one of the world's largest with a staggering 17,974 pipes. Organ recitals are held on weekdays at noon, and on Thursday at 7.30pm from May to October (adult/child €3/1 lunchtime; €5/3 evening).

From the south aisle, a set of corkscrew stairs leads to the New Bishop's Residence, which contains the **Domschatz- und Diözesanmuseum** (Cathedral Treasury & Museum; adult/concession €1.50/0.50; ☼ 10am-4pm Mon-Sat May-Oct). This showcases a range of ecclesiastical finery that nicely illustrates the power and wealth of the Church rulers.

ALTES RATHAUS

The carillon in the colourful **Rathaus** chimes several times daily (hours are listed on the wall alongside the historical flood levels). Inside, the **Grosser Rathaus Saal** (Great Assembly Room; adult/concession €1.50/1; ☼ 10am-4pm Apr-Oct) has wonderful murals by local artist Ferdinand Wagner, showing scenes from Passau's history with a melodramatic flourish. If it's not being used for a wedding, also sneak into the adjacent **Small Assembly Room** for a peek at the ceiling fresco showing buxom beauties and a fierce-looking man – meant as allegories of the three rivers.

Wagner, who used to live in the huge building on the north bank of the Danube, just to the right of where the Luitpoldbrücke suspension bridge is today, threatened to move out of town if the bridge was built. It was, he did, and after viewing the paintings, you wonder whether the city made the right choice.

PASSAUER GLASMUSEUM

A splendid collection of over 30,000 examples of Bohemian glasswork and crystal from over 250 years is on view at the **Passauer Glasmuseum** (Passau Museum of Glass; ☎ 350 71; Hotel Wilder Mann, Am Rathausplatz; adult/concession €5/3; ☼ 1-5pm). Even if you charge through the place, you'll need an hour to view the 36 rooms filled with baroque, classical, Art Nouveau and Art Deco pieces. There's a luxury bedroom chamber right in the museum that's let to visiting VIPs as part of the adjacent Hotel Wilder Mann (p386). Be sure to pick up a floor plan as it's easy to get lost.

BAVARIA

OTHER MUSEUMS

The **Museum Moderne Kunst** (Modern Art Museum; ☎ 383 8790; Bräugasse 17; adult/concession €5/3; ☻ 10am-6pm Tue-Sun) shows an ambitious cycle of temporary exhibits, often of international merit, in a fascinating jumble of buildings.

Across the Fünferlsteg Inn footbridge, in the Kastell Boiotro, is the **Römermuseum** (☎ 347 69; Kastell Boiotro; adult/concession €2/1; ☻ 10am-noon & 2-4pm Tue-Sun Mar-May & Sep-Nov, 10am-noon & 1-4pm Jun-Aug), which depicts Passau's original settlement.

Activities

From March to early November, **Wurm + Köck** (☎ 929 292; www.donauschiffahrt.de; Höllgasse 26; adult/child 45min €6.50/3.50, 2hr €9.50/6.50) runs cruises to the Dreiflusseck from the docks near Rathausplatz.

It's a pleasant, easy hike from town to the Zur Triftsperre (opposite). From the camping ground Zeltplatz Ilzstadt (right), head north and walk 2.8km along Halser Strasse and its extension, Grafenleite Strasse, looking for the beer garden signs. Ask at the tourist office for hiking maps.

Sleeping

Zeltplatz Ilzstadt (☎ 414 57; Halser Strasse 34; adult/child €6/5) This tent-only camping ground has an idyllic spot on the Ilz, about a 15-minute walk from the Altstadt. Catch bus 1, 2, 3 or 4 to Exerzierplatz-Ilzbrücke.

DJH hostel (☎ 493 780; www.djh.de; Veste Oberhaus 125; dm under/over 26yr €17.10/21.10) This beautifully renovated hostel is right in the fortress.

Pension Rössner (☎ 931 350; www.pension-roessner.de; Bräugasse 19; s/d €35/60; Ⓟ) You'll get plenty for your money at this immaculate *pension* in a restored mansion on the eastern tip of the Altstadt. Each room is uniquely decorated and many also have fortress views. Breakfast is €7 extra.

Hotel König (☎ 3850; www.hotel-koenig.de; Untere Donaulände; s €68-85, d €85-130; Ⓟ ✗) Spacious modern rooms, great views over the river and a good central location make this riverside property an excellent choice. The hotel also has a good restaurant with a beautiful dining terrace. There is wheelchair access.

Hotel Wilder Mann (☎ 350 71; www.wilder-mann.com; Am Rathausplatz; s €40-50, d €60-180; Ⓟ) Royalty and celebrities, from Empress Elizabeth of Austria

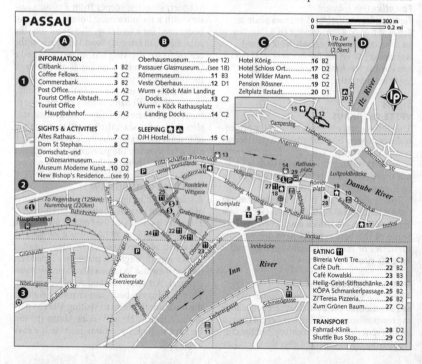

PASSAU

INFORMATION		Oberhausmuseum.............(see 12)		Hotel König........................16 B2
Citibank.....................................1 B2		Passauer Glasmuseum.....(see 18)		Hotel Schloss Ort...............17 D2
Coffee Fellows..........................2 C2		Römermuseum..................11 B3		Hotel Wilder Mann.............18 C2
Commerzbank...........................3 B2		Veste Oberhaus.................12 D1		Pension Rössner................19 D2
Post Office.................................4 A2		Wurm + Köck Main Landing		Zeltplatz Ilzstadt...............20 D1
Tourist Office Altstadt............5 C2		Docks...............................13 C2		
Tourist Office		Wurm + Köck Rathausplatz		SLEEPING
Hauptbahnhof.......................6 A2		Landing Docks.................14 C2		DJH Hostel........................15 C1

SIGHTS & ACTIVITIES		EATING
Altes Rathaus............................7 C2		Birreria Venti Tre................21 C3
Dom St Stephan........................8 C2		Café Duft............................22 B2
Domschatz-und		Café Kowalski.....................23 B3
Diözesanmuseum...................9 C2		Heilig-Geist-Stiftsschänke..24 B2
Museum Moderne Kunst......10 D2		KÖPA Schmankerlpassage..25 B2
New Bishop's Residence....(see 9)		Zi'Teresa Pizzeria...............26 B2
		Zum Grünen Baum............27 C2

| TRANSPORT |
| Fahrrad-Klinik....................28 D2 |
| Shuttle Bus Stop................29 C2 |

BAVARIA

FAVOURITES IN GLASS

Georg Höltl, founder of the Passauer Glasmuseum, named the following works as a few of his favourites:

- Dolphin dinner service (No 262) – A beautiful enamel-and-gold-leaf 170-piece set, all adorned with a happy flopping fish; thought to be a wedding present for the well-to-do.

- A pair of decorative vases (No 288) – Larger-than-life Oriental-style vessels hand-blown in transparent amber for the 1876 Munich Trade Fair (each 1.65m tall).

- Daumengläser (Nos 293–94) – Curious tumblers (literally 'thumglasses') in Old German style that were all the rage in the mid-1800s.

- Sektgläser (Nos 305–08) – Brocaded, barbell-shaped sparkling wine glasses with piercing white-eyed portraits of four poets and artists including Albrecht Dürer.

- Bismarck wine glass (No 311) – Detailed profile of the Iron Chancellor in a Bacchanalian setting.

---

to Mikhail Gorbachev and Henry Kissinger, have stayed at this historic hotel. Rooms seek to recapture a lost grandeur, and some of the carved bedsteads are very grand indeed. The best rooms overlook the garden at the back.

Hotel Schloss Ort (☎ 340 72; www.schlosshotel -passau.de; Im Ort 11; s €54-78, d €88-128; P) Behind the walls of this snug medieval palace awaits a stylish hotel just a hop from the Dreiflusseck. Rooms have wrought-iron beds, modern parquet floors and great river views.

Eating & Drinking

Heilig-Geist-Stiftsschänke (☎ 2607; Heilig-Geist-Gasse 4; mains €8-16) Traditional food is prepared with panache, and served either in the classy walnut-panelled tangle of dining rooms or the leafy beer garden, where hedges create separate dining areas. The candle-lit stone cellar is open from 6pm.

Zi'Teresa Pizzeria (☎ 2138; Theresienstrasse 26; meals €4.80-12.50) Theresienstrasse and its side streets are lined with cafés and restaurants and popular places to just hang out, such as Zi'Teresa. This lively, always-bustling Italian restaurant draws people of all ages to munch on delicious pizzas and pastas as well as the good appetisers and salads.

Zum Grünen Baum (☎ 356 35; Höllgasse 7; mains €6-14) This darling eatery has some eccentric design touches, such as a cutlery chandelier and a toy-filled, smoke-free backroom. Organic beer, wine and lots of vegetarian dishes give this place a healthy bent. For dessert, be sure to ask for the unlisted 'variety platter'.

Café Kowalski (☎ 2487; Oberer Sand 1; dishes €5-11) Chat flows as freely as wine or beer at this gregarious café, a kicker of a night spot. The giant burgers, schnitzels and salads are best sampled on the terrace overlooking the Ilz.

Birreria Venti Tre (☎ 490 5283; Schmiedgasse 23; mains €8-16) This new trattoria has candle-lit ambience and tasty food that blend together as perfectly as a Tuscan stew. The spaghetti *Renate* (with shrimp and tomatoes) is highly recommended. The garden is among Passau's finest.

Zur Triftsperre (☎ 511 62; Triftsperre Strasse 15) A wonderful beer garden and restaurant on a peaceful section of the Ilz.

Other recommendations:

Café Duft (☎ 346 66; Theresienstrasse 22; mains €3.40-8.20) A vaulted chamber with low lights, dark wood and a good range of dishes.

KÖPA Schmankerlpassage (Ludwigstrasse 6) Fruit stalls, meat and fish counters to put together a full meal under €6.

Getting There & Away

TRAIN

Passau is on the main train line going to Nuremberg (€37, two hours), Regensburg (€18, 1½ hours) and Vienna (€38, 3½ hours). There are also direct trains to Munich (€27, 2¼ hours). The trip to Zwiesel (€17, 1½ hours) and other Bavarian Forest towns requires a change in Plattling.

Passau is just off the A3 autobahn from Nuremberg to Regensburg, which links up with the A92 to Munich near Deggendorf.

Getting Around

Central Passau is compact, so most sights are reachable on foot. The CityBus regularly links the Bahnhof with the Altstadt (€0.80). Longer trips within Passau cost €1.50; a day pass costs €3 (€4 for a family).

The walk up the hill to the Veste or the hostel, via Luitpoldbrücke and Ludwigsteig path, takes about 30 minutes. From April to October, a shuttle bus operates from Rathausplatz (€2/2.50 one-way/return).

There are several public car parks near the train station but only one in the Altstadt at Römerplatz (€1.10/€10 per hour/day).

The **Fahrrad-Klinik** (☎ 334 11; Bräugasse 10) hires out bikes from €11 per day.

MARKTL AM INN
☎ 08678 / pop 2700

On a gentle bend in the Inn, some 68km southwest of Passau, sits the prim hamlet of Marktl am Inn. Few people outside of Germany (or indeed Bavaria) had heard of it before 19 April 2005, the day when its favourite son, Cardinal Joseph Ratzinger, was elected as **Pope Benedict XVI**. Literally overnight the village was inundated with reporters, devotees and the plain curious, all seeking clues about the pontiff's life and times. Souvenirs like mitre-shaped cakes, 'Papst-Bier' (Pope's Beer) and religious board games flooded the local shops.

The pope's **Geburtshaus** (Birth House; ☎ 748 820; Marktplatz 11; adult/child €2/free; 🕑 2-5pm Tue-Sun) is the simple but pretty Bavarian home where Ratzinger lived for the first two years of his life before his family moved to Tittmoning, another tiny burg. A tablet commemorates his birth in 1927, and his elevation to honorary citizen half a century later, by which time he was already serving as chief advisor to his predecessor in the Vatican. A Ratzinger museum was expected to open here in late 2006.

The **Heimatmuseum** (Local History Museum; ☎ 7341; Marktplatz 2; adult/child €1.50/1; 🕑 2-4pm Tue-Sat, 2-4.30pm Sun, May-Oct) is in possession of a golden chalice and a skullcap that was used by Ratzinger in his private chapel in Rome. His baptismal font can be viewed at the **Pfarrkirche St Oswald** (Parish Church of St Oswald, ☎ 293; Marktplatz 6), which is open for viewing except during church services.

More papal attractions are sure to be in development, so do check for the latest details at the newly-erected **tourist office** (☎ 748 820; www.markt-marktl.de; Marktplatz 1). Marktl am Inn is best reached by car on the B12 between Munich and Passau.

BAVARIAN FOREST
Together with the Bohemian Forest on the other side of the Czech border, the Bavarian Forest (Bayerischer Wald) forms the largest continuous woodland area in Europe. It's a lovely landscape of rolling hills and tree-covered mountains interspersed with small, little-disturbed valleys. A large area is protected as the surprisingly wild and rugged Bavarian Forest National Park (Nationalpark Bayerischer Wald).

Despite being incredibly good value, the region sees very few international tourists and remains quite traditional. A centuries-old glass-blowing industry is still active in many of the towns along the **Glasstrasse** (Glass Road), a 250km holiday route connecting Neustadt an der Waldnaab with Passau. You can visit the studios, factories and shops and stock up on the magnificent designs.

Orientation
The ranges of the Bavarian Forest stretch northwest to southeast along the German–Czech border, and its wild frontier nature is still the region's chief attribute. One of the bigger towns, and an ideal base for its good train and bus connections, is Zwiesel.

Information
Café Flitzer (☎ 09922-502 160; Dr Schottstrasse 18, Zwiesel; per 10min €0.50; 🕑 11am-10pm) Internet access; about 300m southwest of the main square.
Grafenau tourist office (☎ 08552-962 343; www .grafenau.de; Rathausgasse 1; 🕑 9am-noon & 2-6pm Mon-Thu, 9am-4pm Fri, 10-11.30am Sat) Also has internet access (€2 for 30 minutes).
Zwiesel tourist office Town centre (☎ 09922-840 523; www.zwiesel-tourismus.de; Stadtplatz 27); Zwiesel-Süd (🕑 10am-1pm & 2-5pm Mon-Fri, 10-3pm Sat) The latter has English-speaking staff and is just outside town on the main road towards Regan.

Sights
Forest, local customs and glass making are the main themes of exhibits at Zwiesel's **Waldmuseum** (Forest Museum; ☎ 09922-608 88; Stadtplatz 28; adult/concession €2/1.50; 🕑 9am-5pm Mon-Fri, 10am-noon & 2-4pm Sat & Sun mid-May–mid-Oct, reduced hours in winter). Also in Zwiesel is the **Dampfbier-Brauerei** (☎ 09922-846 60; Regener Strasse 9, Zwiesel; tours €7; 🕑 tours 10am Wed) where you can join a brewery tour and sample its peppery ales.

Frauenau's sparkling new **Glasmuseum** (☎ 09926-9401 020; Am Museumspark 1; adult/child €5/2.50;

☺ 9am-5pm Mon-Fri, 10am-4pm Sat & Sun) covers four millennia of glass-making history, starting with the ancient Egyptians and ending with modern glass art from around the world. Demonstrations and workshops for kids are regular features. The colourful section of designer snuff flasks is a must-see.

On the southern edge of the Bavarian Forest, in Tittling, there's the **Museumsdorf Bayerischer Wald** (☎ 08504-8482; Herrenstrasse 11; adult/child €3.50/free; ☺ 9am-5pm Apr-Oct). This 20-hectare open-air museum features 150 typical Bavarian Forest buildings from the 16th to the 19th centuries, with displays ranging from clothing and furniture to pottery and farming implements. Take RBO bus 8771 to Tittling from Passau Hauptbahnhof.

BAVARIAN FOREST NATIONAL PARK
A paradise for outdoor enthusiasts, the Bavarian Forest National Park stretches for about 24,250 hectares along the Czech border, from Bayerisch Eisenstein in the north to Finsterau in the south. Its thick forest, most of it mountain spruce, is crisscrossed by hundreds of kilometres of hiking, cycling and cross-country skiing trails. The three main mountains, Rachel, Lusen and Grosser Falkenstein, rise up to between 1300m and 1450m and are home to deer, wild boar, fox, otter and countless bird species.

The park's superb visitor centre is housed in the **Hans-Eisenmann-Haus** (☎ 08558-961 50; www.nationalpark-bayerischer-wald.de; Böhmstrasse 35, Neuschönau; ☺ 9am-5pm). You can pick up maps and leaflets (some in English) and see exhibits on the park's flora, fauna and environmental issues; there's also a children's discovery room and a library. See p390 for details about transport in the park.

Activities
Two long-distance hiking routes cut through the Bavarian Forest: the European Distance Trails E6 (Baltic Sea to the Adriatic) and E8 (North Sea to Carpathia). There are mountain huts all along the way. Another popular hiking trail is the Gläserne Steig (Glass Trail) from Lam to Grafenau. Detailed maps and hiking suggestions are available at the local tourist offices and at the Hans-Eisenmann-Haus.

The Bavarian Forest has seven ski areas, but downhill skiing is low-key, even though the area's highest mountain, the Grosser

Arber (1456m), occasionally hosts European and World Cup ski races. The best resorts are in the north, such as Bischofsmais near the Geisskopf (1097m), Bodenmais near the Grosser Arber, and Neukirchen near the Hoher Bogen (1079m). The major draw here is cross-country skiing, with 2000km of prepared routes through the ranges.

Sleeping
Accommodation in this area is a real bargain; Zwiesel and Grafenau have the best choices.

HOSTELS & CAMPING
All hostels close for at least a month around November and December.

DJH hostel (☎ 08553-6000; www.djh.de; Herbergsweg 2; dm under/over 26yr €18.10/22.10) The only hostel right in the national park and an ideal base for hikers.

Azur-Ferienpark Bayerischer Wald (☎ 09922-802 595; www.azur-camping.de; Waldesruhweg 34, Zwiesel; per person €5-7, tent €5.50-8.50) About 500m north of the Hauptbahnhof, near public pools and sports facilities.

PENSIONS & HOTELS
Landgasthaus Karin (☎ 08552-2187; www.schall-fewe -de; Buschweg 24, Grafenau; d €39-44, apt €31-50; P ☒) Run by a delightful young couple, this child- and pet-friendly property sits right on a forest slope, with meticulously kept rooms and apartments. Rates include admission to the local fitness centre.

Hotel-Gasthaus Zum Kellermann (☎ 08552-967 10; www.hotel-zum-kellermann.de; Stadtplatz 8, Grafenau; s/d €31/50; ☺ closed Wed; P) Bright, modern rooms at very reasonable rates make this simple guesthouse in Grafenau a good bet. There's a pretty terrace area outside and the restaurant (mains €6 to €12) serves up tasty traditional dishes.

Hotel Zur Waldbahn (☎ 09922-3001; www.zurwald bahn.de; Bahnhofplatz 2, Zwiesel; s €54-58, d €84-90; P ☒) Tradition and modern comforts blend seamlessly at this friendly inn, conveniently located opposite the Hauptbahnhof. The warm, wood-panelled rooms are tastefully furnished and the restaurant, with an authentic tiled oven, is top-notch (mains €7 to €16).

Hotel Hubertus (☎ 08552-96490; www.hubertus -grafenau.de; Grüb 20, Grafenau; s €46-58, d €72-102; P ☒) This elegant hotel in Grafenau offers incredible value for the weary traveller. The stylish rooms are spacious and most have balconies. Guests are treated to a pool and sauna, and delicious buffet meals.

BAVARIA

Eating

Many of the hotels mentioned in Sleeping also have good restaurants.

Restaurant Nepomuk (☎ 09922-605 30; Stadtplatz 30, Zwiesel; mains €6-13) This place, just off the square opposite the tourist office, is popular with locals. It has a good range of traditional dishes as well as some lighter choices and a few vegetarian options.

Weinanger (☎ 09922-869 690; Angerstrasse 37, Zwiesel; mains €5-9) If your stomach craves lighter fare, try this cheerful wine bistro with brick walls and polished wooden tables. French onion soup, cheeses and baguette sandwiches all feature on the menu, and some Fridays there's live jazz.

Getting There & Around

From Munich, Regensburg or Passau, Zwiesel is reached by rail via Plattling; most trains continue to Bayerisch Eisenstein on the Czech border, with connections to Prague. The Waldbahn shuttles directly between Zwiesel and Bodenmais and Zwiesel and Grafenau.

There's also a tight network of regional buses, though service can be infrequent. The Igel-Bus navigates around the national park on four routes. A useful one is the Lusen-Bus (€4/10 per one-/three-day ticket), which leaves from Grafenau Hauptbahnhof and travels to the Hans-Eisenmann-Haus, the Neuschönau hostel and the Lusen hiking area.

From mid-May to October, the best value is usually the **Bayerwald-Ticket** (€6), a day pass good for unlimited travel on bus and train throughout the forest area. It's available from the visitors centre and tourist offices throughout the national park.

Baden-Württemberg

Baden-Württemberg is one of Germany's most popular holiday regions, rivalled only by Bavaria in its natural landscapes and range of outdoor activities. Most of the state is covered by the fabled Black Forest (Schwarzwald), a vast nature playground whose peaks, lakes and cuckoo clocks are irresistible to hikers, cyclists, bathers, boaters and punctual people who find quarter-hourly mechanical bird calls charming rather than annoying.

One of the country's most prosperous states, Baden-Württemberg was created in 1951 out of three historic regions: Baden, Württemberg and Hohenzollern. Further back in history, much of its southern reaches were part of Swabia (Schwaben) and many people here still speak Swabian (Schwäbisch), a melodic dialect that other Germans find largely incomprehensible.

In the centre, the capital Stuttgart is the home of Mercedes-Benz and Porsche, and a wealth of urban pleasures. A bit to the east are Schwäbisch Hall, a medieval gem, and, on the banks of the Danube, the architecturally audacious city of Ulm. The spas of Baden-Baden have been soothing the stresses of modern and ancient life since Roman times.

The state is also home to three famous and ancient university cities. In Heidelberg, students still gather in ancient beer halls while Tübingen, with its narrow lanes and hilltop fortress, positively oozes charm. Flowery Freiburg, not far from the Swiss border, makes an ideal base for exploring the Black Forest and the rolling vineyards of Breisach, on the French frontier.

Lake Constance (Bodensee), whose southern shore – overlooked by the Alps – is in Switzerland and Austria, is a huge draw, especially in summer.

BADEN-WÜRTTEMBERG

HIGHLIGHTS

- **Art and Automobiles** Explore outstanding museums and classy shops in Stuttgart (p393)
- **Snow and Eis** Admire the snow-capped Alps and savour ice cream (*Eis*) with strudel at a lakefront café on Lake Constance (p452)
- **Warm Watery Indulgence** Soak in an ornate 19th-century Baden-Baden spa (p434)
- **Back to the Middle Ages** Explore the medieval old town and ancient castle in the university city of Tübingen (p423)
- **Hell's Valley** Hoof it, train it or floor it through the Höllental (Hell's Valley, p449) in the Southern Black Forest

★ Baden-Baden ★ Stuttgart
★ Tübingen
★ Höllental
★ Lake Constance

- POPULATION: 10.7 MILLION
- AREA: 35,752 SQ KM

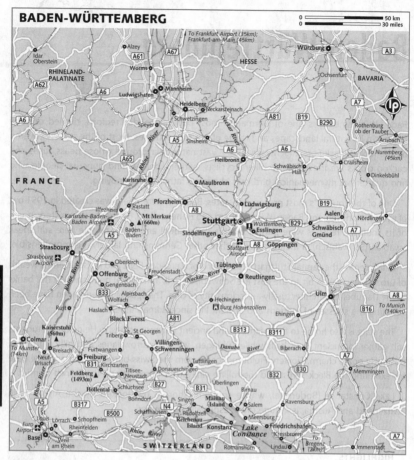

Activities

HIKING

Baden-Württemberg is crisscrossed by walking and hiking trails too numerous to count, many of them through forests, along rivers or around lakes. Local tourist offices sell maps and can suggest suitable day hikes.

CYCLING

Baden-Württemberg is a cyclists' paradise, with thousands of kilometres of paved bike paths. Those with plenty of watery views include the following:

Bodensee-Weg Goes all the way around Lake Constance.

Donautal-Radweg (www.donau-radweg.info, in German) Follows the mighty Danube from the unexciting town of Donaueschingen (65km east of Freiburg) to Ulm (190km northeast of Donaueschingen), Vienna, Budapest and beyond.

Neckartal-Radweg (www.neckartal-radweg.de, in German) Follows the Neckar River for 357km from Villingen-Schwenningen northward (more or less) to Tübingen, Stuttgart and Heidelberg.

Rheintal-Weg Goes along the Rhine from Konstanz westward to Basel and then northward via Freiburg (or Breisach) to Baden-Baden, Heidelberg, Mannheim and beyond.

Veloroute Rhein Follows the Rhine along all of its left bank (in France and then Germany) and most of the right bank from Basel northward to Mannheim (415km).

Getting There & Around

Stuttgart airport (www.stuttgart-airport.com), Baden-Württemberg's largest, is a major hub for the discount airline **German Wings** (www.germanwings .com). Frankfurt airport is about 75km north of Mannheim. Other useful airports include the **EuroAirport** (www.euroairport.com), which serves Freiburg as well as the Swiss city of Basel and the French city of Mulhouse; **Karlsruhe-Baden-Baden airport** (Baden Airpark; www.badenairpark .de); **Friedrichshafen airport** (www.fly-away.de); and **Strasbourg airport** (www.strasbourg.aeroport.fr) in France, across the Rhine from the Northern Black Forest.

Trains, trams and/or buses serve almost every city, town and mountain village in this chapter. Public transport across the Black Forest can be pretty slow, and long-distance trips (such as from Freiburg to Tübingen or Konstanz) may require several changes.

STUTTGART

☎ 0711 / pop 589,000

Perhaps best known as the headquarters of Mercedes-Benz and Porsche, Stuttgart has a number of first-rate art collections and two museums that are sure to set the pulse of the motor-minded racing. Blessed with an air of relaxed prosperity and a keen sense of style, the city is one of the greenest in Europe – not only is it well-endowed with parks, but it even has its own vineyards! The shopping, restaurant, cultural and nightlife scenes are all vibrant, if upmarket.

Stuttgart began as a stud farm ('*Stuotgarten*', hence the name) on the Nesenbach Stream around AD 950. By 1160 it was a booming trade centre, and in the early 14th century it became the royal seat of the Württemberg family. After WWII, the city's architectural treasures were painstakingly reconstructed.

ORIENTATION

The main pedestrian shopping street, Königstrasse, stretches southwest from the well-tended Hauptbahnhof (train station). Public squares on or near Königstrasse include Schlossplatz and Schillerplatz. The three sections of the Schlossgarten (a grassy park) stretch northeastward from Schlossplatz almost 4km to the Neckar River. The district of Bad Cannstatt straddles the Neckar River about 3km northeast of the Hauptbahnhof.

Steep grades are common on Stuttgart's hillsides – more than 500 city streets end in *Stäffele* (staircases).

INFORMATION
Bookshops
Wittwer (☎ 250 70; Königstrasse 30) A bookshop with foreign-language and travel sections.

Cultural Centres
Deutsch-Amerikanisches Zentrum (German-American Center; ☎ 228 180; www.daz.org; Charlottenplatz 17; ☾ 2-6pm Tue-Thu) Promotes German-American relations.

Internet Access
Café Naser (in the Hauptbahnhof; per hr €5; ☾ 6am-10pm) Up the stairs behind track 4.
City Call & Internet Center (Eberhardstrasse 14; per hr €2; ☾ 9am-midnight Mon-Sat, 11am-midnight Sun & holidays)
Cyber Café (Klett Passage; per hr €2; ☾ 9am-11pm)
Level One Cyber Bar (Königstrasse 22; per hr €4.50; ☾ 9am-midnight Mon-Sat, noon-midnight Sun) A stylish internet café in the basement of a cinema.

Laundry
SB-Waschsalon Trieb (☾ 5am-midnight) Self-service laundry in the arcade behind (just south of) the tourist office.

Medical Services
Ärtzliche Bereitschaft (☎ 262 8012; Böheimstrasse 37; ☾ 7pm-7am, 7am-7pm Sat, Sun & holidays) A doctor's office inside Marien-Hospital, which is 3km southwest of

---

DISCOUNT TICKETS

The three-day **Stuttcard** (€12) gets you free entry to most public museums as well as discounts on cultural events and leisure activities, including the tourist office's guided tours. The **Stuttcard Plus** (€17.50) also affords unlimited bus, tram and metro travel within the city, including to and from the airport.

If you have a hotel reservation, for €9 you can get a three-day ticket good for unlimited public transport usage within the city limits (valid for an adult and two children up to age 17). A version good for public transport throughout the entire metropolitan area costs €12.30. They are generally available at hotel reception desks.

All four passes can be purchased at the tourist office, including the airport branch.

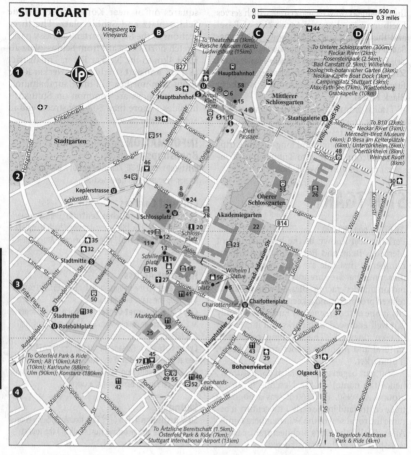

the Hauptbahnhof. Staffed when regular medical practices are closed.

Katharinen Hospital (☎ 2780; Kriegsbergstrasse 60) The city's largest.

Money

American Express exchange bureau (Arnulf-Klett-Platz 1; ☒ 9.30am-noon & 1-6pm Mon-Fri, 10am-1pm Sat)

ATMs There are lots along Königstrasse.

Reisebank & Western Union (in the Hauptbahnhof behind track 11; ☒ 8am-8.30pm, Western Union to 8pm) Currency exchange.

Post

Post office (inside Königsbau Passagen) A bit northwest of the Schlossplatz. There's also a branch in the Hauptbahnhof, up the stairs behind track 4.

Tourist Information

State Tourist Board (www.tourismus-bw.de)

Tourist office (☎ 222 80; www.stuttgart-tourist.de; Königstrasse 1a; ☒ 9am-8pm Mon-Fri, 9am-6pm Sat, 11am-6pm Sun & holidays) The staff can help with room bookings. Has a public transport information desk.

Welcome Information Center (☎ 0711 2228-0; ☒ 8am-8pm) The tourist office branch at Stuttgart International Airport. Situated in Terminal 3, Level 2 (Arrivals).

SIGHTS
City Centre

High above the huge Hauptbahnhof, the 10-storey **Aussichtsplatform** (Viewing Platform; admission free; ☒ 10am-9pm Tue-Sun Apr-Sep, 10am-6pm Tue-Sun, to 9pm Thu Oct-Mar) affords a close-up view of the giant Mercedes logo and, through netting, a wonderful panorama of the surrounding hillsides. It's accessible by lift from the Hauptbahnhof's eastern entrance.

Just east of the train station is the **Mittlerer Schlossgarten** (Middle Palace Garden). Here you'll find meandering walkways, fountains, an excellent **beer garden** and, weather permitting, sunbathing folk watching the world – and the inline skaters – go by. The **Unterer Schlossgarten** (Lower Palace Garden) stretches several kilometres northeast to the Neckar River, where it links up with the **Rosensteinpark**, home of the zoo (see p397). To the south is the **Oberer Schlossgarten** (Upper Palace Garden), ringed by landmark buildings such as the **Staatstheater** (State Theatre) and the **Landtag** (State Parliament).

To the east of the Staatstheater, just across Konrad-Adenauer-Strasse, is the world-renowned **Staatsgalerie** (State Gallery; ☎ 470 400; www.staatsgalerie-stuttgart.de; Konrad-Adenauer-Strasse 30-32; adult/concession €4.50/3, incl special exhibition €8/6; ☼ 10am-6pm Tue-Sun, to 9pm Thu, 10am-midnight 1st Sat of every month), whose collection of 14th- to 20th-century art includes works by masters such as Fra Angelico, Tiepolo, Rembrandt, Rubens, Manet, Monet, Renoir and Cézanne. It occupies two adjacent (and connected) buildings: the neoclassical Alte Staatsgalerie (1843) and the Neue Staatsgalerie (1984), whose pink

tubes and green window frames were designed by James Stirling.

The focus of Stuttgart's commercial life is the pedestrians-only **Königstrasse**, a spotlessly clean and conspicuously well-heeled shopping precinct that stretches for a bit over 1km southwestward from the Hauptbahnhof. Halfway down (and contiguous with the Oberer Schlossgarten) is the **Schlossplatz**, Stuttgart's main public square and a showcase for its cultural riches. In the middle stands the **König Wilhelm Jubilee Column**, flanked by fountains representing the eight rivers of Baden-Württemberg.

Dominating the west side of the square is the new **Kunstmuseum Stuttgart** (☎ 216 2188; www.kunstmuseum-stuttgart.de; Kleiner Schlossplatz 1; adult/student & senior €5/3.50, during special exhibitions around €8/6.50; ☼ 10am-6pm Tue, Thu, Sat & Sun, to 9pm Wed & Fri), by day a semireflective glass cube, by night impressively illuminated from within. Opened in 2005, this municipal art museum features 20th-century and contemporary art; highlights include works by Otto Dix, Dieter Roth and Willi Baumeister.

Out front stands **Alexander Calder's mobile**, bought by the city in 1981 for the equivalent of about €500,000. Stuttgarters, known for what other Germans might call 'miserliness' but which they themselves see as 'thrift',

BADEN-WÜRTTEMBERG

PEDAL TO THE METAL

When Herman the German eases behind the wheel of his jet-black Mercedes, he's revving up for a pleasure as Teutonic as beer and bratwurst: fast driving. In a society famous for its adherence to rules and regulations, and for its passionate environmentalism, the autobahn is one of the few realms where Germans throw all caution to the wind. Where else can you travel at more than 200km (125 miles) per hour with no threat of a fine?

Germans argue vehemently to uphold their command of the autobahn. The magazine *Firmen Auto* has claimed that 'the danger of being overtaken drops sharply at 200km per hour, allowing the driver to concentrate fully on the traffic in front of the vehicle'. The AvD car club argues that 95% of all auto accidents in Germany involve drivers travelling less than 100km per hour.

Ironically, however, all but one-quarter of Germany's 11,000km of autobahns – the second-biggest such network after the USA – have restrictions of 130km per hour or less due to endless construction work, noise pollution regulations for built-up areas and traffic jams. But long stretches remain where the only limits are warp drive and a motorist's own nerve. Here, unwitting foreigners are given a rough lesson in autobahn etiquette every time a Mercedes, BMW or Porsche appears out of nowhere in the rear-view mirror, angrily flashing its lights to press its urgent demand: MOVE OVER!

---

initially went ballistic over the cost but are now quite satisfied as the work's value has gone up considerably.

Just to the north is the classical, colonnaded **Königsbau**, which in 2006 was reborn as an upmarket shopping mall, the **Königsbau Passagen**. On the top two floors of the complex's western **Stilwerk** section are more than a dozen of Germany's most stylish interior-design shops.

On the north side of the Schlossplatz, adjacent to Königstrasse, is the **Olgabau**, a fine example of 1950s architecture that's home to Dresdner Bank. A bit to the east, topped by a copper cupola, is the **Württembergischer Kunstverein** (☎ 223 370; www.wkv-stuttgart.de; Schlossplatz 2; adult/student from €5/3; 11am-6pm Tue-Sun, to 8pm Wed, longer hours for some exhibitions), which puts on temporary exhibitions of contemporary art.

Dominating the east side of Schlossplatz is the late-baroque/neoclassical **Neues Schloss**, once the residence of kings Friedrich I and Wilhelm I and now the home of state government ministries. Just south across the Planie is **Karlsplatz**, where you'll find a statue of Wilhelm looking noble and serious on a bronze steed.

A short block south of Schlossplatz, on the other side of the Renaissance **Alte Kanzlei** (Old Chancellory), is Schillerplatz, named after the poet-dramatist Friedrich Schiller, whose statue stands in the centre. Through the archway just east of the Alte Kanzlei is the **Altes Schloss**, adorned with a large statue of Eberhard, Württemberg's first duke and founder of Tübingen University. Now the old

palace holds the excellent **Württembergisches Landesmuseum** (☎ 279 3400; Schillerplatz 6; adult/student incl audio guide €3/2; 10am-5pm Tue-Sun), with well-presented exhibitions on themes ranging from the material culture of the ancient Celts to the Württemberg crown jewels. A new section displays colourful glass objects. In the ornate arcaded courtyard, rebuilt after the war, the rams above the clock on the tower lock horns on the hour.

In Schillerplatz' southwestern corner – in the **Stiftsfruchtkasten**, a former wine depot topped by a Bacchus statue – is the **Instrumenten Museum** (Schillerplatz 1; admission free with Landesmuseum ticket; 10am-5pm Tue-Sun), which displays all sorts of historic musical instruments. Next to it stands the reconstructed **Stiftskirche**, with its twin 61m-high late-Gothic towers (by law, no Stuttgart building can be built taller).

Motorcar Museums

Housed in a fantastic futuristic structure that seems destined to become a landmark, the new **Mercedes-Benz Museum** (☎ 173 0000; www.mercedes-benz.com/museum; Mercedesstrasse 100; concession €8/4; 9am-6pm Tue-Sun & holidays), opened in 2006, gets rave reviews from locals and visitors alike. A visit begins on the top level and takes you past 180 gleaming vehicles, including various 'firsts' on display in the Legend Rooms. The museum is on the right bank of the Neckar about 4km northeast of the city centre; to get there without wheels take the S1 S-Bahn line to Gottlieb-Daimler-Stadion (€2.20).

The **Porsche Museum** (☎ 911 5685; Porscheplatz 1; admission free; ☺ 9am-4pm Mon-Fri, 9am-5pm Sat, Sun & holidays), 6km northwest of the centre in the district of Zuffenhausen, will also soon be transformed by some bold architecture. With its inauguration set for early 2008 (until which time the old premises will remain open), the new museum – designed to showcase the company's flagship qualities of 'power and passion' – will display 80 vehicles (four times as many as the current exhibition) produced since the company first began making sports cars in 1948. Call ☎ 911 5384 to arrange a factory tour (minimum age: 18). To get to the museum, take the S6 S-Bahn line to Neuwirtshaus (€2.20).

Parks

Animals and plants from around the world feature at the enormously popular **Wilhelma Zoologisch-botanischer Garten** (Zoo & Botanical Gardens; ☎ 540 20; www.wilhelma.de; Rosensteinpark; adult/student under 28yr €10.80/5.40, after 4pm & in winter €7.40/3.70; ☺ 8.15am-nightfall), which is in the **Rosensteinpark** (contiguous with the Unterer Schlossgarten) about 3km northeast of the centre. Founded in 1839, its kid-friendly attractions include bathing elephants and feeding sea lions and penguins. To get there, take the U14 to Wilhelma or the U13 or buses 52, 55 or 56 to Rosensteinbrücke.

On warm summer days, Stuttgarters young and old – including Turkish families with portable barbecue equipment – flock to the **Max-Eyth-See**, a lake and park right on the Neckar (and on the U14 line) about 7km northeast of the Hauptbahnhof (Eyth rhymes with height). The water is hardly pristine, so swimming is out, but there's a great **bike path** here – in fact it's part of the Neckartal-Radweg (see p392). Along the river, the steep hills still have some older terraced-style vineyards;

many of the little **Wengerter Häuschen** (tool sheds) that dot the hillside are more than 200 years old and are protected landmarks.

TOURS
Boat

From late April to late October, **Neckar-Käpt'n** (☎ 5499 7060; www.neckar-kaeptn.de) operates a variety of boat excursions on the Neckar River (from €7.40; free on your birthday) departing from its dock at Wilhelma in Bad Cannstatt (on the U14).

Walking & Bus

The tourist office runs a variety of tours, including the 1½-hour **Stadt-Spaziergang** (City Walk; €7; ☺ 11am, also 5pm Fri Apr-Oct) and the 2½-hour **Stadt-Rundfahrt** (City Coach Tour; adult/concession incl admission to TV Tower €17/13.50; ☺ 1.30pm daily Apr-Oct, Sat & Sun Nov-Mar). Both are in English and German and begin at the tourist office (p394).

Taxi

Many people highly recommend taking a 2½-hour taxi tour (in English, French, Spanish or German) with **Anselm Vogt-Moykopf** (☎ 0172-740 1138; www.stadtrundfahrt-stuttgart.de; for 4 people Mon-Fri €100, Sat, Sun & holidays €125), a knowledgeable and easy-going fellow who really loves the city, its architecture and taking people to beautiful, out-of-the-way spots.

FESTIVALS & EVENTS

Stuttgart plays host to a number of notable annual events.

Sommerfest An open-air festival with live music and food that's held on Schlossplatz, Thursday to Sunday during the second week of August.

Weindorf A 10-day event where wine-makers sell the year's vintages from hundreds of booths on Schlossplatz and the Oberer Schlossgarten. Begins on the last weekend in August.

STUTTGART'S VINEYARD TRAILS

The **Stuttgarter Weinwanderweg** (www.stuttgarter-weinwanderweg.de, in German) is the name given to two walking trails that head through vineyards so lush and pastoral you'll hardly believe that some of the world's most advanced motorcar factories are just over the hill. One begins 3km due north of the Hauptbahnhof at the Pragsattel light rail station (on the U5 or U6 line) and goes northeast to the Max-Eyth-See (above). The other is a circuit that takes you from the Obertürkheim train station (on the S1), 6km east of the Hauptbahnhof, via Uhlbach (served by buses 62 and 65 from Obertürkheim) to Untertürkheim (also on the S1) and, if you like, back to Obertürkheim.

See Besenwirtschaft on p399 for details on dining options.

Cannstatter Volksfest Stuttgart's version of Oktoberfest, this huge event is held over three consecutive weekends in Bad Cannstatt from late September to mid-October.

Weihnachtsmarkt Germany's largest Christmas market is held in the city centre on Marktplatz, Schillerplatz and Schlossplatz from late November to 23 December.

SLEEPING
Budget

Campingplatz Stuttgart (☎ 556 696; www.campingplatz -stuttgart.de; Mercedesstrasse 40, Bad Cannstatt; per person/ tent/car €6/4/2.50; ☼ year-round) A riverside camping ground about 4km northeast of the city centre on the right bank of the Neckar. It's about 1km southeast of the Bad Cannstatt S-Bahn station.

DJH hostel (☎ 664 7470; www.jugendherberge-stuttgart .de; Haussmannstrasse 27; dm 1st/subsequent night €20.30/ 17.10; ☼ 24hr; ✗ ▣) Totally renovated in 2006, this luxurious, 309-bed hostel is 800m southeast (up the hill) from the Hauptbahnhof. Amenities here include two- or four-bed rooms, all with bathroom, and bicycle parking. Reached via a glass-and-steel column with a lift running down the middle, reception is on level 5.

Hostel Alex 30 (☎ 838 8950; www.alex30-hostel.de; Alexanderstrasse 30; dm €19, s €20-29, d €50, with toilet & shower €70, breakfast €6; ℗ ✗) This privately-run hostel, opened in 2004, has colourful and creatively decorated public areas and 32 rooms outfitted with basic furnishings and high school–style lockers for your stuff. Kitchen facilities are available. Bike rental costs €6 per day. From the Hauptbahnhof, take U5, U6 or U7 to the Olgaeck stop.

Museumstube (☎ 296 810; fax 120 4359; www .museumstube.de; Hospitalstrasse 9; d €65, s/d without bathroom €30/45, not incl breakfast; ☼ reception 10am-3pm & 5.30-10pm or 11pm, closed Sun & holidays) A modest, family-run place with 14 spiffy, superclean rooms.

Hotel Centro (☎ 585 3315; www.hotelcentro.de in German; Büchsenstrasse 24; s/d from €55/85, without bathroom €35/65) A very central hotel whose 11 rooms are practical and compact, with nature-themed prints on the wall.

Midrange

Wirt am Berg (☎ 241 865; fax 236 1348; Gaisburgstrasse 12a; s/d from €60/85, s without bathroom €50; ℗ ✗) A statue of a vintner greets you at this family-run hotel, whose 12 rooms are nicely furnished. Situated on a quiet backstreet. The nearest U-Bahn stop is Olgaeck.

InterCity Hotel (☎ 225 00; www.intercityhotel.com; Arnulf-Klett-Platz 2; s €77-136, d €77-151, breakfast €12) Hugely convenient if you're arriving by train (it's in the southwest corner of the Hauptbahnhof), this place has 112 hotel-ish but comfortable rooms. Rates are cheapest on Friday, Saturday and Sunday nights.

Hotel Unger (☎ 209 90; www.hotel-unger.de; Kronenstrasse 17; s/d from €102/125, Fri, Sat & Sun from €79/99; ℗ ✗) A very central 116-room hotel popular with business travellers. It's known for its generous breakfast buffet featuring smoked fish, served in your room for no extra charge. Two additional floors, including a fitness studio, are being added in 2007.

Top End

Der Zauberlehrling (☎ 237 7770; www.zauberlehrling.de; Rosenstrasse 38; d €140-280) This ultrachic 'design hotel' has 17 named rooms, each unique and each a feast for the eyes. It has some pretty far-out bathtubs. The name means 'sorcerer's apprentice'.

Steigenberger Graf Zeppelin (☎ 204 80; www .stuttgart.steigenberger.de; Arnulf-Klett-Platz 7; s/d from €195/220; ℗ ✗ ✗) Facing the Hauptbahnhof, this superluxurious, five-star hotel has 189 rooms in a variety of styles: classical, elegant or avant-garde. Amenities include a pool, sauna, fitness studio, bistro, bar and cigar lounge. The restaurant has one Michelin star.

EATING & DRINKING

There are lots of eateries and pubs – many of them very chic and quite a few with outdoor tables – a few blocks east of the southern end of Königstrasse, along and near Eberhardstrasse. Further east across Hauptstätter Strasse, in the old labourers' quarter Bohnenviertel (between Rosenstrasse and Pfarrstrasse), traditional places with regional specialities predominate. Tiny Geissstrasse, two short blocks west of Eberhardstrasse, has several little café-pubs that spill out onto what's unofficially called Hans-im-Glück Platz – a little square with a fountain depicting the caged German fairytale character 'Lucky Hans'. Theodor-Heuss-Strasse, three blocks west of Königstrasse, has lots of trendy *Szenekneipen* (clubs and bars that cater to style-conscious yuppies). The city's best beer garden is in the Mittlerer Schlossgarten.

Imbiss zum Brunnenwirt (☎ 245 021; Leonhardsplatz 25; ☼ 11am-2am Mon-Thu, 11am-3am Fri & Sat, 4pm-2am

BESENWIRTSCHAFT

From about October to March, wine growers throughout the region attach a broom (Besen) to the front of their homes to indicate that they're open for business as a Besenwirtschaft, a small restaurant where people can drink and purchase the new vintage. They also serve lunch and dinner, usually featuring typical Swabian dishes like Kartoffelsuppe (potato soup), Gaisburger Marsch (a stew of sliced potatoes, noodles and beef) and the evil-sounding Schlachtplatte (sauerkraut with pork belly, liver, lard, sausage and smoked meat, served with peas and other vegetables).

Some Besenwirtschaften open every year, but most don't. Check Lift Stuttgart or S-Trip, published in the Stuttgarter Zeitung on the last Wednesday of the month during vintage times.

Stuttgart-area Besenwirtschaften that operate every year include **Weingut Ruoff** (☎ 321 224; Uhlbacher Strasse 31, Obertürkheim; 🕑 11am-midnight except Sun & holidays mid-Nov–mid- or late Feb), in a fabulous house built in 1550 (take the S1 to Obertürkheim), and **D'Besa am Kelterplätzle** (☎ 331 149; Strümpfelbacher Strasse 40, Untertürkheim; 🕑 11am-midnight Tue-Sat mid-Oct–early Dec & late Jan–mid-Mar), which has a romantic vaulted wine cellar (take the S1 to Untertürkheim).

Sun & holidays) This quirky little Bohnenviertel sausage stand, next door to Gaststätte Brunnenwirt, sells Stuttgart's most famous Currywurst (€2.40 to €3.20). Half-grungy, half-chic, this local institution draws an eclectic crowd – from passing vagrants to Mercedes coupé drivers.

Calwer-Eck-Bräu (☎ 2224 9440; Calwer Strasse 31; 9am or 10am-1am, to 2am Fri & Sat, from 5pm holidays) This Gemütlich (cosy) brewery-pub, up on the 1st floor, serves Swabian-Bavarian fare, including Maultaschensuppe (€3.50; ravioli soup), a Stuttgart speciality. On Sunday there's an all-you-can-eat menu for €9.99 until 5pm.

Amadeus (☎ 292 678; Charlottenplatz 17; mains €7.80-14.90, salads €4.50-8.80; 🕑 noon-midnight Mon-Fri, 10am-midnight Sat & Sun) In the courtyard of a one-time orphanage, this place serves great Swabian-style food and has Dinkel Acker on tap. Sunday brunch, available till 3pm, costs €13.50.

Nirvan (☎ 240 561; Eberhardstrasse 73; mains €3.50-13.80; 🕑 11am-11pm) Dine to the sounds of mellow Persian music at this basement restaurant, where you'll find delicious Persian dishes (lamb, fish and vegetarian). The lunch menu (€5 to €8.50) is served till 3pm.

Weinhaus Stetter (☎ 240 163; Rosenstrasse 32; 🕑 3-11pm Mon-Fri, 11am-3pm Sat) This Bohnenviertel place has solid, good-value regional specialities such as Linsen und Saiten (lentils with sausage) and a great wine selection. The attached Weinhandlung (wine shop) sells 650 different vintages.

Palast der Republik (☎ 226 4887; Friedrichstrasse 27; 🕑 11am-2am, to 3am Fri & Sat) This grandly named beer bar is actually a kiosk – once a public toilet – with signs reading 'Schwaben Bräu' and 'Palast' outside. A real Stuttgart institution, it is hugely popular with young locals, especially students and counter-culture types, who sit at tables or on the ground sipping their brew.

Deli (☎ 236 0200; Geissstrasse 7; mains €6.10-12.90; 🕑 10am-apm, to 2am Thu, to 3am Fri & Sat) A chic café-bar with food.

Self-caterers can try the **food market** (Marktplatz; 🕑 7.30am-1pm Tue, Thu & Saturday) and the **Markthalle** (market hall; Dorotheenstrasse 4; 🕑 7am-6.30pm Mon-Fri, 7am-4pm Sat), which sells picnic fixin's and has Italian and Swabian restaurants.

ENTERTAINMENT

Details on Stuttgart's exceptionally lively cultural scene can be found in Lift Stuttgart (€1.80), an easy-to-use German-language monthly available at the tourist office or news kiosks. **Prinz** (www.prinz.de/stuttgart.html) is another listings magazine (€1.30). Events tickets can be purchased at the **Kartenvorverkauf desk** (☎ 222 8243; inside the tourist office; 🕑 9am-8pm Mon-Fri, 9am-4pm Sat, phone staffed till 6pm Mon-Fri).

Cinemas

Cinemas that screen undubbed (OmU) films:

Ambo (☎ 225 7712; www.kinostar.com, in German; Arnulf-Klett-Platz 3) Facing the Hauptbahnhof. Screens first-run films in four halls.

Kommunales Kino (☎ 3058 9160; www.koki-stuttgart.de, in German; Friedrichstrasse 23a) An art cinema in the old Amerika Haus building.

Clubs

Details on the nightlife and club scene can be found at www.subculture.de (in German).

BADEN-WÜRTTEMBERG

Dilayla (☎ 236 9527; Eberhardstrasse 49; admission free; ⏲ 9pm-4am, to 6am Fri & Sat nights, from 11pm late May-Sep) A laid-back basement music bar with dancing, this dimly lit place has bright orange walls, cosy tables and lots of soft couches for lounging. The soundtrack is mainly from the '70s and '80s. Things get going between midnight and 1am. Attracts a mixed crowd.

Die Röhre (☎ 299 1499; www.die-roehre.com; Willy-Brandt-Strasse 2/1) A hugely popular, industrial-style concert and party venue under the curved ceiling of an aborted vehicle tunnel – a few metres away an identical *Röhre* (tube) takes cars through the hill. Linked to Willy-Brandt-Strasse by a path through the trees.

Zap Club (☎ 235 227; www.zap-club.de, in German; Hauptstätterstrasse 40; admission €4-10; ⏲ 8pm or 9pm-2am Wed, 9pm-2am Thu, 10pm-4am Fri, 10pm-6am or later Sat) In the cellar of the Schwabenzentrum (around the corner from Josef-Hirn-Platz), this sprawling disco has very modern décor and a cocktail bar. Attracts mainly a younger, 18-to-26 crowd. Over-30s get a discount on Wednesday. Hosts live music about once a week.

Gay & Lesbian venues

King's Club (☎ 226 4558; www.kingsclub-stuttgart.de, in German; Calwer Strasse 21; admission Fri & Sat €10; ⏲ 10pm-6am Wed-Sun, to 7am Fri & Sat nights) This gay and lesbian disco has red-carpeted walls, banquettes around the sides and a DJ positioned right in the middle. Heteros are welcome. Gets going after midnight. Enter from Gymnasiumstrasse.

Rock & Jazz

Romeo's Kiste (☎ 553 2805; Hauptstätter Strasse 35; ⏲ 4pm-2am Mon-Thu, to 3am Fri & Sat) This hole-in-the-wall bar, often jam-packed, is the city's leading jazz venue, with concerts nightly except Sunday, starting at 9.30pm or 10pm.

Theaterhaus (☎ 402 0720; www.theaterhaus.com, in German; Siemensstrasse 11) This place, 3km north of the Hauptbahnhof, hosts live rock, jazz and other music genres virtually nightly. Also has theatre and comedy performances. To get there take the U6 to Maybachstrasse.

Theatre & Classical Music

Staatstheater (☎ 203 2220; www.staatstheater-stuttgart.de; Oberer Schlossgarten 6) The city's premier venue for ballet, opera, theatre and Western classical music. Tickets start at just €8. The Stuttgart Ballet (www.stuttgart-ballet.de) is renowned as one of the best companies in Europe.

Variété im Friedrichsbau (☎ 225 7070; www.friedrichsbau.de, in German; Friedrichstrasse 24; tickets €19-40) Famous for its excellent variety shows and cabaret productions. To get there take the U9 or U14 to Friedrichsbau/Börse.

SHOPPING

For outdoor action, there's a **flower market** (Schillerplatz; ⏲ 7.30am-1pm Tue, Thu & Sat) and a **flea market** (Karlsplatz; ⏲ to 4pm Sat).

Many varieties of wine are produced in the Stuttgart region; most are whites, but locals also go for Trollinger, a full-bodied red made from a variety of grape originally from the South Tirol in Austria. Stuttgarters consume wine at a rate twice the national average, so while Trollinger is readily available here, they're not really exporting a lot. The tourist office has lists of vineyards open for tastings.

Stuttgart isn't renowned for bargain shopping. Indeed, upmarket stores predominate in the city centre, where options can be found all along Königstrasse. The new Königsbau Passagen (see p396) has some classy design shops.

GETTING THERE & AWAY
Air

Stuttgart International Airport (STR; ☎ 01805-948 444; www.stuttgart-airport.com), a major hub for **German Wings** (www.germanwings.com), is 13km south of the city. There are four terminals, all within easy walking distance of each other.

Car & Motorcycle

The A8 from Munich to Karlsruhe passes by Stuttgart, as does the A81 from Singen (near Lake Constance) to Heilbronn and Mannheim. Stuttgart is often abbreviated to 'S' on highway signs.

Train

IC and ICE destinations include Berlin (€112, 5½ hours), Frankfurt (€44.60, 1¼ hours) and Munich (€39 to €46, 2¼ hours). There are frequent regional services to Tübingen (€10, one hour), Schwäbisch Hall's Hessental station (€11.70, 69 minutes) and Ulm (€14.70, one hour).

GETTING AROUND
To/From the Airport

S2 and S3 trains take about 30 minutes to get from the airport to the Hauptbahnhof (€2.90).

Bicycle

Rent a Bike (☎ 4207 0833; www.rentabike-stuttgart.de, in German; adult 6hr/full day €9.50/13, student €6/8) delivers and picks up bikes. Word has it that by 2007 a Hauptbahnhof-based rental service, Call-a-Bike, will begin operating.

You can take along your bike free of charge on Stadtbahn lines, except from 6am to 8.30am and 4pm to 6.30pm Monday to Friday. Bikes are allowed on S-Bahn trains (S1 to S6) but you have to buy a Kinderfahrschein (child's ticket) from 6am to 8.30am Monday to Friday. Bikes cannot be taken on buses or the Strassenbahn (tramway).

Car & Motorcycle

Underground parking in the city centre costs about €2 for the first hour and €1.50 for each subsequent hour. Park-and-ride (P+R) options, available in many Stuttgart suburbs, afford cheap parking plus free transport into the city centre for the driver and all passengers; convenient lots include Degerloch Alsbstrasse (on the B27; take the U5 or U6 into town), which is 4km south of the centre; and Österfeld (on the A81; take the S1, S2 or S3 into the centre).

Avis, Budget, Europcar, Hertz, National and Sixt have offices at the airport (Terminal 2, Level 2). Europcar, Hertz and Avis have offices at the Hauptbahnhof (next to track 16).

Public Transport

From slowest to fastest, Stuttgart's **public transport network** (www.ssb-ag.de and www.vvs.de, both in German) consists of a Zahnradbahn (rack railway), buses, the Strassenbahn (tramway), Stadtbahn lines (light rail lines whose names begin with U; underground in the city centre), S-Bahn lines (suburban rail lines named S1 through to S6) and Regionalbahn lines (regional trains whose names begin with R). On Friday and Saturday there are night buses (their names begin with N) with departures from Schlossplatz at 1.11am, 2.22am and 3.33am.

For travel within the city, single tickets are €1.80, and four-ride tickets (*Mehrfahrtenkarte*) cost €6.30. A day pass, good for two zones (including, for instance, the Mercedes-Benz and Porsche Museums), is better value at €5.10 for one person and €8.50 for a group two to five.

Taxi

To order a taxi call ☎ 194 10 or ☎ 566 061.

AROUND STUTTGART

The region around Stuttgart is easily accessible by public transport or, better still, by bicycle.

Württemberg

When Conrad von Württemberg established the Württemberg family dynasty, he built the family castle on this absolutely breathtaking hill southeast of Stuttgart. Covered with vines, it affords sweeping views down into a gorgeous valley.

Katherina Pavlovna, daughter of a Russian tsar and wife of King Wilhelm I of Württemberg (1781–1864), reputedly told her husband that she'd never seen such a beautiful place and hoped to be buried here. When she died, aged just 30, Wilhelm tore down the Württemberg family castle and in its place built a domed, classical-style Russian Orthodox chapel. The **Grabkapelle** (burial chapel; www.schloesser-und-gaerten.de; adult/concession €1.50/0.70; ☽ 10am-noon Wed, 10am-noon & 1-5pm Fri & Sat, 10am-noon & 1-6pm Sun & holidays Mar-1 Nov) is where he was also buried decades later.

The grounds outside afford lovely views of the countryside and are a perfect place for a picnic. To get to Württemberg, 10km east of Stuttgart's city centre, take bus 61 from the Obertürkheim station, served by the S1.

Ludwigsburg

☎ 07141 / pop 88,000

This neat and cultured little place, the childhood home of the dramatist Friedrich Schiller, is named for Duke Eberhard Ludwig, who built the vast, Versailles-inspired Residenzschloss (chateau) in the early 1700s. Just a 20-minute train ride north of Stuttgart, Ludwigsburg – home to Baden-Württemberg's only film academy – is the perfect place to come if you want to 'go for baroque'.

ORIENTATION & INFORMATION

The Bahnhof, served by S-Bahn trains from Stuttgart, is at the southwestern edge of the town centre. The Residenzschloss, on Schlossstrasse (the B27), is at the northeastern edge of the centre. The broad Marktplatz is more or less in the middle, about 750m northeast of the train station and 400m southwest of the chateau entrance.

Ludwigsburg's **tourist office** (☎ 910 2252; www.ludwigsburg.de; Marktplatz 6; ☽ 9am-6pm Mon-Fri, 9am-2pm Sat) has excellent material in English

---

BAROQUE IN BLOOM

The Residenzschloss gardens are transformed into an immaculately trimmed festival of flowers during the annual **Blühendes Barock** (www.blueba.de, in German; adult/student €7/3.30; ☺ tickets sold 9am-6pm, to 7pm Sat & Sun mid-Mar–early Nov). Included in the ticket price is the kids-oriented **Märchengarten** (Fairy Tale Garden), a small Japanese garden and an **aviary** filled with exotic birds. It's a fabulous setting for a picnic!

There's an entrance to the gardens on Schorndorfer Strasse (the eastern continuation of Wilhelmstrasse). Blühendes Barock tickets are *not* sold at the main entrance to the Residenzschloss on Schlossstrasse (the B27). However, combo tickets that include the chateau *are* on sale at the entrances to the gardens.

---

and can provide details on performing arts festivals, jazz performances, cinema-related events and the baroque Weihnachtsmarkt (Christmas market).

SIGHTS & ACTIVITIES

Known as the 'Swabian Versailles', the magnificent, early 18th-century **Residenzschloss** (☎ 182 004; www.schloss-ludwigsburg.de, in German, www.schloesser-und-gaerten.de; Schlossstrasse; tours adult/student to 28yr/family €5/2.50/12.50; ☺ 10am-6pm, last tour at 5pm), with its 18 buildings and 452 rooms, is a symphony of baroque, rococo and Empire decoration. The 90-minute tours (in German with an English text) of the chateau's furnished interior begin every 30 minutes. English-language tours begin at 1.30pm daily; from mid-March to early November there are additional tours held at 11am and 3.15pm on Saturday, Sunday and holidays.

The chateau, refurbished in 2004 in honour of the complex's 300th anniversary, is also home to the **Carl Eugen Appartement**, an impossibly ornate, generously gilded rococo gem, and three new **museums** (adult/student incl audioguide €5/2.50; ☺ 10am-5pm): the **Barockgalerie** (Baroque Gallery), which showcases baroque paintings from the collections of the Staatsgalerie in Stuttgart; the **Modemuseum** (Fashion Museum), which has a fine collection of original clothing and accessories created between 1750 and 1970; and the **Keramikmuseum** (Ceramics Museum), with some pretty spectacular porcelain, faïence and majolica.

Duke Karl Eugen (*oy*-gen), a businessman and *bon vivant*, established a porcelain factory in the castle in 1758. Historic pieces can be seen in the Keramikmuseum, and you can purchase the fine stuff it makes today – by hand, as always – at the **Porzellan-Manufaktur** (www.porzellan-manufaktur-ludwigsburg.de).

A 10-minute walk north of the Residenzschloss, surrounded by a park, is another early 18th-century Württemberg family palace, the baroque **Schloss Favorite** (☎ 182 004; 30min tour adult/concession €2.50/1.20; ☺ 10am-12.30pm & 1.30-5pm mid-Mar–1 Nov, 10am-12.30pm & 1.30-4pm Tue-Sun 2 Nov–mid-Mar). The scene of Duke Eugen's glittering parties, its furnishings date from the Napoleonic period.

About 2km to the northwest on the Schlosspark lake is yet another Württemberg chateau, the rococo **Seeschloss Monrepos** (☎ 221 060; ☺ wine tasting & sales 9am-6pm Mon-Fri, 10am-2pm Sat). Once used as a summer residence, it's still owned by the Württemberg family, which sells the wines it makes – and lets you taste them – on the premises. From mid-March to mid-October you can hire **boats** (from €8 to €10 per hour) to sail on the adjacent lake. Open-air concerts, just a small part of Ludwigsburg's rich cultural offerings, are held here in the summer.

GETTING THERE & AROUND

Stuttgart's S4 and S5 S-Bahn lines go directly to Ludwigsburg's Bahnhof (€2.90), frequently linked to the chateau by buses 421 and 427; buses 422 and 425 go to the Blühendes Barock entrance. On foot, the chateau is about 1km from the train station.

If you come by car, there are two large parking lots 500m south of the Residenzschloss, just off the B27.

From mid-May to late September (and on some days in early May and October), a more relaxing option is to take a boat run by **Neckar-Käpt'n** (☎ 5499 7060; www.neckar-kaeptn.de) from Bad Cannstatt (Stuttgart, see p397) to Ludwigsburg-Hoheneck (one-way/return €14.60/19.60, two hours). From there, the chateau is either a 20- to 30-minute walk or a short ride on bus 427 (every 10 minutes).

NORTHERN BADEN-WÜRTTEMBERG

The northern third of the state has a number of unique and enticing cities. Heidelberg is famed for its mile-long pedestrian precinct, Mannheim for its chessboard street grid, Karlsruhe for its fanlike street layout and Schwäbish Hall for its narrow medieval alleyways. All have fine museums and a wealth of cultural activities.

HEIDELBERG

☎ 06221 / pop 143,000

Heidelberg's baroque old town, lively university atmosphere, excellent pubs and evocative half-ruined castle make it hugely popular with visitors, 3.5 million of whom flock here each year. They are following in the footsteps of the 19th-century romantics, most notably the poet Goethe. Britain's William Turner also loved the city, which inspired him to paint some of his greatest landscapes.

Less starry eyed was Mark Twain (www .mark-twain-in-heidelberg.de), who in 1878 began his European travels with a three-month stay in Heidelberg, recounting his bemused observations in *A Tramp Abroad*. There is speculation that the writer's attraction to the city may have something to do with the fact that the name Heidelberg is derived from Heidelbeerenberg (Huckleberry Hill).

Heidelberg, Germany's oldest and most famous university town, has a red-roofed townscape of remarkable architectural unity. It was created in the 18th century after it had been devastated during the Thirty Years' War and then all but destroyed by invading French troops under Louis XIV. Today the city has a student population of 32,000 (including lots of foreign students), heaps of tradition and nightlife that makes it outstanding for a pub crawl. The city also serves as an important **NATO headquarters** (www.nato.int/lahd).

Orientation

Heidelberg's Altstadt stretches along the Neckar River from Bismarckplatz east to the Schloss. Europe's longest pedestrian zone, the 1600m-long Haupstrasse – the so-called Royal Mile – runs east-to-west through the middle of the Altstadt, about 200m south of the Neckar.

Two bridges link the Altstadt with the Neckar's northern bank: at the western end, north of Bismarckplatz, is Theodor-Heuss-Brücke, while north of the Marktplatz is the Alte Brücke (also known as Karl-Theodor-Brücke).

Information

There are a number of internet cafés on or near Hauptstrasse, such as in the vicinity of the Jesuitenkirche.

Ärztlicher Bereitschaftdienst (☎ 192 92; Alte Eppenheimer Strasse 35; ☻ 8pm-7am, 7am-8pm Sat, Sun & holidays, from 1pm on Wed) For medical care when most doctors' offices are closed. Situated one block north of the Hauptbahnhof. A house call is possible if necessary but for less serious cases just drop by. Costs the same as a regular doctor.

Deutsch-Amerikanisches Institut (☎ 607 30; www .dai-heidelberg.de; Sofienstrasse 12; ☻ library 1-6pm Mon-Fri) Has concerts, films, lectures and occasional exhibits.

Heidelberg Card (2/4 days €14/26, 2-day family card €26) Entitles you to unlimited public transport use and free or discounted admission to museums and some cultural events. Available at the tourist office.

Internet Lounge (per 5min/hr €0.50/6; ☻ 7am-midnight) In the Hauptbahnhof on the way to the tracks, with pricey train station internet access.

Main post office (Hugo-Stotz-Strasse 14) To the right as you exit the Hauptbahnhof.

Post Office (Sofienstrasse 8-10)

Reisebank (☻ 7.30am-8pm Mon-Fri, 9am-5pm Sat, 9am-1pm Sun & holidays) In the Hauptbahnhof building; exchanges currency.

Tourist office (☎ 194 33; www.cvb-heidelberg.de, www.heidelberg.de; ☻ 9am-7pm Mon-Sat, 10am-6pm Sun & holidays Apr-Oct, 9am-6pm Mon-Sat Nov-Mar) Right outside the Hauptbahnhof. Out front is a hotel reservation board with a free telephone. Sells the Heidelberg Card.

Waschsalon (Kettengasse 17; per 7kg €8.50; ☻ 10am-1pm & 2-6pm Mon, Tue, Thu & Fri, 10am-2pm & 3-6pm Wed, 10am-3pm Sat) A laundry where you can DIY or leave your dirty duds and pick them up two hours later.

Wetzlar (☎ 241 65; Plöck 79-81) Specialises in foreign-language books.

Sights

SCHLOSS

Dominating the Altstadt from on high, the partly ruined, red-sandstone **Schloss** (☎ 538 431; adult/student under 28yr admission to courtyard till 5.30pm or 6pm, Deutsches Apothekenmuseum & Grosses Fass €5/1.50, courtyard free from 5.30pm or 6pm till dusk, gardens

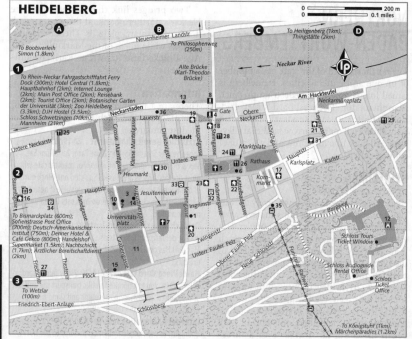

HEIDELBERG

always free; ☼ 8am-dusk) is one of Germany's finest Gothic-Renaissance fortresses. Begun in the 13th century, the oldest surviving bits date from 1400.

The Renaissance **Schlosshof** (courtyard) is so elaborately decorated it often elicits a gasp from visitors (see p406). The **terrace** affords superb views of the town and the Neckar. The only way to see the less-than-scintillating interior is to join a guided **tour** (adult/concession €4/2; ☼ 11.15am, 12.15pm, 2.15pm & 4.15pm daily, also 10.15am Sat & Sun, additional tours at 1.15pm & 3.15pm mid-Apr–mid-Oct). An audioguide of the Schloss costs €4.

Off the courtyard is the **Deutsches Apothekenmuseum** (German Pharmacy Museum; ☎ 165 780; ☼ 10.15am-6pm), which has well-presented exhibits on chemistry and pharmacology in centuries past. Signs are in English. The 18th-century **Grosses Fass** (Great Vat) is said to be capable of holding more than 220,000L. Even the **Kleines Fass** is not exactly tiny.

Behind the castle, the **Schlossgarten** (castle garden) is a delightful place for a stroll. The **Pulver Turm** (Gunpowder Tower) was damaged by French forces in 1693.

To get up to the castle you can either take the **Bergbahn** (funicular railway; www.bergbahn-heidelberg.de; adult/6-14yr one way €3/2, return €5/4; ☼ every 10min), with its spanking new cars, from the Kornmarkt station on Zwingerstrasse; or walk up the steep, cobbled **Burgweg** (about 10 minutes), right next to the Bergbahn station.

KÖNIGSTUHL

The upper section of the Bergbahn (see above) uses rail cars dating from 1907. From the Schloss, it continues up to the **Königstuhl** (altitude 550m – over 400m above the Altstadt), where there's a view and a TV tower. The return fare, with a stop at the Schloss, is adult €8 and child 6 to 14 years €6.

Also at the top of the hill is the **Märchenparadies** (Fairy-Tale Park; ☎ 23 416; www.maerchenparadies.de in German; adult/child 2-12yr €3/2; ☼ 10am-6pm, to 7pm Sun Mar-Jun & Sep–mid-Nov, 10am-7pm Jul-Aug), a mini-theme park with fairy-tale characters, a little train line, play areas and other kiddies' stuff.

UNIVERSITY

Germany's oldest university, **Ruprecht-Karls-Universität** (www.uni-heidelberg.de), was established in 1386 by Count Palatinate Ruprecht I, one of the seven imperial prince-electors. Originally made up of four faculties – philosophy, law, medicine and theology – today it has 18 faculties with more than 30,000 students from 80 nations. Women were first admitted in 1900.

The university's facilities are scattered all over town but some of the most historic are on the Altstadt's **Universitätsplatz**, which is dominated by the 18th-century **Alte Universität** and the **Neue Universität**, the old and new university buildings.

From 1778 to 1914, university students convicted of misdeeds (such as singing, womanising, drinking or just plain goofing around) were tossed into the **Studentenkarzer** (Student Jail; ☎ 543 554; Augustinergasse 2; adult/concession €2.50/2; ☺ 10am-6pm Tue-Sun Apr-Sep, 10am-4pm Tue-Sat Oct-Mar), around the back side of the Alte Universität building. Sentences were generally a minimum of three days and the detainees were fed only bread and water; delinquents serving longer sentences could interrupt their stay for critical reasons (say, to take exams). In some circles, a stint in the Karzer was considered *de rigueur* to prove one's manhood (women were never imprisoned here). Detainees passed their time by carving inscriptions and drawing graffiti, which still covers the walls.

A ticket to the Studentenkarzer also gets you into the **Alte Aula** (Old Assembly Hall; Grabengasse 1; ☺ 10am-6pm Tue-Sun Apr-Sep, 10am-4pm Tue-Sat Oct-Mar, except when in use) and an exhibition on the university's history inside the Alte Universität.

A block to the south, the **Universitätsbibliothek** (University Library; Plöck 107-109; admission free), built from 1901 to 1905, displays rare books and prints from its superb collections in the upstairs corner **Ausstellungsraum** (exhibition room; ☺ 10am-6pm, closed Sun & holidays).

The university's largest campus area is on the north side of the Neckar about 1km due north of the Hauptbahnhof. This is where you'll find the **Botanischer Garten der Universität** (University Botanical Garden; ☎ 545 783; Im Neuenheimer Feld 340; admission free; ☺ outdoor areas open all day, hothouses 9am-4pm Mon-Thu, 9am-2.30pm Fri, 9am-noon & 1-4pm Sun & holidays), one of Germany's oldest. To get there take tram 4 or 5.

The delightful **Zoo Heidelberg** (☎ 645 50; www .zoo-heidelberg.de; Tiergartenstrasse 3; adult/child 3-18yr €6/3; ☺ 9am-7pm Apr-Sep, to 6pm Mar & Oct, to 5pm Nov-Feb), just off the Neckar a bit west of the botanical garden, features animals from five continents. From the Hauptbahnhof or Bismarckplatz take bus 33.

JESUITENKIRCHE

Just east of Universitätsplatz is the **Jesuitenviertel**, an attractive little square dominated by the city's recently renovated former **Jesuitenkirche** (Jesuit church), built of red sandstone between 1712 and 1750. On the façade are statues of Christ, Faith (on the rooftop), St Ignatius Loyola and St Francis Xavier. The **Schatzkammer** (treasury; admission €2; ☺ 10am-5pm Tue-Sat, 1-5pm Sun & holidays Jun-Oct, Sat & Sun Nov-May) displays precious religious objects.

MARKTPLATZ

The **Heiliggeistkirche** (built 1398–1441), on the old market square, is a superb old Gothic church. From 1706 to 1936 there was a wall between the part used by Protestants and that used by Catholics; today, it's a Protestant place of worship. You can climb the 204 steps to the top of the **church spire** (adult/student

BADEN-WÜRTTEMBERG

MARK TWAIN ON THE SCHLOSS

Heidelberg Castle must have been very beautiful before the French battered and bruised and scorched it two hundred years ago. The stone is brown, with a pinkish tint, and does not seem to stain easily. The dainty and elaborate ornamentation upon its two chief fronts is as delicately carved as if it had been intended for the interior of a drawing-room rather than for the outside of a house. Many fruit and flower clusters, human heads and grim projecting lions' heads are still as perfect in every detail as if they were new. But the statues which are ranked between the windows have suffered. These are life-size statues of old-time emperors, electors, and similar grandees, clad in mail and bearing ponderous swords. Some have lost an arm, some a head, and one poor fellow is chopped off at the middle.

Mark Twain, A Tramp Abroad (1880)

€1/0.50; 11am-5pm Mon-Sat, 12.30-5pm Sun & holidays mid-Mar–Oct, 11am-3pm Fri & Sat, 12.30-3pm Sun & holidays Nov–mid-Mar).

In the centre of Marktplatz is the **Hercules fountain**; in medieval times petty criminals were chained to it and left to face the populace. On the south side of the Markt, the lavishly decorated former royal **pharmacy** has been reborn as a McDonald's.

ALTE BRÜCKE

On the Altstadt, at the entrance to the bridge side, is a statue of a **brass monkey** holding a mirror and surrounded by mice: touch the mirror for wealth, the outstretched fingers to ensure you return to Heidelberg and the mice to ensure you have many children. Up on the bridge, through the tower, is the **Karl-Theodor-Statue**, being renovated as we go to press, which makes reference to the local legend that the prince fathered almost 200 illegitimate children. The bridge's foundation bears some pretty hairy high-water marks.

KURPFÄLZISCHES MUSEUM

Tucked in behind a courtyard, the excellent **Kurpfälzisches Museum** (Palatinate Museum; ☎ 583 400; Hauptstrasse 97; adult/concession €3/1.80, on Sun €1.80/1.20; 10am-6pm Tue-Sun) focuses on 15th- to 20th-century paintings and sculptures, and Heidelberg and regional history. Displays include lots of Roman and Merovingian items and a copy of the jawbone of a 600,000-year-old Heidelberg Man (the original is stored across the river at the palaeontology centre).

PHILOSOPHENWEG

A stroll along the **Philosophenweg** (Philosophers' Walk), on the hillside north of the Neckar River, provides a welcome respite from the tourist hordes. Leading through steep vineyards and orchards, the path offers those great views of the Altstadt and the castle that were such an inspiration to the German philosopher Hegel. It's a well-known lovers' haunt, and many a young local is said to have lost their heart (and virginity) along the walkway.

Atop the Heiligenberg is the **Thingstätte**, a Nazi-era amphitheatre. There are several ruins and countless other hiking options in the surrounding hills.

Tours

The tourist office runs English-language **guided tours** (adult/student €7/5; 10.30am Fri & Sat Apr-Dec) that depart from the Löwenbrunnen (Lions Fountain) at Universtätsplatz.

Paddle boats can be hired at **Bootsverleih Simon** (☎ 411 925; 3-/4-person paddle boat per 30min €6/7; 11am-sundown Apr-Sep), on the north shore of the Neckar by the Theodor-Heuss-Brücke.

The following two companies run cruises on the Neckar.

Rhein-Neckar Fahrgastschifffahrt (☎ 201 81; www.rnf-schifffahrt.de, in German; adult/child 4-12yr to Neckarsteinach return €10/6; up to 7 times a day mid-Apr–late Nov) Boats dock on the south bank of the Neckar about midway between the two bridges. It's a nice day trip upriver to Neckarsteinach and its four castles, built by four brothers between 1100 and 1250 as a result of a family feud. Also offers other excursions to towns on the Neckar and Rhine.

Solarschiff (☎ 409 284; www.hdsolarschiff.com; adult/child 3-14yr/student €6/3/4; Tue-Sun Mar-Oct) An ultramodern, glass-topped sightseeing boat whose 50-minute excursions begin next to the Alte Brücke.

Festivals & Events

Heidelberg's most popular annual events include **Heidelberger Herbst** (on the last Saturday in September), a huge autumn festival during which the entire pedestrian zone is closed off for a wild party; and the thrice-yearly **fireworks**

festivals (usually on the first Saturday in June, first Saturday in September and second Saturday in July). For the latter, the best views are from the northern bank of the Neckar, the Philosophenweg and boats floating in the river.

The **Christmas market** (late November to late December), held at five public squares around town (including Universitätsplatz), is a real treat.

Sleeping

BUDGET

Bargains are thin on the ground in Heidelberg. In the high season finding a place to stay can be difficult, so arrive early in the day or book ahead, especially for the hostel. The tourist office charges €3 for a hotel booking.

DJH hostel (☎ 412 066; www.jugendherberge.de; Tiergartenstrasse 5; dm 1st/subsequent night €20.30/17.10; ☒) Situated near the zoo about 2.5km northwest of the Hauptbahnhof, this lively, noisy establishment has 487 beds, most in rooms with toilet and shower. From the Hauptbahnhof or Bismarckplatz take bus 33.

Pension Jeske (☎ 237 33; www.pension-jeske-heidelberg.de; Mittelbadgasse 2; dm not incl breakfast €20-35; ☽ check-in 11am-1pm & 5-7pm; ☒) Large, colourful and decorated with flair, the rooms in this 250-year-old house are the antithesis of cookie-cutter, chain-hotel blandness.

Dubliner (☎ 873 0751; www.dublinerheidelberg .com; Hauptstrasse 93; d €69-85; P ☒) In the heart of Heidelberg's nightlife district, this Irish-style pub has eight basic, newly renovated rooms that are both quiet and clean; three have views of the Schloss. Reception is at the bar.

MIDRANGE

Hotel Zum Pfalzgrafen (☎ 204 89; www.hotel-zum -pfalzgrafen.de; Kettengasse 21; s €69-77, d €89-103; P ☒) Polished pine floors are a nice touch at this family-run place, which has 24 well-appointed rooms.

Hotel Central (☎ 206 41; www.hotel-central-heidelberg .de, in German; Kaiserstrasse 75; s €75-90, d €90-125; ☒) A decent but unexciting 48-room hotel in a rather dull area near the Hauptbahnhof – very convenient if you're arriving by train. The cheery, well-lit rooms have solid pine furniture and dazzling white bathrooms. There's also a nice fitness room.

Hotel Goldener Hecht (☎ 536 80; www.hotel-goldener -hecht.de; Steingasse 2; s/d from €66.50/91) Goethe almost slept here: the hotel would have kept the famous author had the clerk on duty not been quite so uppity. Ever since, guests at this family-run place have received a warm welcome. Some of the 13 rooms, each unique, have views of the Neckar.

Hotel Am Kornmarkt (☎ 905 830; hotelamkorn markt@web.de; Kornmarkt 7; s/d/q from €75/95/140, s/d without bathroom €45/75) Discreet and understated, this Altstadt favourite has 20 pleasant, well-kept rooms. The pricier rooms have great views of the Kornmarkt, while the cheaper ones afford easy access to the spotless hall showers.

Denner Hotel (☎ 604 510; www.denner-hotel.de; Bergheimer Strasse 8; s/d from €82/97, €10 less on Fri, Sat & Sun; ☽ reception 6am-9pm; ☒ ☐) An almost-boutique hotel where the 19 sleek rooms are decked out in modern wooden furniture and have creatively painted walls; some come with neoclassical balconies overlooking bustling Bismarckplatz.

Hotel Vier Jahreszeiten (☎ 241 64; www.4-jahres zeiten.de; Haspelgasse 2; s/d/t/q €69/99/114/155; P) You can hardly get more central than Hotel Vier Jahreszeiten. on the riverfront, the hotel has 22 rooms have blue or red carpets, colourful curtains and white walls.

KulturBrauerei Hotel (☎ 502 980; www.heidelberger -kulturbrauerei.de; Leyergasse 6; s/d from €106/116; P) This 34-room boutique-style hotel greets you with harmonious designer styling and modern art. The rooms are very bright and have pastel walls, wood floors and cheerful décor.

TOP END

Romantik Hotel Zum Ritter St Georg (☎ 1350; www .ritter-heidelberg.de; Hauptstrasse 178; s €90-130, low season €70, d €140-200; P) In an ornate, late Renaissance–style building (1592), this place, right near the Marktplatz, is one of the town's few buildings to have survived the French attacks of 1693. The 37 rooms, dark and Germanic, are very comfortable but are inevitably a bit of a let-down after the fantastic façade and luxurious lobby.

Eating & Drinking

The Altstadt is crammed with eateries, including quite a number on Steingasse (between the Heiliggeistkirche and the Alte Brücke). Quiet a few of Heidelberg's most popular drinking establishments are clustered along Untere Strasse (perpendicular to Steingasse), where bar-hopping is just a matter of walking next door.

Raja Rani (☎ 653 0893; Friedrichstrasse 15; mains from €2) Fast, cheap Indian food. On weekdays students get a free lassi with any order over €2.50.

Mensa Marstall (Neckarstaden) This well-liked student cafeteria is located two blocks north of Universitätsplatz.

Vetter im Schöneck (☎ 165 850; Steingasse 9; ☾ 11.30am-1am, to 2am Fri & Sat) This place serves its own microbrewed beer, made in huge copper vats, and hearty German dishes, including various kinds of sausages (from €5.80). It has a comfy atmosphere and lovely service.

Café Gecko (☎ 604 510; Bergheimer Strasse 8; mains €7.40-13.50; ☾ 7am or 8am-1am, to 3am Fri & Sat) An informal café-restaurant, half a block west of Bismarckplatz and thus a bit away from the tourists, with wicker chairs, off-beat décor and a palmlike canopy of halogen lights. Has a big selection of breakfasts as well as salads, meat, fish and vegetarian dishes.

KulturBrauerei (☎ 502 980; Leyergasse 6; mains €9.50-19.50; ☾ 11am-1am) With rough plank floors, chandeliers and high ceilings, this microbrewery has the feel of an old-time beer hall. It serves regional German cuisine and has a beer garden when it's warm.

Zur Herrenmühle (☎ 602 909; Hauptstrasse 239; mains €8.50-22.50; ☾ 6-11pm Mon-Sat) Serves traditional, classic south German food and international cuisine under the ancient wood beams of a 17th-century mill. Rustically elegant.

MaxBar (☎ 244 19; Marktplatz 5; ☾ 8am-1am, to 2am Fri & Sat) A French-style café with classic views of the Marktplatz. Perfect for a beer or a pastis, it's especially popular on weekend nights.

Zum Sepp'l (☎ 230 85; Hauptstrasse 213; ☾ noon-midnight) One of Heidelberg's most historical student pubs, with frat photos on the dark wood-panelled walls, pilfered signs hanging from the ceiling and heavy wooden tables with names carved into them. Retains the ambience of yesteryear, although these days students are outnumbered by tourists.

Destille (☎ 228 08; Untere Strasse 16; ☾ noon-2am, to 3am Fri & Sat) Known for the tree trunk behind the bar, this mellow and hugely popular pub (no food is served) specialises in drinks such as melon-flavoured schnapps and something called a *Warmer Engel* (schnapps with Tabasco sauce). In the afternoon, patrons can avail themselves of chessboards, playing cards and other games.

Self-caterers could try **Handelshof supermarket** (Kurfürstenanlage 61; ☾ 7am-8pm Mon-Sat), two blocks northeast of the Hauptbahnhof,

or there's an **outdoor food market** (6am-1pm Wed & Sat) on Marktplatz, as there has been for centuries.

Entertainment

Heidelberg has a lively cultural scene, with plenty of concerts and theatre performances. *Meier* (€1.80), a monthly events calendar featuring clubs, pubs, restaurants and gay and lesbian venues, can be found at the tourist office and newsagents. Tickets and details for concerts and other cultural events are available at **Heidelberg Ticket** (☎ 582 0000; Theaterstrasse 4; ☾ 11am-7pm Mon-Fri, 10am-3pm Sat).

Heiliggeistkirche (Marktplatz) Puts on hour-long concerts (adult/student/senior €10/6/8) of sacred organ music every Saturday at 6.15pm. In the warmer months there are 30-minute organ concerts (adult/student €3/2) daily except Saturday at 5.15pm.

Gloria und Gloriette (☎ 253 19; www.cinevent.de, in German; Hauptstrasse 146) A cinema that screens undubbed films three times a week.

Nachtschicht (☎ 438 550, 438 5522; www.nachtschicht .com, in German; Alte Eppelheimer Strasse 5; ☾ 10pm-5am, usually Wed-Sat) Near the Hauptbahnhof, in a warehouse area between Bergheimer Strasse and Alte Eppelheimer Strasse, this is one of the city's largest and most popular discos. It attracts lots of students and admission is often €4.50.

Cave54 (☎ 221 58; www.cave54.de, in German; Krämergasse 2; admission from €5) Opened in 1954, this place is said to be the oldest student jazz club in Germany. Its claim to fame is that Louis Armstrong once played here. It functions as a pub-disco on most nights (10pm to 3am), has concerts (8.30pm to midnight) at least once a week, and has jam sessions every Sunday from 8.30pm.

Getting There & Away

Heidelberg is 21km southeast of Mannheim and 120km northwest of Stuttgart.

Lufthansa's Airport Shuttle (☎ 0621-651 620; www.lufthansa-airportbus.de) links the Crown Plaza Hotel (Kurfürstenanlage 1–3), three blocks southwest of Bismarckplatz, with Frankfurt airport (€18, 1¼ hours, almost hourly).

The north–south A5 links Heidelberg with both Frankfurt and Karlsruhe.

There are at least hourly train services to/from Baden-Baden (€17, one hour), Frankfurt (€13.40, one hour) and Stuttgart (€21, 40 minutes).

(Continued on page 417)

Berlin

RICHARD NEBESKY

Soak up the glamour of 1930s Berlin over cocktails at Reingold (p134)

ANDREA SCHULTE-PEEVERS

Get back to the roots of modern architecture at the Bauhaus Archiv/Museum für Gestaltung (p112)

RICK GERHARTER

Expect nothing but the very latest at Berlin's cutting-edge clubs (p138)

Thuringia

The restored Altstadt of Erfurt (p251) features medieval-style architecture

JOHN BORTHWICK

DAVID PEEVERS

The museum and memorial at Buchenwald (p265) pay tribute to victims of the concentration camp

Wittumspalais (p263), the home of über-arts patron Anna Amalia, is but one of the many intellectual landmarks in Weimar

MARTIN MOOS

Bavaria

MARTIN MOOS

Hike and ski the Bavarian Alps in the pristine Berchtesgaden National Park (p351)

KRZYSZTOF DYDYNSKI

Oktoberfest originated in Munich and is held at its Theresienwiese fair grounds (p304)

Baden-Württemberg

Home of the Brothers Grimm fairy tales, the Black Forest (p430) is great for hiking, cycling, swimming and boating

DAVID PEEVERS

You don't have to be a car-lover to enjoy the new Mercedes-Benz Museum (p396) in Stuttgart

THOMAS WINZ

The town square of Tübingen (p423) has long been a dynamic student hang-out – even Pope Benedict XVI (aka Joseph Ratzinger) spent time here in his university days

Black Forest

ESBIN ANDERSON

CHARLOTTE HINDLE

Standing tall is the red-sandstone town hall of Freiburg (p439), a university town with a lively cultural scene

In a forest setting, Schiltach (p438) is full of half-timbered houses like these

DAVID PEEVERS

Rhine & Moselle Valleys

Muller-Thurgau grapes are a common variety in the Moselle Valley (p495)

Take a winery tour along the Romantic Rhine (p483)

The west portal of the Speyer's Kaiserdom (p474), which is one of the finest examples of Romanesque architecture in the world

Cologne &
the Rhineland

ANDREA SCHULTE-PEEVERS

Bonn's Kunst-und Ausstellungshalle der
Bundesrepublik Deutschland (p564) has
international blockbuster exhibitions

ANDREA SCHULTE-PEEVERS

Cologne's most famous Romanesque church, Gross
St Martin (p552), towers over the medieval Altstadt

Be dazzled by Düsseldorf's electric bar and club scene (p546)

DAVID PEEVERS

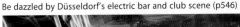

Northern Germany

The Hamburger Dom (p664) is one of Europe's oldest fun fairs

MARTIN LLADÓ

Avoid the crowds and dine at Lübeck's elegant
Markgraf restaurant (p688)

MARTIN LLADÓ

Schnoor (p644), Bremen's former red-light
district, is now a restaurant and café district

RICHARD NEBESKÝ

(Continued from page 408)

Getting Around

Bicycles can be hired from **Eldorado** (☎ 654 4460; www.eldorado-hd.de, in German; Neckarstaden 52; per day €15; ♡ 9am-noon & 2-6pm Tue-Fri, 10am-6pm Sat, 2-6pm Sun), three short blocks west of the Alte Brücke.

Parking in Heidelberg is an expensive proposition. The city's well-marked underground car parks charge around €1.50 per hour and €16 for the whole day.

Tram 5 links the Hauptbahnhof with Bismarckplatz, the main hub for **public transport** (www.vrn.de, in German). Single tickets cost €2; a 24-hour pass (also valid on Sunday if stamped Saturday) for one/five people costs €5/8. Tickets are sold by bus and tram drivers (except on tram line 5) and at ticket machines.

Buses 11, 21, 33, 34, 41 and 42, as well as tram 1, run between Bismarckplatz and the Hauptbahnhof. Buses 11 and 33 go directly from the Hauptbahnhof to Neckarmuntzplatz.

Taxis (☎ 302 030) line up outside the Hauptbahnhof. It costs about €12 from the Hauptbahnhof to the Alte Brücke.

AROUND HEIDELBERG

The apex of German baroque landscaping can be admired at the magnificent **Schloss Schwetzingen** (☎ 06202-128 828; www.schloesser-und-gaerten.de; adult/concession/family €7/3.50/17.50 Apr-Oct, €5.50/2.70/13.70 Nov-Mar, garden only €4/2/10 Apr-Oct, €2.50/1.20/6.20 Nov-Mar; ♡ chateau tours 10am-4pm Tue-Fri, 11am-5pm Sat, Sun & holidays Apr-Oct, 2pm Fri, 11am, 2pm & 3pm Sat, Sun & holidays Nov-Mar, garden 8am-8pm Apr-Sep, to 6pm Oct & Mar, to 5pm Nov-Feb).

When Prince-Elector Carl Theodor (1724–99) inherited the Kurpfalz (Electoral Palatinate) region in the mid-18th century, he made Schwetzingen his summer residence, creating whimsical gardens – inspired by Versailles – that are a jewel. The grounds radiate from a formal French garden and include follies such as **Temple Apollos**, an auditorium built in the columned style of a Greek shrine, and the **Moschee** (Mosque), which sports minarets and a dome above a rather Germanic baroque entrance. One of the paths crosses the **Chinesische Brücke**, an arched Chinese bridge.

Inside the **Jagdschloss** (Hunting Palace) is the **Rokokotheater** (1752), with a deep-set stage that draws on light and a tunnel illusion to enhance its dimensions. The big and little hands of the **clock** on the façade (1700) were reversed so that horsemen could read the time more easily from a distance.

Schloss Schwetzingen is just off the A6 autobahn, 10km west of Heidelberg and 8km south of Mannheim. It's linked to Heidelberg's Hauptbahnhof by bus 717 (€3.30, 30 minutes, twice an hour) and to Mannheim's Hauptbahnhof by bus 710 (€3.30; 35 minutes, twice an hour).

MANNHEIM

☎ 0621 / pop 308,300

Just 21km northwest of Heidelberg, the sprawling industrial centre of Mannheim isn't likely to appear on anyone's list of the Top 10 (or even Top 100) German tourist destinations. It offers visitors few specific attractions or things to do but compensates with its big-city sense of fun, lively cultural scene (it's proud of playing host to Germany's only pop music academy) and decent shopping. Mannheim is famous for its quirky – indeed, unique – street layout.

Orientation

Mannheim's city centre, surrounded by a ring road, is almost round except for a flat stretch along its southwest side. It's sandwiched between the Rhine (to the southwest) and the Neckar (to the northeast), which meet about 5km to the northwest. The Hauptbahnhof is at the southern edge of the centre, near the intersection of Bismarckstrasse and Kaiserring.

The 1.5km-by-1.5km city centre is divided into four quadrants by two perpendicular, largely pedestrianised shopping streets, the more-or-less north–south Breite Strasse and the east–west Planken. Paradeplatz is situated at their intersection.

The city centre's chessboard layout is a trip. The streets, laid out on a grid, have no names; instead, each rectilinear city block has an alphanumeric designation. Starting at the Schloss (at the southern end of Breite Strasse), as you move north the letters go from A up to K west of this artery, and from L to U east of it. The numbers rise from 1 to 7 as you move outwards – either east or west –from Breite Strasse. The result is addresses such as 'Q3, 16' or 'L14, 5' (the latter numeral is the building number) that sound a bit like galactic sectors.

Information

Chat-Corner Internet café (L14, 16-17; ♡ 8am-3am; per hr €3) On the corner of Bismarckstrasse and Kaiserring, a block northeast of the Hauptbahnhof.

Main post office (02) Next to Paradeplatz.
Post office (Willy Brandt Platz) To the right as you exit the Hauptbahnhof.
Tourist office (☎ 101 012, tickets 101 011; www
.tourist-mannheim.de; Willy-Brandt-Platz 3; ✆ 9am-7pm
Mon-Fri, 9am-1pm Sat, to 6pm Sat in Dec) Just outside the
Hauptbahnhof. Sells tickets for cultural events.
Wäsche Insel (Seckenheimer Strasse 8; laundry per 6kg
€6.60; ✆ 8am-8pm Mon-Fri, 9am-4pm Sat) Wash your
stuff yourself or leave it and pick it up two hours later.
Situated four blocks northeast of the Hauptbahnhof behind
the Kunsthalle.

Sights & Activities

The pastel yellow and dark red sandstone
Schloss, at the southern end of Breite Strasse,
is Germany's largest baroque palace and the
focal point of the whole city centre. Soon
after its completion in 1777, Elector Carl
Theodor moved his court to Munich, ren-
dering the complex a bit pointless. Today,
most of it serves as a university campus,
with hundreds of rather ordinary classrooms
and offices. As we go to press, parts of the
palace are under renovation, but from 2007
it will again be possible to see the **Rittersaal**
and other sumptuously decorated bits of the
interior. Elector Carl Philip is splendidly buried in the crypt of the baroque **Schlosskirche**,
rebuilt after the war, which is on the west side
of the **Ehrenhof** (the courtyard at the base of
Breite Strasse).

A block north of the northwestern tip of the
Schloss is Mannheim's most dazzling piece
of architecture, the **Jesuitenkirche** (A4, 2; www
.jesuitenkirchemannheim.de, in German; ✆ 9am-6pm), an
18th-century baroque church with a spectacular and recently renovated interior.

Five blocks northeast of the Hauptbahnhof, on the busy Kaiserring at the western
end of the Planken, is the elegant, 60m-high
Wasserturm (Water Tower), the city's most
recognisable landmark. Built in the 1880s,
it sits in the middle of pretty **Friedrichsplatz**,
surrounded by manicured lawns, flower beds
and two Art Nouveau fountains. A handsome
ensemble of red-sandstone buildings, many
with arcades, lines the perimeter.

On Friedrichsplatz' southern side is the
highly acclaimed **Kunsthalle** (☎ 293 6430; Friedrichsplatz 4; www.kunsthalle-mannheim.de, in German; adult/
student/family €7/5/5; ✆ 11am-6pm Tue-Sun), which
features modern and contemporary art by
masters such as Cézanne, Manet, Klee, Leger,
Kandinsky, Max Ernst and Schlemmer.

Also worth a look is the Protestant **Christuskirche** (Werderplatz), a long block northeast
of Friedrichsplatz. Topped by a green dome,
this neobaroque church has a distinctive
outline and is exactly 5m higher than the
Wasserturm.

Three blocks further to the northeast, along
the Neckar, is the lovely **Luisenpark** (adult/student
€4/3; ✆ 9am-dusk), a sprawling green belt with
hothouses, gardens, a butterfly hall, an aquarium and even a Chinese teahouse. The 212m-
high **Fernmeldeturm** (telecommunications tower; ☎ 419
290; Hans Reschke Ufer; adult/student €3.50/2.50; ✆ 10am-
midnight), built in 1975, has a rotating restaurant
midway up. To get there take tram 5.

Sleeping

Mannheim is primarily a business town, a fact
reflected in its hotel scene.

DJH hostel (☎ 822 718; Rheinpromenade 21; www
.jugendherberge-mannheim.de; dm 1st/subsequent night
€16.80/13.70; P ✗) This 109-bed hostel, for
which renovations are planned, is only a
15-minute walk south of the Hauptbahnhof
towards the Rhine. It's served by bus 7 to
Lindenhofplatz.

Arabella Pension Garni (☎ 230 50; www.pension
-arabella-mannheim.de, in German; M2 12; s €28-35, d €45-55
not incl breakfast; ✆ reception noon-8pm; ✗) Super-
centrally located two blocks north of the
Schloss, the 18 rooms here are simply furnished but practical and bright. Call ahead if
you'll be arriving when reception is closed.

Central Hotel (☎ 123 00; www.centralhotelmannheim
.de, in German; Kaiserring 26-28; s/d Mon-Fri €86/96, Sat & Sun
€65/75; P ✗) Two blocks north of the Haupt-
bahnhof, this 34-room hotel has bright, cheery
rooms of a decent size; those in back are quietest. Reception is at the stylish café-bar.

Maritim Parkhotel (☎ 158 80; www.maritim.de; Friedrichsplatz 2; s/d Mon-Thu & during conventions €146/186,
Fri, Sat & Sun €100/133; ✗ 🏊 ♨) This luxurious,
173-room hotel, built in 1901, offers all the
traditional 1st-class creature comforts plus
pool, sauna, steam bath, fitness gadgets and
live lobby music in the evenings. It faces the
Wasserturm.

Eating & Drinking

Gasthaus Zentrale (☎ 202 43; N4, 15; daily specials
€4.50-7, meat mains €6.30-16.40; ✆ 9.30am-1am) This
pub-restaurant, three short blocks east of
Paradeplatz, is a favourite student hang-out
thanks to its reasonably priced food and
warm-weather beer garden.

Café Klatsch (☎ 156 1033; Hebelstrasse 3; ✆ 6pm-3am Mon-Sat, 4pm-3am Sun & holidays) Facing the Nationaltheater just off Friedrichsring, this sleek bar is Mannheim's best-known gay and lesbian venue. Hetero-friendly, it holds a 'cake and coffee' event every Sunday afternoon. The soundtrack is mellow until 10pm, after which house sets the tone.

Self-caterers could try the **food market** (Marktplatz, block G1; ✆ till 2pm Tue, Thu & Sat) and the **Lidl supermarket** (Tattersall 6; ✆ 8am-8pm Mon-Sat) two blocks northeast of the Hauptbahnhof.

There's a Mensa student cafeteria at the northwestern tip of the Schloss.

Getting There & Around

Mannheim, on the Hamburg–Basel line, is a major rail hub. Destinations include Frankfurt (by RE: €13.40, 70 minutes, hourly; by ICE: €23, 36 minutes, several times an hour), Frankfurt airport (€20, 31 minutes, hourly) and Freiburg (€33 by RE, €39 by ICE, 1½ hours, twice hourly). Various S-Bahn and RE trains link the Hauptbahnhof with Heidelberg (€4.50, 15 minutes).

Mannheim is near the junction of the east–west A6 (here oriented north–south), the A67 north to Frankfurt, and the A656 east to Heidelberg. There's free parking about 1km east of the Wasserturm around the Fernmeldeturm (such as along Hans Reschke Ufer and Ludwig Ratzel Strasse).

KARLSRUHE

☎ 0721 / pop 283,000

Karlsruhe (literally 'Carl's Rest'), just 15km from the northeasternmost tip of France, was dreamt up in 1715 by Margrave Karl Wilhelm of Baden-Durlach as a residential retreat. The city came out of the postwar reconstruction process fairly well, all things considered, and today it's a creative university city with a lively cultural scene. Highlights of a visit include the Schloss, set in a lovely park, and some stellar museums.

Karlsruhe is the seat of the Bundesverfassungsgericht, the Federal Constitutional Court, which is heavily guarded in a harmonious modern building just southwest of the Schloss.

Orientation

From the Schloss and its gardens, 32 streets radiate like the spokes of a wheel. Nine of them, forming a quarter-circle, head south and southwest, delineating the fan-shaped

city centre. Karlsruhe's focal point is the Marktplatz, which is two blocks south of the Schloss gardens at the intersection of the main east–west shopping street, tram-clogged Kaiserstrasse, and the Karl-Friedrich-Strasse, which goes north–south and links the Schloss with the Hauptbahnhof, 2.5km due south (and then a bit west).

The university campus, which extends northward from Kaiserstrasse, begins 500m east of the Marktplatz.

Information

ATMs There are several along Kaiserstrasse near the Marktplatz.

Hauptbahnhof tourist office (Stadt-information; ☎ 3720 5383; www.karlsruhe-tourism.de; Bahnhofplatz 6; ✆ 9am-6pm Mon-Fri, 9am-1pm Sat). Right across the street from the Hauptbahnhof. The City Tour (€8) is a self-guided audio-visual (PDA) walking tour of the city centre lasting up to four hours. Also sells the Karlsruher Welcome-Card and carries *Karlsruhe Extra*, a free trilingual listing of concerts, museum exhibitions, cultural events, etc issued twice a year.

Internet Cafe (Kronenplatz 28; per hr €1.50; ✆ 9am-midnight Mon-Sat, 10am-midnight Sun) Down the block from Kaiserstrasse 95.

Karlsruher WelcomeCard (€9.50) Good for two days (three days including a weekend), entitling you to public transport use and reduced-price entry to museums.

Marktplatz tourist office (Tourist-information; ☎ 3720 5376; Karl-Friedrich-Strasse 9, ✆ 9.30am-7pm Mon-Fri, 10am-3pm Sat) Offers the same services as the Hauptbahnhof tourist office. Sells events tickets and has a public transport information desk.

Post office (Poststrasse) Just east of the Hauptbahnhof.

Sights

SCHLOSS & BADISCHES LANDESMUSEUM

Karlsruhe's **palace** was destroyed in the war but city custodians had enough sense – and money – to rebuild it in the original style, which reflects the transition from baroque to neoclassical. Its dual function as a residence and a retreat is apparent in the layout of the gardens: while the **Schlossplatz** (to the south towards the Marktplatz) is formal, the huge **Schlossgarten** north of the palace has a more relaxed English design. In fine weather, the latter – which has a **Botanischer Garten** and its own miniature train line, the **Schlossgartenbahn** – is a popular hangout for students from the nearby university (the campus, shaped more or less like two slices of pizza, is just to the southeast).

BADEN-WÜRTTEMBERG

BADEN-WÜRTTEMBERG

The Schloss houses the superb collections of the **Badisches Landesmuseum** (Baden State Museum; ☎ 926 6520; www.landesmuseum.de, in German; adult/student €4/3, free after 2pm Fri; 10am-5pm Tue-Thu, 10am-6pm Fri-Sun), which include the dazzling gem-encrusted crown, sceptre and sword of Baden's grand-ducal ruling family; altars, statues and paintings from the Middle Ages (both on the 1st floor), and 'spoils of war' brought back by Margrave Ludwig Wilhelm from his 17th-century campaigns against the Turks. Climbing the **tower** is the best way to appreciate the town's circular layout.

The **Museum in der Majolika** (☎ 926 6583; www .majolika-karlsruhe.com; Ahaweg 6; adult/concession €2/1; 10am-1pm & 2-5pm Tue-Sun, free after 2pm Fri), which displays 1000 ceramic objects made since 1901 by Karlsruhe's Majolika-Manufactur, is linked to the Schloss by the **Blaue Linie**, a line of 1645 blue majolica tiles that lead across the Schlossgarten lawns.

At the northern end of the Marktplatz is the **Museum am Markt** (☎ 926 6578; Karl-Friedrich-Strasse 6; adult/concession €2/1; 11am-5pm Tue-Thu, 10am-6pm Fri-Sun, free after 2pm Fri), a branch of the Badisches Landesmuseum that focuses on post-1900 applied arts, including the delicious objects produced by the Art Nouveau and Art Deco movements.

STAATLICHE KUNSTHALLE

Southwest across the garden from the Schloss, and past the Federal Constitutional Court, is the outstanding **State Art Gallery** (☎ 926 3370; www.kunsthalle-karlsruhe.de, in German; Hans-Thoma-Strasse 2-6; adult/student €6/4; 10am-5pm Tue-Fri, 10am-6pm Sat & Sun). Highlights include works by German masters of the late Gothic period such as Matthias Grünewald and Lucas Cranach the Elder; and canvases by French innovators such as Degas, Manet, Monet, Pissarro, Sisley and Renoir. The modern art section, in the Orangerie, was reopened in 2006 after renovations.

ZENTRUM FÜR KUNST UND MEDIENTECHNOLOGIE

Locals are immensely proud of the **ZKM** (Centre for Art and Media; ☎ 8100 1200; www.zkm.de; Lorenzstrasse 19; 10am-6pm Wed-Fri, 11am-6pm Sat & Sun), a huge exhibition, research and documentation complex that brings together art and emerging electronic media technologies. Housed in the vast halls of a historic munitions factory, it includes several cafés and restaurants. The

website has details on special exhibitions, concerts and other events.

The **Medienmuseum** (Media Museum; adult/child 7-18yr/student & senior €5/2/3, free after 2pm Fri) focuses on interactive media art, while the **Museum für Neue Kunst** (Museum for Contemporary Art; adult/ child 7-18yr/student & senior €5/2/3, incl the Medienmuseum €8/3/5, free after 2pm Fri) hosts first-rate temporary exhibitions of art created after 1960.

Next to the ZKM is the **Städtische Galerie** (☎ 133 4401; www.staedtische-galerie.de, in German; Lorenzstrasse 27; permanent collection adult/student & senior €2.60/1.80), which showcases local art as well as postwar German art.

The ZKM is located in the southwest corner of the city centre, a bit over 2km southwest of the Schloss and a similar distance northwest of the Hauptbahnhof; it's served by tram 2.

Sleeping

DJH hostel (☎ 282 48; www.jugendherberge.de; Moltke-strasse 24; dm 1st/subsequent night €17.90/14.70;) A few blocks due west of the Schloss, this hostel has 167 beds, most in rooms with shower and toilet. From the train station, take tram 2, 4 or 6 to Europaplatz and then walk five blocks north along Karlstrasse and its continuation.

Hotel Avisa (☎ 349 77; www.hotel-avisa.de; Am Stadtgarten 5; s/d from €67/97;) Two blocks northeast of the Hauptbahnhof at the southern edge of the Stadtgarten-Zoo, this place has 27 hotel-ish but perfectly decent rooms. A solid choice.

Eating

Karlsruhe has a wide selection of beer gardens and eateries.

Café Salomon (☎ 921 2080; Hans-Thoma-Strasse 3; 8.30am-7pm Mon-Fri, 10am-6pm Sat & Sun) Facing the Staatliche Kunsthalle, this is the best place in town for bagels (€1.40 to €4.20).

Krokodil (☎ 1208 4790; Waldstrasse 63; mains €5.90-12.50; 7.30am-1am, to 3am Fri & Sat) A popular café-restaurant, right at Ludwigsplatz, with soaring ceilings and walls covered with wood panelling, tiles, mirrors and yellow smoke-stained paint. There's a brunch buffet (€10) on Sunday and holidays from 10am to 2pm.

Alte Bank (☎ 183 2818; Herrenstrasse 30-32; salads €4.80-8.90, mains around €8.50; 10am-1am) A block south of Kaiserstrasse, this cultured but informal café-restaurant has two rows of columns and chandeliers overhead.

Entertainment

Club le Carambolage (☎ 373 227; www.club-caram bolage.de, in German; Kaiserstrasse 21; ☺ 9pm-4am or later) A hugely popular *Musikklub* facing the university campus. It has free billiards from 9pm to 11pm.

Getting There & Away

Destinations well-served by rail include Baden-Baden (€5, more by IC or ICE, 15 to 30 minutes) and Freiburg (€24 to €29, one hour).

Karlsruhe is on the A5 (Frankfurt–Basel) and is the starting point of the A8 to Munich.

Getting Around

The Hauptbahnhof is linked to the Marktplatz (just two blocks south of the Schloss gardens) by tram and light rail lines 2, 3, S1, S11, S4 and S41. Single tickets cost €2 for an adult and €1 per child between six and 14 years of age; a 24-Stunden-Karte, good for 24 hours, costs €4.20 (€6.50 for up to five people).

There are park-and-ride options outside of the city centre; look for 'P+R' signs.

KLOSTER MAULBRONN

This one-time **Cistercian monastery** (☎ 07043-926 610; www.schloesser-und-gaerten.de; adult/concession/family €5/2.50/12.50; ☺ 9am-5.30pm Mar-Oct, 9.30am-5pm Tue-Sun Nov-Feb), a Unesco World Heritage Site since 1993, is one of the best-preserved medieval monasteries anywhere north of the Alps. Founded by monks from Alsace around 1140, it became a Protestant school in 1556. Famous graduates include the astronomer Johannes Keppler.

Features of architectural interest include the **monastery church**, but it's the insights into the spirit of monastic life, with its mixture of contemplation and labour, that make this place so culturally important and interesting.

Maulbronn, in the Salzach Valley, is 30km east of Karlsruhe and 33km northwest of Stuttgart, not far from the Pforzheim Ost exit on the A8. To get there by public transport from Karlsruhe, take the S4 light rail line to Bretten Bahnhof and from there the hourly bus 700 (€4, one hour); from Stuttgart, take the train to Mühlacker and then bus 700.

SCHWÄBISCH HALL

☎ 0791 / pop 36,000

Home of the Schwäbisch Hall banking and insurance company, this easy-to-like, picture-perfect Swabian river town – which celebrated its 850th anniversary in 2006 – is known for its ancient riverside cityscape, innovative museums and open-air theatre performances. An aimless amble will take you along narrow stone alleys, among half-timbered hillside houses, over covered bridges and up slopes overlooking the tranquil Kocher River. The islands and grassy riverbank parks are perfect for picnics.

Orientation & Information

The Kocher River runs south-to-north through Schwäbisch Hall, separating the Altstadt, on the right (east) bank, from the Neustadt (New Town), on the left (west) bank. The Altstadt's main commercial street, Neue Strasse, links Am Markt (the Marktplatz) with the river.

PTT-Tele-Cafe (Marktstrasse 15; per hr €1.50; ☺ 10am-10pm Tue-Sat, noon-10pm Sun & Mon) Internet access a block north of Am Markt.

Tourist office (☎ 751 246; www.schwaebischhall.de; Am Markt 9; ☺ 9am-6pm Mon-Fri, 10am-3pm Sat & Sun May-Sep, 9am-5pm Mon-Fri Oct-Apr) On the Altstadt's main square.

Sights

ALTSTADT

Am Markt, which still hosts markets on Wednesday and Saturday mornings, boasts the **Rathaus** (town hall), reconstructed in baroque style after a town fire in 1728 and again after WWII. The centrepiece of the Markt, however, is the late-Gothic **Kirche St Michael**, begun in 1156 but mainly constructed during the 15th and 16th centuries. Note the classical net vaulting on the ceiling of the choir.

The majestic staircase out the front has been used to stage **Freilichtspiele** (open-air theatre performances; www.freilichtspiele-hall.de, in German) every summer since 1925.

Next to the tourist office is the **Gotischer Fischbrunnen** (1509), a large iron tub once used for storing river fish before sale.

Two short blocks south of the church, at the end of Pfarrgasse, is the massive **Neubau**, a steep-roofed 16th-century structure built as an arsenal and granary and now used as a theatre; walk up the stone staircase on its south side for a wonderful view of the city's red-roofed houses. Looking down toward the river, you can see the former **city fortifications**, the covered **Roter Steg** bridge and, at the western end of Neue Strasse, the **Henkerbrücke** (Hangman's Bridge).

Housed in seven old buildings down by the river, the outstanding **Hällisch-Frankisches Museum** (☎ 751 289; Im Keckenhof 6; adult/student €2.50/1.50; ☯ 10am-5pm Tue-Sun year-round, until 8pm Fri early Jun–mid-Aug) has well-presented collections covering the history of Schwäbisch Hall and nearby areas. Exhibits include artwork and crafts from the 17th century, painted wooden targets shot through with holes and an extremely rare hand-painted wooden **synagogue interior** from 1738.

KUNSTHALLE WÜRTH

Founded in 2001 by the industrialist Reinhold Würth, this **art museum** (☎ 946 720; www .kunst.wuerth.com; Lange Strasse 35; adult/student & senior €5/3; ☯ 10am-6pm), a block up the hill from the Roter Steg bridge, puts on intriguing temporary exhibitions that change every four or five months (it closes for two weeks between exhibits). An audioguide may be available for €4. It is housed in a striking ultramodern building, faced with rough-hewn local stone that preserves part of a century-old brewery, the **Sudhaus**, where you'll find a brasserie that often hosts live music in the evenings.

Sleeping

Campingplatz Am Steinbacher See (☎ 2984; www .camping-schwaebisch-hall.de; Mühlsteige 26; tent/adult €5.10/4.80; ☯ year-round) An idyllic lakeside camping ground with a washer-dryer and communal kitchen. Take bus 4 to Steinbach Mitte.

DJH hostel (☎ 410 50; www.jugendherberge.de; Langenfelder Weg 5; dm 1st/subsequent night €17.90/14.70; ☒) This friendly 133-bed hostel, just 10 minutes on foot east from Am Markt, has bathrooms in some rooms.

Hotel Garni Sölch (☎ 518 07; www.hotel-soelch.de, in German; Hauffstrasse 14; s/d €43/63, extra for stays of 1 night €5; ℗ ☒) This hotel, about 20 minutes on foot from the centre, is modern with a rustic-themed interior.

Hotel Garni Scholl (☎ 975 50; www.hotel-scholl.de; Klosterstrasse 2-4; s €64-74, d €88-104; ☒) Behind Kirche St Michael, this family-run hotel has homely, well-designed and fastidiously kept rooms with hardwood floors and marble bathrooms.

Hotel Hohenlohe (☎ 758 70; www.hotel-hohenlohe .de in German; Weilertor 14; s €101-132, d €126-184; ℗ ☒ ▣ ▨) This extremely comfortable hotel, where many of the 114 rooms afford superb river views, has four saltwater pools, a sauna, a large wellness centre and politically incorrect statuary in the lobby. The rooms

have sleek wooden furniture and are decorated in warm Mediterranean tones of yellow, orange and pastel green.

Eating

Eateries can be found on or near Haalstrasse, a bit southwest of Am Markt. There's a brasserie at Kunsthalle Würth (left).

Hespelt (☎ 930 220; Am Spitalbach 17; lunch plate from €3.60; ☯ 8.30am-6pm Mon-Fri, 8am-12.30pm Sat) This butcher-deli, two blocks northwest of Am Markt, puts together great hot lunches.

Weinstube Würth (☎ 6636; Im Weiler 8; mains €5-13; ☯ 11pm-midnight Tue-Sun) Across the river from the Altstadt, this veteran serves delicious Swabian and vegetarian specialities, including *Maultaschen*, and has a lovely beer garden.

Gasthaus Sonne (☎ 970 840; Gelbinger Gasse 2; ☯ closed 2-5.30pm & Mon) This historic restaurant has been serving local specialities since 1903.

Getting There & Around

The town is served by two train stations: trains from Stuttgart (€11.70, 1¼ hours, hourly) arrive at Hessental, on the right bank about 7km south of the centre and linked to the Altstadt by bus 1; trains from Heilbronn go to the left-bank Bahnhof Schwäbisch Hall, a short walk along Bahnhofstrasse from the centre. Trains and buses run regularly between the two.

Outfits hiring out bikes include **2-Rad Zügel** (☎ 971 400; Johanniterstrasse 55; per day €10; ☯ 9am-12.30pm & 2-7pm Mon-Fri, 9am-2pm Sat), north of the centre on the B19.

AROUND SCHWÄBISCH HALL

The open-air **Hohenloher Freilandmuseum** (Farming Museum; ☎ 971 010; adult/student €5.50/3.50; ☯ 9am-6pm Tue-Sun May-Sep, 10am-5pm Tue-Sun Mar, Apr, Oct & Nov) in Wackershofen, 6km northwest of Schwäbisch Hall, has ancient farmhouses hosting demonstrations of pre-20th-century farming methods and equipment – we nearly got blisters just watching. From Schwäbisch Hall, it's an easy ride out here on bus 7.

SCHWÄBISCHE ALB

The hilly area south of Stuttgart and east of the Black Forest, sometimes known in English as the Swabian Alp, is crossed by two major rivers that rise in the Black Forest. The mighty Danube moseys through Ulm, with its daring modern architecture, before heading to Budapest and beyond. The Neckar flows through the university city of Tübingen on its way to Stuttgart and Heidelberg, eventually joining the Rhine at Mannheim.

TÜBINGEN

☎ 07071 / pop 83,000

Tübingen, 40km south of Stuttgart, mixes all the charms of a late-medieval city – such as a hilltop fortress, cobbled alleys and lots of half-timbered houses – with the erudition and mischief of a real college town. A seat of higher learning since the university was founded in 1477 by Count Eberhard VI of Württemberg, Tübingen was a favoured haunt of Goethe, who published his first works here; famous graduates include the philosopher Hegel, the lyric poet Friedrich Hölderlin (1770–1843) and the astronomer Johannes Keppler.

Today, Tübingen is a lovely place to relax for a few days, hit some pubs and paddle your way down the Neckar River. If you'd like to hang out in a German university town but are wary of Heidelberg's mass tourism, Tübingen is an excellent choice.

Orientation

The Neckar River flows through Tübingen from east to west. From Eberhardsbrücke (Neckarbrücke), the city centre's only bridge, Karlstrasse leads south to the Hauptbahnhof (500m). Going north up the hill is Mühlstrasse, to the left (west) of which lies the Altstadt. The main university area is further north (about 1km from the river) along Wilhelmstrasse, the northern continuation of Mühlstrasse.

Most of Tübingen's sights are in the Altstadt. The northern bank of the Neckar leads steeply up to a ridge, at (or near) the top of which you'll find (from east to west) the Stiftskirche, the pedestrianised Kirchgasse, Am Markt (the Altstadt's main public square) and the Schloss. The northern half of the Altstadt, including most of the shopping (such as on Hirschgasse), is on the slope leading down to the tiny Ammer River.

Information

ATMs There's one in the Hauptbahnhof, another at the southern end of Eberhardsbrücke and yet another at Am Markt.

Frauenbuchladen Thalestris (☎ 265 90; www .frauenbuchladen.net, in German; Bursagasse 2; ☼ 10am-7pm Mon-Fri, 10am-2pm Sat) Stocks books related to women. It's a women's information centre, too, and men aren't allowed inside. Situated right behind the Hölderlinturm, half a block up from the river.

N-Telecenter (Wilhelmstrasse 3/1; per hr €2; ☼ 8.30am-10.30pm Mon-Sat, 11am-10.30pm Sun) Internet access.

Osiander (☎ 920 10; Wilhelmstrasse 12-14) A purveyor of books since 1596.

Post office (cnr Hafengasse & Neue Strasse) In the Altstadt.

Tourist office (☎ 913 60; www.tuebingen.de; An der Neckarbrücke 1; ☼ 9am-7pm Mon-Fri, 9am-5pm Sat) At the south end of Eberhardsbrücke. Has a board with hotel details outside and can provide details on hiking options (for example to Bebenhausen or Wurmlingerkapelle).

Vu-Tel (Mühlstrasse 14; per hr €2.50; ☼ 10am-10pm Mon-Sat, noon-10pm Sun) Two other internet cafés are located on the same block.

Waschsalon (Mühlstrasse 18; ☼ 7am-10pm Mon-Sat) Self-service laundry.

BADEN-WÜRTTEMBERG

TÜBINGEN AND THE POPE

In the late 1960s Tübingen, like university towns around the globe, was swept by a wave of student radicalism. Among those who experienced those tumultuous times was a forty-ish Catholic theology lecturer, known as a church reformer for his role in the Second Vatican Council (1962–65), named Father Joseph Ratzinger.

The students were revolting – about that, and perhaps that alone, Ratzinger was in full agreement with his liberal rivals within the Church, who saw in the spirit of the times the glowing idealism of youth. Ratzinger, on the other hand, detected in the Marxist-influenced radicals a tendency towards totalitarianism that reminded him of what he had seen growing up in Nazi-era Bavaria. His conclusion was that only unswerving adherence to Church doctrine could save humanity from barbarism.

That clear-cut view of Catholicism has been pursued by Ratzinger ever since his time in Tübingen: as a theologian, as Archbishop of Munich, as prefect of the Congregation for the Doctrine of the Faith and now as Pope Benedict XVI.

Sights & Activities

Entered through an ornate Renaissance gate (1606), **Schloss Hohentübingen** (Burgsteige 11), at the western edge of the Altstadt, affords fine views over the steep, red-tiled rooftops of the Altstadt. This mostly 16th-century castle houses various university institutes, including the **museum of archaeology & Egyptology** (☎ 297 7384; adult/student & senior €4/2; ☼ 10am-6pm Wed-Sun, to 5pm Oct-Apr). The gardens around the Schloss afford ample options for romantic strolling.

Surrounded by towering half-timbered houses, **Am Markt**, the Altstadt's main public space, is a much-loved student hang-out; in summer it overflows with geraniums and café tables. Presiding over the hullabaloo is the **Rathaus** (1433), with a riotous 19th-century baroque façade and, way up top, an astronomical clock (1511). The four women of the **Neptune Fountain** represent the seasons; note that the city council members who approved funds for the fountain modestly placed themselves in the decorative ironwork.

On the northern side of the Markt is the **Lammhofpassage**, an erstwhile watering hole for many of Tübingen's leading figures; today it's owned by the Protestant church. Walk through the little passageway to see the beer garden and a very original **bronze statue**, the meaning of which you may end up arguing with your friends about.

Walking two blocks east along Kirchgasse will take you to the late-Gothic, late-15th-century **Stiftskirche** (Am Holzmark), which houses tombs of the Württemberg dukes and has excellent original medieval stained-glass windows. It hosts concerts every Saturday evening.

Facing the church's west façade is the **Cottahaus**, one-time home of Johann Friedrich Cotta, who first published the works of both Schiller and Goethe. Goethe, who was known to find inspiration at the local pubs, stayed here for a week in September 1797. One night he apparently staggered home, missed the front door and wrote a technicolour poem on the wall next door. If you look up at the 1st-floor window of the building – now a grungy student dorm – you'll see a little sign: 'Hier kotzte Goethe' (Goethe puked here).

In centuries past, delinquent students as young as 14 were given the choice of losing their wine ration or being sent to the city's **Karzer** (student jail; Münzgasse 20), just up the block.

From the east end of Holzmarkt, Neckargasse leads down to the Neckar where – right next to **Eberhardsbrücke** – you'll find **Neckarmüller** (p426), Tübingen's best beer garden.

From the middle of the bridge, stairs lead down to the **Platanenallee**, a long sliver of an island that's perfect for a plane tree–shaded stroll. On the Thursday of the Feast of Corpus Christi (late May or early June), the Burschenschaften (fraternities) – who own many of the mansions along the river and high up on the hill – hold their wildly popular **Stocherkahn races** (punt races) here, drawing thousands of spectators. A two-week festival takes over the island every August.

Facing the Platanenallee about 150m west of Eberhardsbrücke is the **Hölderlinturm**, a riverside tower in which the poet Friedrich Hölderlin lived from 1807 until his death in 1843. Right nearby, on the banks of the Neckar, you can hire a **Stocherkahn** (per hr up to 16 people €60-65; ☼ mid-Apr–Oct). Students often bring along a case of beer, which weighs down the boat and, by contributing to various phenomena often associated with the consumption of brewed liquids, occasionally causes a *Stocherkahn* to sink amid much beery merriment.

Across the river just east of the bridge (behind and below the tourist office), **Bootsvermietung Märkle** (☎ 315 29; www.bootsvermietung -tuebingen.de in German; Eberhardsbrücke 1; ☼ 11am-7pm Apr-Oct, to 9pm in summer) hires out rowboats, canoes, pedal-boats and 12-person *Stocherkähne* for €7.50, €7.50, €10 and €48 per hour respectively.

Just northeast of the Altstadt is the **Alter Botanischer Garten** (Old Botanical Garden), a grassy park that's hugely popular with students because it's sandwiched between the eateries of the Altstadt, where they nourish their stomachs, and the **Universität district**, where they nourish their minds (or at least jump through the hoops to get that all-important piece of paper). The neoclassical **Neue Aula** (cnr Wilhelmstrasse & Gmelinstrasse), built in 1832, is the main university administration building.

The university's absolutely delightful **Botanischer Garten** (Botanical Garden; ☎ 297 8822; www .botgarden.uni-tuebingen.de, in German; Hartmeyerstrasse 123; ☼ 8am-4.45pm, till 7pm Sat & Sun in summer) has hothouses, a Tropicarium and some lovely outdoor gardens. Situated 2km northwest up the hill from the centre, it's served by buses 5, 13, 15 and 17.

MAULTASCHEN

Sometimes referred to as 'Swabian pockets' or 'German ravioli', *Maultaschen* are pasta pillows that are traditionally filled with ground meat or sausage, preboiled spinach, bits of damp bread and eggs. Once an efficiency food for the poor, who could wring one more meal out of leftovers by chopping them up and concealing them in a boiled noodle-dough pocket, they are now acknowledged as one of the glories of Swabian cuisine. *Maultaschen*, if prepared properly (fiendishly difficult to do, according to true connoisseurs), can hold their own in any competition with dim sum, pirogi and ravioli.

The origins of *Maultaschen* are shrouded in steaming broth. According to one legend, they were invented by the Cistercian monks of Maulbronn Monastery – thus the name. Another story making the rounds is that some Swabians figured they could get away with eating meat during Lent by hiding it inside pasta and further camouflaging it with spinach, thus keeping their culinary misdemeanours from the prying eyes of the parish priest (if not from higher authorities). What is clear is that at sporting events, fans wishing to insult their Swabian rivals sometimes call them *Maultaschenfresser* – uncouth devourers of *Maultaschen*.

An excellent place to sample first-rate *Maultaschen* – 60 to 70 varieties, some of them seasonal, are available over the course of the year – is Tübingen's Hotel am Schloss restaurant (see p426).

Sleeping

Neckar Camping Tübingen (☎ 431 45; www.neckarcamping.de; Rappenberghalde 61; adult/tent/car €5.30/4.10/2.60; ⊙ Apr-Oct) A grassy and nicely shaded camping ground on the north bank of the Neckar about 2km west of the Hauptbahnhof. Bus 9 has a stop nearby.

DJH hostel (☎ 230 02; www.jugendherberge.de; Gartenstrasse 22/2; dm 1st/subsequent night €20.30/17.10; ✗) This 159-bed hostel has a pretty location on the north bank of the Neckar about 300m east of Eberhardbrücke. It's linked to the Hauptbahnhof by bus 22.

Viktor-Renner-Haus (☎ 559 020; viktor-renner-haus-tuebingen@internationaler-bund.de; Frondsbergstrasse 55; s/d €40/52, s without bathroom €30) A young people's hostel that rents out basic rooms to travellers. It has cooking facilities and you get fridge space. Situated 800m northwest of the city centre up Schnarrenbergstrasse; it's served by buses 5, 13, 14 and 18 to Breiter Weg or Frondsbergstrasse.

Hotel Hospiz Tübingen (☎ 9240; www.hotel-hospiz.de; Neckarhalde 2; s €59-76, d €92-110, s/d without bathroom €30.45/72; P ✗) Just a block up the hill from Am Markt, this friendly hotel – painted a shocking ochre-pink colour – has 50 attractive medium-sized rooms, some with rather odd colour schemes. By car, take Neckarhalde from the B28.

Hotel am Schloss (☎ 929 40; www.hotelamschloss.de; Burgsteige 18; s €55-82, d €98-118; P 🖳) Just 50m down the hill from the Schloss, this superbly situated hotel is ensconced in a 16th-century building where Keppler used to drop by for

wine. The 33 comfortable rooms have bright, shiny bathrooms, pillows arranged to look like swans and, in many cases (such as room 30), great views. By car, take Neckarhalde from the B28.

Hotel Krone Tübingen (☎ 133 10; www.krone-tuebingen.de; Uhlandstrasse 1; s €87-107, d €125-155; P ✗ 🖳) A very swish place at the southern end of Eberhardsbrücke and just two blocks northeast of the Hauptbahnhof. Run by the same family since 1885, it has 43 elegant, understated rooms, all with superb soundproofing.

Eating & Drinking

In the northeast corner of the Altstadt, several cafés and ice-cream places cluster along the tiny Ammer River on Beim Nonnenhaus, linked to the Alter Botanischer Garten by a tunnel under Am Stadtgraben.

Locals disagree as to which of the two Turkish takeaways – at opposite ends of Eberhardsbrücke – is better, Kalender (on the north side) or Istanbul (on the south side).

A number of popular student bars can be found west of Am Markt along Haaggasse.

X (☎ 249 02; Kornhausstrasse 6; snacks under €3; 11am-1am) The region's best chips/French fries are right here, along with good-value bratwurst and burgers (both from €2.20).

Hades (☎ 228 18; Hafengasse 8; ⊙ 5pm-2am, to 3am Fri & Sat) A *Bierlokal* (bar-restaurant) whose edible specialities include *Flammkuche* (€3.60 to €7.50), homemade soups and, each Tuesday, pasta (first/subsequent portions cost just €2/1). It's pronounced *ha*-dess.

BADEN-WÜRTTEMBERG

Neckarmüller (☎ 278 48; Gartenstrasse 4; mains €6.50-13.50; ⏰ 10am-1am) Tübingen's best-loved beer garden, overlooking the Neckar at the northern end of Eberhardsbrücke, is also a microbrewery. Shaded by giant chestnut trees (there's also an inside section), it serves Swabian dishes, including *Maultaschen*, at all hours.

Collegium (☎ 252 223; Lange Gasse 8; mains €8-14.50; ⏰ 11am-2.30pm & 4.30pm-midnight, closed Sun evening) A cosy restaurant whose good-sized Swabian and vegetarian dishes, prepared with fresh local products, can be washed down with reasonably priced beer and local wine.

Restaurant Museum (☎ 228 28; Wilhelmstrasse 3; mains €10-22; ⏰ 11am-2pm & 6pm-midnight) An elegant, very modern restaurant that specialises in fresh, light Swabian and French cuisine.

Hanseatica (☎ 269 84; Hafengasse 2; ⏰ 8.30am-5.30pm Mon-Fri, to 4.30pm Sat) Come here for super sip-it-standing coffee.

Tangente Jour (☎ 245 72; Münzgasse 17; 9am or 10am-1am) A sleek, modern café-bar near the Stiftskirche. It has six local beers on tap and serves breakfast (€4.60 to €9.90) as well as light meals, including quiche and bagels.

Tangente (☎ 230 07; Pfleghofstrasse 10; ⏰ 10am-3am) Popularly known as Tangente Night (to avoid confusion), this laid-back bar, two blocks northeast of the Stiftskirche, has karaoke on Monday from 9pm. Popular with students.

JazzKeller (☎ 550 906; www.jazzkeller.eu, in German; Haaggasse 15/2; concert admission €3-15; ⏰ 7pm-2am, to 3am Fri & Sat) This Tübingen institution (it's been around since 1958), three blocks west of Am Markt, has a mellow bar upstairs and hosts DJs and live music (there's jazz every Wednesday from 9pm) in the cellar.

Getting There & Around

By train, Tübingen is an easy day trip from Stuttgart (€10, 45 to 60 minutes, two or more an hour).

Central Tübingen is a maze of one-way streets with little parking. There's a taxi stand at Wilhelmstrasse 3 or call ☎ 243 01.

Radlager (☎ 551 651; Lazarettgasse 19-21; ⏰ 9.30am-6.30pm Mon, Wed & Fri, 2-6.30pm Tue & Thu, 9.30am-2.30pm Sat, to 1pm Sat in winter) has a few bikes for rent.

BURG HOHENZOLLERN

Hohenzollern Castle (☎ 07471-2428; www.preussen.de), about 25km south of Tübingen, is the ancestral seat of the Hohenzollern family, the first and last monarchical rulers of the short-lived second German Empire (1871–1918). The neo-Gothic castle you see now (built 1850–67) is impressive from a distance – rising dramatically from an exposed crag, its vast medieval battlements often veiled in mist – but up close it looks more contrived.

The interior, with its artwork, stained glass and fabulous **Schatzkammer** (treasury), can be seen on a 35-minute **tour** (in German; adult/child 6-18yr/student/senior €5/2.50/3.50/4.50; ⏰ 9am-5.30pm, to 4.30pm Nov–mid-Mar). You can view the **grounds** (without tour €2.50) at your leisure. On clear days you can see the Swiss Alps.

Frequent trains link Tübingen with Hechingen (€4, 20 minutes, one or two an hour), about 4km northwest of the castle.

ULM

☎ 0731 / pop 120,000

On the Danube (Donau) River, Ulm is one of the region's most audacious and creative-thinking cities. How many other municipalities would dare to erect a startling piece of modern architecture next to their most famous medieval landmark? It's somehow fitting, then, that the founder of modern physics, Albert Einstein, was born here.

In 1811, a highly sceptical public watched as Albrecht Berblinger, a tailor who had invented a flying machine similar to a hang-glider,

---

THE AUTHOR'S CHOICE

Hotel am Schloss restaurant (☎ 929 40; www.hotelamschloss.de; Burgsteige 18; Maultaschen €7.40-9.50; ⏰ 11.30am-2.30pm & 5.30-10.30pm) This place is renowned among locals for making Tübingen's finest *Maultaschen* (see p425). Indeed, the owner, Herbert Rösch Sr, literally wrote the book on this Swabian delicacy – look for the *Schwäbisches Maultaschenbuch* around town.

About 23 types of *Maultaschen*, many of them seasonal (eg asparagus or trout), are available here at any one time. The menu, partly in Swabian (English version available), promises that *'älle Mauldasche geits au mit vegetarischer Gmüsfüllung'* (all *Maultaschen* are also available with vegetarian filling). Also on offer are *Spätzle* (type of pasta) and light meals for those with merely a *gloina Honger* (small appetite). The terrace has great views.

attempted to fly across the Danube after leaping (some say he was kicked) from the city wall. The 'Tailor of Ulm', as the locals called him, made an embarrassing splash landing but his design was later shown to be workable.

Orientation

Ulm's Altstadt, on the north bank of the Danube, is inside a 1300m-by-700m oval delineated by the river (to the south), the Hauptbahnhof (to the west) and Olgastrasse (to the north). In the centre of the oval lies the Münster, surrounded by a pedestrian shopping precinct. The tiny Blau River's two channels, lined with quaint houses, meet the Danube about 300m south of the Münster.

On the south side of the Danube, in Bavaria, is the city of Neu-Ulm, a rather bland, modern city. The two cities share transport systems and important municipal facilities.

Information

Eco-Express SB-Waschsalon (Wielandstrasse 29; 6am-11pm Mon-Sat) A self-service laundry four blocks northeast of Willy-Brandt-Platz, in the northeast corner of the city-centre oval.

Global Internetcafé (Neue Strasse 86; per hr €2; � 10am-11pm Mon-Sat, 11am-10pm Sun & holidays)

Herwig (☎ 962 170; Münsterplatz 18) A bookshop with a good selection of travel guides and maps.

Intercall (Neue Strasse 101; per hr €2; � 9.30am-11pm Mon-Sat, 10am-10pm Sun & holidays) Internet access.

Post office (Bahnhofplatz 2) To the left as you exit the Hauptbahnhof.

Tourist office (☎ 161 2830; www.tourismus.ulm.de; Stadthaus bldg, Münsterplatz 50; � 9am-6pm Mon-Fri, 9am-4pm Sat, 11am-3pm Sun Apr-Oct, 9am-6pm Mon-Fri, 9am-1pm Sat Nov-Mar) Sells the Ulm Card.

Ulm Card (1/2 days €8/12) Offers discounted museum admission and public transport.

Sights

MÜNSTER

Ulm's outstanding architectural landmark is the towering **Münster** (Cathedral; Münsterplatz; admission free; � 9am-4.45pm Jan & Feb, to 5.45pm Mar & Oct, to 6.45pm Apr-Jun & Sep, to 7.45pm Jul & Aug), celebrated for its 161.53m-high steeple – the tallest in the world. Though the first stone was laid in 1377, it took over 500 years for the structure to be completed. A **bronze plaque** embedded in the pavement out front shows directions and distances to cities around Europe. Note the **hallmarks** on each stone, inscribed by cutters who were paid by the block.

Only by climbing the **tower** (adult/student €4/2.50; � last admission 1hr before closing) – up 768 spiral steps to the 143m-high viewing platform – can you fully appreciate the tower's dizzying height. As they climb up, romantically minded local couples have a tradition of kissing at each landing. Up top there are unparalleled views of the Black Forest and the Schwäbische Alb, and on clear days you can even see the Alps.

As you enter the church, note the **Israelfenster**, a stained-glass window above the west door that serves as a memorial to Jews killed during the Holocaust. The Gothic-style wooden **pulpit canopy**, as detailed as fine lace, eliminates echoes during sermons; a tiny spiral staircase leads to a mini-pulpit for the Holy Spirit. On the 15th-century oak **choir stalls**, the top row depicts figures from the Old Testament, the middle from the New Testament, and the bottom and sides show historical characters, such as the Roman playwright Lucius Seneca and Pythagoras, who strums a lute. The impressive **stained-glass windows** in the choir, dating from the 14th and 15th centuries, were removed during WWII.

The Münster's regular **organ concerts** (Sat/Sun €2.50/4.50; � noon-12.30pm Sat Easter-Christmas, 11.30am most Sun year-round) are a real treat.

STADTHAUS

The other highlight of Münsterplatz – from a completely different era – is the white-and-glass **Stadthaus** (1993), designed by the American architect Richard Meier. He caused an uproar by erecting a postmodern building next to the city's Gothic gem but the result is both gorgeous and functional. The structure stages art exhibitions and special events, and also houses the tourist office and a café.

RATHAUS

The 14th-century **Rathaus** (Town Hall) has an ornately painted Renaissance façade and a gilded **astrological clock** (1520); bells count off every quarter-hour. Inside you can see a replica of **Berblinger's flying machine**.

In the Marktplatz to the south is the **Fischkastenbrunnen**, a fountain where fishmongers kept their river fish alive on market days. That striking all-glass pyramid behind the Rathaus (28m by 28m at its base and 36m high) is the city's main library, the **Zentralbibliothek** (2004), designed by Gottfried Böhm.

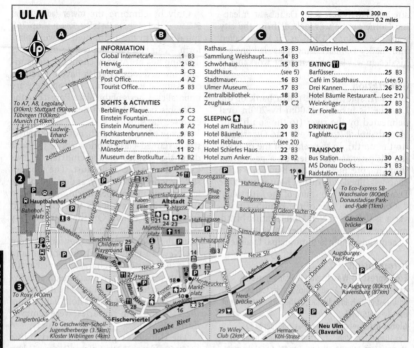

ULM

0   300 m
0   0.2 miles

INFORMATION
Global Internetcafe...............1 B3
Herwig.................................2 B2
Intercall..............................3 C3
Post Office..........................4 A2
Tourist Office......................5 B3

SIGHTS & ACTIVITIES
Berblinger Plaque.................6 C3
Einstein Fountain.................7 C2
Einstein Monument..............8 A2
Fischkastenbrunnen.............9 B3
Metzgerturm.....................10 B3
Münster.............................11 B2
Museum der Brotkultur......12 B2

Rathaus.............................13 B3
Sammlung Weishaupt.........14 B3
Schwörhaus.......................15 B3
Stadthaus.......................(see 5)
Stadtmauer.......................16 A3
Ulmer Museum..................17 B3
Zentralbibliothek...............18 B3
Zeughaus..........................19 C2

SLEEPING
Hotel am Rathaus...............20 B3
Hotel Bäumle.....................21 B2
Hotel Reblaus.................(see 20)
Hotel Schiefes Haus............22 B3
Hotel zum Anker................23 B3

Münster Hotel....................24 B2

EATING
Barfüsser...........................25 B3
Café im Stadthaus...........(see 5)
Drei Kannen.......................26 B2
Hotel Bäumle Restaurant..(see 21)
Weinkrüger.......................27 B3
Zur Forelle........................28 B3

DRINKING
Tagblatt............................29 C3

TRANSPORT
Bus Station........................30 A3
MS Donau Docks................31 B3
Radstation.........................32 B3

To A7, A8, Legoland (30km); Stuttgart (90km); Tübingen (100km); Munich (140km)

Ludwig-Erhard-Brücke

Hauptbahnhof
Bahnhof-platz

To Roxy (400m)

To Geschwister-Scholl-Jugendherberge (3.5km); Kloster Wiblingen (4km)

Zinglerbrücke

Children's Playground Blau

Fischerviertel

Danube River

Altstadt

Münster-platz

Neue Str

To Eco-Express SB-Waschsalon (800m); Donaustadion Park-and-Ride (1km)

Gänstor-brücke

Augsburger-Tor-Platz

To Augsburg (80km); Ravensburg (87km)

Neu Ulm (Bavaria)

To Wiley Club (2km)

Hermann-Köhl-Strasse

FISCHERVIERTEL & CITY WALL

On the first Monday of each July, the mayor swears allegiance to the town's 1397 constitution from the 1st-floor loggia of the early 17th-century baroque **Schwörhaus** (Oath House; Weinhof), three blocks west of the Rathaus.

Just to the southwest is the **Fischerviertel**, the city's old fishers' and tanners' quarter. This charming area of half-timbered houses is built along the two channels of the tiny Blau River – crossed by a series of footbridges – which are confluent with the Danube nearby. Here you'll find several art galleries, a number of restaurants and the crookedest hotel in the world (see opposite).

Along the south side of the Fischerviertel, along the north bank of the Danube, runs the **Stadtmauer** (city wall), the height of which was reduced in the early 19th century after Napoleon decided that a heavily fortified Ulm was against his best interests. Note the **Metzgerturm** (Butcher's Tower), leaning 2m off-centre.

East of the Herdbrücke (the bridge leading to Neu Ulm) is a **bronze plaque** marking the spot where Albrecht Berblinger attempted his flight (his failure was later determined to

have been caused by a lack of thermals on that particular day).

EINSTEIN FOUNTAIN & MONUMENT

About 750m northeast of the Münster in front of the 16th-century Zeughaus (arsenal), at the northern end of Zeughausgasse, stands a fiendishly funny **fountain** dedicated to Albert Einstein, who was born in Ulm but left aged one year. The nearby health administration building, at Zeughaus 14, bears a single stone attached to the wall with the inscription *Ein Stein* (One Stone).

Over near the Hauptbahnhof, on Bahnhofstrasse, is Max Bill's **monument** (1979) to the great physicist, a stack of staggered granite pillars on the spot where Einstein's babyhood home once stood.

MUSEUMS

The **Museum Card** (€6), which gets you into eight local museums, is sold at the tourist office and participating museums.

The **Ulmer Museum** (☎ 161 4330; www.museum.ulm.de, in German; Marktplatz 9; adult/concession €3/2, free admission to permanent collection Fri; 11am-5pm Tue-Sun,

11am-8pm Thu) houses a collection of ancient and modern art, including icons, religious paintings and sculptures. A highlight is the 20th-century **Kurt Fried Collection**, with works by artists such as Klee, Kandinsky, Picasso, Lichtenstein and Macke.

Across the street, a brand new building housing the **Sammlung Weishaupt** (Neue Strasse), spotlighting modern and pop art, is set to open in the spring of 2007. This impressive structure is the latest in a series of bold and ac-claimed modern buildings that have injected new dynamism into Ulm's Altstadt.

The **Museum der Brotkultur** (Museum of Bread Culture; ☎ 699 55; www.museum-brotkultur.de; Salz-stadelgasse 10; adult/student & senior €3/2; 10am-5pm Thu-Tue, 10am-8.30pm Wed) celebrates bread as the staff of life, taking a look at the process of growing grain and making bread over millennia and across cultures. No actual bread is on display because, as a brochure solemnly explains, bread is food and must be respected as such, not collected in museums.

KLOSTER WIBLINGEN

This one-time Benedictine **monastery** (☎ 502 8975; www.schloesser-und-gaerten.de; adult/concession/family €3.50/1.70/8.70; ⏰ 10am-1pm & 2-5pm Tue-Fri, 10am-5pm Sat & Sun Apr-Oct, 1-5pm Sat, Sun & holidays Nov-Mar), about 4km south of the city centre, was founded in 1093 and rebuilt in the baroque style in the 1700s. Highlights of a visit include the splendid **Bibliothekssaal** (library hall), a rococo master-piece in pink and green (in 1757 the monastery was in possession of 15,000 volumes, a huge number for the time). The late baroque–early classical **Klosterkirche** (Monastery Church) and a **museum** opened in 2006. An audioguide is available. The monastery is linked to Ulm by bus 3 and 8; get off at Pranger.

LEGOLAND

Legoland Deutschland (☎ 08221-700 700; www .legoland.de; adult/child 3-11 & senior €29/25; ⏰ 10am-btwn 6pm & 10pm mid-Apr–early Nov) is a Lego-themed amusement park in Günzburg, about 30km northeast of Ulm just off the A8. Bus 850 links Ulm with Günzburg's train station; from there a shuttle goes to the park.

Tours

The 20m-long **MS Donau** (☎ 627 51; adult/child €7/4; ⏰ May–mid-Oct) cruises the Danube at 2pm, 3pm and 4pm daily, and also at 5pm on weekends and holidays. The docks are on the Ulm side, just south of the Metzgerturm.
Sportiv Touren (☎ 970 9298; www.sportivtouren.de in German; adult/child under 14yr €24/16) runs 2½-hour *Kanutouren* (canoe tours) from various points on the Danube and Iller Rivers.

Sleeping

Geschwister-Scholl-Jugendherberge (☎ 384 455; www.jugendherberge.de; Grimmelfinger Weg 45; dm 1st/subsequent night €17.90/14.70) This 126-bed youth hostel is named after Hans and Sophie Scholl, Ulm-born student activists who were ex-ecuted for the incredibly brave act of dis-tributing anti-Nazi handbills in Munich in 1943. It's situated 3.5km southwest of the Hauptbahnhof on bus lines 4 and 8; get off at Schulzentrum.

Münster Hotel (☎ 641 62; www.muenster-hotel.de; Münsterplatz 14; s/d from €40/60, without bathroom €30/55; P ✗) Friendly and very central, this 20-room hotel offers excellent value for money, with simply furnished, well-maintained rooms.

Hotel zum Anker (☎ 632 97; fax 603 1925; Rabengasse 2; s/d from €48/65, without bathroom €35/55; P ✗) This well-kept family-run hotel is a popular stop for cyclists doing the Danube – on rainy days staff will even dry out your cycling clothes. The 12 rooms are bright and cheerful, if a bit small – not surprising since the building is six centuries old.

Hotel am Rathaus & Hotel Reblaus (☎ 968 490; www.rathausulm.de, in German; Kronengasse 10; s/d/q from €57/87/120, s/d without bathroom €45/65; P ✗) Behind the Rathaus, these family-run twin hotels – the former postwar, the latter built in 1651 – have 33 rustic rooms with lots of character and rather small bathrooms. They have bicycle parking.

Hotel Bäumle (☎ 622 87; www.hotel-baeumle.de, in German; Kohlgasse 6; s/d/q from €65/85/120; P ✗) In a 500-year-old building, this snug 15-room place affords leafy views of the Münster – ask for a room at the back. It was totally renovated in 2006.

Hotel Schiefes Haus (☎ 967 930; www.hotelschiefes hausulm.de; Schwörhausgasse 6; s/d €108/140) This ro-mantic half-timbered house (built in 1443) on the Blau River is listed in the *Guinness Book of Records* as the 'most crooked hotel in the world' (the building, that is). Rooms have ancient wood-beam ceilings and floors with a grade of up to 8%; beds have specially-made height adjusters and spirit levels so you won't roll out at night. Discounts are available on some weekends.

Eating & Drinking

There are quite a few pubs and restaurants along the two channels of the Blau River, south across Neue Strasse from the Münster.

Tagblatt (☎ 746 78; Insel 1, Neu Ulm; ☺ 7am-2am Mon-Fri, 5am-2am Sat, Sun & holidays) A bright, cheerful place on the banks of the Danube with a beer garden and a wide selection of salads. Weekend breakfasts begin at 5am, perfect after a late-late club crawl. Just across the river from central Ulm.

Drei Kannen (☎ 677 17; Hafenbad 31/1; Mon-Sat lunch special €5.50, mains from €8.50; ☺ 11am-midnight) A German and Swabian restaurant whose courtyard beer garden is overlooked by an Italian-style loggia. Serves a strong malty beer – not to everyone's taste – available only here. The Friday speciality is fresh trout; extra Swabian dishes are featured on Thursday.

Café im Stadthaus (☎ 600 93; Münsterplatz 50; salads €5.60-8.80; mains €7.50-15.40; ☺ 8am-10pm Mon-Sat, 10am-10pm Sun) A modern, airy café-restaurant with great views of the Münster through the bay windows and from the terrace.

Barfüsser (☎ 602 1110; Lautenberg 1; mains €6.50-12.80; ☺ 10am-1am, to 2am Thu-Sat) This restaurant-bar is very popular thanks in part to its three kinds of prize-winning beer (microbrewed at its second location in New Ulm). Tuesday is karaoke night (from 10pm). Edible options include salads and vegetarian dishes.

Weinkrüger (☎ 649 76; Weinhofberg 7; mains €7.50-14.90; ☺ 11am-midnight, to 1am Fri & Sat) A rustic wine tavern in a five-century-old bathhouse and tannery between the two channels of the Blau River. It has a good selection of traditional Swabian dishes and offers 90 different wines, 16 of them by the glass.

Hotel Bäumle (☎ 622 87; www.hotel-baeumle.de, in German; Kohlgasse 6; mains from €8.60; ☺ 4pm-midnight Mon-Fri) A rustic *Weinstube* (wine bar) with loads of 19th-century wood panelling, a ceramic stove, good wines and creative Swabian fare. One especially tasty option is the *Ulmer Laubfrösche,* filled with spinach or *Mangold* (a kind of beet).

Zur Forelle (☎ 639 24; Fischergasse 25; mains €9.50-21.50; ☺ 11am-2.30pm & 5.30pm-midnight) A rustic restaurant, awash with flowers in the spring, whose speciality is trout, kept fresh in a cage under the bridge. In a 15th-century building with low ceilings and a Napoleon-era cannonball lodged in the wall outside. It also serves Swabian dishes. Einstein ate here and is said to have gone home relatively satisfied.

Entertainment

Details on cultural events appear in the free monthly *Spazz,* available at the tourist office and some cafés. Events tickets are sold by the tourist office.

Roxy (☎ 968 620; www.roxy.ulm.de in German; Schillerstrasse 1) A huge cultural venue, housed in a former industrial plant 1km south of the Hauptbahnhof, with a concert hall, cinema, disco, bar and special-event forum. Take tram line 1 to Ehinger Tor.

Wiley Club (☎ 867 04; www.wiley-club.de, in German; Wileystrasse 4, Neu Ulm; ☺ 11am-1am, to 2am Fri & Sat) On a former US military base, this one-time canteen has a restaurant, café-bar and stage, and hosts live music and disco events. Situated 2.5km south of the Altstadt; to get there take bus 6 to the Wiley Club stop.

Getting There & Away

Ulm, about 90km southeast of Stuttgart and 140km west of Munich, is near the intersection of the north–south A7 and the east–west A8.

Ulm is well-served by ICE trains; major destinations include Stuttgart (€14.70 to €22, one hour, several hourly) and Munich (€22.10 to €30, 1½ hours, several hourly).

Getting Around

There's a local **transport information counter** (☎ 166 2120; www.swu-verkehr.de, in German) in the tourist office.

Except in parking garages (per half-hour €0.60), the whole city centre is metered; many areas are limited to one hour. There's a park-and-ride lot at Donaustadion, a stadium 1.5km northeast of the Münster that's on tram line 1.

You can hire bikes, including tandems, from **Radstation** (☎ 150 0231; Friedrich-Ebert-Strasse; ☺ 6am-8pm Mon-Fri, 9am-7pm Sat, Sun & holidays), between the Hauptbahnhof and the bus station. Bike paths go along the Danube.

It's easy to order a **taxi** (☎ 660 66).

NORTHERN BLACK FOREST

The hills, valleys, rivers and forests of Germany's famed Schwarzwald (Black Forest) stretch from the swish spa town of Baden-Baden south to the Swiss border, and from the Rhine – the west bank of which is in the

---

VISITORS PASSES

In most Schwarzwald localities your hotel or B&B host will issue you with a Schwarzwald-Gästekarte (Guest Card; formerly known as a Kurkarte) that gets you discounts – or even freebies – on museums, ski lifts, cultural events and attractions. Versions of the card with the Konus symbol (showing a bus, a train and a tram), known as the Konus-Gästekarte, entitle you to free use of trains, trams and buses throughout the Black Forest region, and are intended to encourage holidaymakers to use environmentally friendly public transport even if they arrive in the area by private car.

Almost all tourist offices in the Black Forest sell the three-day **SchwarzwaldCard** (adult/child 4-11yr/family €37/27/113 incl 1 day at Europa-Park €47/37/153), which gets you free admission to about 150 attractions in the Black Forest, including museums, ski lifts, boat trips, spas and swimming pools.

Details on both cards are available at www.blackforest-tourism.com.

French region of Alsace – east almost to Lake Constance. The northern section, with its hilly but relatively gentle terrain, includes the Kinzig Valley, home to several charming towns. Freudenstadt makes a good base for exploring the area.

BADEN-BADEN

☎ 07221 / pop 54,000

From Queen Victoria to the Vanderbilts, from Bismarck to Brahms and Berlioz, they all came to Baden-Baden – the royal, the rich, the renowned and the moneyed wannabees – to take the waters or lose their fortunes in the casino.

Today Baden-Baden, at the foot of the Black Forest, is the grande dame of German spas, ageing but still elegant. Sophisticated yet relaxed, it offers a *belle époque* townscape of palatial villas, stately hotels, tree-lined avenues, groomed parks and chic boutiques. Many of the most delightful activities, such as strolling, are free, and even the famous spas don't necessarily require deep pockets to enjoy (at one of them, deep pockets are banned entirely).

Orientation

The heart of Baden-Baden is Leopoldsplatz, which is surrounded by pedestrianised shopping streets. Most sights – including Lichtentaler Allee, on the west bank of the gurgling Oosbach – are within easy walking distance.

The Bahnhof is in the suburb of Oos, about 4km northwest of the town centre, with the central bus station right out the front.

Information

Branch tourist office (Kaiserallee 3; ◷ 10am-5pm Mon-Sat, 2-5pm Sun) In the Trinkhalle. Sells events tickets.

Internet Café (Lange Strasse 54; per hr €2; ◷ 10am-10pm) Internet access at the northern edge of the pedestrianised town centre.

Main tourist office (☎ 275 200; www.baden-baden .com; Schwarzwaldstrasse 52; ◷ 9am-6pm Mon-Sat, 9am-1pm Sun) Situated 2km northwest of the town centre. If you're driving from the northwest (from the A5) this place is on the way into town. Sells events tickets.

Post office (Lange Strasse 44) Inside Kaufhaus Wagener.

Waschsalon SB (☎ 248 19; Scheibenstrasse 14; ◷ 7.30am-10pm Mon-Sat) A self-service laundry, three blocks east (up the hill) from Leopoldsplatz.

Weblounge (Eichstrasse 3; per hr €2.40; ◷ 10am-midnight Mon-Thu, 10am-10pm Fri-Sun) Internet access in a mellow atmosphere.

Sights

KURHAUS & CASINO

In the heart of Baden-Baden, two blocks southwest of Leopoldsplatz and just west of the Oos River, looms the palatial **Kurhaus** (☎ 3530; www.kurhaus-baden-baden.de, in German; Kaiserallee 1), set in an impeccably groomed garden. Corinthian columns and a frieze of mythical griffins grace the august exterior of the structure, designed by Friedrich Weinbrenner in 1824. An alley of chestnut trees – flanked by two rows of elegant mini-shops – links the Kurhaus with Kaiserallee.

Inside – besides lavish festival halls used for balls, conventions, concerts, dance competitions and weddings – is the opulent **casino** (☎ 302 40; www.casino-baden-baden.de; admission €3; ◷ 2pm-2am Sun-Thu, 2pm-3am Fri & Sat, baccarat tables open 8pm-5am Fri & Sat), opened in 1838 and reminiscent of the 19th century or a 1970s James Bond film, depending on your proclivities. Its décor, which seeks to emulate – indeed, outdo – the splendour of France's famed chateaux, such as Versailles, led Marlene Dietrich to

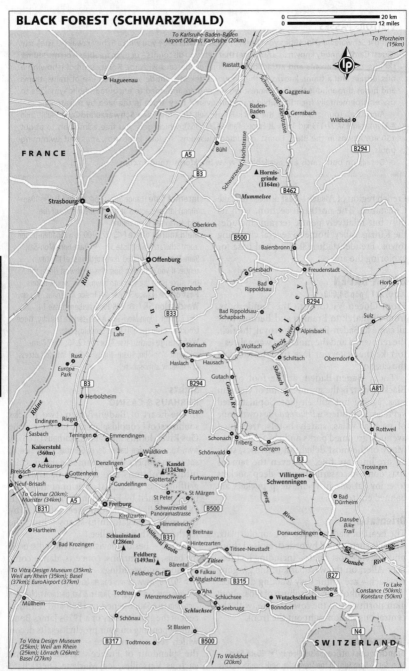

BLACK FOREST (SCHWARZWALD)

0 — 20 km
0 — 12 miles

To Karlsruhe-Baden-Baden
Airport (20km); Karlsruhe (20km)

To Pforzheim
(15km)

Rastatt

Gaggenau

Hagueenau

Baden-Baden

Gernsbach

Wildbad

FRANCE

A5

Bühl

B3

B294

Schwarzwald-Hochstrasse

Schwarzwald-Täterstrasse

▲Hornis-
grinde
(1164m)

B462

Strasbourg

Kehl

Mummelsee

Oberkirch

B500

Baiersbronn

Offenburg

Griesbach

Freudenstadt

Gengenbach

Bad
Rippoldsau

Horb

River

K
i
n
z
i
g

B33

Bad Rippoldsau-
Schapbach

B294

Sulz

Lahr

Steinach

Wolfach

Alpirsbach

Kinzig River

Schiltach

Oberndorf

Rust

Haslach

Hausach

Schiltach Rv.

A81

Europa
Park

B3

B294

Gutach

Herbolzheim

Gutach Rv.

Elzach

Rhine

Endingen

Riegel

Schonach

Triberg

Rottweil

Sasbach

Teningen

Emmendingen

Waldkirch

Schönwald

St Georgen

B3

Kaiserstuhl
(560m)
▲

Denzlingen

Kandel
▲(1243m)

Furtwangen

Villingen-
Schwenningen

Trossingen

Achkarren

Gottenheim

Glottertal

Breisach

Gundelfingen

St Peter

St Märgen

Breg River

Bad
Dürrheim

Neuf-Brisash

To Colmar (20km);
Münster (34km)

A5

Freiburg

Kirchzarten

Schwarzwald
Panoramastrasse

B500

B31

Hartheim

Himmelreich

Danube
Bike
Trail

Bad Krozingen

Schauinsland
(1286m)
▲

Höllental Route

Breitnau

B31

Hinterzarten

Titisee-Neustadt

Donaueschingen

Titisee

Danube River

Feldberg
(1493m)▲

Feldberg-Ort

Bärental

Falkau

B27

Müllheim

Todtnau

Altglashütten

B315

Blumberg

To Lake
Constance (50km);
Konstanz (50km)

Menzenschwand

Aha

Schluchsee

Wutachschlucht

Schönau

Schluchsee

Seebrugg

Bonndorf

St Blasien

To Vitra Design Museum
(25km); Weil am Rhein
(25km); Lörrach (26km);
Basel (27km)

B317

Todtmoos

B500

N4

SWITZERLAND

To Waldshut
(20km)

call it 'the most beautiful casino in the world'. After observing the action here, Dostoevsky was inspired to write *The Gambler*.

You need your passport or European national ID card to enter, and cell phones must be switched off. Games include French and American roulette, blackjack and poker (Friday and Saturday only). Minimum stakes range from €2 to €50. You do not have to gamble but men must wear a jacket and tie, rentable for €8 and €3 respectively. The rules for women are more relaxed but nothing too sporty (for example shorts) is permitted. But the times they are a-changin', even here: jeans, so long as they are neat, clean and without holes, are now permitted for both sexes. Sports shoes remain forbidden, however.

A more casual way to see the interior is to take a **guided tour** (€4; in German with guides who speak English), offered every half-hour from 9.30am (10am from October to March) until 11.30am daily.

In the leafy park just north of the Kurhaus stands the **Trinkhalle** (Pump Room; Kaiserallee 3), which houses a branch of the tourist office. Here you can amble beneath a 90m-long portico decorated with 19th-century frescoes of local legends and myths. Inside you can get a free glass of hot, salty and reputedly curative mineral water from a tap (accessible from 10am to 2am, and until 3am Friday and Saturday) linked to the springs below. The café, which has leather wing chairs and a terrace, is open the same hours and sells plastic cups for €0.20.

LICHTENTALER ALLEE

This elegant park promenade, planted with vegetation from around the world, follows the flow of the sprightly Oosbach from Goetheplatz, adjacent to the Kurhaus, to Kloster Lichtenthal about 3km south. Even today, it's not hard to imagine the movers and shakers of 19th-century Europe – aristocrats, diplomats, artists and writers – taking leisurely strolls along this fragrant avenue.

The gateway to Lichtentaler Allee is formed by the **Baden-Baden Theater**, a neobaroque confection of white-and-red sandstone whose frilly interior looks like a miniature version of the Opéra-Garnier in Paris.

Nearby stands the **Staatliche Kunsthalle** (State Art Gallery; ☎ 300 763; Lichtentaler Allee 8a; adult/concession €5/4; ☼ 11am-6pm Tue-Sun, 11am-8pm Wed), which features temporary international exhibits, mainly of contemporary art.

Next door is **Museum Frieder Burda** (☎ 398 980; www.museum-frieder-burda.de; Lichtentaler Allee 8b; adult/student/family €8/6/18; ☼ 11am-6pm Tue-Sun), opened in 2004 in a striking modern building designed by Richard Meier. The collections focuses on modern and contemporary art, particularly from the USA and Germany.

A bit further south is the new home of the **Stadtmuseum** (City History Museum; ☎ 932 272; Lichtentaler Allee 10; adult/child €4/2; ☼ 10am-6pm Tue-Sun, to 8pm Wed), also opened in 2004, where highlights include historic roulette wheels and other gambling paraphernalia, as well as furnishings, photos and paintings from Baden-Baden's *belle époque*.

About 1km south of here is the **Gönneranlage**, a rose garden ablaze with more than 400 varieties that thrive in the local microclimate, said to be almost Mediterranean. Said to be almost Siberian is the **Russische Kirche** (Russian Church; 1882; Maria-Victoria-Strasse; admission €0.50; ☼ 10am-6pm, may be closed Dec-Jan), just east of here. Built in the Byzantine style, it is topped with a brilliantly golden onion dome.

Lichtentaler Allee concludes at the **Kloster Lichtenthal**, a Cistercian abbey founded in 1245, with an **abbey church** (☼ daily) where generations of the margraves of Baden lie buried.

ALTSTADT & PANORAMAS

Two blocks northeast of Leopoldsplatz is the **Stiftskirche** (Marktplatz), whose foundations incorporate part of the ruins of the former Roman baths. Elsewhere, it's a hotchpotch of Romanesque, Gothic and baroque styles. Inside, look for the crucifix by Nicolaus Gerhaert, with a heart-wrenchingly realistic depiction of the suffering Christ.

For wonderful views over Baden-Baden, climb up to the terrace of the Renaissance **Neues Schloss** (Schlossstrasse). Until 1995 the palace was one of the residences of the margravial family of Baden-Baden, but acute cash-flow problems forced them to auction off the furnishings and artworks. It's now being turned into a five-star hotel. The terrace is linked to the Marktplatz by a narrow, vine-enveloped and very romantic staircase.

Four short blocks east of the church, right underneath the Friedrichsbad complex (p434), are the **Römische Badruinen** (Roman Bath Ruins; Römerplatz; adult/child under 15yr €2/1; ☼ 11am-1pm & 2-5pm mid-Mar–mid-Nov, 2-5pm Fri, Sat & Sun mid-Nov–mid-Mar, 2-5pm 25 Dec–mid-Jan), where, thanks to some well-preserved remains, you can get a sense of how the Romans relaxed.

For another panoramic vista of Baden-Baden, head to the **Rosenneuheitengarten** (Rose Novelty Garden; Moltkestrasse; ☺ 9am-sundown mid-Apr–early Oct), on the Beutig hilltop 800m southwest of the Kurhaus.

Activities

SPAS

The famed **Friedrichsbad** (☎ 275 920; www.roemisch-irisches-bad.de; Römerplatz 1; ☺ 9am-10pm, last admission 7pm), its focal point an ornate circular pool ringed by columns, looks more like a neo-Renaissance palace than a bathhouse. Built in 1877, it has lots of small pools with water temperatures ranging from 18°C to 36°C. The **Roman-Irish Bath** (admission €21, incl a soap-and-brush massage €29), three hours of humid bliss, consists of a timed series of hot and cold showers, saunas, steam rooms and baths that leave you feeling scrubbed, lubed and loose as a goose.

No clothing is allowed inside so leave your modesty at the reception desk. Most pools and baths are mixed except on Monday and Thursday, when men and women are separate except in the big pool. A towel, shoes, skin creme etc are provided so you can walk in off the street with no special preparation. Children under 14 are not admitted; children over 14 are admitted with their parents.

Owned by the same company, the modern **Caracalla-Therme** (☎ 275 940; www.caracalla.de; Römerplatz 11; 2/3/4hr €12/14/16; ☺ 8am-10pm, last admission 8pm), which opened in 1985 and is named for a Roman emperor, has more than 900 square metres of outdoor and indoor pools, hot and cold water grottoes, various whirlpools, therapeutic water massages, a surge channel and a range of saunas, including a new log-cabin sauna. Bathing suits (available for purchase) must be worn everywhere except in the upstairs sauna; towels can be rented. Children are admitted from age three.

HIKING

Popular hiking destinations include the **Altes Schloss**, 2.5km north of the centre; **Geroldsauer waterfalls**, 6km south of Leopoldsplatz; and the **Yburg castle ruin**, in the wine country southwest of the centre.

A **Standseilbahn** (cable car; ☎ 2770; www.stadtwerke-baden-baden.de, in German; adult/child 6-15yr one-way €2/1.30, return €4/2; ☺ 10am-10pm Apr-Dec), opened in 1913, whisks you up to the 668m-high summit

of **Mt Merkur**, east of the centre. To get there take bus 204 or 205 from Leopoldsplatz.

Sleeping

Baden-Baden is choc-a-block with hotels but there aren't many bargains. The tourist office has a room-reservation service; the 10% fee is deducted from the cost of the room.

DJH hostel (☎ 522 23; www.jugendherberge-baden-baden.de; dm 1st/subsequent night €17.80/14.70; ☒) The local hostel, 2.5km northwest of the branch tourist office, has rather outdated facilities. To get there from the Bahnhof or the town centre, take bus 201 to Grosse Dollenstrasse and walk 750m up the hill from the church with the big green dome.

Hôtel-Gästehaus Löhr (☎ 3060; bcs@brandau-catering.de; Lichtentalerstrasse 19; d €55-75, s without bathroom €25-40) This centrally located, 28-room guesthouse (two blocks south of Leopoldsplatz) is one of the cheapest options in town. Passable if you're on a tight budget.

Hotel am Markt (☎ 270 40; www.hotel-am-markt-baden.de; Marktplatz 18; s/d €47/80, without bathroom €30/62; ☒) A family-run hotel right next to the Stiftskirche that's got 23 lovingly kept, comfortable rooms with minimalist décor. Overall, excellent value.

Rathausglöckel (☎ 906 10; www.rathausgloeckel.de; Steinstrasse 7; d €70-90) Half a block down the hill from the Stiftskirche, this family-run hotel has 11 bright, cheerful rooms, some with rooftop views that are half *belle époque*, half Mary Poppins.

Am Friedrichsbad (☎ 396 340; www.hotel-am-friedrichsbad.de; Gernsbacher Strasse 31; s/d from €89/119; ☒) Right across the street from the Friedrichbad complex, this comfortable place, in a classic 1920s building, has 22 large quiet rooms, many decorated with prints and paintings of the Jewish ghetto in Prague, the owner's hometown.

Steigenberger Badischer Hof (☎ 9340; www.badischer-hof.steigenberger.com; Lange Strasse 47; s €120-154, d €180-248; ☒ ☒ ☒) A great place for splashing out, with plush, spacious quarters, attentive staff, its own spa and droves of bathrobed guests shuffling to and from the indoor and outdoor thermal baths. In some rooms you can choose between mineral water and tap water in your bathtub.

Eating

There are a number of restaurants in the pedestrianised zone around Leopoldsplatz.

Leo's (☎ 380 81; Luisenstrasse 10; mains €9.50-21.50; ☺ 8am-3am) Near Leopoldsplatz, Leo's is a trendy and hugely popular bistro and wine bar that serves up large salads, creative pasta dishes, meat and fish.

Rathausglöckel (☎ 906 10; www.rathausgloeckel.de; Steinstrasse 7; mains €15-18; ☺ 6-9pm Wed, 11.30am-2pm & 6-9pm Thu-Sun) This rustic restaurant, in a 16th-century building, is a good place to sample local Baden cuisine, including vegetarian options, to the accompaniment of relaxing Western classical music. Has salads in summer.

La Provence (☎ 216 515; Schlossstrasse 20; mains €13.50-21.50; ☺ noon-11pm, to 1am Fri & Sat) In the Neues Schloss' one-time wine cellar, the vaulted ceilings, Art Nouveau mirrors and French sense of humour go well with the French and German cuisine (including vegetarian options).

Kaiser Früchte (Langestrasse; ☺ 9am-7pm Mon-Fri, 9am-6pm Sat) Self-caterers can buy fresh fruits and veggies at this place at the northern end of the pedestrianised zone, facing Lange Strasse 44 (the post office).

Entertainment

Ensconced in an historic train station, the **Festspielhaus** (☎ 301 3101; www.festspielhaus.de; Beim Alten Bahnhof 2, Robert-Schumann-Platz) hosts concerts, opera and ballet.

The **Baden-Badener Philharmonie** (☎ 932 791; www.philharmonie.baden-baden.de) often performs in the Kurhaus.

Getting There & Away

Karlsruhe-Baden-Baden airport (Baden Airpark; www.badenairpark.de), 15km west of town, is linked to London and Dublin by Ryanair.

Buses to a variety of Black Forest destinations depart from the bus station, situated next to the Bahnhof.

Baden-Baden is close to the A5 (Frankfurt–Basel autobahn) and is the northern starting point of the scenic Schwarzwald-Hochstrasse (see p436), also known as the B500.

Baden-Baden is on a major north–south rail corridor. Twice-hourly destinations include Freiburg (€15.70 to €24, 45 to 80 minutes) and Karlsruhe (€5, more by IC or ICE, 15 to 30 minutes).

Getting Around
BUS

Local buses, run by **Stadtwerke Baden-Baden** (☎ 2771; www.stadtwerke-baden-baden.de), cost €1.50 for a one-zone single ticket, and €2 for a two-

zone ticket, but the 24-hour pass, valid for three zones, is a better deal at €4.20 (€6.50 for two to five people).

Bus 201 (every 10 minutes) and other lines link the Bahnhof with Leopoldsplatz. Bus 205 links the Bahnhof with the airport from Monday to Friday.

CAR & MOTORCYCLE

Much of the centre is either pedestrianised or blocked off to traffic, so it's best to park and walk.

Michaelstunnel, a 2.5km tunnel on the D500, routes traffic away from the town centre, ducking underground just west of the Festspielhaus (at the northern entrance to town) and popping to the surface just south of the Russische Kirche.

FREUDENSTADT
☎ 07441 / pop 23,000

A good base for exploring the northern Black Forest, this spa town was the brainchild of Duke Friedrich I of Württemberg, who in 1599 decided to build a new capital. Together with his favourite architect, Heinrich Schickardt, he scoured Bologna and Rome for inspiration and came back with the idea for a town laid out like a spider web.

At Freudenstadt's centre is a gigantic market square, Germany's largest, measuring 216m by 219m. Friedrich hoped to adorn the square with a palace but this grandiose plan was never realised. The town fell into obscurity after the duke's death in 1610, not rising again until the mid-19th century, when a rail link brought the first waves of tourists. The French wreaked havoc here at the end of WWII, but thanks to postwar restoration Freudenstadt retains some of its unique, quasi-urban charm.

Orientation & Information

Freudenstadt's focal point is the Marktplatz, which is on the B28. The town has two train stations: the Stadtbahnhof, centrally located about five minutes' walk north of the Marktplatz, and the Hauptbahnhof, about 2km southeast of the Marktplatz at the end of Bahnhofstrasse. The central bus station is right outside the Stadtbahnhof.

ATMs There are several on the Marktplatz.
Post office (Marktplatz 64)
Tourist office (☎ 864 730, hotel reservations 864 733; www.freudenstadt.de; Marktplatz 64; ☺ 9am-6pm

TOP FIVE SCENIC DRIVES IN THE BLACK FOREST

More than just pretty drives, many of these routes focus on a theme, such as Franco–German friendship, wine growing, clock-making and spas. Details and brochures are available at local tourist offices.

■ Schwarzwald-Hochstrasse (Black Forest Hwy): officially known as the B500, this connects Baden-Baden with Freudenstadt, 60km to the south. The oldest tourist road in the Black Forest, it affords expansive views of the Upper Rhine Valley and, further west, the Vosges Mountains in Alsace (France) and skirts a number of lakes, of which the Mummelsee is the best known. There are plenty of hotels en route and a **DJH hostel** (☎ 07804-611; www .jugendherberge.de; dm 1st/subsequent night €17.90/14.70; ✗) in Zuflucht, about 19km north of Freudenstadt. From May to October you can get there by bus twice a day.

■ Schwarzwald-Bäder-Strasse (Black Forest Spa Road): a loop connecting all of the region's spa towns including, of course, Baden-Baden and Freudenstadt.

■ Badische Weinstrasse (Baden Wine Road): an oenologists delight. From Baden-Baden south to Lörrach, this 160km route winds through the red-wine vineyards of Ortenau, the Pinot Noir of Kaiserstuhl and Tuniberg, and the white-wine vines of Markgräflerland.

■ Deutsche Uhrenstrasse (German Clock Road): a 320km-long loop starting in Villingen-Schwenningen that revolves around the story of clock-making in the Black Forest. Stops include Triberg and Furtwangen.

■ Grüne Strasse (Green Road): links the Black Forest with the Rhine Valley and the Vosges Mountains in France. It was developed to highlight and strengthen the cultural links between the two countries. Popular with hikers and cyclists, this 160km route takes you through Kirchzarten, Freiburg, Breisach, Neuf-Brisach, Colmar and Munster.

Mon-Fri, 10am-2pm Sat, Sun & holidays May-Oct; 10am-5pm Mon-Fri, 10am-1pm Sat, 11am-1pm Sun & holidays Nov-Apr) Has an internet terminal (per 5/60min €0.50/6) Hotel reservations are free.

Sights & Activities

The Marktplatz is too huge to really feel like a square, especially since it's chopped into three parts by a T-junction of heavily trafficked roads. Along the perimeter are Italianate arcades providing weatherproof access to dozens of shops.

In its southwestern corner, the Marktplatz is anchored by the Protestant **Stadtkirche** (☉ 10am-5pm), built in 1608, whose two naves are at right angles to each other – yes, another unusual design by the geometrically minded duke. It's a potpourri of styles, with Gothic windows, Renaissance portals and baroque towers. Of note inside is a stone Cluniac-style **baptismal font** (early 12th century) with intricate animal ornamentations, a wall-mounted Ulm-school Gothic **crucifix** (c 1470) and a painted wooden **lectern** (from 1140) that looks like it's being carried on the shoulders of the four Evangelists.

Near the church is a **children's playground**. Kids may also enjoy the **Panorama-Bad** (☎ 921 300; www.panorama-bad.de, in German; Ludwig-Jahn-Strasse 60; adult/child 6-17yr all day €8/6.50, incl sauna €13/10; ☉ 9am-10pm Mon-Sat, 9am-8pm Sun & holidays), a huge complex of indoor and outdoor swimming pools at the northern edge of town.

Biking options include cycling down the Kinzigtal or the Murgtal – both valleys have bike paths – and returning to Freudenstadt by train. Maps with details on the area's myriad **hiking options** are available at the tourist office.

Sleeping & Eating

Outside the tourist office there's a hotel board with a free phone.

Camping Langenwald (☎ 2862; www.camping -langenwald.de; Strasburger Strasse 167; person/tent/car €5.50/4/3; ☉ Easter-1 Nov) This excellent camping ground, about 3km west of town along the B28, even has a heated outdoor swimming pool. It's served by bus 12 to Kniebis.

DJH hostel (☎ 7720; www.jugendherberge.de; Eugen-Nägele-Strasse 69; dm 1st/subsequent nights €18.30/15.10; ✗) Freudenstadt's 130-bed hostel is located about 1km northeast of the Stadtbahnhof at the end of Gottlieb-Daimler-Strasse. The nearest bus stop is Berufsschule, served by lines that include bus 15 from the Hauptbahnhof.

Hotel Adler (☎ 915 20; www.adler-fds.de; Forststrasse 15-17; s/d from €40/66, without bathroom from €33/52; **P** **⊠**) Located midway between the Stadt-bahnhof and Markt, this no-nonsense family-run hotel has 16 cheery and spotless rooms. The restaurant, open from 11.30am to 2pm and 5pm to 10pm daily except Wednesday, has tasty international, German and regional (Badisch and Swabian) cuisine; mains cost €7 to €18.

Hotel Schwanen (☎ 915 50; www.schwanen -freudenstadt.de, in German; Forststrasse 6; s/d from €38/78; **⊠**) Family-run and friendly, this hotel has 17 rooms that are tidily outfitted with wooden furniture. The daily three-course lunch special costs €8 to €11.

Turmbräu (☎ 905 121; www.turmbraeu.de, in German; Marktplatz 64; mains €5.20-14.80; ☯ 10am-1am, to 3am Fri & Sat) Right next to the tourist office, this rustic-style microbrewery does double duty as a beer garden and restaurant, and is probably the most happening place in town. Details on events (such as concerts, guest DJs and disco parties, held on Friday and Saturday from 9pm and Sunday from 5pm) appear on the website.

Self-caterers could check out the **food market** (Marktplatz; ☯ Fri mornings year-round, Tue morning in warm season).

Getting There & Away

Trains on the Kinzigtal rail line, which goes to Offenburg, leave hourly from the Haupt-bahnhof. The hourly Murgtalbahn (the S41 suburban rail line) goes to Karlsruhe (€13.40, 1½ hours) from both the Stadtbahnhof and the Hauptbahnhof.

Bus 178 makes two trips a day east to Tübingen and west to the train station in Strasbourg, France.

Freudenstadt marks the southern end of the Schwarzwald-Hochstrasse (see opposite). It's also a terminus of the Schwarzwald-Tälerstrasse (Black Forest Valley Road, ie the B462), which runs from Rastatt via Alpirsbach.

Getting Around

Freudenstadt's **bus network** (☎ 07443-247 340; www.vgf-info.de, in German) consists of five local routes (A, B, C, D and 15); a ticket for travel anywhere within town costs €1.30. Some trains and lots of local and regional buses link the two train stations. The Hauptbahnhof is linked to the Marktplatz by various local and regional buses.

There's a **bike rental station** (☎ 864 732; Lauter-badstrasse 5) in the Kurhaus, 400m south of the tourist office.

KINZIG VALLEY

The horseshoe-shaped Kinzig Valley begins south of Freudenstadt and follows the little Kinzig River south to Schiltach, then west to Haslach and north to Offenburg. Near Stras-bourg, 95km downriver, the Kinzig is eventu-ally swallowed up by the mighty Rhine.

A 2000-year-old trade route through the valley links Strasbourg with Rottweil, where that feared canine breed, the Rottweiler, evolved from Roman cattle dogs. The valley's inhabitants survived for centuries on mining and shipping goods by raft.

Getting There & Away

BUS

Bus 7160 traverses the valley on its route be-tween Offenburg and Triberg. From Monday to Friday, bus 7161 links Freudenstadt with Alpirsbach, Schiltach, Wolfach, Gutach and Hausach.

CAR & MOTORCYCLE

The B294 follows the Kinzig from Freuden-stadt to Haslach, from where the B33 leads north to Offenburg. If you're going south, you can pick up the B33 to Triberg and beyond in Hausach.

TRAIN

The hourly Kinzigtal rail line links Freu-denstadt's Hauptbahnhof with Offenburg (on the Karlsruhe–Freiburg line), stopping in the Kinzig Valley villages of Alpirsbach, Schiltach, Wolfach, Hausach, Haslach and Gengenbach.

From Hausach, trains go southeast to Triberg, Villingen and Donaueschingen, where you can change for Konstanz.

Alpirsbach

☎ 07444 / pop 7000
Alpirsbach, 18km or so south of Freudenstadt, has a small medieval centre, but the main attraction is the 11th-century **Klosterkirche St Benedict** (☎ 951 6281; www.schloesser-und-gaerten.de; Freudenstädterstrasse; adult/student €3/2.30; ☯ 10am-5.30pm mid-Apr–1 Nov, 10am-4.30pm mid-Mar–mid-Apr, 1.30-3.30pm Wed, Sat & Sun 2 Nov–mid-Mar), once the centrepiece of a Benedictine monastery. Ro-manesque in style, its has a red-sandstone

façade and an almost unadorned interior with a flat, wood-beam ceiling. The Gothic **cloister** dates from 1480, and the **museum** showcases bits and bobs from the 16th century, accidentally discovered in 1958, that illustrate everyday monastic life. The complex plays host to concerts on Saturday at either 5pm or 8.30pm.

The town is best known around the Schwarzwald area for the locally brewed Alpirsbacher Klosterbräu. Guided tours of the **brewery museum** (€6; ☺ tours at 2.30pm), next to the Klosterkirche, are in German, though guides may speak English.

The **tourist office** (☎ 951 6281; www.alpirsbach .de; Hauptstrasse 20) is next to the train station, inside Haus des Gastes, a multipurpose events venue. It can supply maps detailing the area's many hiking options and, for cyclists, information on the **Kinzigtalradweg** from Offenburg to Lossburg.

The 122-bed **DJH hostel** (☎ 2477; www.jugend herberge.de; Reinerzauer Steige 80; dm 1st/subsequent night €18.30/15.10; ✕) is located above the town, about 1.5km north (up the hill) from the train station.

Schiltach

☎ 07836 / pop 4100

If you like half-timbered houses, you'll love Schiltach, about 18km south of Alpirsbach at the confluence of the Kinzig and Schiltach Rivers. Set amid forests, this picture-perfect village is at its most scenic along the Schiltach River and around the triangular **Marktplatz**, built on a pretty steep slope. Take a closer look at the step-gabled **Rathaus**, built in the late 1500s; the murals, painted in 1942, illustrate the town's history.

The **tourist office** (☎ 5850; www.schiltach.de; Hauptstrasse 5; ☺ 9am-noon & 2-5pm Mon-Fri, 10am-noon Sat May-Sep, 9am-noon & 2-5pm Mon-Thu & Fri morning Oct-Apr), across the Schiltach River from the Marktplatz, can help find accommodation. Various hiking options appear on an enamel sign across the street from the tourist office. There's an ATM just below the Marktplatz.

Gutach

pop 4500

A 4km detour south of the Kinzig Valley along the B33 (which follows the Gutach River) is one of the Black Forest's biggest tourist draws, the **Schwarzwald Freilicht Museum** (Black Forest Open-Air Museum; ☎ 07831-935 60;

www.vogtsbauernhof.org, in German; adult/child 6-17yr/ student/family €5/2.50/3/11; ☺ 9am-6pm early Apr-early Nov, to 8pm Aug). It's centred on the **Vogtsbauernhof**, a traditional farming hamlet that has stood in the valley since 1570. Other farmhouses – along with a bakery, sawmill, chapel and granary – have been moved here from their original locations around the region. The complex is not entirely kitsch-free but the houses are authentically furnished and the craftspeople inside know what they're doing.

Haslach

☎ 07832 / pop 6900

Back in the Kinzig Valley, Haslach prospered from silver mines in the Middle Ages but when these shut down it became a simple market town. These days it has a pretty Altstadt with some half-timbered houses, but the most interesting building is the 17th-century former Capuchin monastery, which now houses the **Schwarzwälder Trachtenmuseum** (Museum of Black Forest Costumes; ☎ 706 172; www.trachtenmuseum-haslach .de.vu, in German; Im Alten Kapuzinerkloster; admission €2; ☺ 9am-5pm Tue-Sat, 10am-5pm Sun & holidays Apr–mid-Oct, 9am-noon & 1-5pm Tue-Fri mid-Oct–Dec & Feb-Mar). Among the featured traditional women's headdresses is the Bollenhut, a straw bonnet festooned with woollen pompons – red for unmarried women, black for married. Originally from Gutach, it's now a symbol of the entire Black Forest. And there's the Schäppel, a fragile-looking crown made from hundreds of beads that can weigh as much as 5kg. Around the Schwarzwald, traditional costumes are still worn on important holidays, during religious processions and, occasionally, at wedding ceremonies.

The **tourist office** (☎ 706 170; www.haslach.de, in German; ☺ 8am-noon & 1.30-5pm Mon, 9am-5pm Tue-Sat, 10am-5pm Sun & holidays Apr–mid-Oct, 8am-noon & 1-5pm Mon-Fri mid-Oct–Mar) is in the same building as the museum.

Gengenbach

☎ 07803 / pop 11,000

This romantic village, about 11km south of Offenburg, has remained relatively unspoiled by mass tourism. You can stroll through its narrow lanes, past handsome patrician townhouses with crimson geraniums spilling out of flower boxes, and wander down to the **Stadtkirche**, with its lovely baroque tower, or to the **Rathaus** (1780s), about midway between the town's two tower-topped gates. On the triangular **Marktplatz** you'll find a fountain with a statue of a knight, a symbol of the village's medieval status as a Free Imperial City. Masks and costumes worn during **Fasend** (the local version of Carnival, held over six days about seven weeks before Easter) can be admired on the seven floors of the **Narrenmuseum** (☎ 5749; Niggelturm, Hauptstrasse; admission €2; ☒ 2-5pm Wed & Sat, 10am-noon & 2-5pm Sun Apr-Oct).

The **tourist office** (☎ 930 143; www.stadt-gegenbach .de, in German; Im Winzerhof; ☒ 9am-12.30pm & 1.30-5pm Mon-Fri Sep-Jun, no midday closure Jul & Aug, also open 10am-noon Sat May-Oct), in the courtyard across from Hauptstrasse 21, rents out bicycles – three-speed bikes cost €5.50 a day; mountain bikes are €9.50 a day.

There are several places to eat and drink in the courtyard around the tourist office.

SOUTHERN BLACK FOREST

Many of the Schwarzwald's most impressive sights are in the triangle delimited by the lively university city of Freiburg, 15km east of the Rhine in the southwest; Triberg, cuckoo-clock capital, in the north; and the charming river-valley city of St Blasien in the southeast.

Getting Around
Various public-transport groupings offer extensive, reasonably priced bus and rail links to towns and villages throughout the southern Black Forest. See p444 for details. You can plan your journey with the help of www.efa-bw.de.

FREIBURG
☎ 0761 / pop 213,000
Freiburg, western gateway to the Southern Black Forest, has the happy-go-lucky attitude of a thriving university community. Framed by the velvety hills of the Black Forest, it is endowed with a wealth of historical attractions, led by the superb Münster. Add to this a lively cultural scene and an excellent range of restaurants, bars and clubs, and it's easy to understand why Freiburg is such a terrific place to visit and to base yourself while exploring the Schwarzwald.

Orientation
The Altstadt's focal point, situated two blocks southwest of the Münster, is the intersection of

Kaiser-Joseph-Strasse, the centre's main north–south artery, with east–west Bertoldstrasse. About 600m west is the Hauptbahnhof and the adjacent bus station, which define the western edge of the Altstadt. The Dreisam River runs along the Altstadt's southern edge.

Information
Buchhandlung Rombach (☎ 4500 2400; Bertoldstrasse 10) A huge bookshop with English titles.
Herder (☎ 282 820; Kaiser-Joseph-Strasse 180; ☒ 9.30am-7pm Mon-Fri, 9.30am-6pm Sat) Stocks a good assortment of foreign-language books and maps.
Police station (Rotteckring)
Post office (Eisenbahnstrasse 58-62)
Shake-n-Surf (Bismarckallee 5; per hr €3; ☒ 10am-10pm) Cheery internet access and fruit shakes next to the Hauptbahnhof, on the ground floor of the InterCity Hotel.
Tee-Online (Grünwälderstrasse 19; per hr €3.50; ☒ 11am-9pm Mon-Thu, 11am-8pm Fri & Sat, 11am-7pm Sun) Internet access.
Tourist office (☎ 388 1885/6; www.freiburg.de, www .baden24.de; Rotteckring 14; ☒ 9.30am-8pm Mon-Fri, 9.30am-5pm Sat & 10am-noon Sun & holidays Jun-Sep, 9.30am-6pm Mon-Fri, 9.30am-2.30pm Sat, 10am-noon Sun & holidays Oct-May) Friendly and well stocked, this place sells 1:50,000-scale cycling maps (€4.50 to €10) and the useful booklet *Freiburg – Official Guide* (€4). The *Hotelinformation* kiosk out front indicates room availability.
Wasch & Fun Laundry (Egonstrasse 25; ☒ 9am-10pm Mon-Sat)
Wash & Tours (Salzstrasse 22; per hr €3, laundry per machine €4; ☒ 9am-7pm Mon-Fri, 9am-6pm Sat) Why didn't someone think of this before – a self-service laundry that's also an internet café?! Duds hit suds in the cellar while upstairs electrons zip to the far corners of the globe. Laundry customers get 10 free online minutes.

Sights
MÜNSTER
Freiburg's townscape is dominated by its marvellous Münster, begun in 1200 and now (as then) surrounded by the city's bustling market square. Its **main portal** is adorned with a wealth of sculptures depicting scenes from the Old and New Testaments – look for allegorical figures such as Voluptuousness (the one with snakes on her back) and Satan himself. Nearby are medieval wall markings used to make sure that merchandise (eg loaves of bread) were of the requisite size.

The sturdy **tower**, square at the base, becomes an octagon higher up and is crowned by a filigreed 116m-high spire. An **ascent of the tower** (adult/student €1.50/1; ☒ 9.30am-5pm Mon-Sat,

BADEN-WÜRTTEMBERG

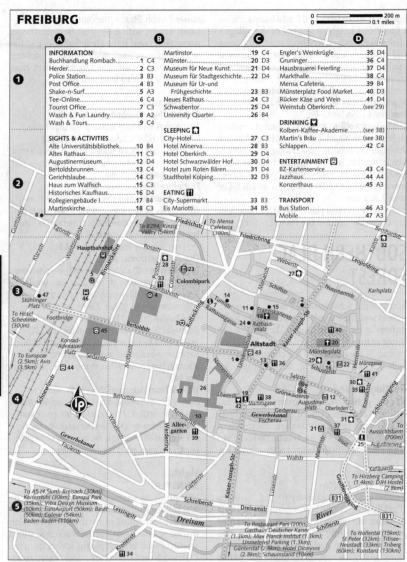

FREIBURG

0 — 200 m
0 — 0.1 miles

INFORMATION
Buchhandlung Rombach..............1 C4
Herder..2 C3
Police Station..........................3 B3
Post Office................................4 B3
Shake-n-Surf.............................5 A3
Tee-Online.................................6 C4
Tourist Office............................7 C3
Wasch & Fun Laundry..............8 A2
Wash & Tours............................9 C4

SIGHTS & ACTIVITIES
Alte Universitätsbibliothek......10 B4
Altes Rathaus..........................11 C3
Augustinermuseum...................12 D4
Bertoldsbrunnen........................13 C4
Gerichtslaube............................14 C3
Haus zum Walfisch....................15 C3
Historisches Kaufhaus...............16 D4
Kollegiengebäude I....................17 B4
Martinskirche.............................18 C3

Martinstor................................19 C4
Münster.....................................20 D3
Museum für Neue Kunst...........21 D4
Museum für Stadtgeschichte....22 D4
Museum für Ur-und
    Frühgeschichte......................23 B3
Neues Rathaus...........................24 C3
Schwabentor..............................25 D4
University Quarter......................26 B4

SLEEPING
City-Hotel..................................27 C3
Hotel Minerva...........................28 B3
Hotel Oberkirch.........................29 D4
Hotel Schwarzwälder Hof.........30 D4
Hotel zum Roten Bären.............31 D4
Stadthotel Kolping.....................32 D3

EATING
City-Supermarkt.........................33 B3
Eis Mariotti................................34 B5

Engler's Weinkrügle..................35 D4
Gruninger.................................36 C4
Hausbrauerei Feierling..............37 D4
Markthalle.................................38 C4
Mensa Cafeteria.......................39 B4
Münsterplatz Food Market.......40 D3
Rücker Käse und Wein..............41 D4
Weinstub Oberkirch..............(see 29)

DRINKING
Kolben-Kaffee-Akademie......(see 38)
Martin's Bräu.......................(see 38)
Schlappen.................................42 C4

ENTERTAINMENT
BZ-Kartenservice.....................43 C4
Jazzhaus..................................44 A4
Konzerthaus............................45 A3

TRANSPORT
Bus Station..............................46 A3
Mobile.....................................47 A3

1-5pm Sun & holidays), for which you pay at the top, provides an excellent view of the church's intricate construction; on a clear day you can see the Vosges Mountains in France.

Inside the Münster, the kaleidoscopic **stained-glass windows** are dazzling. Many were financed by various guilds – in the bottom panels look for a pretzel, scissors and other symbols of various medieval trades. The **high altar** features a masterful triptych of the coronation of the Virgin Mary by Hans Baldung, best viewed on a **guided tour** (€2; ☼ at 2pm).

SOUTH OF THE MÜNSTER

Facing the Münster's south side is the arcaded brick-red **Historisches Kaufhaus** (Münsterplatz), a merchants' hall built in 1530. The coats of arms on the oriels and the four figures above the balcony represent members of the House of Habsburg and indicate Freiburg's allegiance.

The sculptor Christian Wentzinger built himself a **baroque townhouse** a bit east of the Kaufhaus in 1761. Inside is a wonderful staircase with a wrought-iron railing which guides the eye to the elaborate ceiling fresco. Nowadays, the building is occupied by the **Museum für Stadtgeschichte** (Municipal History Museum; ☎ 201 2515; Münsterplatz 30; adult/concession €2/1; ☺ 10am-5pm Tue-Sun), where you can learn all about Freiburg's eventful past.

Admission to this museum also covers entrance to the **Augustinermuseum** (☎ 201 2531; Augustinerplatz 1; adult/concession €2/1; ☺ 10am-5pm Tue-Sun). Housed in a former monastery, its extensive collection of medieval art includes paintings by Baldung, Matthias Grünewald and Cranach, while its collection of stained glass from the Middle Ages to the present ranks as one of the most important in Germany.

The **Museum für Neue Kunst** (Museum of Modern Art; ☎ 201 2581; Marienstrasse 10; adult/concession €2/1, incl special exhibition €7/5; ☺ 10am-5pm Tue-Sun, special exhibitions to 8pm Thu), about 200m further south in a century-old school building, leaps into the 20th century with its collection of expressionist and abstract art.

Following the little canal west through the **Fischerau**, the former fishing quarter, will soon get you to the landmark **Martinstor** (Kaiser-Joseph-Strasse), one of Freiburg's two surviving town gates. Heading north along Kaiser-Joseph-Strasse leads you to the **Bertoldsbrunnen**, a statue-fountain marking the spot where the city's two main thoroughfares have crossed since the city's founding in 1091.

A long block east of the Museum für Neue Kunst, at the southeastern end of Salzstrasse, is the muralled, 13th-century **Schwabentor**, a massive city gate with tram tracks running under its two arches. From just east of here, trails lead up the forested **Schlossberg**, which dominates the town (that's why the French built a fort there in the late 1600s) and is topped by the ice cream–cone-shaped **Aussichtsturm** (lookout tower); the views are fantastic!

WESTERN ALTSTADT

The **university quarter**, in the area west of Martinstor, consists of an eclectic mix of old and

The **Museumticket** (€4), valid for one day, gets you into all five of Freiburg's municipal museums (www.museen.freiburg.de, in German).

new buildings. The **Kollegiengebäude I** has Art Nouveau elements, while the **Alte Universitätsbibliothek** (Old University Library) is resolutely neo-Gothic.

A bit north is the chestnut-shaded Rathausplatz, with another fountain that's a popular gathering place. On its western side stands the red sandstone **Neues Rathaus** (New City Hall), a symmetrical structure composed of two Renaissance town houses flanking a newer, arcaded section that leads to a cobblestone courtyard. The little tower contains a carillon, played at noon daily.

Linked to the Neues Rathaus by an over-the-street pedestrian bridge is the **Altes Rathaus** (Old City Hall; 1559), also the result of merging several smaller buildings and a good example of successful postwar reconstruction. Freiburg's oldest town hall, the **Gerichtslaube** (13th century), is a bit west along Turmstrasse.

The northern side of Rathausplatz is taken up by the medieval **Martinskirche**, once part of a Franciscan monastery. Severely damaged in WWII, it was rebuilt in the ascetic style typical of this mendicant order. Virtually across the street on Franziskanergasse stands its architectural antithesis, the extravagant **Haus zum Walfisch** (House of the Whale), whose gilded late-Gothic oriel is garnished with two gargoyles. This building served as a temporary refuge for the philosopher Erasmus von Rotterdam after his expulsion from Basel in 1529.

Further west, in a delightful little park across the street from the tourist office, is the neo-Gothic **Colombischlössle**, a villa housing the **Museum für Ur- und Frühgeschichte** (Museum of Pre- & Early History; ☎ 201 2571; www.museen.freiburg.de, in German; Rotteckring 5; adult/concession €2/1; ☺ 10am-5pm Tue-Sun). Via the cast-iron staircase, you'll reach an eclectic bunch of archaeological exhibits stretching from the Stone Age up through the Celtic and Roman periods.

Tours

Freiburg Kultour (☎ 290 7447; www.freiburg-kultour.com, in German; Rotteckring 14), based in the tourist office (where tours start), offers 1½- to two-hour

FREIBURG BENEATH YOUR FEET

As you stroll around Freiburg's mostly pedestrianised Altstadt, be sure to look down at the pavement for the cheerful mosaics found in front of many shops. A diamond marks a jewellery shop, a cow is for a butcher, a pretzel for a baker, and so on.

Be careful not to step into the Bächle, the permanently flowing rivulets that run along many footpaths. Originally part of an elaborate system to deliver nonpotable water, these literal 'tourist traps' now provide welcome relief for hot feet on sweltering summer days. It's said that if you fall into one you'll marry a Freiburger or a Freiburgerin.

All around Freiburg (as in many other German cities and towns), square brass plaques bearing names and dates, embedded in the sidewalk, indicate houses where Jews lived before being deported to concentration camps.

walking tours (adult/child 12-18yr €7/6; ☽ 10.30am Mon-Fri & 10am Sat Apr-Oct, 10am Sat & 10.30am Sun Nov-Mar) of the Altstadt and the Münster in German and English.

Velotaxi (☎ 0172-768 4370; ☽ mid-Apr–Oct) charges €6.50 for a 20-minute, two-person tour of the Altstadt in a rain-protected pedicab. Order by phone or look for one at Rathausplatz or Münsterplatz.

Sleeping

The tourist office can help with a hotel booking for €3.

Hirzberg Camping (☎ 350 54; www.freiburg-camping .de; Kartäuserstrasse 99; adult/site €5.50/3; ☽ year-round; ▣) A lovely camping ground at the base of a forested slope 1.5km east of the Schwabentor. Has cooking and laundry facilities and rents out tents, caravans and bikes. Take tram 1 to Stadthalle, walk north and cross the river.

DJH hostel (☎ 676 56; www.jugendherberge-freiburg.de; Kartäuserstrasse 151; dm 1st/subsequent night €20.30/17.10; ▣ ☒) Freiburg's 394-bed hostel, often brimming with German students, is 3km east of the Schwabentor along the Dreisam. It's a good idea to phone ahead for reservations. To get there take tram 1 to Römerhof and follow the signs down Fritz-Geiges-Strasse and across the river – it's an 800m walk.

Hotel Dionysos (☎ 293 53; www.hoteldionysos.de, in German; Hirschstrasse 2, Günterstal; d with shower €45, s/d with washbasin €28/40) Situated 3km south of the Altstadt, in the idyllic streamside village of Günterstal, this friendly family-run hotel has a guesthouse atmosphere, basic spotless rooms and a Greek restaurant. It's an easy ride from town on tram line 4.

Hotel Schemmer (☎ 207 490; www.hotel-schemmer .de, in German; Eschholzstrasse 63; s/d from €39/62, without bathroom €34/51) On a nondescript street 800m southwest of the Hauptbahnhof, this 18-room

pension-style place is a good budget option. There's free parking across the street. By car, get off the B31 at Eschholzstrasse.

Gasthaus Deutscher Kaiser (☎ 749 10; www.hotel -deutscher-kaiser.com in German; Günterstalstrasse 38; s/d €50/70, without bathroom €45/60; ⓟ) This old-time family-run hotel, a 1.5km walk south of Martinstor and across the street from the Max Planck Institut, has 15 simple but spacious rooms.

Hotel Schwarzwälder Hof (☎ 380 30; www.schwarz waelder-hof.eu; Herrenstrasse 43; s/d/5-person ste from €55/89/150, s/d without bathroom from €38/65) A circular staircase with a wrought-iron railing leads from the lobby, entered via tiny Münzgasse, to the 45 rooms, which are simply furnished and very white; some have charming views of the old town.

Hotel Minerva (☎ 386 490; www.minerva-freiburg .de, in German; Poststrasse 8; s €75-90, d €105-115; ⓟ ☒) In an Art Nouveau–influenced building just a five-minute walk from the train station and the city centre. The 26 comfortable rooms are sleek and modern, with a different colour scheme on each floor. Amenities include a sauna.

City-Hotel (☎ 388 070; www.cityhotel-freiburg.de; Weberstrasse 3; s/d from €85/114; ⓟ ☒) This sleek place is a good showcase for the charms of practical, modern German design. The 42 rooms are large, clean and orderly.

Stadthotel Kolping (☎ 319 30; www.stadthotel-kolp ing.de; Karlstrasse 7; s €72-82, d €114-124; ⓟ ☒) Just north of the Altstadt, this four-star place has 94 comfortable rooms furnished in a business-like style. Extras include a spacious lobby and two different massage studios; a fitness room is planned.

Hotel Oberkirch (☎ 202 6868; www.hotel-oberkirch .de; Münsterplatz 22 & Schusterstrasse 11; s €92-115, d €115-156; ⓟ) Facing the Münster – you can't get any more central than this. The tasteful rooms have flowery wallpaper and the latest mod-cons; some also come with half-canopies over the beds. Small singles start at €62.

Hotel zum Roten Bären (☎ 387 870; www.roter
-baeren.de; Oberlinden 12; s/d from €105/145; **P**)) Just inside the Schwabentor, this place dates back to 1120 and claims to be the oldest guesthouse in Germany. But though the cellar is medieval, the 25 rooms have sleek wooden furnishings. The back rooms look out on a quiet garden.

Eating & Drinking

As a university town, Freiburg has all sorts of cheap eats options, quite a few of them around Martinstor (for example on Univer-sitätsstrasse and Gartenstrasse) and, several blocks east, along Konviktstrasse.

Mensa cafeterias (11.30am-2pm & 5.20-7.30pm Mon-Fri) Stefan-Meier-Strasse 28 (on the campus at the northern end of Hebelstrasse; may be closed for dinner during holiday periods); Rempartstrasse 18 (also 11.30am-1.30pm Sat) If you can produce student ID, a world of salad buffets and other filling fodder will open before you at these locations.

Markthalle (Martinsgasse 235 & Grünewalderstrasse 4; 8am-7pm) A food court whose Mexican, Italian, Indian, Korean and French counters offer fast, tasty lunches.

Martin's Bräu (☎ 387 0018; Kaiser-Joseph-Strasse 237; mains €5.10-15.10; 11am-midnight, to 2am Fri & Sat) Down the alley from Martinstor, this rustic cellar microbrewery has a good selection of home-brewed beers, some of them seasonal, and serves up hearty Baden-style specialities – some porcine, others bovine and yet others with *Spätzle*. Warm dishes are available until 11.30pm.

Restaurant Pars (☎ 712 21; cnr Turnseestrasse & Tal-strasse; mains €5.35-11.30; 11am-10pm) A favourite with locals who live and work nearby, this place serves delicious and reasonably priced Persian dishes, including lots of vegetarian op-tions, to the accompaniment of mellow Persian music. It's situated across the Dreisam from the Altstadt, 600m south of Martinstor.

Hausbrauerei Feierling (☎ 243 480; Gerberau 46; mains €6-12; 11am-midnight, to 1am Fri & Sat) A styl-ish microbrewery with Freiburg's best beer garden. Serves up some good vegetarian op-tions and absolutely enormous schnitzels with salad and *Brägele* (chipped potatoes). If you drink one too many, be extra careful not to fall in the adjacent stream or you may become dinner for the open-jawed *Krokodil*.

Englers Weinkrügle (☎ 383 115; Konviktstrasse 12; mains €7.60-13.50; 11am-2pm & 5.30-9.30pm Tue-Sun) A warm, woody Baden-style *Weinstube* with wisteria growing out front and traditional regional specialities on the menu.

Weinstub Oberkirch (☎ 202 6868; Münsterplatz 22; main meals served noon-2pm & 6.30-10pm Mon-Sat) Fac-ing the Münster, this traditional restaurant, with its dark wood-panelled walls, is known among locals for its highly professional service and excellent Black Forest trout (€17). Serves light meals all day long (8am to 12.30am).

Kolben-Kaffee-Akademie (☎ 387 0013; Kaiser-Joseph-Strasse 233; large coffee €1.60; 8am-7pm Mon-Fri, 8am-5pm Sat & 10am-5pm Sun) An old-fashioned stand-up coffee house with fresh pastries and sandwiches.

Schlappen (☎ 334 94; Löwenstrasse 2; 11am-1am Mon-Thu, 11am-3am Fri & Sat, 3pm-1am Sun & holidays) With its jazz-themed back room, its poster-plastered walls and its mirrored urinal, this is one of Freiburg's most popular and relaxed pubs. Light meals (such as Flammkuche) are on offer and you can try 10 different types of absinthe (€3).

Eis Mariotti (☎ 707 5061; Kronenstrasse 9; 10am-11pm late Feb–mid-Oct) An unpretentious, reason-ably priced place considered by many to be Freiburg's best homemade ice-cream parlour. Situated 600m southwest of Martinstor.

Self-caterers can pick up picnic fixin's at the following places:

City-Supermarkt (Eisenbahnstrasse 39; 7.30am-8pm Mon-Sat)

Gruninger (Kaiser-Joseph-Strasse 201; 8.30am-7pm Mon-Fri, 8am-5pm Sat) An award-winning meat shop with lots of Black Forest specialities available in a bun.

Münsterplatz food market (until 1pm Mon-Fri, to 1.30pm Sat) Local farmers come to sell local produce. Stalls are particularly numerous and varied on Saturday. On a per-calorie basis, the least expensive meals in town are the various versions of wurst-in-a-bun (€2), topped with fried onions (a Freiburg tradition), sold here.

Rücker Käse und Wein (Münzgasse 1; 9am-6.30pm Mon-Fri, 9am-3pm Sat) For wine and cheese.

Entertainment

Get the free listings monthly, *Freiburg Aktuell*, at hotels and the tourist office.

BZ-Kartenservice (☎ 01805-55 66 56; www.badische
-zeitung.de, in German; Bertoldstrasse 7; 9am-7pm Mon-Fri, 9am-4pm Sat) Click on 'Termine' for events tickets.

Jazzhaus (☎ 349 73; www.jazzhaus.de; Schnewlin-strasse 1) Under the arches of an old brick wine cellar, this first-rate venue hosts jazz rock, pop, blues, hip-hop and world music concerts (€10 to €30) at 8pm at least three nights a week (less frequently from June to August; see the website for details). It becomes a disco (admission about €6) from 11pm to 3am or 4am on Friday and Saturday nights, and is popular with people of all ages.

Konzerthaus (☎ 388 1552; www.konzerthaus.freiburg .de, in German; Konrad-Adenauer-Platz 1) A hulking modern concert hall that doubles as a convention and cultural events centre. Don't miss the tornado sculptures out front.

Getting There & Around
AIR
Freiburg shares an airport, **EuroAirport** (www .euroairport.com), with Basel (Switzerland) and Mulhouse (France). Destinations include London and Luton with EasyJet.

BUS
The **Airport Bus** (☎ 500 500; www.freiburger-reisedienst .de, in German) goes from Freiburg's bus station to EuroAirport (€16, 55 minutes, every hour or two).

SüdbadenBus and **RVF** (☎ 01805-77 99 66; www .suedbadenbus.de, www.rvf.de, both in German) offer extensive, reasonably priced bus and rail links to towns and villages throughout the southern Black Forest. Single tickets for one/two/three zones cost €2/3.40/4.80 (half that for children age six to 14); a Regio24 ticket, good for 24 hours, costs €4.80/9.60/9.60 for one person and €7.20/14.40/14.40 for two to five people. If you'll be using lots of public transport it's worth picking up one of the detailed *Fahrplan* timetables (€1).

From Freiburg, bus 1066 travels once a day Monday to Friday to Haslach, Hausach and Schiltach (2¼ hours) in the Kinzig Valley. See the various town listings in the Southern Black Forest section for other bus options to/from Freiburg.

Bus and tram travel within Freiburg (www .vag-freiburg.de) is charged at the one-zone rate. Buy tickets from the red vending machines or from the driver and be sure to validate upon boarding.

CAR & MOTORCYCLE
The Frankfurt–Basel A5 passes just west of Freiburg. The scenic B31 leads east through the Höllental to Lake Constance. The B294 goes north into the Black Forest.

Car-hire agencies include **Europcar** (☎ 515 100; Löracherstrasse 10) and **Avis** (☎ 197 19; St-Georgener-Strasse 7).

About 1.5km south of Martinstor, around the **Max Planck Institut** (Günterstalstrasse 73), there's unmetered parking on some of the side streets (eg Türkenlouisstrasse) – to get there from the Altstadt drive south on Günterstalstrasse (the southern continuation of Kaiser-Joseph-Strasse).

TRAIN
Freiburg is on a major north–south rail corridor so there are frequent departures for destinations such as Basel (€12.80 to €19.80, 50 to 80 minutes) and Baden-Baden (€15.70 to €24, 45 to 80 minutes). Freiburg is also the western terminus of the Höllentalbahn to Donaueschingen via Titisee-Neustadt (€4.80, 38 minutes, twice an hour). There's a local connection to Breisach (€4.80, 27 minutes, at least hourly).

BICYCLE
Bike paths run along both banks of the Dreisam River, leading westward to Breisach and then into France.

Mobile (☎ 292 7998; www.mobile-freiburg.com, in German; Wenzingerstrasse 15; 3hr/day/week €5/12.50/50, under 17yr half price; ◷ 24hr), in a round, glass-enclosed pavilion just over the bridge from the Hauptbahnhof, rents bikes and sells cycling maps (€6.80).

AROUND FREIBURG
Schauinsland
Year-round, a ride on the 3.6km **Schauinslandbahn** (cabin ski lift; adult/child 6-14yr/student & senior return €10.70/6.50/9.50, one-way €7.50/4.50/6.50; ◷ 9am-5pm, to 6pm Jul-Sep) to the 1286m **Schauinsland peak** (www.bergwelt-schauinsland.de, in German), topped by a striking lookout tower, is an easy and very popular way to get from Freiburg to the Black Forest highlands. Numerous well-marked trails make the Schauinsland area ideal for walks. To get to the lift from town, take tram 4 south to Günterstal and then bus 21 to Talstation. Ring ☎ 0180-5019 703 to check weather conditions.

WEST OF FREIBURG
Breisach
☎ 07667 / pop 14,000
About 27km west of Freiburg, Breisach is separated from France by the Rhine, and nothing else. It is an ancient town that has often been

caught in the crossfire of conflict, including during WWII, when it was 85% destroyed. The star-shaped French fortress-town of **Neuf Brisach** (New Breisach), designed by Vauban, is 4km west of Breisach – both towns are candidates for Unesco World Heritage status.

On the hilltop, the Romanesque and Gothic **St Stephansmünster**, built between the 12th and the 15th centuries, towers over the commercial centre on the flats below. Inside there's a faded fresco cycle, *The Last Judgment* (1491) by Martin Schongauer (at the west end), a delicate Flamboyant Gothic rood loft from around the same period, and a magnificent **high altar triptych** (1526) made of linden wood. The Schänzletreppe (stairs) lead from the church down to Münsterbergstrasse, at the bottom of which is the **Gutgesellentor**, a town gate built in 1402 and rebuilt in the 1950s. This is where the scandalous Pope John XXIII was caught in 1415 while fleeing the Council of Constance.

Briesach's main commercial area is between the Gutgesellentor and the Markplatz. The **tourist office** (☎ 940 155; www.breisach.de; Marktplatz 16; ☼ 9am-5pm Mon-Fri & 10am-1pm Sat Apr-Dec, also 1-4pm Sun May-Oct, 9am-12.30pm & 1.30-5pm Mon-Fri Jan-Mar) has accommodation options posted out the front and can provide details on visiting local wine growers.

DJH hostel (☎ 7665; www.jugendherberge-breisach.de; Rheinuferstrasse 12; dm 1st/subsequent night €20.30/17.10; ✗) Situated on the Rhine just south of a bridge over the tiny Möhlin River, this 164-bed hostel is 1.1km south and then west from the train station. A camping ground and swimming pool are right next door.

You'll find a number of restaurants and some food shops between the Gutgesellentor and the tourist office. There's a **Minimal supermarket** (Bahnhofstrasse; ☼ 8am-8pm Mon-Sat) across the street from the train station.

Breisach is an excellent base for **cycling**; the many options include an international bike ride across the Rhine, perhaps taking advantage of the new bridge 9km south of Breisach (near Hartheim) opened to French and German fanfare in 2006. Bikes can be hired from **Funbike** (☎ 7733; Metzgergasse 1; 1/3 days €10/25; ☼ 9am-noon & 6-7pm Apr-Oct), across the street from the tourist office.

Boat excursions along the Rhine (eg to Colmar) are run by **BFS** (☎ 924 010; www.bfs-info .de in German; Rheinuferstrasse; ☼ Apr-Sep); the dock is 500m southwest of the tourist office.

Local trains link Breisach's train station (Bahnhofstrasse), 500m southeast of the Marktplatz, with Freiburg (€4.80, 27 minutes, at least hourly) and towns around the periphery of the Kaisterstuhl. Buses go to the delightful French town of Colmar, 22km to the west.

Kaiserstuhl

The Kaiserstuhl, a 560m-high mountain that, somewhat unexpectedly, is volcanic in origin, begins a few kilometres northeast of Breisach. Its inelegantly terraced slopes constitute one of Germany's finest wine-growing areas, noted especially for its production of *Spätburgunder* (Pinot Noir); another locally popular variety is *Grauburgunder* (Pinot Gris). The wines owe their quality to an ideal microclimate (said to be the warmest and sunniest in Germany) and the fertile loess (clay and silt) soil that retains heat during the night. The area of **fruit orchards** between Breisach and the Kaiserstuhl is a riot of blossoms in the spring.

The Breisach tourist office has details on cellar tours, wine tastings, bike paths such as the 55km **Kaiserstuhltour** circuit, and walking trails such as the 15km **Winzerweg** (Wine Growers' Trail) from Achkarren (5km northeast of Breisach) to Riegel. Bikes can be hired in Breisach.

The **Kaiserstuhlbahn** rail loop goes all the way around the Kaiserstuhl; stops (where you may have to change trains) include Sasbach, Endingen, Riegel and Gottenheim (on the Freiburg–Breisach line).

Europa Park

Germany's largest **theme park** (☎ 01805-776 688; www.europapark.de; adult/child 4-14yr & senior €28.50/25.50; ☼ 9am-6pm early Apr-early Nov & early Dec-early Jan, later in peak season) is about 35km north of Freiburg near the village of Rust. It brings together thrilling rides, including nine roller coasters, with 'villages' designed to look – and be shopped – like they're typically Italian, Swiss, Dutch and so on. A short stroll is like a quick trip around Europe – if we left the half-scale model of Rome's Colosseum at 2pm and now it's 2.05pm this must be Mykonos! Keen to brush up on German architectural styles? Just head to 'Germany', where you'll find it all, from Gothic red brick and cute half-timber to curvaceous baroque. This place even has a big mouse walking around – sound familiar? OK, so he's got small ears and is called Euromaus, but still…

BADEN-WÜRTTEMBERG

Shuttle buses (hourly in the morning) link the Ringsheim train station, on the Freiburg–Offenburg line, with the park. By car, take the A5 to Herbolzheim (exit 58).

Vitra Design Museum

The **Vitra Design Museum** (☎ 07621-702 3200; www.design-museum.de; Charles-Eames-Strasse 1; adult/concession €7.50/6; ⌚ 10am-6pm, to 8pm Wed), 50km south of Freiburg in Weil am Rhein (just across the Rhine from Basel, Switzerland, and St-Louis, France), hosts thought-provoking temporary exhibitions of contemporary design. The museum's striking modern building – all angles and curves – was designed by Frank Gehry. Nearby buildings – on the campus of the Swiss furniture manufacturer Vitra – by architects such as Tadao Ando, Nicholas Grimshaw, Zaha Hadid and Alvaro Siza, can be visited on a two-hour **architectural tour** (admission €9, incl the museum €13; ⌚ noon & 2pm). Taking the tour is the only way to see 100 chairs from Vitra's collection.

To get there by car, get off the A5 at Weil am Rhein (exit 69). By public transport, take bus 55 from Basel's Badischer Bahnhof, linked to Freiburg (€10 or €17, 35 or 63 minutes, hourly in each price category). You can also walk (it takes about 15 minutes) from the Weil am Rhein train station, an easy trip from Freiburg (€9.10, 50 minutes, hourly).

BADEN-WÜRTTEMBERG

NORTHEAST OF FREIBURG

St Peter

☎ 07660 / pop 2500

The folk of the bucolic village of St Peter, on the southern slopes of Mt Kandel (1243m), are deeply committed to their ancient traditions and customs. On religious holidays and Sunday mornings you can see the villagers, from young boys and girls to grey-haired pensioners, proudly sporting their colourful, handmade *Trachten* (folkloric costumes).

The most outstanding local landmark is the **former Benedictine abbey**, a rococo jewel designed in the 1720s by the masterful Peter Thumb of Vorarlberg. Many of the period's top artists collaborated on the sumptuous interior decoration of the twin-towered red-sandstone **church** (⌚ open daily), including Joseph Anton Feuchtmayer, who carved the gilded statues of various Zähringer dukes affixed to the pillars. Guided tours (€4; in German) take you inside the monastery complex, including the rococo library. Secularised in 1806, the complex served as a Catholic seminary from 1842 to 2006 and is now a Catholic-run spiritual centre.

The **tourist office** (☎ 910 224; www.st-peter-schwarzwald.de, in German; Klosterhof 11; ⌚ 9am-noon & 2-5pm Mon-Fri Easter-Oct, 10am-noon Sat Jul & Aug, 9am-noon Mon-Fri, 2-5pm during school holidays Nov-Easter) is under the archway leading to the **Klosterhof** (the abbey courtyard) and the church. A nearby information panel shows room availability.

By public transport, the best way to get from Freiburg to St Peter is to take the train to Kirchzarten (13 minutes, two or three an hour) and then bus 7216 (24 minutes, two or three an hour); a few buses on the 7216 run begin at Freiburg's bus station.

St Peter is on the **Schwarzwald Panoramastrasse** (Black Forest Panorama Road; www.schwarzwald-panoramastrasse.de), a 50km-long scenic route from Waldkirch (26km northeast of Freiburg) to Hinterzarten (5km west of Titisee) with dreamy mountain views.

Triberg

☎ 07722 / pop 5400

Wedged into a narrow valley and framed by three mountains (hence the name), Triberg is the undisputed capital of cuckoo-clock country. Numerous shops sell the rustic but annoying timepieces – one place (at Hauptstrasse 79) is proud of having over a thousand cuckoo clocks on hand, all locally made except for a few from Switzerland. The latest commercial quartz models are equipped with a sensor that puts the cuckoo to sleep when the lights in the room are off.

Two local structures claim the title of the *weltgröste Kuckucksuhr* (world's largest cuckoo clock), giving rise to the 'War of the Cuckoos', with Triberg in one corner and Schonach in the other. In fact, both places look pretty much like the same village, except perhaps to those who live there.

Attractions unconnected to timekeeping include Germany's highest waterfall and an excellent museum of local culture.

ORIENTATION & INFORMATION

Triberg's main drag is the B500 – known in town as Hauptstrasse and Wallfahrtstrasse – which runs more-or-less parallel to the Gutach River except around the waterfall, where it does some fancy switchbacks. The town's focal point is the Marktplatz, a steep 1.2km uphill from the Bahnhof, which is at Hauptstrasse's northeastern (lower) end, not far from where the B500 meets the B33.

The Triberg area markets itself as **Ferienland** (Holidayland; www.dasferienland.de) to visitors.

Post office On Marktplatz next to the Rathaus.

Tourist office (☎ 866 490; www.triberg.de, in German; Wahlfahrtstrasse 4; ☺ 10am-5pm) On the B500, 50m uphill from the river, inside the Schwarzwald-Museum.

SIGHTS

For a well-presented overview of the Triberg region's history and customs, head for the **Schwarzwald-Museum** (☎ 4434; www.schwarzwald museum.de; Wallfahrtstrasse 4; adult/child 5-13yr/child 14-17yr/family €4.50/2.50/3/10; ☺ 10am-5pm). Exhibits include a clockmaker's shop, a mock mineral mine, mechanical musical instruments and some outrageous hats, must-have accessories for the well-dressed local *Fraülein* of the 1850s.

Yosemite Falls they ain't but Germany's tallest **Wasserfälle** (waterfalls) do exude their own wild romanticism. Fed by the Gutach River, they plunge 163m in seven cascades bordered by mossy rocks. Energy has been generated here since 1884, when the elevation differential was first harnessed to power the town's electric street lamps. There are five access points to the lushly wooded **gorge** (☎ 2724; adult/child 8-16yr/family €2/0.70/4.50), and one of them is just down the hill from the Schwarzwald-Museum. It's annoying to have to pay to experience nature but in this case the fee is worth it. The gorge is officially open (depending on the weather) from March or April to October or early November, and from 25 to 30 December. The rest of the time there's no fee but you enter at your own risk because of the snow and ice.

The **Naturerlebnispark** (admission free), almost across the street from the Schwarzwald-Museum, is a children's playground with imaginative, mostly wooden constructions.

Triberg's underdog **World's Biggest Cuckoo Clock**, complete with oversized gear-driven innards, can be found about 1km further up the hill in Schonach, inside a snug little **house** (☎ 4689; www.dold-urlaub.de; Untertalstrasse 28; admission €1, ☺ 9am-noon & 1-6pm). Its commercially savvy **rival** (☎ 962 20; www.uhren-park.de; Schonachbach 27; admission €1.50; ☺ 9am-6pm Mon-Sat, 10am-6pm Sun Easter-Oct), listed in *Guinness*, is at the other end of town, integrated into a large clock shop on the B33 between Triberg and Hornberg.

SLEEPING & EATING

DJH hostel (☎ 4110; www.jugendherberge-triberg.de; Rohrbacher Strasse 35; dm 1st/subsequent night €17.90/14.70; ☒) Triberg's 125-bed hostel is on a scenic ridge on the southeastern edge of town. It's a steep 45-minute (3km) walk from the Hauptbahnhof but you can take any bus to the Marktplatz, from where it's just 1200m uphill.

Hotel Central (☎ 4360; hotel-central-triberg@online .de; Hauptstrasse 64; s/d/tr from €30/55/70; Ⓟ) Facing the Rathaus, this 14-room hotel has a late-'70s vibe and smallish rooms with all the amenities tightly packed in. There's an elevator from the bank's fore-lobby.

Parkhotel Wehrle (☎ 860 20; www.parkhotel-wehrle .de; Hauptstrasse 51; s €74-84, d €109-129; Ⓟ 🖳 🐾) A haven of style in Triberg's sea of exuberant kitsch – even well-travelled Ernest Hemingway, in Triberg to check out the local trout streams, was enchanted by his stay here. The 50 rooms have classic décor, including touches such as bevelled glass, and sexy transparent shower stalls. The main building, just down the hill from the Rathaus, will turn 400 in 2008. A new pool and 'wellness clinic' are set to open in 2007. In the kitchen, the chef works his magic with creativity and panache; mains cost €16 to €22.

GETTING THERE & AWAY

The Schwarzwaldbahn railway line goes southeast to Villingen (25 minutes) and Konstanz (€19.10, 1½ hours) to the northwest Offenburg (€9.10, 45 minutes, hourly) is on the Frankfurt–Freiburg line.

DEMOCRACY, PEACE & CUCKOO CLOCKS

In Italy for 30 years under the Borgias they had warfare, terror, murder and bloodshed, but they produced Michelangelo, Leonardo da Vinci and the Renaissance. In Switzerland they had brotherly love, they had 500 years of democracy and peace, and what did that produce? The cuckoo clock.

Harry Lime (played by Orson Welles) in The Third Man

Welles apparently ad-libbed the scene that produced this famous quote in the classic 1949 film. In fact, cuckoo clocks, as we know them, originated in Germany's Black Forest sometime in the 1700s.

Bus 7160 travels north through the Gutach and Kinzig valleys to Offenburg; bus 7265 heads south to Villingen via St Georgen (one hour).

GETTING AROUND

There's a bus service between the Bahnhof and the Marktplatz, and on to the nearby town of Schonach, about once an hour (€1.65).

Villingen-Schwenningen

☎ Villingen 07721, Schwenningen 07720 / pop 82,000

When Villingen and Schwenningen (VS for short) were joined in 1972, the union couldn't have been more unlikely. Villingen is a spa town with a medieval layout; Schwenningen is a clock-making centre less than a century old. What's worse, Villingen used to belong to the Grand Duchy of Baden, while Schwenningen – more or less where the Neckar River begins – was part of the duchy of Württemberg, conflicting allegiances that apparently can't be reconciled.

From the tourist's point of view, Villingen definitely has more to offer, though Schwenningen has a couple of museums devoted to clock-making.

ORIENTATION & INFORMATION

Villingen's Altstadt, surrounded by a ring road, is crisscrossed by two wide and mostly pedestrianised main streets: north–south Obere Strasse and its continuation, Niedere Strasse, and east–west Bickenstrasse and its continuation, Rietstrasse. The Bahnhof and the regional bus station are just east of the ring on Bahnhofstrasse. Schwenningen's centre is about 5km east of Villingen's Altstadt.

Post office (Bahnhofstrasse 6, Villingen)

Schwenningen tourist office (in the Bahnhof; ☼ 9am-5pm Mon-Fri, 9am-noon Sat)

Villingen tourist office (☎ 822 340; www.tourismus -vs.de, www.villingen-schwenningen.de, in German; Rietgasse 2, ie Rietstrasse 35; ☼ 9am-5pm Mon-Sat, 11am-5pm Sat) In the Franziskaner Museum.

SIGHTS

The focal point of Villingen's Altstadt, still protected by ramparts and three towers, is the mostly Gothic **Münster** (Münsterplatz). Situated a block north of Rietstrasse, it has a striking pair of disparate spires, one overlaid with coloured tiles, the other thin and spiky. The west and south portals are Romanesque and both have modern bronze *haut-relief* doors showing dramatic Biblical scenes. Inside, the nave is baroque. Old-style buildings around **Münsterplatz** include the **Altes Rathaus** (old town hall).

The **Franziskaner Museum** (☎ 822 351; Rietgasse 2; adult/concession €3/2; ☼ 1-5pm Tue-Sat, 11am-5pm Sun & holidays), just inside the Riettor (a city gate), is housed in a former Franciscan monastery. The collections illuminate the town's art and culture through the centuries. Tickets to cultural events are sold at the desk next to the café. Enter via Rietstrasse 35.

Also run by the museum is **Magdalenenberg** (☎ 822 351; Rietgasse 2; adult/concession €3/2; ☼ 1-5pm Tue-Sat, 11am-5pm Sun & holidays), an *in situ* Celtic burial chamber in Villingen's southwestern outskirts, 30 minutes on foot from the centre.

Schwenningen's main draw is the extremely well-presented **Uhrenindustriemuseum** (Clock Industry Museum; ☎ 380 44; www.uhrenindustriemuseum .de; Bürkstrasse 39, Schwenningen; adult/concession €3/2; ☼ 10am-noon & 2-6pm Tue-Sun), situated in an old clock factory four blocks northwest of Schwenningen's Bahnhof.

At the eastern edge of Schwenningen, the **Internationales Luftfahrt-Museum** (☎ 663 02; Spittelbronner Weg 78, Schwenningen; ☼ 9am-7pm Mar-Oct, 9am-5pm Nov-Feb), at the airfield, displays 50 old aircraft ranging from biplanes to MiGs. It's served by buses 8 and 8a.

Villingen-Schwenningen is the southern terminus of the **Neckartal-Radweg** (see p392), one of Baden-Württemberg's premier bike trails.

SLEEPING & EATING

There are several food shops and inexpensive eateries along Niedere Strasse and Obere Strasse.

DJH hostel (☎ 541 49; www.jugendherberge.de; St-Georgener Strasse 36; dm 1st/subsequent night €18.30/15.10; ✗) This 128-bed hostel is at the northwestern edge of town. Take bus 3 or 4 to Triberger Strasse.

Hotel Bären (☎ 206 9690; www.hotel-baeren.biz; Bärengasse 2, Villingen; s/d from €52/80; P ✗) This friendly and central Villingen hotel, recently renovated, has 16 spacious rooms with high-quality modern furnishings.

Vitala (Obere Strasse 11; ☼ 9am-6.30pm Mon-Fri, 8am-2pm or 6pm Sat) is an organic grocery, and there's also a **Plus supermarket** (Obere Strasse 16) for picnic supplies.

GETTING THERE & AROUND

Villingen's Bahnhof is on the scenic Schwarzwaldbahn railway line from Konstanz and

Donaueschingen to Triberg (25 minutes) and Offenburg. Schwenningen's Bahnhof is on the secondary line to Rottweil, where you can change for Stuttgart. To get to Freiburg change in Donaueschingen.

From Villingen, bus 7265 makes regular trips north to Triberg via St Georgen.

Villingen-Schwenningen is just west of the Stuttgart–Singen A81 and is also crossed by the B33 to Triberg and the B27 to Rottweil.

Frequent buses (for example lines 1 and 1S) link Villingen with Schwenningen.

Bikes can be hired from **Hermann Fleig** (☎ 24 687; Rietgasse 5, Villingen), near the tourist office.

SOUTHEAST OF FREIBURG

Höllental

Jagged, near-vertical rock faces, alternating with tree-covered hillsides, dwarf everything beneath them along the wildly romantic Höllental (Hell's Valley). It begins about 15km east of Freiburg and stretches along (and above) the serpentine B31 and the tracks of the Höllentalbahn, which passes through nine tunnels on its way from Freiburg to Donaueschingen. The best way to experience the gorge is on foot – a trail goes all the way from Freiburg to Titisee.

Fans of wordplay will note that the Höllental's western gateway is the village of **Himmelreich** (Kingdom of Heaven), from where the valley continues east to Hinterzarten, 5km west of Titisee. Somewhere in the middle, not far from a death-defying hairpin curve, is a rest stop called **Teufelsschwänzli** ('devil's tail' in the local dialect).

At the **Hirschsprung** (Stag's Leap), the narrowest point of the valley, a male deer being pursued by hunters is said to have saved itself by leaping across the abyss. The stag there now – a statue – looks a bit hesitant, as if he's having second thoughts about trying anything fancy. The canyon is so deep here that the bottom is in deep shade until mid-morning – if you've recently been told to go somewhere 'where the sun don't shine', this might be a good choice.

Titisee-Neustadt

☎ 07651 / pop 12,000

Named for the glacial lake on the northern tip on which the town sits, Titisee is a cheerful and hugely popular resort with souvenir shops, cafés and restaurants lining its flowery waterfront promenade, the **Seestrasse**. The lake itself (2km long and 750m wide) is reasonably scenic and is perhaps best appreciated from the relative quiet of a rowing boat or pedal boat.

Heading off on foot is one way to escape the crowds. Walking all the way around the lake is an easy 6km trek. Scenic destinations include the 1192m **Hochfirst**, which overlooks Titisee from the east and is topped by an outlook tower.

The Titisee area is a popular centre for **Nordic walking**, which – for the uninitiated – is like cross-country skiing without the skis or the snow. In other words, it's walking with ski poles, whose sole purpose is to exercise the upper body.

The town bills itself as a *Bikerparadies* (that's a paradise for cyclists, not for the Hell's Angels) and indeed, paths and routes head – literally – in every direction.

The **tourist office** (☎ 980 40; www.titisee-neustadt.de; Strandbadstrasse 4; 🕑 9am-6pm Mon-Fri, 10am-1pm Sat, Sun & holidays May-Oct, 9am-noon & 1.30-5pm Mon-Fri Nov-Apr) is in the Kurhaus building, 500m southwest of the train station.

SLEEPING & EATING

Titisee-Neustadt and its surrounds have tonnes of hotels, *pensions* and camping grounds to choose from.

DJH hostel (☎ 238; www.jugendherberge-titisee-veltishof.de; Bruderhalde 27; dm 1st/subsequent night €18.30/15.10; ⊠) The fabulous Titisee-Veltishof hostel is at the lake's western tip, 2km southwest of the tourist office. To get there from the train station take bus 7300, or it's 30 minutes on foot.

Hotel Sonneneck (☎ 8246; fax 881 74; Parkstrasse 2; s/d €45/72, low season €39/64) A modest, family-run hotel that's just 250m from the train station and a three-minute walk from the beach. The 18 rooms have furniture made of local spruce.

Self-caterers should try **Gutscher** (cnr Strandbadstrasse & Seestrasse; 🕑 daily) for local food specialities including meats, cheeses, schnapps and bread loaves the size of car tires, or **Edeka supermarket** (Jägerstrasse).

GETTING THERE & AROUND

Rail routes include the Höllentalbahn to Freiburg and Donaueschingen (twice an hour; stops at both Titisee and Neustadt), the Dreiseenbahn to Feldberg and Schluchsee (hourly; stops at Titisee) and the Donautalbahn to Ulm (stops at Neustadt).

From both the Neustadt and Titisee train stations, bus 7257 goes to Schluchsee (three or four times a day). Bus 7300 links the Titisee train station with Feldberg-Bärental (15 minutes; at least seven Monday to Saturday, three on Sunday and holidays).

In its local version, bus 7257 connects Titisee with Neustadt every hour.

Bikes (and in winter, ski equipment) can be hired from **Ski-Hirt** (☎ 922 80; Titiseestrasse 26, Neustadt), which can also supply details on local cycling options.

Feldberg
☎ 07655 / pop 1800

At 1493m the Feldberg is the highest mountain in the Black Forest – no surprise, then, that it's the region's premier downhill skiing area. The actual mountaintop is treeless and not particularly attractive, looking very much like a monk's tonsured skull, but on clear days the view southward towards the Alps is stunning.

Feldberg is also the name given to a cluster of five villages, of which **Altglashütten**, a one-time glass-blowing centre, is the administrative centre. Its Rathaus plays host to the **tourist office** (☎ 8019; www.feldberg-gipfeltreffen.de, in German; Kirchgasse 1; ⏰ 8.30am-5.30pm Mon-Fri, also 10am-noon Sat in the warmer months, 10am-noon Sun Jul & Aug), which has a wealth of information about outdoor activities.

About 2km north is **Bärental**, site of Germany's highest train station (967m), where traditional Black Forest farmhouses snuggle against the hillsides. East of Bärental in the Haslach Valley is **Falkau**, a family-friendly resort with a cute waterfall. **Windgfällweiher**, a good lake for swimming or rowing, is 1km southeast of Altglashütten.

About 9km west of Altglashütten is **Feldberg-Ort**, right in the heart of the 42-sq-km nature preserve that covers much of the mountain. Almost all the ski lifts are here, as is the popular **Feldbergbahn chairlift** (one-way/return €5.40/6.90) to the **Bismarckdenkmal** (Bismarck monument), where there are wonderful panoramic views. The **tourist office** (☎ 07676-933 666) is in the **Haus der Natur**, where you'll find exhibits on local flora and fauna.

ACTIVITIES
The Feldberg area is great for **hiking**. The most strenuous route takes you to the top of the Feldberg. The **Westweg** trail, which links Pforzheim with Basel, crosses the area. Since much of the Feldberg is part of a nature preserve, you may very well come across rare wildflowers or animal species such as mountain hens and chamois.

The **Feldberg ski area** (adult/child under 15yr per day €23/12, from 1pm €16/8) has a network of 28 lifts, all accessible with the same ticket. Four groomed cross-country trails are also available. For the latest snow conditions, ring ☎ 07676-1214. Eight ski schools offer a variety of packages. If you want to hire skis, look for signs reading 'Skiverleih' – one reliable option is **Skiverleih Schubnell** (☎ 560; www.skiverleih-feldberg.de, in German; Bärentaler Strasse 1, Altglashütten).

SLEEPING
DJH hostel (☎ 07676-221; www.jugendherberge.de; Passhöhe 14; dm 1st/subsequent night €19.70/16.50; ✗) The 267-bed Hebelhof Hostel, perched at 1234m in Feldberg-Ort, is served by bus 7300 from the Bärental train station to Hebelhof (15 minutes, hourly).

Sonneck Hotel (☎ 211; www.sonneck-feldberg.de; Schwarzenbachweg 5, Altglashütten; s/d from €30/58) Facing the tourist office, this modest place has 11 modern rooms with chalet-style wooden balconies and a rustic restaurant.

GETTING THERE & AWAY
Bärental and Altglashütten are stops on the Dreiseenbahn (named for three lakes), which links Titisee with Seebrugg (on the Schluchsee). From the train station in Bärental, bus 7300 makes direct trips at least hourly to Feldberg-Ort.

From late December until the end of the season shuttle buses, run by Liftverbund Feldberg (look for red-on-yellow signs), link all the Feldberg communities and Titisee and with the ski lifts (free with a lift ticket or Gästekarte).

If you're driving, take the B31 (Freiburg–Donaueschingen) to Titisee, then the B317. To get to Altglashütten, head down the B500 from Bärental.

Schluchsee
☎ 07656 / pop 2600

The town of Schluchsee (930m), named after the nearby lake, is about 10km south of Titisee. Less commercial than its bigger neighbour, it's also a popular summer holiday-resort area and a centre for outdoor activities of all kinds, especially swimming, windsurfing, sailing and scuba diving. Thanks to its location at the foot of the Feldberg, the forests around Schluchsee offer some wonderful hiking.

Bathing options include **Aqua Fun Strandbad** (☎ 7732; Strandbadstrasse; adult/student €3.80/2.20; 🕑 9am-7pm late May–mid-Sep), a seaside swimming-pool complex with lots of grass and a narrow sandy beach.

T Toth (☎ 9230; www.seerundfahrten.de, in German) offers a boat service around the Schluchsee, with stops in Aha, at the dam (Staumauer), in Seebrugg and in Schluchsee town (hourly from 10am or 11am to 5pm May to late October). You can get on and off as you please; the whole round trip takes one hour and costs €6 (less for single stops).

ORIENTATION & INFORMATION

The railway tracks and the B500 run along the lake's eastern shore between the lakefront and the Schluchsee's hillside town centre. The community of Aha caps the northwestern end of the lake; Seebrugg is at the lake's southeastern tip. The western shore of the lake is accessible only by bike or on foot (the lake's circumference is 18.5km).

ATMs At Kirchplatz and on nearby Fischbacherstrass.

Tourist office (☎ 7732; www.schluchsee.de; Haus des Gastes, Fischbacher Strasse 7; 🕑 8am-6pm Mon-Thu, 9am-6pm Fri, also 10am-noon Sat Jul, 10am-noon Sat & Sun Aug & holiday weekends) Situated 150m uphill from the church, next to the Rathaus. Maps and room availability details are posted out front.

SLEEPING & EATING

DJH hostel (☎ 329; www.jugendherberge-schluchsee -wolfsgrund.de; Im Wolfgrund 28; dm 1st/subsequent night €18.30/15.10; 🗙) On a peninsula jutting into the lake, this 117-bed hostel is about a 10-minute walk west along the lakefront from the Schluchsee train station.

Hotel Schiff (☎ 975 70; www.hotel-schiff-schluchsee.de; Kirchplatz 7; s from €35, d €54-104; mains €9.60-22.50; ℗ 🗙) Next to the church. The 27 rooms here are cosy but a bit out of date. The restaurant serves local, Austrian and vegetarian dishes; the best seats are on the terrace overlooking the lake.

Hotel Sternen (☎ 251; Dresselbacher Strasse 1; s/d from €40/72) The hall wallpaper is a crime against good taste but the 34 rooms are spacious. The restaurant serves solid regional fare (mains €12 to €20.50; closed Thursday); specialities include venison (in season) and Black Forest fish. The rustic Rumpelfass bar (open 8pm to 3am) dispenses good beer and cheer.

There's a supermarket, **Isele Markt** (Kirchplatz 2; 🕑 8am-12.30pm & 2.30-6.30pm Mon-Fri, 8am-1pm Sat), across the square from the church.

GETTING THERE & AROUND

The hourly Dreiseenbahn train goes to Feldberg and Titisee. Bus 7257 links Schluchsee with the Neustadt and Titisee train stations (three or four times a day).

Hotel Schiff hires out **bicycles** (per day €7.70) year-round. The tourist office sells a good cycling map (€3.10).

St Blasien

☎ 07672 / pop 4100

St Blasien, a bucolic but substantial settlement in a lush river valley about 8km south of Schluchsee town, has long been a political and cultural heavyweight thanks to its Benedictine monastery, founded in the 9th century. This august institution reached its zenith in the 18th century under the prince-abbot Martin Gerbert, who built the town's most outstanding landmark, the magnificent Dom. The monastery was turned into a boarding school by the Jesuits in 1933, and today **Kolleg St Blasien** ranks as one of Germany's top *Gymnasiums* (private schools), perhaps because parents feel that high school kids couldn't possibly get into too much trouble in such a remote, healthy little town – yeah, right!

Thanks to its healthy, fogless climate, St Blasien has been a popular spa resort since the late 19th century and today its radon-laced waters continue to attract visitors who come to take the waters. **Menzenschwand**, about 8km northwest of St Blasien, has three ski lifts.

St Blasien's public spaces are adorned with lots of **modern wood sculptures**, a legacy of the town's annual *Holzskulpturen* (wood sculpture) competition, established in 1995.

ORIENTATION & INFORMATION

St Blasien's small centre, bisected by the Alb River, is dominated by the Dom and the adjacent former monastery complex.

The **tourist office** (☎ 414 30; www.st-blasien.de; Haus des Gastes, Am Kurgarten 1-3; 🕑 10am-noon & 3-5pm Mon-Fri, also 10am-noon Sat May-Sep) is between the arch at the entrance to the town centre and the Dom.

SIGHTS

Crowned by an enormous greenish-copper cupola, **Dom St Blasien** (🕑 8am-6.30pm May-Sep,

BADEN-WÜRTTEMBERG

8.30am-5.30pm Oct-Apr) has a light-flooded rotunda of dazzling symmetry, harmony and whiteness. A giant sphere 36m in diameter would fit neatly under the cupola, whose interior is as high as it is wide (as measured just above the 20 Corinthian columns). The rectangular choir, adorned with some very convincing fake marble (in fact expertly painted stucco), is the same length as the cupola's diameter. The patterns in the marble floor mirror the cupola's interior features, including its 18 windows. In July and August, the Dom hosts free concerts of Western classical music.

The adjacent former **Kloster** (monastery), now home to the town's famous boarding school, is of equally generous proportions, measuring 105m by 195m. Free guided tours (in German) of the Kloster's historic baroque rooms are held at 10.15am on Tuesday, except during school holiday periods. The best views of the Dom are from across the river.

Museum St Blasien (adult/student €1.60/0.50; ⏲ 2.30-5pm Tue-Sun), above the tourist office, takes a charmingly eclectic look at local history and culture, and includes scale models of locally-made Schmidt snow-clearing equipment.

SLEEPING & EATING
St Blasien and its affiliated towns, Menzenschwand and Albtal, have a wide variety of accommodation options.

DJH hostel (☎ 07675-326; www.jugendherberge-menzenschwand.de; Vorderdorfstrasse 10, Menzenschwand; dm 1st/subsequent night €18.30/15.10; ✗) A 104-bed hostel ensconced in a gorgeous Black Forest–style, all-wood farmhouse.

Hotel Klostermeisterhaus (☎ 848; www.kloster meisterhaus.de, in German; Im Süssen Winkel 2; s/d €65/95; ✗) Smack in the centre of town, this riverside place – built in 1826 – has eight spacious rooms with wicker and bare wood furnishings. The cosy, wood-panelled restaurant serves excellent cuisine made with all-fresh ingredients (mains €9.50 to €25.50); the delightful terrace affords great Dom views.

Lidl supermarket (Friedhofstrasse; ⏲ 8am-8pm Mon-Sat) From the tourist office, go through the arch and then another 200m.

GETTING THERE & AROUND
St Blasien is linked to the train station in Seebrugg, on the Schluchsee, by bus 7319 (20 minutes, hourly). Bus 7321 shuttles between St Blasien and Menzenschwand (almost hourly). If you need a taxi, ring ☎ 907 090.

Bikes (and ski equipment too) can be rented from **Sport Gfrörer** (☎ 07675-923 810; Hinterdorfstrasse 8, Menzenschwand).

St Blasien is about 4km west of the B500.

Wutachschlucht
Wutach Gorge, sometimes billed as the 'Grand Canyon of the Black Forest', is a lovely ravine whose craggy rocks rise almost vertically. Below, along the **Wutach** ('angry river' in loose translation), which rises almost at the summit of the Feldberg, lies a fertile habitat harbouring a huge variety of wildflowers, including orchids, as well as rare birds and countless species of butterflies, beetles and lizards. The Wutach flows into the Rhine near Waldshut, on the Swiss frontier.

To appreciate the Wutachschlucht in all its splendour, you can take a 13km hike from **Schattenmühle** to **Wutachmühle** (or vice versa). If you have the energy, you can add the romantic, 2.5km-long **Lotenbach-Klamm** (Lotenbach Glen) to your tour.

In Bonndorf, 15km east of Schluchsee town, the **tourist office** (☎ 07703-7607; www.bonndorf .de, in German; Schlossstrasse 1; ⏲ 9am-noon & 2-6pm Mon-Fri, 10am-noon Sat May-Oct, 9am-noon & 2-5pm Mon-Fri except Wed afternoon Nov-Apr) has hiking information and maps.

To get to Bonndorf from the train station in Neustadt, take bus 7258 (40 minutes, hourly Monday to Saturday, every two hours Sunday and holidays). To get to Schattenmühle or Wutachmühle, take bus 7344 from Bonndorf (runs every hour or two Monday to Friday when school is in session but may stop at Schattenmühle and Wutachmühle only a few times a day).

LAKE CONSTANCE

The watery expanses of Lake Constance (Bodensee), framed – if you're on the German shore – by a row of breathtaking snow-capped Swiss peaks, is the perfect tonic if you're feeling a bit landlocked. Sometimes called the 'Swabian Sea', this giant bulge in the sinewy course of the Rhine offers a choice of relaxation, cultural pursuits, hiking, cycling and water sports.

Lake Constance has a circumference of some 273km, of which the southern 72km belong to Switzerland, the eastern 28km to Austria and the remaining northern and western

173km to Germany (including a little strip in Bavaria). It measures 14km at its widest point and is up to 250m deep. The distance from Konstanz to Bregenz (Austria) is 46km. During stormy weather, Lake Constance can get quite dangerous, with huge waves crashing onto the shoreline. Visibility is especially good when the Föhn – a warm dry wind that's common in March, April and October – is blowing northward from the Alps.

April and May are among the best times to visit Lake Constance because that's when the fruit trees are flowering. Summers are humid but at least the lake is warm enough for swimming (around 20° to 23°C). The autumn wine harvest is also a pleasant time to come. Winters are often foggy, or misty at best. The area gets extremely crowded in July and August, when it may be hard to find a room for the night and the roads are constantly choked.

Cycling

An international bike track, the 268km **Bodensee-Radweg** (www.bodensee-radweg.com, in German), circumnavigates Lake Constance, tracing the shoreline between vineyards and beaches. The route is well signposted but RegioCart's 1:50,000 *Rund um den Bodensee* cycling-hiking map is useful, and is available in bookshops and some tourist offices. In general, bikes can be taken on both ferries and trains, making it possible to cycle one way and take public transport the other.

Getting There & Around

Ryanair flies from London Stansted and Dublin to **Friedrichshafen** (www.fly-away.de).

By far the most enjoyable way to get around, or to cross the lake for a quick peak at Switzerland, is by ferry. Konstanz is the main hub; Meersburg and Friedrichshafen also have a good variety of ferry options.

The public transport system is well-organised and is a good alternative to driving. Although most of the towns on Lake Constance have a train station (Meersburg is an exception), in some cases buses provide the only land connections. **Euregio Bodensee** (www.euregiokarte.com, in German), which groups all Lake Constance–area public transport providers, publishes a free *Fahrplan* book with schedules for all train, bus and ferry services in tiny type.

The **Euregio Bodensee Tageskarte** (1 land zone plus lake €24, all 7 zones plus lake €27, half-price for children

6-15yr) gets you all-day access to all land and sea transport on and around Lake Constance, including areas deep in Austria, Switzerland and even Liechtenstein. It is sold at tourist offices, train stations and ferry docks.

PASSENGER FERRIES

The **Weisse Flotte** (☎ 281 389), a grouping of six German, Swiss and Austrian companies with a total of 31 passenger ferries and three car ferries, runs a variety of ferry lines that hop from town to town along the Lake Constance coastline, and link towns on opposite shores. Holders of rail passes get a 50% discount on certain services.

The most useful line, run by **BSB** (☎ 07531-364 0389; www.bsb-online.com, in German) and **OBB** (www.bodenseeschifffahrt.at in German) – the former is German, the latter Austrian – links Konstanz with ports such as Meersburg (€4.20, 30 minutes), Friedrichshafen (€8.80, 2¾ hours), Lindau (€11.20, three hours) and Bregenz (€12, 3½ hours); children age six to 15 pay half price. There are seven daily runs from early July to early September, five from late May to early July and early September to early October, and three from early April to late May, making it possible to visit several places in a single day.

Other ferry runs, mostly operated by BSB, link Konstanz with Reichenau Island, and both Konstanz and Meersburg with Mainau Island and Überlingen.

Der Katamaran (☎ 07541-971 0900; www.der-katamaran.de; adult/child 6-14yr & dogs €8.50/4.30) is a sleek new passenger service that takes 50 minutes to make the Konstanz–Friedrichshafen crossing (hourly from 5am or 6am to 8pm or 9pm).

CAR FERRIES

The roll-on roll-off **Konstanz–Meersburg car ferry** (☎ 07531-8030; www.sw.konstanz.de; car up to 4m incl driver/bicycle/pedestrian €7.20/1.50/2) runs 24 hours a day (except when the lake's water level is especially high, in which case it can't dock properly). The frequency is every 15 minutes from 5.30am or 6am to 9pm, every 30 minutes from 9pm to midnight and every hour from midnight to 5.30am or 6am. The new **Mini-Maxi Ticket** (one-way/return €3.60/7.20) gets pedestrians a ferry ride plus bus transport on either end (to and from the centres of Meersburg and Konstanz). The crossing, which affords superb views (especially from the top deck), takes 15 minutes.

The dock in Konstanz, served by local bus 1, is about 4km northeast of the city centre along Mainaustrasse. In Meersburg, car ferries leave from a dock 400m northwest of the old town.

KONSTANZ

☎ 07531 / pop 81,000

Konstanz (Constance), right on the Swiss border, is the cultural and economic centre of the Bodensee. Its picturesque Altstadt has never suffered fire or war damage, making it a rarity among Germany's oft-ravaged cities. During WWII it was too close to neutral Switzerland to be bombed by the Allies.

Konstanz was settled by the Romans and played a leading role in the area during the Middle Ages, when it was a Free Imperial City and grew rich from trade. The town reached its historical apex when the Council of Constance convened here from 1414 to 1418, choosing a single pope (replacing three others) and healing the 'Great Schism' in the Catholic Church.

Today, Konstanz is a liberal university town with little industry, though its shops attract hordes of Swiss shoppers drawn by 'bargain' German prices. About one in seven inhabitants – affectionately known as *Seehas* (sea hares) – is a student at the local university, founded in 1966. The student presence is palpable in the lively pub and restaurant scene, unique in the otherwise rather staid Lake Constance region.

Orientation

Konstanz is bisected by the Rhine, from the left (south) bank of which the Altstadt stretches southward. The imposing imperial-style Deutscher Bahnhof (German train station) and the ugly Schweizer Bahnhof (Swiss train station) – little more than a shed – are adjacent to each other on Bahnhofplatz, at the eastern edge of the Altstadt across the tracks from the harbour. Delineating the southern edge of the Altstadt is Bodanstrasse; a few blocks farther south is the Swiss frontier, complete with the kind of border crossings with uniformed guards that have almost disappeared elsewhere in Europe.

Information

Clixworx (Bodanstrasse 21; per 15min €1; ⏰ 10am-7pm Mon-Fri, 10am-4pm Sat) Internet access.

English Bookshop (☎ 150 63; Münzgasse 10) Stocks a good selection.

BODENSEE ERLEBNISKARTE

The three-day **Bodensee Erlebniskarte** (adult/child 6-15yr €69/35, not incl ferries €39/19), available at area tourist and ferry offices from early April to October, allows free travel on almost all boats and mountain cableways on and around Lake Constance (including its Austrian and Swiss shores) and gets you free entry to around 170 tourist attractions and museums. There are also seven-day (adult/child €89/45) and 14-day (adult/child €119/59) versions.

Reisebank (Hauptbahnhof; ⏰ 8am-12.30pm & 1.30-6pm Mon-Fri, 8am-3pm Sat) Currency exchange, including Swiss francs.

Schweizer Bahnhof (Swiss train station; ⏰ 6.50am-7pm Mon-Sat, 8.50am-12.10pm & 1.40-6pm Sun & holidays) The ticket counter changes currency at good rates.

Tel Center (per hr €4.20) Bahnhofplatz 6 (⏰ 9am-10pm); Marktstätte 30 (⏰ 9am-10pm Mon-Sat, noon-10pm Sun) Internet access.

Tourist office (☎ 133 030; www.konstanz.de/tour ismus; Bahnhofplatz 13; ⏰ 9am-6.30pm Mon-Fri, 9am-4pm Sat & 10am-1pm Sun & holidays Apr-Oct, 9am-12.30pm & 2-6pm Mon-Fri Nov-Mar) Just north of the train stations. Inside you can pick up a walking-tour brochure (€1), outside there's a hotel reservation board and free hotel telephone.

Waschsalon und Mehr (Hofhalde 3; ⏰ 10am-7pm Mon-Fri, 10am-4pm Sat) A self- or full-service laundry.

Sights

WATERFRONT

Konstanz' delightful **seafront promenade**, between the train tracks and the lake, is lined with gardens, statues, ferry docks and old warehouses, some housing restaurants. It's linked to the Altstadt by a passageway under the train tracks at the eastern end of Marktstätte.

Just past the passageway, the white dormered **Konzilgebäude** (Council Building), built in 1388, served as a granary and warehouse before making its mark in history as the place where Pope Martin V was elected in 1417. Today it's a conference and concert hall.

At the end of the pier facing the Konzilgebäude – welcoming incoming ferry passengers on a perpetually turning pedestal – stands **Imperia**, a 9m-high sculpture of a very voluptuous woman, a prostitute who is said to have plied her trade in the days of the Council of

Constance; she was immortalised in a novel by Honoré de Balzac.

A few steps from here is the **Zeppelin Monument**, honouring the airship inventor Count Ferdinand von Zeppelin. He was born in 1838 on the **Insel**, a tiny island a short stroll north through the **Stadtgarten** park. The Stadtgarten has a **children's playground**.

Practically across the street from the Insel is the **Stadttheater** (Inselgasse 2), whose façade sports a comical scene depicting the Fool's banishment from the theatre.

Just north of the Insel, the **Rheinbrücke** links the Altstadt with newer quarters across the Rhine. On the opposite bank, Seestrasse has a row of handsome **Art Nouveau villas** just east of the bridge. Further east, at No 21, is the **Casino**.

MÜNSTER

At the Altstadt's highest point stands the **Münster** (9am-6pm Mon-Sat, 10am-6pm Sun). The crypt, built in 1000, is Carolingian, but the core of today's structure is Romanesque. Between the 12th and 15th centuries, the Gothic vaulted side aisles were added, as was the masterfully carved oak main portal and the choir stalls. The Renaissance brought the organ, perched on an elaborate stone balcony above the west entrance; the high altar dates from the baroque era. The neo-Gothic spires were added in the 19th century. Made of soft sandstone from the nearby Swiss town of Rorschach, the Münster has not been without scaffolding since 1961 and is likely to be under repair forever.

The **Schnegg** (literally 'snail'; 1438), in the northern transept, is a vividly decorated spiral staircase, to the left of which a door leads down to the **crypt**, adorned with gilded copper medallions. From the crypt's polychrome chapel, a door leads to the Gothic cloister and, in one corner, the **Mauritius Rotunda**, with its 13th-century **Heiliges Grab** (Holy Sepulchre), inspired by Christ's tomb in Jerusalem.

You can climb the recently restored **tower** (adult/child €2/1; 10am-5pm Mon-Sat, noon or 12.30-5pm Sun & church holidays).

NIEDERBURG

Stretching north from the Münster to the Rhine, the Niederburg is Konstanz' oldest quarter. The site of a Roman settlement, it later housed craftspeople and small merchants. An almost medieval atmosphere still permeates this maze of alleyways (such as Niederburg-

gasse), which are lined with centuries-old houses. Some contain lovely antiques shops, snug wine bars and lively restaurants.

Kloster Zoffingen (Brückengasse 15), founded in 1257, is the only convent left in Konstanz. It is still in the hands of Dominican nuns, whose predecessors founded the city's first girls' school in 1775.

On the Rheinsteig, which runs along the Rhine west of the bridge, stands the 15th-century **Rheintorturm** (Rhine Gate Tower), a defensive tower with a wooden upper section and a pyramid-shaped red-tile roof. About 200m to the west, also on the river bank, is the squatter **Pulverturm** (Gunpowder Tower; 1321), with 2m-thick walls.

Almost across the street is the bright orange-red **Domprobstei** (Rheingasse 20), a baroque structure that was built in 1609 and was once the residence of the cathedral provosts.

MUSEUMS

The former guildhall of the town's butchers is now occupied by the **Rosgartenmuseum** (900 246; www.rosgartenmuseum-konstanz.de in German; Rosgartenstrasse 3-5; adult/student €3/1.50, free 1st Sun of the month & after 2pm Wed; 10am-6pm Tue-Fri, 10am-5pm Sat, Sun & holidays), founded in 1871 and dedicated to regional art and history.

The **Archäologisches Landesmuseum** (Archaeological State Museum; 980 40; www.konstanz.alm-bw.de, in German; Benediktinerplatz 5; adult/concession €3/2, free 1st Sat of month; 10am-6pm Tue-Sun), located inside a former monastery just north of the Rheinbrücke, has three floors of exhibits that go from the Stone Age through the Middle Ages.

Sea Life (128 270; www.sealifeeurope.com; Hafenstrasse 9; adult/child €11.75/8.50; 10am-7pm Jul–mid-Sep, 10am-6pm May, Jun & mid-Sep–Oct, 10am-5pm Mon-Fri, 10am-6pm Sat & Sun Nov-Apr) is a privately run aquarium. Ecologically educational but verging on the kitsch, it runs a drag net through your wallet but presents a realistic portrait of the underwater life of the Rhine, which means that the fish are mostly grey and silver and there's lots of 'authentic' human detritus decorating the aquariums. Greenpeace has a permanent exhibition space.

Sleeping

There are several so-so hotels west of the train stations along Bodanstrasse.

Campingplatz Bruderhofer (31 388; www.campingplatz-konstanz.de; Fohrenbühlweg 45; adult/car/tent €3.50/2.60/3.10) This modern camping ground,

BADEN-WÜRTTEMBERG

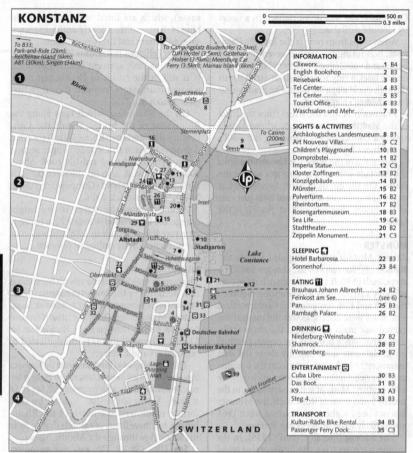

KONSTANZ

0 ——————— 500 m
0 ——————— 0.3 miles

To B33;
Park-and-Ride (2km);
Reichenau-Island (6km);
A81 (30km); Singen (34km)

Reichenaustr

To Campingplatz Bruderhofer (2.5km);
DJH Hostel (3.5km); Gästehaus
Holzer (3.5km); Meersburg Car
Ferry (3.5km); Mainau Island (6km)

INFORMATION
Clixworx...........................1 B4
English Bookshop..............2 B3
Reisebank.........................3 B3
Tel Center.........................4 B3
Tel Center.........................5 B3
Tourist Office....................6 B3
Waschsalon und Mehr.......7 B3

SIGHTS & ACTIVITIES
Archäologisches Landesmuseum..8 B1
Art Nouveau Villas............9 C2
Children's Playground.......10 B3
Domprobstei.....................11 B2
Imperia Statue...................12 C3
Kloster Zoffingen..............13 B2
Konzilgebäude...................14 B3
Münster............................15 B2
Pulverturm.......................16 B2
Rheintorturm....................17 B2
Rosengartenmuseum.........18 B3
Sea Life............................19 C4
Stadttheater......................20 B2
Zeppelin Monument..........21 C3

SLEEPING
Hotel Barbarossa...............22 B3
Sonnenhof.........................23 B4

EATING
Brauhaus Johann Albrecht..24 B2
Feinkost am See.............(see 6)
Pan...................................25 B3
Rambagh Palace................26 B2

DRINKING
Niederburg-Weinstube........27 B3
Shamrock..........................28 B3
Wessenberg........................29 B2

ENTERTAINMENT
Cuba Libre.........................30 B3
Das Boot...........................31 B3
K9....................................32 A3
Steg 4...............................33 B3

TRANSPORT
Kultur-Rädle Bike Rental....34 B3
Passenger Ferry Dock.........35 C3

Rhein

Benediktiner-
platz

Sternenplatz

To Casino
(200m)

Seestr

Niederburg

Konradigasse

Rheinsteig

Inselgasse

Untere Laube

Münsterplatz

Torgasse

Altstadt

Hofhalde

Stadtgarten

Hohenhausgasse

Salmannsweiler Gasse

Obermarkt

Münzgasse

Kanzleistr

Markstätte

Obere Augustinergasse

Bahnhofpl

Deutscher Bahnhof

Bodanstr

Schweizer Bahnhof

Kreuzlinger Str

Otto-Raggenbass-Str

Hafenstr

Wiesenstr

Lago
Shopping
Mall

Lake
Constance

Swiss Frontier

SWITZERLAND

Konstanzer Str

---

in Konstanz' northeastern suburb of Staad, is
3km northeast of the Altstadt and 800m south
of the Meersburg car-ferry dock.

DJH hostel (☎ 322 60; www.jugendherberge-konstanz
.de; Zur Allmannshöhe 18; dm 1st/subsequent night
€20.80/17.60; ✗) This newly renovated, 178-
bed hostel, in a white cylindrical one-time
water tower, is in Allmannsdorf, 4km northeast of the Altstadt and 1.2km northwest of
the Meersburg car-ferry dock. It's served
by bus 4 (to Jugendherberge) and bus 1 (to
Allmannsdorf).

Gästehaus Holzer (☎ 315 46; www.gaestehaus-holzer
.de, in German; Fischerstrasse 6; s/d from €43/78; ✗) This
13-room pension, near the Meersburg car-
ferry landing, has simple but well-outfitted
rooms. It's served by bus 1.

Sonnenhof (☎ 222 57; www.hotel-sonnenhof-konstanz
.de, in German; Otto-Raggenbass-Strasse 3; s/d €53/78, s with
shower €44) This comfortable family-run guesthouse is on a quiet residential street midway
between Bodanstrasse and the Swiss border.

Hotel Barbarossa (☎ 128 990; www.barbarossa
-hotel.com, in German; Obermarkt 8-12; s €50-68, d €95-
125; P ✗) Beautifully located on a central
square, this place has 55 rooms that mix class
with whimsy. Some of the bathrooms are a
tight fit.

Eating & Drinking

There are quite a few places to eat and drink
in the pedestrians-only area south of the Münster, such as along narrow Salmannsweiler
Gasse.

Pan (☎ 254 78; cnr Salmannsweiler & Hohenhausgasse; mains €6.50-14.50; ✆ noon-2.30pm & 5.30pm-midnight Mon-Fri, noon-midnight Sat, 5.30pm-midnight Sun, noon-midnight Mon-Fri Jun–mid-Sep) This place looks like a beer hall but the good-value menu is decidedly Greek. It's deservedly popular.

Brauhaus Johann Albrecht (☎ 250 45; Konradigasse 2; mains €7.50-13.50) A rambling beer hall with a rustic menu featuring daily specials. The food here offers good value and the beer, brewed on the premises in copper vats, gets excellent reviews.

Rambagh Palace (☎ 254 58; Brückengasse 1, 1st fl; veggie/meat mains €8/13; ✆ noon-2pm & 6-11pm Tue-Sun; ✗) Exotic spices tickle the nostrils at this colourful north Indian place, named after a palace in Jaipur.

Niederburg-Weinstube (☎ 213 67; Niederburggasse 7; ✆ 5pm-midnight except Sun & holidays, also open 10am-2pm Wed) This rustic, hole-in-the-wall wine tavern has 400 regional wines on offer.

Wessenberg (☎ 919 664; Wessenbergstrasse 41; ✆ 9am-1am Mon-Thu, 9am-2am Fri, 9am-3am Sat, 10am-1am Sun) This chichi bar, decked out with modern art, attracts an 'in' crowd with its sleek bar, spacious inner courtyard and good food – its specialities include ravioli (€9) and tiramisù (€5).

Shamrock (☎ 246 22; Bahnhofstrasse 4; ✆ 7pm-1am Sun-Fri, 2pm-3am Sat) An Irish pub that's very popular with English speakers and serves as a sort of home base for the local rugby team. On Monday there's bingo and student discounts on food and beer, Tuesday is quiz night and on Thursday there's karaoke.

Feinkost am See (Bahnhofplatz 25; ✆ 7am-6pm) This little grocery is right next door to the tourist office.

Entertainment

For details on the local nightlife scene see www.party-news.de (in German).

K9 (☎ 167 13; www.k9-kulturzentrum.de, in German; Obere Laube 71) A happening cultural-events venue with concerts of every imaginable sort, from klezmer to traditional Mongolian, as well as disco nights and salsa parties.

Cuba Libre (☎ 567 03; www.cuba-libre-kn.de, in German; Hussenstrasse 4; ✆ from 9pm Wed-Sun) A popular salsa club and cocktail bar that sometimes has concerts.

Steg 4 (☎ 174 28; Hafenstrasse 8; ✆ closed Jan) This restaurant, in a revamped warehouse facing the ferry harbour, becomes a disco on Friday and Saturday nights.

Das Boot (☎ 0172-724 2031; www.dasboot.de, in German; Am Hafen) A docked BSB ferry transmogrifies into a disco on many Saturday and some Friday nights from 11pm to 4am.

Getting There & Away

Konstanz is Lake Constance's main ferry hub – for details on ferry options see p453.

By car, Konstanz can be reached via the B33, which links up with the A81 to and from Stuttgart near Singen. To get to Konstanz you can also take the B31 to Meersburg and then catch a car ferry.

Konstanz' Hauptbahnhof is the southern terminus of the scenic Schwarzwaldbahn, which travels hourly through the Black Forest, linking Offenburg with towns such as Triberg and Villingen. To get to towns on the northern shore of Lake Constance by rail, you generally have to change in Radolfzell. The Schweizer Bahnhof (Swiss train station) offers connections to destinations all over Switzerland.

Getting Around

The city centre is a traffic nightmare, especially on Saturday and Sunday. Your best bet may be to park in the free Park & Ride lot 3km northwest of the Altstadt, near the Flugplatz (airfield) at the northwestern end of Max-Stromeyer-Strasse, where your only outlay will be for a bus day pass.

Local buses (www.sw.konstanz.de) cost €1.80 for a single ticket (€3 for night buses); day passes are €3.50 for one person and €5.80 for a family. Bus 1 links the Meersburg car-ferry dock with the Altstadt. If you stay in Konstanz for at least two nights, your hotelier will give you a Gästekarte entitling you to free local bus travel.

For a taxi, ring ☎ 222 22.

Bicycles can be hired from **Kultur-Rädle** (☎ 273 10; Bahnhofplatz 29; per day €10; ✆ 9am-12.30pm & 2.30-6pm Mon-Fri, 10am-4pm Sat year-round, also 10am-12.30pm Sun & holidays Easter-Sep), 50m south of the tourist office.

AROUND KONSTANZ
Mainau Island

Perennially one of the most popular attractions in the Lake Constance region, delightful **Mainau** (☎ 07531-3030; www.mainau.de; adult/child 6-15yr/student/family €11.90/3.90/5.90/23.90, winter adult/child 6-15yr/student €6/free/3; ✆ 7am-8pm late Mar-late Oct, 9am-6pm late Nov -late Mar) has been transformed into a vast Mediterranean garden complex by the Bernadotte family, who are related to the royal house of Sweden.

More than two million visitors a year make their way over a narrow causeway to stroll around 45 hectares of splendid gardens, hothouses and fountains, visit the baroque church and castle, and attend special events and concerts. Highlights include the **Butterfly House**, where butterflies flit and dart around your head; a **petting zoo**; and the **Italian Cascade**, which integrates bursting patterns of flowers with waterfalls. In the warm season you can stay on the island straight through till dusk.

To get to Mainau, you can drive (the causeway is about 6km north of Konstanz), take bus 4 from Konstanz' train station or, in the warm season, hop aboard a passenger ferry on the line linking Meersburg and Konstanz with Überlingen.

Reichenau Island
☎ 07534 / pop 5100

In AD 724 a hard-working missionary named Pirmin founded a Benedictine monastery on **Reichenau**, (www.reichenau.de), a 4.5km-by-1.5km island (Lake Constance's largest) located in the Untersee about 10km west of Konstanz. During its heyday, from around 820 to 1050, it had one of the largest libraries anywhere. The so-called Reichenauer School produced stunning illuminated manuscripts and vivid frescoes.

Today, three surviving churches provide silent testimony to the Golden Age of Reichenau, and it is thanks to them that the island was declared a Unesco World Heritage Site in 2000. About two-thirds of the island is taken up by vegetable cultivation.

A 2km-long tree-lined causeway connects the mainland with the island, which is served by bus 7372 from Konstanz (most runs begin at Wollmatingen-Urisberg). The Konstanz–Schaffhausen and Konstanz–Radolfzell ferries stop off at Reichenau.

MEERSBURG
☎ 07532 / pop 5500

Meersburg is a postcard-perfect romantic village, scenically perched on a rocky outcrop overlooking Lake Constance and surrounded by vineyards and orchards. Its historic **Oberstadt** (Upper Town) has a labyrinth of narrow, pedestrian-only lanes that are lined with half-timbered houses and stately baroque

buildings; some have their construction dates carved into their lintels. Two castles lord over the bustling **Unterstadt** (Lower Town) and its seafront promenade, where the touristic overload is even more pronounced than up top.

Orientation & Information

Walking downhill from the church, across the street from the tourist office, will take you to the Marktplatz, the heart of the Oberstadt. Go through the Rathaus arch and you're at the castles. Steigstrasse will take you down to the Unterstadt and the harbour.

Post office (Am Bleicheplatz) Across the intersection from the church.

Schickeria (☎ 6887; Stettener Strasse 3; per hr €4; ☼ noon–midnight) Internet access.

Tourist office (☎ 431 110; Kirchstrasse 4; www .meersburg.de; ☼ 9am–12.30pm & 2–6pm Mon–Fri, 10am–1pm Sat May–Sep, 9am–noon & 2–4.30pm Mon–Fri Oct–Apr) Housed in a one-time Dominican monastery. Internet access costs €3 per hour.

Sights
ALTES SCHLOSS

Overlooking Lake Constance from its lofty Oberstadt perch, the **Altes Schloss** (Burg; ☎ 800 00; adult/child 6–13yr/youth 14–18yr/student €8/5/6/6.80, without tour €6/3/4/5.10; ☼ 9am–6.30pm Mar–Oct, 10am–6pm Nov–Feb) is a quintessential medieval castle, complete with defensive walkways, a knights' hall, moats, dungeons and a pretty grim vibe. Its origins supposedly go back to the 7th-century Merovingian king Dagobert I, after whom the massive central keep is named (the oldest extant sections date from the 1200s). Between 1268 and 1803, the bishops of Konstanz used the castle as a summer residence.

Purchased in 1838 by Baron Joseph von Lassberg, the castle became something of an artists' colony. For many years it was home to his sister-in-law, the celebrated German poet Annette von Droste-Hülshoff (1797–1848), whose portrait, along with several Meersburg landmarks, once graced the DM20 note (her prim, Biedermeier quarters can be visited). Visitors included the Brothers Grimm and Ludwig Uhland. Today the castle remains a private residence.

NEUES SCHLOSS

In 1710, Prince-Bishop Johann Franz Schenk von Stauffenberg decided that the Altes Schloss was no longer suitable as a residence (you'll see why if you visit) and began building the pink baroque **Neues Schloss** (☎ 440 4900; www.schloesser-und-gaerten.de; adult/child/family €4/1/8; ⏰ 10am-1pm & 2-6pm Apr-Oct) just east of the old castle. The elegant staircase is the work of Bathasar Neumann. The back garden, a favourite site for weddings, affords a superb sea panorama.

Now state-owned, the castle houses the **Städtische Galerie**, which hosts temporary exhibits. On the 1st floor, the interesting **Dornier Museum** is dedicated to Claude Dornier, the inventor of the seaplane.

Sleeping

Gasthaus zum Letzten Heller (☎ 6149; www.zum-letzten-heller.de, in German; Daisendorfer Strasse 41; s/d from €35/55; **P**) This simple and welcoming place, 800m north of the old town, has plenty of parking. An excellent choice if you're on a budget; payment is in cash only.

Haus Säntisblick (☎ 9277; info@tp-meersburg.de; Von-Lassberg-Strasse 1; s/d from €42/56, off-season €30/48; ⏰ closed winter to mid-Feb; **P** ✖ 🐾) This pension, named after an Alpine peak you can see across the lake, has five cheery rooms and is also home base for the local scuba school (www.tauchschule-meersburg.de, in German). It's situated off Daisendorfer Strasse, 400m north of the old town.

Gasthof zum Bären (☎ 432 20; www.baeren-meersburg.de, in German; Marktplatz 11; s/d from €48/79; ⏰ closed Jan; **P**) Housed in three 13th- to early-17th-century buildings, this historic hotel has 20 classic but cheery rooms. The two huge corner rooms, 13 and 23, are particularly romantic. It's situated in the Altstadt just inside the Obertor (the burnt-orange clock tower). The same family also rents out Unterstadt holiday apartments for two to five adults (€48 to €105; minimum three-day stay).

Eating & Drinking

Felchen (whitefish) is a local speciality.

Gasthaus zum Letzten Heller (☎ 6149; www.zum-letzten-heller.de, in German; Daisendorfer Strasse 41; mains €8.20-12.50; ⏰ closed Wed & Nov) An unpretentious restaurant where the good-value regional dishes have long been favourites with locals.

Gasthof zum Bären (☎ 432 20; www.baeren-meersburg.de, in German; Marktplatz 11; mains €8.95-17.50 ⏰ closed Dec-Feb & Mon) The south German specialities here include lots of fish options, including whitefish in grapefruit sauce.

Alemannen-Torkel (☎ 1067; Steigstrasse 16-18; meals €9.50-17.50) This 300-year-old, barrel-vaulted

wine tavern has lots of local vintages. You'll feast like Prince von Stauffenberg in the restaurant upstairs.

Winzerstube zum Becher (☎ 9009; Höllgasse 4; mains €10.50-25.80; ⏰ closed Mon) This wood-panelled restaurant, run by the same family since the late 1800s, has a classy chef who infuses traditional Bodensee fish dishes with an international flavour. Situated half a block from the Neues Schloss.

Café im Barockschloss (☎ 800 00; inside Altes Schloss; ⏰ 10am-6.30pm, closed Nov-Mar & Mon Oct & Apr) Savour your coffee, ice cream, or apple strudel with whipped cream (€3.60) on the Neues Schloss' panoramic terrace.

Edeka City Markt (Daisendorfer Strasse) Self-caterers can stock up on supplies at this supermarket 100m north of the old town.

Getting There & Away

For details on the many ferry options from here, see p453.

Meersburg, which lacks a train station, is 17km west of Friedrichshafen.

From Monday to Friday, seven times a day, express bus 7394 makes the trip to Konstanz (45 minutes) and Friedrichshafen; the latter city is also served almost hourly, including weekends, by bus 7395. Bus 7373 connects Meersburg with Ravensburg (45 minutes, four daily Monday to Friday, two Saturday). Meersburg's main bus stop is next to the church.

Getting Around

The best – in fact the only – way to get around Meersburg is on foot. Even the large pay parking lot near the car-ferry port is often full in the high season. Free parking might be findable north of the old town along Daisen-dorfer Strasse.

Bikes can be hired at **Hermann Dreher** (☎ 5176; Stadtgraben 5; per day €4.50; ⊗ rental 8am-noon Mon-Sat, 9-11am Sun & holidays), down the alley next to the tourist office; you can return them anytime before 8pm.

AROUND MEERSBURG
Birnau
The exuberantly rococo **Birnau church** (admission free), a favourite for weddings, is one of the true architectural highlights of the Lake Constance region. Sitting majestically on a bluff overlooking the lake and surrounded by lush vineyards, it was built by the rococo master Peter Thumb of Vorarlberg.

When you walk in, the décor is so intricate and profuse you don't know where to look first. At some point your gaze will be drawn to the ceiling, where Gottfried Bernhard Göz worked his usual magic – look for whimsical details such as the tiny mirror in the cupola fresco.

Birnau is just off the B31, about 8km northwest of Meersburg and 5km southeast of **Überlingen**, which has one of the region's loveliest seafront promenades. Twice-hourly bus 7395 from Friedrichshafen (50 minutes) and Meersburg (20 minutes) stops near the church. You can also take a ferry (p453) to Überlingen and then walk to Birnau and back (10km return).

Schloss Salem
The **Prälatenweg** (Prelates' Path) connects the church at Birnau with the former Cistercian abbey of Salem, 7km to the northeast. Once the largest and richest monastery in southern Germany, the huge complex (founded in 1137) is now known as **Schloss Salem** (☎ 07553-814 37; www.salem.de in German; adult/child 6-16yr/student/senior €5.50/3/3.50/4.50; ⊗ 9.30am-6pm Mon-Sat, 10.30am-6pm Sun & holidays Apr-1 Nov). It became the property of the Grand Duchy of Baden after secularisation and is still the main residence of the family's descendants. The west wing is occupied by an elite boarding school that was briefly attended by Prince Philip (Duke of Edinburgh and husband of Queen Elizabeth II).

The focal point is the 14th-century **Münster**, whose Gothic purity is somewhat marred by the 26 early neoclassical-style alabaster altars. Certain parts of the complex (such as some of the rococo rooms) can only be seen

on two different guided tours in German (€3 or €4 extra each, free for children aged six to 16). The complex, which often hosts music festivals, also has a fire-fighting museum, old-time artisans' workshops, gardens and various restaurants.

Bus 7397 links Salem with Meersburg (20 or 30 minutes; via Oberuhldingen) every hour or two. The Bodensee-Gürtelbahn train goes to Friedrichshafen hourly.

FRIEDRICHSHAFEN
☎ 07541 / pop 58,000
Founded in 1811, Friedrichshafen stretches for 11km along the placid shore of Lake Constance and is surely one of Germany's nicer industrial towns. Its name will forever be associated with the Zeppelin airships, first built here under the stewardship of Count Ferdinand von Zeppelin (1838–1917) at the turn of the 20th century and now the focus of a fine museum.

Orientation & Information
There are two train stations, the main-line Stadtbahnhof, 200m north of the waterfront, and, 800m southeast, the Hafenbahnhof, next to the Zeppelin Museum and the ferry port. Going east to west, the seafront promenade is called Seestrasse and then Uferstrasse. Friedrichstrasse runs between the train tracks and the lakefront, linking the Stadtbahnhof with the commercial zone just inland from Seestrasse.

ATMs Near the seafront on Schanzstrasse.
City Wash laundrette (Schwabstrasse 16; ⊗ 8am-10pm Mon-Sat) About 1km north of the Zeppelin Museum.
Internet & Tele Cafe (Schanzstrasse 16; per hr €2; ⊗ 10am-10pm Mon-Sat, 11am-10pm Sun & holidays, to 9pm Nov-Apr) Two blocks inland from the Gondelhafen.
Post office (Bahnhofplatz) To the right as you exit the Stadtbahnhof.
Tourist office (☎ 300 10; www.friedrichshafen.ws; Bahnhofplatz 2; ⊗ 9am-6pm Mon-Fri, 9am-1pm Sat May-Sep, 9am-noon & 2-5pm Mon-Thu, 9am-noon Fri Apr & Oct, 9am-noon & 2-4pm Mon-Thu, 9am-noon Fri Nov-Mar) On the square right outside the Stadtbahnhof, in the corner of the SeeHotel.

Sights
Near the eastern end of Friedrichshafen's pleasant promenade, Seestrasse, lined with cafés and ice creameries, is the **Zeppelin Museum** (☎ 380 10; www.zeppelin-museum.de; Seestrasse 22; adult/student/senior/family €7.50/3/6.50/13; ⊗ 9am-5pm Tue-Sun May-Oct, 10am-5pm Tue-Sun Nov-Apr, also Mon Jul & Aug),

housed in the sleek, Bauhaus-style former Hafenbahnhof, built in 1932. Just for the record:
the Nazis hated Bauhaus architecture.

The museum's centrepiece is a full-scale
mock-up of a 33m section of the *Hindenburg*
(see the boxed text, p462), made of the light-
est materials available in the 1930s. Exhibits
(including an original motor gondola from
the *Graf Zeppelin*), models, touch-screen information terminals (in German and English)
and a series of four short movies (in German)
provide technical and historical insights. An
audioguide (€3) gives 1½ hours of English
commentary (most of the signage is in German). The eclectic art collection on the top
floor includes works by Otto Dix.

Children will have fun playing on the stainless-steel **Zeppelin sculpture** outside the museum
on Buchhornplatz. Lots more creative modern
sculptures are sprinkled around town, including in the grassy lakefront **Stadtgarten** along
Uferstrasse. **Boats** (row, pedal, motor and electric) can be rented at the Gondelhafen, at the
park's eastern end (€5 to €17 per hour).

The western end of Friedrichshafen's seafront promenade is anchored by the twin
onion-towered, baroque **Schlosskirche** (Klosterstrasse; ☯ 9am-6pm Mon, Tue, Thu & Sat, 9am-2.30pm Wed,
11am-6pm Fri, about noon-6pm Sun mid-Apr–Oct), built
between 1695 and 1701 by Christian Thumb.
It's the only accessible part of the Schloss,
and is still inhabited by the ducal family of
Württemberg. Note the lavish ceiling and the
vividly carved choir stalls. For details on concerts see www.kirchenmusik-freundeskreis-fn
.de (in German).

Sleeping & Eating

The tourist office has a free booking terminal
outside. Numerous eateries, including pizzer-
ias, line the Seestrasse promenade.

DJH hostel (☎ 724 04; www.jugendherberge.de;
Lindauer Strasse 3; dm 1st/subsequent night €20.80/17.60;
✗) Named (like seemingly everything else
here) after Graf Zeppelin, this 235-bed hostel
is on the Rotach River near the lakefront 2km
east of the Hafenbahnhof and 3km east of the
Stadtbahnhof. Bus 7587 comes here from both
train stations almost hourly from Monday to
Friday, and on Saturday morning; you can
also take local bus 7 to Eberhardstrasse.

Gasthof Rebstock (☎ 216 94; www.gasthof-rebstock
-fn.de, in German; Werastrasse 35; s/d €50/70; P) One of
Friedrichshafen's better deals, with wooden
furnishings inside and a beer garden outside,

this is situated 750m northwest of the Stadtbahnhof (take Eugenstrasse).

Hotel Schwanen (☎ 385 50; www.hotel-schwanen
-fn.de; Friedrichstrasse 32; s €50-65, d €80-100; ✗) An
unpretentious, family-run hotel with 20 modern rooms at the edge of the pedestrianised
city centre. The restaurant (mains €8.80 to
€14.80) serves traditional German and Swabian dishes, including Maultaschen.

Buchhorner Hof (☎ 2050; www.buchhorn.de, in German; Friedrichstrasse 33; summer s/d from €85/140, winter from
€75/85; P ✗ ❄) This old-time, four-star place
has a very Germanic lobby, 98 cleverly decorated rooms, and a sauna, steam bath and whirlpool. The restaurant (mains €18.50 to €23.50)
serves regional and international dishes.

Fehl supermarket (Karlstrasse 36; ☯ 8am-6.30pm
Mon-Fri, 8am-4pm Sat) There's an entrance from
Seestrasse opposite the skeletal steel lookout
tower.

Getting There & Around

Ryanair flies from London Stansted and Dublin to **Friedrichshafen's airport** (www.fly-away.de),
which is frequently linked to the city centre
by buses 7586 and 7394. **InterSky** (www.intersky.biz)
flies mainly to cities in Germany and Italy.

For details on ferry options, including
the catamaran to Konstanz, see p453. Sailing times are posted on the waterfront just
outside the Zeppelin Museum.

From Monday to Friday, seven times a day,
express bus 7394 makes the trip to Konstanz
(1¼ hours) via Meersburg (30 minutes). The
latter city and Birnau are also served almost
hourly, including on weekends, by bus 7395.

Friedrichshafen is on the Bodensee–
Gürtelbahn rail line, which runs along or near
the lake's northern shore from Radolfzell to
Lindau. It's also served by the Südbahn, which
goes to Ravensburg (15 minutes) and Ulm
(€15.70, 1¼ hours).

RAVENSBURG
☎ 0751 / pop 48,500
Ravensburg, situated 18km inland from
Friedrichsburg, was a Free Imperial City in
medieval times and became exceedingly rich
from the linen trade. It was also one of the
first German cities to mass-produce paper,
an industry that would later spawn the Raven-
sburger publishing house, famed for its games
and children's books. Today, Ravensburg is a
cosy town with an attractive Altstadt centre
that serves as something of a shopping hub.

BADEN-WÜRTTEMBERG

OH THE HUMANITY!

Unlike today's nonrigid airships (such as the Goodyear blimp), Zeppelins had an aluminium frame-work covered by a cotton-linen fairing. The cigar-shaped behemoths, the first of which flew in 1900, were soon used for passenger flights, outfitted as luxuriously and comfortably as ocean liners but made of superlightweight materials. The most famous of them all, the *Graf Zeppelin* (LZ 127), made 590 trips, including 114 across the Atlantic, and in 1929 she travelled around the world in just 21 days. By the mid-1930s Zeppelins, bearing swastikas on their fins, had become instantly recognisable symbols of Nazi power.

The *Hindenburg* (LZ 129), the largest airship ever built, was a whopping 245m long, more than three times the length of Airbus' new A380. In 1937, while landing in Lakehurst, New Jersey, the hydrogen-filled craft burst into flames, killing 36 passengers and crew (61 others survived). Horror-struck, the radio journalist Herbert Morrison – in a segment broadcast the next day – wailed 'Oh the humanity!', three of the most famous words in the history of broadcast journalism. The first album released by Led Zeppelin (in 1969) featured a photo of the disaster on the cover.

These days the **Zeppelin company** (www.zeppelin.de) is still around, though its Friedrichshafen-built airships are now filled with the inert gas helium. During certain periods of the year, you too can float over Lake Constance on a 12-passenger **Zeppelin NT** (☎ 0700-9377 2001; www.zeppelinflug .de). Trips of 30/40/60/120 minutes cost €190/250/335/675. NT, in case you were wondering, stands for *neue Technologie* (new technology). Take-off and landing are in Friedrichshafen.

Orientation & Information

The heart of Altstadt is the pedestrianised Marienplatz, which is more a long, wide street than a proper public square; almost all of Ravensburg's sights are right nearby. The train station is six blocks to the west along Eisenbahnstrasse.

Ravensbuch (☎ 163 88; Marienplatz 34) Has a bookshelf of English-language books.

Stadtbücherei (city library; Marienplatz 12; per hr €2; ⏰ 10am-7pm Tue-Fri, 10am-1pm Sat) Internet access for all is upstairs. On the ground floor people under 27 can go online for free for a half-hour.

Tourist office (☎ 828 00; www.ravensburg.de; Kirchstrasse 16; ⏰ 9am-5.30pm Mon-Fri, 10am-1pm Sat) A block northeast of Marienplatz. The entrance is on Herrenstrasse.

Sights & Activities

A number of imposing monuments from centuries past are arrayed along the central section of lively **Marienplatz**. The white, 51m-high **Blaserturm** (adult/child €1/0.50; ⏰ 2-5pm Mon-Fri, 11am-4pm Sat Apr-Oct), part of the original city fortifications, affords superb views of the Altstadt and the Alps from up top. Adjacent is the late-Gothic **Waaghaus**, with its stepped gable. Across Marktstrasse is the burnt-orange **Rathaus**, with some lovely stained glass. On the other side of Marienplatz, the 16th-century **Lederhaus**, once the domain of tanners and shoemakers (the ground floor is now a post office), has an elaborate Renaissance façade.

Three blocks east of Marienplatz stand seven exceptional late-medieval houses set around a courtyard. These are being trans-formed into **Museum Humpis** (Marktstrasse 45), set to open in 2010, and are worth a look for the architecture in the meantime.

At the far northern end of Marienplatz is the round **Grüner Turm** (Green Tower), with its intricate tiled roof, and the weighty, late-Gothic **Liebfrauenkirche**.

At the Altstadt's southern edge stands the **Mehlsack** (Flower Sack), a white, round tower the same height as the Blaserturm. From there a steep staircase leads up to the **Veitsburg**, a hillside castle founded in the 11th century that offers a fine panorama.

Sleeping

DJH hostel (☎ 253 63; www.jugendherberge-ravensburg.de; Veitsburg Castle; dm 1st/subsequent night €18.10/15.10; ✗) This quaint little hostel, recently renovated, is perched on the hillside above the Mehlsack tower, southeast of the Altstadt. It's about 25 minutes on foot from the train station.

Hotel Garni Baur (☎ 256 16; fax 132 29; Marienplatz 1; s/d €38/70; P ✗) This place, in an undersized building on the site of a medieval city gate, is at the far southern end of Marienplatz. The very reasonable rooms are decorated in a modern style. The entrance is around back and up the stairs.

Hotel Residenz (☎ 369 80; www.residenz-ravensburg .de; Herrenstrasse 16; s/d from €75/99; P ✗) In a modern building 100m east of the tourist office, just behind the Liebfrauenkirche. The 33 light-yellow rooms, reached via creaky stairs, are dull but spacious.

Eating & Drinking

There are lots of eateries along Marienplatz.

Humpisgaststätte (☎ 256 98; Marktstrasse 47; mains €6.60-15; ☐ 9am-1am, meals till 11pm) A down-to-earth pub-eatery whose edibles include schnitzel and Swabian dishes such as *Maultaschen*.

Central (☎ 325 33; Marienplatz 48; ☐ 9-1am) This trendy café-restaurant offers reasonably priced Italian and local fusion dishes in chic bistro surrounds.

Food market (Marktstrasse & Gespinstmarkt; ☐ 8am-1pm Sat) This superlively outdoor market stretches eastwards from Marienplatz. It has everything from local asparagus to Ghanaian pineapples.

Bauern Markt (Marktstrasse 6; ☐ 9am-6pm Mon-Fri, 8am-1pm Sat) An indoor food market.

Balthes (Marktstrasse 31) A very modern café-bar that's perfect for a coffee, beer or glass of wine.

Getting There & Away

Ravensburg is on the rail line linking Friedrichshafen (15 minutes, twice an hour) with Ulm (€13.40, 50 minutes, at least hourly) and Stuttgart (€25.20 to €33, two hours, at least hourly).

LINDAU

☎ 08382 / pop 24,300

Lindau, on a snippet of coastline that belongs to Bavaria, occupies a flowery little island in the northeastern corner of Lake Constance. In the Middle Ages, as a Free Imperial City, it enjoyed a heady prosperity thanks to its location on a major north–south trading route.

Today Lindau, whose views of the Alps are worth a thousand postcards, exudes old-world wealth and romance. Since 1951, Nobel Prize winners have gathered here for a week at the end of June to rub elbows and minds and meet with students from around the world.

Orientation

The *Insel* (island), where the town centre and harbour are to be found, is connected to the mainland by the Seebrücke, a road bridge at its northeastern tip, and by the Eisenbahndamm, a rail bridge open to cyclists

and pedestrians. The Hauptbahnhof is in the eastern part of the island, a block south of the western end of the main east–west thoroughfare, the pedestrianised, shop-lined Maximilianstrasse.

Information

ATMs There are several along the western section of Maximilianstrasse.

Lindauer Telecenter (Bahnhofplatz 8; per hr €4; ☐ 10am-7pm Mon-Fri, 11am-5pm Sat & Sun) Internet access; 100m to the left as you exit the Hauptbahnhof.

Post office (cnr Maximilianstrasse & Bahnhofplatz)

Tourist office (☎ 260 030; www.prolindau.de, in German; Ludwigstrasse 68; ☐ 9am-6pm Mon-Fri, 10am-2pm Sat & Sun mid-Jun–mid-Sep, 9am-6pm Mon-Fri & 9.30am-4pm Sat Apr–mid-Jun & mid-Sep–mid-Oct, 9am-noon & 3-5pm Mon-Fri mid-Oct–Mar)

Wasch-Center Lindau (Holdereggenstrasse 21) A self-service laundry on the mainland, about 1km north of the Seebrücke.

Sights

In the warm season the **Seepromenade** along the harbour offers an almost Mediterranean scene, with a sky bluer than blue, bobbing white boats, upmarket hotels and lots of well-heeled tourists soaking up the sun. Sipping something here is the consummate Lake Constance summer experience.

Out at the harbour gates is Lindau's signature 33m-high **Neuer Leuchtturm** (New Lighthouse) and, just in case you forget which state you're in, a statue of the Bavarian lion. The square tile-roofed, 13th-century **Alter Leuchtturm** (Old Lighthouse), also known as the Mangturm, is on the northern edge of the sheltered port.

The Marktplatz, at the eastern edge of the pedestrianised town centre, is dominated by **Haus zum Cavazzen**, a baroque construction of 1729, decorated with a riot of trompe l'oeil lions and voluptuous human forms. Inside, the attractive **Stadtmuseum** (☎ 944 073; Marktplatz 6; adult/child €2.50/1; ☐ 11am-5pm Sun & Tue-Fri, 2-5pm Sat) has a fine collection of furniture, weapons and paintings. The section dedicated to **mechanical musical instruments** (adult/child incl museum €4/2; ☐ tours at 2.15pm & 3pm Tue-Sun Apr-Oct) can only be visited on a tour.

The 15th-century **Altes Rathaus** (Bismarckplatz), with its stepped gable, is adorned with murals based on 19th-century designs, which were added only in 1975. Alongside stands the **Diebsturm** (Brigand's Tower), once a tiny jail.

Three blocks north of the tourist office, the former **Peterskirche** (Schrannenplatz; ☼ daily), a millennium-old church that's now a war memorial, is decorated with frescoes of the Passion of Christ by Hans Holbein the Elder.

Sleeping

DJH hostel (☎ 967 10; www.lindau.jugendherberge.de; Herbergsweg 11; dm 1st/2nd/4th night €20.50/19.90/19.35, a bit less in low season; ☼ closed early Dec-early Feb except Christmas school holidays; ✗) An attractive 240-bed hostel 2km northeast of the Hauptbahnhof, on the mainland near the Lindau-Park shopping mall. To get there by bus, take line 1 or 2 from the Hauptbahnhof and then transfer to bus 3 at ZUP.

Gasthof Inselgraben (☎ 5481; www.inselgraben.de, in German; Hintere Metzgergasse 4-6; s/d without bathroom from €40/60; ☼ closed Nov-late Mar) A no-frills guesthouse a block and a half from the Seepromenade, with 17 cheaply furnished rooms. A reasonable choice if you're on a tight budget.

Gasthof Engel (☎ 5240; fax 5644; Schafgasse 4; s/d €47/84, s without bathroom €28; ☼ closed Jan) This guesthouse, in a centuries-old half-timbered house, offers modern, stylish rooms with smallish bathrooms. It's a block north of Maximilienstrasse.

Alte Post (☎ 934 60; www.alte-post-lindau.de, in German; Fischergasse 3; s €44-52, d €88-108; ☼ closed late Dec-late Mar) In a 300-year-old coaching inn that was once a stop on the Frankfurt–Milan mail run, this delightful place has 11 spacious and lovingly kept rooms with antique touches. Situated midway between the port and the Seebrücke.

Eating

Seepromenade is lined with cafés that have views.

Il Cappuccino (☎ 946 484; Maximilienstrasse 16) Known for its excellent Italian ice cream, it also has lasagna (€7.50), pasta (€5.60 to €8.40), pizza and meat dishes.

Kederer's Leuchtturm (☎ 942 167; Vordere Mezgergasse 18; mains €6.80-13.30; ☼ 9.30am-midnight, food till

10pm, closed Wed in winter) A decent place for an inexpensive, hearty meal under an ancient wooden ceiling.

Alte Post (☎ 934 60; www.alte-post-lindau.de, in German; Fischergasse 3; mains €7.50-16.50) This welcoming and highly civilised restaurant, whose specialities include local whitefish, *Maultaschen* and Austrian dishes, has had the same chef since 1985. It offers excellent value.

Gasthaus zum Sünfzen (☎ 5865; Maximilianstrasse 1; mains €9.90-18.90) An island institution whose Swabian-Bavarian fare includes homemade wurst (including *Schübling*), locally caught whitefish and lots of dishes made with fresh seasonal veggies.

Getting There & Away

For details on ferry services, see p453.

Lindau is on the B31 and is connected to Munich by the A96. The scenic **Deutsche Alpenstrasse** (German Alpine Road), which winds eastward to Berchtesgaden, begins in Lindau.

Lindau is located at the eastern terminus of the Bodensee–Gürtelbahn rail line, which goes along the lake's north shore via Friedrichshafen (€4.60, 15 minutes) westward to Radolfzell; and the southern terminus of the Südbahn to Ulm (€19.30, 1¾ hours) via Ravensburg (€7.60, 45 minutes).

Getting Around

The island is tiny and ideal for walking.

Buses 1 and 2 link the Hauptbahnhof to the main bus hub, known as ZUP. A single ticket costs €1.50, a 24-hour pass is €3.50.

To get to the island by car follow the signs to 'Lindau-Insel'. There's a large metered car park at the western end of the island, beyond the train tracks, but your best bet may be to park on the mainland and either walk or catch a bus over.

Bikes can be rented inside the Hauptbahnhof at **Fahrrad Station** (☎ 212 61; ☼ 9am-1pm & 2-6pm Mon-Fri, 9.30am-12.30pm Sat), which also opens 9am until noon Sunday and holidays May to September in good weather.

Rhineland-Palatinate & Saarland

The state of Rhineland-Palatinate (Rheinland-Pfalz), patched together by the French after WWII, united historically disparate bits of Bavaria, Hesse and Prussia that had only one thing in common – the Rhine (Rhein). The river meanders for 1390km from the Swiss Alps to Rotterdam, but nowhere else has it shaped the land and its people more profoundly than along the 290km stretch traversing Rhineland-Palatinate.

Some of Europe's largest corporations dominate the Rhine banks south of Mainz, the state capital. But along here there's also a grand legacy of the Middle Ages: the magnificent Romanesque cathedrals of Mainz, Worms and Speyer. Northwest of Mainz is the river's most picturesque stretch, the storied Romantic Rhine, whose vine-clad slopes, medieval hilltop castles and snug wine villages have drawn artists and tourists since the early 19th century.

Most of Germany's wine is grown in Rhineland-Palatinate's six wine regions: the Ahr Valley, Moselle-Saar-Ruwer, Middle Rhine, Nahe, Rheinhessen and, famed for its German Wine Road, the Rheinpfalz. The region's wonderful wines can all be sampled in a multitude of ambience-laden wine taverns. The local people's *joie de vivre* finds expression in the many town and village wine festivals, held from August to October.

Tiny Saarland, in the southwest, was once a centre for heavy industry but these days it's better known for Saarbrücken's Frenchified urbane charms, and its verdant forests and fields.

HIGHLIGHTS

- **Riverine Scenery** Cruise, cycle or ramble along the castle-studded Romantic Rhine (p483) between Koblenz and Bingen
- **Architectural Stunners** Marvel at the Romanesque cathedrals in Mainz (p467), Worms (p472) and Speyer (p474)
- **Roman Relics** Explore the remarkable ruins of Roman Trier (p497)
- **Romantic Bargain** Dream about knights and damsels – in your bunk and over a muesli breakfast – at the DJH Burg Stahleck hostel (p492) in Bacharach
- **Thrill Ride** Take a high-speed spin around the Nürburgring race track (p482)
- **Cultural Moment** Listen to jazz at the Saarland's historic Völklinger Hütte ironworks (p508) in Völklingen

★ Nürburgring ★ Koblenz

Bacharach ★
Bingen ★ ★ Mainz

★ Trier

Worms ★

★ Völklingen

Speyer ★

- RHINELAND-PALATINATE POPULATION: 4 MILLION
- SAARLAND POPULATION: 1.06 MILLION
- RHINELAND-PALATINATE AREA: 19,853 SQ KM
- SAARLAND AREA : 2569 SQ KM

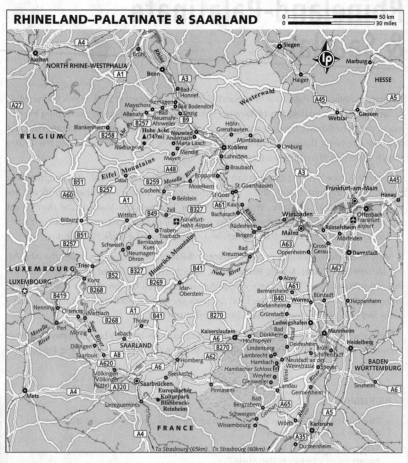

RHINELAND–PALATINATE & SAARLAND

Accommodation

Accommodation is scarce and most expensive in September and October (especially on the weekends), when visitors are attracted by the grape harvest, the many village wine festivals and the red and gold tones of the changing autumn leaves. Also busy are May and June, with their spring weather and long days; August, also a time of wine festivals; and, in some locales, from late November to late December (especially weekends), when Christmas markets take place. During high season, some places enforce a two-night minimum stay.

Getting There & Away

People complain that **Frankfurt-Hahn Airport** (☎ 06543-509 200; www.hahn-airport.de), a Ryanair

hub, is misleadingly named because it's nowhere near Frankfurt, and they have a point. But it *is* near many of the cities and towns covered in this chapter and is linked by bus to destinations including Bernkastel-Kues (€8, 30 minutes, two or three daily Monday to Friday), Bingen (€8.90, one hour, three daily), Idar-Oberstein (€5.60, 50 minutes, five daily Monday to Friday, two or three Saturday and Sunday), Koblenz (Bus 610; €12.30, 65 minutes, six daily), Mainz (€10.50, 70 minutes, 11 times daily), Traben-Trarbach (€6, 25 minutes, twice daily Monday to Saturday), Trier (€12, 80 minutes, seven daily) and Saarbrücken (€15, six daily).

The *real* Frankfurt airport (p524) is also a good option, especially if you're headed by public transport to places such as Mainz, Worms, Speyer, the German Wine Road (be prepared to transfer a few times) and some of the Romantic Rhine villages, especially right-bank ones served by direct trains from Wiesbaden.

Getting Around

With the Rheinland-Pfalz-Ticket (RP-Ticket; €23), up to five adults (or parents or grandparents with an unlimited number of their own children or grandchildren) can take any regional train (RE, IRE, RB and S-Bahn), tram, intercity bus or local bus anywhere within Rhineland-Palatinate and the Saarland for a full day – an unbeatable price for environmentally friendly transportation!

The ticket also lets you take the train along the right bank of the Rhine between Wiesbaden and St Goarshausen (this bit of track is officially in Hesse) and as far afield as Bonn, Mannheim, Karlsruhe and Wissembourg in the French region of Alsace. The RP-Ticket, valid from 9am to 3am Monday to Friday and all day long on Saturdays. Sundays and holidays, is available from train station ticket machines, at local public transport offices and on buses.

RHINE-HESSE & PALATINATE

MAINZ

☎ 06131 / pop 185,500

Mainz, the capital of Rhineland-Palatinate, is a lively locale thanks to its sizable university, a large media presence and a certain savoir-vivre whose origins go back to Napoleon's occupation (1798–1814). Strolling along the Rhine and sampling local wines in a half-timbered Altstadt (old town) tavern are as much a part of any Mainz visit as viewing the fabulous Dom, Chagall's ethereal windows in the St-Stephan-Kirche (St Stephen's Church) or the first printed Bibles in the Gutenberg Museum.

The Romans were the first to take advantage of Mainz' strategic location at the confluence of the Main and Rhine Rivers. In 12 BC, under Emperor Augustus, they founded a military camp called Moguntiacum as a base for the invasion of Germania. After the Romans, Mainz took a 250-year nap before being

awoken by English missionary St Boniface, who established an archbishopric here in AD 746. In the 15th century, native son Johannes Gutenberg ushered in the information age by perfecting moveable type (see boxed text, p470).

Orientation

The mostly pedestrianised Altstadt is centred on the Dom (cathedral) and the adjacent Marktplatz (Domplatz), which are 1km east of the Hauptbahnhof (central train station). Pedestrians-only thoroughfares include east–west Ludwigsstrasse and north–south Augustinerstrasse.

Information

ConAction Internetcafé (Grosse Bleiche 25; per 30/60min €1/1.70; ☽ 24hr)

Eco-Express (Parcusstrasse 12; ☽ 6am-11pm except Sun & holidays) Laundry.

Gutenberg Buchhandlung (☎ 270 330; Grosse Bleiche 27-31) Bookshop.

Internet Center (Bahnhofstrasse 11; per hr €1.50; ☽ 9am-11pm) There are several other internet cafés right nearby.

Post office (Bahnhofstrasse 2) Has an ATM.

Reisebank Currency exchange in the Hauptbahnhof.

Tourist office (☎ 286 210; www.info-mainz.de/tourist; Brückenturm am Rathaus; ☽ 9am-6pm Mon-Fri, 10.30am-2.30pm Sat) Signposted as 'Touristik Centrale Mainz', this place is across the pedestrian bridge (ie over the highway) from the Rathaus (town hall). The MainzCard (individual/family €6/10) gets you admission to museums (some are free anyway), a walking tour, unlimited public transport plus discounts for boat tours, plays and other events.

Sights

DOM

Mainz' famed **cathedral** (☽ 9am-6.30pm Mon-Fri, 9am-4pm Sat, 12.45-3pm & 4-6.30pm Sun, to 5pm Sun-Fri Nov-Feb), entered from the Marktplatz, is one of Germany's most magnificent houses of worship. The focal point of the Altstadt, this richly detailed 'mountain' of reddish sandstone, topped by an octagonal tower, went through a literal 'baptism by fire' when the original burned down just one day before its consecration in 1066. Most of what you see today is quintessential 12th-century Romanesque.

Inside, a solemn ambience pervades the nave which, surprisingly, has a choir at each end. The grandiose, wall-mounted **memorial tombstones** form a veritable portrait gallery of

MAINZ

0   200 m
0   0.1 miles

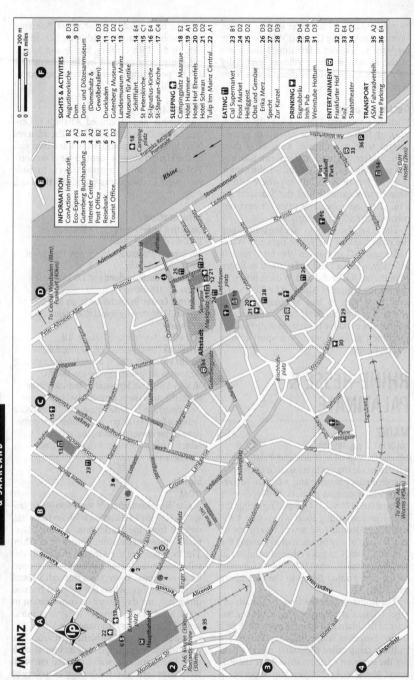

archbishops and other 13th- to 18th-century power mongers, many portrayed alongside their private putti.

Off the late-Gothic cloister, accessible from inside the Dom, is the **Dom- und Diözesanmuseum** (Cathedral & Diocesan Museum; ☎ 253 344; www .dommuseum-mainz.de in German; ☺ 10am-5pm, to 6pm Sat & Sun, closed Mon & Catholic holidays). The **Domschatz** (adult/student/family €3/2.50/6) features bejewelled ritual objects from as far back as the 10th century and 15th- and 16th-century tapestries (English guide pamphlet available). Across the cloister, the **Gewölbehallen** (adult/student/family €2.50/2/5, combination ticket €5/4/10) has artwork from the cathedral, including sculptures from the rood screen (1239) – the work of the renowned Master of Naumburg – that portray the saved and the, well, not-so-saved.

OTHER CHURCHES

On a hill, **St-Stephan-Kirche** (Kleine Weissgasse 12; ☺ 10am-noon & 2-5pm Mon-Sat, till 4.30pm Dec & Jan) would be just another Gothic church rebuilt after WWII were it not for the nine brilliant, stained-glass windows created by the Russian-Jewish artist Marc Chagall (1887–1985) in the final years of his life. Bright blue and imbued with a mystical, meditative quality, they serve as a symbol of Jewish-Christian reconciliation.

Mainz also has a trio of stunning baroque churches which illustrate the evolution of this often over-the-top architectural style. Part of the local Catholic seminary, the classically baroque **Augustinerkirche** (Augustinerstrasse 34; ☺ 8am-5pm Mon-Fri, 9am-5pm Sat & Sun when the seminary is in session), built in 1768, features an elaborate organ loft and a delicate ceiling fresco by Johann Baptist Enderle. Unlike so many other such structures in Germany, it has never been destroyed. **St Peterskirche** (Petersstrasse 3; ☺ 9am-6pm) shows off the sumptuous glory of the rococo style and is noted for its richly adorned pulpit and altars. **St-Ignatius-Kirche** (Kapuzinerstrasse 36; ☺ 9am-6pm) marks the transition from rococo to neoclassicism. The sculpture outside is a copy of one made by Hans Backoffen (the original is in the Dom- und Diözesanmuseum).

GUTENBERG MUSEUM

A heady experience for anyone excited by books, the **Gutenberg Museum** (☎ 122 644; Liebfrauenplatz 5; adult/student & senior/family €5/3/10; ☺ 9am-5pm Tue-Sat, 11am-3pm Sun) chronicles the history of the technology that made the world as we know it –

including this guidebook – possible. Besides historical presses, old typesetting machines and several rooms on pre-Gutenberg printing in Korea, Japan and China, you can admire hand-copied manuscripts as well as printed masterpieces such as Gutenberg's original Bible. For a 1925 re-creation of Gutenberg's print shop, head to the basement. More English signs are planned.

In the museum's **Druckladen** (print shop; ☎ 122686; www.druckladen.mainz.de; group admission per person €3-5, individuals are asked for a donation; ☺ 9am-5pm Mon-Fri, 10am-3pm Sat), across tiny Seilergasse, you can try out Gutenberg's technology yourself – on the condition that you're at least five years old. You'll be issued with a smock (the unique odour of printers' ink may, for many, conjure up the nobility of making the written word available to the masses – but the goop is hell to get out of fabric) and instructed in the art of hand-setting type – backwards, of course. Nearby, master craftsmen produce elegant posters, certificates and cards using the labour-intensive technologies of another age. Fascinating, especially in an era when 'print' usually means tapping a few computer keys. Hands-on kids-oriented activities are a speciality.

LANDESMUSEUM MAINZ

The rich and far-reaching collection of the **Landesmuseum Mainz** (State Museum; ☎ 285 70; Grosse Bleiche 49-51; adult/student & senior €2/1.50, more during special exhibitions, free on Sat; ☺ 10am-8pm Tue, 10am-5pm Wed-Sun), housed in the former prince-elector's stables, traces the region's cultural history from the Stone Age to the present. Treasures include the famous **Jupitersäule**, a Roman triumphal column from the 1st century. The richly festooned façade of the **Kaufhaus am Brand**, a 14th-century trading house, is scheduled to go back on display in 2007 (renovations are scheduled to continue through 2009). Also of interest: Dutch and Flemish paintings, faïence and Art Nouveau glass.

MUSEUM FÜR ANTIKE SCHIFFFAHRT

In 1981 excavations for a hotel spectacularly unearthed the remains of five wooden ships of the Romans' Rhine flotilla, once used to thwart Germanic tribes trying to intrude upon Roman settlements. They are now on display, along with two full-size replicas, in the **Museum für Antike Schiffahrt** (Museum of Ancient Shipping; ☎ 286 630; Neutorstrasse 2b; admission free; ☺ 10am-6pm Tue-Sun).

FORTY-TWO LINES THAT CHANGED THE WORLD

Johannes Gutenberg, the inventor of printing with moveable type, is one of those rare epochal figures whose achievements changed the course of human history. The Chinese came up with printing using a press long before Gutenberg but they used it to print designs on silk rather than spread the word, any word. Without Gutenberg, Martin Luther's career as a religious revolutionary might never have got off the ground.

Little is known about Gutenberg the man, who was born in Mainz in the very late 1300s, trained as a goldsmith and then, in the late 1420s, left for Strasbourg, where he first experimented with printing technology. By 1448 he was back in Mainz, still working on his top-secret project and in debt to some rather impatient 'venture capitalists'. But eventually his perseverance paid off and he perfected a number of interdependent technologies: metal type that could be arranged into pages; precision moulds to produce such type in large quantities; a metal alloy from which type could be cast; a type of oil-based ink suitable for printing with metal type; and press technology derived from existing wine, paper and bookbinding presses.

Despite several lawsuits, by 1455 Gutenberg had produced his masterpiece, the now-legendary Forty-Two-Line Bible, so-named because each page has 42 lines. Thus began a new era in human history, one in which the printed word – everything from lyrical poetry to Nazi propaganda – was to become almost universally accessible.

Tours

Walking tours of the city (€5) in German and English begin at the tourist office at 2pm on Saturday; in the warm season, tours also begin at 2pm on Wednesday and Friday.

Festivals & Events

The **Mainzer Johannisnacht** (www.mainz.de /johannisnacht), held from Friday to Monday around 24 June, is one of Germany's largest street festivals, attracting more than half-a-million revellers. The 3.5km of city-centre festivities, which include the ceremonial initiation of printers' apprentices, also has music, theatre and folklore performances and a thousand street stalls, 150 of them dedicated to beer.

Sleeping

The tourist office has a **room reservations hotline** (☎ 286 2128; 9am-6pm Mon-Fri, 10.30am-2.30pm Sat); bookings can also be made via the tourist office website (www.info-mainz.de/tourist).

Campingplatz Maaraue (☎ 06134-4383; www .krkg.de/camping.html; Auf der Maaraue; adult/tent/car €4.20/3.20/2.70) Situated across the Rhine from the city centre at the confluence of the Rhine and Main, this grassy riverside camping ground is not far from an outdoor swimming pool. From the Hauptbahnhof take bus 6 or 6A to Brückenkopf; from there it's a 10-minute walk south.

DJH hostel (☎ 853 32; www.jugendherberge.de; Otto-Brunfels-Schneise 4; dm from €17.50; P) A modernised 166-bed hostel near a city park with two- and four-bed rooms, all with private bathroom. About 3.5km from the Hauptbahnhof; take bus 62 or 63.

Hotel Hof Ehrenfels (☎ 971 2340; www.hof-ehrenfels .de; Grebenstrasse 5-7; s/d/tr €55/78/95) Just steps from the cathedral, this 22-room place, housed in a 15th-century, one-time Carmelite nunnery, has prices and Dom views that are hard to beat. A real treat if you love the sound of church bells; consider bringing earplugs if you don't.

Tulip Inn Mainz Central (☎ 2760; www.goldentulip .com; Bahnhofplatz 8; s €72-110, d €85-155; P) An air of faded glamour envelops this 58-room hotel, built in 1871, which in the heyday of rail travel hosted stars of film and stage. The spacious rooms are unexciting but the bathrooms come in tile colours they don't make anymore and you can still sit down in the lift.

Hotel Schwan (☎ 144 920; www.mainz-hotel-schwan .de; Liebfrauenplatz 7; s/d €84/110) You can't get any more central than this family-run place, which has been around since 1463. The 22 well-lit rooms have baroque-style furnishings.

Hotel Hammer (☎ 965 2828; www.hotel-hammer .com; Bahnhofplatz 6; s/d from €90/112, in low season from €71/86;) With contemporary furnishings and an upbeat colour scheme, the Hammer is a pleasing place to camp out, close to the train station. The attractively designed sauna is a welcome bonus.

Eating & Drinking

Cheap eateries are near the Hauptbahnhof and south of the Dom along Augustinerstrasse.

Weinstube Hottum (☎ 223 370; Grebenstrasse 3; dishes €4-10; ☼ 4pm-midnight, to 1am Sat) One of the best of the Altstadt wine taverns, Hottum has a cosy, traditional atmosphere, delectable wines and a menu – half of which appears on a tiny slate tablet – with regional dishes such as *Pfälzer Pfannkuchen* (pancakes) and *Winzersteak* (vintner-style pork steak).

Eisgrubbräu (☎ 221 104; Weissliliengasse 1a; mains €4-14; ☼ 9am-1am, to 2am Fri & Sat) Grab a seat in this down-to-earth micro-brewery's warren of vaulted chambers, order a mug of *Schwarz* (dark) or *Hell* (light) – or even a 3/5L *Bierturm* (beer tower; €16/26) – and settle in for people-watching. The Monday-to-Friday, all-you-can-eat lunch buffet (€5), the Sunday buffet dinner (€8.50) and the Saturday and Sunday breakfast buffet (€3.90) are good value. Call two or three days ahead to arrange a free, 20-minute tour of the beer-making facilities.

Heiliggeist (☎ 225 757; Mailandsgasse 11; mains €6-15; ☼ 4pm-1am Mon-Fri, 9am-2am Sat, Sun & holidays) Sit beneath the soaring Gothic vaults of a 15th-century hospital and enjoy a drink, snack or full meal from a menu with lots of Italian-inspired options.

Specht (☎ 231770; Rotekopfgasse 2; mains €9-14 ☼ 5pm-midnight Sun-Fri, 11.30am-midnight Sat, also 11.30am-midnight Sun Jun-Aug) Thanks to its ancient wood beams, smoked walls and Fastnacht (carnival) medals, 'Woodpecker' has a 19th-century feel though the building itself is much older. Serves German and regional cuisine made with fresh products from the nearby market. If the ceiling *doesn't* look uneven and wavy, you've drunk too much.

Zur Kanzel (☎ 237 137; Grebenstrasse 4; mains €15.50-22.50; ☼ closed Sun) A classy place with a distinctly French flair and a nice courtyard, this *Weinstube* (wine bar) serves up-market French and regional cuisine, including *pot au feu* (boiled meat and vegetables) and dishes made with *grüne Sosse* (a light sauce made with half-a-dozen fresh herbs, sour cream and soft white cheese). All products are fresh so the menu evolves with the seasons. From May to September, the chef-owner takes small groups on half-day wine and food cruises aboard a one-time police boat (€500 for eight to 10 people).

Irish Pub (☎ 231 430; Weissliliengasse 5; ☼ 5pm-1am, to 2am Fri & Sat) An unpretentious watering hole with karaoke on Monday, solo musicians Tuesday to Thursday, bands on Friday and Saturday and an open-mic night on Sunday (all from 9.30pm). Attracts a very international crowd that often includes US soldiers from nearby Wiesbaden.

Self-catering options:

Cial supermarket (Grosse Bleiche 41; ☼ 8am-8pm Mon-Sat)

Food market (Marktplatz & Liebfrauenplatz; ☼ 7am-2pm Tue, Fri & Sat) Along the north and east sides of the Dom.

Obst und Gemüse Erika Merz (Augustinerstrasse 18; ☼ 9am-7pm Mon-Fri, 9am-5pm Sat) Fresh fruit and vegetables.

Entertainment

Two free monthly mags, *Fritz* and *Der Mainzer*, available at the tourist office and in cafés and pubs, have details on cultural events. Tickets are available at the tourist office.

KuZ (☎ 286 860; www.kuz.de, in German; Dagobertstrasse 20b) Dance parties, live concerts, a summer beer garden with al fresco movie screenings, a world-music summer festival, kids' theatre… the happening Kulturzentrum (cultural centre) has something for everyone. It's housed in a neat red-brick building that began life in the 19th century as a military laundry.

Staatstheater (☎ 285 1222; www.staatstheater-mainz .de in German; Gutenbergplatz 7) Mainz' theatre stages plays, opera and ballet. Students get significant discounts.

Frankfurter Hof (☎ 220 438; www.frankfurter-hof -mainz.de, in German; Augustinerstrasse 55) In the late 1980s a group of preservation-minded citizens saved this historical building from demolition and turned it into a hugely popular performance venue. Since 1991 it has hosted everyone from up-and-comers to big-name acts such as Joe Jackson and Wir sind Helden.

Getting There & Away

Frankfurt Airport, 30km northeast of Mainz, is linked to the Hauptbahnhof by S-Bahn line 8 (€3.40, several times hourly).

Mainz, a major IC rail hub, has frequent regional services to Bingen (€5.30, 35 minutes) and other Romantic Rhine towns, Koblenz (€14.70, 1½ hours), Idar-Oberstein (€9.80, one hour), Saarbrücken (€24.30, two hours) and Worms (€7.60, 26 to 44 minutes).

Mainz is encircled by a ring road with connections to the A60, A63 and A66.

City-centre parking options are limited to pricey underground garages and street spots with one- or two-hour time limits. On the southeast edge, there's free parking on Am

Winterhafen, just east of KuZ. You could also design your own Park & Ride schedule by leaving your vehicle outside the centre along a tram line.

For details on cruising to villages down the Romantic Rhine, see p484.

Getting Around

Mainz operates a joint bus and tram system with Wiesbaden (www.mvg-mainz.de, in German). Single tickets cost €2.10; day passes are €4.90/8 for individuals/groups of up to five. Tickets are available from vending machines and must be stamped before boarding.

ASM Fahrradverleih (☎ 238 620; Binger Strasse 19; 3-speed/mountain bike/tandem per day €5.50/8/14; ☺ 7am-8pm Mon-Fri, 10am-4pm Sat Apr-Sep) hires out bikes on the ground level of CityPort Parkhaus, near the Hauptbahnhof.

WORMS
☎ 06241 / pop 81,000

Worms (rhymes with 'forms'), one of Germany's oldest cities, has played a pivotal role at various moments in European history. In AD 413 it became capital of the legendary, if short-lived, Burgundian kingdom whose rise and fall was creatively chronicled in the 12th-century *Nibelungenlied*, featured in a local museum and the annual **Nibelungen-Festspiele** (www.nibelungenfestspiele.de, in German), a two-week festival held in mid-August.

After the Burgundians, just about every other tribe in the area had a go at ruling Worms, including the Huns, the Alemans and finally the Franks, under whose leader, Charlemagne, the city flourished. The most impressive reminder of Worms' medieval heyday is its majestic, late-Romanesque Dom. A Jewish community, renowned for the erudition of its rabbis, thrived here from the 10th century until the 1930s, earning Worms the moniker 'Little Jerusalem'.

In the Middle Ages, Worms hosted more than 100 sessions of the imperial parliament (Diet), including one in 1521 at which Luther famously refused to recant his views and was declared an outlaw. An impressive memorial now honours the Protestant reformer.

Orientation

From the Hauptbahnhof and adjacent bus station, pedestrianised Wilhelm-Leuschner-Strasse leads 500m southeast to Lutherplatz, on the northwest edge of the half-oval-shaped Altstadt. From there, it's 150m southeast to Kämmererstrasse, the old city's main commercial thoroughfare, and 300m south to the Dom. A plane-shaded promenade runs along the Rhine about 800m east of the Dom.

Information

There are ATMs inside the Hauptbahnhof and along nearby Wilhelm-Leuschner-Strasse.

Gerhard Neef (Neumarkt 14; ☺ 4.30am-6.30pm Mon-Fri, 5.30am-3.30pm Sat) A newsagent that sells events tickets; also carries brochures from the tourist office, which is next door.

Internet und Telefonhaus (Hardtgasse 7; per hr €1; ☺ 10am-11pm or midnight) Across the street from Woolworth's.

Post office (Kaiserpassage)

TeleBistro (per hr €1) Kämmererstrasse 50 (☺ 9.30am or 10am-11pm); Neumarkt 3-5 (☺ 9am-11pm) Internet access.

Tourist office (☎ 250 45; www.worms.de; Neumarkt 14; ☺ 9am-6pm Mon-Fri year-round, 9.30am-1.30pm Sat, 10am-2pm Sun Apr-Oct) Sells events tickets and can supply you with a walking-tour brochure in English.

Sights
KAISERDOM

Worms' skyline, such as it is, is dominated by the four towers and two domes of the magnificent **Dom St Peter und St Paul** (☺ 9am-5.45pm Apr-Oct, to 4.45pm Nov-Mar), built in the 11th and 12th centuries in the late-Romanesque style. Inside, the lofty dimensions impress as much as the lavish, canopied **high altar** (1742) in the east choir, designed by the baroque master Balthasar Neumann. In the south transept, a **scale model** shows the enormity of the original complex. Nearby stairs lead down to the stuffy **crypt**, which holds the stone sarcophagi of several members of the Salian dynasty of Holy Roman emperors.

In the *Nibelungenlied,* the **Kaiserportal** (open only during services) on the north side was the setting of a fierce quarrel between the Burgundian queens Kriemhild and Brunhilde about who had the right to enter the Dom first. Trivial as it may seem, this little interchange ultimately led to their kingdom's downfall. Today, the main entrance is through the Gothic **Südportal** (south portal; 1300), richly decorated with biblical figures.

JEWISH SITES

Starting in the 900s, the Jewish community of Worms – known as Varmaiza in medieval

Jewish texts – was centred on the northeast corner of the Altstadt along Judengasse and its side streets. Before 1933 1100 Jews lived in the city; a Jewish community – now numbering 130 souls, almost all of them from the former USSR – was re-established in the late 1990s.

Worms' most ancient synagogue, founded in 1034, was destroyed by the Nazis but in 1961 a new **Alte Synagoge** (Synagogenplatz; admission free; 🕑 10am-12.30pm & 1.30-5pm Apr-Oct, to 4pm Nov-Mar, closed to visitors Sat morning) rose from its ashes. Men are asked to cover their heads. Around the side, stone steps lead down to the 12th-century, Romanesque **Mikwe** (ritual bath).

Behind the synagogue is the modern **Raschi Haus**, built on the 14th-century foundations of a community wedding hall. It is named after Rashi (Rabbi Shlomo Yitzhaqi), a brilliant 11th-century Talmudic scholar who studied in Worms. Inside is the **Jüdisches Museum** (Jewish Museum; 🕾 853 4707; Hintere Judengasse 6; adult/student €1.50/0.80; 🕑 10am-12.30pm & 1.30-5pm Tue-Sun Apr-Oct, to 4.30pm Nov-Mar), which illustrates Jewish customs, ceremonies and festivals and tells the history of the local Jewish community. The singed Torah fragments were burnt on Reichspogromnacht (Kristallnacht; literally 'Night of Broken Glass'; see boxed text, p35).

Just east of here is the arched **Raschitor**, a city gate that's part of the wall that still partially encircles the Altstadt.

A bit outside the southwest corner of the Altstadt is the peaceful **Alter Jüdische Friedhof** (Old Jewish Cemetery; Willy-Brandt-Ring 21; 🕑 9am-dusk, to 8pm Jul-Aug), also known as the Heiliger Sand, opened in 1076. The most revered gravestone – it's one of two topped with especially large piles of pebbles, left by visitors as tokens of respect – is that of Rabbi Meir of Rothenburg (1215–93), who died in captivity after being imprisoned by King Rudolf of Habsburg for attempting to lead a group of persecuted Jews to Palestine.

NIBELUNGEN MUSEUM

The *Nibelungenlied* is the ultimate tale of love and hate, treasure and treachery, revenge and death, with a cast including dwarves, dragons and bloodthirsty *Überfraus* (superwomen). Richard Wagner set it to music, Fritz Lang turned it into a masterful silent movie and the Nazis abused its mythology, seeing in Siegfried the quintessential German hero.

The state-of-the-art **Nibelungen Museum** (🕾 202 120; www.nibelungen-museum.de; Fischerpförtchen 10; adult/child €5.50/3.50; 🕑 10am-5pm Tue-Thu, Sat & Sun, 9am-10pm Fri) brings the epic to life in a highly entertaining, multimedia exhibit set up in two towers and along the ramparts of the medieval town wall. In the first tower you can listen to the anonymous poet tell his tale (in flawless English) via a wireless headset while watching excerpts from Lang's movies.

OTHER MUSEUMS

Two blocks south of the Dom, the **Museum der Stadt** (City Museum; 🕾 946 390; Weckerlingplatz 7; adult/student/family €2/1/5, more during special exhibitions; 🕑 10am-5pm Tue-Sun), housed in the handsome Andreasstift Kirche, chronicles Worms' turbulent history from Neolithic and (especially) Roman times onward.

In the corner of a pretty park just north of the Dom, on the grounds of the former imperial and bishop's palace, is the **Museum Heylshof** (🕾 220 00; Stephansgasse 9; adult/student/family €2.50/1/5; 🕑 11am-5pm Tue-Sun May-Sep, 2-5pm Tue-Sat & 11am-5pm Sun Oct-Dec & mid-Jan–Apr). Its important private art collection includes Italian, Dutch, French and German paintings from the 15th to the 19th centuries, including works by such heavyweights as Tintoretto, Rubens and Lenbach. The Frankenthaler porcelain, Venetian, Bohemian and German glass and beer steins (in the basement) are also worth a look.

Sleeping

DJH hostel (🕾 257 80; www.jugendherberge.de; Dechaneigasse 1; dm €18, s/d €23.50/47; 🕑 reception 7.30am-11pm; �) In an unbeatable location facing the south side of the Dom. The recently renovated rooms have two to six beds and private bathrooms.

Hotel Lortze-Eck (🕾 263 49; 273 70; Schlossergasse 10-14; s/d €44/70) This family-run, 14-room hotel is a fairly stylish choice, particularly suitable if you like fake, well-intentioned flowers. Bright colours and tasteful knick-knacks brighten up the public areas. The attached restaurant serves German classics as well as vegetarian dishes (mains €9 to €14).

Hotel Kriemhilde (🕾 911 50; www.hotel-kriemhilde.de; Hofgasse 2-4; s/d €48/70) Wake up to the peal of the Dom bells at this unassuming inn. It's a mere stone's throw from the mighty cathedral, which is visible from the top-floor rooms and audible everywhere.

Parkhotel Prinz Carl (🕾 3080; www.parkhotel-prinzcarl.de; Prinz-Carl-Anlage 10-14; s/d from €75/115; P �) Housed in one-time barracks built –

and built to last – during the reign of the last Kaiser, this place has 90 pastel rooms that are spacious, comfortable and impersonal. From the Hauptbahnhof, the hotel, just off Pforten-Ring, is a 500m walk north through the chestnut-shaded park.

Eating & Drinking
Several Italian restaurants can be found a block southeast of the Dom on Gerberstrasse. Cheap eats are available up towards the Hauptbahnhof along Wilhelm-Leuschner-Strasse. The Hotel Lortze-Eck has a restaurant.

Trattoria-Pizzeria Pepe e Sale (☎ 258 36; Wollstrasse 12; pizzas €2.60-5.70; ⏰ 11am-midnight) Serves more than 200 different kinds of pizzas as well as pastas, including Spaghetti Robinson (tuna and garlic). Excellent value.

Café TE (☎ 234 65; Bahnhofstrasse 5; mains €2.60-10.60; ⏰ 8am or 9am-1am, to 2am Sat) A trackside bar-café and beer garden half-a-block south of the Hauptbahnhof that's especially popular with students. Chic in an Italian sort of way, it features 16 breakfast options and a different dinner special each night. Local bands sometimes play here.

Café Ohne Gleichen (☎ 411 177; Kriemhildenstrasse 11; light meals €4-8; ⏰ 9am-1am, to 2am on Fri, Sat & holidays) A long block south of the Hauptbahnhof, this eclectic, student-oriented café-bar has off-the-wall art on the arty walls and serves drinks, cheap meals and, on Saturday, Sunday and holidays, brunch (€6.90). Occasionally hosts live bands.

Marktkauf supermarket (Schönauerstrasse 3; ⏰ 8am-8pm Mon-Sat) Self-caterers will find the entrance to this supermarket two blocks south of the tourist office on Gerberstrasse.

Along the Rhine to the north of the bridges, along the riverfront promenade known as Am Rhein, are several hugely popular beer garden–type eateries, including **Hagenbräu** (Am Rhein 5; mains €5-10), a microbrewery that serves hearty German fare.

Getting There & Around
Worms is about 50km south of Mainz and has frequent train connections with Mannheim (€4.50), a major rail hub, as well as Mainz (€7.60, 26 to 44 minutes, twice hourly) and Bingen (€18.30, 70 minutes). Going to Speyer (€7.20) requires a change in Ludwigshafen.

There's free parking in a huge lot just north of the Nibelungsbrücke, Worms' Rhine bridge, which is currently being doubled.

Bicycles can be rented at **Radhaus-Mihm** (☎ 242 08; Von Steubenstrasse 8; 3-speed/all-terrain per day €5/12.50, weekend €7.50/19, tandem per day €12.50; ⏰ 9.30am-12.30pm & 1.30-6pm Mon-Fri, 10am-1pm Sat), across the tracks from the Hauptbahnhof. The local **ADFC club** (www.adfc-worms.de, in German) organises group rides. The tourist office sells cycling maps.

SPEYER
☎ 06232 / pop 50,000
Speyer, about 50km south of Worms, is a dignified town with a compact, mostly-modern centre distinguished by a magnificent Romanesque cathedral, a couple of top-rate museums and a respected culinary scene.

First a Celtic settlement, then Roman market town, Speyer gained prominence in the Middle Ages under the Salian emperors, hosting 50 imperial parliament sessions (1294–1570).

In 1076 the king and later Holy Roman Emperor Heinrich IV – having been excommunicated by Pope Gregory VII – launched his penitence walk to Canossa in Italy from Speyer. He crossed the Alps in the middle of winter, an action that warmed even the heart of the pope, who revoked his excommunication. He lies buried in the Kaiserdom.

Orientation
Majestic Maximilianstrasse, the city centre's main commercial street, extends from the Altpörtel (a medieval city gate) 800m east to the Dom. The numbering of the buildings along Maximilianstrasse begins at the Dom, runs along the south side to the Altpörtel, then it continues along the north side back to the Dom - be prepared for confusion! The Hauptbahnhof is about 1km north of the Altpörtel.

Information
ATM (Maximilianstrasse 47) Near the Altpörtel.
Post office (Wormser Strasse 4) A block northeast of the Altpörtel.
Silver Surfer (Schulergasse 2, Königsplatz; per hr €3; ⏰ 11am-midnight Mon-Sat, 1pm-midnight Sun) Internet access a block south of Maximilianstrasse.
Tourist office (☎ 142 392; www.speyer.de; Maximilianstrasse 13; ⏰ 9am-5pm Mon-Fri year-round, 10am-3pm Sat, 10am-2pm Sun Apr-Oct, 10am-noon Sat Nov-Mar) Inside the historic Rathaus.

Sights
KAISERDOM
In 1030 Emperor Konrad II of the Salian dynasty laid the cornerstone of the majestic

Romanesque **Kaiserdom** (🕙 9am-7pm Apr-Oct, to 5pm Nov-Mar, closed Sun morning), whose square towers and green copper dome float above Speyer's rooftops. A Unesco World Heritage site since 1981, its interior is startling for its awesome dimensions (it's an astonishing 134m long) and austere, dignified symmetry; walk up to the elevated altar area to get a true sense of its vastness. Another set of steps leads down to the darkly festive **crypt**, whose candy-striped Romanesque arches – like those on the west front – recall Moorish architecture. Stuffed into a side room are the granite sarcophagi of eight Salian emperors and kings, along with some of their queens. The most scenic way to approach the Dom is from Maximilianstrasse.

Behind the Dom, the large **Domgarten** (cathedral park) stretches towards the Rhine.

MAXIMILIANSTRASSE

Roman troops and medieval emperors once paraded down 'Via Triumphalis'. Now known as Maximilianstrasse, Speyer's pedestrian-only commercial main drag links the Dom with the 55m-high, 13th-century **Altpörtel** (adult/concession €1/0.50; 🕙 10am-noon & 2-4pm Mon-Fri, 10am-5pm Sat & Sun Apr-Oct), the city's western gate and the only remaining part of the town wall. The clock (1761) has separate dials for minutes and hours. The views from up top are superb.

A favourite with window-shoppers and strollers alike, Maximilianstrasse is lined with baroque buildings of which the **Rathaus** (at No 13), with its red façade and lavish rococo interior, and the **Alte Münze** (Old Mint; at No 90) are worth a look. The 18th-century writer **Sophie von la Roche** (1730–1807), founder of the first magazine for women, lived in the light blue building at No 99 (almost across the street from the tourist office); a new **exhibit** (admission free; 🕙 10am-5pm Mon-Fri, 10am-4pm Sat) illustrates her life and work. The same building houses two antiquarian bookshops.

A block south of the Rathaus is the **Judenhof** (Jews' Courtyard; ☎ 291 971; Kleine Pfaffengasse 21; adult/youth aged 7-17yr €2/1; 🕙 10am-5pm, closed Nov-Mar), where, in the courtyard, the excavated remains of a 12th-century synagogue and ritual bath hint at the glories of the city's storied medieval Jewish community. Signs are in English. A curious fact: everyone with the surname of Shapira (or Shapiro) is descended from Jews who lived in Speyer during the Middle Ages.

HISTORISCHES MUSEUM DER PFALZ

The truly superb **Historisches Museum der Pfalz** (Historical Museum of the Palatinate; ☎ 620 222; Domplatz; adult/student €4/3, during special exhibitions €8/6; 🕙 10am-6pm Tue-Sun), in addition to hosting world-class special exhibitions, has a permanent collection that values quality over quantity. One of the highlights is the **Goldener Hut von Schifferstadt**, an incredibly ornate, perfectly preserved gilded hat, shaped like a giant thimble, that dates back to the Bronze Age. The **Wine Museum** features a bottle containing an unappetizing jellied substance from the 3rd century AD, purported to be the world's oldest wine. Two floors below is the **Domschatz** (cathedral treasury), whose prized exhibit is Emperor Konrad II's surprisingly simple bronze crown.

TECHNIK MUSEUM

It's easy to spend an entire day wandering around this amazing **museum** (☎ 670 80; Am Technik Museum 1; adult/child under 14yr €12/10, IMAX €8/6, combined ticket €16/12; 🕙 9am-6pm, to 7pm Sat & Sun), 1km south of the Dom (on the other side of the A61 highway). You can explore – and even climb aboard – a variety of aeroplanes, trains and vintage vehicles, including a genuine Boeing 747 (how in the world did they get it here and then mount it 28m off the ground?), a U9 submarine and an Antonov-22, the world's largest prop plane. Kids will love the playgrounds, various motion simulators, the 54m slide and two Imax theatres.

SEALIFE SPEYER

Situated on the Rhine 700m northeast of the Dom, this somewhat kitschy **aquarium** (☎ 697 80; www.sealifeeurope.com; Im Hafenbecken 5; adult/child 3-14yr/senior & student/family €12/8.50/9.50/38; 🕙 10am-7pm Jul-Sep, 10am-5pm Mon-Fri, 10am-6pm Sat, Sun & holidays Apr-Jun & Oct, 10am-5pm Nov-Mar), which is privately run with input from Greenpeace, and one of nine ecologically-minded Sea Life aquariums around Germany. For details see p455.

Sleeping

DJH hostel (☎ 615 97; www.jugendherberge.de; Geibstrasse 5; dm €18, d €47; 🕙 reception 7.30am-8pm; 🗶) A modern hostel on the Rhine, a bit east of the Technik Museum. Has 48 rooms, including 13 doubles, all with private bathroom. Linked to the Hauptbahnhof by the City-Shuttle bus.

Maximilian (☎ 622 648; info@café-maximilian.de; Korngasse 15; apt €45-50) Also a café-bistro, Maximilian rents out two-person apartments.

Hotel Zum Augarten (☎ 754 58; www.augarten .de, in German; Rheinhäuser Strasse 52; s €44-54, d €65-75; P X) A cosy, family-run, family-friendly hotel where you'll enjoy German guesthouse hospitality and observe suburban German life up close. Situated 1.7km south of the Dom – from the Technik Museum take Industrie- strasse and turn right on Am Flugplatz.

Hotel Trutzpfaff (☎ 292 529; www.trutzpfaff-hotel.de, in German; Webergasse 5; s/d €54/74; reception 8am-8pm; P X) Centrally situated just a block south of the tourist office, this unassuming hostelry has eight pretty average rooms and a tavern (open Monday to Friday; mains cost €6.80 to €15.90) serving Palatine specialities such as *Saumagen* (a pig's stomach stuffed with meat, potatoes and spices that's boiled, sliced and then briefly fried).

Hotel am Technik Museum (☎ 671 00; www.hotel-am -technik-museum.de; Am Technik Museum 1; s/d €55/80; P X) Part of the Technic Museum complex, this place has 108 charmless, institutional rooms with adequate comforts. Those trav- elling by campervan or with a tent can stay at the adjacent Stellplatz (€19 per site), open year-round.

Hotel Domhof (☎ 132 90; www.domhof.de in Ger- man; Bauhof 3; s €92, d €112-122, cheaper Sun night; P X X 🖳) A hotel has stood on this spot next to the Dom – which is an unbeatable location – since the Middle Ages, once host- ing emperors, kings and councillors. The 49 rooms, wrapped around an ivied, cobbled courtyard, are very 1990s.

Eating & Drinking

A selection of eateries can be found along Maximilianstrasse and nearby streets. The Hotel Trutzpfaff has a restaurant.

Maximilian (☎ 622 648; Korngasse 15; mains €6- 16) Just inside the Altpörtel, this convivial café-bistro serves up 12 different breakfasts, salads, lots of Italian options and cheap dinner specials (€5.80).

Domhof-Hausbrauerei (☎ 740 55; Grosse Him- melsgasse 6; mains €6-15; 11am-midnight, to 1am Fri & Sat) Speyer's loveliest beer garden, shaded by chestnut trees, is just steps west of the Dom and has its own children's playground. The menu features Palatine and international favourites, some prepared using beer brewed on the premises.

Zweierlei (☎ 611 10; Johannesstrasse 1, cnr Salzgasse; mains €6-19; lunch & dinner Tue-Sat) This trendy bistro-restaurant, a block north of the tourist office, serves German nouvelle cuisine amid minimalist, ultra-modern décor. If you go for the 'Tender' dinner offer, the chef will randomly assign you an hors d'oeuvre, a main dish and a dessert (€6 each).

Backmulde (☎ 715 77; Karmeliterstrasse 11-13; mains €12-28; lunch & dinner) Owner-chef Gunter Schmidt has a knack for spinning fresh, local products into gourmet dishes with a Medi- terranean flavour. With an epic wine list, it's considered one of Speyer's finest restaurants. A block south of the Altpörtel.

Picnic supplies are available at **Tengelmann supermarket** (Maximilianstrasse 50; 8am-8pm Mon- Sat), next to the Altpörtel.

Getting There & Around

A new S-Bahn line links the Hauptbahnhof with Ludwigshafen and Mannheim, both key rail hubs. Buses (eg bus 717 to Heidelberg) depart from the Hauptbahnhof but the train is usually faster.

Parking costs €2 per day at the Festplatz, 500m south of the Dom and just under the A61 from the Technik Museum.

The City-Shuttle minibus (bus 565; day pass €1) links the garden behind the Dom, the Festplatz, the Technik Museum, Sealife and the youth hostel at 10- or 15-minute intervals from 6am (9am on Sunday) to 8pm.

Bikes can be hired from **Radsport Stiller** (☎ 759 66; Gilgenstrasse 24; bike/tandem per day €10/20; 9.30am-6pm Mon-Fri, 9am-2pm Sat), a block south- west of the Altpörtel. The **Kaiser-Konrad-Radweg** (35km; Kaiser Konrad bicycle path) links Sp- eyer's Dom with Bad Dürckheim's Rathaus.

GERMAN WINE ROAD

The **Deutsche Weinstrasse** (www.deutsche-weinstrasse .de, in German) traverses the heart of the Palatinate (Pfalz), a region of gentle forests, ruined cas- tles and Germany's largest contiguous wine- growing area. Starting in Bockenheim, about 15km west of Worms, it winds south 85km to Schweigen on the French border. Hiking and cycling options are legion.

Blessed with a moderate climate that allows almonds, figs, kiwi fruit and even lemons to thrive, the German Wine Road is especially pretty during the spring bloom. The **wine festival season** from May to October is also a good time to visit, especially around the grape harvest (September and October).

In part because of its proximity to France, the Palatinate is a renowned culinary destination, with restaurants serving everything from gourmet New German cuisine to traditional regional specialities such as *Saumagen*. In the **Pfälzerwald** (the hilly forest west of the Wine Road), locals often plan a day out-of-doors in order to dine in a Waldhütte, a traditional Palatine eatery found along forest trails.

GETTING THERE & AWAY

Neustadt an der Weinstrasse, a central hub from which to start exploring the German Wine Road, is on the twice-an-hour Heidelberg–Mannheim–Kaiserslautern railway line and also has twice-hourly train links to Saarbrücken (€15.50, 1½ hours) and Karlsruhe (€9.10, one hour). The trip from Speyer requires a change at Schifferstadt. The Rhein-Haardtbahn (RHB) light rail line links Bad Dürkheim with Mannheim (€4.50, 50 minutes, at least hourly).

GETTING AROUND

The German Wine Road is most easily explored by car or bicycle (look for the yellow signs sporting a cluster of grapes). Area tourist offices sell the 1:50,000-scale *Deutsche Weinstrasse* cycling map (€6.50), which details a multitude of *Radwanderwege* (bike paths and cyclable back roads).

Thanks to Germany's superb public transport system, it's possible to get almost everywhere – including *to* trailheads and *from* hike destinations – by public transport. Twice an hour, local trains that take bicycles head from Neustadt north to Deidesheim and Bad Dürkheim and south to Landau. Bus options

(every half-hour Monday to Friday, hourly on Saturday, Sunday and holidays) from Neustadt include bus 512 to Deidesheim and Bad Dürkheim and bus 501 to Landau via wine villages such as Hambach, Weyher and Gleisweiler. From Landau, buses continue south to Bad Bergzabern and Schweigen. A number of Pfälzerwald villages west of Neustadt, including Lindenberg, are served by bus 517.

Neustadt an der Weinstrasse

☎ 06321 / pop 54,000

The busy, modern town of Neustadt has preserved a rather charming, largely pedestrianised **Altstadt** teeming with half-timbered houses. It is anchored by the **Marktplatz**, an attractive square flanked by the baroque **Rathaus** and the 14th- and 15th-century Gothic **Stiftskirche** (open only during services), a red-sandstone structure that's been shared by Protestant and Catholic congregations since 1708.

About 4km south of the centre is the **Hambacher Schloss** (Hambacher Castle; ☎ 308 81; admission to grounds free, exhibit adult/student €4.50/1.50; ☺ 10am-6pm Mar-Nov), known as the 'cradle of German Democracy'. It was here that students held massive protests for a free, democratic and united Germany on 27 May 1832, during which the German tricolour flag of black, red and gold was raised for the first time. Today an exhibition commemorates the event, known to history as the Hambacher Fest. Views over the vineyards and the Rhine plains are best from the tower. Bus 502 makes the trip here hourly.

ROAD-TRIP RADIO IN ENGLISH

While tooling around Rhineland-Palatinate, the Saarland and much of Baden-Württemberg, you can crank up the car radio and tune in to a variety of often surprising programmes in English.

When atmospheric conditions are right (as they almost always are at night), the **BBC World Service** can be picked up on 648 kHz AM (medium wave) and, if you're lucky, **BBC Radio 4** can be heard on 198 kHz longwave.

To feel like you're in Middle America, just tune to a station run by the **AFN** (American Forces Network; www.afneurope.net), whose intended audience is US military personnel serving at places like Ramstein Air Base near Kaiserslautern and the Wiesbaden US Army Garrison. Programming you might come across includes NPR (National Public Radio) favourites such as *Car Talk*, pearls of populism from Rush Limbaugh, and news from AP Radio News, CNN Radio and something called the Pentagon Channel. One music show boasts that it plays 'music worth fighting for'. The public service advertisements, peppered with unfathomable acronyms, give a flavour of US military life in Germany. The most powerful relay frequencies to check are 873 kHz AM (transmission from Frankfurt), 1107 kHz (from Kaiserslautern) and 1143 kHz (from Stuttgart). There are also a variety of local FM options.

INFORMATION

ATM Across the street from the tourist office in the shopping mall.

Internet café (Friedrichstrasse 8; per hr €1; ☯ 11am-10pm) Around the corner from the tourist office.

Tourist office (☎ 926 892; www.neustadt.pfalz.com, in German; Hetzelplatz 1; ☯ 9.30am-6pm Mon-Fri, 9.30am-noon Sat Apr-Oct, 9.30am-5pm Mon-Fri Nov-Mar) Across the parklike Bahnhofplatz from the Hauptbahnhof. Has ample information on hiking and cycling options.

SLEEPING & EATING

Neustadt's nicest lodging options are in Haardt, a suburb northwest of the town centre. There are quiet a few restaurants in Neustadt's Altstadt.

DJH hostel (☎ 2289; www.jugendherberge.de; Hans-Geiger-Strasse 27; dm €18; ☒) A modern facility with 122 beds in rooms for one, two and four people, all with private bathroom. A 15-minute walk south of the Hauptbahnhof.

Hotel Tenner (☎ 9660; www.hotel-tenner.de in German; Mandelring 216, Haardt; s/d from €64/89; Ⓟ ☒) Surrounded by vineyards, this 32-room hotel, on a quiet suburban street, offers sweeping views of the Hambacher Schloss. In fine weather, breakfast is served on the pebbly panoramic patio. To get there from the town centre, take bus 512 or drive northeast on Maximilianstrasse and hang a left onto Haardter Strasse.

Pelgen's Worschtstubb (☎ 34 420; Hintergasse 14; Saumagen €7.50) Serves prize-winning *Saumagen* and other Palatine delicacies. Situated two blocks east of the Stiftskirche on a street lined with half-timbered houses, many sheltering restaurants.

Liebstöckl (☎ 313 61; Mittelgasse 22; meat mains from €10; ☯ lunch & dinner Wed-Mon) Has a beer garden and a hearty meat-heavy menu complemented by a few vegetarian choices (€8).

Mandelhof (☎ 882 20; www.mandelhof.de in German; Mandelring 11, Haardt; 3-course meals €18.90; ☯ restaurant & perhaps hotel closed Wed; Ⓟ ☒) Up on a hill overlooking the town, this gourmet restaurant has a delightful terrace and several lovely rooms (singles/doubles from €50/80). A leisurely walk leads to the Wolfsburg ruin.

The Marktplatz hosts a **food market** (mornings Tue & Sat year-round, morning Thu May-Oct).

GETTING AROUND

The bus station is next to the Hauptbahnhof. Bikes can be rented from **Fahrrad Trimpe** (☯ 487 070; Branchweilerhofstrasse 11; per day €10), 10 blocks east of the Hauptbahnhof.

Deidesheim

☎ 06326 / pop 3800

Diminutive Deidesheim, awash in wisteria and one of the German Wine Road's most picturesque villages, is home to about 30 wine-makers; look for signs reading *Weingut* (winery), *Verkauf* (sale) and *Weinprobe* (wine tasting). The helpful **tourist office** (☎ 967 70; www.deidesheim.de; Bahnhofstrasse 5; ☯ 9am-noon & 2-5pm Mon-Fri year-round, 10am-noon Sat Apr-Oct) is 150m across the car park from the Hauptbahnhof.

Deidesheim is centred on the historic Marktplatz, where you'll find a Gothic church, **Pfarrkirche St Ulrich** (open daily), and the 16th-century **Altes Rathaus**, noted for its canopied open staircase. Inside is the three-storey **Museum für Weinkultur** (Wine Museum; ☎ 981 561; Marktplatz 8; admission free; ☯ 3-6pm Wed-Sun & holidays Mar-Dec), whose displays include naive art portrayals of the German Wine Road (English brochure available).

Down an alleyway across from the Rathaus, the **Deutsches Film- und Fototechnik Museum** (Film & Photography Museum; ☎ 6568; Weinstrasse 33; adult/student & senior €3/2.50; ☯ 4-6.30pm Wed-Fri, 2-6.30pm Sat & Sun Mar-Dec) has a truly impressive collection of historical photographic equipment. Veteran shutterbugs may be able to spot every camera they've ever used.

Galleries and studios can be visited along the **Rundgang Kunst und Kultur** (art and culture trail); look for the black-on-yellow 'K' signs. A leaflet available at the tourist office has details and opening hours.

Near the tourist office, the whimsical **Geissbockbrunnen** (Goat Fountain), erected in 1985, celebrates a quirky local tradition. For seven centuries, the nearby town of Lambrecht has had to pay an annual tribute of one goat for using pastureland belonging to Deidesheim. The presentation of this goat, which is auctioned off to raise funds for local cultural activities, culminates in the raucous **Geissbockfest** (Goat Festival), held on Pentecost Tuesday.

SLEEPING & EATING

Gästehaus Ritter von Böhl (☎ 972 201; www.ritter-von-boehl.de in German; Weinstrasse 35; s €45, d €70-85; ☯ reception 9am-6pm, sometimes closed Sun; Ⓟ ☒) This 27-room guesthouse, set around a delightful, wisteria-wrapped courtyard, belongs to, and occupies part of the grounds of, a charity hospital (now an old-age home) founded in 1494.

Deidesheimer Hof (☎ 968 70; www.deidesheimerhof .de; Am Marktplatz; s/d from €120/165, low season from €95/125; **P** ✕ ✕) One of the region's few hotels with five coveted stars, this renowned hostelry has 28 elegant rooms, each unique, and two fine restaurants: St Urban (four-course meals €39), whose regional offerings include *Saumagen*, made with chestnuts in autumn; and the gourmet Schwarzer Hahn (five-/six-/ seven-course meals €75/85/95; open for dinner Tuesday to Saturday), which specialises in creative French- and Palatinate-style dishes.

Turmstüb'l (☎ 981 081; Turmstrasse 3; mains €5-14) This contemporary, artsy wine-café, down an alley from the church, serves tasty hot dishes, including regional specialities such as *Saumagen*.

Gasthaus zur Kanne (☎ 966 00; Weinstrasse 31; mains €8-20; ⊗ noon-2pm & 6-10pm Wed-Sun, noon-9pm Sun & holidays) Serves refined regional cuisine. You can sit inside at hand-painted tables or in the leafy courtyard.

GETTING AROUND
Steinweg (☎ 982 284; www.gepaeckservice-pfalz.de in German; Kirschgartenstrasse 49), 200m from the tourist office, rents bikes (€6.50 per day) and arranges cycling tours with Olympic cycling champion Stefan Steinweg.

Bad Dürkheim
☎ 06322 / pop 18,600
Bad Dürkheim is a handsome, easily walkable spa town as famous for its salty thermal springs as for the annual **Dürkheimer Wurstmarkt** (sausage market; www.duerkheimer-wurstmarkt.de), held in the second and third weeks of September, which bills itself as the world's largest wine festival. Most of the action takes place around the **Dürkheimer Riesenfass**, a gargantuan wine cask that's had a restaurant inside since a master cooper built it in 1934.

INFORMATION
Spielotek (Kurgartenstrasse 10; per hr €2; ⊗ 9am-10pm Mon-Sat, 11am-10pm Sun & holidays) Internet access – but only if you're over 18.
Tourist office (☎ 956 6250; www.bad-duerkheim .de in German; ⊗ 9am-7pm Mon-Fri, 11am-1pm or 3pm Sat & Sun). In the Kurzentrum building. Has a town map in English.

SIGHTS
Between the Hauptbahnhof and the tourist office lies the **Kurpark**, a grassy, azalea-

and wisteria-filled park where you'll find a **children's playground** (in the corner nearest the Hauptbahnhof) and most of the town's spa and wellness facilities. Classic and exotic treatments range from a full-body massage (30 minutes for €24) to Nuad Tao (Thai foot massage). For reservations (required for all but the thermal baths and sauna) stop by the **Kurzentrum** (spa centre; ☎ 9640; www.kurzentrum-bad -duerkheim.de in German; Kurbrunnenstrasse 14). **Vitalis**, another spa run by the same company, is next door.

The city-run **Salinarium** (☎ 935 865; www .salinarium.de in German; adult/child over 6yr €5.50/3, saunas €11.50/9), a year-round complex of indoor and outdoor swimming pools (only one of which is saltwater) and saunas, is a few hundred metres to the northeast.

Hiking options include **Weinwanderwege** (vineyard trails) from St Michaelskapelle, a chapel atop a little vine-clad hill a bit northeast of the tourist office, to Honigsäckel and Hochmess; and forest trails to two historic ruins, **Limburg** (1½ hours) and **Hardenburg** (two hours). The **Kaiser-Konrad-Radweg** (35km) links Bad Dürkheim's Rathaus with Speyer's Dom.

SLEEPING & EATING
Several restaurants with warm-season terraces can be found on Römerplatz and along nearby Kurgartenstrasse.

Knaus Camping Park (☎ 613 56; www.knauscamp.de in German; In den Almen 3; site €6-11, person €6) A lakeside camping ground about 3.5km northeast of the centre.

Marktschänke (☎ 952 60; www.bd-marktschaenke .de in German; s/d from €47/72; **P**) An especially friendly, family-run hotel with seven extralarge rooms and a playfully cluttered, rustic restaurant specialising in regional dishes (mains €6 to €18). About 250m southwest of the Hauptbahnhof.

Hotel Weingarten (☎ 940 10; www.hotelweingarten .de in German; Triftweg 11a-13; s/d from €57.50/82; ⊗ reception closed after 2pm Sun; **P** ✕) This aptly named, 18-room place, 1km northeast of the Bahnhof, offers excellent value. Most of the lovingly cared-for rooms have balconies. Welcome extras include a sauna (€6).

GETTING AROUND
Bikes can be rented around the corner from the tourist office at a **house** (☎ 63447; Schlossgartenstrasse 3; per day €8) with no sign out front. It's best to phone ahead.

AHR VALLEY & THE EIFEL

The Eifel, a rural area of gentle hills, tranquil villages and volcanic lakes, makes for a great respite from the mass tourism of the Moselle and Rhine Valleys. Its subtle charms are best sampled on a bike ride or a hike, though it also has a few headline attractions, including a world-class car-racing track, a stunning Romanesque abbey and a lovely wine region, the Ahr Valley.

The Ahr River has carved a scenic 90km valley stretching from Blankenheim, in the High Eifel, to the Rhine, with which it is confluent near Remagen. This is one of Germany's few red-wine regions – growing *Spätburgunder* (Pinot Noir), in particular – with vineyards clinging to steeply terraced slopes along both banks. The quality is high but the yield small, so very few wine labels ever make it beyond the valley – all the more reason to visit and try them for yourself.

Getting Around

The best way to travel through the Ahr Valley is on the Ahrtalbahn, an hourly train serving most of the villages between Altenahr and Remagen (35 minutes), and, Monday to Saturday, Bonn. Bus 841 also travels the route but takes twice as long and is rather infrequent. If you're driving, make your way to the B266/B267, which traverses the valley.

The scenic **Rotweinwanderweg** (Red Wine Hiking Trail; www.ahr-rotweinwanderweg.de in German), marked by small signs with grape icons, takes hikers though vineyard country on its 35km route from Bad Bodendorf to Altenahr via the hills above Bad Neuenahr and Ahrweiler. You can walk as far as you like and then return on the Ahrtalbahn. Tourist offices have a detailed trail description and maps.

Cycling options include the 46km-long **Ahrradweg**, which runs parallel to the Ahr and links Sinzig (on the Rhine) with Blankenheim. Bikes can be taken on the Ahrtalbahn free-of-charge.

REMAGEN

☎ 02642 / pop 16,000

Remagen, 20km south of Bonn, was founded by the Romans in AD 16 as Rigomagus, but the town would hardly figure in the history books were it not for one fateful day in early March 1945. As the Allies raced across France and Belgium to rid Germany of Nazism, the *Wehrmacht* (armed services of the Third Reich) tried frantically to stave off defeat by destroying all bridges across the Rhine. But the steel rail bridge at Remagen lasted long enough for Allied troops to cross the river, contributing significantly to the collapse of Hitler's western front. One of the bridge's surviving basalt towers now houses the **Friedensmuseum** (Peace Museum; ☎ 201 46; www.bruecke-remagen.de; adult/concession €3.50/1; ⌚ 10am-5pm early Mar-late Nov, to 6pm May-Oct), with an exhibit about Remagen's pivotal role in WWII.

BAD NEUENAHR & AHRWEILER

☎ 02641 / pop 28,000

Bad Neuenahr and Ahrweiler are a bit of an odd couple. Bad Neuenahr is an elegant spa town whose healing waters have been sought out by the moneyed and the famous (including Karl Marx and Johannes Brahms) for a century and a half. Ahrweiler, by contrast, is a dreamy medieval village encircled by a town wall and crisscrossed by narrow, pedestrianised lanes that are lined with half-timbered houses. What the two do have in common, however, is wine, which can be enjoyed in both towns at taverns and restaurants.

Orientation

From Ahrweiler's Hauptbahnhof, walk 600m west along Wilhelmstrasse to get to the old town; more convenient is the Ahrweiler Markt train stop, just north of the old town.

From the Hauptbahnhof in Bad Neuenahr, it's a five-minute walk to the centre, which is around car-free Poststrasse.

Information

Let's Play (Ahrhutstrasse 23, Ahrweiler; per hr €3; ⌚ 9am-11pm) Internet access near the tourist office; you must be over 18.

Post office (cnr Hauptstrasse & Kölner Strasse, Bad Neuenahr)

Tourist offices (☎ 91710; www.ahrtaltourismus.de in German) Ahrweiler (Blankartshof 1; ⌚ 9.30am-1pm & 2-5.30pm Mon-Fri, 10am-3pm Sat & Sun mid-Apr–mid-Nov, 10am-1pm & 2-5pm Mon-Fri, 10am-1pm Sat & Sun mid-Nov–mid-Apr); Bad Neuenahr (Hauptstrasse 114; ⌚ 9.30am-5.30pm Mon-Fri, 10am-1pm Sat & Sun) Both sell walking and cycling maps of the area.

Sights & Activities

AHRWEILER

Ahrweiler preserves a delightful, pedestrianised **Altstadt** almost entirely encircled by a medieval **town wall** with four surviving gates. The focal point is the Marktplatz and its yellow Gothic church, **Pfarrkirche St Laurentius**, beautifully decorated with floral frescoes from the 14th century and luminous stained-glass windows, some of which show farmers working their vineyards. Of the many half-timbered buildings, pride of place goes to **Haus Wolff** (Niederhutstrasse 42), a block east of the church, which is festooned with a knock-out octagonal oriel.

Ahrweiler's Roman roots spring to life at the **Museum Roemervilla** (Roman Villa Museum; ☎ 5311; Am Silberberg 1; adult/student/family €3.60/1.80/7.20; ☼ 10am-5pm Tue-Sun late Mar–mid-Nov) on the northwest edge of town. Protected by a lofty glass and wood structure are 1st- to 3rd-century ruins – a veritable Rhenish Pompeii – that reveal the remarkable standard of living enjoyed by wealthy Romans. A detailed English pamphlet is included in the price.

BAD NEUENAHR

The focal point of Bad Neuenahr, bisected by the Ahr, is the stately **Kurhaus**, an Art Nouveau structure built in 1903 that houses the **Spielbank** (casino; ☎ 757 50; www.spielbank-bad-neuenahr.de, in German; Felix-Rütten-Strasse 1; ☼ 2pm-2am), the first to open in post-WWII Germany. Night after night, an elegant crowd (jacket required for men) mingles among the roulette and blackjack tables or tries its luck at the 'one-armed bandits'. Bring your passport and a lucky charm. The nearby **river banks** are great for strolling.

Neuenahr owes its 'Bad reputation' (ie its spa status) to its mineral springs, whose soothing qualities can be experienced in the **Ahr-Thermen** (☎ 801 200; www.ahrthermen.de, in German; Felix-Rütten-Strasse 3; per 2hr €10, day pass €14, sauna extra €4; ☼ 9am-11pm). Besides swimming pools, options include a surge channel, massage jets and all sorts of saunas. Various discounts are available.

Sleeping & Eating

The town centres of Bad Neuenahr and Ahrweiler teem with traditional German restaurants.

DJH hostel (☎ 349 24; www.jugendherberge.de; St-Pius-Strasse 7; dm €18, d per person €23.50; ☒) This modern, 140-bed hostel is on the south bank

of the Ahr about midway between Ahrweiler and Bad Neuenahr (1.5km from each). All rooms have private bathrooms.

Hotel Garni Schützenhof (☎ 90283; www.schuetzenhof -ahrweiler.de, in German; Schützenstrasse 1, Ahrweiler; s/d from €46/70; ℗ ☒) Facing the Ahrtor, one of Ahrweiler's landmark town gates, this unpretentious family-run hotel has 14 spacious rooms. Offers excellent value.

Hotel-Restaurant Hohenzollern (☎ 4268; www .hotelhohenzollern.com; Am Silberberg 50, Ahrweiler; s €65-80, d €108-143; ℗ ☒) This elegant hillside hotel, right on the Rotweinwanderweg, has unbeatable valley views and a gourmet restaurant (mains €16 to €28). From Ahrweiler's Museum Roemervilla, head up the 1½-lane road through the forest.

Apbell's (☎ 900 243; Niederhutstrasse 27a, Ahrweiler; mains €7-15.50; ☼ closed Mon & Jan) The menu here has something in store for all tastes and budgets, including *Haxe* (leg of pig) and five options for kids. In fine weather, the chestnut-shaded beer garden has the nicest tables.

Eifelstube (☎ 348 50; Ahrhutstrasse 26, Ahrweiler; mains €9.50-15, 3-course lunch €14.50; ☼ closed Tue & Wed) In the same family since 1905, this is one of Ahrweiler's best restaurants. Sample upmarket German and regional specialities while seated in the cosy dining room with beam ceiling and tiled stove. Around the corner facing the tourist office, the affiliated Bistro (closed Tuesday) has cheaper fare such as *Flammkuchen* (Alsatian-style pizza), salads and cakes.

Getting There & Away

Rail travel from the Ahrweiler Markt, Ahrweiler and Bad Neuenahr train stations to Koblenz (€11 or €12, 42 to 67 minutes, hourly) requires a change at Remagen. Direct trains from all three stations serve Bonn (€6.20, 40 minutes, hourly).

ALTENAHR

☎ 02643 / pop 1700

Hemmed in on all sides by craggy peaks giving way to rolling hills and steep vineyards, Altenahr wins top honours as the most romantic location in the Ahr Valley. The landscape is best appreciated by taking a 10-minute uphill walk to the 11th-century **Burgruine Are**, a ruined hilltop castle, whose weather-beaten stone tower stands guard over the valley.

Altenahr is the western terminus of the **Rotweinwanderweg** (opposite). A dozen more trails can be picked up either in the village centre or at the top of the **Ditschardhöhe**, whose 'peak', at 354m, is most easily reached by **chairlift** (☎ 8383; up/return adult €3/4.50, child 3-14yr €2/2.50; ☷ 10am-5pm or later, closes earlier in stormy weather, Easter-Oct). Kids may enjoy the summer **Rodelbahn** (toboggan run).

Altenahr's **tourist office** (☎ 8448; www.altenahr-ahr.de in German; ☷ 9am-noon & 12.30-4pm or 4.30pm Mon-Fri, to 3.30pm Fri, also 10am-1pm Sat mid-Apr–May & Aug-Oct) is inside the Bahnhof (train station).

Sleeping & Eating

Campingplatz Altenahr (☎ 8503; www.camping-altenahr.de; Im Pappelauel; per tent & car/person €7/4.50; ☷ Apr-Oct). A green, grassy camping ground.

DJH hostel (☎ 1880; www.jugendherberge.de; Langfigtal 8; dm €17; ✖) Altenahr's 92-bed hostel, completely renovated in 2006, is beautifully located in the Langfigtal nature park.

Hotel-Restaurant Zum Schwarzen Kreuz (☎ 1534; www.zumschwarzenkreuz.de; Brückenstrasse 5-7; s €38-70, d €58-100; [P] ✖) In a neat half-timbered building in the heart of town, this 60-bed place offers original retro flair with flowery wallpaper; some rooms even have groovy tapestries. The restaurant does regional specialities (mains €9 to €18) and *Flammkuchen*.

Getting There & Away

The Ahrtalbahn train serves villages between Altenahr and Remagen (35 minutes, hourly); on Monday to Saturday it goes to Bonn. Bus 841 also travels the route but takes twice as long and is rather infrequent.

NÜRBURGRING

This historic **Formula One race car track** (☎ 02691-302 630; www.nuerburgring.de) has hosted many spectacular races with legendary drivers since its completion in 1927. Its 20.8km, 73-curve **Nordschleife** (North Loop) was not only the longest circuit ever built but also one of the most difficult, earning the respectful moniker 'Green Hell' from racing legend Jackie Stewart. After Niki Lauda's near-fatal crash in 1976, the German Grand Prix moved to the Hockenheimring near Mannheim but in 1995 Formula One returned to the 5km South Loop, built in 1984.

If you have your own car or motorbike, you can discover your inner Michael (Schumacher, that is) by taking a spin around the North Loop for €14 per round. Those who lack a really fast vehicle and/or prefer to let someone else do the driving can take the **BMW Ring-Taxi** (☎ 932 020, staffed 10am-noon Mon-Fri; http://ring-taxi.bmw-motorsport.com; ☷ Mar-Nov, call for exact days). For €175, up to three people (children must be at least 150cm tall) pile into a 507hp BMW M5, which goes from 0km/h to 100km/h in under five seconds, and are 'chauffeured' around the North Loop by a professional driver at speeds of up to 320km/h. It's hugely popular so make reservations early.

Right by the track is the **Erlebniswelt** (☎ 302 698; adult/child 6-14yr €11/7.50; ☷ 10am-6pm), an automotive theme park where you'll learn about the history and mythology of the Nürburgring and can participate in interactive entertainments and simulators. One hall houses the 450m **Kartbahn** (www.karterlebniswelt.de; per 10/30min €11/26; ☷ 11am-8pm, shorter hours in winter), a go-kart track where you get to experience what 60km/h feels like with your tail just 3cm above the asphalt.

The Nürburgring is off the B258, reached via the B257 from Altenahr.

MARIA LAACH

About 25km northwest of Koblenz, **Abteikirche Maria Laach** (Maria Laach Abbey Church; ☎ 02652-590; www.marialaach.de, in German; admission free; ☷ 5am-8pm) is one of the finest examples of Romanesque architecture in Germany. It's part of a nine-century-old Benedictine abbey, and sits at the edge of a forest and next to a volcanic lake, the **Laacher See**, which is surrounded by a 21-sq-km nature reserve.

You enter the church via a large portico, a feature not usually found north of the Alps. Note the quirky carvings on and above the capitals and the Löwenbrunnen (Lion Fountain), reminiscent of Moorish architecture. The interior is surprisingly modest, in part because the original furnishings were lost during the 1800s. In the west apse lies the late-13th-century tomb of abbey founder Henry II of Palatine (laminated information sheets are available nearby), while the east apse shelters the high altar with its wooden canopy; overhead is an early-20th-century Byzantine-style mosaic of Christ donated by Kaiser Wilhelm II. The entrance to the 11th-century **crypt** (☷ 9-11am & 12.30-5pm Mon-Sat, 12.30-2pm & 3.30-5pm Sun & holidays) is to the left of the choir.

The abbey itself is not open to the public but across the path from the **Gaststätte** (restaurant), a free 20-minute **film** (☷ 9.30-11am & 1-4.30pm except Sun & holiday mornings) looks at the life of the 55 monks, who take the motto 'Ora et Labora' (pray and work) very seriously indeed. They earn a living from economic activities such as running the abbey's hotel, growing organic apples and raising houseplants (available for purchase in the **hothouses**); and they pray five times a day. Attending **Gottesdienst** (prayer services; hours posted in the church) is worthwhile if only to listen to the ethereal chanting in Latin and German.

Various **trails** take walkers up the hill into the forest; options for circumambulating the Laacher See include the lakefront **Ufer-Rundweg** (8km) and two hillier trails (15km and 21km). You can swim near the camping ground.

Next to the car park is a **grocery** (☺ 9am-6pm Mon-Sat year-round, 10am-6pm Sun except sometimes in Jan, Feb, Jul & Aug) selling organic fruits, veggies, cheese and meat grown or prepared by the monks.

Maria Laach is served hourly by bus 312 from Mendig, the nearest town with a train station. By car, get off the A61 at the Mendig exit (No 34), 2km from Maria Laach. The car park (€1.50) is across the road from the church.

THE ROMANTIC RHINE

Between Koblenz and Bingen, the Rhine carves deeply through the Rhenish slate mountains, meandering between hillside castles and steep fields of wine to create a magical atmosphere mixing wonder and legend. This is Germany's landscape at its most dramatic – muscular forested hillsides alternate with craggy cliffs and nearly-vertical terraced vineyards. Idyllic villages appear around each bend, their neat half-timbered houses and proud church steeples seemingly plucked from the world of fairy tales.

High above the river, busy with barge traffic, and the rail lines that run along each bank are the famous medieval castles, some ruined, some restored, all mysterious and vestiges of a time that was anything but tranquil. Most were built by a mafia of local robber barons – knights, princes and even bishops – who extorted tolls from merchant ships by blocking their passage with iron chains. Time and French troops under Louis XIV laid waste to many of the castles but several were restored in the 19th century, when Prussian kings, German poets and British painters discovered

the gorge's timeless beauty. Today, some have been reincarnated as hotels and, in the case of Burg Stahleck, as a hostel (p492).

In 2002 Unesco designated these 65km of riverscape, more prosaically known as the **Oberes Mittelrheintal** (Upper Middle Rhine Valley; www .welterbe-mittelrheintal.de), as a World Heritage Site. One of Germany's most popular tourist destinations, the area is often deluged with visitors, especially in summer and early autumn, but it all but shuts down in winter.

Activities
CYCLING
The **Rhein-Radweg** runs along the left (west) bank of the Romantic Rhine and along some sections of the right bank. It links up with two other long-distance bike paths, the **Nahe-Hunsrück-Mosel-Radweg** (www.naheland-radtouren.de in German), which follows the Nahe River from Bingen southwest to Idar-Oberstein and beyond; and the 311km **Mosel-Radweg** (www.mosel -radweg.de in German), which runs along one or the other banks of the Moselle River from Koblenz to the French city of Metz, passing through Bernkastel-Kues, Trier and Luxembourg.

Bicycles can be taken on most regional trains, making it possible to ride one way (eg down the valley) and take the train the other way.

HIKING
The Rhine Valley is great hiking territory. Each tourist office can supply suggestions and maps for superb local walks.

Four long-distance trails parallel the Rhine between Koblenz and Bingen, continuing downriver to Bonn and upriver to Mainz and beyond. Each bank has a **Rheinhöhenweg** (Rhine Heights Trail), which takes you from hill top to hill top – a bit away from the river – and affords spectacular views. Closer to the Rhine, along the riverbank or on the hillsides just above it, run the new **Rhein-Burgen-Wanderweg** (on the left bank, ie Bingen and Boppard) and the **Rheinsteig** (on the right bank, ie Loreley; www.rheinsteig.de); the latter links Bonn with Wiesbaden, a distance of 320km.

Festivals & Events
Every river village holds at least one wine festival each year, with most of them crammed into August and September, just before harvest time. The Rhineland-Palatinate *Veranstaltungskalender* (events calendar), which

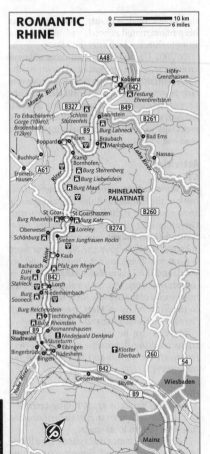

ROMANTIC RHINE

0 _____ 10 km
0 _____ 6 miles

details all the festivals, is available from tourist offices.

During **Rhein in Flammen** (Rhine in Flames), the region's most famous and spectacular festival series, castles, boats and the river banks, all swathed in glowing illumination, form the backdrop to gargantuan firework displays, best viewed from a **boat** (www.rhine-river-lights .com for reservations). Events are held every year in five locations:

Siebengebirge (seven hills between Linz & Bonn) First Saturday in May.

Bingen/Rüdesheim First Saturday in July.

Koblenz to Braubach/Spay Second Saturday in August.

Oberwesel Second Saturday in September.

Loreley rock (St Goar/St Goarshausen) Third Saturday in September.

Getting There & Away

Koblenz (for transport details see p487) and Mainz (p471) are good starting points for touring the region. If you're pressed for time, you can get a glimpse of the Romantic Rhine on a long day-trip from Frankfurt.

Getting Around

BOAT

River travel is a relaxing and very romantic way to see the castles, vineyards and villages of the Romantic Rhine. A boat trip in one direction can be combined with a hike or train trip in the other.

Because of fast currents, shallows, narrow channels and the many passing barges (the Rhine is still an important trade artery), manoeuvring a passenger ferry is a very tricky business – and a fascinating one to see up close. Vessels zipping downriver have priority over those steaming slowly upriver.

From about April to October (winter services are very limited), boats that are run by **Köln-Düsseldorfer** (KD; ☎ Mon-Fri 0221-2088 318, daily 06742-2232; www.k-d.com) link villages such as Bingen, St Goar and Boppard on a set timetable. You can travel to the next village or all the way from Mainz to Koblenz (one-way/return €44.10/50.10, downstream/upstream 5½/8½ hours). Within the segment you've paid for (for example, Boppard-Rüdesheim, which costs €18.80 return), you can get on and off as many times as you like, but make sure to ask for a free stopover ticket each time you disembark.

Many rail passes (such as Eurail) will get you a free ride on normal KD services. However, you still need to obtain a ticket. Children up to the age of four travel for free, while those up to age 13 are charged a flat fee of €3.50. Students under 27 get a 50% discount. Travel on your birthday is free. Return tickets usually cost only slightly more than one-way tickets. There's a €1.50 supplement for travel on the *Goethe*, a Mississippi-style paddle-wheeler.

Several smaller companies, including **Bingen-Rüdesheimer** (☎ 06721-14140; www.bingen -ruedesheimer.com) and **Rössler Linie** (☎ 06722-2353; www.roesslerlinie.de), also run passenger boats up and down the Romantic Rhine.

BUS & TRAIN

Bus and train travel, perhaps combined with minicruises by boat and car ferry, is a convenient way to go village-hopping along the

Rhine, to get to a trailhead, or to return to your lodgings at the end of a hike or bike ride. All local trains take bicycles for no charge.

Villages on the Rhine's left bank (eg Bingen, Boppard and St Goar) are served hourly by local trains on the Koblenz–Mainz run. Right bank villages such as Rüdesheim, Assmannshausen and St Goarshausen are linked every hour or two by Koblenz–Wiesbaden services. It takes about 1½ hours to travel by train from Koblenz to either Mainz or Wiesbaden.

CAR & MOTORCYCLE

The B9 highway travels along the left bank of the Rhine from Koblenz to Bingen, from where the A60 leads on to Mainz. On the right bank, the B42 hugs the river.

CAR FERRY

Since there are no Rhine bridges between Koblenz and Mainz (though many locals would like there to be; environmentalists and the ferry companies are, predictably, opposed), the only way to cross the river along this stretch is by **Autofähre** (car ferry). Services operate between Boppard and Filsen/Kamp Bornhofen (runs until 9pm or 10pm, to 8pm in winter); St Goar and St Goarshausen; Bacharach and Kaub; Niederheimbach and Lorch (till 8pm, 7pm in winter); and Bingen and Rüdesheim (till midnight, 10pm in winter).

Prices vary slightly but you can figure on paying about €3 per car, including the driver; €1.30 per foot passenger (€0.70 for a child); and €0.50 for a bicycle. This being well-organised Germany, the fare tables take into account the possibility, however remote, that you might want to bring along a dog (€0.50), cattle (€3 each) or a horse-drawn cart (€4.50, including the driver).

KOBLENZ

☎ 0261 / pop 108,000

Koblenz is a modern town with ancient roots that go all the way back to the Romans, who founded a military stronghold here around 10 BC. They called it, quite appropriately, Confluentes for its supremely strategic value at the spot where the Moselle is confluent with the Rhine.

Today, Koblenz is the economic and commercial centre of the Upper Rhine region. The eminently strollable town, home to two fabulous castles, is the northern gateway to the Romantic Rhine and also affords access to the

outdoor charms of three low mountain ranges – the Hunsrück, the Eifel and the Westerwald – which converge here.

Orientation

Koblenz' core is shaped like the bow of a ship seen in profile, with the Rhine to the east, the Moselle to the north and the Deutsches Eck right where Leonardo DiCaprio would be kissing Kate Winslet if this were the Titanic. The area's southern border is Friedrich-Ebert-Ring; to the west it's delineated by Hohenfelderstrasse, which leads north to the Balduinbrücke (a bridge spanning the Moselle). The Altstadt is around the northern end of shop-lined, pedestrians-only Löhrstrasse, whose southern, cars-admitted section leads 500m to the Hauptbahnhof.

Information

ATM Inside the Hauptbahnhof.

Main tourist office (☎ 313 04; www.touristik -koblenz.de; Bahnhofsplatz 17; ☯ 9am-7pm May-Sep, to 6pm Apr & Oct, 9am-6pm Mon-Fri, 9am-2pm Sat Nov-Mar) Across the square and a bit to the right as you exit the Hauptbahnhof. Has an excellent map in English and sells events tickets.

Post office (Bahnhofsplatz 16; ☯ 7am-7pm Mon-Fri, 7am-2pm Sat)

Rathaus tourist office (☎ 130 920; Jesuitenplatz 2; ☯ 9am-7pm Mon-Fri, 10am-7pm Sat & Sun May-Sep, to 6pm Apr & Oct, 9am-6pm Mon-Fri, till 4pm Sat Nov-Mar)

Reuffel (Löhrstrasse 62; per 30min €0.60; ☯ 9.30am-7pm Mon-Wed & Fri, to 8pm Thu, to 6pm Sat) A bookshop with English-language books and an internet café upstairs.

Waschsalon (Bahnhofstrasse 22; ☯ 6am-11pm) Self-service laundry 400m north of the Hauptbahnhof.

Sights

CITY CENTRE

Löhrstrasse, Koblenz' main shopping drag, is lined primarily with chain and department stores. Its intersection with Altengraben is known as **Vier Türme** (Four Towers) because each of the 17th-century corner buildings sports a richly detailed façade and an ornately carved and painted oriel.

Turning east on Altengraben takes you to **Am Plan**, a broad square that has undergone various incarnations – as a butchers' market, a stage for religious plays, a place of execution and an arena for medieval tournaments.

The arched walkway at Am Plan's northeastern corner leads to the **Liebfrauenkirche** (☯ 9am-6pm), in the heart of the Altstadt, which was built in a harmonious hotchpotch of styles: of Romanesque origin, it has a Gothic choir and baroque onion-domed turrets. Note the painted vaulting above the central nave.

A block to the north, **Florinsmarkt** is dominated by the **Florinskirche** (☼ 11am-5pm Jun-Aug) and is home to the **Mittelrhein-Museum** (☎ 129 2520; Florinsmarkt 15; adult/concession €2.50/1.50, during special exhibitions €4/2.50; ☼ 10.30am-5pm Tue-Sat, 11am-6pm Sun & holidays), with eclectic displays reflecting the region's history. The collection of 19th-century landscape paintings of the Romantic Rhine by German and British artists is worth a look. For a bit of whimsy, look for the **Augenroller** (eye-roller) figure beneath the façade clock, which rolls its eyes and sticks out its tongue on the hour and half-hour.

Stroll a block north to the Moselle, turn right and follow the riverbank to the **Deutsches Eck**, a promontory built on a sandbank right at the two rivers' point of confluence. It derives its name from the Deutscher Ritterorden (Order of Teutonic Knights), which had its headquarters in the 13th-century building now occupied by the Ludwig Museum. A **statue of Kaiser Wilhelm I** on horseback, in the bombastic style of the late 19th century, dominates the spot. After the original was destroyed in WWII, the empty stone pedestal served as a memorial to German unity – until reunification was achieved in 1990. Bus 1 links the Deutsches Eck with the Hauptbahnhof.

Just south, not far from the riverfront promenade, is the **Deutschherrenhaus**, which once belonged to the Teutonic Knights. Today it's home to the **Ludwig Museum** (☎ 304 040; www .ludwigmuseum.org in German; Danziger Freiheit 1; adult/concession €2.50/1.50; ☼ 10.30am-5pm Tue-Sat, 11am-6pm Sun & holidays), whose emphasis is on post-1945 and contemporary art from France and Germany. Just beyond are the slender towers of 12th-century **Basilika St Kastor** (☼ 9am-6pm).

Two blocks to the southwest, at **Josef-Görres-Platz**, the captivating **Historiensäule** (History Column) portrays 2000 years of Koblenz history in 10 scenes perched one atop the other – the WWII period, for instance, is represented by a flaming ruin. A nearby panel explains all (in English).

FESTUNG EHRENBREITSTEIN

On the right bank of the Rhine looming above the Deutsches Eck, the mighty **Ehrenbreitstein Fortress** (☎ 974 2440; fortress only adult/student & senior €1.10/0.50; ☼ 10am-5pm) proved indestructible to

all but Napoleonic troops, who levelled it in 1801. A few years later, the Prussians took this as a challenge to build one of Europe's mightiest fortifications, completed in 1832.

Behind the stone bulwarks you'll find a DJH hostel, two restaurants and the **Landesmuseum** (☎ 66 750; www.landesmuseumkoblenz.de in German; adult/student & senior incl fortress admission €4/3; ☼ 9.30am-5pm mid-Mar–mid-Nov), with exhibits on the region's economic history, local industries such as tobacco, wine and pumice, and photography. There's also a section about August Horch, founder of the Audi automotive company, who was born in nearby Winningen on the Moselle.

Festung Ehrenbreitstein is accessible by motorcar (it doesn't have to be an Audi). You can also take bus 9 or 10 to the Obertal bus stop, where you can hop on the **Sesselbahn** (chairlift; adult/child 4-14yr & hostel guest €4.20/2.50, return €5.80/3.50). Alternatively, take bus 9 to the Neudorf/Bergstrasse stop, from where it's a 20-minute walk uphill (follow the signs to the DJH hostel). A tiny **passenger steamer** (adult €1.30; ☼ till 6pm or 7pm approx Easter–mid-Nov) links the right-bank Ehrenbreitstein quarter, below the fortress, with the left-bank's Rheinpromenade.

SCHLOSS STOLZENFELS

With its crenellated towers, ornate gables and medieval-style fortifications, **Schloss Stolzenfels** (☎ 516 56; adult/concession obligatory guided tour €2.60/1.30; ☼ 9am-6pm Apr-Sep, 9am-5pm Jan-Mar & Oct-Nov, closed on the 1st work day of each week), 5km south of the town centre, exudes the timeless, sentimental beauty for which the Romantic Rhine is famed. In 1823, the future Prussian king Friedrich Wilhelm IV fell under its spell and had the castle – ruined by the French – rebuilt as his summer residence; during the Victorian era, guests included Queen Victoria. Today, the rooms remain largely as the king left them, with paintings, weapons, armour and furnishings from the mid-19th century.

To get there, take bus 650 from the Hauptbahnhof to the castle car park, from where it's a 15-minute walk.

Sleeping

Campingplatz Rhein-Mosel (☎ 827 19; www.camping -rhein-mosel.de; Schartwiesenweg 6; per adult/tent/car €4.50/2.50/3; ☼ Apr–mid-Oct) On the north bank of the Moselle, right opposite the Deutsches Eck. Linked to the city centre by a passenger ferry.

DJH hostel (☎ 972 870; www.jugendherberge.de; dm €17, d €47; P ⊠) A modern, 183-bed place inside historic Ehrenbreitstein Fortress. Some rooms have private bathroom. See Festung Ehrenbreitstein (opposite) for transport details.

Hotel Jan van Werth (☎ 36 500; www.hoteljanvan werth.de, in German; Von-Werth-Strasse 9; s/d €41/62, without bathroom €23/48) A favourite with backpackers on a budget, this guesthouse-like establishment has a lobby that feels like someone's living room and 16 rooms with 22 beds. Offers exceptional value – no surprise that it's often booked-out, especially when the weather's good. Situated four blocks north of the Hauptbahnhof and one block south of Friedrich-Ebert-Ring.

Hotel Hamm (☎ 303 210; www.hotel-hamm.de; St-Josef-Strasse 32-34; s €52-64, d €65-93, q €120; P ⊠ ▣) Unpretentious and unsurprising, this 35-room hotel, while hardly exhilarating, is popular with businesspeople and offers good value. In a residential area three blocks south of the Hauptbahnhof and 1.5km from the Altstadt, to which it's linked by bus 1.

Contel Koblenz (☎ 406 50; www.contel-koblenz.de; Pastor-Klein-Strasse 19; s/d from €71/76, buffet breakfast €10; P ⊠) This 185-room hotel's exuberant bad taste begins with the electric blue façade and gets wilder inside – some new outrage against bourgeois good taste awaits around every corner! About a third of the rooms have kitchenettes with tiny fridges and three come with waterbeds. Situated 1km west along the Moselle from the Altstadt; served by bus 3, whose nearest stop is Ludwig-Erhard-Strasse.

Diehl's Hotel (☎ 970 70; www.diehls-hotel.de; Rheinsteigufer 1; s €57-95, d €74-120, breakfast €12.50; P ⊠ ▣) A family-run hotel on the Rhine's east bank. Has a 1980s vibe and 57 comfortable rooms, all offering watery views of Koblenz. The restaurant has a gorgeous terrace overlooking the Rhine – perfect for a romantic sunset dinner. Situated about 1km south of Festung Ehrenbreitstein.

Eating & Drinking

Many of Koblenz' restaurants and pubs are in the Altstadt, eg around and northeast of Münzplatz, and along the Rhine. Diehl's Hotel has a romantic restaurant.

Kaffeewirtschaft (☎ 914 4702; Münzplatz 14; mains €5.50-12.50, salads €4.50-8.50; ⏱ 9am-midnight Mon-Fri, 9am-2am Sat, 10am-midnight Sun) A hip café with minimalist designer décor, old marble tables and daily specials, including vegetarian options, that take advantage of whatever's in season.

Cafe Miljöö (☎ 142 37; Gemüsegasse 12; salads €6-8; ⏱ 9am-2am Sun-Fri, 8am-2am Sat) Miljöö, pronounced like the French word milieu, is a cosy bistrolike café, decorated with changing exhibits of original art and fresh flowers. It serves a wide selection of coffees, teas and homemade cakes. Breakfast is available until 5pm.

Weindorf (☎ 133 7190; Julius-Wegeler-Strasse 2-4; mains €6-17; ⏱ 10am-1am, warm food till 11pm, from 4pm Nov-Apr) Sure, this little 'wine village', with its four cute, half-timbered German-style restaurants, is a post-WWII reconstruction of a 1925 replica of the 'real thing' (whatever that is), but the quality of the food remains high and prices are fair. Only the service needs improving.

Elsa's Cuisine (☎ 133 8868; Paradies 2; mains €12.50-26; ⏱ 6pm-midnight, last order 10pm) Provence meets Joburg at this homy, welcoming restaurant, which serves up innovative French cooking with South African flair. Carnivorous options include crocodile, ostrich, kangaroo and bison.

Irish Pub (☎ 973 7797; www.irish-pub-koblenz.de; Burgstrasse 7; ⏱ 4pm-2am or 3am Mon-Fri, 1pm-2am or 3am Sat & Sun) A Koblenz institution since 1985, this place is a favourite with English speakers. Monday is quiz night (from 9pm) and there's karaoke every Wednesday (from 9pm). Screens major sports events and hosts live music six to eight times a month, usually on Friday or Saturday (9pm to 1am).

Self-catering options:

Aldi supermarket (Bahnhofstrasse 50; ⏱ 8am-8pm Mon-Fri, 8am-6pm Sat) Two blocks north of the Hauptbahnhof.

Rizza (Rizzastrasse 49; ⏱ 7.30am-7pm Mon-Fri, 7.30am-4pm Sat) Fresh fruit and veggies three blocks north of the Hauptbahnhof.

Getting There & Away

Koblenz' Hauptbahnhof is served by frequent IC trains going north to such cities as Bonn and Cologne and south to Mainz, Frankfurt and beyond. Regional trains go to Trier and villages on both banks of the Romantic Rhine, including Bingen (€10, 50 minutes). Some of the Rhine villages are also served by buses that stop outside the Hauptbahnhof – bus 650 goes to Boppard via Schloss Stolzenfels while bus 570 goes to Braubach/Marksburg.

Several boat operators have docks along Konrad-Adenauer-Ufer, on the Rhine just south of the Deutsches Eck.

A number of highways converge in Koblenz, including the B9 from Cologne/Bonn. The nearest autobahns are the A61 (Koblenz-Nord exit) and the A48/A1 to Trier.

Getting Around

To avoid parking fees you can leave your vehicle at a Park & Ride lot – options include Sporthalle-Stadion Oberwerth, 2.5km south of the Hauptbahnhof next to the stadium, from where bus 1 goes to the city centre.

Bus trips in the city centre cost €1.40; longer trips (eg to the hostel or Schloss Stolzenfels) are €2.10. Day passes cost €3.15/4.20 for one/ two zones.

BRAUBACH

☎ 02627 / pop 3200

Framed by vineyards and rose gardens, the snug 1300-year-old town of Braubach, about 8km south of Koblenz on the right bank, unfolds against the dramatic backdrop of the **Marksburg** (☎ 206; www.marksburg.de; adult/ student/child €4.50/4/3.50; ☉ 10am-5pm Apr-Oct, 11am-4pm Nov-Mar). This hilltop castle's main claim to fame is that it has never been destroyed, thanks in large part to several layers of forti-fication added by a succession of counts and landgraves. The tour takes in the citadel, the Gothic hall and the large kitchen plus a grisly torture chamber, with its hair-raising assort-ment of pain-inflicting nasties.

Bus 570 goes from Koblenz' Hauptbahnhof to Braubach, from where it's a 20-minute uphill walk to the castle.

BOPPARD

☎ 06742 / pop 16,000

Thanks to its outdoor options, historic sites and scenic location on a horseshoe bend in the river, Boppard (bo-*part*), about 20km south of Koblenz, is a very worthwhile stop. A gateway to lots of great hikes in the Hunsrück, it's also a real town complete with a small cinema and travel agencies where locals can book flights to where you're from. Be sure to sample the excellent riesling from grapes grown near here in some of the Rhine's steepest vineyards.

Information

ATMs On the Marktplatz behind the tourist office.
Call-Shop (Oberstrasse 99; per hr €2; ☉ 10.30am-

8.30pm or later Mon-Sat, 2-8.30pm Sun) Has internet access.
Post office (Heerstrasse 177)
Tourist office (☎ 3888; www.boppard.de; Marktplatz; ☉ 8am-6pm Mon-Fri, 9am-1pm Sat May-Sep, 8am-4pm Mon-Fri Oct-Apr) Inside the Altes Rathaus. Lists of hotels and cultural events and a map are posted outside.

Sights

Just off Boppard's main commercial street, the pedestrianised, east–west oriented **Oberstrasse**, is the ancient **Marktplatz**, whose fountain is a favourite local hang-out. Still home to a market on Friday mornings, it's dominated by the twin towers of the late Romanesque **Severuskirche**, an elegant 13th-century church built on the site of Roman military baths. In-side are polychrome wall paintings, a hanging cross from 1225 and spiderweb-like vaulted ceilings.

Half-a-block east of the church, the cutest of Boppard's half-timbered buildings, built in 1519, now houses a tearoom called **Teehäusje** (☎ 5798; Untere Marktstrasse 10; ☉ 9.30am-12.30pm Mon-Sat, 2.30pm or 3-6pm daily).

A couple of blocks east, in a 14th-century palace, the **Museum der Stadt Boppard** (☎ 103 69; Burgstrasse; admission free; ☉ 10am-12.30pm & 1.30-5pm Tue-Sun Apr-Oct) has displays on local history and an entire floor dedicated to bentwood furniture (see boxed text, opposite).

Along the riverfront is the **Rheinallee**, a promenade lined with ferry docks, neatly painted hotels and wine taverns. There are grassy areas and a **children's playground** a bit upriver from the car-ferry dock.

A block south of the Marktplatz, the **Römer-Kastell** (Roman Fort; cnr Angertstrasse & Kirchgasse; admission free; ☉ 24hr), also known as the Römerpark, has 55m of the original 4th-century Roman wall and graves from the Frankish era (7th century). A wall panel shows what the Roman town of Bodobrica looked like 1700 years ago.

Activities

For a spectacular view that gives you the illu-sion of looking at four lakes instead of a single river, take the 20-minute **Sesselbahn** (☎ 2510; up/return €4.20/6.20; ☉ 9.30am-6.30pm Apr-Oct) from the downriver edge of town up to the **Viersee-nblick** viewpoint. The nearby **Gedeonseck** affords views of the Rhine's hairpin curve.

The new **Klettersteig** (admission free; ☉ 24hr), which begins near the Sesselbahn, is a 2½- to

---

CLASSIC, MODERN & TIMELESS

Faced with fickle fashion trends, few furniture styles retain their freshness and popularity for long. A rare exception is bentwood furniture, invented by a Boppard-born cabinetmaker named Michael Thonet (1796–1871; *tone*-et).

Whether in modern-day Paris-style cafés or Toulouse Lautrec paintings of real *fin de siècle* Paris cafés, we've all seen Thonet's minimalist Chair Number 14 looking curvaceous, elegant and sturdy. The secret of this model, of which tens of millions have been produced, and all other bentwood pieces, lies in a production process that involves stacking strips of veneer, soaking them in hot glue so they become pliable, and then drying them in the desired shape in metal moulds. Thonet began his experiments in his Boppard shop in about 1830 but it was the 1851 Great Exhibition in London's Crystal Palace that catapulted him and his Vienna-based firm, soon to be known as Gebrüder Thonet, into prominence.

Exquisite bentwood furniture produced by Thonet during the 19th century can be seen in the **Museum der Stadt Boppard** (opposite). **Gebrüder Thonet** (www.thonet.de) is now run by its founders' great-great grandchildren.

---

three-hour cliffside adventure hike. Decent shoes are a must. If you chicken out at the critical vertical bits – some with ladders – less vertiginous alternatives are available. It's possible to walk back to town via the Vierseenblick.

Even more memorable is the dramatically steep **Hunsrückbahn** train that travels through five tunnels and across two viaducts on its 8km journey from Boppard's Bahnhof to Buchholz (adult/child up to 11 years one-way €2.10/1.20, 15 minutes). Many people hike back to Boppard from here, but Buchholz is also the starting point of an excellent 17km hike via the romantic **Ehrbachklamm Gorge** to Brodenbach, from where you can get back to Boppard by taking bus 301 to Koblenz and then bus 650 to Boppard. Another option: take the hourly bus 626 from Brodenbach to Emmelshausen, and then the Hunsrückbahn back to Boppard (adult/child €3.45/1.75).

The tourist office organises **wine tastings** (5 wines €5; ☾ 8pm Thu Apr–Oct), hosted each month by a different *Weingut* (wine-growing estate).

Bikes can be hired from **Fahrrad Lüdicke** (☎ 4736; Oberstrasse 105; per day €6.50; ☾ 9am-6pm Mon-Fri, 9am-1pm Sat). The tourist office has lots of material on cycling options.

Sleeping & Eating

Hotels, cafés and restaurants line the Rheinallee, Boppard's riverfront promenade. To get there by car, follow the signs on the B9 to the *Autofähre* – that is, turn onto Mainzer Strasse at the upriver (eastern) edge of town.

Campingpark Sonneneck (☎ 2121; www.campingpark -sonneneck.de; B9 hwy; person/site/car €5.70/3.20/3.20;

☾ Easter–mid-Oct; ⌘) Stretching for 2km along the riverfront about 5km downriver from Boppard, this camping ground has modern facilities and a large pool. From Boppard take bus 650 towards Koblenz.

Hotel Rebstock (☎ 4876; www.rheinhotel-rebstock.de; Rheinallee 31; s €31-46, d €46-77; ☾ reception 7am-10pm Wed-Sun, 7am-4pm Mon & Tue; ✗) This family-run hotel, on the Rhine facing the car-ferry landing, has 10 bright, spacious rooms, many with river views and some with balconies. The restaurant is top-notch.

Hotel Günther (☎ 890 90; www.hotelguenther.de; Rheinallee 40; s €50-82, d €62-98; ☾ closed most of Dec; ✗ ▱) Watch boats and barges glide along the mighty Rhine from your balconied room at this bright, welcoming waterfront hotel. It's owned by an American fellow and his German wife, which makes communication a cinch – and explains why the breakfast buffet includes peanut butter.

Hotel Bellevue (☎ 1020; www.bellevue-bop pard.de; Rheinallee 41; s/d from €86/120, cheaper in winter; P ✗ ☾ ▱) This luxurious, Best Western– affiliated hotel, built in grand style in 1910, has 94 highly civilised rooms, most with views of the Rhine.

Weinhaus Heilig Grab (☎ 2371; Zelkesgasse 12; snacks €3.50-7; ☾ 3-11pm or later, closed Tue & Christmas–mid-Jan) Across the street from the Hauptbahnhof, Boppard's oldest wine tavern offers a cosy setting for sipping the local rieslings. In summer, you can sit outside under a leafy chestnut canopy. Also has five rooms for rent (doubles €56 to €66).

Weingut Felsenkeller (☎ 2154; Mühltal 21; snacks €4-7; ☾ 3-10pm or later, closed Tue) Across the street

RHINELAND-PALATINATE & SAARLAND

from the chairlift station and next to a little stream, this place serves its own and other local growers' wines.

Severus Stube (☎ 3218; Untere Marktstrasse 7; mains €7-12.50; ⊗ closed Thu) Serves up good-value German food under rustic beam ceilings.

The **Penny Markt supermarket** (Oberstrasse 171; ⊗ 7am-8pm Mon-Sat) sells picnic supplies.

ST GOAR

☎ 06741 / pop 3100

St Goar, 10km upriver of Boppard and 28km downriver from Bingen, is lorded over by the sprawling ruins of **Burg Rheinfels** (☎ 383; Schlossberg; adult/child 6-14yr €4/2; ⊗ 9am-6pm Apr–mid-Oct, to 5pm mid-Oct–early Nov, 10am-5pm Sat & Sun in good weather early Nov-Mar), once the mightiest fortress on the Rhine. Built in 1245 by Count Dieter V of Katzenelnbogen as a base for his toll-collecting operations, its size and labyrinthine layout is truly astonishing. Not only kids will love exploring the subterranean tunnels and galleries. To get there, you can walk for 20 minutes up the hill from the youth hostel, drive (parking fee required) or, from April to October, take the Burgexpress tourist train (€3 return, every 25 minutes).

Another kid-pleasing stop is the **Deutsches Puppen- und Teddymuseum** (German Doll & Teddy Bear Museum; ☎ 7270; Sonnengasse 8; adult/child 4-11yr/youth 12-17yr €3.50/1.50/2.50; ⊗ 10am-5pm Apr-Dec).

The Protestant **Stiftskirche** (Am Marktplatz), across the street from the Bahnhof, is known for its late Gothic murals, neat vaulting and Romanesque crypt.

Walking options include the **Panoramaweg** – follow the signs from the Rathaus.

The **tourist office** (☎ 383; www.st-goar.de; Heerstrasse 86; ⊗ 9am-12.30pm & 1.30-6pm Mon-Fri, to 5pm Oct-Apr, closes 2pm Fri Nov-Mar, also open 10am-noon Sat May-Sep), on the pedestrianised main street, can supply you with a map for the Via Sancti Goaris city-centre walking tour.

Sleeping & Eating

DJH hostel (☎ 388; www.jugendherberge.de; Bismarckweg 17; dm €13.50; ⊗ reception 7am-10pm; ✗) This old-style hostel is at the northern end of town, on the hillside below Burg Rheinfels.

Hotel Zur Loreley (☎ 1614; www.hotel-zur-loreley.de; Heerstrasse 87; s €35-45, d €50-68, apt €58-74, all incl breakfast; P ✗) A central and welcoming place to hang your hat, this seven-room hotel has tasteful, modern décor in natural colours; a garage and repair centre for bicycles, and a

variety of lodging options, including eight holiday apartments. Just off the B9 near the Marktplatz.

Hotel Hauser (☎ 333; www.hotelhauser.de; Heerstrasse 77; s €26-30, d €52-58; ⊗ reception closed Mon Nov-Mar, hotel closed mid-Dec–mid-Jan) Graced with an air of slightly faded gentility, this informal, 13-room hotel, situated next to the Stiftskirche, feels lived-in – and lived-in well, with humour and *joie de vivre*. The restaurant serves regional specialities, including fish.

ST GOARSHAUSEN & LORELEY

☎ 06771 / pop 1600

St Goar's twin town on the right bank of the Rhine – the two are connected by car ferry – is St Goarshausen, gateway to the most fabled spot along the Romantic Rhine, the **Loreley**. This enormous slab of slate owes its fame to a mythical maiden whose siren songs are said to have lured sailors to their death in the treacherous currents, as poetically portrayed by Heinrich Heine in 1823. At the very tip of a narrow strip of land jutting into the Rhine, a sculpture of the blonde buxom beauty perches lasciviously.

The Loreley outcrop can be reached by car, by shuttle bus (one-way €1.45, hourly from April to October) or via the **Treppenweg** (a steep stairway). At the **Loreley Besucherzentrum** (Visitor Centre; ☎ 599 093; adult/student €2.50/1.50; ⊗ 10am-6pm Mar–mid-Nov), which has a tourist office branch inside, exhibits (including an 18-minute 3D film) examine the region's geology, flora and fauna, shipping, wine making, the Loreley myth and the beginnings of Rhine tourism in an engaging, interactive fashion. To the left as you approach the centre, a gravel path leads through the forest to the **Loreleyspitze** (the tip of the Loreley outcrop; admission free; ⊗ 24hr), where you'll find spectacular panoramic views, pay-per-view telescopes and a café. Far below, teeny-tiny trains slither along both banks of the Rhine while miniature barges negotiate its waters.

St Goarshausen is also home to two castles. **Burg Maus** (Mouse Castle; www.burg-maus.de, in German), originally called Peterseck, was built by the archbishop of Trier in an effort to counter Count Dieter's toll practices. In a show of medieval muscle-flexing, the latter responded by building a much bigger castle, calling it **Burg Katz** (Cat Castle; closed to the public). And so, to highlight the obvious imbalance of power between count and archbishop, Peterseck soon came to be known as Burg Maus. These days, Burg Maus (interior closed) houses the **Adler- und Falkenhof** (Eagle & Falcon House; ☎ 7669; adult/child over 6yr/family €6.50/5.50/20; ☺ falconry show 11am & 2.30pm Tue-Sun, also 4.30pm Sun & holidays mid-Mar–early Oct), reached by a 20-minute walk from St Goarshausen-Wellmich.

St Goarshausen has its own **tourist office** (☎ 9100; www.loreley-touristik.de; Bahnhofstrasse 8; ☺ 9am-5pm Mon-Fri, 10am-noon Sat Apr-Oct).

OBERWESEL
☎ 06744 / pop 3200

Oberwesel has lost some of its 'romantic' feel to modern construction and the railway, built in 1857, which runs between the river and a section of the impressive, 3km-long medieval **town wall**. The latter, sporting 16 guard towers, wraps around much of the Altstadt; you can stroll on top of much of it.

Easily spotted on a hillside at the northern end of town is the 14th-century **St-Martins-Kirche**, known as the 'white church', which has painted ceilings, a richly sculpted main altar and a tower that once formed part of the town's defences. In the southern Altstadt, the **Liebfrauenkirche**, known as the 'red church' for the colour of its façade, is older by about 100 years and boasts an impressive carved gold altar.

Each April, Oberwesel crowns, not a *Weinkönigin* (wine queen) as in most towns, but a *Weinhexe* (wine witch) – a good witch, of course, who is said to protect the vineyards. Photos of all the *Weinhexen* crowned since the 1940s are on display in the new **Kulturhaus** (☎ 714 726; Rathausstrasse 23; adult/student €2.50/1.50; ☺ 10am-noon & 2-5pm Tue-Fri, 2-5pm Sat, Sun & holidays), whose well-presented local history museum displays 19th-century engravings of the Romantic Rhine and models of Rhine riverboats. An excellent English visitors' guide is available at reception.

High above the town's southeastern edge is the majestic **Schönburg** castle, saved from total ruin when a New York real estate millionaire purchased it in 1885 (it's now a hotel). Legend has it that this was once the home of seven beautiful but haughty sisters who ridiculed and rejected all potential suitors until they were turned into stone and submerged in the Rhine. If you look closely, you can spot the **Sieben Jungfrauen** (Seven Virgins rocks) from a viewpoint reached via a lovely vineyard trail beginning at the town's northwestern edge.

The **tourist office** (☎ 710 624; www.oberwesel.de; Rathausstrasse 3; ☺ 9am-1pm & 2-6pm Mon-Fri, to 5pm Nov-Mar, 10am-2pm Sat Jul-Aug) is across the street from the Rathaus.

Half-timbered **Hotel Römerkrug** (☎ 7091; www.hotel-roemerkrug.rhinecastles.com; Marktplatz 1; s/d €47.50/77.50), run by two generations of a friendly local family, is in the most picturesque part of town, facing the Rathaus. The seven rooms have an antique feel. The restaurant (mains €12 to €24) is closed on Wednesday; in January and February it's only open on the weekend.

Picnic supplies are available at the **Aktiv Markt supermarket** (Koblenzstrasse 1; ☺ 8am-7pm Mon-Fri, 8am-4pm Sat).

Bicycles can be rented from **Höhn** (☎ 336; Liebfrauenstrasse 38).

BACHARACH
☎ 06743 / pop 2200

One of the prettiest of the Rhine villages, tiny Bacharach – 24km downriver from Bingen – conceals its considerable charms behind a time-worn, 14th-century wall. From the B9, go through one of the thick arched gateways under the train tracks and you'll find yourself in a medieval village that has exquisite half-timbered mansions such as the **Altes Haus**, the **Posthof** and the off-kilter **Alte Münze** – all are along Oberstrasse, the main street, which runs parallel to the Rhine.

Also on Oberstrasse is the late Romanesque **Peterskirche** (☺ 9.30am-6pm Apr-Oct) with some particularly suggestive capitals. Look for the naked woman with snakes sucking her breasts (a warning about the consequences of adultery) at the end of the left aisle. A path that begins in between the church and the tourist office takes you uphill for 15 minutes to the 12th-century **Burg Stahleck**, now a hostel, and past the filigree ruins of the Gothic **Wernerkapelle**.

The best way to get a sense of the village and its surrounds is to take a walk atop the ramparts – a complete circuit should be possible by 2008. The lookout tower on the upper section of the wall affords panoramic views.

Bacharach's **tourist office** (☎ 919 303; www.rhein-nahe-touristik.de; Oberstrasse 45; ☺ 9am-5pm Mon-Fri, 10am-1pm Sat, Sun & holidays Apr-Oct, 9am-noon Mon-Fri Nov-Mar) has handy information about the entire area. There's an ATM across Oberstrasse from the church.

RHINELAND-PALATINATE & SAARLAND

Sleeping & Eating

There are places to eat all along Oberstrasse.

Campingplatz Sonnenstrand (☎ 1752; www.camping-sonnenstrand.de; Strandbadweg 9; per person/tent/car €5/3/3; ☻ Apr-Oct) On the Rhine about 500m south of (upriver from) town.

DJH Burg Stahleck (☎ 1266; www.jugendherberge.de; Burg Stahleck; dm €17; ☒) In a dream setting inside the medieval Burg Stahleck, this hostel has 166 beds in rooms for one to six people, almost all with private bathrooms.

Rhein Hotel (☎ 1243; www.rhein-hotel-bacharach.de; Langstrasse 50; €48-57, d €76-90; P ☒) This homy, family-run hotel, right on the town's medieval ramparts, has 14 well-lit, medium-sized rooms with compact bathrooms and original artwork. Those facing the river, and thus the train tracks, have double double-glazing. The restaurant (mains €9 to €17; closed Tuesday) serves regional dishes.

Zum Grünen Baum (☎ 1208; Oberstrasse 63; snacks & light meals €3-7.50) An unpretentious wine tavern serving some of the best wine in town. Try the *Weinkarussel*, a 15-wine sampler (€13.50).

Posthof (☎ 599 663; Oberstrasse 45; mains €7.50-16) In the same building as the tourist office, this restaurant serves German and vegetarian dishes, all made with fresh, local products. On balmy summer nights the most coveted tables are in the ancient courtyard.

You can stock up for a picnic at the **Rewe grocery** (Oberstrasse 66; ☻ 8am-12.30pm & 2-6pm Mon-Fri, 8am-12.30pm Sat).

BACHARACH TO BINGEN

Along the southernmost stretch of the Romantic Rhine, three impressive castles affording spectacular views grace the craggy left-bank slopes. First up (if you're coming from the north) is the state-owned **Burg Sooneck** (☎ 06743-6064; adult/concession guided tour €2.60/1.30; ☻ 9am-6pm, to 5pm Oct-Mar, closed 1st workday of each week, usually Mon & in Dec), carefully restored in the 19th century and filled with neo-Gothic and Biedermeier furniture and paintings.

Looming above the village of Trechtingshausen, the mighty **Burg Reichenstein** (☎ 06721-6117; www.burg-reichenstein.de in German; adult/child under 12yr €3.50/2.50; ☻ 10am-6pm Mar–mid-Nov, closed Mon except Jul & Aug) now harbours a museum with a prized collection of cast-iron oven slabs, hunting trophies, armoury and furnishings. There's also a restaurant.

The most picturesque of the three is the privately owned **Burg Rheinstein** (☎ 06721-6348;

www.burg-rheinstein.de; adult/child €3.80/2.70; ☻ 9.30am-5.30pm mid-Mar–mid-Nov, 2-5pm Mon-Thu & 10am-5pm Sun mid-Nov–mid-Mar), which in the 1820s became the first Rhine castle to be converted – by Prussian royalty – into a romantic summer residence. The still-functional drawbridge and a portcullis evoke medieval times but the interior is mostly neo-Gothic.

BINGEN

☎ 06721 / pop 24,700

Thanks to its strategic location at the confluence of the Nahe and Rhine Rivers, Bingen has been coveted by warriors and merchants since its founding by the Romans in 11 BC. Scarred by war and destruction many times, these days it's an attractive town and is considerably less touristy than some of its neighbours.

Bingen was the birthplace of the writer Stefan George (1868–1933) and, more notably, the adopted home of Hildegard von Bingen (see boxed text, opposite).

Locals are immensely proud that between mid-April and mid-October 2008, Bingen has been selected to host Rhineland-Palatinate's quadrennial **Landesgartenschau** (State Garden Show; www.landesgartenschau-bingen-2008.de).

Orientation & Information

Bingen's centre is along the left (south) bank of the Rhine just east of where it is joined by the Nahe River. The town has two train stations: the Hauptbahnhof, a bit west of the Nahe in Bingerbrück; and the smaller Bahnhof Bingen Stadt, a bit east of the town centre.

Post office (Am Fruchtmarkt)

Tourist office (☎ 184 205; www.bingen.de; Rheinkai 21; ☻ 9am-6pm Mon-Fri, 9am-12.30pm Sat Easter-Oct, 10am-1pm Sun May-Oct, 10am-12.30pm & 1.30-4pm Mon-Thu, 10am-1pm Fri Nov-Easter) Facing the Rhine 250m west of Bahnhof Bingen Stadt. Has brochures and maps for hikers and cyclists.

Sights

Bingen's commercial centre is on and around pedestrians-only Basilikastrasse, named after **Basilika St Martin**, a 15th-century, Gothic-style church – built on the site of a Roman temple – at its western end. Up the hillside is the town's most prominent landmark, **Burg Klopp**, an imposing castle restored in the late 19th century. The views are superb and the terrace is the perfect spot for a first kiss – or a 10,000th. To get a bit higher you can climb the **tower** (admission free; ☻ 8am-6pm in the warm months), which proudly flies the town's red-and-white flag. The old Roman well seems bottomless (it's actually 52m deep).

The modern **Historisches Museum am Strom** (☎ 991 531; Museumsstrasse 3; adult/concession €3/2; ☽ 10am-5pm Tue-Sun) occupies a former power station right on the Rhine. One section traces the life and achievements of Hildegard von Bingen (see boxed text below); there are few actual objects on display but the panelling, in German and English, is informative. Another highlight is a set of surgical instruments – from scalpels and cupping glasses to saws – left behind by a Roman doctor in the 2nd century AD. Idealised visions of the Rhine area, both engraved and painted, are the focus of several rooms dedicated to Rhine romanticism.

High atop the **Rochusburg** (Rochus Hill), 2.5km southeast up Rochusallee from the tourist office, is the neo-Gothic **Rochuskapelle**, a pilgrimage church – last rebuilt in the late 1800s – with a very sharp steeple and a splendid canopied altar showing scenes from the life of Hildegard von Bingen. About 400m nearer Bingen is the **Hildegard Forum** (☎ 181 0012; Rochusweg 1; admission free; ☽ 11am-6pm Tue-Sun), run by nuns in black-and-white habits, which houses Hildegard exhibits, a medieval herb garden and a **restaurant** (☽ lunch 11.30am-2pm, café 2-5pm Tue-Sun) serving wholesome foods prepared just the way Hildegard liked them, including dishes made with spelt, her favourite grain. The area is linked to Bahnhof Bingen Stadt at least hourly by City-Linie bus 607.

On an island near the confluence of the Nahe and Rhine is the **Mäuseturm** (Mouse Tower; closed to the public) where, according to legend, Hatto II, the 10th-century archbishop of Mainz, was devoured alive by mice as punishment for his oppressive rule. In reality, the name is a mutation of *Mautturm* (toll tower), which was the building's medieval function.

The monumental statue on the wine slopes across the Rhine portrays a triumphant **Germania** (see p494).

Activities

Eight short **day-hike circuits**, including several through the vineyards, begin at the car park across Rosegartenweg from the Hildegard Forum. Possible walking destinations from Bingen include **Trechtingshausen** (11km). You can also explore the **Binger Stadtwald**, a large forested area northwest of Bingerbrück.

Bingen is the meeting point of two major long-distance bike paths, the **Rhein-Radweg**, which hugs the Rhine's left bank, and the **Nahe-Hunsrück-Mosel-Radweg**, which follows the Nahe River to Idar-Oberstein.

Sleeping

Quite a few inexpensive places to sleep can be found on and around Basilikastrasse.

DJH hostel (☎ 32 163; www.jugendherberge.de; Herterstrasse 51, Bingerbrück; dm €18; ✗) Totally renovated in 2006, this 119-bed hostel is a 10-minute walk from the Hauptbahnhof. It has rooms for one to six people, all with bathrooms.

HILDEGARD VON BINGEN

She's hip and holistic, a composer, a dramatist and a courageous campaigner for the rights of women. She heals with crystals and herbs, her music frequently hits the New Age charts…and she's been dead for more than 800 years.

Hildegard von Bingen (1098–1179) was born in Bermersheim (between Worms and Alzey), the 10th child of a well-off and influential family. At the age of three she experienced the first of the visions that would occur over the course of her extraordinary – and extraordinarily long – life. As a young girl she entered the convent at Disibodenberg on the Nahe River and eventually became an abbess, founding two abbeys of her own: Rupertsberg, above Bingen, in 1150; and Eibingen, across the Rhine near Rüdesheim, in 1165. During her preaching tours – an unprecedented activity for women in medieval times – she lectured both to the clergy and the common people, attacking social injustice and ungodliness.

Pope Eugen III publicly endorsed Hildegard, urging her to write down both her theology and her visionary experiences. This she did in a remarkable series of books that encompass ideas as diverse as cosmology, natural history and female orgasm. Her overarching philosophy was that humankind is a distillation of divinity and should comport itself accordingly. Her accomplishments are even more remarkable considering her life-long struggle against feelings of worthlessness and the physical effects of her mysterious visions, which often left her near death.

Hotel-Café Köppel (☎ 147 70; www.hotel-koeppel .de; Kapuzinerstrasse 12; s €45-55, d €65-78, s/d without bathroom €30/50; ☐) In the heart of town across from the Kapuzinerkirche, this place has a stylish, cheerful café whose cakes will make your eyes go wide; its rooms are modest but spotless and well-kept.

Hotel Martinskeller (☎ 134 75; www.hotel-bingen -rhein.com; Martinsstrasse 1-3; s €67-74, d €85-103; ☐ ☒) Creative use of some rather odd spaces gives this family-run, 15-room hotel, two blocks up the hill from the tourist office, a quirky but personal vibe. The comfortable rooms are big and each is unique – one is African-inspired, another a bit English.

Eating & Drinking

Gaggianer (☎ 14882; Badergasse 36; mains from €6; ☿ 4-11pm, closed Tue) This friendly, informal restaurant, a block east of the Nahe, serves salads and full meals in a leafy beer garden and a rustic dining room, the latter chock full of antique kitchen utensils donated by friends and clients. A speciality is *Zipfelchen* (potato dough filled with fresh white cheese, cream cheese and herbs).

Burg Klopp Restaurant (☎ 156 44; Burg Klopp 1; mains €12.50-19.50; ☿ lunch & dinner) One of Bingen's most elegant restaurants. Right in the castle with lovely city and Rhine views, it serves Mediterranean-inspired cuisine, including fish and vegetarian options.

Zum Alten Simp'l (Salzgasse; ☿ from 6pm or 7pm, closed Tue) A pub especially beloved by local students.

Getting Around

Bicycles can be rented from **Fahrrad Becker** (☎ 922 110; www.fahrradbecker.de in German; Koblenzer Strasse 43-45, Bingerbrück; ☿ 10am-6.30pm Mon-Fri, 10am-4pm Sat, shorter hours in winter).

RÜDESHEIM

☎ 06722 / pop 9900

Rüdesheim, capital of the Rheingau (famous for its superior riesling), is on the Rhine's right bank just across from Bingen, to which it's connected by passenger and car ferries. Administratively part of Hesse, it is deluged by day-tripping coach tourists – three million a year – and for some its most famous feature, Drosselgasse, brings to mind the words 'tourist nightmare from hell'. If you're looking for a souvenir thimble, this is definitely the place to come. That said, the exuberance can be

fun, at least for a while, and the town is also a good place to begin a variety of delightful vineyard walks.

At Rüdesheim's renowned **Weihnachtsmarkt** (Christmas Market), with its huge Nativity scene, you can stroll among 120 stalls from a dozen countries. It's held from late November to 23 December.

The **tourist office** (☎ 194 33; www.ruedesheim .de; Geisenheimer Strasse 22; ☿ 9am-6.30pm Mon-Fri & 11am-5pm Sat & Sun mid-Apr–1 Nov, 11am-5pm Mon-Fri 2 Nov–mid-Apr, also Sat & Sun late Nov-late Dec) is 600m east of Drosselgasse.

Sights & Activities

The focus of most visits to Rüdesheim is **Drosselgasse**, a tunnel-like alley so overloaded with signs that it looks like it might be in Hong Kong. This is the Rhine at its most colourfully touristic – bad German pop hits waft out from the pubs, which are filled with rollicking crowds. The **Oberstrasse**, at the top of Drosselgasse, is similarly overloaded with eateries and drinkeries, though to get away from the drunken madness all you have to do is wander a few blocks in any direction.

One island of relative calm, just 50m to the left from the top of Drosselgasse, is **Siegfried's Mechanisches Musikkabinett** (☎ 492 17; Oberstrasse 29; adult/child €5.50/3; ☿ 10am-6pm Mar-Dec), a fun collection of mechanical musical instruments, such as pianolas, from the 18th and 19th centuries. Many are demonstrated during the frequent guided tours (in English at 11am and 1pm; English text always available).

Near the Bingen car-ferry dock in the 800-year-old Brömserburg castle is the **Weinmuseum** (Wine Museum; ☎ 2348; Rheinstrasse 2; adult/student incl audio-guide €5/3; ☿ 10am-6pm Apr-Oct), where you'll find lots of wine paraphernalia from Roman times onwards. The tower affords great town and river views.

For an even better panorama, head up to the **Niederwald Denkmal** (1883), a bombastic monument on the wine slopes west of town starring **Germania** and celebrating the creation of the German Reich in 1871. You can walk up via the vineyards (trails are signposted) but it's faster to glide above the vineyards aboard the **Seilbahn** (cable car; ☎ 2402; Oberstrasse; adult/child €4.50/2, return €6.50/3; ☿ late Mar-Oct & late Nov-late Dec).

From the monument, a network of trails leads to destinations such as the romantic **Burg Ehrenfels** ruin and the **Jagdschloss** (hunting lodge). Down below, along the river, is

Assmannshausen, 5km downriver from Rüdesheim, which is known for its red wines. From near the lodge you can catch a trail or the **Sesselbahn** (chairlift; adult/child incl the Seilbahn €6.50/3.50) down to Assmannshausen and then head back to Rüdesheim either by train or passenger ferry (adult/child including the two lifts €10/5); the latter also goes to Bingen.

AROUND RÜDESHEIM
Eibingen

About 2km north of Rüdesheim, the wine village of Eibingen is the burial place of medieval power woman **Hildegard von Bingen** (see boxed text, p493). Her elaborate reliquary shrine, containing her heart, hair, tongue and skull, is prominently displayed inside the **parish church** (Marienthaler Strasse 3; ☙ daily). It attracts pilgrims from around the world, especially on 17 September, the day of her death, when a procession makes its way from Rüdesheim. The church stands on a site once occupied by the second of the abbeys founded by Hildegard. Nearby, the new St Hildegard Convent, with around 60 nuns, dates back to 1904.

Kloster Eberbach

If you saw the 1986 film *The Name of the Rose*, starring Sean Connery, you've already seen much of this one-time Cistercian **monastery** (☎ 06723-917 80; www.kloster-eberbach.de; adult/student €3.50/1.50; ☙ 10am-6pm Apr-Oct, 11am-5pm Nov-Mar), where a number of scenes were shot. Dating from as far back as the 12th century and secularised in the early 1800s, this graceful complex went through periods as a lunatic asylum, a jail, a sheep pen and accommodation for WWII refugees. Visitors can explore the monks' refectory and dormitory as well as the austere Romanesque basilica.

Eberbach is about 20km northeast of (ie towards Wiesbaden from) Rüdesheim. If you're not driving, the only way to get here is to take the train or bus to Eltville, followed by a one-hour signposted walk.

THE MOSELLE VALLEY

While plenty of places in Germany demand that you hustle, the Moselle (in German, Mosel; *moze*-l) suggests that you should, well…just mosey. The German section of the river, which rises in France and then traverses Luxembourg, runs 195km from Trier to Koblenz on a slow, serpentine course, revealing new scenery at every bend. Unlike the Romantic Rhine, it's spanned by plenty of bridges.

Exploring the vineyards and wineries of the Moselle Valley is an ideal way to get to know German culture, meet German people and, of course, acquire a taste for some wonderful wines. Slow down and experience sublime serial sipping.

Europe's steepest vineyards (the Bremmer Valmont, with a 72% grade) and Germany's most expensive vineyards (the Bernkasteler Doctor in Bernkastel-Kues) are both on the Moselle.

Activities
CYCLING

With its gentle curves, the Moselle is great for exploration by bicycle – see p483 for information on long-distance bike paths along the Moselle and the Rhine. Tourist offices and bookshops can supply maps.

The **Mosel-Maare-Radweg** (www.maare-moselradweg .de, in German) links Lieser, on the Moselle's left bank and about 5km towards Trier from Bernkastel-Kues, with Daun in the Eifel. From mid-April or May to 1 November, you can take Regiolinie bus 300 up (per person €8, per bike €2, hourly) and ride the 55km back to Bernkastel-Kues.

On weekends and holidays from May to October and daily from mid-July to August and during two weeks in mid-October, it costs €2 to bring your bike on a limited number of **Moselbahn 'RadelBus' buses** (☎ 0651-96 800; www .moselbahn.de) plying the route between Trier, Bernkastel-Kues and Bullay.

HIKING

The Moselle Valley is especially scenic walking country. Expect some steep climbs if you venture away from the river but the views are worth a few sore muscles. A popular long-distance hike is the **Moselhöhenweg**, running on both sides of the Moselle for a total of 390km. Good hiking maps are available at most good bookshops and tourist offices – the *Moselland-Wanderführer* (€6.60) is a comprehensive guide.

Getting There & Away

The closest airport to this region is **Frankfurt-Hahn** (☎ 06543-509 200; www.hahn-airport.de), only 20km from Traben-Trarbach and 30km from Bernkastel-Kues.

RHINELAND-PALATINATE & SAARLAND

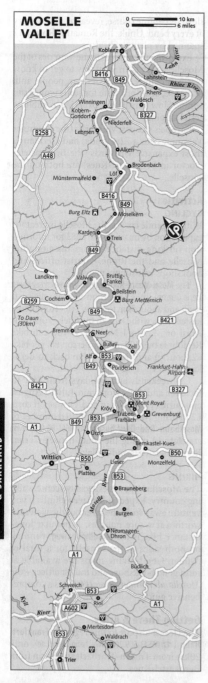

MOSELLE VALLEY

Most people start their Moselle exploration either in Trier or in Koblenz. If you have private transport and are coming from the north, you might head up the Ahr Valley and cut through the Eifel Mountains. If you're coming from the Saarland, your route will take you through the Hunsrück Mountains.

Getting Around

BOAT

The river's winding course and a fair number of locks make water travel rather slow. In any case, passenger boats don't run frequently enough to make it practicable to hop from village to village.

From late April to early October, **Köln-Düsseldorfer** (KD; ☎ Mon-Fri 0221-20 88 318, daily 06742-2232; www.k-d.com) links Koblenz with Cochem (5¼ hours upriver, 4¼ hours downriver) with stops in seven villages (no cruises from Tuesday to Thursday until mid-June).

Personen-Schifffahrt Gebrüder Kolb (☎ 02673-1515; www.moselfahrplan.de in German) links Trier with Bernkastel-Kues (about 4½ hours each way) once a day, except Monday, from early May to October. The company also has a number of short-haul options that can be picked up in Bernkastel-Kues and Traben-Trarbach.

In many villages, local boat operators offer additional cruising options.

BUS & TRAIN

The at-least-hourly rail line linking Koblenz with Trier (1½ to two hours) follows the river and serves its villages, but only as far up the Moselle as Bullay. From there, hourly Moselwein-Strecke shuttle trains head to Traben-Trarbach (€6, 25 minutes). **Moselbahn buses** (☎ 0651-96 800; www.moselbahn.de) serve all the river villages between Bullay and Trier (eight daily weekdays, five Saturday, three Sunday).

CAR & MOTORCYCLE

Driving is the easiest way to see the Moselle. From Trier, the B53 and then, from Bullay, the B49 follow the river all the way to Koblenz, crossing it several times.

TRIER

☎ 0651 / pop 100,000

A Unesco World Heritage Site since 1986, Trier is home to an outstanding assortment of Roman monuments as well as architectural gems from later ages. Its proximity to both Luxembourg and France can be tasted in the cuisine and felt in the local esprit. About 18,000 students do their part to contribute to the lively atmosphere.

Trier was founded by the Romans as Augusta Treverorum in 15 BC, becoming capital of the Western Roman Empire by the 3rd century AD. A second heyday arrived in the 13th century, when its archbishops acquired the rank and power of prince-electors. In the following centuries, the city seesawed between periods of prosperity and poverty. Karl Marx (1818–83) lived here until age 17.

In 2007 the Luxembourg region, including Trier, will serve as a European Capital of Culture (www.luxembourg2007.org). Local events include a major **exhibition** (www.konstantin-ausstellung.de), held from June to November, on the Roman emperor Constantine the Great (AD 275–337) and his role in European history, to be held at the city's leading museums.

Trier is an excellent base for day trips along the Moselle River and to Luxembourg, where quite a few locals, attracted by higher pay, have found employment.

Orientation

The Hauptbahnhof, in a rather seedy area, is about 600m southeast of the landmark Porta Nigra (Black Gate) and the adjacent tourist office. From there, the pedestrianised Simeonstrasse leads southwest to the Hauptmarkt. The Olewig (oh-*leh*-vig) Wine District is about 2km southeast of the centre.

Information

ATMs Several are situated at Am Kornmarkt and in the Hauptbahnhof.

ES-Telecom (Bahnhofplatz 1; per hr €1; ☒ 9am-10pm) Internet access next to the Hauptbahnhof.

Internet-Café (Karl-Marx-Strasse 32; per hr €1; ☒ 10am-10pm Mon-Fri, 11am-9pm Sat & Sun)

Mehrfachkarte (adult/child/senior & student/family €6.20/1.50/3.10/14.80) A discount card good for the Porta Nigra, Kaiserthermen, Amphitheater and Barbarathermen. Sold at the tourist office.

Post office (Bahnhofplatz) Just north of the Hauptbahnhof.

Tourist office (☎ 978 080; www.trier.de; An der Porta Nigra; ☒ 9am-6pm Mon-Thu, to 7pm Fri & Sat, to 5pm Sun May-Oct, 9am or 10am-5pm or 6pm Mon-Sat, 10am-1pm or 3pm Sun Nov-Apr) Has a hotel vacancies board outside and sells Moselle-area walking maps.

Trier-Card (individual/family €9/15) For three consecutive days this card will get you 50% off museum and monument admissions, unlimited use of public transport

and various other discounts. It's only sold at the tourist office.

Waschsalon (Brückenstrasse 19-21; ☒ 8am-10pm) Self-service laundry.

Sights & Activities

Top billing among Trier's Roman monuments goes to the **Porta Nigra** (☎ 754 24; Porta-Nigra-Platz; adult/child to 18yr/senior & student/family €2.10/1/1.60/5.10; ☒ 9am-6pm Apr-Sep, to 5pm Mar & Oct, to 4pm Nov-Feb), a brooding 2nd-century city gate that's been blackened by time (hence the name, Latin for 'black gate'). A marvel of engineering and ingenuity, it's held together by nothing but gravity and iron rods. In the 11th century, Archbishop Poppo converted the structure into St Simeonkirche, a church named in honour of a Greek hermit who spent a stint holed up in its east tower.

The church spawned a monastery whose erstwhile home is now the **Städtisches Museum Simeonstift** (☎ 718 1459; An der Porta Nigra). Set to reopen in May 2007 after extensive renovations, it illustrates eight centuries of city history and also has collections of Coptic textiles and East Asian sculpture.

A block southwest is the 13th-century **Dreikönigenhaus** (Simeonstrasse 19; closed to public), a late Gothic residence with a geometrically painted façade. Originally, the entrance was up on the 1st floor, reachable by stairs that could be retracted in case of danger. Two blocks further on is the **Hauptmarkt**, where a farmers' market is still held daily except Sunday. Anchored by a festive fountain dedicated to St Peter and the Four Virtues, it's hemmed in by medieval and Renaissance architectural treasures such as the **Rotes Haus** (Red House) and the **Steipe**, a former banqueting hall that's now the home of the **Spielzeugmuseum** (Toy Museum; ☎ 758 50; adult/youth 11-18yr/child €4/2/1.50; ☒ 11am-6pm Apr-Oct, 11am-5pm Tue-Sun Nov-Mar), a major draw for fans of miniature trains, mechanical toys, dolls and other childhood delights. The Gothic **St-Gangolf-Kirche** (☒ daily) is reached via a flowery portal.

A block east of Hauptmarkt looms the fortresslike **Dom** (☒ 6.30am-6pm Apr-Oct, 6.30am-5.30pm Nov-Mar), built above the palace of Constantine the Great's mother, Helena. The present structure is mostly Romanesque with some Gothic and baroque embellishments. To see some dazzling ecclesiastical equipment and peer into early Christian history, head upstairs to the **Domschatz** (cathedral treasury; adult/child

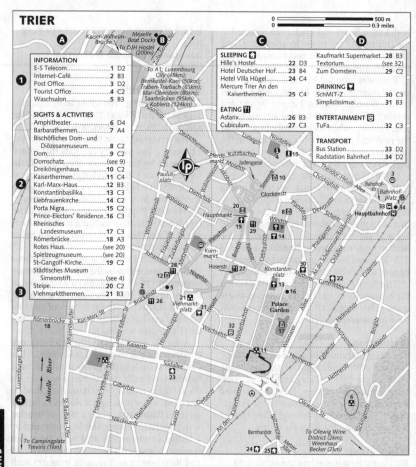

TRIER

0 | 500 m
0 | 0.3 miles

INFORMATION
E-S Telecom.................................1 D2
Internet-Café..............................2 B3
Post Office..................................3 D2
Tourist Office.............................4 C2
Waschsalon................................5 B3

SIGHTS & ACTIVITIES
Amphitheater.............................6 D4
Barbarathermen.........................7 A4
Bischöfliches Dom- und
   Diözesanmuseum...................8 C2
Dom..9 C2
Domschatz............................(see 9)
Dreikönigenhaus.......................10 C2
Kaiserthermen...........................11 C4
Karl-Marx-Haus.........................12 B3
Konstantinbasilika.....................13 C3
Liebfrauenkirche.......................14 C2
Porta Nigra................................15 C2
Prince-Electors' Residence.......16 C3
Rheinisches
   Landesmuseum....................17 C3
Römerbrücke.............................18 A3
Rotes Haus...........................(see 20)
Spielzeugmuseum..................(see 20)
St-Gangolf-Kirche.....................19 C2
Städtisches Museum
   Simeonstift.......................(see 4)
Steipe...20 C2
Viehmarktthermen....................21 B3

SLEEPING
Hille's Hostel.............................22 D3
Hotel Deutscher Hof.................23 B4
Hotel Villa Hügel.......................24 C4
Mercure Trier An den
   Kaiserthermen......................25 C4

EATING
Astarix..26 B3
Cubiculum..................................27 C3

DRINKING
SchMIT-Z...................................30 C3
Simplicissimus............................31 B3

ENTERTAINMENT
TuFa..32 C3

TRANSPORT
Bus Station................................33 D2
Radstation Bahnhof..................34 D2

Kaufmarkt Supermarket...28 B3
Textorium..........................(see 32)
Zum Domstein.................29 C2

€1.50/0.50; 10am-5pm Mon-Sat, 2-5pm Sun & religious holidays, to 4pm Nov-Mar) or go straight to the **Bischöfliches Dom- und Diözesanmuseum** (710 5255; Windstrasse 6-8; adult/student €2/1; 9am-5pm Tue-Sat, 1-5pm Sun & religious holidays, also open Mon Apr-Oct), just north of the Dom. The prized exhibit here is a 4th-century ceiling fresco from Helena's palace that was pieced together from countless fragments.

Just to the south is the **Liebfrauenkirche** (7.30am-6pm Apr-Oct, to 5.30pm Nov-Mar), one of Germany's earliest Gothic churches. The cruciform structure is supported by a dozen pillars symbolising the 12 apostles and, despite its strict symmetry, has a light, mystical quality.

Liebfrauenstrasse leads south to another architectural masterpiece, the brick-built **Konstantinbasilika** (Konstantinplatz; 10am-6pm Mon-Sat,

noon-6pm Sun & holidays Apr-Oct, 11am-noon & 3-4pm Tue-Sat, noon-1pm Sun & holidays Nov-Mar), built in AD 310 as Constantine's throne hall. Its dimensions (67m long and 36m high) are truly mind-blowing considering how long ago it was built. Later part of the residence of Trier's prince-electors, it is now a Protestant church.

The adjacent **prince-electors' residence**, a pink rococo confection, looks south over the lawns, pools and fountains of the formal **Palastgarten** (palace garden), in the middle of which stands the **Rheinisches Landesmuseum** (Roman Archaeological Museum; 977 40; Weimarer Allee 1; adult/child incl audio-guide €5.50/1.50; 9.30am-5pm Mon-Fri, 10.30am-5pm Sat, Sun & holidays, closed Mon Nov-Apr). The rich collections provide an extraordinary look at local Roman life – highlights include a scale model of 4th-century Trier and rooms filled

RHINELAND-PALATINATE & SAARLAND

with tombstones, mosaics, rare gold coins and some fantastic glass. Renovations of parts of the complex are set to be completed by June 2007.

From the museum, it's just a coin's toss south to the **Kaiserthermen** (☎ 442 62; Weimarer Allee 2; adult/child to 18yr/senior & student/family €2.10/1/1.60/5.10; ☒ 9am-6pm Apr-Sep, to 5pm Mar & Oct, to 4pm Nov-Feb), a vast thermal bathing complex created by Constantine. The striped brick-and-stone arches, once part of the Caldarium, may make you feel like you're at the Forum in Rome. You can get a sense of the layout from the lookout tower.

A 700m walk southeast is the Roman **Amphitheater** (☎ 730 10; Olewiger Strasse; adult/child to 18yr/senior & student/family €2.10/1/1.60/5.10; ☒ 9am-6pm Apr-Sep, to 5pm Mar & Oct, to 4pm Nov-Feb), once capable of holding 20,000 spectators during gladiator tournaments and animal fights. The dank cellars were once used to keep prisoners, caged animals and corpses.

For more Roman baths, head to the **Viehmarktthermen** (☎ 994 1057; Viehmarktplatz; adult/senior/student €2.10/1.60/1; ☒ 9am-5pm, closed 1st week day of each week). Found by accident in the 1980s during the construction of a parking garage, the excavations are sheltered by a dramatic glass cube designed by the Cologne architect Oswald M Ungers.

Diehard thermal bath devotees still have the **Barbarathermen** (cnr Südallee & Friedrich-Wilhelm-Strasse), closed for renovations until at least 2008. In the meantime you can look over the fence at the foundations, cellars and floor-heating system, all of which survived a 17th-century raid for stones to build a school.

Two blocks northwest is the **Römerbrücke**, successor to a 2nd-century bridge, five of whose original seven pylons are still extant.

The respectable bourgeois townhouse in which the author of *Das Kapital* was born and, quite comfortably, grew up is now the **Karl-Marx-Haus** (☎ 970 680; Brückenstrasse 10; adult/concession €3/1.50; ☒ 1-6pm Mon, 10am-6pm Tue-Sun Apr-Oct, 10am-1pm & 2-5pm Tue-Sun Nov-Mar), whose exhibits take a look at the man and his oeuvre. Interestingly, early 19th-century Trier was no Dickensian industrial nightmare but rather a small town with just 10,000 residents.

Tours

City Walking Tour (adult/child €6/3; ☒ 1.30pm Sat approx Apr-Oct) A two-hour tour in English that begins at the tourist office.

Wine Tastings (4/6/8 wines €4.50/6.50/8.50; ☒ 10am-6pm) Four local vintners take turns as hosts – contact the tourist office for a schedule.

Sleeping

Campingplatz Treviris (☎ 820 0911; www.camping-treviris.de; Luxemburger Strasse 81; per adult/tent €6/4; ☒ campers year-round, tents late Mar-late Oct) On the Moselle's left bank 1.5km south of the Römerbrücke.

Hille's Hostel (☎ 710 2785, 0171-329 1247; www.hilles-hostel-trier.de; Gartenfeldstrasse 7; dm from €15, s/d €32/38; ☒ reception 8-11am & 4-6pm; ☒) An independent hostel with colourful artwork, a piano in the kitchen and spacious, brightly decorated rooms with private bathrooms.

DJH hostel (☎ 146 620; www.jugendherberge.de; An der Jugendherberge 4; dm €18; Ⓟ ☒) Spick-and-span, 242-bed hostel right on the Moselle, about 1km northeast of the tourist office. Rooms have bathrooms and up to six beds. Take bus 12 from the Hauptbahnhof.

Weinhaus Becker (☎ 938 080; www.weinhaus-becker.de in German; Olewiger Strasse 206; s/d from €50/80; Ⓟ) About 2km east of the centre in the wine district of Olewig, this 18-room hotel pairs down-to-earth accommodation with a Michelin-starred restaurant (open for dinner Tuesday to Saturday, for lunch Wednesday to Sunday).

Hotel Deutscher Hof (☎ 977 80; www.hotel-deutscher-hof.de; Südallee 25; s €60-90, d €90-120, q €130; Ⓟ ☒) An international-standard business and tourist hotel whose 102 rooms come with sound-proof windows and pretty convincing fake orchids. Has a genuine nine-pin *Kegelbahn* (bowling alley; €6per hour) in the basement.

Hotel Villa Hügel (☎ 330 66; www.hotel-villa-huegel.de; Bernhardstrasse 14; s €79-99, d €99-149; Ⓟ ☒ ☒) At this stylish hillside villa you can begin the day with a lavish champagne breakfast buffet and end it luxuriating in the 12m indoor pool and Finnish sauna. Views are great from the terrace and from many of the 30 rooms. Served by buses 2 and 82.

Mercure Trier An den Kaiserthermen (☎ 937 70; www.mercure.com; Metzer Allee 6; s €70-95, d €80-105; Ⓟ ☒ ☒) Modern, well-run business hotel with 105 rooms and weekend and seasonal specials. A bit out of the centre. Breakfast is €14.

Eating & Drinking

Weinhaus Becker has an excellent restaurant.

Cubiculum (☎ 451 27; Hosenstrasse 2; light meals €2.50-6.50; ☒ 7pm-1am or 2am) This beer hall and restaurant, in a medieval cellar, serves light meals such as casserole but the unique speciality here is *Pizzasalat* (€5.50) – you guessed it, a pizza topped with a pile of salad. Occasionally has live music on Friday or Saturday.

Astarix (☎ 722 39; Karl-Marx-Strasse 11; pizza from €5) Popular student hang-out with good pizza and casseroles (€4.20 plus €0.30 for each added ingredient). Extra-cheap on Monday. Enter through the arcade.

Textorium (☎ 474 82; Wechselstrasse 4-6; meals from €6) A very popular, industrial-chic restaurant with outdoor seating and daily specials. Located inside the TuFa cultural events venue.

Zum Domstein (☎ 744 90; Am Hauptmarkt 5; mains €9.50-18.50, Roman dinner €15-33) A German-style bistro where you can either feast like the ancient Romans or dine on more conventional German and international fare. A cookbook printed in Venice in 1498 is on display downstairs.

Simplicissimus (Viehmarktplatz 11; ☯ 10am-2am Mon-Sat, 2pm-2am Sun & holidays) An unpretentious café-bar with interesting old photos on the walls, rock on the PR system and waiters who've been known to get sloshed. Several other places to drink are right nearby.

SchMIT-Z (☎ 42 514; www.schmit-z.de in German; Mustorstrasse 4; ☯ 8pm-midnight Thu, 9pm-2am Sat, 4-8pm Sun) A mellow gay and lesbian information centre with a bar.

Picnic supplies are available at the **Kaufmarkt supermarket** (Brückenstrasse 2; ☯ 8am-8pm Mon-Fri, 8am-4pm Sat).

Entertainment

Click 'events' on the tourist office website (www.trier.de) for details on concerts and other cultural activities.

TuFa (☎ 718 2412; Wechselstrasse 4-6) This vibrant cultural events venue, housed in a former *Tuchfabrik* (towel factory) – thus the name – hosts cabaret, live music of all sorts, theatre and dance performances. It is home to the Textorium (see above).

Getting There & Away

Trier has several hourly train connections to Saarbrücken (€13.40, one to 1½ hours) and Koblenz (€17, 1½ to two hours). There are also frequent trains to Luxembourg (€8.40, 50 minutes), with onward connections to Paris. Regional buses to the Eifel and Hunsrück Mountains leave from the bus station outside the Hauptbahnhof.

Getting Around

Trier has a comprehensive **bus system** (☎ 01801-993366; www.vrt-info.de, in German) but the city centre is easily explored on foot. Single tickets/day passes, sold by drivers, cost €1.55/4.25. The Olewig Wine District is served by buses 6, 16 and 26.

Bikes can be rented at **Radstation Bahnhof** (☎ 148 856; per day €7.50-10; ☯ 9am-7pm Apr-Oct, 10am-6pm Mon-Fri Nov-Mar), inside the Hauptbahnhof next to track 11.

BERNKASTEL-KUES
☎ 06531 / pop 6900

This charming twin town, some 50km downriver from Trier, is the hub of the middle Moselle region. Bernkastel, on the right bank, is a symphony in half-timber, stone and slate and teems with wine taverns. Kues (pronounced *koos*), the birthplace of theologian Nicolas Cusanus (1401–64), has little fairy-tale flair but is home to the town's most important historical sights.

The **tourist office** (☎ 4023/24; www.bernkastel.de; Am Gestade 6, Bernkastel; ☯ 8.30am-12.30pm & 1-5pm Mon-Fri, 10am-5pm Sat, 10am-1pm Sun & holidays May-Oct, to 3pm Fri & closed weekends & holidays Nov-Apr), 100m downriver from the bridge, sells hiking and cycling maps, offers internet access (per half-hour €0.50) and has an ATM. A hotel reservation board with a free telephone is just up Am Gestade (the road running along the river), near the bridge.

The bus station is next to the boat docks in Bernkastel.

Sights & Activities

Bernkastel's pretty **Marktplatz**, a block inland from the bridge, is a romantic ensemble of half-timbered houses with beautifully decorated gables. Note the medieval iron rings, to which criminals were attached, on the façade of the old **Rathaus**.

On Karlsstrasse, the alley to the right as you face the Rathaus, the tiny **Spitzhäuschen** resembles a giant bird's house, its narrow base topped by a much larger, precariously leaning, upper floor. More such crooked gems line Römerstrasse and its side streets. Facing the bridge is the partly 14th-century **Pfarrkirche St Michael**, whose tower, ringed by a crown of turrets, was originally part of the town's fortifications.

A rewarding way to get your heart pumping is by hoofing it up to **Burg Landshut**, a ruined

13th-century castle – framed by vineyards and
forests – on a bluff above town; allow 30 to
60 minutes. You'll be rewarded with glorious
river valley views and a cold drink at the **café-
beer-garden** (☉ 10am-6pm mid-Feb–mid-Dec). The
less robust can catch a ride from Bernkastel's
waterfront on the yellow **Burg Landshut-Express**
(up/down/return €3.50/2.50/5; ☉ 10am-6pm on the hour
approx Easter-Oct).

In Kues, most sights are conveniently
grouped next to the bridge in the **St-Nikolaus-
Hospital** (☎ 2260; Cusanusstrasse 2; admission free;
☉ 9am-6pm Sun-Fri, 9am-3pm Sat), an old-age home,
founded in 1458 by Cusanus, for 33 men (one
for every year of Christ's life). You're free to
explore the inner courtyard, Gothic chapel
and cloister at leisure but the treasure-filled
library can only be seen on a **guided tour** (€4;
☉ 10.30am Tue & 3pm Fri Apr-Oct), sometimes held
in English.

The complex also houses the small **Mosel-
Weinmuseum** (☎ 4141; adult/child under 12yr €2/1;
☉ 10am-5pm mid-Apr–Oct, 2-5pm Nov–mid-Apr) and the
Vinothek (admission free; ☉ 10am-5pm mid-Apr–Oct, 2-
5pm Nov–mid-Apr). Here, in the hospice's historic
cellars, you can get thoroughly acquainted
with Moselle wines during an 'all-you-can-
drink' wine tasting (€9).

Sleeping & Eating

In Bernkastel, places to eat can be found along
the waterfront and in the Alstadt's narrow,
pedestrians-only streets. In Kues there are
several restaurants near the bridge.

Campingplatz Kueser Werth (☎ 8200; www
.camping-kueser-werth.de; Am Hafen 2, Kues; site/person/car
€4/4.50/1.50; ☉ Apr-Oct) About 2km upriver from
the bridge, next to the yacht harbour.

DJH hostel (☎ 2395; www.jugendherberge.de;
Jugendherbergsstrasse 1, Bernkastel; dm €15; ✗) Fairly
basic by today's standards. Scenically but
inconveniently located above town next to
Burg Landshut.

Hotel-Restaurant Weinhaus St Maximilian (☎ 965
00; www.hotel-sankt-maximilian.de in German; Saarallee 12,
Kues; s €34-44, d €58-72; ✗) Run by a family of
wine makers, this place has 12 quiet rooms,
many with balconies, that look out on the
courtyard of the restaurant, where you can
dine on German and *moselländische* dishes
(mains €8.50 to €14).

Hotel Moselblümchen (☎ 2335; www.hotel
-moselbluemchen.de; Schwanenstrasse 10, Bernkastel; s €39-
63, d €64-98; ✗) A traditional, family-run hotel
on a narrow old-town alley behind the tourist

office. Has 20 tasteful rooms and a small sauna
and can arrange bike rental. The restaurant's
German and local specialities include sauerkraut and homemade wurst.

Getting Around

Hire bikes at **Fun Bike Team** (☎ 940 24; Schanzstrasse
22, Bernkastel), 500m upriver from the bridge.

TRABEN-TRARBACH
☎ 06541 / pop 6000

It's hard to imagine today that this peaceful
twin town, 24km downriver from Bernkastel-
Kues (but just 7km by foot over the hill), was
once in the crosshairs of warring factions during the late-17th-century War of the Palatine
Succession. Two ruined fortresses are all that
survive from those tumultuous times, which
were followed by a long period of prosperity
as the town became a centre of wine making
and trade.

Traben lost its medieval look to three major
fires but was well compensated with beautiful
Jugendstil (Art Nouveau) villas – and lots of
wisteria. It joined with Trarbach in 1904.

Orientation & Information

Traben, on the Moselle's left bank, is where
you'll find the tourist office, the end-of-the-
line train shelter (linked to Bullay), the adjacent bus station and the commercial centre.
Trarbach is across the bridge on the right
bank.

The **tourist office** (☎ 839 80; www.traben-trarbach
.de in German; Am Bahnhof 5, Traben; ☉ 10am-6pm Mon-Fri
Jul-Oct, to 5pm Apr-Jun & Nov, 10am-noon & 2-4pm Dec-
Mar, also 11am-3pm Sat May-early Nov), in the Alter
Bahnhof (old train station) 100m west along
Bahnhofstrasse from the train shelter, sells the
excellent *Mittelmosel Rad- und Wanderkarte*
(€2.95), a map of area walking and cycling
trails, and has two internet terminals (per
hour €2). There are several ATMs in the immediate vicinity.

Sights & Activities

The ruined medieval **Grevenburg**, which unlike
its Cochem cousin survived the 19th century without being 'restored', sits high in the
craggy hills above Trarbach and is reached
from the Markt via a steep footpath. Because
of its strategic importance, the castle changed
hands 13 times, found itself under siege six
times and was destroyed seven times. No
wonder two walls are all that are left! Across

the river, the vast Vauban-style **Mont Royal** fortress, built in the late 1600s under Louis XIV as a base from which to project French power in the Rhineland, proved ruinously expensive and was soon dismantled by the French themselves.

Learn more about these castles and their historical significance at the **Mittelmosel-Museum** (☎ 9480; Casinostrasse 2, Trarbach; adult/youth €2.50/1; ⏰ 10am-5pm Tue-Sun Apr-Oct), housed in a furnished baroque villa proud of once having hosted Johann Wolfgang von Goethe.

The new **Haus der Ikonen** (☎ 812 408; Mittelstrasse 8, Trarbach; adult/11-17yr €2/0.50; ⏰ 10am-5pm Tue-Sun Easter-1 Nov, 10am-5pm Sat, Sun & holidays 2 Nov-Palm Sunday) displays modern Russian Orthodox icons and tries to promote intercultural dialogue. The adjacent, 14th-century **Stadtturm** (admission free; ⏰ daily), which can be climbed, has a 24-bell **glockenspiel** (carillon) that was installed in 2004 to commemorate the twin towns' centenary together.

Of Traben's sinuous **Art Nouveau villas**, the most seductive – and the only one open to the public – is the **Hotel Bellevue** (Am Moselufer), easily recognised by its champagne-bottle-shaped slate turret. The oak-panelled lobby and stained-glass windows in the restaurant typify the style, brought to town by Berlin architect Bruno Möhring. He also designed the 1898 **Brückentor**, above the bridge on the Trarbach side, now home to an excellent restaurant, Brücken-Schenke.

Traben-Trarbach is also a spa town, with hot mineral springs in Trarbach's southern district of Bad Wildstein. The **Moseltherme** (☎ 830 30; www.moseltherme.de; Wildsteiner Weg; adult/child 6-15yr pool all-day €9/5, with sauna €11/7, cheaper for 1-3hr & Jun-Aug; ⏰ pool 9am-9pm Mon-Fri, 9am-6pm Sat & Sun, sauna 3-9pm Mon, 3-10pm Tue, 3pm-midnight Wed-Fri, 10am-6pm Sat & Sun) has saunas (women-only on Tuesday) and pools and also offers massages and beauty treatments.

The tourist office organises daily **wine tastings** (4/6/8 wines €4/6/8) and cellar tours with various vintners.

Sleeping & Eating

Trarbach has quite a few restaurants in the area upriver from the bridge.

DJH hostel (☎ 9278; jh-traben-trarbach@djh-info.de; Hirtenpfad 6, Traben; dm €17; ✗ ▢) All rooms at this modern, 172-bed hostel have private bathrooms. It's a 1.2km, signposted walk up from the train station, past the fire station.

Central Hotel (☎ 6238; www.central-hotel-traben.de; Bahnstrasse 43, Traben; s €30-35, d €56-66) In the same family for three generations, this 32-room hotel has modest rooms with compact bathrooms. The owner, Iris, lived in Texas for eight years but somehow returned twang-less.

Hotel Bellevue (☎ 7030; www.bellevue-hotel.de; Moselufer, Traben; s €80-110, d €125-180; P ✗ ▢ ⌨) Classy, romantic and historic, this exquisite Art Nouveau hotel, facing the river, offers perks that include bike and canoe hire, pool and sauna. The stained-glass-adorned gourmet restaurant (mains €12.50 to €24.50) serves regional and Mediterranean-inspired cuisine.

Weingut Caspari (☎ 5778; Weiherstrasse 17-19, Trarbach; mains €7-12; ⏰ 5pm-midnight Mon & Wed, 11.30am-midnight Thu-Sun Easter-Oct) Six short blocks inland from the bridge, this rustic, old-time *Strausswirtschaft* (a winery that serves its own products as well as hearty local cuisine) offers excellent value.

Brücken-Schenke (☎ 818 435; in the Brückentor, Trarbach; meat mains €9.50-14.5, veg mains €6-12; ⏰ 2-11pm Mon & Wed-Sat, 11am-10pm Sun; ✗) A range of solid, good-value German and regional favourites are served up inside the tower at the Trarbach end of the bridge. Great views.

There is an **Edeka Neukauf supermarket** (Am Bahnhof 44, Traben; ⏰ 8am-8pm Mon-Sat) across the tracks from the train shelter.

Getting There & Around

You can hire bikes at **Zweirad Wagner** (☎ 1649; Brückenstrasse 42, Trarbach; per day €7.50; ⏰ 8am-12.30pm & 1.45-6pm Mon-Fri, 8.30am-1pm Sat, also 10-11am Sun & holidays in summer), next to the Brückentor.

COCHEM

☎ 02671 / pop 5200

Cochem, a picture-postcard village 40km downriver from Traben-Trarbach, spends much of the year overrun with day-trippers. If you're after narrow alleyways and half-timbered houses – well, there are less jaded locales to find them.

But Cochem does have a couple of unique sights. Towering above steep vineyards, the city-owned **Reichsburg** (☎ 255; www.reichsburg -cochem.de; adult/child 6-17yr €4.50/2.50; ⏰ 9am-5pm mid-Mar–Nov) – everyone's idealised version of a turreted medieval castle – is actually a neo-Gothic pastiche built in 1877, making it a full 78 years older than Disneyland (the 11th-century original fell victim to frenzied Frenchmen in 1689). It can be seen on a 40-minute guided tour (ask for a sheet in English). The walk up from town takes about 15 minutes.

For great views of the town and river, you can catch the **Sesselbahn** (☎ 989 063; Endertstrasse 44; 1-way/return €4/5.50; ☷ 9.30am-7.30pm mid-Jul–Aug, 10am-6pm Easter–mid-Jul & Sep–mid-Nov), which begins a few blocks west of the tourist office, up to the **Pinner Kreuz**. It's a pleasant walk back down through the vineyards.

From the train station, on the left bank at the downriver edge of town, it's only a short walk down Ravenéstrasse to the **tourist office** (☎ 600 40; www.cochem.de; Endertplatz 1; ☷ 9am-5pm Mon-Fri, closed 1-2pm Nov-Mar, 9am-3pm Sat May–mid-Jul, to 5pm mid-Jul–Oct, 10am-noon Sun Jul-Oct).

Tucked away uphill from the Markt and its fountain, **Zom Stüffje** (☎ 7260; Oberbachstrasse 14; mains €7.50-16.50; ☷ lunch & dinner, closed Tue) is richly decorated with dark timber and murals and serves classic German fare as well as four meat-free options.

AROUND COCHEM
Beilstein
pop 170

On the right bank of the Moselle about 12km upriver from Cochem, Beilstein (www .beilstein-mosel.de, in German) is a pint-size village right out of the world of fairy tales. Little more than a cluster of houses surrounded by steep vineyards, its romantic, half-timbered townscape is enhanced by the ruined **Burg Metternich**, a hill-top castle reached via a staircase. During the Middle Ages, the **Zehnthauskeller** was used to store wine delivered as a tithe; it now houses a romantically dark, vaulted wine tavern.

Burg Eltz

Victor Hugo thought this fairy-tale castle, hidden away in the forest above the left bank of the Moselle, was 'tall, terrific, strange and dark'. Indeed, **Burg Eltz** (☎ 02672-950 500; www .burg-eltz.de; tour adult/student €6/4.50, treasury adult/child €2.50/1.50; ☷ 9.30am-5.30pm Apr-1 Nov), owned by the same family for almost 1000 years, has a compact and impenetrable exterior softened by scores of turrets crowning it like candles on a birthday cake. The **treasury** features a rich collection of jewellery, porcelain and weapons.

By car, you can reach Burg Eltz, which has never been destroyed, via the village of Münstermaifeld; the castle is 800m from

the car park (shuttle bus €1.50). Trains link Koblenz and Cochem with Moselkern, where a 35-minute trail to the castle begins at the Ringelsteiner Mühle car park.

HUNSRÜCK MOUNTAINS

IDAR-OBERSTEIN
☎ 06781 / pop 33,000

Agate mining in Idar-Oberstein goes back to at least 1454 but the industry really took off in the early 19th century after local adventurers left for South America (especially Brazil), where they harvested raw stones and sent them back home to be processed. The local mines have long since been exhausted, but Idar-Oberstein has remained a major gemcutting and jewellery-manufacturing centre. If crystals really do have mysterious powers, you'd expect that a town with so many would look a lot better than this one does.

Scores of Idar-Oberstein shops have signs reading 'Schmuck' – whether you are one (in Yiddish and American English) or just looking for some (in German), following them is the best way to find jewellery, minerals and gemstones.

Along the **Nahe-Hunsrück-Mosel-Radweg**, it's a 75km bike ride to Bingen, on the Rhine.

Orientation & Information

Idar-Oberstein is an unwieldy town, stretching for about 20km along a narrow, forested valley carved by the Nahe River. Hauptstrasse runs for about 6km (it's numbered from 1 up to about 500) but the interesting, pedestrianised bit – where you'll find the Marktplatz – is in Oberstein a few blocks northeast of the Bahnhof.

The **tourist office** (☎ 56 390; www.idar-oberstein .de; Hauptstrasse 419, Oberstein; ☷ 9am-7pm Mon-Fri, 10am-4pm Sat, Sun & holidays mid-Mar–Oct, 10am-5pm Mon-Fri Nov–mid-Mar) is near Oberstein's Marktplatz.

Sights & Activities

Museum Idar-Oberstein (☎ 246 19; Hauptstrasse 436, Oberstein; adult/child €3.60/2.10; ☷ 9am-5.30pm, to 7.30pm Jul, Aug & mid-Oct), 50m off the Marktplatz, has an impressive collection of minerals and crystals, including a model of Manhattan made of rock crystal.

Tucked in a niche in the rock face above the museum is the 15th-century **Felsenkirche** (Chapel in the Rocks; ☎ 228 40; adult/child €2/0.50;

10am-6pm Apr-Oct), said to have been built by a local knight in atonement for the murder of his brother. It's a 216-step climb from the Marktplatz.

From the church it's a 20-minute uphill hike through a beech forest to the twin castles of **Burg Bosselstein**, a ruin dating from 1196, and **Schloss Oberstein**. At the top, you'll be rewarded with great views over the town, the Hunsrück Mountains and the Nahe Valley.

Industriedenkmal Bengel (☎ 27 030; Wilhelmstrasse 42a, Oberstein; adult/student €3/1.50; 10am-noon & 2-4pm Tue-Fri) is in the charmingly decrepit Jacob Bengel jewellery factory, built more than a century ago. It once serviced the Russian market (before the Revolution) and, later, made sleek Art Deco pieces. Now it's a jerry-rigged but engaging museum, where you can watch ancient machines click-clack as they transform spools of wire into chains. To get there from the tourist office, cross the pedestrian bridge at Hauptstrasse 466.

In a nature park west of Idar are the **Edelsteinminen Steinkaulenberg** (☎ 474 00; 30min tour adult/child €4/2.50; 9am-5pm mid-Mar–mid-Nov), the only visitable gemstone mine in Europe. You can dig for your own agate, amethyst, jasper and quartz in an **outdoor mining area** (adult/student €13/5; 3hr sessions at 9am & 1pm) but reservations are required and you must bring your own hammer, chisel and protective glasses (or purchase them). To get there, take bus 303 to Strassburgkaserne.

Cutters lying belly-down atop tilting benches demonstrate how gemstones used to be processed at the 17th-century **Historische Weiherschleife** (Historical Pond Mill; ☎ 901 918; Tiefensteiner Strasse 87, Tiefenstein; 40min tour adult/child €3/2; 10am-6pm mid-Mar–mid-Nov), the last of nearly 200 such water-powered gem-cutting mills that once stood along the Idarbach creek. It's situated northwest of Idar in Tiefenstein; take bus 1 to the Weiherschleife stop.

The **Deutsches Edelsteinmuseum** (☎ 900 980; www.edelsteinmuseum.de in German; adult/child under 14yr €4.20/1.60; 9am-6pm, to 5pm Nov-Apr, closed Mon in Nov, Jan & Feb) should dazzle even the most, well, jaded of visitors. Highlights include a 12.555-carat topaz from Brazil. Take bus 301 or 302 to Börse.

Sleeping & Eating

The local meat speciality, *Spiessbraten*, consists of a hunk of beef or pork marinated in raw onion, salt and pepper and then grilled over a beechwood fire, giving it a spicy, smoky taste. It's available at restaurants around Oberstein's Marktplatz.

DJH hostel (☎ 243 66; www.jugendherberge.de; Alte Treibe 23, Oberstein; dm €17; P X) All the rooms in this modern, 128-bed hostel have a private bathroom. Situated on the hillside southeast of the Bahnhof.

Edelstein-Hotel (☎ 502 50; www.edelstein-hotel.de; Hauptstrasse 302, Oberstein; s/d/tr from €45/60/87; P) It's not terribly stylish, but the owners of this 18-room place are enthusiastic and helpful, and the 30°C pool and sauna area offer a perfect retreat on a rainy day. Situated about 600m towards Idar from Oberstein's pedestrian zone.

Gästehaus Amethyst (☎ 700 01; www.gaestehaus-amethyst.de; Hauptstrasse 324, Oberstein; s/d €49/66; P) This pocket-sized, bike-friendly *pension*, 200m from Oberstein's pedestrian zone, has delightful owners, nicely furnished rooms, a spanking-clean sauna and a fitness room (both free).

Getting There & Around

Idar-Oberstein, about 80km east of Trier and about 90km northeast of Saarbrücken, is connected by train with Saarbrücken (€11.70, one hour) and Mainz (€10, one hour). The B41 and the B422 cross in Idar-Oberstein.

Local bus 301 regularly shuttles between Oberstein and Idar.

KAISERSLAUTERN

☎ 0631 / pop 99,000

Better known as a perennial football contender (though its once-vaunted team was relegated in 2006) – and, more recently, as a World Cup host – than as a tourist magnet, Kaiserslautern does have a few worthwhile sights.

The city's Hauptbahnhof, on the southern edge of the commercial centre, was recently spruced up to welcome the 2006 World Cup hordes. About 1km to the north, on the northern edge of the downtown, is the spacious **tourist office** (365 2316; www.kaiserslautern.de; Fruchthallstrasse 14; 9am-6pm Mon-Fri, 10am-4pm Sat), also a World Cup legacy.

Next door to the tourist office is the mid-19th-century **Fruchthalle** (market hall), which looks like it was beamed in from Florence (in fact, it was modelled on that city's Palazzo Medici) and is now used as a cultural events venue. Across the street are the ruins of the 16th-century **Casimirbau**, built on the site of Emperor Barbarossa's 12th-century palace. The 19th-century, neo-Renaissance **Pfalzgalerie** (Palatinate Gallery of Art; ☉ 11am-8pm Tue, 10am-5pm Wed-Sun), whose focus is on paintings and sculptures, is a few blocks to the north.

About 1.5km northwest of the tourist office is the peaceful **Japanischer Garten** (Japanese Garden; www.japanischergarten.de, in German; Lauterstrasse 18; adult/child 12-17yr €3/1; ☉ 10am-7pm mid-Apr–early Oct, 11am-5pm early Oct–mid-Apr), opened in 2000. Approximately 1.5km further west is the **Gartenschau** (☎ 710 0700; Turnerstrasse 2; ☉ 9am or 10am-7pm Apr-Oct), a 22-hectare garden exhibition that springs to flowery life each year in the warm months.

Some 34,000Americans live in and around Kaiserslautern (nicknamed 'K-Town'), forming the largest US military community outside the United States. The area's best-known installation is **Ramstein Air Base**, used by both NATO and the US Air Force. That's where the huge C-17 cargo planes you sometimes see over Kaiserslautern are heading, perhaps on a direct five-hour medical evacuation flight from Iraq.

The family-run **Hotel Pfälzer Hof** (☎ 362 400; www.pfaelzer-hof-kl.de, in German; Fruchthallstrasse 15; s/d €45/70; ✕), almost across the street from the tourist office, is a modest, old-time place with 18 rooms.

SAARLAND

The tiny federal state of Saarland, long a land of coal and heavy industry, has in recent decades cleaned up its air and streams and reoriented its struggling economy towards hi-tech and tourism. The capital, Saarbrücken, is a vibrant city with good museums and an excellent culinary scene. Rolling hills and forest cover much of the countryside, which can be explored not only by car but also on foot or bicycle along sign-posted long-distance routes, including the 362km, circular **Saarland-Radweg**. In places such as the historic Völklinger Hütte ironworks, the region's industrial heritage is celebrated rather than downplayed.

Over the centuries, France and Germany have played Ping-Pong with the Saarland, coveting it for its valuable natural resources. In the 20th century, the region came under French control twice – after each of the world wars – but in both cases (in referendums held in 1935 and 1955) its people voted in favour of rejoining Germany.

Although now solidly within German boundaries, the influence of the land of the baguette is still felt in all sorts of subtle ways. Many locals are bilingual and the standard greeting is not '*Hallo*' but '*Salü*', a variation of the French '*salut*'. Their French heritage has softened the Saarlanders, who tend to be rather relaxed folk with an appreciation of good food, wine and company – *saarvoir vivre*, it's been called.

SAARBRÜCKEN

☎ 0681 / pop 200,000

The Saarland capital, Saarbrücken, though a thoroughly modern city, is not without considerable charms. Vestiges of its 18th-century heyday as a royal residence under Prince Wilhelm Heinrich (1718–68) survive in the baroque townhouses and churches designed by his prolific and skilled court architect, Friedrich Joachim Stengel. The historic centre around St Johanner Markt brims with excellent restaurants and cafés, and there's a pleasant promenade for strolls along the Saar River.

Orientation

Central Saarbrücken is bisected by the Saar River and the A620, an ugly autobahn that disfigures the river's left bank. From the Hauptbahnhof, at the northwestern end of the commercial centre, pedestrians-only Reichstrasse and Bahnhofstrasse lead 1km to St Johanner Markt, the city's nightlife hub.

Information

Several ATMs can be found along Kaiserstrasse.

Discount Waschsalon (Blumenstrasse 42; ☉ 7am-11pm) Self-service laundry.

Evangelisches Krankenhaus (EvK; ☎ 38 860; Grossherzog Friedrich Strasse 44) A hospital whose main entrance is on Niekestrasse.

Police station (☎ 962 2233; Karcherstrasse 5)

Post office (Hauptbahnhof; ☉ 8am-6.30pm Mon-Fri, 9am-1pm Sat)

Reisebank (Hauptbahnhof) Exchanges currency.

Telecenter (Dudweilerstrasse 26; per hr €1.50; ☉ 9am-midnight) Internet access.

Telehouse (per hr €1.50) Kaiserstrasse (☉ 9am-midnight); Obertorstrasse 1 (☉ 9am-midnight Mon-Sat, noon-midnight Sun) Internet access.

TOURISM WITHOUT BORDERS

Astride the frontier between Germanic and Romantic Europe, the Saarland, neighbouring Luxembourg and the French *département* of Moselle (part of Lorraine) promote themselves to visitors as a single, culturally diverse area known as the **Grossregion** (Greater Region). The word *grenzenlos* (without borders, boundless) is often bandied about and this will be especially true in 2007, when the whole region – sometimes referred to as **SaarLorLux** or **QuattroPole** (www.quattropole.org) – plus Trier will serve as a **European Capital of Culture** (www.luxembourg2007.org).

It's remarkably easy to add an international flavour to your stay in the Saarland. From Saarbrücken's Hauptbahnhof, you can pop over to **Luxembourg** by bus (€13 return, 1¼ hours, four daily), rail it south to the French cathedral city of **Metz** (€13.30, 70 minutes, hourly) or hop on the S1 tram line to the French town of **Sarreguemines** (Saargemünd; €3.90), which has a delightful farmers market every Tuesday morning. Cyclists can take advantage of the 340km, trans-frontier **VeloRoute SaarLorLux**.

Thalia Bücher (☎ 388 30; Bahnhofstrasse 54) Bookshop.

Tourist office (☎ 938 090; www.die-region-saarbruecken.de; Saar-Galerie, Reichsstrasse 1; ☼ 9am-6pm Mon-Fri, 10am-4pm Sat) Facing the bus station outside the Hauptbahnhof. Sells tickets for cultural events.

Waschhaus (Nauwieserstrasse 22; per wash €3; ☼ 8am-10pm Mon-Sat) Self-service laundry.

Sights
NORTHERN SAAR BANK

The heart of Saarbrücken (and its nightlife hub) is the historic **St Johanner Markt**, a long, narrow public square anchored by an ornate fountain designed by Stengel and flanked by some of the town's oldest buildings. The city's main commercial street, pedestrianised Bahnhofstrasse, heads northwest – as you cross Betzenstrasse, look to the northeast and you'll spot the cathedral-like **Rathaus**, a red-brick neo-Gothic structure.

At the southern end of St Johanner Markt is the **Stadtgalerie** (☎ 936 8321; www.stadtgalerie.de in German & French; St Johanner Markt 24; admission free; ☼ 11am-7pm Tue & Thu-Sun, noon-8pm Wed), which puts on temporary exhibitions of the latest in contemporary art, including video and performance art. Another example of Stengel's work awaits a block east and north on Türkenstrasse, in the form of the Catholic **Basilika St Johann**.

Heading south on Türkenstrasse will bring you to the massive yellow **Staatstheater** (☎ 30 920; www.theater-saarbruecken.de in German; Schillerplatz), a grandiose Nazi-era structure with neoclassical touches. It opened in 1938 with Richard Wagner's *The Flying Dutchman* and today presents opera, ballet, musicals and drama.

A short walk southeast is one of Saarbrücken's cultural highlights, the **Saarland Museum** (☎ 996 40; www.saarlandmuseum.de; Bismarckstrasse 11-19;

adult/student €1.50/1, more for special exhibitions; ☼ 10am-6pm Tue & Thu-Sun, 10am-10pm Wed). The **Moderne Galerie** tracks the development of European art over the course of the 20th century and is especially noteworthy for its German impressionists (eg Slevogt, Corinth and Liebermann) and expressionist works (eg by Kirchner, Marc and Jawlensky). The **Alte Sammlung** (Old Collection) across the street, goes back further in history with a millennium's worth of paintings, porcelain, tapestries and sculptures from southwest Germany and the Alsace and Lorraine regions of France.

SOUTHERN SAAR BANK

Crossing the Saar River via the pedestrians-only Alte Brücke takes you over the autobahn and up to the Stengel-designed baroque **Schlossplatz**. The dominant building here is the **Saarbrücker Schloss**, which mixes elements of several architectural styles, from Renaissance to baroque to neoclassical; the modern glass tower was added in the 1980s and, alas, doesn't do for the Schloss what IM Pei's pyramid did for the Louvre. Its basement and a modern annex house the **Historisches Museum Saar** (☎ 506 4501; Schlossplatz 15; adult/concession €2.50/1.50; ☼ 10am-6pm Tue, Wed, Fri & Sun, 10am-8pm Thu, noon-6pm Sat), which has interesting exhibits about the region in the 20th century, with a focus on WWI, the Third Reich and the post-WWII years. Fans of the Romans, the Celts and their predecessors won't want to miss the **Museum für Vor- und Frühgeschichte** (Museum of Early History & Prehistory; ☎ 954 050; www.historisches-museum.org in German; Schlossplatz 16; admission free; ☼ 9am-5pm Tue-Sat, 10am-6pm Sun).

The late Gothic **Schlosskirche** (☎ 950 7638; Am Schlossberg 6; admission free; ☼ 10am-6pm Tue & Thu-Sun,

10am-10pm Wed) is now a museum whose focus is religious art from the 13th to 19th centuries; highlights include statuary from the 15th and 16th centuries and the elaborate tombs of three local, 17th- and 18th-century princes. The original stained-glass windows were destroyed in WWII and – as is obvious from the style – replaced in the late 1950s. Some of the panes had to be repaired after being blown out in 1999 by a bomb – presumably planted by extreme right-wing militants – aimed at a controversial historical exhibition on the role of *Wehrmacht* soldiers in WWII atrocities.

To the northwest is Stengel's handsome Ludwigsplatz, flanked by stately baroque townhouses. **Ludwigskirche** (⊗ 10am-4.30pm Tue-

Sun), built in 1775, sports a façade festooned with Biblical figures and a brilliant white interior with stylish stucco decoration. If the church is closed, you can sneak a peek through the windows of the vestibule.

Sleeping

DJH hostel (☎ 330 40; www.jugendherberge.de; Meerwiesertalweg 31; dm €18; ✗) Near the university northeast of the centre, on the Prinzenweiher lake in Saarbrücken's green belt. Served by bus 19 from the Rathaus and, Monday to Friday, by buses 49 and 69 from the Hauptbahnhof.

Hotel Schlosskrug (☎ 36 735; www.hotel-schlosskrug .de in German; Schmollerstrasse 14; s/d €39/66) A rather ordinary hotel with some of the cheapest rooms in the city. Just a short walk from the centre.

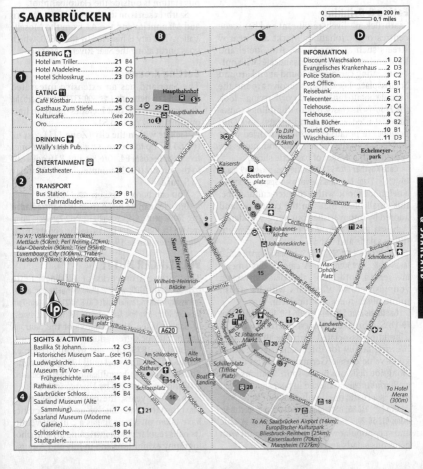

SAARBRÜCKEN

0 ———— 200 m
0 ———— 0.1 miles

SLEEPING 🏠
Hotel am Triller.................**21** B4
Hotel Madeleine................**22** C2
Hotel Schlosskrug **23** D3

EATING 🍴
Café Kostbar....................**24** D2
Gasthaus Zum Stiefel.......**25** C3
Kulturcafé......................(see 20)
Oro................................**26** C3

DRINKING 🍸
Wally's Irish Pub..............**27** C3

ENTERTAINMENT 🎭
Staatstheater..................**28** C4

TRANSPORT
Bus Station.....................**29** B1
Der Fahrradladen.............(see 24)

INFORMATION
Discount Waschsalon **1** D2
Evangelisches Krankenhaus **2** D3
Police Station........................**3** C2
Post Office............................**4** B1
Reisebank.............................**5** B1
Telecenter.............................**6** C2
Telehouse.............................**7** C4
Telehouse.............................**8** C2
Thalia Bücher........................**9** B2
Tourist Office........................**10** B1
Waschhaus...........................**11** D3

SIGHTS & ACTIVITIES
Basilika St Johann.................**12** C3
Historisches Museum Saar...(see 16)
Ludwigskirche......................**13** A3
Museum für Vor- und
  Frühgeschichte..................**14** B4
Rathaus...............................**15** C3
Saarbrücker Schloss.............**16** B4
Saarland Museum (Alte
  Sammlung)........................**17** C4
Saarland Museum (Moderne
  Galerie)............................**18** D4
Schlosskirche........................**19** B4
Stadtgalerie.........................**20** C4

RHINELAND-PALATINATE & SAARLAND

Hotel Madeleine (☎ 322 28; www.hotel-madeleine.de; Cecilienstrasse 5; s €61-69, d €69-79; ✗ 🖳) This central and friendly family-run hotel has 28 recently renovated rooms that are smallish but bright and comfortable.

Hotel Meran (☎ 653 81; www.hotel-meran.de in German; Mainzer Strasse 69; s €55-66, d €74-95; 🕭 ✗) Despite its plain beige façade, this 43-room hotel, about 500m southeast of St Johanner Markt, has some nice touches, such as an 11m pool, sauna, and fireplace lounge. Rooms are fairly standard.

Hotel am Triller (☎ 580 000; Trillerweg 57; www .hotel-am-triller.de, in German; s/d from €108/146, Fri-Sun from €69/105; Ⓟ ✗ 🖳 🕭) This 114-room, almost-boutique hotel, on a quiet street uphill from Schlossplatz, has airy and artsy public areas and a Franco-German restaurant.

Eating & Drinking

Saarbrücken's lively restaurant and bar scene centres on St Johanner Markt and nearby streets such as Saarstrasse, Am Stiefel and Kappenstrasse. Several pleasant cafés with outdoor seating can also be found at and around Schlossplatz. Local dishes revolve around the humble potato but are well worth trying – look for *Hoorische* (tasty potato dumplings sometimes stuffed with ground meats) and *Dibbelabbes* (a potato casserole with dried meat and leeks). In the French tradition, meals are served with a basket of baguette slices.

Café Kostbar (☎ 93 86 366; Nauwieserstrasse 19; mains €6-10; ⏱ 11am-1am, meals served noon-3pm & 6-11pm) In a neighbourhood with a counter-culture vibe, this small place that's in the courtyard and adored by impoverished but hungry students, serves a small selection of inexpensive but filling salads and mains.

Kulturcafé (☎ 379 9200; St Johanner Markt 24; light meals €6-8; ⏱ 9.30am-1am) A café by day (meals are served until 6pm), this place attracts a youngish crowd after dark with its stylish minimalism-meets-gothic décor.

Gasthaus Zum Stiefel (☎ 936 450; Am Stiefel 2; mains €9-19) Saarbrücken's oldest microbrewery, in a building associated with the Bruch beer-brewing family for three centuries, features good-value classic German and local dishes alongside delicious home-spun creations such as *Bierhähnchen* (chicken in beer sauce). Next door is a rustic brew-pub, Stiefelbräu.

Oro (⏱ 938 8663; St Johanner Markt 7-9; daily specials €6, mains €12.50-20; ⏱ 10am-1am, to 3am Fri & Sat) A chic and very popular wine bar and restaurant with generous salads and a leafy courtyard.

Wally's Irish Pub (☎ 938 0587; Katolisch-Kirch-Strasse 1; ⏱ noon-2am or later 365 days a year) A welcoming pub, popular with English-speakers, that's owned by an Irish fellow whose name is *not* Wally. Monday is quiz night (9pm) and there's whiskey tasting on Sunday (7pm).

Getting There & Away

Saarbrücken Airport (☎ 06893-832 72; www.flughafen -saarbruecken.de), about 14km east of the city, offers mainly holiday charters and short hops within Germany, many operated by locally-based **Cirrus Airlines** (0180-444 4888; www.cirrus-airlines.de).

Saarbrücken's Hauptbahnhof has at least hourly rail connections to Trier (€13.40, one hour), Idar-Oberstein (€11.70, 50 minutes) and Mainz (€24.30, 1¾ hours). The city's main bus station is outside the Hauptbahnhof.

Saarbrücken is on the A6 from Kaiserslautern and Mannheim and the A1 from the Moselle Valley. The city is bisected by the A620, which goes north along the Saar River to Merzig.

Getting Around

The Saarland has an extensive integrated **bus and rail network** (☎ 500 3377; www.saarbahn .de, www.vgs-online.de) that includes one tram line, optimistically named S1.

Tickets within the city (Zone 111) cost €2 (€1.60 for up to six stops); a day pass for one/ five people costs €4.10/6.80. Bus R10 goes out to the airport (€2, 20 minutes, hourly Monday to Saturday).

You can book a taxi on ☎ 330 33.

Bicycles can be hired from **Der Fahrradladen** (☎ 370 98; per day €15, weekend €30; ⏱ 2-7pm Mon, 10am-7pm Tue-Fri, 10am-2pm or 3pm Sat) in the courtyard at Nauwieserstrasse 19.

VÖLKLINGER HÜTTE

The former ironworks of **Völklinger Hütte** (☎ 06898-910 0100; www.voelklinger-huette.org; adult/ concession/family incl audio-guide €10/8.50/21; ⏱ 10am-7pm May-Oct, 10am-6pm Nov-Apr), about 10km northwest of Saarbrücken on the banks of the Saar, is one of Europe's great industrial monuments. Opened in 1873, this vast foundry complex produced iron and steel until 1986. In recognition of its historical significance, it was declared a World Heritage Site by Unesco in 1994.

In recent years, the complex's towering blast furnaces and massive smelting facilities have taken on a new life as a cultural venue. Its halls regularly host intriguing art and photography exhibitions and in July and August, the sweet sounds of jazz ring out every Friday night from 6pm to 7pm at Zimmerplatz. The Gebläsehalle (blowing hall), with its original red-and-white tiled floor, is also used for concerts. At night the compound is often lit up like a vast science-fiction set.

Trains link the town of Völklingen with Saarbrücken (€2.70, nine minutes, several times an hour) and Trier (€11.70, one hour, at least hourly); the ironworks are only a three-minute walk from the Bahnhof.

METTLACH

☎ 06864 / pop 11,500

Mettlach, on the Saar River about 50km northwest of Saarbrücken, is at the heart of the prettiest section of the Saarland. For the last 200 years its history has been tied to the ceramics firm of Villeroy & Boch, which moved its factory and administrative headquarters into the **Alte Abtei**, a former Benedictine abbey, in 1809. Today, the abbey houses a predictably commercial, though not uninteresting, multimedia exhibit called **Keravision** (☎ 811 020; ☻ 9am-6pm Mon-Fri, 9.30am-4pm Sat, Sun & holidays, closed Sun Nov-Mar), which introduces the company's history and products. Also here is the **Keramikmuseum** (☎ 811 294; ☻ 9am-6pm Mon-Fri, 9.30am-4pm Sat, Sun & holidays, closed Sun Nov-Mar), with its collection of historical porcelain. Beside it, the millennium-old **Alter Turm** (Old Tower), burial place of the town's founder, Merovingian Duke Luitwin, is a refreshingly quirky piece of walk-in public art called **Living Planet Square**. As you walk through the installation – a giant bird topiary called the Earth Spirit which overlooks six giant-tile walls representing the continents in a rather, shall we say, explicit fashion – your movement activates jungle noises.

The **tourist office** (Saarschleife Touristik; ☎ 06864-8334; www.tourist-info.mettlach.de; Freiherr-vom-Stein-Strasse 64; ☻ 8.30am-4.30pm Mon-Fri), has information about the town and region.

Frequent regional trains link Mettlach with Saarbrücken's Hauptbahnhof (€6.50, 40 minutes). By car, take the Merzig-Schwemlingen exit off the A8 and then follow the B51 north.

AROUND METTLACH

The most scenic spot along the Saar River is the **Saarschleife**, where the river makes a spectacular hairpin loop. It's in the community of **Orscholz**, in a large nature park about 5km west of Mettlach. The best viewing point is **Cloef**, just a short walk through the forest from the village.

To experience the loop from the river, you can take a 1½-hour cruise from Mettlach offered by **Mettlacher-Personenschifffahrt** (☎ 06864-802 20; www.saar-schifffahrt.de, in German; adult/concession €7/3.50), with several daily departures from March to December.

PERL-NENNIG

☎ 06866 / pop 6350

Perl-Nennig, on the Luxembourg border about 20km west of Mettlach and 40km south of Trier, is the Saarland's only wine-growing community; the local specialities are made with grape varieties from Burgundy, introduced after the war when the region was under French control. On weekends between April and October, wine growers open up their cellars for tastings on a rotating basis.

The main historical sight here is a stunning 160-sq-metre floor **mosaic** in the reconstructed 3rd-century **Römische Villa** (Roman villa; ☎ 1329; Römerstrasse 11; adult/child €1.50/0.75; ☻ 8.30am-noon & 1-6pm Tue-Sun Apr-Sep, 9-11.30am & 1-4.30pm Tue-Sun Oct, Nov & Mar). Composed of three million tiny chips of coloured stone, it's the largest and best-preserved such mosaic north of the Alps.

The **tourist office** (☎ 1439; www.nennig.de, in German; Bübinger Strasse 1a, Nennig; ☻ 9.30am-12.30pm & 2-5pm Mon-Fri), right by the Bahnhof in Nennig, can provide information on the villa, wine tastings and accommodation. It also hires out bicycles.

Perl-Nennig can be reached from Merzig by bus 6300. The train to/from Trier runs every hour or two (€6.20, 40 minutes). By car take the A8 from Saarbrücken or the B419 from Trier.

EUROPÄISCHER KULTURPARK BLIESBRUCK-REINHEIM

Flanking the Franco–German border about 25km southeast of Saarbrücken in the charming Blies Valley, the **Europäischer Kulturpark Bliesbruck-Reinheim** (European Archaeological Park; ☎ 06843-900 221; www.kulturpark-online.de, in German, www.archeo57.com, in French; Robert-Schuman-Strasse 2; adult/student €4.60/3.10; ☻ 10am-6pm Tue-Sun mid-Mar–Oct) showcases the ruins of a 1st- to 4th-century Gallo-Roman crafts town. Most of the artisans' houses, with their ovens, cellars and heating systems, as well as the thermal baths, are on the French side, but the area's most spectacular discovery, the **tomb of a Celtic princess** from AD 400, was discovered on the German side of the line. In 2007 the park will host an exhibit on life in Roman Europe.

From Saarbrücken, take bus R10 to Blieskastel (€4.60, one hour) and then bus K501.

Hesse

Though relatively small in surface area, Hesse (Hessen in German) is Germany's economic powerhouse, with the highest per capita income of all German states.

Originally part of what is now Thuringia, Hesse won independence in the mid-13th century and in the Middle Ages was influenced by one figure – the margrave Philip I (Philip the Magnanimous). A bigamist who sired 19 children, Philip embraced the Reformation early, but two distinct entities emerged after his death, the resulting carve-up between his sons: Lutheran Darmstadt-Hesse in the south, and Calvinistic Kassel in the north. During the Thirty Years' War these two principalities fought on opposite sides. For most of its history, Frankfurt was either a free imperial city or, following the Napoleonic wars, an independent city state.

About two-thirds of Hesse's population lives in the Rhine-Main region, a large basin and urban conglomeration that includes Wiesbaden, Darmstadt, Frankfurt-am-Main and lots of smaller towns. Wiesbaden is the political capital, but Frankfurt wields the economic clout. In fact, Wiesbaden's parliament was where the taxi-driving former foreign minister, Joschka Fischer, rocked boats by taking his first ministerial oath wearing tennis shoes, and Frankfurt was a hotbed of student politics and the squatting movement in the 1960s and '70s. Ironically, Frankfurt is the most un-German city, but the first contact many will have with Germany.

Although the cities are the main attraction for visitors, the Rhön and Odenwald mountain ranges, as well as the picturesque Lahn River valley, are also splendid places to explore and get to know in this interesting part of Germany.

HIGHLIGHTS

- **City Chic** Check Frankfurt-am-Main's trademarks: apple wine, smelly cheese, first-class museums and a big-city skyline (opposite)

- **Heroes and Villains** Stand at the feet of Hercules in Kassel and set off down the Fairy-Tale Road (p535)

- **Nightlife** Watch the sun rise with students, night owls and drunks in Marburg's hilly Oberstadt (p530)

- **Best Baths** Saunter between the saunas and pools of Wiesbaden's historic Kaiser-Friedrich-Therme (p529)

- **Artistic Pursuits** Relax in the luscious surrounds of an Art Nouveau artist colony, or gape at Joseph Beuys' chair of fat in Darmstadt (p525)

- **Waterworks** Paddle along the Lahn River, a world away from urban sprawl (p530)

★ Kassel

★ Marburg

★ Lahn River

Wiesbaden ★ ★ Frankfurt-am-Main

★ Darmstadt

- POPULATION: 6 MILLION
- AREA: 21,114 SQ KM

HESSE

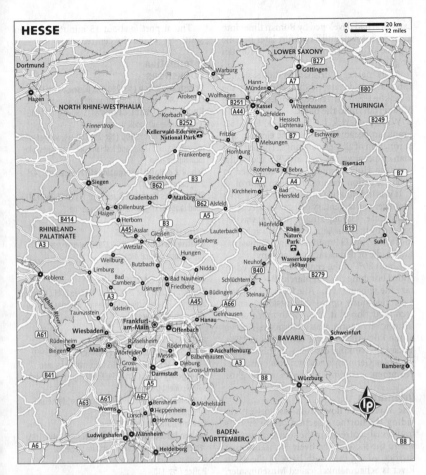

HESSE

FRANKFURT-AM-MAIN

☎ 069 / pop 660,000

Unlike any other German city, Frankfurt-on-the-Main (pronounced 'mine') is unashamedly high-rise. It bristles with jagged skyscrapers that rise up from the Rhine–Main basin and alongside a restored Altstadt (Old Town). As a business capital, it attracts thousands of foreign expats and exiles from other German cities who have come here to work. It is home to one of Europe's largest stock exchanges, the Bundesbank (Germany's central bank), and the European Central Bank, the regulating bank for member countries of the European Single Currency. Its enormous airport is the region's largest employer and, after Heathrow, Europe's second-largest airport, handling over 50 million passengers each year. Frankfurt also hosts a string of important trade events, including the world's largest book, consumer-goods and musical-instrument fairs.

Frankfurt has a rich collection of museums, second only to Berlin's. In nightlife, too, it is the capital's only serious rival, especially when it comes to the dance-music scene, centred on the ever-popular techno beat.

Avoid the trade fairs and the transport masses and join the increasing number of travellers dropping into Frankfurt for a city-break or a longer stay.

History

First mentioned in 794, an original stone age settlement near present-day Frankfurt's

HESSE

cathedral had developed by Roman times into a garrison town, and Frankfurt later became a place of importance in the Holy Roman Empire.

As its market flourished, so did its significance as a trade city; by the 12th century the 'Frankfurt Fair' attracted business from the Mediterranean to the Baltic.

With Frederick I (Barbarossa) in 1152, Frankfurt became the site of the election and coronation of all German kings. The last German emperor was elected in 1792, and by the time the Holy Roman Empire collapsed in 1806 the region was under French control.

It was in Frankfurt in 1848 that Germany's first-ever parliamentary delegation met at the Paulskirche. Although this parliament was disbanded by the Prussians, Frankfurt was hailed, much later, by US President John F Kennedy as the 'cradle of democracy in Germany'.

About 80% of the centre was destroyed by Allied bombing raids in March 1944. Plans to raze the remains of the Alte Oper (old opera) were vigorously opposed by residents and a reconstruction of it, along with much of the historic city centre, was undertaken. Known as the Römerberg, it was completed in 1983. Today its banking district – a shimmering symbol of Germany's post-war economic redevelopment – continues to reach new heights.

Orientation

The Main River flows from east to west, dividing the northern section of the city, its traditional centre, from the southern section, where the focus is the lively Sachsenhausen district. Along the south bank of the Main River is Schaumainkai, called Museumsufer, or the Museum Embankment, for the high concentration of museums there.

The Hauptbahnhof is on the western side of the city, about 800m from the Römerberg, the historic centre. A large square, An der Hauptwache, is northeast along Kaiserstrasse. The Hauptwache itself is a lovely baroque building that was once the local police station.

The pedestrianised Zeil, Frankfurt's main shopping street, runs west to east between the Hauptwache U/S-Bahn station and the Konstablerwache U/S-Bahn.

The area near the Alte Opera, Bornheim and Sachsenhausen have the largest concentration of eating and drinking places, whereas the serious nightclubbing district is along Hanauer Landstrasse.

The airport is about 15 minutes by train southwest of the city centre.

Information

BOOKSHOPS

British Bookshop (☎ 280 492; Börsenstrasse 17) Largest selection of English-language books in town.
Hugendubel (☎ 01801 4844 84; Steinweg 12) Multi-level, multilingual book store.
Oscar Wilde Bookshop (☎ 281 260; www.oscar-wilde .de; Alte Gasse 51) Gay and lesbian books and tapes, plus local information.
Schmitt & Hahn Internationale Presse (☎ 2425 230; Hauptbahnhof)
Süssmann's Presse & Buch (☎ 131 0751; Zeil 127) Good range of English-language magazines.

CULTURAL CENTRES

Goethe Institut (☎ 961 2270; Diesterwegplatz 72) The German cultural organisation.

DISCOUNT CARDS

FrankfurtCard (per 24/48hr €8/12) Free public transport and up to 50% reduction at museums, galleries, zoo and airport visitor terraces.

EMERGENCY

AG36 Schwules Zentrum Frankfurt (☎ 295 959; Alte Gasse 36) Advice and AIDS help, mainly for men.
Emergency clinic (☎ 4750; Friedberger Landstrasse 430) Accident treatment.
English hotline (☎ 192 92) Advice, assistance and information for English speakers.
Fire/ambulance (☎ 112)
Lesben Informations- und Beratungsstelle (LIBS; ☎ 282 883; www.libs.w4w.net; Alte Gasse 38) Information and assistance for lesbians.
Police (☎ 110)
Women's hotline (☎ 709 494; www.frauennotrufe -hessen.de)

INTERNET ACCESS

CyberRyder (☎ 9139 6754; Töngesgasse 31; per 15min €1.60; ◷ 9.30-10pm Mon-Fri, 10am-10pm Sat, noon-10pm Sun)
Internet@Game Café (☎ 2878 52; Grosse Friedberger Strasse 37-39; per 30min €2; ◷ 9.30am-midnight Mon-Sat, noon-11pm Sun) Central and modern internet café.

INTERNET RESOURCES

Frankfurt.de (www.frankfurt.de) Official Frankfurt website.
frankfurt-handicap.de (www.frankfurt-handicap.de, in German) Excellent city guide giving detailed information on disabled access to many of Frankfurt's attractions and venues.

LAUNDRY
SB Waschsalon (Wallstrasse; wash €3, dry €0.50; ☻ 6am-11pm Mon-Sat) With a second branch in Bockenheim (Grosse Seestrasse 46).
Wasch-Center (Sandweg 41; wash/dry €3/0.50; ☻ 6am-11pm Mon-Sat)

LIBRARIES
Central library (☎ 2123 8080; Zeil 17)
Stadt- und Universitätsbibliothek (☎ 2123 9205; Bockenheimer Warte U-Bahn)

MEDICAL SERVICES
Pharmacies that are open all night are listed in the window or *Frankfurter Rundschau*.
24-hour doctor service (☎ 192 92)
Krankenhaus Sachsenhausen (☎ 660 50; Schulstrasse 31)
Uni-Klinik (☎ 630 11; Theodor-Stern-Kai 7, Sachsenhausen; ☻ 24hr)

MONEY
International ATM (Platform 15, Hauptbahnhof) Others are located around the station.
Reisebank (☎ 2427 8591; South exit, Hauptbahnhof; ☻ 7am-9pm) Exchanges cash and cheques; makes advances on cards.

POST
Post Office Karstadt (Zeil 90; ☻ 9.30am-8pm Mon-Fri, 9.30am-4pm Sat); Hauptbahnhof (1st fl, Hauptbahnhof; ☻ 7am-7.30pm Mon-Fri, 8am-4pm Sat); Airport (Departure hall B; ☻ 7am-9pm); Goetheplatz (Goetheplatz 4; ☻ 9.30am-8pm Mon-Fri, 9.30am-2pm Sat)

TOURIST INFORMATION
German National Tourist Office (☎ 974 640; www.germany-tourism.de; Beethovenstrasse 69)
Infoline (☎ 2123 8800) Event information in English.
Tourismus + Congress (☎ 2123 8800, room reservations ☎ 2123 0808; www.tcf.frankfurt.de; Kaiserstrasse 56; ☻ 8am-9pm Mon-Fri, 9am-6pm Sat & Sun) Services for tourists with particular needs and long-stay visitors.
Tourist office Hauptbahnhof (☎ 2123 8849; www.frankfurt.de; ☻ 8am-9pm Mon-Fri, 9am-6pm Sat & Sun); Römer (☎ 2123 8708; Römerberg 27; ☻ 9.30am-5.30pm Mon-Fri, 9.30am-4pm Sat & Sun)
Verkehrsinsel (☎ 01805-069 960; Zeil; ☻ 9am-8pm Mon-Fri, 9.30am-6pm Sat) Public transport and general information, plus transport tickets.

TRAVEL AGENCIES
Hapag-Lloyd Reisebüro (☎ 216 216; Kaiserstrasse 14) Travel service with money transfer and travellers cheque/cash exchange services.

Lufthansa City Center (☎ 9133 700; Kirchnerstrasse 3)
STA Travel (☎ 703 035; Bockenheimer Landstrasse 133); Bornheim (☎ 9043 6970; Berger Strasse 118)

UNIVERSITIES
Johann Wolfgang von Goethe Universität (☎ 7981; Bockenheimer Warte & Westend)

Dangers & Annoyances
The area around the Hauptbahnhof is a base for Frankfurt's trade in sex and illegal drugs, and has *Druckräume*, special rooms where needles are distributed and the drug dependent can shoot up. Women in particular might want to avoid Elbestrasse and Taunusstrasse, the main sex drags. Frequent police and private security patrols of the station and the surrounding Bahnhofsviertel keep things under control, but it's always advisable to use big-city common sense.

Sights & Activities
MAIN TOWER
A good place to start seeing the sights of Frankfurt is from the **Main Tower** (☎ 3650 4740; www.maintower.helaba.de; Neue Mainzer Strasse 52-58; adult/concession €4.50/3; ☻ 10am-9pm Sun-Thu, 10am-11pm Fri & Sat Apr-Oct, 10am-7pm Nov-Mar, weather permitting), Frankfurt's highest public viewing platform. At 200m tall, the tower offers spectacular views of the city. To the southeast you can see the Römerberg, a remake of the original city centre; beyond it, across the river, is Sachsenhausen, an entertainment area with lots of pubs, bars and restaurants. To the north and northwest is the banking district with its ever-changing vista of towers, including the 256m-high peak of the elegant **Messeturm**, which locals call the *Bleistift* (pencil). Europe's tallest office block, the 258m-high (298m including the antenna) **Commerzbank Tower**, stands aloof at Kaiserplatz, a stone's throw from the Main Tower, which has a restaurant and cocktail bar.

RÖMERBERG
The Römerberg, west of the Dom, is Frankfurt's old central square, where restored 14th- and 15th-century buildings, including the **Paulskirche** (☻ 10am-5pm Mon-Fri), provide a glimpse of how beautiful the city once was. It's especially lovely during December's Weihnachtsmarkt.

The old town hall, or **Römer**, in the northwestern corner of Römerberg, consists of three

CENTRAL FRANKFURT

recreated step-gabled 15th-century houses. The Römer was the site of celebrations during the election and coronation of emperors in the Holy Roman Empire; today it's the registry office and the office of Frankfurt's mayor. Inside, there are portraits of 52 rulers in the **Kaisersaal** (Imperial Hall; ☎ 2123 4919; adult/concession €2/1; ⏰ 10am-1pm & 2-5pm). Right in the centre

of Römerberg is the **Gerechtigkeitsbrunnen**, the 'Font of Justice'. In 1612, at the coronation of Matthias, the fountain ran with wine!

FRANKFURTER DOM

East of Römerberg, the **Frankfurter Dom** (☎ 1310 467; ⏰ 9am-noon Mon-Thu, 2.30-6pm Fri, Sat & Sun) sits behind the **Historischer Garten** (Histori-

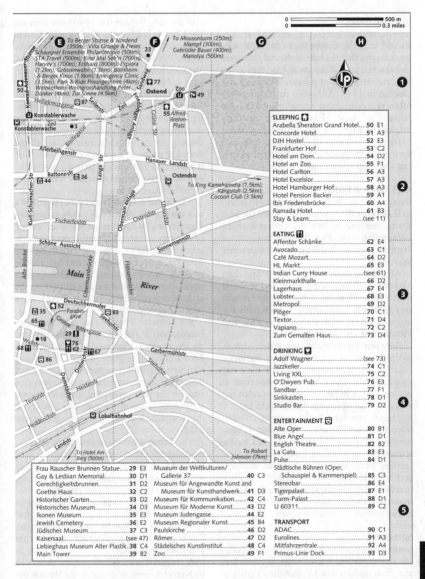

To Berger Strasse & Nordend (350m); Villa Orange & Freies Schauspiel Ensemble Philanthropin (500m); STA Travel (500m); Kino Mal Seh'n (700m); Harvey's (700m); Eckhaus (800m); Explora (1.2km); Grössenwahn (1.5km); Bornheim & Berger Kinos (1.8km); Emergency Clinic (3.5km); Park & Ride Preungesheim (4km); Weinkellerei-Weingrosshandlung Peter Dünker (4km); Zur Sonne (4.5km)

To Mousonturm (250m); Mampf (300m); Gebrüder Bauer (400m); Manolya (500m)

To King Kamehameha (1.5km); Känguruh (2.5km); Cocoon Club (3.5km)

To Hotel Am Berg (500m)

To Robert Johnson (7km)

SLEEPING
Arabella Sheraton Grand Hotel	**50**	E1
Concorde Hotel	**51**	A3
DJH Hostel	**52**	E3
Frankfurter Hof	**53**	C2
Hotel am Dom	**54**	D2
Hotel am Zoo	**55**	F1
Hotel Carlton	**56**	A3
Hotel Excelsior	**57**	A3
Hotel Hamburger Hof	**58**	A3
Hotel Pension Backer	**59**	A1
Ibis Friedensbrücke	**60**	A4
Ramada Hotel	**61**	B3
Stay & Learn	(see 11)	

EATING
Affentor Schänke	**62**	E4
Avocado	**63**	C1
Café Mozart	**64**	D2
HL Markt	**65**	E3
Indian Curry House	(see 61)	
Kleinmarkthalle	**66**	D2
Lagerhaus	**67**	E4
Lobster	**68**	E3
Metropol	**69**	D2
Plöger	**70**	C1
Textor	**71**	D4
Vapiano	**72**	C2
Zum Gemalten Haus	**73**	D4

DRINKING
Adolf Wagner	(see 73)	
Jazzkeller	**74**	C1
Living XXL	**75**	C2
O'Dwyers Pub	**76**	E3
Sandbar	**77**	F1
Sinkkasten	**78**	D1
Studio Bar	**79**	D2

ENTERTAINMENT
Alte Oper	**80**	B1
Blue Angel	**81**	D1
English Theatre	**82**	B2
La Gata	**83**	E3
Pulse	**84**	D1
Städtische Bühnen (Oper, Schauspiel & Kammerspiel)	**85**	C3
Stereobar	**86**	E4
Tigerpalast	**87**	E1
Turm-Palast	**88**	D1
U 60311	**89**	C2

TRANSPORT
ADAC	**90**	C1
Eurolines	**91**	A3
Mitfahrzentrale	**92**	A4
Primus-Linie Dock	**93**	D3

Frau Rauscher Brunnen Statue	**29**	E3	Museum der Weltkulturen/	
Gay & Lesbian Memorial	**30**	D1	Gallerie 37	**40** C3
Gerechtigkeitsbrunnen	**31**	D2	Museum für Angewandte Kunst and	
Goethe Haus	**32**	C2	Museum für Kunsthandwerk	**41** D3
Historischer Garten	**33**	D2	Museum für Kommunikation	**42** C4
Historisches Museum	**34**	D3	Museum für Moderne Kunst	**43** D2
Ikonen Museum	**35**	E3	Museum Judengasse	**44** E2
Jewish Cemetery	**36**	E2	Museum Regionale Kunst	**45** B4
Jüdisches Museum	**37**	C3	Paulskirche	**46** D2
Kaisersaal	(see 47)		Römer	**47** D2
Liebieghaus Museum Alter Plastik	**38**	C4	Städelsches Kunstinstitut	**48** C4
Main Tower	**39**	B2	Zoo	**49** F1

cal Garden), where you can wander through excavated Roman and Carolingian foundations. Dominated by the elegant 15th-century Gothic-style **tower** (95m; completed in the 1860s), the Dom was one of the few structures to survive the 1944 bombing. The **Dommuseum** (☎ 1337 6816; www.dommuseum-frankfurt.de; ☒ 10am-5pm Tue-Fri, 11am-5pm Sat & Sun; tour adult/concession

€2/1) has a valuable collection of reliquaries and liturgical objects; it conducts tours of the Dom at 3pm daily.

On the cathedral's southern side is the small **Wahlkapelle** (Voting Chapel), where seven electors of the Holy Roman Empire chose the emperor from 1356 onwards. Adjoining it is a **choir** with beautiful wooden stalls.

HESSE

GOETHE HAUS

Anyone with an interest in German literature should visit the **Goethe Haus** (☎ 138 800; www .goethehaus-frankfurt.de; Grosser Hirschgraben 23-25; adult/ concession €5/2.50; 🕑 10am-6pm Mon-Sat, 10am-5.30pm Sun), the birthplace of Johann Wolfgang von Goethe in 1749. Although furnishings are often reproductions, some original pieces remain on show. Highlights are Goethe's original writing desk and the library. Guided tours are conducted in German at 2pm and 4pm; English tours can be arranged, but staff can also help you along.

ALTE OPER & BÖRSE

Inaugurated in 1880, the lovely Renaissance-style **Alte Oper** (Old Opera House; ☎ 134 0400; Opernplatz 8) was designed by Berlin architect Richard Lucae and stylistically influenced by Gottfried Semper, creator of the famous Semperoper in Dresden.

After being destroyed in WWII, and then narrowly avoiding being razed and replaced with 1960s cubes, the Alte Oper was rebuilt and its façade reconstructed to resemble the original, graced with statues of Goethe and Mozart. The interior is modern.

Between Opernplatz and Börsenstrasse is the section of street known as **Fressgasse** (Munch Alley), a somewhat overrated dining area lined with snack bars and restaurants. If you're visiting in September, try to catch the very nice Rheingau wine festival held here.

The old city **Börse** (Stock Exchange; ☎ 2111 1515; visitors.centre@deutsche-boerse.com; Börsenplatz; 🕑 10am-6pm Mon-Fri) is open to visitors, who can view a semi-active trading floor from an observation section. Book at least an hour in advance, and bring ID with you. Most of the Börse's functions and electronic trading systems have moved to new headquarters in the northwestern suburb of Frankfurt-Hausen.

MUSEUMS

Most museums open from 10am to 5pm Tuesday to Sunday and 10am to 8pm Wednesday, and close on Monday. In most places entry is free on the last Saturday of the month.

Museumsufer

A string of museums lines the southern bank of the Main River, also known as Museum Embankment. The pick of the crop is the **Städelsches Kunstinstitut** (Städel Art Institute; ☎ 605 0980; www.staedelmuseum.de; Schaumainkai 63; adult/ concession €6/5; 🕑 10am-5pm Tue & Fri-Sun, 10am-9pm Wed & Thu). It holds a world-class collection of works by various artists including Botticelli, Dürer, Van Eyck, Rembrandt, Renoir, Rubens, Vermeer and Cézanne, plus Frankfurt natives such as Hans Holbein.

The **Museum für Kommunikation** (☎ 606 00; Schaumainkai 53; adult/concession €2/1; 🕑 9am-6pm Tue-Fri, 11am-7pm Sat & Sun) is a touchy-feely museum displaying the history of communication, including tips on how to make invisible ink and decipher codes. It's a winner with kids, and it won't cost you a penny unless you visit the excellent café – on Wednesday and Sunday even the tours are free.

The **Deutsches Architekturmuseum** (☎ 2123 8844; www.dam-online.de; Schaumainkai 43; adult/concession €6/3; 11am-6pm Tue & Thu-Sun, 11am-8pm Wed) is something of a disappointment: the permanent collection is just a series of models showing settlements from the Stone Age to the present day, and the rotating exhibits tend to fail on their English translations. Without a single display on the architecture of Frankfurt itself, this is really a missed opportunity.

By contrast, you'll find the **Deutsches Filmmuseum** (☎ 2123 8830; www.deutsches-filmmuseum .de; Schaumainkai 41; adult/concession €2.50/1.30) next door a fascinating place. It has a library and film history exhibit, constantly changing exhibitions and extensive archives, plus premieres and special film events (all in their original languages) in the Kommunales Kino; check the programme in any listings magazine (see p522).

The **Ikonen-Museum** (Icon Museum; ☎ 2123 6262; www.ikonenmuseumfrankfurt.de; Brückenstrasse 3-7; adult/ concession €3/2) houses a collection of Russian religious paintings. Admission includes entry to the neighbouring Russian church.

The **Museum für Angewandte Kunst** (Museum of Applied Arts; ☎ 2123 4037; Schaumainkai 15-17; adult/ concession €5/2.50; 🕑 10am-5pm Tue & Thu-Sun, 10am-9pm Wed) is set in lovely gardens with a smart café and outdoor seating.

A favourite with school parties, thanks to its Native American displays, the **Museum der Weltkulturen/Gallerie 37** (Museum of World Cultures/ Gallery 37; ☎ 2123 5391; www.mdw-frankfurt.de; Schaumainkai 29-37; adult/concession €3.60/2; 🕑 10am-5pm Tue, Thu, Fri & Sun, 10am-8pm Wed, 2-8pm Sat) has lots of fascinating ethnological exhibits.

The **Liebieghaus Museum Alter Plastik** (Museum of Ancient Sculpture; ☎ 2123 8615; www.liebieghaus.de; Schaumainkai 71; adult/concession €4/2.50) has classical, medieval, baroque and Renaissance sculptures and an exhibition of Egyptian art. Close by is the **Museum Giersch** (☎ 6330 4128; www .museum-giersch.de; Schaumainkai 83; adult/concession €4/2; ☺ noon-7pm Tue-Fri, 11am-5pm Sat & Sun), a regional museum with regular exhibitions of works by lesser-known Hesse artists.

Other Museums

The triangular **Museum für Moderne Kunst** (Museum of Modern Art; ☎ 2123 0447; www.mmk-frankfurt .de; Domstrasse 10; adult/concession €6/23), dubbed the 'slice of cake' by locals, is an excellent and imaginatively run exhibition space with a permanent collection containing works by Roy Lichtenstein, Claes Oldenburg and Joseph Beuys. Temporary exhibits showcase local, national and international artists.

The **Historisches Museum** (☎ 2123 5599; www .historisches-museum.frankfurt.de; Saalgasse 19; adult/concession €4/2), just south of Römerberg, is worth visiting, even if you skip the uninspiring permanent exhibition on the Middle Ages in favour of the spectacular model (€1) of the city from the 1930s in the foyer.

The city has two notable museums on Jewish life in Frankfurt, reminding visitors that the Jewish community here, with 35,000 people, was once one of the largest in Europe. The main **Jüdisches Museum** (☎ 2123 5000; www .juedischesmuseum.de; Untermainkai 14-15; adult/concession €2.60/1.30), in the former Rothschildpalais, is a huge place with an exhibit of Jewish life in the city from the Middle Ages to present day, with good detail on well-known Frankfurt Jews persecuted, murdered or exiled by the Nazis. Religious items are also displayed.

The **Museum Judengasse** (☎ 297 7419; Kurt-Schumacher-Strasse 10; adult/concession €1.50/0.70, incl Jüdisches Museum €3/1.50), along the northeastern boundaries of the old city fortifications, is the annexe to the Jüdisches Museum. On display here are remains of ritual baths and houses from the Jewish ghetto, which was destroyed by the Nazis.

Behind the Museum Judengasse, the western wall of the **Jewish Cemetery** is a remarkable **memorial** studded with metal cubes bearing the names of all the Frankfurt-born Jews murdered during the Holocaust. The cubes allow visitors to place stones or pebbles, a Jewish tradition that shows that a grave is tended and the person not forgotten.

Further north is the interactive **Explora** (☎ 788 888; www.exploramuseum.de; Glauburgplatz 1,

Nordend; adult/concession €9/7; ☺ 11am-6pm Tue-Sun), a family-oriented science and technology museum. The 3D photos of turn-of-the-century Frankfurt are a definite highlight. To get there, get off at Glauburgstrasse U-Bahn.

PALMENGARTEN & IG-FARBENHAUS

A nice place to relax is in the botanical **Palmengarten** (Palm Garden; ☎ 2123 6689; www.palmengarten -frankfurt.de; Siesmayerstrasse 61; adult/child €5/2). It has rose and formal gardens, a playground for kids, a little pond with rowing boats and a mini-gauge train that puffs round the park (€1/0.50).

Nearby is the monumental **IG-Farbenhaus**, now part of the university's Westend campus (see the boxed text, p518)

MONUMENTS

On the corner of Alte Gasse and Schäfergasse, at the heart of the city's main gay and lesbian area, is a **gay and lesbian memorial** (one of only three in Europe) to the many homosexuals persecuted and killed by the Nazis during WWII. It is deliberate that the statue's head is nearly severed from the body.

South of the river, the **Frau Rauscher Brunnen** statue on Klappergasse in Sachsenhausen is a rather less poignant figure: a bulky, bitchy-looking Hausfrau who periodically spews a stream of water about 10m onto the footpath. When the street's busy you'll undoubtedly see pedestrians get drenched. The idea is based on a popular Frankfurt song about apple wine.

FRANKFURT ZOO & AIRPORT

The **zoo** (☎ 2123 3735; Alfred-Brehm-Platz 16; adult/concession €8/4; ☺ 9am-7pm Apr-Oct, 9am-5pm Nov-Mar), with its creative displays, signs and exhibits, is a relief from the cosmopolitan chaos, and even has scheduled tropical storms (11.30am and 3.30pm). Take the U6 to Zoo station.

Just as creative, and beloved by children, is the visitor terrace at **Frankfurt airport**. The platform, on Level 3, Terminal 1, was being upgraded in 2006. The airport's only 11 minutes away from the Hauptbahnhof by S-Bahn (see p525).

SKATING

Every Tuesday from April to October, thousands of inline skaters hit the streets for a sociable 33km to 42km road circuit with a police escort. For more information visit www .tns-frankfurt.de.

Courses

Due to the large number of foreign residents in
Frankfurt-am-Main, there are many language
schools in the city. The most respected, and
expensive, option is the **Goethe Institut** (☎ 961
2270; frankfurt@goethe.de; Diesterwegplatz 72); call for
accommodation options.

Inlingua (☎ 242 9200; www.inlingua-frankfurt.de;
Kaiserstrasse 37) and **Language Alliance** (☎ 253 952; www
.languagealliance.de; Kaiserstrasse 74) offer a wide range
of intensive afternoon and evening courses,
starting from around €320 a month for 80
tuition hours. Accommodation is offered at
Stay & Learn (see opposite).

Tours

Between 1.30pm and 5.30pm during weekends and holidays, the city's **Ebbelwei-Express**
(☎ 2132 2425; www.vgf-ffm.de; adult/concession €5/2.50)
tram circles Frankfurt. Jump on at any stop –
the zoo, Hauptbahnhof, Südbahnhof, Frankensteiner Platz (near the Haus der Jugend) are
convenient ones.

Kulturothek Frankfurt (☎ 281 010; www.kulturothek
.de; adult/concession €8/6) runs 2½-hour German-
language walking tours on a variety of subjects
every Sunday. Show up at 2pm at the agreed
meeting point. The price is €90 to €120 for
groups of up to 25 people.

The **tourist offices** offer excellent 2½-hour
city tours, which include visits to the Goethe
Haus (10am or winter tours) and a ride up to
the Main Tower gallery (2pm, summer only),
leaving at 10am April to October and 2pm daily
from the Römer and Hauptbahnhof (15 minutes later) offices. The cost is €25 per adult, €20
on a concession and €10 per child. There are
also themed excursions, like Jewish Frankfurt,
Frankfurt architecture and Goethe tours.

Elisabeth Lücke (☎ 06196-457 87; www.elisabeth
-luecke.de; per hr €50) is a private guide who runs

tours for individuals or groups in English,
German and Spanish on various themes such
as architecture, the finance world and Jewish
life in Frankfurt.

Primus Linie (☎ 133 8370; www.primus-linie.de;
☑ May-Oct) operates short cruises along the
Main River (€6.20 to €8.20) and longer Rhine
trips to Rüdesheim, Loreley, Seligenstadt and
Aschaffenburg, leaving from the docks on
the northern embankment near the Eiserner
Steg bridge.

Festivals & Events

Frankfurt festivals include the following:
Dippemess A fun fair with apple wine and food; held in
March and September.
Illuminale When artists surrealistically illuminate buildings
and public spaces; held in April.
Kunsthandwerk Heute An arts and handicrafts festival
held on Paulsplatz in late May/early June.
Sound of Frankfurt Takes place along the Zeil, with local
and visiting groups playing everything from techno to soul,
blues and rock; held in July.
Frankfurt Book Fair (Frankfurter Buchmesse) World-
famous publishing event; held in autumn.
Weihnachtsmarkt A Christmas fair on Römerberg with
mulled wine, choirs and traditional foods; held in December.

Sleeping
BUDGET
Prices in Frankfurt fluctuate considerably
according to whether it's a weekend (usually
cheaper) or a weekday. The real crunch is
caused by the trade fair, however, when the
price can double, even for modest rooms.

The tourist offices can usually book singles from about €20 to €50. They only book
private rooms (from €40 per person) during trade
fairs. At other times you can contact one of
the **Mitwohnzentrale offices** City (☎ 299 050; www
.city-mitwohnzentrale.de; Hanseallee 2); Mainhattan (☎ 597

IG-FARBENHAUS – THE HEADQUARTERS OF HORROR

Set in Frankfurt's tranquil Westend, the monumental IG-Farbenhaus is now part of the university. This long, arcing stone building was erected in 1931 as the prestigious headquarters of
IG-Farben, the German chemicals conglomerate that produced Zyklon-B, the deadly gas used in
the concentration camps. After the war, the USA moved in and used IG-Farbenhaus as a military
command centre and CIA office – one obvious reason why the Red Army Faction (p40) detonated
a bomb in the foyer during the 1970s. When German occupation ended in the early 1990s, US
forces handed over the building and the university's drama department took up residence as
one of the first departments to move from the old campus near Bockenheimer Warte. There was
much debate about whether to change the name, but in the end the university decided to retain
IG-Farbenhaus as a reminder of the building's dubious past.

5561; www.mitwohnzentrale-mainhattan.de; Fürstenberger Strasse 145); Allgemeine Mitwohnzentrale (☎ 9552 0892; www .allgemeine-mitwohnzentrale.de). The city branch also has its own apartments.

Most of Frankfurt's low-end accommodation is in the Bahnhofsviertel, the rather sleazy area surrounding the Hauptbahnhof.

DJH hostel (☎ 610 0150; www.jugendherberge-frankfurt .de; Deutschherrnufer 12; dm €16.50-28.50; s €35-39.50, d €25-34.50; ⏰ 6am-2am; **P** ✗) Advance bookings are advisable for the big, bustling DJH Haus der Jugend on the south side of the Main River; it's within walking distance of the city centre and Sachsenhausen's nightspots. From the Hauptbahnhof, take bus 46 to Frankensteiner Platz or S-Bahn lines 2, 3, 4, 5, or 6 to Lokalbahnhof.

Stay & Learn Residence (☎ 253 952; www.frankfurt -hostel.com; Kaiserstrasse 74; dm €16-20, s €35-40, d €55-60; ✗ 💻) Students doing courses mainly use these rooms at the busy Language Alliance language school, but travellers are welcome here too; it has a choice of private and shared bathrooms and small shared kitchens (there's no on-site catering).

Hotel Pension Backer (☎ 747 992; Mendelssohnstrasse 92; r €25-50; **P**) A favourite for visitors seeking a safe, clean place to stay away from the Hauptbahnhof, this pension has plain rooms with shared bathrooms on each floor.

Hotel Hamburger Hof (☎ 2713 9690; www.hamburger hof.com; Poststrasse 10-12; s €69, d €85) Located alongside some illustrious companions on the (northern) side of the Hauptbahnhof, rooms in this comfortable hotel are well-priced, with cheaper deals on the internet.

Hotel Carlton (☎ 241 8280; Karlstrasse 11; s/d €45/60; **P** 💻) A smart little townhouse, the Carlton is one of the best options in this area, with cheaper summer rates, TV, phone, nice linen and even minibars in the rooms.

Hotel Excelsior (☎ 256 080; www.hotelexcelsior -frankfurt.de; Mannheimer Strasse 7-9; s €57, d €67; **P** ✗ 💻) Alongside the Hauptbahnhof in an ugly building, the Excelsior offers excellent value, especially for business travellers on a tight travel allowance. There's internet access, a free minibar and phone calls throughout Germany.

Ibis Friedensbrücke (☎ 273 030; www.ibishotel.de; Speicherstrasse 3-5; s €81, d €90; **P** ✗ 🐾) You won't be swinging cats in the rooms of this chain hotel, but they are chirpy and some have nice views to the nearby Main River or the quiet yard. Breakfast is extra.

Hotel Am Berg (☎ 660 5370; www.hotel-am-berg-ffm .de; Grethenweg 23; s €58-73, d €75-99; ✗) Located in a

sandstone building in the quiet backstreets of Sachsenhausen, this hotel close to Südbahnhof has very decent rooms (without breakfast).

MIDRANGE

Ramada City Center (☎ 310 810; ramada-frankfurt@ t-online.de; Weserstrasse 17; s €65-92, d €107; **P** ✗ 💻) Though unspectacular, this chain hotel offers all the fundamentals in rooms that are good value for Frankfurt.

Concorde Hotel (☎ 242 4220; www.hotelconcorde .de; Karlstrasse 9; s/d €93/113; ✗ 🐾 💻) Understated and friendly, this establishment in a restored Art Deco building near Hauptbahnhof is a good choice any time, but especially on weekends.

Hotel am Dom (☎ 138 1030; Kannengiessergasse 3; s €85-90, d €110, apt €115) This unprepossessing hotel offers immaculate rooms, suites and apartments just a few paces from the Frankfurter Dom. The high standard makes it popular, so book well in advance.

Falk Hotel (☎ 7191 8870; www.hotel-falk.de; Falkstrasse 38; s/d €65/85; ✗) This small hotel located on a quiet street in Bockenheim is popular for its pleasant, nicely appointed rooms. It's near the Bockenheim shops, and also a hop from Palmengarten and the upper reaches of Grüneburg Park. Take the U-Bahn to Leipziger Strasse.

Hotel am Zoo (☎ 949 930; www.hotel-am-zoo.com; Alfred-Brehm-Platz 6; s/d €72/106; **P** ✗ 💻) Unpretentious and situated in two buildings, this is a comfortable option near the Zeil and (obviously) the zoo.

Hotel Liebig (☎ 241 829 90; www.hotelliebig.de; Liebigstrasse 45; s €103-152, d €128-179; **P** ✗) Set in Frankfurt's leafy Westend district, this Italian-run hotel has stylish rooms, some with fabric wallpaper; it's near the beautiful Grüneburg Park and within easy walking distance of Opernplatz.

Hotel Palmenhof (☎ 7530 060; www.palmenhof.com; Bockenheimer Landstrasse 89-91; s €110-140, d €150-170) Another excellent option in Westend, this hotel in a historic building offers modern, fair-sized rooms with tasteful furnishings and has friendly, efficient staff. It also rents residential apartments nearby.

TOP END

Even prices of the top-flight options usually double during important fairs – business travellers take note, lest receipts are sent directly to the Raised Eyebrow Department.

EBBELWOI & HANDKÄSE MIT MUSIK

Frankfurt delicacies are best experienced in the city's traditional taverns, which serve *Ebbelwoi* (Frankfurt dialect for Apfelwein), an alcoholic apple cider, along with local specialities like *Handkäse mit Musik* (hand-cheese with music) and *Frankfurter Grüne Sosse* (Frankfurt green sauce).

Definitive Ebbelwoi joints include **Adolf Wagner** (☎ 612 525; www.apfelwein-wagner.com; Schweizer Strasse 69) and the **Affentor Schänke** (☎ 9819 0881; Neuer Wall 9), with its tree-shaded terrace. **Zur Sonne** (☎ 459 396; Berger Strasse 312) is widely considered the best in town.

Handkäse mit Musik is a name you could only hear in Germany. It describes a round cheese marinated in oil and vinegar with onions, served with bread and butter and no fork. As you might imagine, this potent mixture tends to give one a healthy dose of wind – the release of which, ladies and gentlemen, is the 'music' part.

Frankfurter Grüne Sosse is made from parsley, sorrel, dill, burnet, borage, chervil and chives mixed with yoghurt, mayonnaise or sour cream; it's served with potatoes and ox meat or eggs, and was Goethe's favourite food.

Villa Orange (☎ 405 840; www.villa-orange.de; Hebelstrasse 1, Nordend; s €120-220, d €140-270; P ⊗) This attractive Italian-style 'country' villa, with 38 spacious rooms, offers all facilities (including a library and patio) without the drawbacks of large hotels.

Radisson SAS Hotel (☎ 770 1550; www.frankfurt.radissonsas.com; Franklinstrasse 65; r €185, ste €450-950; P ⊗ ⊗ ⊟ ⊕) A new-kid in town, this business hotel looks like a futuristic Ferris wheel that someone has tried to square. It has four comfortable room designs: 'fashion', 'chic', 'at home' and 'fresh'. It's a short ride to the fair grounds (by tram 17) but is most suitable if you have a car or can take taxis. Prices vary from day to day.

Arabella Sheraton Grand Hotel (☎ 298 10; grandhotel.frankfurt@arabellasheraton.com; Konrad-Adenauer-Strasse 7; s €219-294, d €244-319, ste €575-1225; P ⊗ ⊗ ⊟ ⊛) The service, location and facilities make this a good choice for business travellers, even if the furnishings lag somewhat with the times. Breakfast is extra, but check for weekend and internet deals.

Frankfurter Hof (☎ 215 920; www.frankfurter-hof.steigenberger.de; Kaiserplatz; s €289-590, d €499-590, ste €650-1290; P ⊗ ⊗ ⊟) This is one of the best addresses in town and for good reason – its rooms and suites are tastefully furnished and the service here is excellent. There is also a choice of four exquisite restaurants. The corner suites (usually suite numbers ending with 16 on each floor) are secluded and bright, with windows on two sides. Rooms usually come without breakfast, but inclusive weekend deals start at almost half-price, and there are internet-only offers that are well worth exploring.

Eating

BAHNHOFSVIERTEL & MESSE

The area around the Hauptbahnhof is dominated by southern European, Middle Eastern and Asian eateries. The station itself has plenty of snack and fast-food options.

Indian Curry House (☎ 230 690; Weserstrasse 17; dishes €3-7) This popular sit-down/takeaway spice-house serves unpretentious and very tasty dishes, a cut above the rest in the lowlife Bahnhofsviertel.

Vapiano (☎ 9288 7888; Goetheplatz 1-3; ☯ 10am-midnight; €5-8) In this bustling Italian eatery you get an electronic card at the door, and let one of the frisky young just-off-the-bus chaps swipe it through the till after he's dashed together your dish before your very eyes. You pay when you leave. The pasta and salads are very decent. Wash them down with an Italian red or white from the bar. Keep your card in your pocket and not on your tray, lest it gets whisked away.

Orfeos Erben (☎ 7076 9100; www.orfeos.de; Hamburger Allee 45; mains €9-16; ☯ noon-3pm & 6pm-1am Mon-Fri, dinner Sat & Sun) Orfeos is an art house cinema, a restaurant and a bar rolled into one. If the feet are sore or your spirit is in need of a shot of cinematic art, the distances won't kill you – it's about 10 paces between table, bar and arthouse cinema, all in an ambience dominated by timbers.

FRESSGASSE & NORTHERN CENTRE

Known to locals as Fressgasse (Munch Alley), the stretch of Kalbächer Gasse and Grosse Bockenheimer Strasse between Rathenauplatz and Opernplatz has lots of mid-priced restaurants and fast-food places with outdoor tables.

Look around (especially on the northern side streets) and take your pick. The quality is fairly uniform, if not startling.

Plöger (☎ 1387 1123; www.ploeger.de; Grosse Bockenheimer Strasse 30) Tempting, titillating and tasting as delicious as it all looks, the finest tinned, smoked and bottled goodies can be found here to bend the will of the most tempered self-caterer.

Avocado (☎ 294 642; www.restaurant-avocado.de; Hochstrasse 27; mains €26-35; ✆ noon-2.30pm Tue-Sat, 6-10.30pm Mon-Sat) This French bistro is something very special. Treat yourself to a five-course menu (€57) or a lunch menu (€30). The champagne list sparkles with class, and the little outside garden area, completely enshrouded in vines, is as romantic as anything on a summer's night.

ZEIL & RÖMERBERG

Café Mozart (☎ 291 954; Töngesgasse 23; cakes from €1) Join Frankfurt's 'granny scene', or the travellers who beat a path to this popular café for cakes and coffee.

Kleinmarkthalle (Off Hasengasse; ✆ 7.30am-6pm Mon-Fri, 7am-3pm Sat) This huge covered hall was the first food market in post-war Frankfurt selling fruit, vegetables, meats, fish and hot food. Stalls sell Italian, Turkish, Chinese and German food, and you can get salads and fresh fruit juices as well as wine and beer. The *Gref Völsings Rindswurst* (beef sausage) stand is an institution. At the western end of the hall is a large mural depicting impressions of Frankfurt.

Metropol (☎ 288 287; Weckmarkt 13-15; ✆ 10am-1am Tue-Thu, 10am-2am Fri, 9am-2am Sat, 9am-midnight Sun; mains €11-13) In the long shadow of the Dom and with a lovely courtyard out the back where children can chill out away from the city heat, Metropol serves dishes from a changing menu that fluctuates between the inspired and bistro staples. It's a great place for coffee or a drink too.

SACHSENHAUSEN

Sachsenhausen is fairly safe and everyone-friendly (gays, lesbians, heteros, students, naked men with Walkmans, baked sun-studio worshippers). Virtually every building in the pedestrian area between Grosse Rittergasse and Darmstädter Landstrasse is a bar, restaurant or takeaway; Schweizer Strasse and Textorstrasse also have many taverns and eating places.

Zum Gemalten Haus (☎ 614 559; Schweizer Strasse 67; mains €6-12; ✆ 10am-midnight Tue-Sun) The colourful façade, and the paintings inside, give this apple wine tavern the edge on many others. Try local specialities like *Handkäse mit Musik* (see boxed text, opposite), the smelly cheese that keeps reminding you, and everyone around you, just how charming Frankfurt can be.

Textor (☎ 622 299; Textorstrasse 38; ✆ 10am-1am; meals €7-14) The wine prices can gnaw into your wallet here, but outdoor summer seating, a kitchen producing reliable German nosh and the voluble crowds make this a lively option away from Sachsenhausen's traditional quarter.

Lagerhaus (☎ 628 552; Dreieichstrasse 45; mains €6-13) Tradition dances to the tune of the modern in this colourful restaurant and bar that has vegetarian dishes as well as a bevy of traditional staples. Weekend brunches are especially lively.

NORDEND & BORNHEIM

Berger Strasse – Frankfurt's longest street – is the main drag here, hosting a wealth of cafés and bars.

Manolya (☎ 494 0162; Habsburger Allee 6; mains €8-15; ✆ 5pm-1am Sun, Mon & Tue, 11am-1am Wed & Thu, 11am-2am Fri & Sat) Frankfurt's favoured Turkish restaurant dishes up killer-bee starters and pleasing mains in a convivial atmosphere. There's outdoor tent seating for cool or balmy nights.

Gebrüder Bauer (☎ 4059 2744; www.gebrueder-bauer .de; Sandweg 113; mains €7.50-15; ✆ 11.30am-3.30pm Mon-Fri, 10.30am-3pm Sun, 6pm-late) Yes, there really are two *Gebrüder* (brothers), and they look pretty much the spitting image of each other. This place established itself quickly on the Frankfurt scene because the food, wine and other drinks are delicious. It's very gay and everyone-else friendly, and the brothers do a take-along picnic basket from €9.50 (order ahead).

Eckhaus (☎ 491 197; Bornheimer Landstrasse 45; mains €7.50-14; ✆ 5pm-1am Mon-Sat, 5pm-midnight Sun) The smoke-stained walls, the iron fan above the door and those ancient floorboards all suggest an inelegant, long-toothed past. We love this place, others say the noise level snaps their nerves. The hallmark *Rösti* (shredded potato pancake), large servings of tasty salads and other main courses have been served in this restaurant-bar for over 100 years.

Grössenwahn (☎ 599 356; www.cafe-groessenwahn .de; Lenaustrasse 97; mains €9-20) The name translates as 'megalomania' and it's a snorting treat. The food in this upmarket pub-restaurant relies on pure flavours and the wine seduces your tongue into parts of your mouth you didn't know were there. The downside of this wonderful Frankfurt institution is that the air can be shocking at times, especially if someone's tugging on a cigar or a pipe at the next table. Stylish modern German cuisine with plenty of international extras are the order of the day. Take the U-Bahn to Glauburgstrasse.

Tiger-Restaurant (☎ 920 0220; www.tigerpalast.com; Heiligkreuzgasse 16-20; menus €90-110; ☺ 6pm-midnight Tue-Sat) Culinary guru Martin Göschel concocts delicious Italian and French-inspired cuisine in what many consider to be the best nosh address in town. It's part of the Tigerpalast cabaret venue (opposite).

BOCKENHEIM

Many university faculties have now moved to Westend, but Bockenheim retains a string of cheap eating places in what was – and still is to some extent – the stamping ground of Frankfurt students' Green student (or taxing driving) movement. Take the U6 or U7 to Bockenheimer Warte or Leipziger Strasse.

Prielok (☎ 776 468; Jordanstrasse 3; mains €8-13; ☺ 11am-3pm & 5.30pm-midnight Mon-Fri, 5.30pm-midnight Sat) Without claiming to be special, this place somehow is: loyal regulars, students and workers tread a path here for traditional fare.

Bastos (☎ 7072 0004; Gräfstrasse 45; mains €6.50-14; ☺ 10am-late Mon-Sat, 10am-6pm Sun) A restaurant, café and night-owl drinking spot, this dark tavern does good salads, pasta and more substantial dishes for students. Against all odds, some even do their homework or huddle together in work groups here. The clientele ebbs and flows. The terrace is nice, especially on a sizzling hot day.

Andalucia (☎ 773 730; www.restaurante-andalucia.de; Konrad-Brosswitz-Strasse 41; mains €11.50-30; ☺ 6pm-1am) A meal can easily be made of the delicious tapas here; there's also a weekly-changing menu, or order from a regular menu that's strong on red meat and seafood dishes. Book in advance.

SELF-CATERING

Fresh produce markets are held from 8am to 6pm on Thursday and Friday at Bockenheimer Warte and Südbahnhof respectively. There are supermarkets in the basements of Galeria Kaufhof and Hertie on Zeil, and an **HL Markt** (Elisabethenstrasse 10-12) near the hostel in Sachsenhausen.

Drinking

Studio Bar (☎ 1337 9225; www.studiobar.de; Katharinenpforte 6) You might wonder, 'Whatever happened to the revolution?' on entering this joint. The décor is very in-your-face 1960s, with decorative shots of glam pop and enough mirrors and plush sofas to make a hedonist scream uncontrollably with delight. Great drinks are served over two levels plus an outdoor terrace that becomes wall-to-wall in summer.

Sandbar (☎ 4908 3695; Sandweg 6) If the Studio Bar gets too cramped, or the glam too ragged round the edges, dive into the Sandbar as a chic alternative. The minimalist interior and soft bar stools invite a long evening or a short repose between clubs.

Harvey's (☎ 497 303; www.harveys-frankfurt.de; Bornheimer Landstrasse 64) This relaxed café-bar and restaurant is a favourite – for gays and lesbians especially, but anyone will feel fine here.

Bockenheimer Weinkontor (☎ 702 031; Schlossstrasse 92) A mixed crowd of the young, middle-aged and business-suited all come here to quaff various European wines. Sometimes they also come here to pick each other up. The building, a 19th-century workshop, has a lovely summer courtyard, but the long window ledge and the bar are the places to hang your buttocks and start talking.

O'Dwyers Pub (☎ 9620 1413; Klappergasse 19) There are lots of Irish pubs in Frankfurt. This one features on the drinking topography because it's livelier than many others – even hellish sometimes – and near the youth hostel.

Weinkellerei-Weingrosshandlung Peter Dünker (☎ 451 993; Bergerstrasse 265; ☺ noon-1am Mon-Sat, 6pm-1am Sun) There's only one of these. Located to the right as you enter the yard, this musty little Frankfurt wine cellar/dealer in Nordend is not retro, it's real. Descend, rub your eyes and try some of Germany's finest here. A snack is always sold for €1 to prime the palate.

Entertainment

Frankfurt is not just 'Mainhattan' – it's a magnet for the whole Rhine-Main region and this is reflected in the number, velocity and depth of its clubs and cabaret scene. Oddly, Thursday is often dynamite night for those working in Frankfurt, because lots of commuting workers go 'home' on Friday – with tired eyes, crushed dance toes and wretched hangovers.

The best information source is the German-language *Journal Frankfurt* (€1.50), available at newsstands and kiosks, with comprehensive monthly listings in German. It also has a section for lesbians and gays. *Frizz, Prinz* and *Strandgut* are free listings magazines that are available throughout the city. *Partysan* has news on club events in the Rhein-Main-Saar area.

Also check listings for beach clubs along the Main River – several of the dance clubs have them.

CABARET

Tigerpalast (☎ 920 0220; www.tigerpalast.com; Heiligkreuzgasse 16-20) Cabaret and other performances are staged here in one of Frankfurt's top venues. For a great night out, eat in the restaurant (opposite) or cosy bistro, and after the show drop into the bar for a tipple.

Mousonturm (☎ 4058 9520; www.mousonturm.de; Waldschmidtstrasse 4) There's lots to explore in this rambling converted soap factory – dance, politically-oriented cabaret and a bistro that serves food until midnight.

CINEMAS

Films screened in the original language are denoted by 'OF' or 'OmU'. Look for posters in U-Bahn stations; if the description is in English, so is the movie. Listings can also be found at www.kinoservice.de.

Turmpalast (☎ 281 787; Grosse Eschenheimer Strasse 20) The toilets can be a bummer in this otherwise good multiscreen cinema, showing mostly English current releases.

Berger Kinos (☎ 945 0330; Berger Strasse 177) A good arthouse venue in Bornheim, with regular festivals and special screenings.

Kino Mal Seh'n (☎ 597 0845; www.malsehnkino.de; Adlerflychtstrasse 6) This tiny repertory cinema shows all kinds of offbeat movies; its wine bar and living room are equally engaging.

There's an art-house cinema located at Orfeos Erben (p520).

CLUBS

King Kamehameha (☎ 480 0370; www.king-kamehameha.de; Hanauer Landstrasse 192) A strapping Leonardo DiCaprio–type guy might dash out and unexpectedly plough the length of the ornamental pool (clothed, take note) – it's been known to happen here. And much more too, for 'KingKa' is legendary, with its own live club band on Thursday, dance beats on weekends, private rooms and that tempting watercourse in one bar. But while you're here, explore the yard and neighbouring buildings. In summer, the magic words will be 'Sansibar Roofgarden'.

U 60311 (☎ 2970 60311; www.u60311.net; Rossmarkt) Any underground station with this many numbers deserved to be recycled into a club – and so it was. Now it's one of the best stops in town for techno beats, in a unique location deep in the concrete bowels of the city.

Stereo Bar (☎ 617 116; www.stereobar.de; Abtsgässchen 7) You'll need to get this right if you want to be in the right shirt: Studio Bar (opposite) is 1960s, Stereo Bar is 1970s. This one's a bit more eclectic, and more off-beat in character without fudging on hedonism.

Cocoon Club (☎ 900 200; www.cocoonclub.de; Carl-Benz-Strasse 21; ☾ closed Mon) This postmodern pulsating membrane-like miracle is the home of techno legend Sven Väth; it throbs with music from the man himself or his guests Friday and Saturday, and other days in smaller format. The screen, which is everything but small, is a delight.

Living XXL (☎ 242 9370; www.livingxxl.de; Kaiserstrasse 29) If the euro goes into freefall, it'll land here – Frankfurt's large, bustling and highly popular club has three bars and a gallery dining room at the foot of the European Central Bank.

Robert Johnson (☎ 821 123; Nording 131) Beside the river in the swampy primeval soup of Offenbach, this club attracts the best names in German electronic music and also has regular nights from the thriving Frankfurt-based Playhouse label.

GAY & LESBIAN VENUES

The monthly *Frizz* has gay listings in every issue Pick up *Frankfurt von Hinten* (Frankfurt from Behind), a good gay guide, or check out www.frankfurt.gay-web.de, which has some English in its city guide. The gay scene is concentrated around Alte Gasse and Schäfergasse, with a bevy of clubs, cafés and bathhouses.

Blue Angel (☎ 282 772; www.blueangel-online.de; Brönnerstrasse 17) This is a popular, strictly gay club (men only) with outrageous events for the party-minded.

Pulse (☎ 1388 6802; www.pulse-frankfurt.de; Bleichstrasse 38a) The only thing this *isn't* is a hotel – it's a restaurant, a bar and a nightclub all rolled into one. It's mainly a guys' place, but many lesbians also come here. Check out the wonderful conservatory/patio out the back. Also see Harvey's (p514).

Switchboard (☎ 283 535; Alte Gasse 36) is the info-café downstairs from the gay and lesbian advice centres (see p512).

La Gata (☎ 614581; Seehofstrasse 3) This is Frankfurt's only women-only bar for Lesbians.

ROCK & JAZZ

Batschkapp (☎ 9521 8410; www.batschkapp.de; Maybachstrasse 24) In its 30-plus years of staging live bands, the 'Batsch' has seen 'em come, go, burn out, gloriously self-destruct or simply rust to dust. There are also club nights.

Festhalle (☎ 757 50; Ludwig-Erhard-Anlage 1) The venue for major international acts.

Sinkkasten (☎ 280 385; www.sinkkasten-frankfurt.de, in German; Brönnerstrasse 5) From Bollywood to Bon Jovi and everything beyond or between – the Sinkkasten has lots of live music as well as entertaining vinyl to dance to, especially if you love 1980s flavours.

Jazzkeller (☎ 288 537; www.jazzkeller.com; Kleine Bockenheimer Strasse 18a) Look hard to find this place – a great jazz venue with mood – hidden in an alley parallel to Goethestrasse.

Mampf (☎ 448 674; www.mampf-jazz.de, in German; Sandweg 64) This place used to be a nosh house where apprentice butchers took their tipple. Today you'll hear great jazz sounds in this jazz club-cum-pub that has a lot of surprises up its sleeve, especially during sessions.

THEATRE & CLASSICAL

The Frankfurt theatre scene has all the hallmarks of high art – it bites backs, it bitches, and occasionally an offended ego spontaneously and publicly explodes. There are over 30 different venues around town. **Frankfurt Ticket** (☎ 134 0400) takes bookings for the theatres Kammerspiel and Schauspiel Frankfurt – part of the **Städtische Bühnen** (☎ 2123 7101; www.schauspielfrankfurt.de; Neuer Mainzer Strasse 17) – as well as for the **Oper** (www.oper-frankfurt.de; Willy-Brandt-Platz) and the three stages at the **Alte Oper** (www.oper-frankfurt.de; Opernplatz 8).

English Theatre (☎ 2423 1620; www.english-theatre.org; Kaiserstrasse 34) The quality of the favourites rolled out at this theatre for English-language plays and musicals is surprisingly high.

Freies Schauspiel Ensemble Philanthropin (☎ 596 9490; www.freiesschauspiel.de; Hebelstrasse 15-19, Nordend) This is the kind of offbeat and alternative venue where an ego could explode spontaneously on-stage and find its way into the script for the next performance.

TAT (☎ 2123 7555; Bockenheimer Warte) This former tram depot offers some of the most innovative stuff around, and children usually have a rollicking time in the ample space.

Shopping

Frankfurt is not Milan or Berlin when it comes to shopping – it's more the place to satisfy any souvenir or last-minute inspirations before boarding the plane or train home. Zeil is the main shopping street, but the serious splurging takes place on the streets immediately south of Fressgasse, where you'll find upmarket fashion boutiques and jewellery stores.

There's a great **flea market** (Schaumainkai; ⏰ 8am-2pm Sat) along Museumsufer. You'll also find plenty of private art galleries south of the museums, selling work by local and international artists.

Getting There & Away

AIR

Flughafen Frankfurt-am-Main (☎ 01805-372 4636; www.frankfurt-airport.de) is Germany's largest airport, amd has the highest freight and passenger turnover in continental Europe (London's Heathrow just beats it on passenger numbers).

This high-tech sprawl has two terminals, linked by an elevated railway called the Sky Line. Departure and arrival halls A, B and C are in the old Terminal 1, which handles Lufthansa and Star Alliance flights. Halls D and E are in the newer Terminal 2.

Regional train and S-Bahn connections are deep below Terminal 1 in Hall B. IC/EC and ICE trains depart from the Fernbahnhof, connected to the main terminal building by a walkway. ICE trains run between Hamburg (€94, four hours) and Stuttgart (€49, 1¼ hours) via Hanover (€72, 2½ hours) and the airport every two hours, to Cologne (€53, one hour) and Dortmund (€72, 2¼ hours), and south to Basel (€65, three hours). Trains service Berlin (€98, four hours) from Hauptbahnhof. Platforms 1 to 3 are in the regional station and platforms 4 to 7 are in the long-distance train station, where there's also a DB ticket office and service point. Train services from the regional station run between 5am and 12.30am.

The terminals have a wide range of (horribly expensive) cafés and bars, as well as Dr Müller's – Germany's only airport sex shop/adult movie theatre.

If you're in transit, you can enjoy a hot shower (or a cold one, after Dr Müller) for €4.09 in Hall B; ask at the information counter.

From the UK, Ryanair offers cheap flights to Frankfurt-Hahn airport but, despite the name, this is not even in Hesse but in Rhineland-Palatinate, not far from Koblenz! See p466 for details. It's a 110km, 1¾-hour bus journey to Frankfurt city from the terminal (€12).

BUS

Long-distance buses leave from the south side of the Hauptbahnhof, where there's a **Eurolines office** (☎ 230 331; Mannheimerstrasse 15) catering for most European destinations; an interesting domestic option is the Europabus that plies the Romantic Road (see p763 and p326). German Eurolines services are operated by **Deutsche Touring** (☎ 790 350).

CAR & MOTORCYCLE

Frankfurt features the Frankfurter Kreuz, Germany's biggest autobahn intersection – modelled, it would seem, after the kind you might find in Los Angeles. All major (and some minor) car-rental companies have offices in the Hauptbahnhof and at the airport.

Känguruh (☎ 596 2035; Intzestrasse 20a) rents out older-model cars from around €20 per day, including insurance and a 200km kilometre allowance; call in advance. **ADAC** (☎ 01805-101 112; Schillerstrasse 12) has useful information for drivers.

The **Mitfahrzentrale** (☎ 194 40; Baselerplatz; 9am-6.30pm Mon-Fri, 9am-4pm Sat, 10am-4pm Sun) arranges lifts; typical all-up fares are Berlin €30, Cologne and Kassel €14, and Munich €23.

TRAIN

The Hauptbahnhof, west of the centre, handles more departures and arrivals than any other station in Germany. The information office for connections and tickets is at the head of platform 9; for train information call ☎ 01805-996 633.

Deutsche Bahn's regional saver comes in the form of the Hessenticket (€25), which gives a full day of regional train travel for up to five people.

Getting Around
TO/FROM THE AIRPORT

S-Bahn lines 8 and 9 shuttle between the airport and the Hauptbahnhof (€3.35, 15 minutes), usually continuing to Offenbach, via Hauptwache and Konstablerwache.

Bus 61 runs to the Südbahnhof in Sachsenhausen from Terminal 1, level 1.

Taxis charge about €25 for the trip into town.

BICYCLE

Frankfurt is good for cyclists, with designated bike lanes on most streets, but few people in town rent bikes. **Günter Storch** (97843194; www.fahrrad-storch.de; Alexanderstrasse 1; at Rödelheim train station) does for €12 from 10am to 6.30pm (bring your passport). Deutsche Bahn's remote-operated **Call-a-Bike** scheme (☎ 07000-522 5522; www.callabike.de) costs from €0.07 a minute or €15 per day for 24 hours, making it a better deal.

CAR & MOTORCYCLE

Traffic flows smoothly in central Frankfurt, but the one-way system can be extremely frustrating. You're better off parking your vehicle in one of the many car parks (€2 per hour, €2.50 overnight) and proceeding on foot. Throughout the centre you'll see signs giving directions and the number of places left in nearby car parks. A free Park & Ride parking garage is in Preungesheim next to the exit from the A 661 and the tram stop Preungesheim.

PUBLIC TRANSPORT

Frankfurt's excellent – if expensive – transport network (RMV) integrates all bus, tram, S-Bahn and U-Bahn lines. Single or day tickets can be purchased from the machines at almost any stop. Press *Einzelfahrt Frankfurt* for destinations in zone 50, which takes in most of Frankfurt, excluding the airport. *Kurzstrecken* (short-trip tickets; consult the list on machines) cost up to €1.60, single tickets €2.10 and a *Tageskarte* (24-hour ticket) €4.90. Weekly passes cost €19.

TAXI

Taxis are quite expensive. There's a €2 hire charge, plus a minimum of €1.53 per kilometre. There are taxi ranks throughout the city, or you can call ☎ 250 001, ☎ 792 020, ☎ 634 800 or ☎ 230 01.

DARMSTADT
☎ 06151 / pop 139,000

The beautiful Mathildenhöhe artist's colony, *Jugendstil* (Art Nouveau) and a technical university are hallmarks of this modest but interesting city about 35km south of Frankfurt. The technical university is one of Germany's most respected and makes for a lively student scene. Despite being architecturally patchy, Darmstadt is a pretty city in areas east of the Altstadt (Old Town) and is well-worth an excursion from Frankfurt or an overnight stay in any season.

Orientation

The Hauptbahnhof is flanked by Europaplatz on the western side and Platz der Deutschen Einheit on the city side. It is connected to the Altstadt (Old Town), to the east, by a long walk or a short ride along Rheinstrasse, the major street to the right as you exit at Platz der Deutschen Einheit. Bus H from the station, or any tram or bus from the first stop on Rheinstrasse, runs to Luisenplatz, the French-style square at the heart of the city. The main museums are in the centre and Mathildenhöhe is about 1km east of Luisenplatz.

Information

Gutenberg Buchhandlung (☎ 202 02; Am Luisenplatz 4) Bookshop.

On-Game (☎ 870 0651; www.multimedia-bistro.de; Europaplatz 1; per hr €3.60) Internet access.

Post office (Luisenplatz)

ProRegio (☎ 951 5013; www.proregio-darmstadt.de; Luisinplatz 5; ⏰ 9.30am-7pm Mon-Fri, 9.30am-4pm Sat) Tourist information and concert tickets.

Reisebank (☎ 136 5678; Luisenstrasse 10)

Sights

Established in 1899 at the behest of Grand Duke Ernst-Ludwig, the former artists' colony at **Mathildenhöhe** is Darmstadt's biggest attraction, having churned out fascinating works of German Art Nouveau until 1914. The **Museum Künstlerkolonie** (Artists' Colony Museum; ☎ 133 385; Alexandraweg/Bauhausweg; adult/concession €3/2; ⏰ 10am-5pm Tue-Sun) displays some of these works in its beautiful grounds. Take bus F from the Hauptbahnhof. Also in the grounds is the **Ausstellungsgebäude Mathildenhöhe**, an art gallery with changing exhibitions (€5/3), and a stunning Russian Orthodox **chapel** (1897-99; ☎ 424 235; donation €0.75; ⏰ 9am-6pm Apr-Sep, 9am-5pm Oct-Mar), built and designed by Louis Benois for the Russian Tsar Nicholas II after he married Princess Alexandra of Hesse in 1894.

Back in the centre, the highlight of the **Hessisches Landesmuseum** (Hesse State Museum; ☎ 165 703; www.hlmd.de; Friedensplatz 1; adult/concession/child €2.50/1.20/0.50, free after 4pm; ⏰ 10am-5pm Tue & Thu-Sat, 10am-8pm Wed, 11am-5pm Sun) is less its natural science objects (though they are good) than the fascinating collection of art – especially in the seven rooms dedicated to Joseph Beuys (p53). The museum has about 250 of his sculptures

as well as lots of drawings, so it's probably good to its claim of having the largest collection of his work anywhere.

The **Schlossmuseum** (☎ 240 35; Marktplatz; adult/concession €2.50/1.50; ⏰ 10am-1pm & 2-5pm Mon-Thu, 10am-1pm Sat & Sun) is in a former margrave's residence with an 18th-century castle. It is packed with ornate furnishings, carriages and paintings, including *The Madonna of Jakob Meyer, Mayor of Basle* by Hans Holbein the Younger. The building is now part of the Technische Universität.

Tours

ProRegio (☎ 951 5013; www.proregio-darmstadt.de; Luisinplatz 5; ⏰ 9:30am-7pm Mon-Fri, 9:30am-4pm Sat) organises thematic city tours in German (€5/7 per one/two hours; check ahead) and sells a great tourist guide (€1).

Sleeping & Eating

DJH hostel (☎ 452 93; darmstadt@djh-hessen.de; Landgraf-Georg-Strasse 119; dm/s €22/34; ✗) This hostel is a short dash from the shores of the Woog lake (take bus L from anywhere in the centre of town).

Hotel Prinz Heinrich (☎ 813 70; www.hotel-prinz-heinrich.de; Bleichstrasse 48; s €48-58, d €62; ✗) Traditional flair, old-fashioned furniture and the overall comfort of rooms make this classic establishment – with its own *Weinstube* (wine bar) – a premier choice in town.

Hotel Ernst-Ludwig (☎ 271 90; www.hotel-ernstludwig .de; Ernst-Ludwig-Strasse 14; s €49-51, d €69-73) Plain but comfortable, this is a very convenient pension just off Luisenplatz on a main shopping street.

City Braustübl (☎ 255 11; Wilhelminerstrasse 31; mains €9-18; ⏰ 11am-midnight Mon-Fri, 11am-1am Sat & Sun) A classic brewery outlet restaurant, strong on regional dishes that can be washed down with one of the many offerings of local beer.

Drinking & Entertainment

Centralstation (☎ 366 8899; www.centralstation -darmstadt.de; Im Carree) This venue is legendary throughout the Rhine–Main region as a three-level party paradise and cultural haunt, with a cocktail lounge (happy hour from 9pm), a venue for live music and an excellent midday buffet restaurant. Next door is also a food hall for a selection of nibbles and tipples.

An Sibin (☎ 204 52; www.ansibin.com; Landgraf-Georg-Strasse 25) An Irish pub and live concert venue good for a few rounds and a yarn or four.

Goldene Krone (☎ 213 52; www.goldene-krone
.de; Schustergasse 18) This multimedia diehard
would survive a nuclear direct attack without
looking any different – it's a refuge with a
cinema, piano room, pool table, club nights,
live music and toilets that are already the
day after.

Getting There & Away
Frequent S-Bahn trains serve Frankfurt's
Hauptbahnhof (€6.25, 30 minutes). The A5
connects Frankfurt and Darmstadt.

AROUND DARMSTADT
Kloster Lorsch
Founded in the 8th century, and Unesco-listed
in 1991, **Kloster Lorsch** (Lorsch Abbey; ☎ 06251-103 820;
www.kloster-lorsch.de; Nibelungenstrasse 35, Lorsch; adult/
concession €3/2; ⏲ 10am-5pm Tue-Sun) was an important religious site in its heyday, especially for
the Carolingian dynasty. A visit to the monastery makes a nice excursion from Darmstadt,
despite few of the original buildings having
been preserved (the Königshalle and Altenmünster are the most accessible). The complex
has three museum sections – one on the history of the abbey, the second on life in Hesse,
and a third on tobacco, which was cultivated
in Lorsch in the late 17th century.

Lorsch is easily reached from Darmstadt
along the A5 or the A67 south, or via the picturesque Bergstrasse (B3). The train from Darmstadt goes via Bensheim (€7, 25 minutes). The
abbey is a 10-minute walk from the station.

Messel
Another Unesco monument, the Grube Messel (Messel Pit) fossil site contains a wealth
of well-preserved animal and plant remains
from the Eocene era, around 49 million years
ago. It's best known for the specimens of early
horses found here, which illustrate the evolu-
tionary path towards the modern beast.

The most interesting fossils excavated are
now held in the Hessisches Landesmuseum
(see opposite), in Darmstadt, the **Senckenberg
Museum** (☎ 069-754 20; www.senckenberg.uni-frankfurt.
de; Senckenberganlage 25; adult/concession €5/4; ⏲ 9am-
5pm Mon, Tue, Thu & Fri, 9am-8pm Wed, 9am-6pm Sat &
Sun) in Frankfurt, and Messel's own **museum**
(☎ 06159-5119; www.messelmuseum.de; Langgasse 2; ⏲ 2-
5pm Tue-Sun Apr-Oct, 2-4pm Sat & Sun Nov-Mar, 10am-noon
Sun year-round) in a pretty half-timbered house.
For tours of the site itself, call ☎ 06159-71570
or contact the Messel museum.

Messel is about 10km northeast of Darm-
stadt and is served by city trams 4 and 5 from
Hauptbahnhof to Siemenstrasse (direction
Kranichstein), where the bus U to Messel-
Oberach departs.

WIESBADEN
☎ 0611 / pop 275,000
The capital of Hesse is an attractive spa town
west of Frankfurt and a stone's throw from
Mainz, with a handful of historic attractions,
luscious green parks to calm the weariest of
urban eyes, and an attractive historic thermal
bath. Wiesbaden has always lured the literary
big game. Goethe spent time here in 1814,
and Russian writers have swooned in over
the centuries to gamble, experience the rich
green shadows of this spa town, and depart
with empty pockets. Dostoevsky messed himself up badly here in the 1860s (where didn't
he, though?) when he amassed huge debts at
the city's gambling tables. The Russians still
come here, as do the wealthy, the ailing or
simply the travelling. And for good reason –
Wiesbaden has a lot of provincial charm for a
state capital and is a nice respite from bustling
Frankfurt.

Orientation
The city centre is a 15-minute walk north from
the Hauptbahnhof along Bahnhofstrasse, or
you can take bus 1 or 8.

The cable car up the Neroberg is on the
northern edge of the city; the Kurhaus is northeast of the centre; bus 1 goes to both.

Information
Doctor (☎ 461 010)
Jawz (☎ 308 8715; www.jawz.de; Am Michelsberg 3;
per 20min €1; ⏲ 24hr) BYO laptop costs €2 per hour.
Nemesis (☎ 308 8850; Luisenstrasse 17; per hr €3;
⏲ 10am-4am) Internet access.
Post office (Kaiser-Friedrich-Ring 81)
Reisebank (☎ 743 19; Hauptbahnhof)
Tourist office (☎ 172 9930; www.wiesbaden.de;
Marktstrasse 6; ⏲ 10am-6.30pm Mon-Fri, 9am-6pm Sat,
11am-5pm Sun Apr-Dec, 10am-6pm Mon-Fri, 9am-3pm
Sat Jan-Mar) Helpful office with plenty of English material.

Sights & Activities
A nice place to start exploring the city is
Schlossplatz, spiked with the **Marktbrunnen**
(market fountain; 1537) and flanked by the
stunning Gothic **Marktkirche** (1852–62) and
the **Neues Rathaus** (New Town Hall; 1884–87).

HESSE

On the northern side is the neoclassical **Stadtschloss** (1840), built for Duke Wilhelm von Nassau and now the Hessian parliament.

A restored 1888 **cable car** (€1.30) makes the trip up the Neroberg to the **Russian Orthodox Church** (adult/child €0.60/0.30; 10am-5pm), often mistakenly called the 'Greek Chapel'. It was built between 1847 and 1855 as the burial place of Elizabeth Mikhailovna, wife of Duke Adolf of Nassau; Elizabeth died here during childbirth in 1845 and Adolf built this five-domed church in her honour, modelled on the Church of the Ascension in Moscow. An impressively bearded custodian turns on atmospheric music when you enter.

Also on the hill are a war memorial, a large swimming pool complex, a café and one of the oldest vineyards in the area (open to visitors). The grassy expanse overlooking the pool and the town is a popular sun-bathing spot.

Back in town, **Museum Wiesbaden** (335 2170; www.museum-wiesbaden.de; Friedrich-Ebert-Allee 2; adult/concession/child €2.50/1.25/0.50, free from 4pm Tue; 10am-8pm Tue, 10am-5pm Wed-Sun) houses many paintings by Russian expressionist Alexei Jawlensky, who lived in Wiesbaden from 1921 until his death in 1941.

The **Kurhaus Wiesbaden** (172 90; Kurhausplatz 1) is a restored classical building (1907) that's been converted into the city's main theatre, convention centre and casino. To do a gambling Dostoevsky, men will need a jacket and tie.

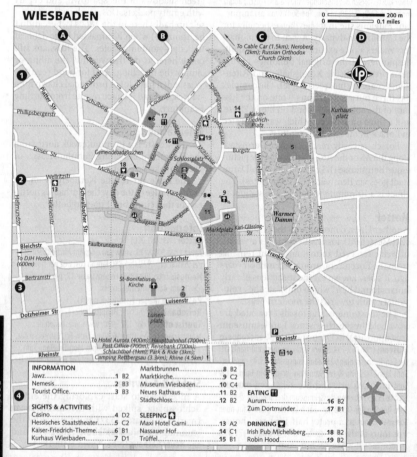

INFORMATION			
Jawz	1 B2	Marktbrunnen	8 B2
Nemesis	2 B3	Marktkirche	9 C2
Tourist Office	3 B3	Museum Wiesbaden	10 C4
		Neues Rathaus	11 B2
SIGHTS & ACTIVITIES		Stadtschloss	12 B2
Casino	4 D2	SLEEPING	
Hessisches Staatstheater	5 C2	Maxi Hotel Garni	13 A2
Kaiser-Friedrich-Therme	6 B1	Nassauer Hof	14 C1
Kurhaus Wiesbaden	7 D1	Trüffel	15 B1

EATING		
Aurum	16 B2
Zum Dortmunder	17 B1

DRINKING		
Irish Pub Michelsberg	18 B2
Robin Hood	19 B2

WIESBADEN

If the historic **Kaiser-Friedrich-Therme** (☎ 172 9660; kft@wiesbaden.de; Langgasse 38-40; 4hr €17.50; ⏱ 10am-10pm Sat-Thu, 10am-midnight Fri) had been around in Dostoevsky's day, maybe he'd have written a story called *The Sauna* and not *The Gambler*. For many this spa complex, dating from 1913, is Wiesbaden's finest attraction. Tuesday is for women only; nudity is de rigueur all days of the week.

Tours

The tourist office runs bus and walking tours on Saturday, leaving from the Theatre Colonnade in front of the Hessisches Staatstheater. Most take in the Kurhaus, Neroberg and the castle at Biebrich, and sometimes include a glass of wine. Bus tours cost €10/5 per adult/child; walks are €6/3. Tours in English are available.

Sleeping

Dostoevsky's wallet had a date with destiny at the casino; yours could at Wiesbaden's hotels if care isn't taken. Rates rise during Frankfurt trade fairs, too, but weekends are cheaper.

DJH hostel (☎ 486 57; Blücherstrasse 66; dm/s €19/27; ✗) The DJH Jugendherberge is 10 minutes on foot west of the city centre, or take bus 14 to Gneisenaustrasse. It's unattractive exterior belies clean rooms and helpful staff.

Camping Rettbergsau (☎ 215 51; camp sites €4.50; ⏱ Apr-Sep) This camping ground is on the island in the middle of the Rhine. The island is off-limits to cars; take bus No 3, 4 or 38 from anywhere in the centre to Rheinufer Biebrich, then catch the ferry (€2).

Hotel Aurora (☎ 373 728; Untere Albrechtsstrasse 9; s/d €55/80; ✗) Very friendly, bright, quiet and Italian-run, this rare gem situated near the Hauptbahnhof offers free wireless internet access from some rooms and doesn't hike its prices during trade fairs.

Maxi Hotel Garni (☎ 945 20; www.hotel-maxi.de; Wellritzstrasse 6; s/d €70/95; P) Recently renovated, these are simple but very tasteful rooms in a convenient, if unexciting, location just outside the Altstadt.

Trüffel (☎ 990 550; www.trueffel.net; Webergasse 6-8; s/d €110/145; ✗ ⌨ ▣) Although on Wiesbaden's conference circuit, this hotel offers a very high level of comfort as well as a restaurant with a nice terrace and a moderately priced bistro downstairs – it's a stylish place for sleeping and eating.

Nassauer Hof (☎ 1330; www.nassauer-hof.de; Kaiser-Friedrich-Platz 3-4; s €228-288, d €278-338, ste €410-1350; P ✗ ⌨ ▣) This elegant old dame is one of Europe's few remaining full-service grand hotels, with a prestigious location and total luxury throughout.

Eating & Drinking

Aurum (☎ 360 0877; Goldgasse 16; pizzas €4.50-9-50, mains €8.50-16; ⏱ 9am-1am Mon-Sat, 10am-1am Sun) One of a number of nosh places along the dog-legged Goldgasse, this restaurant and bar has very good stone oven pizza and quite good main dishes with a Mediterranean flavour – almost as good as the décor promises. You can also drink here comfortably.

Zum Dortmunder (☎ 302 096; Langgasse 34; mains €8-18; ⏱ 11am-midnight) A long-standing local favourite in Wiesbaden, this restaurant serves traditional cuisine in a pub atmosphere. The streetside tables (in summer), free-flowing beer and convivial ambience make it well worthwhile.

Irish Pub Michelsberg (☎ 300 849; Michelsberg 15) Verging on the grungy, this German rendition of an Irish pub gets an expat and student crowd.

Robin Hood (☎ 301 349; www.robin-wi.de; Häfnergasse 3) They may not be stealing from the rich, but you'll certainly find a bunch of merry men in this well-frequented gay bar-bistro. There's a sauna next door.

Schlachthof (☎ 974 450; www.schlachthof-wiesbaden .de; Gartenfeldstrasse 57) Live music, top-name DJs and a rich and tumultuous program make this venue, one block east of the train station, a Mecca for party animals. Nothing happens here before 10pm.

Getting There & Around

S-Bahn trains leave every 20 minutes from Frankfurt's Hauptbahnhof (€6.25, 45 minutes). The S8 runs via Frankfurt airport.

Passenger boats on Cologne–Mainz routes stop at Wiesbaden, as do cruises to and from Frankfurt and other local destinations.

Wiesbaden is connected to Frankfurt by the A66 Autobahn and is just off the A3, which leads to the Ruhr region.

City buses cost €1.95 for a single ticket or €4.50 for a day pass. There's parking near the Rhein-Main-Halle and a Park & Ride on Berlinerstrasse about 2km east of the Hauptbahnhof. The train station is a major hub for buses; buy tickets from the machines.

HESSE

LAHN VALLEY

Popular with cyclists, this majestic valley carved by the Lahn River acts as a natural border between the Taunus and Westerwald hills, north of Wiesbaden. It links such eye-catching places as the peninsula town of Weilburg and the historic town of Limburg, before spilling into the Rhine at Lahntal, south of Koblenz. The 44km stretch between Weilburg and Limburg is a particular attraction, both for its cultural and sporting offerings.

Weilburg, almost entwined by the river, is dominated by the 16th-century **Schloss** (☎ 06471-912 70; adult/concession €3.50/2.50; ☒ 10am-5pm Tue-Sun, 10am-4pm Nov-Feb), a sprawling rococo complex whose splendid gardens stretch 400m from the craggy hilltop right down to the Lahn River bank. Weilburg is also home to Germany's only **ship tunnel**, a 195m-long structure built in 1847 to save river traffic having to sail around the peninsula. It's a perfect point to embark on a paddle downstream.

Limburg has a timber-framed core that is preserved as a historic monument. Its striking orange-and-white 13th century **Dom** (☎ 06431-295 327; ☒ tours at 11am & 3pm Mon-Fri, 11am Sat, 11.45am Sun) is visible from far away, perched on a rocky precipice overlooking the Lahn to the north and the beautiful Altstadt to the south. The **Rathaus** is a well-preserved 14th-century masterpiece and the **Lahnbrücke**, a former toll bridge, is testament to the days when Limburg was a rich merchant town.

Velociped (☎ 06421-245 11; www.velociped.de) organises cycling tours for individuals, with maps, lodging arrangements and of course the bicycle from €410 per person. It begins in Marburg. **Lahntours** (☎ 06426-928 00; www.lahntours .de; Lahntalstrasse 45; in Roth an der Lahn) has other great options, including a combination of three days cycling, two days kayaking and two days hiking, from €470. Book well in advance for weekend trips.

MARBURG

☎ 06421 / pop 79,000

Historic, half-timbered and buzzing any time of day or night, Marburg is a university town some 90km north of Frankfurt. Narrow streets and lanes wind through its vibrant Altstadt (Old Town), and it is also blessed with the Elisabethkirche, Germany's oldest pure Gothic cathedral. Established in 1527, the Philipps-Universität is Europe's oldest Protestant university; even the bookish Brothers Grimm studied here for a short time. When the toil of hilly, cobblestoned and half-timbered history becomes too much, you'll find plenty of bars and cafés to relax in.

Orientation

The Lahn River flows south between the Altstadt and the Hauptbahnhof area. The Altstadt rises up the hill on the west bank of the river, divided into a fairly bland Unterstadt at the bottom and the charming old-fashioned Oberstadt on the hillside.

Bahnhofstrasse leads from the Hauptbahnhof to Elisabethstrasse, which takes you south past the Elisabethkirche to a fork in the road; bear right for the Oberstadt and left for the Unterstadt. The university campus is spread throughout the city, but the Old University building is on the edge of the Altstadt.

Information

Internet TREFF (☎ 175 0630; Pilgrimstein 29; per 30min €1.50; ☒ 10am-1am Mon-Fri, noon-1am Sun)
Marburg Information (☎ 991 20; www.marburg.de; Pilgrimstein 26; ☒ 9am-6pm Mon-Fri, 10am-2pm Sat)
Post office (Bahnhofstrasse 6)
Sparkasse (Barfüsser Strasse) Bank.
Uni-Klinikum (☎ 283 697; Baldingerstrasse) Medical services.
Universitätsbuchhandlung (☎ 170 90; Reitgasse 7-9) Bookshop.

Sights

ELISABETHKIRCHE

Built between 1235 and 1283 (the twin spires were a later addition), this is considered to be Germany's best pure Gothic **cathedral** (adult/concession €2/1.50; ☒ 9am-6pm Apr-Sep, 10am-4pm Nov-Mar, 9am-5pm Oct). The highlight inside is the Hohe Chor (High Choir), where you can see a decorative celebratory stool and beautiful stained glass behind an astounding stone Hochaltar (High Altar). The cathedral also houses an elegant Elisabethschrein (Elisabeth Shrine) and gravestones. You can join a German-language **tour** (adult/concession €2/1) at 3pm, or an attendant might take you around for the same fee.

OBERSTADT

Just a short stroll along Steinweg from the cathedral, the historic **Markt** is elegantly adorned with a stone fountain and flanked on the south side by the historic **Rathaus** (1512), which was used in the mid-16th century as a

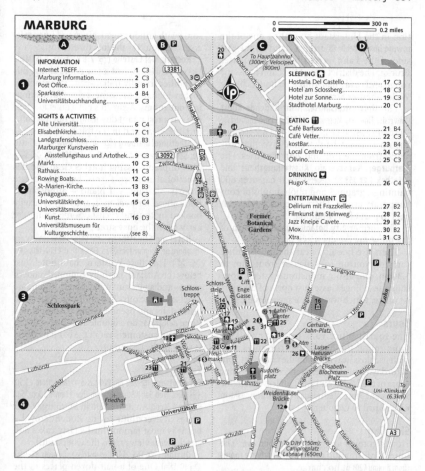

MARBURG

meat market. Today a produce market is held every Saturday morning here. From Markt it's a steep climb to the **St-Marien-Kirche**, an imposing red-brick church on a terrace with great views over the lower town. This is the place to come at sunrise, particularly on weekends, when you'll often be joined by a motley crowd of students, late-night drinkers, early morning dog walkers, rough sleepers and anyone else wandering past.

Perched on a hill at the highest point in town, the massive stone **Landgrafenschloss** (Landgraves' Castle; ☎ 282 2355; Schloss 1; adult/concession €3/1; 10am-6pm Tue-Sun Apr-Oct, 11am-5pm Tue-Sun Nov-Mar) was built between 1248 and 1300 as the administrative seat of Hesse. The vantage point offers uninterrupted views over the bucolic landscape, jumbled Marburg rooftops

and the **Schlosspark**, where concerts are held throughout the year. The **Universitätsmuseum für Kulturgeschichte** (University Cultural History Museum; included in castle admission) inside the castle has five rooms with exhibits covering cultural history from prehistoric times through Christian artefacts, and decoration to (relatively) modern local Hesse furniture.

At the foot of the Schloss and back near Markt are the excavated remains of a medieval **synagogue** under glass.

UNTERSTADT

If the legs are not too tired, it's worth the stroll down Reitgasse to the **Universitätskirche** (1300), a former Dominican monastery, and the **Alte Universität** (1891), still a bustling part of the campus. Or swing the arms into ac-

HESSE

tion in the Unterstadt by renting one of the **rowing boats** (per hr €8) from a stand on the east side of the Lahn, across the Weidenhäuser Brücke. The district east of the Lahn has some rough and ready half-timbered houses lining Weidenhäuser Strasse.

The **Universitätsmuseum für Bildende Kunst** (University Fine Arts Museum; ☎ 282 2355; Biegenstrasse 11; adult/concession €2/1; ☒ 11am-1pm & 2-5pm Tue-Sun) on the east bank of the river has artworks from the 19th and 20th centuries. The **Marburger Kunstverein Ausstellungshaus und Artothek** (☎ 258 82; Biegenstrasse 1) has over 600 paintings, graphics and photographs of contemporary artists. There's a commercial cinema in part of the building.

The former city **botanical gardens**, north of the museum, are open as a public park.

There are free lifts near the tourist office carrying you up to Reitgasse from 7am to 1.30am, and also a monstrously steep stone staircase at Enge Gasse, just north of the tourist office, which was once a sewage sluice.

Tours

The tourist office runs two-hour walking tours round the Elisabethkirche and Landgrafenschloss, leaving from the church at 3pm Saturday (adult/concession €3/2). One-hour tours of the Markt and Altstadt leave from the Rathaus at 3pm Wednesday (adult/concession €3/2; April to October).

Sleeping

Hotels in town are generally expensive. The tourist information office books **private rooms** (from around €20) at no charge.

DJH hostel (☎ 234 61; marburg@djh-hessen.de; Jahnstrasse 1; dm/s €18.50/30; ☒) Downstream from Rudolphsplatz, this is a clean and well-run establishment; staff can help plan outings, rent out canoes and arrange bike hire. Take Bus C to the Auf der Weide bus stop, follow the street left and cross the small bridge; the hostel is straight ahead on the left.

Campingplatz Lahnaue (☎ 213 31; Trojedamm 47; per adult/child €4/3, per car/tent €2/4) South of the hostel, this is a fine camping ground right on the river, with plenty of sports facilities in the immediate vicinity.

Hotel zur Sonne (☎ 171 90; fax 171 940; Markt 14; s €41-51, d €77-87) Small, Italian-run and right in the heart of the Altstadt, this hotel with a restaurant downstairs is not for the noise-sensitive but it does offer comfortable rooms,

some with antique furnishings and huge rafters; watch out for the low thresholds.

Hostaria Del Castello (☎ 258 84; fax 132 25; Markt 19; s €47-72, d €67-93) Just a few doors along, this is another friendly Italian-run establishment that even shares the same style of furnishings in some rooms. Again, it's not a quiet location and has a restaurant downstairs, but it is comfortable, clean and in the thick of things.

Stadthotel Marburg (☎ 685 880; www.village-hotels .de; Bahnhofstrasse 14; s €64-89, d €84-105; P ☒ ☐) This unprepossessing hotel is clean and has functional modern furnishings that create a fairly pleasant – if bland – atmosphere. Book ahead for weekends, and May is heavily booked by touring cyclists. Some rooms are away from the busy street.

Hotel am Schlossberg (☎ 9180; www.schlossberg -marburg.de; Pilgrimstein 29; s €90-110, d €110-130; P ☒ ☒) This Best Western chain hotel, just below the Altstadt, has fully-equipped modern rooms and a pleasant atmosphere. Rooms are quiet and spacious. The midrange restaurant downstairs and pseudo-rustic, pastel-painted Pinte cellar bar do a double act – one is always open, and customers eat in the bar if business is slow in the restaurant.

Eating

Café Vetter (☎ 258 88; Reitgasse 4; cakes from €1.50; ☒ Mon, Wed-Sat 8.30am-6.30pm, Tue 11am-6.30pm, Sun 9.30am-6.30pm) An institution in Marburg, Vetter tosses in everything for its student crowd – but it is most famous for its tasty cakes and snacks with views from the Oberstadt.

Olivino (☎ 163 251; Biegenstrasse 4; meals €5-7.50; ☒ 10-1am) One of a half-dozen places in the Lahn-Center that serves sit-down and take-away light meals and snacks, this stylish Italian eatery specialises in pizzas, Flammkuchen and pasta – all of which can be washed down with a refreshing beer or wine.

Café Barfuss (☎ 253 49; Barfüsserstrasse 33; meals €3-7; ☒ 10am-1am) This loud, off-beat place attracts a sociable student crowd and serves up good light and vegetarian dishes, and a killer Currywurst (curry sausage).

Local Central (☎ 253 90; Markt 11; mains €9.50-16; ☒ 10am-1am) The service here is young and friendly, the steaks are especially delicious, and the room warbles with the sounds of lively conversation – this is a comfortable favourite for locals of all ages who come to eat and imbibe from a good selection of wine and beers, or just to ponder next moves from the bar.

kostBar (☎ 161 170; Barfüsserstrasse 7; mains €6.50-
14; ☓ 10am-1am) This modern restaurant and
bar aims at the gourmet and vegetarian end
of the market, but charges very reasonable
prices for its soups, salads, pastas and fish or
red-meat dishes concocted from a creative
blend of ingredients.

Drinking & Entertainment

For listings look no further than the free
Marburger Magazin Express, or the *Kino-
Programm* for film schedules. Both are in
German, but are pretty easy for English speak-
ers to decipher.

Filmkunst am Steinweg (☎ 672 69; www.marburger
-filmkunst.de; Steinweg 4) Arthouse cinemas might
be having a tough time elsewhere, but in Marburg this one lives on – its Kammer, Palette
and Atelier screens show blockbusters, classics
and offbeat treats.

Hugo's (☎ 130 00; www.hugos-marburg.de; Gerhard-
Jahn-Platz 21a) Hugo has a finger in lots of pies.
This Latin-inspired bar, tapas and finger-food
place trawls for a young working crowd morning until late. Right on the Lahn, it has views
through glass walls to the river and lots of
seating outside for balmy summer nights.

Xtra (☎ 130 00; www.xtra-marburg.de; Pilgrimstein 29)
You guessed it – Hugo again. This time with a
dark and moody club that swings and has DJs
spinning real vinyl. The club takes pride in
being open every night of the week and later
than most others. You'll find house and other
styles here, depending on the night.

Delirium mit Frazzkeller (☎ 649 19; Steinweg 3) Delirium is upstairs, Frazzkeller is downstairs –
both sigh under the weight of grunge and
have great views over the Unterstadt (yes,
even from the cellar). A classic haunt that also
stays open later than most.

Jazz Kneipe Cavete (☎ 661 57; www.jazzini.de;
Steinweg 12) This is the prime port of call for
jazz lovers. Monday and Thursday are often
session nights without a cover charge.

Mox (☎ 690 0161; www.moxclub.de; cnr Keizerbach
& Pilgrimstein) Back on the grunge circuit, this
hang-out has lots of house and independent
music.

Getting There & Around

The best train connections are with Frankfurt
(€18, one hour) and Kassel (€15, 1¼ hours).
From/to Fulda is slow and expensive (€30,
three hours). By car, the quickest way to reach
Marburg from Frankfurt is via the A5 head-

ing north towards Giessen. Marburg lies on
the B3. See p538 for a route by car between
that city and Marburg via Kellerwald-Edersee
National Park.

Velociped (☎ 245 11; www.velociped.de; Alte Kasseler
Strasse 43) hires out bicycles from €10 per day
or €50 per week and can help organise trips to
nearby towns, including accommodation.

Buses 1/A3, 6/A1 and 7 operate from the
Hauptbahnhof to Rudolphsplatz; tickets cost
€1.35.

FULDA

☎ 0661 / pop 64,000

Founded in 744 by Benedictine monks as
a monastery town at the behest of the English missionary St Boniface, Fulda remains
strongly influenced by its religious roots. With
many fine churches, an interesting grand palace and a large baroque district, it rewards
even a flying visit. Those who like hang-
gliding, skiing or rock-climbing will enjoy
the beautiful Rhön nature park and its highest mountain, the Wasserkuppe, accessible
from Fulda.

The Hauptbahnhof is at the northeastern
end of Bahnhofstrasse, five minutes from the
baroque Altstadt (Old Town), which begins
just west of Universitätsplatz. Turn right at
the corner of Universitätsplatz and Rabanusstrasse to get to the Stadtschloss, at the
northern end of the Altstadt. The Dom and
Michaelskirche are just west of the Stadtschloss. The bus station is at the southern end
of the Hauptbahnhof.

Information

Ärztlicher Notdienst (☎ 840; Pacelliallee 4)
Emergency doctors.
Commerzbank (Bahnhofstrasse 11a)
Lellau (☎ 235 83; Peterstor 21; per 30min €1.50)
Internet access.
Post office (Heinrich-von-Bibra-Platz)
Tourist Information (☎ 102 1813; www.tourismus
-fulda.de; Bonifatiusplatz 1; ☓ 8.30am-6pm Mon-Fri,
9.30am-4pm Sat, 10am-2pm Sun)

Sights

The **Stadtschloss** (Town Castle; ☎ 1021 814; adult/
concession €3/2; ☓ 10am-6pm Sat-Thu, 2-6pm Fri), built in
1707, was the former residence of the prince
abbots. It now houses the city administration and function rooms, including the baroque Fürstensaal, a grandiose banquet hall
decorated with frescos, portraits of abbots

and bishops, and reliefs of tipsy-looking wine queens. It's possible to climb the tower for views over town, and from the Green Room there are also pretty views over the palace gardens to the **Orangerie**, now part of the Maritim Hotel. On the hill is the baroque Frauenberg Franciscan Friary; the **church** (☎ 109 50; ☷ 7.30am-6.30pm) of this functioning friary is open to the public.

West of the gardens is the remarkable **Michaelskirche** (☎ 820 22; ☷ 10am-6pm Apr-Oct, 2-4pm Nov-Mar, closed January), the burial chapel of the Benedictine monastic cemetery, with its classic witch's-hat towers. The rotunda and crypt are Carolingian from the 9th century.

The baroque **Dom** (Cathedral; ☎ 872 07; ☷ 10am-6pm Mon-Fri, 10am-3pm Sat, 1-6pm Sun Apr-Oct, closes one hr earlier Nov-Mar), built 1704–12, is across the street on the grounds of the Ratgar Basilica, which stood here from 819 to 1700. Inside is the tomb of St Boniface – who died a martyr in 754 – plus amazing paintings of the Assumption of Mary and the Holy Trinity, and a Gothic relief of Charlemagne (15th century). There are **organ recitals** (adult/concession €3/2) here every Saturday at noon during May, June, September, October and December.

The **Dommuseum** (Cathedral Museum; ☎ 872 07; adult/concession €2.10/1.30; ☷ 10am-5.30pm Tue-Sat, 12.30-5.30pm Sun Apr-Oct, 10am-12.30pm & 1.30-4pm Tue-Sat, 12.30-4pm Sun Nov-Mar, closed Jan 15-Feb 15) is a highlight of any visit to Fulda. The museum's treasures include Jewish gravestones (in the artefact-packed front yard), the painting *Christus und die Ehebrecherin* by Lucas Cranach the Elder (1512), the spectacular Silver Altar and a spooky thing reported to be part of the skull of St Boniface (it even wears headdress). In the cloakroom, look through the glass floor to the foundations of the original basilica.

Sleeping & Eating

Book ahead in May, when Fulda has a spate of trade fairs. Many traditional eating options are located in the winding streets directly south of the tourist office.

DJH hostel (☎ 733 89; Schirrmannstrasse 31; fulda@djh-hessen.de; dm from €17; ☒) Clean and friendly, this hostel is southwest of the centre – take bus 3 to Am Stadion.

Hotel Peterchens Mondfahrt (☎ 902 350; www.hotel-peterchens-mondfahrt.de; Rabanusstrasse 7; s €60-70, d €80-100; ☒ ☒ ☒) This hotel, close to the Stadtschloss, offers spacious rooms in subdued pastel colours for tourists and business

visitors. Breakfast is bountiful, rooms are spacious and some have double doors from the hallway and are especially quiet.

Hotel Goldener Karpfen (☎ 868 00; www.hotel-goldener-karpfen.de; Simpliziusbrunnen 1-15; s €95-155, d €130-230, ste €1250-2450; ☒ ☒ ☒ ☒) With antiques and contemporary furniture throughout, rooms in this elegant hotel playfully blend old and new. The restaurant is a great option for upmarket local specialities, with various set lunch and dinner menus and delicious à la carte dishes (€14 to €28).

Viva Havanna (☎ 227 11; Bonifatiusplatz 2; mains €5-15; ☷ 11am-1am) Revolutionaries like Fidel, Ché and Alfred (Hitchcock) adorn the walls of this lively little baroque former watch house at the foot of the cathedral. Depending on the hour, it's a generous restaurant (the kitchen closes at 10pm), bar, cocktail bar and even salsa venue on big nights, with outdoor seating in summer.

Getting There & Away

Regular (but not all) ICEs plying the main north–south and Frankfurt–Erfurt lines stop at Fulda from Frankfurt (€26, one hour) or Kassel (€26, 30 minutes). Fulda can be reached by the A7, which runs north towards Kassel and south to Würzburg. There's plenty of secure garage parking around town, and metered parking that's free from 6pm to 8am alongside the post office on Heinrich-von-Bibra-Platz.

KASSEL

☎ 0561 / pop 199,000

The term 'architectural crimes' could well have been coined to describe the reconstruction of Kassel, nestled on the Fulda River, 1½ hours north of Frankfurt. The label still fits some parts of town, but Kassel has gradually reinvented its cityscape over the past few years, and it also has some wonderful parkland.

Attractions include the city's unusual Museum of Death, and the Wilhelmshöhe – a glorious baroque park. There's also a museum dedicated to Wilhelm and Jakob Grimm, who were born in Hesse and began compiling folk stories while living in Kassel.

Every five years Kassel is host to one of Western Europe's most important contemporary art shows, the **Documenta**, founded by art professor Arnold Bode in 1955; lasting 100 days, it attracts up to 700,000 visitors. If you don't catch Documenta in 2007, the one after is in 2012.

Orientation

There are two main train stations. ICE and IC trains use Wilhelmshöhe Bahnhof (known as the ICE-Bahnhof), 3km west of the city centre. The Hauptbahnhof (central train station in name only) at the western end of the centre has regional connections; it's also a cultural centre.

The mostly pedestrianised centre of the city focuses on Königsplatz and Friedrichsplatz. Wilhelmshöhe and its attractions are all at the western end of Wilhelmshöher Allee, which runs straight as an arrow from the centre to the castle.

Information

Doom's World (☎ 7392 030; Obere Königsstrasse 3-5; per hr €2) Internet access.

Hugendubel (☎ 01801 484 484; Königsplatz 61) Bookshop in City-Point shopping centre.

Kassel Card (1/3 days €10/13) Discounts on attractions for one to two people.

Kassel Tourist ICE-Bahnhof (☎ 340 54; www.kassel -tourist.de; ⏲ 9am-6pm Mon-Fri, 9am-1pm Sat); Rathaus (☎ 707 707; Obere Königsstrasse 8; ⏲ 9am-6pm Mon-Fri, 9am-2pm Sat) Tourist information.

Post office (Untere Königsstrasse 95)

Reisebank (☎ 7015 958; Untere Königsstrasse 91) Bank and money services.

Sparkasse (ICE-Bahnhof, north side) Bank.

Wasch-Treff (Friedrich-Ebert-Strasse 81; ⏲ 5am-midnight) Laundry.

Sights

WILHELMSHÖHE

Seven kilometres west of the centre, within the enchanting Habichtswald (Hawk Forest) nature park, the baroque **Schlosspark Wilhelmshöhe** (☎ 3168 0223) was created in the early 18th century. It's replete with castles, fountains and grottos, a spectacular cascade, and the city's symbol: the massive Herkules statue, atop a huge stone pyramid atop an octagonal amphitheatre atop an impressive hill. You can spend an entire day here walking through the forest, down the hiking paths (all levels of difficulty) and enjoying a romantic picnic among grottos. A single Wilhelmshöhe museum ticket (adult/concession €3.50/2.50) gives entry to the museums and castle Weissensteinflügel (the south wing), but not Herkules.

Herkules

This **statue** (adult/concession €2/1.50; ⏲ 10am-5pm Mar-Nov), 600m above sea level, was built between 1707 and 1717 as a symbol of regional power. The scantily clad mythical hero leans nonchalantly on his big club and looks down at the defeated Encelados, but the main attraction here (after 449 steps to the top) is an unbelievable view in all directions.

Facing the town, you'll see Wilhelmshöhe Allee running due west towards the town; until reunification, the hills here formed the border with the GDR. To the south and northwest is the Habichtswald, with over 300km of hiking trails. At the bottom of the hill you'll see Schloss Wilhelmshöhe and, to its south, Löwenburg.

Take tram 3 from the ICE-Bahnhof or town to the terminus, and change for bus 43, which goes right up to the top once or twice an hour from 8am to 8pm.

Schloss Wilhelmshöhe

Home to Elector Wilhelm and later Kaiser Wilhelm II, this palace (1786–98) houses the **Gemäldegalerie Alte Meister** (Old Masters Gallery; ☎ 316 800; ⏲ 10am-5pm Tue-Sun). It has one of Germany's best collections (especially of Flemish and Dutch baroque painting), featuring works by Rembrandt, Rubens, Jordaens, Lucas Cranach the Elder, Dürer and many others.

To reach Schloss Wilhelmshöhe from the ICE-Bahnhof, take tram 1 to the last stop. From there you can take bus 23, which makes a loop around the lower regions of the park, or walk to the top, following the well-marked trails.

The **Weissensteinflügel** (☎ 3168 0200; last tour 4pm) dates from 1790 and today has 23 rooms filled with original furnishings and paintings, which are open for viewing on a guided tour.

Schloss Löwenburg

Modelled on a medieval Scottish castle, the **Schloss Löwenburg** (☎ 3168 0244; ⏲ 10am-5pm Tue-Sun) is also open on guided tours, taking in the castle's Rüstkammer (Museum of Armaments) and Ritterzeitsmuseum (Museum of Chivalry).

Fountains

Every Wednesday, Sunday and public holiday from May to 3 October, the **Wasserspiel** takes place along the hillside. At 2.30pm the water begins its cascade from Herkules, from where you can walk down to the **Grosse Fontäne** and

HESSE

FAIRY-TALE ROAD

The 600km *Märchenstrasse* (Fairy-Tale Road) is one of Germany's most popular tourist routes. It's made up of cities, towns and hamlets in four states (Hesse, Lower Saxony, North Rhine-Westphalia and Bremen), many of them associated with the works of Wilhelm and Jakob Grimm.

The brothers travelled extensively through central Germany in the early 19th century documenting folklore. Their collection of tales – *Kinder- und Hausmärchen* – was first published in 1812 and quickly gained international recognition. It includes such famous tales as *Hansel and Gretel, Cinderella, The Pied Piper, Rapunzel* and scores of others.

Every town, village and hamlet along the Fairy-Tale Road has an information office of sorts. For advance information, contact the **central information office** (☎ 0561-707 707; www.deutsche -maerchenstrasse.de; Obere Königsstrasse 15, Kassel); also helpful is the tourist office in Hamelin.

For an organised tourist route, Fairy-Tale Road transport isn't very well organised. There's no equivalent of the Romantic Road bus and, because the route covers several states, local bus and train services outside the major cities aren't coordinated. The easiest way to travel is by car; the ADAC Weserbergland map covers the area in detail.

There are over 60 stops on the Fairy-Tale Road. Kassel aside, major ones include the following.

Hanau

The route kicks off east of Frankfurt, in the birthplace of Jakob (1785–1863) and Wilhelm (1786–1859) Grimm. A statue honours the town's most famous sons, and there's also a puppet museum featuring some recognisable characters.

Steinau

The Grimm brothers spent their youth here, and the Renaissance Schloss contains exhibits on their work. The Amtshaus, Renaissance palace of the counts of Hanau, was their grand home, and the puppet theatre stages some of their best-known tales.

Marburg

This university town on the Lahn River (see p530) was where the Grimms were educated and began their research into folk tales and stories.

Göttingen

The brothers were professors at the university here (see p625) before being expelled in 1837 for their liberal views. In the summer months, versions of the tales are performed at the woodland stage in Bremke, southeast of Göttingen.

Bad Karlshafen

This meticulously planned white baroque village (see p606) is a major highlight.

Bodenwerder

The rambling Münchhausen Museum here has three buildings dedicated to the legendary Baron von Münchhausen, who was born in Bodenwerder and became (in)famous in his own lifetime for telling outrageous tales (see p605).

Hamelin

The biggest stop on the Fairy-Tale Road is the quaint city of Hamelin (Hameln, p603), forever associated with the legend of the Pied Piper.

Bremen

The route ends in this old Hanseatic city, at the statue of the famous *Town Musicians of Bremen* (see p644).

watch the water emerge in a 52m-high jet one hour later (3.30pm). The cascade itself is a 12km network of surface and subterranean channels. On the first Saturday of the month from June to September, the cascades are illuminated at dusk.

MUSEUMS & GALLERIES

Billed as 'a meditative space for funerary art', Kassel's riveting **Museum für Sepulkralkultur** (Museum of Sepulchral Culture; ☎ 918 930; www.sepulkral museum.de; Weinbergstrasse 25-27; adult/concession €4/2.50; ⊗ 10am-5pm Tue & Thu-Sun, 10am-8pm Wed) is certainly an interesting way to become familiar with German death rituals. Designed to end the taboo of discussing death, the museum's permanent collection consists of headstones, hearses, dancing skeleton bookends and sculptures depicting death.

The **Brüder-Grimm-Museum** (Brothers Grimm Museum; ☎ 103 235; grimm-museum@t-online.de; Schöne Aussicht 2; adult/concession €1.50/1; ⊗ 10am-5pm), in the Palais Bellevue, has displays on the brothers' lives, their work (they were well-respected grammarians before turning to fairy stories) and the famous tales themselves, with original manuscripts, portraits and sculptures. *Grimm's Fairy Tales* is now available in almost 200 languages and is read to children all over the world.

Across the street is the **Neue Galerie** (New Gallery; ☎ 3168 0400; www.museum-kassel.de; Schöne Aussicht 1), which has displays of paintings and sculptures by German artists from 1750 to the present day, as well as exhibits from past Documenta. It was closing for restoration at the time of writing, so check with the tourist office before visiting.

The sharply contoured **Documenta Halle** (☎ 707 270; www.documentahalle.de; Du-Ry-Strasse 1) houses changing modern art exhibitions between five-yearly Documenta exhibitions (next ones held in mid-2007 and mid-2012).

Tours

From April to December, there are two-hour city bus tours – which include Wilhelmshöhe – at 2pm on Saturday (adult/concession €13/9.50), leaving from the Staatstheater bus parking area. The tourist office also organises a wide range of thematic **walking tours** (adult/ concession €6.50/4.50).

Rehbein-Linie (☎ 185 05; www.fahrgastschiffahrt .com) and **Söllner** (☎ 774 670; www.personenschiffahrt .com) run cruises Easter to October to destina-

tions along the Fulda River. Prices start at €5/4 return per adult/child, or €17/11 Hann-Münden return.

Sleeping

The tourist office books **private rooms** (from around €20).

Fulda-Camp (☎ 224 33; www.fulda-camp.de; Giessenallee 7; per adult/child €4/2, per car/tent €3/6). Situated 3.5km south of town on the Fulda River, this is a very pleasant camping ground. Bus 25 stops right outside.

DJH hostel (☎ 776 455; kassel@djh-hessen.de; Schenkendorfstrasse 18; dm/s €19.50/29.50; ✗) Kassel's hostel is one of the best in the country, with real plants in its multilevel foyer, a bright atmosphere, and a leafy location in the suburbs. It's 10 minutes' walk from the Hauptbahnhof, or take tram 4 or 8 to Annastrasse.

Hotel Garni Kö 78 (☎ 716 14; www.koe78.de; Kölnische Strasse 78; s €41-51, d €61-74; P) Although the furnishings don't live up to the wonderful exterior and location, rooms are comfortable in this excellent hotel, and there's a peaceful back garden. Front-facing rooms have balconies.

Hotel Domus (☎ 703 330; www.hotel-domus-kassel.de; Erzbergerstrasse 1-5; s €71-86, d €87-108; P ✗) Beyond the stunning Art Nouveau foyer – with atrium, bar and billiard table – are excellent rooms in three classes, with the Bel Etage top floor offering views over town or to the Herkules statue. Prices include an evening buffet.

City Hotel (☎ 728 10; www.city-hotel-kassel.de; Wilhelmshöher Allee 38-42; s €60-142, d €85-178; P ✗) The unpromising exterior here conceals a class act. The mirrored lift has infinite lines of flight, double doors in most rooms keep out hallway sounds, and the windows are well-insulated against traffic noise. The Thai restaurant next door, and its proximity to eating and drinking dens just north of here, are other plusses.

Schlosshotel Wilhelmshöhe (☎ 308 80; www .schlosshotel-kassel.de; Schlosspark; s €58-102, d €86-132, ste €380-750; P) This building is Bauhaus gone stark raving 'bow-wow' with shocking concrete walls, but inside it's an absolutely charming hotel; the parkland location near Schloss Wilhelmshöhe, the casino and the balconies are other attractions here.

Eating

Many of Kassels best eating places aren't open for lunch – so it might pay to snack by daylight and eat at night.

Cook (☎ 710 818; Goethestrasse 31; mains €7-16; ⓨ 11am-1am Mon-Thu, 11am-2am Fri, 10am-2am Sat, 10am-1am Sun) As in 'Captain' – multilevel South Sea decor meets steak, salad and pasta on this epicurean island with outdoor decking. Sunday brunch is served here.

Gutshof (☎ 325 25; www.restaurant-gutshof.de; Wilhelmshöher Allee 347a; mains €10-19; ⓨ noon-1am) Local Hessian TV doesn't have to go far to hook a TV chef – this quality establishment serves international cuisine right next door to the studio in a quiet yard with outdoor seating, set at the foot of Wilhelmshöhe.

Podium (☎ 104 693; Kölnische Strasse 48; mains €5-9; ⓨ noon-1am Mon-Fri, 6pm-2am Sat, 11am-1am Sun) As much a place to drink a beer or wine as to enjoy German bistro fare, Podium has a rich wooden interior for winter warmth and a raised terrace area with outdoor summer seating.

Enchilada (☎ 703 3791; www.enchilada.de; Opernstrasse 9; mains €7-15; ⓨ 5pm-late) One of several Tex-Mex places in town that does *ensaladas*, *enchiladas* and various *especialadas* for Kassel's hot *chicas y chicos*.

El Erni (☎ 710 018; Parkstrasse 42; mains €12-18; ⓨ 6pm-1am) Kassel's finest Spanish restaurant has lots of fish dishes and a stupendously romantic atmosphere, with chandeliers creating the right mood and a wonderful shrub-shrouded front garden area with flaming torches to eat by.

Drinking & Entertainment

As a cultural venue, the Hauptbahnhof, called the Kultur Bahnhof (or KüBa), has waned of late, what with the closure of its No 1 nightspot and all the digging outside in 2007; but check it out – its star is certain to rise again. For listings, *Frizz* is one of the best free magazines in town.

Lolita Bar (☎ 713 147; Werner-Hilpert-Str 22) A quirky but popular night café, bar and club with weird karaoke nights and dance events, plus a beer garden – all in one murky heap, with affiliated and similar places around it.

New York (www.nytd.de; Obere Königsstrasse 4; ⓨ 11pm-6am Fri & Sat) The most central of the happening house venues in Kassel, mostly for a crowd in their 20s.

Cafe-Bar Suspekt (☎ 104 522; Fünffensterstrasse 14) This small gay bar is the place to embark on an exploration of the scene. They have a fold-out brochure to help.

Getting There & Away

Regional trains leave from Hauptbahnhof and Kassel-Wilhelmshöhe, but ICE and IC trains only go from Kassel-Wilhelmshöhe. Kassel is on the north–south ICE line with frequent connections via Göttingen to and from Hamburg (€61, 2¼ hours), Frankfurt-am-Main (€43, 1½ hours) and Munich (€84, 3¾ hours). Regional trains connect both stations with Marburg (€16, 1 to 1½ hours). Regional direct trains to and from Fulda (€17, 1½ hours) leave every two hours from Hauptbahnhof, and twice-hourly from Kassel-Wilhelmshöhe (€26, 30 minutes).

If you have your own transport, it's possible to meander on the backroads to Marburg via the **Kellerwald-Edersee National Park**. Take the B251 (Wolfhager Strasse) northwest out of Kassel for about 60km towards Korbach. Turn south onto the B252 just outside Korbach and follow this towards Frankenberg and to Marburg (about 120km from Kassel), making side trips into the national park on the way.

Getting Around

The local transport authority NVV operates a transport network connecting the entire north Hesse region, with Kassel at its centre. Tickets are available from bus and tram drivers as well as at machines and kiosks (single €2.50, MultiTicket day pass €5). Tram 1 runs from the ICE-Bahnhof to the centre.

Kassel is one city where a bike saves sore feet. You can rent city bikes from **Fahrradhof** (☎ 313 083; Wilhelmshöher Allee 253) for €10 per day.

North Rhine-Westphalia

With a population greater than that of Austria and Switzerland combined, North Rhine-Westphalia feels almost like a country unto itself. Cobbled together in 1946 by the Allies from two Prussian provinces and a little fiefdom called Lippe-Detmold, it harbours within its boundaries flat, windswept expanses and forested hills high enough to hold onto snow during winter. Villages sweetly lost in time contrast with frenzied metropolises habitually on fast-forward. There are places whose looks have remained largely unchanged since the Middle Ages and others fashioned completely from scratch in the wake of WWII. And through it all carves the muscular Rhine, fed by tributaries such as the Ruhr that gave an entire region its name.

The industrial age has shaped North Rhine-Westphalia more than any other German region. For about a hundred years, coal and steel fuelled the growth of Germany into one of Europe's most powerful nations. But starting in the mid-1960s, lower demand forced the region to focus its energies elsewhere. And so it did, banking instead on hi-tech, media, retail and culture.

Must-sees include Cologne with its lofty Dom (cathedral), Bonn with its Beethoven legacy and fabulous museums, the Unesco-listed baroque palaces in Brühl, and Charlemagne's imperial capital of Aachen. The lively Ruhrgebiet and placid Lower Rhine are best for off-beat experiences. There are historical cities like Münster, where the treaty that ended the Thirty Years' War was signed, and elegant ones like Düsseldorf, the state capital. Paderborn and Soest are treasured for their churches and the Sauerland is the place to get your nature fix.

HIGHLIGHTS

■ **Spiritual Delight** Feel like an ant when looking up at the majestic loftiness of Cologne's Dom (cathedral; p551)

■ **Party Town** Toast your health with a glass or 10 of refreshing *Altbier* (old beer) in a characterful and character-filled Altstadt beer hall (p546) in Düsseldorf

■ **Palace Dreams** Learn about life at court on a tour of Schloss Augustusburg (p561) in Brühl

■ **Off-Beat Adventure** Free-climb and dive in a former iron works in Duisburg, now the Landschaftspark Duisburg-Nord (p579)

■ **Quirk Factor** Visit a Rapunzel-style palace and a nuclear power plant turned theme park in Kalkar (p549)

■ **Culture Fix** Visit Bonn (p561) to pay your respects to Beethoven and see how Germany's old capital has reinvented itself

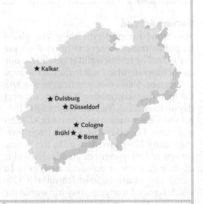

★ Kalkar

★ Duisburg
★ Düsseldorf

★ Cologne
Brühl ★
★ Bonn

■ POPULATION: 18.07 MILLION   ■ AREA: 34,080 SQ KM

NORTH RHINE–WESTPHALIA

Getting Around

For getting around North Rhine-Westphalia by public transport several ticket deals are available. The **SchönerTagTicket** is valid for one day of travel anywhere within the state on local and regional public transport from 9am to 3am the following day (midnight to 3am the next day on weekends). You can only use RE, IRE, RB and S-Bahn trains as well as buses, U-Bahn and trams. The ticket costs €21 for single travellers and €27 for groups of up to five people (or one or both parents or grandparents plus all their children or grandchildren up to 14 years). There's also the **SchöneFahrtTicket** (€13.20), which is good for any one-way trip within the state. Tickets are available at train station ticket offices and from vending machines.

THE RHINELAND

DÜSSELDORF

☎ 0211 / pop 572,000

Düsseldorf, the state capital, dazzles with boundary-pushing architecture, zinging nightlife and an art scene to rival many larger cities. It's a posh and modern city that seems all business at first glance: banking, advertising, fashion and telecommunications are among the fields that have made Düsseldorf one of Germany's wealthiest cities. Yet all it takes is a few hours of bar-hopping around the Altstadt, the historical quarter along the Rhine, to realise that locals have no problem letting their hair down once those Armani ties come off.

The Altstadt may still be the 'longest bar in the world' but it's increasingly getting competition from the Medienhafen, a redeveloped harbour area about 1km further south. Not only is this a feast of international avant-garde architecture by the genre's boldest and brightest (Frank Gehry among them), the area is also evolving into a chic and sleek place to hang out after dark.

If you're more into high-brow culture, you'll likely more than get your fill at the many top-notch art museums and the renowned opera house, theatre and orchestra hall.

Orientation

The airport is about 7km north of the Altstadt (old quarter), see p547 for details about getting into town. The Hauptbahnhof (main train station) is on the southeastern edge of the city centre. From here it's about a 20-minute walk along Bismarckstrasse and Blumenstrasse to the Königsallee, with the Altstadt just beyond. Alternatively, take any U-Bahn (underground train) from the Hauptbahnhof to the Heinrich-Heine-Allee stop to be right in the heart of things.

Information

BOOKSHOPS
Buchhaus Stern-Verlag (☎ 388 10; Friedrichstrasse 24-26; ☻ 9.30am-8pm Mon-Fri, 9.30am-6pm Sat) Three floors of books, with a café and internet access.

DISCOUNT CARDS
Düsseldorf Welcome Card (single per 24/48/72hr €9/14/19, group €18/28/38) Available at hotels and the tourist offices, this card buys unlimited public transport and discounts for museums, tours and cultural venues.

EMERGENCY
After-hour medical emergencies (☎ 192 92)
Dental emergencies (☎ 666 291)
Municipal Lost & Found (☎ 899 3285)

INTERNET ACCESS
Buchhaus Stern-Verlag (☎ 388 10; Friedrichstrasse 24-26; per 15min €1; ☻ 9.30am-8pm Mon-Fri, 9.30am-6pm Sat)

MONEY
American Express (☎ 385 0069; Immermannstrasse 65b; ☻ 9.30am-5.30pm Mon-Fri, 10am-1pm Sat) Inside the Hauptbahnhof tourist office.
Reisebank (☎ 364 878; Hauptbahnhof; ☻ 7am-10pm Mon-Sat, 8am-9pm Sun)

POST
Post office (Konrad-Adenauer-Platz 1; ☻ 8am-8pm Mon-Fri, 8am-2pm Sat)

TOURIST INFORMATION
Extended hours apply during major trade shows.
Altstadt tourist office (☎ 1720 2840; Burgplatz; ☻ 11am-6pm)
Finanzkaufhaus tourist office (☎ 1720 2841; Berliner Allee 33; ☻ 10am-6pm)
Hauptbahnhof tourist office (☎ 1720 2844; Immermannstrasse 65b; ☻ 9.30am-6.30pm)

Dangers & Annoyances

Düsseldorf is a safe city overall, although the area around the Hauptbahnhof attracts a murky element, especially after dark. The same is true of the city parks. Just pay extra attention and you should be fine.

Sights

ALTSTADT

Düsseldorf's quaint Altstadt, a mostly pedestrianised web of lanes hugging the Rhine, is rightly (in)famous for its raucous nightlife. Fortunately, it also brims with charming and quiet corners, a smattering of museums and historical sights, and good shopping.

At its centre is the historic Marktplatz, framed by the Renaissance **Rathaus** (town hall; 1573) and accented by an equestrian **statue of Jan Wellem**. The art-loving elector lies buried nearby in the early baroque **Andreaskirche** (Andreasstrasse 27; ☻ church 7.30am-6pm, mausoleum 3-5.30pm Mon-Fri), a bright, galleried church founded by Jesuits in 1629. The mausoleum, life-size apostle sculptures and fanciful stucco-ornamented ceiling are all fine features. Free organ concerts take place on Sundays at 4.30pm.

A few steps west is the memorial **Mahn-und Gedenkstätte für die Opfer des Nationalsozialismus** (Memorial Exhibit to the Victims of the Nazi Regime; ☎ 899 6205; Mühlenstrasse 29; admission free; ☻ 11am-5pm Tue-Fri & Sun, 1-5pm Sat), with an important but academic exhibit on local persecution and resistance during the Third Reich. Leaflets in English may be borrowed at no charge.

North of here looms the twisted tower of the 14th-century **St Lambertuskirche** (Church of St Lambert; Stiftsplatz), which is filled with treasures from several centuries. Look for the Gothic tabernacle, the Renaissance marble tombs, baroque altars and modern windows.

NORTH RHINE-WESTPHALIA

DÜSSELDORF

0 ———— 500 m
0 ———— 0.3 miles

INFORMATION
Altstadt Tourist Office....................1 B4
American Express.......................(see 4)
Buchhaus Stern-Verlag....................2 C6
Finanzkaufhaus Tourist Office............3 C5
Hauptbahnhof Tourist Office..............4 D6
Post Office................................5 D5
Reisebank................................6 D6

SIGHTS & ACTIVITIES
Andreaskirche.............................7 B4
Filmmuseum..............................(see 11)
Goethe Museum...........................8 D4
Heine Birth House.........................9 B5
Heinrich Heine Institut...................10 B5
Hetjens Museum..........................11 A5
K20 Kunstsammlung am
    Grabbeplatz...........................12 B4
K21 Kunstsammlung im
    Ständehaus...........................13 B6
Kaufhof..................................14 C5
Kunsthalle...............................15 B4
Mahn-und Gedenkstätte für die Opfer
    des Nationalsozialismus...............16 B4
museum kunst palast......................17 B3

NRW-Forum Kultur & Wirtschaft..18 B3
Rathaus..................................19 A5
Rheinturm...............................20 A6
St Lambertuskirche.......................21 B4
Schiffahrt Museum.......................22 A4
Schloss Jägerhof.......................(see 8)
Schlossturm............................(see 22)
Statue of Jan Wellem....................23 B5
Theatermuseum.........................24 C4
Triton fountain..........................25 C5

SLEEPING
Burns Art Hotel..........................26 C6
Easy Living Schaper Apartment....27 B6
Hotel Alt-Düsseldorf....................28 B4
Hotel Berial.............................29 C3
Hotel Orangerie.........................30 A5
Ibis Hotel...............................31 B5
Max Hotel Garni.........................32 C6
Sir & Lady Astor........................33 D5

EATING
Bäckerei Hinkel.........................34 B5
Bim's Marktwirtschaft..................35 B5
En de Canon.............................36 A5

Im Füchschen...........................37 B4
Libanon Express........................38 B5
Ohme Jupp..............................39 B4
Op de Eck...........................(see 12)
Pia Eis.................................40 B5
Waffelladen............................41 B5
Zum Schiffchen.........................42 B5
[Q]üche.............................(see 44)

DRINKING
Melody Bar.............................43 B4
Q-stall.................................44 B5
Salon des Amateur......................45 B4
Zum Uerige.............................46 B5

ENTERTAINMENT
Deutsche Oper am Rhein................47 C4
Marionetten-Theater....................48 B5
Pretty Vacant..........................49 B5
Roncalli's Apollo Varieté..............50 A6
Schauspielhaus.........................51 C4
Tonhalle................................52 B3

TRANSPORT
Central Bus Station.....................53 D5

To Hotel Ashley's Garden (1.5km)

To Düsseldorf International Airport (6km)

Fischerstr
Sittarder Str
Scheibenstr
Arnoldstr
Inselstr
Inselstr
Joseph-Beuys-Ufer
Ehrenhof
Oederallee
Oberkasseler Brücke
Hofgartenrampe
Fritz-Roeber-Str
Reutterstr
Ratinger Str
Altstadt
Stiftsplatz
Ritterstr
Mühlenstr
Burgplatz
Kurze Str
Andreasstr
Marktplatz
Bolkerstr
Flinger
Schneider-Wibbel-Gasse
Flingerstr
Zollstr
Rheinuferpromenade
Rheinuferstr
Wallstr
Grabenstr
Karlplatz
Benrather Str
Bilker Str
Medienplatz
Bastionstr
Hohe Str
Postr
Südstr
Haroldstr
Neubrückstr
Kavallerstr
Reichstr
Fürstenwall
Elisabethstr
Friedrichstr
Herzogstr
Luisenstr

Duisburger Str
Stockkämpstr
Nordstr
Kaiserstr
Sternstr
Rochusstr
Prinz-Georg-Str
Bagelstr
Franklinstr
Flinghorstr
Humboldtstr
Rethelstr
Mozartstr
Rosenstr
Gartenstr
Jägerhofstr
Jacobistr
Pempelforter Str
Düsseldorfer Str
Maltakerstr
Scheurenstr
Grafenberger Allee
Am Wehrhahn
Maxim-Weyhe-Allee
Hofgarten
Hofgarten
Gustav-Gründgens-Platz
Jan-Wellem-Platz
Cornelius-platz
Schadow-platz
Oststr
Ostr
Schadowstr
Liesegangstr
Kölner Str
Stephanienstr
Worringer-platz
Klosterstr
Marienstr
Charlottenstr
Kurfürstenstr
Karlstr
Pionierstr
Friedrich-Ebert-Str
Worringer Str
Blumenstr
Steinstr
Königsallee
Königsallee
Königsstr
Berliner Allee
Hofgartenstr
Platz der Deutschen Einheit
Mintropstr
Graf-Adolf-Platz
Adersstr
Graf-Adolf-Str
Graf-Adolf-Str
Alexanderstr
Ernst-Reuter-Platz
Konrad Adenauer Platz
Hauptbahnhof
Bahnhofstr
Eisenstr
Ellerstr
Oststr
Kasernenstr
Breite Str
Kreuzstr

Altstadt

Rhine

Hofgarten

To Landtag (50m);
Medienhafen (100m);
Curry (100m);
Robert's Bistro (100m);
Radisson SAS Media
Harbour Hotel (200m);
3001; Harpune (300m)

To DJH
Hostel
(2km)

Horion-platz

To Backpackers
Düsseldorf (200m)

To Zakk (2.3km);
Tor 3 (3km);
Stahlwerk
(3km)

To Schloss
Benrath (10km)

Ständehausstr

Just beyond, on Burgplatz, the **Schlossturm** (Palace Tower) is all that's left of the electors' palace, which burned down in 1872. It now houses the **Schifffahrt Museum** (Navigation Museum; ☎ 899 4195; adult/child/concession €3/free/1.50; ☽ 11am-6pm Tue-Sun) with neat multimedia exhibits chronicling Rhine shipping from Roman days until today. The 4th-floor café offers panoramic views.

Burgplatz marks the beginning of the **Rheinuferpromenade** (river walk), whose cafés and benches fill with people in fine weather, creating an almost Mediterranean flair. It follows the Rhine all the way to the Rheinpark and the 240m **Rheinturm** (Rhine Tower; Stromstrasse 20; lift €3.30) with a viewing platform and revolving restaurant at 172m. Just beyond are the **Landtag** (the state parliament) and the old harbour, which has been redeveloped into the Medienhafen (Media Harbour; see right), a spectacular showcase of contemporary architecture.

Along the Rheinuferpromenade you'll pass the ornate Palais Nesselrode (Nesselrode Palace), where the **Hetjens Museum** (☎ 899 4210; Schulstrasse 4; adult/concession €4/2; ☽ 11am-5pm Tue & Thu-Sun, 11am-9pm Wed) provides a survey of 8000 years of ceramic art from around the world. An extension houses the **Filmmuseum** (☎ 899 2232; adult/concession €3/1.50; ☽ 11am-5pm Tue & Thu-Sun, 11am-9pm Wed), which trains the spotlight on the technology, history and mystery of movie-making. The integrated Black Box art-house cinema presents cutting-edge films in the original language (separate admission).

For a literary kick swing by the **Heinrich Heine Institut** (☎ 899 5571; Bilker Strasse 12-14; adult/concession €3/1.50; ☽ 11am-5pm Tue-Fri & Sun, 1-5pm Sat), where letters, portraits, first editions and manuscripts document this famed Düsseldorfer's career. **Heine's birth house** at Bolkerstrasse 53 now contains a literary bookshop, café and reading room.

ART MUSEUMS

Düsseldorf has long had a love affair with art and has several high-calibre museums to prove it.

If you only have time for one museum, zero in on the **K20 Kunstsammlung am Grabbeplatz** (☎ 838 1130; Grabbeplatz 5; adult/concession/family €6.50/4.50/15; ☽ 10am-6pm Tue-Fri, 11am-6pm Sat & Sun), housed behind an undulating shiny black façade. Walls brim with post-WWII art, most notably a stunning Paul Klee collection along with select works by Picasso, Matisse, Robert Rauschenberg, Jasper Johns and Düsseldorf's own Joseph Beuys. The biggest crowds turn out for the top-notch temporary exhibitions. A combination ticket with K21 (below) costs €10/8, including audio-guide.

Immediately south, the **Kunsthalle** (Art Hall; ☎ 899 6243; www.kunsthalle-duesseldorf.de; Grabbeplatz 4; admission prices vary; ☽ noon-7pm Tue-Sat, 11am-6pm Sun) is renowned for its outstanding temporary art and photography shows.

Never mind the dull name, the **NRW-Forum Kultur und Wirtschaft** (NRW Forum for Culture & Economics; ☎ 892 6690; www.nrw-forum.de; adult/concession €5.50/3.50; ☽ 11am-8pm Tue-Thu, Sat & Sun, 11am-midnight Fri) targets the lifestyle-savvy crowd with exhibits on fashion, media, design and architecture. Hip factors: palmtop-sized audio-guides and a video lounge.

Nearby, the once stuffy **museum kunst palast** (☎ 892 4242; www.museum-kunst-palast.de; Ehrenhof 5; admission varies; ☽ 11am-6pm Tue-Sun) now takes an unconventional approach to presenting its well-respected collection. Old masters find themselves juxtaposed with contemporary young dogs and non-Western works to reveal unexpected connections between the ages and artistic trends. Temporary exhibitions further reinforce the theme.

For art so new that the paint has barely dried, you have to travel south to the **K21 Kunstsammlung im Ständehaus** (☎ 838 1630; Ständehausstrasse 1; adult/concession/family €6.50/4.50/15; ☽ 10am-6pm Tue-Fri, 11am-6pm Sat & Sun). The former 19th-century state parliament building brims with canvasses, photographs, installations and video art ranging from fabulous to frivolous. The international cast of artists includes Sigmar Polke, local boy Thomas Schütte and the late Nam June Paik. Combination tickets with the K20 (left) are €10/8, including audio-guide.

MEDIENHAFEN

South of the Altstadt, the once-dead old harbour area has been reborn as the **Medienhafen** (Media Harbour), an increasingly lively quarter filled with bold architecture, restaurants, bars and clubs. Crumbling warehouses turned hi-tech office buildings rub shoulders with bold new structures by celebrated international architects. The most eye-catching is the **Neuer Zollhof**, an ensemble of three warped and dynamically curving buildings typical of Frank Gehry's sculptural approach. Moored nearby is Claude Vasconi's **Grand Bateau**, built to resemble an ocean liner. A new pedestrian bridge links to another quay where William Alsop has created **Colorium** with its Mondrian-inspired façade and springboardlike red roof. A few doors down a plain structure is enlivened by an 'invasion' of **Flossies** – giant candy-coloured stick figures clambering all over its façade. Ask about an information booklet (€5) or guided tours at the tourist offices.

KÖNIGSALLEE & HOFGARTEN

The main *raison d'être* of Düsseldorf's most famous thoroughfare, the **Königsallee** (Kö for short) is to help you spend your hard-earned cash in its exclusive boutiques and department stores. Otherwise there's little of actual merit here, although the Art Nouveau façade of the **Kaufhof** department store and the landmark **Triton fountain** deserve a glance.

When you've had your shopping fill, head on over to the pleasant **Hofgarten** (palace garden) dotted with statues of Heinrich Heine, Robert Schumann and other German greats. Thespians might get a kick out of the **Theatermuseum** (☎ 899 4660; Jägerhofstrasse 1; adult/concession €3/1.50; ⊗ 1-8.30pm Tue-Sun), which looks back on Düsseldorf's centuries-old theatre tradition and has a collection of marionettes and paper toy theatres. Enter from the park side.

Painted piglet-pink, but otherwise very dignified, the nearby **Schloss Jägerhof** (Jägerhof Palace) is a rococo confection dreamed up by leading 18th-century architect Johann Joseph Couven. Inside is the eclectic **Goethe Museum** (☎ 899 6262; Jacobistrasse 2; adult/concession €3/1.50; ⊗ 11am-5pm Tue-Fri & Sun, 1-5pm Sat), whose exhibits capture the spirit of this complex genius and his time. Putting the 'trip' in triptych is Paul Struck's epic oil painting (1974) depicting the Walpurgisnacht scene from *Faust II*.

SCHLOSS BENRATH

Elector Carl Theodor was a man of deep pockets and good taste, as reflected in his exquisite **pleasure palace and gardens** (☎ 899 3832; Benrather Schlossallee 104; adult/concession per museum €4/2, for all 3 €6.50/3.75, child under 18yr free; ⊗ 10am-6pm Tue-Sun mid-Apr–Oct, 11am-5pm Nov–mid-Apr). About 10km south of the city centre, this is where the ruler came to relax and frolic in the wonderfully harmonious complex designed by Frenchman Nicolas de Pigage.

At the centre of the three-winged palace is the **Corps de Logis**, a fancy name for the former

residential tract, where tours (in German) offer a glimpse of the elector's lifestyle. The west wing contains a missable natural history museum, while the east wing houses the moderately interesting **Museum für Europäische Gartenkunst** (Museum of European Garden History).

Take tram 701 from Jan-Wellem-Platz (near Altstadt and Kö).

Sleeping

Düsseldorf hotels cater primarily to the business brigade, which explains why prices spike during big trade shows held not only here but as far away as Cologne and Essen. On the bright side, bargains abound at weekends and in summer. Prices quoted here are applicable outside trade-show times. The tourist offices (p541) can help with **reservations** (☎ 01805-172 020; www.duesseldorf-tourismus.de) for partner hotels only.

BUDGET

Backpackers Düsseldorf (☎ 302 0848; www.backpackers -duesseldorf.de; Fürstenwall 180; dm incl linen & breakfast €20; P ⊠ 🖵) Düsseldorf's first indie hostel sleeps 44 in appealing and clean four- to six-bed dorms outfitted with individual backpack-sized lockers. It's a low-key place with a homy kitchen and a relaxed lounge where cultural and language barriers melt quickly. Free wi-fi. The reception is generally staffed from 8am to 9pm.

DJH hostel (☎ 557 310; www.djh.de; Düsseldorfer Strasse 1; dm/s/d €21/26/48 Jan-Jul, €22/27/52 Aug-Dec; P ⊠ 🖵) Across the Rhine from the Altstadt, this megahostel is being overhauled while remaining partially open for business. When completed in late 2007 it will put heads on 386 beds in 69 rooms, each with its own shower and toilet.

Hotel Berial (☎ 490 0490; www.hotel-berial.de; Gartenstrasse 30; s/d from €40/60; ⊠ 🖵) A recent top-to-bottom renovation has spruced up this hotel right by the Hofgarten, even though it didn't completely banish 1970s stodginess from its 40 rooms. Still, all the main amenities, including free wi-fi, are there.

Hotel Alt-Düsseldorf (☎ 133 604; www.alt-duessel dorf.de; Hunsrückenstrasse 11; s €50-115, d €70-160) If you're happy to trade generic-ness for centrality, this family-run hotel should do in a snap. It's a small, good-value place where days start with a big breakfast buffet served in sun-yellow surroundings.

THE AUTHOR'S CHOICE

Sir & Lady Astor (☎ 173 370; www.sir-astor.de; Kurfürstenstrasse 18 & 23; s/d €83/103; P ☒ ☒ ☐) Never mind the ho-hum setting on a residential street near the Hauptbahnhof: this unique twin boutique hotel brims with class, originality and charm. The reception is at the Sir Astor, whose 21 rooms are decked out in one of four colour schemes – grey, mandarin, vanilla and red – and furnished in 'Scotland-meets-Africa' style. Every detail speaks of refinement, from the hand-picked furniture to the textured wallpaper and tactile bedspreads. The 16 rooms at the Lady Astor across the street are even more adventurously decorated and have names evoking dreams of faraway places (eg Madame Butterfly, Marco Polo, Auguste Renoir). Only the gamut of communication devices, including free wi-fi, will keep you grounded in the here and now. This place has a huge fan base, so book early.

Max Hotel Garni (☎ 0211-386 800; www.max -hotelgarni.de; Adersstrasse 65; s/d/tr €63/75/87; ☐) Upbeat, contempo and run with personal flair, this 11-room hotel offers exceptional value and is one of our Düsseldorf favourites. Rates include coffee, tea, soft drinks and a regional public transport pass. The reception isn't always staffed, so call ahead to arrange an arrival time.

Ibis Hotel (☎ 167 20; www.ibishotel.com; Konrad-Adenauer-Platz 14; r €57-72; P ☒) Offers the usual amenities and is perfectly located for catching an early train.

MIDRANGE

Easy Living Schaper Apartment (☎ 8622 1100; www .schaper-apartment.com; Hohe Strasse 37-41; apt €95-230; ☒) If you're in town for three or more nights, you might opt for one of these bright, furnished apartments with pantry kitchens in surroundings of galleries and antique shops. The Roof Garden Suite (€275) is the ultimate retreat.

Hotel Orangerie (☎ 866 800; www.hotel-orangerie -mcs.de; Bäckergasse 1; s €100-165, d €125-210; ☒) Ensconced in a neoclassical mansion in a quiet corner of the Altstadt, this place puts you within staggering distance of the pubs yet offers a quiet and stylish oasis to retire to in the wee hours. Rooms are as bright, modern and uncluttered as the lobby and breakfast room.

Hotel Ashley's Garden (☎ 516 1710; www.ashleys garden.de; Karl-Kleppe-Strasse 20; d €130-170; P ☒) You'll feel like an English country squire at this adorable property run by a couple fancying all things British. Public areas and rooms brim with shiny antiques, thick rugs and enough Laura Ashley fabrics to drape the nearby fairgrounds. It's about 4km north of the city centre; from the Hauptbahnhof take the U78 to Reeser Platz.

Radisson SAS Media Harbour Hotel (☎ 311 1910; www.mediaharbour.duesseldorf.radissonsas.com; Hammerstrasse 23; s €110-485, d €130-505; P ☒ ☒ ☐) This hipster haven in the Medienhafen has 135 rooms flaunting the cutting-edge cool of Italian designer Matteo Thun. Even the 'standard' rooms are anything but, given the flat-screen TVs, walk-in showers, full-length windows and other *Zeitgeist*-capturing features. Bonus: free wi-fi throughout.

Burns Art Hotel (☎ 779 2910; www.hotel-burns .de; Bahnstrasse 76; s €125-270, d €145-290, ste €170-350; P ☒) Near the Hauptbahnhof, this cheery hotel is great for stretching out in 35 spacious rooms in the main house as well as 26 suites with pantry kitchens in a separate building. All feature modern furniture, natural stone floors and mostly tasteful original art; courtyard-facing rooms also have balconies.

Eating

Curry (☎ 303 2857; Hammerstrasse 2; meals under €6) In this vibrant little kitchen, sausage is king. Get them big, spicy, hot and paired with your choice of gourmet sauce and possibly a mountain of fresh French fries. At lunchtime trendy types from the nearby Medienhafen offices invade.

Im Füchschen (☎ 137 470; Ratinger Strasse 28; snacks €3, mains €6-12; ☾ 9am-1am) Boisterous, packed and drenched with local colour – the Füchschen (which translates as 'Little Fox') is all you expect a Rhenish beer hall to be. The kitchen makes a mean Schweinshaxe (roast pork leg).

Bim's Marktwirtschaft (☎ 327 185; Benrather Strasse 7; mains €8-15) With its horseshoe-shaped bar, big mirrors and red banquettes, this Altstadt classic may flaunt a retro look but won't go out of fashion any time soon. Come for breakfast, solid German fare or just drinks.

ALTSTADT SNACK FAVES

The Altstadt is chock-full of *Imbisse* (snack bars), mostly of the pizza-by-the-slice and doner-kebab variety, which are fine but nothing to write home about. We've ferreted out a few of the places where in-the-know locals feed their cravings. Those with a sweet tooth can't escape the magnetism of **Pia Eis** (Kasernenstrasse 1), the best ice-cream parlour around, bar none, with an incredible selection, quick service and modest prices. Another great sugar fix is the **Waffelladen** (Bolkerstrasse 8), an unimaginably tiny waffle kitchen in business for more than 40 years. Try one with a little powered sugar or drenched in cherries or other toppings.

Bäckerei Hinkel (several branches, incl Hohe Strasse 31) is another institution that has people queuing patiently for its excellent breads and cakes. A great way to prepare the stomach for an extended pub crawl is by filling up on superb falafel sandwiches at **Libanon Express** (Berger Strasse 21). Trendy types, meanwhile, are drawn to **[Q]üche** (Kurze Strasse 3) for its fresh and healthful soups, salads and sandwiches.

Op de Eck (☎ 328 838; Grabbeplatz 5; mains €8-20; ⏱ 5pm-1am Mon, 11am-1am Tue-Sun) Sheltered by the K20 art museum, this uncluttered bistro draws office folk, tourists and art lovers with its intriguing crossover menu. Breakfast is served until 3pm and in summer the terrace tables are the most coveted.

Zum Schiffchen (☎ 132 421; Hafenstrasse 5; mains €9-19) History pours from every nook and cranny in this almost ridiculously cosy Altstadt restaurant specialising in gut-busting German and Rhenish meals. Were portions as huge when Napoleon dropped by a couple of centuries ago? Reservations recommended.

Robert's Bistro (☎ 304 821; Wupperstrasse 2; mains €10-18; ⏱ Tue-Sat) Tables are squished together as tightly as lovers at this *très* French restaurant. Bring an appetite for hearty Gallic fare, a tolerance for smoke, and patience – there are no reservations and a queue is guaranteed.

Other recommendations:

Ohme Jupp (☎ 326 406; Ratinger Strasse 19; dishes €4-8; ⏱ 8am-1am) Casual, slightly artsy café serving breakfast and mouth-watering blackboard specials.

En de Canon (☎ 329 798; Zollstrasse 7; mains €10-19; ⏱ noon-3pm & 5.30pm-1am Mon-Sat) Similar to Zum Schiffchen with a jovial beer garden in summer.

For tapas, paella and other Iberian fare, head to Schneider-Wibbel-Gasse, just off Bolkerstrasse, which is almost completely given over to Spanish restaurants; prices go from rock-bottom to stratospheric.

Drinking

At night, especially in good weather, the atmosphere in the Altstadt is electric and often raucous. The beverage of choice is *Altbier*, a dark and semisweet beer typical of Düsseldorf.

Zum Uerige (☎ 866 990; Berger Strasse 1; ⏱ 10am-midnight) This cavernous warren is the best place to soak it all up. The beer flows so quickly from giant copper vats that the waiters – called '*Köbes*' – simply carry huge trays of brew and plonk down a glass whenever they spy an empty.

Salon des Amateurs (☎ 899 6243; Grabbeplatz 4; ⏱ noon-1am Tue-Sun) Tucked under the Kunsthalle, this tunnel-shaped café-lounge pulls off an artsy vibe without a single canvas. Museum-goers arrive in the afternoon for tea and chat, while after dark a young, hip crowd keeps the bar and little dance floor hopping.

Melody Bar (☎ 329 057; Kurze Strasse 12; ⏱ Tue-Sun) On most nights you'll have to shoehorn your way into this jewel of a cocktail bar, an island of sophistication in the rowdy Altstadt. The drinks are excellent, the owner couple gracious and the crowd mixed.

Q-Stall (☎ 836 9058; Kurze Strasse 3; ⏱ Fri & Sat) If Melody Bar is too packed, head across the street to Q-Stall with its circle bar and danceable music in the back.

Entertainment

Check the listings magazines *Prinz* and *Überblick* or the free *Coolibri* for current goings-on in 'D-Town'. Gays and lesbians should look for *Rik Magazin*. All are in German only.

CLUBS & LIVE MUSIC

Harpune (☎ 688 1490; Speditionstrasse 15a) At this highly rated club the dance floor hums with a mixed bag of globally influenced techno, House and electronica. Fridays are dedicated to other music styles, from hip-hop to reggae. The door policy is pretty relaxed, but don't show up drunk or dishevelled.

Pretty Vacant (Mertensgasse 8; ☿ from 8pm) It may be named for a Sex Pistols song, but this Altstadt haunt ain't no punk club. It's a shape-shifter really, whose cellar walls vibrate to different sounds nightly – glam rock to Britpop, electronica to R&B. Live bands, too.

Zakk (☎ 973 0010; Fichtenstrasse 40; ☿ Mon-Sat) Parties, concerts, readings, theatre, discussions – the menu sure varies at this well-established cultural centre in a former factory. A couple of kilometres east of the Hauptbahnhof, the beer garden is a convivial place to spend a balmy summer night.

Tor 3 (☎ 733 6497; www.tor3.com; Ronsdorfer Strasse 143; ☿ Fri & Sat) Massive Attack has played here, as has Radiohead and even Robbie Williams, but now this mega-sized old factory venue draws mostly unshowy party people ready to soak up house, techno, punk, rock or other sounds. It's in the suburb of Flingern, east of the Hauptbahnhof (take the U75).

Other recommendations:

3001 (☎ 6882 4960; Franziusstrasse 7; ☿ Thu-Sat) Hi-tech electronica club in the Medienhafen with giant dance floor, sizzling light and video projections and celebrity DJs.

Stahlwerk (☎ 730 350; Ronsdorfer Strasse 134; ☿ Fri & Sat) Huge dance hall with industrial flair, different sounds and theme parties; near Tor 3.

THEATRE & CLASSICAL MUSIC

D:ticket (☎ 01805-644 332; www.dticket.de) is the central booking hotline.

Schauspielhaus (☎ 369 911; www.duesseldorfer -schauspielhaus.de; Gustaf-Gründgens-Platz 1) The main venue for drama and comedies, the Schauspielhaus enjoys a solid reputation nationwide.

Marionetten-Theater (☎ 328 432; www.marionetten theater.duesseldorf.de; Bilker Strasse 7) For something entirely different, catch a show at this theatre, which presents charming and beautifully orchestrated operas and fairy tales, many geared to an adult audience.

Roncalli's Apollo Varieté (☎ 828 9090; Haroldstrasse 1) Another popular diversion where you'll be entertained by acrobats, comedians and other variety acts under the faux night sky of a nostalgic theatre hall.

Opera and musicals make it to the stage of the **Deutsche Oper am Rhein** (☎ 890 8211; www .rheinoper.de; Heinrich-Heine-Allee 16a), while the imposing domed **Tonhalle** (☎ 899 6123; www.tonhalle -duesseldorf.de; Ehrenhof 1) is the home base of the Düsseldorfer Symphoniker.

Getting There & Away

AIR

Many domestic and international carriers serve the recently revamped **Düsseldorf International Airport** (☎ 4210; www.duesseldorf-international.de) whose infrastructure includes a 24-hour left-luggage office, a Reisebank and car-rental desks.

BUS

Eurolines runs daily buses to Paris (one-way/ return from €50/92, seven hours) and Warsaw (€58/95, 20 hours) and once-weekly buses to Prague (€58/103, 13 hours).

CAR & MOTORCYCLE

Autobahns from all directions lead to Düsseldorf, including the A3 from Cologne and the A46 from Wuppertal and the eastern Ruhrgebiet.

TRAIN

Düsseldorf is part of a dense S-Bahn network in the Rhine-Ruhr region (see p572) and regular services run to Cologne and Aachen as well. There are frequent ICE trains to Frankfurt (€65, 1¾ hours), Berlin (€89, four hours) and Munich (€115, five hours).

Getting Around

TO/FROM THE AIRPORT

S-Bahns 1 and 7 shuttle between the airport and the Hauptbahnhof every few minutes. Long-distance trains also stop at the airport, significantly cutting travel time to the Rhine-Ruhr region and beyond. The free SkyTrain takes you from the station to the terminals. A taxi into town costs about €16.

PUBLIC TRANSPORT

An extensive network of U-Bahn trains, trams and buses operates throughout Düsseldorf. Most trips within the city cost €2, longer trips to the suburbs are €3.80. Day passes are €4.70/8.90. Tickets are available from bus drivers and orange vending machines at U-Bahn stops, and must be validated upon boarding.

TAXI

For a taxi, call ☎ 333 33 or ☎ 212 121.

AROUND DÜSSELDORF

If you're the kind of person that enjoys tracking down great art and architecture in unusual places, the **Langen Foundation** (☎ 02182-57010;

www.langenfoundation.de; Raketenstation Hombroich; adult/concession €7.50/5; ☯ 10am-6pm Tue-Sun) should fit the bill. The location: a former NATO missile base where Pershings armed with nuclear warheads held the line against the Soviet Union during the Cold War. The architecture: a minimalist glass, steel and concrete box by current Japanese meister Tadao Ando. The art: a private, top collection of Japanese art and modern European and American art. It's in the rural flatlands near the town of Neuss, about 20km west of Düsseldorf. Catch a train to Neuss Hauptbahnhof, then bus 860 or 877. By car, exit the A57 at Neuss-West and follow the signs to Raketenstation Hombroich.

LOWER RHINE

North of Düsseldorf, the Rhine widens and embarks on its final headlong rush towards the North Sea traversing the flat and sparsely populated Lower Rhine (Niederrhein). It's a flat, windswept and sparsely populated plain that feels like Holland without the windmills and yields a number of off-beat surprises.

The region has its own airport, the tiny **Niederrhein airport** (☎ 02837-666 000) in Weeze, which is used by RyanAir.

Xanten

☎ 02801 / pop 24,500

Xanten, some 60km north of Düsseldorf, is the largest town of the Lower Rhine region. It is one of Germany's oldest settlements, founded by the Romans around AD 100 as Colonia Ulpia Traiana in support of their mission to subjugate the Germanic tribes. At its peak, some 15,000 people milled about the town, enjoying a surprisingly high standard of living. Xanten's medieval heyday is best symbolised by the majestic Dom and nicely restored centre. The town is also the mythological birthplace of Siegfried, the hero of the 12th-century Nibelungen epic and immortalized 700 years later in the *Ring* opera cycle by Richard Wagner.

ORIENTATION

The Altstadt is about a 10-minute walk northeast of the Bahnhof (train station) via Hagenbuschstrasse or Bahnhofstrasse. The Archäologischer Park (Archaeological Park) is a further 15 minutes north of here.

INFORMATION

The **tourist office** (☎ 983 00; www.xanten.de; Kurfürstenstrasse 9; ☯ 9am-6pm Mon-Fri, 10am-4pm Sat & Sun Apr-Oct; 10am-5pm Mon-Fri, 10am-noon Sat & Sun Nov-Mar) is right in the Altstadt, close to the Markt (market square) and Dom.

SIGHTS

Altstadt

The crown jewel of Xanten's Altstadt is the **Dom St Viktor** (Propstei-Kapitel 8; ☯ 10am-6pm Mar-Oct, 10am-5pm Nov-Feb), which has Romanesque roots but is now largely Gothic. It is framed by a walled close, called an 'Immunity', which can only be entered from the Markt.

The soaring five-nave interior brims with treasures, reflecting the wealth Xanten enjoyed in the Middle Ages. Foremost among them is the **Marienaltar**, halfway down the right aisle, whose base features an intricately carved version of the *Tree of Jesse* by Heinrich Douvermann (1535). The candelabrum in the central nave, with its **Doppelmadonna** (Double Madonna, 1500), is another masterpiece. A stone sarcophagus in the crypt holds the remains of St Viktor, the Roman martyr who became Xanten's patron saint.

Archäologischer Park

Colonia Ulpia Traiana was the only Roman settlement north of the Alps that was never built upon. What's left of it can now be seen at the **Archäologischer Park** (Archaeological Park; ☎ 2999; Wardter Strasse 2; adult/child/family Mar-Nov €6.50/2.50/13, Dec-Feb €5.50/2/11; ☯ 9am-6pm Mar-Nov, 9am-5pm Nov, 10am-4pm Dec-Feb). To help amateurs visualise what a Roman town looked like, the park doesn't merely preserve the ancient foundations and ruins but features faithfully reconstructed buildings and roads. Critics have ridiculed the results, and the place does indeed feel a bit like a Roman theme park – especially in the restaurant where toga-clad staff serve 'Roman' meals. But overall, it's been nicely done and is well worth a visit.

A self-guided tour begins at the **Herberge**, an inn that, along with the restaurant, snack bar and furnished rooms, also contains an info-centre with models and explanatory panels. The **Badehaus** (bathhouse) next door points to the fairly high standard of hygiene enjoyed 2000 years ago. Accessible from a nearby portico are two new **workshops**, where you can observe craftsmen create bone carvings and leather shoes and even buy the finished products. To give you a sense of what the **private homes** of such workers looked like, three of them are being constructed nearby.

Other highlights include the **Amphitheatre**, which seats about 12,000 people during Xanten's summer festival, and the partly rebuilt **Hafentempel**. Be sure to walk around the back for a glimpse of the original foundation. At the **Spielehaus** you can play a round of authentic antique board games. Kids will also enjoy the two imaginative **playgrounds**, including the new water-themed one with little canals, locks and other unusual features (bring a towel).

Grosse Thermen & Regionalmuseum

Just west of the park, and included in the admission, are the **Grosse Thermen** (☼ 9am-6pm Mar-Oct, 9am-5pm Nov, 10am-4pm Dec-Feb), extensive Roman thermal baths sheltered by an extravagant glass-and-steel construction.

The similarly daring structure taking shape next door is the future home of the **Regionalmuseum** where Roman treasures excavated in the area will be presented along suspended ramps spiralling down from the ceiling. The opening is scheduled for 2008.

SLEEPING

DJH hostel (☎ 985 00; www.xanten.jugendherberge.de; Bankscher Weg 4; dm under/over 26yr €17.30/20.30; P ✗) This brand-new hostel has a pretty lakeside setting but is 3km from the Altstadt.

Klever Tor (☎ 983 00; Klever Strasse; apt €42, 2-night minimum) A romantic place to spend the night is inside the most striking of Xanten's surviving medieval town gates, now converted into holidays flats with small kitchens. Book through the tourist office.

Hotel van Bebber (☎ 6623; www.hotelvanbebber.de; Klever Strasse 12; s €68-100, d €110-135; P ✗) Queen Victoria and Churchill have slept in this old-school hotel where waiters wear tuxedoes and the reception is reached via a gallery of mounted animal heads.

EATING

Café de Fries (☎ 2068; Kurfürstenstrasse 8; dishes €3.50-8; ☼ 8.30am-9.30pm Tue-Fri, 9am-6pm Sat & Sun) It's a bit stuffy, but this little café has been a Xanten institution for 180 years and is famous for its filled pancakes. Kids love the 'chocolate fountain' and the Easter-bunny centrifuge in the one-room museum (admission free; open 11am to 5pm) at the back.

Gotisches Haus (☎ 706 400; Markt 6; mains €7-15; ☼ 9am-1am) Xanten's prettiest restaurant offers creative German cuisine and artsy design

flourishes within the wood-panelled walls of a nook-and-cranny Gothic merchant house.

GETTING THERE & AWAY

Getting to Xanten from the Niederrhein airport (opposite) involves taking a bus to Duisburg Bahnhof, then catching the hourly train (€8.40, 45 minutes). Xanten is on route B57. If travelling on the A57, take the Alpen exit, then route B58 east to B57 north.

Kalkar & Around

☎ 02824 / pop 11,500

About 15km north of Xanten, Kalkar boasts a pretty medieval core centred on a proud **Rathaus** and the **St Nikolaikirche** (Jan-Joest-Strasse 6; ☼ 10am-noon & 2-6pm Mon-Fri, 10am-noon & 2-5pm Sat & Sun Apr-Oct, 2-5pm daily Nov-Mar), famous for its nine masterful altars chiselled by members of the Kalkar woodcarving school. This was essentially a 15th-century vanity project funded by local burghers who'd grown rich on the wool trade.

Top billing goes to the **High Altar**, which depicts the Passion of Christ in heart-wrenching detail. For a little comic relief, lift the first seat on the left in the back row of the choir chairs (with you facing the altar) to reveal a **monkey on a chamberpot**. Another eye-catcher is the **Seven Sorrows Altar** by Henrik Douvermann at the end of the right aisle. Note the oak-carved *Jesse's root*, which wraps around the entire altar.

Bus 44 makes regular trips from Xanten's Bahnhof to the Markt in Kalkar but service is infrequent at weekends.

SCHLOSS MOYLAND

With its Rapunzel towers, Romeo-and-Juliette balcony and creeping ivy, **Schloss Moyland** (☎ 02824-95100; Am Schloss 4; www.moyland .de; adult/concession/family €5.50/3/12; ☼ 11am-6pm Tue-Fri, 10am-6pm Sat & Sun Apr-Sep, 11am-5pm Tue-Sun Oct-Mar) looks like something from your childhood dreams. It's also a most unexpected sight amid the sweeping pastures and sleepy villages around here. Medieval in origin, it got its fairy-tale looks in the 19th century and since 1997 has housed a private modern-art collection, including one of the largest assortments of Joseph Beuys works in the world. 'Less is more' is definitely not a curatorial concept here, as every wall of the labyrinthine interior is smothered in drawings, paintings and etchings. If you need to clear your head, take a spin around the lovely park with its old trees and wacky sculptures.

The Schloss is about 4km northwest of Kalkar off the B57 and well sign-posted. Bus 44 heads out here from the Xanten Bahnhof or the Markt in Kalkar, but service is sketchy at weekends.

WUNDERLAND KALKAR
What do you do with a decommissioned nuclear power plant? Turn it into a convention hotel and amusement park, of course. So was the vision of a wily Dutchman who, in 1995, bought the so-called *Schneller Brüter* (Fast Breeder) reactor on a field in Kalkar. Thankfully, the behemoth had never gone live thanks to opposition from environmentalists who convinced the authorities that it was unsafe. Reborn as **Wunderland Kalkar** (☎ 02824-9100; www.wunderland-kalkar.de) it offers utterly bizarre cruise-ship-meets-Vegas ambience. You can free-climb the cooling tower, admire the concrete complex from atop a Ferris wheel or enjoy drinks in a Wild West saloon. A **day pass** (11am-6pm), including park access, meals and drinks, costs €30 for adults and €22.50 for kids aged three to 12 (€25/17.50 November to March). Various hotel and dinner packages are also available. The plant is about 6km northeast of Kalkar and not served by public transport.

COLOGNE
☎ 0221 / pop 969,000
Cologne (Köln) is like a three-dimensional textbook on history and architecture. Drifting about town you'll stumble upon an ancient Roman wall, medieval churches galore, nondescript postwar buildings and avant-garde museums and concert halls. Germany's fourth-largest city, founded by the Romans in 38 BC, has a long list of sightseeing attractions, led by its famous Dom whose filigree twin spires dominate the impressive Altstadt skyline. The Altstadt is also the best place to sample *Kölsch*, the refreshing local brew, in beer halls rivalling those in Bavaria in rollicking intensity. Those with more refined tastes have numerous museums – art to chocolate to sports – to explore or concerts to attend.

Orientation
Cologne Bonn Airport is southeast of the city; see p560 for details on transport to/from the airport. Cologne's Hauptbahnhof is practi-

cally on the Rhine's western bank, right next to the landmark Dom. The pedestrianised Hohe Strasse – the main shopping street – runs south of the Dom, as does the Altstadt, which hugs the river bank between the two bridges, Hohenzollernbrücke and Deutzer Brücke. Student-flavoured Zülpicher Viertel and the more grown-up Belgisches Viertel about 1.5km west of here are also zinging bar and pub quarters.

Information
BOOKSHOPS
Gleumes (Map p556; ☎ 211 550; Hohenstaufenring 47-51) Travel and map specialist.
Gonski (Map p552; ☎ 209 090; Neumarkt 18a)
Mayersche Buchhandlung (Map p552; ☎ 203 070; Neumarkt 2) There's another branch at Schildergasse 31-37.

DISCOUNT CARDS
Köln Welcome Card (per 24/48/72hr €9/14/19) Offers free public transport and admission discounts; also available for groups (€18/28/38). It's available at the tourist office and participating venues.

EMERGENCY
Dental emergencies (☎ 01805-986 700)
Gay Attack Hotline (☎ 192 28)
Medical emergencies (☎ 192 92)

INTERNET ACCESS
Internet Café Colony (Map p556; ☎ 272 0630; Zülpicher Strasse 38-40; per 10min €0.40; ⏰ 10am-2am Mon-Sat, 11am-2am Sun)
Surf Inn (Map p552; ☎ 925 3301; 3rd fl, Galeria Kaufhof, Hohe Strasse 41-53; per 15min €1; ⏰ 9.30am-8pm Mon-Sat)

LAUNDRY
Cleanicum (Map p556; ☎ 869 0638; Brüsseler Strasse 74-76; ⏰ 10am-1am) Also a bar (p558).
Eco-Express Waschsalon (per load from €1.50, per 10min of dryer time €0.50; ⏰ 6am-11pm Mon-Sat) Has branches at Friedrichstrasse 12 (Map p556), Richard-Wagner-Strasse 2 (Map p556) and Hansaring 68 (Map p552).

MEDICAL SERVICES
Universitätskliniken (☎ 4780; Josef-Stelzmann-Strasse 9) Located 1.6km southeast of Zülpicher Viertel.

MONEY
American Express (Map p552; ☎ 257 5186; Burgmauer 14; ⏰ 9am-6pm Mon-Fri, 10am-1pm Sat) Also a travel agency.

Reisebank (Map p552; ☎ 134 403; Hauptbahnhof; ☻ 7am-10pm)

Travelex (Map p552; ☎ 925 2596; Unter Fettenhennen 19; ☻ 9am-10pm Mon-Sat Jul-Sep, 9am-9pm Mon-Sat Oct-Jun, 10am-6pm Sun year-round) Inside the tourist office.

POST
Post office (Map p552; ☎ 925 9290; WDR Arkaden shopping mall, Breite Strasse 6-26; ☻ 9am-7pm Mon-Fri, 9am-2pm Sat)

TOURIST INFORMATION
Tourist office (Map p552; ☎ 2213 0400; www .koelntourismus.de; Unter Fettenhennen 19; ☻ 9am-10pm Mon-Sat Jul-Sep, 9am-9pm Mon-Sat Oct-Jun, 10am-6pm Sun year-round)

Sights
KÖLNER DOM
Cologne's geographical and spiritual heart – and its main tourist draw – is the magnificent **Kölner Dom** (Map p552; ☎ 1794 0200; ☻ 6am-7.30pm). With its soaring twin spires, this is the Mt Everest of cathedrals, packed with an astonishing array of art treasures. Its loftiness and dignified ambience leave only the most jaded of visitors untouched.

Building began in 1248 in the French Gothic style but was suspended in 1560 when funds ran out. The structure lingered half-finished for nearly 300 years and was even demoted to a horse stable and prison by Napoleon's troops. Finally, a generous cash infusion from Prussian King Friedrich Wilhelm IV led to its completion in 1880. Luckily, it escaped WWII bombing raids with nary a shrapnel wound and has been a Unesco World Heritage Site since 1996.

The Dom is Germany's largest cathedral. Circle it before heading inside to truly appreciate its dimensions. Note how its lacy spires and flying buttresses create a sensation of lightness and fragility despite its impressive mass and height.

This sensation continues inside where a phalanx of pillars and arches supports the lofty central nave. Soft light filters through the radiant **stained-glass windows**. Other highlights include the **Gero Crucifix** (970), notable for its monumental size and an emotional intensity rarely achieved in those early medieval days; the **choir stalls** from 1310, richly carved from oak; and the **altar painting** by local artist Stephan Lochner from around 1450.

The *pièce de résistance*, though, is the **Shrine of the Three Magi** behind the main altar, a richly bejewelled and gilded sarcophagus said to hold the remains of the kings who followed the star to the stable in Bethlehem where Jesus was born. It was spirited out of Milan in 1164 as spoils of war by Emperor Barbarossa's chancellor and instantly turned Cologne into a major pilgrimage site.

To get more out of your visit, invest €0.70 in a pamphlet with basic information, or join a **guided tour**. These are offered in English (adult/concession €4/2) at 10.30am and 2.30pm (2.30pm only on Sunday) and more frequently in German. Tours include a 20-minute slide show with music presented at the **Domforum** information centre opposite the main portal.

For an exercise fix, climb the 509 steps up the Dom's **south tower** (adult/concession €2/1, combination ticket with treasury €5/2.50; ☻ 9am-6pm May-Sep, 9am-5pm Mar-Apr & Oct, 9am-4pm Nov-Feb) to the base of the steeple that dwarfed all buildings in Europe until Gustave Eiffel built a certain tower in Paris. A good excuse to take a breather on your way up is the 24-tonne **Peter Bell** (1923), the largest working bell in the world. As you might imagine, views from the 95m platform are fabulous…

Cologne is justifiably proud of its **Domschatzkammer** (Cathdral Treasury; ☎ 1794 0300; adult/concession €4/2; ☻ 10am-6pm), whose reliquaries, robes, sculptures and liturgical objects are handsomely presented in 13th-century vaulted rooms. One item to keep an eye out for is the Gothic bishop's staff from 1322.

In 2007, yet another repository of religious art is set to open in an edgy new building by Swiss architect Peter Zumthor which will be cleverly fused to the ruin of the late-Gothic church St Kolumba. Called **Kolumba** (Map p552; ☎ 257 7672), the museum will present treasures from nearly 2000 years. For the latest information, call or check with the tourist office.

ROMANESQUE CHURCHES
Cologne's medieval heyday is reflected in its wealth of Romanesque churches, which were constructed between 1150 and 1250 and survived largely intact until WWII. About a dozen have been rebuilt since and offer many unique architectural and artistic features. Even if you're pushed for time, try seeing at least a couple of the ones mentioned here.

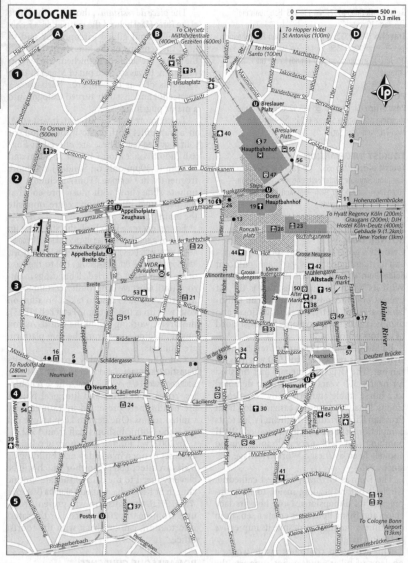

Winning top honours for most handsome exterior is **Gross St Martin** (Map p552; ☎ 1642 5650; An Gross-St-Martin 9; ⏱ 10am-noon & 3-5pm Tue-Sat, 2-4pm Sun), whose ensemble of four slender turrets grouped around a central spire towers above Fischmarkt in the Altstadt. Inside, it has a striking clover-leaf choir, an architectural style pioneered by **St Maria im Kapitol**

(Map p552; ☎ 214 615; Marienplatz 19; ⏱ 9.30am-6pm), whose stand-out treasures include a carved door from the original 11th-century church and a spectacularly ornate Renaissance rood screen.

The most eccentric-looking church is **St Gereon** (Map p552; ☎ 134 922; Gereonsdriesch 2-4; ⏱ 10am-noon & 3-5pm Mon-Fri, 10am-noon Sat, 3-5pm

Sun), which grew from a late-Roman chapel into a massive complex with a soaring decagonal dome with delicate ribbed vaulting.

If you look at Cologne's coat of arms, you'll see what looks like 11 apostrophes but in fact represents the Christian martyrs St Ursula and 10 virgins. The church of **St Ursula** (Map p552; ☎ 133 400; Ursulaplatz; usually 10am-noon & 3-5pm Mon-Sat) stands atop the Roman cemetery where the virgins' remains were allegedly found. In the 17th century, the richly ornamented baroque **Goldene Kammer** (Golden Chamber; adult/child €1/0.50) was built to house their relics.

ROMAN COLOGNE

Anyone even remotely interested in Roman history should not skip the extraordinary **Römisch-Germanisches Museum** (Roman Germanic Museum; Map p552; ☎ 2212 4438; Roncalliplatz 4; adult/concession €6/3.50; 10am-5pm Tue-Sun), adjacent to the Dom. Sculptures and ruins displayed outside and in the lobby are merely the (free)

overture to a full symphony of Roman artefacts found along the Rhine. Highlights include the giant **Poblicius tomb** (AD 30–40), the magnificent 3rd-century **Dionysus mosaic** around which the museum was built, and astonishingly well-preserved glass items. Insight into daily Roman life is gained from such items as toys, tweezers, lamps and jewellery, the designs of which have changed surprisingly little since.

Near the museum's southern wall are remains of the **Roman harbour street** and two **Roman wells**. Other vestiges from the ancient settlement include a **Roman arch** (Map p552) from the former town wall outside the Dom; the **Römerturm** (Map p552), a tower standing among buildings at the corner of St-Apern-Strasse and Zeughausstrasse; and the **Praetorium** (Map p552; ☎ 2212 2394; adult/concession €1.50/0.75; 10am-5pm Tue-Sun), a Roman governor's palace below the Renaissance **Rathaus** (Map p552). Enter from Kleine Budengasse.

NORTH RHINE-WESTPHALIA

MUSEUM LUDWIG

The distinctive building façade and unorthodox roofline signal that the **Museum Ludwig** (Map p552; ☎ 2212 6165; Bischofsgartenstrasse 1; adult/concession/family €7.50/5.50/18; ☼ 10am-6pm Tue-Sun) is no ordinary museum. Considered a European mecca of postmodern art, it also offers a thorough overview of all genres – traditional to warped – generated in the 20th century. There's plenty of American pop art, including Roy Lichtenstein's *Maybe* and Andy Warhol's *Brillo Boxes* alongside a large Picasso collection covering all of his major creative phases. Fans of German expressionism will get their fill here as much as those with a penchant for such Russian avant-gardists as Kasimir Malewitsch and Ljubow Popowa.

Admission is also good for the **Foto-Museum Agfa Foto-Historama**, an unusual collection of historic photographs and equipment, housed under the same roof.

WALLRAF-RICHARTZ-MUSEUM & FONDATION CORBOUD

A famous collection of art from the 13th to the 19th centuries, the **Wallraf-Richartz-Museum** (Map p552; ☎ 2212 1119; Martinstrasse 39; adult/concession €8/5; ☼ 10am-8pm Tue, 10am-6pm Wed-Fri, 11am-6pm Sat & Sun) occupies a postmodern cube that was designed by Cologne's own OM Ungers. Works are presented chronologically, with the oldest on the 1st floor where standouts include brilliant examples from the Cologne School, known for its distinctive use of colour. Upstairs are Dutch and Flemish artists like Rembrandt and Rubens, Italians such as Canaletto and Spaniards including Murillo. The 3rd floor focuses on the 19th century with evocative works by Caspar David Friedrich and Lovis Corinth. Thanks to a permanent loan from Swiss collector Gèrard Corboud, there's now also a respectable collection of impressionist paintings, including some by heavyweights Monet and Cézanne.

MUSEUM SCHNÜTGEN

The beautifully restored church of St Cäcilia provides a magical setting for the medieval church treasures of the **Museum Schnütgen** (Map p552; ☎ 2212 3620; Cäcilienstrasse 29; adult/concession €3.20/1.90; ☼ 10am-5pm Tue-Fri, 11am-5pm Sat & Sun), including wooden and stone sculptures, manuscripts, textiles and ivory carvings.

SCHOKOLADEN MUSEUM

Anyone with a sweet tooth will likely enjoy the **Schokoladen Museum** (Chocolate Museum; ☎ 931 8880; Rheinauhafen 1a; adult/concession €6/3.50; ☼ 10am-6pm Tue-Fri, 11am-7pm Sat & Sun), a hi-tech temple to the art of chocolate-making. Exhibits on the origin of the 'elixir of the gods', as the Aztecs called it, and the cocoa-growing process are followed by a live-production factory tour and a stop at a chocolate fountain for a sample. Upstairs are departments on the cultural history of chocolate, advertising, and porcelain and other accessories. Stock up on your favourite flavours at the downstairs shop.

DEUTSCHES SPORT & OLYMPIA MUSEUM

In a 19th-century customs building near the Schokoladen Museum, the **Deutsches Sport & Olympia Museum** (German Sport & Olympic Games Museum; Map p552; ☎ 336 090; Rheinauhafen 1; adult/concession/family €5/2.50/12; ☼ 10am-6pm Tue-Fri, 11am-7pm Sat & Sun) is an imaginative, if Germany-focused, tribute to the sporting life from antiquity to today. There are exhibits on the 1936 Berlin and 1972 Munich Olympic Games and on such modern-day heroes as Steffi Graf and Michael Schumacher. Interactive displays allow you to experience a bobsled run or a bike race, and on the miniature football field on the rooftop you can kick with a view of the river and Dom.

EL-DE HAUS

Cologne's Third Reich history is poignantly documented in the **EL-DE Haus** (Map p552; ☎ 2212 6332; Appellhofplatz 23-25; adult/concession €3.60/1.50; ☼ 10am-4pm Tue-Fri, 11am-4pm Sat & Sun), which takes its curious name from its builder Leopold Dahmen. In 1935 it became the local Gestapo prison where scores of people were interrogated, tortured and killed. Inscriptions on the basement cell walls offer a gut-wrenching record of the emotional and physical pain endured by inmates.

OTHER MUSEUMS

Inside a bank branch is the **Käthe-Kollwitz-Museum** (Map p552; ☎ 227 2899; Neumarkt 18-24; adult/concession €3/1.50; ☼ 10am-6pm Tue-Fri, 11am-6pm Sat & Sun), with graphics and a few sculptures by the acclaimed socialist artist. A highlight is the haunting cycle called *Ein Weberaufstand* (A Weavers' Revolt, 1897). Enter through the arcade, then take the glass-bubble lift to the 4th floor.

FOOLS, FLOATS & REVELRY

Carnival in Cologne is one of the best parties in Europe and a thumb in the eye of the German work ethic. Every year at the onset of Lent (late February/early March), a year of painstaking preparation culminates in the 'three crazy days' – actually more like six.

It all starts with *Weiberfastnacht*, the Thursday before Ash Wednesday, when women rule the day (and do things like chop off the ties of their male colleagues/bosses). The party continues through the weekend, with more than 50 parades of ingenious floats and wildly dressed lunatics dancing in the streets. By the time it all comes to a head with the big parade on *Rosenmontag* (Rose Monday), the entire city has come unglued. Those still capable of swaying and singing will live it up one last time on Shrove Tuesday before the curtain comes down on Ash Wednesday.

'If you were at the parade and saw the parade, you weren't at the parade', say the people of Cologne in their inimitable way. Translated, this means that you should be far too busy singing, drinking, roaring the Carnival greeting *'Alaaf!'* and planting a quick *Bützchen* (kiss) on the cheek of whoever strikes your fancy, to notice anything happening around you. Swaying and drinking while sardined in a pub, or following other costumed fools behind a huge bass drum leading to God-only-knows-where, you'll be swept up in one of the greatest parties the world knows.

The **Kölnisches Stadtmuseum** (Cologne City Museum; Map p552; ☎ 2212 5789; Zeughausstrasse 1-3; adult/concession €4.20/2.60; ⏰ 10am-8pm Tue, 10am-5pm Wed-Sun), in the former medieval armoury, explores all facets of Cologne history. There are exhibits on Carnival, *Kölsch* (the local beer), eau de Cologne and other things that make the city unique.

The **Museum für Angewandte Kunst** (Museum of Applied Arts; Map p552; ☎ 2212 6714; An der Rechtschule; adult/concession €3/1.50; ⏰ 11am-5pm Tue-Sun) consists of a series of period rooms tracing European design from the Middle Ages to today. Keep an eye out for a 15th-century Venetian wedding goblet, a silver service by Henry van de Velde and life-sized animals made of Meissen porcelain.

Tours

Guided two-hour city **bus tours** (☎ 979 2570; adult/child 6-12yr €14/4) in German and English depart from the tourist office up to three times daily.

Rent-A-Bike (Map p552; ☎ 0171-629 8796; Marksmanngasse) runs German/English three-hour bicycle tours (€15) daily at 1.30pm from April to October. Tours start in the Altstadt right below the Deutzer Brücke.

In the warmer months, several boat companies offer one-hour spins taking in the splendid Altstadt panorama (adult/child €7/3.50). Other options include sunset cruises and all-day trips to Königswinter.

Dampfschifffahrt Colonia (Map p552; ☎ 257 4225) Board below the Hollenzollernbrücke.

KD Köln (Map p552; ☎ 208 8318) Boats leave from Frankenwerft, north of the Deutzer Brücke.

Köln-Tourist Personenschifffahrt (Map p552; ☎ 121 600) Leaves from Konrad-Adenauer-Ufer, north of the Hohenzollernbrücke.

Sleeping

Cologne is not a cheap city, especially during major trade shows (mostly in spring and autumn) when prices can be triple the standard rate.

BUDGET

Station – Hostel for Backpackers (Map p552; ☎ 912 5301; www.hostel-cologne.de; Marzellenstrasse 44-56; dm €16-19, s/d/tr/q with bathroom €35/50/66/78; ☒ 🖳) This recently expanded and upgraded hostel is a great budget base close to the Hauptbahnhof. A lounge gives way to clean, colourful rooms sleeping one to six people. The helpful staff speak fluent English, and there's lots of free stuff, including linen, internet access, lockers, city maps and guest kitchen. Breakfast is à la carte, meaning you only pay for what you eat.

DJH hostel Köln-Deutz (☎ 814711; www.koeln-deutz .jugendherberge.de; Siegesstrasse 5; dm €23.50, s/d €40/60; 🅿 ☒ 🖳) As far as DJH hostels go, this 506-bed behemoth is state-of-the-art, with each room sporting its own bathroom. It's only a three-minute walk from the Köln-Deutz train station. The Hauptbahnhof is a 10-minute walk across the river.

Pension Jansen (Map p556; ☎ 251875; www.pension jansen.de; Richard-Wagner-Strasse 18; s €31-45, d €62-65) Privacy is at a premium in this six-room *pension* located in a big apartment that's also shared by the owners. Still, it's cheap, close to restaurants and nightlife, and its rooms are colourful, comfortable and decorated with imagination.

Artisthotel Montechristo (Map p552; ☎ 277 4883; www.artisthotelmontechristo.com; Grosse Sandkaul 24-26; s/d from €50/70) 'Camp' rules at Cologne's trippiest hotel whose 12 rooms are brightly pigmented and outfitted with lava lamps and Madonnas. It's close to nightlife, but the buzzy in-house cocktail bar and techno-House cellar club bring the party home. Check-out is a hangover-friendly 5pm. Breakfast is €8.

Hotel Allegro (Map p552; ☎ 240 8260; www.hotel -allegro.com; Thurnmarkt 1-7; s €50-125, d €70-160; P ✗) This is a pleasant option just south of the Altstadt with rooms that sport either a rustic Bavarian, modern or cheerful Mediterranean look. Some have river views, but those at the back are quieter.

MIDRANGE
Hotel Chelsea (Map p556; ☎ 207 150; www.hotel-chelsea .de; Jülicher Strasse 1; s €70-130, d €90-150, r €95-180; P ✗ 🖳) Those fancying an artsy vibe will be well sheltered in this self-proclaimed 'hotel different'. Originals created by inter-

national artists in exchange for lodging grace the public areas and 38 rooms and suites. The eye-catching deconstructivist rooftop extension houses a spectacular penthouse. There's free wi-fi.

Hotel Cristall (Map p552; ☎ 163 00; www.hotelcristall .de; Ursulaplatz 9-11; s €72-184, d €95-235; P ✗ 🖳) This laid-back yet stylish hotel manages to appeal both to the suit brigade and city-break types. Rooms won't fit a ton of luggage but all are appealingly designed and quite comfortable. Light sleepers should get one facing away from the busy street.

Hopper Hotel Et Cetera (Map p556; ☎ 924 400; www.hopper.de; Brüsseler Strasse 26; s €70-175, d €100-230; P ✗ 🖳) A waxen monk welcomes you to this former monastery whose 49 rooms sport eucalyptus floors, cherry furniture and marble baths along with lots of little pampering touches. The sauna and bar, both in the vaulted cellars, are great places for reliving the day's exploits.

INFORMATION	
Cleanicum	1 A1
Eco-Express Waschsalon	2 A2
Eco-Express Waschsalon	3 B3
Gleumes	4 B3
Internet Café Colony	5 A3

SLEEPING 🛏	
Hopper Hotel Et Cetera	6 A2
Hotel Chelsea	7 A2
Hotel Leonet	8 B2
Pension Jansen	9 A2

EATING 🍴	
Alcazar	10 A1
Barflo	11 B2
Brennerei Weiss	12 B2
Café Feynsinn	13 A3
Café Fleur	14 B3
Engelbät	15 B2
Falafel Salem	16 B3
Fischermann's	17 A3
Sumo	18 A2

DRINKING 🍷	
Cleanicum	19 A1
Hallmackenreuther	20 A2
Päffgen	21 B1
Rosebud	22 B3
Scheinbar	23 A2
Shepheard	24 B3
Six Pack	25 A2

ENTERTAINMENT 🎭	
Lauschgift	26 A2
Roonburh	27 B3
Stadtgarten	28 A1

TRANSPORT	
Hertz	29 A1

ZÜLPICHER VIERTEL & BELGISCHES VIERTEL

0 — 100 m
0 — 0.1 miles

Hotel Santo (☎ 913 9770; www.hotelsanto.de; Dago-bertstrasse 22-26; s €80-130, d €100-150; P ✗) This hotel's location near the Hauptbahnhof may be drab, but this 69-room boutique hotel is an island of sassy sophistication. The design flaunts an edgy, urban feel tempered by playful light effects, soothing colours and natural materials. Gourmet breakfast and free wi-fi in the public areas.

New Yorker (☎ 473 30; www.thenewyorker.de; Deutz-Mülheimer Strasse 204; s €95-125, d €115-145; P ✗ ✗) This snazzy lifestyle hotel is a charming surprise in an industrial neighbourhood about 3km east of the Hauptbahnhof. Standard rooms are dressed in virginal white, while upper categories boast bold colour accents and parquet floors. Breakfast is €13.

Other recommendations:

Lint Hotel (Map p552; ☎ 920 550; www.lint-hotel.de; Lintgasse 7; s €70-155, d €100-210; ✗) Ecologically correct, contemporary hotel in the heart of the Altstadt.

Hotel Leonet (Map p556; ☎ 272 300; www.leonetkoeln.de; Rubensstrasse 33; s €90-155, d €115-215; P ✗ 🖳) Modern hotel with good-sized rooms and extensive wellness area.

TOP END

Mauritius Hotel & Therme (Map p556; ☎ 924 130; www.mauritius.de, Mauritiusplatz 3-11; s €130-160, d €150-180; P ✗ ✗ 🖳 ✈) This would be just another three-star hotel were it not for the vast wellness area, perfect for getting off weary feet after a long day on the tourist track. Rooms come in three sizes, but all have a kitchenette, cable TV and sound system.

Hopper Hotel St Antonius (☎ 166 00; www.hopper.de; Dagobertstrasse 32; s €100-240, d €150-260; P ✗ 🖳) History and hi tech mix nicely at this posh retreat with plenty of eye candy for the style-conscious. The romantic courtyard garden and small wellness area in the brick-vaulted cellar are great bliss-out spots. Main drawback: the bland location near the Hauptbahnhof.

Hyatt Regency Köln (☎ 828 1234; www.cologne.regency.hyatt.com; Kennedy-Ufer 2a; s €150-280, d €175-305; P ✗ ✗ 🖳 ✈) This ultra-posh abode is a favourite with celebrities, politicians and anyone in need of feeding their luxury cravings. If you go for it, get a room facing the river and the Altstadt skyline.

Hotel Im Wasserturm (Map p552; ☎ 200 80; www.hotel-im-wasserturm.de; Kaygasse 2; s €180-265, d €210-335; P ✗ ✗ 🖳) This is an extremely classy designer hotel cleverly converted from an old water tower, south of Neumarkt.

Eating
RESTAURANTS

Cologne's multiculturalism makes it possible to take a culinary journey around the world. Rhenish specialities and typical German food are best sampled in the beer halls (see p558).

Sumo (Map p556; ☎ 222 1590; Aachener Strasse 17-19; nigiri €1.50-3.50, maki €3-6.50; ☽ noon-2.30pm & 6-11pm, closed Sun lunch) This small and simple Japanese-run sushi parlour also serves soups, teriyaki, *yakitori* and other dishes. The lunch combinations are especially good.

Falafel Salam (Map p556; ☎ 240 2933; Zülpicher Platz 7; falafels €2.60-5; ☽ 11.30am-2am or later) This is Col-ogne's mother of all falafel snack bars. There's almost always a queue for the freshly made and nicely spiced garbanzo (chickpea) balls paired with your choice of sauce. The late hours make it a popular refuelling stop for night owls.

Engelbät (Map p556; ☎ 246 914; Engelbertstrasse 7; dishes €3.50-7) This woodsy restaurant-pub is famous for its habit-forming crepes which come in 30 varieties – sweet, meat or vegetarian. From October to April it presents free concerts at noon on Sunday. Also popular for breakfast.

Alcazar (Map p556; ☎ 515 733; Bismarckstrasse 39; snacks €4-10, mains €9-17) This is the kind of place that never goes out of fashion, thanks to its winning combination of freshly prepared international dishes, unpretentious ambience and chirpy service. No food service in the afternoon.

Fischermann's (Map p556; ☎ 801 7790; Rathenauplatz 21; mains €9.50-18, 3-course dinners €26; ☽ dinner) This perennial favourite has minimalist décor, all the better so as not to distract you from the delicious crossover cuisine mixing German, Mediterranean and Asian flavours. Regulars often treat the place as a launch pad for a night on the razzle. Nice terrace in summer.

Graugans (☎ 8281 1771; Kennedy-Ufer 2a; mains €20-35; ☽ closed lunch Sat & all day Sun) Fans of 'wok-meets-Western' cuisine – expertly prepared and beautifully presented – will be in culinary heaven at this elegant restaurant inside the Hyatt Regency Köln. Views of the Dom and the Altstadt skyline are gratis.

Osman 30 (☎ 5005 2080; Im Mediapark 8; 3-course menu €39; ☽ 6-11.30pm Mon-Sat, 11am-6.30pm Sun) The setting alone of this made-to-impress newcomer on the 30th floor of the KölnTurm would be spectacular, but fortunately the Mediterranean food can more than hold its own with the views. Cap your meal with liba-tions served in the wine salon with its stylish white leather armchairs. High romance factor. Reservations essential.

CAFÉS
Café Fleur (Map p556; ☎ 244 897; Lindenstrasse 10; dishes €4-10; ⏰ 9am-1am) This small and romantic café with its chandeliers and large gilded mirrors is a great place to linger over breakfast, cakes and light dishes or simply while away the time pouring over the free periodicals.

Café Feynsinn (Map p556; ☎ 240 9209; Rathenauplatz 7; mains €6-10; ⏰ 9am-1am) Eccentric glass-chard chandeliers, a painted-sky ceiling and a mirror-backed bar festooned with twinkling lights give this neighbourhood favourite its own, easy-going charm. Come for great breakfast, homemade dishes or your favourite libation (50 malt whiskeys!).

Drinking
Cologne brims with bars, pubs and clubs ranging from grungy and relaxed to upmarket chic. Centres of action include the Altstadt, with its rollicking pubs and beer halls; the Friesenviertel along Friesenwall and Friesen-strasse; the 'Kwartier Lateng' (Cologne dialect for Latin Quarter, or student quarter), also known as Zülpicher Viertel, along Zülpicher, Roon- and Kyffhäuser Strasse; and the Bel-gisches Viertel (Belgian Quarter), which has a more grown-up yet still somewhat alterna-tive feel, along Bismarck-, Flandrische- and Maastrichter Strasse.

BEER HALLS
Beer reigns supreme in Cologne with more than 20 breweries producing a variety called *Kölsch*, which is relatively light and slightly bitter. Many run their own beer halls where the brew comes in skinny glasses called *Stan-gen* that hold a mere 200mL. They also serve a selection of stout Rhenish dishes to keep you grounded.

Früh am Dom (Map p552; ☎ 261 30; Am Hof 12-14; breakfast €4-10, mains €5-14) This beer-hall warren near the Dom is also a good stop for a hearty breakfast.

Schreckenskammer (Map p552; ☎ 132 581; Ursula-gartenstrasse 11; mains €7-14; ⏰ 11am-1.45pm & 4.30-10.30pm Mon-Fri, 11am-2pm Sat) This locals' favourite has better food than your average beer hall. Empty chairs are a rare sight, especially on Friday potato pancake nights.

Malzmühle (Map p552; ☎ 210 117; Heumarkt 6; mains €8-15; ⏰ 10am-midnight) At this convivial beer hall off the beaten tourist track you can enjoy *Kölsch* brewed with organic ingredients in a setting of deer antlers, pewter plates and conversation-happy locals.

Päffgen (Map p556; ☎ 135 461; Friesenstrasse 64-66; mains €8.50-14; ⏰ 10am-midnight) Busy, loud and boisterous, Päffgen has been pouring *Kölsch* since 1883 and hasn't lost a step since. In summer you can enjoy the refreshing brew and local specialities underneath starry skies in the beer garden.

Brauhaus Peters (Map p552; ☎ 257 3950; Müh-lengasse 1; snacks €2.50-8, mains €9-17) This relative newcomer gets a slightly less raucous crowd holding forth in six highly individualistic nooks, including a small chapel and a room lidded by a kaleidoscopic stained-glass ceiling.

PUBS & BARS
Scheinbar (Map p556; ☎ 923 9048; Brüsseler Strasse 10) If you needed any proof that Cologne's nightlife is smoking hot, simply stop by this bar that's dressed in red satin, lava lamps and has sitting areas perfect for chilling.

Six Pack (Map p556; ☎ 254 587; Aachener Strasse 33; ⏰ 9am-5am) This is a must-stop on any Belgian Quarter pub crawl. Belly up to the super-long bar and pick from several-dozen varieties of beer, all served by the bottle from a giant fridge. Things can get seriously jammed after midnight.

Hallmackenreuther (Map p556; ☎ 517 970; Brüsseler Platz 9) This trendy Belgian Quarter hangout went 1960s retro-style long before the look became all the rage. Most patrons, though, weren't born until after that particular decade. Come here any time of day, breakfast to late-night cocktails.

Cleanicum (Map p556; ☎ 869 0638; Brüsseler Strasse 74-76; ⏰ 10am-1am) You can wash your smalls, surf the internet, check out the original art on the walls, and chill to mellow sounds with reasonably priced drinks (there are nightly specials) at this retro-styled lounge-meets-Laundromat.

Shepheard (Map p556; ☎ 331 0994; Rathenauplatz 5) Cocktail connoisseurs should descend into this elegant cellar bar, which was named Playboy's Bar of the Year in 2006. Named for a colonial hotel in Cairo, it offers 190 different cocktails, including 40 original creations concocted by bar chef Mirko himself.

Also worth a stop:

Rosebud (Map p556; ☎ 240 1455; Heinsbergstrasse 20) American-style cocktail bar for the fat-wallet crowd.

Flanagans (Map p552; ☎ 257 0674; Alter Markt 36) Irish pub. Enough said.

Sky Beach (Map p552; Galeria Kaufhof, Hohe Strasse 41-53; ☼ from 11am, weather permitting) Beach bar on the upper park deck of this department store with great views and chill ambience.

Entertainment

For an overview of Cologne's main nightlife quarters, see Drinking (opposite). Major listings magazines are *Monatsvorschau* (bilingual, mainstream), *Kölner Illustrierte* (mainstream), *Prinz* (trendy) or *StadtRevue* (alternative), available at newsagents and bookshops.

CLUBS & LIVE MUSIC

Gebäude 9 (☎ 814 637; Deutz-Mülheimer Strasse 127) This ex-factory is one of the most essential indie-rock concert venues in town. DJs take over at other times, and there's also an eclectic programme of edgy plays and films. Take tram 3 or 4 to KölnMesse/Osthallen. Check out the wacky toilets.

Stadtgarten (Map p556; ☎ 9529 9421; Venloer Strasse 40) Surrounded by a small park, this Belgian Quarter favourite hosts vibrant dance parties and live concerts in its cellar hall, but is also a great spot for drinks (summer beer garden) and tapas (€6 to €12).

Lauschgift (Map p556; ☎ 550 0060; Aachener Strasse 50) This three-part fun zone is tailor-made for those nights when you're not sure whether you simply want to chill or hit the dance floor. If you fancy a spin, expect different sounds nightly – electro to funk, soul to trip-hop.

Underground (☎ 542 326; Vogelsanger Strasse 200; ☼ closed Mon) This complex combines a pub and two concert rooms where indie and alternative rock bands hold forth several times a week. Otherwise it's party time with different music nightly (no cover). There's a beer garden in summer. To get here take U3 or U4 to Venloer Strasse/Gürtel.

Alter Wartesaal (Map p552; ☎ 912 8850; Johannisstrasse 11) In a former train station waiting hall, this is a stylish bar-disco-restaurant combo. Themed nights range from the erotic KitKat-Club to Depeche Mode parties, '80s nights and the legendary free Monday dance parties with go-go dancers.

Papa Joe's Em Streckstrump (Map p552; ☎ 257 7931; Buttermarkt 37) This hot spot for live jazz has

been packing 'em in nightly since 1976. Since concerts are always free, we don't mind the slightly higher drinks prices. Try the wicked herb liquor available only here.

Other recommendations:

Roonburg (Map p556; ☎ 240 3719; Roonstrasse 33; ☼ Tue & Thu-Sat) High-octane party den with cheap beers and student crowd.

Papa Joe's Klimperkasten (Map p552; ☎ 258 2132; Alter Markt 50) A piano player tickles the ivories nightly in this museum-like place with 1920s-style décor.

THEATRE & CLASSICAL MUSIC

Kölner Philharmonie (Map p552; ☎ 204 080; www.koelner -philharmonie.de; Bischofsgartenstrasse 1) This grand and modern space is the city's premier venue for classical music; it's below the Museum Ludwig. Buy tickets at the tourist office (p541).

Repertory theatre is based at the **Schauspielhaus** (Map p552; ☎ 2212 8400; www.buehnenkoeln .de; Offenbachplatz), in the same complex as the Opernhaus. The box office for both is in the Opernhaus foyer.

Shopping

Cologne is a fantastic place to shop, with lots of eccentric boutiques, designer stores and trendy secondhand shops, plus the usual selection of chain and department stores. You'll find plenty of the latter along Hohe Strasse, one of Germany's oldest pedestrianised shopping strips, and its side street, In der Höhle (Map p552). Schildergasse has smaller fashion and shoe shops and culminates in the Neumarkt (Map p552), where the Neumarkt-Galerie is easily recognised by the upturned ice-cream cone designed by Claes Oldenburg and Coosje van Brugge. The best streets for maxing out your credit card are Mittelstrasse and Pfeilstrasse (Map p556), lined with exclusive fashion, jewellery and home-accessory shops. For a more youthful, creative flair hit Ehrenstrasse (Map p556), which also has some secondhand boutiques.

A classic gift for mum is a bottle of eau de Cologne, the not terribly sophisticated but refreshing perfume created – and still being produced – in its namesake city. **4711 Perfumery & Gift Shop** (Map p552; cnr Glockengasse & Schwertnergasse) The most famous brand of eau de Cologne is called 4711, named after the number of this house where it was invented. The shop also has a carillon with characters from Prussian lore parading hourly from 9am to 9pm.

The shops in the Hauptbahnhof stay open until 10pm.

Getting There & Away

AIR

Cologne Bonn Airport (☎ 02203-404 001; www.airport -cgn.de) has direct flights to 130 cities, including New York City on Continental. Discount carriers flying here include Germanwings, Deutsche BA, Hapag-Lloyd Express and easyJet. See p754, for airline contact details. There's a **tourist office** (☺ 9am-8pm) on the arrival level of terminal two.

BUS

The central bus station (Busbahnhof) is northeast of the Hauptbahnhof, on Breslauer Platz. Eurolines has daily buses to Paris (one way/return from €37/66, eight hours) and Warsaw (from €55/76, 21 hours). Trips to Prague (from €47/85, 12 hours) are scheduled three times a week.

CAR & MOTORCYCLE

Cologne is encircled by the heavily trafficked Kölner Ring, with exits to the A1, A3, A4, A57, A555 and A559 leading in all directions.

If you'd like to hitch a ride, contact **Citynetz Mitfahrzentrale** (☎ 194 44; www.citynetz -mitfahrzentrale.de; Kiosk EGE 1, Krefelder Strasse 21).

TRAIN

Regional trains travel several times hourly to Bonn (€6.10, 25 minutes), Brühl (€3.10, 15 minutes), Düsseldorf (€9, 30 minutes) and Aachen (€12.50, one hour). Cologne is also a major main-line hub with direct ICE service to Berlin (€93, 4¼ hours), Frankfurt (€55, 1¼ hours) and Munich (€112, 4½ hours).

Getting Around

TO/FROM THE AIRPORT

The S13 train connects the airport and the Hauptbahnhof every 20 minutes (€2.20, 15 minutes). Taxis charge about €25.

BICYCLE

Rent-A-Bike (Map p552; ☎ 0171-629 8796; Marksmanngasse) hires out bikes for €2/10/20 per hour/day/three days and also does tours (see p555).

Radstation (Map p552; ☎ 139 7190; Breslauer Platz), at the Hauptbahnhof, has the same rates as Rent-A-Bike.

CAR & MOTORCYCLE

Driving around Cologne can be an absolute nightmare. Unless you're careful, you could easily end up in a tunnel or on a bridge going across the Rhine. Most streets in the centre of the city are restricted to residents, so often your only option is an expensive parking garage (from €1.25 an hour).

Avis (Map p552; ☎ 2723 4730; Clemensstrasse 29-31) and **Hertz** (Map p556; ☎ 515 084; Bismarckstrasse 19-21) are among the international car-rental agencies that have branches at the airport and in town.

GAY & LESBIAN COLOGNE

Next to Berlin, Cologne is Germany's gayest city with the rainbow flag flying especially proudly in the so-called 'Bermuda Triangle' around Rudolfplatz, which explodes into a nonstop fun zone at weekends. Another major romping ground is the Heumarkt area (especially Pipinstrasse), which draws more sedate folks and leather and fetish lovers. The **Gay & Lesbian Street Festival** in June basically serves as a warm-up for the **Christopher Street Party & Parade** (usually in July), which brings more than a million people to Cologne.

A good place to start plugging into the scene is the information and health centre **Checkpoint** (Map p552; ☎ 9257 6868; www.checkpoint-cologne.de; Pipinstrasse 7; ☺ 5-9pm Mon-Fri, 1-9pm Sat). The listings magazine **Rik** (www.rik-magazin.de) has good info and a database of hangouts, unfortunately in German only.

Places worth checking out include: **Blue Lounge** (Map p552; ☎ 271 7117; Mathiasstrasse 4-6; ☺ Wed-Sun), a smooth dance and cocktail bar for a mixed crowd; **Barflo** (Map p556; ☎ 257 3239; Friesenwall 24d), a perennially popular all-day café with great breakfasts and cakes; **Brennerei Weiss** (Map p556; ☎ 257 4638; Hahnenstrasse 22; mains €6.50-14), a no-nonsense restaurant serving delicious German and regional cuisine; **Gezeiten** (☎ 474 7703; Balthasarstrasse 1), which is favoured by lesbians and has a nice terrace and cabaret stage; and the men-only **Chains** (Map p552; ☎ 238 730; Stephanstrasse 4), the city's largest leather-and-fetish bar with House and techno on the turntable and an active darkroom.

PUBLIC TRANSPORT

Cologne's mix of buses, trams, and U-Bahn and S-Bahn trains is operated by the **Verkehrsverbund Rhein-Sieg** (VRS; ☎ 01803-504 030; www .vrsinfo.de) in cooperation with Bonn's system.

Short trips (up to four stops) cost €1.30, longer ones €2.20. Day passes are €6 for one person and €9 for up to five people travelling together. Buy your tickets from the orange ticket machines at stations and aboard trams; be sure to validate them.

TAXI

Taxis cost €2.20 at flag fall, plus €1.45 per kilometre (€1.55 between 10pm and 6am and at weekends); add another €0.50 if you order by phone (☎ 2882 or ☎ 194 10).

BRÜHL

☎ 02232 / pop 40,000

Brühl, halfway between Cologne and Bonn, wraps an astonishing number of riches into a pint-size package. The town languished in relative obscurity until the 18th century when archbishop-elector Clemens August (1723–61) – friend of Casanova and himself a lover of women, parties and palaces – made it his residence. His two made-to-impress rococo palaces, at opposite ends of the elegant Schlosspark, landed on Unesco's list of World Heritage Sites in 1984.

The larger and flashier of the two, **Schloss Augustusburg** (☎ 440 00; Schlossstrasse 6; tours adult/ student/family €4/3/9; 9am-noon & 1.30-5pm Tue-Fri, 10am-5pm Sat & Sun, closed Mon & Dec-Jan) is a little jewel box designed by François Cuvilliés. On guided tours you'll learn fascinating titbits about hygiene, dating and other aspects of daily life at court. The architectural highlight is a ceremonial staircase by Balthasar Neumann, a dizzying symphony in stucco, sculpture and faux marble.

Cuvilliés also dreamed up **Jagdschloss Falkenlust** (☎ 440 00; Schlossstrasse 6; adult/concession €3/2; 9am-noon & 1.30-5pm Tue-Fri, 10am-5pm Sat & Sun, closed Mon & Dec-Jan), a hunting lodge where Clemens August liked to indulge his fancy for falconry. Though small, it's almost as opulent as the main palace. A particular gem is the adjacent chapel, which is awash in shells, minerals and crystals.

Since autumn of 2005, the palaces have a worthy new neighbour in the **Max Ernst Museum** (☎ 579 3110; www.maxernstmuseum.com; Comesstrasse 42; adult/concession/family €5/3/10; 11am-6pm Tue-Sun),

where nine rooms trace all creative phases of the Brühl-born Dadaist and surrealist (1891–1976). We especially enjoyed examples of his artistic innovations such as frottage (floor-board rubbings) and the spooky collage novels, which are graphic works exploring the darkest crevices of the subconscious.

Brühl's other big drawcard is **Phantasialand** (☎ 362 00; Berggeiststrasse 31-41; www.phantasialand.de; adult/child €28/24.50; 9am-6pm Apr-Oct, last admission 4pm, extended hours possible in summer), one of Europe's earliest Disneyland-style amusement parks (since 1967). The park has seven themed areas – Chinatown, Old Berlin, Wild West, Mexico, Fantasy, Mystery and, new in 2006, Deep in Africa whose Black Mamba roller coaster will take your breath away. The others also have coasters along with gondolas, flight simulators, water rides and other thrills, plus song and dance shows. To be admitted as a child you have to be shorter than 145cm; if you're under 1m or it's your birthday, admission is free.

Brühl is regularly served by regional trains from Cologne (€3.10, 15 minutes) and Bonn (€4, 10 minutes). The Hauptbahnhof is opposite Schloss Augustusburg, with the compact town centre behind the palace. Shuttle buses to Phantasialand leave from outside the station. If you're driving, exit Brühl-Ost/ Wesseling off the A553 or Godorf/Brühl off the A555, then follow the signs.

BONN

☎ 0228 / pop 309,000

When this friendly, relaxed city on the Rhine became West Germany's 'temporary' capital in 1949 it surprised many, including its own residents. When in 1991 a reunited German government decided to move back to Berlin, it shocked many, *especially* its own residents. More than 15 years later, no-one need feel sorry for Bonn. Change brings opportunity, and rather than plunge into the dark depths of provincialism, the ex-capital has reinvented itself with creativity and vigour. Its cosmopolitan openness has attracted an international cast of businesses, students, scientists and even such world organisations as the UN.

For visitors, the birthplace of Ludwig van Beethoven has plenty in store, not the least the great composer's birth house, a string of top-rated museums, a lovely riverside setting and the nostalgic flair of the old government quarter. Bonn can be seen on an easy day trip from Cologne but also makes for an excellent jumping-off point to the Siebengebirge nature reserve and other attractions that can be found in the area.

Orientation

Cologne Bonn Airport is about 15km north of the city centre (see p567 for information on getting to/from the airport). The Altstadt extends north of the Hauptbahnhof with the Nordstadt just beyond, while the Museums-meile (Museum Mile) and Bundesviertel (former government district) are south along the Rhine; Poppelsdorf is also south of the station but away from the river.

Information

Bonn hospital (Uniklinikum Bonn; ☎ 2870; Sigmund-Freud-Strasse 25) Emergency-room hospital, 4km south of the Hauptbahnhof.

Bonn Regio WelcomeCard (per 24/48/72hr €9/14/19) Unlimited public transport, admission to 20 museums, plus discounts on tours, thermal baths and more. The group (three adults) or family (two adults, two kids) version is €18/28/38.

Bouvier (☎ 729 010; Am Hof 28) Bookshop.

Internet Several call shops near the Hauptbahnhof offer internet access.

Post office (Münsterplatz 17; ☺ 9am-8pm Mon-Fri, 9am-4pm Sat)

Reisebank (☎ 632 958; Hauptbahnhof; ☺ 9am-7pm Mon-Fri, 9am-3pm Sat)

Tourismus & Congress GmbH (www.bonn-region.de) Excellent pretrip planning source.

Tourist office (☎ 775 000; www.bonn.de; Windeckstrasse 1; ☺ 9am-6.30pm Mon-Fri, 9am-4pm Sat, 10am-2pm Sun)

Sights

ALTSTADT

A good place to start exploring Bonn's historic centre is on Münsterplatz, where the landmark **Münster Basilica** (☺ 7am-8pm) was built on the graves of the two martyred Roman soldiers who became the city's patron saints. It's been mostly Gothic since the 13th century, but the Romanesque style survives beautifully in the ageing cloister. Outside the church, in front of a buttercup-yellow Palais that's now the post office, stands the **Beethoven Monument** (1845), which was largely financed by Franz Liszt.

Beethoven (1770–1827) first saw the light of day in the rather modest **Beethoven Haus** (Beethoven House; ☎ 981 7525; Bonngasse 20; adult/ concession/family €4/3/10; ☺ 10am-6pm Mon-Sat, 11am-6pm Sun Apr-Oct, to 5pm Nov-Mar). It now houses a rather static array of letters, musical scores, instruments and paintings. The highlights – his last grand piano, the huge ear trumpets to combat his growing deafness and a famous portrait – are all on the 2nd floor. Tickets are also good for the **Digitales Beethoven-Haus** next door, where you can experience the composer's genius during a spacey, interactive 3D multimedia show or deepen your knowledge in the digital archive.

In the Altstadt's other main square, the triangular Markt, the baroque **Altes Rathaus** (old town hall) stands pretty in pink with silver and gold trim. Politicians from Charles de Gaulle to John F Kennedy have waved to the crowds from its double-sided staircase.

To the south is the palatial 1705 **Kurfürstliche Residenz** (Electoral Residence; Regina-Pacis-Weg), once the immodest home of the archbishop-electors of Cologne and part of Bonn's university since 1818. Its south side opens up to the expansive **Hofgarten** (Palace Garden), a popular gathering place for students. At its far end, the recently renovated **Akademisches Kunstmuseum** (Academic Art Museum; ☎ 737 738; Am Hofgarten 21; admission €1.50, student free; ☺ 10am-1pm Sun-Fri & 4-6pm Thu, closed Aug) presents plaster casts of antique sculptures in a former anatomy institute designed by Prussian master builder Karl Friedrich Schinkel.

Considerably more intriguing is the nearby **Arithmeum** (☎ 738 790; www.arithmeum.uni-bonn.de; Lennéstrasse 2; adult/concession €3/2; ☺ 11am-6pm Tue-Sun), which explores the symbiosis of science, technology and art. On view are hundreds of mechanical calculators and historic mathematics books but also an out-there exhibit on the aesthetics of microchips. Design your own or study their beauty through a polarisation microscope. Work your way down from the top floor of this minimalist glass-and-steel cube.

South of the Hauptbahnhof, the completely revamped **Rheinisches LandesMuseum** (Rhineland Regional Museum; ☎ 207 00; www.rlmb.lvr.de; Colmant-strasse 14-18; adult/student/family €5/3.50/10; ☺ 10am-6pm Tue & Thu-Sun, 10am-9pm Wed) now presents its rich collections in such themed exhibits as Epochs, Gods, and Power. Highlights include a 40,000-year-old Neanderthal skull and a rare blue Roman glass vessel from the 1st century AD. The museum restaurant, **DelikArt** (mains €11 to €17), enjoys a fine reputation.

BUNDESVIERTEL

About 1.5km south of the Altstadt along the B9, Bonn's former government quarter was, from 1949 to 1999, the nerve centre of West German political power. These days the Bundesviertel has reinvented itself as the home of the UN and other international and federal institutions (see boxed text, p564). The airy

and modern **Plenary Hall** where the Bundestag (German parliament) used to convene, now hosts international conferences. Nearby, the high-rise nicknamed **Langer Eugen** (Tall Eugen), where members of parliament kept their offices, is now a UN campus. Officially retaining their former purposes are the stately **Villa Hammerschmidt**, still a secondary official

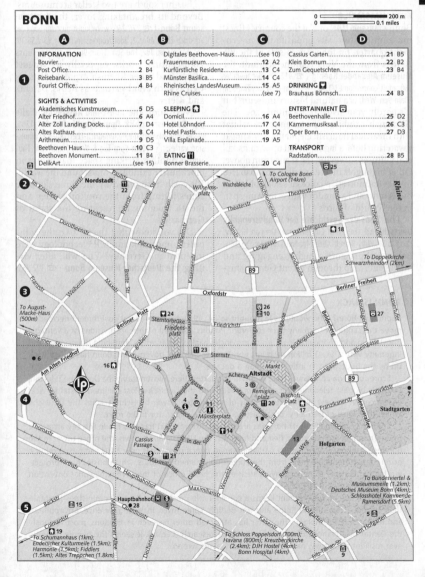

BONN		
INFORMATION	Digitales Beethoven-Haus........(see 10)	Cassius Garten.............................21 B5
Bouvier.................................1 C4	Frauenmuseum.......................12 A2	Klein Bonnum..........................22 B2
Post Office............................2 B4	Kurfürstliche Residenz............13 C4	Zum Gequetschten..................23 B4
Reisebank.............................3 B5	Münster Basilica......................14 C4	
Tourist Office........................4 B4	Rheinisches LandesMuseum....15 A5	**DRINKING**
	Rhine Cruises.........................(see 7)	Brauhaus Bönnsch....................24 B3
SIGHTS & ACTIVITIES		
Akademisches Kunstmuseum....5 D5	**SLEEPING**	**ENTERTAINMENT**
Alter Friedhof........................6 A4	Domicil....................................16 A4	Beethovenhalle........................25 D2
Alter Zoll Landing Docks.........7 D4	Hotel Löhndorf.......................17 C4	Kammermusiksaal....................26 C3
Altes Rathaus.........................8 C4	Hotel Pastis............................18 D2	Oper Bonn...............................27 D3
Arithmeum............................9 D5	Villa Esplanade.......................19 A5	
Beethoven Haus....................10 C3		**TRANSPORT**
Beethoven Monument............11 B4	**EATING**	Radstation...............................28 B5
DelikArt...............................(see 15)	Bonner Brasserie.....................20 C4	

residence of the federal president, and the neoclassical **Palais Schaumburg**, now serving as the chancellor's Bonn office.

An easy way to explore the district is by following the new **Weg der Demokratie** (Path of Democracy), a self-guided walking tour taking in 18 key historic sites. Explanatory panelling in English is provided.

MUSEUMSMEILE

Bonn's **Museum Mile**, one of the country's finest museum clusters, sits opposite the government quarter, on the western side of the B9. Across from the Villa Hammerschmidt, the **Museum Alexander Koenig** (☎ 912 20; Adenauerallee 160; adult/concession €3/1.50; ⊗ 10am-6pm Tue, Thu-Sun, 10am-9pm Wed) is a natural history museum but it's hardly your usual dead-animal zoo. The 'Savannah' exhibit re-creates an entire habitat with theatrical flourish: elephants drinking at a watering hole, a jaguar holed up with its kill and vultures surveying the scene from above. Other highlights include a talking baobab tree in the 'Rainforest', a colossal sea elephant in the 'Arctic' and a condor with a 3m wingspan in the 'World of Birds'.

The **Haus der Geschichte der Bundesrepublik Deutschland** (Forum of Contemporary German History; ☎ 916 50; Willy-Brandt-Allee 14; admission free; ⊗ 9am-7pm Tue-Sun) presents a highly engaging and intelligent romp through recent German his-

tory, starting when the final bullet was fired in WWII. Walk through the fuselage of a Berlin Airlift '*Rosinenbomber*', watch classic clips in a 1950s movie theatre, examine Erich Honecker's arrest warrant, stand in front of a piece of the Berlin Wall or see John F Kennedy's famous '*Ich bin ein Berliner*' speech.

Further south are two stellar art museums. Beyond its breathtaking foyer, the **Kunstmuseum Bonn** (☎ 776 260; www.kunstmuseum-bonn.de; Friedrich-Ebert-Allee 2; adult/concession/family €5/2.50/10; ⊗ 11am-6pm Tue, Thu-Sun, 10am-9pm Wed) presents 20th-century works, especially by August Macke and other Rhenish expressionists, as well as such avant-gardists as Beuys, Baselitz and Kiefer.

Next door, the **Kunst-und Ausstellungshalle der Bundesrepublik Deutschland** (☎ 917 1200; www.bundeskunsthalle.de; Friedrich-Ebert-Allee 4; admission varies; ⊗ 10am-9pm Tue & Wed, 10am-7pm Thu-Sun) is another striking space that brings in blockbuster exhibits from around the world. It's easily recognised by the three sky-blue cones jutting from the rooftop garden and the 16 columns representing the states of Germany.

Did you know that the air bag, the computer tomograph and MP3 technology were invented in Germany? You will, after visiting the **Deutsches Museum Bonn** (☎ 302 255;

BONN IS BACK

Boomtown Bonn? Who would have thought so in 1991 when the federal government decided to move the capital of Germany back to Berlin? Pundits conjured nightmarish visions of a veritable ghost town and an inevitable return to provincial backwater. Hardly. Combining drive, vision and ingenuity with a €1.43 billion cash infusion from the federal government, Bonn has pulled itself up by the bootstraps in little more than a decade.

Scores of mega-companies have set up headquarters here, most notably the Deutsche Telekom, Europe's biggest telecommunications provider, and the Deutsche Post (German postal service) ensconced in its new skyline-dominating glass-and-steel tower by Helmut Jahn. The Deutsche Welle, the 'voice of Germany' broadcasting company, is just down the road.

Bonn may be small but its horizons are big, an attitude that has also made the city attractive to international organisations, first and foremost the UN. The *Bundeshaus*, the office tower in the Bundesviertel once occupied by parliamentarian pencil pushers, is now a UN campus. Around a dozen departments are here, from the endearingly named Eurobats, which busies itself protecting bats in Europe, to major players such as the head office of the UN Framework Convention on Climate Change (UNFCCC).

Even the federal government keeps a considerable presence in Bonn. Six ministries maintain their headquarters on the Rhine and not Berlin's Spree River, including Defence, Environment and Research & Technology. The latter has attracted other research institutions, most famously the Center of Advanced European Studies and Research (Caesar). It seems the people of Bonn, ever resilient and savvy, have proved the naysayers wrong.

www.deutsches-museum-bonn.de; Ahrstrasse 45; adult/child/family €4/2.50/10; ☺ 10am-6pm Tue-Sun), about 2km further south. This subsidiary of the Munich mother-ship (p304) highlights German technology since WWII with plenty of buttons to push and knobs to pull. Look for the Transrapid train outside the entrance.

NORDSTADT

Northwest of the Altstadt, this former working-class quarter with its cobweb of narrow streets is growing pockets of casual hipness. Cafés, restaurants, boutiques and galleries are sprouting especially along Breite Strasse and its side streets. It's prettiest in spring when the cherry trees are in bloom.

The expressionist painter August Macke (1887–1914) lived in this neighbourhood during the three years before his untimely death on the battlefields of WWI in 1914. At his neoclassical home, now the **August-Macke-Haus** (August Macke House; ☎ 655 531; www.august-macke-haus.de; Bornheimer Strasse 96; adult/concession €4/3; ☺ 2.30-6pm Tue-Fri, 11am-5pm Sat & Sun), you can see his re-created studio and some originals; the finest works, though, are at the Kunstmuseum Bonn (opposite).

Nordstadt is also home of the **Frauenmuseum** (Women's Museum; ☎ 691 344; www.frauenmuseum.de; Im Krausfeld 10; adult/concession €4.50/3; ☺ 2-6pm Tue-Sat, 11am-6pm Sun), which supports and showcases the art of women through exhibits, lectures, readings and performances.

POPPELSDORF & AROUND

South of the Altstadt, elegant and leafy Poppelsdorf is anchored by **Schloss Poppelsdorf**, another electoral palace now used by the university. Students and neighbourhood folk populate the bars and restaurants along Clemens-August-Strasse, which runs south of the palace towards the hillside **Kreuzbergkirche** (Stationsweg 21; ☺ 9am-5pm). This rococo gem is lavishly decorated with gilded faux marble, frescoes and a Balthasar Neumann–designed version of the Holy Steps.

Fans of Robert Schumann (1810–56) might enjoy the small memorial exhibit in the **Schumannhaus** (Schumann House; ☎ 773 656; Sebastianstrasse 182; admission free; ☺ 11am-1.30pm & 3-6pm Mon & Wed-Fri). It's in the former sanatorium he checked into following a suicide attempt in 1854. He and his wife Clara are buried in **Alter Friedhof** (Old Cemetery) on Bornheimer Strasse in the Nordstadt.

DOPPELKIRCHE SCHWARZRHEINDORF

Across the river in the suburb of Schwarzrheindorf, the 12th-century **Doppelkirche Schwarzrheindorf** (☎ 461 609; Dixstrasse 41; ☺ 9am-6.30pm Tue-Sat, noon-6.30pm Sun; upper church Sat & Sun only) is a magnificent 'double church' where the nobility sat on the upper level and the parishioners on the lower. The beautiful Romanesque architecture is impressive, as is the restored Old Testament fresco cycle in the lower church. Take bus 550 and 640 from the Hauptbahnhof to Schwarzrheindorf-Kirche.

Tours

The tourist office runs two English-language tours. The **Big City Tour** (adult/concession €14/7; ☺ 2pm Wed-Sun mid-Apr–Oct, daily Jul & Aug, Sat only Nov–mid-Dec & Jan–mid-Apr) is a combined 2½-hour bus-walking tour. The **Altstadt Walking Tour** (adult/concession €7/4; ☺ 11am Sat mid-Apr–May, 11am & 3pm Sat Jun-Oct) takes 1½ hours.

Boats heading upriver to Königswinter and beyond leave from the Alter Zoll landing docks at the Brassertufer between April and October. **Bonner Personen Schiffahrt** (☎ 0228-636 363) and **KD** (☎ 0221-208 8318) are the main operators.

Sleeping

For phone bookings, call ☎ 0180-500 3365 or ☎ 775 000; for online bookings go to www.bonn-region.de. Bargains abound in summer and at weekends.

DJH hostel (☎ 289 970; bonn@jugendherberge.de; Haager Weg 42; dm/s/d €22/27/30; P ✗) About 4km south of the city centre (bus 621).

Hotel Pastis (☎ 969 4270; Hatschiergasse 8; s/d €55/85) This little hotel-restaurant combo is so fantastically French, you'll feel like the Eiffel Tower is just around the corner. After dining on unfussy gourmet cuisine – paired with great wines, *bien sûr* – you'll sleep like a baby in snug, cosy rooms.

Schlosshotel Kommende Ramersdorf (☎ 440 734; www.schlosshotel-kommende-ramersdorf.de; Oberkasseler Strasse 10; s €55-80, d €85-105; P) Despite the unfortunate autobahn-adjacent setting, you'll feel like a prince when approaching this towered and turreted fairy-tale palace from 1220. It's considerably less grand on the inside, though, so you can leave your tux at home.

Hotel Löhndorf (☎ 634 726; www.hotel-loehndorf-bonn.de; Stockenstrasse 6; s/d €70/80; ✗ ▢) This 13-room (all nonsmoking) property puts you close to the Hofgarten and the Rhine, but is surprisingly quiet despite the central location. The cheery breakfast room with its new flower-festooned winter garden is a good place to greet the day.

Altes Treppchen (☎ 625 004; www.treppchen.de; Endenicher Strasse 308; s/d €70/100; P) In the suburb of Endenich, this rustic inn is a true gem that's been in the same family for 500 years. The nine rooms don't spoil you with space but all are fresh, bright and recently renovated. The restaurant, all warm and snug with its woodsy booths, is great for dinner but, alas, only open weekdays.

Villa Esplanade (☎ 983 800; www.hotel-villa -esplanade.de; Colmantstrasse 47; s/d/tr €70/100/120; P ✗) Inside a stately late-19th-century building, this charming hotel has 17 bright rooms with soft, feminine décor: think wicker chairs, pink bedspreads and lacy curtains. Days start with a heaping breakfast buffet served in a lovely room with ornate stucco ceilings.

Domicil (☎ 729 090; www.domicil-bonn.bestwestern .de; Thomas-Mann-Strasse 24/26; s/d €133/160; P ✗) This classy hotel sprawls over several buildings grouped around a central courtyard. For something a little special, book the larger deluxe rooms, some of which have romantic stucco ceilings or a courtyard-facing terrace. The Jacuzzi and sauna are good unwinding options after a day of turf-pounding.

Eating & Drinking

You'll find some traditional Rhenish restaurants in the Altstadt and plenty of cafés and international restaurants in the Nordstadt, Poppelsdorf and along Frongasse in Endenich, the so-called Endenicher Kulturmeile (literally 'Endenich Cultural Mile'). Endenich is about 1.5km west of the Altstadt; take bus 634 from Hauptbahnhof to Frongasse.

Harmonie (☎ 614 042; Frongasse 28-30; mains €4-12; ☽ 5pm-1am Mon-Sat, 10.30am-1am Sun) This historic dance hall is a beloved pub and cultural venue in the heart of the Endenicher Kulturmeile. A low-key, all-ages crowd feasts on delicious German and Mediterranean dishes inside or in the idyllic beer garden.

Brauhaus Bönnsch (☎ 650 610; Sterntorbrücke 4; mains €4-12; ☽ 11am-1am) The unfiltered ale is a must at this congenial brew-pub adorned with photographs of famous politicians: Willy Brandt to, yes, Arnold Schwarzenegger. The menu is full of hearty snacks, but the *Flammekuche* (a pizzalike French dish) is a speciality.

Havana (☎ 721 8884; Clemens-August-Strasse 1; mains €6-12; ☽ 10am-1am) This friendly contender in Poppelsdorf always hums with activity. The cooking may not indulge in flights of fancy, but the cocktails are strong and the chicken dishes, pizzas and pastas fill the tummy nicely.

Klein Bonnum (☎ 638 104; Paulstrasse 5; mains €7-14; ☽ 6pm-midnight) Klein Bonnum was a Nordstadt institution long before the quarter became up-and-coming. It's sort of a grown-up student pub where you can stick to the basics – salads, pizzas, nachos – or go fancy with such dishes as black linguine with salmon and tiger shrimp.

Bonner Brasserie (☎ 655 559; Remigiusplatz 5; mains €8-15; ☽ 9am-1am) This bustling place manages to be all things to all people, from the breakfast crowd to business lunchers, from cake-craving shoppers to late-night cocktail swillers. In summer, tables spill out onto the square.

Zum Gequetschten (☎ 638 104; Sternstrasse 78; mains €8-15; ☽ noon-midnight) This traditional restaurant-pub is festooned with eye-catching blue tiles and is one of the oldest inns in town. The menu is back-to-basics German, but it's all delicious and portions are huge.

Other recommendations:

Fiddlers (☎ 614 161; Frongasse 9; dishes €4-16; ☽ 4pm-1am) Near Harmonie, Bonn's best Irish pub is famous for its fish and chips.

Cassius Garten (☎ 652 429; Maximilianstrasse 28, Cassius-Passage; dishes per 100g €1.50; ☽ 11am-8pm Mon-Fri, 11am-6pm Sat) Self-service vegetarian buffet.

Entertainment

De Schnüss and *BonnJour* are the main listings magazines, available at newsagents. The central ticket hotline is ☎ 910 4161.

Bonn's entertainment scene is especially strong in the field of classical music. A calendar highlight is the Beethovenfest in late September with several dozen concerts held in venues around town. These include the intimate **Kammermusiksaal** (☎ 981 7515; Bonngasse 24-26) next to the Beethoven Haus; the **Beethovenhalle** (☎ 722 20; Wachsbleiche 17), Bonn's premier concert hall; and the **Oper Bonn** (Bonn Opera; ☎ 778 000; Am Boeselagerhof 1), which also hosts theatre, dance and opera.

Getting There & Away

Bonn shares its **Cologne Bonn Airport** (☎ 02203-404 001; www.airport-cgn.de) with Cologne and offers connections within Germany, Europe and beyond as well as direct flights from New York on Continental.

Regional trains to Cologne (€6, 30 minutes) leave several times hourly, and there are also frequent trains to the Ruhrgebiet cities and Koblenz (€9.10, 45 minutes).

Bonn is at the crossroads of the A59, A555 and A565. The B9 highway cuts north–south through the city.

Getting Around

Airport-Bus 670 makes the trip from the airport into town every 20 or 30 minutes between 5.30am and 12.30am (€5.45, 35 minutes). A taxi to/from the airport costs from €35 to €40.

Buses, trams and the U-Bahn make up the public transport system, which is operated by the **VRS** (☎ 01803-504 030). It extends as far as Cologne and is divided into zones. All you need to travel within Bonn is a City Ticket for €2.10 per trip or €5.70 for the 24-hour pass. All tickets must be validated when boarding.

For a taxi, ring ☎ 555 555. Bikes may be hired at **Radstation** (☎ 981 4636; Quantiusstrasse 26; per day €7; ☺ 6am-10.30pm Mon-Fri, 7am-10.30pm Sat, 8am-10.30pm Sun), on the south side of the Hauptbahnhof via the subterranean passageway.

AROUND BONN

Steeped in legend, the densely forested hills of the **Siebengebirge** (Seven Mountains) rise above the right bank of the Rhine, just a few kilometres south of Bonn. Closer inspection actually reveals about 40 peaks, but only the seven most prominent give the region its name.

At 461m, the Ölberg may be the highest, but the 321m **Drachenfels** is the most heavily visited of these 'mountains'. Since 1883, some 32 million peak-baggers have reached the top aboard the **Drachenfelsbahn** (☎ 02223-920 90; Drachenfelsstrasse 53; uphill/downhill/both directions €6.50/6.50/8; ☺ 9am-7pm May-Sep, shorter hours Oct-Apr), a nostalgic cogwheel train chugging along for 1.5km. Prices are a bit steep, but so is the paved path should you prefer to walk.

The walking route leads past restaurants and various attractions, including the 1913 **Nibelungenhalle** (☎ 02223-241 50; adult/child €4/3; ☺ 10am-6pm daily mid-Mar–mid-Nov, Sat & Sun mid-Nov–mid-Mar), a templelike shrine to the composer Richard Wagner decorated with scenes from his opera cycle *Ring of the Nibelungen*. Tickets include access to the **Drachenhöhle**, a

cave inhabited by a 13m-long stone dragon, and a small **reptile zoo**.

Further uphill loom the fairy-tale turrets of the neo-Gothic **Schloss Drachenburg** (☎ 02223-901 970; adult/concession €2.50/1; ☺ 11am-6pm Tue-Sun Apr-Oct), which is being restored and will remain mostly under wraps for the foreseeable future. Eventually, it will house a museum on the *Gründerzeit* period (late 19th century); the current exhibit details the restoration process. Views are pretty nice from here but even better from the medieval **Burg Drachenfels** at the top of the mountain, ruined since feuding troops came through during the Thirty Years' War (1618–48).

The Drachenfels rises above the town of Königswinter, which is served by the U66 from Bonn Hauptbahnhof. A more atmospheric approach is by boat, which leave from the Brassertufer in Bonn between April and October. **Bonner Personen Schiffahrt** (☎ 0228-636 363; one-way/return €6/8) and **KD** (☎ 0221-208 8318; one-way/return €6.70/8.80) are the main operators.

While in Königswinter, you might also want to check out **SeaLife** (☎ 02223-297 297; Rheinallee 8; adult/child/concession €12/9/11; ☺ 10am-6pm), a brand-new walk-through aquarium with a legend and fairy-tale theme.

AACHEN

☎ 0241 / pop 248,000

The Romans nursed their war wounds and stiff joints in the steaming waters of Aachen's mineral springs, but it was Charlemagne who put the city firmly on the European map. The emperor too enjoyed a dip now and then, but it was more for strategic reasons why, in 794, he made Aachen the geographical and political capital of his vast Frankish Empire. The thermal waters remain a prime attraction to this day, but Aachen's main lure really is the stunning Dom, which incorporates Charlemagne's original palace chapel. In 1978, it became Germany's first monument to be included on Unesco's list of World Heritage Sites.

Aachen shares borders with the Netherlands and Belgium, giving it a distinctly international and lively vibe that's further enhanced by a large student population.

Orientation

Aachen's centre is contained within two ring roads and is best explored on foot. The inner ring road encloses the Altstadt proper and is called Grabenring because it's composed of segments all ending in *graben* (meaning 'moat'). The outer ring is known as Alleenring, even though only some of its segments end in *allee* (meaning 'avenue'). The Hauptbahnhof is just south of this outer ring, on Römerstrasse. To get to the Altstadt and the tourist office, head north from the Hauptbahnhof for about 10 to 15 minutes. The main bus station, called Bushof, is in the centre at the corner of Kurhausstrasse and Peterstrasse.

Information

Aachen University hospital (Universitätsklinikum Aachen; ☎ 800; Pauwelsstrasse 30) Major hospital, 2km northwest of the city centre.

Mayersche Buchhandlung (☎ 477 199; Buchkremerstrasse 1-7) Books galore. Also at Pontstrasse 131.

Post office (☎ 01802-3333; Kapuzinerkarree, Kapuzinergraben 19) Inside a shopping mall.

Reisebank (☎ 912 6872; Lagerhausstrasse 9; ⌚ 9.45am-5.45pm Mon-Fri)

Tourist office (☎ 180 2960/1; www.aachen-tourist .de; Elisenbrunnen, Friedrich-Wilhelm-Platz; ⌚ 9am-6pm Mon-Fri, 9am-2pm Sat year-round, 10am-2pm Sun Easter-Dec)

Web (☎ 997 9210; Kleinmarschierstrasse 74-76; per hr €3; ⌚ 11am-11pm Mon-Thu, 11am-3am Fri & Sat, noon-10pm Sun) Internet access.

Sights

The tourist office runs **English-language tours** (⌚ tours 11am Sat Apr-Oct) that cost €4.

DOM

The oldest and most precious section of the **Dom** (☎ 477 090; www.aachendom.de; Münsterplatz; ⌚ 7am-6pm Jan-Mar, 7am-7pm Apr-Dec) is Charlemagne's **Pfalzkapelle** (palace chapel), an exquisite example of Carolingian architecture. Completed in 800, the year of the emperor's coronation, it's an octagonal dome encircled by a 16-sided, two-storey ambulatory supported by antique pillars from Italy. Suspended from the 31m-high dome hangs a colossal brass **chandelier**, donated by Emperor Friedrich Barbarossa during whose reign Charlemagne was canonised in 1165.

Pilgrims have poured into town ever since, drawn as much by the cult surrounding Charlemagne as by the prized relics – said to include Christ's loincloth – he had brought to Aachen. These are still displayed every seven years; the next time in 2007. To accommodate the flood of the faithful, a Gothic

choir was fused to the chapel in 1414 and filled with priceless treasure. Highlights include the **pala d'oro**, a gold-plated altar-front depicting Christ's Passion, and the jewel-encrusted gilded copper **pulpit**, both fashioned in the 11th century. At the far end is the **shrine of Charlemagne**, a golden extravaganza that has held the emperor's remains since 1215. In 1239 it was joined by the equally fanciful **shrine of St Mary**, which shelters the cathedral's four premium relics.

Unless you join a German-language tour (€2.50, 45 minutes), you'll only catch a glimpse of Charlemagne's white marble **imperial throne** in the upstairs gallery. Reached via six steps – just like King Solomon's throne – it served as the coronation throne of 30 German kings between 936 and 1531.

DOMSCHATZKAMMER

If you were awed by the Dom, don't miss the **cathedral treasury** (☎ 4770 9127; Klostergasse; adult/concession €4/3; ⌚ 10am-1pm Mon, 10am-5pm Tue-Sun Jan-Mar, 10am-1pm Mon, 10am-6pm Tue, Wed, Fri-Sun, 10am-10pm Thu Apr-Dec), a veritable mother lode of gold, silver and jewels. Besides numerous reliquary shrines, focus your attention on the **Lotharkreuz**, a 10th-century processional cross, and the **marble sarcophagus** that held Charlemagne's bones until his canonisation; the relief shows the rape of Persephone.

RATHAUS

Aachen's **Rathaus** (☎ 432 7310; Markt; adult/concession €2/1; ⌚ 10am-1pm & 2-5pm) is an imposing Gothic edifice festooned with 50 life-size statues of German rulers, including 31 kings crowned in town. It was built in the 14th century atop the foundations of Charlemagne's palace of which only the eastern tower, the **Granusturm**, survives. Inside, check out the **Kaisersaal** with its epic 19th-century **frescoes** by Alfred Rethel depicting scenes from the emperor's life, and the replicas of the **imperial insignia**: a crown, orb and sword (the originals are in Vienna).

MUSEUMS

Of Aachen's two art museums, the **Suermondt Ludwig Museum** (☎ 479 800; www.suermondt-ludwig -museum.de; Wilhelmstrasse 18; adult/concession €3/1.50; ⌚ noon-6pm Tue & Thu-Sun, noon-9pm Wed) surveys art from the Middle Ages to modern times. Highlights include portraits by Lucas Cranach and Rubens, and sculptures from the late

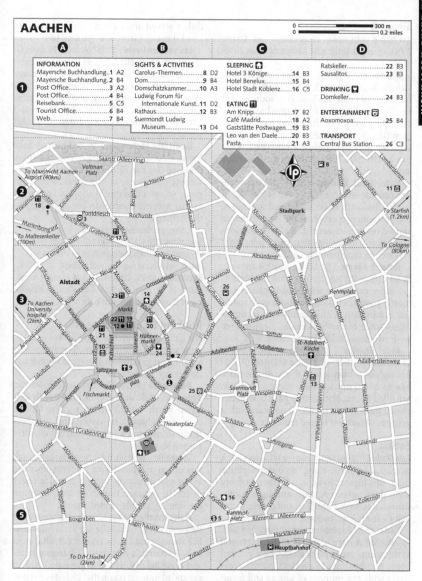

AACHEN

0 — 300 m
0 — 0.2 miles

INFORMATION
Mayersche Buchhandlung..1 A2
Mayersche Buchhandlung.2 B4
Post Office.....................3 A2
Post Office.....................4 B4
Reisebank.......................5 C5
Tourist Office.................6 B4
Web.............................7 B4

SIGHTS & ACTIVITIES
Carolus-Thermen............8 D2
Dom.............................9 B4
Domschatzkammer......10 A3
Ludwig Forum für
   Internationale Kunst..11 D2
Rathaus.......................12 B3
Suermondt Ludwig
   Museum...................13 D4

SLEEPING
Hotel 3 Könige..............14 B3
Hotel Benelux...............15 B4
Hotel Stadt Koblenz.......16 C5

EATING
Am Knipp.....................17 B2
Café Madrid..................18 A2
Gaststätte Postwagen....19 B3
Leo van den Daele........20 B3
Pasta...........................21 A3

Ratskeller......................22 B3
Sausalitos.....................23 B3

DRINKING
Domkeller.....................24 B3

ENTERTAINMENT
Aoxomoxoa..................25 B4

TRANSPORT
Central Bus Station.......26 C3

Middle Ages. In a former umbrella factory, the **Ludwig Forum für Internationale Kunst** (Ludwig Forum for International Art; ☎ 180 7104; www.ludwigforum .de; Jülicherstrasse 97-109; adult/concession €5/2.50; ☼ noon-6pm Tue-Sun) is a treasure trove of modern and contemporary art. Exhibits draw from a respectable collection that includes works by Andy Warhol and Jörg Immendorff.

CAROLUS-THERMEN

Oriental pools, honey rubs, deep-tissue massages and soothing saunas are just some of the relaxation zones at the **Carolus-Thermen** (Thermal Baths; ☎ 182 740; www.carolus-thermen.de; Passstrasse 79, Stadtgarten; admission with/without sauna from €19/9.50; ☼ 9am-11pm), a snazzy bathing complex on the edge of the city park.

Sleeping

To make your room reservation call ☎ 180 2950, or do it online at **aachen.de** (www.aachen -tourist.de).

DJH hostel (☎ 711 010; www.jgh-aachen.de; Maria-Theresia-Allee 260; dm/s/d €21.90/35.40/54; **P** ✕) This modernised hostel is about 2km southwest of the Hauptbahnhof in a park overlooking the city. Only a third of the rooms have private facilities, but there are special rooms for families and the mobility-impaired. Take bus 2 (direction Preuswald) to the Ronheide stop.

Hotel Stadt Koblenz (☎ 474 580; www.hotel -ambahnhof.de; Leydelstrasse 2; s/d from €47/67; ✕) If you're fine with basic décor and amenities, this 16-room property near the Hauptbahnhof should be an adequate fit. Budget-conscious families will appreciate that kids under eight stay free in their parents' room.

Hotel 3 Könige (☎ 483 93; www.h3k-aachen.de; Büchel 5; s/d/ste €80/110/125; ✕) With its doesn't-get-more-central location and 10 cheery and mostly good-sized Mediterranean-style rooms (all nonsmoking), this family-run favourite offers some of the best value in town. Free wi-fi sweetens the deal even more.

Hotel Benelux (☎ 400 030; www.hotel-benelux .de; Franzstrasse 21-23; s €88-103, d €103-148; **P** ✕) Though on a busy street, this well-run place has 33 quiet, uncluttered rooms and classy, art-filled floors. The rooftop garden with enclosed gazebo is a bonus. Days start with a generous breakfast served tableside.

Eating

Café Madrid (☎ 160 5201; Pontstrasse 141; dishes €2-9) A perennial favourite along this buzzy nightlife drag, this hipster joint in a former clothing shop does tapas, cocktails and light meals. Breakfast is served until late and cocktails cost just €4 from 5pm to 8pm.

Pasta (☎ 28891; Jakobstrasse 1; mains €5-10; ⊙ 9.30am-7pm Mon-Sat) A haze of good smells greets you at this teensy fresh-pasta shop where you can enjoy the handmade product paired creatively with any number of sauces and farm-fresh ingredients. Avoid the lunch-hour rush, however.

Am Knipp (☎ 331 68; Bergdriesch 3; mains €6-15; ⊙ 5pm-midnight Wed-Mon) Hungry eaters have stopped by since 1698, making this Aachen's oldest restaurant. You too will have a fine time sending your cholesterol levels through the roof with the first-rate traditional German

dishes served amid a flea market's worth of knick-knacks. Great beer garden, too.

Leo van den Daele (☎ 357 24; Büchel 18; dishes €7-11; ⊙ 9am-6.30pm Mon-Sat, 11am-6.30pm Sun) Even if you don't feel like trying its divine cakes or no-nonsense German dishes, have a look inside this dark and cosy nook-and-cranny café. Leather-covered walls, tiled stoves and antique furniture create a quintessential old-world atmosphere.

Gaststätte Postwagen (☎ 350 01; Krämerstrasse 2; mains €7.50-18; ⊙ noon-midnight) You can enjoy the same German dishes – schnitzel, sausages, veal etc – in plenty of other restaurants, but rarely will you find one as snug and convivial as this historic double-decker right next to the Rathaus.

Other recommendations:

Sausalitos (☎ 401 9437; Markt 45-47; mains €6-13; ⊙ noon-1am) Lively cantina with quasi-Mexican fare, serious cocktails and nice courtyard seating.

Ratskeller (☎ 350 01; Markt 40; 3-/4-/5-course menu €32/40/48; ⊙ noon-3pm & 6-9.30pm Mon-Sat) Michelin-starred silver-service restaurant in the historic town hall.

Drinking & Entertainment

For listings pick up the free *Klenkes* in cafés, pubs and the tourist office. The main bar-hopping drag is student-flavoured Pontstrasse (locals say 'Ponte').

Aoxomoxoa (☎ 226 22; Reihstrasse 15; ⊙ Mon-Sat) This laid-back dance club hums with different music nightly (from rock to Gothic to metal), charges no cover, and numbers cheap drinks and a friendly, mixed clientele among its assets.

Domkeller (☎ 342 65; Hof 1) Near the cathedral, this casual pub has drawn students since the 1950s with its woodsy ambience and fair beer prices. In summer, the action spills out onto the sloping, cobble-stoned square.

Malteserkeller (☎ 257 74; www.malteserkeller.de; Malteserstrasse 14; ⊙ usually Tue-Sat) Elvin Jones and Bill Ramsey used to be regulars at what used to be a venerable jazz venue. Changing tastes and financial realities have translated into an expanded musical menu that includes electro-funk, House, Nu Skool and punk.

Starfish (☎ 938 900; www.starfish-aachen.de; Liebigstrasse 17-19; ⊙ Fri & Sat) A cornerstone of Aachen's dance-club scene, Starfish keeps things interesting with four different dance floors playing House and charts, rock and pop, soul, and dance floor. It's northeast of the city centre.

Shopping

Aachen is known for its *Printen,* a crunchy spiced cookie similar to gingerbread. Traditionally log-shaped, Aachen bakeries now churn it out in various shapes, from the Easter Bunny to Santa Claus. A good spot to buy them is Leo van den Daele café (opposite).

Getting There & Away

The tiny **Maastricht Aachen Airport** (MAA; ☎ 0031-43-358 9898 in Holland; www.maa.nl), about 40km northwest of the city, is served once daily by easyJet from Berlin. Flights are met by the Airport Shuttle (per trip €10) with service to the centre.

Regional trains to Cologne (€12.50, one hour) run several times hourly, with some proceeding to Dortmund and other Ruhrgebiet cities. Trips to most cities south of Aachen require a change in Cologne.

For drivers, Aachen is easily reached via the A4 (east–west) from Cologne and the A44 (north–south) from Düsseldorf. The B57, B258 and B264 also meet here.

Getting Around

Bus tickets for travel within the area bounded by Alleenring cost a flat €1.45. All of Aachen and the adjoining Dutch communities of Vaals and Kelmis can be covered with a Zone 1 ticket for €2 (day pass €5.50). Drivers sell tickets.

For a taxi, call ☎ 344 41.

EIFEL NATIONAL PARK

Established in 2004, the **Eifel National Park** (☎ 02444-95100; www.nationalpark-eifel.de), some 45km southeast of Aachen near the border with Belgium, is North Rhine-Westphalia's first national park. It protects about 100 sq km of majestic beech forest, rivers and lakes along with plenty of plant- and wildlife, including wild cats, beavers, kingfishers, bats and owls. In spring, a sea of wild narcissus floods the valleys.

It's hard to imagine now that, until recently, Belgian troops used much of the area for military exercises. Also here is **Vogelsang** (☎ 02444-915 790; www.vogelsang-ip.de, www.serviceagentur -vogelsang.de; admission free; ☾ 10am-dusk), a vast complex built by the Nazis as a party leadership training centre. German-speakers should join a €3 **guided tour** (☾ 2pm) to learn more about the place, its history and architecture.

There are **visitors centres** (☾ 10am-5pm) in Rurberg, Gemünd and Heimbach.

Getting to the park without your own wheels is complicated. At weekends from Easter to October, bus 63 travels to Vogelsang from Aachen's central bus station (Map p569). Otherwise you can reach Heimbach on the park's northern perimeter by train via Düren. Call ☎ 0180-504 030 for specifics.

THE RUHRGEBIET

Densely populated and with a legacy as Europe's largest industrial and mining region, the Ruhrgebiet doesn't show up in glossy brochures promoting German *Gemütlichkeit* (a convivial, cosy ambience). But to travellers with an open mind, a sense of adventure and a desire to get off the beaten track, it offers a treasure trove of surprises and unique experiences: a former gas tank reborn as a cutting-edge exhibit space; free-climbing around a blast furnace; a turbine house turned trendy restaurant; dancing in a boiler room; and collieries designed by Art Nouveau and Bauhaus architects are just a few of the quirky things that give the Ruhrgebiet its edge.

Culture is king in the Ruhrgebiet, which is well known for lavish musical productions, top-notch orchestras, playhouses and cultural celebrations. No surprise then, that the entire region has been named the Cultural Capital of Europe 2010.

Discount Cards

The **RuhrTop-Card** (adult/child €33/23) gives free public transport and free or discounted admission to 120 attractions, including theme parks, museums and tours, on any three days. It's available from tourist offices and other outlets. For information call ☎ 01805-181 6180 or check www.ruhrtopcard.de.

Entertainment

For listings, check *Coolibri* or *Prinz*.

Industrial Heritage Trail

Most of the smokestacks and mines are quiet today, but the Ruhrgebiet has embraced its heritage by cleverly converting many of its 'cathedrals of industry' into museums, concert halls, cinemas, restaurants, lookouts, playgrounds and other venues. About 25 of them are linked along the 400km Industrial

Heritage Trail that takes in such cities as Dortmund, Essen, Duisburg and Bochum. Most sites are also served by public transport.

Details are at www.route-industriekultur .de, or stop by the route's **central visitors' centre** (☎ 0180-400 0086; Hall 2; 10am-7pm Apr-Oct, 10am-5pm Nov-Mar) at the Zollverein colliery complex (opposite) in Essen.

Getting Around

Each Ruhrgebiet city has an efficient and comprehensive public transport system, usually composed of U-Bahns, buses and trams. Cities are also connected to each other by S-Bahn and regional trains. The same tariffs apply within the entire region, which is divided into three zones. Look at the displays on orange ticket vending machines to see which price applies in your case. Single tickets are €2.10/4/8.70 for one/two/three zones. Single day passes are €4.90/9.30/20.30; group day passes for up to five people travelling together are €10.60/14.50/26.90.

ESSEN

☎ 0201 / pop 585,000

When the decision came down that Essen had beat historic Görlitz in Saxony to become Cultural Capital of Europe in 2010, eyebrows were raised around the land. What kind of 'culture' could there possibly be in this city of steel and coal?

Plenty.

Van Gogh anyone? Go to the Folkwang Museum. Fancy a look at Emperor Otto III's gem-studded childhood crown? Head for the cathedral treasury. A Bauhaus-style colliery on the list of Unesco's World Heritage Sites? Look no further than the Zollverein colliery complex. Need we go on?

It's taken a few decades, but Germany's seventh-largest city has mastered the transition from industrial powerhouse to city of commerce and culture like few others. Add to that a verdant green belt and half-timbered medieval quarters and you may find it hard to believe you're in the Ruhrgebiet. Old images die hard, but even cynics would find lots to like about Essen – if only they'd come and see for themselves.

Orientation

The Hauptbahnhof Nord (North) exit drops you right onto the centre's main artery, the pedestrianised Kettwiger Strasse. Essen's major sights are rather spread out, but all are accessible by U-Bahn, S-Bahn or trams. The handiest line is tram 107, which connects the centre with Zollverein colliery complex in the north and the museum complex and Rüttenscheid entertainment mile in the south. The Baldeneysee and the Werden suburb are further south and served by S-Bahn.

Information

Mayersche Buchhandlung (☎ 365 670; Markt 5-6) Bookshop.
Medical emergencies (☎ 192 92)
Police headquarters (☎ 8290; Büscherstrasse 2)
Post office (Willy-Brandt-Platz 1; 8am-7pm Mon-Fri, 8.30am-3.30pm Sat) Outside the Hauptbahnhof.
Reisebank (☎ 202 671; Hauptbahnhof; 7.15am-7.45pm Mon-Fri, 8.15am-4pm Sat, 9.45am-1.15pm Sun)
Stadtbibliothek (9am-6pm Mon-Fri, 10am-2pm Sat) Internet access.
Tourist office (☎ 194 33, 887 2048; www.essen.de; Am Hauptbahnhof 2; 9am-5.30pm Mon-Fri, 10am-1pm Sat)

Sights

CITY CENTRE

Essen's medieval **Dom** (☎ 220 4206; Burgplatz 2) is an island of quiet engulfed by the commercialism of pedestrianised Kettwiger Strasse, the main shopping strip. It has a magnificent collection of Ottonian works, all about 1000 years old. Most prized is the **Golden Madonna**, set in its own midnight-blue chapel matching the colour of her eyes. More highlights await in the **treasury** (adult/concession €3/2; 10am-5pm Tue & Thu-Sat, 10am-7pm Wed, 11.30am-5pm Sun), including a crown worn by Holy Roman Emperor Otto III and gemstone-encrusted processional crosses.

East of the cathedral, the **Alte Synagoge** (☎ 884 5218; Steeler Strasse 29; admission free; 10am-6pm Tue-Sun) is Germany's largest synagogue and miraculously survived WWII largely intact. Today it's a memorial site with exhibits on Jewish life, persecution and resistance during the Third Reich.

MUSEUM COMPLEX

One of Germany's most prestigious collections of 19th- and 20th-century art awaits at the **Museum Folkwang** (☎ 884 5314; Goethestrasse 41; adult/concession/family €5/3.50/10.50, child under 14yr free; 10am-6pm Tue-Thu, Sat & Sun, 10am-midnight Fri). From brooding landscapes by Caspar David Friedrich to light-hearted impressionist works by Monet and Renoir and abstract classics by Mark Rothko and Jackson Pollock, you'll find hardly a big name missing.

The **Ruhrlandmuseum** (Ruhr Regional Museum; ☎ 884 5200; Goethestrasse 41; adult/concession/family €5/3.50/10.50, child under 14 free; ⏱ 10am-6pm Tue-Thu, Sat & Sun, 10am-midnight Fri) next door is a traditional regional history museum. In late 2007, however, a completely revamped presentation is expected to open in the former coal wash house in the Zollverein complex as the rebaptised Ruhrmuseum.

Catch tram 107 or the U11 to Rüttenscheider Stern, then follow the signs.

ZOLLVEREIN

A key site along the Industrial Heritage Trail, the former **Zollverein colliery complex** (☎ 830 3636; www.zollverein.de; Gelsenkirchener Strasse 181; ⏱ visitors centre 10am-7pm Apr-Oct, 10am-5pm Nov-Mar) is a marvel of efficiency while in operation from 1932 until 1986. In 2001 Unesco declared the Bauhaus-style colliery a World Heritage Site. In a shining example of how to recycle an industrial waste heap, it is now a cultural centre with performance venues, a restaurant, artist studios and exhibition spaces. Unique experiences include a ride aboard the Ferris wheel–like **Sonnenrad** (Sun Wheel) through the smelters of the coking plant and a dip into a **pool** wrought from shipping containers (both free). In winter, it's possible to **ice skate** (€6) around the coking plant.

Another highlight is the **Red Dot Design Museum** (☎ 301 040; adult/concession €5/3, child under 12 free; ⏱ 11am-6pm Tue-Thu, 11am-8pm Fri-Sun) in the former boiler house, creatively adapted by Lord Norman Foster. In a perfect marriage of space and function, this four-storey maze showcases the best in contemporary design right amidst the original fixtures: bathtubs balance on grated walkways, bike helmets dangle from snakelike heating ducts, and beds perch atop a large oven.

In late 2007, the **Ruhrmuseum** (currently called Ruhrlandmuseum, above) is expected to take up residence in the former coal wash house.

A variety of German-language **guided tours** (€4.50-15), some led by former miners, take you around the grounds. Call or check www .zollverein.de for details.

The 107 tram travels here from the Hauptbahnhof.

BALDENEYSEE & VILLA HÜGEL

South of the city centre is Essen's sprawling green belt, which follows the flow of the Ruhr River to the large **Baldeneysee**. It's not quite the Med, but on hot summer days there's an undeniable holiday feeling at the **Seaside Beach** (Freiherr-vom-Stein-Strasse 384), a 250m-long stretch of sand where you can swim, windsurf and play beach volleyball.

On the lake's north shore looms the imposing **Villa Hügel** (☎ 188 4823; www.villahuegel.de; Hügel 1; adult/concession €1/free; ⏱ 10am-6pm Tue-Sun), where the Krupp dynasty made its home from 1873 to 1945. You can wander around the partially furnished private quarters of the Grosses Haus (Large House), which also hosts the occasional concert and internationally acclaimed art show (call or check the website for hours and admission). The Kleines Haus (Small House), a former guesthouse, is currently under renovation but will eventually house an exhibit on the history of the family and the company. The lavish **park** (⏱ 8am-8pm) is a pleasant place for a picnic or relaxing.

The lake and Villa Hügel are served by the S6 from the Hauptbahnhof.

WERDEN

On the southern Ruhr bank, across from Villa Hügel, the half-timbered houses and cobbled lanes of the suburb of Werden give you a sense of what a pre-industrial Ruhrgebiet must have looked like. Students of the prestigious Folkwang School for Music, Dance and Drama fill the many pubs, cafés and restaurants, and the DJH hostel is here as well.

Werden's main sight is the 1175 **Abteikirche St Liudger** (☎ 491 801; Brückstrasse 54; ⏱ 10am-noon & 3-5pm Tue-Sun), a beautiful late-Romanesque church named for the Frisian missionary buried here. It has an impressive exterior as well as a commendable **treasury** (admission €2).

The S6 goes straight to Werden from the Hauptbahnhof.

Sleeping

Hotels in the centre cater for the suit brigade and are mostly nondescript and overpriced. The more charming places are in the suburbs.

DJH hostel (☎ 491 163; www.jugendherberge.de/jh /essen; Pastoratsberg 2; dm/s/tw €19.80/24.90/30; Ⓟ ✕) Essen's expanded and updated hostel is nicely located in Werden. Many rooms have private

THE KRUPP DYNASTY – MEN OF STEEL

Steel and Krupp are virtual synonyms. So are Krupp and Essen. For it's this bustling Ruhrgebiet city that is the ancestral seat of the Krupp family and the headquarters of one of the most powerful corporations in Europe. (To avoid confusion, Krupp has nothing to do with the company that produces coffee-makers and other appliances – that's Krups.)

Through successive driven and obsessive generations, the Krupps amassed a huge private fortune, provided the German weaponry for four major wars and manipulated world economics and politics for their own gain. At the same time, however, they established a relationship between workers and management that's still the basis for today's social contract in industrialised Germany.

It all began rather modestly in 1811 when Friedrich Krupp and two partners founded a company to process 'English cast steel' but, despite minor successes, he left a company mired in debt upon his death in 1826. Enter his son Alfred, then a tender 14, who would go on to become one of the seminal figures of the industrial age.

It was through the production of the world's finest steel that the 'Cannon King' galvanised a company that – by 1887 – employed more than 20,000 workers. In an unbroken pattern of dazzling innovation, coupled with ruthless business practices, Krupp produced the wheels and rails for America's railroads and the stainless steel plating on New York's Chrysler building. Krupp gave the world the first diesel engine and the first steam turbine locomotive. And – ultimately – it produced the fearsome weapons that allowed the Wehrmacht to launch the horror of the Blitzkrieg in WWII.

But in another pioneering move, Krupp also provided womb-to-tomb benefits to its workers at a time when the term 'social welfare' had not yet entered the world's vocabulary. Alfred realised that his company's progress and profit came at a price largely borne on the backs of his workers. He created a variety of measures, including company health insurance, a pension scheme, subsidised housing estates and company-owned retail shops.

Krupp will forever be associated, however, with the disastrous period in German history when a maniac from Austria nearly brought the world to its knees. Not only did the corporation supply the hardware for the German war machine, but it also provided much of the financial backing that Hitler needed to build up his political power base. Krupp plants were prime targets for Allied bombers. When the dust had settled, about two-thirds of its factories had either been destroyed or damaged. An American military court sentenced Alfried Krupp von Bohlen und Halbach (Alfred's great-grandson) to prison, releasing him in 1951. He resumed the management of the firm in 1953.

An excellent source for an understanding of what the Krupp family has meant to Germany is William Manchester's brilliant chronicle The Arms of Krupp (1964).

bathrooms. Take the S6 to Essen-Werden, then bus 190 to Ruhrlandklinik.

Hotel Zum Deutschen Haus (☎ 232 989; www .hotel-zum-deutschen-haus.de; Kastanienallee 16; s €42-46, d with/without bathroom €77/46) This central, family-operated hotel offers pleasant if plain rooms and home-cooked meals in the restaurant (mains €6 to €12).

Hotel Résidence (☎ 02054-955 90; www.hotel -residence.de; Auf der Forst 1; s/d €100/125; P) Posh and petite, this 18-room hotel in an Art Nouveau villa in the historic suburb of Kettwig appeals to refined tastes. Its gourmet restaurant ranks among Germany's finest (mains around €35), but the food's almost as good at its second eatery, Püree (opposite).

Hotel Margarethenhöhe (☎ 438 60; www .margarethenhoehe.com; Steile Strasse 46; s €100-135, d €130-165; P ✗) A former Krupp guesthouse has morphed into this colourful hotel, filled with youthful flair, art and designer touches. It's about 5km south of the centre in the Margarethenhöhe, a gardenlike workers' colony of small and trim houses. Take the U17 to Laubenweg.

Eating

Skip Essen's city centre and head straight to the Rüttenscheid district ('Rü' for short; U11 or tram 107 to Martinstrasse). Here pubs and bars rub shoulders with restaurants of all kinds.

Zodiac (☎ 771 212; Witteringstrasse 41; mains €8-16; ✆ dinner Fri-Wed) People sharing laughs over dinner are a common sight at this jungly vegetarian restaurant where you'll munch on creative foods inspired by the world's cuisines. Some dishes are suitable for vegans, and organic pizza is available too.

raum.eins (☎ 455 3747; Rüttenscheider Strasse 154; business lunch €8, mains €10-23; ✆ lunch Mon-Fri & dinner Mon-Sat) The purist look, trendy crowd and crossover food could be warning signs, but not at this perennial favourite whose chef puts substance before culinary pyrotechnics. Nice terrace.

Casino Zollverein (☎ 830 240; Gelsenkirchener Strasse 181; mains €12-20; ✆ closed Mon) Cast iron, concrete and candlelight characterise this eccentric, even romantic, restaurant inside the colliery's former turbine house. The menu advertises 'new world cuisine' but in reality sticks mostly to new spins on regional and German faves. Not bad, though.

Püree (☎ 02054; Auf der Forst 1; mains €13-19; ✆ dinner Tue-Fri) A godsend for budget gourmets, the second – but by no means secondary – restaurant of the Hotel Résidence (opposite) presents tummy tantalisers that you'll remember long after the bill's been paid.

For the creamiest ice cream, stop by **Mörchens Eiscafé** (☎ 422 538; Rüttenscheider Strasse 202).

Entertainment

Zeche Carl (☎ 834 4410; Wilhelm-Nieswandt-Allee 100; ✆ nightly) The machine hall and washrooms of this former colliery have been reborn as an alternative cultural centre with live concerts, parties, cabaret, theatre and art exhibits. Take U11 or U17 to Karlsplatz.

Mudia Art (☎ 235 028; Frohnhauser Strasse 75; ✆ Sat) This sexy dance temple in an old factory has been a sizzling Ruhrgebiet hot spot since 1993. It's high-style, high-energy and high-attitude.

GOP Varieté (☎ 247 9393; Rottstrasse 30) At this crowd-pleaser, jugglers, acrobats, ventriloquists and other artistes seize the stage in monthly changing programmes.

Colosseum (☎ 887 2333; Altendorfer Strasse 1) Musical theatre is presented at this handsomely converted late-19th-century factory.

Philharmonie Essen (☎ 812 2200; Huyssenallee 53) Classical, jazz and other concerts take place in this beautiful space, which combines a historical section with a new glass pavilion.

Grillo-Theater (☎ 812 2200; Theaterplatz) Come here for classic and contemporary drama and comedies.

Aalto-Theater (☎ 812 2200; Operplatz 10) Designed by the late Finnish star architect Alvar Aalto, this is Essen's main venue for opera and ballet.

Getting There & Away

ICE trains leave in all directions hourly for such cities as Frankfurt (€72, 2¼ hours) and Berlin (€83, 3¾ hours). Essen is also efficiently linked to other Ruhrgebiet cities, as well as to Düsseldorf and Cologne.

The local autobahns A40, A42 and A52 are often clogged during rush-hour. For ride-shares contact the **Citynetz Mitfahrzentrale** (☎ 194 44; www.citynetz-mitfahrzentrale.de; Freiheit 5) outside the Hauptbahnhof's south exit.

BOCHUM
☎ 0234 / pop 389,000

Industrial cities are not exactly the stuff of heartfelt anthems, but that didn't stop singer-songwriter Herbert Grönemeyer from rhapsodising about his home town in the 1984 song 'Bochum'. The homage not only boosted Grönemeyer's career but also the image of this classic Ruhrgebiet city, halfway between Essen and Dortmund.

Though indeed no beauty, as one of the lyrics says, Bochum still makes for a worthwhile stop thanks to a couple of interesting museums and one of the buzziest nightlife districts in the entire Ruhrgebiet.

The **tourist office** (☎ 963 020; Huestrasse 9; ✆ 10am-7pm Mon-Fri, 10am-6pm Sat) is a short walk north of the Hauptbahnhof main exit.

Sights
DEUTSCHES BERGBAU-MUSEUM

The enormous **Deutsches Bergbau-Museum** (German Mining Museum; ☎ 587 70; Am Bergbaumuseum 28; adult/concession/family €6.50/3/14; ✆ 8.30am-5pm Tue-Fri, 10am-5pm Sat & Sun) thoroughly documents life *unter Tage* (below ground). Admission includes a trip beneath the earth's surface to a demonstration pit, which will help you imagine the merciless working conditions coal miners endured. Only weekday visits are guided (in German). Another highlight is a ride up the landmark winding tower, a turquoise metal construction once used for transporting men and equipment down the shaft and bringing the full wagons back up. Views are commanding from the 62m platform. The U-Bahn 35 goes here from the Hauptbahnhof.

NORTH RHINE-WESTPHALIA

EISENBAHNMUSEUM
Fans of historic 'iron horses' should make the pilgrimage to the **Eisenbahnmuseum** (☎ 492 516; Dr-C-Otto-Strasse 191; adult/child/family €5/2.50/13; ☷ 10am-5pm Tue-Fri & Sun Mar-late Nov). It displays around 180 steam and electric locomotives, coaches and wagons dating back as far as 1853. From the Hauptbahnhof take tram 318 to Bochum-Dahlhausen, then walk for 1200m or take the historic shuttle (Sundays only).

Sleeping & Eating
Aleppo (☎ 588 380; www.hotelaleppo.de; Nordring 30; dm €21-22, s/d €36/46; ✕) After a night of partying in the Bermuda Triangle (see below), you'll get a good night's sleep at this friendly hotel-hostel combination opposite the Bergbau-Museum. Bonuses include free wi-fi and public transport tickets, but bathrooms are shared.

Art Hotel Tucholsky (☎ 964 360; www.art-hotel-tucholsky.de; Viktoriastrasse 73; s €55-80, d €99-109; Ⓟ) Right in the Bermuda Triangle, this designer hotel has smallish but stylish rooms and a nice café (mains €6 to €13) that pulls in a good crowd all day long.

Entertainment
Bochum rightly enjoys a reputation as a Ruhrgebiet entertainment hub. Most people come to get lost in the city's infamous Bermuda Triangle of bars, clubs and restaurants. The three streets in question are the Kortumstrasse, Viktoriastrasse and Brüderstrasse, all within a five-minute walk of the Hauptbahnhof.

Starlight Express (☎ 963 020; www.starlight-express-musical.de) This musical has been playing to capacity crowds since 1988.

Schauspielhaus (theatre; ☎ 333 311; Königsallee 15) Bochum's theatre ranks among the best in Germany.

Getting There & Around
Bochum is efficiently linked by direct train to major cities such as Hamburg (€56, three hours), Berlin (€82, 3½ hours) and Frankfurt (€73, 2½ hours). Getting to other Ruhrgebiet towns is a snap using the S-Bahn or RE trains with multiple departures hourly. The A43 and A40 intersect in Bochum.

Public transportation within the city is composed of a small U-Bahn network, trams and buses.

DORTMUND
☎ 0231 / pop 591,000
Dortmund, the largest city in the Ruhrgebiet, once built its prosperity on coal, steel and beer. These days, the mines are closed, the steel mills quiet and more *Zeitgeist*-compatible hi-tech industries have taken their place. Only the breweries are going as strong as ever, churning out huge quantities of delicious beer and ale, much of it for export. Trading has always been big in Dortmund, which was a major stop on the Hellweg, a medieval trading route, and a big player in the Hanseatic League. Even today, the city centre is tops for shopping. Football (soccer) is another major passion. Borussia Dortmund, the city's *Bundesliga* (Germany's first league) team, has been national champion six times, although not since the 2001–2 season. Its home base, the 67,000-seat Westfalenstadion (now Signal-Iduna Park) was one of a dozen FIFA World Cup venues in 2006.

Orientation
The airport is east of the city (see p579 for transport to/from the airport). Most sights cluster within the city centre bounded by a ring road consisting of segments all ending in 'wall'. The Hauptbahnhof, bus station and tourist office are on Königswall on the north side of this ring. Just south of here, the pedestrianised Westenhellweg (which turns into Ostenhellweg further east) is the centre's main thoroughfare and heart of a bustling shopping district. The Kreuzviertel student quarter, the trade fair grounds and the famous football stadium are all south of the centre and easily reached by public transport.

Information
Dortmund hospital (Klinikum Dortmund; ☎ 9530; Beurhausstrasse 40) Centrally located hospital.

Dortmund Tourist-Card (1/3 days per person €8/14, up to 5 persons €14/24) Unlimited public transport, free or reduced museum admission and other discounts on one day or three consecutive days.

Mayersche Buchhandlung (☎ 809 050; Westenhellweg 37-41) Bookshop.

Post office (☎ 01802-3333; Kurfürstenstrasse 2; ☷ 8am-7pm Mon-Fri, 9am-2pm Sat) About 75m to the west of the Hauptbahnhof north exit.

Reisebank (☎ 138 8946; Königswall 18a; ☷ 10am-6pm Mon-Fri, 10am-3pm Sat) Next to the tourist office.

Stadtbücherei (public library; ☎ 502 3209; Königswall 18; per 30min €1; ☷ 10am-6.30pm Tue-Fri, 10am-2pm Sat) Internet access.

Tourist office (☎ 1899 9222; www.dortmund-tourismus .de; Königswall 18a; ◷ 9am-6pm Mon-Fri, 9am-1pm Sat) Opposite the Hauptbahnhof south exit.

Web M@nia Café (☎ 189 1848; Westenhellweg 136; per min €0.07; ◷ 10am-1am Mon-Sat, noon-1am Sun) Full-service internet café.

Sights

CITY CENTRE

Although its streets still follow a medieval layout, Dortmund's city centre is essentially a creation of modern times and among the Ruhrgebiet's most popular shopping districts. However, commerce coexists beautifully with church treasures here, especially along the main artery, the pedestrianised Westenhellweg.

Near the Hauptbahnhof is the 14th-century **Petrikirche**, a Gothic hall church. Its showstopper is a massive Antwerp **altar** (1520), featuring 633 individually carved and gilded figurines in scenes depicting the Easter story. Note that the altar is closed in summer, exposing only the panels' painted outer side.

East along Westenhellweg, past the **Krügerpassage**, a shopping arcade built in 1912 in exuberant neo-Renaissance style, is the **Reinoldikirche** (1280), named after the city's patron saint. After he was martyred in Cologne, the carriage containing his coffin rolled all the way to Dortmund stopping on the spot of the church – or so the story goes. A life-sized statue of the saint flanks the choir with another of Charlemagne just opposite. Of outstanding artistic merit is the late Gothic **high altar** (ask nicely in the sacristy for a close-up look). The bell tower can be climbed.

Across the street, **Marienkirche** is the oldest of Dortmund's churches, and its Romanesque origins are still visible in the round-arched nave. The star exhibit here is the **Marienaltar** (1420), with a delicate triptych by local son Conrad von Soest. In the northern nave is the equally impressive **Berswordt Altar** (1385). Also note the rather frivolous wood reliefs on the choir stalls and the ethereal St Mary statue.

The **Museum am Ostwall** (☎ 502 3247; www .museumdortmund.de; Ostwall 7; adult/concession €3/1.50, Sat free; ◷ 10am-5pm Sun, Tue, Wed & Fri, 10am-8pm Thu, noon-5pm Sat) specialises in 20th- and 21st-century art and is especially proud of its collection of paintings by Alexej von Jawlensky. Admission is more expensive for special exhibits.

An Art Deco former bank building houses the **Museum für Kunst & Kulturgeschichte** (Museum of Art & Cultural History; ☎ 502 6028; www.museen dortmund.de; Hansastrasse 3; adult/concession €3/1.50, free Sat; ◷ 10am-6pm Tue-Sun, to 8pm Thu). Exhibits take visitors from the Stone Age to the present. Highlights include re-created period rooms, a Roman gold treasure trove, a Romanesque triumphal cross and paintings by Caspar David Friedrich, Lovis Corinth and other outstanding artists.

North of the Hauptbahnhof, just beyond the multiplex cinema, is the **Mahn-und Gedenkstätte Steinwache** (☎ 502 5002; Steinstrasse 50; admission free; ◷ 10am-5pm Tue-Sun). A former Gestapo prison, it now houses a memorial exhibit about Dortmund during the Third Reich. A free English-language pamphlet is available.

Since 2006, Dortmund's beer tradition is creatively documented in the revived **Brauerei-Museum** (Brewery Museum; ☎ 840 0200; Steigerstrasse 14; adult/concession/family €1.50/0.75/4; ◷ 10am-5pm Tue, Wed & Fri-Sun, 10am-8pm Thu, noon-5pm Sat) inside the former Hansa brewery. Exhibits are an interesting hybrid of city history and the mysteries of commercial beer brewing. It's about 2km north of the Hauptbahnhof (U-Bahn 41 to Lortzingstrasse, then a 10-minute walk).

BEYOND THE CENTRE

Outside of the city centre are these two excellent Industrial Heritage Trail sites.

The **Zollern II/IV Colliery** (☎ 696 1111; www .industriemuseum.com; Grubenweg 5; adult/child/student €3.50/2/2.10; ◷ 10am-6pm Tue-Sun) is one of eight industrial sites that form the Westphalian Industrial Museum. Considered a 'model mine' when operation began in 1902, it boasted state-of-the-art technology and fantastic architecture, including an Art Nouveau machine hall and an office building adorned with gables and onion-domed towers. An innovative exhibit documents the harsh realities of life as a miner, with plenty of interactive and children-oriented programmes. To get here, take the U47 to Huckarde Bushof, then bus 462 direction Dortmund-Marten to 'Industriemuseum Zollern'.

Never mind the unwieldy name, the **Deutsche Arbeitsschutzausstellung** (German Occupational Safety & Health Exhibition; ☎ 9071 4645; Friedrich-Henkel-Weg 1-25; admission free; ◷ 9am-5pm Tue-Sat, 10am-5pm Sun) is a surprisingly fun and interactive museum that lets you experience working conditions of the past, present and future. Walk through a 'noise tunnel', sit in the cockpit of an Airbus, crank up an old printing machine and learn what steps can be taken to ensure health and safety in the workspace. To get here take the S1 to Dortmund-Dorstfeld-Süd.

Sleeping

The tourist office makes free room reservations – call ☎ 1899 9111.

Ruhgebiet International Hostel (☎ 952 9977; www .ruhgebiet.de; Lindemannstrasse 78; dm €17-22, s/d without bathroom €35/48, d with bathroom €50; P ⊠ ☐) The young owners have poured their cash and hearts into making this sparkling new indie hostel a clean and comfortable hospitality zone. Up to 56 guests can stretch out in large rooms sleeping two to eight. It's steps away from the football stadium and close to the Kreuzviertel pub quarter. From the Hauptbahnhof, take any U-Bahn to Stadtgarten, then catch the U42 to Kreuzstrasse.

Ibis Dortmund (☎ 185 770; www.ibishotel.com; Märkische Strasse 73; r €47-62; P ⊠ ⊠) This is one of the nicer contenders in this good-value chain. It's a 10-minute walk from the city centre and close to a supermarket and beer garden.

Cityhotel Dortmund (☎ 477 9660; www.cityhotel dortmund.de; Silberstrasse 37-43; s €70-80, d €87-99; P ⊠) A mousy grey façade hides this jewel of a hotel where a palette evoking the ocean, sun and sand gives rooms and public areas a cheerful and fresh look. Nonsmoking rooms facing the courtyard are quietest, but noise isn't really an issue here, even though the city's hip party zone is only a short walk away.

Eating

Dortmund brims with pubs and restaurants, making it ideal for sampling the local brews and cuisine. Centres of action include Kleppingstrasse and Alter Markt. Southeast of here is the student-flavoured Kreuzviertel, with Arneckestrasse being one of the main drags (U42 to Möllerbrücke).

BarRock (☎ 206 3221; Kreuzstrasse 87; dishes €5-13; ⊙ noon-1am Mon-Sat, 10am-1am Sun) Painted cherubs frolicking on the ceiling survey the scene at this charismatic locals' café in the Kreuzviertel. The food – baguettes to roast chicken – won't win awards but fills the tummy nicely. Reservations are advised for BarRock's famous Sunday brunch.

Rigoletto (☎ 150 4431; Kleppingstrasse 9-11; pizza & pasta €7-11, mains €11-15; ⊙ 8.30am-1am Mon-Fri, 8.30am-3am Sat, 10am-midnight Sun) Sure, it's popular with the see-and-be-seen crowd, but this

high-energy restaurant also delivers substance with reliable Mediterranean classics and operatic décor mixing wood, wrought-iron and chandeliers. It's also a good place for breakfast, afternoon coffee or a drink at the bar.

Hövel's Hausbrauerei (☎ 914 5470; Hoher Wall 5-7; mains €8-15) A complete overhaul has turned this classic into a brew-pub for the 21st century, adding a touch of sleekness without sacrificing the characteristic rustic flair. The menu is custom-made for meat lovers and the libation of choice is, of course, the tasty house-brewed Bitterbier.

Ristorante Bei Marija (☎ 751 9571; Am Beilstück 48; mains €10-20; ⊙ 6pm-midnight Tue-Sat) Like a hug from an old friend, Marija is warm and welcoming. The place looks like an overstuffed living room, the owner is a character and the Italian country fare mouth-watering. It's way off the tourist track; catch the U42 to An der Palmweide. Reservations recommended.

Other recommendations:

Am Alten Markt (☎ 572 217; Markt 3; mains €5-15; ⊙ 11am-midnight Mon-Sat, 3pm-midnight Sun) Traditional Westphalian fare served in belt-loosening portions amid smokey ambience.

Liv'Inn Room (☎ 144 043; Augustastrasse 1; mains €8-13; ⊙ dinner Mon-Sat, 10am-10pm Sun) Cosy resto-pub furnished grandma-style and serving wholesome salads, casseroles, crepes and other simple fare. Interesting toilets.

Drinking

Some of the places mentioned under Eating also make good drinking destinations.

Spirit (☎ 527 225; Helle 9; ⊙ Mon-Sat) Don't show up early at this cultish rock haunt run by a local biker club (the nice kind, we're told). DJ Mimi plays whatever strikes his fancy but no pop or techno.

Live Station (☎ 914 3625; Königswall 15, Hauptbahnhof; ⊙ Fri & Sat) This scene dinosaur still packs them in with various theme parties on Fridays and classic and contemporary chart busters on Saturdays, plus regular live gigs.

Domicil (☎ 862 9030; www.domicil-dortmund.de; Hansastrasse 7-11) Jazz, world and avant-garde music are the focus of this internationally renowned music club that's been booking promising newcomers and bona fide greats since 1969.

Entertainment

Signal Iduna Park (☎ 01805-309 000; www.bvb.de; tickets €11-50) A German insurance giant may have bought the naming rights, but that hasn't changed the fact that Dortmund's Westfalen-stadion (home base of the Borussia Dortmund team) is still one of the best football stadiums in the country.

Theater Dortmund (☎ 01805-517 0517; Hiltropwall 15) High-brow drama, opera and musicals are staged by this theatre. It has a second location at Hansastrasse 7.

Konzerthaus (☎ 01805-448 044; Brückstrasse 21) This snazzy new place presents top-flight classical concerts starring Dortmund's Philharmonic Orchestra or international guest performers.

On Friday and Saturday night hipsters gravitate to the new fun zone on the grounds of the former Thier brewery between Martinsstrasse and Hövelsstrasse in the centre. Half-a-dozen bars and clubs have set up shop here, including **Mendoza** (☎ 233 3239), an artsy cocktail bar; **Blauer Raum** (☎ 226 6504), a black music lounge and club; and **Sixx.pm** (☎ 9419 9888), a largish electronica club.

Getting There & Away
Air Berlin and easyJet are among the carriers serving **Dortmund Airport** (☎ 921 301; www.flughafen-dortmund.de), connected to the centre by the Airport Express bus (€5, 4.30am to 10.30pm, mostly hourly). Buses stop outside the Hauptbahnhof, a major hub with frequent ICE and IC trains in all directions and RE and S-Bahn trains to other Ruhrgebiet cities departing every few minutes.

Dortmund is on the A1, A2 and A45. The B1 runs right through the city and is the link between the A40 to Essen and the A44 to Kassel. It's very busy and often clogged.

Getting Around
For public transport, see p572. For a taxi call ☎ 144 444 or ☎ 194 10. The tourist office rents bikes for €4 per hour or €12 per day with a €30 deposit.

ELSEWHERE IN THE RUHRGEBIET
The Ruhrgebiet has plenty of other places of interest, many of them on the Industrial Heritage Trail (p571).

Oberhausen
☎ 0208 / pop 219,000
The city of Oberhausen has one of Germany's most unusual exhibit spaces, the **Gasometer** (☎ 850 3730; www.gasometer.de; Am Grafenbusch 90; adult/concession €6/4; ☼ 10am-6pm Tue-Sun). The giant barrel-shaped structure that once stored gas to

power blast furnaces now hosts *Feuer-Licht-Himmel* (Fire-Light-Sky) in the upper section; it's a light and sound installation by Berlin artist Christina Kubisch. Downstairs is a documentary exhibit about the history of the building and its transformation into an art space. You can also ride the glass elevator to a 117m platform with views over the entire western Ruhrgebiet.

Next door is the **CentrO**, one of Europe's largest shopping malls with more than 200 shops, some 20 restaurants and entertainment venues, including a multiplex cinema. Little kids will likely be tempted by the **CentrO Adventure Park** (☎ 456 780; unlimited rides adult/concession €12/8.50; ☼ 10am-6pm mid-Mar–Oct, days vary, call for details), a small amusement park. Also here is the largest **SeaLife** (☎ 4448 8444; Zum Aquarium 1; adult/child/concession €13/11/12; ☼ from 10am, closing time varies), yet another instalment in this chain of walk-through aquariums that seems to be proliferating faster than sea slugs on Viagra.

Take any bus or tram that's going in the direction of Neue Mitte Oberhausen from platform one outside the Oberhausen Hauptbahnhof. By car, take the Oberhausen Osterfeld/Neue Mitte exit off the A42.

Oberhausen is well connected to other Ruhrgebiet cities, including directly by S-Bahn from Essen (€4, 17 minutes) and by RE train from Dortmund (€8.70, 40 minutes).

Duisburg
☎ 0203 / pop 500,000
Molten iron used to flow 24/7 from the fiery furnaces of the iron works, now creatively recycled into a unique adventure playground, the **Landschaftspark Duisburg-Nord** (Emscherstrasse 71; admission free, activities vary; ☼ 24hr). You can free-climb its ore bunkers, take a diving course in the former gas tank, climb to the top of the blast furnace or balance on tightropes suspended between buildings. There's plenty of green space for drifting around, picnics or play, along with flower gardens and even a small farm with a petting zoo. At the **visitors centre** (☎ 429 1942; ☼ 10am-5pm Mon-Thu, 10am-9pm Fri-Sun Apr-Oct, reduced hours in winter) you can pick up information about the entire Industrial Heritage Trail and find out about guided tours, concerts and other events at the park. Next door, a restaurant-bar serves drinks, snacks and full meals.

Just outside the complex is the newish **DJH hostel** (☎ 417 900; www.djh.de; Lösorter Strasse 133; dm under/over 26yr €20/23; P ⊠). From Duisburg Hauptbahnhof take tram 902 (direction Duisburg-Walsum) or 903 (direction Dinslaken) to Landschaftspark-Nord; from here it's a seven-minute walk via Emscherstrasse.

Duisburg is on a major rail line and served by ICE, IC and regional trains. The trip from either Düsseldorf or Essen costs €4 on RE or S-Bahn trains and takes about 15 minutes.

Bottrop
☎ 02041 / pop 120,000

TETRAEDER
Egypt has them, so does Mexico and now there's one in the Ruhrgebiet: a pyramid, right here in the town of Bottrop. The **Tetraeder** (Tetrahedron; admission free; ☼ 24hr) is a 50m-high skeletal construct made from steel pipes and open space. It graces the top of a former slag heap turned attractive landscape park, complete with trees, trails and benches. You can climb the Tetraeder via 'floating' staircases suspended from steel cables (yes, they swing when the wind's up), which lead to three viewing platforms, an experience not recommended for vertigo sufferers. Views of the surprisingly green yet undeniably industrial landscape are impressive rather than conventionally beautiful. At night, the Tetraeder becomes a light installation that you can see glowing from afar. Right next to it, the **alpincenter Bottrop** (☎ 70950; www.alpincenter.com; Prosperstrasse 299; day pass adult/concession from €33/22; ☼ 9.30am-midnight) is the world's longest indoor alpine ski run (630m). Take bus 262 from Bottrop Hauptbahnhof to Brakerstrasse.

JOSEF ALBERS MUSEUM
Fans of this famous Bauhaus artist won't want to miss the **Josef Albers Museum** (☎ 297 16; Im Stadtgarten 20; admission free; ☼ 10am-6pm Tue-Sun). Albers, who fled the Nazis for the US in 1933, is especially famous for his explorations of colour and spatial relationships, especially of squares. The works are housed in a starkly minimalist space that's like a visual metaphor for his works. Displays include examples from his famous series Homage to the Square as well as early lithographs from the Bottrop period such as Arbeiterhäuser (workers' homes).

MOVIE PARK GERMANY
The Ruhrgebiet's answer to Disneyland Paris, the sprawling **Movie Park Germany** (☎ 02045-8990; www.moviepark.de; Warner Allee 1; adult/senior & child 4-11yr €25.50/22, parking €5; ☼ at least 10am-5pm Mon-Fri, 10am-6pm Sat & Sun Apr-Oct; closed Nov-Mar) presents an entertaining mix of thrill rides, live-action shows, restaurants and shops. The High Fall Tower, which has you free-falling from a height of 65m, should satisfy even the most speed-crazed teen, while Wonderland Studios is a fantasyland for the little ones with fanciful rides and friendly animal characters. Actual opening hours vary; those shown here are the minimum.

The park is in Bottrop-Kirchhellen, about 15km north of Essen. There are direct RE connections hourly from Essen; get off at the Feldhausen stop. If you're driving, take the Kirchhellen-Nord exit off the A31, then follow the signs.

GETTING THERE & AWAY
Bottrop is served by the A2 and A42 autobahns and the B223. S-Bahn and RE trains link it to other Ruhrgebiet cities such as Essen (€4, 15 minutes). The trip to/from Düsseldorf requires a change in Oberhausen or Duisburg (€8.70, one hour).

Gelsenkirchen
☎ 0209 / 270,000

To football fans Gelsenkirchen is synonymous with Schalke 04, the legendary club that's long been a mainstay in the *Bundesliga*. In 2006, the city hosted five World Cup games in its spectacular new **Arena AufSchalke** (☎ 36180; www .schalke04.de; Ernst-Kuzorra-Weg 1), aka Veltins Arena, a multifunction stadium that counts a retractable glass roof and disappearing grass floor among its state-of-the-art features. Tours are offered only by prior arrangement; call ☎ 389 2900. Schalke fans can check out the new **club museum** (adult/youth €4/2; ☼ 10am-7pm Tue-Fri, 10am-5pm Sat & Sun). Take tram 302 from the Gelsenkirchen Hauptbahnhof.

Gelsenkirchen's other major new draw is **Zoom Erlebniswelt** (☎ 954 50; www.zoom-erlebniswelt .de; Bleckstrasse 47; adult/child/student €12/8/9, parking €3; ☼ 9am-6pm Mar & Oct, 9am-6.30pm Apr-Sep, 9am-5pm Nov-Feb), an imaginatively landscaped zoo where animals don't roam in cages but in habitats that re-create their natural surroundings as closely as possible. Rivers, a gushing waterfall, canyons and rock formations characterise the Alaska section, where grizzly bears lumber, timber wolves prowl, otters tumble and elks strut. Denizens of the Africa exhibit, which opened in 2006, include lions, giraffes and zebras. Fencing is minimal and unobtrusive, yet you can get surprisingly close to even the fiercer animals thanks to ditches and glass walls. Asia is set to follow in 2007. Tram 301 goes straight to the zoo from the Gelsenkirchen Hauptbahnhof.

Gelsenkirchen is bisected by the A2 and A42 but only served by a minor rail line. The S-Bahn 2 makes frequent direct trips from Dortmund (€4, 34 minutes). Coming from Bochum, the best way to travel between the cities' main train stations is by tram 302 (€4, 30 minutes).

WESTPHALIA

MÜNSTER

☎ 0251 / pop 269,000

When strolling around Münster's Altstadt, it's hard to imagine that nearly everything you see is only 60 years or so old. After near total destruction in WWII, the cultural capital of Westphalia opted for creating a carbon copy of its medieval centre rather than embracing the ideas of modern town planning. Although the decision epitomises the conservative mindset of locals, Münster is not mired in nostalgia. Its 50,000 students definitely keep the cobwebs out and help make a success out of alternative projects such as the Hafenviertel (old harbour quarter) redevelopment. More than anything, though, it's the 100,000 bicycles – called *Leeze* in local dialect – that quite literally bring energy and movement to this pretty and inviting city.

Orientation

Münster's tiny airport is about 20km north of town in Greven (see p584 for travel between the airport and town). Many of the city's main sights are within the confines of the easy-to-walk Altstadt, a short walk northwest of the Hauptbahnhof via Windhorststrasse. The bus station is right outside the station's west exit. The Altstadt is encircled by the 4.8km Promenade, a car-free ring trail built on top of the former city fortifications; it's hugely popular with bicyclists.

Information

There are several banks in the centre, including a Sparkasse in the Münster Arkaden.

Altes Rathaus tourist office (☎ 492 2724; Prinzipalmarkt 10; ☺ 10am-5pm Tue-Fri, 10am-4pm Sat & Sun)

Main tourist office (☎ 492 2710; www.tourismus .muenster.de; Heinrich-Brüning-Strasse 9; ☺ 9.30am-6pm Mon-Fri, 9.30am-1pm Sat)

Poertgen Herder (☎ 490 140; Salzstrasse 56) Good selection of English books.

Post office (☎ 01802-3333; Domplatz) There's another branch at the Hauptbahnhof.

Raphaelsklinik (☎ 500 70; Klosterstrasse 72) Medical services.

Stadtbücherei (☎ 492 4242; Alter Steinweg 11; per hr €0.50; ☺ 10am-7pm Mon-Fri, 10am-3pm Sat) Public library with internet access, international newspapers and magazines and clean toilets.

Sights
DOM ST PAUL

The two massive towers of Münster's cathedral, **Dom St Paul** (Domplatz; ☺ 10am-6pm), match the proportions of this 110m-long structure and the vast square it overlooks. It's a three-nave construction built at a time when Gothic architecture began overtaking the Romanesque style in popularity. Enter from Domplatz via a porch (called the 'Paradise'), richly festooned with apostle sculptures. Inside, pay your respects to the **statue of St Christopher**, the patron saint of travellers, then make your way to the southern ambulatory with its **astronomical clock**. This marvel of 16th-century ingenuity indicates the time, the position of the sun, the movement of the planets, and the calendar. Crowds gather daily at noon (12.30pm Sunday) when the carillon starts up.

The **Domkammer** (cathedral treasury; ☎ 495 587; admission €1; ☺ 11am-4pm Tue-Sun), which is reached via the cloisters, counts an 11th-century gem-studded golden head reliquary of St Paul among its finest pieces.

AROUND DOMPLATZ

Northwest of the Dom, the **Überwasserkirche** (officially known as Liebfrauenkirche) is a 14th-century Gothic hall church with handsome stained-glass windows. The nickname was inspired by its location right by the Aa, a tiny stream whose tree-lined promenade makes for lovely strolling.

In the 16th century, the iconoclastic Anabaptists 'cleansed' this church of all sculptures, but miraculously many ended up at the **Westfälisches Landesmuseum** (Regional Museum; ☎ 590 701; Domplatz 10; adult/concession €3.50/2.10; ☺ 10am-6pm Tue-Sun). Its well-respected art collection spans from the Middle Ages to modern times and includes works by the famous Westphalian

NORTH RHINE-WESTPHALIA

painter, Conrad von Soest. Fans of August Macke and other expressionists should make a beeline to the 2nd floor.

For an in-depth study of the lithographic work of another 20th-century master, head to the **Graphikmuseum Pablo Picasso** (☎ 414 4710; www.graphikmuseum-picasso-muenster.de; Königsstrasse 5; adult/concession €5/4; ☒ 11am-6pm Tue-Fri, 10am-6pm Sat

& Sun), the first German museum dedicated to the Spanish artist. It shows rotating selections drawn from among nearly 800 graphics, including still life and bull-fighting scenes.

PRINZIPALMARKT

Münster's main artery is the Prinzipalmarkt, lined by restored Patrician town houses with

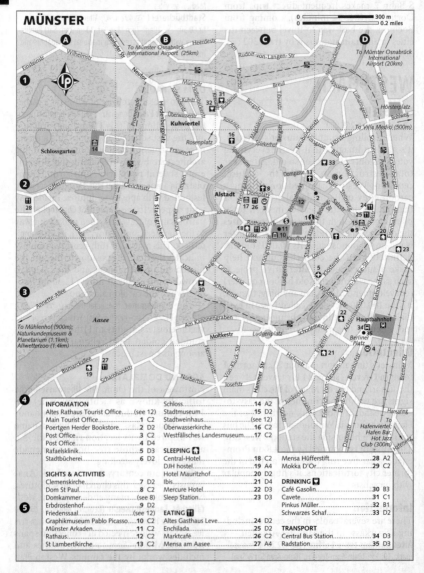

MÜNSTER

0 —————— 300 m
0 —————— 0.2 miles

arcades sheltering elegant boutiques and cafés. At its centre stands the Gothic **Rathaus**, site of the signing of the Peace of Westphalia in 1648, which marked the first step in ending the calamitous Thirty Years' War. The signing took place in the **Friedenssaal** (Hall of Peace; ☎ 492 2724; adult/concession €1.50/1; ☽ 10am-5pm Tue-Fri, 10am-4pm Sat & Sun), a spectacular hall with intricately carved wood panelling. There's also an odd display of a golden drinking vessel in the shape of a rooster, a mummified hand and a slipper. As you exit, note the adjacent **Stadtweinhaus** (City Wine House), a Renaissance gem with porticoes that was once used for wine storage and now contains a restaurant.

Further north is the late-Gothic **St Lambertikirche** (1450) with its landmark openwork spire from which dangle three wrought-iron cages. These once held the corpses of the Anabaptist leader Jan van Leyden and his deputies. This Protestant sect, which believed in adult baptism, polygamy and communal property, was routed in 1535 by troops of the prince-bishop. Van Leyden and his co-horts were publicly tortured with red-hot tongs – now among the treasures on view at the **Stadtmuseum** (☎ 492 4503; Salzstrasse 28; admission free; ☽ 10am-6pm Tue-Fri, 11am-6pm Sat & Sun) – then stuck in the cages as a warning to all wannabe Protestants.

Just south of Prinzipalmarkt is the **Münster Arkaden**, a gorgeous new shopping mall with patterned marble flooring and a central glass dome.

BAROQUE BUILDINGS

The architect that left his mark on Münster more than any other was Johann Conrad Schlaun (1695–1773). He was a master of the Westphalian baroque, a more subdued, less exuberant style than in southern Germany. A most exquisite example of Schlaun's vision is the 1757 **Erbdrostenhof** (Salzstrasse 38), a lavish private mansion. Nearby, the equally stunning 1753 **Clemenskirche** (Klemensstrasse) boasts a domed ceiling-fresco supported by turquoise faux-marble pillars. Less pristinely preserved is the 1773 **Schloss** (Schlossplatz), the former residence of the prince-bishops and now the main university building.

OUTSIDE THE ALTSTADT

A 10-minute walk southeast of the Hauptbahnhof takes you to the **Hafenviertel** (aka Kreativkai), Münster's revitalised old harbour.

Old halls and brick warehouses now house a theatre, artists studios, a children's book publisher and other offices alongside a fun mixture of restaurants, bars and dance clubs. Its edgy charms are best sampled sitting outdoors and watching cargo barges cutting along the Dortmund-Ems canal. In summer, there's swimming in the canal. To get to the Hafenviertel, exit the Hauptbahnhof to the east via Bremer Platz, follow Bremer Strasse south, cross Hansaring and it will be on your left.

Another recreational area is the Aasee lake, southwest of the Altstadt, where you can picnic and enjoy water sports. Halfway down its western shore is the **Mühlenhof** (☎ 981 200; www.muehlenhof-muenster.de; adult/child/student/family €4/2/2.50/10; ☽ 10am-6pm daily mid-Mar–Oct, 1-4.30pm Mon-Sat, 11am-4.30pm Sun Nov–mid-Mar), an open-air cluster of historical Westphalian buildings, including a mill and bakery. Dinosaurs and the universe are among the attractions at the **Naturkundemuseum & Planetarium** (Natural History Museum; ☎ 591 05; Sentruper Strasse 285; adult/concession €5.50/3; ☽ 9am-6pm Tue-Sun), while highlights of the **Allwetterzoo** (☎ 890 40; Sentruper Strasse 315; adult/concession €11.50/5.75; ☽ 9am-6pm Apr-Sep, 9am-5pm Oct & Mar, 9am-4pm Nov-Feb) include the dolphin show and the horse museum with fun exhibits about the region's equestrian heritage.

Sleeping

The tourist office operates a **reservation hotline** (☎ 492 2726; ☽ 8am-10pm).

Sleep Station (☎ 482 8155; www.sleep-station.de; Wolbecker Strasse 1; dm €14-20, s/d €28/44, linen €3; ☒ 🖳) This colourful hostel is about 200m from the Hauptbahnhof. Facilities are shared in all but two of the carpeted rooms outfitted with one to eight beds. There's free coffee and tea, and a guest kitchen. Check-in is from 5pm to 8pm.

Mercure Hotel (☎ 41710; www.mercure.com; Engelstrasse 39; s €70-130, d €90-150; ℗ ☒ 🖳) It's a chain so don't expect too much personality from this one. What you will find are 156 handsome rooms with a bevy of mod cons. The appealing public areas invite lounging and the sauna and steam bath are welcome relaxation zones after a busy day of sightseeing. Breakfast is €15.

Central-Hotel (☎ 510 150; www.central-hotel-muenster.de; Aegidiistrasse 1; s €85-105, d €105-130, tr €115-150; ℗ ☒ 🖳) This small and personally run 20-room hotel has so many admirers that it's often fully booked. The owners are avid art

NORTH RHINE-WESTPHALIA

supporters who don't mind sharing views of their originals with guests.

Hotel Mauritzhof (☎ 417 20; www.mauritzhof.de; Eisenbahnstrasse 17; s €101-158, d €116-173, ste €188-203; ☒ ☒) Bold colours, plenty of glass and natural wood and extravagant designer furniture turn this 37-room property into a mod hotspot. The generous lobby-lounge is a good spot for a healthful breakfast (€15) or for winding down the day with a snack or glass of wine. There's free wi-fi.

Also recommended:

DJH hostel (☎ 530 280; www.djh.de; Bismarckallee 31; dm/d €22.50/60; ☒ ☒ ☐) Take bus 10 or 34 to Hoppendamm, followed by a 500m walk.

Ibis (☎ 481 30; www.ibishotel.com; Engelstrasse 53; r €61-78; ☒ ☒ ☒ ☐) Good-value cookie-cutter property.

Eating

Mokka D'Or (☎ 482 8591; Rothenburg 14-16; mains €5-12; ☒ 9am-1am Mon-Sat, 11am-1am Sun) Perhaps it's the breezy urbanity, or the Italian breakfasts, or the yummy pizzas delivered piping hot from the wood stove. Fact is, this convivial noshery has been a local bestseller for years. That's *dolce vita*, Westphalian style. Enter via the alleyway.

Marktcafé (☎ 575 85; Domplatz 7; mains €5-13; ☒ 9am-1am) Views of the Dom are gratis at this contemporary café, which draws everyone from students to suits, tourists to punters, especially on market days (Wednesday and Saturday). The food is fresh and tasty, and Sunday's brunch buffet (€8.95) an institution.

Altes Gasthaus Leve (☎ 455 95; Alter Steinweg 37; mains €6-16; ☒ 11.30am-11pm) Münster's oldest inn (since 1607) is a trippy time-warp where painted tiles, oil paintings and copper etchings form a suitably rustic backdrop to the hearty Westphalian fare. Dishes such as lima bean stew or sweet and sour beef sound more challenging than they are.

Enchilada (☎ 455 66; Artzkarrengasse 12; mains €8-15; ☒ dinner) The spectacular setting in a resurrected medieval ballroom, two happy hours (6pm to 8pm and after 11pm) and tasty Tex-Mex ensure that this place is never without a crowd. Nice terrace in summer.

Villa Medici (☎ 342 18; Ostmarkstrasse 15; mains €25-40, menu around €40; ☒ dinner Tue-Sat) If you're in need of a first-class culinary journey, book a table at this Italian gourmet temple whose reputation extends well beyond city borders. It's a fairly formal affair, but even first-timers are greeted warmly by the charming owners.

Not only students will enjoy a meal at one of Münster's superb *Mensen* (university cafeterias) where you can fill up for €5 or less. Our favourites:

Mensa am Aasee (Bismarckallee 11; ☒ lunch Mon-Sat, dinner Mon-Sat) Huge, modern with lake views, salad and vegetable bars and grill and wok stations.

Mensa Hüfferstift (Hüfferstrasse 27; ☒ 7.30am-2.30pm Mon-Fri) Paella, pasta, fish, schnitzel, salad and more with views over Münster's rooftops.

Drinking

Münster's party-happy students fuel an eclectic pub and club scene.

Hafen Bar (☎ 289 7810; Hafenweg 26a) Hipsters flock to this bar in Hafenviertel. It's a stylish glass cube with complexion-friendly lighting and is a great place to sip cocktails.

Hot Jazz Club (☎ 6866 7909; Hafenweg 26b) Also in the trendy Hafenviertel, this subterranean bar hosts live music of all stripes, not only jazz.

Café Gasolin (☎ 510 5897; Aegidiistrasse 45; ☒ 11am-3am) Snazzily converted from a '50s gas station, Café Gasolin is a good spot for a nightcap. In the afternoon, their yummy cakes and latte macchiatos make for a great sugar fix. Prices are low, quality is not.

North of the Dom, the traditional student quarter – the Kuhviertel – teems with such time-honoured classics as **Cavete** (☎ 457 00; Kreuzstrasse 38) and the brew-pub **Pinkus Müller** (☎ 451 51; Kreuzstrasse 4; ☒ closed Sun) with its typical Westphalian décor. The **Schwarzes Schaf** (☎ 484 3577; Alter Fischmarkt 26; ☒ Mon-Sat) is mostly a regular pub, but at weekends the attached historic ballroom morphs into a full-on party den with several dance floors.

Getting There & Away

The **Münster Osnabrück International Airport** (☎ 02571-943 360; www.fmo.de) has low-cost flights on Air Berlin from London, Rome, Barcelona and other destinations.

Münster is on an IC line with regular links to points north and south and frequent trains to the Ruhrgebiet cities. The city is on the A1 from Bremen to Cologne and is near the starting point of the A43 direction Wuppertal. It is also at the crossroads of the B51, B54 and B219.

Getting Around

Buses connect the airport and the Hauptbahnhof every half-hour (€5, 40 minutes). Drivers should take the B219.

Bus drivers sell single tickets for €1.30 or €1.90, depending on the distance. Day passes are €3.45 (valid after 9am). For information, call ☎ 01803-504 030.

Hire bikes (€7/16 per one/three days) at **Radstation** (☎ 484 0170; Berliner Platz 27a; ⏱ 5.30am-11pm Mon-Fri, 7am-11pm Sat & Sun) outside the Hauptbahnhof. The tourist office has cycling maps.

AROUND MÜNSTER

Münster is surrounded by the **Münsterland**, home to about 100 well-preserved castles and palaces, many of them protected by moats. In these rural flatlands, water was often the only way for local rulers to keep out the 'rabble' and rebels.

The region is a dream for cyclists, with over 4500km of well signposted trails (called *Pättkes* in local dialect), including the 100 Schlösser Route (Route of 100 Palaces) that allows you to hop from one castle to the next. Bicycles may be hired in Münster (above) and at practically all local train stations. Many castles are also served by public transport, though service can be sketchy or cumbersome, especially at weekends.

For route planning, lodging and general information, call tollfree ☎ 0800-939 2919, check www.muensterland-tourism (in German) or contact the Münster tourist office (p581).

The following are snapshots of a quartet of castles that offer the greatest tourist appeal and, except for Schloss Nordkirchen, are relatively accessible from Münster.

Burg Hülshoff

About 10km west of Münster, **Burg Hülshoff** (☎ 02534-1052; Schonebeck 6; adult/concession €3.50/3; ⏱ 9.30am-6pm Feb–mid-Dec) is the birthplace of one of Germany's pre-eminent women of letters, Annette von Droste-Hülshoff (1797–1848). The red-brick Renaissance chateau is embedded in a lovely – partly groomed, partly romantic – park (admission free). The interior, which consists of period rooms furnished in the style of the poet's day, can be explored with an audio-guide. Bus 564 makes the trip out here from Münster's Hauptbahnhof (€1.85, 22 minutes).

Haus Rüschhaus

Annette von Droste-Hülshoff did some of her finest writing at the smaller **Haus Rüschhaus** (☎ 02533-1317; Am Rüschhaus 81; adult/concession €3/2;

⏱ tours hourly 10am-noon & 2-5pm Tue-Sun May-Oct, fewer tours Nov-Apr) where she lived for 20 years from 1826. The building was once the private home of star architect Johann Conrad Schlaun, who magically morphed a farmhouse into a baroque minimansion backed by a formal garden (always open). It's in the suburb of Nienberge, about 3km north of Burg Hülshoff, and served by bus 5 from Münster's Hauptbahnhof (€1.85, 20 minutes).

Burg Vischering

The quintessential medieval moated castle, **Burg Vischering** (☎ 02591-799 00; Berenbrok 1) is Westphalia's oldest (1271), and the kind that conjures romantic images of knights and damsels. Surrounded by a system of ramparts and ditches, the complex consists of an outer castle and the main castle, now a **museum** (adult/concession €2.50/2; ⏱ 10am-noon & 1.30-5.30pm Tue-Sun Apr-Oct, until 4.30pm Nov-Mar).

Burg Vischering is in Lüdinghausen, about 30km south of Münster. Catch bus S90/91 or S92 at the Hauptbahnhof to Lüdinghausen (€5, 45 minutes), then walk for about 10 minutes.

Schloss Nordkirchen

On an island surrounded by a sprawling, manicured park, **Schloss Nordkirchen** (☎ 02596-9330; ⏱ 11am-5pm Sun May-Sep, 2-4pm Sun Oct-Apr & by prior arrangement) is an imposing baroque red-brick structure nicknamed the 'Westphalian Versailles'. On a nice day, the palace is well worth visiting for the gardens and the exterior alone. Since it's used as a state college for financial studies, the interior – with its stuccoed ceilings, festival hall and dining room – can only be seen on guided tours (tours €2).

Schloss Nordkirchen is 8km southeast of Lüdinghausen in the hamlet of Nordkirchen, which is incredibly poorly served by public transport. Consult your bike map to find the route between Burg Vischering and Schloss Nordkirchen.

SOEST
☎ 02921 / pop 48,000
Soest is a quiet, spire-studded town of half-timbered houses lining a maze of idyllic, crooked lanes. It lies about 45km east of Dortmund and is the northern gateway to the Sauerland. Although devastated by WWII bombing raids, it has miraculously preserved much of its medieval character. Soest is a

'green' town, not only because of its many parks and gardens but also for the colour of the local sandstone used in building its town wall, churches and other structures. Brimming with treasure, these churches reflect the wealth Soest enjoyed during its medieval heyday as a member of the Hanseatic League. Its romantic looks have also charmed modern artists, including expressionists Emil Nolde, Karl Schmidt-Rottluff and native son Wilhelm Morgner.

Orientation

The train and bus stations are on the north side of the ring road enclosing Soest's centre. Follow the pedestrianised Brüderstrasse south to the Markt, tourist office, Dom and the churches.

Information

There are several banks with ATMs around Markt.

Post office (Hospitalgasse 3)
Tourist office (☎ 6635 0050; www.soest.de; Teichmühlengasse 3; ☼ 9.30am-4.30pm Mon-Fri, 10am-3pm Sat year-round, 11am-1pm Sun Apr-Oct)

Sights

Much of Soest's historic centre is still encircled by a moated **defensive wall**, which today has a parklike appearance and is great for strolling and picnicking.

Fans of medieval churches have plenty to keep them busy in Soest. Closest to the Hauptbahnhof is the exquisite late-Gothic hall church, **St Maria zur Wiese** (Wiesenstrasse; ☼ 11am-4pm Mon-Sat, noon-4pm Sun), also known as Wiesenkirche and easily recognised by its lacy neo-Gothic twin spires. These are undergoing restoration and will remain under wraps until at least 2023 (!). Inside, it's the delicate proportions and vibrant stained-glass windows that create an ethereal atmosphere. An endearing feature is the window above the north portal, which shows Jesus and his disciples enjoying a **Westphalian Last Supper** of ham, beer and rye bread.

On Hohe Gasse, **St Maria zur Höhe** (☼ 10am-5.30pm Mon-Fri, 10am-5pm Sat, noon-5pm Sun Apr-Sep, to 4pm Oct-Mar), better known as Hohnekirche, is a squat, older and architecturally less accomplished hall church. Its sombreness is brightened by beautiful ceiling frescoes, an altar ascribed to the Westphalian painter known as the Master of Liesborn, and the *Scheibenkreuz*,

a huge wooden cross on a circular board more typically found in Scandinavian churches; in fact, it's the only such cross in Germany. Look for the light switch on your left as you enter to shed a little light on the matter.

Three more churches are near Markt, a short walk west via the **Grosser Teich**, a placid duck pond and park where the tourist office is now housed in an old water mill. The dignified tower of **St Patrokli** (Propst-Nübel-Strasse 2; ☼ 10am-6pm), a three-nave Romanesque structure partly adorned with delicate frescoes, looks down upon the **Rathaus**, a baroque confection with an arched portico on the western side.

Adjacent to this ensemble is the **Petrikirche** (Petrikirchhof 10; ☼ 9.30am-noon & 2-5.30pm Tue-Fri, to 4.30pm Sat, 2-5.30pm Sun), with Romanesque origins in the 8th century and a choir from Gothic times, all topped by a baroque onion dome. It's adorned with wall murals and features an unusual modern altar made from the local green sandstone, glass and brushed stainless steel.

The tiny **Nikolaikapelle** (Thomästrasse; ☼ 11am-noon Tue, Wed & Sun) is a few steps southeast of St Patrokli. It's a pity it's rarely open, for its almost mystical simplicity is enlivened by a masterful altar painting that may be the work of 15th-century artist Conrad von Soest (born in Dortmund).

Sleeping

DJH hostel (☎ 162 83; www.jugendherberge.de; Kaiser-Friedrich-Platz 2; dm under/over 26yr €15.60/18.60; Ⓟ ☒) Wallet watchers should check out this pleasantly renovated hostel.

Hotel Stadt Soest (☎ 362 20; www.hotel-stadt-soest .de; Brüderstrasse 50; s €45, d €75-90; Ⓟ ☒) At this low-key property, rooms pair a hodgepodge of old-fashioned furniture with such modern amenities as in-room DVDs (on request) and free wi-fi. It's in the pedestrian zone, just south of the train station.

Hotel Im Wilden Mann (☎ 150 71; www.im-wilden -mann.de; Am Markt 11; s €49, d €78-85) This central landmark hotel in a portly half-timbered town house has comfortable rooms furnished in rustic country style, as well as a fine restaurant.

Eating

Local specialities include the Soester *pumpernickel,* a rough-textured rye bread made entirely without salt, and the *Bullenauge* (bull's eye), a creamy mocha liqueur.

Der Kater (☎ 135 44; Nöttenstrasse 1; dishes €3-8; ☽ 10am-midnight) For more youthful flair try Der Kater, a bistro-pub with good pizza, salads and other casual fare.

Bontempi im Park (☎ 166 31; Im Theodor-Heuss-Park; pizza & pasta €6-10, mains €10-15; ☽ 10am-10pm) In fine weather, the idyllic park setting next to a duck pond is the biggest selling point of this popular bistro, but the Mediterranean menu convinces too. Come for breakfast, snacks, ice cream, coffee or a full meal.

Pilgrim Haus (☎ 1828; Jakobistrasse 75; snacks €6-10, mains €14-20; ☽ dinner Mon & Wed-Fri) This charming restaurant is similar but more upmarket than Brauerei Christ and claims to be Westphalia's oldest inn (since 1304).

Brauerei Christ (☎ 155 15; Walburger Strasse 36; mains €8-18; ☽ noon-11pm) History oozes from every nook and cranny of this warren of living-room-style rooms stuffed with musical instruments, oil paintings and unique knick-knacks. Hunker down at polished tables for Westphalian specialities or any of its 14 schnitzel variations. Nice beer garden.

Getting There & Away
Soest is easily reached by train from Dortmund (€9, 40 minutes) and is also regularly connected to Paderborn (€9, 35 minutes) and Münster (€12.10, 50 minutes). If you're driving, take the Soest exit from the A44. Soest is also at the crossroads of the B1, B229 and B475.

PADERBORN
☎ 05251 / pop 140,000

About 50km east of Soest, Paderborn is the largest city in eastern Westphalia and offers an intriguing blend of medieval marvels and hi-tech. It derives its name from the Pader which, at 4km, is Germany's shortest river. About 200 springs surfacing in the Paderquellgebiet, a landscaped park in the city centre, spurt out an average of 5000L per second.

Charlemagne used the royal seat and bishopric he had established here to control the Christianisation of the Saxon tribes. A visit by Pope Leo III in 799 led to the establishment of the Western Roman Empire, a precursor to the Holy Roman Empire, and Charlemagne's coronation as its emperor in Rome the following year. Paderborn remains a pious place to this day – churches abound, and religious sculpture and motifs adorn façades, fountains and parks. Many of the city's 14,000 students

are involved in theological studies (economics and technology are other major fields).

Orientation
Tiny Paderborn-Lippstadt Airport is 18km southwest of town. Most sights are conveniently bunched up in the largely pedestrianised Altstadt, which is encircled by a ring road and small enough to explore on foot. The Hauptbahnhof is just outside this ring. To get to Marienplatz (with the tourist office), the Dom and other sights, exit right onto Bahnhofstrasse and continue straight via busy Westernstrasse, the main shopping street. Alternatively, you can take bus 2, 4, 8 or 9 to Rathausplatz.

Information
Several banks with ATMs can be found along Westernstrasse and around the Dom and Rathaus.

Linnemann (☎ 285 50; Westernstrasse 31) Bookshop.

Post office (☎ 01802-3333; Liliengasse 2) Off Westernstrasse.

Raffles Internet Bar (☎ 282 507; 1st fl, Libori-Galerie, Kamp 30-32; per hr €2; ☽ 9.30am-1am)

St-Vincenz Hospital (☎ 860; Busdorf 2)

Tourist office (☎ 882 980; www.paderborn.de; Marienplatz 2a; ☽ 10am-6pm Mon-Fri, 10am-2pm Sat Apr-Oct, 10am-5pm Mon-Fri, 10am-2pm Sat Nov-Mar)

Sights
CITY CENTRE
Paderborn's massive **Dom** (Markt 17; ☽ 10am-6.30pm), a three-nave Gothic hall church, is a good place to start exploring the city. Enter through the southern portal (called 'Paradies'), adorned with delicate carved figures, then turn your attention to the **high altar** and the pompous **memorial tomb of Dietrich von Fürstenberg**, a 17th-century bishop. Signs point the way to the Dom's most endearing feature, the so-called **Dreihasenfenster**, a unique trompe l'oeil window in the cloister. Its tracery depicts three hares, ingeniously arranged so that each has two ears, even though there are only three ears in all.

The hall-like **crypt**, one of the largest in Germany, contains the grave and relics of St Liborius, the city's patron saint. To see the famous Liborius shrine, though, visit the **Erzbischöfliches Diözesanmuseum** (☎ 125 1400; Markt 17; adult/concession €2.50/1.50; ☽ 10am-6pm Tue-Sun), housed in an incongruously modernist structure outside the Dom. Its surprisingly attractive interior brims with church treasures, the most precious of which are kept in the basement, including the gilded shrine and prized portable altars. Upstairs, the one piece not to be missed is the Imad Madonna, an exquisite 11th-century lindenwood statue.

Paderborn's proud **Rathaus** (1616) with ornate gables, oriels and other decorative touches is typical of the Weser Renaissance architectural style. South of the Rathaus is the **Marktkirche** (Rathausplatz; ☺ 9am-6pm), a largely baroque galleried basilica, where pride of place goes to the dizzying high altar. A soaring symphony of wood and gold, it is an exact replica of the 17th-century original destroyed in WWII. Completely rebuilt using photographs and ingenuity, it only returned to this spot in 2004.

Rathausplatz blends into Marienplatz with its delicate **Mariensäule** (St Mary's Column) and **Heising'sche Haus**, an elaborate 17th-century patrician mansion that shares a wall with the tourist office. The **Abdinghofkirche** (Am Abdinghof; ☺ 11am-6pm May-Sep) is easily recognised by its twin Romanesque towers. Once a Benedictine monastery, it's been a Protestant church since 1867 and is rather austere with whitewashed and unadorned walls and a flat wooden ceiling.

At the foot of the Abdinghofkirche lies the **Paderquellgebiet**, a small park perfect for relaxing by the gurgling springs of the Pader and with nice views of the Dom. This is also the starting point of a lovely walk along the little river to **Schloss Neuhaus**, a moated palace about 5km northwest, which hosts frequent cultural events in summer.

East along Am Abdinghof to the north of the Dom are the remnants of the **Carolingian Kaiserpfalz**, Charlemagne's palace where that fateful meeting with Pope Leo took place. It was destroyed by fire and replaced in the 11th century by the **Ottonian-Salian Kaiserpfalz**, which has been reconstructed as faithfully as possible atop the original foundations. Inside is the **Museum in der Kaiserpfalz** (☎ 105 110; Am Ikenberg 2; adult/concession €2.50/1.50; ☺ 10am-6pm Tue-Sun), which presents excavated items from the early Middle Ages. Immediately adjacent is the tiny and beautiful **Bartholomäuskapelle** (☺ 10am-6pm), built in 1017 and the oldest hall church north of the Alps, with otherworldly acoustics.

HEINZ NIXDORF MUSEUMSFORUM (HNF)

Not only techies will enjoy the **HNF** (☎ 306 600; www.hnf.de; Fürstenallee 7; adult/concession €4/2; ☺ 9am-6pm Tue-Fri, 10am-6pm Sat & Sun), a fascinating romp through 5000 years of information technology, from cuneiform to cyberspace. Established by the local founder of the Nixdorf Computer AG (since swallowed by bigger corporations), it displays calculating machines, typewriters, cash registers, punch-card systems, manual telephone exchanges, accounting machines and other time-tested gadgets, although the heart of the museum clearly belongs to the computer age. Most memorable is the full-scale replica of **Eniac**, a room-sized vacuum-tube computer developed for the US Army in the 1940s that became the forerunner of the modern computer. These days, the data it held fits onto a teensy microchip.

There are plenty of machines to touch, push and prod as well as computer games and a virtual-reality theatre. English-language explanatory panels are only sporadic, but a comprehensive museum guide in English is available for €5. To get here, catch bus 11 from the Hauptbahnhof to Museumsforum.

Sleeping

Galerie-Hotel Abdinghof (☎ 122 40; www.galerie-hotel.de; Bachstrasse 1; s/d €75/92; Ⓟ ✗) In a 1563 stone building overlooking the Paderquellgebiet, this is Paderborn's most unconventional hotel. Rooms are named after famous artists and decorated in styles ranging from country-rustic to elegant-feminine. Original art graces the downstairs café-restaurant.

Hotel Stadthaus (☎ 188 9910; www.hotel-stadthaus.de; Hathumarstrasse 22; s/d €86/103; ✗ ✗) An air of quiet elegance pervades this 34-room hotel spread over two separate but equally delightful buildings. Free wine and bottled water are welcome perks, and so is the sauna for relaxing. The restaurant serves light meals.

Also recommended:

DJH hostel (☎ 220 55; Meinwerkstrasse 16; dm under/over 26yr Mar-Oct €15.60/18.60, Nov-Feb €14/17; Ⓟ ✗) Well-run and central hostel. Take bus 2 to Detmolder Tor.

Hotel Campus Lounge (☎ 892 070; www.campus-lounge.de; Mersinweg 2; s/d €80/90; Ⓟ ✗) Warm and welcoming property near the university with great views from the 'panorama rooms' and free DSL and wi-fi.

Krawinkel Hotel (☎ 693 990; www.hotel-krawinkel.de; Karlstrasse 33; s/d €90/100; Ⓟ ✗) Comfortable, contemporary suite with small kitchens, plenty of work space and sofabeds.

Eating

Curry Company (☎ 387 7414; Kamp 10; dishes €2-8; ☺ 11am-midnight) 'Gourmet snack' is not an oxymoron at this artsy sausage parlour where you can pair your wurst with such delicious homemade sauces as truffle mayonnaise, coriander-chilli sauce and classic curry.

Café Central (☎ 296 888; Rathauspassage; mains €4-9) This local favourite recently went sophisticated with shiny leather seating, a long bar and an elegant frieze. Fortunately, it hasn't sacrificed its laid-back vibe and is still a great hang-out for breakfast, a light meal or a drink. It's in the Rathauspassage (enter from Rosenstrasse).

Deutsches Haus (☎ 221 36; Kisau 9; mains €7-19; ⊙ 8.30am-1am) Rustic beams and woodsy booths combine with colourful Art Deco lamps at this popular German restaurant. All the classics are here, including 10 schnitzel variations.

Trattoria Il Postino (☎ 296 170; Rathauspassage; mains €9-19; ⊙ lunch & dinner Mon-Sat) Locals intent on superior Italian food flock to this snazzy, glass-fronted restaurant with fresh flowers, crisp tablecloths and a big central bar. The chef does creative things with fresh pasta, but it's the meat and fish dishes that reveal the full extent of his skills. Enter from Jühenplatz.

Getting There & Away

AirBerlin offers direct flights between London-Stansted and the tiny **Paderborn-Lippstadt Airport** (☎ 02955-770; www.flughafen-paderborn-lippstadt .de), which is connected to the Hauptbahnhof by bus 400 and 460.

Paderborn has direct IC or ICE trains every two hours to Kassel-Wilhelmshöhe (€21 to €23, 1¼ hours) and regional connections to Dortmund (€17.60, 1¼ hours) and other Ruhrgebiet cities. Trains to Soest (€9, 35 minutes) leave several times hourly.

Paderborn is on the A33, which connects with the A2 in the north and the A44 in the south. The B1, B64 and B68 also go through Paderborn.

Getting Around

Bus rides cost €1.15 for short trips, €1.70 for longer ones and €4.60 for a day pass. **Radstation** (☎ 870 740; Bahnhofstrasse 29; ⊙ 5.30am-10.30pm) at the Hauptbahnhof rents bicycles for €9 per 24 hours.

SAUERLAND

Even if you've never heard of the Sauerland, you're probably familiar with its most famous product: beer – or Warsteiner Pils to be precise – made by Germany's largest brewery in the town of Warstein. Otherwise, this forested upland region in the southeast of North Rhine-Westphalia serves mostly as an easy getaway for Ruhrgebiet residents. There are a few museums and castles, but the Sauerland's primary appeal lies in nature. Nordic walking and hiking are big here, with some 20,000km of marked trails, mostly through beech and fir forest. For cyclists, Bike Arena Sauerland covers 1400km on 37 routes. Reservoirs and lakes are popular with swimmers, windsurfers and boaters, and in winter the higher elevations often get enough snow to allow for decent downhill and Nordic skiing. The area is also rich in caves filled with bizarrely shaped formations.

The Sauerland is best explored under your own steam, although even the smallest towns are served by buses or trains. Local tourist offices abound or call the central hotline at ☎ 0180-509 6980. Staff here can also book private rooms and hotels.

ALTENA

☎ 02352 / pop 22,200

In a steep, narrow valley carved by the Lenne River, Altena has built its fortune on producing industrial wire since making mail-shirts for medieval knights. Despite its scenic setting, it wouldn't be worth a stop were it not for the majestic **Burg Altena**, a quintessential medieval castle and 1912 birthplace of the youth hostel movement. The world's first hostel, with dark dorms sporting wooden triple bunks, now forms part of the newly revamped **castle museum** (☎ 966 7034; Fritz-Thomee-Strasse 80; adult/concession/family €5/2.50/10; ⊙ 9.30am-5pm Tue-Fri, 11am-6pm Sat & Sun). This is a series of 28 themed rooms, each zeroing in on a different aspect of regional history, often in a visually pleasing and engaging fashion. You'll see some fancy historic weapons and armour, but also an exhibit on the Sauerland under the Nazis. Plan on spending at least 90 minutes to see it all.

Admission is also good at the **Deutsches Drahtmuseum**, about 300m downhill. It has hands-on displays on the many facets of wire from its manufacture to its use in industry, communications and art.

Altena's **tourist office** (☎ 209 295; www.altena -tourismus.de; Lüdenscheider Strasse 22) keeps erratic hours, so call ahead if possible.

You won't have to sleep in triple bunks but staying at Altena's **DJH hostel** (☎ 235 22; www.djh.de;

Fritz-Thomee Strasse 80; dm under/over 26yr €15.60/18.60; ⊗), which is inside the old castle, is still a nostalgic treat.

The castle and hostel are about a 15-minute walk from the train station. Altena is served by regional train from Hagen.

ATTENDORN
☎ 02722 / pop 24,500

The main attraction of Attendorn, a typical Sauerland town on the northern shore of the Biggesee lake, is the **Atta-Höhle** (☎ 937 50; Finnentroper Strasse 39; tours adult/child €6/4.50; ☺ 9.30am-4.30pm May-Sep, reduced hours Oct-Apr), one of Germany's largest and most impressive caves. The 40-minute tour takes you past a subterranean lake and stalagmites and stalactites shaped into curtains, domes, columns and shields.

The Biggesee lake is great for water sports as well as lake cruises, which are operated by **Personenschifffahrt Biggesee** (☎ 02761-965 90; www .personenschifffahrt-biggesee.de; €8/4.50; ☺ Apr-Oct).

Attendorn's **tourist office** (☎ 4897; www .attendorn.net; Rathauspassage; ☺ 9am-5.30pm Mon-Fri year-round, 10am-1pm Sat Jun-Sep) can help out with accommodation.

A memorable place to spend the night is **Burg Schnellenberg** (☎ 6940; www.burg-schnellenberg .de; s €87-107, d €125-170; P ⊗), a 17th-century castle-hotel with gourmet restaurant perched high above town. It's pretty formal, so bring your manners. The cheapest rooms are very small.

To get to Attendorn by regional train requires changing in Hagen and in Finnentrop.

WINTERBERG
☎ 02981 / pop 14,500

Winterberg, the region's winter sports centre, is overlooked by the Kahler Asten, at 842m the Sauerland's highest mountain. Besides skiing, attractions include a 1600m-long bobsled run and an indoor skating rink. In good winters, the season runs from December to March, often helped along by snowmaking machines if nature fails to perform. In summer, there's lots of good hiking, including a popular and moderately strenuous 5km trail to the top of the Kahler Asten.

For more ideas, stop by the **tourist office** (☎ 925 00; www.winterberg.de; Am Kurpark 6).

Winterberg is served directly by trains from Dortmund every two hours.

SIEGERLAND

The hills and mountains of the Sauerland continue southward into the Siegerland region, with the city of Siegen as its focal point. Frankfurt, the Ruhrgebiet and Cologne are all about 100km away.

SIEGEN
☎ 0271 / pop 106,000

Wedged into a valley hemmed by dense forest, Siegen is the commercial hub of the Siegerland. For centuries it was ruled by the Counts of Nassau-Oranien, the family that ascended to the Dutch throne in 1813. Two palaces from those glory days survived the bombing squadrons of WWII, but in every other respect Siegen is a thoroughly modern city. The hilly Altstadt is the most scenic part of it, but its streets are increasingly quiet as two new giant shopping malls down by the Hauptbahnhof zap away the bulk of the business. Siegen was the birthplace of the painter Peter Paul Rubens (1577–1640).

Orientation
Siegen's Altstadt slopes up from the Hauptbahnhof via pedestrianised Bahnhofstrasse and Kölner Strasse. If you're driving, the main artery through town is Koblenzer Strasse (B54/62).

Information
Banks with ATMs are right outside the Hauptbahnhof along Bahnhofstrasse.
Post office (Hindenburgstrasse 9)
Siegen tourist office (☎ 404 1316; www.tourismus .gss-siegen.de; Rathaus, Markt 2; ☺ 8am-4pm Mon & Tue, 8am-noon Wed & Fri, 8am-6pm Thu, 9am-noon Sat)
Siegerland tourist office (☎ 333 1020; Koblenzer Strasse 73; www.siegerland-wittgenstein-tourismus.de; ☺ 8.30am-5pm Mon-Fri)

Sights
A hardened criminal arriving in prison might well gripe: 'This sure ain't no palace'. Well, in Siegen, it is. The **Unteres Schloss**, a mustard-coloured baroque palace, now houses the local jail along with other city-government offices. The elegant three-wing structure originally served as the residence of the Protestant princes of Nassau-Oranien, who had split off from the family's Catholic branch in 1623.

Right next to the prison wing, the **Museum für Gegenwartskunst** (Museum of Contemporary Art; ☎ 405 770; Unteres Schloss 1; adult/concession €3.90/2.60; ⏲ 11am-6pm Tue, Wed & Fri-Sun, 11am-8pm Thu) occupies a 19th-century telegraph office with a modern annex. The permanent exhibit includes works by Francis Bacon, Lucian Freud and Cy Twombly, all of them recipients of the Rubenspreis (Rubens Prize) awarded by the city to an international artist every five years.

In the Markt you'll find the late Romanesque **Nikolaikirche** (⏲ 10am-6pm Mon-Fri, 10am-noon Sat May-Oct), which has a unique hexagonal floor plan but is otherwise quite plain on the inside. The golden, filigree crown atop the steeple is the city emblem. It was put there in 1652 to commemorate the local ruler's promotion from count to prince.

From Markt, Burgstrasse slopes up to the **Oberes Schloss**, a classic medieval fortress and the ancestral home of the rulers of Nassau-Oranien. Its labyrinth of rooms now houses the **Siegerlandmuseum** (☎ 230 410; Burgstrasse; adult/concession €2/1; ⏲ 10am-5pm Tue-Sun), which would be a mediocre collection of old paintings were it not for its eight Rubens originals, including a self-portrait and a large-scale work viscerally depicting a lion hunt.

Sleeping

The local and the regional tourist offices can help with room reservations.

Berghotel Johanneshöhe (☎ 310 008; www.johann eshoehe.de; Wallhausenstrasse 1; s €51-67, d €71-89; **P**) If you're motorised, this hilltop hotel will treat you to sweeping views (somewhat marred by the autobahn) and immaculate if rather stuffy quarters. The stiff-white-linen restaurant makes upscale German dishes (mains €11 to €23).

Park Hotel (☎ 338 10; www.bestwestern.de; Koblenzer Strasse 135; s/d €81/96; **P** **✗**) This modern 88-room property offers four-star amenities at three-star prices. Although it goes mostly after the business brigade, it offers such welcome leisure facilities as a sauna and steam room.

Eating

9Bar (☎ 313 9169; Markt 27; mains €6-8; ⏲ 10am-midnight Mon-Sat, 2pm-midnight Sun) Pasta paired with classic and creative sauces is the main draw at this little urban bistro across from the Nikolaikirche. At night, it morphs into a bar-lounge.

Laternchen (☎ 231 8000; Löhrstrasse 37; mains €10-20; ⏲ dinner Thu-Tue) For classic German cuisine, book a table at this elegantly rustic restaurant. It's in one of Siegen's few historic buildings with neat leaded-glass windows and slate-covered façade.

Piazza (☎ 303 0856; Unteres Schloss 1; lunch €6-11, dinner €12-22; ⏲ 11am-11pm) Next to the Museum für Gegenwartskunst, this is a surprisingly urban restaurant with sleek décor, a terrace with teak furniture and a menu that mixes German and Mediterranean flavours and techniques.

Getting There & Away

Direct trains depart for Cologne hourly (€16.30, 1½ hours) and to Frankfurt (€21, 1¾ hours) every two hours. Change in Hagen for Dortmund (€22, two hours). Siegen is off the A45 connecting the Ruhrgebiet with Frankfurt and is also easily reached from Cologne via the A4.

AROUND SIEGEN
Freudenberg

☎ 02734 / pop 18,600

About 12km north of Siegen, Freudenberg would be unremarkable without its amazing **Altstadt** (called 'Alter Flecken', meaning Old Borough), the 17th-century equivalent of a planned community. Built in tidy rows, these half-timbered houses all point in the same direction, are approximately the same height and sport the same white façades, the same pattern of wooden beams and the same black-slate roofs. Follow signs to *Historischer Stadtkern* (historic town centre). For panoramic views head to the Kurpark, best accessed from the intersection of Am Kurpark and Kölner Strasse.

Lower Saxony

Confusingly, Lower Saxony lies in the north and evinces the sort of character opinion pollsters would describe as 'Middle Germany'. Yes, Niedersachsen, as it's called in German, lacks the big set-piece or bold image of some fellow states, but that doesn't make it uninteresting. Instead, it presents a mosaic, a panoply, a potpourri. With an array of wildly different attractions, visitors can certainly mix it up in Germany's second biggest state: steer a Volkswagen over an obstacle course in Wolfsburg's Autostadt theme park, smell the roses in Hanover's Herrenhäuser Gardens, or even pay a sobering visit to Bergen-Belsen.

The capital, Hanover, has a workaholic reputation as a host of trade fairs, especially the enormous communications show, CeBit. But cute medieval towns, cutting-edge science centre Phaeno, and a park of life-size dinosaur models make it a perfect state for relaxation and families. Cycling the Fairy-Tale Road to Hamelin's engaging Renaissance museum or visiting the archaeological site of a Roman defeat at Osnabrück's 'Varusschlacht' will appeal to young and old.

Culture vultures will be kept happy, with an early example of Daniel Libeskind's striking architecture in Osnabrück's Felix-Nussbaum-Haus. Plus, beautiful Celle is so keen about its art it's launched the 'world's first 24-hour museum' (of sorts).

With a varied landscape of coast, river plains, moor and heath, there's also plenty of stuff for nature lovers. In how many places can you say that you've walked to an island? Head north to where Deutschland meets the North Sea, and Lower Saxony offers that opportunity too.

HIGHLIGHTS

- **Adrenaline Rush** Test your driving skills at Volkswagen's Autostadt theme park (p622) in Wolfsburg
- **Quirky Old Town** Fall head over heels for the wobbly city of Lüneburg (p611)
- **Living History** Travel back in time to the Renaissance, in the Pied Piper's town of Hamelin (p603)
- **Pilgrimage** Pay your respects to Anne Frank at the Bergen-Belsen concentration camp (p610)
- **Green Haven** Admire the Niki de Saint Phalle grotto at Hanover's Herrenhäuser Gärten (p595)
- **Off-beat Experience** Walk to an East Frisian island across the seabed at low tide (p637)

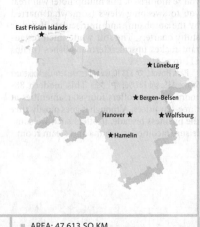

East Frisian Islands

★ Lüneburg

★ Bergen-Belsen

Hanover ★   ★ Wolfsburg

★ Hamelin

■ POPULATION: 8 MILLION ■ AREA: 47,613 SQ KM

HANOVER

☎ 0511 / pop 515,800

Hanover gets a bad rap. Local comedians dismiss it as 'the Autobahn exit between Göttingen and Walsrode'. News magazine *Der Spiegel* has written it off as having 'the most boring parties', and the rest of the world knows it as the host of the not particularly sexy CeBit communications trade show.

However, things aren't really so grim up north in Lower Saxony's state capital. The city also boasts acres of greenery. Its baroque Herrenhäuser Gärten (gardens) are a mini-Versailles, featuring a sparkly Niki de Saint Phalle Grotto. The compact centre, only partially reconstructed in a medieval style after WWII bombing, is adjoined to the east by the Eilenreide forest, and you can enjoy a few museums en route to the southern Maschsee (lake).

History

Hanover was established around 1100 and became the residence of Heinrich der Löwe (see boxed text, p619) later that century. An early Hanseatic city, it developed into a prosperous seat of royalty and a major power by the Reformation.

It has links with Britain through a series of marriages. In 1714 the eldest son of Electress Sophie of Hanover, a granddaughter of James I of England (James VI of Scotland), ascended the British throne as George I while simultaneously ruling Hanover. This British–German union lasted until 1837.

In 1943, up to 80% of the centre and 50% of the entire city was destroyed by Allied bombing. The rebuilding plan included creating sections of reconstructed half-timbered houses and painstakingly rebuilding the city's prewar gems, such as the Opernhaus (Opera House), the Marktkirche and the Neues Rathaus (New Town Hall).

A few years ago, Hanover was hoping to be at the centre of world attention as the host of Expo 2000. However, only 18 million visitors turned up – less than half the number expected. Having been one of the 12 German host cities for the FIFA Football World Cup in 2006 at least gives the city something new to boast about.

Orientation

The Hauptbahnhof (central train station) is located on the northeastern edge of the city centre. The centre contains one of the largest pedestrianised areas in Germany, focusing on Georgstrasse and Bahnhofstrasse. Bahnhofstrasse heads southwest from the Hauptbahnhof, and Georgstrasse runs west–east from Steintor via the Kröpcke square to Georgsplatz. There's a subterranean shopping strip running below Bahnhofstrasse, from the Hauptbahnhof to just south of Kröpcke, called the Niki de Saint Phalle Promenade.

The Herrenhäuser Gärten are situated about 4km northwest of the city centre. The Messegelände, the main trade fairgrounds, are in the city's southeast (see boxed text, p596).

Information

DISCOUNT CARDS

HannoverCard (per 1/3 days €9/15) Available from the tourist office, this card offers unlimited public transport and discounted or free admission to museums etc. Group tickets for five available, too.

EMERGENCY

Medical emergency service (☎ 314 044)

Police (☎ 110; Raschplatz) Beneath the overpass on the north side of the Hauptbahnhof.

INTERNET ACCESS

Teleklick Hannover (Schillerstrasse 23; per hr €3; ☺ 10am-11pm Mon-Sat, noon-10pm Sun)

LAUNDRY

Waschsalon (cnr Friesenstrasse & Eichstrasse; per wash €3.50; ☺ 6am-11pm)

MEDICAL SERVICES

Hospital (☎ 304 31; Marienstrasse 37)

MONEY

There are several ATMs and a late-opening Reisebank in the Hauptbahnhof.

POST

Main post office (Kurt-Schumacher-Strasse 4; ☺ 9am-8pm Mon-Fri, to 4pm Sat)

TOURIST INFORMATION

Tourist brochures are also available from the Neues Rathaus (see p594).

Hannover Tourismus (☎ information 1234 5111; room reservations 1234 555; www.hannover.de, www .hannover-tourism.de; Ernst-August-Platz 8; ☺ 9am-6pm Mon-Fri, to 2pm Sat)

LOWER SAXONY

LOWER SAXONY

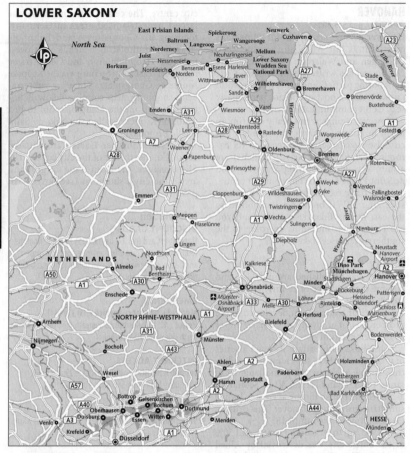

Dangers & Annoyances

The area around the Hauptbahnhof feels a bit dodgy after dark; there's a huge police presence there, but you should still use common sense. The red-light districts around Steintor to the southwest of the station and Ludwigstrasse to its north have been partly reclaimed by clubs and hotels, but it's still a good idea to stay reasonably vigilant in these areas at night.

Sights & Activities
ROTER FADEN

The city has painted a *Roter Faden* (red line) on pavements around the centre. Follow it with the help of the multilingual *Red Thread Guide* (€2), available from the tourist office,

for a quick 4.2km, do-it-yourself tour of the city's main highlights.

NEUES RATHAUS

An excellent way to get your bearings in Hanover is to visit the Neues Rathaus (built in 1901–13) and travel 98m to the top in the **curved lift** (elevator; adult/concession €2.50/1.50; ☉ 10am-6pm Apr-Nov) inside its green dome. There are several viewing platforms here, and while it's a novelty taking a lift that slants to stay within the dome, it's only on descent that you feel any gravitational swing. The cabin can take only five people at a time, so queues are inevitable.

In the downstairs lobby are four city models showing Hanover from the Middle Ages

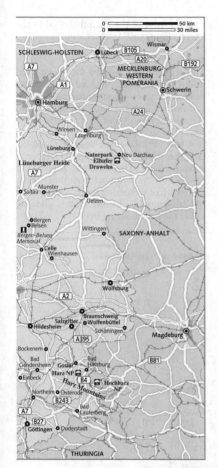

to today. Comparing the models from 1939 and 1945 drives home the dramatic extent of WWII devastation.

HERRENHÄUSER GÄRTEN

Largely modelled on the gardens at Versailles, the **Herrenhäuser Gärten** (☎ 1684 7576, 12345-333; www.herrenhaeuser-gaerten.de; ⏰ 9am-sunset; 🚇 4 or 5 to Herrenhäuser Gärten) truly rank among Hanover's most memorable attractions. You need a couple of hours to do them justice, but they combine a couple of treats.

On the one hand, the Grosser Garten (Large Garden), Berggarten (Mountain Garden) and Georgengarten (Georgian Garden), are prime examples of why Hanover calls itself a city 'in green'. On the other, the statues, fountains

and coloured tile walls of the **Niki de Saint Phalle Grotto** (opened after her death in 2002) provide a magical showcase of the artist's work that could one day outshine Die Nanas (see below).

With its fountains, neat flowerbeds, trimmed hedges and shaped lawns, the 300-year-old **Grosser Garten** (admission €3, combined admission with Berggarten €4, child free Apr-early Oct, free mid-Oct–Mar) is the centrepiece of the experience. There's a maze near the northern entrance, while the **Grosse Fontäne** (Big Fountain; the tallest in Europe) at the southern end jets water up to 80m high. In summer, there are **Wasserspiele** (Water games; ⏰ 11am-noon & 3-5pm Mon-Fri, 11am-noon & 2-5pm Sat & Sun Apr-early Oct) when all fountains are synchronised. During the **Illuminations** (adult/concession €4/3; ⏰ approximately 10pm Thu-Tue Jun-Aug, call for exact times) the gardens and fountains are atmospherically lit at night. Meanwhile there are summer concerts, Shakespearean dramas and more. Call or check the Herrenhäuser website for details.

North of the Grosser Garten lies the **Berggarten** (admission €2, combined admission with Grosser Garten €4, child free Apr-early Oct), with its great assortment of flora from around the world. Also here is the **Regenwaldhaus** (Tropical Rainforest House; ☎ 126 0420; www.regenwaldhaus.de; Herrenhäuser Strasse 4a; adult/concession €4.50/1.50; ⏰ 9am-7pm, later on weekends in summer). Inside there's a fairly gimmicky and contrived virtual 'journey' to the Amazon. Things are much more pleasant in the attached tropical greenhouse.

Amid the lake-dotted Georgengarten (admission free), you'll find the **Wilhelm-Busch-Museum** (☎ 1699 9916; www.wilhelm-busch-museum .de; adult/concession €4.50/2.50; ⏰ 10am-5pm Tue-Fri, to 6pm Sat & Sun) containing a wealth of caricature, including works by Busch, Honoré Daumier and William Hogarth.

DIE NANAS

The city government was inundated with nearly 20,000 letters of complaint when these three earth-mama **sculptures** were first installed beside the Leine River in 1974. Now, the voluptuous and fluorescent-coloured 'Sophie', 'Charlotte' and 'Caroline' by French artist Niki de Saint Phalle are among the city's most recognisable, and most loved, landmarks.

Indeed the Nanas helped make De Saint Phalle famous. Devout fans of her work will find that a direct trip to Leibnizufer (U-Bahn:

Markthalle Landtag) rewarding. Others could be left thinking 'Is that it?' In that case, wait until Saturday, when the extra attraction of a flea market takes place at the Nanas' feet.

SPRENGEL MUSEUM

It's the building as much as the curatorial policy that puts the **Sprengel Museum** (☎ 1684 3875; www.sprengel-museum.de; Kurt Schwitters Platz; adult/ child under 12yr/concession €7/free/4; ♥ 10am-6pm Wed-Sun, 10am-8pm Tue) in such high esteem. Its huge interior spaces are brilliant for displaying its modern figurative, abstract and conceptual art, including a few works by Nolde, Chagall and Picasso. At the core of the collection are 300 works by Niki de Saint Phalle, a selection of which is usually on show. Take bus 131

from in front of the Hauptbahnhof to the Sprengelmuseum/Maschsee stop.

MASCHSEE

This artificial lake, built by the unemployed in one of the earliest Nazi-led public works projects, is now a favourite spot for boating and swimming. It's certainly the most central at just half an hour's walk away; otherwise take bus 131 to Sprengelmuseum/Maschsee.

A **ferry** (☎ 0172-541 5525; adult/child €3/1.50, tour €6/3) plies the lake from Easter to October in good weather, and there are sailing, pedal and rowing boats for hire. On the southeast bank, there's a free swimming beach, or **Strandbad** (♥ May-Aug), while in-line skaters glide by under the neighbouring trees.

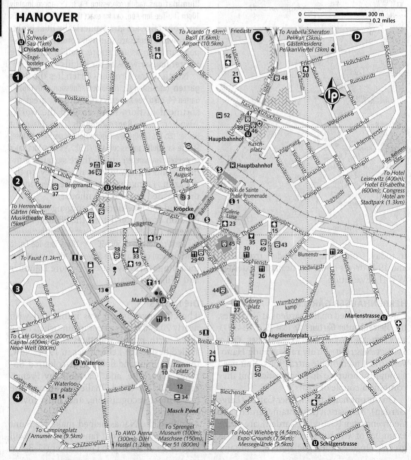

HANOVER

ALTSTADT

Some of it is a postwar fake, but parts of Hanover's Altstadt (old town) still look appealingly quaint. The red-brick, Gothic **Marktkirche** (1349–59) in the market square has original elements, as do both the **Altes Rathaus** (begun 1455) across the market, and the nearby **Ballhof** (1649–64), a hall originally built for 17th-century badminton-type games.

However, the city re-created an entire row of **half-timbered houses** lining Kramerstrasse and Burgstrasse near the Marktkirche. The Renaissance façade of the **Leibnizhaus** is also a reconstruction; the house was once the home of mathematician and philosopher Gottfried Wilhelm Leibniz (1646–1716).

In front of the Leibnizhaus is the **Oskar-Winter-Brunnen** (Oskar Winter Fountain). If you make a wish and turn the small brass ring embedded in the ironwork three times, local lore has it that the wish will come true.

OTHER MUSEUMS

It's always worth checking listings for the **Kestner Gesellschaft** (Kestner Society; ☎ 701 200; www.kestner.org; Goseriede 11; adult/concession €5/2.50; ☽ 10am-7pm Tue, Wed & Fri-Sun, to 9pm Thu). Having exhibited works by Otto Dix, Georg Grosz, Wassily Kandinsky and Paul Klee before they became famous, the society is still originating shows that later tour Europe. Its wonderfully light, high-ceilinged premises were once a bathhouse.

Decorative arts through the ages are covered at the **Kestner Museum** (☎ 1684 2120; Trammplatz 3; adult/concession €4/3, Fri free; ☽ 11am-6pm Tue & Thu-Sun, to 8pm Wed), where you'll see everything from Bauhaus-style cutlery to a very impressive collection of Greek and Egyptian antiquities.

WAR MEMORIALS

In a city so devastated by war, it's not surprising to find a **peace bell**. Donated by sister city Hiroshima, it lies inside a steel-cross **Memorial to Our Dead** on Breite Strasse near the corner of Osterstrasse. Every 6 August at 8.15am, the date and time of the atomic detonation at Hiroshima, a delegation from both cities meets here to ring the bell. The neighbouring **Aegidienkirche Memorial** (1350) was bashed by artillery in 1943.

The winged angel **Waterloo Memorial** you see south of the Altstadt and west of the Neues Rathaus commemorates the German forces who fought at Waterloo.

Festivals & Events

The annual **Maschsee festival**, which includes drinking, performances and an enormous fireworks display, runs annually in early August. The international **fireworks festival** and competition at Herrenhäuser Gärten is another big summer event. People also come to Hanover from afar for the **International Jazz Festival**, held around Ascension Day in May/June.

INFORMATION		Etap Hotel	18 B1	Café Caldo	37 A2
Hannover Tourismus	1 C2	Hanns Lilje-Haus	19 B3	Café Konrad	38 B3
Hospital	2 D3	Hotel Alpha	20 C1	Diablo Latino	39 C2
Teleklick Hannover	3 B2	Hotel Königshof am Funkturm	21 C1	Eve Club	(see 41)
Waschsalon	4 D1	Hotel Stella	22 D4	GOP Varieté	40 B3
		Kastens Hotel Luisenhof	23 C2	Heartbreak Hotel	41 A2
SIGHTS & ACTIVITIES		Lühmanns Hotel am Rathaus	24 C4	Intensivstation	(see 42)
Aegidienkirche Memorial	5 B3			Kiez Club	42 A2
Altes Rathaus	6 B3	EATING 🍴		Marlene Bar &	
Ballhof	7 B3	Besitos	25 B2	Bühne	43 C3
Die Nanas	8 A3	Biesler	26 C3	Neues Theater	44 C3
Kestner Gesellschaft	9 A2	Georxx	27 C3	Opernhaus	45 C3
Kestner Museum	10 B4	Hiller	28 D3	Osho Diskothek	46 C1
Leibnizhaus	(see 13)	Holländische Kakaostube	29 B3	Palo Palo	47 C1
Marktkirche	11 B3	Maestro	30 C3	Pavilion	48 C1
Neues Rathaus	12 B4	Markthalle	31 B3	Sansibar	(see 42)
Oskar-Winter-Brunnen	13 A3	Mr Phung Kabuki	32 C4	Schauspielhaus	49 C3
Peace Bell	(see 5)			Theater am	
Waterloo Memorial	14 A4	DRINKING 🍷🍸		Aegi	50 C4
		Brauhaus Ernst August	33 B3		
SLEEPING 🛏		Der Gartensaal	34 B4	SHOPPING 🛍	
City Hotel am		HeimW	35 C3	Flea Market	51 A3
Thielenplatz	15 C2				
City Hotel Flamme	16 C1	ENTERTAINMENT 🎭		TRANSPORT	
CVJM City Hotel	17 B3	Anzeiger Hochhaus	36 A2	Central Bus Station	52 C1

LOWER SAXONY

LOWER SAXONY

ALL THE FUN OF THE TRADE FAIR

Coming to Hanover for a trade fair or Messe? You're part of a time-honoured tradition. The first export fair was held in August 1947 in the midst of all the rubble from WWII. As most hotels had been destroyed, the mayor made an appeal to citizens to provide beds for foreign guests. The people did, the money came and it's become a tradition; about a third more beds are available in private flats at fair-time (the only time they're offered) than in hotels.

The pre-eminent fair today is CeBit, a telecommunications and office information gathering that organisers claim is 'the largest trade show of any kind, anywhere in the world'. It's held every March and during the dotcom boom of the late 1990s had as many as 800,000 attendees. (More recent shows have attracted smaller crowds of around half a million visitors.) Another biggie is Hannover Messe, an industrial show in late April.

The Messegelände, the main trade fairgrounds, are in the city's southeast, served by tram/U-Bahn 8 (and during fair times 18) as well as IC and ICE trains. Tram/U-Bahn 6 serves the eastern part of the fairgrounds near the former Expo site.

During major fairs there's a full-service tourist office at the airport and an information pavilion at the fairgrounds, in addition to the main tourist office (see Information, p585).

Pressure on accommodation means you really need to book ahead – and be prepared for phenomenal price hikes too. Indeed some visitors choose to stay instead in Hildesheim, Celle (both of which up their own prices during these times) or even in Hamburg, and commute. To organise a private room or hotel in Hanover, call ☎ 1234 5555.

Sleeping

The tourist office books rooms, but for a pretty hefty €6.50 fee. Prices given here are those outside trade-show periods. During shows, they can double, triple and even quadruple. Check on the city website (www.hannover.de) or better yet ask the tourist office directly to ensure you're not unintentionally arriving during a trade-fair period.

BUDGET

Campingplatz Arnumer See (☎ 05101-3534; http://camping-hannover.de; Osterbruchweg 5, Arnum-Hemmingen; adult/car €5/2, tent €3-5; ☐) In a pleasant leafy lakeside location south of the city, this extremely well-equipped camping ground has modern washing facilities, a restaurant, internet access, a playground and a separate areas for tents and caravans. Take bus 300 to Arnum Mitte, from where it's a five-minute walk. By road take A7 south to Laatzen, or B3 from Arnum and follow the signs.

DJH hostel (☎ 131 7674; www.jugendherberge.de/jh/hannover; Ferdinand-Wilhelm-Fricke-Weg 1; dm under/over 26yr from €18/21; Ⓟ ☒ ☐ ; Ⓞ 3 or 7 to Fischerhof) This huge, space-lab-looking structure houses a modern hostel with breakfast room and terrace bar overlooking the river. You feel like you're out in the surburbs when you arrive, but soon realise it's only a short walk to the Maschsee. All mod cons are provided.

Etap Hotel (☎ 235 5570; www.etaphotel.com; Runde Strasse 7; s/d €40/50; Ⓟ ☒ ☐) This garish but comfortable chain hotel is not in particularly salubrious surroundings, but is handy for the train station.

City Hotel am Thielenplatz (☎ 327 691; www.smartcityhotel.de; Thielenplatz 2; s €40-50, d €50-60; Ⓟ ☒) This central place is metamorphosing from boring cheapie to 'budget boutique' beauty. The reception and bar have already spread their butterfly wings, having been remodelled in opulent style with red leather wall panels, black-and-white leaf-patterned wallpaper and lots of wood laminate. The rooms are expecting a 1950s-style retro refit, but were previously no-irony-intended, humble 1980s, so check the latest when booking.

Hotel Leisewitz (☎ 288 7940; www.hotel-leisewitz.de; Leisewitzerstrasse 11; s €50-90, d €75-115; Ⓟ) Grannies on acid alert! A psychedelic mishmash of chintzy patterns – florals, stripes and checks – is crammed into a small space in this friendly, family-run hotel. Fans of minimalism will hate it, but it's got bags of character and is pleasantly located on a leafy residential street. To get here take bus 128 to Plathnerstrasse.

GästeResidenz PelikanViertel (☎ 399 90; www.gaesteresidenz-pelikanviertel.de; Pelikanstrasse 11; s €40-230, d €60-260, tr €80-280; Ⓟ ; Ⓞ 9 to Pelikanstrasse) Upmarket student residence meets budget hotel, this huge complex alongside the Arabella Sheraton has a wide range of very pleasant Ikea-ish rooms. Some are split over two levels, with the bathroom and cupboard at hall level, and stairs to the bed, desk and kitchenette. Prices fluctuate wildly according to trade fair periods, but in quieter seasons it's excellent value indeed.

MIDRANGE

CVJM City Hotel (☎ 360 70; www.cityhotelhannover.de; Limburgstrasse 3; s €45-70, d €65-100; ✗) Deliciously candy-striped curtains and bed bases (eg, yellow and green in some rooms) add a touch of elegance and chic to this quiet but central hotel. Be warned, however, that while doubles are perfectly adequate in size, the singles are a little too small.

City Hotel Flamme (☎ 388 8004; www.cityhotelflamme.de; Lammstrasse 3; s €50-65, d €75-90, q €120-140; P ✗) The rooms of this relaxed hotel-*pension* open onto balconies facing a large internal courtyard, which has an eating area and glassed-in front wall. If you don't like the area around the train station, they will pick you up from there for free, and you can forego breakfast if you wish to pay slightly less.

Hotel Stella (☎ 811 2050; www.hotelstella.de; Adelheidstrasse; s/d from €60/80; P ✗) Pleasant if unspectacular, the Stella is a small hotel with a big heart and decent-sized rooms (plus odd floor numbering and a jolting lift). With luggage, it's a short U-Bahn ride from the Hauptbahnhof, but once you've dropped your bags, you can easily walk into town.

Hanns Lilje-Haus (☎ 124 1698; www.hanns-lilje-haus.de; Knochenhauerstrasse 33; s/d from €65/80, breakfast per person €6; ✗) No-one could take offence at the recently renovated rooms of this church-run hotel, which are decorated in the most neutral tones. However, they are quite spacious for such a central establishment and offer a good degree of comfort.

Lühmanns Hotel am Rathaus (☎ 326 268; www.hotelamrathaus.de; Friedrichswall 21; s €60-85, d €80-120, ste €150; ✗ 💻) Posters from the nearby Kestner Museum adorn the halls here, and the rooms themselves are tastefully decorated with liberal use of reds, blues and black, as well as the occasional bit of original art. Although the hotel's on a busy street, double-glazing keeps noise at bay.

Hotel Wiehberg (☎ 879 990; www.hotel-wiehberg.de; Wiehbergstrasse 55a; s/d €70/90; P ✗ ; 🚍 1 or 2 to Dorfstrasse) The patterned carpets mean the rooms of this historic villa could never be described as Zen. However, they do feature low Japanese-style beds, set on rails so that guests can indulge in a little feng shui of their own by repositioning them. The hotel's in a leafy residential neighbourhood.

Hotel Königshof am Funkturm (☎ 339 80; www.koenigshof-hannover.de; Friesenstrasse 65; s €70-110, d €100-125; P ✗) An eclectic mix of religious statues and ethnic sculptures (plus an old Rolls Royce) greet you as you roll your suitcase onto the Persian carpets here. This rambling abode has an older, cheaper wing out the back – where the bathrooms are huge – and a modern wing with corporate-oriented 'comfort', 'business' and 'deluxe' rooms. The location is handy for the train station, if somewhat sleazy.

Hotel Alpha (☎ 341 535; www.hotelalpha.de; Friesenstrasse 19; s/d €95/125; ✗) Although it's in a less grotty part of the same street, the Alpha is like Hotel Königshof in having quirky decorations. Here, however, the statues and marionettes are sweeter and more bucolic. There's a trompe l'oeil of an Italian piazza in the breakfast room and the rooms are lovely and homy.

TOP END

Arabella Sheraton Pelikan (☎ 909 30; pelikanhotel@arabellasheraton.com; Podbielskitrasse 145; s €100-125, d €130-155; P ✗) Fat beds with thick mattresses and plump cushions dominate the rooms of this luxury hotel, although the high ceilings alleviate any feeling of being cramped. It's easy to see why celebrities love the place. Set on a redeveloped factory site in the suburbs, it feels like a hideaway village, with the renowned restaurant 5th Avenue and Harry's New York bar. There's a fitness centre next door, too. Take tram 9 to Pelikanstrasse.

Kastens Hotel Luisenhof (☎ 304 40; www.kastens-luisenhof.de; Luisenstrasse 1-3; s €155-185, d €180-220, ste from €250; P ✗ ✗ 🖥) Obviously extremely well cared for, this *grande dame* looks pretty good for having recently turned 150 years old. Rooms reflect a timeless elegance, but there's a stylish new addition in the upper-level spa and fitness centre. The extremely central location is another selling point.

Eating

RESTAURANTS

Maestro (☎ 300 8575; Sophienstrasse 2; mains €4.50-8) This atmospheric subterranean restaurant offers an all-you-can-eat vegetarian buffet (€7) at lunch daily. Its tucked-away courtyard beer garden (ask the staff) is perfect in summer.

Georxx (☎ 306 147; Georgsplatz 3; dishes €5.50-14.50) Arty types come to lounge around this upmarket bistro, with a wine, beer or coffee, but the changing menu, which runs the gamut from European to Asian to Caribbean, is also worth savouring. Breakfast is a staple, and served until 5pm.

Pier 51 (☎ 807 1800; Rudolf von Bennigsen Ufer 51; mains €6-18) One of Hanover's loveliest restaurants, and very romantic at sundown, Pier 51 is walled with glass and juts out over the Maschsee. The menu is strong on fish, although you can also choose pasta or meat. In summer, there's an outside 'Piergarten', decked out with the old-fashioned *Strandkörbe* (straw basket seats) that you see on German beaches. Book at least a few days ahead if you want a window seat at dinner.

Mr Phung Kabuki (☎ 215 7609; Friedrichswall 10; sushi €2-6, mains €7-14) Boats bob by on the water-based sushi train, but you can order all manner of pan-Asian and wok dishes at this airy, trendy restaurant with an enormous range of spirits.

Hiller (☎ 321 288; Blumenstrasse 3; mains €7.50-14, set menus €8-21.50; ☽ closed Sun) Germany's oldest vegetarian restaurant is such an institution it even has its logo – a carrot – carefully embroidered on to every linen napkin. Despite the modern interior, with swirly green painting and mustard-coloured walls, the atmosphere is quite hushed and the food a tad old-fashioned. That said, come with an appetite if ordering a set menu.

Besitos (☎ 169 8001; courtyard, Goseriede 4; tapas €2-4, mains €8-14; ☽ from 5pm) Locals come to this warehouse-sized place to enjoy the city's best tapas under high ceilings and the watchful eye of gaucho and matador murals on the Mediterranean-coloured walls.

Basil (☎ 622 636; Dragonerstrasse 30; mains €12-23, menus around €25; ☽ dinner Mon-Sat) This former stables to the north of town now houses a fabulous fusion restaurant, with a high arched ceiling and pressed tablecloths. It serves imaginative concoctions, such as coffee-marinated duck breast with chicory and pear ragout, to an in crowd. Take tram 1, 2 or 8 to Dragonerstrasse.

Biesler (☎ 321 033; Sophienstrasse 6; mains €14-19; ☽ closed Sun year-round & Mon Nov-Mar) One of the oldest eateries in the city likes to mix the ancient and the modern on its menu. So each day it serves a different traditional German dish, such as roast calves' livers with apple

and onion, alongside international fare such as lamb on mushroom 'parfait' with rosemary and fennel.

CAFÉS & QUICK EATS

Holländische Kakaostube (☎ 304 100; Ständehausstrasse 2-3; ☽ 9am-7.30pm Mon-Fri, 8.30am-6pm Sat) With the blue-and-white square-patterned floor matching the Delft pottery, and a curved ship's staircase and maritime paintings creating a subtle nautical feel, this historic Dutch coffee house has many fans, young and old. Stained glass, windmill figures, daintily swirled cakes and great hot chocolate all contribute to the atmosphere.

Markthalle (☎ 341 410; Kamarschstrasse 49; dishes €3.50-8; ☽ 7am-8pm Mon-Wed, to 10pm Thu & Fri, to 4pm Sat) This huge covered market of food stalls and gourmet delicatessens is a no-nonsense place for a quick bite – both carnivorous and vegetarian.

Drinking

CAFÉS

Der Gartensaal (☎ 1684 8888; Neues Rathaus, Trammplatz 2; ☽ 11am-6pm) A great place to sit and have a summer afternoon coffee overlooking the central *Stadtpark*, this venue now hosts occasional club evenings, too. Keep an eye out for flyers.

BARS

Many of the cultural centres, clubs and rock and jazz venues listed under Entertainment (opposite) are also good places to go just for a drink.

Brauhaus Ernst August (☎ 365 950; Schmiedestrasse 13) A Hanover institution, this sprawling brewpub makes a refreshing unfiltered Pilsner called Hannöversch. A party atmosphere reigns nightly, helped along by a varied roster of live bands.

HeimW (☎ 235 2301; Theaterstrasse 6; ☽ from 9am) Hanover's hipsters flock to this long, narrow bar, and not just for the cocktails, vodkas and whiskeys. How could you resist a place with lights shaped like huge droplets of water about to land on your head, a ceiling of blue sky and white clouds, potted palms beside cream leather banquettes, and intriguing photos of Hanover landmarks? Small meals are also served.

Acanto (☎ 391 030; Dragonerstrasse 28; ☽ Thu-Sat) Next door to the restaurant Basil, you'll find one of Hanover's trendiest DJ bars, where fashionably dressed beautiful people sip caipirinhas under chandeliers and mirror balls. Take tram 1, 2 or 8 to Dragonerstrasse.

Entertainment

For listings, check out the local edition of *Prinz*, in German.

CLUBS

Hanover has two main clusters of clubs and bars. Increasingly, the place to head is the red-light district of Steintor (cheekily nicknamed Stöhntor by locals, meaning 'Moaning Gate'), in a former strip and sex club stronghold.

Eve Klub (Reuterstrasse 3-4; ☿ Fri & Sat) For many, this small club is not only the best in Hanover, but one of Germany's best, too. A former striptease bar, it's kept the red lamps over the tables and red corduroy sofas, and added mirror balls, red hearts and retro trimmings. Reasonably priced drinks, a mixed crowd (mostly over 20) and a melange of funk, soul and party tunes from the 1970s and '80s keep things going to 6am on weekends.

Kiez Club (☎ 353 5699; Scholvinstrasse 4; ☿ Wed, Fri & Sat) Minimal house, techno house, electro house – it's all house within the red walls here. Beck's beer costs less than €1 on Wednesdays.

Sansibar (☎ 0177-500 6006; Scholvinstrasse 7) Its roster of 1960s soul, combined with classic tunes from the 1970s and '80s, make this another Steintor favourite.

Intensivstation (☎ 301 59; Scholvinstrasse 9; ☿ Fri & Sat, plus some Wed & Thu) This place has staff dressed as nurses and medically themed surrounds and drinks. Kinky.

Traditionally, the other main clubbing destination has been the concrete environs of Raschplatz (the so-called 'golden triangle') behind the train station. For years, this is where you've found **Osho Diskothek** (☎ 342 217; Raschplatz 7l), or 'Baggi' as Hanoverians fondly call it, playing a mix of classic disco hits for the over-25s. Latin club **Diablo Latino** (☎ 341 025; Raschplatz 1h) is also based here, as well as the see-and-be-seen **Palo Palo** (☎ 331 073; Raschplatz 8a). However, with Raschplatz due to be renovated in 2007, the future of all these clubs has been thrown into doubt. Check local listings before heading in this direction.

CINEMAS

Anzeiger Hochhaus (☎ 144 54; Goseriede 9) This spacious, art-house cinema is on the top floor of a magnificent expressionist building designed by Fritz Höger, the architect of Hamburg's Chilehaus (see p655). Check listing times, as the box office only opens just before screenings.

GAY & LESBIAN VENUES

More information can be found at http://hannover.gay-web.de, or head to the lesbian and gay hang-outs **Café Konrad** (☎ 323 666; Knochenhauerstrasse 34) or **Café Caldo** (☎ 151 73; Bergmanstrasse 7) where the staff will be able to fill you in on the scene.

Schwule Sau (☎ 700 0525; Schaufelder Strasse 30a; ⊖ U6 or 11 to Kopernikusstrasse) This alternative gay and lesbian centre regularly hosts concerts, theatre and club nights.

Otherwise the scene tends to revolve more around individual party nights, such as **Peppermint Pavilion** (www.hannover-gay-night.de) or **Der Blaue (B)Engel** (www.thenextgeneration.net). Check the websites for details.

THEATRE & CLASSICAL MUSIC

Opernhaus (☎ 268 6240; Opernplatz 1) The star in Hanover's cultural firmament, the 19th-century Opera House was lovingly restored after suffering WWII damage and now hosts classical music performances as well as opera.

GOP Varieté (☎ 301 8760; Georgstrasse 36) This is an old-school type of variety theatre with dancing, acrobatics, circus-style acts, magic, music and more, housed in the Georgspalast. It also boasts a much-lauded restaurant.

Those interested in seeing some cabaret should make tracks for **Marlene Bar & Bühne** (☎ 368 1687; cnr Alexanderstrasse & Prinzenstrasse), while German speakers into more serious drama should check out what's on at **Schauspielhaus** (☎ 168 6710; Prinzenstrasse 9) or the **Neues Theater** (☎ 363 001; Georgstrasse 54). Comedies and musical theatre are performed at **Theater am Aegi** (☎ 989 3333; Aegidientorplatz).

LIVE MUSIC

Café Glocksee (☎ 161 4712; Glockseestrasse 35) Part live-music venue, part club, the Glocksee has everything from techno and trance DJs to grungy gigs. Friday nights go electronic.

Capitol (☎ 444 066; Schwarzer Bär 2) This former movie theatre has rock, pop, house, soul and more on weekends and frequently during the week. Take tram 3, 7 or 9 to Schwarzer Bär.

Heartbreak Hotel (☎ 328 061; Reuterstrasse 5) You have to smile at a place that reserves a parking space for Elvis outside, which is just one reason why this scurrilous little live-music venue and not-just-for-old-rockers club managed to become so cool.

Gig Neue Welt (☎ 453 486; Lindener Markt 1) This chi-chi venue in a historic house is divided into three spaces: the Jazz-Café, as well as serving food, has black music, funk and jazz evenings; the Gig-Lounge specialises in soul; and the main room downstairs is for major events. To get here take tram 9 to Lindener Marktplatz.

Faust (☎ 455 001; Zur Bettfedernfabrik 1-3, Linden; ⓔ Leinaustrasse) Ska from Uruguay, Chinese new year festivals, disco, reggae, heavy metal gigs, multimedia installations, quiz evenings, book readings – this all happens, and more, in this former factory complex. The 1960s concert hall is complemented by a pub-bar, Mephisto.

Musiktheater Bad (☎ 169 4138; Am Grossen Garten 60) In this large old building and its surrounding grounds, you'll find a mixed bag of live music and dance offerings. It's great in summer when there's an outdoor stage.

Pavilion (☎ 344 558; Lister Meile 4) The café-bar of this huge circular venue swarms with customers all the day through, while evenings see a wide programme of jazz, off-beat rock, world music and even theatre.

SPORT

AWD Arena (www.awdarena.de) Given a major makeover for the FIFA Football World Cup in 2006, this stadium with a capacity of 44,000 is top-class. If you're going to a football match, it's just west of the Maschsee. Take bus 131 to the AWD Arena stop. Alternatively, take U-Bahn 3, 7 or 9 to Waterloo and follow the signs for about 500m.

Shopping

Hanover's compact city centre makes it ideal for shopping, although most of what you will find is modern, international fashion. A pedestrianised zone full of shops extends south from the Hauptbahnhof, along Bahnhofstrasse, Georgstrasse and Karmarschstrasse. The Niki de Sainte Phalle Promenade, a subterranean shopping strip running below Bahnhofstrasse, is also recommended as a good place for browsing.

There's a regular **flea market** (Hohen Ufer; ☼ 7am-1pm Sat) behind the Historisches Museum, along the Leine River Canal near Die Nanas.

Getting There & Away

AIR

Hanover Airport (HAJ; ☎ 977 1223; www.hannover -airport.de) has many connections, including with low-cost carrier **Air Berlin** (☎ 01805-737 800; www.airberlin.com), **British Airways** (☎ 721 076) and **Lufthansa** (☎ 0180-380 3803).

The S-Bahn (S5) takes 16 minutes from the airport to the Hauptbahnhof (€3.20).

CAR

Nearby autobahns run to Hamburg, Munich, Frankfurt and Berlin, with good connections to Bremen, Cologne, Amsterdam and Brussels. Major car rental firms are in the Hauptbahnhof, including **Sixt** (☎ general reservation 01805-252 525, local 363 830) and **Avis** (☎ general reservation 0180-555 77, local 322 610).

TRAIN

Hanover is a major rail hub, with frequent ICE trains to/from Hamburg (€36, 1¼ hours), Munich (€101, five hours), Cologne (€56, three hours) and Berlin (€53, 1½ hours), among others.

Getting Around

The transit system of buses and tram/U-Bahn lines is run by **Üstra** (☎ 01803-194 49). Most U-Bahn lines from the Hauptbahnhof are boarded in the station's north (follow signs towards Raschplatz), including U-Bahn 8 to the Messe (fairgrounds, 17 minutes). Lines U10 and U17 are different. These are overground trams leaving south of the station near the tourist office.

Most visitors only travel in the central 'Hannover' zone, where single tickets are €1.90 and day passes €3.60. If you wish to venture further into the Umland/Region zones, singles cost €2.60/3.20, while day passes cost €4.80/6.

For taxis call ☎ 8484. From the centre to the fairgrounds a taxi costs about €35; to the airport it's about €20.

AROUND HANOVER

Nobles the world over will tell you that ancestral homes can be *such* a huge financial burden to maintain, especially when they're turreted castles. In late 2005, the family of Prince Ernst August of Hanover (Princess Caroline of Monaco's husband) auctioned off some 25,000 household objects to raise money for the upkeep of their 130-room neo-Gothic fancy. Now a small part of the palace, **Schloss Marienburg** (☎ 05069-407; www .schloss-marienburg.de; tour adult/under 16yr €6/4.50; ☺ 10am-6pm Apr-Oct), is open to members of the public interested in a *Hello!* magazine-style behind-the-scenes glimpse. Admission is by a 45-minute tour only (leaving half-hourly), which includes the Knight's Hall, Queen's Library and more.

From Hanover, take the A7 and exit 62 for Hildesheim. Take the B1 out of Hildesheim and continue 7km until you come to Mahl-ehrten. Turn right for Nordstemmen and you should see the castle. By public transport, you can take a train from Hanover as far as Nordstemmen (€4.60) or bus 300 to Pattensen (€4.80 day card), but you'll have to walk or catch a taxi over the last few kilometres. If this sounds too complicated, ask the Hanover Tourist Office (p593) about guided tours to the castle.

Meanwhile, for something completely different, a wonderful family outing from Hanover is to **Dino Park Münchehagen** (Dinosaur Open Air Museum; ☎ 05037-2073; www.dinopark.de; adult/under 12yr €8.50/7; ☺ 9am-7pm Mar-Oct, 10am-4.30pm Nov-Feb, last entry 1 hr before closing). This is *Jurassic Park* brought to life, with more than 200 life-size dinosaurs (brontosauruses, T-rexes, raptors and so on) arranged around a walking trail where real dinosaurs once roamed. There are even genuine dino footprints!

By car, follow the A2 west of Hanover and take the No 40 exit to Wunstorf-Luthe. Continue along the 441 out of Wunstorf and you'll reach the park before Locum. By public transport, take S-Bahn 1 or 2 from Hanover to Wunstorf (€6 day pass, 19 minutes), then bus 716 to Dino Park (€3.50 return, 15 minutes). Buses run more frequently at weekends; for timetable information check www.regiobus .de or call ☎ 0511-3688 8723.

FAIRY-TALE ROAD – SOUTH

This stretch of the **Märchenstrasse** (Fairy-Tale Road; ☎ 0561-707 707; www.deutsche-maerchenstrasse.de) is one of the prettiest. Connecting Hamelin, Bodenwerder and Bad Karlshafen, it hugs the Weser River for much of the way and is one of Germany's most popular cycling routes. South of Bodenwerder, the river is flanked

to the east by the Solling-Vogler Naturpark, which is a great spot for hikers, too.

Hamelin is charming, if touristy, Bodenwerder is worth a quick stopover and Bad Karlshafen's a sleepy beauty.

See the boxed text on p536 for more information about this part of the Fairy-Tale Road.

Getting There & Away

What is a simple journey by car – take the B83 to/from Hamelin or Bad Karlshafen – requires a little planning with public transport. From Hamelin's Hauptbahnhof, bus 520 follows the Weser to/from Holzminden (€10.25) via Bodenwerder (€5.15) hourly from 6am to 8pm during the week and every couple of hours on weekends. From Holzminden trains leave hourly to Bad Karlshafen (€6.75), via Ottbergen. Direct trains run every two hours from Bad Karlshafen to Göttingen (€7.95, one hour).

From April to October, boats operated by **Flotte Weser** (☎ 05151-939 999; www.flotte-weser.de, in German) also travel from Hamelin to Bodenwerder on Wednesday, Friday, Saturday and Sunday (€12, 2½ hours). Very occasional cruises go as far as Bad Karlshafen.

Details of the much-loved **Weser Radweg** (Weser Cycle Path; www.weser-radweg.de, in German) can be found online. See Getting There & Around, p605, for details on bike hire.

HAMELIN
☎ 05151 / pop 58,800

If you were to believe *The Pied Piper of Hamelin* fairy tale, this quaint, ornate town on the Weser River ought to be devoid of rats and children. According to legend, the Pied Piper (*Der Rattenfänger*) was employed by Hamelin's townsfolk to lure their pesky rodents into the river in the 13th century. When they refused to pay him, he picked up his flute again and led their kids away.

However, it is a bedtime story, after all; international tourism means the reality is very different. Everywhere you look along Hamelin's cobbled streets are – you guessed it – fake rats and happy young children. Hamelin (Hameln) positively revels in its folklore with a plague of fluffy rat toys, rat-shaped bread…rat everything really. Even the Pied Piper himself can be seen in various tourist-guide guises, mesmerising onlookers with haunting tunes.

Orientation

On the eastern bank of the Weser River lies Hamelin's circular Altstadt. The main streets are Osterstrasse, which runs east–west, and Bäckerstrasse, the north–south axis.

The Hauptbahnhof is about 800m east of the centre. Turn right out of the station square (past the roundabout), follow Bahnhofstrasse to Diesterstrasse and turn left. Diesterstrasse becomes Diesterallee, where you'll find the tourist office, and then Osterstrasse. Buses 3, 4, 5 and 6 are just some of the lines that will take you into town.

Information

Hameln Tourist Information (☎ 957 823, 0180-551 5150; www.hameln.de; Diesterallee 1; ☒ 9am-6.30pm Mon-Fri, 9.30am-4pm Sat, 9.30am-1pm Sun May-Sep, 9am-6pm Mon-Fri, 9.30am-1pm Sat Oct-Apr) On the eastern edge of the Altstadt.

Sights & Activities

ALTSTADT

The best way to explore is to follow the **Pied Piper trail** – the line of white rats drawn on the pavements. There are information posts at various points. They're in German, but at least you know when to stop to admire the various restored 16th- to 18th-century half-timbered houses.

The ornamental Weser Renaissance style prevalent throughout Hamelin's Altstadt has a strong Italian influence. The **Rattenfängerhaus** (Rat Catcher's House; Osterstrasse 28), from 1602, is the finest example, with its typically steep and richly decorated gable.

Also not to be missed is the **Hochzeitshaus** (1610–17) at the Markt (square) end of Oster-strasse; see the following section for details on its interior. The **Rattenfänger Glockenspiel** at the far end of the building chimes daily at 9.35am and 11.35am, while a **carousel of Pied Piper figures** twirls at 1.05pm, 3.35pm and 5.35pm.

During summer, ask the tourist office about the **open-air light displays** at noon on Sunday and the comic musical *Rats* on Wednesday at 4.30pm.

From May to September, there are **one-hour cruises** (adult/child €6/3) on the Weser River. They run five times daily between 10am and 3pm, with an additional departure at 4.15pm according to demand. Contact **Flotte Weser** (☎ 939 999), upstairs from the tourist office, to arrange. Cruises leave from the far west of the old town.

ERLEBNISWELT RENAISSANCE

Clever use of modern media delivers a genu-inely exciting history lesson in Hamelin's **Erlebniswelt Renaissance** (Renaissance Experience; ☎ 403 680, 01805-013 330; www.erlebniswelt-renaissance .de; Hochzeitshaus, Osterstrasse 2; adult/child/concession €9/5.40/7.20; ☒ 10am-6pm). The upper floor, where you start, is probably the weakest, although it features a handy timeline. However, stick with it because as you descend through the build-ing it gets much, much better. A computer lays a table with three types of Renaissance meals, and a wall of 1000 masterpieces is presented alongside sections on the calendar and time, exploration and travel, fashion, trade and much more.

The history of the period is later presented as the evening news, while four great astrono-mers (Ptolemy, Copernicus, Kepler and Gali-leo) meet on an evening chat show. While it's obviously aimed at school-age children, adults will get a kick out of the exhibition, and learn from it, too, as it demonstrates how the Renaissance period laid the groundwork for the world we live in today.

Audio guides provide a narrative (in Ger-man only at the time of research, but in Eng-lish and French soon), which automatically synchronises with the main displays. Mean-while interactive features provide more detail on the subjects that interest you. Colum-bus, da Vinci, Dürer, Gutenburg, Luther and Shakespeare are just some of the major players waiting to tell their stories.

There's a Hamelin angle, of course – you can spy through a telescope at what's going on in the animated 17th-century town. Further sites in the surrounding countryside continue the 'Renaissance experience'; ask at the cash desk for details.

GLASHÜTTE HAMELN

Another Pied-Piper-free zone is the **Glashütte Hameln** (Glass-Blowing Factory; ☎ 405 571; www .glasblaeserei-hameln.de; Am Pulverturm/Kastanienwall; adult/child under 6yr/student €2.50/free/1.05; ☒ 10am-1pm & 2-6pm Mon-Sat, 10am-5pm Sun). Learn about glass-blowing throughout Hamelin's history and see the experts at work; you can even try it yourself, under supervision (€9). Don't worry if your own creation doesn't turn out quite as you'd hoped: there are plenty of covetable glassworks in the accompanying shop. The 35-minute glass-blowing demonstrations start every 30 minutes.

Sleeping & Eating

Fährhaus an der Weser (☎ 611 67; www.campingplatz -faehrhaus-hameln.de, in German; Uferstrasse 80; per adult/ tent & car €4/6; ☒) Although catering mainly to caravans, this year-round camping ground does have a few places for tents. It's across the river from the Altstadt and 10 minutes' walk north. Facilities are reasonably new, plus there's a beer garden, heated swimming pool and Greek restaurant.

DJH hostel (☎ 3425; www.jugendherberge.de/jh /hameln; Fischbeckerstrasse 33; dm under/over 26yr €15.30/ 18.30; ☒) This hostel is clean and relatively modern. Although there's not a lot of space in the dorms or bathrooms, the place does enjoy excellent river views out the back. Take bus 2 from the Hauptbahnhof to Wehler Weg.

Hotel Garni Altstadtwiege (☎ 278 54; www.hotel -altstadtwiege.de; Neue Marktstrasse 10; s/d/tr from €45/ 75/100; ℗) This unprepossessing red-brick building actually contains charming, individually decorated rooms. Most have stained-glass windows, while there's a four-poster bed in No 14. Kids will love No 12, which features a raised single bed, where you climb a stool to retire for the night.

Hotel zur Krone (☎ 9070; www.hotelzurkrone.de, in German; Osterstrasse 30; s €65-85, d €90-95, ste from €130; ℗ ☒) The rooms in the old, half-timbered part of this hotel are creaky, but have exposed ceiling beams, bags of character, and some even have bathtubs. Those in the modern wing are slightly more up to date and occasionally boast balconies. Take your pick.

Hotel-Garni Christinenhof (☎ 950 80; www .christinenhof-hameln.de; Alte Marktstrasse 18; s/d €70/90; ℗ ☒ ☒) Historic on the outside, but totally modern in attitude, this hotel likes to pamper its guests, providing a small swimming pool in the vaulted cellar, a sauna, a generous buffet breakfast and compact but uncluttered rooms.

Shaki Sushi Bar (☎ 783 839; Osterstrasse 38; mains €4-11.50) The small ground-floor café here opens into a bright, black, red and yellow restaurant upstairs, with a fairly select menu of Japanese dishes. There's a small area where you can sit on cushions at low tables, and sushi is half-price after 10pm.

Rattenfängerhaus (☎ 3888; Osterstrasse 28; mains €5-20) Hamelin's restaurants are unashamedly touristy and sometimes it's best to just give in to it. This cute half-timbered tavern's speciality is 'rats' tails' flambéed at your table (fortunately, like most of the theme dishes

here, this one's based on pork). Schnitzels, herrings, vegie dishes and 'rat killer' herb liquor are also offered.

Ambrosia (☎ 253 93; Neu Marktstrasse 18; mains €6-22) The aromas of this restaurant's Italian and Greek food waft down the street, mesmerising diners just as the Pied Piper's tunes do.

Museumscafé im Stiftsherrenhaus (☎ 215 53; Osterstrasse 8; dishes €7-15) The must-munch here is the marzipan-filled *Rattenfängertorte* (rat-catcher, or Pied Piper, cake). However, there are also sandwiches and light seasonal meals available, served in a tearoom atmosphere.

Getting There & Around

Frequent S-Bahn trains (S5) head to Hamelin from Hanover's Hauptbahnhof (€9.10, 45 minutes). You can also travel direct from Hanover's airport to Hamelin by train. By car, take the B217 to/from Hanover. See Getting There & Away on p603 earlier in this section for bus and boat links.

Bikes can be hired from the **Troches Fahrrad Shop** (☎ 136 70; Kreuzstrasse 7).

BODENWERDER

☎ 05533 / pop 6800

If Bodenwerder's most famous son were to have described his hometown, he'd probably have painted it as a huge, thriving metropolis on the Weser River. But then Baron Hieronymous von Münchhausen (1720–1797) was one of history's most shameless fibbers. He gave his name to a psychological condition – Münchhausen's syndrome, or compulsive exaggeration of physical illness – and inspired Terry Gilliam's cult movie *The Adventures of Baron Munchhausen*.

Really just a small village, Bodenwerder's principal attraction is the **Münchhausen Museum** (☎ 409 147; Münchhausenplatz 1; adult/child €2/1.50; ☒ 10am-noon & 2-5pm Apr-Oct), which struggles a little with the difficult task of conveying the chaos and fun associated with the 'liar baron' – a man who liked to regale dinner guests with his Crimean adventures, claiming he had, for example, tied his horse to a church steeple during a snow drift and ridden around a dining table without breaking one teacup.

The museum does its best, housing a cannonball to illustrate the baron's most famous tale, in which he claimed to have hitched a lift on one similar in an attempt to spy on a battlefield enemy. It also has paintings and displays of Münchhausen books in many languages.

It's all definitely more enjoyable if you first arm yourself with the English-language book, *Tall Tales of Baron Münchhausen*, available at the museum shop.

In the garden by the museum, the simple **fountain** showing the baron riding half a horse relates to one such tale, where the baron noticed his horse seemed a bit thirsty, and then realised the animal had been cut in two by a descending town gate, so the water was pouring right through it. (In the story the horse is sewn back together and lives happily ever after.)

From April to October, things become livelier in Bodenwerder, as German storytellers relate Münchhausen tales for €1 (10am to noon and 2pm to 4pm daily). English stories can only be arranged for groups; ask at **Tourist Information Bodenwerder** (☎ 405 41; www .muenchhausenland.de, in German; Münchhausenplatz 3; ☺ 9am-12.30pm & 2.30-6pm Mon-Fri year-round, 9am-1pm Sat Apr-Oct), which can also arrange accommodation and answer other queries.

No trains travel to Bodenwerder; see Getting There & Away on p603 for transport information. The village is small and walkable.

BAD KARLSHAFEN
☎ 05672 / pop 4700

You'd be forgiven for thinking you'd stumbled into 18th-century France in this sleepy spa town. Little wonder, for Bad Karlshafen's orderly streets and whitewashed baroque buildings were built at that time for the local earl Karl by Huguenot refugees. The town was planned with an impressive harbour and a canal connecting the Weser with the Rhine to attract trade. But the earl died before his designs were completed and all that exists today is a tiny *Hafenbecken* (harbour basin) trafficked only by white swans. Add the town's

Gradierwerk, a large pine-twig contraption poured with saltwater to create 'healthy' air, and this is the perfect place to escape the worries of the world for a few days.

Bad Karlshafen is strictly in Hesse, but it's at the end of the Fairy-Tale Road, just across the Lower Saxony border. For transport information, see Getting There & Away, p603.

The town is small and easily covered on foot. Most of it lies on the south bank of the Weser River, with the *Hafenbecken* and surrounding square, Hafenplatz, at its western end. To reach the **tourist office** (☎ 999 922; kurverwaltung@bad-karlshafen.de; Hafenplatz 8; ☺ 9am-5.30pm Mon-Fri, 9.30am-noon Sat, 2.30-5pm Sun May–mid-Oct, 9am-noon & 2-4pm Mon-Fri mid-Oct–Apr) from the Hauptbahnhof, follow the only road exiting the station for a few minutes and cross the bridge, right, over the river. Turn right again on the other side and continue straight ahead to Hafenplatz.

While here, take a stroll around the *Hafenbecken* and pop into the **Deutsches Huguenotten Museum** (German Huguenot Museum; ☎ 1410; Hafenplatz 9a; adult/concession €2/1; ☺ 9am-1pm & 2-6pm Tue-Sat, 11am-6pm Sun mid-Feb–Dec), which explains the history of the Huguenots in Germany.

The *Gradierwerk* lies to the left as you cross the bridge.

Sleeping
Am Rechten Weserufer (☎ 710; www.campingplatz -bad-karlshafen.de, in German; per adult/tent & car €3.50/3) This camping ground enjoys a prime position on the northern riverbank, just south of the train station. It overlooks the town centre.

Hermann Wenning DJH hostel (☎ 338; bad -karlshafen@djh-hessen.de; Winnefelder Strasse 7; dm €17, s/d €20/36.50; P ✗) A genuinely lovely and quite healthy-feeling hostel, this place attracts lots of cyclists, has table tennis and other nearby sporting opportunities and an excellent breakfast, with freshly sliced fruit. (Other meals are available on request.) It's a short, uphill walk from the train station; some of its clean modern rooms enjoy dreamy views over Bad Karlshafen and the surrounding hills.

Hotel-Pension Haus Fuhrhop (☎ 404; www.hotel -fuhrhop-karlshafen.de; Friedrichstrasse 15; s/d €35/65) The style of this charming *pension* is no-style. The spacious rooms are decorated with a mishmash of furniture, seemingly as pieces have come into the owners' possession, which gives the place a homy, relaxed atmosphere. It's on the first street left after you've crossed the bridge.

Hotel zum Schwan (☎ 104 445; fax 1046; Conradis-trasse 3-4; s/d €40/80; **P**) Although Earl Karl's former hunting lodge is now a bit creaky, this atmospheric hotel is still one of the town's best. It overlooks the *Hafenbecken* and its rococo dining room is a perfect museum piece.

LÜNEBURGER HEIDE

North of Hanover along the sprawling Lüneburger Heide lies a land of attractive, historic villages and natural allure. Lower Saxony was ruled from here before the court moved to Hamburg, so royal treasures and exquisitely preserved buildings await you in Celle. In Lüneburg, you can observe the quirky side-effects of the salt-mining that made the town rich in the Middle Ages (the town visibly leans).

The area in between, along the Lüneburger Heide, can be covered on foot, by bike or in a boat, and there are hay hotels (see boxed text, p614) and camp sites along the way.

CELLE
☎ 05141 / pop 71,400
Celle's old town is an object of beauty, like a Fabergé egg, built by hard-working, pious folk who ironically had no truck with such frippery. In the 16th century, they lined their cobbled streets with ornate half-timbered buildings and then decorated them with stern mottos like 'Don't let widows and orphans suffer or you'll face the wrath of God', and 'This house was built from necessity not desire'. (What would they make of the one that now blares 'Sex Shop Kino'?)

The white-and-pink Ducal Palace is another historic landmark, passed down from the Middle Ages. However, Celle is also looking to the future with its new '24-hour' art museum.

Orientation
The mainly pedestrianised Altstadt is about a 15-minute walk east of the Hauptbahnhof, reached by the rather unattractive Bahnhofstrasse. Turning left at the street's end will take you to the palace after 100m. From here, Stechbahn leads east (right) to the nearby tourist office. The Aller River flows around the northern section of the Altstadt, with a tributary encircling it to the south. Just south of the Altstadt is the Französischer Garten (French Garden).

Information
Adunni Callshop & Internet (Bahnhofstrasse 38; internet per hr €3; ☽ 10am-10pm Mon-Sat, noon-10pm Sun)
Main post office (Rundstrasse 7; ☽ 8.30am-6pm Mon-Fri, to 1pm Sat) Diagonally opposite the Schloss.
Tourismus Region Celle (☎ 1212; www.region-celle .com; Markt 14; ☽ 9am-6pm Mon-Fri, 10am-4pm Sat, 11am-4pm Sun May-Oct, 9am-5pm Mon-Fri, 10am-1pm Sat Nov-Apr) Runs guided tours (€4; in German) at 2.30pm Monday to Saturday and 11am on Sunday from May to October (during other months at 2pm Saturday and 11am Sunday), and organises horse-drawn carriage rides (from €5 per person).

Sights
ALTSTADT
With row upon row of ornate half-timbered houses, all decorated with scrolls and allegorical figures, Celle is a perfect place for a stroll. Even the tourist office is located in a striking building, the **Altes Rathaus** (1561–79), which boasts a wonderful Weser Renaissance stepped gable, topped with the ducal coat of arms and a golden weather vane.

At the tourist office door, on the building's south side, there are two **whipping posts** with shackles; these were used from 1786 to 1850 to punish minor offenders. Prisoners weren't whipped but merely left here for 12 hours, to allow their neighbours to spit at them or throw insults and eggs. Opposite, the statue of a man in shackles recreates the scene.

Jousting tournaments were held a little further west on **Stechbahn**. The little horseshoe on the corner of the street's north side marks the spot where a duke was slain during a

LOWER SAXONY

tournament; step on it and make a wish, and local lore holds that the wish will come true.

If you walk south from the tourist office, straight down Poststrasse, you'll find one of Celle's most magnificent buildings, the ornate **Hoppener Haus** (1532), one block along on the corner of Runde Strasse.

Continue another block southwards and stop in the square in the corner. Look up, and in the tiny alley between the two buildings you'll see a little box with a window. This was a **baroque toilet**. It's less glamorous than the name implies; waste would flush directly down into the alley.

Retrace your steps to the corner of Poststrasse and Zöllnerstrasse, and turn right into Zöllnerstrasse. This way, you'll pass **No 37** (built in 1570, now the shop Reformhaus), with its heart-warming inscription on the upper gable, 'Work! No chatting, talking or gossiping!'. Turn left into Rabengasse, and you'll come to Neue Strasse. Highlights here include the **Green House** (1478) with the crooked beam at No 32 and the **Fairy-Tale House** at No 11. The façade of the latter is decorated with characters, such as a jackass crapping gold pieces.

The tourist office has booklets describing various houses in German, but unfortunately nothing in English.

If you'd like to continue walking, double back south, where Celle also has a lovely **French Garden** at the edge of the Altstadt.

SCHLOSS

Beautifully proportioned and magnificently restored is Celle's wedding-cake **Schloss** (Ducal Palace; ☎ 123 73; Schlossplatz; tours adult/concession €3/2; ☉ tours hourly 11am-4pm Tue-Sun Apr-Oct, 11am & 3pm Tue-Sun Nov-Mar). Built in 1292 by Otto Der Strenge (Otto the Strict) as a town fortification, the building was expanded and turned into a residence in 1378. The last duke to live here was Georg Wilhelm (1624–1705), and the last royal was Queen Caroline-Mathilde of Denmark, who died here in 1775.

The Schloss can only be visited on guided tours (in German), but there are explanatory brochures in English for sale. Highlights include the magnificent baroque theatre, the private apartment of Caroline-Mathilde and, above all, the chapel. Its original Gothic form is evident in the high windows and vaulted ceiling, but the rest of the intricate interior is pure Renaissance. The duke's pew was

above; the shutters were added later so his highness could snooze during the three-hour services.

Rehearsals permitting, some tours do venture into the baroque **Schlosstheater** (☎ tickets 127 14; www.schlosstheater-celle.de; Schlossplatz; ☉ closed Jul & Aug). However, the only guaranteed way to peek inside is to attend one of the performances here. The tourist office can provide details.

KUNSTMUSEUM & BOMANN MUSEUM

Across from the palace stands Celle's **Kunstmuseum** (Art Museum; ☎ 123 55; www.kunst.celle.de; Schlossplatz 7; adult/concession incl Bomann Museum €3/2; ☉ 10am-5pm Tue-Fri, to 6pm Sat & Sun), due to have reopened in the latter half of 2006, supposedly as 'the world's first 24-hour museum'. It's claiming this after a €4 million refurbishment has created a transparent glass façade and a showcase for electric-light installations right through the evening. During the day, you can visit the contemporary German paintings, sculptures and objects of collector Robert Simon – all the while thanking the heavens you're not paying the museum's electricity bill.

In the older building adjacent, you'll still find the regional history **Bomann Museum** (☎ 125 44; www.bomann-museum.de; Schlossplatz 7; adult/concession incl Kunstmuseum €3/2; ☉ 10am-5pm Tue-Sun, last entry 4.15pm). Here, among other things, you can wander through rooms furnished in 19th-century style.

STADTKIRCHE

Just west of the Rathaus is the 13th-century **Stadtkirche** (☎ 7735; tower admission adult/concession €1/0.50; ☉ 10am-6pm Tue-Sat, tower 10am-noon & 1-6pm Tue-Sat Apr-Oct). You can climb up the 235 steps to the top of the church steeple for a view of the city, or just watch as the city trumpeter climbs the 220 steps to the white tower below the steeple for a trumpet fanfare in all four directions. The ascent takes place at 5.15pm and 7.30pm Monday to Friday, 9.30am and 7.15pm on Saturday and either 9.30am or 7.15pm on Sunday (ask the tourist office closer to the time).

SYNAGOGUE

Dating back to 1740, Celle's **synagogue** (☎ 550 714; Im Kreise 24; admission free; ☉ noon-5pm Tue-Thu, 9am-2pm Fri, 11am-4pm Sun) is the oldest in northern Germany. Partially destroyed during Kristallnacht (see boxed text, p35), it looks just like any other half-timbered house from the outside, but a new Jewish congregation formed in 1997 and services are held regularly. Changing exhibitions on Jewish history take place next door.

The synagogue is at the southeastern end of the Altstadt, in the town's former ghetto.

Sleeping

Camping Silbersee (☎ 312 23; www.campingpark -silbersee.de; Zum Silbersee 19; per adult €3, per tent/tent & car €2.60/4.10) On the shore of a lake with plenty of tree cover, this camping ground has older buildings, but nevertheless plenty of facilities. About 4km from the centre, it can be reached by bus 1 to Am Tierheim.

DJH hostel (☎ 532 08; www.jugendherberge.de/jh /celle; Weghausstrasse 2; dm under/over 26yr €15/18; P ⊠) For a place so large and rambling, this hostel doesn't have especially spacious rooms and the lighting in the public areas can be a little gloomy. It's also very popular with school groups. On the edge of town, it's reached by bus 3 (alight at Boye) or by following the signs from the train station.

Hotel Zur Herberge (☎ 208 141; www.nacelle.de; Hohe Wende 14; s/d/tr €38/58/85; P) Seemingly straight from the Ikea showroom – with blonde-wood furnishings and yellow and blue fabrics – this small, charming hotel offers excellent value. En suite rooms have TV, phone and bathroom, and you can help yourself to coffee and beer in the communal kitchen corner. Reception isn't always staffed, so ring ahead. Bus 12 to Harburger Herrstrasse will get you here.

Hotel St Georg (☎ 210 510; www.hotel-st-georg.de; St Georg Strasse 25-27; s/d €60/80; P) A short walk from the old town, this family-run hotel offers a lovely mix of historic façade, modern rooms and friendly atmosphere. Amuse yourself at breakfast by checking out all the pictures on the restaurant walls.

Celler Hof (☎ 911 960; www.cellerhof.de; Stechbahn 11; s €65, d €90-100; P ⊠) You're mainly paying for the super-central location here – opposite the Stadtkirche and minutes from the Schloss. Although the design is modern and extremely comfortable, the rooms are reasonably small. A fitness room and sauna add value.

Hotel Utspann (☎ 927 20; www.utspann.de; Im Kreise 13; s €80, d €85-95; P) Under new management – reduced in size to 10 rooms in two half-timbered houses and a little less cluttered than previously – this historic place still evokes a staying-with-friends atmosphere. Individually

sized rooms variously feature exposed wooden beams, antique desks and even a few alcove beds. The guest living room backs onto a leafy garden.

Hotel Fürstenhof (☎ 2010; www.fuerstenhof.de; Hannoversche Strasse 55/56; s €135-185, d €185-255, ste from €225; P ⚑) A converted baroque palace, this renowned five-star hotel has given each of its floors a subtle theme, from golf, hunting and horses to romance and heath (where, for example, the carpet features sheep and the pillow cases a leaf pattern). That the place still feels extremely elegant says something about the quality furnishings and the deft touch of the interior designer.

Eating

Pasta (☎ 483 460; Neue Strasse 37; mains €4.50-6.50; ⏲ 9am-10pm Mon-Fri, to 4pm Sat May-Sep, 9am-5pm Mon-Fri, to 4pm Sat Oct-Apr) Behind this instant Celle hit lies one of those ideas that is so simple it's genius. Mix your favourite pasta (tagliatelle, penne rigate, gnocchi, ravioli etc) with a sauce that takes your fancy (from bolognese or pesto to tuna and capers, or salmon cream). Crucially, it's all freshly homemade.

Schlosscafé Vis à Vis (☎ 925 790; Schlossplatz; mains €3.50-12; ⏲ 8am-6pm) The interior is overwhelmingly green and during the week this place can be filled with bus tour groups. However, Sundays are fantastic, when a huge brunch buffet is laid out, or you can choose the usual pasta, salads or other light meals.

Zum Ältesten Haus (☎ 246 01; Neue Strasse 27; mains €7.50-18) German to the neat fringes of its pink tablecloths, this is the best place in town to try local specialities such as *Celler Rohe Roulade*, rolled, thinly sliced raw beef in a mustard marinade, or *Herzogen Pfanne*, Heide-style roast lamb with cranberries, stuffed pears, green beans and fried potatoes.

India Haus (☎ 485 152; Neue Strasse 34; mains €8-16) The combination of subcontinental interior décor and traditional, exposed medieval beams creates a surprisingly harmonious atmosphere in this half-timber house. The food might not meet exacting Londoners' standards (and we heard the occasional microwave ping), but it's excellent for provincial Germany. Lunch specials cost €5 to €5.50.

Getting There & Away

Celle is within easy reach of Hanover, with three trains an hour making the trip (from €7.60) in anything from 19 minutes (ICE) to

45 minutes (S-Bahn). There are also IC (€17, 40 minutes) and regional (€13.40, 1½ hours) services to/from Lüneburg.

If you're driving, take the B3 straight into the centre.

Getting Around

City buses 2, 3 and 4 run between the Haupt-bahnhof and Schlossplatz, the two main stations. Single tickets are €1.50 and day passes €4.20.

For a taxi call ☎ 444 44 or ☎ 280 01. Bicycle hire is available at **Fahrradverleih am Bahnhof** (☎ 901 3377; Bahnhofstrasse 26-27; 🕑 9am-1pm & 3-6pm Mon-Fri, 9am-1pm Sat).

BERGEN-BELSEN

Many concentration camps move you with their buildings, exhibitions and museums. **Bergen-Belsen** (☎ 05051-6011; www.bergenbelsen .de; Lohheide; admission free; 🕑 9am-6pm) provides a horrifying punch to the stomach through the sheer force of its atmosphere.

Unlike Auschwitz in Poland, none of the original buildings remain from the most infamous concentration camp on German soil. Yet the large, initially peaceful-looking lumps of grassy earth – covered in beautiful purple heather in summer – soon reveal their true identity as mass graves. Signs indicate approximately how many people lie in each – 1000, 2000, 5000, an unknown number…

In all, 70,000 Jews, Soviet soldiers, political hostages and other prisoners died here. Among them was Anne Frank, whose post-humously published diary became a modern classic.

Inside the **Documentation Centre** just outside the cemetery gates, there's a small exhibition outlining the history of the concentration camps in general and of Bergen-Belsen in particular, plus a theatre showing a 25-minute documentary. Both include awful scenes of the several thousand unburied bodies and emaciated survivors who greeted the British forces when they liberated the camp in April 1945. The film includes a moving testimony from one of the cameramen. Screenings are hourly from 10am to 5pm daily, but rotate between different languages.

Also inside the centre, there's a book of names of those who were interned here, as well as guides and books for sale – including *The Diary of Anne Frank* (1947) – plus the free *Guide for Visitors to the Belsen Memorial*.

In the several hectares of cemetery within the gates is a large stone **obelisk and memorial**, with inscriptions to all victims, a **cross** on the spot of a memorial initially raised by Polish prisoners and the **Haus der Stille**, where you can retreat for quiet contemplation.

A **gravestone for Anne Frank** and her sister, Margot, has also been erected (not too far from the cemetery gates, on the way to the obelisk). The entire family was initially sent to Auschwitz when their hiding place in Amsterdam was betrayed to police, but the sisters were later transferred to Belsen. Although no-one knows where Anne lies exactly, many pay tribute to their 15-year-old heroine at this gravestone. Other monuments to various victim groups, including a **Soviet memorial**, are dotted across the complex.

Bergen-Belsen began its existence in 1940 as a POW camp, but was partly taken over by the SS from April 1943, to hold Jews hostage in exchange for German POWs held abroad. Many Russian and Allied soldiers, then later Jews, Poles, homosexuals and Romanian Gypsies all suffered here – beaten, tortured, gassed, starved or worked to death, and used as medical guinea pigs.

Tens of thousands of prisoners from other camps near the front line were brought to Belsen in the last months of WWII, causing overcrowding, an outbreak of disease and even more deaths. Despite the best attempts of the SS to hide the evidence of their inhumane practices, by forcing prisoners to bury or incinerate their deceased colleagues, thousands of corpses still littered the compound when British troops arrived.

After WWII, Allied forces used the troop barracks here as a displaced persons' (DP) camp, for those waiting to emigrate to a third country (including many Jews who went to Israel after its establishment in 1948). The DP camp was closed in September 1950.

Getting There & Away

Driving from Celle, take Hehlentorstrasse north over the Aller River and follow Harburger Strasse north out of the city. This is the B3; continue northwest to the town of Bergen and follow the signs to Belsen.

By public transport the journey is considerably trickier and only possible Monday to Friday, so you'll need to be particularly determined to visit.

From the ZOB (central bus station), under the huge car park opposite the Celle Hauptbahnhof, you need to catch bus 12 (leaving 12.05pm, 1.40pm and 3.40pm) and change to bus 11 in the town of Bergen. Alternatively, take bus 80 (departing 1.35pm) from the ZOB and change to 11 in Winsen. The journey costs €4.80 each way and takes one hour. Beware that the 12.05pm and 1.40pm buses don't run during school holidays.

The last buses back from the camp are at 4.50pm and, requiring two changes, 5.29pm. A **taxi** (☎ 05051-5555) to the camp from the village of Bergen will cost about €15. There's a phone at the camp to call a taxi when leaving.

For further details, ask at the Celle tourist office.

LÜNEBURG

☎ 04131 / pop 71,500

An off-kilter church steeple, buildings leaning on each other and houses with swollen 'beerbelly' façades: in parts it looks like the charming town of Lüneburg has drunk too much of the Pilsener lager it used to brew.

Of course, the city's wobbly angles and uneven pavements have a more prosaic cause. For centuries until 1980, Lüneburg was a saltmining town, and as this 'white gold' was extracted from the earth, shifting ground and subsidence caused many buildings to tilt sideways. Inadequate drying of the plaster used in the now-swollen façades merely added to this asymmetry.

However, knowing the scientific explanation never detracts from the pleasure of being on Lüneburg's comic-book crooked streets. The lopsidedness of its pretty stepped gables and Hanseatic architecture make it a destination in its own right, not just the gateway to the surrounding heath.

Orientation

The Ilmenau River sits between the Hauptbahnhof, which is on its eastern bank, and the city centre to its west. To reach the Markt by foot from the train station, turn left when leaving the station, and take the first right into Altenbrückertorstrasse. This street leads across the river to Am Sande. From here, you'll find lots of billboard maps all over town.

Information

Lüneburg Tourist-Information Office (☎ 207 6620; www.lueneburg.de; Rathaus, Am Markt; ☼ 9am-6pm

Mon-Fri, to 4pm Sat & Sun May-Oct, 9am-6pm Mon-Fri, to 2pm Sat Nov-Apr) Arranges city tours and trips to the surrounding Lüneburger Heide.

Post office (☎ 7270; Sülztorstrasse 21; ☼ 8.30am-6pm Mon-Fri, 9am-1pm Sat)

Spielhalle Westbahnhof (Westbahnhof; per hr €3; ☼ 7am-11pm Mon-Thu, to midnight Fri, 9am-midnight Sat, 10am-11pm Sun) Internet access.

Stadt Krankenhaus (Hospital; ☎ 770; Bögelstrasse 1)

Sights & Activities

ST JOHANNISKIRCHE

At the eastern edge of the square called Am Sande stands the clunky 14th-century **St Johanniskirche** (☎ 435 94; Am Sande; 10am-5pm Sun-Wed, to 6pm Thu-Sat Apr-Oct, 9am-6pm Thu-Sat, to 4pm Sun Nov-Mar), whose 106m-high spire leans 2.2m off true. Local legend has it that the architect was so upset by this crooked steeple that he tried to do himself in by jumping off it. He fell into a haycart and was saved, but celebrating his escape later in the pub drank himself into a stupor, fell over, hit his head and died after all.

The inside of the church is, well, a lot more believable than the legend; there's an impressive organ and stained-glass windows, both ancient and modern. Explanatory leaflets are provided in many languages.

AM SANDE

Moving westwards, the cobbled, slightly wobbly Am Sande is full of red-brick buildings with typically Hanseatic stepped gables. Even among these striking buildings, the black-and-white **Industrie- und Handelskammer** (Trade and Industry Chamber) at the far western end stands out; it's undoubtedly the most beautiful. Continue one block past the Handelskammer and turn right into restaurant-lined Schröderstrasse, which leads to the Markt.

RATHAUS & MARKT

The name Lüneburg hails from the Saxon word *hliuni* (refuge), which was granted at the Ducal Palace (p612) to those fleeing other territories. However, many sources mistakenly assume the town's name has something to do with Luna, the Roman goddess of the moon. The city authorities at one time seem to have been among these misguided souls, erecting a **fountain** with a statue of the Roman goddess in the town's Markt.

The statue sits in front of the medieval **Rathaus**, which has a spectacular baroque façade,

LOWER SAXONY

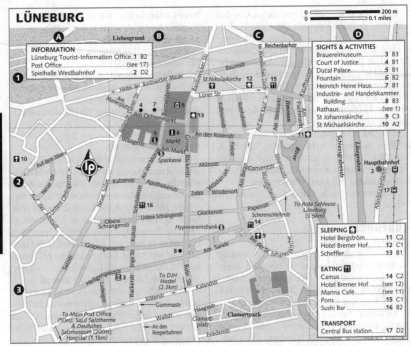

added in 1720, decorated with coats of arms and three tiers of statues. The top row of statues on the façade represents (from left to right): Strength, Trade, Peace (the one with the big sword), Justice and Moderation. The steeple, topped with 41 Meissen china bells, was installed on the city's 1000th birthday in 1956.

Tours of the building's interior leave daily at 11am, 12.30pm and 3pm (€4.50/3.50/11.50 per adult/concession/family) from the entrance on Am Ochsenmarkt.

Other buildings around the Markt include the **Court of Justice**, the little gated-in, grotto-like area with paintings depicting scenes of justice being carried out throughout the centuries; and the former **Ducal Palace**, now a courthouse. West of that, on the corner of Burmeisterstrasse and Am Ochsenmarkt, is the **Heinrich Heine Haus**, the home of the poet's parents. Heine, who hated Lüneburg, wrote the *Loreley* here (for more on the Loreley rock, see p490).

AUF DEM MEERE & ST MICHAELISKIRCHE

If you continue west along Waagestrasse from the Markt and veer left, you'll come to

Auf dem Meere, a particularly striking Lüneburg street. Here the wavy pavements have pushed façades sideways or made buildings buckle in the middle. All the way to **St Michaeliskirche** (Johann-Sebastian-Bach-Platz; ☺ 9am-4pm Mon-Sat), the street feels like something from the 1919 German expressionist movie *The Cabinet of Dr Caligari*, or as if you're in a Tim Burton film. Just look at the steps leading to the church!

SPA BATHS

With Lüneburg having made its fortune from salt, where better to try the mineral's therapeutic properties than at the town's **SaLü Salztherme** (Spa Baths; ☎ 723 110; www.kurzentrum.de; Uelzener Strasse 1-5; admission from €7.70; ☺ 10am-11pm Mon-Sat, 8am-9pm Sun). You can bathe in 4% saltwater at 36°C, and try out the sauna, water fountains and whirlpool.

CARRIAGE RIDES & CYCLING

Traditional **horse-drawn carriage rides** (☎ 04178-8542; adult/child €9/4.50; ☺ at 11.30am, 1pm & 2.30pm Tue, Thu & Fri) leave from the Markt. Call ahead or simply turn up.

Many tourists come to the Lüneburger Heide to go **cycling**; Lüneburg's tourist office has dozens of different pamphlets outlining routes.

MUSEUMS

The **Deutsches Salzmuseum** (☎ 450 65; Sülfmeisterstrasse 1; adult/child/student €4/2.50/2.70; ☺ 9am-5pm Mon-Fri, 10am-5pm Sat & Sun May-Sep, 10am-5pm Oct-Apr) explains (in German only) how Lüneburg's precious food preservative made the town such an important player in the Hanseatic League.

There's also a **Brauereimuseum** (☎ 448 04; Heiligengeiststrasse 39; admission free; ☺ 1-4.30pm Tue-Sun) looking at the history of beer-making in this city, which once housed more than 80 breweries.

Sleeping

Rote Schleuse Lüneburg (☎ 791 500; www.camproteschleuse.de; per adult/car & tent €4.80/5.70) This camping ground is about 3.5km south of the centre and offers a woodsy terrain scattered with fruit trees. Take bus 5600 to Rote Schleuse.

DJH hostel (☎ 418 64; www.jugendherberge .de/jh/lueneburg; Soltauer Strasse 133; dm under/over 26yr €16.50/19.50; Ⓟ Ⓧ 😐) After sundown, the lights glow a warm welcome from the glass-walled stairwell of this spacious, modern and relatively luxurious hostel in the town's south, right near the university. However, do call ahead as reception is not always staffed. Bus services – 5011 or 5012 from the train station to Scharnhorststrasse/DJH – don't run very late, either.

Scheffler (☎ 200 80; www.hotel-scheffler.de; Bardowicker Strasse 7; s/d €55/85; Ⓟ Ⓧ) The hotel most in keeping with Lüneburg's quirky character, this place just off the Markt greets you with brickwork, stained glass, carved wooden stair-rails, animal trophies and indoor plants. The rooms are low-ceilinged and cosy, and there's a restaurant on site.

Hotel Bremer Hof (☎ 2240; www.bremer-hof.de; Lüner Strasse 12-13; s €50-100, d €80-125; Ⓟ) Choose older, cheaper rooms in the 1970s concrete block at the courtyard's rear, or plump for more comfortable accommodation in the historic main house. Room 76 is particularly striking, with huge exposed ceiling beams.

Hotel Bergström (☎ 3080; www.bergstroem.de; Bei der Lüner Mühle; s €125-145, d €160-195; Ⓟ Ⓧ 😺) A little bit of New York loft living can be had in the 'Lüner Mühle' section of this luxury hotel, spread across half a dozen warehouse buildings and an old mill around a weir in the Ilmenau River. Other rooms are more traditional and romantic.

Eating & Drinking

Camus (☎ 428 20; Am Sande 30; mains €6-18) Despite the heavy wooden beams and winding stairs to the two upper floors, this central establishment somehow manages to feel like a brasserie. Jazz is on the stereo (maybe that helps), while Tuscan and Provençale mains, and pizza and pasta are on the menu.

Hotel Bremer Hof (☎ 2240; Lüner Strasse 12-13; mains €6-22) Light and airy, with a lot of blue, the atmospheric restaurant here is strong on local specialities, including lamb from the heath, or *Heidschnucke*, which comes in all shapes and sizes.

Sushi Bar (☎ 248 348; Schröderstrasse 8; sushi €1.70-9.50, mains €7-29) All gleaming red-and-black lacquer, with blue up-lighting behind the bar, this chic restaurant obviously serves sushi. However, it's often the regularly changing supplementary menu of various Asian cuisines (Thai one week, Korean the next and so on) that offers up the truly delicious choices.

Marina Café (☎ 3080; Bei der Lüner Mühle; mains €25-35) The view over the Ilmenau is reason enough for coming to the upmarket restaurant of the Hotel Bergström, but the daily changing menu of international cuisine is also pretty good. For those who want to spend a little less but enjoy the views, there's also a pleasant warehouse coffee shop attached to the hotel.

Pons (☎ 224 935; Salzstrasse am Wasser 1; ☺ from 5pm Mon-Sat, from 3pm Sun) If Pons looks this cracked, crooked and uneven when you walk in of an evening, just imagine how it will seem when you stagger out after a few drinks. A hippy hangover from the 1970s, it fortunately has much, much better musical taste and a small menu of cheap food served from 6pm (from €3.50). It's on the corner of the student drinking strip known as the 'Stint' (Am Stintmarkt).

Getting There & Away

There are frequent train services to Hamburg (€11, 30 minutes), Hanover (€23, one hour) and Schwerin (€16 to €30, one hour 20 minutes). There are also IC (€17, 40 minutes) and regional (€13.40, 1½ hours) services to/from Celle.

LOWER SAXONY

A ROLL IN THE HAY

Like several other German states, Lower Saxony has an excellent network of farm accommodation and several **Heu Hotels** (literally 'hay hotels'), where farmers set up straw bunks in their barns so they can rent them out for a small fee. It's an interesting way to spend time in the countryside, and they are usually much more comfortable (if odorous) than they sound. Some have horse riding, swimming lakes, sledding in winter and other activities. While some are bare-bones, all are heated in winter and many get downright luxurious. Check with tourist offices in the region for listings. The two best centres for finding country accommodation in the Lüneburger Heide are Celle and Lüneburg itself.

If you read German, visit www.heuhotel.de for further details.

If you're driving from Hamburg, take the A7 south to the B250. From Schwerin take the B6 south to the A24 west and then exit No 7 (Talkau). From there, turn south on the B209, and you'll eventually get to town. From Hanover, take the A7 north to the B209.

Getting Around

Buses leave from the ZOB central bus station at the Hauptbahnhof and from the busy bus stop on Am Sande. Most services stop running at around 7pm. Single tickets are €1.60; day tickets cost €3.20.

For a taxi, call ☎ 194 10. You can hire bicycles at the **Hauptbahnhof** (☎ 557 77).

NATURPARK ELBUFER-DRAWEHN

The Bleckede and the Biosphärenreservat Niedersächsische Elbtalaue (Lower-Saxony Elbe Floodplain Biosphere) are located some 20km east of Lüneburg, in a wetland area of the Lüneburger Heide. The reserve is a haven for birdlife such as white storks, wild geese and cranes, and runs for 85km along the Elbe River. Cyclists and hikers will be well rewarded by this picturesque and interesting wetland, which is all part of the **Elberadweg** (www.elberadweg.de; p216). If you intend to come out here, make sure you drop by the tourist office in Lüneburg first. You should find that it is well stocked with brochures on accommodation and activities that are available in the area.

For more information, you should contact the **tourist information office** (☎ 05852-958 458; www.elbtalaue-touristik.de, in German; Breite Strasse 10; ☻ 10am-6pm Tue-Sat Apr-Oct, 10am-5pm Sun Nov-Mar) in Bleckede. The **Elbschloss Bleckede** (☎ 05852-951 40; www.elbschloss-bleckede.de, in German; Schlossstrasse 10; adult/child €4/2; ☻ 10am-6pm Tue-Sat Apr-Oct, 10am-5pm Wed-Sun Nov-Mar) also has plenty of information on the biosphere.

Getting There & Around

No trains run to Bleckede, but buses leave at least hourly from Lüneburg at Am Sande or the Hauptbahnhof.

If you're going by car, the B216 leads to the turn-off to Bleckede. A car ferry crosses the river at the turn-off and in Neu Darchau to the south.

SOUTH & EAST OF HANOVER

HILDESHEIM

☎ 05121 / pop 102,700

Two things in particular have visitors flocking to this former bishopric and market city: a picture-book 'medieval' town centre that's a glorious fake, and the genuinely ancient cathedral door bas-reliefs, which were cleverly saved from the WWII firebombing that razed Hildesheim to the ground on 22 March 1945. A legendary '1000-year-old' rosebush that re-emerged from the ashes of this attack also attracts pilgrims.

Orientation

The central Markt is 750m south of the Hauptbahnhof. To walk there from the station, take the pedestrianised Bernwardstrasse, which becomes Almsstrasse and Hoher Weg. Turning left, or east, from Hoher Weg into either Markstrasse or Rathausstrasse will lead you to Hildesheim's stunning centre, and the tourist office.

Continuing along Hoher Weg, instead of turning left for the tourist office, you hit Schuhstrasse, a central bus stop. To the right (west), the road heads to the cathedral and the Roemer- und Pelizaeus-Museum. Straight ahead across Schuhstrasse you'll find the drinking strip of Friesenstrasse and, 10 minutes further south, the old Jewish quarter.

Information

Main post office (Bahnhofsplatz 3-4; ☎ 8.30am-6pm Mon-Fri, to 1pm Sat)

Tele.Net.Journal (☎ 697 2088; Friesenstrasse 20; per hr €1.50; ☎ 10am-midnight) Internet access.

Tourist Office Hildesheim (☎ 179 80; www .hildesheim.com; Rathausstrasse 20; ☎ 8.30am-6pm Mon-Fri, to 3.30pm Sat) Office renovations mean this office might still be in temporary lodgings at Rathausstrasse 18 into 2007.

Sights & Activities

For just €1, the tourist office sells the *Hildesheimer Rosenroute*, a very comprehensive guide to all Hildesheim's sights. It's available in several languages, including English, and is particularly useful if you're staying a few days.

MARKT

The town's central market place was reconstructed in traditional style during the 1980s, after locals decided they could no longer stand the typical 'German postwar hideous' style in which the town was originally repaired. However, knowing that the **Markt** is about as old as *The Simpsons* barely tempers its appeal. People still 'ooh' and 'aah' as they gaze around, particularly at the (clockwise from north) **Rokokohaus**, **Wollenweberhaus**, **Wedekindhaus**, **Knochenhauerhaus** (Butchers' Guild Hall) and **Bäckeramtshaus** (Bakers' Guild Hall). In many cases, you can see behind the façade, too: the Rokokohaus is now home to the Meridien Hotel, and the Knochenhauerhaus houses a restaurant and there's also a local history **museum** (☎ 301 163; Markt 7-8; adult/concession €2/1; ☎ 10am-6pm Tue-Sun).

One original feature is the **Marktbrunnen**, the fountain in front of the **Rathaus** on the east side of the square (bells play folk songs at noon, 1pm and 5pm daily).

DOM

There's a tiny entrance fee to see the **Tausendjähriger Rosenstock** (1000-year-old rosebush; adult/concession €0.50/0.30) in the cloister of the **Hildesheimer Dom** (Hildesheim Cathedral; ☎ 179 1760; Domhof; ☎ 9.30am-5pm Mon-Sat, noon-5pm Sun May-Oct, 10am-4.30pm Mon-Sat, noon-5pm Sun Nov-Apr). However, the bas-reliefs on the cathedral's almost 5m-high **Bernwardstüren** (Bernward bronze doors) have much greater visual impact, and they aren't pay-per-view.

The allure of the rosebush lies in its supposed history as the very one on which Emperor Ludwig the Pious left his cloak and other effects in AD 815, where they miraculously stayed safe from theft. Its phoenix-like rise from the burnt-out cathedral remains after 1945 has only added to the bush's mystique.

Ultimately, though, it looks much like any other rose: something you wouldn't say about the bronze cathedral doors, which are Unesco-protected. Dating from 1015 and saved only because a concerned WWII prelate insisted they be stashed in a basement, they depict scenes from the Bible's Old and New Testaments in three-dimensional reliefs. A plaque to the left describes each scene in German, however, it's easy to identify each one yourself: from the creation of man, Adam and Eve's banishment from the garden of Eden, and Cain and Abel, to the three wise men attending the birth of Christ, and Mary Magdalene attending his crucified body (no *Da Vinci Code* conspiracy theories here, please!).

The church's **wheel-shaped chandelier** and the **Christussäule** (Column of Christ) are also original, and if you're really keen, there's an attached **Dom-Museum** (☎ 179 1640; Domhof; adult/concession €3.50/2; ☎ 10am-1pm & 1.30-5pm Tue-Sat, noon-5pm Sun), with rotating exhibitions and the cathedral treasury.

OTHER CHURCHES

Like the cathedral doors, the Romanesque **St Michaeliskirche** (☎ 344 10; Michaelisplatz; admission free; ☎ 8am-6pm Mon-Sat, noon-6pm Sun Apr-Oct, 9am-4pm Mon-Sat, noon-4pm Sun Nov-Mar) is under Unesco protection. Built in 1022 and reconstructed after extensive war damage, it has been undergoing another makeover and should be seen in yet more gleaming new detail from 2007.

Off Hoher Weg is **St Andreaskirche** (☎ 124 34; Andreasplatz; adult/concession €1.50/1; ☎ tower 11am-4pm Mon-Sat, noon-4pm Sun) whose lofty spire offers a sweeping view. There are 364 steps to the top.

LAPPENBERG

The former **Jewish Quarter** in and around Lappenberg Square is the oldest section of town. Most of it remains because, while local fire crews let the synagogue burn to the ground on Kristallnacht in November 1938, they rescued other houses around the square. These included the former **Jewish school**, now owned by St Godehard's Church, on the corner. In 1988, on the 50th anniversary, a memorial was installed on the site of the synagogue, following the outline of its foundations and topped by a model of Jerusalem.

While down this way, take time to check out the quaint **Wernesches Haus** on Hinterer Brühl, which is one of the oldest buildings in Hildesheim.

ROEMER- UND PELIZAEUS-MUSEUM

One of Europe's best collections of Egyptian art and artefacts is found in the **Roemer- und Pelizaeus-Museum** (☎ 936 90; www.rpmuseum.de, in German; Am Steine 1-2; adult/concession/family €8/6/14; ◷ 10am-6pm). There are dozens of mummies, scrolls, statues and wall hangings, but the life-size re-creation of an Egyptian tomb (of Sennefer) is a particular highlight.

Sleeping

Its proximity to Hanover means Hildesheim often takes overspill guests during trade fairs, when accommodation prices rise phenomenally.

DJH hostel (☎ 427 17; www.jugendherberge.de/jh /hildesheim; Schirrmannweg 4; dm under/over 26yr €16.50/ 19.50; (P) (X) (▣)) In the morning, guests here often act as though they've just had an embarrassing one-night stand. It's a great hostel, really, with modern facilities and a good breakfast. But it's just so inconveniently located that many seem to be wondering what they're doing here and look in a hurry to leave. To get here catch bus 1 or 2 to Schuhstrasse and change to 4 in the direction of Im Koken-Hof. Get off at the Triftstrasse stop and walk the remaining 750m uphill.

Gästehaus Klocke (☎ 179 213; www.gaestehaus -klocke.de; Humboldtstrasse 11; s €45-55, d €75-80) This is a quirky gem, which feels a bit like a mini-castle upon entering, as its high-ceilinged stairwell has a landing with a stained-glass window, chess set and chairs. The rooms aren't quite as amazing but have character nevertheless. The hotel is just south over the canal from the Jewish quarter.

Gästehaus-Café Timphus (☎ 346 86; www.timphus -conditorei-hotel.de; Braunschweiger Strasse 90/91; s €50-62, d €72-82, tr €108; (X)) Walls here are bedecked with photos of artful chocolate displays, which might mean you keep going next door to the

associated café for supplies. The 10 rooms are otherwise fairly generic, but spotless. The place has its own apartment-style entrance; you need to arrive between 8am and 6pm to collect the key from the patisserie.

Hotel Bürgermeisterkapelle (☎ 140 21; www .hotelbuergermeisterkapelle.de; Rathausstrasse 8; s €55-85, d €80-135; (P) (X)) Old meets new at this midrange hotel. The lobby has been nicely renovated and most of the rooms done up in blonde wood and green tones, but the restaurant and dim-lit halls remain rustic, with ancient wood-cut pictures, flower pots and bookshelves. The unrenovated rooms can cost as much as the refurbished ones, but don't offer the same quality.

Dorint Novotel Hotel (☎ 171 70; www.accorhotels .com; Bahnhofsallee 38; s €120-130, d €140-165; (P) (X)) Furnishings in black and beige, and warm touches like superior sea grass–style carpet, have been added to the exposed brick walls of this spacious stone cloister building to imbue it with cosy designer-chic style. Summer discounts are offered.

Meridien Hotel (☎ 300 600; www.starwoodhotels .com/lemeridien; Markt 4; s €135-155, d €155-175; (X) (▣)) Behind its historic frontage on the central market place, this luxury hotel opens out into a surprisingly large building. Through the flagstone-floored atrium entrance, you'll find upbeat rooms decorated in shades of yellow and red. Prices are cheaper in summer.

Eating & Drinking

Café Desseo (☎ 399 27; Hindenburgplatz 3; tapas €3-9, other dishes €4.40-14) Generally billed as a tapas bar, this excellent venue is actually much more of an all-rounder – the one catch-all Hildesheim address to file in your little black book. All-you-can-eat breakfasts (€6) and lunches (€6.90 – with jelly!) are joined by sandwiches, delicious wraps, pasta, pizza and other dishes. In addition to all this there's a large nonsmoking area and good cocktails of an evening.

Die Insel (☎ 145 35; Dammstrasse 30; mains €8-20; ◷ closed Mon) With its trimmed hedges, hanging pots of blazing geraniums, blue tablecloths and Tiffany lampshades, it's not surprising this cute restaurant in a former mill is a hit with Hildesheim's more mature citizens. Its location on a small, leafy 'island' in the middle of one of the town's canals means its terrace is an ideal spot to enjoy coffee and cake in summer.

Noah (☎ 691 530; Hohnsen 28; mains €8-19) Well worth the short journey out of town, this airy, glass-walled bistro enjoys great views of a peaceful lake. The normal fare is Mediterranean-influenced modern cuisine, including fish. However, in summer there are sometimes barbecues. Take bus 2 to Theodor Storm Strasse/Ochtersum.

Schlegels Weinstuben (☎ 331 33; Am Steine 4-6; mains €12.50-24.50; ☽ dinner Mon-Sat) The lopsided walls of this rose-covered, 500-year-old house hunkering beside the Roemer- und Pelizaeus-Museum just add to the sheer magic of the place. Inside, there's a group of historic rooms and, in one corner, a round, glass-topped table fashioned from a well, where you can dine overlooking the water far beneath. As the ever-changing international cuisine is also exceptional, it's advisable to book ahead.

For further options, there's a popular strip along **Friesenstrasse** (just behind Schuhstrasse), where the pubs and bars usually sell cheap meals.

Getting There & Around

Frequent regional train services operate between Hildesheim and Hanover (€6.20, 30 minutes), while ICE trains head to Braunschweig (€13, 25 minutes) and Göttingen (€22, 30 minutes).

For those driving, the A7 runs right by town from Hanover, while the B1 goes to Hamelin.

Most sights in Hildesheim are within walking distance, but buses will take you to outlying restaurants and accommodation, as indicated. Single tickets cost €1.80, daily city tickets €5.15.

BRAUNSCHWEIG

☎ 0531 / pop 245,800

Still famous as the city of Heinrich der Löwe (Henry the Lion) nine centuries after this powerful medieval duke made it his capital, Braunschweig (Brunswick) reveals its past as five separate settlements with a slightly meandering and confusing but pleasant historic old town.

Having spent most of the post-WWII period near the Iron Curtain, it doesn't have a great reputation for sightseeing, but with a couple of glittering collections of artefacts, cobbled streets and its quaint Magniviertel district it can soon grow on you.

Orientation

Most sights are in the historic town centre, a distorted rectangle bounded by Konrad-Adenauer-Strasse to the south, Güldenstrasse to the west, Lange Strasse to the north and Bohlweg to the east. However, the arty quarter of the Magniviertel and the Herzog Anton Ulrich Museum lie just to the old town's east. A moat surrounds the centre, lending it the compact character of an island. One-way systems may cause problems if you're driving.

Information

Main post office (Berliner Platz 12-16) Near the Hauptbahnhof.
Post (Friedrich-Wilhelm-Strasse 3; ☽ 9am-7pm Mon-Fri, to 1pm Sat)
Tourist Service Braunschweig (☎ 470 2040; www .braunschweig.de; Vor der Burg 1; ☽ 10am-7pm Mon-Fri, to 4pm Sat)

Dangers & Annoyances

The city's red-light district is in the alley connecting Wallstrasse with the intersection of Leopoldstrasse and Friedrich-Wilhelm-Strasse. It's not considered unsafe, but women who go there might be whistled at and generally harassed.

Sights & Activities

Braunschweig's identity is so tied up with Heinrich der Löwe, it's best not to fight it and to learn a little about the duke (see boxed text, p619). The **Braunschweiger Löwe** (Brunswick lion) statue you see replicated around town, but most prominently on Burgplatz, is the city's symbol. Heinrich ordered the original to be built in 1166 as a symbol of his power and jurisdiction; you can see the original at Burg Dankwarderode (p618).

DOM ST BLASII

Heinrich's tomb is in the crypt of **Dom St Blasii** (St Blasius Cathedral; ☎ 243 350; www.braunschweigerdom .de; Domplatz 5; crypt admission €1; ☽ 10am-1pm & 3-5pm), where he lies alongside his wife Mathilde. In a macabre postscript to the duke's life, the Nazis decided to coopt his image and in 1935 exhumed his tomb to conduct an 'archaeological investigation'. Even Hitler paid a visit. However, the corpse found inside had one leg shorter than the other (it's known that Heinrich suffered a terrible horse-riding accident late in life) and dark hair, and the master-race propagandists went very quiet on the subject after that. There were also questions over the body's gender and some doubt as to whether it's really Heinrich in the sarcophagus.

On the cathedral's northern side is the largely Gothic building's only remaining Romanesque door, which sports so-called 'claw marks'. Legend has it these were left by the duke's pet lion, trying to get to its master when he lay in the cathedral after his death. A more realistic explanation is that soldiers sharpened their swords here.

BURG DANKWARDERODE

Heinrich's former **castle** (☎ 122 50; www.braun schweig-museum.de; Burgplatz; adult/concession incl Herzog Anton Ulrich Museum €3/1.50; ⏱ 10am-5pm Tue & Thu-Sun,

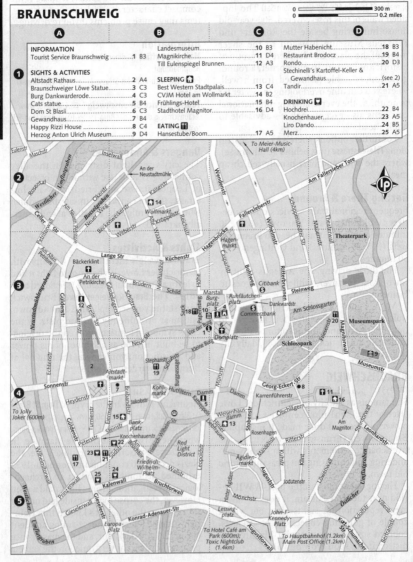

BRAUNSCHWEIG

0 ━━━━━ 300 m
0 ━━━━━ 0.2 miles

INFORMATION
Tourist Service Braunschweig 1 B3

SIGHTS & ACTIVITIES
Altstadt Rathaus 2 A4
Braunschweiger Löwe Statue 3 C3
Burg Dankwarderode 4 C3
Cats statue 5 B4
Dom St Blasii 6 C3
Gewandhaus 7 B4
Happy Rizzi House 8 C4
Herzog Anton Ulrich Museum 9 D4

Landesmuseum 10 B3
Magnikirche 11 D4
Till Eulenspiegel Brunnen 12 A3

SLEEPING
Best Western Stadtpalais 13 C4
CVJM Hotel am Wollmarkt 14 B2
Frühlings-Hotel 15 B4
Stadthotel Magnitor 16 D4

EATING
Hansestube/Boom 17 A5

Mutter Habenicht 18 B3
Restaurant Brodocz 19 B4
Rondo 20 D3
Stechinelli's Kartoffel-Keller &
 Gewandhaus ....(see 2)
Tandir 21 A5

DRINKING
Hochdrei 22 B4
Knochenhauer 23 A5
Liro Dando 24 B5
Merz 25 A5

SOUTH & EAST OF HANOVER •• Braunschweig

1-8pm Wed) is now a museum. It houses a glittering **medieval collection** (🕑 11am-5pm Tue & Thu-Sun, 1-2.30pm & 4-8pm Wed), including golden sculptures of arms, medieval capes, and the original bronze lion statue cast in 1166.

Upstairs is a huge, spectacularly adorned **Knights' Hall** (🕑 10am-11am Tue & Thu-Sun, 2.30-4pm Wed).

HERZOG ANTON ULRICH MUSEUM

Braunschweig is not always about Heinrich der Löwe. Another duke, Anton Ulrich (1633–1714) left Braunschweig with an impressive legacy too. Like Bruce Chatwin's compulsive collector *Utz*, Anton Ulrich had an eye for miniature porcelain figures – as well as for crockery, furniture and all types of painting, from Chinese to European. Now the thousands of pieces he assembled in his lifetime are found in the **Herzog Anton Ulrich Museum** (☎ 122 50; www.braunschweig-museum.de; Museumstrasse 1; adult/concession incl Burg Dankworderode €3/1.50; 🕑 10am-5pm Tue & Thu-Sun, 1-8pm Wed). Artefacts, including an ancient Roman onyx cup that survived some escapades through the years, and the most complete museum collection of Fürstenburg porcelain anywhere, are here. Unfortunately, lack of funding often means that opening times for different floors are staggered (as at Burg Dankworderode), so ring ahead.

LANDESMUSEUM

The city's **Landesmuseum** (State Museum; ☎ 121 50; Burgplatz; adult/concession €2.50/1.30; 🕑 10am-5pm

Tue, Wed & Fri-Sun, to 8pm Thu) covers German history from a local perspective. It's particularly engaging if you understand German, but also has some visual displays, such as the *zweihundert Milliarden* (200 billion) and *zwanzig Millionen* (20 million) mark notes from the inflationary days of the Weimar Republic and the huge statue of Heinrich der Löwe made from nails, that will appeal to all.

OLD TOWN

Of the several market places in Braunschweig, each representing an original township, the Altstadtmarkt is arguably the most appealing, with the step-gabled Renaissance **Gewandhaus** (1303, façade 1590) and the Gothic **Altstadt Rathaus**. Inside the Rathaus is the magnificent Dronse meeting hall. The tourist office can help with individual details on other buildings.

Kids will like the playful **cats statue** on the corner of Damm and Kattreppeln and the lovely **Till Eulenspiegel Brunnen** at Bäckerklint, with Till sitting above owls and monkeys.

MAGNIVIERTEL

Don't miss this arty quarter around the 11th-century **Magnikirche** (Am Magnitor). Restaurants and bars have colonised the area's many restored half-timbered houses and there are some great boutique stores. Particularly eye-catching is the **Happy Rizzi House** (Ackerhof, cnr Georg-Eckert-Strasse & Schlossstrasse), actually three colourful buildings decorated by American

---

THE LION KING

Legendary in Germany, Heinrich the Löwe (1129–1195) is relatively unknown outside its boundaries. Yet, until his cousin and Holy Roman Emperor Frederick Barbarossa engineered his downfall, he was one of the most powerful nobles in 12th-century Europe.

The duke of both Saxony and Bavaria, Heinrich founded not only Braunschweig, but Munich, Lübeck and Lüneburg too. At the height of his reign, his domain stretched from the north and Baltic coasts to the Alps, and from Westphalia to Pomerania (in Poland).

Part of the Welfen clan, Heinrich's family connections no doubt helped him ascend to such heights. His father and grandfathers were dukes and his second, English wife, Mathilde, was Richard the Lionheart's sister. However, his military ability and acumen were also renowned, as were his greed and ambition.

Heinrich oversaw a period of *Ostkolonisation,* when German settlers moved east of the Elbe and Saale rivers. But then he refused to help Barbarossa on an ill-fated incursion into Lombardy – he wanted Goslar in exchange, Barbarossa refused – and the emperor took him to court and had him convicted of disobedience.

Stripped of his lands, Heinrich spent three years in exile (1182–1185) in Normandy with his father-in-law, Henry II (King of England). After another brief exile in 1188, he died in Braunschweig in 1195 and was entombed in its cathedral.

pop artist James Rizzi. Hearts are a recurring theme on the façade, while curved windows form integral parts of facial murals.

Sleeping

Budget accommodation is both scarce and frequently disappointing in Braunschweig. There is no longer a hostel, so ask the tourist office about private rooms.

Hotel Café am Park (☎ 730 79; www.hotel -cafeampark.de; Wolfenbüttler Strasse 67; s/d from €32/50; P) This pleasant enough, slightly granny-style Hotel Garni is near a park to the south of town and relatively handy for the train station. The café serves homemade cakes.

CVJM Hotel am Wollmarkt (☎ 244 400; www .hotelamwollmarkt.de; Wollmarkt 9-12; s €55-60, d €85-95, tr €110; P) This YMCA-run hotel is just north of the centre and has pretty standard, but clean and comfortable rooms. The staff are welcoming and there's a nice breakfast bar and guest lounge, with a mural of historic Braunschweig, plus table football.

Frühlings-Hotel (☎ 243 210; www.fruehlingshotel .de; Bankplatz 7; s €65-110, d €85-145; P) Friendly staff with a good sense of humour, a stylish ground floor with reception and guest lounge plus three categories of pleasant bedrooms make this an excellent choice. Some of the cheaper accommodation on the top floor is a little old-fashioned, but still livable, while stunning room 407 has good rooftop views. There's even a tiny gym of sorts – a step-machine left in a corridor niche as a present from a regular guest.

Best Western Stadtpalais (☎ 241 024; www.palais -braunschweig.bestwestern.de; Hinter Liebfrauen 1a; s €70-140, d €90-155; P ✕) This former 18th-century palace is now a hotel that really works, striking a good balance between historic and modern. Lots of cream, gilt and blue furnishings create interest, while great care has been taken to ensure that the place is comfortable and

functional. The central, but fortunately not too noisy, location is another plus.

Eating

Tandir (☎ 165 67; Südstrasse 24; dishes €2-5.50) Its lavish displays of *pide* (flat bread), salads, doners, fried vegetable dishes and baklava have guaranteed this place an enduring position in the city's panoply of Turkish fast-food outlets.

Mutter Habenicht (☎ 459 56; Papenstieg 3; mains €5.50-15, weekday lunch menus €5.50) This 'Mother Hubbard' sure doesn't have a bare cupboard, as she dishes up filling portions of schnitzels, potatoes, steaks, spare ribs and the occasional Balkan dish. Seasonal specialities like *Spargel* (white asparagus) are also served in the dimly lit, bric-a-brac-filled front room, or in the small beer garden out the back.

Restaurant Brodocz (☎ 422 36; Stephanstrasse 1; mains €6.50-15; ⏱ 11am-10.30pm Mon-Fri, to 5pm Sat) Long a vegetarian restaurant, this Braunschweig institution now specialises in piscine delights, with everything from English-style fish and chips to dorade, perch and salmon on the menu. For old times' sake, though, it still serves ratatouille.

Stechinelli's Kartoffel-Keller & Gewandhaus (☎ 242 777; Altstadtmarkt 1-2; dishes €4-26) In the basement of the Rathaus, these adjacent restaurants are reasonably touristy, but handy as they open daily. Should you wish, you can indulge in potatoes over three courses in casual Stechinelli's, from potato soup to potato waffles for dessert. Gewandhaus specialises in schnitzel, although you're generally given a menu that covers both restaurants.

Rondo (☎ 123 4595; Magnitorwall 18; lunch mains €3-6, dinner mains €7-20; ⏱ lunch Tue-Fri, dinner Tue-Sun) A great find on the top floor of the Stadttheater building, Rondo has a modern bistro-style room decorated with dramatic photos of opera diva Maria Callas, plus a roof terrace offering city views. The food is plain and

---

THE AUTHOR'S CHOICE

Stadthotel Magnitor (☎ 471 30; www.stadthotel-magni.de, in German; Am Magnitor 1; s €55-80, d €80-110, ste €100-160) Easily the best of several half-timbered hotels in town, this place succeeds because of its location and interior. The historic black-and-white façade looks as it would have centuries ago, but up-to-date rooms have been painted white to create a sense of space and light unusual in such claustrophobic buildings. Furnishings keep things chic by rarely straying from the white, grey and black theme, although a touch of colour is added by the hall paintings. Two or three rooms do have very low ceilings, but these are cheaper than the rest. To cap it all, the place has a trendy bar and restaurant, right in the charming Magniviertel.

simple at lunch, but steps up a notch at dinner, with an array of fish, meat, vegetarian and seasonal specialities. Coffee and cake can be had in between times.

Hansestube/Boom (☎ 243 900; Güldenstrasse 7; mains €9-17) Widely regarded as Braunschweig's leading restaurants, these sister establishments in a renovated half-timbered house serve a seasonally changing menu of modern international cuisine. Or enjoy the *Braunschweiger Mummbraten,* a roast stuffed with mincemeat and served in a sauce based on Mumme, a local non-alcoholic malt extra. The room is divided into an elegant dining area with lots of glass and dark wood (Hansestube) and a more informal bistro (Boom).

Drinking

The Magniviertel is a good district to head for drinks, with several traditional pubs. More listings can be found in *Cocktail* or *Subway,* the tourist office's *Braunschweig Bietet* or the quarterly *Hin & Weg.*

Knochenhauer (☎ 480 3503; Altes Knochenhauerstrasse 11; ☽ from 6pm) The bistro/bar of choice among Braunschweig's hip, casual set, Knochenhauer buzzes on a summer eve with friends getting together for drinks or light snacks. There are also DJs on Friday and Saturday night.

Merz (☎ 181 28; Gieselerstrasse 3) Spacious and relaxed, with table football, an attached weekend club (Schwanensee) playing house and soul classics, and a beer garden, Merz is a long-standing favourite. Snacks are also served.

Liro Dando (☎ 157 09; Kalenwall 3) A slightly trendier and older crowd can be found here, just around the corner from Merz.

Hochdrei (Südstrasse 31; ☽ from 10am) This young, upbeat café bar is the place to come for cheap drinks, with vodka kicking off at €1.

Entertainment

Jolly Joker (☎ 0800-244 255, 281 4660; Broitzemerstrasse 220; ☽ from 10pm Tue-Sat) Other Braunschweig clubs come and go, but the Jolly Joker is not just here after more than 20 years, it's still being voted the city's best by local punters. Since a major overhaul in 2001, this venue with a capacity of 4000 features four separate dance spaces, 10 bars including a huge cocktail bar, and several food outlets. Expect top 100 dance-chart hits. The same complex also houses a cinema.

You probably don't need to know about anything other than the Jolly Joker, but if that's not to your tastes, other popular, mainstream clubs include **Toxic** (☎ 618 3399; www.toxic-bs.de; Böcklerstrasse 30-31; ☽ Fri & Sat) and **Meier-Music-Hall** (☎ 232 050; www.meier-music-hall.de; Schmalbachstrasse; ☽ Fri & Sat plus special events).

Getting There & Away

There are regular IC and RE services to Hanover (from €14, 35 to 45 minutes) and IC trains to Leipzig (€35, two hours). ICE trains go to Berlin (€46, one hour 20 minutes) or Frankfurt (€68, 2¾ hours).

The A2 runs east–west between Hanover and Magdeburg across the northern end of the city. This connects with the A39 about 25km east of the city, which heads north to Wolfsburg. The A39 also heads south from the city.

Getting Around

Braunschweig is at the heart of an integrated transport network that extends throughout the region and as far south as the Harz Mountains. Bus and tram ticket prices are determined by time, not distance: 90-minute tickets cost €1.90, 24-hour tickets €4.20.

Any bus or tram going to 'Rathaus' from the Hauptbahnhof will get you to the centre in 10 minutes; these leave from the same side as the public transport information booth just outside the train station. Trams 1 or 2 and buses 419 and 420 are among these.

If driving, be aware that there are one-way systems all around the Altstadt. Alternatively, there's parking by the train station.

WOLFENBÜTTEL

☎ 05331 / pop 54,500

'Alles mit Bedacht' (take your time) is the motto of this friendly, charming little city, about 10 minutes by train from Braunschweig, but worlds away in attitude. First mentioned in 1118, Wolfenbüttel was virtually untouched by WWII, and it's almost a time capsule of half-timbered houses – there are over 600 of them, nearly all beautifully restored.

Orientation & Information

The Hauptbahnhof is a five-minute walk southwest of Stadtmarkt, the town centre. To get to **Tourist Information Wolfenbüttel** (☎ 862 80; www.wolfenbuettel.com; Stadtmarkt 7; ☽ 9am-6pm Mon-Fri, to 1pm Sat), in Stadtmarkt, take Bahnhofstrasse north to Kommisstrasse. This joins Kornmarkt, the main bus transfer point. Stadtmarkt is just to the north. The Schloss and Herzog August Bibliothek are west of here.

Sights

The free tourist office brochure *A walk through historic Wolfenbüttel* is an excellent guide. It starts at Wolfenbüttel's pretty **Schloss Museum** (☎ 924 60; Schlossplatz 13; adult/concession/family €3/2/4; ◷ 10am-5pm Tue-Sun), where the living quarters of the Braunschweig-Lüneburg dukes have been preserved in all their glory of intricate inlaid wood, ivory walls, brocade curtains and chairs.

However, it's the **Herzog August Bibliothek** (☎ 808 214; Lessingplatz 1; adult/concession €3/2; ◷ 10am-5pm Tue-Sun), across the square, that will most interest bibliophiles. Not only is this hushed place one of the world's best reference libraries for 17th-century books (if you're a member that is), its collection of 800,000 volumes also includes what's billed as the 'world's most expensive book' (€17.50 million). This is the *Welfen Evangelial*, a gospel book once owned by Heinrich der Löwe. The original is only on show sporadically, as taking it out inevitably causes slight damage. However, an impressive facsimile is permanently displayed in the vault on the first floor.

From Schlossplatz, the walk suggested in the brochure continues east along Löwenstrasse to Krambuden and north up Kleiner Zimmerhof to **Klein Venedig** (Little Venice), one of the few tangible remnants of the extensive canal system built by Dutch workers in Wolfenbüttel in the late 16th century. From there the brochure continues to guide you past historic courtyards, buildings and squares. The entire walk takes around one hour (2km), excluding visits.

Getting There & Away

Trains connect Wolfenbüttel with Braunschweig's Hauptbahnhof (€2.35, 10 minutes) twice an hour.

WOLFSBURG

☎ 05361 / pop 121,800

All is not well in the 'capital of Volkswagen', but from the outside you wouldn't realise it. In a scene that could have come from Fritz Lang's classic film *Metropolis*, a huge VW emblem still adorns the company's nation-sized global headquarters – and the same insignia is repeated in solidarity on almost every vehicle.

Behind the scenes, the company wants to scale down operations in high-wage 'Golfsburg' (as Wolfsburg is nicknamed after one of VW's most successful models). Conversely, however, more visitors want in. Besides the increasingly successful theme park of Autostadt, the town now boasts the Phaeno science centre, a sleek piece of futuristic architecture by celebrity architect Zaha Hadid.

Orientation

Wolfsburg's centre is just southeast of the Hauptbahnhof. Head diagonally left out of the train station to the partly pedestrianised main drag, Porschestrasse, and continue south. The Phaeno centre is impossible to miss, just to the left of the station. To get to Autostadt, walk under Phaeno and continue until you see the stairs across the railway tracks. These lead to the theme park.

Information

Babylon Tele- and Internet Shop (Porschestrasse 23; per hr €2; ◷ 10am-11pm) Internet access.
Main post office (Porschestrasse 22-24)
Wolfsburg tourist office (☎ 899 930; www .wolfsburg.de; Willy Brandt-Platz 3; ◷ 9am-7pm) In the train station.

Sights & Activities

AUTOSTADT

Spread across 25 hectares, **Autostadt** (Car City; ☎ 0800-288 678 238; www.autostadt.de; Stadtbrücke; adult/child/concession/family €14/6/11/38; ◷ 9am-8pm Apr-Oct, to 6pm Nov-Mar) is a celebration of all things VW – so no muttering about the company's recent boardroom scandals up the back there, please! Conceived as a luxury centre for customers to collect new vehicles, it soon developed into a theme park with broad family appeal.

Things kick off with a broad view of automotive design and engineering in the Konzernforum, while the neighbouring Zeithaus looks back at the history of the Beetle (see boxed text, p624) and other VW models. Then, in various outlying pavilions you can learn more about individual marques, including VW itself, Audi, Bentley, Lamborghini, Seat and Skoda. Many exhibits are interactive and most have signage in German and English.

Many people will be keener to do something more active, and Autostadt doesn't disappoint here. Included in the entrance price is a 45-minute trip into the neighbouring Volkswagen factory, bigger than Monaco and the world's largest car plant. These leave at 15-minute intervals from Monday to Friday only, and there's a daily tour in English (at 1.30pm at the time of research, but check the latest details on the website). Queues can be long, so heed the staff's advice if they ask you to come back later. Be aware that because the factory is so large, tours rotate through different workshop sections, so it's pot luck whether you'll see one of the 3000 cars produced each day roll off the assembly line or something less interesting, such as metal-pressing.

For a pure, competitive adrenaline rush, ring ahead to organise an English-speaking instructor for the park's **obstacle courses** and **safety training** (€25 each). You'll need a valid licence, of course, and to be comfortable with a left-hand-drive car. The park even has a **mini-course**, with toy models that can be driven by kids.

AUTOMUSEUM

After the whizz-bang, showbiz aplomb of Autostadt, its sister **AutoMuseum** (☎ 520 71; Dieselstrasse 35; adult/concession/family €6/3/15; ☼ 10am-5pm, closed 24 Dec-1 Jan) is pretty low-key. You proceed through a hallway of ads (in German), which make you realise how central its 'cheeky chappie' persona was to the Beetle's success. Then you turn the corner and a room full of that personality confronts you.

The museum often lends its cars to other exhibitions, so it's impossible to list exactly what you'll see. However, its collection does include a vehicle used in the *Herbie, the Love Bug* movie, a Beetle built from wood, the original 1938 Cabriolet presented to Adolf Hitler on his 50th birthday, and (our favourite) a white, see-through, iron-lace Beetle built by Mexican factory workers for the wedding of some colleagues. Amphibious Beetles and a few Passats and Golfs complete the show.

Take bus 208 to Automuseum.

PHAENO

The glass-and-concrete building that houses the science centre **Phaeno** (☎ 0180-106 0600; www.phaeno.de; Willy Brandt-Platz 1; adult/concession/family €11/7/25; ☼ 10am-6pm Tue-Sun, last entry 1hr before closing) is truly cutting edge. Sleek, curved and thin, it looks like a stretchy spaceship from Planet Minimalism.

Inside, however, you rarely have time to appreciate the design by British-based Iraqi architect Zaha Hadid. The place is full of 250 hands-on physics exhibits and experiments (with instructions and explanations in both German and English) and, frequently it seems, 10 times as many schoolchildren all pulling at them. You can wind up your own rocket, check your eyes by looking at bunnies, build an arched polystyrene bridge, watch thermal images of your body – and so on and so on. Indeed, the place is quite physically, as well as mentally, absorbing, so it helps to set yourself some time or other limits.

If you speak German, an excellent idea is to pick up the brochure that poses a list of questions and try to answer them during your visit. For the one really peaceful chance to savour the building's architecture, head to the canteen. Look for the window at the far end to see how it cleverly frames Porschestrasse.

CITY CENTRE

As you walk south down Porschestrasse, you'll come to another great building, the **Kunstmuseum** (Art Museum; ☎ 266 90; Porschestrasse 53; adult/concession €6/3; ☼ 11am-8pm Tue, to 6pm Wed-Sun), which is home to temporary exhibitions of modern art. On the hill just southwest of the southern end of Porschestrasse is **Planetarium Wolfsburg** (☎ 219 39; Uhlandweg 2; adult/concession/family €5/3/10), built in 1982 after VW bartered Golfs for Zeiss projectors with the GDR. It's got laser and rock shows, star shows and spoken-word performances set to the stars. Call ahead, as show times vary.

Next to it is the city's historic landmark, the **Esso Station**, built in 1951 and now restored to its original splendour.

SCHLOSS WOLFSBURG

In historic contrast to Autostadt's space-age sheen, Wolfsburg's castle dates from 1600 and today houses the **Stadt Museum** (☎ 828 540; Schlossstrasse 8; adult/concession €2.50/1.50; ☼ 10am-6pm Tue-Fri, 1-6pm Sat, 11am-6pm Sun). It has a rundown of the city's history from 1938, when the VW plant was founded, to the present day. There's also a small regional history museum and two **art galleries** that host rotating exhibitions. The Schloss is five minutes northeast of Autostadt. Several buses, including 160, 201, 202, 208, 211 and 380 will get you here.

FALLERSLEBEN

Keen history students who speak German might want to visit this historic part of town to see **Fallersleben Schloss** and its **Hoffmann Museum** (☎ 05362-526 23; adult/concession/family €1.50/0.50/3; ☺ 10am-5pm Tue-Fri, 1-6pm Sat, 10am-6pm Sun). In 1841, Fallersleben native August Heinrich Hoffman (1798–1874) wrote the lyrics to what would become the German national anthem (music courtesy of Joseph Hayden). Here you'll find discussion of how his words '*über alles*' (above everything) were simply a call for an end to petty inter-German fiefdoms, and how they were expunged after the Third Reich's nationalistic excesses. Take bus 206 or 214 to Fallersleben.

Sleeping

Most tourists who come to Wolfsburg tend to be day-trippers, and the city's accommodation is geared towards business travellers. Facilities like modem ports are standard, but single rooms far outnumber doubles.

DJH hostel (☎ 133 37; www.jugendherberge.de/jh/wolfsburg; Lessingstrasse 60; dm under/over 26yr €16.50/19.50; P X 🖵) Slightly cramped and fairly old, with pine furniture and checked linen, this hostel is nevertheless friendly and extremely central.

Hotel Wolf (☎ 865 60; www.alterwolf.de; Schlossstrasse 21; s/d from €35/50, f €75-85; P) A good-value option for families travelling by car, this attractive, black-and-white half-timbered house is located in a quiet, leafy part of town just behind Autostadt and the city castle. Rooms aren't particularly fashionable, but some are huge.

Cityhotel Journal (☎ 292 662; www.cityhotel-journal.de; Kaufhofpassage 2; s/d from €40/70) Better in winter than summer, as it's on the city's main drinking strip, this place is friendly, homy and convenient for automotive fans in town for one night.

Global Inn (☎ 2700; www.globalinn.de; Kleistrasse 46; s €45-65, d €90; P X) While very much aimed at the corporate customer, this place's comfortable furnishings and facilities, including an

---

BITTEN BY THE BUG

Cast-iron proof that Germans *do* have a sense of humour, the Volkswagen Beetle is truly greater than the sum of its parts. After all, the parts in question initially comprised little more than an air-cooled, 24-horsepower engine (maximum speed: 100km/h) chucked in the back of a comically half-egg-shaped chassis. Yet somehow this rudimentary mechanical assembly added up to a global icon – a symbol of Germany's postwar *Wirtschaftswunder* (economic miracle) that owners the world over fondly thought of as one of the family.

Indeed, it's a testament to the vehicle's ability to run on the smell of an oily rag while rarely breaking down that few would even begrudge its Nazi provenance. Yes, in 1934 Adolf Hitler asked Ferdinand Porsche to design a 'Volkswagen' (people's car) affordable for every German household and, yes, the *Käfer* (bug) was the result. However, Beetle production only really began in the new Wolfsburg factory under British occupation in 1946.

Did the company realise then what a hit it had on its hands? By the early 1960s, the chugging, spluttering sound of VW engines could be heard across 145 nations.

Urged on by ads to 'Think Small', North Americans were particularly bitten by the bug, and this durable, cut-price vehicle became a permanent fixture on the hippie scene. Later in Europe, the Golf model cars that superseded the Beetle in the 1970s and 1980s would prove a phenomenal success. (While Douglas Coupland talked about *Generation X*, the German equivalent, as identified by best-selling author Florian Illies in 2000, is *Generation Golf*). However the US never warmed to the usurper, pushing VW to introduce a sleek, trendy, state-of-the-art New Beetle in 1998.

Long after VW withdrew its bucket-of-bolts old Beetle (essentially the same beast despite improvements) from Western markets, the car remained a best-seller in the developing world. Only on 31 July 2003 did the last one roll off the assembly line in Mexico, the 21,529,464th of its breed.

But the secondhand market remains strong. In 2005, online auction site eBay sold Pope Benedict XIII's old Volkswagen Golf to a US casino for about €189,000. Newspapers since have said Volkswagen has now contacted the former Cardinal Joseph Ratzinger; it reportedly wants to build the next Pope-mobile.

excellent Italian restaurant, deliver the goods for leisure travellers, too. Book ahead.

Penthouse Hotel (☎ 2710; www.penthouse-hotel.de; Schachtweg 22; s €60-65, d €80-95, f €95) With basic kitchens, these central, although quite plain-Jane apartments, are also suitable for families or longer-stay business travellers. Discounts are given for extended stays.

Ritz-Carlton (☎ 607 000; www.ritzcarlton.com; Stadtbrücke; rooms from €280; P ⊠ ⊠ ⊠) This stunning ring-shaped building in the heart of Autostadt is Wolfsburg's only five-star hotel. It has elegant rooms decorated in natural tones of camel, cream and brown, a sauna, and a Michelin-starred restaurant. Naturally, if you stay here admission to Autostadt is free.

Eating & Drinking

Atelier Café (☎ 122 19; An der St Annenkirche; dishes €4.50-16; ⊙ closed Tue) Summer breakfasts are the best here, because you can sit in the lovely courtyard in the historic inner-city district of Hesslingen, five minutes east of Porschestrasse. You can also head inside the half-timbered house, where three meals a day are served in a modern industrial-style bistro of concrete, glass and steel. Ask the tourist office for a map and directions.

Altes Brauhaus (☎ 053362-3140; Schlossplatz, Fallersleben; mains €7-15) If you're visiting the Hoffman Museum in Fallersleben or simply dying for some genuine German beer-hall atmosphere, come here. There's a good house brew and hearty fare including salads, sausages, potatoes and sauerkraut.

Aalto Bistro (☎ 891 689; Porschestrasse 1; mains €10.50-15; ⊙ from 6pm Mon-Sat) This is the only part of the Kulturhaus, designed by star Finnish architect Alvar Aalto, that most visitors will get to see. It serves pasta and seafood in a modern bistro environment.

Walino (☎ 255 99; Kunstmuseum, Porschestrasse 53; mains €16-17.50, per person 3-course meal for 2 €18.50; ⊙ closed Mon) The menu of international cuisine always changes in the Kunstmuseum's loft-style restaurant – including dishes such as corn-fed chicken breast on polenta, and fish on truffle risotto – while the pleasant outlook over town makes it a perennial.

Some of the eight **Autostadt restaurants** (☎ 406 100) stay open later than the park itself, so within two hours of the park's closing time, you can buy an *Abendticket* (evening ticket, €6) and your admission fee is credited towards your restaurant meal. The restaurants

are all operated by Mövenpick, but have different cuisines. Options range from a cheap American diner to a sushi bar and an upmarket Mediterranean restaurant. Ask for details at the park's main cash desk.

Wolfsburgers do much of their drinking in **Kaufhof** – not the department store, but a small strip of bars, pubs and a few eateries west of Porschestrasse. The best thing is to wander along and see what appeals.

Getting There & Away

Frequent ICE train services go to Berlin (€39, one hour) and Hanover (€19, 30 minutes), the latter passing through Braunschweig (€11, 16 minutes). Regional trains are cheaper, especially to Braunschweig (€3.50, 24 minutes).

From Braunschweig, take the A2 east to the A39 north, which brings you right into town. Alternatively, take the B248 north to the A39.

Getting Around

Single bus tickets, valid for 90 minutes, cost €1.90 and a day pass costs €4.20. The major bus transfer point (ZOB) is at the northern end of Porschestrasse. Buses 206 and 214 go regularly to Fallersleben from here.

A free shuttle called City Mobil runs from the Hauptbahnhof down Porschestrasse with stops at Kaufhof, the Südkopf Center (a shopping centre) and the Kunstmuseum from 8am to 5.30pm Monday to Friday and 10am to 4pm Saturday.

Once you leave the pedestrianised centre, distances become difficult to cover easily by foot. In every sense, Wolfsburg was built for cars. The car park behind the Planetarium is free. Vehicles can be hired from **Europcar** (☎ 815 70; Dieselstrasse 19).

There are taxi ranks at the Hauptbahnhof and at the northern end of Porschestrasse. Alternatively, call **City Taxi** (☎ 230 223).

GÖTTINGEN

☎ 0551 / pop 121,800

Germans sometimes take the mickey out of themselves as a nation of *Besserwissers* (know-it-alls), and few places know better than this famous university town. With the Georg-August Universität a pillar of the community since 1734, Göttingen has sent more than 40 Nobel Prize winners into the world. And, as well as all those award-winning doctors and scientists, the fairy-tale writing Brothers

Grimm (as German linguistic teachers) and Prussian chancellor Otto von Bismarck (as a student) could also be expected at a timeless alumni evening.

Despite such a formidably pointy-headed reputation, Göttingen is actually an atmospheric and typical student haunt. Much is made of the iconic statue of Gänseliesel (the little goose girl) being the most kissed in the world, thanks to the custom among graduating doctoral students to peck her on the cheek. For most of the year, however, Gänseliesel remains unmolested, while the university's 25,000 students major in having a good time.

Orientation

The circular city centre is surrounded by the ruins of an 18th-century wall and is divided by the Leinekanal (Leine Canal), an arm of the Leine River. The centre has a large pedestrianised mall, the hub of which is the Markt, a 10-minute walk east of the Hauptbahnhof.

Information

Gö-Card (one/two days €5/9) Discount card offering free public transport and discounts on tours and museums.
Post office (Heinrich von Stephanstrasse 1-5) Near the Hauptbahnhof.
Post office (Groner Strasse 15)
Tourist-Information Göttingen (☎ 499 800; www.goettingen.de; Altes Rathaus, Markt 9; ⏲ 9.30am-6pm Mon-Fri, 10am-4pm Sat & Sun Apr-Oct, closed Sun Nov-Mar)
Universitätsklinikum (University hospital; ☎ 390; Robert-Koch-Strasse 40) Medical services.

'STADT, DIE WISSEN SCHAFFT'

Göttingen is so damn pointy-headed that even its clever-clever tourist office slogan takes a bit of explaining to translate into English. A play on words, its straightforward meaning is 'the town that forges knowledge'. However, Wissenschaft (as one word, with one f) also means science – one of Göttingen's strengths.

Vitamin D was discovered here and aluminium first developed. Meanwhile, famous names to have worked at the university include physicists Niels Bohr, Max Planck and Otto Hahn, as well as astronomist Carl Friedrich Gauss. David Hilbert and Hermann Minkowski also laid down the mathematical groundwork for Einstein's theory of relativity.

Waschsalon (Ritterplan 4; per wash from €3; ⏲ 7am-10pm Mon-Sat) Laundry.

Sights & Activities

Rather than having any urgent must-sees, Göttingen is a mosaic of attractions that you'll most appreciate by walking around. Having existed since 953 at least, the town long had a protective network of walls and moats, and a walk around the 18th-century ramparts is recommended. These are not brick constructions, but rather earthy hummocks left from that time. It takes less than an hour to circumnavigate the city, the best starting point being the entrance near Cheltenham Park. This takes you past **Bismarckhäuschen** (Bismarck Cottages; ☎ 485 844; Im Hainberg; admission free; ⏲ 10am-1pm Tue, 3-5pm Thu & Sat), where the town fathers reputedly banished 18-year-old Otto for rowdy behaviour in 1833. This incident is probably apocryphal, but it's a matter of historical record that the future Iron Chancellor was later found guilty of witnessing an illegal duel. Nearby are two old **water mills**. The walk ends near the **Deutsches Theater** (☎ 496 90; Theaterplatz 11).

AROUND THE MARKT

The city's symbol, the **Gänseliesel** statue and fountain remains a handy meeting point for locals and most visitors will soon head this way after arrival, if for no other reason than to see the Markt and visit the tourist office. Close up, the demure little goose girl (with geese) isn't exactly a show stopper. After all you hear about her being the 'most kissed girl in the world', the bronze statue doesn't even have particularly shiny cheeks from all that human contact. There's nothing here to compare with the gleaming right breast of the statue of Juliet in Verona, Italy.

While you're here, however, pop into the nearby **Altes Rathaus** (⏲ 9.30am-6pm Mon-Fri, 10am-4pm Sat & Sun Apr-Oct, closed Sun Nov-Mar) for a quick look at the interior. Built in 1270, the structure once housed the merchants' guild, and the rich decorations later added to its Great Hall include frescoes of the coats of arms of the Hanseatic cities and local bigwigs, grafted onto historic scenes.

BUILDINGS

Looking at some of Göttingen's half-timbered buildings is a pleasant way to while away some time. **Junkernschänke** (Barfüsserstrasse 5) is the prettiest, thanks to its colourful 16th-century

Renaissance façade. Just down the road is another ornate number, **Haus Börner** (Barfüsserstrasse 12); built in 1536 it has the busy **Börnerviertel** alley behind it. Kurze Strasse and Paulinerstrasse are also worth exploring.

Among Göttingen's six Gothic churches, the most interesting is the **St Jakobikirche** (1361) on Weender Strasse. With eye-catching red, white and grey angular striped columns, it also features some contemporary stained-glass windows.

PARKS & GARDENS

In the shadow of the old ramparts, the small **Botanische Gärten** (Botanical Gardens; ☎ 395 753; Untere Karspüle 2; admission free; 🕑 8am-6pm Mon-Fri, to 3pm Sat & Sun) were Germany's first, and there's a section devoted to mountain plants – the Andes, the Alps etc. The **tropical greenhouses** (🕑 9am-noon & 1.30-2.45pm) are highly recommended in winter.

A 20-minute walk east of the Markt is the **Schillerwiese**, a large park that backs onto forest. To reach it, follow Herzberger Landstrasse east, then turn right into Merkelstrasse.

To enter **Göttinger Wald** (Göttinger Forest), continue along Herzberger Landstrasse near where it forms a hairpin bend, and turn into Borheckstrasse. From there, a bitumen track open to hikers and cyclists winds towards Hainholzhof-Kehr, 45 minutes away, where there's a Bavarian-style beer garden in summer. Another option is to take bus 1 or 7 to Zietenterrassen and walk northwest back through

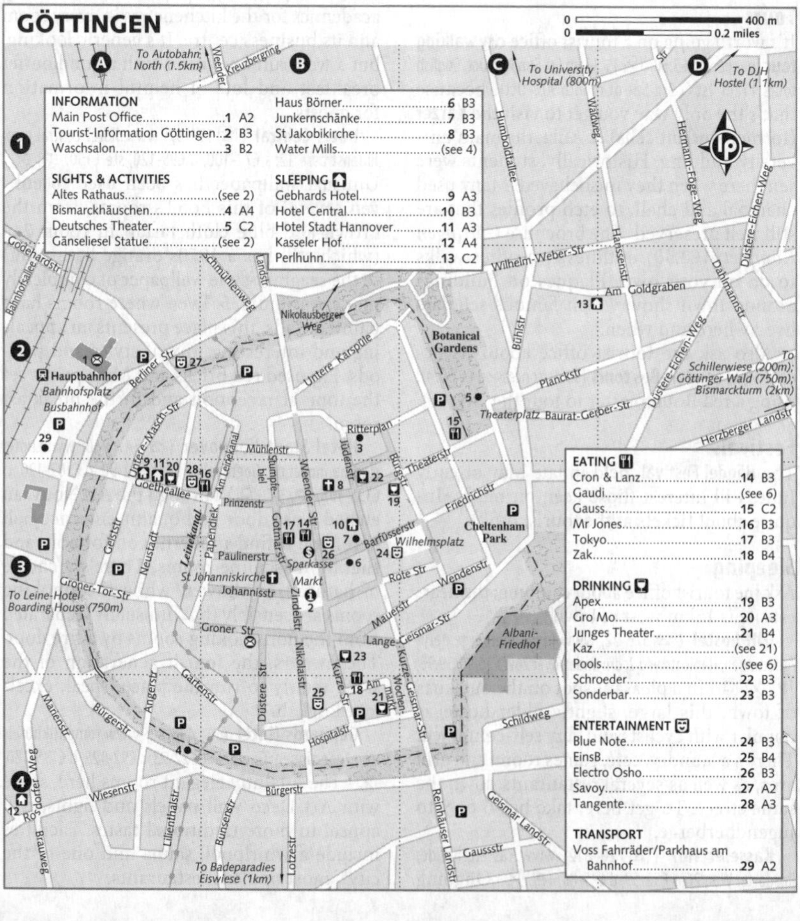
GÖTTINGEN
0 400 m
0 0.2 miles
To Autobahn North (1.5km)
To University Hospital (800m)
To DJH Hostel (1.1km)
To Schillerwiese (200m); Göttinger Wald (750m); Bismarckturm (2km)
To Leine-Hotel Boarding House (750m)
To Badeparadies Eiswiese (1km)
Hauptbahnhof
Bahnhofsplatz
Busbahnhof
Botanical Gardens
Cheltenham Park
Albani-Friedhof
Markt
Wilhelmsplatz
Theaterplatz
Sparkasse
St Johanniskirche
INFORMATION
Main Post Office 1 A2
Tourist-Information Göttingen 2 B3
Waschsalon 3 B2
SIGHTS & ACTIVITIES
Altes Rathaus (see 2)
Bismarckhäuschen 4 A4
Deutsches Theater 5 C2
Gänseliesel Statue (see 2)
Haus Börner 6 B3
Junkernschänke 7 B3
St Jakobikirche 8 B3
Water Mills (see 4)
SLEEPING
Gebhards Hotel 9 A3
Hotel Central 10 B3
Hotel Stadt Hannover 11 A3
Kasseler Hof 12 A4
Perlhuhn 13 C2
EATING
Cron & Lanz 14 B3
Gaudi (see 6)
Gauss 15 C2
Mr Jones 16 B3
Tokyo 17 B3
Zak 18 B4
DRINKING
Apex 19 B3
Gro Mo 20 A3
Junges Theater 21 B4
Kaz (see 21)
Pools (see 6)
Schroeder 22 B3
Sonderbar 23 B3
ENTERTAINMENT
Blue Note 24 B3
EinsB 25 B4
Electro Osho 26 B3
Savoy 27 A2
Tangente 28 A3
TRANSPORT
Voss Fahrräder/Parkhaus am Bahnhof 29 A2

the forest into town. From the terminus a path leads to the **Bismarckturm** (adult/concession €1.70/0.70; ☉ 11am-6pm weekends & holidays Apr-Sep). This stone tower has spectacular views over the Leine Valley.

BATHS

If all the walking through parks has knotted your muscles, unwind in **Badeparadies Eiswiese** (☎ 507 090; Windausweg 6; adult/concession from €12/8; ☉ 10am-10.30pm Mon-Fri, 9am-10.30pm Sat & Sun). This huge swimming/spa complex has pools from 28°C to 34°C, with the usual assortment of massaging underwater jets, geysers and currents. While kids enjoy the water slides, there are massages (book in advance), a solarium and a sauna for adults.

Tours

It's worth going on a tourist office **city walking tour** (per person €5.50; ☉ 11.30am Fri-Sun Apr-Oct, English tours 11am 1st & 3rd Sat of month Apr-Oct), because that's the only way you get to visit the **Karzer** (former student cells) at Aula, the main university building. Historically, students were sent here when they misbehaved. Many used charcoal and chalk to etch profiles that are still well preserved. The brochure *Göttingen Komplett* (€2.50) outlines two other walks to do on your own. Plaques on buildings around town show which famous scholars lived where and when.

Also ask the tourist office about its occasional **London-Bus tours** (adult/concession €6.50/4), using a red Routemaster to tour the city.

Festivals

The **Händel Festival**, held in late May or early June, will interest those keen on music. Inquire about tickets at the tourist office.

Sleeping

Ask the tourist office about camping; the nearest site is 15km west of town.

DJH hostel (☎ 576 22; www.jugendherberge.de/jh/goettingen; Habichtsweg 2; dm under/over 26yr €16.90/19.90; P ✗ ☐) In a pleasant spot on the outskirts of town, this large, slightly older hostel is popular with cyclists and very self-contained. There's a laundry, café, games room, and grill area, as well as several restaurants down the same street. To get here, take bus 6 or 9 to Jugendherberge.

Kasseler Hof (☎ 720 812; www.kasselerhof.de; Rosdorfer Weg 26; s €52-59, d €75-89; P ✗) Ongoing

renovations are turning a chintzy budget hotel into something a little more appealing, with newer rooms decorated in a simple Ikea style. All rooms have en suite bathrooms. Tucked away in a quiet corner not far from town, the hotel has its own restaurant.

Perlhuhn (☎ 551 10; www.perlhuhn.de; Am Gold-graben 22; s/d €55/80; ✗) This tiny B&B offers two unforgettable apartments themed from the golden age of travel. One combines an aircraft living room with an African bedroom, the other a captain's living room (with a ship's propeller as an elegant table base) and a pirate's bedroom.

Leine-Hotel Boarding House (☎ 505 10; www.leinehotel-goe.de; Groner Landstrasse 55; s €55-70; d €85-110; P ✗ ☐) A 10-minute walk from the centre, this place is popular with visiting academics for the kitchenettes in every room and its business centre. It's generic looking, but a well-run operation with a good buffet breakfast and lots of helpful information for guests.

Hotel Central (☎ 571 57; www.hotel-central.com; Jüdenstrasse 12; s €72-100, d €95-120, ste €150; P ✗) Unusual wallpaper has been used to enliven several of this hotel's rooms, from the brown-and-blue cloth tartan in room 245 (which still has a 1970s orange bathroom) to the seagrass-style wallpaper of completely modern room 135. Even where rooms have painted walls, this place presents an appealing and interesting mix of styles and periods. Exposed red bricks and Miró prints set the tone at reception and in the breakfast room.

Hotel Stadt Hannover (☎ 547 960; www.hotel stadthannover.de; Goetheallee 21; s €72-90, d €102-120, tr €135-155; P ✗ ☐) Through the Art Nouveau etched glass door and quaint entrance hall here, you'll find modern, comfortable and slightly masculine rooms. There's a choice of bathtub or shower, while the smoking rooms are sensibly (but unusually) separated from the nonsmoking rooms by a fire door. The owners, the fourth generation of the same family to run the place, speak excellent English.

Gebhards Hotel (☎ 496 80; www.romantikhotels.com/goettingen; Goetheallee 22-23; s €92-125, d €135-180; ✗) The quaintly elegant rooms here, some with Art Deco wall panels and lights, will appeal to more traditional tastes. Facilities include a whirlpool, sauna and one of the city's most opulent restaurants.

Eating

Cron & Lanz (☎ 560 22; Weender Strasse 25; coffee/cake from €2/2.50, snacks €2.50-6.50) The windows of this ornate Viennese-style café will tempt you in with their artful arrangements of chocolates and cakes. Once inside, you may have to wrestle with your conscience to ignore the healthier light snacks of toasted sandwiches, quiches and casseroles.

Zak (☎ 487 770; Am Wochenmarkt 22; mains €5-9.90) This ivy-covered pub-café-bar is a relaxed popular meeting spot, thanks in part to its excellent location opposite the Junges Theater. But do try to keep a straight face when ordering. Dishes, from bagels to potatoes to meat, all carry film-title names, so you'll have to ask for the likes of a *Natürlich Blond* (Legally Blond) or a *Findet Nemo* (Finding Nemo)!

Tokyo (☎ 999 5735; Gotmarstrasse 16; sushi €2-9, mains €8-14; �) closed Mon) In the simple exposed-pine and bamboo interior here, the lone sushi chef works hard to turn out customers' orders, including the usual *maki* and *nigiri* sushi, tempura and *gyoza*. Tofu and vegetarian options are available, and there's even Korean beef and *kimchi*.

Gaudi (☎ 531 3001; Börnerviertel, Barfüsserstrasse 12-13; mains €10-22) Stained glass and other Iberian-style splashes of colour give this restaurant its name. The menu, however, would be better described as Mediterranean or modern international, with dishes such as beef roulades with spinach, ratatouille chutney and grated polenta, and rack of lamb in garlic sauce with spinach and gnocchi.

Gauss (☎ 566 16; Oberer Karspüle 22, enter on Theaterstrasse; mains €16-24; ☉ dinner, closed Sun) Renowned TV chef Jacqueline Amirfallah upholds this cellar restaurant's reputation as Göttingen's best gourmet experience with exquisite (and changing) *haute cuisine*, such as souffléed fillet of North Sea flounder on lemon sauce with endives and asparagus risotto. There's a noticeable concentration on seasonal ingredients.

Drinking

Pools (☎ 820 7472; Börnerviertel, Barfüsserstrasse 12-13) Göttingen's contribution to the spate of funky 'second-hand bars' (with recycled furniture) currently popular in Germany, Pools features '70s arc lamps, potted plants and chairs rescued from the rubbish, including four ripped-out bus seats. The toilets are upstairs;

outside a cool, relaxed crowd hangs out in the courtyard.

Schroeder (☎ 556 47; Jüdenstrasse 29) This hip, studenty place touts itself as a 'bar-café-living room', and some patrons do seem to treat it as their second home, spending hours drinking and chatting. There's a TV screen used for watching football, some DJ evenings, and pavement tables in summer.

Mr Jones (☎ 531 4500; Goetheallee 8) Waiters zip to and fro with milkshake-sized cocktails in Day-Glo colours at this relaxed, slightly American-style bar. The €4 happy hour lasts all evening (despite what the menu says) and punters are keen to taste everything, including the 'surprise' Mr Jones and Mrs Jones drinks.

Gro Mo (☎ 488 9232; Goetheallee 13a) Patrons nurse huge mugs of coffee or even bigger steins of beer at this funky Goetheallee hangout. As they're strewn all over the place, it's a great spot to pick up flyers and local magazines.

Apex (☎ 447 71; Burgstrasse 46) A refined, academic and generally older crowd (40s to 50s) comes to sup a range of wines or even Sion Kölsch in this dark-wood bistro, attached to a cabaret venue and art gallery.

Sonderbar (☎ 431 43; Kurze Strasse 9) If you're after a late-night watering hole, head to Sonderbar, which is open until 5am daily.

Combined with Zak, **Junges Theater** (☎ 495 0150; Hospitalstrasse 6) draws a large crowd to Am Wochenmarkt. The theatre's bar, **Kaz** (☎ 530 62), is also an enduringly popular place to drink.

Entertainment

German-language *Pony* is your best bet for information about individual gigs and club nights.

Savoy (☎ 531 5353; Berliner Strasse 5) Dress up, for only sleek and trendy beings are waved through easily at Göttingen's leading and most glamorous club. Playing mainstream and house music, it's spread over a couple of levels, with a chilled-out lounge below the main floor (with bar and go-go podium).

EinsB (☎ 820 7799; Nikolaistrasse 1b) Friday nights concentrate on new-wave guitar music, Brit-pop etc, while on Saturday things take a turn for the electronic in this laid-back, younger club above a pipe-smoking Turkish lounge.

Electro Osho (☎ 517 7976; Weender Strasse 38) This small club, at the end of an arcade next to a mobile-phone shop, focuses on drum 'n' bass and techno.

Tangente (☎ 463 76; Goetheallee 8a) The long-standing punters at Tangente just keep getting older with it and its famous 'Zartbitter' rock parties (which are quite heavy metal).

Blue Note (☎ 469 07; Wilhelmsplatz 3) Right next to the university *Mensa* (canteen), the Blue Note has regular live bands and theme dance nights, including salsa, tropical and even Persian.

Getting There & Away

There are frequent direct ICE services north to Hanover (€28, 30 minutes) and Hamburg (€54, two hours) or south to Frankfurt (€51, 1¾ hours) and Munich (€87, four hours). ICE services also go to Berlin-Hauptbahnhof (€63, two hours 20 minutes). Direct regional services go to Kassel (€11.70, one hour) and Weimar (€23.10, two hours), but you'll have to change trains to get to Goslar (€13.40, 1¼ hours).

Göttingen is on the A7 running north–south. The closest entrance is 3km southwest along Kasseler Landstrasse, an extension of Groner Landstrasse. The Fairy-Tale Road (B27) runs southwest to the Weser River and northeast to the Harz Mountains.

Getting Around

Single bus tickets cost €1.70, while 24-hour tickets are €4.

There are taxi ranks at the Hauptbahnhof and behind the Altes Rathaus. To call one, ring ☎ 340 34.

Bikes can be hired from **Voss Fahrräder/Parkhaus am Bahnhof** (☎ 599 94; Am Bahnhof).

WEST OF HANOVER

OSNABRÜCK

☎ 0541 / pop 163,000

'Zum Glück komm' ich aus Osnabrück', locals boast of their good luck to come from this city; and that's something you most understand at night, wandering the winding lamp-lit streets of the old town, past ornate half-timbered houses.

But this historic heartland is now offset by a contemporary building that has overtaken interest in native son Erich Maria Remarque, author of the WWI classic *All Quiet on the Western Front*, and truly eclipsed Osnabrück's claim to be where the Thirty Years' War ended

in 1648. The construction in question is the Felix-Nussbaum-Haus, by leading world architect Daniel Libeskind.

Orientation

Osnabrück's egg-shaped city centre is divided into the northern Altstadt and the southern Neustadt, with the east–west Neumarkt drawing a line across the middle. The Hauptbahnhof is on the town's eastern edge. To reach the centre from the station takes about 15 minutes, going straight ahead along Möserstrasse, turning left at the Kaufhof building into Wittekindstrasse and then right into Grosser Strasse. When you come to the Domhof, continue left along Krahnstrasse to the tourist office.

Information

There's an ATM in the Hauptbahnhof.

Main post office (Theodor-Heuss-Platz 6-9; 🕑 8am-7pm Mon-Fri, to 2pm Sat)

Marketing & Tourismus Osnabrück (☎ 323 2202; www.osnabrueck-tourism.de, in German; Bierstrasse 22/23; 🕑 9.30am-6pm Mon-Fri, 10am-4pm Sat)

Sights

FELIX-NUSSBAUM-HAUS

Shaped like an interconnected series of concrete shards, with slit windows and sloping floors, the **Felix-Nussbaum-Haus** (☎ 323 2207, 323 2237; Lotter Strasse 2; adult/concession €5/3; 🕑 11am-6pm Tue-Fri, 10am-6pm Sat & Sun) is an older, slightly more neglected sister to Libeskind's famous Jewish Museum Berlin. The Osnabrück-born Jewish painter Felix Nussbaum (1904–44) wasn't a great original; his work has shades of Van Gogh and Henri Rousseau. However, Libeskind's 1988 building was deliberately designed to show it at its best.

When first opened, the building conveyed Nussbaum's changing life circumstances and moods, for example, using a long, darkening corridor to convey the period of despairing wartime exile before the painter was finally arrested and sent to Auschwitz.

However, the collection has since been rehung to drive you into the adjacent Kulturgeschichtliche Museum (don't bother going in) and now isn't such a powerful experience. All the same, it remains an interesting insight into the life of a German-Jewish artist, as well as Libeskind's architecture.

MARKT & AROUND

It was on the **Rathaus** (admission free; 🕑 9am-5pm Mon-Fri, to 4pm Sat, 10am-4pm Sun) steps that the

Peace of Westphalia was proclaimed on 25 October 1648, ending the Thirty Years' War. The preceding peace negotiations were conducted partly in Münster, about 60km south, and partly in the Rathaus' **Friedenssaal** (Peace Hall). On the left as you enter the Rathaus are portraits of the negotiators. Also have a look in the **Schatzkammer** (Treasure Chamber) opposite, especially at the 13th-century *Kaiserpokal* (Kaiser goblet).

The four richly ornamented cross gables of the **Marienkirche** loom above the square, painstakingly rebuilt after burning down during WWII. Opposite, the small **Erich Maria Remarque Friedenszentrum** (Erich Maria Remarque Peace Centre; ☎ 323 2109; Markt 6; admission free; ☟ 10am-1pm & 3-5pm Tue-Fri, 11am-5pm Sat & Sun) uses photos and documents to chronicle the writer's life (1898–1970) and work.

Various **half-timbered houses** survived WWII. At Bierstrasse 24 is the baroque **Walhalla** (right), with a portal flanked by cheeky cherubs. At Krahnstrasse 4 you'll find a beautiful house (1533), with **Café Läer** taking up the ground floor (see below). The best of the bunch is the Renaissance **Haus Willmann** (1586) at No 7, with its carved circular motifs and small relief of Adam and Eve.

Ask the tourist office about the **Bocksturm**. The oldest tower of the former city wall contains torture implements dating from Osnabrück's medieval witch trials, but at the time of research it was due to be restored, so it might not be open.

Sleeping

Ask the tourist office about camping, about 5km northeast of town.

Penthouse Backpackers (☎ 600 9606; www .penthousebp.com; Möserstrasse 19; dm €14-15; ☐) The furniture looks like it's been cobbled together from friends of the owner (because it has been!) and the reception has limited hours (so call ahead), yet you can't beat the warmth of the welcome here, from a well-travelled proprietor who understands the backpacker scene. Handily located for the train station, this 4th-floor establishment has a kitchen, big guest lounge room and a leafy terrace great for summer barbecues.

DJH hostel (☎ 542 84; www.jugendherberge.de /jh/osnabrueck; IIburger Strasse 183a; dm under/over 26yr €15.40/18.10; ☒) This modern, if somewhat nondescript hostel, is something of a schlep from the centre, so you might be lucky

enough – providing no school groups are booked in – to get a dorm to yourself. Take bus 62, 643 or 468 to Kinderhospital.

Intour Hotel (☎ 963 860; www.intourhotel.de; Maschstrasse 10; s €30-50, d €67-80; ℗) From the squat building's exterior, you wouldn't expect the rooms here to be as modern and comfortable as they are; it's an excellent deal. If the owner is on duty, remember to give her lovely dog – half German Shepherd, half terrier – a pat.

Dom Hotel (☎ 358 350; www.dom-hotel-osnabrueck .de; Kleine Domsfreiheit 5; s €45-60, d €70-100; ℗) Rooms here are comfortable and cheery in Mediterranean yellowy-orange, but they don't exude bags of atmosphere. That's left to the friendly owner, who always seems ready to help and chat, even when busy.

Romantik Hotel Walhalla (☎ 349 10; www.hotel -walhalla.de; Bierstrasse 24; s €80-85, d €100-110; ℗) If you're looking for historic atmosphere, this hotel has it aplenty. The half that's housed in a traditional half-timbered building has higgledy-piggledy rooms with low-beamed ceilings and rustic features. Even rooms in the more modern half continue the theme.

Steigenberger Hotel Remarque (☎ 609 60; www .osnabrueck.steigenberger.de, in German; Natruper-Tor-Wall 1; s/d from €110/120, weekends €90/110; ℗ ☒) Overlooking the old town from a small hill just across from it, this modern four-star hotel offers the unusual combination of quiet and convenience. A glass lift takes you up to tasteful rooms decorated in Mediterranean-style sienna and blues, with portraits and mementos of Erich Maria Remarque dotted around for local colour.

Eating

Bagels (☎ 260 363; Osterberger Reihe 12; bagels from €0.80, dishes €3-10) With a wide range of sandwich fillings you'd expect to find in a New York deli, coupled with the usual German breakfasts and light meals, customers often settle in for a couple of hours here. You can also get your bagel to go, and be out of there in minutes.

Café Läer (☎ 222 44; Krahnstrasse 4; snacks €4-4.50) The stone walls inside this historic building lend the place a surprisingly modern feel. The mezzanine floor is a great place to sit while having coffee and cake.

Pferde haben keine Flügel (☎ 202 7910; Am Kamp 81-83; tapas €2-8, platter for 2 €18) Candlelight and rough-hewn stone walls create a romantic atmosphere at 'Horses Have No Wings' (don't ask), so it's hardly surprising so many couples

LOWER SAXONY

flock to this tapas bar during the evenings. Still, there are enough bigger groups of friends to put other customers at ease and the food is extremely tasty, especially the dates in bacon.

Arabesque (☎ 260 363; Osterberger Reihe 12; mains €5.50-14.50) Settle yourself into a private niche and smoke a hookah. Or take your place on the low Arabic seating and tuck into kebabs and falafel. Alternatively, park yourself at a table, drink an Afri-Kola and admire the desert wall painting. It's all possible at this relaxed friendly restaurant; no wonder it's become such an Osnabrück hit.

Hausbrauerei Rampendahl (☎ 245 35; Hasestrasse 35; lunch €6, mains €10-20) The restaurant here serves one set dish from noon, before breaking out the other traditional German food after 6pm. Special beers are brewed on the premises, including the potent Rampendahl Spezial.

Osnabrück has a wonderful range of pubs (most open in the evening only) that also serve simple, inexpensive food. These include the traditional food haven of **Grüne Gans** (☎ 239 14; Grosse Gildewart 15; mains €3.50-7.50).

Drinking

Grüner Jäger (☎ 273 60; An der Katherinenkirche 1) Right near Arabesque is this popular student hang-out, with a covered-in beer garden and table football.

Zwiebel (☎ 236 73; Heger Strasse 34) 'Onion' does sell onion cake, but it's the quirky decoration in the room out the back, with a rocking horse, old metal-plate ads for coffee and even a Marx Brothers photo, that makes this place stand out.

Getting There & Away

The low-cost carrier **Air Berlin** (www.airberlin.com) is among those with services to **Münster-Osnabrück airport** (FMO; www.flughafen.fmo.de). The airport is 30km southwest of the centre, and reached by Schnellbus X150 (€8.50, 40 minutes), which leaves the airport roughly hourly between 6am and 8pm, with reduced services on weekends.

RE (€20.20, 1½ hours) and IC (€24, 1¼ hours) trains to Hanover leave twice an hour. Various services go to Hamburg (€39, one hour 50 minutes), Cologne (€35, two hours 10 minutes) and Dortmund (€25, 55 minutes). Osnabrück is well connected by road via the A1 (Bremen to Dortmund) and the B51, B65 and B68.

Getting Around

Single tickets cost €1.80 and day tickets €3.10 (so buy a day ticket).

Call a taxi on ☎ 277 81 or ☎ 320 11.

VARUSSCHLACHT MUSEUM & PARK KALKRIESE

You needn't be a history buff to come to the **Varusschlacht Museum & Park Kalkriese** (☎ 05468-920 40; www.kalkriese-varusschlacht.de; Bramsche-Kalkriese; ☻ 10am-6pm Apr-Oct, 10am-5pm Tue-Fri, to 6pm Sat & Sun Nov-Mar), although by the time you leave you'll have probably acquired an interest. It was long known that a ragtag bunch of rebellious Germanic tribes had won a major victory over their Roman masters somewhere in the Osnabrück region in AD 9 – defeating three of military commander Publius Quinctilius Varus' legions.

However, only in 1987 was the exact site of the so-called 'Battle of Teutoberg Forest' uncovered near Kalkriese. In 2000, the battlefield was opened as an archaeological park to display the Germans' dirt ramparts and explain how they did it. Two years later, a funky new steel-clad museum was built by famous Swiss architectural duo Annette Gigon and Mike Guyer.

This museum, rising in a 40m rectangular tower, showcases coins, battle masks, bells, spearheads and other finds. And it tells the story in an incredibly engaging manner, at one point using film and sound to evoke the feeling of battle. Elsewhere, the Doors song 'The End' (famous from *Apocalypse Now*) accompanies a short video on the mysterious identity of the victorious German commander, and national hero, Arminius. The site was discovered by an amateur British archaeologist, so there are English annotations.

The surrounding park and battlefield now features three quirky pavilions, called 'seeing', 'hearing' and 'questioning'. Using a camera obscura, huge ear trumpet and video technology respectively, they give you an unusual perspective on the battlefield.

Unless you have your own car, you must plan your visit carefully, as bus services are sparse. Take bus X275 from Osnabrück's main train station (€2.90, 50 minutes). Sometimes you will need to change at Herringhausen Leckermühle, but the bus driver will make an announcement. Check return bus times when you arrive. At least if you come in summer, there's a restaurant and beer garden where you can while away any waiting time.

LOWER SAXONY

OLDENBURG

☎ 0441 / pop 162,400

Being shuffled between Danish and German rule has left the relaxed capital of the Weser-Ems region with a somewhat difficult-to-pin-down identity. Most of its medieval buildings were destroyed in a huge fire in 1676, while others were later refashioned at various stages according to the prevailing architectural style of the time. Count Peter Friedrich Ludwig began redecorating the town in a neoclassical style in 1785, evidence of which still survives in the Schlosspark, its promenade and other nearby buildings.

Today it's principally a business destination, but you might make a day-trip from Bremen if you're a mummy fan, or stop over on the way to the East Frisian Islands.

Orientation

Oldenburg's pedestrianised core is bounded by Heiligengeistwall to the north, Theaterwall to the west and Schlosswall to the south. Turn right after you exit from the 'Stadtmitte' side of the Hauptbahnhof (Bahnhof Sud), which takes you along Moslestrasse. Turn left into Osterstrasse, which takes you to Achternstrasse in the city centre. Turn left and continue until you come to the Markt. The tourist office is in a street one block northwest of this; look for the signs.

Information

Main post office (Bahnhofsplatz 10; ☺ 8am-6pm Mon-Fri, 9am-1pm Sat)

Oldenburg Tourismus (☎ 01805-938 333, 361 6130; www.oldenburg-tourist.de; Kleine Kirchenstrasse 14; ☺ 10am-6pm Mon-Fri, to 2pm Sat)

Sights

The pale-yellow Renaissance-baroque **Schloss** (1607) at the southern end of the Altstadt shopping district (on Schlossplatz, just south of the Markt) was once home to the counts and dukes of Oldenburg. Part of the same family governed Denmark briefly in the 15th century.

Inside is the **Landesmuseum für Kunst und Kulturgeschichte** (Museum of Art & Cultural History; ☎ 220 7300; adult/concession incl Augusteum €3/1.50; ☺ 9am-5pm Tue, Wed & Fri, to 8pm Thu, 10am-5pm Sat & Sun), which chronicles the area's history from the Middle Ages to the 1950s. On the 1st floor, you'll find the remarkable Idyllenzimmer with 44 paintings by court artist Heinrich Wilhelm Tischbein, a friend of Goethe.

Behind the Schloss is the sprawling English-style **Schlosspark**. The neoclassical building you see across the square from the Schloss is **Die Neue Wache** (1839), once a city guardhouse but now part of a bank.

The museum's collection of 20th-century art has been farmed out to the **Augusteum** (☎ 220 7300; Elisabethstrasse 1; adult/concession incl Landesmuseum €3/1.50; ☺ 9am-5pm Tue, Wed & Fri, to 8pm Thu, 10am-5pm Sat & Sun). Showcased here are works by Erich Heckel, Ernst Ludwig Kirchner, August Macke and others.

However, skip all this if time is tight. The best museum in Oldenburg is the **Landesmuseum Natur und Mensch** (Natural History Museum; ☎ 924 4300; www.naturundmensch.de; Damm 38-44; adult/concession €4/2; ☺ 9am-5pm Tue & Wed, to 3pm Fri, 10am-8pm Thu, 10am-5pm Sat & Sun). Covering the ecology of Lower Saxony's various landscapes, its highlight is a huge chunk (or wall) of peat bog, with three niches containing bodies from the Roman period originally found preserved in surrounding moors in the 1930s and '40s. Damm runs southeast from Schlossplatz and this museum is not far from the Augusteum. Alternatively, take bus 289, 270, 314, 315 or 316 from the train station to the Staatsarchiv stop.

Sleeping & Eating

The tourist office can help with private rooms or provide information on camping, north of town.

DJH hostel (☎ 871 35; www.jugendherberge.de/jh/oldenburg; Alexanderstrasse 65; dm under/over 26yr €15/17.70; Ⓟ ☒) Large and rambling, this hostel is rather old and very dimly lit. However, the staff is helpful and it atones for its shortcomings by having a few comfy bathrooms with tubs. It's about 20 minutes by foot north of the Hauptbahnhof, or take bus 302 or 303 to Von-Finckh-Strasse.

Hotel Tafelfreuden (☎ 832 27; www.tafelfreuden-hotel.de; Alexanderstrasse 23; s €60-70, d €85-95, apt €115; Ⓟ ☒) Really the only interesting hotel in town, this has seven distinctively themed rooms, plus an apartment. Some of the singles, such as England and Japan are tiny, if cleverly organised, but larger boudoirs like the 'Orient', 'Afrika' and 'Unter Wasser' (underwater) are real treasures. There's an upmarket organic restaurant on the ground floor.

For eating options simply cruise along pedestrianised **Wallstrasse**, north of the Markt.

LOWER SAXONY

Getting There & Around

There are trains at least once an hour to Bremen (€5.80, 30 minutes) and Osnabrück (€17.20, 1¼ hours). From Oldenburg, there are trains north to Emden and beyond.

Oldenburg is at the crossroads of the A29 to/from Wilhelmshaven and the A28 (Bremen–Dutch border).

Single bus tickets (valid for one hour) for the entire city cost €1.75; short trips are only €1.30, and day passes €4.80. Buy your tickets from the driver.

EMDEN & AROUND

☎ 04921 / pop 51,700

You're almost in Holland here, and it shows – from the flat landscape, dikes and windmills around Emden to the lackadaisical manner in which locals pedal their bikes across canal bridges and past red-brick Lego-like houses. People greet you with a 'Moin', or 'Moin Moin', and they're generally proud of the local *Plattdütsch* dialect, even if they don't always speak it. It sounds like a combination of English, German and – guess what? – Dutch.

Orientation

Emden's train and bus stations are about a 10-minute walk west of the city centre. As you exit, take the road heading right, which will lead to Grosse Strasse and the small medieval harbour called Ratsdelft.

Information

Tourist-Information Emden Pavilion (☎ 974 00; www.emden-touristik.de; Am Stadtgarten; 9am-6pm Mon-Fri, 10am-1pm Sat, 11am-1pm Sun May-Sep, 9am-1pm & 3-5.30pm Mon-Fri, 10am-1pm Sat Oct-Apr) Just north of the central Ratsdelft harbour, near the car park and taxi stand.

Sights & Activities

Most people visit Emden en route to the East Frisian Islands, although there are lots of relaxing pursuits here and a few surprisingly good museums.

For starters, Emden has an unusually good **Kunsthalle** (☎ 975 050; Hinter dem Rahmen 13; adult/concession €4.50/2.50; 10am-8pm Tue, to 5pm Wed-Fri, 11am-5pm Sat & Sun), thanks to local boy Henri Nannen. The founder of the magazine *Stern* (a glossy newsweekly à la *Time* or *Newsweek*), he made his private collection available to the town when he retired. Focusing on 20th-century art, its white-and-exposed-timber, light-flooded rooms show off a range of big, bold canvases. There are some works by Max Beckmann, Erich Heckel, Alex Jawlensky, Oskar Kokoschka, Franz Marc, Emil Nolde and Max Pechstein, although most of the artists are more obscure. Three times a year, the museum closes its doors for a week while exhibitions are changed. Follow the signs from the tourist office.

The revamped **Ostfriesisches Landesmuseum** (Regional History Museum; ☎ 872 057; www.landesmuseum-emden.de; Rathaus, Neutorstrasse; adult/child €6/3; 10am-6pm Tue-Sun) now has an impressive new entrance, through which you'll find a gallery of old Dutch masters and one of the biggest armouries in Germany.

The labyrinth of WWII civilian air-raid shelters at the **Bunkermuseum** (☎ 322 25; www.bunkermuseum.de; Holzsägerstrasse; adult/child €2/1; 10am-1pm & 3-5pm Tue-Sun May-Oct) includes testimonies from those who sheltered here, offering a moving insight into part of recent history.

Some 6km north of Emden, along the B70, stands what claims to be the world's most crooked church. That's nothing to do with the administration of the church of **Suurhusen** (1262), but a comment on its tilting tower. Currently leaning 2.43m off true, it allegedly outdoes even the famous tower in Pisa by 4.7cm. The overhang is the result of the decreasing groundwater levels in the peat-rich soil.

Harbour cruises run by **EMS** (☎ 890 70; www.ag-ems.de, in German) leave several times daily between March and October from the Delfttreppe steps in the harbour (adult/child €6.50/3). The company also runs services to the East Frisian Island of Borkum (see p640) and North Frisian Island of Helgoland (see p702).

Canal tours (adult/child €10/5) leave from the quay at the Kunsthalle between April and October on weekdays at 11am and 3pm, and on Sunday at noon and 3pm.

The flatlands around Emden are perfect for **cycling**, and the tourist office has plenty of maps.

Another good way to travel is by water. **Kanuverlieh am Wasserturm** (☎ 04921-974 97; Am Wasserturm) has canoes for hire, or ask at the tourist office.

Sleeping & Eating

DJH hostel (☎ 237 97; www.jugendherberge.de/jh/emden; An der Kesselschleuse 5, off Thorner Strasse; dm under/over 26yr €16.50/19.50; closed Dec & Jan; P ⊠) With some

EAST, WEST, FRIESLAND'S BEST

Like Bavarians, the people in northwest Germany have a reputation for being 'different'. Frieslanders, as they're called, have their own language – Plattdütsch – and are rather partial to a cup of tea (reputedly drinking 25% of Germany's tea imports). Although merely a geographical area today, Friesland was once a political entity, a league of seven states stretching from the northern Netherlands to the Danish coast. Roughly speaking, the eastern part of the Netherlands was Westfriesland (Western Frisia), northwest Germany was Ostfriesland (Eastern Frisia) and the area around the Danish border was Nordfriesland (Northern Frisia).

In the 16th century, Jeverland, the region around Jever, seceded from Ostfriesland and remained separate as it fell into the hands of the Dukes of Oldenburg and subsequently Russia. In modern times, however, Jeverland was rechristened Friesland, leading to the odd situation today where Ostfriesland (Eastern Frisia), around Emden, actually lies *west* of Friesland.

dorms in stand-alone bungalows, this place feels more like a holiday camp than a hostel. Popular with schools and other groups, its canal-side location offers plenty of swimming, canoeing and cycling opportunities. Take bus 3003 to Realschule/Am Herrentor.

Hotel am Boltentor (☎ 972 70; fax 972 733; Hinter den Rahmen 10; s/d €65/85; P) Hidden by trees from the main road nearby and just a minute from the Kunsthalle, this homy red-brick hotel has possibly the best location in town, plus comfy and well-equipped rooms.

Heerens Hotel (☎ 237 40; www.heerenshotel.de; Friedrich-Ebert-Strasse 67; s €50-80, d €90-105; P) The generously sized rooms here are slightly older, but the hotel comes highly rated for its service and restaurant.

Other recommendations:

Alt Emder Bürgerhaus (☎ 976 100; www.alt-emder -buergerhaus-emden.de; Friedrich-Ebert-Strasse 33; s/d from €50/70; P) Friendly, family-run hotel and restaurant in traditional building in the centre.

Goldener Adler (☎ 927 30; Neutorstrasse 5; s/d from €65/85) Central and modern, with an excellent local restaurant.

Getting There & Around

Emden is connected by rail to Oldenburg (€13.40, one hour) and Bremen (€19.10 to €23, 1¾ hours). Despite its relative remoteness, the town is easily and quickly reached via the A31, which connects with the A28 from Oldenburg and Bremen. The B70/B210 runs north from Emden to other towns in Friesland and to the coast.

Emden is small enough to be explored on foot but also has a bus system (€1 per trip). The best transport method is the bicycle; to hire one contact **Oltmanns** (☎ 314 44; Grosse Strasse 53-57; per day €8).

JEVER

☎ 04461 / pop 13,000

Famous for its Pilsener beer, the capital of the Friesland region also has a secondary motif. The face of 'Fräulein Maria' peers out from attractions and shop windows alike. She was the last of the so-called *Häuptlinge* (chieftains) to rule the town in the Middle Ages, and although Russia's Catherine the Great got her hands on Jever for a time in the 18th century, locals always preferred their home-grown queen. Having died unmarried and a virgin, Maria is the German equivalent of England's (in truth more worldly) Elizabeth I.

With its Russian-looking castle, Jever is worth a brief visit, probably en route to the East Frisian Islands.

Orientation

Most of Jever's attractions are within a few hundred metres of each other in the eastern section of the Altstadt around the Schloss. There are map boards at the small train station. Follow the signs to the centre along Schlossstrasse to the beginning of the pedestrianised streets. Continue along the cobbled streets until you come across yet more signposts.

Information

Tourist Information Jever (☎ 710 10; tourist-info@stadt-jever.de; Alter Markt 18; ⏰ 10am-6pm Mon-Fri, 9am-1pm Sat Apr-Oct, 9am-5pm Mon-Thu, 9am-4pm Fri Nov-Mar)

Sights & Activities

SCHLOSS

Looking like a prop from the film *Doctor Zhivago*, the onion-shaped dome is the first thing that strikes you about Jever's 14th-century

Schloss (☎ 969 350; adult/concession €3/2; ☺ 10am-6pm Mon-Sat year-round, 10am-6pm Sun Jul & Aug). The town's 18th-century Russian rulers added it to a building built by Fräulein Maria's grandfather, chieftain Edo Wiemken the Elder. Today the palace houses the **Kulturhistorische Museum des Jeverlandes**, a mildly diverting cultural-history museum with objects chronicling the daily life and craft of the Frieslanders, including a vast porcelain collection.

The *pièce de résistance* is the magnificent **audience hall**, with a carved, coffered, oak ceiling of great intricacy. Fräulein Maria retained the Antwerp sculptor Cornelis Floris to create this 80-sq-metre Renaissance masterpiece.

FRIESISCHES BRAUHAUS ZU JEVER

A brewery that has been producing dry Pilsener since 1848 is worth a visit, and the **Friesisches Brauhaus** (☎ 137 11; www.jever.de; Elisabethufer 18; tours €6.50; ☺ tours hourly 9.30am-4.30pm Mon-Fri, 9.30am-12.30pm Sat) allows visitors a peek behind the scenes. The two-hour tours travel through the production and bottling facilities, as well as a small museum. Reservations are essential.

OTHER ATTRACTIONS

Many of Jever's sights are in some way connected to Fräulein Maria. The most spectacular is in the **Stadtkirche** (☎ 933 80; Am Kirchplatz 13; ☺ 8am-6pm), where you'll find the lavish memorial tomb of her father, Edo von Wiemken (1468–1511). The tomb is another opus by Cornelis Floris and miraculously survived eight fires. The church itself succumbed to the flames and was rebuilt in a rather modern way; the main nave is opposite the tomb, which is now behind glass.

Near the tourist office, you'll see a **statue of Fräulein Maria**. Her image also joins that of her father and other historic figures in the town's **Glockenspiel** (☺ 11am, noon, 3pm, 4pm, 5pm & 6pm), opposite the tourist office on the façade of the Hof von Oldenburg.

Alternatively, an interesting Frisian craft is on show at the **Blaudruckerei shop** (☎ 713 88; www.blaudruckerei.de; Kattrepel 3; ☺ 10am-1pm & 2-6pm Mon-Fri, 10am-2pm Sat). This is owned by former teacher Georg Stark, who 20 years ago revived the long-lost art and tradition of Blaudruckerei, a printing and dying process whose results vaguely resemble batik.

Sleeping

DJH hostel (☎ 909 202; www.jugendherberge.de/jh/jever; Dr-Fritz-Blume-Weg 4; dm under/over 26yr €17.70/20.70; P ☒ ☐) Jever's new *Jugendherberge* is like a little village, with a series of green and red-brick bungalows grouped around the reception. Dorms are as clean, modern and comfortable as you would expect from buildings only opened in 2006.

Am Elisabethufer (☎ 949 640; www.jever-hotel-pension.de; Elisabethufer 9a; s €35-40, d €60-70; P) Frilly lampshades and floral duvet covers are par for the course in Jever's *pensions*, and also what you'll find in this steep-roofed Frisian brown-brick building. There are nice garden views from its breakfast window.

Hotel Pension Stöber (☎ 5580; www.hotel-stoeber.de, in German; Hohnholzstrasse 10; s €35-40, d €60-70; P) In a leafy neighbourhood south of the centre, this whitewashed building has traditionally German rustic rooms.

Im Schützenhof (☎ 9370; www.schuetzenhof-jever.de, in German; Schützenhofstrasse 47; s €45-50, d €75-80; P) For something a little more upmarket, this hotel, just south of the centre, has comfortable modern rooms. It's favoured for local celebrations because of its excellent restaurant, Zitronengras.

Eating & Drinking

Balu (☎ 700 709; Kattrepel 1a; mains €9-17.50) Whitewashed walls and tasteful ethnic decoration give this African restaurant understated style. Tex-mex and Italian fare are also on the menu, for those unfamiliar with the *joliffe* rice, *jambo*, yams and plantains.

Haus der Getreuen (☎ 3010; Schlachtstrasse 1; mains €10-20) With a historic dining room and outside seating, Haus der Getreuen is famous for regional dishes, especially fish.

Bier Akademie (☎ 5436; Bahnhofstrasse 44) Although it's located on the corner of a rather unattractive shopping centre, inside the wood-lined Bier Akademie turns out to be an excellent place to educate yourself in the ways of Jever Pilsener and dozens of other beers.

Getting There & Around

The train trip to Jever from Bremen (€15.70, two hours) involves at least one change, in Sande, and sometimes one in Oldenburg, too. By road, take the exit to the B210 from the A29 (direction: Wilhelmshaven).

Jever is small enough to explore on foot.

EAST FRISIAN ISLANDS

Trying to remember the sequence of the seven East Frisian Islands, Germans – with a wink of the eye – recite the following mnemonic device: 'Welcher Seemann liegt bei Nanni im Bett?' (which translates rather saucily as 'Which seaman is lying in bed with Nanni?').

Lined up in an archipelago off the coast of Lower Saxony like diamonds in a tiara, the islands are (east to west): Wangerooge, Spiekeroog, Langeoog, Baltrum, Norderney, Juist and Borkum. Their long sandy beaches, open spaces and sea air make them both a nature lovers' paradise and a perfect retreat for those escaping the stresses of the world. Like their North Frisian cousins Sylt, Amrum and Föhr (see p696), the islands are part of the Wadden Sea (Wattenmeer) National Park.

The main season runs from mid-May to September. Beware, however, that the opening hours of tourist offices in coastal towns change frequently and without notice. Call ahead if possible.

Resort Tax

Each of the East Frisian Islands charges a *Kurtaxe* (resort tax), entitling you to entry onto the beach and offering small discounts for museums etc. It's a small amount, typically €3 a day, and if you're staying overnight it's simply added to your hotel bill. Remind your hotel to give you your pass should they forget.

Getting There & Away

Most ferries sail according to tide times, rather than on a regular schedule, so it's best to call the ferry operator or **Deutsche Bahn** (DB; www.bahn.de/nordseeinseln, in German) for information on departure times on a certain day. Tickets are generally offered either as returns for those staying on the island (sometimes valid for up to two months) or cheaper same-day returns.

In most cases (apart from Borkum, Norderney and Juist) you will need to change from the train to a bus at some point to reach the harbour from where the ferry leaves. Sometimes those are shuttle buses operated by the ferry company, or scheduled services from **Weser-Ems Bus** (☎ 01805-194 49; www.weser-ems-bus.de, in German). For more details, see Getting There & Away for each island.

Light aircraft also fly to every island except Spiekeroog. Contact **Luftverkehr Friesland Harle** (☎ 04464-948 10; www.inselflieger.de, in German).

Getting Around

Only Borkum and Norderney allow cars, so heading elsewhere means you'll need to leave

---

WALKING TO THE ISLANDS

When the tide recedes on Germany's North Sea coast, it exposes the mudflats connecting the mainland to the East Frisian Islands, and that's when hikers and nature lovers make their way barefoot to Baltrum and its sister 'isles'. It's a minimum two-hour journey, wallowing in mud or wading knee-deep in seawater, but it's one of the most popular outdoor activities in this flat, mountainless region.

Wattwandern, as such trekking through the Wadden Sea National Park is called, can be dangerous. You need to know which fordable channels are left by the receding sea, and must be able to cope with the enveloping fog that, even in summer, can blow in within minutes. Therefore, the crossing should only be undertaken with a guide. Once you've safely reached your destination – and can now boast that you've walked to an island – you get to wait for the ferry to take you back while watching the sea rise swiftly over your trail.

As a kind of 'horizontal alpinism', *Wattwandern* (*Wadlopen* in the Netherlands) is far too dirty and strenuous to really be compared to walking on water. But the fresh sea air and the workout you've given your body does make you feel pretty holy.

Tourist offices in Jever and Emden can provide details of state-approved guides, including **Martin Rieken** (☎ 04941-8260; www.wattfuehrer-rieken.de, in German), or **Eiltraut and Ulrich Kunth** (☎ 04933-1027; www.wattwanderung-kunth.de, in German). English-speaking guides can be contacted at info@wattwandern.de.

Tours cost about €20, including the ferry ride back. Necessary gear includes shorts or short trousers and possibly socks or trainers (although many guides recommend going barefoot). In winter, gumboots are necessary.

your vehicle in a car park near the ferry pier (about €3.50 per 12 hours).

WANGEROOGE

A famous German novel is called *Die Entdeckung der Langsamkeit* (The Discovery of Slowness). That's what the marketing folks have cleverly said about this island, and it's true. Crunching sand between your toes and watching huge tanker ships lumber in and out of the ports at Bremerhaven, Hamburg and Wilhelmshaven, it's easy to feel like a willing castaway.

There are two information centres: the **Kurverwaltung** (spa administration; ☎ 04469-990; www .wangerooge.de; Strandpromenade 3; ☼ 9am-3.30pm Mon-Fri, to noon Sat & Sun Apr-Oct, 9am-noon Mon-Fri Nov-Mar) and the **Verkehrsverein** (☎ 04469-9480; info@westturm.de; Hauptbahnhof), which handles room reservations as well.

If you're feeling active you can climb the historic 39m-tall **lighthouse**, take to the sea-water adventure pool or indulge in a long list of sports activities. For more of a learning experience, head to the **Nationalparkhaus** (☎ 04469-8397; admission free; ☼ 9am-1pm & 2-6pm Tue-Fri, 10am-noon & 2-5pm Sat & Sun) in the Rosenhaus; opening hours are reduced in winter, so call ahead.

Getting There & Away

The ferry to Wangerooge leaves from Harlesiel two to five times daily (1½ hours), depending on the tides. An open return ticket costs €26.90 (two-month time limit), and a same-day return ticket is €25. This includes the tram shuttle to the village on the island (4km). Large pieces of luggage are an extra €2.50 each, and a bike €10 each way. The ferry is operated by **DB** (☎ in Harlesiel 04464-949 411, in Wangerooge 04464-947 411).

To reach Harlesiel, take bus 211 from Jever train/bus station (30 minutes).

SPIEKEROOG

Rolling dunes dominate the landscape of min-uscule Spiekeroog; about two-thirds of its 17.4 sq km is taken up by these sandy hills. It's the tranquillity of this rustic island that draws people, although you can distract yourself with the **Pferdebahn** (☎ 04976-910 120; Inselmuseum, Nooderloog 1; adult/child return €3/2; ☼ 2pm, 3pm & 4pm Tue-Sun Apr-Sep), a horse-drawn train that runs on rails and dates back to 1885. There are also plenty of baths for swimming.

The **tourist office** (☎ 04976-919 3101; www .spiekeroog.de, in German; Noorderpad 25; ☼ 9am-12.30pm & 2-5pm Mon-Fri, 9am-1pm Sat Apr-Oct, 9am-12.30pm Mon-Fri Nov-Mar) is in the 'Haus Kogge', where there's also a **Mussel Museum** (☎ 04976-919 3225; admission €1; ☼ 9am-12.30pm & 2-5pm Mon-Fri) with more than 3000 shells of all varieties.

Spiekeroog is not only car-free but discourages bicycles too.

Getting There & Away

From the ferry departure point in Neuharlingersiel it takes 40 to 55 minutes to reach Spiekeroog. Ferry times depend on the tides, so same-day returns aren't always possible. Prices are €10 each way or €17 for same-day return tickets. Each piece of luggage over the two-bag limit costs an extra €2 return. Call ☎ 04974-214 or ☎ 04976-919 3133, or email reederei@spiekeroog.de for details and tickets.

To get to the ferry, catch a train to Esens (coming from Jever, 22 minutes) or Norden (from Emden, 15 minutes), and change there for a bus. Not all buses from Esens to Neuharlingersiel run daily, so check with the Jever tourist office beforehand.

LANGEOOG

Floods and pirates make up the story of Langeoog, whose population was reduced to a total of two following a horrendous storm in 1721. But by 1830 it had recovered sufficiently to become a resort town.

The island boasts the highest elevation in East Friesland – the 20m-high **Melkhörndüne** – and the **grave** of Lale Anderson, famous for being the first singer to record the WWII song 'Lili Marleen'. Nautical tradition is showcased in the **Schiffahrtsmuseum** (☎ 04972-693 211; adult/concession €1.50/0.75; ☼ 10am-noon & 3-5pm Mon-Thu, 10am-noon Fri & Sat), although the original **sea rescue ship** (admission free; ☼ 3-5pm Tue & Thu, 10am-noon Sat) also on view is perhaps more interesting. In sunshine, the 14km-long **beach** is clearly the biggest attraction.

Langeoog's **tourist office** (☎ 04972-6930; kurverwaltung@langeoog.de; Hauptstrasse 28; ☼ 8am-12.30pm & 2-5pm Mon-Thu, 8am-12.30pm Fri year-round, 3-5pm Fri, 10am-noon Sat Jul & Aug) is in the Rathaus, while **room reservations** (☎ 04972-693 201; zimmern achweis@langeoog.de; ☼ 9am-6.30pm Mon-Fri, 10am-3pm Sat & Sun) can be dealt with on the 1st floor of the island's 'train station' or ferry landing stage.

Getting There & Away

The ferry shuttles between Bensersiel and Langeoog up to nine times daily. The trip takes about one hour and costs €21 return, or €18.50 for a same-day return. Luggage is €2.50 per piece, bikes €15 return. For details, call ☎ 04971-928 90 or email schiffahrt@langeoog.de.

To get to Bensersiel, take the train to Esens or Norden, and change to a shuttle bus.

BALTRUM

The smallest inhabited East Frisian Island, Baltrum is just 1km wide and 5km long and peppered with dunes and salty marshland. It's so tiny that villagers don't bother with street names but make do with house numbers instead. Numbers have been allocated on a chronological basis; house Nos 1 to 4 no longer exist so the oldest is now No 5.

There's little to do except go on walks or to the beach, or visit the exhibition on the National Park environment in **house No 177** (☎ 04939-469; admission free; 9am-noon & 2-7pm Mon-Fri). As the island closest to the mainland, Baltrum is the most popular destination for *Wattwanderungen* guided tours (see boxed text, p637).

The **Kurverwaltung** (☎ 04939-800; www.baltrum.de; house No 130; 8.30am-noon & 2-4pm Mon-Thu, 8.30am-noon Fri) can provide information. For room reservations, call ☎ 01805-914 003 or email zimmernachweis@baltrum.de.

Getting There & Away

Ferries (and *Wattwanderungen*) leave from Nessmersiel. Ferries take 30 minutes. Departures depend on the tides, which means day trips aren't always possible. Tickets are €12.50 one way or €16/22 for a same-day/open return. Bikes cost €4 each way and luggage is usually free. More details are available from **Reederei Baltrum** (☎ 04939-9130; www.baltrum-linie .de, in German).

To get to Nessmersiel change from the train in Norden to a bus (€6.50/10 per same-day/open return).

NORDERNEY

'Queen of the East Frisian Islands', Norderney was Germany's first North Sea resort. Founded in 1797 by Friedrich Wilhelm II of Prussia, it became one of the most famous bathing destinations in Europe, after Crown Prince Georg V of Hanover made it his summer residence, and personalities such as Chancellor Otto von Bismarck and composer Robert Schumann visited in the 19th century.

Now 'Lüttje Welt' – little world, as the islanders call Norderney for the way fog makes it seem like it's the only place on earth – is trying to regain its pre-eminence. It has a new designer spa, an upcoming five-star hotel, and 21st-century refurbishments of its lighthouse and church. All these add to its wonderful Art Deco **Kurtheater** and other historic buildings to make this a great time to visit.

The jewel in the crown is indisputably the new **Bade:haus** (☎ 04932-891 162, 891 141; Am Kurplatz 3; adult/child from €6/3.50; 9.30am-9.30pm, women only from 2pm Wed), opened in 2006 in the old Art Nouveau seawater baths. This sleek stone-and-glass complex is now the biggest thalassotherapy centre in Germany, with warm and cold swimming pools, a roof-top sauna with views over the island, relaxation areas where you can lie back on loungers and drink Frisian tea, and much more – all split between the 'Spa' and 'Spass' (fun) zones.

Norderney's **tourist office** (☎ 04932-918 50, room reservations 01805-667 331; www.norderney.de; Bülowallee 5; 9am-6pm mid-May–Sep, 9am-12.30pm & 2-6pm Mon-Fri, 9am-12.30pm Sat Oct–mid-May) can provide more details or book rooms.

There's also an outdoor pool at Weststrand. The **Nationalpark-Haus** (www.nationalpark-haus -norderney.de; admission free; 9am-6pm Tue-Sun) is directly on the harbour.

Getting There & Away

To get to Norderney you have to catch the ferry in Norddeich. **Reederei Frisia** (☎ 04931-9870; www.reederei-frisia.de, in German; adult/child return €15/7.50, bikes €5.50) offers roughly hourly departures from 6am to 6pm daily (to 8pm in summer). The journey takes 50 minutes and any DB office can provide details.

There are trains (€6.90 to €9.70) from Emden to Norddeich Mole, the ferry landing stage.

JUIST

Juist, shaped like a snake, is 17km long and only 500m wide. The only ways to travel are by bike, horse-drawn carriage or on your own two feet. What makes Juist special is what is not here: no high-rises, cars or shopping malls. Instead, you're often alone with the screeching seagulls, the wild sea and the howling winds. Forest, brambles and elderberry bushes blanket large sections of the island.

One peculiarity of Juist is the idyllic **Hammersee** – the only freshwater lake on all the islands, and also a bird sanctuary. There's also the **Juister Küstenmuseum** (Coastal Museum; ☎ 04935-1488; adult/concession €2/1.25; ⏲ 9am-12.30pm & 2.30-5.30pm Mon-Sat) on Loogster Pad.

Juist's **tourist office** (☎ 04935-8090; www.juist .de, in German; Friesenstrasse 18; ⏲ 8.30am-5pm Mon-Fri, 10am-noon Sat) has a separate number for room reservations (☎ 04935-809 222).

Getting There & Away

Reederei Frisia (☎ 04931-9870; www.reederei-frisia.de, in German) operates the ferries from Norddeich to Juist (adult day/normal return €17.50/27.50, 1½ hours); children are half-price and bikes cost €9.50. You can also ask any DB office for details.

Trains from Emden (€6.90 to €9.70) travel straight to the landing dock in Norddeich Mole.

BORKUM

The largest of the East Frisian Islands – once even larger before it was ripped apart by a flood in the 12th century – has a tough seafaring and whaling history. Reminders of those frontier times are the whalebones that you'll occasionally see, stacked up side by side, or as unusual garden fences. In 1830, however,

locals realised that tourism was a safer way to earn a living. Recently, the island has been hoping for an extra spike in interest since former Chancellor Gerhard Schröder and his wife Doris bought a holiday home here.

To learn about the whaling era and other stages in the life of Borkum, visit the **Heimatmuseum** (Local History Museum; ☎ 04922-4860; adult/concession €3/1.50; ⏲ 10am-noon & 3-5pm Tue-Sun) at the foot of the old lighthouse. Also of interest is the museum fire ship *Borkumriff*, with its exhibition on the Wadden Sea National Park.

Borkum has a **Kurverwaltung** (☎ 04922-9330; kurverwaltung@borkum.de; Goethestrasse 1). It's open on weekdays, timed to coincide with ferry arrivals/departures. There's a **tourist office** (☎ 04922-933 117; Hauptbahnhof; ⏲ 9am-5.30pm Mon-Fri, 10am-noon & 2-4pm Sat & Sun), which also handles room reservations.

Getting There & Away

The embarkation point for ferries to Borkum is Emden. **AG-Ems** (☎ 01805-024 367; www.ag-ems .de, in German) has both car ferries (adult sameday/open return €16/29.50, two hours) and faster catamarans (€24.80/38.30, one hour). Transporting a car costs from €70 to €150 return (depending on size), while a bike costs €10.50.

Bremen

Small is beautiful? Bremen is delicious proof of that particular pudding. Officially, the name describes a Hanseatic city and Germany's tiniest state, but most visitors – shh, don't mention it to the locals – would recognise it as more of a town really.

Or they might call it two towns, for the state of Bremen consists of a pair of distinct flecks of land dotted across the Lower Saxony landscape: industrial Bremerhaven at the Weser River's mouth and riverside Bremen, 65km south. They've been linked politically since 1827, when Bremen's mayor cleverly bought the river delta from Hanover.

And yet, despite its diminutive dimensions as both a state and a city, Bremen is a winner. Compact and easy to get to know in a weekend, it's a perfect example of what's called *schön klein* – the German equivalent of good things coming in small packages.

The picturesque red-brick capital will take you from an unusual Art Nouveau street to a quaint district of winding medieval lanes and on to an alternative student quarter, all within minutes. Imbibing the local Beck's beer on the waterfront 'Schlachte' promenade, Bremers might even talk of their oyster-shaped science centre as one of several modernising features.

To the north, Bremerhaven is reinventing itself with an impressive Emigration Centre that's a perfect companion piece to New York's Ellis Island. Meanwhile, back in the capital, Bremen has long settled on its unique brand image, courtesy of fairy-tale writers the Brothers Grimm. Everywhere you move, the picture of four animals riding piggyback – *The Town Musicians of Bremen* – stares out from statues, souvenirs and shop windows.

BREMEN

HIGHLIGHTS

- **Grand Designs** Marvel at the golden archangel and red-brick angles of Böttcherstrasse (p644)
- **Window shopping** Check out the quaint outlets of the medieval Schnoor district (p644)
- **Prost!** Make merry on the Schlachte promenade with a Beck's beer (p648)
- **Off-beat Experience** Peek in at the blackened mummies in the Dom St Petri's lead cellar (p645)
- **Living History** Follow an ancestor across the ocean at the German Emigration Centre (p650) in Bremerhaven

★ German Emigration Centre

★ Dom St Petri
Böttcherstrasse ★
Schlachte ★ ★ Schnoor

- POPULATION: 668,000 MILLION
- AREA: 404 SQ KM

CITY OF BREMEN

☎ 0421 / pop 550,000

When you think about going to Bremen, the name seems somehow comfortingly familiar. A background character in a famous fairytale, it's a place many people have heard about on their mother's knee. After which, never have they devoted a second thought to it.

Which is a shame, because the little city on the Weser River offers a wonderfully relaxing short break, with its unexpectedly impressive old town centre, shop-lined mini-maritime quarter and unique Art Nouveau laneway.

As they mingle in the bars along the waterfront Schlachte promenade, Bremers can toast their perfectly-judged pace of life – not too fast, not too slow, just right.

That's another fairytale, of course, but in Bremen's case the reality is better than any fiction.

HISTORY

Bremen was known as the 'Rome of the North' during its early history, because after its establishment by Charlemagne in 787, it was used as the main base for Christianising Scandinavia. The city grew by leaps and bounds in the following centuries, and by 1358 was ready to join the Hanseatic League. In 1646 it became a free imperial city, a status it – sort of – still enjoys today as a 'Free Hanseatic City'.

ORIENTATION

Bremen's compact centre is easy to get around on foot, but trams cover most of the city. The Altstadt lies south of the Hauptbahnhof (central train station), on the north bank of the Weser River. The Art Nouveau Böttcherstrasse lies directly south of the central Markt, and the popular Schlachte promenade southwest of this.

The Schnoor maritime quarter is found to the southeast, and the art galleries and studenty Das Viertel nightlife district lie to the east along Ostertorsteinweg (also known, for obvious reasons, as O-Weg).

INFORMATION

ErlebnisCARD (1 adult & 2 children for 1/2 days €6.50/8.50) Free public transport and discounts on sights; available from tourist office.

Internet.Center Bremen (☎ 277 6600; Bahnhofsplatz 22-28; per hr €3; ⊙ 10am-10pm Mon-Sat; noon-8pm Sun)

Main post office (Domsheide 15; ⊙ 8am-7pm Mon-Fri, 9am-1pm Sat)

Police (☎ 3621; Am Wall 201)

Post office (Bahnhofplatz 21; ⊙ 9am-7pm Mon-Fri, 9am-1pm Sat)

Schnell und Sauber (Vor dem Steintor 105; per wash €3.50; ⊙ 6am-11pm) Laundry, just east of centre.

Tourist Office branch (Obernstrasse/Liebfrauenkirchhof; ⊙ 10am-6.30pm Mon-Fri, to 4pm Sat & Sun)

Tourist Office Hauptbahnhof (☎ 01805-101 030; www.bremen-tourism.de; Hauptbahnhof; ⊙ 9am-7pm Mon-Fri, to 6pm Sat & Sun)

DANGERS & ANNOYANCES

Incredibly, little Bremen has witnessed serious violence along the club mile of Rembertiring in recent years (hence the dubious 'Bremen Fight Club' T-shirts sold in Das Viertel). A couple of people have been fatally shot or stabbed, as rival gangs fight over who installs doormen at individual clubs. A strong police presence has removed most of the danger, but it pays to be mindful of the problem when queuing here.

SIGHTS & ACTIVITIES
Markt

With tall, old buildings looming over a relatively small space, Bremen's Markt is one of the most remarkable in northern Germany. The twin towers of the 1200-year-old **Dom St Petri** (St Petri Cathedral; see also p645) dominate the northeastern edge, beside the ornate

BREMEN

0 _____ 20 km
0 _____ 12 miles

To Cuxhaven (35km)

North Sea

Bremerhaven
Bremervörde

B74
B71
B74
B71

Brake
A27
B74
B71
Zeven

B212

Hamme River

Worpswede

A1

Blumenthal
Vegesack
Ritterhude
To Hamburg (65km)

Oldenburg
Burglesum

Bremen

A29
A28
B75

Airport

B215

Weser River

B213
B51
Weyhe

LOWER SAXONY
Syke
Verden
A27

A1
Wildeshausen
To Düsseldorf (260km)
Bassum
B6
To Hanover (90km)
To Hanover (85km)

BREMEN

0 _____ 300 m
0 _____ 0.2 miles

INFORMATION
Internet.Center Bremen.....................1 C4
Post Office...2 C4
Tourist Info Branch...............................3 B5
Tourist Info Hauptbahnhof..................4 C3

SIGHTS & ACTIVITIES
Bleikeller...5 B5
Dom St Petri..6 B5
Dommuseum....................................(see 6)
Gerhard Marcks Haus...........................7 C6
Glockenspiel.................................(see 15)
Hal Över Schreiber Reederei................8 B6
Haus Atlantis..9 B6
Haus der Bürgerschaft.......................10 B5
Kirche Unser Lieben Frauen...............11 B5
Knight Roland Statue.........................12 B5
Kunsthalle..13 C6
Neues Museum Weserburg.................14 A5
Paula Modersohn-Becker Haus...........15 B5
Rathaus..16 B5
Roselius Haus................................(see 15)
Schnoor..17 B6
Town Musicians of Bremen Statue....18 B5
Übersee Museum..................................19 C4

Wilhelm-Wagenfeld Haus...................20 C6
Windmill...21 B4

SLEEPING
Bremen Hilton...............................(see 9)
Bremer Backpacker Hostel.................22 C4
Hochzeitshaus.....................................23 B6
Hotel Bölts am Park............................24 D3
Hotel Lichtsinn....................................25 C5
Hotel Residence..................................26 D3
Hotel Stadt Bremen............................27 A4
Hotel Überfluss...................................28 A5
Jugendherberge Bremen....................29 A4

EATING
Café Engel..30 D6
Casablanca...31 C4
Delano..32 B5
Energie Café...33 B5
Katzen Café..34 B6
Luv..35 A5
Restaurant Flett..................................36 B5
Salomon's...37 C6
Schnoor Teestübchen...................(see 23)
Schröter's...38 B6

Stromburg.....................................(see 14)
Überfluss.......................................(see 28)

DRINKING
2raumlounge..39 D5
Airport...(see 41)
Bodega Del Puerto...............................40 A5
Feldmann's...41 A5
Lemon Lounge......................................42 C5
Room...43 B5

ENTERTAINMENT
Die Glocke..44 B5
La Viva..45 C4
NFF Cream Club...................................46 B5
Schauspielhaus..............................(see 48)
Stubu Dancehouse..............................47 C5
Theater am
  Goetheplatz......................................48 C6

SHOPPING
Hachez...49 B5

TRANSPORT
Central Bus Station.............................50 C4

BREMEN

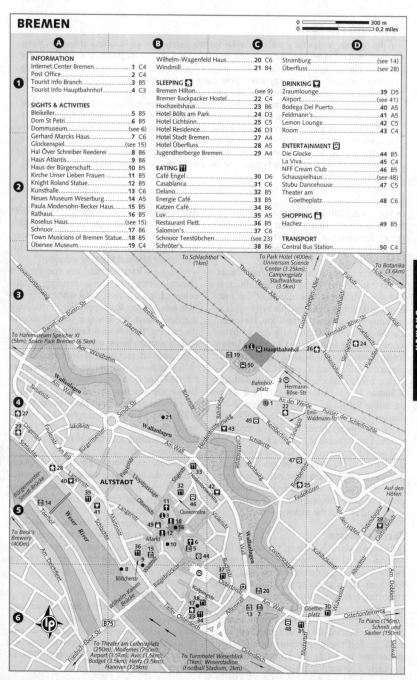

THE FANTASTIC FOUR

In the Brothers Grimm fairy tale, the *Bremer Stadtmusikanten* (Town Musicians of Bremen) never actually make it to Bremen, but when you do arrive in the city, you might enjoy a quick reminder of what the fuss is about. Starting with a donkey, four overworked and ageing animals, fearing the knacker's yard or the Sunday roasting pan, run away from their owners. They head for Bremen intending, like many young dreamers, to make their fortune as musicians.

On their first night on the road, they decide to shelter in a house. It turns out to be occupied by robbers, as our heroes discover when they climb on the donkey to peer through the window. The sight of a rooster atop a cat, perched on a dog, which is sitting on a donkey – and the 'musical' accompaniment of braying, barking, meowing and crowing – startles the robbers so much, they flee. The animals remain and make their home 'where you'll probably still find them today'.

On Sunday from May to early October, this story is charmingly re-enacted (at noon and 1.30pm) in Bremen's Markt.

and imposing **Rathaus** (town hall). Although the Rathaus was first erected in 1410, the Weser Renaissance balcony in the middle, crowned by three gables, was added between 1595 and 1618.

Bremen boasts that the 13m-high **Knight Roland statue** (1404) in front of the Rathaus is Germany's tallest representation of this just, freedom-loving knight, and his belt buckle is certainly in an interesting position. However, it's the statue tucked away on the Rathaus' western side, in front of the **Kirche Unser Lieben Frauen** (Church of our Beloved Lady) that people more readily identify with this city. Sculptor Gerhard Marcks has cast the **Town Musicians of Bremen** (1951) in their famous pose – one on top of the other, on the shoulders of the donkey (see boxed text). The donkey's nose and front legs are incredibly shiny after being touched by visitors for good luck.

The one obviously modern building on the Markt is the **Haus der Bürgerschaft** (State Assembly; 1966), whose geometrical steel-and-concrete structure features artfully moulded pieces of metal attached to its façade, helping it to blend in with the historic square.

Böttcherstrasse

If Bremen's Markt is striking, the nearby Böttcherstrasse (1931) is unique. A charming laneway with a golden entrance, staggered red-brick walls and a spiral staircase with colourful inlaid glass, it's a superb example of expressionist–Art Nouveau styling.

This 110m-long street was commissioned in 1931 by Ludwig Roselius, a merchant who made his fortune by inventing decaffeinated coffee and founding the company Hag in the early 20th century. Most of the street's

design was by Bernhard Hoetger (1874–1959), including the **Lichtbringer** (Bringer of Light), the golden relief at the northern entrance, showing a scene from the Apocalypse with the Archangel Michael fighting a dragon.

Hoetger's **Haus Atlantis** (now the Bremen Hilton) features a show-stopping, multi-coloured, glass-walled **spiral staircase** (☯ tours 10am-noon & 2-4pm Mon); peek at it through the doors anytime. Hoetger worked around the existing, 16th-century **Roselius Haus**, but the **Paula Modersohn-Becker Haus**, with its rounded edges and wall reliefs, is his design too.

Today these two houses adjoin **museums** (☎ 3365077; combined ticket adult/concession €5/3; ☯ 11am-6pm Tue-Sun). The first showcases the art of the eponymous painter, Paula Modersohn-Becker (1876–1907), an early expressionist and member of the Worpswede colony (see p651). The second contains Roselius' private collection of medieval art.

Outside, the **Glockenspiel** (Carillon; ☯ hourly noon-6pm May-Dec; noon, 3pm & 6pm Jan-Apr) chimes while a panel honouring great sea explorers, such as Leif Eriksson and Christopher Columbus, rotates.

Böttcherstrasse is all the more enjoyable for having survived a Nazi destruction order. Roselius convinced the authorities to save the 'degenerate' street as a future warning of the depravity of 'cultural Bolshevism'.

Der Schnoor

Over the years, Bremen's former maritime and then red-light district has transmogrified into a quaint maze of restaurants, cafés and boutique shops. It's a honey-pot for tourists, but its restaurants are also popular with locals in the evenings.

The name Schnoor is north German for 'string', and refers to the way the 15th- and 16th-century cottages – once inhabited by fisherfolk, traders and craftspeople – are 'strung' along the alleyways.

Cathedral Cellar

What's most unusual about Bremen's cathedral (Dom St Petri) is what lies beneath. In the incredibly dry air of its **Bleikeller** (Lead Cellar; ☎ 365 0441; adult/concession €1.40/1; ☼ 10am-5pm Mon-Fri, 10am-2pm Sat, noon-5pm Sun Easter-Oct) corpses mummify, and you can still spy eight preserved bodies in open coffins here. The figures include a Swedish countess, a soldier with his mouth opened in a silent scream, and a student who died in a duel in 1705. It's slightly macabre and uncomfortable viewing, though, and not for the very squeamish.

The Bleikeller has its own entrance, to the south of the main door. The 265 steps to the top of the cathedral's **tower** (adult/child €1/0.70; ☼ Easter-Oct) can also be climbed.

Beck's Brewery

You have to feel a little sorry for Beck's. Its once distinctive brand name is now more readily associated with a certain English footballer who's a regular in international gossip magazines. Still, the firm is far from crying into its – light, refreshing – beer, and is happy to show you what pumps that smell of hops out over Bremen during a two-hour tour of the **brewery** (☎ 5094 5555; Am Deich; tours €7.50; ☼ hourly 10am-5pm Tue-Sat, 10am-3pm Sun). A tour in English leaves at 2pm daily. Take tram 1 or 8 to Am Brill. *Prost!*

Museums

Bremen has a strong aerospace industry, and space buffs will enjoy the eye-catching, oyster-shaped **Universum Science Center** (☎ 334 60; www.universum-bremen.de; Wiener Strasse 2; adult/child €12/8; 9am-6pm Mon-Fri, to 7pm Sat & Sun), where you can make virtual trips to the stars, as well as to the ocean floor or the centre of the earth. Take tram No 6 from the main train station to Universität/NW1 stop.

The renovated **Übersee Museum** (Overseas Museum; ☎ 1603 8101; www.uebersee-museum.de; Bahnhofplatz 13; adult/concession €6/2.50; ☼ 10am-6pm Tue-Sun) offers to take you 'around the world in 80 minutes' with its dazzling collection of exotic artefacts from abroad. These include African art, tropical plants and gold from South America.

Meanwhile, the **Hafenmuseum Speicher XI** (Harbour Museum Warehouse 11; ☎ 303 8279; www.speicherelf.de; Am Speicher XI; adult/concession €3.50/2.50; ☼ 11am-6pm Tue-Sun; Bus 26 to Speicher XI) expounds on Bremen's waterside history.

For art, the rather short Kulturmeile (Cultural Mile) boasts the excellent modern collection of the **Kunsthalle** (☎ 329 080; www.kunsthalle-bremen.de; Am Wall 207; adult/concession €5/2.50, special exhibitions €9/6; ☼ 10am-9pm Tue, 10am-5pm Wed-Sun) and two other galleries devoted to Bremen-born lads – the Kunsthalle's café alone is worth visiting. The **Gerhard Marcks Haus** (☎ 327 200; Am Wall 208; adult/concession €3.50/2; ☼ 10am-6pm Tue-Sun) showcases sculpture, while the **Wilhelm Wagenfeld Haus** (☎ 338 8116; Am Wall 209; adult/concession €3.50/1.50; ☼ 3-9pm Tue, 10am-6pm Wed-Sun) features household objects from this Bauhaus luminary.

Across from the Schlachte, above a sign reading 'Auf Sand gebaut, tatsächlich (aus) auf anderem Grund; Built on sand, actually on another base (basis)', is the **Neues Museum Weserburg** (☎ 598 390; www.nmwb.de; Teerhof 20; adult/concession €5/3; ☼ 10am-6pm Tue-Fri, 11am-6pm Sat & Sun) with changing exhibitions of art hot off the press.

Other Attractions

The city's typical Dutch **windmill** (Am Wall; admission free; ☼ 9.30am-midnight May-Sep, 10am-11pm Oct-Apr) houses a restaurant. Plant-lovers shouldn't miss a trip to **botanika** (Rhododendronpark; free Jul-Mar, adult/child €8/5 Apr-Jun; ☼ 9am-5pm) and its replicated landscapes from Borneo, the Himalayas and Japan. To get here, take tram 4 to Horner Kirche.

TOURS

Leaving from the Hauptbahnhof, the tourist office runs a **city bus tour** (adult/child under 12 €15.50/10; ☼ 10.30am Tue-Sun) which offers English and German commentary. Otherwise, ask the office about its plethora of German-language tours.

Hal Över Schreiber Reederei (☎ 338 989; www.hal-oever.de; Martinianleger, Schlachte 2) operates a 75-minute **Weser and harbour tour** (adult/child €8.50/4.50) up to five times daily between April and October. The tourist office has a full schedule of candlelight cruises, weekend party cruises and boat trips to the islands of Helgoland and Sylt. Scheduled services also ply the river (see Getting There & Away, p649).

BREMEN

SLEEPING
Budget
Camping Stadtwaldsee (☎ 841 0748; www.camping
-stadtwaldsee.de; Hochschulring 1; per adult/tent/car €7/4/1.50)
Rebuilt in late 2005, this features modern
amenities, a supermarket and a café with a
lakeside terrace. By car, take the A27 to the
university exit in Bremen Nord. Tram 6 will get
you close, and bus 28 goes past the doorstep.

Jugendherberge Bremen (☎ 163 820; www
.jugendherberge.de/jh/bremen; Kalkstrasse 6; dm under
26yr/over 26yr €21/24, s/d €32/56; ☒ ☐) Like a work
of art from the exterior, with a yellow and
orange Plexiglas façade and slit rectangular
windows, this refurbished building is even
better inside. Comfortable dorms all have
bathrooms, while there's a bar-breakfast
room with huge glass windows overlooking
the Weser River, and a rooftop terrace.

Bremer Backpacker Hostel (☎ 223 8057; www
.bremer-backpacker-hostel.de; Emil-Waldmann-Strasse
5-6; dm/s/d €16/27/44; ☐ ☐) At this place, five
minutes from the train station and tucked
away on a quiet street, you'll find simply
furnished but spotless rooms, a kitchen and
living room. The communal showers are all
on the ground floor – thanks to low water
pressure, we presume from the slow-running
taps on the first floor.

Midrange
Hotel Bölts am Park (☎ 346 110; www.hotel-boelts.de;
Slevogtstrasse 23; s/d €50/80; ☐) This family-run
hotel in a leafy neighbourhood has real character, from the wonderfully old-fashioned
breakfast hall to its well-proportioned rooms.
A few singles with hall showers and toilets
cost €40.

Hotel Residence (☎ 348 710; www.hotelresidence
.de; Hohlenstrasse 42; s €65-100, d €80-140; ☐ ☒) This
century-old terrace has been converted to
a charming hotel. The cheaper rooms are a
bit snug, but the best doubles (rooms 12 and
22) have balconies overlooking a quiet street.
A sauna, solarium, bar, dining room and
London black cab (parked on the forecourt)
complete the package.

Hotel Lichtsinn (☎ 368 070; www.hotel-lichtsinn
.com; Rembertistrasse 11; s/d €80/105; ☐ ☒) Wooden
floorboards, Persian carpets and vaguely
Regency-style furniture characterise most of
this hotel's rooms, although one has an old
German-style four-poster bed. A favourite with
the theatre world (and even a NASA astronaut
or two), it's a very civilised experience.

Hotel Stadt Bremen (☎ 949 410; www.hotelgruppe
-kalber.de; Heinkenstrasse 3-5; s €75-85, d €100, tr €105;
☐ ☒) Very popular, although this is prob-
ably as much as for its convenient location
as its keep-it-simple modern décor. Surprisingly, some rooms come with a TV in the
bathroom.

Turmhotel Weserblick (☎ 949 410; www.hotelgruppe
-kalber.de; Osterdeich 53; s €75-85, d €90-100; ☐ ☒ ; tram
2, 3, or 10 to Sielwall) Another outlet from the same
local group as Hotel Stadt Bremen, this looks
like an atmospheric old pile from the exterior.
However, inside there are renovated and extremely spacious rooms, with bare floorboards
and Persian carpets. The tower rooms overlook the river and have a kitchen.

Top End
Hotel Überfluss (☎ 322 860; www.hotel-ueberfluss.com;
Langenstrasse 72/Schlachte; s/d €135/180; ☒ ☒ ☒ ☒)
Dragging quaint Bremen into the 21st century is this stunning design hotel, with green-
tinted windows overlooking the Weser River,
black bathrooms and glowing fibre-optic curtains imported from Las Vegas. However,
the friendly staff prevent it from becoming
too snooty.

Park Hotel (☎ 340 80; www.park-hotel-bremen.de;
Im Bürgerpark; s €185-280, d €235-330; ☐ ☒ ☒) This
domed mansion, surrounded by parkland and
overlooking a lake, is pure extravagance. It has
excellent spa and beauty facilities, and there's
a bathroom where you can watch the world
below through the window beside the tub.

EATING
Town Centre
Energie Café (☎ 277 2510; Cnr Sögestrasse & Am Wall;
mains €3.50-12.50; ☒ 9am-8pm Mon-Sat) A delightfully
upbeat café run by a local power company,
this serves delicious cut-price lunches and
solid early-evening meals. Amuse yourself
while waiting by watching the model surfer
on the wave-motion display, or whatever is
their latest energy-related gimmick.

Delano (☎ 338 7400; Queerenstrasse 1; mains €5-
18.50) The black wood furniture, fat columns,
ringed black-and-white lampshades and high
density of men in shirt collars give this Italian brasserie a sophisticated air, but you can
eat very cheaply here. Each menacingly large
pizza (€7 to €10) comes in an elongated oval
shape and is *meant* to be eaten between two.

Restaurant Flett (☎ 320 995; Böttcherstrasse 3-5; most
mains €7-15) Come here for local specialities like

THE SMALLEST HOTEL IN THE WORLD...PROBABLY

If you've ever struggled to open a suitcase in a hotel room where you can touch all four walls from your bed, Bremen's claim to having possibly the world's tiniest hotel won't immediately impress you. Small isn't usually beautiful in the world of tourist accommodation, but in the Schnoor quarter's **Hochzeitshaus** (Wedding House; ☎ 0170-461 8333; www.hochzeitshaus-bremen.de, in German; Wüste Stätte 5; 1/2 nights €320/520) it is. Aimed at loved-up couples willing to pay to have an entire hotel to themselves, this renovated medieval house has just one bedroom, occupying the entire upper floor, with a bathroom and whirlpool tub on the level below, and a kitchen beneath (should you really want to come back to earth during your romantic sojourn).

According to the owners, wedding houses were common in medieval cities, because couples coming from the country to get married in the cathedral needed somewhere to stay – and consummate the marriage – before returning home. So as they hang out the 'Do not disturb' sign on their narrow three-storey abode, guests can take extra pleasure in the knowledge that they're carrying on a long tradition.

Labskaus (a hash of beef or pork with potatoes, onion and herring) or *Knipp* (fried hash and oats) or try the Schweinhaxe or Alsatian, pizza-style *Flammkuchen*. Touristy it might be, but it's hard to dislike the photo-bedecked room, featuring first-hand snaps of celebs from Elvis to Clinton to Gerhard Schröder.

Salomon's (☎ 244 1771; Ostertorstrasse 11-13; mains €12-20) This designer restaurant in a former law courts building is smart enough to impress a business partner or date, but there are a few bench seats where you won't feel alone dining on the Eurasian cuisine. A bar, courtyard and club are found in the same complex.

Schlachte & Around

Luv (☎ 165 5599; Schlachte 15-18; most mains €6-15) A friendly, upbeat atmosphere reigns in this large bistro with comfy cushioned banquettes arranged on staggered levels. The menu criss-crosses the globe, from Texas burgers to *Wiener Schnitzel* and back.

Stromburg (☎ 240 2100; Teerhof 21; snacks €4.50-9.50, mains €9-22) This retro restaurant is relaxed and chilled, with pink, purple and beige overtones, plus tasty international cuisine. Try the king prawns on Asian greens with mushrooms, mint, coriander and lime sauce, or see if they're still offering the Sunday evening 'surprise' menu, where you can pay only what you think their invention was worth.

Überfluss (☎ 322 860; Langenstrasse 72/Schlachte; mains €11-23) Fibre-optic curtains glow in the background as you savour skilful Eurasian dishes under low-hanging, silver globe lights. Yet, despite such cutting-edge chic, kids are obviously welcome here, particularly on the cowhide chairs in the informal lounge

area. Toilets are divided into men, women and children's – with the last appropriately downsized!

Schnoor

Katzen Café (☎ 326 621; Schnoor 38; mains €8.50-16.50, 3-course menu €19.50) This Moulin Rouge–style restaurant opens out into a rear sunken terrace bedecked with flowers. The menu runs the gamut from Alsatian to Norwegian, with seafood a strong theme.

Schröter's (☎ 326 677; Schnoor 13; mains €11-18) A modern bistro with artful decoration, Schröter's is known for its antipasti and has plenty of Mediterranean mains, from risotto to fish. The Toulouse-Lautrec room upstairs, decorated with plenty of copies of the painter's pictures, is more formal.

Das Viertel

This arty, student neighbourhood is where to head for cheap eats.

Casablanca (☎ 326 429; Ostertorsteinweg 59; meals €3-11) The emphasis is on the 'Casa' in this homey Bremen institution, where goths, grannies and particularly students while away the hours within scuffed walls painted to look like marble, and under a ceiling that's a trompe l'oeil jungle canopy.

Piano (☎ 785 46; Fehrfeld 64; mains €5.50-9.50) Another enduringly popular café, this serves pizza, pasta, steaks and vegie casseroles to a broad neighbourhood mix, from ad types checking proofs to young mums. Breakfast can also be ordered until 4pm.

Café Engel (☎ 766 15; Ostertorsteinweg 31; meals €6-12) Housed in a former pharmacy, this is a popular hang-out that matches black-and-white tiled floors with dark wood furniture. In summer, tables spill onto the pavement.

Cafés

Schnoor Teestübchen (☎ 326 091; Wüste Stätte 1) If you can ignore the hint of twee tourist shop about it, this is a great place to indulge in Frisian tea-drinking rituals – putting huge crystals of sugar into your cup with tongs, or twirling honey into your char. Some local blends are wonderfully smooth, too.

DRINKING

The waterfront Schlachte promenade is wall-to-wall bars catering to all tastes. For a grungy student vibe, head to Das Viertel and just walk along O-weg. Check listings mags, such as *Prinz Bremen4U* or *Port01*, for more details.

Lemon Lounge (☎ 514 8855; Am Wall 164; ☺ from 5pm) Don't spend too much thought on the fact that this is a one-time *Playboy* bar of the year. Up the galleried metal stairs there are no bunnies, just friendly staff mixing up great cocktails from the 30-page drinks list. Join the cool but unpretentious crowd of early 20s to early 40s, by planting yourself on a red leather sofa and enjoying the loungey house music.

2raumlounge (☎ 745 77; Auf den Höfen; ☺ from 7pm) Another lounge, another great bar and the reliable lynchpin of the somewhat flagging Auf den Höfen scene. Sitting in the space-age orange chairs, you have photos of groups of friends looking down on you, and real people on the mezzanine above. A variety of theme evenings – Desperate Housewives, Oriental and student – brighten up the early part of the week.

Bodega Del Puerto (☎ 178 3797; Schlachte 31a) Essentially, the point of the Schlachte is to walk along it and see which bar you most like the look of. However, should you be in the mood for a Spanish-style place that's a bit quieter than most, pop in here.

Feldmann's (☎ 168 9192; Schlachte 19/20a) A slightly older crowd can be found chatting and lingering over the wide range of Haake-Beck beers in this modern *Bierhaus*, which also sells food.

Room (☎ 276 5945; Herdentorsteinweg 2-3; ☺ from noon Mon-Sat, from 5pm Sun) This trendy new downtown bar, with red crocodile leather seats and a tiny dance floor, also hosts some gay evenings.

Airport (☎ 745 12; Am Dobben 70; ☺ closed Sun) A small 1970s retro bar in Das Viertel.

ENTERTAINMENT

Clubs

Clubbing in Bremen is relatively cheap; expect to pay €4 to €8 at the door for regular nights, although special events may cost more.

Modernes (☎ 505 553; Neustadtwall 28; ☺ from 11pm Fri & Sat, plus special events) South of the river in Neustadt, this converted old movie theatre also hosts live music, and remains Bremen's best club bar none. The centrepiece is the domed roof that can be opened to let in some much-needed air towards the end of the evening.

NFF Cream Club (☎ 345 199; Katherinenstrasse 12-14; ☺ Fri & Sat, plus special events) With a futuristic looking bar, a chic dance-floor and lots of cocktails, Nur Für Freunde (Just for Friends) is the place for house, dance and electro. It's also where famous German and international DJs come to spin the tunes.

Stubu Dancehouse (☎ 321 423; Rembertiring 21; ☺ from 9pm nightly) This long-term Bremen institution has spread its wings and now offers five different spaces over three floors, from the traditional 'music club' in the basement to the new Skyline area, with house, funk and chart hits.

Stubu is on a street of wall-to-wall clubs, including the huge, ex-multiplex **La Viva** (cnr Rembertiring & Auf der Brake). Many Bremers, however, dismiss this area as largely for 'teenies'. See also Dangers and Annoyances (p642).

Theatre & Music

Die Glocke (☎ 336 699; Domsheide) Bremen's concert hall has two house orchestras and welcomes visiting performers with its excellent acoustics.

Schlachthof (☎ 377 750; Findorffstrasse 51; bus 25 to Theodor-Heus-Allee) Ethnic and world-music concerts, theatre, cabaret and variety are all complemented here by art exhibitions and a café.

Theater am Leibnizplatz (☎ 500 333; www .shakespeare-company.com; Am Leibnizplatz; tram 4, 5 or 6 to Leibnizplatz) The highly acclaimed Bremer Shakespeare Company mixes the Bard (in German) with fairy tales and contemporary works.

Theater am Goetheplatz (☎ 365 30; Goethe-platz) The famous 1970s film director, Rainer Werner Fassbinder, honed his craft with this company. The main theatre stages opera, operettas and musicals.

In the attached **Schauspielhaus** (☎ 365 3333; Ostertorsteinweg 57a) you'll find updated classics and avant-garde drama.

Sport

After the FIFA Football World Cup 2006, local team **Werder Bremen** (☎ 01805-937 337; www .werder.de) became hugely popular, thanks to its inclusion of Miroslav Klose, the winner of the tournament's 'Golden Boot' award for most goals. National footballers Torsten Frings and Tim Borowski also play for Werder Bremen, whose home games are at the **Weser Stadion** (www.weserstadion.de; Franz-Böhmert-Strasse 1a; tram 3 to Weserstadion, tram 2 & 10 to St Jürgen-Strasse). Sadly, at the time of writing, these were virtually sold out for a year.

SHOPPING

It's fun to reacquaint yourself with the fairy tale of *The Town Musicians of Bremen* (see the boxed text on p644) via one of the many English-language editions. Otherwise, the most obvious buy in Bremen is sweets. **Hachez** (☎ 339 8898; Am Markt 1) is a good port of call, as the local purveyor of chocolate and specialities like *Kluten* (peppermint sticks covered in dark chocolate).

Both Böttcherstrasse and the Schnoor Viertel are full of interesting jewellery, from antique silver and oodles of amber to modern designer pieces. Ostertorsteinweg, in Das Viertel, is the place to look for funky streetwear.

There's also a renowned flea market on the Bürgerweide, north of the Hauptbahnhof (open 7am to 2pm most Sundays; check exact dates at the tourist office).

GETTING THERE & AWAY
Air

Bremen's **airport** (☎ 559 50; www.airport-bremen .de) is about 3.5km south of the centre and has flights to destinations in Germany and Europe. Airline offices here include **Air Berlin** (☎ 0421-552 035) and **Lufthansa Airlines** (☎ 01803-803 803). Low-cost carrier **easyJet** (www.easyjet.com) flies from here to London Luton airport.

Boat

Hal Över Schreiber Reederei (☎ 338 989; www .hal-oever.de, Martinianleger, Schlachte 2) operates scheduled services along the Weser between

April and September. Boats from Bremen to Bremerhaven (one-way/return €13.50/21.50, 3½ hours), with numerous stops en route, depart at 8.30am every Wednesday, Thursday and Saturday, and 9.30am on Sunday. Shorter trips ending at Brake (€9/14.50, 2½ hours) depart on Tuesday at 12.30pm. Students and children pay half-price.

Bus

Eurolines (☎ 040-247 160; www.eurolines.com) runs from Bremen to Amsterdam (five hours), and other European destinations. Check prices online as they are extremely variable.

Car & Motorcycle

The A1 (from Hamburg to Osnabrück) and the A27/A7 (Bremerhaven to Hanover) intersect in Bremen. The city is also on the B6 and B75. All major car-rental agencies have branches at the airport, including **Avis** (☎ 558 055), **Hertz** (☎ 555 350) and **Budget** (☎ 597 0016).

Train

Frequent trains go to Hamburg (€18.30 to €22, one hour), Hanover (€18.70 to €27, one hour to one hour, 20 minutes) and Cologne (€52, three hours). Some IC trains run direct to Frankfurt-am-Main (€76, 3¾ hours) and Munich (€100, six hours) daily.

GETTING AROUND

Tram 6 travels between the Hauptbahnhof and the airport (€2.90, 15 minutes). A **taxi** (☎ 140 14, 144 33) costs about €15.

buses and trams are operated by **Verkehrsverbund Bremen/Niedersachsen** (☎ 01805-826 826; www .bsag.de). Main hubs are in front of the Hauptbahnhof and at Domsheide near the Rathaus. A €2.05 single covers most of the Bremen city area, while a day pass (Tageskarte) costs €5.

For bike rental, contact the **Fahrradstation** (☎ 302 114; ⏰ 6am-10pm Mon-Fri, 9am-8pm Sat) just outside the Hauptbahnhof (bring your passport).

AROUND BREMEN

BREMERHAVEN
☎ 0471 / pop 130,000

Ship ahoy! Bremerhaven is a bit of a boy's-own adventure for anyone who likes industrial machinery and has dreamt of running away to sea. Although it could never be called charming and is definitely best seen on a day trip, the city has an unusual zoo and many boats you can clamber over, so it's a hit with kids.

Most of all, Bremerhaven's new emigration centre is worth coming to see. Of the millions who landed at New York's Ellis Island, a large proportion sailed from here, and this enticing exhibition allows you to share their history.

A new climate house (looking in plan a bit like the bubbly Kunsthaus in Graz, Austria) and the new Atlantic SailCity hotel (like a mini-version of Dubai's Burj Al-Arab) should open in 2008, giving 'Fishtown' (as it's nicknamed for all its fresh fish) some much-needed pulling power.

Orientation

Before coming here, ask the Bremen tourist office for a free map of Bremerhaven. Alternatively, the bus office outside Bremerhaven's train station sells them for a small fee.

The city is essentially one long streak, running southwest to northeast, a kilometre or so north of the train station. Most attractions – the emigration centre, zoo and ship museum – are clustered around the Alter and Neuer Hafen, northeast of the train station. The Fischereihafen lies to the northwest of the station. See opposite for more details.

Information

Bremerhaven Touristik (☎ 414 141; www .bremerhaven-tourism.de; H-H-Meier-Strasse 6; 8.30am-6pm Mar-Oct, 9am-5pm Mon-Fri, 10am-4pm Sat & Sun Nov-Feb) When you cross from the bridge behind the Auswandererhaus, this is in the building ahead, but is unhelpfully hidden on the far side.
Tourist Info Colombus Center (Columbus-Center, Obere Bürger 17; 9.30am-6pm Mon-Wed, 9.30am-8pm Thu & Fri, 9.30am-4pm Sat)
Tourist Info Schaufenster Fischereihafen (9am-7pm mid-Mar–Oct) Fischkai, near the FMS 'Gera' ship. Also rents bicycles.

Sights & Activities
GERMAN EMIGRATION CENTRE

'Give me your tired, your poor, your huddled masses,' invites the Statue of Liberty in New York harbour. Well, Bremerhaven is one place that most certainly did. Millions of those landing at Ellis Island departed from here, and the **Deutsches Auswandererhaus** (☎ 902 200; www.dah-bremerhaven.de; Columbusstrasse 65; adult/concession/child/family €8.50/7.50/6/22; 10am-

6pm, to 7pm Sat Apr-Oct, 10am-5pm, to 6pm Sat Nov-Mar) now chronicles and commemorates some of their stories.

Opened in late 2005, this is Europe's largest exhibition on emigration, and it does a superb job of conjuring up the experience. For added piquancy, it's on the very spot where more than 7 million people set sail, for the USA and other parts of the world, between 1830 and 1974.

The exhibition recreates their travelling conditions, as you move from a third-class passengers' waiting room, to dockside, to the gangway, into the bowels of a ship. You also stop in the huge 'Gallery of the 7 Million', which contains emigrants' personal details (a few thousand of them) in pull-out drawers and tries to explain why people left home. Your electronic entry card contains the biographical details of one particular traveller, whom you can follow throughout the exhibition. Everything is available in both German and English.

Later sections land you in the reception centre at Ellis Island, and show a film of emigrants talking about their new homeland and discussing the migration today. If your forebears moved from Germany to the States, you can start doing research here; although some trips must be investigated at the **Historisches Museum Bremerhaven/Morgenstern Museum** (☎ 201 38; An der Geeste; www.historisches -museum-bremerhaven.de; adult/concession €3.20/2.50; 10am-6pm Tue-Sun).

Unfortunately, information about emigrants to other countries is sketchier.

OTHER SIGHTS

Behind the Deutsches Auswandererhaus, the **Zoo am Meer** (☎ 308410; www.zoo-am-meer -bremerhaven.de; H-H-Meier-Strasse 6; adult/concession/child €6.50/3.50/3.50, slightly cheaper on Mon; 9am-7pm Apr-Sep, 9am-6pm Mar & Oct, 9am-4.30pm Nov-Feb, last entry 30 mins before closing) isn't quite as spectacular inside as it looks in photos. Still, young families seem to love watching the polar bear, polar foxes, seals, penguins, pumas and chimpanzees in enclosures built into one big artificial 'rock' formation. Windows below water level allow you to watch creatures swim. Check the website or ask the tourist office for feeding times.

A highlight of the **Deutsches Schiffahrtsmuseum** (German Maritime Museum; ☎ 482 070; www .dsm.de; Hans-Scharoun-Platz 1; adult/concession €5/3.50;

🕙 10am-6pm daily Apr-Oct, closed Mon Nov-Mar, last entry 30min before closing) is the reconstructed *Bremer Hansekogge,* a merchant boat from 1380. Partly reassembled from pieces rescued from the deep, it's the German equivalent of the famous *Mary Rose* in England. The collection of 500 boats inside is complemented by a harbour full of museum ships – and a submarine – which you can explore. Some have small additional entrance fees.

Succulently fresh fish is served at the many restaurants of the remodelled **Fischereihafen** (Fishery Harbour) complex. There's also an aquarium and puppet theatre; the on-site tourist office can help with details.

A **Hafenbus** (adult/child €9.50/6.50) does a circuit of town, passing the impressive container terminal. It runs daily all year, and between April and October it runs two or three times a day.

Getting There & Around
Frequent trains from Bremen to Bremerhaven take about one hour. Singles cost €9.60, but for day trips a €17 return Niedersachsen ticket is cheaper.

Travelling by car, Bremerhaven is quickly reached via the A27 from Bremen; get off at the Bremerhaven-Mitte exit. An alternative is a leisurely boat ride from Bremen (see Getting There & Away p649).

Within Bremerhaven, single tickets/day passes cost €1.95/4.80. From the train station, buses 502, 504, 505, 506, 508 and 509 make the 1.3km journey to Alte Kirche, near the Alter and Neuer Hafen. Buses 504, 505 and 506 also go to Schaufenster Fischereihafen, in the other direction.

WORPSWEDE
☎ 04792 / pop 9000
Originally an artists' colony esatblished by the expressionist–Art Nouveau architects and painters later associated with Bremen's Böttcherstrasse, Worpswede has, like so many of its ilk, developed into one of those cutesy artisans' towns where nearby city-dwellers come to mooch around on weekends. Outside Germany, the community's most famous member was the poet Rainer Maria Rilke, who dedicated several books to this pretty Niedersachsen village. Other major names involved include Paula Modersohn-Becker (see p644) and her husband Otto Modersohn, plus the future designer of Böttcherstrasse, Bernhard

Hoetger, architect and painter Heinrich Vogeler, and painter Fritz Mackensen.

They weren't the first writers and artists to be attracted to the stark, melancholic landscape here. Earlier individuals had drawn inspiration from the dramatic clouds and moody light over the **Teufelsmoor** (Devil's Moor) peat bog. But from the end of the 19th century, this group made the place their own. Today, not only can you visit their buildings and view their art in some seven museums, but you can also shop for porcelain, jewellery, posters, soap made from moor products and other trinkets.

Add plenty of opportunities to stop for coffee and cakes, enjoy a spa, go hiking, cycling or canoeing, and even younger visitors not particularly attracted by the expressionist–Art Nouveau style will find Worpswede a pleasant outing.

The **tourist office** (☎ 935 820; www.worpswede.de; Bergstrasse 13; 🕙 9am-5pm Mon-Fri, 10am-2pm Sat & Sun) can provide more details, but one highlight is the short stroll to the 55m-tall **Weyerberg dune** at the heart of the moor, where Hoetger's **Niedersachsenstein** sculpture looms like a giant eagle. A memorial to the fallen of WWI, it's a controversial beast for both the way it 'spoils' the natural landscape and its original purpose as a victory column.

The creative heart of the colony was the **Barkenhoff** (☎ 3968; Ostendorfer Strasse 10; adult/ concession €4/2; 🕙 10am-6pm), a half-timbered structure remodelled in Art Nouveau style by its owner Heinrich Vogeler. Today, it's a museum. Meanwhile, Vogeler's beautiful **Art Nouveau train station** (www.worpsweder-bahnhof.de) has been transformed into a restaurant. Another eaterie worth stopping at is Hoetger's **Café Worpswede**. Looking part half-timbered house, part Art Deco-style building and part tepee, it's locally known as Café Verrückt (Café Crazy).

Sleeping
Worpswede has several charming hotels, often integrated with art galleries.

DJH (☎ 1360; www.djh.de; Hammeweg 2; dm under/ over 26yr €15.80/18.80, s/d from €23.80/39.60; P ✕) This hostel is located in a brick farm-style building, one bus stop (800m) from the village centre.

Haus im Schluh (☎ 950 061; www.haus-im-schluh .de; Im Schluh 37a; s/d/tr from €60/75/100; P ✕) Sleep among Art Nouveau furnishings in a former

Vogeler residence, down a leafy winding lane.

Hotel Village (☎ 935 00; www.village-worpswede.de; Bergstrasse 22; s/d/tr from €80/125/145; P ✗) Split-level units are divided into ground floor living and mezzanine sleeping areas, above a restaurant and basement art gallery.

Hotel Worpsweder Tor (☎ 989 30; www.hotel -worpsweder-tor.de; Finddorfstrasse 3; s €95-125, d €115-145; P ✗ ✈) This new four-star establishment near the main bus stop subtly harks back to the Art Deco era, with fat-armed lounge chairs, dark wood and four circular 'tower' rooms.

Getting There & Around

From Bremen's central bus station, bus 670 (€3.30 one-way) makes the 50-minute trip to 'Worpswede Insel' 21 times a day during the week and every two hours on weekends. The vintage **Moor Express** (☎ 04761-993 116; www .moorexpress.net; one-way adult/child/family €9/4.50/19) train has been resurrected between Worpswede and Bremen (and on to Stade), but still only operates three daily return trips on Saturdays and Sundays.

Fahrradladen Eckhard Eyl (☎ 2323; Finddorfstrasse 28) hires out bikes from €6 a day.

Hamburg

Water, water everywhere – Germany's biggest port has always been outward-looking. Its dynamism, multiculturalism and hedonistic red-light district, the Reeperbahn, all arise from its maritime history. Joining the Hanseatic League trading bloc in the Middle Ages, this long-standing duty-free port has been enthusiastically doing business with the world ever since. In the 1960s, it nurtured the talent of the Beatles. In the 21st century, it's also a media capital and the wealthiest city in Germany.

Still overshadowed internationally by Berlin and Munich, domestically Hamburg is known as a natural achiever. Rarely prone to the self-doubt that's wracked the rest of Germany since reunification, this thriving 'harbourpolis' has seen its container ports growing like topsy thanks to new Eastern European business. 'Boomtown Hamburg', *Stern* magazine declared in 2006 – with a beautiful cover of the night-time harbour lights twinkling.

Such easygoing self-confidence makes Germany's second-largest city wonderful to visit. Immigrant workers mingle with students among the Portuguese, Turkish and Asian eateries of vibrant St Pauli and Schanzenviertel. Shipping, TV and newspaper magnates drive their Porsches up to mansions in leafy Blankenese. Defying the city's renowned *Schmuddelwetter* (drizzly weather), Hamburg's hipsters lounge on artificial river beaches, while visitors cruise around the Alster Lakes and the neo-Gothic Speicherstadt warehouses, or haggle at the rowdy fish market as cargo ships navigate the Elbe River.

And if this isn't enough, there are buildings shaped like ocean liners, plus an all-new waterside HafenCity district. The Philharmonic hall being built there is tipped to rival the Sydney Opera House. In which case, the world might finally return some of Hamburg's attentions.

HAMBURG

HIGHLIGHTS

- **Boating** Float through the Speicherstadt canals (p655) or on the Alster lakes (p663)

- **Dining** Munch your way along the Elbmeile (p670), Hamburg's new gastro strip

- **Shopping** Catch the sights, sounds and smells on Sunday morning at the boisterous Fischmarkt (p662) in St Pauli

- **Grand Designs** Admire the ship shape of elegant Chilehaus (p655)

- **Off-beat** Follow a 'Hafenklang' podcast tour around HafenCity (p659) or head for a city beach (p673) in summer

★ Alster Lakes
★ Chilehaus
Elbmeile ★ ★
Fischmarkt ★ Speicherstadt & HafenCity

■ TELEPHONE CODE: 040   ■ POPULATION: 1.7 MILLION   ■ AREA: 755 SQ KM

HISTORY

In the mid-19th century, one admiring Glaswegian treasurer described Hamburg as the world's 'most mercantile city'. That commercial character was forged early in the city's history, in 1189, when local noble Count Adolf III persuaded Emperor Friedrich I (Barbarossa) to grant the city free trading rights and an exemption from customs duties. It was this step that turned the former missionary settlement and 9th-century moated fortress of Hammaburg into an important port and member of the Hanseatic League.

The city prospered for centuries on the banks of the Elbe before suffering a major setback in 1842, when the Great Fire destroyed one-third of its buildings. While it managed to recover in time to join the German Reich in 1871, this saw it involved in two world wars even less kind than the Great Fire. After WWI, most of Hamburg's merchant shipping fleet (almost 1500 ships) was forfeited to the Allies as reparation. During WWII, more than half of Hamburg's housing, 80% of its port and 40% of its industry were left as rubble, and tens of thousands of civilians were killed.

In the postwar years, Hamburg showed its usual resilience to participate in Germany's economic miracle or *Wirtschaftswunder*. Its harbour and media industries are now the backbone of its wealth. More than 6200 companies in the fields of publishing, advertising, film, radio, TV and music are based in the city. The print media are especially prolific: 15 out of 20 of the largest German publications are produced here, including news magazines *Stern* and *Der Spiegel* and the newspaper *Die Zeit*.

The city is also a major Airbus base, manufacturing parts of the now much delayed A380 super-jumbo.

About 15% to 20% of the population are immigrants, giving the city an exciting, international flavour.

ORIENTATION

Hamburg is as watery as Venice and Amsterdam. Three rivers – the Elbe, the Alster and the Bille – traverse it, as does a grid of narrow canals called *Fleete*. The Binnenalster and Aussenalster (Inner and Outer Alster lakes) in the city centre accentuate the maritime feel.

The half-moon-shaped city centre arches north of the Elbe and is bisected diagonally by the Alsterfleet, the canal that once separated the now almost seamless Altstadt (old town) and Neustadt (new town).

The Hauptbahnhof (central train station) is on Glockengiesserwall on the centre's northeastern edge; the ZOB (Central Bus Station) is behind it to the southeast. Three other stations lie west (Altona), south (Harburg) and north (Dammtor) of the centre.

This sprawling city consists of distinct neighbourhoods. East of the Hauptbahnhof is St Georg, a gradually gentrifying red-light district. It's also the hub of the city's gay scene. West of the centre lies St Pauli, home to the Reeperbahn, as well as lots of mainstream clubs and bars. Further west St Pauli merges with the lively Altona district; to its north you'll find its trendy and creative neighbour, the Schanzenviertel.

Select neighbourhoods hug the 160-hectare Aussenalster north of the city centre, with Winterhude and Uhlenhorst on the eastern and Harvestehude and Rotherbaum on the western shores. The Universitätsviertel (University Quarter) takes up the western section of Rotherbaum.

INFORMATION
Bookshops

Dr Götze Land & Karte (Map pp656-7; ☎ 357 4630; www.mapshop-hamburg.de; Alstertor 14-18) An enormous range of guidebooks and maps.

Thalia Bücher (Map pp656-7; ☎ 3020 7160; Grosse Bleichen 19) Also has English books.

Discount Cards

The tourist office, some hostels and hotels all sell Hamburg discount cards.

Hamburg Card (per 1/3 day €7.50/15) Free public transport and museum discounts.

Power Pass (1st day €7, each extra day up to 1 week €3) For under-30s, this offers free public transport, reduced rates for museums and sightseeing tours, some free club entries and a free listings magazine.

Emergency

Fundbüro (Lost Property; ☎ 428 113 501; Bahrenfelder Strasse 254-260, Altona)

Police Hauptbahnhof (Map pp656-7; Kirchenallee exit); St Pauli (Davidwache; Map pp656-7; Spielbudenplatz 31, cnr Davidstrasse)

Internet Access

Internet Café (Map p665; ☎ 2800 3898; Adenauerallee 10; per hr €2; ⊙ 10am-midnight Mon-Sat, 10am-1pm Sun)

Tele-Time (☎ 4131 4730; Schulterblatt 39; per hr €3; ⊙ 10am-midnight)

Laundry

Schnell und Sauber (Map pp656-7; Neuer Pferdemarkt 27; ⊙ 6am-11pm)

Waschbar (☎ 8972 6425; Ottenser Hauptstrasse 56, Altona; ⊙ 10am-midnight)

Medical Services

Ärztlicher Notfalldienst (☎ 228 022) For 24-hour medical advice.

Emergency Doctor Service Hamburg (☎ 228 022)

Internationale Apotheke (Map pp656-7; ☎ 309 6060; Ballindamm 39) Pharmacy.

Money

There are ATMs at the Hauptbahnhof, the airport and all over town.

American Express (Map pp656-7; ☎ 3039 3811; Rathausmarkt 10; ⊙ 9.30am-6pm Mon-Fri, 10am-3pm Sat)

Post

Post Office (Map pp656-7; ☎ 01802-3333; Dammtorstrasse14; ⊙ 8.30am-6pm Mon-Fri, 9am-noon Sat)

Post Office (Map pp656-7; ☎ 01802-3333; Möncke-bergstrasse 7; ⊙ 9am-7pm Mon-Fri, to 3pm Sat)

Tourist Information

Hamburg Tourismus (www.hamburg-tourismus.de) airport (☎ 5075 1010; ⊙ 5.30am-11pm); Hauptbahnhof (Map p665; ☎ information 3005 1200, hotel bookings 3005 1300; Kirchenallee exit; ⊙ 8am-9pm Mon-Sat, 10am-6pm Sun); Landungsbrücken (Map pp656-7; btwn piers 4 & 5; ⊙ 8am-6pm Mon, Wed & Sun, to 7pm Tue, Thu, Fri & Sat Apr-Sep, 10am-6pm Oct-Mar; ⊙ Landungsbrücken)

Information booth (Map pp656-7; Dammtor train station, Dag Hammarskjöld Platz; ⊙ 8am-7.45pm Mon-Fri, 10am-4pm Sat) No hotel bookings.

DANGERS & ANNOYANCES

Although safe and wealthy, Hamburg is also undeniably sleazy in parts, with red-light districts around the train station and Reeperbahn. Junkies and drunks also congregate at the Kirchenallee exit of the Hauptbahnhof and at Hansaplatz in St Georg. Fortunately, there's a strong police presence in these areas, too.

SIGHTS

Altstadt & Merchant's District

Hamburg's baroque **Rathaus** (Map pp656-7; Town Hall; ☎ 428 312 010; adult/concession tour €2/1; ⊙ English tours hourly 10.15am-3.15pm Mon-Thu, to 1.15pm Fri-Sun) is one of Europe's most opulent, renowned for the Emperor's Hall and the Great Hall, with its spectacular coffered ceiling. Indeed, there are 647 rooms here, but the guided 40-minute tours only take in a small number.

North of the Rathaus, you can wander through the **Alsterarkaden**, where the elegant Renaissance-style arcades shelter shops and cafés alongside a canal.

For some visitors the city's most remarkable building isn't the Rathaus, but another that lies south in the Merchant's District. The brownbrick **Chilehaus** (www.chilehaus.de; cnr Burchardstrasse & Johanniswall) is shaped like an ocean liner, with remarkable curved walls meeting in the shape of a ship's bow and staggered balconies to look like decks.

Designed by architect Fritz Höger for a merchant who derived his wealth from trading with Chile, the 1924 building is a leading example of German Expressionist architecture. It's situated in an interesting quarter of town, the Kontorhausviertel, alongside other so-called 'Backsteingotik' buildings (*Backstein* refers to a specially glazed brick; *gotik* means Gothic).

Hamburg's Great Fire of 1842 broke out further west in **Deichstrasse**, which features a few restored 18th-century homes.

Speicherstadt

The seven-storey red-brick warehouses lining the **Speicherstadt** (Map pp656–7) archipelago, across from the Deichtorhallen exhibition space, are a well-recognised Hamburg

HAMBURG

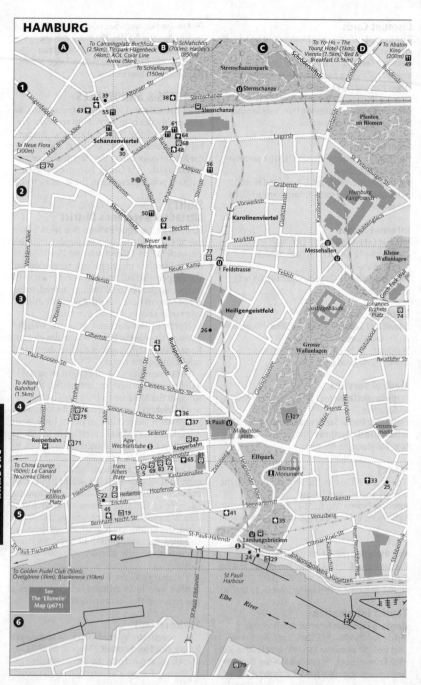

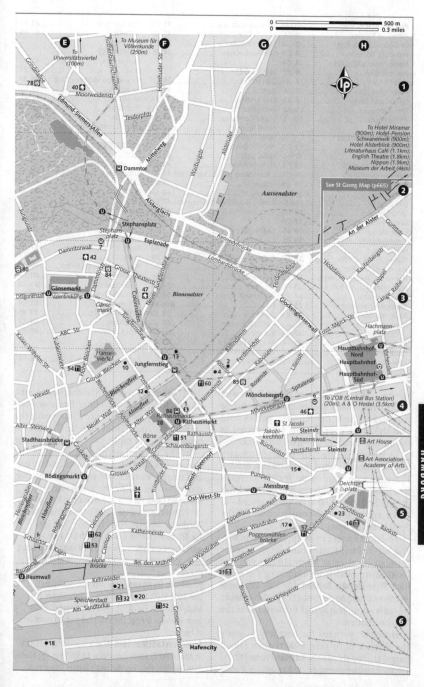

INFORMATION
American Express........1 F4
Dr Götze Land & Karte........2 G4
Hamburg Tourismus........3 C5
Internationale Apotheke........4 G4
Police Station........5 B5
Post Office........6 H4
Post Office........7 E3
Schnell und Sauber........8 B2
Tele-Time........9 B2
Thalia Bücher........10 F4

SIGHTS & ACTIVITIES
Abicht........11 C5
Alsterarkaden........12 F4
ATG Alster-Touristik........13 F4
Cap San Diego........14 D6
Chile Haus........15 G5
Condomerie........(see 72)
Davidwache........(see 5)
Deichtorhallen........16 H5
Dialog im Dunkeln........17 G5
Elbphilharmonie........18 E6
Erotic Art Museum........19 B5
Hadag........(see 11)
HafenCity InfoCenter........20 F6
Hamburg Dungeon........21 F6
Harry's Hamburger Hafenbasar..22 A5
High Flyer Hot-Air-Balloon........23 H5
Kapitän Prüsse........24 C5
Krameramtswohnungen........25 D5
Millerntor-Stadion........26 B3
Museum für Hamburgische Geschichte........27 C4
Rathaus........28 F4
Rickmer Rickmers........29 C5
Rote Flora........30 B2
Speicherstadtmuseum........31 G6
Spicy's Gewürzmuseum........32 F6
St Michaeliskirche........33 D5
St-Nikolai-Kirche........34 F5

SLEEPING
DJH Hostel........35 C5
East........36 B4
Etap Hotel........37 B4
Fritz Hotel........38 B1
Home Company........39 A1
Hotel Bellmoor........(see 40)
Hotel Fresena........40 E1
Hotel Hafen........41 C5
Hotel SIDE........42 E3
Hotel St Annen........43 B3
Instant Sleep Backpacker Hostel..44 A1
Kogge........45 A5
Park Hyatt........46 G4
Raffles Hotel Vier Jahreszeiten..47 F3
Schanzenstern........48 B2

EATING
Balutschi........49 D1
Bok........50 B2
Café Paris........51 F4
Chilli Club........52 F6
Deichgraf........53 E5
Die Bank........54 E4
Die Herren Simpel........55 A1
East........(see 36)
Erikas Eck........56 B2
Fleetschlösschen........57 G5
Kumpir........(see 38)
Made in Portugal........58 A1
Shikara Quick........59 B1
Sushi for Friends........60 F4
Thai Cowboys........61 B1
'Ti Breizh........62 E5

DRINKING
Central Park........63 A1
Dual........64 B1
Meanie Bar/Molotow Club........65 B4
Nachtasyl........(see 85)
Nouar........(see 44)
StrandPauli........66 B5
Tower Bar........(see 41)
Zoë 2/Summun Bonum........67 B2

ENTERTAINMENT
3001........68 B2
Angie's Nightclub........69 B5
Astra Stube........70 A2
Cult........71 A4
Docks........72 B5
EDK........73 B5
Frauencafé endlich........74 D3
Funky Pussy Club........75 A4
Grosse Freiheit 36/ Kaiserkeller........76 A4
Knust im Schlachthof........77 B3
Logo........78 E1
Musicaltheater im Hafen........79 C6
Musikhalle........80 E3
Operettenhaus........81 B4
Quatsch Comedy Club im Café Keese........82 B4
Schmidt Theater........83 B5
Staatsoper........84 E3
Thalia Theater........85 G4

TRANSPORT
Rathaus Bus Station........86 F4

symbol, stretching as they do to Baumwall in the world's largest continuous warehouse complex. Their neo-Gothic gables and (mostly) green copper roofs are reflected in the narrow canals of this free-port zone.

Such a separate free port became necessary when Hamburg joined the German Customs Federation on signing up for the German Reich in 1871. An older neighbourhood was demolished – and 24,000 people displaced – to make room for the construction of the Speicherstadt from 1885 to 1927.

Today, the area can be appreciated in several ways. Firstly, you can simply wander through its streets. Alternatively, you can look down on it from Hamburg's moored **High Flyer Hot-Air-Balloon** (☎ 3008 6968; www.highflyer-hamburg.de; per 15min €15; 🕒 10am-midnight, to 10pm in winter), just across the water near the Deichtorhallen.

However, perhaps the best way to enjoy the district is to take a *Barkassen* (small barge) trip up its canals. **Kapitän Prüsse** (☎ 313 130; www.kapitaen-pruesse.de; Landungsbrücken 3; adult/child €12/6) offers regular Speicherstadt tours, leaving from the port. Other *Barkassen* operators simply tout for business opposite the archipelago, near Hohe Brücke. The area is beautifully lit at night.

In the postindustrial age, many of the warehouses have been put to a secondary use, and there are now some eight Speicherstadt museums, including the following:

Dialog im Dunkeln (Dialogue in Darkness; Map pp656-7; ☎ 0700-443 3200; www.dialog-im-dunkeln.de; Alter Wandrahm; adult/concession €10/7; 🕒 9am-5pm Tue-Fri, noon-7pm Sat & Sun) A pitch-black journey with a blind guide through re-created natural and urban landscapes gives a memorable impression of what it's like not to see.

Hamburg Dungeon (Map pp656-7; ☎ information 3600 5500, tickets 3005 1512; Kehrwieder 2; adult/child €13.95/10.95; 🕒 11am-6pm last entry, from 10am Jul & Aug) The usual camped-up chamber of horrors.

Speicherstadtmuseum (Map pp656-7; ☎ 321 191; St Annenufer 2; adult/concession €2.50/1.50; 🕒 10am-5pm Tue-Sun) Relating the area's history (in German).

Spicy's Gewürzmuseum (Map pp656-7; ☎ 367 989; Am Sandtorkai 32; adult/concession €3/2; ☺ 10am-5pm Tue-Sun) This spice and herb museum invites you to exercise your olfactory sense to the fullest.

HafenCity

The Speicherstadt merges into Europe's biggest building site, otherwise known as **HafenCity**. Here a long-abandoned area of 155 hectares is being redeveloped with restaurants, shops, apartments and offices in an enormous inner-city regeneration project. In the next 20 years, it's planned that some 40,000 people will work and 12,000 will live here. There are even plans for a primary school and a university.

The jewel in the crown should be ready much sooner, however, as early as 2009. If you walk to the back of the Speicherstadt and keep going along Grosser Grasbrook, you'll see it. The squat brown-brick former warehouse at the far west of the zone is being transformed into the new **Elbphilharmonie** (Elbe Philharmonic Hall). Pritzker prize-winning Swiss architects Herzog & de Meuron are responsible for the design, which, like their Tate Modern building in London, boasts a glass top. This time, however, they're being far more ambitious, as the glass façade should be taller than its brick base and the roofline will rise in wave-like peaks to reflect the waterfront location. Boosters are already comparing it to the Museo Guggenheim Bilbao and the Sydney Opera House.

For information on this and other plans for the district, pop into the **HafenCity Info-Center** (☎ 3690 1799; www.hafencity.com; Am Sandtorkai 30; admission free; ☺ 10am-6pm Tue-Sun), where you'll find brochures (in German and English), and architectural models and installations, as well as a café. And if travel podcasts are all the rage (at least among publishers), the Hafen-City InfoCenter offers one that's quite trippy and unusual. **Hafenklang** is a 55-minute MP3 'soundscape' tour through HafenCity's streets. The loan of the MP3 player is free, but you need to leave your passport as a deposit.

Port of Hamburg

South of St Pauli lies one of the largest ports in Europe. Each year about 12,000 ships deliver and take on some 70 million tonnes of goods here. The port sprawls over 75 sq km, accounting for 12% of Hamburg's entire surface area.

Climbing the steps above the Landungsbrücken U/S-Bahn station to the Stintfang stone balcony offers an interesting snapshot, while dozens of **port and Elbe River cruises** put you right in the middle of the action. They start at the St Pauli Landungsbrücken. **Abicht** (☎ 317 8220; www.abicht.de; Brücke 1; adult/child €10/5; ☺ noon Mar-Nov) offers English commentary, while one of the cheapest operators is **Hadag** (☎ 311 7070; www.hadag.de; Brücke 2; adult/child 1hr harbour trip from €9/4.50).

At the piers, you'll also find the **Rickmer Rickmers** (☎ 319 5959; www.rickmer-rickmers.de; Brücke 1; adult/concession €3/2.50; ☺ 10am-6pm), a three-masted steel windjammer from 1896 that is now a museum ship and restaurant. The 10,000-tonne **Cap San Diego** (☎ 364 209; adult/child €4/2) nearby hosts some interesting temporary exhibitions on immigration and shipping.

Just west of the St Pauli landing piers stands a grey structure topped by a copper cupola. This is the entrance to the **St Pauli Elbtunnel** (1911), a 426m-long passageway beneath the Elbe River. It is still used by vehicles and pedestrians, although most cars take the New Elbe Tunnel further west.

Reeperbahn

Sex sells, and they're hyper-aware of this along Hamburg's vast red-light thoroughfare of the **Reeperbahn**. Sure, it's tamer than the Amsterdam scene, but it's still Europe's biggest – a kind of Champs-Elysées of sex shops, peep shows, dim bars, raucous clubs and in-the-gutter-looking-at-the-stars life stories.

It slowly starts to awaken about 4pm, and over the next few hours crowds of thousands stream in (see boxed text, p661).

Just north of the S-Bahn station is the **Grosse Freiheit** (literally 'great freedom') street, with its bright lights, dark doorways and live sex nightclubs. Smarmy doormen try to lure the passing crowd into clubs; if you're interested, ask about the conditions of entry. Admission tends to be fairly low (around €5), but it's the mandatory drink minimum (usually at least €20) that drives up the cost. Ask at the bar how much drinks cost; we've heard reports of people being charged nearly €100 for a couple of watery cocktails.

South of the Reeperbahn stands the **David-wache** (Map pp656-7; Spielbudenplatz 31, cnr Davidstrasse). This brick building festooned with ornate ceramic tiles is the base for 150 police officers,

---

THE BEST HAMBURG BOAT TRIP?

Hamburg offers so many boat trips, it's difficult to know which to choose. Certainly, highlights include tours of the canals of the Alster lakes and *Barkassen* trips up the Speicherstadt. However, locals will tell you that you don't have to book a cruise to see the port – the city's harbour ferries will take you up the river on a cheap and ordinary public transport ticket.

One oft-recommended route is to catch ferry 62 from Landungsbrücken towards Finkenwerder and change there for the 64 to Teufelsbrücke. From here you can wander along the Elbe back towards town, eastwards to Neumühlen.

Stop for a drink at Strandperle (p673) or book a meal beforehand at Das Weisse Haus (p672) or Le Canard Nouveau (p672). From Neumühlen, you can catch bus 112 back to Altona S- and U-Bahn station or ferry 62 back to Landungsbrücken.

---

who maintain St Pauli's reputation as the safest area in Hamburg.

People gather outside the nearby **Condomerie** (Spielbudenplatz 18), with its extensive collection of prophylactics and sex toys. They're usually gawping at the gargantuan (and nowadays slightly grubby) condom in the window, to which the shop owner has appended a €100 gift voucher offer to any gentleman who can properly fit it. They say the prize has been awarded twice. Ouch.

Some 50m south along Davidstrasse, you'll see a painted tin wall on the right. This bars views into **Herbertstrasse**, a block-long bordello that's off-limits to men under 18 and to women of all ages.

Further west lies **Harry's Hamburger Hafenbasar** (☎ 312 482; www.hafenbasar.de; cnr Balduinstrasse & Erichstrasse; adult/child €2.50/1.50, redeemable against any purchase; ⌚ noon-6pm Tue-Sun) bursting with African statues, Asian masks and other paraphernalia shipped back from abroad by now deceased collector Harry Rosenberg. The shop is now run by his daughter; ask her about insider tours, in English, of the secrets of the St Pauli district.

The **Erotic Art Museum** (☎ 317 4757; www.erotic artmuseum.de; Bernhard-Nocht-Strasse 69; adult/concession €8/5; ⌚ noon-10pm, to midnight Fri & Sat) does exactly what it says on the tin: presents erotic art from S&M to (mainly) soft porn.

Schanzenviertel & Karolinenviertel

North of St Pauli lie the **Schanzenviertel** and **Karolinenviertel** districts. Once home to Hamburg's counterculture scene, they have been gentrified in recent years. You'll probably visit this area (bordered by the U-Bahn Feldstrasse, S-/U-Bahn Sternschanze and Stresemannstrasse) because you're staying here, shopping or enjoying one of its restaurants or bars. However, if you just want to explore, you'll find two lively quarters, where creative media types mix with students among a landscape of doner kebab shops, Italian and Portuguese cafés and funky clothing stores.

One of the most outstanding remnants of the area's rougher days is the graffiti-covered building on Schulterblatt that looks one step away from demolition. This is the **Rote Flora**, now an alternative culture centre, but once the famous Flora Theatre.

Blankenese

The people of Hamburg say that the better you're doing in life, the further west in the city you live. If those who reside in Övelgönne are making it, those in **Blankenese** (☒ Blankenese, then bus 48 to Krögers Treppe or Weseberg) have arrived. Once a former fishing village and haven for cut-throats, the suburb now boasts some of the finest and most expensive houses in Germany.

For visitors, the area's attraction lies in its hillside labyrinth of narrow, cobbled streets, with a network of **58 stairways** (4864 steps in total!) connecting them.

The best views of the Elbe (nearly 3km wide here) and the container ships putting out to sea are enjoyed from the 75m-high **Süllberg** hill (head through the restaurant at the summit).

Getting off bus 48 at Weseberg – having passed the clutch of beachfront restaurants and cafés and reached the summit of the following hill – you'll see a sign pointing to the nearby Süllberg. If you alight at Krögers Treppe, head up the Bornholldt Treppe and Süllbergweg. Alternatively, you can get off once the road starts winding and just explore.

SEX AND THE HANSEATIC CITY

Even those not interested in strip shows usually pay a quick trip to the Reeperbahn just to see what the fuss is all about. You can certainly imagine writers like Charles Bukowski (*Post Office, Tales of Ordinary Madness*), Nelson Algren (*Walk on the Wild Side*) and Damon Runyon (*Guys & Dolls*) giving it the treatment. It has the seedy, lowlife quality needed.

On a busy night there might be as many as 40,000 people cruising the rip-roaring collection of bars, sex clubs, variety acts, restaurants, pubs and cafés collectively known as the 'Kiez'. The abstemious and celibate St Paul, for whom Hamburg's 'sin centre' is named, wouldn't have taken kindly to such displays, but the sightseers come from all walks of life.

Long established as a party place for incoming sailors, the area's popularity peaked in the swinging 1960s when the Beatles cut their musical teeth at the legendary – now defunct – Star Club. Prostitution boomed along the lurid, spidery streets spilling off the Reeperbahn. But then a wave of hard crime and drugs sent St Pauli on a downward spiral, and rip-offs became commonplace (with cheap wine served from expensive bottles, as just one example). Germany's *Sündenmeile* (Sin Mile) had to reinvent itself to survive – which it did.

The answer, as always in Hamburg, was greater commercialisation, as another layer of attractions was added as the No 1 attraction for tourists. In recent years, musicals like *Cats* and *Mamma Mia* have played to sold-out houses on the eastern edge, and stylish nightclubs, bars and even restaurants keep a hip, moneyed clientele entertained until dawn.

The sex industry is still in full swing as girls line up along some streets. However, some of the rougher edges are gone; for example, pimps no longer loiter and leer. With its flashing neon lights and raucous crowds, the Reeperbahn today seems nothing more than a nightly carnival to some visitors. For others, it's a place to observe the *Taxi Driver* underbelly of Germany's wealthiest city.

Museums

The Hamburger **Kunsthalle** (Map p665; ☎ 428 131 200; www.hamburger-kunsthalle.de; Glockengiesserwall; adult/concession €8.50/5; ☺ 10am-6pm Tue, Wed & Fri-Sun, to 9pm Thu) consists of two buildings – one old, one new – linked by a memorable underground passage. The main building houses works ranging from medieval portraiture to 20th-century classics, such as Klee, Kokoschka and Munch. There's also a memorable room of 19th-century landscapes by Caspar David Friedrich. The stark white new building, the **Galerie der Gegenwart** (Map p665) showcases German artists like Rebecca Horn, Georg Baselitz and Gerhard Richter, alongside international stars like Nan Goldin, David Hockney, Jeff Koons, Barbara Kruger and Gillian Wearing. The view out of the gallery's huge picture windows is also wonderful.

The **Museum für Kunst und Gewerbe** (Museum of Arts & Crafts; Map p665; ☎ 428 542 732; www.mkg-hamburg.de; Steintorplatz 1, St Georg; adult/concession €8/5, from 4pm Tue & 5pm Thu €5; ☺ 10am-6pm Tue, Wed & Fri-Sun, to 9pm Thu) isn't quite so exalted, but its posters, ornaments and temporary exhibitions are always lots of fun. Its vast collection of sculpture, furniture, jewellery, porcelain, musical instruments and household objects runs the gamut from Italian to Islamic, from Japanese to Viennese and from medieval to pop art eye-candy.

There are period rooms, including an Art Nouveau salon from the 1900 Paris World Fair and a room designed by Belgian architect Henry van de Velde, plus sections on modern poster design, graphic design and Italian design from the 1950s to 1990s (with Bakelite, space age–shaped TVs!). The museum café is integrated into the exhibition space.

The **Museum für Völkerkunde** (Museum of Ethnology; ☎ 01805-308 888; www.voelkerkundemuseum.com; Rothenbaumchaussee 64; adult/concession €6/3, Fri €3/3; ☺ 10am-6pm Tue, Wed & Fri-Sun, to 9pm Thu; ☻ Hallerstrasse) demonstrates seagoing Hamburg's acute awareness of the outside world. The exhibits themselves are stunning, particularly the domed room at the top of the entrance hall's steps, with its carved wooden canoes and giant sculptures from Papua New Guinea. The approach is also refreshingly open-minded and not at all patronising. Modern artefacts and issues from Africa, Asia and the South Pacific are presented alongside traditional masks, jewellery, costumes and musical instruments. There's also a complete, intricately carved Maori meeting hall open from 1.30pm.

HAMBURG

HAMBURG'S UNIQUE FISH MARKET

Every Sunday morning, in the wee hours, an unusual ritual unfolds along the banks of the Elbe, just a few hundred metres south of the Reeperbahn. A fleet of small trucks roars onto the cobbled pavement. Hardy types with hands the size of baseball gloves emerge from the drivers' cabins and set out to turn their vehicles into stores on wheels. They artfully arrange their bananas, apples, cauliflower and whatever else the earth has yielded that week. Others pile up slippery eels, smoked fish fillets and fresh shrimp in tasteful displays. In another corner, cacti, flowers and leafy plants begin to wait for customers. It's not yet 5am as the first of them begin to trundle in, their brains boozy, their eyes red, their moods hyper from a night of partying in St Pauli. May the trading begin.

The Fischmarkt in St Pauli has been a Hamburg institution since 1703 and still defines the city's life and spirit. Locals of every age and walk of life join curious tourists as the beer flows, and you can buy everything from cheap sweatshirts and tulips to a hearty breakfast or a scorched bratwurst.

The undisputed stars of the event – and great, free entertainment – are the boisterous *Marktschreier* (market criers) who hawk their wares at the top of their lungs. With lascivious winks and leering innuendo, characters like Aal-Dieter or Banana-Harry boast of the quality and size of their product. 'Don't be shy, little girl,' they might say to a rotund 60-year-old, waggling a piece of eel in front of her face. But nobody minds the vulgar come-ons. Almost always, the 'girl' blushes before taking a hearty bite as the crowd cheers her on. It's all just part of the show.

More entertainment takes place in the adjoining Fischauktionshalle (Fish Auction Hall), where a live band cranks out cover versions of ancient German pop songs to which everyone seems to know the words. Down in the pit, the beer flows and sausage fumes waft through the air as if it were 8pm and not just past dawn. For those who actually know what time it is, breakfast is served on the gallery, away from the crooners.

Hamburg life thrives here – at the edge of the river – in the good stink of mud and oil and fish. If Bruegel were to paint a picture of Hamburg life, this is where he'd set up his easel.

The Fischmarkt takes place from 5am to 9.30am on Sunday (from 7am October to March).

The **Museum für Hamburgische Geschichte** (Museum of Hamburg History; Map pp656–7; ☎ 428 412 380; www.hamburgmuseum.de; Holstenwall 24; adult/concession €7.50/4, Fri €4/4; ⏰ 10am-5pm Tue-Sat, to 6pm Sun) is a bit of a boy's own dream. It's chock-full of intricate ship models, has a large model-train set (only open at certain times; ring ahead) and even includes the actual bridge of the steamship *Werner*, which you can clamber over. Furthermore, it chronicles the city's evolution, revealing little titbits about its Masonic societies and the fact that the Reeperbahn was once the home of ropemakers (*Reep* means rope). Most exhibits have English annotations.

The **Museum der Arbeit** (Museum of Work; ☎ 428 322 364; Maurienstrasse 19; adult/concession €4/3, Fri half-price; ⏰ 1-9pm Mon, 10am-5pm Tue-Sat, 10am-6pm Sun; ⊕ 2 & 3 to Barmbek, ⊠ 1 to Barmbek) chronicles the development of the workplace in the Hamburg area, with a focus on the changing rights and roles of working men and women. There's also a section on printing, appropriate for this media city. The museum is on the grounds of the former New York-Hamburg Rubber Company.

Keep an eye out for special exhibitions in the other smaller museums along Hamburg's **Kunstmeile** (Art Mile), extending from Glockengiesserwall to Deichtorstrasse between the Alster lakes and the Elbe. In particular, the converted market halls of the wonderful **Deichtorhallen** (Map pp656–7; ☎ 321 030; Deichtorstrasse 1-2; ⏰ 11am-6pm Tue-Fri, 10am-6pm Sat & Sun) show international touring exhibitions of contemporary art (Warhol, Lichtenstein, Haring etc) as well as photography by Helmut Newton, Annie Leibowitz and other prominent shooters.

Churches

The **St Michaeliskirche** (Map pp656–7; ☎ 3767 8100; adult/concession tower €2.50/1.25, tower & crypt €3/1.50; ⏰ 10am-5.30pm Apr-Oct, to 4.30pm Nov-Mar), or 'Der Michel' as it's commonly called, is one of Hamburg's most recognisable landmarks and northern Germany's largest Protestant baroque church. From its tower you can better understand the layout of this jigsaw city.

Below the church, in a tiny alley off Krayenkamp 10, are the **Krameramtswohnungen** (Map pp656-7; ☎ 3750 1988; adult/concession €1/0.50, Fri half-price; ☺ 10am-5pm Tue-Sun), a row of tiny half-timbered houses from the 17th century that, for nearly 200 years, were almshouses for the widows of members of the Guild of Small Shopkeepers. Taken over by the city in 1863, they became seniors' homes until 1969 and are now just a tourist attraction. Only one home is a museum; others are shops or restaurants.

The WWII-damaged **St-Nikolai-Kirche** (Map pp656-7; Ost-West-Strasse; adult/child €2.50/1.50; ☺ 11am-5pm) is now an antiwar memorial, with some chilling photos of the then bombed-out city.

Zoo & Parks

Hamburgers prefer not to call **Tierpark Hagenbeck** (☎ 5400 0147/8; Lokstedter Grenzstrasse 2, Hamburg-Stellingen; adult/child under 16yr €14.50/8.50; ☺ 9am-sunset; ⓘ Hagenbecks Tierpark) a zoo. That's because its 2500 animals are housed in very open enclosures spread across 27 hectares. It's not only elephants, tigers, orang-utans, toucans and other creatures you'll find here, either. There's a replica Nepalese temple, Japanese garden, Art Deco Tor (gate) and similar attractions. A petting zoo, horse-carriage rides and a children's playground mean you'll probably have to drag the kids away at the end of the day.

Closer to the centre is the much-loved **Planten un Blomen**, a landscaped park where there are water and light displays in summer.

ACTIVITIES

The paved path around the Aussenalster is a popular **jogging** route because it measures nearly exactly 8km, a handy guideline for those checking their performance. It's also suitable for **inline skating** or **cycling**.

Head to Dr Götze Land & Karte (p654) for a wide range of local cycling maps and itineraries. For bike hire, try **Fahrradladen St Georg** (Map p665; ☎ 243 908; Schmilinskystrasse 6).

Hamburg was one of the host cities for the FIFA Football World Cup in 2006, for which its **AOL Color Line Arena** (Sylvesterallee 7, Bahrenfeld) was extensively refurbished. Since declared a five-star stadium by FIFA, it boasts 51,000 fully covered seats and is home to Bundesliga club Hamburger SV.

The stadium lies in the city's northwest, just off the E45/7/27 by car. Alternatively, take S-Bahn 21 or 3 to 'Stellingen' (for the east and north terrace). From Altona station, take S-Bahn 1 or 11 to 'Othmarschen'. Free buses link these stations with the stadium.

Favourite local team FC St Pauli plays at home in the **Millerntor-Stadion** (Map pp656-7; ☎ tickets 3179 6112; Heiligengeistfeld).

TOURS
Alster Lake Cruises

Taking a cruise on Binnenalster and Aussenalster is not only one of the least stressful ways to appreciate the city, but also one of the most revealing, as you cruise past its elegant buildings. **ATG Alster-Touristik** (Map pp656-7; ☎ 3574 2419; www.alstertouristik.de; adult/child 2hr round-trip €10/5) offers regular trips from April to October. The company also offers a wonderful two-hour **canal tour** (€11; ☺ 3-6 times daily, depending on season), which floats past stately villas and gardens; and a two-hour **Fleet tour** (€13; ☺ 3 times daily Apr-Oct), which heads from the Binnenalster to the Elbe and Speicherstadt. Free English-language pamphlets and taped commentaries are available for the Alster and Fleet tours.

If you're the DIY kind, hire your own rowboat or canoe; some travellers tell us it's the most fun they've had in Hamburg. Head to **Segelschule Pieper** (Map p665; ☎ 247 578; www.segelschule-pieper.de; An der Alster; per hr from €12), opposite the Atlantic Hotel, or ask the tourist office about other rental outlets.

Bus Tours

As with boats, there is a confusing array of bus tours, although these aren't quite such a quintessential Hamburg experience. **Top-Tour Hamburg** (☎ 641 3731, 672 0394; www.top-tour-hamburg .de) offers a choice of four tours, the most popular being the eponymous **Top-Tour** (adult/child under 14yr €14/7; ☺ every 30min 9.30am-4.30pm, hourly in winter). This passes all the leading sights in a double-decker bus during jump-on, jump-off 1½-hour sightseeing tours. You can board at the Kirchenallee exit of the train station and Landungsbrücken, plus the Rathaus, St Michaeliskirche, the Reeperbahn or Speicherstadt. Commentary is in German and English.

HHB (☎ 792 8979; www.hummelbahn.de) offers much the same deal, but distinguishes itself with its vehicles, including red London double-decker buses and the 1920s **Hummelbahn Trolley** (adult/child under 12yr/teenager €13/free/11). Bus times are pretty much the same as for Top-Tour and you can board at the Kirchenallee exit of the train station or Landungsbrücken.

Ask the tourist office about other deals.

HAMBURG

FESTIVALS & EVENTS

While Hamburg is not a particularly festival-orientated city, the **Hafengeburtstag** (Harbour Birthday) is one enthusiastically celebrated highlight. It commemorates the day Emperor Barbarossa granted Hamburg customs exemption (see p654) and runs for five days from 7 May.

Another major event – or series of events – is the **Hamburger Dom**, held in late March, late July and late November. Established in 1329, it is one of Europe's largest and oldest fun fairs. Today, it's held on Heiligengeistfeld, between St Pauli and Schanzenviertel (site of the FIFA Fan Fest during the 2006 World Cup).

SLEEPING

Long-term room rentals should cost from €350 to €500 per month. Furnished apartments start at €500, including commission and tax (although this might increase soon). Agencies worth trying are **Bed & Breakfast** (☎ 491 5666; www.bed-and-breakfast.de; Müggenkampstrasse 35) and **HomeCompany** (Map pp656-7; ☎ 194 45; hamburg@homecompany.de; Schulterblatt 112).

Budget

ST GEORG

Hotel Pension Annenhof (Map p665; ☎ 243 426; www.hotelannenhof.de; Lange Reihe 23; s/d €40/70) Behind this place's grubby façade lie 13 simple but attractive rooms, with polished wooden floorboards and walls in different, bright colours. Even though a few have shower cabins rather than proper bathrooms, they're still a great deal. Breakfast isn't served, but there are dozens of cafés in this increasingly gentrified part of St Georg.

SCHANZENVIERTEL & ST PAULI

Instant Sleep Backpacker Hostel (Map pp656-7; ☎ 4318 2310; www.instantsleep.de; Max-Brauer-Allee 277; dm €15-20, s/d €28/44, linen €2; 🖵) Brightly painted murals, from green stripes to golden Buddhas, distract you from this place's relatively spartan surrounds. It's friendly, though, and handily located in the happening Schanzenviertel.

DJH hostel (Auf dem Stintfang; Map pp656-7; ☎ 313 488; www.jugendherberge.de/jh/hamburg-stintfang; Alfred-Wegener-Weg 5; dm €18.80-21.80, d €46.60; 🅿 🗙 🖵) Convenient, modern and clean, this large hostel overlooks the Elbe and the harbour from its newly refurbished lounge area. With lots of large, noisy school groups, however, it's very keen on security and rules, and you're

locked out part of the day during cleaning. The entrance is at the top of the 100 stairs from Landungsbrücken U-Bahn station. There's another DJH hostel in town (see www.jugendherberge.de/jh/hamburg-horn) but it's nowhere near as convenient.

Schanzenstern Altona (Map p671; ☎ 3991 9191; Kleine Rainerstrasse 24-26; dm €18, s/d/tr €40/60/75; 🗙 🖵) You'll like this place the moment you enter its cheery, light-infused reception. Large *National Geographic* prints decorate the yellow walls, while wooden chairs are painted in similar parrot colours. A mix of families and slightly more grown-up backpackers inhabit the sparklingly clean en suite rooms. (As a slight warning, though, there are no lockers.)

Schanzenstern (Map pp656-7; ☎ 439 8441; www.schanzenstern.de; Bartelsstrasse 12; dm €18, s/d/tr €36/52/62; 🗙 🖵) This is the original Schanzenstern, but its accommodation is more worn than its Altona counterpart.

Kogge (Map pp656-7; ☎ 312 872; www.kogge-hamburg.de; Bernhard-Nocht-Strasse 59; s/d €30/50) Budget doesn't have to mean boring. At this quirkily themed rock'n'roll pub deep in noisy, grungy Reeperbahn territory, sleepyhead young partygoers can check out as late as 5pm from their 'Bollywood', 'Punk Royal', 'Erich Honecker' or other ingeniously decorated rooms.

Etap Hotel (Map pp656-7; ☎ 3176 5620; www.etaphotel.com; Simon-von-Utrecht-Strasse 64; s/d €44/52; 🖵) Two minutes from the Reeperbahn, this hotel is unusually central for this budget chain outlet.

UNIVERSITÄTSVIERTEL

Hadley's (☎ 417 871; www.bed-and-breakfast-hamburg.de; Beim Schlump 85; s/d with shared bathroom from €60/70, breakfast €5; 🅿 ; 🚇 Schlump) With mattresses set on tall mezzanine platforms, there's enough space for you to have your own living room in this B&B in a former hospital wing. In return, be prepared to climb a ladder into bed every evening. Shared bathrooms are lined with grey slate and there's a communal wine cooler fridge. While you can have breakfast in your room, Hadley's fantastic café (p670) is also on your doorstep.

ALTONA

Seemannsheim Altona (Seaman's Home Altona; ☎ 306 220; www.seemannsmission.de; Grosse Elbestrasse 132; s/d with shared bathroom €35/60) Christian sailors lodge here between trips and it's possible for you to stay too, overlooking the river at the start of the Elbmeile. Although its hostel-like rooms have become a little run-down recently, it's due to be progressively refurbished during 2007. Even some women stay here, but if you are female, do *not* confuse this with the Seemannsheim near St Michaeliskirche, which can feel intimidating. Take bus 112 to Fischmarkt.

OUT OF TOWN

Campingplatz Buchholz (☎ 540 4532; www.camping -buchholz.de; Kieler Strasse 274, Stellingen; per person/car €4.80/5, tent €8-11; ❸ Hagenbecks Tierpark) This small, family-run camping ground has decent washing facilities, lots of shade and now some private hotel rooms. It's well connected to the city. When driving, take the A45/E45 then exit 26 to Hamburg-Stellingen.

A & O Hostel (☎ 2104 0294; www.aohostel.com; Hammer Landstrasse 170; dm €12, breakfast €5, linen €3, s/d incl breakfast & linen €29/32; Ⓟ ✖ 🖳) Typical of the A & O chain – new and bland, but a trifle bland – this Hamburg branch has a slightly out-of-the-way location.

Midrange

ST GEORG

Hotel Village (Map p665; ☎ 480 6490; www.hotel -village.de; Steindamm 4; s €65-70, d €90-95) Tickle Hamburg's seedy underbelly in this edgy gem, wedged between the sex shops and leering of Steindamm. A former bordello going straight, its boudoirs feature various kitsch mixes of red velvet, gold flock wallpaper, leopard prints and sometimes even blue-neon-lit bathrooms

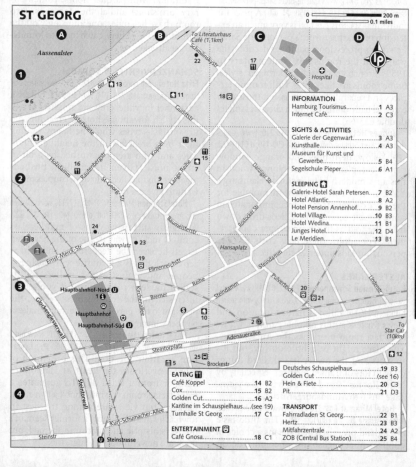

ST GEORG

0 ——— 200 m
0 ——— 0.1 miles

To Literaturhaus
Café (1.1km)

Aussenalster

Hospital

INFORMATION
Hamburg Tourismus....................1 A3
Internet Café.............................2 C3

SIGHTS & ACTIVITIES
Galerie der Gegenwart..................3 A3
Kunsthalle................................4 A3
Museum für Kunst und
  Gewerbe................................5 B4
Segelschule Pieper.......................6 A1

SLEEPING 🏠
Galerie-Hotel Sarah Petersen..........7 B2
Hotel Atlantic............................8 A2
Hotel Pension Annenhof.................9 B2
Hotel Village.............................10 B3
Hotel Wedina.............................11 B1
Junges Hotel.............................12 D4
Le Meridien..............................13 B1

EATING 🍴
Café Koppel..............................14 B2
Cox.......................................15 B2
Golden Cut...............................16 A2
Kantine im Schauspielhaus.........(see 19)
Turnhalle St Georg......................17 C1

ENTERTAINMENT 🎭
Café Gnosa..............................18 C1

Deutsches Schauspielhaus..............19 B3
Golden Cut............................(see 16)
Hein & Fiete.............................20 C3
Pit.......................................21 D3

TRANSPORT
Fahrradladen St Georg..................22 B1
Hertz.....................................23 B3
Mitfahrzentrale..........................24 A2
ZOB (Central Bus Station).............25 B4

To Star Car (10km)

Hauptbahnhof-Nord
Hauptbahnhof
Hauptbahnhof-Süd

Steinstrasse

HAMBURG

or mirrors above the bed. The place attracts a mix of gay and straight guests.

Hotel Wedina (Map p665; ☎ 280 8900; www.wedina .de; Gurlittstrasse 23; main bldg s/d from €70/90, others from €95/115; **P**) You might find a novel instead of a chocolate on your pillow at Wedina, a hotel that's a must for bookworms and literary groupies. Margaret Atwood, Jonathan Safran Foer, Jonathan Franzen, Michel Houellebecq, Vladimir Nabokov and J K Rowling are just some of the authors who've stayed and left behind signed books. Young and friendly, the hotel's spread over four buildings, offering a choice of traditional décor in the main red building or modern, urban living in its green, blue and yellow houses.

Galerie-Hotel Sarah Petersen (Map p665; ☎ 249 826, 0173 200 0746; www.galerie-hotel-sarah-petersen.de; Lange Reihe 50; s €70-140, d €85-150; 𝌆 🖵) A place for individualists, this *pension* is very much an extension of its artist owner's personality. Sarah Petersen's professional paintings decorate the walls, and the rooms mix contemporary to 1950s French to classic Biedermeier styles. Some rooms are like suites, with rooftop terraces and separate living areas, but those with external bathrooms are much cheaper (single/ double €55/65).

Junges Hotel (Map p665; ☎ 419 230; www.junges -hotel.de; Kurt-Schumacher-Allee 14; s €90-110, d €110-120; **P**) Yellow, flesh-pink and orange window panels complement lots of blonde wood in this airy, modern hotel (actually Hamburg's YMCA). However, it's most memorable for the way extra guests can be accommodated in some double rooms, where beds drop down from the wall as in a train sleeper compartment. For adults, these beds costs €25 per person, but kids under 12 stay free.

ALSTER LAKES

Hotel-Pension Schwanenwik (☎ 220 0918; www.hotel -schwanenwik.de; Schwanenwik 29; s/d €70/90, with shared bathroom €46/66) Enjoy a luxury location and views for less at this humble *pension*, whose breakfast room overlooks the Aussenalster. The place might be a little dowdy, but it's spotless and the owner has cheered things up with lots of framed pictures, especially by Miró. Rooms 19 and 20 also have lake views. Take bus 6 to Mundsburger Brücke.

Hotel Miramar (☎ 220 9395; www.hotelmiramar.de; Armgartstrasse 20; s/d €80/100; **P**) The little taste of England promised here means a choice of quintessential English rose or colonial décor,

plus the 50-something owners' irreverent sense of humour. It's a mix you'll either love or hate, but it has its confirmed fans. Bus 6 to Mundsburger Brücke will get you here.

Nippon (☎ 227 1140; www.nippon-hotel-hh.de; Hofweg 75; s/d from €95/115, breakfast €10) White walls, low futon beds, rice-paper screens, tatami flooring and occasional splashes of cherry red create a Zen recipe here. Take bus 6 to Zimmerstrasse.

Hotel Alsterblick (☎ 2294 8989; www.hotel-alsterblick .de; Schwanenwik 30; s €65-125, d €110-145, ste €160-180) Staff here take some pride in the stained-glass windows and historic lift in the entrance to this terrace building, and even more in the excellent lake view from the breakfast room. Accommodation blends modern and traditional with parquet floors, contemporary furnishings and all the mod cons. Two rooms have balconies, one amusingly off the bathroom. To get here, catch bus 6 to Mundsburger Brücke.

SCHANZENVIERTEL & ST PAULI

Fritz Hotel (Map pp656-7; ☎ 8222 2830; www.fritzhotel .com; Schanzenstrasse 101-103; s/d €60/90) Cool as a cucumber in white, grey and splashes of red, this stylish townhouse hotel is great for solo urbanistas – types who'll be happy finding their own breakfast in the neighbourhood cafés and who aren't perturbed by a bit of street noise. Given its smallish, pushed-together 'double' beds, though, couples might want to give it a miss.

Hotel St Annen (Map pp656-7; ☎ 3177130; www.stannen .de; Annenstrasse 5; s €80-100, d €90-140; **P** 𝌆 🖵) A slightly surprising oasis of middle-class comfort tucked away in one of the few quiet streets between the Reeperbahn and Schanzenviertel, this is a favourite with business-people and mainstream travellers for its stylish modern rooms. Even if you're not interested in the free business centre, the pleasant back garden and terrace make a perfect summer retreat.

Hotel Hafen (Map pp656-7; ☎ 311 1370; www.hotel -hamburg.de; Seewartenstrasse 9; r €100-200; **P**) Location, location, location. This behemoth of a hotel overlooks the heart of Hamburg's harbour from a small hill. To guarantee a front-facing room you must book a two-night package, but views are among the best in town. The main building, a former seaman's home, is historic and maritime-themed, but there are newer modern wings, too.

UNIVERSITÄTSVIERTEL

Schlafschön (☎ 4135 4949; www.schlafschoen.de; Monetastrasse 4; s with shared bathroom €55-75, d with shared bathroom €85; (P) ; ⊙ Schlump) Set in the same former hospital as Hadley's, albeit in another wing, this B&B mixes sunny beach-house colours with Turkish throws and Moroccan tiles. The centrepiece is the huge breakfast room, with a balcony overlooking the inner courtyard. Look for the door saying 'Schwesterhaus' on the left side of the street.

Hotel Fresena (Map pp656-7; ☎ 410 4892; www .hotelfresena.de; 3rd fl, Dammtorpalais, Moorweidenstrasse 34; s €60-80, d €82-106, tr €93-108, q €124-144, breakfast €9; (P) ✕) 'Fresena' sounds fresh and citrusy, and this tidy, well-kept hotel is. You're greeted with African sculptures and interesting photos, but the main impression is how nice the place smells (helped by a largely nonsmoking policy). Several people with minor physical and mental disabilities work here, and between them they speak German, English, French, Russian and North African Arabic.

Schlaflounge (☎ 3868 5387; www.schlaflounge.de; Vereinstrasse 54b; s/d €70/92; ✕ ; ⊙ Christuskirche) Live like a local in this stylish, streamlined B&B. With lots of blonde wood throughout and extremely attractive rooms in either brown and ochre or dark red and aqua, few guests find it necessary to stray far from home here. Organic fruit, homemade jam at breakfast and home-baked cakes on weekends are extra bonuses.

YoHo – The Young Hotel (☎ 284 1910; www.yoho -hamburg.de; Moorkamp 5; s/d €80/95, under 26yr €55/65, breakfast €10; (P)) The superlative YoHo could teach low-cost airline easyJet something about the use of orange. Its tasteful splashes – the winged retro chairs and walls in reception and the burnt-sienna blankets draped across the beds – don't detract from its minimalist feel. Rooms are Zen-like; the only outrageous eyecandy is found in its Syrian restaurant, Mazza, and the 'Occidental' breakfast room.

Hotel Bellmoor (☎ 413 3110; www.hotel-bellmoor .de; 4th fl, Dammtorpalais, Moorweidenstrasse 34; s/d €80/100; (P)) White embossed wallpaper and vintage advertising posters line the halls of this pleasant, traditional hotel. Amazingly, it used to be one apartment and many of the bedrooms have been converted from other uses. Singles really stand out here: rooms 14 and 34 in particular feature Art Nouveau-ish bathrooms with stained-glass windows and tiled tubs.

From the breakfast lounge there are good views over Hamburg's rooftops.

ALTONA

25 Hours (☎ 855 870; www.25hours-hotel.de; Paul-Dessau-Strasse 2; d under/over 26yr €61/101; (P) ✕ ; ⓡ 1 or 11 to Bahrenfeld) A budget design hotel aimed at a younger market, 25 Hours attracts many models and fashion types with its funky décor and upbeat atmosphere. The reception features bright pink chairs and a reception desk that looks like it's wearing a studded belt, but the rooms are a little less Barbie-meets-Barbarella, with white, blues and exposed concrete. The biggest drawback is the location, in a suburban business park. There's a fitness centre nearby, though.

Clipper Elb Lodge (☎ 809 010; www.clipper-hotels .de; Carsten-Rehder-Strasse 71; r from €120, with river view from €165; (P) ✕) These spacious designer apartments are kitted out with cream stone bathrooms, black kitchen cupboards and clever LCD TVs that swivel in the wall between the sleeping and living areas. As often happens in Hamburg though, if you're staying in a room at the front of the building, your gaze will be drawn outwards to the Elbe River at the start of the gastronomic Elbmeile. Take bus 112 to Fischmarkt to get here.

Top End

Gastwerk Hotel (☎ 890 620; www.gasthof-hotel.de; Beim Alten Gaswerk 3, Daimlerstrasse, Altona; r €130-170, breakfast €16; (P) ✕ ✕ ⊡ ⓡ) Hamburg's original design hotel is fashioned from a former gasworks, but warmly coloured furnishings and touches of humour – like the clock in reception stuck at five to 12 and the huge milling chute above the bar – offset the exposed steel and concrete. Located in a suburban business park, the place feels a little stranded, but it's fine if you have your own car or just want to cocoon. To get here, catch bus 2 from Altona to Stresemannstrasse.

Hotel SIDE (Map pp656-7; ☎ 309 990; www.side -hamburg.de; Drehbahn 49; r €190-230; (P) ✕) There's nothing shy and retiring about this Matteo Thun–designed beauty, from its eight-storey triangular atrium with colourful light strips to its pale minimalist rooms. Splashes of colour are found in the suites' bathtubs (variously yellow, green-blue or blood-red) and the 1950s-style saucers-from-outer-space sofas strewn across the 8th-floor lounge.

Raffles Hotel Vier Jahreszeiten (Map pp656-7; ☎ 349 40; www.raffles-hvj.de; Neuer Jungfernstieg 9-14; s €220-295, d €270-345, ste €475-4000, breakfast €14-22; P ✗ ✗ ⌨) This venerable hotel's fame stretches well beyond the shores of the Binnenalster, which it overlooks. With bags of history, it hasn't forgotten to move with the times. Its classic rooms were recently refurbished, while the 100-year-old *Wohnhalle*, where Hamburg society takes afternoon tea, is getting some competition from its own trendy Doc Cheng's restaurant.

Hotel Atlantic (Map p665; ☎ 288 80; www.kempinski .atlantic.de; An der Alster 72-79; r per person from €155, breakfast €22; P ✗ ✗ ⌨) Imagine yourself aboard a luxury ocean liner in this see-and-be-seen grand hotel. Built for cruise passengers, it has ornate stairwells, wide hallways and subtle maritime touches. 'Modernised' rooms – still classic-looking – are a big leap up from the standard accommodation. There are BMW and James Bond suites.

Other recommendations:

Le Meridien (☎ 210 00; www.lemeridien.com; An der Alster 52-56; r from €210 P ✗ ✗ ⌨) The 'chic' design here is pretty ho-hum formulaic, but the restaurant's front-row lake views are mesmerising, and the beds famously comfortable.

Park Hyatt (Map pp656-7; ☎ 3332 1234; www .hamburg.park.hyatt.de; Bugenhagenstrasse 8; s/d from €185/210; P ✗ ✗ ⌨) Huge horizontal spaces make up for the low ceilings in this exquisite, Asian-feeling hotel tucked away in a central *Kontorhaus* (an old-fashioned name for a certain type of clinker-brick office building).

EATING
City Centre

Sushi for Friends (Map pp656-7; ☎ 2091 1000; Ballindamm; sushi plates €3-11; ☽ lunch & dinner Mon-Fri, dinner Sat & Sun) Handy after an Alster cruise or some shopping around Jungfernstieg, this restaurant serves spicy-tuna-and-rocket rolls, mango chutney sushi and other innovative

Japanese dishes. Stay downstairs, where it's all white leather banquettes and dark wood – although the colourful cushions strewn across the mezzanine area look enticing, it can get muggy up there, especially in summer.

Café Paris (Map pp656-7; ☎ 3252 7777; Rathausstrasse 4; mains €6.50-15) This otherwise quintessentially French brasserie has a very 'Hamburg' lid in the form of its spectacular maritime-and-industry-themed ceiling murals. Come to admire its Art Deco interior and busy but down-to-earth atmosphere.

Die Bank (Map pp656-7; ☎ 238 0030; Hohe Bleichen 17; mains €16-28; ☽ closed Sun) Hamburg's most *schmicki-micki* (chichi) downtown eatery is about conspicuous consumption – of 'banker's platters' (prawns, crabs, more prawns and lobster) and 'Bourse toast' (salmon tartare, poached egg, potato purée and caviar). The bar's huge sepia photo of piles of coins had us thinking we'd stumbled back into the 1980s, but the marble columns, lofty ceiling and generally opulent surrounds do impress, and the place buzzes even on a Monday night. Some comfort dishes, such as Wiener schnitzel and *pot au feu* (beef and vegetable stew), are on the menu, too.

St Georg

Kantine im Schauspielhaus (Map p665; ☎ 2487 1239; Kirchenallee 39; meals €4.50-6.50; ☽ noon-3pm Mon-Fri) There's as much theatre in this cheap, bustling basement restaurant as there is on the stage in the theatre above, as waiters patrol between the tables calling out ready orders of cheap pasta, salad or meat, and thespians gossip between rehearsals.

Café Koppel (Map p665; ☎ 249 235; Lange Reihe 66; dishes €3.50-7.50) Set back from busy Lange Reihe, with a garden in summer, this largely veggie café is a refined oasis where you can hear the tinkling of spoons in coffee cups mid-morning on the mezzanine floor (although they're *still*

THE AUTHOR'S CHOICE

East (Map pp656-7; ☎ 309 930; www.east-hamburg.de; Simon-von-Utrecht-Strasse 31; r €150-375, breakfast €14; P ✗) Even those who've seen a few design hotels in their time will be impressed by East. Not for it the oft-used template of pale colours and minimalist lines, or the attention-grabbing device of bright retro hues. Rather the walls, lamps and huge pillars of this hotel's public areas all tastefully emulate organic forms – droplets, flowers, trees – giving it an incredibly warm, rich and enveloping feel. Floors are themed by plants and spices, and rooms have open bathroom areas, divided off by flowing curtains. Its Japanese garden and sunken restaurant (p670) are simply stunning.

playing the Buena Vista Social Club some evenings!). The menu includes great breakfasts, lots of salads, stews, jacket potatoes, curries and pasta.

Turnhalle St Georg (Map p665; ☎ 2800 8480; Lange Reihe 107; mains €12-20) Intimate is not a word you could use for this converted gymnasium of a local girls' school, but you still sometimes have trouble getting a seat. Exercise rings and ropes remain hanging from one of the thick white beams under the vaulted A-line roof, but designer lampshades and huge, potted trees have been added to the mix. The happy crowd tucks into modern international cuisine.

Golden Cut (Map p665; ☎ 8510 3532; Holzdamm 61; sushi €2.50-13, mains €13-25; ☉ dinner Mon-Sat) Hamburg scenesters love this restaurant for three reasons. Firstly, the well-executed menu runs the gamut from carrot-coconut soup with baked black tiger prawns in tempura to French black pudding with truffles. Secondly, patrons can show off in the high-ceilinged room with its olive-green leather chairs and copper-plated leaf chandeliers. Thirdly, and most importantly, they can bypass the strict person on the door and walk straight into the exclusive adjoining club (p673).

Cox (Map p665; ☎ 249 422; Lange Reihe 68; mains lunch €9-12, dinner €16-20; ☉ closed lunch Sat & Sun) This upmarket French-style bistro was in the vanguard of the gentrification of sleazy St Georg, and some long-term residents find it a bit snobby. Even they will admit, though, that the changing menu is delicious. Dishes include things like red snapper with basil pesto and Provençale potato salad, or veal in balsamic *jus* with ratatouille and gnocchi.

Alster Lakes

Literaturhaus Café (☎ 220 1300; Schwanenwik 38; dishes €4-15, 3-course menus from €21) If you're strolling around the Outer Alster, don't forget to stroll in here, where creaky parquet floors lead you to a slightly shabby but spectacular baroque café. It's like a charming old Viennese coffee house, with golden walls, cherubs, marble columns, huge chandeliers and leafy garden views. Bistro fare – antipasto, risotto, tarts, salads and roasts – is served.

Port & Speicherstadt

Fleetschlösschen (Map pp656-7; ☎ 3039 3210; Brooktorkai 17; snacks €4-7.50; ☉ 11am-6pm) One of the cutest little cafés you ever saw, this former customs post overlooks a Speicherstadt canal and has a narrow, steel spiral staircase to the toilets. There's barely room for 20 inside, but its several outdoor seating areas are brilliant in sunny weather. Hamburg is into *Kleinods* (small treasures, in this case buildings) at the moment, and this one is the business.

Ti Breizh (Map pp656-7; ☎ 3751 7815; Deichstrasse 39; mains €5-11; ☉ closed Mon) Even if you don't like crepes, this simple Breton restaurant will have you thinking you do. Tuck into a thin, delicious savoury number folded into a perfect square.

Chilli Club (Map pp656-7; ☎ 3570 3580; Am Sandtorkai 54; dishes €4-20) This trendy noodle bar is tucked away in the industrial-looking HafenCity. Asian tapas, dim sum and sushi are also served within the restaurant's red-and-black interior. Main meals are served at dinner only.

Schanzenviertel & St Pauli

Made in Portugal (Map pp656-7; ☎ 4319 0991; Schulterblatt 3; snacks €0.60-3.50; ☉ 8am-8pm) The Schanzenviertel teems with Portuguese eateries, especially around the 'piazza' just to the south of this tiny tiled café. This place produces the creamiest custard tarts, as well as simple snacks.

Die Herren Simpel (Map pp656-7; ☎ 3868 4599; Schulterblatt 75; dishes €4-8) The sky-blue mural with huge white flowers has become this café's signature. Its tiny entrance opens into an unexpectedly spacious series of retro rooms, plus a small winter garden niche. The range of breakfasts, from the fishy *Sylter* (from Sylt) to the healthy *Frucht* (fruit), is fantastic, and there are also sandwiches and light meals on offer.

EEL SOUP, ANYONE?

As in any port city, Hamburg's restaurants offer an international mix, which is lucky because the local specialities are something of an acquired taste. More adventurous gourmands might like to sample *Labskaus*, a dish of boiled marinated beef put through the grinder with mashed potatoes and herring and served with a fried egg, red beets and pickles. Or perhaps you'd prefer *Aalsuppe* (eel soup) spiced with dried fruit, ham, vegetables and herbs? **Deichgraf** (Map pp656-7; ☎ 364 208; Deichstrasse 23; mains €14-22; ☉ lunch Mon-Sat, dinner Sat) is one leading local restaurant that can acquaint you with these and other local dishes.

Erikas Eck (Map pp656-7; ☎ 433 545; Sternstrasse 98; mains €5.50-10; ⏲ 7-2pm Mon-Fri, 7pm-9am Sat, midnight-9am Sun) Traditional, wood-lined Erikas has been serving up red-eye specials since the golden oldies always on its radio were first-time hits. Fare includes schnitzels, herrings and *Schweinebraten* (roast pork), and an array of breakfasts – the *belegte Brötchen* (sandwiches) plus accompaniments – from midnight.

Bok (Map pp656-7; ☎ 4318 3597; Schulterblatt 3; mains €9-15) What the famous Wagamama is to London, Bok is to the Schanzenviertel. A local mini-chain, it has at least four outlets, however, this one has the nicest ambience. The food is mild and aimed at German palates; duck makes a frequent appearance on the pan-Asian (Thai, Korean and Japanese) menu.

East (Map pp656-7; ☎ 309 930; Simon-von-Utrecht-Strasse 31; mains €18-22.50; ⏲ lunch & dinner Mon-Fri, dinner Sat & Sun) This design hotel's euro-Asian restaurant is its most breathtaking feature. Huge fat white columns, slightly wavy and striated like trees, stretch from the basement floor to the high ceiling above the mezzanine Yakshi's bar. Private lounges are hidden in the white honeycomb wall.

Universitätsviertel

Hadley's (☎ 450 5075; Beim Schlump 84a; dishes €4.50-9; ⓟ Schlump) It's hard to believe this warm, enveloping café was once an ER (emergency room). Through the door curtains, there's a subtle retro mix of olive-green, brown and sienna-coloured fabric lampshades, but the most eye-catching feature is the sunken winter garden, where a buffet breakfast is laid out on Sundays.

Balutschi (Map pp656-7; ☎ 452 479; Grindelallee 33; meals €7.50-14) Out the back here, there's an over-the-top *Arabian Nights*-style grotto, where

you remove your shoes and sit on carpets and low benches. At lunch (specials around €5), however, most customers seem to devour the very tasty Pakistani cuisine at tables in the more plain main room.

Vienna (☎ 439 9182; Fettstrasse 2; mains €8.50-19; ⏲ bistro service from 2pm, meals from 7pm Tue-Sun) Neighbours whisper proudly that this is Hamburg's best German-Austrian restaurant. Even though it looks like a French country-cottage restaurant, particularly with the overgrown garden hiding its outdoor terrace, the schnitzels, venison and fish are distinctly authentic.

Altona

Schweizweit (Map p671; ☎ 3990 7000; Grosse Rainstrasse 2; mains €4.50-13; ⏲ closed Mon dinner) The strong smell of Swiss cheese might alert you to this small basement bistro's presence before you spot it. Watched over by a cable-car triptych (more *Wallpaper** than Heidi), you can enjoy its changing noodle and meat dishes, as well as delicious homemade chocolate mousse.

Filmhauskneipe (Map p671; ☎ 393 467; Friedensallee 9; mains €6-11) This relaxed café-cum-bistro wouldn't be out of place on Paris' left bank, with its arty clientele and simple but wholesome food.

Eisenstein (Map p671; ☎ 390 4606; Friedensallee 9; mains €17.50) This hip international restaurant inside Altona's Zeisehallen is a postmodern symphony of stone, steel and wood wrapped around the brick chimney of an old ship propeller factory. The menu runs the gamut from homemade pasta to fish couscous.

The 'Elbmeile'

In the last few years, Hamburg's western riverfront, from Altona to Övelgönne, has metamorphosed into one of Germany's hottest

---

CHEAP EATS IN THE SCHANZE

The streets of the Schanzenviertel are lined with so many restaurants it's impossible for us to cover even a tenth of them, really. However, if you're on a budget, walk along Susannenstrasse in particular, or Schulterblatt and Schanzenstrasse, and you're sure to find something you like. Seriously cheap eateries include the following:

■ **Kumpir** (Map pp656-7; Schanzenstrasse; meals €2.90-3.30) The best outlet of this jacket potato chain; near the Fritz Hotel.

■ **Shikara Quick** (Map pp656-7; ☎ 430 2353; Susannenstrasse 20; meals €4.50-7.50) Tasty Indian curries.

■ **Thai Cowboys** (Map pp656-7; ☎ 430 8025; Susannenstrasse 18; meals €5.50-9.50) Cheap stand-up Thai fare.

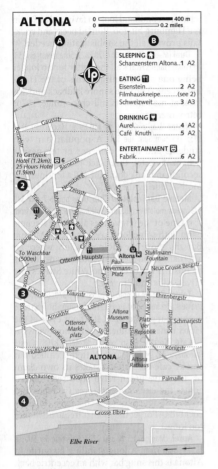

ALTONA

SLEEPING 🏠
Schanzenstern Altona..1 A2

EATING 🍴
Eisenstein.................2 A2
Filmhauskneipe.........(see 2)
Schweizweit..............3 A3

DRINKING 🍷
Aurel.......................4 A2
Café Knuth 5 A2

ENTERTAINMENT 🎭
Fabrik......................6 A2

sometimes both – is certainly memorable. The following only represent a portion of what's on offer.

Oh, It's Fresh (Map p671; ☎ 3803 7861; Carsten-Rehder-Strasse 71; dishes €2.50-12; ⏰ 7am-7pm Mon-Fri, 8.30am-5.30pm Sat & Sun; 🚇 Königstrasse) California meets New York meets Hamburg in this chain outlet, which rates a mention not only for its waterfront location and groovy swinging-London logos, but also for its array of healthy salads, bagels, focaccias and international breakfasts. Flock retro wallpaper, a lounge area and a series of world clocks decorate this light-filled, airy space.

Lust auf Italien (Map p671; ☎ 382 811; Grosse Elbstrasse 133; mains €7-18.50) If you just can't be bothered to dress up for an Elbmeile evening, the communal wooden benches of this rustic, unpretentious Italian restaurant are the best place to plonk yourself. The pasta and fish dishes are homy rather than gourmet, but the seafood usually tastes like it's just leapt from the sea. Take a post-prandial stroll for a proper look at the river.

La Vela (Map p671; ☎ 3869 9393; Grosse Elbstrasse; mains €9.50-19) Cruise and container ships glide by just outside the window of this buzzing, semiformal Italian restaurant. With such unusually close-up views, it keeps most other things simple: the red-brick interior is uncluttered and the menu is sparse, with about a dozen main choices. The only complicated thing is the enormous wine list. To get here, take the S-Bahn to Königstrasse or bus 112 to Hafentreppe/Fischmarkt.

Henssler & Henssler (Map p671; ☎ 3869 9000; Grosse Elbstrasse 160; mains €13-21; ⏰ closed Sun) This smart-casual sushi bar doesn't really 'do' views; it's across the road from the water and has an opaque frontage. However, couples, business-people and young families all come here for the food, and seem perfectly content with the milieu of black wooden chairs, white table-cloths and concrete flooring.

dining scenes. None of the restaurants along the so-called 'Elbmeile' (Elbe Mile) has been awarded a Michelin star (at least not at the time of writing). However, the sheer concentration of eateries and the setting – sometimes stunning, sometimes laughably industrial,

HAMBURG

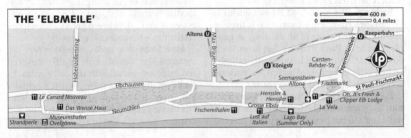

THE 'ELBMEILE'

Fischereihafen (Map p671; ☎ 381 816; Grosse Elbstrasse 143; mains €13-40) The hokey sea captain's uniform worn by the doorman is the only jarring note at this incredibly elegant, traditional restaurant. It's subtly maritime themed and serves Hamburg's best fish as well as some regional dishes to a mature, well-heeled clientele. Windows overlook the Elbe and a remarkable new ship-shaped office building. Reservations are recommended.

Das Weisse Haus (Map p671; ☎ 390 9016; Neumühlen 50; menus €28 & €36; ☒ lunch & dinner Mon-Fri, dinner Sat) A converted fisherman's cottage, this White House would look tiny beside its US namesake, and it's surprisingly cramped given its status as a major culinary player. Chef Tim Mälzer is Germany's answer to Jamie Oliver, so people book a month ahead to submit themselves to his team's 'surprise' dinners. (Vegetarian and other dietary requirements can be accommodated to a limited degree.) Alternatively you can book ahead for a simple lunch (€7 to €9); the best seats among the artfully low-key rooms are in the front winter garden. To get here, catch bus 112 to Neumühlen.

Le Canard Nouveau (Map p671; ☎ 8812 9531; Elbchaussee 139; mains €16-28, menus €48-99; ☒ lunch & dinner Tue-Fri, dinner Sat) Above the main Elbmeile strip, this swish contemporary place has a bird's-eye view of the river and imposing container port opposite – all from the curved glass frontage of its white modernist building. Chef Ali Güngörmüs prepares changing dishes such as lamb with a mustard crust and goat-cheese and fig tortellini, tuna with saffron potatoes and crispy capers, and Valrhona chocolate cake, while sated critics tip him as a contender for a Michelin star. Reserve for dinner; lunch tables are freer. Take Schnellbus 36 to Hohenzollernring Süd.

DRINKING

For a fuller assessment of the enormous bar scene, check out *Prinz*, *Oxmox* or *Szene*.

Nachtasyl (Map pp656-7; ☎ 814 444; Alstertor 1; ☒ from 7pm) Hamburg's inner city is usually like the *Marie Celeste* of an evening, as people head to St Pauli to drink. Yet downtown does boast this unusual beauty, with its high-arched ceiling, embossed wallpaper, reasonably priced drinks and arty clientele.

Zoë 2/Summun Bonum (Map pp656-7; Neuer Pferdemarkt 17; ☒ from noon) The battered sofas, rough walls and old lampshades here prove that the ad hoc, secondhand look so favoured in Berlin is a Hamburg hit, too. Bottled beers and cocktails provide all the sophistication needed.

Dual (Map pp656-7; ☎ 4320 8829; Schanzenstrasse 53; ☒ from 11am) Dual's all the better for no longer being one of the central pivots of the Hamburg scene. The vibe's more laidback and less look-at-me within its still-chic orange, 1970s retro interior.

Nouar (Map pp656-7; ☎ 430 8949; Max-Brauer-Allee 275; ☒ from 8pm Tue-Sat) A popular bar with students and other denizens of the nearby Schanzenviertel, this place has that relaxed secondhand look going on and a fondness for football during the week.

Meanie Bar/Molotow Club (Map pp656-7; ☎ 310 845; www.molotowclub.com; Spielbudenplatz 5; ☒ from 6pm) One of the few venues along the Reeperbahn with some local cred, the retro Meanie Bar sits above the Molotow Club, where an alternative, independent music scene thrives by hosting the likes of the White Stripes, the Hives, Kills and Bravery.

Tower Bar (Map pp656-7; ☎ 311 1370; Seewartenstrasse 9; ☒ from 6pm) For a more elegant, mature evening, repair to this 14th-floor eyrie at the Hotel Hafen for unbeatable harbour views.

Café Knuth (Map p671; ☎ 4600 8708; Grosse Rainstrasse 21; ☒ from 10am) With this chilled but smoky café-bar, Altona stakes its own claim on the olive-green retro style seen dotted across the city. Students, creative types and work colleagues come to chat over coffee or cocktails. (Forget the food; it frequently takes too long.)

Aurel (Map p671; ☎ 390 2727; Bahrenfelder Strasse 15; ☒ from 11am) A long-standing favourite in Altona is this snug bar with an eccentric back room where Stone Age meets baroque.

ENTERTAINMENT
Clubs

Angie's Nightclub (Map pp656-7; ☎ 3177 8816; Spielbudenplatz 27; ☒ from 10pm Wed-Sat) When many visitors think of Hamburg nightlife, they immediately think of Angie's. Floy, 'the white queen of soul', plays live as guests – sometimes celebrities – sip cocktails genteelly.

Astra Stube (Map pp656-7; Max-Brauer-Allee 200; ☒ from 9.30pm Mon-Sat) This graffiti-covered red building underneath the railway tracks looks totally unpromising, but it's actually a pioneer of the underground scene, with DJs playing experimental electro, techno and drum 'n' bass. It's also in a growing cluster of

HAMBURG'S UNLIKELY BEACH BARS

When it comes to city beaches, you have to hand it to Hamburg's hardy hipsters for their can-do spirit – or perhaps just sheer obstinacy. Undeterred by the cranes, shipbuilding docks and steel containers decorating their city's workaholic port, they've begun shipping in tonnes of artificial sand to the industrial waterfront, giving these newly created party zones wildly optimistic names like Hamburg del Mar.

The city beach season kicks off in spring and lasts until at least September, as patrons come to drink, listen to music, dance and generally hang out. Ibiza it ain't, but it does have its own special buzz. Here are some of the leading venues, open daily, Hamburg's intemperate weather permitting.

- **Central Park** (Map pp656-7; ☎ 433 684; www.centralpark-hamburg.de in German; Max-Brauer-Allee 277) A beach bar without water? No problem, said the owners of the Waagenbau club who built this summer garden smack bang in the grungy Schanzenviertel. Music, snacks, massages and a kid's playground have been joined by sculpture exhibitions in some years.

- **Lago Bay** (www.lago.cc, in German; Grosse Elbstrasse 150) Lago Bay is wedged between Hamburg del Mar (which looks like a pirates' cove with its famous St Pauli skull-and-crossbones flags) and Hamburg City Beach Club (with its Moroccan lounge). Refreshingly, you can actually swim at this chic retreat. Sun-loungers are arranged around the outdoor pool, while free exercise classes will help you keep fit, er, between cocktails. S-Bahn Königstrasse will get you here, or catch bus 112 to Hafentreppe/Fischmarkt and walk for five minutes straight ahead or west from Hafentreppe; downhill from Fischmarkt to the riverbank and then right or west.

- **StrandPauli** (Map pp656-7; www.strandpauli.de, in German; St-Pauli Hafenstrasse 84) Tuesday is tango night at this *Gilligan's Island* stretch of sand overlooking the heart of the busy docks. The reed-thatched shack looks a bit out of place, but the beer, cocktails and sausages hit the spot. Take bus 112 to St-Pauli-Hafenstrasse.

- **Strandperle** (Schulberg 2) The mother of Hamburg's beach bars is little more than a kiosk, but the people-watching is tops, as patrons linger over the MOPO (*Hamburger Morgenpost* newspaper) with a snack, coffee, beer or local Fritz-Kola. Take bus 112 to Neumühlen, then walk for five minutes straight ahead (west).

clubs, with the popular Waagenbau just next door.

China Lounge (☎ 3197 6622; Nobistor 14; ☾ from 11pm Thu-Sat) If you go to one mainstream club in Hamburg, this leading venue probably should be it. Stylish without being snootily exclusive, it boasts four areas playing electro, house, hip-hop and R&B. A huge laughing Buddha looks down on the main floor.

Cult (Map pp656-7; ☎ 2982 2180; Grosse Freiheit 2; ☾ from 11pm Thu-Sat) Claiming to be Hamburg's most beautiful club, Cult serves up an unintimidating, good-time mix of '70s and '80s music in its shiny, cathedral-like main room.

Funky Pussy Club (Map pp656-7; ☎ 314 236; Grosse Freiheit 34; ☾ from 11pm Thu-Sat) Despite the dreadful name, this artistically decorated place is a hit for its mainstream chart-toppers and hip-hop, dance and house.

Golden Cut (Map p665; ☎ 8510 3532; Holzdamm 61; ☾ from 10pm Fri & Sat) Hamburg's beautiful people clamber – stylishly of course – to get past the city's most difficult door scene into this exclusive club, where video projections spin over the dance floor while DJs spin soul, funk and house. Eating in the adjoining restaurant (p669) is – no pun intended – a sure entrée.

Golden Pudel Club (☎ 3197 9930; Fischmarkt 27; ☾ from 10pm) In a ramshackle fisherman's hut near the waterfront, this underground bar-club plays an eclectic mix of electronic, hip-hop, R&B and reggae to a mixed crowd. There was some building work going on when we visited, however, so double-check listings magazines to make sure it's still there. Take bus 112 to Hafentreppe.

Cinemas

Several cinemas screen movies in the original language with subtitles. Look for the acronym 'OmU' (Original mit Untertiteln). Venues include **Abaton Kino** (☎ 4132 0320; cnr Grindelhof & Allende Platz, Universitätsviertel) and **3001** (Map pp656-7;

GAY & LESBIAN HAMBURG

Hamburg has a thriving gay and lesbian scene; find out more at the gay centre **Hein & Fiete** (Map p665; ☎ 240 333; Pulverteich 21; ☻ 4-9pm Mon-Fri, to 7pm Sat), or look for free listings magazine *hinnerk* (found in many venues listed in this section).

Café Gnosa (Map p665; ☎ 243 034; Lange Reihe 93) This attractive olde-worlde café, with its vaguely erotic, vaguely abstract art, is hugely popular and an excellent starting point for gay and lesbian visitors to Hamburg. It stocks *hinnerk*.

Frauencafé endlich (Map pp656-7; ☎ 351 616; Dragonerstall 11) This modern, wood-lined café is a top meeting spot for lesbians. It's located in a women-only hotel (www.hotel-hanseatin.de).

EDK (Map pp656-7; ☎ 312 914; Gerhardstrasse 3) 'Small is beautiful' says the sign outside, and for the gays, lesbians and friends who come to this techno-house club it certainly is.

Pit (Map p665; ☎ 280 3056; Pulverteich 17) Hamburg's first gay disco, founded more than 30 years ago, has managed to keep up with the times and is still one of the favourite clubs for men.

☎ 437 679; Schanzenstrasse 75, Schanzenviertel). Movies usually cost €5.50 during the week, €7.50 at weekends.

Theatre

Deutsches Schauspielhaus (Map p665; ☎ 248 713; www .schauspielhaus.de in German; Kirchenallee 39) Germany's largest and most important theatre stage, the Schauspielhaus presents imaginative interpretations of the classics (by Shakespeare, Goethe, Chekhov etc) alongside new works such as *Nipple Jesus*, from *High Fidelity* author Nick Hornby.

Thalia Theater (Map pp656-7; ☎ 3281 4444; www .thalia-theater.de in German; Alstertor 1) This intimate, galleried venue with a central stage is fond of cutting-edge adaptations of classics. Interestingly, it's recently been adapting cinema – for example, from Krystof Kieslowski and Lars von Trier – for the stage.

English Theatre (☎ 227 7089; www.englishtheatre .de; Lerchenfeld 14; ⊙ Mundsburg) For more than 30 years now, a cast of predominantly British actors has been performing mysteries, comedies and the occasional classic, such as Tennessee Williams' *The Glass Menagerie*, at this venue in Winterhude.

Schmidt Theater (Map pp656-7; ☎ 3177 8899; www .tivoli.de; Spielbudenplatz 24) This plush former ballroom now stages a cornucopia of very saucy musical reviews, comedies, soap operas and variety shows. Midnight shows follow the main performance, and there's a smaller cabaret-comic venue, Schmidt's Tivoli, attached.

Quatsch Comedy Club im Café Keese (Map pp656-7; ☎ 0180-544 4411; www.quatschcomedyclub.de; Reeperbahn 19) The Keese has had a chequered career. It went from being a dance hall to pick-up bar with table telephones. Now it's a comedy club

run by Thomas Hermann, a (smiling) face frequently seen on German TV.

Live Music

Grosse Freiheit 36/Kaiserkeller (Map pp656-7; ☎ 3177 7811; Grosse Freiheit 36; ☻ from 10pm Tue-Sat) Among live sex theatre and peep shows, this alternative venue hosts an eclectic mix of pop and rock concerts. The Beatles once played in the basement Kaiserkeller (see boxed text, opposite), where there's now a range of student nights.

Docks (Map pp656-7; ☎ 3178 8311; Spielbudenplatz 19; ☻ from 10pm Thu-Sun) Although it's officially now called D-Club, everyone still calls this place by its former name Docks. It has less than perfect acoustics, but an excellent roster of guitar-led bands and reasonably cheap drinks.

Knust im Schlachthof (Map pp656-7; ☎ 8797 6230; Neuer Kamp 30) Many muso types rate this live venue in a former slaughterhouse as the best in town, principally for its atmosphere. Not just gigs, but spoken word, football fan parties, puppet shows and other events are held here.

Logo (Map pp656-7; ☎ 362 622; Grindelallee 5) This concrete block of a building in the Universitätsviertel is a great place to catch touring American or British alternative-underground bands.

Fabrik (Map p671; ☎ 391 070; Barnerstrasse 36, Altona) Fabrik is an unusual venue in a former foundry, famous for its pink exterior and crane jutting from the roof. It's aimed at a slightly older crowd, with jazz, blues and over-30s disco evenings.

Musicals

Mainstream musicals are seemingly as popular in Hamburg as they were in London during the 1990s.

THE BEATLES IN HAMBURG – FOREVER

'I was born in Liverpool, but I grew up in Hamburg.' – John Lennon

It was the summer of 1960 and a fledgling band from Liverpool had been assured a paying gig in Hamburg, if only they could come up with a drummer. After a frantic search, Pete Best joined John, Paul, George and Stuart (Sutcliffe) in August that year.

Within days, the band opened at the Indra Club on the notorious Grosse Freiheit to a seedy crowd of drunks and whores. After being egged on by the club's burly owner to 'Put on a show', John went wild, screaming, leaping and shouting, even performing in his underwear and with a toilet seat around his neck.

After 48 consecutive nights of six-hour sessions, the Beatles' innate musical genius had been honed. The magnetism of the group that would rock the world began drawing huge crowds. When police shut down the Indra they moved a block south to the Kaiserkeller – and the crowds moved with them.

At the Kaiserkeller, the Beatles alternated with a band called Rory Storm and the Hurricanes, whose drummer was one Ringo Starr. But they hardly had time to get to know each other before an underage George was deported in November, and Paul and Pete were arrested for attempted arson. All three escaped the German authorities and returned to England. There, as 'The Beatles: Direct from Hamburg', they had their Merseyside breakthrough.

In 1961 the Beatles returned to Hamburg, this time to the Top Ten Club on the Reeperbahn. During their 92-night stint here, they made their first professional recording. Around this time, manager extraordinaire Brian Epstein and the recording genius (now Sir) George Martin arrived on the scene. The Beatles' recording contract with German producer Bert Kaempfert was bought out and they began their career with EMI, with one proviso: exit Pete Best, enter Ringo, a more professional drummer. Stuart Sutcliffe had also quit the band, and sadly not long afterwards died of a brain haemorrhage.

In the spring of 1962 the final constellation of the Beatles was to log 172 hours of performance over 48 nights at Hamburg's Star Club (once at Grosse Freiheit 39, but now long gone). But with their increasing fame in England, they began to shuttle off more regularly for home and foreign shores. To usher in the new year of 1963, the Beatles gave their final concert at the Star Club, immortalised in what would become known as the 'Star Club Tapes'.

The Beatles returned occasionally to Hamburg in later years. But it was the combined 800 hours of live performance on grimy German stages in the city's red-light district that burned away the rough edges of four Liverpool boys to reveal their lasting brilliance.

Operettenhaus (Map pp656-7; ☎ 01805-114 113; Spielbudenplatz 1) The big glossy musicals, such as *Mamma Mia*, are staged here at Operettenhaus.

Neue Flora (☎ 0180-544 44; Stresemannstrasse 159a) One of Europe's largest theatres, Neue Flora was constructed so as to bring Andrew Lloyd Webber's *Phantom of the Opera* to Hamburg. In more recent times, it has reverberated to the strains of *Titanic* and the love-it-or-hate-it piece that brought the world Patrick Swayze, *Dirty Dancing*.

Musicaltheater im Hafen (Map pp656-7; ☎ 0180-544 44; www.loewenkoenig.de, in German; Norderelbstrasse 6) The yellow tent resembling a giant bee situated across the harbour hosts *The Lion King*. To get there take the shuttle from Landungsbrücke 1.

Opera & Classical Music

Staatsoper (Map pp656-7; ☎ 356 868; Dammtorstrasse 28) Among the world's most respected opera houses, the Staatsoper has been directed by the likes of Gustav Mahler and Karl Boehm during its 325-year-plus history. Performances often sell out, but try the Hamburg Hotline (☎ 3005 1300) or visit the box office at Grosse Theaterstrasse 25, about 50m from the opera house.

Musikhalle (Map pp656-7; ☎ 346 920; Dammtorwall 46) The premier address for classical concerts is this splendid neobaroque edifice, home to the State Philharmonic Orchestra, among others. Along with the opera house, it's now artistically directed by the world's leading female conductor Simone Young, formerly of Opera Australia and a real star in the classical world.

HAMBURG

SHOPPING

Central Hamburg has two main shopping districts. West of the Hauptbahnhof, along Spitalerstrasse and Mönckebergstrasse (known as the 'Mö'), you'll find the large department stores and mainstream boutiques. However, more elegant shops are located within the triangle created by Jungfernstieg, Fuhlentwiete and Neuer Wall. Most of them are in a network of 11 shopping arcades.

For secondhand shopping, try the Schanzenviertel or Karolinenviertel, particularly Marktstrasse.

In Altona, along Ottenser Hauptstrasse, hip clothing stores mingle with Turkish vendors.

GETTING THERE & AWAY

Air

Hamburg Airport (HAM; ☎ 507 50; www.flughafen-hamburg.de) has frequent flights to domestic and European cities, including on **Lufthansa** (☎ 01803-803 803; Terminal 4), **British Airways** (☎ 01805-735 522; Terminal 4), **Air France** (☎ 5075 2325; Terminal 4) and low-cost carrier **Air Berlin** (☎ 01801-737 800; www.airberlin.com; Terminal 1).

For flights to/from Ryanair's so-called 'Hamburg-Lübeck', see p688.

Bus

The **ZOB/Busbahnhof** (Central Bus Station; ☎ 247 5765; www.zob-hamburg.de; Adenauerallee 78; ⏰ 6.30am-9pm) is southeast of the Hauptbahnhof and most popular for services to central and Eastern Europe, particularly Poland. **Eurolines** (☎ 4024 7106; www.eurolines.com) has buses to Prague (one-way/return €55/98) and Warsaw (€55/86), for example. Check the Eurolines website for other destinations, including Amsterdam, Copenhagen and Paris.

Gulliver's (☎ 253 289 278; www.gullivers.de) goes all over Europe and has a website you can search in English. **Polen Reisen** (☎ 241 427) is one of several Eastern European specialists you'll find in the building.

Autokraft (☎ 208 8660; www.autokraft.de) goes to Berlin frequently and charges €24/39 one-way/return.

Car & Motorcycle

The autobahns of the A1 (Bremen–Lübeck) and A7 (Hanover–Kiel) cross south of the Elbe River. Three concentric ring roads manage traffic flow. For ride-shares, try the **Mitfahrzentrale** (☎ 194 40; Ernst-Merck-Strasse 8).

Train

Hamburg has four train stations: the Hauptbahnhof, Dammtor, Altona and Harburg. Many of the long-distance trains originate in Altona and stop at both Dammtor and the Hauptbahnhof before heading out of the city. Remember this as you read the timetables or you may end up at the wrong station.

There are several trains hourly to Lübeck (€10.30, 45 minutes), Kiel (from €17.20, 1¼ hours), Hanover (€36, 1¼ hours) and Bremen (€18.30 to €22, one hour). A direct service to Westerland on Sylt Island leaves every two hours (€29, three hours).

There are direct IC connections to Berlin-Hauptbahnhof (€48 to €58, 1½ hours) and Cologne (€68 to €78, four hours). Frankfurt is served hourly by the ICE train (€82, 3½ hours), as is Munich (€111, six to nine hours). There's a direct service to Copenhagen several times a day, but the only direct train to Paris is the night train (otherwise, change in Cologne).

GETTING AROUND

To/From the Airport

The **Airport Express** (☎ 227 1060; www.jasper-hamburg.de; ⏰ 6am-11pm) runs between the Hauptbahnhof and airport (€5, 25 minutes, every 15 to 20 minutes). You can also take the U1 or S1 to Ohlsdorf, then change to bus 110.

Car & Motorcycle

Driving around Hamburg is easy. Major thoroughfares cutting across town in all directions are well signposted. Parking is expensive, however, especially in the city centre.

All major car-hire agencies have branches in Hamburg. **Budget** (☎ 01805-244 388) and **Europcar** (☎ 01805-5000) are both at the train station and airport. The city office of **Hertz** (Map p665; ☎ 01805-333 535; Kirchenallee 34-36) is just opposite the Hauptbahnhof. Local agencies include **Star Car** (☎ 468 8300; Jenfelder Alle 2-4), with cars available from around €30 per day or €50 per weekend.

Public Transport

The **HVV** (☎ 194 49; www.hvv.de) operates buses, ferries, U-Bahn and S-Bahn, and has several offices, including at the Hauptbahnhof and at Jungfernstieg station.

The city is divided into zones. The Nahbereich (central area) covers the city centre, roughly between St Pauli and the Hauptbahnnhof. The Grossbereich (Greater Hamburg area) covers the city centre plus outlying communities like Blankenese, and is the ticket you'll most commonly need. The Gesamtbereich covers the entire Hamburg State.

S-/U-Bahn tickets must be purchased from machines at station entrances; bus tickets are available from the driver. Only single tickets (€1.55) are available in the Nahbereich. Ticket types include the following:

Ticket	Grossbereich	Gesamtbereich
Single	€2.50	€6.50
Day Pass (after 9am)	€4.90	€12.50
Day Pass (all day)	€5.80	€14.30
3-Day Pass	€14.40	-
Group Day Pass (up to 5 people)	€8.10	€19.90

If you catch an express bus or Schnellbus, it costs an extra €1.20. The fine for riding without a valid ticket is €50 and checks are fairly frequent.

Services run around the clock on weekends, but between 1am and 4am Sunday to Thursday the night bus network takes over, converging on Rathausmarkt.

Bikes may be taken onto S-/U-Bahn trains, buses and ferries outside rush hours (6am to 9am and 4pm to 6pm).

Taxi

Taxis can be found at the Hauptbahnhof, Dammtor and Altona, and at some larger S-Bahn and U-Bahn stations. You can book one by calling ☎ 441 011 or ☎ 666 666.

AROUND HAMBURG

Hamburg State also boasts the so-called **Altes Land** south of the Elbe, a fertile area of orchards reclaimed from marshy ground by Dutch experts in the Middle Ages. Towns here include Stade, Buxtehude and Jork.

Hamburg Wadden Sea National Park is found at the mouth of the Elbe River. This is the smallest of Germany's three mud-flat national parks, in the same vein as the Schleswig-Holstein Wadden Sea National Park (p696) and the Lower Saxony Wadden Sea National Park (p637), where you can climb dunes, hike along dykes, seal-spot, take a horse-and-carriage ride across the seabed or, at low tide, *Wattwandern* (see p637). In the Hamburg Wadden Sea National Park, you can also hunt for amber.

Ask the Hamburg tourist office for more information if you like the sound of either of these options.

However, with Germany's great train system, destinations in surrounding states often make better day trips. For example, Lüneburg (p611) in Lower Saxony is within easy reach, as is Bremen (p641) and Lübeck (p683) in Schleswig-Holstein.

Among Germans, one very popular day trip from Hamburg is by boat to Helgoland (p702). **Förde Reederei Seetouristik** (☎ 0180-320 2025; www.frs.de) operates these services. From April to November, you can catch the fast 'Halunder Jet' (return €55 to €70) from Landungsbrücken 3 or 4. Every Saturday in July and August, the larger 'Wappen von Hamburg' makes a 'traditional' day trip (€44 return).

HAMBURG

Schleswig-Holstein

Cows and coastline – these are the two faces of Schleswig-Holstein's split personality. But while this flat peninsula between the North and Baltic Seas is 70% covered in farmland, it's the other 30% that interests most visitors.

Sandy beaches, jaunty red-and-white striped lighthouses, fjords, sandpipers and seals have traditionally made this Germany's stay-at-home summer retreat. Since reunification in 1990 more adventurous souls have been heading to Mecklenburg-Western Pomerania (p703). However, the islands off Schleswig-Holstein's western coast remain the country's answer to the Côte d'Azur. Of course, the northern European weather makes for a funny sort of answer, as cold winds and dark clouds periodically drive the hardiest holidaymakers from their *Strandkörbe* (sheltered straw seats). Yet, there's something unusually beguiling about the state's wide horizons, grass-covered dunes and meandering canals. Snuggled up against Denmark, Schleswig-Holstein belonged solely to that country until 1864 and you'll find Scandinavian overtones and remnants of a Viking past, particularly in the town of Schleswig, which also boasts the state's best art museum.

Local artists are among the few to have positively embraced the moodier side of Schleswig-Holstein's beauty. At home in Seebüll, Emil Nolde swirled his brushes into stormy oil-paint waves; Theodor Storm set his novella, *Der Schimmelreiter* (The Rider on the White Horse), along the Husum coast; and contemporary literary giant Günter Grass moved to Lübeck years ago.Lübeck is a story unto itself, as memorable as one of Grass' thumping great tomes. The former headquarters of the medieval Hanseatic League, it's one of Germany's best-preserved medieval towns – and reason alone to visit the region.

HIGHLIGHTS

- **Historic City** Feast on Lübeck's fairy-tale skyline (p683), as well as its delicious marzipan
- **Nordic Walking** Hike among the otherworldly dune landscape near List (p698) on Sylt
- **Adrenaline** Go windsurfing (p697) off Sylt's North Sea coast
- **Planet Watch** See the 17th-century night sky spin at Schleswig's Schloss Gottorf (p690)
- **Highbrow** Read up on both Thomas Mann and Günter Grass in their Lübeck museums (p686)
- **Offbeat Experience** Celebrate a Midsummer's Day evening at Schleswig's Wikinger Museum (Viking Museum; p691)

- POPULATION: 2.7 MILLION
- AREA: 15,729 SQ KM

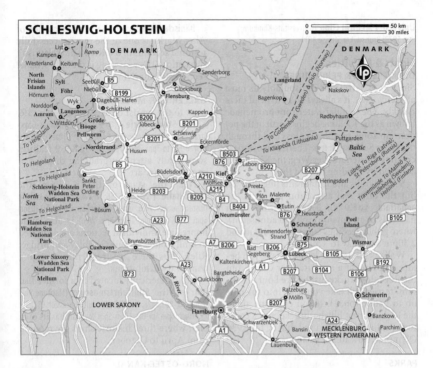

KIEL

☎ 0431 / pop 233,800

Rebuilt in a hurry after its U-Boot (submarine) base meant that it was shattered during WWII, modern Kiel has the sort of face only a mother could love. But then what an unfeasible number of mothers it turns out to have too! Yes, some locals admit, the Schleswig-Holstein capital is *grottenhässlich* (ugly as sin) downtown, but they staunchly defend the place for its location on an 18km-long *Förde* (firth) and its friendly, relaxed personality. The waterfront Kiellinie is its most popular promenade, and there are some pretty quarters inland (if you look hard enough).

Whether visitors leave convinced depends on whom they meet and their fascination for places where you have to scratch below the surface. There's little debate that 'Kiel Sailing City's' most romantic aspect is the water, where huge ferries transport millions of passengers to and from Scandinavia during the year and the international Kieler Woche regatta fills the city with sailing ships and merrymakers every June.

Orientation

Kiel's main thoroughfare is the pedestrianised Holstenstrasse, about 100m inland from the firth. It runs between the Sophienhof, a huge indoor shopping mall opposite the Hauptbahnhof (central train station) on Sophienblatt, to Kieler Schloss (Kieler Castle) about 1.5km north. The central bus station is just to the north of the Hauptbahnhof, through the 'City/Fernbus' exit leading to Auguste-Viktoria-Strasse.

The Deutsche Bahn (DB) service counter inside the Hauptbahnhof has central Kiel maps.

Information

There's an ATM inside the Hauptbahnhof.

Kiel tourist office (☎ 01805-656 700, 679 1024; www.kiel-tourist.de; Neues Rathaus, Andreas-Gayk-Strasse 31; ⏱ 9am-6pm Mon-Fri, 10am-2pm Sat)

Post office (Stresemannplatz 5; ⏱ 9am-7pm Mon-Fri, 9am-2pm Sat) Around the corner from the tourist office.

Schnell und Sauber (Knooper Weg 27; per load €3.50; ⏱ 6am-11pm) Laundry.

Silver Angel Café (☎ 888 1919; Schlossstrasse 16; per hr €3-4; ⏱ 10am-10pm Mon-Sat, noon-10pm Sun) Internet access.

University Medical Clinic (Universitäts-Klinikum; ☎ 5970; Brunswiker Strasse 10)

Sights & Activities

DIE KIELLINIE & FERRY RIDES

Since its waterfront is indisputably its most attractive side, it's always good to head there quickly. The popular waterfront promenade known as the Kiellinie begins north of the pedestrian zone, past the Schloss and through the green Schlossgarten. There's an overpass crossing Düsternbrooker Weg; the Kiellinie is accessed by heading behind this.

Sailing clubs and restaurants line the way, but the only real attraction per se is the **aquarium** (☎ 600 1637; Düsternbrooker Weg 20). It has seals in an outside tank (no admission), where public feedings take place at 10am and 2.30pm Saturday to Thursday.

Walk as far as your legs will take you before stopping at a restaurant or café. From the Revenloubrücke just before Louf restaurant, ferries will take you back into town or on to Laboe (p682). If you continue along the Kiellinie past Blücherbrücke, you'll come to the sailing harbour used during the 1936 Olympics, now full of yachts.

PARKS

Kiel also has several attractive parks, including the **Schrevenpark** and **Old Botanical Gardens**. One of the few picture-postcard views of Kiel city (as opposed to Kiel firth) can be enjoyed from the intersection of Lorenzdamm and Legienstrasse, situated between the two **Kleiner Kiel** lakes. Children will love the playful **Jeppe Hein Fountain** in the **Hiroshimapark** next to the westerly lake and behind the Opera House.

DOWNTOWN

The pedestrian zone is unattractive but usually unavoidable. You'll have to traverse it to get to the Kiellinie. As you wander from the Sophienhof, through Holstenplatz and along Holstenstrasse, you'll pass the **Altes Rathaus** (old town hall) to your left down Fleethörn, with its 106m tower.

Outside the **Nikolaikirche** (Church of St Nicholas) on the Alter Markt (old square) stands a striking Ernst Barlach statue. **Der Geistkämpfer** (Ghost Fighter) was removed during the Third Reich as 'degenerate art', but was later found buried in the Lüneburg Heath.

Dänische Strasse, at the far left corner of Alter Markt, is one of the more successfully restored sections of old Kiel. The **Schloss** isn't so exciting. The west wing is the only original section still surviving.

GALLERIES & MUSEUMS

Next to the tourist office, with its own café, Kiel's **Stadtgalerie** (☎ 901 3400; Andreas-Gayk-Strasse 31; adult/concession €3/1.50; ☉ 10am-5pm Tue & Wed-Fri, to 7pm Thu, 11am-5pm Sat & Sun) features some really attention-grabbing displays of contemporary art.

Near the start of the Kiellinie, the **Kunst-halle** (☎ 880 5756; www.kunsthalle-kiel.de; Düsternbrooker Weg; adult/concession €5/3; ☉ 10am-6pm Tue & Thu-Sun, 10am-8pm Wed) is also quite impressive. Individual sections are dedicated to Emil Nolde, Antony Gormley and Bridget Riley, plus there are frequently changing temporary exhibitions.

Atmospherically located in a former fish market, the **Schiffahrtsmuseum** (Maritime Museum; ☎ 901 3428; Am Wall 65; adult/concession €3/1.50; ☉ 10am-6pm Apr-Oct, 10am-5pm Nov-Mar) has its own pier, where three historic ships are moored from April to October.

NORD-OSTEE-KANAL

Kiel lies at the point at which the 99km-long Nord-Ostsee-Kanal enters the Baltic Sea from the North Sea. Inaugurated in 1895, the canal sees some 60,000 ships pass through it every year, and is the third most trafficked canal in the world, after Suez and Panama.

Between June and September, boats will take you along the canal to Rendsburg and back, from Bahnhofsbrücke in Kiel. These run on Wednesday and Sunday, cost €31.50/19 per adult/child and take about eight hours. On certain days, the historic steamship **Rad-dampfer Freya** (☎ 04651-987 00; www.raddampfer-freya .de) also runs trips. The tourist office is your best contact for all bookings.

If you don't have time for such a trip, but would like a closer look at the canal, you can see the *Schleusen* (locks) at Holtenau, north of Kiel. There's a **museum** (☎ 360 30; adult/concession €2.30/1.50) on the southern side of the canal. **Tours of the locks** (☎ 360 30; adult/concession €2.30/1.50) depart at 9am, 11am, 1pm and 3pm daily from the northern side. To get to the locks, take bus 11 to Wik, Kanal. A free ferry shuttles back and forth between the southern and northern banks.

Festivals & Events

Kiel's most famous event is **Kieler Woche** (Kiel Week; ☎ 679 100) traditionally held during the last full week of June, although sometimes earlier. It's a giant festival revolving around a series of yachting regattas, and attended by more than 4000 of the world's sailing elite and half a million spectators. Even if you're not into boats, it's one nonstop party – so you need to book ahead.

Sleeping

Kiel long concentrated on business travellers, but new hostels and a nice cheap hotel are making it a backpacker mecca.

DJH hostel (☎ 731 488; www.jugendherberge.de/jh /kiel; Johannesstrasse 1; under/over 26yr €16.80/18.80, s/d €25/42; P ✕) On a hill across the firth from the Hauptbahnhof, this 30-year-old red-brick hostel has great night-time views of Kiel. Take bus 11 or 12 to Kieler Strasse.

Peanuts Hostel (☎ 364 2208; www.peanuts-hostel .de; Harriesstrasse 2; dm €17, d per person €20; ☽ reception 8.30-11am & 5-10pm) This humble but central and pleasant hostel – with just eight beds in three rooms and a homy living space – is in one of Kiel's few historic buildings and run by one of the city's most staunch defenders. She'll point out all the city's attractive features.

Bekpek Kiel (☎ 888 8009; www.bekpek-kiel.de; Kronshagener Weg 130a; dm €21, d €54; ☽ reception 8am-noon & 4-9pm; P ✕ 💻) To get here, you have to take a bus from the centre (No 34, 100 or 101 to Dehnckestrasse). However, it's worth it for the friendly atmosphere and nice, modern rooms, painted in yellow, with turquoise lockers. Bekpek is also run by knowledgeable locals and offers a laundry, kitchen and more. Little extras include homemade jam and fresh peppermint tea courtesy of the plant on the balcony.

Hotel Garni am Schrevenpark (☎ 915 57; www .am-schrevenpark.de; Goethestrasse 7; s/d from €30/55) This lovely budget hotel is set back from the street in a courtyard, and has only a handful of rooms. Most are decorated in a simple white, blue and grey Nordic style, but one has an interesting beach mural. The breakfast room is in a separate building, across the small garden.

Hotel Nordic (☎ 986 800; www.nordic-hotels.com; Muhliusstrasse 95; s €55-60, d €80-85; P 💻) Rooms here are modern and spacious, with Picasso tribute paintings. Nothing is too much for the friendly staff, whether organising a courier or feeding a hungry guest after hours. There are

several other recommendable Kiel branches, including the 2004-renovated Am Sophienhof (☎ 626 78) at Königsweg 13.

Hotel Berliner Hof (☎ 663 40; www.berlinerhof-kiel .de; Ringstrasse 6; s €70-75, d €90-95; P ✕) Although completely modern, this central hotel has a touch of old-world class. Above the faux-marble floor, red leather lounges and Persian rugs in reception, there are two main types of room: a newer, lighter variety, and a cheaper, slightly older type. Accommodation for those with disabilities is available.

For good views of the firth, try the centrally located and upmarket **Steigenberger Hotel Conti-Hansa** (☎ 511 50; www.kiel.steigenberger.de; Schlossgarten 7; s €95-145, d €120-175; P ✕) or the **Hotel Maritim Bellevue** (☎ 389 40; www.maritim.de; Bismarckallee 2, Kiel-Düsternbrook; s €95-225, d €120-290; P).

Eating

For a quick bite, head to the north of Europaplatz, where there is a series of popular if not particularly distinguished eateries. (And we don't mean the McDonald's, but those opposite.)

Club 68 (☎ 617 39; Ringstrasse 68; mains €7-15; ☽ dinner) This scurrilous little *urige Kneipe* (down-to-earth and authentic pub) is decked out like the local in popular cartoon *Werner*. Even those unfamiliar with the strip will enjoy the unusual décor, including old Mercedes car seats with wooden armrests. Food runs from pasta to schnitzel.

Louf (☎ 551 178; Reventloualle 2, cnr Kiellinie; mains €8-16) In summer, Kiel's hipsters lounge around on the deckchairs on the lawn, while behind them a distinctly mixed crowd – from young mothers to skiving businessmen – lap up the delicious smell of waffles, and the taste of pasta, Thai curries, meat dishes, wine, beer and aperitifs. Outdoor heaters and blankets keep things going in cooler seasons.

Ratskeller (☎ 971 0005; Rathaus; mains €9-18.50) Freshly caught fish in summer and artery-choking warming meals in winter make Kiel's Ratskeller much better than most. It's conveniently located and is open every day of the week.

Fuego del Sur (☎ 364 6036; An der Halle 400, Willy-Brand-Ufer; mains €9-19) Its open grill means this Argentine *parilla* (grill) establishment is as steaming as the pampas it evokes. So in summer the huge noisy crowd totally ignores the indoor tables and chairs – plus the area of low gaucho-style seating – and decamps to the

SCHLESWIG-HOLSTEIN

terrace. Big bloody steaks are accompanied on the menu by pasta, pizza, polenta and crème caramel made from *dulce de leche* (a thickened condensed-milk confection).

Lüneburg-Haus (☎ 982 600; Dänische Strasse 22; mains €10-22; ☯ closed Mon) Despite the designer touches, there are still historic hints in this lovely century-old restaurant, and the mix of delicious regional cuisine and modern international dishes leaves lasting culinary memories.

Drinking

Prinz Willy (Lutherstrasse 9; ☯ 2-10pm Tue-Sat, 10am-10pm Sat) A cool little café-bar patronised by book-reading arty types and students, this is located in one of Kiel's tucked-away historic quarters.

Two Irish pubs, **O'Dwyer's Irish Pub** (☎ 556 227; Bergstrasse 15) and **Mc Lang´s Irish Pub** (☎ 828 456; Lange Reihe 17), are local stalwarts. Everyone seems to have their favourite of the two; you'll have to pop in for a Guinness in each to discover yours.

You'll pick up reasonably priced meals at many of Kiel's numerous watering holes, such as the traditional brewery **Kieler Brauerei** (☎ 906 290; Alter Markt 9), the legendary student pub **Oblomov** (☎ 801 467; Hansastrasse 82) or **Forstbaumschule** (☎ 333 496; Dvelsbeker Weg 46), which is a huge beer garden in a park about 3.5km north of the city centre.

Getting There & Away
AIR

The bus service **Kielius** (☎ 666 2222; www.kielius .de) shuttles 36 times a day (18 times in each direction) between Hamburg airport and Kiel's central bus station (one-way/return €16/27). Lübeck airport is also quite close (see p688).

BOAT

See p760 for details of ferry services to Kiel from Gothenburg, Oslo and Klaipeda in Lithuania.

BUS

Interglobus Reisen (☎ 666 1787; ☯ 2-5pm Mon-Fri), located in the central bus station, has daily buses to Poland. Many other services head from the central bus station to towns in Schleswig-Holstein, although the train is often more convenient.

CAR & MOTORCYCLE

Kiel is connected with the rest of Germany via the A210 and A215, which merge with the A7 to Hamburg and beyond. The B4, B76, B404, B502 and B503 also converge here.

TRAIN

Numerous trains shuttle between Kiel, Hamburg-Altona and Hamburg Hauptbahnhof (€15.20, 1½ hours). Trains to Lübeck leave hourly (€13.40, 1¼ hours). There are regular local connections to Schleswig, Husum, Schwerin and Flensburg.

Getting Around

Bus trips cost from €2 one-way or €6.60 for a day card. For a taxi, call ☎ 680 101.

A **ferry service** (☎ 594 1263) along the firth operates daily until around 6pm (to 5pm on weekends) from the Bahnhofbrücke pier behind the Hauptbahnhof. Short journeys cost €2.40 and the trip to Laboe is €3.40.

AROUND KIEL
Laboe
☎ 04343 / pop 5300

At the mouth of the Kiel Firth, on its eastern bank, lies the village of Laboe. It is home to a

---

A MUSICAL INTERLUDE

The gentle lowing of cattle is the sound one most expects to hear emanating from a barn, but during the state-wide **Schleswig-Holstein Music Festival** (www.shmf.de) in late summer you might find yourself down on the farm listening to a chamber orchestra instead. Over seven weeks, leading international musicians and promising young talents perform some 150 concerts in 55 venues throughout Schleswig-Holstein and Hamburg, ranging from the castle in Kiel and music academy in Lübeck to churches, warehouses and animal stalls, and sometimes even ferries to the North Frisian Islands.

Each year, the festival takes a different country as a theme (in 2006, for example, the Netherlands) and, although performances are largely classical, you'll also find pop, rock and jazz on the menu. Tourist offices throughout the state, and in Hamburg, can help with details.

THE FIRST EUROPEAN UNION

A trading bloc capable of raising an army to safeguard its commercial interests, the medieval Hanseatic League was a more pugnacious version of the EU and NATO combined. Formed before the era of the nation state, it united more than 150 merchant cities – from Novgorod to London, and as far south as the German Alps – in an 'association' (for which the medieval German word was 'Hanse').

The league wasn't so much born; rather, it grew organically. In the mid-12th century, rich merchants in Northern Germany began signing deals to safeguard each other's commercial shipping, and in 1241 Lübeck and Hamburg completed a mutual protection treaty. Other towns, including Bergen, Bruges, Riga, Tallinn, Braunschweig, Cologne, Dortmund, Lüneburg, Magdeburg, Rostock and Stralsund, subsequently joined the compact, which lasted some 500 years.

While its initial aim was to ensure that neither war nor piracy interrupted trade in the North and Baltic Seas, its collective power soon made the Hanseatic League a dominant political force. Through its meetings in Lübeck, it dictated policy by fixing the prices of commodities such as grain, fur and ore, or by threatening to withhold trading privileges. In 1368 it even went to war. Challenged by Danish King Valdemar IV for control of the southwestern Baltic, the league's members raised an army and comprehensively defeated the Danes.

Mostly, however, the Hanseatic League was a bastion of stability in a time of endless feudal squabbles and religious ruptures. Commercial prosperity sat well with its citizens. Plus, its far geographical reach fostered political exchange between different societies. Even author Thomas Mann, born in Lübeck, admired its power in creating 'a humane, cosmopolitan society'.

The league began to crumble in the 16th century, with the rise of strong English and Dutch authorities and an increasing focus on national interests. The ruin and chaos of the Thirty Years' War in the 17th century delivered the final blow.

Although the league met for the last time in 1669, three members still call themselves Hanseatic cities: Bremen, Hamburg and Lübeck.

U-Boot (☎ 427 00; adult/child €2.50/1.50; ⏰ 9.30am-6pm Apr-Oct, 9.30am-4pm Nov-Mar) and associated **Marine Ehrenmal** (adult/child €4/2.50, combined entry with U-Boot adult/child €5/3.50). The sub is the kind featured in Wolfgang Petersen's seminal film *Das Boot* (1981), and actually served during WWII. It's now a museum where you can climb through its claustrophobic interior. Next to the sub is a naval memorial built in the shape of a ship's stern and housing a **navigation museum**. From Kiel, take the ferry (see opposite) or bus 100 or 101.

Schleswig-Holsteinisches Freilichtmuseum

South of Kiel, in Molfsee, is the **Schleswig-Holsteinisches Freilichtmuseum** (Schleswig-Holstein Open-Air Museum; ☎ 0431-659 660; Alte Hamburger Landstrasse 97; adult/child/family €6/2/13; ⏰ 9am-6pm Apr-Oct, 9am-8pm mid-Jun–mid-Aug, 11am-4pm Sun & holidays Nov-Mar) This open-air museum features some 70 traditional houses typical of the region, relocated from around the state and providing a thorough introduction to the northern lifestyle. Take bus 500/504 from Kiel's central bus station.

LÜBECK

☎ 0451 / pop 213,000

Oh, how the mighty are fallen. But Lübeck doesn't look like she cares. The centre of the powerful Hanseatic League, or 'Queen of the Hanse' (see boxed text, above), is now merely a provincial city, albeit with a picture-book appearance.

Yet what a fairy tale it seems. The two pointed cylindrical towers of the landmark Holstentor (gate) lean together across the stepped gable that joins them, behind which the streets are lined with medieval merchants' homes and spired churches forming Lübeck's so-called 'crown'. It's no surprise to learn that this 12th-century gem, including more than 1000 historical buildings, has been on Unesco's World Heritage List since 1987. It looks so good you could eat it – especially the red-foil-wrapped displays of its famous marzipan, which you actually can.

Orientation

Lübeck's Altstadt (old town) is located on an island that's ringed by the Trave River, which has been canalised. The Holstentor

LÜBECK

0 ————— 300 m
0 ————— 0.2 miles

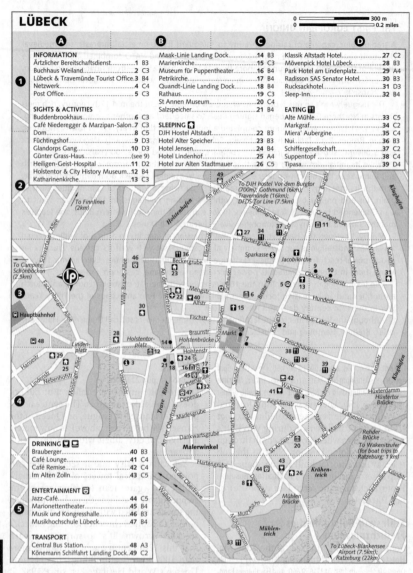

INFORMATION
Ärztlicher Bereitschaftsdienst............1 B3
Buchhaus Weiland.................................2 C3
Lübeck & Travemünde Tourist Office.3 B4
Netzwerk..4 C4
Post Office...5 C3

SIGHTS & ACTIVITIES
Buddenbrookhaus...................................6 C3
Café Niederegger & Marzipan-Salon.7 C3
Dom..8 C5
Füchtingshof...9 D3
Glandorps Gang....................................10 D3
Günter Grass-Haus.........................(see 9)
Heiligen-Geist-Hospital 11 D2
Holstentor & City History Museum..12 B4
Katharinenkirche..................................13 C3

Maak-Linie Landing Dock..................14 B3
Marienkirche..15 C3
Museum für Puppentheater...............16 B4
Petrikirche...17 B4
Quandt-Linie Landing Dock..............18 B4
Rathaus...19 C3
St Annen Museum...............................20 C4
Salzspeicher...21 B4

SLEEPING 🏠
DJH Hostel Altstadt............................22 B3
Hotel Alter Speicher..........................23 B4
Hotel Jensen...24 B4
Hotel Lindenhof...................................25 A4
Hotel zur Alten Stadtmauer..............26 C5

Klassik Altstadt Hotel.........................27 C2
Mövenpick Hotel Lübeck...................28 B3
Park Hotel am Lindenplatz................29 A4
Radisson SAS Senator Hotel.............30 B3
Rucksackhotel......................................31 D3
Sleep-Inn..32 B4

EATING 🍴
Alte Mühle..33 C5
Markgraf...34 C4
Miera' Aubergine.................................35 C4
Nui..36 B3
Schiffergesellschaft............................37 C4
Suppentopf...38 C4
Tipasa..39 D4

DRINKING 🍷 🍺
Brauberger..40 B3
Café Lounge..41 C4
Café Remise..42 C4
Im Alten Zolln......................................43 C5

ENTERTAINMENT 🎭
Jazz-Café...44 C5
Marionettentheater.............................45 B4
Musik und Kongresshalle....................46 B3
Musikhochschule Lübeck....................47 B4

TRANSPORT
Central Bus Station..............................48 A3
Könemann Schiffahrt Landing Dock.49 C2

forms the western gateway to the Altstadt, with the Hauptbahnhof and central bus station conveniently located only several hundred metres west of here. You will find there's a map on a billboard just across from the Hauptbahnhof exit, and others dotted around town, and this really makes it difficult to get lost.

Information

The Lübeck-Travemünde tourist office sells a German-language book of tours and tips called *Lübeck rundum* (€2.90). There's also a pocket-sized map in English (€0.90) with a walk, museums and other basic details.
Ärztlicher Bereitschaftsdienst (☎ 710 81; An der Untertrave 98) Medical services.

Buchhaus Weiland (☎ 160 060; Königstrasse 67a)
Stocks a selection of foreign-language books.
Happy Day Card (per 1/3 days €5/10) Free public
transport and museums discounts.
Lübeck & Travemünde tourist office (☎ 01805-
882 233; www.luebeck-tourism.de; Holstentorplatz 1;
☽ 9.30am-7pm Mon-Fri, 10am-3pm Sat, 10am-2pm Sun
Jun-Sep, 9.30am-6pm Mon-Fri, 10am-3pm Sat Oct-May)
With café, and internet terminals.
Netzwerk (☎ 396 8060; Wahmstrasse 58; per hr €3;
☽ 10am-10pm Mon-Sat, to 8pm Sun) Internet access.
Post office (Königstrasse 46)

Sights & Activities

Lübeck has good English signposting, with
information on the sides of landmarks and
in museums. Some churches also have multilingual electronic information points.

HOLSTENTOR & AROUND

Lübeck's small Holstentor city gate really is
quite stunning. It captivated Andy Warhol
(his print of it is in the St Annen Museum)
and it's a sight where people sit and stare. Its
twin pointy-roofed circular towers, tilting
together across a stepped gable, have made it
a true German icon, which has graced postcards, paintings, posters, marzipan souvenirs
and even the old DM50 note, as you'll discover
in the engaging **City History Museum** (☎ 122 4129;
adult/concession €5/3; ☽ 10am-5pm Tue-Sun Apr-Sep, 10am-
4pm Tue-Sun Oct-Mar) inside. Built in 1464, the
gate has been under renovation recently, but
should be out of its trompe l'oeil wraps by
now, so that its famous Latin inscriptions are
visible: 'Concordia Domi Foris Pax' (roughly
translated as 'Harmony within, peace abroad')
on one side, and 'SPQL' (Senate and People
of Lübeck) on the reverse.

Just behind the Holstentor (to the east)
stand six gabled brick buildings. These are the
Salzspeicher, once used to store salt transported
from Lüneburg, which was then bartered for
furs from Scandinavia and used to preserve
the herrings that formed a substantial chunk
of Lübeck's Hanseatic trade.

BOAT TOURS

Just behind the Salzspeicher lies the Trave
River, which forms a moat around the old
town; and if you arrive between April and
September one of the first things to do is to
take a boat tour. Sure, you start off viewing
an industrial harbour, but the trips soon start
passing beautiful leafy surrounds. **Maak-Linie**
(☎ 706 3859; www.maak-linie.de) runs good one-
hour tours, leaving from the north of the Hol-
stentorbrücke. **Quandt-Linie** (☎ 777 99; www.quandt
-linie.de) leaves from just south of the bridge.
Boats are scheduled to leave every half-hour,
although many wait until they're half-full.
Prices are adult/concession €8/5.50.

MARKT & AROUND

Sometimes described as a 'fairy tale in stone',
Lübeck's 13th- to 15th-century **Rathaus** (☎ 122
1005; Breite Strasse; guided tours in German only €3/2; ☽ tours
11am, noon & 3pm Mon-Fri) is regarded as one of the
most beautiful in Germany. Unfortunately,
it's become a little grubby and its impact is
somewhat limited by new buildings around
the marketplace, which block previously open
views. Inside, a highlight is the Audienzsaal
(Audience Hall), a light-flooded hall decked
out in festive rococo.

To be brutally honest, however, the attention of most people is going to be drawn
across the street to **Café Niederegger** (☎ 530 1126;
Breite Strasse 89; ☽ 7am-7pm Mon-Fri, 9am-6pm Sat, 10am-
6pm Sun). This is Lübeck's mecca of marzipan,
the almond sweet from Arabia, which Lübeck
confectioners have excelled in making for centuries. Even if you're not buying, the stop is a
feast for the eyes. In the upstairs **Marzipan-Salon**
you'll learn that in medieval Europe marzipan
was thought of as medicine, not a sweet.

CHURCHES

Each of Lübeck's churches offers something
different. Near the Markt rise the 125m twin
spires of Germany's third-largest church, the
Marienkirche (Schüsselbuden 13; ☽ 10am-6pm Apr-Sep, to
5pm Oct, 10am-4pm Tue-Sun Nov-Mar). It's most famous
for its shattered bells, which have been left
where they fell after a WWII bombing raid, as
a peace memorial. Turn left upon entering the
church and go to the end of the aisle. There's
also a little devil sculpture outside, with an
amusing folk tale (in German and English).

If you want panoramic views over the city,
head for the **Petrikirche** (Schmiedstrasse; lift adult/
concession €2.50/1.50; ☽ 11am-4pm Tue-Sun, to 6pm mid-
Nov–mid-Dec, closed Feb), which has a tower lift to
the 7th floor.

The **Dom** (Cathedral; ☽ 10am-6pm Mon-Sat, noon-
6pm Sun) was founded in 1173 by Heinrich der
Löwe (see boxed text, p619) when he took
over Lübeck. Hence it's the oldest church
in town. Locals like to joke that if you approach the Dom from the northeast, you

SCHLESWIG-HOLSTEIN

have to go through *Hölle* (hell) and *Fegefeuer* (purgatory) – the actual names of streets – to see **Paradies**, the lavish vestibule to the Dom. Otherwise, the building is quite spartan.

Art lovers will enjoy the towerless **Katharinenkirche** (cnr Glockengiesserstrasse & Königstrasse; admission €0.50; ☺ 10am-1pm & 2-5pm Tue-Sun Apr-Sep). It houses sculptures by Ernst Barlach and Gerhard Marcks, plus *The Resurrection of Lazarus* by Tintoretto.

COURTYARDS & MEWS

In the Middle Ages, Lübeck was home to numerous craftspeople and artisans. Their influx soon meant demand for housing outgrew the available space, so tiny single-storey homes were built in courtyards behind existing rows of houses. These were then made accessible via little walkways from the street.

Almost 90 such *Gänge* (walkways) and *Höfe* (courtyards) still exist, among them charitable housing estates built for the poor, the so-called *Stiftsgänge* and *Stiftshöfe*. The most famous of the latter are the beautiful **Füchtingshof** (Glockengiesserstrasse 25; ☺ 9am-noon & 3-6pm) and the **Glandorps Gang** (Glockengiesserstrasse 41-51), which you can peer into.

If you head south along An der Obertrave, you pass the idyllic **Malerwinkel** (Painters' Quarter), where people sit on garden benches among blooming flowers in summer, looking out at the houses and white picket fences across the water. This is one of Lübeck's most lovely corners, and shouldn't be missed.

LITERARY MUSEUMS

There must be something in the water in Lübeck, or maybe it's all that marzipan, for the city has connections to two Nobel Prize–winning authors (as well as Nobel Peace Prize–winning former chancellor Willy Brandt).

The winner of the 1929 Nobel Prize for Literature, Thomas Mann, was born in Lübeck in 1875 and his family's former home is now the **Buddenbrookhaus** (☎ 122 4190; www.buddenbrookhaus.de; Mengstrasse 4; adult/concession €5/2.60; 'Kombi' card with Günter Grass Museum €7/4; ☺ 10am-6pm Apr-Dec, 11am-5pm Jan-Mar). Named after Thomas' novel of a wealthy Lübeck family in decline, *The Buddenbrooks* (1901), this award-winning museum is a monument not only to the author of such classics as *Der Tod in Venedig* (Death in Venice) and *Der Zauberberg* (The Magic Mountain), but also to his

brother Heinrich, who wrote the story that became the Marlene Dietrich film *Der Blaue Engel* (The Blue Angel). There's a rundown of the rather tragic family history, too.

While born in Danzig (now Gdansk), Günter Grass had been living just outside Lübeck for 13 years when he collected his Nobel Prize in 1999. But Germany's postwar literary colossus – the author of, among many other works, 1959's searing *Die Blechtrommel* (The Tin Drum) – initially trained as an artist, and has always continued to draw and sculpt. So the **Günter Grass-Haus** (Günter Grass House; ☎ 122 4192; www.guenter-grass-haus.de; Glockengiesserstrasse 21; adult/concession €4/2.20; 'Kombi' card with Günter Grass Museum €7/4; ☺ 10am-6pm Apr-Dec, 11am-5pm Jan-Mar) is one the most aesthetically inviting literary museums you'll ever see. The author's leitmotifs – flounders, rats, snails and eels – are brought to life in bronze and charcoal, as well as in prose, offering a fascinating insight into his creative genius. Here, you can view a copy of the first typewritten page of *Die Blechtrommel*, while the man himself occasionally appears for readings.

Both museums have extensive English annotations and the Buddenbrookhaus in particular houses a great shop.

OTHER MUSEUMS

If you're travelling with children – or have a particular interest in marionettes – don't miss the **Museum für Puppentheater** (☎ 786 26; Am Kolk 14; adult/concession/child €4/3/1.50; ☺ 10am-6pm). It's a private collection of some 1200 puppets, props, posters and more, from Europe, Asia and Africa.

You're most likely to enter the four bare walls of the former **Heiligen-Geist-Hospital** (Königstrasse; admission free; ☺ 10am-5pm Tue-Sun, to 4pm Dec-Feb) if you're coming to Lübeck's superlative **Christmas Market**. Although the building is largely an elegant shell these days, there are resonances of Germany's first hospital (dating back to 1227). Through an early-Gothic hall church, you'll come to the hospital hallway, where you'll see the little chambers that were built around 1820 to give the sick and old a certain degree of privacy.

The **St Annen Museum** (☎ 122 4137; St-Annen-Strasse 15; adult/concession €4/3.50; ☺ 10am-5pm Tue-Sun Apr-Sep, 10am-4pm Tue-Sun Oct-Mar) houses a browsable mish-mash of ecclesiastical art (including Hans Memling's 1491 Passion Altar), historical knick-knacks and contemporary art in its modern Kunsthalle wing. The latter houses the Andy Warhol print of Lübeck's Holstentor.

Sleeping

If you want to experience historic Lübeck, stay in one of the restored *Gänghäuser* (mews houses), in the Stiftsgänge courtyards (see opposite) away from the street. They usually cost €50 to €70 per night for two people, but there's often a three-night minimum. The tourist office can help with bookings, but there aren't many so ring ahead.

BUDGET

Campingplatz Schönböcken (☎ 893 090; fax 892 287; Steinrader Damm 12; per tent/person/car €4.50/3.50/1; ☺ Apr-Oct) This modern camping ground has a kiosk, entertainment room and children's playground. It's a 15-minute bus ride west of the city centre (take bus 7).

DJH hostel Vor dem Burgtor (☎ 334 33; www.jugendherberge.de; Am Gertrudenkirchhof 4; junior/senior dm €16.80/19.80; P 🖳) Those fussy about their furnishings might like this huge, modern hostel. However, it's popular with school groups, and outside the old town – just.

DJH hostel Altstadt (☎ 702 0399; www.jugendherberge.de; Mengstrasse 33; dm under/over 26 yr €17.90/20.90) If you prefer convenience, opt for this central hostel. It isn't particularly new, but it's cosy and comfortable enough.

Hotel zur Alten Stadtmauer (☎ 737 02; www.hotelstadtmauer.de; An der Mauer 57; s/d with shared bathroom from €38/65, with private bathroom from €45/75; P) With pine furniture and splashes of red or yellow, this simple 25-room hotel is bright and cheerful. The wooden flooring means sound carries, but customers tend not to be the partying type. Back rooms overlook the river.

Two very cheap and basic places are **Sleep-Inn** (☎ 719 20; www.cvjm-luebeck.de/cvjm; Grosse Petersgrube 11; dm €12.50; ☺ mid-Jan–mid-Dec) and the **Rucksackhotel** (☎ 706 892; www.rucksackhotel-luebeck.de; Kanalstrasse 70; dm €13-15, d €34-40, linen €3, 🖳). The latter has a vegetarian café open to the public and serves breakfast for €3 to €5.

MIDRANGE

Hotel Lindenhof (☎ 872 100; www.lindenhof-luebeck.de; Lindenstrasse 1a; s €65-80, d €85-110, f €100-135; P ✗) Its rooms are businesslike and small, but a healthy breakfast buffet, friendly service and little extras (such as free biscuits, newspapers and snack service) propel the Lindenhof into a superior league.

Park Hotel am Lindenplatz (☎ 871 970; www.parkhotel-luebeck.de; Lindenplatz 2; s €65-80, d €85-110; P) Art Deco overtones distinguish the public areas of this small, friendly hotel. With their low lighting, the rooms, like Lübeck itself, are ideal for a romantic interlude.

Hotel Jensen (☎ 702 490; www.hotel-jensen.de; An der Obertrave 4-5; s €65-85, d €85-110) Classic and romantic, this old *Patrizierhaus* (mansion house) is conveniently located facing the Salzspeicher across the Trave River. Its seafood restaurant, Yachtzimmer, is also excellent.

Klassik Altstadt Hotel (☎ 702 980; www.klassik-altstadt-hotel.de; Fischergrube 52; s/d €75/130, ste from €135; P) Each room here is dedicated to a different, mostly German writer or artist (somehow Russia's Nikolai Gogol creeps in). It's a token gesture, though, and the overwhelming impression is of a decent, traditionally furnished hotel. Some cheaper singles (€45) at the back share bathrooms.

Hotel Alter Speicher (☎ 710 45; www.hotel-alter-speicher.de; Beckergrube 91-93; s €65-100, d €75-125; P ✗) Well located and comfortable, this also benefits from friendly service. However, the brightly patterned carpet (red and yellow splotches on a dark blue background) in most rooms might give design-conscious guests a headache.

TOP END

Mövenpick Hotel Lübeck (☎ 150 40; www.moevenpick-luebeck.com; Willy-Brandt-Allee 1-5; s €140-145, d €180-190; P ✗ ✗ 🖳) Although it might be a chain with an ugly concrete exterior, this hotel's renovated superior rooms are startling stylish and designer-y. Decorated in tones of either slate grey or burnt sienna, they even feature tasteful abstract works from local artists. Ordinary rooms are, well, more ordinary, but the location near the Holstentor and tourist office couldn't be more convenient.

Radisson SAS Senator Hotel (☎ 1420; www.senatorhotel.de; Willy-Brandt-Allee 6; s €140-145, d €180-190; P ✗ ✗ 🖳 🕿) The Lübeck option that really wows, the Senator resembles something from *War of the Worlds* with its three parallel rectangular wings cantilevered out into the Trave River. Plate-glass windows in the riverfront restaurant and the lofty atrium ensure front-row views of the old town (beautiful at night or in winter), while in 2006 rooms were renovated in a Southeast Asian colonial style.

SCHLESWIG-HOLSTEIN

Eating

Suppentopf (☎ 400 8136; Fleischhauerstrasse 36; soups €3.50; ☽ 11am-4pm Mon-Fri Sep-Jun) Join Lübeck's office workers for a stand-up lunch of delicious, often spicy soup, in this progressive modern kitchen.

Tipasa (☎ 706 0451; Schlumacherstrasse 12-14; mains €3.60-16) Pizzas, curries and other budget meals are served below the faux caveman frescos of animals and Australian Aboriginal dot paintings.

Alte Mühle (☎ 707 2592; Mühlendamm 24; mains €4.50-23; ☽ from 3pm Mon-Sat, from 12.30pm Sun) Located, as the name suggests, in an historic old mill on the banks of the Trave River, this atmospheric wood-lined bistro attracts a savvy mix of Lübeck citizens with its *Flammkuchen* (Alsatian pizzas), chilli con carne, steaks, seasonal specialities, beer and wine. Well worth the detour.

Nui (☎ 203 7333; Beckergrube 72; sushi €1.80-15.50, mains €8.50-17; ☽ dinner only Sat, closed Sun) Tempting smells waft from the artfully organised designer plates in this trendy but relaxed Thai-cum-Japanese restaurant.

Miera' Aubergine (☎ 772 12; Hüxstrasse 57; mains €9-20; ☽ delicatessen-bistro 10am-midnight, restaurant Tue-Sat evenings) Eat antipasti for lunch in the delicatessen-bistro or dine in the restaurant on more formal Italian food.

Markgraf (☎ 706 0343; Fischergrube 18; mains €9.50-21.50; ☽ dinner Tue-Sun) While Schiffergesellschaft (following) can be touristy, this similarly historic restaurant is the epitome of elegance, with white tablecloths and silverware laid out under the chandeliers and black ceiling beams of this 14th-century house. The cuisine displays Mediterranean and Asian influences, with dishes such as pumpkin soup with coconut, and ginger-spiced perch.

Schiffergesellschaft (☎ 767 76; Breite Strasse 2; mains €10-23) Ships' lanterns, models of 17th-century ships and orange Chinese-style lamps with revolving maritime silhouettes hang from the painted and wooden-beamed ceiling in this low-lit former sailors' guildhall. As you sit on long benches resembling church pews, staff in long white aprons bring you Frisian specialities.

Drinking

Café Lounge (☎ 307 2950; Wahmstrasse 40; ☽ from 11am Mon-Sat, from 3pm Sun) Turntables hang like paintings on the wall and you have a choice of viewing – the aquarium or TV – in this hip, narrow bar, where you have to squeeze past your neighbours to get to your seat.

Café Remise (☎ 777 73; Wahmstrasse 43-45) This cult café does serve humble fare, but it's far better to pop into its courtyard instead for its wide range of teas, coffees, beer and wine.

Im Alten Zolln (☎ 723 95; Mühlenstrasse 93-95) Classic, slightly alternative pub, where patrons people-watch from the terrace in summer and watch bands inside in winter.

Brauberger (☎ 702 0606; Alfstrasse 36; ☽ closed Sun) This traditional German brewer has been serving its own golden amber since 1225.

Entertainment

Local listings magazines include *Piste* and *Ultimo*. The tourist office's *Lübeck rundum* (€2.90, German only) is also useful.

MUSIC

Ask the tourist office about church organ concerts.

Musikhochschule Lübeck (☎ 150 50; Grosse Petersgrube 17-29) This music academy puts on a number of high-calibre concerts throughout the summer and winter semesters, and these are mostly free.

Musik und Kongresshalle (☎ 790 40; Willy-Brandt-Allee 10) This concrete monolith across from the Altstadt – notable for the colourful statues on its roof – is where big international names play when in town.

Jazz-Café (☎ 707 3734; Mühlenstrasse 62) Jam sessions and a wide programme of concerts make this slick, sleek place Lübeck's top meeting spot for jazz lovers.

THEATRE

Marionettentheater (☎ 700 60; Am Kolk 20-22; ☽ Tue-Sun) This terrific puppet theatre puts on a children's show at 3pm, and another for adults on some Thursdays and every Saturday at 7.30pm.

Getting There & Away

AIR

Low-cost carrier **Ryanair** (www.ryanair.com) flies from London to Lübeck-Blankensee, calling it Hamburg-Lübeck. Synchronised shuttle buses take passengers straight to Hamburg (one-way €8, 1¼ hours). Alternatively, scheduled bus 6 (€2.15) takes passengers into Lübeck's Hauptbahnhof and central bus station.

BOAT

DFDS Tor Line (☎ 399 270; www.dfdstorline.de; Lübeck Siems pier, Unter der Herrenbrücke 21) sails to Riga, and **Finnlines** (☎ 150 70; www.finnlines.de; Nordlandkai, Einsiedelstrasse 43) to St Petersburg. See p760 for details.

Könemann Schiffahrt (☎ 0451-280 1635; www.koene mannschiffahrt.de; Teerhofinsel14a) has ferries to and from Travemünde (one-way/return €8/14) three times daily in season.

BUS

Regional buses stop opposite the local buses on Hansestrasse, around the corner from the Hauptbahnhof. Kraftomnibusse services to/from Wismar terminate here, as do the Autokraft buses to/from Hamburg, Schwerin, Kiel, Rostock and Berlin.

CAR & MOTORCYCLE

Lübeck is reached via the A1 from Hamburg. The town also lies at the crossroads of the B75, the B104 to Schwerin, the B206 to Bad Segeberg and the B207 to Ratzeburg.

TRAIN

Lübeck has connections every hour to Hamburg (€10, 45 minutes), Kiel (€13.40, 1¼ hours) and Rostock (€18.80, two hours) via Bad Kleinen.

Getting Around

Lübeck's centre is easily walkable, and since some streets (Königstrasse and all the Altstadt streets to the east of it) are pedestrianised and off limits to all but hotel guests' vehicles between 11.30am and 6pm (from 10am on Saturday), many people just park their cars and go on foot.

Bus tickets for a few stops cost €1.40, ordinary singles €1.90 and day cards €5.60. The last two are valid for Travemünde and Gothmund.

AROUND LÜBECK
Travemünde
☎ 04502

Writer Thomas Mann declared he spent his happiest days in Travemünde just outside Lübeck and many German holidaymakers feel the same way. Bought by Lübeck in 1329 to control the shipping coming into its harbour, this is now a popular coastal playground. With 4.5km of sandy beaches at the point where the Trave River flows into the Baltic Sea, beach sports are the main draw. There's an annual **sand sculpture festival** (www .sandworld.de) in July and August, a **sailing regatta** (www.travemuenderwoche.de) in the last week of July and much more.

The town takes great pride in its historic sailing ship, **Passat** (☎ 122 5202), which used to do the run around South America's Cape Horn in the earlier part of the 20th century. Now it's a living museum. The **Passat Choir** (www.passatchor.de) performs concerts of sea shanties and other appropriate tunes, on board the ship itself or sometimes on land. If you want to hear it for free, it practises most Thursdays at 7.30pm in the Pommernzentrum at Europaweg 3. Ask **Lübeck & Travemünde tourist office** (☎ 01805-882 233; www .travemuende-tourismus.de; Strandbahnhof; ☺ 9.30am-7pm Mon-Fri, 10am-3pm Sat, 10am-2pm Sun Jun-Sep, 9.30am-6pm Mon-Fri, 10am-3pm Sat Oct-May) for more details.

The tourist office can also help with accommodation. Camping is particularly fun, with a couple of beachfront sites, but there's the usual range of accommodation. The town's two most famous hotels are the luxurious **Columbia Hotel Casino Travemünde** (☎ 3080; www.columbia-hotels.de; Kaiserallee 2) and the brand-new spa resort **A-Rosa** (☎ 307 00; www.a-rosa.de; Aussenallee 10), where you have to book a package; it specialises in preventative medicine and youth-giving treatments. Both hotels are in historic, 19th-century buildings.

Könemann Schiffahrt (☎ 0451-280 1635; www .koenemannschiffahrt.de; Teerhofinsel 14a) has ferries going to and from Lübeck (one-way/ return €8/14) three times daily in season. Otherwise, regular trains connect Lübeck to Travemünde, which has three train stations: Skandinavienkai (for ferries), Hafenbahnhof and Strandbahnhof (for the beach and tourist office). Buses 30 and 31 provide direct services from Lübeck's central bus station. The B75 leads northeast from Lübeck to Travemünde.

Travemünde is as much a gateway to Scandinavia as Kiel, with three major ferry lines sailing from its Skandinavienkai, as follows:

Finnlines (☎ 150 70; www.finnlines.de) To Helsinki.
Finnlines Nordö-Link (☎ 805 20; www.nordoe-link .com) To Malmö, Sweden.
TT-Line (☎ 801 81; www.ttline.de) To Trelleborg, Sweden.

SCHLESWIG-HOLSTEIN

Ratzeburg

☎ 04541 / pop 13,700

An historic town scenically located on an island and connected to the surrounding land by three narrow causeways, Ratzeburg makes another idyllic day trip. Highlights in town include the **Dom** built by Heinrich der Löwe (see boxed text, p619) and a former **residence of the Dukes of Mecklenburg**. However, it's the surrounding waterways that are most interesting in this so-called 'Amazon of the north'. While that moniker is rather optimistic, there is a lush variety of plants, animals and landscapes – deciduous trees, water lilies, herons, swans, marsh and fen – and as the area was in the shadow of the Iron Curtain it was virtually untouched for half a century.

These days, **boat tours** (☎ 0451-793 885; www .wakenitz-schiffahrt-quandt.de; Wakenitzufer 1c) sail from Lübeck up the 14.5km Wakenitz River to the Ratzeburger Lake (one-way/return €11/17.50, four departures daily each way between May and September).

If you're interested in spending more time in the town itself, ask the Lübeck & Travemünde tourist office (p685) or **Ratzeburg Information** (☎ 858 565; info@ratzeburg.de; Schlossweise 7; ☻ 9am-5pm Mon-Fri, 11am-4pm Sat & Sun May-Sep, reduced hours in winter).

Gothmund

Lined with fishermen's cottages, this charming village on Lübeck's outskirts hasn't changed for years. Stroll along Fischerweg, a path running in front of the cottages, or take the same path west, which leads through a nature reserve beside the Trave River.

Take bus 12 (leaving three times an hour from Lübeck's central bus station) to the last stop.

SCHLESWIG

☎ 04621 / pop 25,000

Still some 45km to go before the Danish border, but Scandinavia feels much nearer in Schleswig, the 'Viking town' on the longest Baltic Sea fjord. Suburban red-brick houses and well-kept lawns give the place a Nordic look, while the tall cathedral spire stands proudly above the water, hinting that little Schleswig wasn't always this sleepy.

This is certainly true. Founded in 804, after a major Viking community put down roots across the Schlei fjord, it was the continent's economic hub for some 200 years.

A lot of other people have since come and gone, including the Dukes of Gottorf (who made Schleswig their power base from the 16th to 18th centuries) and later generations of humble fishers. But all have left remarkable reminders, making Schleswig a charming stopover. As host of the 2008 *Landesgartenschau* (State Garden Show) it hopes to build on that legacy.

Orientation

Schleswig's Hauptbahnhof is about 1km south of Schloss Gottorf and 3km from the town. Most buses from the Hauptbahnhof will take you into town, and the long footpath from the Hauptbahnhof to the Schloss, and onwards into town, is very clearly marked. In town, the central bus station is on the corner of Königstrasse and Plessenstrasse, with the tourist office, Dom and Altstadt just to the southeast.

Information

There are late-opening internet cafés in the Hauptbahnhof and bus station.

Post office (Poststrasse 1a)
Tourist office (☎ 981 616; touristinformation@ schleswig.de; Plessenstrasse 7; ☻ 9.30am-5.30pm Mon-Fri, 9.30am-12.30pm Sat May-Sep, 10am-4pm Mon-Thu, 10am-1pm Fri Oct-Apr) There's a hotel board and phone outside this office for late arrivals.

Sights & Activities
SCHLOSS GOTTORF

Wartime destruction of Kiel meant that the **Schleswig-Holstein Landesmuseum** (☎ 8130; www .schloss-gottorf.de, adult/concession/family €6/3/13; ☻ 10am-6pm Apr-Oct, 10am-4pm Tue-Sun Nov-Mar) was moved to the Dukes of Gottorf's 12th-century castle in Schleswig. The collection fitted perfectly and has stayed here ever since. Its sterling reputation brings visitors from Scandinavia and even Russia to view its treasures, and Schloss Gottorf certainly doesn't disappoint.

The Historischer Rundgang (historical tour) creates a memorable first impression with a roomful of paintings by Lucas Cranach the Elder and a wood-panelled 17th-century wine tavern from Lübeck. There's also the rococo **Plöner Saal**, with faïence from the Baltic region; the stunning **Schlosskapelle** (room 26); and the elegant **Hirschsaal**, the former banquet hall named for the bas-reliefs of deer on the walls.

The more contemporary collection is equally noteworthy. There's an entire **Jugendstil Abteilung** (Art Nouveau department; 😊 closed 1-2pm), featuring chairs by Henry van de Velde and Joseph Hoffman, among others. Plus the **Stiftung Rolf Horn**, in one of the smaller buildings, has outstanding 20th-century paintings, sketches, lithographs and woodcuts from German artists such as Emil Nolde and Ernst Balach (as well as Ludwig Kirchner, Erich Heckel, Christian Rohlfs and Otto Müller).

And we haven't even reached the museum's two main highlights!

The first is the **Nydam-Boot**, a reconstructed and preserved 28-oar rowing boat from 350 BC, which is housed in its own hall (and sometimes goes on loan to other museums).

More recently, a reconstruction of the famous **Gottorfer Globus** (Gottorf Globe; adult/child Mon-Fri €10/6.50, Sat & Sun €13/10.50; 😊 10am-6pm Apr-Oct, to 4pm Nov-Mar) has been placed in its own house a five-minute walk behind the castle grounds. The original 17th-century globe was lauded as one of the wonders of the world – its first planetarium – but through war ended up being taken from Schleswig to St Petersburg. It's still there in the Lomonosov Museum (although it's fire-damaged).

The exterior of the 3m-diameter reconstruction shows how the continents and seas were thought to look in the 17th century. The real magic is inside, however. Several people can fit on a bench inside the globe and watch the Renaissance night sky change as the globe spins around them; it takes eight minutes to simulate a day.

Russian president Vladimir Putin accompanied his pal (and then Chancellor) Gerhard Schröder on a state visit to inaugurate the replica globe at the end of 2004.

There are English-language guides to the entire museum, as well as a café and restaurant on site. You'll need at least half a day to do the place justice.

WIKINGER MUSEUM

It would have been rather dangerous venturing into this area some 1000 to 1200 years ago, when Vikings ruled the roost from their base here at Haithabu, across the Schlei from Schleswig. Fortunately, these days the local warriors are a lot less fearsome, being merely actors or exhibits at the **Wikinger Museum** (Viking Museum; 😊 813 222; www.haithabu.de; adult/concession/ family €4/2.50/9; 😊 9am-5pm daily Apr-Oct, 10am-4pm Tue-Sun Nov-Mar).

Located just outside the historic settlement (now an archaeological site), this engrossing museum features replica huts showing how the Vikings lived *en famille*. There are also seven exhibition halls (designed to resemble Viking boat sheds) with multilingual multimedia displays and artefacts discovered nearby. One of these includes a 30m longboat, since reconstructed.

Kids love the place and seasonal events include an autumn *Messe* (fair) of Viking crafts. Other good times to come are at Midsummer's Day eve, New Year's Eve and during Schleswig's 'Viking Days' every second August (held in 2006 and 2008).

The museum lies east of the B76 that runs between Schleswig and Kiel, about 3km from Schleswig's Hauptbahnhof. Between May and September, the easiest way to arrive is by ferry (see p693).

Otherwise, bus 4810 to Kiel runs all year. Alight at Haddeby.

HOLM

This traditional fishing village southeast of the Altstadt looks even cuter than it sounds – a kind of mini-me of medieval towns. It sits on a peninsula that until 1935 was an island, and its centrepiece is an almost **toy-sized chapel** in the middle of a small cemetery, which is in turn ringed by a cobbled road and tiny fishermen's houses. Only residents of Holm may be buried at the cemetery.

A handful of men still fish here, and their colourful nets hanging out to dry are a favourite photo opportunity. Continue further east, and you'll come to the **Johanniskloster** (Convent; 😊 242 36; Süderholmstrasse).

DOM ST PETRI & AROUND

With its steeple towering above the town, the **Dom St Petri** (😊 253 67; Süderdomstrasse 2; 😊 9am-5pm Mon-Sat, 1.30-5pm Sun May-Sep, 10am-4pm Mon-Sat, 1.30-4pm Sun Oct-Apr) provides an excellent point of orientation. It's also home to the intricate **Bordesholmer Altar** (1521), a carving by Hans Brüggemann. The 12.6m by 7.14m altar, on the wall furthest from the entrance, shows more than 400 figures in 24 scenes relating the story of the Passion of Christ – the result of extraordinary craftsmanship and patience. English pamphlets (€0.30) describe lesser cathedral features.

While here, don't forget to explore the cobbled cluster of streets behind the cathedral, especially **Rathhausmarkt**. The **Königswiese meadow** south of Königstrasse will be the main site of the 2008 State Garden Show and is currently being redeveloped.

Tours

Three different companies offer a vast array of boat trips up the 40km Schlei between April and October. The leading operator is **Schleischiffahrt A Bischoff** (☎ 233 19; www.schleischiff fahrt.de, in German). Check the website if you read German, or ask the tourist office for more details. Services leave from downtown Schleswig on Tuesday and near Schloss Gottorf on other days.

Sleeping

Many hotels in Schleswig close their reception at 10pm or even as early as 6pm. You can still contact them by phone after closing time, but it's always better to call at least half a day ahead.

Campingplatz Haithabu (☎ 324 50; per adult/tent/car €3.50/6/2; ☼ Mar-Oct) This camping ground is right on the southern shore of the Schlei in Haddeby, with a great view of the Schleswig skyline. Take bus 4810 or catch a ferry (see opposite) in summer.

DJH hostel (☎ 238 93; www.jugendherberge.de/jh /schleswig; Spielkoppel 1; under/over 26yr €14.10/17.10; ✗) Grab an early night in this pleasant, renovated hostel that's popular with families and school groups. (Noise is an afternoon phenomenon here.) It's wise to grab an early breakfast, too, before the locusts – your fellow guests – move in. The nearest bus stop is Stadttheater, from where it's a 10- to 15-minute walk.

B&B Schleswig (☎ 485 992; www.bb-schleswig.de; Töpferstrasse 9; s/d €60/80; Ⓟ) You'd scarcely credit there's a building behind all the ivy, let alone one this spacious. From the long, narrow dining room, the six bedrooms and guest lounge stretch back to the private garden, where the Sinram family's two dogs roam around the teahouse. Décor combines historic, romantic and design touches, but is all very much the individual taste of the owner, who (unusually for a continental B&B) lives on the premises.

Zollhaus (☎ 239 47; www.zollhaus-schleswig.de; Lollfuss 110; s €65-75, d €80-95; Ⓟ ✗) Culture vultures coming to neighbouring Schloss Gottorf will enjoy the refined but totally unstuffy

atmosphere here. The 200-year-old customs house building was given a designer makeover in 2000, with a handful of stylish and comfortable rooms renovated in varying colours. The restaurant's good, too (closed Monday).

Hotel Alter Kreisbahnhof (☎ 302 00; www.hotel -alter-kreisbhahnhof.de; Königstrasse 9; s/d €52/90; Ⓟ) A former local train station, this new hotel-restaurant is an all-round winner. Just across from the bus station, its stylish modern rooms are light-filled and spacious, and some have water views. As a matter of policy, the hotel employs some staff with minor disabilities, and rooms can be equipped for special needs. You'll certainly never want for electricity sockets; we counted 10 in one room (all tastefully arranged, mind).

Eating & Drinking

Panorama (☎ 245 80; Plessenstrasse 15; mains €4.50-13.50) The tasty wood-fired pizza provides an antidote for vegetarians or those tired of seafood. There are some Asian and even Persian dishes, too.

Schleimöve (☎ 243 09; Süderholmstrasse 8; mains €11-20) This maritime restaurant rounds off the perfect Schleswig morning or afternoon. On the edges of the main 'square' in pint-sized Holm, it serves platters combining different types of fresh fish, from salmon and perch to North Sea shrimp and, for more adventurous gourmets, eel.

Senatorkroog (☎ 222 90; Rathausmarkt 9-10; mains €10-18.50) If Schleimöve is booked out, this also gives you the chance to sample a melange of different local fish as well as good old German staples. The 1884 building creates an interesting atmosphere.

Café im Wikingturm (☎ 330 40; 26th fl, Wikingturm, Wikingeck 5) For coffee and cake, guess what? This hulking great ugly tower across the Schlei enjoys the best regional views.

Schleswig also boasts a **brewery** (☎ 292 06; Königstrasse 27; ☼ from 5pm Sun-Fri, from 11am Sat, closed Sun & Mon Oct-Mar).

Getting There & Away

In one respect, it's more convenient to catch a bus from neighbouring towns, such as Kiel (bus 4810; €6.10, 1½ hours), Flensburg (bus 4810; €5.65, 50 minutes) and Husum (bus 1046, sometimes requires a change; €5.65, one hour), because the buses land you downtown, whereas the train is 3km from the centre. However, bus services are less frequent than the train, particularly on weekends.

Direct trains to Hamburg (€19.30, 1½ hours) run every two hours, while trains to Flensburg (€6.10, 30 minutes) leave several times hourly. There's also an hourly link to Husum (€6.10, 30 minutes) and Kiel (€8.70, 50 minutes).

If you're driving, take the A7 (Hamburg–Flensburg) to the Schuby exit, then continue east on the B201.

Getting Around

Tickets for Schleswig's bus system cost €1.25 per trip, or €6.15 for a six-ticket strip. If you're arriving by train, you can pick up a bicycle near the Hauptbahnhof, at **Fahrrad Verleih am Bahnhof** (☎ 335 55; www.fahrradverleih-schesswig.com, in German; Husumer Baum 36; per day from €5).

Between May and September, ferries cross the Schlei from Schleswig Hafen (just south of the Dom) between 11.30pm to 5.30pm daily (adult one-way/return €2/3.50).

FLENSBURG

☎ 0461 / pop 90,000

Whereas Schleswig is situated on a fjord, Flensburg is on a firth and the small name change seems to make the world of difference. Flensburg is industrial and much less pretty than its southern neighbour. However, it's a handy and lively staging point en route to nearby Denmark, and it does boast an interesting past.

Still sometimes called 'Rumstadt' for its prosperous 18th-century trade in liquor with the Caribbean, it was also the Third Reich's last seat of power, when shortly before VE Day in WWII a cornered Hitler handed power to Flensburg-based Admiral Karl Dönitz. Unsurprisingly, Flensburg makes nothing of this dark snippet, but reminders of its sea-faring, rum-trading days are found across town.

Orientation

Most attractions run north–south parallel to the western bank of the firth. The tourist office is in the northwestern corner of the central bus station, with the firth lying straight ahead along Norderhofenden (which becomes Schiffsbrücke). The pedestrian zone is just inland; turn left at the tourist office into Rathausstrasse and right into Grosse Strasse (which becomes Norderstrasse).

Information

For late arrivals, there's a hotel board and map at the Hauptbahnhof.

Flensburg tourist office (☎ 909 0920; www .flensburg-tourismus.de; Europa-Haus; ⏰ 9am-6pm Mon-Fri year-round, 10am-2pm Sat May-Sep, to Sat 4pm Jul-Aug) Located beside the central bus station.
Media Speicher (☎ 840 1188; Grosse Strasse 69; per hr €3; ⏰ 10am-10pm Mon-Sat, noon-10pm Sun) In the courtyard; an excellent all-bells-and-whistles internet café.
Post office (Schiffsbrückstrasse 2)

Sights

A Flensburg highlight, literally as well as figuratively, is the hill-top **Museumsberg Flensburg** (Municipal Museum; ☎ 852 956; Museumsberg 1; adult/child/family €4/1.50/8, extra for special exhibitions; ⏰ 10am-5pm Tue-Sun Apr-Oct, 10am-4pm Tue-Sun Nov-Mar). The museum is divided into two sections: the Heinrich-Sauermann-Haus and the Hans-Christiansen-Haus. The first contains a collection of rooms and furniture from Schleswig-Holstein history, including a remarkably painted cembalo (early piano covered in murals; room 25). In the second building, you'll find excellent Art Nouveau works by Flensburg-born painter Hans Christiansen, as well as an Emil Nolde room. Keep your ticket, as it's good for all city museums.

The other thing to do in Flensburg is to check out the town's *Kaufmannshöfe* (merchants' courtyards). These date from the 18th century, when Danish-ruled Flensburg provided supplies to the Danish West Indies (St Thomas, St Jan and St Croix) in exchange for sugar and rum. Designed to make it easier to load goods into ships, they typically consisted of a tall warehouse on the harbour side, behind which was a series of low workshops, wrapped around a central courtyard and leading to the merchant's living quarters.

The tourist office gives out free town maps marking nearly every *Hof,* or ask for its similarly free *Käpitans Weg* brochure, which follows a captain's route around town as he was preparing for a trip.

Just off Grosse Strasse 24 is a courtyard that houses the attractive **Westindienspeicher** (West Indian warehouse). If you continue south along Grosse Strasse it becomes Holm, where at No 17 you also find the **Borgerforeningen Hof**.

The prettiest courtyards can be found off picturesque **Rote Strasse** (continue south along Holm through Südermarkt). While here, you have a chance to buy some rum at **Weinhaus Braasch** (☎ 141 600; www.braasch-rum.de; Rote Strasse 26-28).

For more about the rum trade, head to the **Schiffahrtsmuseum** (☎ 852 970; Schiffbrücke 39; adult/concession €4/1.50; ☑ 10am-5pm Tue-Sun Apr-Oct, 10am-4pm Tue-Sun Nov-Mar), where there's a small but unremarkable **Rum Museum** in the basement.

Activities

Today, when most of us fly across borders, it's fun to have the opportunity to openly cross one on foot. Just north of Flensburg you can do exactly this, by hiking along the so-called **Gendarmenpfad** trail, where the **Schusterkate**, northern Europe's smallest border post, sits on the only bridge connecting Germany and Denmark.

Ask the tourist office for its Gendarmenpfad pamphlet. It's in German and Danish only, but the maps are easily understandable. The tourist office can help (in English) with any more details you need. Remember to take your passport.

Tours

Nordlicht Reisen (☎ 500 8990; www.nordische-seetouristik.de; adult/child return €5/3.50) operates cruises to Glücksburg on MS *Nordertor*, departing from where Norderhofenden meets Schiffbrücke. Boats leave five times daily from June to September and less frequently in winter.

A little bit closer to the bus station, the **MS Möwe** (☎ 629 45; www.ms-moewe.net; adult/child €5/3) offers one-hour cruises around the firth. Check the board for current sailing times.

Sleeping

Generally, hotels in nearby Schleswig are nicer and provide better value for money than in Flensburg. The Strandhotel Glücksburg is a luxurious exception.

DJH hostel (☎ 377 42; www.jugendherberge/jh/flensburg; Fichtestrasse 16; under/over 26yr €15.40/18.40; ℗ ☒) Hidden down a leafy lane near the local football stadium, this is very popular with school sporting teams, so brace yourself for lots of noise and restless activity. Facilities are tip-top, though, and the ride from town (on bus 3, 5 or 7 to Stadion) only takes about five minutes.

Etap Hotel (☎ 480 8920; www.etaphotel.com; Süderhofenden 14; s/d/tr €36/42/50; ℗ ☒ ▢) This McDonald's of the hotel world provides a less stressful budget option. The décor is garish and the bathrooms are plastic capsules, but the place is clean, comfortable and central – right near the bus station.

Hotel Dittmer's Gasthof (☎ 240 52; www.dittmers gasthof.de; Neumarkt 2-3; s/d/tr €50/85/150; ℗) This flower-festooned historic inn has been run by the same family for more than 100 years. Rooms are cosy, the welcome warm, and the restaurant serves fish specialities.

Hotel Flensburger Hof (☎ 141 990; www.flensburger-hof.de; Süderhofenden 38; s €75-80, d €100, tr €120, q €140; ℗ ☒) Subtly decked out with historic Frisian touches, the breakfast room here provides a wonderful start to the day. Upstairs, some of the bedrooms are starting to look a little tired, but minibars, hairdryers, wi-fi and friendly service all help atone for that.

Strandhotel Glücksburg (☎ 04631-614 10; www.strandhotel-gluecksburg.de; Kirstenstrasse 6; s/d €90/120, ste from €150; ℗ ☒ ☒) The 'white castle by the sea' is the sort of hotel around which people will organise their itinerary. A historic villa where author Thomas Mann used to holiday, its rooms are now decked out in a modern designer style, with a spa and gourmet restaurant to boot. The ferry from Flensburg brings you nearest or get off the bus at Kurpark.

Eating & Drinking

For everyday options, simply walk down Grosse Strasse, or pick a restaurant off Rote Strasse or in Holm Passage (the courtyard, not the shopping mall).

Hansens Brauerei (☎ 222 10; Schiffbrücke 16; meals €8-14) Simple but hearty German fare is served here, although most people order their food to accompany the wide range of beers.

Piet Henningsen (☎ 245 76; Schiffbrücke 20; mains €11-38) Flensburg's most famous restaurant is cosily stuffy with exotic souvenirs brought home by its sailors, including African statues and ceramics, Indonesian wall hangings, ship models, empty rum bottles, a leopard skin and a stuffed crocodile. Argentine steaks aside, the menu is a smorgasbord of seafood. The prices can very occasionally seem jacked up on account of the place's fame (ie €17.50 for a prawn sandwich with fried eggs). But, hey, you're on holiday, and as the local saying has it: *Wer dat Piet nicht kennt, hat de Tied verpennt* (He who doesn't know Piet's has missed the tide).

Getting There & Away

Flensburg has rail connections with Kiel (€16.20, 1½ hours), Hamburg (€30, 1¾ hours) and Schleswig (€6.10, 30 minutes). Trips to Husum (€9.10, 1½ hours) require a change at Jübek.

Autokraft (☎ 690 69; www.autokraft.de, in German) has regular buses to Husum (€6.10, one hour), Niebüll (€6.10, one hour) and Kiel (€8.70, two hours); all leave from the central bus station.

Flensburg is at the beginning of the A7, which leads south to Hamburg, Hanover and beyond. The town can also be reached via the B76, B199 and B200.

Getting Around

Buses cost €1.50/4.50 for a single/day pass, but you can easily cover Flensburg on foot.

To walk from the Hauptbahnhof, which takes 10 to 15 minutes, take the exit straight ahead on your left, past the statues carved from tree trunks. Follow Bahnhofstrasse round to the left until you reach the first major crossroad. Veer left (west) across the street towards Rote Strasse. This leads into Südermarkt, which becomes Holm and then Grosse Strasse.

GLÜCKSBURG

☎ 04631 / pop 5985

This small spa town is renowned for its horseshoe-shaped Renaissance **Wasserschloss** (Moated Palace; ☎ 2213; adult/concession €5/3.50; ☒ 10am-5pm May-Sep), which appears to float in the middle of a large lake, and thus appears in many historical TV soap operas too. Even after a recent, much-needed paint job was begun in 2006, it remains a pretty rather than stunning sight, but the rest of this town 10km northeast of Flensburg is equally charming, and it's nice to stroll around the lake up to the beach.

Bus 21 goes hourly between to Glücksburg (€2.10/3.80 one-way/return) from Flensburg's central bus station. For boat services to Glücksburg, see Tours (opposite).

HUSUM & THE HALLIGEN

☎ 04841 / pop 21,000

The 19th-century German novelist and poet Theodor Storm (1817–88) called his hometown 'the grey town by the sea'. That's a little harsh, especially in late March and early April when millions of purple crocuses bloom in Husum's Schlosspark. However, Storm did have a point, especially when Husum is competing with other more attractive destinations. The author's fans will want to see where some of his books were written, including the seminal North Frisian novella *Der Schimmelreiter* (The Rider on the White Horse). Most,

though, will only visit Husum as a launching pad for explorations of the islets known as Halligen.

Orientation

Husum is compact and extremely well signposted. The Hauptbahnhof lies 700m south of the city centre. Head north along Herzog-Adolf-Strasse (passing the library and the central bus station) and turn left at Ludwig-Nissen-Strasse, following the sign saying Zentrum, to the *Binnenhafen* (inner harbour); the *Aussenhafen* (outer harbour) is just west of here. Alternatively, continue north along Herzog-Adolf-Strasse and turn left into Nordstrasse for the Markt, Grossstrasse and tourist office.

Information

Husum tourist office (☎ 898 70; www.tourismus -husum.de; Historisches Rathaus, Grosstrasse 27; ☒ 9am-6pm Mon-Fri, 10am-4pm Sat Apr-Oct, 9am-5pm Mon-Fri, 10am-4pm Sat Nov-Mar)

Sights

HALLIGEN

Is it an island? Is it a sandbank? No, it's a *Hallig*, one of about 10 tiny wafer-flat 'islets' scattered across the Schleswig-Holstein Wadden Sea National Park (Nationalpark Schleswig-Holsteinisches Wattenmeer). In the Middle Ages, some 50 Halligen existed, but the sea has swallowed up most. Life here is rough and in constant conflict with the tides. Up to 60 times a year, floods drown the beaches and meadows, leaving the few reed-thatched farms stranded on the artificial knolls, or 'wharves', that they're built on. An aerial shot of such stranded farms is a favourite postcard image.

Most people experience the islets on day excursions. The prettiest destination is **Hallig Hooge**, which once sheltered a Danish king from a storm in the handsome **Königshaus**, with its blue and white tiles and baroque ceiling fresco. Other popular Halligen include Langeness and Gröde.

From Husum, **Wilhelm Schmid GmbH** (☎ 201 416; www.wef-schmid-husum.de) offers boat tours (€8 to €16) to the Halligen during the high season. The ride can be quite rough on windy days. Boats leave from the Aussenhafen in Husum. Some boats pass sandbanks with seal colonies. Ring and book the day before you need to travel as departure times vary.

The Husum tourist office has brochures on various other operators, some of whom leave from Schlüttsiel, about 35km north. If you're driving to Schlüttsiel, take the B5; bus 1041 makes several runs daily from Husum to the landing docks.

Some Halligen can also be reached from the North Frisian Islands (p699).

OTHER SIGHTS

Even if you've never before heard of the author, the **Theodor-Storm-Haus** (Theodor Storm House; ☎ 666 270; www.storm-gesellschaft.de; Wasserreihe 31; adult/concession €2.50/1; ⏰ 10am-5pm Tue-Fri, 11am-5pm Sat, 2-5pm Sun & Mon Apr-Oct, 2-5pm Tue, Thu & Sat Nov-Mar) will whet your appetite. Well-placed literary snippets and biographical titbits fill in the life of this novelist, poet and proud Schleswig-Holstein citizen. A pamphlet in English provides a brief commentary.

Ask the tourist office about other museums, including a ship museum and a couple of good options for kids. The *Kulturpfad der Stadt Husum* brochure has a handy map and short description of the town's main sights. Many focus on Theodor Storm, right down to the **fountain** in the Markt, which shows Tine, a young Frisian woman who figures in a Storm novella. Even the **Marienkirche** (1829) featured in a couple of his novellas. The church tower is supposed to symbolise a lighthouse.

In early spring, the **Schlosspark**, with millions of blooming crocuses, is the town's most colourful sight.

Sleeping

Holiday apartments, easily booked through the tourist office, are generally cheaper than hotels, though some have minimum three-night stays in the high season (April to October), when prices also rise. Private rooms are available.

DJH hostel (☎ 2714; www.jugendherberge.de/jh /husum; Schobüller Strasse 34; dm under/over 26yr €15.10/18.10; P ✗) Husum's hostel is set in a typical and very atmospheric Frisian building northwest of the city centre; take bus 1051 from the central bus station to Westerkampweg. It closes during the off season, so ring ahead.

Hotel Hinrichsen (☎ 890 70; www.hotel-hinrichsen .de; Süderstrasse 35; s €45-50, d €65-75; P) There's a warm welcome at this privately run hotel, with modern rooms. Even if the bathrooms are largely moulded-plastic constructions, but the friendly welcome makes up for it.

Hotel am Schlosspark (☎ 202 224; www.hotel-am -schlosspark-husum.de; Hinter der Neustadt 76-86; s/d €55/95; P) Whitewashed and laid out like a sprawling motel, this modern hotel is popular with groups.

Hotel Altes Gymnasium (☎ 8330; www.altes -gymnasium.de; Süderstrasse 6; s €115-135, d €140-200; P) This five-star hotel is a splendidly atmospheric former high school, with Persian carpets, flagstones, tapestries and chandeliers in the entrance hall, plus spacious luxury rooms. But it's hardly worth it unless you can get accommodation in the older building, rather than the new wing. There are plenty of eating options around the Binnenhafen (inner harbour).

Getting There & Away

There are direct hourly train connections to Kiel (€16.20, 1½ hours), Hamburg-Altona (€24.50, 2½ hours) and Schleswig (€6.10, 30 minutes), plus several links daily to Westerland on Sylt (€14.70, one hour).

Husum has many bus connections with other towns in North Friesland, but the service is irregular. For detailed information, call ☎ 7870.

Husum is at the crossroads of the B5, the B200 and the B201.

There are high-speed boats from Amrun to Nordstrand (€18.50) and from Sylt to Nordstrand (€25) daily from April to October. They connect by bus to Husum.

NORTH FRISIAN ISLANDS

Germany's North Frisian Islands are a strange proposition. Hearing of their grass-covered dunes, shifting sands, birds, seal colonies, jaunty lighthouses and rugged cliffs, you'd imagine them as the domain of hardy nature-lovers. Instead, these North Sea islands are a favourite of the German jet-set and parts of them feel more like Martha's Vineyard. Traditional reed-thatched cottages now house luxury goods stores such as Cartier and Louis Vuitton, while car parks on Sylt are frequently crammed with Mercedes and Porsches.

Still, bicycle-riding nobodies can still – thankfully – be seen taking in the pure sea air in the more remote corners of glamorous Sylt. Amrum and Föhr, the latter across the tidal Schleswig-Holstein Wadden Sea, are more peaceful still.

Note, however, that while most of Germany is very reasonably priced, on Sylt you will pay a premium for the experience, especially in Kampen.

SYLT

☎ 04651 / pop 21,000

The island of Sylt is shaped a bit like an anchor attached to the mainland. On its west coast, the fierce surf of the North Sea gnaws mercilessly at the changing shoreline. The wind can be so strong that the world's best windsurfers meet here each September for the final Surf World Cup of the tour. By contrast, Sylt's eastern Wadden Sea shore is tranquil and serene. The shallow ocean retreats twice daily with the tides, exposing the muddy sea bottom. On Sylt's north, you'll find wide expanses of shifting dunes with candy-striped lighthouses above fields of gleaming yellow rape flower, as well as expanses of heath.

For the past 40 years, Sylt has been the preferred playground of the German jet set, providing gossip for Germany's tabloid press. These days, the couplings and triplings are more discreet than they once were, but the glut of fancy restaurants, designer boutiques, ritzy homes and luxury cars prove that the moneyed set has not disappeared.

It's easy enough, though, to leave the glamour and crowds behind and get comfortably lost on the beach, in the dunes or on a bike trail.

Orientation

Sylt is 38.5km long and measures only 700m at its narrowest point. The largest town, commercial hub and train terminus is Westerland in the centre. At the northern end is List, Germany's northernmost town, while Hörnum is at the southern tip. Sylt is connected to the mainland by a train-only causeway; for details, see p701.

Information

All communities on Sylt charge visitors a *Kurtaxe* (resort tax), usually €2.50 to €3.50. In return you receive a *Kurkarte* (resort card), which you need to get onto the beach but also entitles you to small discounts at museums. If you're staying overnight, your hotel will automatically obtain a pass for you (adding the *Kurtaxe* to the room rate). Day-trippers

will need to buy a *Tageskarte* (day pass) from the kiosks at entrances to the beach.

Note that many tourist office times change from year to year, but calling around 10am or 11am is usually a safe bet.

There are various ATMs situated around Westerland.

DomAlly Internet Café (☎ 967 411; Strandstrasse 22-24, Westerland; per hr €6; ⏰ 9am-11pm Mon-Fri, 10.30am-11pm Sat & Sun) Enter from Bomhoffstrasse.

Post office (Kjeirstrasse 17, Westerland)

Westerland

People have been complaining about the over-development of Westerland ever since it became Sylt's first resort in the mid-19th century. Their protestations seem to have gone unheeded, for the largest town on the island is now a forest of concrete towers, often blocking sea views.

Yes, in some ways, this is the Miami Beach of Sylt (albeit somewhat older and without the body fascism). But it has its attractions, mostly ones of convenience. The pedestrianised Friedrichstrasse is handily lined with shops and restaurants; and if you want to go anywhere else on the island, this is the easiest place to reach it from.

Windsurfing off Sylt is known as the most radical you'll get on the World Cup tour, with gnarly winds and waves. Yet, it's not so difficult that beginners should be deterred. **Surf Schule Westerland** (☎ 271 72; Brandenburger Strasse 15) can help you take your first steps and also rents out equipment.

Alternatively, the water park and health spa **Sylter Welle** (☎ 0180-500 9980; Strandstrasse; admission with/without sauna €16.50/9.50; ⏰ 10am-9pm Mon, 10am-10pm Tue-Sun) has several saunas – Aroma, Viking or one overlooking the dunes.

Both the **Westerland tourist office** (☎ 9980; www.westerland.de; Strandstrasse 35; ⏰ 9am-5pm Mon-Thu, to 2pm Fri) and its **Zimmernachweise** (☎ 9988; ☎ 10.30am-5.30pm Mon-Fri, 9.30am-5.30pm Sat, 11am-4pm Sun, reduced hours in winter) can help with accommodation; there's also a large after-hours hotel board, with phone, just outside the Hauptbahnhof.

Kampen

If Westerland is the Miami Beach of Sylt, Kampen is its St Tropez. This quiet little village is the island's ritziest, as you immediately realise by the Hermès, Cartier, Joop! and Louis Vuitton boutiques ensconced in the traditional reed-thatched houses. Kampen attracts aristocrats and celebrities, from megastars such as Boris Becker, Claudia Schiffer and Ralf Schumacher to German TV stars such as Dieter Böhlen (a judge on popular talent show *Deutschland sucht den Superstar*). All come to see and be seen in summer along the main promenade of Stroenwai, which is better known as Whiskey Alley.

Apart from people-watching the principle reason to visit Kampen is the stunning **Uwe Dune**, at 52.5m Sylt's highest natural elevation. You can climb the wooden steps to the top for a 360-degree view over Sylt and, on a good day, to the neighbouring islands of Amrum and Föhr.

Kampen tourist office (☎ 469 80; www.kampen .de; Hauptstrasse 12; ☺ 10am-5pm Mon-Fri, 10am-1pm Sat & Sun, reduced hours in winter) produces a quirky illustrated map of the 'in' restaurants, bars and clubs.

Keitum

Historic reed-thatched houses bedecked with ivy, lush gardens of colourful blooms, stone walls and the occasional garden gate made from two curving whalebones all combine to create the island's prettiest village.

In the old days, Keitum was Sylt's most important harbour, and there's plenty of nautical history. The late-Romanesque sailors' church of **St Severin** is known for its Gothic altar and chancel, as well as for its cemetery. Some of the gravestones are even heritage-listed.

Another notable attraction is the historic **Altfriesisches Haus** (Old Friesian House; ☎ 328 05; Am Kliff 13; admission €2.50; ☺ 10am-5pm Apr-Oct, 1-4pm Thu-Sun Nov-Mar).

The **Keitum tourist office** (☎ 337 33; www.sylt-ost .de; Am Tipkenhoog 5; ☺ 9am-noon & 2-5pm Mon-Fri year-round, 9.30am-12.30pm Sat & Sun Apr-Oct) can help with further details.

List

According to the tourist brochures everything here is 'Germany's northernmost' – harbour, beach, restaurant etc… It's a windswept, tranquil land's end, but things usually liven up in the harbour when the ferry from Rømø (Denmark) deposits its load of day-tripping Danes in search of cheap drink. Looking towards Denmark, you can also see one of the many wind farms taking advantage of the stiff breezes in this part of the world.

Towards List is the extremely popular and attractive **Wanderdünengebiet**, where people hike between the grass-covered dunes. Here,

---

AT HOME WITH EMIL NOLDE

Bright flowers, stormy seas, red-lipped women with jaunty hats and impressionistic seaside watercolours: these are some of the recurring themes of great Schleswig-Holstein painter Emil Nolde. Born in 1867 in Nolde village near the Danish border (from whence he took his name), he first gained fame for producing postcards in which he gave mountains human features. In 1906, after spending much of his early life in Berlin, Munich and Karlsruhe, he joined the expressionist group Die Brücke.

In 1927 Nolde and his wife Ada built their own home and studio in Seebüll. Here, banned from working by the Nazis, he proceeded to produce 1300 'unpainted pictures' in secret. He died in 1956.

Nowadays considered one of the great 20th-century watercolourists, Nolde's work is found across Schleswig-Holstein (and beyond), including in Kiel's Kunsthalle (p680), the Schleswig-Holstein Landesmuseum in Schleswig (p690) and the Museumsberg Flensburg (p693). However, by far the biggest and most impressive collection is in his former atelier at Seebüll, now the **Emil Nolde Stiftung** (☎ 04664-364; www.nolde-stiftung.de; Neukirchen bei Seebüll; adult/child €4/1; ☺ 10am-6pm Apr-Oct, to 5pm Nov).

Recently renovated, the exhibition is worth a half- to whole-day's excursion, which is lucky because that's what it will take you, depending on where you're coming from (Westerland or Husum are the best jumping-off points). Catch the train to Klanxbüll, and continue on scheduled bus 1001 to Seebüll (13 minutes). In summer, there's also a dedicated Nolde shuttle. Check with the Bahnhof from which you're departing for exact schedules. A 10am start is needed from Westerland.

By road, follow the B199 and then the B5 from Niebüll.

---

as over the rest of the island, Nordic walking is popular; don't be surprised to see people walking with poles, using them to propel their upper body forward, as if they were skiing.

North of List is the privately owned Ellenbogen (literally 'elbow'). It boasts 35m-high moving dunes and beaches that are unfortunately off limits for swimming because of dangerous currents. En route to Ellenbogen – take the road branching off the main route about 4km southwest of List – you'll pass the **beach-side sauna** (☎ 877 174; admission €16; 🕑 11am-5pm Easter-Oct). The idea here is to heat up and then run naked into the chilly North Sea! To enter the Ellenbogen area by car, you must pay a €5 toll.

Information is available from the **Kurverwaltung List** (spa resort administration; ☎ 952 00; www.list .de, in German; Am Brünk 1; 🕑 9am-noon & 2-5pm Mon-Fri year-round, 9am-noon Sat Apr-Sep).

Wenningstedt

Sylt has several Stone Age graves, but the town that's just north of Westerland houses the best. You can enter its 4000-year-old **Denghoog** (Am Denghoog; 🕑 10am-5pm May-Sep), next to the town church, which measures 3m by 5m and is nearly 2m tall in parts. The outer walls consist of 12 40-tonne stones. How Stone Age builders moved these, well, it's a Stonehenge kind of mystery.

Find out more from the **Kurverwaltung** (☎ 4470; www.wenningstedt.de; Strandstrasse 25; 🕑 8.30am-4pm Mon-Fri, 9am-4pm Sat & Sun Apr-Oct, 8.30am-12.30pm & 2-4pm Mon-Thu, 8.30am-12.30pm Fri Nov-Mar).

Tours

BOAT

There is a frankly head-spinning array of boat cruises, mostly operated by **Adler-Schiffe** (☎ 987 00; www.adler-schiffe.de; Boysenstrasse 13, Westerland), but you can always get details and tickets from the **Info-Pavillon** (☎ 846 1029; 🕑 9am-4pm Jun-Aug, reduced hours in winter) on the Westerland Hauptbahnhof forecourt. Destinations and offers include the following:

Amrun & Föhr (adult/child €22/12.50; 🕑 10.05am daily from Hörnum) Choose one or both islands and a stay of between 1½ and six hours.

Hallig Hooge (adult/child €20.50/12; 🕑 11.55am daily from Hörnum) On the quicker Adler Express; other Halligen can be combined with Amrun/Föhr tours.

Helgoland (adult/child €32.50/20; 🕑 9am Mon & Thu from Hörnum)

Seal Colonies (adult/child €12.50/9.50; 🕑 2pm daily from Hörnum) See seals bask in the sun on their regular sand bank. The tour takes 1½ hours.

Wattwandern tours (adult/child/family €25.50/15/62; 🕑 10.05am or 11.55am on allocated days only) At low tide wander across the seabed between Amrum and Föhr. Ring for precise times or ask at the Westerland Hauptbahnhof Info-Pavilion.

BUS

SVG (☎ 836 100; www.svg-sylt.de) has two choices:

Grosse Inselrundfahrt (Big Island Tour; adult/child €13/9; 🕑 2pm Feb-Nov, 1pm Dec-Jan) Duration of the tour is 3¼ hours.

Grosse Rundfahrt (Small Island Tour; adult/child €11/9; 🕑 11am Mar-Nov) This is a two-hour tour. You can also add boat tours to the Halligen. Buy tickets at the pavilion outside the Hauptbahnhof.

Sleeping

If you're planning a stay of three days or longer, renting a holiday flat can cost as little as €50 to €60 in the high season (May to September). Private rooms are another option – contact the tourist office. Note that few hotels on Sylt accept credit cards, so check beforehand.

Campingplatz Kampen (☎ 420 86; Möwenweg 4, Kampen; per person/tent/car €3.50/4.50/1.50; 🕑 Easter-Oct) Of Sylt's half-a-dozen camping grounds, Campingplatz Kampen is one of the nicest, even if it has more caravans than tents. It's located among dunes at the southern end of Kampen.

Campingplatz Westerland (☎ 994 499; Rantumer Strasse, Westerland; per person/tent/car €3.50/8/2.50; 🕑 Apr-Oct) The largest camping ground on Sylt; has a popular restaurant.

DJH hostel (☎ 870 397; www.jugendherberge/jh /list; List-Mövenberg; dm under/over 26yr €15.60/18.60; 🕑 closed Nov-Dec; 🅿 ✗) A beach rustic idyll, this hostel is nestled among the dunes about 2km northeast of List and just 800m from the North Sea. Buses run from Westerland to List-Schule, and between April and September there's a shuttle to the hostel itself. Otherwise, it's a 2.5km trek. It's not always open from January to April, so you'll need to ring ahead.

DJH hostel (☎ 880 294; www.jugendherberge/jh /hoernum; Friesenplatz 2, Hörnum; dm under/over 26yr €15.60/18.60; 🅿 ✗) Scenically located among dunes and extensively renovated in 2000, this hostel is very handy for ferries and day cruises. Take the bus from Westerland to the

SCHLESWIG-HOLSTEIN

THE AUTHOR'S CHOICE

Long Island House Sylt (☎ 04651-995 9550; www.sylthotel.de; Eidumweg 13, Westerland; s €85, d €125-145, ste €165; P ⊠) Although Sylt has hundreds of hotels and holiday apartments, only the most expensive are truly stylish. Or at least that used to be the case, before Martina Blum and Lars Poppe arrived with their young and fresh Long Island House Sylt. It's a perfect mix of 'pure' modern design and subtle maritime themes.

Mirrors like portholes, unpolished wood hinting at ship's timbers and a carved Moby Dick hanging above one bed are joined by brown quilted or white fake-fur throws, painted cane chairs, orchids and green apples. Most of the individually decorated rooms are small but well equipped, plus there's a spacious garden and a sleek Scandinavian fireplace for winter. (Oh, but the fireplace is the only thing they like smoking here.)

Hörnum-Nord stop, from where it's about a 10-minute walk.

Single Pension (☎ 920 70; www.singlepension.de; Trift 26, Westerland; s €37.50-46, d €50-75; P) Not only for singles, the proprietor is keen to stress, but single-friendly, where young and old can strike up a rapport over tea or during the walking and cycling tours offered. The rooms are humble, but the location central and the atmosphere relaxed, with breakfast served to 1pm (or 4pm on request). Cheaper rooms share bathrooms.

Hotel Gutenberg (☎ 988 80; www.hotel-gutenberg .de; Friedrichstrasse 22, Westerland; s €65-85, d €115-135; P ⊠) Pleasantly decorated in a subtle maritime style, with either blonde or sea-green stained wooden furniture, this hotel often has late availability. We can only presume that's thanks to its very central but not particularly atmospheric location in the main pedestrian zone. Otherwise, it's brilliant quality. The cheaper rooms share spotless bathrooms.

Raffelhüschen Hotel (☎ 836 210; www.sylthotel -raffelhueschen.de; Boysenstrasse 8, Westerland; s €95, d €140-160; P ⊠) Ground-floor rooms in this modern, stylish hotel have wooden floors and garden terraces with *Strandkörbe*. Upstairs, there's carpet and balconies. All guests are free to use the three saunas and solarium. Book well ahead.

Eating

Kupferkanne (☎ 410 10; Stapelhooger Wai, Kampen; meals €5.50-10.50) Giant mugs of coffee and huge slices of cake are served outdoors at this *Alice in Wonderland*–style café, where wooden tables surrounded by a maze of low bramble hedges overlook the Wadden Sea and the Braderup Heide (heath). Meals are also served in the attached Frisian house.

Sansibar (☎ 964 646; Hörnumer Strasse 80, Rantum; mains €6-32) Dine among the dunes in this large grass-roof pavilion on the beach. Or, as tables are hard to come by unless you book, opt for a drink on its terrace at sunset, with a view of the crashing waves.

Alte Friesenstube (☎ 1228; Gaadt 4, Westerland; mains €9.50-20; ☾ Tue-Sun) The interior of this 17th-century reed-thatched cottage is lined with decorative wall tiles and tiled ovens, or in summer you can choose to eat in the surrounding garden. While the handwritten menu is in largely incomprehensible *platt-düütsch* dialect, the staff can explain most of it in English.

Grande Plage (☎ 886 078; Riperstig, Weststrand, Kampen; snacks €2.50-11.50, mains €12-26) This casual bistro overlooking the western Kampen beach serves both oysters and *Currywurst* (curried sausage), plus a range of Mediterranean cuisine and seafood. The on-site sauna is also popular, although if you've just eaten the thought might give you indigestion.

Gogärtchen (☎ 412 42; Stroenwai, Kampen; mains €18-32) *The* place to see and be seen on Sylt, thatch-roofed Gogärtchen is renowned as a favourite of the nation's holidaying glitterati. But even if your knowledge of German celebrity starts and ends at the Shumachers and Schiffers, the modern German cuisine is a gourmet experience worth coming for in itself.

Getting There & Away

Air Berlin (www.airberlin.com) has services from Berlin and Düsseldorf to Sylt/Westerland airport (www.flughafen-sylt.de); **Hapag-Lloyd Express** (www .hlx.com) flies from Hannover, Köln-Bonn and Stuttgart and **Lufthansa** (www.lufthansa.com) arrives from Frankfurt, Hamburg and Munich, among others. Flights are more frequent in summer.

Otherwise, Sylt is connected to the mainland by a narrow causeway exclusively for trains. Regular services travel from Hamburg (Altona and Hauptbahnhof) to Westerland (€39, three hours).

If driving, you must load your vehicle onto a **car train** (☎ 995 0565; www.syltshuttle.de; return €86) in Niebüll near the Danish border. There are constant crossings (usually at least once an hour) in both directions, and no reservations can be made.

An alternative is to catch the **car ferry** (☎ 0180-310 3030; www.sylt-faehre.de) from Rømø in Denmark to List on the island's north (one-way per person/car €5.75/38.50).

For ships to/from Amrun and Föhr, see Tours (p699).

Getting Around

Sylt is well covered by **buses** (☎ 836 100; www .svg-sylt.de). The two main north–south connections run at 20-minute intervals during the day; these are Line 1 (Westerland–Wenningstedt–Kampen–List) and Line 2 (Westerland–Rantum–Hörnum). There are four other lines, and prices are calculated by zone, ranging from €1.45 to €5.95. Tell the driver your destination. Some buses have bicycle hangers.

Cycling is extremely popular and *Fahrradverleih* (bike-hire) outlets abound. In Westerland, the most convenient place is **Fahrrad am Bahnhof** (☎ 5803; Platform No 1, Hauptbahnhof); **Tieves** (☎ 870 226; Listlandstrasse 15, List), at the north of the island, also offers bike hire.

FÖHR

☎ 04681 / pop 10,000

Föhr is known as the green isle, although there's also a good sandy beach in the south. Its main village, Wyk, has plenty of windmills. In the north you'll find 16 tiny Frisian hamlets tucked behind dikes that stand up to 7m tall.

In the old days, Föhr's men went out to sea to hunt whales, an epoch you can learn more about at the **Friesenmuseum** (☎ 2571; Rebbelstieg 34, Wyk; adult/concession €3.50/2; ✆ 10am-5pm Tue-Sun Mar-Oct, 2-5pm Tue-Sun Nov-Feb).

The church of **St Johannis** in Nieblum dates from the 12th century and is sometimes called the 'Frisian Cathedral' because it seats up to 1000 people (ask about guided tours at the tourist office).

The **Föhr tourist office** (☎ 300, 3040; fax 3068; Wyk harbour) can help with accommodation. Föhr does not have a camping ground.

Getting There & Around

To get to Föhr from the mainland, you catch a ferry (one-way €5.50) operated by **WDR** (☎ 01805-080 140, 800; www.wdr-wyk.de, www.faehre.de) from Dagebüll Hafen (reached via Niebüll). Up to 13 boats make the trip daily in the high season, taking 45 minutes to Wyk. Bikes are an extra €4, while cars (prior reservation necessary) cost €50.

For information on getting to Föhr from Sylt, see Tours (p699).

There's an hourly bus service to all villages on Föhr (less frequent in winter). There are bike-rental outlets in every village.

AMRUM

☎ 04682 / pop 2100

Amrum is the smallest North Frisian Island; you can walk around it in a day. It is also, arguably, the prettiest, blessed with glorious Kniepsand – 12km of fine, white sand, sometimes up to 1km wide – that takes up half the island. The island's harmonious patchwork of dunes, woods, heath and marsh make it the perfect place for a relaxing day trip or longer retreat. Besides the central village of Wittdün, there are Nebel, Norddorf, Odde, Steenodde and Süddorf, many boasting typical reed-thatched Frisian houses.

GOSCH: A SYLT SUCCESS STORY

You might have walked past its outlets as far afield as Berlin, Hamburg and Hanover, but you can't come to Sylt without trying some of Gosch's fish. This chain of 'fast-fish' outlets is the best-known local institution and the seafood tastes particularly fresh here.

All around Westerland and Wenningstedt, you'll find kiosks offering the usual range – from fish sandwiches and seafood pasta to smoked salmon and *Rösti* (potato cakes), lobster and caviar (most dishes €3.20 to €12.50). The best place to visit, however, is the original kiosk in List harbour or the maritime-themed **Alte Bootshalle** (☎ 870 383; Hafenstrasse 16, List; ✆ from 11am). In summer come outside main meal times to avoid a crush.

Wittdün has northern Germany's tallest **lighthouse** which, at 63m, affords a spectacular view of the island and across to Sylt and Föhr.

Much of Amrum is under protection, so you must stick to the marked paths. There are some fine walks, including the 10km walk from the lighthouse to Norddorf through the pine forest, or the 8km return hike from Norddorf along the beach to the tranquil **Ood Nature Reserve**, an ideal place to observe bird life. Alternatively you can just go swimming off the beach.

The **tourist office** (☎ 940 30; ferry landing, Wittdün) can provide information on accommodation on the island, which offers **camping** (☎ 2254; fax 4348; Wittdün), a **hostel** (☎ 2010; fax 1747; Mittelstrasse 1) and several hotels.

Getting There & Around

To reach Amrum from the mainland, take the ferry (one-way €7.80) operated by WDR (☎ 01805-080 140, 04681-800; www.wdr-wyk.de, www.faehre.de) from Dagebüll Hafen (change in Niebüll). The trip to Wittdün frequently goes via Wyk in Föhr and takes 1½ hours.

For information on getting to Amrum from Sylt, see Tours (p699).

The touristy **Inselbahn** (day card per adult/child €7/3.50) will take you around the island. There are also regular buses and bike-rental places in every village.

HELGOLAND

☎ 04725 / pop 1650

Its former rulers, the British, really got the better part of the deal in 1891 when they swapped Helgoland for then German-ruled Zanzibar, but Germans today are very fond of this North Sea outcrop. They laud its fresh air and warm weather, courtesy of the gulf stream, and even cynics have to admit there's something impressive about this lonesome wedge of red rock.

The 80m-tall 'Lange Anna' (Long Anna) rock on the island's southwest edge is a compelling sight, standing alone in the ocean like one of Australia's famous 12 Apostles that's been separated from its flock. There are also WWII bunkers and tunnels to explore. And as the island is still covered by an agreement made in 1840 and economically isn't part of the EU, most visitors indulge in a little duty-free shopping in the outlets lining the main drag, Lung Wai (literally 'long way'). To swim, they head to neighbouring **Düne**, a blip in the ocean that is popular with nudists. Little boats make regular trips from the landing stage on Helgoland.

The **Kurverwaltung** (☎ 814 30, room reservations 01805-643 737; www.helgoland.de, room reservations zimmervermittlung@helgoland.de; Im Rathaus, Lung Wai 28; ☒ 9am-5pm Mon-Fri, 11.30am-5pm Sat & Sun May-Sep, reduced hours winter) can help find a room.

Adler Schiffe (☎ 987 00; www.adler-schiffe.de) has day cruises that leave from Hörnum on Sylt (p699). For services from Hamburg, see p677.

Mecklenburg-Western Pomerania

Mecklenburg-Western Pomerania (Mecklenburg-Vorpommern), sparsely populated and refreshingly unurbanised, hasn't enjoyed a high profile internationally, although it's starting to attract some press attention as the scheduled host to a G8 summit of world leaders in 2007. Plus, anyone in Germany will fill you in with glee – the state is Germany's finest domestic holiday spot, much like Blackpool in the UK but with more sun, better beaches and fewer piers.

In summer thousands of visitors descend on the resort islands of Rügen and Usedom to enjoy the sparkling sand, brisk sea air and all-too-brief swimming season, as well as touring pretty coastal towns such as Wismar and Warnemünde.

Unlike Blackpool, however, the region has a lot more to offer than a bit of quality sun-lounger time. The state capital, Schwerin, has an incredible castle at its heart and is among the most striking little cities in the country; the historical centres of Stralsund and Wismar were Unesco-listed in 2002; even Rostock, once a gritty shipbuilding town, is building a reputation as a party city. Elsewhere, you can get off the beaten track into the area's delightfully wild national parks or sail into the sunset with any number of fishing, diving, cruise and ferry companies.

Thanks to Mecklenburg's long tradition of hospitality it's generally easy to get around the state. There's also a solid tourist infrastructure, particularly around the well-frequented coastal towns and resorts. Trust the southerners' judgment and spend some quality holiday time in a corner of Germany that is only going to get more popular.

HIGHLIGHTS

- **Castle** Circumnavigate Schwerin's fairy-tale Schloss (castle; p706), stopping to enjoy its *orangerie*
- **Culture** Listen to open-air opera near the water in Schwerin (p707) or Stralsund (p723)
- **Beach Party** Enjoy a GDR-meets-Ibiza vibe, sipping cocktails on Warnemünde's beach (p714)
- **Natural Sight** Admire the white chalk cliffs of the Jasmund National Park (p732) on Rügen
- **Boating** Paddle and camp through the peaceful waterways of Müritz National Park (p711)
- **Off-beat Experience** Book yourself into a 'swimming holiday home' in Lauterbach (p732) on Rügen

- POPULATION: 1.82 MILLION
- AREA: 23,170 SQ KM

MECKLENBURGER SEENPLATTE

At the doorstep of the state capital, Schwerin, the Mecklenburg Lake Plains is one of the area's prettiest regions. A wilderness spreading across the centre of the state, the area may well become one of the most popular outdoor and sport destinations for visitors looking for some peace, quiet and reasonably pristine wilderness.

The plains are crisscrossed by roads and highways that make getting around very easy if you're travelling under your own steam. The roads (often canopied by trees planted by medieval fish merchants to shield wagons from the heat of the summer sun) meander through charming little villages and hamlets.

SCHWERIN
☎ 0385 / pop 97,700
Schwerin is an unusual beauty. No photo could convey the charming architectural mishmash of its landmark castle, while its

watery landscape of seven lakes – or possibly more depending on how you tally them – is not what you'd expect from this nook of northeastern Europe.

More than this, in its rush to forget its 45 years of communist rule, parts of Schwerin seem to be in denial about the past, oh, 300 years. This former seat of the Grand Duchy of Mecklenburg is an interesting mix of 16th- to 19th-century architecture, and in some of its restaurants you'll find yourself thinking you've slipped back in time to that era.

Orientation
The Altstadt (old town) sits south of the rectangular Pfaffenteich (a pretty, artificial pond) and northwest of Burg Island (Castle Island). Burg Island is connected to two gardens further south – the Schlossgarten and the lesser-known Grüngarten.

Information
In-Ca (☎ 500 7883; Wismarsche Strasse 123; per hr €3; ☺ 1pm-midnight) Internet access.
Main post office (Mecklenburgstrasse 4-6; ☺ 9am-6pm Mon-Fri, to noon Sat)

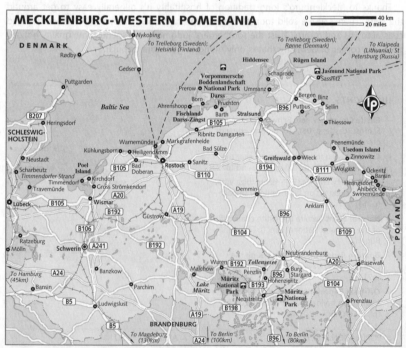

SCHWERIN

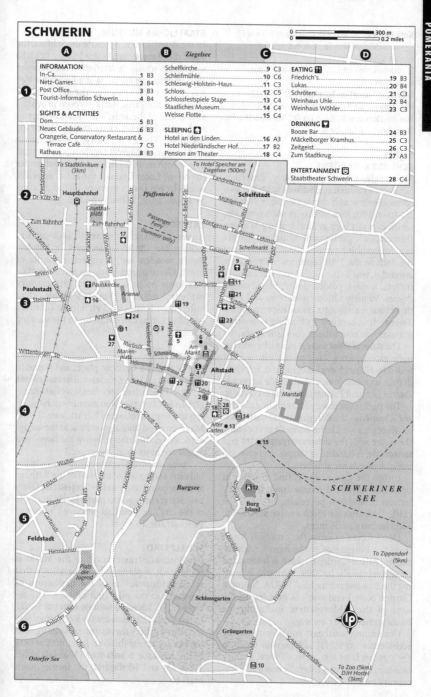

0 — 300 m
0 — 0.2 miles

INFORMATION
In-Ca...1 B3
Netz-Games................................2 B4
Post Office.................................3 B3
Tourist-Information Schwerin.....4 B4

SIGHTS & ACTIVITIES
Dom...5 B3
Neues Gebäude..........................6 B3
Orangerie, Conservatory Restaurant &
  Terrace Café............................7 C5
Rathaus......................................8 B3

Schelfkirche................................9 C3
Schleifmühle.............................10 C6
Schleswig-Holstein-Haus...........11 C3
Schloss.....................................12 C5
Schlossfestspiele Stage..............13 C4
Staatliches Museum...................14 C4
Weisse Flotte............................15 C4

SLEEPING
Hotel an den Linden..................16 A3
Hotel Niederländischer Hof........17 B2
Pension am Theater...................18 C4

EATING
Friedrich's.................................19 B3
Lukas..20 B4
Schröters..................................21 C3
Weinhaus Uhle..........................22 B4
Weinhaus Wöhler......................23 C3

DRINKING
Booze Bar.................................24 B3
Mäckelborger Kramhus..............25 C3
Zeitgeist...................................26 C3
Zum Stadtkrug..........................27 A3

ENTERTAINMENT
Staatstheater Schwerin..............28 C4

Netz-Games (☎ 593 6960; Ritterstrasse 1; per hr €3; ⊗ noon-midnight Mon-Sat, 4pm-midnight Sun) Internet access.

Stadtklinikum (☎ 5200; 397 Wismarsche Strasse) Medical services.

Tourist-Information Schwerin (☎ 592 5212; www.schwerin.de; Rathaus, Am Markt 14; ⊗ 9am-7pm Mon-Fri, 10am-6pm Sat & Sun Apr-Oct, 9am-6pm Mon-Fri, 10am-4pm Sat & Sun Nov-Mar)

Sights

SCHLOSS & GARDENS

No single adjective properly describes Schwerin's multifaceted **Schloss** (☎ 525 2920; www .schloss-schwerin.de; adult/concession €4/2.50; ⊗ 10am-6pm mid-Apr–mid-Oct, 10am-5pm Tue-Sun mid-Oct–mid-Apr), which earns its keep as Mecklenburg-Western Pomerania's parliament building. Its six façades combine various styles mainly from the 16th to the 19th centuries. As you walk around it, you'll spot Gothic and Renaissance turrets, a main golden dome, Slavic onion domes, vaguely Ottoman features and even three square terracotta Hanseatic step gables. Twenty-first century scaffolding is another mainstay, as renovations continue apace.

The **statue of Niklot** you see in a niche over the main gate depicts a Slavic prince, who was defeated by Heinrich der Löwe in 1160. Schwerin derives its name from a Slavic castle known as *Zuarin* (Animal Pasture) formerly on this site.

The park immediately surrounding the palace is known as the Burggarten and most notably features a wonderful **orangerie** overlooking the water with the **conservatory restaurant** and **terrace café**. A handful of statues, a grotto and outlook points are also here.

Inside the castle, you'll find a series of opulently furnished rooms and a huge collection of Meissen porcelain. In 2007, the castle celebrates its 150th anniversary as the Mecklenburg Parliament.

Don't forget to cross the causeway south from the Burggarten to the baroque **Schlossgarten** (Palace Garden), which is intersected by several canals. In 2009, Schwerin is hosting the Bundesgartenschau (BUGA; National Garden Show) and work is ongoing to the west of the Schlossgarten, including the establishment of a new stage.

Continuing southeast you'll come to the **Schleifmühle** (☎ 562 751; adult/concession €2.50/1.50; ⊗ 10am-5pm Easter-Nov), a small local history museum located in a carefully restored 19th-century mill.

STAATLICHES MUSEUM

In the Alter Garten, opposite the Schloss, the **Staatliches Museum** (State Museum Schwerin; ☎ 595 80; www.museum-schwerin.de; Alter Garten 3; adult/concession €6/4; ⊗ 10am-6pm Apr-Oct, to 5pm Tue-Sun Nov-Mar) has a collection spanning the ages. The 15 statues in the Ernst Barlach room provide a small taste of the artist's work, allowing you to decide whether to visit Güstrow (see p708) for more. There's also a typically amusing and irreverent Marcel Duchamp collection. Those with more traditional tastes will prefer the oils by Lucas Cranach the Elder, as well as works by old Dutch masters, including a few by Rembrandt, Rubens and Brueghel.

CATHEDRAL

Above the Markt rises the tall 14th-century Gothic **Dom** (☎ 565 014; Am Dom 4; ⊗ 10am-5pm Mon-Fri, noon-5pm Sun), a superb example of north German red-brick architecture. Locals hotly point out that its 19th-century cathedral tower (118m) is a whole 50cm taller than Rostock's Petrikirche (church, see p714). You can climb up to the viewing platform (€1).

ALTSTADT

The Markt is a bustling place, and home to the **Rathaus** and the neoclassical **Neues Gebäude** (1780–83), which houses the classy Café Röntgen. In front of it is a lion monument honouring the town's founder, Heinrich der Löwe. Make sure you take a good look at the scenes depicted on the column below the lion – you might see more than you expect!

There are several architectural styles in the old city, and a walk southwest of the Rathaus to the appropriately named **Engestrasse** (Narrow Street) brings you past a lovely example of the city's earliest half-timbered houses at Buschstrasse 15.

SCHELFSTADT

Up Puschkinstrasse north of the Markt is Schelfstadt, a planned baroque village that was autonomous until the expansion of Schwerin in the mid-19th century. The restored 1737 **Schleswig-Holstein-Haus** (☎ 555 527; Puschkinstrasse 12; adult/concession €3/2; ⊗ 10am-6pm) contains a gallery that features changing contemporary art exhibitions. Just north of here is the baroque **Schelfkirche** (Nikolaikirche; 1708–13) and **Schelfmarkt**, the former town market.

Tours

From May to September, you can join the lucky locals messing about in boats by taking a cruise on the Schweriner See. **Weisse Flotte** (☎ 557 770; www.weisseflotteschwerin.de) operates a regular Inseltour (island tour; €9.50) leaving eight times a day from the quay between the Schloss and the Marstall. From Tuesday to Sunday, there are longer additional tours (€12 to €13). A reduced service runs in April and October.

The tourist office organises several guided tours, including 90-minute **city tours** (per person €4.50; ☙ 11am & 2pm) and **evening walks** (per person €4; ☙ 8.30pm Thu) from Weinhaus Wöhler (right).

Festivals & Events

The highlight of the cultural calendar is the **Schlossfestspiele** (www.theater-schwerin.de), open-air opera concerts performed on a stage erected in front of the theatre and state museum in June and July. Punters gather across the water in the Burggarten to listen in to the likes of performances such as *Aida*, *Nabucco* and *La Traviata*.

The programme is part of the larger **Festspiele Mecklenburg-Vorpommern** (☎ 591 8585; www.festspiele-mv.de) held throughout the state.

Sleeping

DJH hostel (☎ 326 0006; www.djh-mv.de; Waldschulweg 3; dm under/over 26yr €14.50/17.50; ✗) This hostel is about 4km south of the city centre, just opposite the zoo. Take bus 14. It's in a leafy location and popular with school groups.

Pension am Theater (☎ 593 680; www.pensionamtheater.m-vp.de; Theaterstrasse 1-2; s €50-60, d €70-85, apt 65-80; P) In the shadow of the huge theatre building and (just) within sight of the castle, this privately run establishment boasts cheerful, stylish and spacious rooms, although you may miss little things like soap in the bathrooms.

Hotel an den Linden (☎ 512 084; Franz-Mehring-Strasse 26; s/d €65/80; P) Handily located between the train station and the old town, this dignified midrange option has comfortable accommodation and a breakfast room with winter garden. There's a sauna, plus reiki massages on request.

Hotel Speicher am Ziegelsee (☎ 500 30; www.speicher-hotel.de; Speicherstrasse 11; s €80-100, d €100-120; P ✗) This striking, heritage-listed former warehouse on the waterfront has been kitted out with modern Mediterranean-style rooms. You'll also discover a sauna, solarium, gym, English bar, restaurants and private pier.

Hotel Niederländischer Hof (☎ 591 100; www.niederlaendischer-hof.de; Karl-Marx-Strasse 12-13; s/d from €85/120; P) You can't beat the Pfaffenteich location or the swanky rooms and marble bathrooms at this exceedingly classy hotel. There's a library with an open fire, and a much lauded restaurant.

Eating

Friedrich's (☎ 555 473; Friedrichstrasse 2; mains €8-15) Overlooking the Pfaffenteich, this Parisian-style café has a nice casual atmosphere and an uncomplicated selection of salads, fish, grills and vegetarian dishes.

Lukas (☎ 565 935; Grosser Moor 5; mains €8-16) Seafood lovers should head straight to this top conservatory restaurant, with a great range of dishes and some extravagant prawn and lobster options. If the aquarium makes you feel guilty, there are some steaks and schnitzels on the menu.

Weinhaus Wöhler (☎ 555 830; Puschkinstrasse 26; mains €8-16) With wood-lined rooms dating back to the 19th century, a courtyard and a tapas/cocktail bar, this sprawling historic house attracts a broad mix of people. Although the Hammond organ covers of the Beatles in the courtyard won't be to everyone's taste, the six luxury double rooms (€80 to €130) probably will.

Weinhaus Uhle (☎ 562 956; www.weinhaus-uhle.de; Schusterstrasse 13-15; mains €9-18) Step back in time at this traditional family wine merchants, where the pianist plays beneath stained-glass windows and barrel-vaulted ceilings in the formal restaurant and the occasional customer still wears an opera cloak in the wood-lined Weinstube. Dishes include Chateaubriand, carved at the table, venison and fish – all much cheaper in 1930, as you can see from the vintage menu in the hall. In business since 1740, the place has a practically encyclopaedic wine list.

Schröters (☎ 550 7698; Schliemannstrasse 2; set menus €35-140; ☎ from 6pm Mon-Sat) Run by Erik Schröter, Mecklenburg's No 1 chef, this place is way out of everything else's league, offering incredible regional cooking with a French twist.

Finally, don't forget to pay a visit to the Schloss' Orangerie Café (see Schloss & Gardens, opposite) for coffee and cake.

Drinking

Zum Stadtkrug (☎ 593 6693; Wismarsche Strasse 126) A central, traditional microbrewery pub, the homebrew here was declared among the best in Germany by *Stern* magazine, no less.

Mäckelborger Kramhus (☎ 581 3105; Puschkinstrasse 15) Art gallery, café, bar, jazz club…you'll find it all here.

Booze Bar (☎ 562 576; Arsenalstrasse 16; ⊙ from 5pm) Connected to the somewhat cheesy Madison Club, this central cocktail bar has an eye-catching Marc Chagall–style mural behind the bar and an extensive and inventive drinks list.

Zeitgeist (Puschkinstrasse 22; ⊙ from 5pm Tue-Sun) This modern, young and hip bar offers tapas (€2.50 to €7.95) and football viewing in the historic Schelfstadt. There's a terrace next door in summer.

Entertainment

Staatstheater Schwerin (☎ 530 00; www.theater -schwerin.de; Alter Garten) The state theatre offers an impressive range of concerts as well as varied theatrical performances.

Getting There & Around

Trains arrive regularly from Hamburg (from €19.10, one hour), Rostock (from €13.40, one hour), Stralsund (from €23.30, two hours) and Berlin (€2939, 1½ to 2½ hours). Direct trains run to/from Wismar (€6.20, 45 minutes) throughout the day.

By road from Rostock, head southwest on the B105 (E22), then follow the signs in Wismar.

City buses and trams cost €1.50/6.10 for a single/day pass. In summer a ferry crosses the Pfaffenteich (€1).

LUDWIGSLUST

☎ 03874 / pop 12,500

While it can't compete with Schwerin's Schloss, the sturdy **ducal residence** (☎ 571 90; www.schloss -ludwigslust.de; adult/child €3/2; ⊙ 10am-6pm Tue-Sun mid-Apr–mid-Oct, to 5pm mid-Oct–mid-Apr) at Ludwigslust is a popular day trip from the capital. It's hardly surprising. Such was the charm of this place that when the ducal seat moved 36km north to Schwerin in 1837, some family members continued to live here until 1945. Now part of the Schwerin State Museum, its rooms are being progressively renovated. The stately, gilt-columned, high-ceilinged **Golden Hall** is the unrivalled high point.

Baroque Ludwigslust is a planned town, and its appealing, orderly layout is an attraction in itself.

Trains run from Schwerin every two hours (€6.20, 30 minutes). To get to the castle from Ludwigslust station, walk south on Bahnhofstrasse to Platz des Friedens, cross the canal to Kanalstrasse and turn right on Schlossstrasse.

GÜSTROW

☎ 03843 / pop 32,000

Another town, another castle museum, you might think when you see posters advertising Güstrow. Not quite so. This charming town, more than 775 years old, does have a small but stately Renaissance Schloss housing a historical exhibition, but it also boasts a unique selling point. As the place where sculptor Ernst Barlach spent most of his working life, it invites you to view dozens of his works, including in his former atelier.

The city's Markt is at the centre of the Altstadt; the Schloss is southeast, the Dom southwest and the Barlach museum northwest.

Güstrow Information (☎ 681 023; www.guestrow .de; Domstrasse 9; ⊙ 9am-6pm Mon-Fri, 9.30am-1pm Sat & Sun, closed Sun Oct-Apr) can help with accommodation.

Sights & Activities

The Gothic **Dom** (☎ 682 433; www.dom-guestrow.de; Philipp-Brandin-Strasse 5; ⊙ 10am-5pm Mon-Sat, 2-4pm Sun mid-May–mid-Oct, reduced hours rest of year) contains a copy of Ernst Barlach's *Hovering Angel*, a memorial for the fallen soldiers of WWI; this copy was made secretly from the original mould after the Nazis destroyed the original sculpture.

The Barlach memorial in the **Gertrudenka-pelle** (☎ 844 000; Gertrudenplatz 1; adult/concession €3/2; ⊙ 10am-5pm Tue-Sun Apr-Oct, 11am-4pm Tue-Sun Nov-Mar) displays many of his original works. More of his bronze and wood carvings are housed along with a biographical exhibition at his former studio, the **Atelierhaus** (☎ 822 99; www .ernst-barlach-stiftung.de; Heidberg 15; adult/concession €4/3; ⊙ 10am-5pm Tue-Sun Apr-Oct, 11am-4pm Tue-Sun Nov-Mar), 4km south of the city at Inselsee (take bus 204).

The 16th-century **Schloss** (☎ 7520; www.schloss -guestrow.de; adult/concession €6/4; ⊙ 9am-5pm) is one of several museums in town. It also offers a cultural centre, art exhibitions and occasional concerts.

ERNST BARLACH

One of the most important German expressionists, Ernst Barlach's sculptures and drawings are found across Germany, but it's especially hard not to notice him in Güstrow, where he spent the last 28 years of his life.

Born in 1870 outside Hamburg, Barlach made a trip to Russia in 1906, soon after finishing his art studies, which was to forever influence his work. Based on sketches he made there, his squarish sculptures began bearing the same expressive gestures and hunched-over, wind-blown postures of the beggars and farmers he met.

Barlach greeted WWI with enthusiasm, but soon came to realise the horrors of war, which also became a recurring theme in his work. He gained great fame executing, among other works, the WWI memorial in Magdeburg's cathedral (p208).

However, his profoundly humanist approach did not sit well with Nazi aesthetics. He was declared a degenerate artist in the 1930s and banned from working, while 381 of his works were destroyed.

Sadly he died in 1938 in Rostock at the peak of the ideological frenzy, without ever seeing his work resurrected, as it was, after WWII. He is buried in Ratzeburg (p690).

Getting There & Around

Trains leave for Güstrow once or twice an hour from Rostock's Hauptbahnhof (central train station; €5, 25 minutes) and hourly from Schwerin (€11.70, one hour).

NEUBRANDENBURG

☎ 0395 / pop 69,000

Neubrandenburg has few pretensions. It bills itself as 'the city of four gates on the Tollense (Tollensesee) Lake', and that's pretty well what it is. A largely intact medieval wall – with four gates – circles the 13th-century Altstadt, although you have to peer hard through some harsh GDR architecture to see it. The town's other main asset is its location on Tollense Lake, on the edge of the Mecklenburger Seenplatte, which has made it a boating mecca.

While building a parking station beneath its Markt in 2006, Neubrandenburg unearthed some precious archaeological remnants. The whole square has since been cordoned off and is likely to remain so until 2009.

Orientation

Consider the circular city wall as the outside of a clock face. The train station is at 12 o'clock, and to get to the tourist office and the middle of the Altstadt, you simply have to walk straight down Stargarder Strasse to the middle of the face. The four gates are located as follows: Friedländer Tor at 2 o'clock, Neues Tor at 3 o'clock, Stargarder Tor at 6 o'clock and Treptower Tor at 9 o'clock. Inside the walls is a grid of north–south and east–west streets with the Marktplatz in the centre.

The wall effectively creates the largest roundabout outside Britain; it's circled by Friedrich-Engels-Ring.

Information

Main post office (Marktplatz 2; ☼ 9am-8pm Mon-Fri, to noon Sat)

Stadt Info (☎ 194 33; www.neubrandenburg.de; Stargarder Strasse 17; ☼ 10am-7pm Mon-Fri, to 6pm Sat May-Sep, 11am-4pm Sun Jul-Sep, reduced hours Oct-Apr) Tourist information.

Sights & Activities

CITY WALL

The city was founded in 1248 by Herbord von Raven, a Mecklenburg knight granted the land by Brandenburg Margrave Johann I, and building progressed in the usual order: defence system, church, town hall, pub. The security system was the 2.3km-long, 7.5m-high stone wall that survives today, with four city gates and 56 sentry posts built into it.

The best way to appreciate the wall is to walk around the inside. The **Friedländer Tor**, begun in 1300 and completed in 1450, was the first gate. **Treptower Tor** is the largest and contains the **Regional History Museum** (☎ 555 1271; adult/concession €2/1; ☼ 10am-5pm), which is really more of an archaeological collection.

At the southern end of the city is the gaudy **Stargarder Tor**; the simple brick **Neues Tor** fronts the east side of the Altstadt and houses a small exhibition on writer and satirist Fritz Reuter (1810–74).

Southwest of the train station (at about 11 o'clock) is the city's former dungeon, the **Fangelturm**. You'll recognise it by its pointy tower.

Perhaps even more striking than the city gates are the 27 sweet **half-timbered houses** wedged into the stone circumference. These are what remain of the 56 original sentry posts. When firearms rendered such defences obsolete in the 16th century, the guardhouses were converted into *Wiekhäuser*, homes for the poor, disadvantaged and elderly. The surviving homes have been rebuilt and most are now craft shops, galleries and cafés.

TOLLENSESEE

In the summer months, people flock to this large lake southwest of the centre for swimming, boating, camping and sunbathing.

The best swimming places are both fun and free: Strandbad Broda at the northwest tip of the lake and Augustabad on the northeastern side.

Ferries (☎ 350 0524; www.neu-sw.de; one-way €4) circumnavigate the lake three times daily, going as far as Klein Nemerow (45 minutes one-way), Nonnehof (one hour) or Prillwitz (1½ hours). Ask the tourist office for the latest timetable, which also lists lakeside attractions. **Cruise boats** (☎ 584 1218; www.fahrgastschiff -mudderschulten.de; tours €8; ☼ Tue-Sun) also circumnavigate the lake.

You can hire all kinds of boats, including canoes, from several operators, such as **Bootsvermietung Wassersportzentrum** (☎ 401 3488; Augustastrasse 7; per hr €4.50-25; ☼ 10am-7pm Mon-Fri, 9am-8pm Sat & Sun Apr-Oct) and **Freizeittreff am Kulturpark** (☎ 566 5352; www.freizeittreff-behn.de; Parkstrasse 15; per hr €4.50-20; ☼ 9am-8pm Apr-Oct).

CYCLING

As many people cycle through the region, the tourist office publishes a *Radwandern* pamphlet, which details 60 tours. Several moderate and clearly marked bicycle routes are near the town, and there are cheap overnight accommodation options on routes south of the city.

Bikes can be hired from the two boat rental places in Tollensesee. Prices start from about €8 per day.

CONCERTS

Since 2001, Neubrandenburg has been receiving kudos for its **Konzertkirche** (☎ tickets 559 5127; www.konzertkirche-nb.de; cnr Stargarder Strasse & Grosse Wollweberstrasse). The hall is essentially the converted interior of the 13th-century Marienkirche and has goose pimple–creating acoustics. The ticket service in the tourist office handles bookings.

Sleeping

Camping Gatsch-Eck (☎ 566 5152; www.camping-gatsch -eck.de; per adult/car €4.50/2, tents €3.50-4.50) Down the western side of the lake, this leafy site has new bathroom facilities, and a laundry hut with washing machines and dryers. There's a ferry landing nearby and lots of sports facilities.

Wiekhaus 49 (☎ 581 230; www.hotel-weinert.de; 4th Ringstrasse; d €40; P) This former sentry post near the Neues Tor requires a minimum four-night stay. The hotel leasing it, Hotel Weinert, also has clean and pleasant if not particularly atmospheric rooms (singles/doubles from €45/65) at Ziegelbergstrasse 23.

Wiekhaus 28 (☎ 566 6571; www.wiekhaus.ws; 3rd Ringstrasse; d €50) Another one of the city wall's former sentry posts, this place has a minimum two-night stay. It's a homy little flat with old-fashioned furniture.

Parkhotel Neubrandenburg (☎ 559 00; www .parkhotel-nb.de; Windbergsweg 4; s/d €65/85; P ☒ ⌨) One of the few larger hotels in town that doesn't betray its GDR roots, this place has stylish and well-planned modern rooms, with doubles boasting two bathrooms to save domestic arguments. Located in the Kulturpark between the old town and the Tollensesee, rooms at the front have the best views.

Radisson SAS (☎ 558 60; Treptower Strasse 1; s €80-95, d €95-110; P ☒ ☒) This hotel is handily located on the Markt, but doesn't have the best Radisson rooms you'll ever see.

Eating & Drinking

Café im Reuterhaus (☎ 582 3245; Stargarder Strasse 35; mains €5-9) Formerly home to Fritz Reuter for two years, this simple café serves light meals, snacks and soups during the day. When it closes, the smoky but cosy *Bierstube* (traditional beer pub) next door swings into action.

Wiekhaus 45 (☎ 566 7762; 4th Ringstrasse; mains €7-14; ☼ 11.30am-2pm & 5-10pm Tue-Sun) This is a lovely example of a renovated guardhouse, with huge portions of tasty Mecklenburg specialities and athletic waiters who zip up and down the narrow stairwell carrying them. You can sit outside in summer.

THE AUTHOR'S CHOICE

Koni Kneipe & Ostmuseum (☎ 582 3620; 14th floor, Marktplatz 1; ⌣ from 4pm) This GDR bar on the 14th floor of Neubrandenburg's Haus der Kultur und Bildung (House of Culture and Education) more than atones for the communist-era building's obnoxious aesthetics. Run by a former GDR citizen, and housing more than the usual mix of Lenin and Honecker portraits, it's stuffed with 1950s, '60s and '70s chairs, photos and more retro light fixtures and clocks than is strictly necessary. While much *Ostalgie* (a romanticised yearning for the GDR era) is a case of false-memory syndrome on the part of those who never actually lived under the Communist regime, this place feels more wistful and genuine.

Teens sip daiquiris from enormous cocktail glasses, while genuinely nostalgic *Ossis* (East Germans) drink coffee from similarly *Alice in Wonderland*–sized cups and a cosmonaut's suit hangs from the ceiling. The views over town and the Tollensesee are impressive too.

Getting There & Away

Trains leave every two hours for Berlin (€22.50, two hours). There are also services every two hours to/from Rostock (€19.50, two hours), via Güstrow, and Stralsund (€13.40, 1¼ hours).

By road from Berlin take the A10 northwest to Neuruppin, then head east towards Löwenberg, where you catch the B96 north; follow the signs for Stralsund. From Stralsund or Greifswald, head south on the B96. From Rostock, take the A19 south to Güstrow then follow the B104 east all the way.

MÜRITZ NATIONAL PARK

Müritz is commonly known as the land – or paradise – of a thousand lakes. That's an exaggeration, but there are at least more than 100, as well as countless other ponds, streams and rivers. The national park's two main sections sprawl over 300 sq km to the east and (mainly) west of the lakeside town of Neustrelitz, about 35km south of Neubrandenburg. Declared a protected area in 1990, the park consists of bog and wetlands, and is home to a wide range of waterfowl, including ospreys, white-tailed eagles and cranes. Tourist offices throughout the region offer various recommendations for the main activity: **paddle-and-camp trips**.

The park's waterway begins on the Zierker See, west of Neustrelitz. The main information centre is the **Nationalparkamt** (National Park Office; ☎ 039824-2520; www.nationalpark-mueritz.de; Schlossplatz 3, Hohenzieritz) between Neustreulitz and Brandenburg, reached via either the westerly B196 or the easterly B96 and taking the L34 from either. Tourist offices, hostels and camp sites in the area have trail and park maps, and also sell travel passes for bus and ferry services.

Canoeists should pick up the brochure *Paddeln im Land der Tausend Seen* (Paddling in the Land of 1000 Lakes) from the Neubrandenburg tourist office. This includes tips for 13 tours and places to stay along the way; although it's in German, essential information such as maps, distances, camp site icons and telephone numbers are easy to read.

When camping, you must use designated sites, of which there are more than a dozen within the park, including two FKK (naturist) sites. **Haveltourist** (☎ 03981-247 90; www.haveltourist .de; adult/tent from €5/4) operates camp sites throughout the park. The company also hires out kayaks from €10/15/70 per half-day/day/week and runs organised canoe tours.

COASTAL MECKLENBURG-WESTERN POMERANIA

ROSTOCK

☎ 0381 / pop 197,000

First impressions count and unfortunately Rostock doesn't always make a good one. There is a small but very attractive historic core – red-brick and pastel-coloured buildings harking back to the 14th and 15th century Hanseatic era – but you generally have to wade past a gritty landscape of concrete and industrial eyesores to get to it. As a major port and shipbuilding centre, the city was devastated in WWII and later pummelled by socialist architectural 'ideals'. It is, as someone who knows both cities well remarked to us dryly, 'not to be compared with Hamburg'.

MECKLENBURG-WESTERN POMERANIA

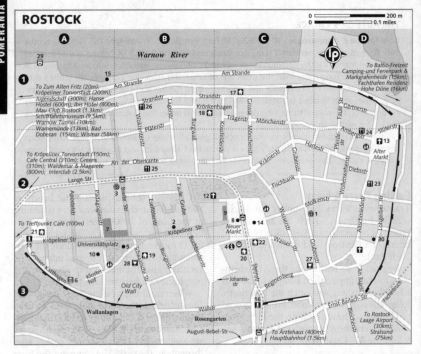

However, the largest city in northeastern Germany does have several winning cards up its sleeves. Its seaside suburb of Warnemünde is really quite stunning, Rostock's nightlife is the best north of Berlin and the city is a good base for several day trips. Most of all, things are getting better all the time, as buildings and streets are continually refurbished, and the city's venerable university helps biotech replace its uncompetitive shipyards.

Orientation

Rostock is located on the last stretch of the Warnow River before it flows into the Baltic Sea. The egg-shaped Altstadt sits below an east–west bend in the river. West of the Altstadt lies the student and nightlife district Kröpeliner Torvorstadt, most commonly known as KTV. The harbour is north along the top of the Altstadt and KTV. From this point, both the river and the city head north to Warnemünde and the sea. Most of Rostock is on the western riverbank, including Warnemünde, although some of Warnemünde's accommodation lies across the river mouth at Hohe Düne.

The train station is about 1.5km south of the Altstadt. Rosa-Luxemburg-Strasse runs north from the station to Steintor, in the old town's southeast corner. The airport is about 30km south of town.

Information

Ärztehaus (☎ 456 1622; Paulstrasse 48) Medical services.

Das Netz (☎ 490 0270; Grubenstrasse 49; per hr €2; ☺ 2-8pm Tue-Thu & Sun, 2pm-midnight Fri & Sat) Internet access.

Main post office (Neuer Markt 3-8; ☺ 9am-6pm Mon-Fri, to noon Sat)

Stadtbibliothek (☎ 381 2840; Kröpeliner Strasse 82) Library.

Surf Inn (☎ 375 6216; Galeria Kaufhof, Lange Strasse; per 15 min €1) Internet access.

Tourist-Information Rostock (☎ 381 2222; www .rostock.de; Neuer Markt 3; ☺ 10am-7pm Mon-Fri, to 4pm Sat & Sun May-Sep, 10am-7pm Mon-Fri, to 4pm Sat Oct-Apr)

Tourist office Warnemünde (☎ 548 000; www .warnemuende.de; Am Strom 59, cnr Kirchstrasse; ☺ 10am-6pm Mon-Fri, to 3pm Sat & Sun)

Treffpunkt Café (☎ 643 8062; www.e-treffpunkt.de; Am Vögenteich 23; ☺ 9am-8pm Mon-Fri) Twenty minutes' free internet access with any order.

Sights

It takes just an hour or two to see the city sights, after which we recommend making a beeline for Warnemünde. The way to the sea is lined with *Plattenbauten,* stunningly ugly concrete apartment blocks, built to house GDR workers, but the beachside is very different.

MARIENKIRCHE

Central Rostock's pride and joy is the 13th-century **Marienkirche** (☎ 453 325; Am Ziegenmarkt; admission €1; ⏱ 10am-6pm Mon-Sat, 11.15am-5pm Sun May-Sep, 10am-noon & 2-4pm Mon-Sat, 11.15am-noon Sun Oct-Apr). It features a 12m-high **astrological clock** (1470–72), which locals optimistically compare to the more famous example in Prague's Old Town Square.

Rostock's clock is a bit more hidden, however, being behind the church's main altar.

(You actually have to walk around the altar to see it.) At the very top is a series of doors, and at noon and midnight the innermost right door opens and six of the 12 apostles march out to parade around Jesus. Note that Judas is locked out. The lower section has a disc that tells the exact day on which Easter falls in any given year. The replaceable discs are accurate for 130 years – the current one expires in 2017, and the university already has a new one ready.

Another highlight of the Marienkirche – the only main Rostock church to survive WWII unscathed – is the unusually tall, organically shaped **baroque organ** (1770).

NEUER MARKT

Just around the corner from the Marienkirche is this open square, dominated by the splendid and rather pink 13th-century **Rathaus**. The building's baroque façade was added in 1727 after the original brick Gothic structure collapsed.

Opposite the Rathaus is a lovely series of restored **gabled houses** and a stylised, sea-themed **fountain** (2001) by artist Waldemar Otto. The explanatory plaque says the four figures are Neptune and his sons, although locals seem to think they represent the four elements.

KRÖPELINER STRASSE & UNIVERSITÄTSPLATZ

Kröpeliner Strasse, a broad, lively, cobblestone pedestrian mall lined with 15th- and 16th-century burghers' houses, runs from Neuer Markt west to Kröpeliner Tor.

At the centre of the mall is **Universitätsplatz**, positively swarming with people year-round, and its centrepiece, the crazy rococo **Brunnen der Lebensfreude** (Fountain of Happiness). True to its name, the square is lined with university buildings, including the handsome terracotta **Hauptgebäude** (1866–70), which replaced the famous 'White College'. The university itself is the oldest on the Baltic (founded in 1419), and currently has about 11,000 students.

At the northern side of Universitätsplatz are the **Five-Gables Houses**, modern interpretations of the residences that lined the square before WWII.

At the southwestern end is the Kloster Zum Heiligen Kreuz, a convent established in 1270 by Queen Margrethe of Denmark. Today it houses the **Cultural History Museum** (☎ 203 590; Klosterhof 18; admission free; ⏱ 1.30-6pm

Tue-Sun), with an interesting collection including Victorian furniture and a few sculptures by Ernst Barlach.

CITY WALLS & GATES
Today only two of 32 gates, plus a small brick section, remain of the old city wall. The 55m-high **Kröpeliner Tor** stands at the western end of Kröpeliner Strasse. From here, you can follow the *Wallanlagen* (city walls) through the pleasant park to Wallstrasse and the other surviving gate, the **Steintor**.

PETRIKIRCHE
The Gothic **Petrikirche** (☎ 211 01; Alter Markt; tower admission €2; ☉ 9am-noon & 2-5pm Mon-Fri, 11am-5pm Sat & Sun) has a 117m-high steeple – a mariner's landmark for centuries – that was restored in 1994, having been missing since WWII. You can climb the steps or take the lift up to the viewing platform.

SCHIFFFAHRTSMUSEUM
Rostock's **Ship Museum** (☎ 1283 1364; www .schifffahrtsmuseum-rostock.m-vp.de; MS Dresden, IGA Park, Liegeplatz Schmarl; admission €3; ☉ 10am-6pm Tue-Sun) has been relocated to the shores of the park that hosted the International Garden Exhibition in 2003, on the northwest riverbank. On board, there's a rundown on shipping from the Hanseatic period to today, plus the chance to play captain and other hands-on activities.

Take the S-Bahn to Lütten Klein and then bus 31 or 35 to IGA Park. Alternatively, see Tours (right).

WARNEMÜNDE
The jewel in Warnemünde's crown is its long, wide expanse of startlingly white beach. Even the butt-ugly concrete block that's the Hotel Neptun (see opposite) can't spoil it, while the mollusc-shaped **Teepott** building (think the TWA terminal at New York's JFK airport) and 19th-century **lighthouse** positively add to its quirky appeal.

Walking from the train station along **Alter Strom**, the boat-lined main canal of this 'fishing village' (now officially a Rostock suburb), you'll pass a row of quaint cottages housing restaurants, but you might still wonder what the fuss is about.

Then you turn the corner into Am Leuchtturm and Seestrasse and – bam! – it hits you. Forget museums and the like,

Warnemünde is all about sunbathing, promenading, eating fish and afterwards sipping cocktails on the beach. Sundown, when the crowds have abated slightly, is a memorable time to be here.

Tours
The tourist office runs 90-minute guided walking tours (€4) at 2pm daily in summer (11am Sunday). English-language tours can be arranged for groups.

Reederei Schütt (☎ 690 953, 0173-917 9178; www .hafenrundfahrten-in-rostock.de) offers round-harbour trips (€4) and services from Rostock's harbour to Warnemünde, stopping at the Ship Museum, between May and October.

Festivals & Events
In the second weekend in August, **Hanse Sail Rostock** (☎ 208 5233; www.hanse-sail.com) is the biggest of the city's many regattas, bringing countless sailing ships to the city and Warnemünde harbours.

Rostock is also one of the venues for the classical music **Festspiele Mecklenburg-Vorpommern** (☎ 0385-591 8585; www.festspiele-mv.de), held annually from June to September.

Sleeping
ALTSTADT
Hotel Kleine Sonne (☎ 497 3153; www.die-kleine-sonne .de; Steinstrasse 7; s €50-70, d €55-75; P ⌨) This lovely place lives up to its sunny name with lots of red and yellow detailing, as well as jaunty paintings by Berlin artist Nils Ausländer dotted around. There's no denying that the bedrooms are plainer than the public areas, but at least you can learn semaphore from the Ausländer print in each.

City-Pension (☎ 252 260; www.city-pension-rostock .de; Krönkenhagen 3; s €45-55, d €70-90; P) This is a small family *pension* occupying a lovely quiet street near the harbour and in the heart of the old-fashioned northern Altstadt.

Altes Hafenhaus (☎ 493 0110; www.alteshafenhaus .de; Strandstrasse 93; s €70, d €75-85; ✂) Stained-glass windows, wooden floors and embroidered towels give the 10 rooms in this converted baroque villa an air of elegance (slightly spoiled by the kitsch toilet seats in the newer rooms, however). It's very handy for the old town and some rooms overlook the water, although this is not the most scenic stretch of river.

Steigenberger Hotel Sonne (☎ 497 30; www.hotel -sonne-rostock.de; Neuer Markt 2; s €120-130, d €140-160;

P X ⌐) It's hard for the interior to compete with the ornate façade at this hotel – a confection of stepped gables and iron lacework topped with a golden 'sun'. However, the rooms do their best in tones of brown, red and yellow and there's a clutch of classy restaurants.

Other recommendations:

Radisson SAS (☎ 375 00; www.rostock.radissonsas .com; Lange Strasse 40; s/d from €105/115; P X) Fabulous new hotel opened in 2005.

Courtyard by Marriott (☎ 497 00; reservation .rostock@courtyard.com; Schwaansche Strasse 6; s/d from €120/140; P X X) Right near pretty Kröpeliner Strasse.

KRÖPELINER TORVORSTADT

Hanse Hostel (☎ 128 6006; www.hanse-hostel.de; Doberaner Strasse 136; dm €12-17, s/d €24/44, breakfast €4, bedding €2; ⌐) On the edge of Rostock's trendy bar district, the KTV, this family-run operation is clean and friendly, with a kitchen, laundry and loads of other facilities – although it is on a busy street. Hosts Iris and Gerd are always ready to help with local tips and you'll feel like one of the family by the time you leave (which for some guests turns out to be many days later than they'd planned).

Ibis Hotel (☎ 038204-122 22; Am Handelspark 5, Broderstorf; r from €54; P X X) One of the first midrange hotels to begin filling a severe gap in the Rostock market, this new business-class hotel is near the Stadthafen. It's generic but comfortable.

DJH hostel (Jugendgästeschiff Georg Buchner; ☎ 670 0320; www.djh-mv.de; Am Stadthafen 72-3; dm under/over 26yr €15/18, d €58; X) A hostel onboard a 1950s cargo ship sounds unusual and interesting. In reality, the dorms are slightly old-fashioned and claustrophobic, and the service gruff. Nevertheless, keen sailors might want to give it a whirl. There's a Hotel Garni here too (singles/doubles €50/75) with slightly better standards. Take tram 4 or 5 to Kabutzenhof.

Jugendschiff (☎ 495 8107; r €50-60) In the next berth to the DJH hostel, the Jugendschiff is a much smaller boat with some nice doubles.

WARNEMÜNDE

DJH hostel Warnemünde (☎ 548 170; www.djh-mv.de; Parkstrasse 47; dm under/over 26yr €21.15/24.15; P X ⌐) Opened in 2001, this fantastic hostel is in a converted weather station, just minutes from the western end of the Warnemünde beach, near Diedrichshagen. The tower rooms are

particularly popular with families, who tend to predominate in July and August holiday period.

Baltic-Freizeit Camping- und Ferienpark (☎ 04544-800 313; www.baltic-freizeit.de; Dünenweg 27, Markgrafenheide; sites €13-35) On the east side of the Warnow River, across from Warnemünde, this is an enormous city-run affair with 1200 pitches. Take tram 4 to Dierkower Kreuz, then bus 18 (45 minutes).

Hotel-Pension Kater (☎ 548 2422; www.pension -zum-kater.de; Am Strom 71 & Alexandrinenstrasse 115; s €50-75, d €70-95, breakfast €8; P) This *pension* manages to be cute and homy without straying into Laura Ashley territory. It's attached to a wood-lined pub selling Irish beer and a small fish restaurant. Look out for the sweet blackcat logo and ask about holiday apartments if you're interested.

Strandhotel Residenz (☎ 548 060; www.residenz -strandhotel.de; Seestrasse 6; s €75, d with/without sea view from €125/100, ste €150-210; P X X ⌐) The exterior of this new hotel reflects and updates the fishermen's cottages along Alter Strom, with a roof terrace above the first level and balconies above this. Inside, you'll find stylish, soundinsulated rooms with flat-screen TVs, plus a library. Spa treatments and physiotherapy are on offer, as is free 'energised' water.

Hotel Neptun (☎ 7770; www.hotel-neptun.de; Seestrasse 19; s €100-220, d €150-250; P X ⌐) As hideous as this concrete GDR monolith is, its balconies have always been cleverly angled so that each room has a beach view, and it's now been completely renovated inside. It has an interesting background too, with past guests as diverse as Fidel Castro and Franz Beckenbauer.

Strand-Hotel Hübner (☎ 543 40; www.hotel-huebner .de; Seestrasse 12; s €115-160, d €140-185; P X) This stylish, modern hotel has balconies overlooking the beach. A highlight is the guest lounge overlooking the Baltic Sea. In winter, you can enjoy coffee, cakes, fondue, baked apples or even *Feuerzangenbowle* punch (see boxed text, p79) here.

Yachthafen Residenz Hohe Düne (☎ 504 00; www .yhd.de; Am Yachthafen 1-8; s/d from €115/160, ste from €240; P X ⌐) Located at the enclosed yacht harbour across the river mouth from the main beach, this huge luxury hotel development is one of those all-inclusive affairs – with 368 rooms and suites, a kids' club and conference centre. You'll need to catch a ferry or shuttle to go to and fro.

Hotel am Leuchturm (☎ 543 70; www.hotel-am -leuchturm.de; Am Leuchturm 16; s €120, d €150-195; P ⊠) The oft-used colours of yellow and blue are given a delicious designer twist in the spacious, light-filled accommodation here. Right near the lighthouse, most rooms enjoy spectacular views, especially the corner panorama ones.

Eating

ALTSTADT

Zur Kogge (☎ 493 4493; Wokrenterstrasse 27; mains €8-15) Touristy but still unmissable, this is Rostock's oldest restaurant. Cosy wooden booths are lined with stained-glass decorations of Hanseatic coats of armour and monster fish threatening sailing ships, while life preservers hang from the walls. The menu is dominated by fish, but you can enjoy coffee and cake between meal times if you want to avoid the crowds.

Tre Kronor (☎ 490 4260; Hansepassage, Lange Strasse; mains €8-16) Set in a strange split-level glass-fronted pillar box at the back of a shopping centre, the 'Three Crowns' serves up interesting Swedish dishes, including elk steak with mushrooms.

Am Berg 13 (☎ 490 6262; Amberg 13; mains €10-15; ☼ from 5pm Tue-Sun) This relaxed, unassuming restaurant is locally renowned for its ambitious and creative cuisine, with dishes such as *Kalbshaxe* (knuckle of veal) accompanied by polenta and capsicum, onion, rosemary and sherry ragout, or rabbit with chanterelle mushrooms, garlic gnocchi and green beans.

Albert & Emile (☎ 493 4373; Altschmiedestrasse 28; mains €15-22; ☼ from 6.30pm Mon-Sat) Up the road from the Petrikirche, an ivy-covered façade conceals this very posh two-storey French restaurant, which offers some of Rostock's finest *haute cuisine*.

KRÖPELINER TORVORSTADT

Waldemar & Margarete (☎ 200 5500; Budapesterstrasse 16; dishes €4-10) This popular café-cum-restaurant and pub has a friendly atmosphere, with its range of TV sports and film evenings. It serves huge portions of hearty meals, which you can enjoy in the beer garden in summer.

Green's (☎ 496 5172; Leonhardstrasse 22; mains €6-10) Paninis, smoothies as well as delicious Thai-influenced curries attract a hip, discerning crowd here. For those in a hurry, there's a weekday 'quick lunch', which has to be on your table in 15 minutes or it's free.

Zum Alten Fritz (☎ 208 780; Warnowufer 65; mains €8-15) One of four establishments in an expanding local brewery chain, this is a big pub-restaurant down on the docks with a good range of standards, plus organic meats and specials like turkey in beer.

WARNEMÜNDE

Both fresh fish and freshly smoked fish are available in abundance here. Somewhat touristy restaurants fill the old fishermen's cottages lining the western bank of Alter Strom. There's a new development on the eastern bank, where the restaurants are less atmospheric, but arguably do better food and have great views of the cottages opposite.

Fischerhaus (Am Strom; mains €8-13) This relaxed canteen-style place serves simple fish dishes, including delicious salmon in beer batter.

La Villa (☎ 510 9944; Am Bahnhof 1b; mains €12-19) In an old white villa with a chequered history, this designer restaurant and café gives its fish dishes a modern, Mediterranean twist. Try the freshly made strawberry punch, too.

Atlantic (☎ 526 55, 526 74; Am Strom 107; mains €11-24) One of the better-regarded fish restaurants on the western bank of the canal, Atlantic offers just about every type of fish downstairs, and Italian gourmet cuisine on the floor above.

Drinking

Szene and *Piste* are the main free monthlies, geared predominantly towards music.

Krahnstöver Likörfabrik (☎ 4377 7654; Grubenstrasse 1) Rostock's oldest family-run wine merchant owns this multifaceted bistro-bar-café, next to an artificial stream near the city wall. They also have a brasserie in the Steigenberger Hotel Sonne.

Studentenkeller (☎ 455 928; Universitätsplatz 5; ☼ Tue-Sat) This cellar and garden joint has been rocking Rostock's learned youth for years.

Café Central (☎ 490 4648; Leonhardstrasse 20) Students and hipsters loll around sipping long drinks on the banquette seats below black-and-white photos or enjoy a tall beer over a game of backgammon at the tables in the middle. One of Rostock's prime meeting places, this is right in the heart of the scene.

The best bars from which to enjoy the Warnemünde sunset include **Schuster's** (☎ 700 7835; Im Teepott; ☼ from 11am), which also has a hip summer pavilion on the beach a few metres away from its main Teepott building location, and the ritzier **Sky-Bar** (☎ 700 7835; 19th fl, Hotel Neptun; ☺ from 9pm Mon-Sat). The Hotel Neptun has a panoramic café, too, open from 1pm to 6pm daily.

Entertainment

MS Stubnitz (☎ 490 7475; www.stubnitz.com; Stadthafen, Liegeplatz 82) A former fishing trawler has been converted into Rostock's most unusual and popular venue, with bands, DJs and performances over three decks. The tone is alternative and often a bit grungy. Beware that the boat sometimes sails off to entertain other cities, too.

Mau Club Rostock (☎ 202 3576; Warnowufer 56; ☺ Fri, Sat & other special dates) Everything from indie to punk to disco attracts a wide-ranging crowd to this former storage hall opposite the Jugendherberge. Well known for its support of up-and-coming acts, it hosts many free local band evenings.

Interclub (☎ 377 8737; Erich-Schlesinger-Strasse 19a, Südstadt; ☺ Fri & Sat) Come here for serious dance music of various shades and flavours.

Getting There & Away

AIR

Rostock's airport, **Rostock-Laage** (RLG; ☎ 01805-007 737; www.rostock-airport.de), has a sparse number of scheduled services to Cologne-Bonn, Dortmund, Munich and Zürich, plus charter flights to holiday resorts in Crete, Spain, Turkey etc.

BOAT

There are ferry services to Denmark, Sweden and Latvia, as well as to Estonia and Finland in summer. Fares are quite complicated depending on the season and the number of people travelling, so the following are provided as rough high-season guides only.

Scandlines (☎ 01805-116 688, 673 1217; www .scandlines.de) travels to Gedser, Denmark (walk-on passenger €10, car with passengers from €75, 1¾ hours, six daily), Trelleborg in Sweden (walk-on €24, car from €126, cabins €45 to €85, 5¾ to 7½ hours, three daily) and Ventspils, Latvia (car without passengers from €80, cabin from €270, 26 hours, four weekly).

TT-Line (☎ 670 790; www.ttline.de) sails to/from Trelleborg (walk-on €30, car with passengers from €100, 5½ hours, three daily).

Boats depart from the overseas seaport (Überseehafen), which is on the east side of the Warnow; take tram 2 to Dierkower Kreuz, then change for bus 49 to Seehafen. There is an S-Bahn to Seehafen, but it's a 20-minute walk from the station to the piers.

CAR & MOTORCYCLE

To reach Rostock from Berlin, head north or south out of the city to the A10. Follow it northwest to the A24, which leads straight into the A19 running directly north to Rostock (2½ hours). From Neubrandenburg, take the B104 west to the A19 and turn north (1½ hours).

For a lift, get in touch with the **Mitfahrzentrale** (☎ 194 40; Lohgerberstrasse 1), a ride-sharing agency.

TRAIN

There are frequent direct trains to Rostock from Berlin (from €31.90, three hours) and hourly services to Stralsund (€11.70, one hour), Wismar (€9.10, 1¼ hours) and Schwerin (€13.40, one hour).

Getting Around

TO/FROM THE AIRPORT

An airport shuttle bus (€5) runs from the train station to the airport, timed with plane departures. A taxi should cost around €35.

BICYCLE

Cycling isn't much fun in the centre because of heavy traffic, but things quickly improve outside the city. Rental stations include **Radstation Rostock** (☎ 240 1153; Rostock main train station) and **Holiday & Mehr** (☎ 700 7060; Warnemünde train station).

CAR & MOTORCYCLE

With complicated one-way systems, confusing street layouts and dedicated parking-ticket police, Rostock is not a driver-friendly city. There are several convenient parking lots off Lange Strasse. The **Warnow Tunnel** (www.warnowtunnel .de; toll €2.50), completed in 2002, crosses beneath the river in the north of the city and links to the A19.

PUBLIC TRANSPORT

Journeys within Rostock city, including Warnemünde, cost €1.50/3.20 for a single/day pass, valid on the Warnow ferries as well as land transport. The surrounding area is zoned; a single/day pass costs €1.50/2.80 for one zone or €5/10 for all zones.

The double-decker S-Bahn has frequent services to Warnemünde (€1.50); some continue to Güstrow (€5) or Berlin (€31.90).

Trams 2, 11 and 12 travel from the Hauptbahnhof up Steinstrasse, around Marienkirche and down Lange Strasse. Take tram 11 or 12 to get from the Hauptbahnhof to the university. Lines 4 and 5, which go from the train station to the KVT district, have been out of operation but *should* be back in service by 2007.

TAXI

For a taxi, ring **Hanse-Taxi** (☎ 685 858) or **FunkTaxi** (☎ 761 1176).

BAD DOBERAN & COASTAL RESORTS

☎ 038203 / pop 11,600

The former summer ducal residence of Bad Doberan, about 15km west of Rostock, was once the site of a powerful Cistercian monastery. Today, it's a tourist town with an impressive *Münster* (large church) and horse races in July and August.

Bad Doberan is also the starting point for the Molli Schmalspurbahn, a popular narrow-gauge steam train that travels to the coastal resorts of Heiligendamm and Kühlungsborn. Catching the train and walking along the coast between some stops makes for a pleasant and undemanding day trip from Rostock.

The Bad Doberan **tourist office** (☎ 621 54; www.bad-doberan-heiligendamm.de; Severinstrasse 6) is five minutes' walk from the train station.

Sights & Activities

MÜNSTER

On the eastern side of town is the **Münster** (☎ 627 16; www.doberanermuenster.de; Klosterstrasse 2; adult/concession €3/2, tour adult €2.50-4, concession €2-3; ✆ 9am-6pm Mon-Sat, 11.30am-6pm Sun May-Sep, 9am-5pm daily Apr & Oct, to 4pm Tue-Sun Nov-Feb), a stunning brick Gothic hall church typical of northern Germany. Its chief treasures include a lovely high altar and an ornate pulpit. The Münster's 1.2 million bricks are being cleaned, while the rest of the monastery complex and grounds is filling up with craft shops, galleries and cafés.

ZAPPA MEMORIAL

Bad Doberan's racecourse is the unlikely venue for the **Zappanale** (☎ 598 207; www.arf -society.de), Germany's only Frank Zappa

festival, which has been held here every July since 1989 and now attracts audiences of up to 3000, as well as several of the great man's former bandmates. In 2002 a **Zappa memorial** was erected in the centre of town amid much psychedelic rejoicing.

MOLLI SCHMALSPURBAHN

In 1886, 'Molli', as she's affectionately known, began huffing and puffing her way to Heiligendamm, carrying Germany's elite. Then in 1910, the line was extended west along the coast to Kühlungsborn. Today the train goes by the full name of **Mecklenburger Bäderbahn Molli** (☎ 4150; www.molli-bahn.de), with services departing Bad Doberan's train station on average 11 times a day (but up to 13).

With a maximum speed of 45km/h, the journey takes 15 minutes to reach the coast at Heiligendamm (single/return €3.50/6) and 45 minutes in total to Kühlungsborn/West (€5.50/10), with interim stops in Steilküste, Kühlungsborn/East and Kühlungsborn/Mitte. Concessions and family fares are also available. Children love the dinky engine and carriages. There's a salon car on many journeys and the scenery is lovely.

To help plan your day, pick up a pocket-sized timetable when you buy your ticket at Bad Doberan's train station.

For a particularly easy walk, get off at Heiligendamm and walk to the Steilküste station before picking up the train again.

HEILIGENDAMM

The 'white town on the sea' is Germany's oldest seaside resort, founded in 1793 by Mecklenburg duke Friedrich Franz I and fashionable throughout the 19th century as the playground of nobility. Since 2003 it's been reborn, with the opening of the exclusive **Kempinski Grand Hotel Heiligendamm** (☎ 7400; www.kempinski-heiligendamm.com; s/d with park view from €250/285, with sea view from €435/470; P X X Q R).

With modern rooms housed in five gleaming white, heritage-listed buildings, the Kempinski is continuing the resort's noble tradition, even proving grand enough to accommodate US President George W Bush on a state visit and to be chosen to host a G8 summit in summer 2007. Even for those not staying here, the hotel is an attraction, with a restaurant, pristine beach and lovely surrounding parkland.

Bad Doberan **tourist information** (☎ 4150) has an outlet in the Heiligendamm Molli-Bahn station.

KÜHLUNGSBORN

The biggest Baltic Sea resort, with 7300 inhabitants, Kühlungsborn is known for its lovely Art Deco buildings and its green surroundings, as it backs onto a 130-hectare forest. The east and west parts of town are linked by the Ostseeallee promenade, lined with hotels and restaurants. In the eastern part of town you'll find a pier running 240m out to sea and a newly built yacht harbour.

All water sports, including diving, are on offer. For more information, contact the **Kurverwaltung** (spa resort administration; ☎ 8490; www .kuehlungsborn.de; Ostseeallee 18).

Getting There & Away

Trains serve Rostock Hauptbahnhof (€2.60, 25 minutes) and Wismar (€6.20, 45 minutes) roughly hourly. By car, take the B105 towards Wismar.

WISMAR

☎ 03841 / pop 46,500

The many colourful 'Swedish Heads' you see across town are the most obvious but not the only mementos of Swedish rule in Wismar. This small, pretty town joined the Hanseatic trading league in the 13th century and looks essentially Hanseatic, with its gabled façades and cobbled streets. However, it spent most of the 16th and 17th centuries as part of Sweden and various buildings, a clock, a tomb and more still hint at this period.

Wismar's picture-postcard looks have always made it popular with filmmakers. Its *Alter Hafen* (old harbour) featured in the 1922 Dracula movie *Nosferatu*, and it's not unusual for day-trippers from Schwerin or Rostock to still stumble across movie crews.

Orientation

The Unesco-listed Altstadt is the city centre, built up around the Markt, said to be the largest medieval town square in northern Germany. The Bahnhof is at the northeastern corner of the Altstadt and the *Alter Hafen* port is at the northwestern corner; a canal runs from *Alter Hafen* almost due east across the northern half of the Altstadt. The streets around the Markt are pedestrianised and

the main night-time entertainment area is around *Alter Hafen*.

Information

Main post office (Mecklenburger Strasse 18-20; ☉ 9am-6pm Mon-Fri, to noon Sat)

Tourist-Information (☎ 251 3025; www.wismar.de; Am Markt 11; ☉ 9am-6pm)

Sights

MARKT

Two things dominate the Markt. The first is the **Wasserkunst** (waterworks) in the middle. This ornate, 12-sided well, completed in 1602, supplied Wismar's drinking water until 1897. Today it remains the town's landmark.

Behind it stands the building and restaurant known as **Alter Schwede**. This has a characteristic step gabled façade, with a copy of one of the two so-called 'Swedish Heads' set in it (see boxed text, p720).

Other gabled houses around the Markt have been lovingly restored. The large Rathaus (1817–19) at the square's northern end houses an excellent **Historical Exhibition** (adult/concession €1/0.50; ☉ 10am-6pm) in its basement. Displays include an original 15th-century *Wandmalerei* (mural) uncovered by archaeologists in 1985, a glass-covered medieval well, and the Wrangel tomb, the coffin of influential Swedish General Helmut V Wrangel and his wife – with larger-than-life wooden figures carved on top of it.

CHURCHES

Of the three great red-brick churches that once rose above the rooftops before WWII, only the **St-Nikolai-Kirche** (☎ 1381-1487; admission €1; ☉ 8am-8pm May-Sep, 10am-6pm Apr & Oct, 11am-4pm Nov-Mar) was left intact. Today it contains a font from its older sister church, the St-Marien-Kirche.

Otherwise, all that remains of this, the 13th-century **St-Marien-Kirche** (admission by donation; ☉ 8am-8pm May-Sep, 10am-6pm Apr & Oct, 11am-4pm Nov-Mar), is its great brick steeple (1339), which still rises above the city. The clock on the tower was donated by the same General Wrangel whose tomb lies in the Rathaus basement. A multimedia exhibit on medieval church-building techniques is housed in the tower's base.

The massive red shell of the **St-Georgen-Kirche** (admission by donation; ☉ 8am-sunset or 8pm, whichever comes sooner) is being restored for use

A SWEDISH HEADS-UP

No, a Swedish head is not what you need to successfully assemble a flat-pack Ikea bookcase. A Swedish Head in the Wismar sense is one of two baroque busts of Hercules, which once stood on mooring posts at the harbour entrance.

Semi-comical, with great curling moustaches and wearing lions as hats, the statues' origins are much debated. However, it's believed they marked either the beginning of the harbour or the navigable channels within it. It's also thought that before this they were simply ships' figureheads.

Either way, they've proved to be a boon for Wismar's souvenir manufacturers, adorning all manner of gifts. The originals were damaged when a Finnish barge rammed them in 1902, at which time replicas were made. One original is now in the Schabbellhaus (see Historical Museum, below), while two replicas guard the Baumhaus in Wismar's *Alter Hafen*.

as a church, concert hall and exhibition space, and was partially opened in 2002 (completion by 2010). In 1945 a freezing populace was driven to burn what was left of the church's beautiful wooden statue of St George and the dragon.

FÜRSTENHOF

Between the St-Marien- and St-Georgen-churches lies the Italian Renaissance **Fürstenhof** (1512–13), now the city courthouse, largely restored. The façades are slathered in terra-cotta reliefs depicting episodes from folklore and town history.

HISTORICAL MUSEUM

The town's historical museum is in the Renaissance **Schabbellhaus** (☎ 282 350; www .schabbellhaus.de; Schweinsbrücke 8; admission free; ☑ 10am-8pm Tue-Sun May-Oct, to 5pm Nov-Apr) in a former brewery (1571), just south of St-Nikolai-Kirche across the canal. One of the original Swedish Heads can still be seen here.

Regional artist Christian Wetzel's four charming **pig statuettes** grace the **Schweins-brücke** between the church and the museum.

Activities

Clermont Reederei (☎ 224 646; www.reederei-clermont .de) operates hour-long harbour cruises five times daily from May to September, leaving from *Alter Hafen* (adult €7). Boats also go to nearby **Poel Island** once a day (adult one-way/return €7/11), which has the atmosphere of a remote fishing community. Various other companies run tours on historic ships during summer; contact the **harbour** (☎ 389 082; www .alterhafenwismar.de) for details. **Fritz Reuter** (☎ 05254-808 500; www.ms-fritz-reuter.de) also organ-ises wreck dives along the Baltic coast.

The huge indoor water park **Wonnemar** (☎ 327 623; www.wonnemar.de; Bürgermeister-Haupt-Strasse 38; day ticket adult/child/concession €9.50/7.50/8.50) has several pools, tennis, bowling, badminton, massage, sauna, steam baths and six (count 'em!) water slides.

Hanse-Sektkellerei (☎ 636 282; www.altes-gewoelbe -wismar.de; Turnerweg 4b), the champagne factory south of the city centre, produces several va-rieties – from dry (Hanse Tradition) to extra dry (Hanse Selection). Tours are offered to groups of at least 15.

Tours

In summer there are 1½-hour walking tours of the city, in German, leaving the tourist of-fice at 10.30am (adult/concession €4/3; also 2pm Saturday, Sunday and holidays). English-language tours are available on request for groups of 20 or more.

Festivals & Events

Annual events include the **Hafenfest** (Harbour Festival) in mid-June, featuring old and new sailing ships and steamers, music and food, and a free **street theatre** festival in July/August. Wismar also holds a **Schwedenfest** on the third weekend of August, commemorating the end of Swedish rule in 1903.

Sleeping

Reserve well ahead for the peak summer season, when Wismar fills up quickly. **Pri-vate rooms** start at €20 through the tourist office.

DJH hostel (☎ 326 80; www.jugendherbergen-mv.de; Juri-Gagarin-Ring 30a; dm under/over 26yr €17.25/20.25; P ⊗) The city's Jugendherberge Am Schwe-denstein is in a pretty, old brick building west of town, not far from the water park. The

Schwedenstein (Swedish Stone) next door is another reminder of Swedish hegemony.

Pension Chez Fasan (☎ 213 425; www.pension-chez-fasan.de; Bademutterstrasse 20a; s €26-30, d €55; P) The en suite rooms in these three linked houses are relatively new (less than 10 years old) and great value for money, although we're not 100% sure about the service. Call ahead to make sure someone's around to let you in.

Bio Hotel Reingard (☎ 284 972; www.reingard.de; Weberstrasse 18; s €50-70, d €80-120; P) Foodies should dump their luggage quickly in their charming room – individually decorated with antique furnishings – before heading straight to the lauded organic restaurant here. Adjoining there's even a small museum and shop (only open Tuesday or on request) dedicated to the *Sanddorn*, a distinctive, citrusy Mecklenburg berry.

Hotel Reuterhaus (☎ 222 30; www.hotel-reuterhaus.de; Am Markt 19; s/d from €60/80) This is a family-run historic establishment with views of the Markt and the Wasserkunst.

Hotel Stadt Hamburg (☎ 2390; www.wismar.steigenberger.de; Am Markt 24; s/d from €85/110; P ☒ ☒) Lots of abstract sculptures decorate the lobby, restaurant and spa of this flash place on the market. The rooms are a lot more generic, but extremely comfortable, and some enjoy great views.

Eating

If you're feeling adventurous, try *Wismarer Spickaal* (young eel smoked in a way unique to the region). Wismar's picturesque 'restaurant row' is along the pedestrianised Am Lohberg, near the *Alter Hafen*.

To'n Zägenkrog (☎ 282 716; Ziegenmarkt 10; mains €7-13; ☉ from 5pm) This popular pub, crammed with maritime mementos and boasting harbour views, serves excellent fish dishes.

Brauhaus am Lohberg (☎ 250 238; Kleine Hohe Strasse 15; mains €7-13) This building was once home to the town's first brewery; restored in 1995, it's now brewing again, taking up three floors and offering a good seafood menu. Look out for the painted penguins.

Fischerklause (☎ 252 850; Fischerreihe 4; mains €7-13; ☉ closed Sun & Mon) This is a tiny but characterful fish restaurant with a mainly local crowd, just off the Altstadt ring road near the *Alter Hafen*.

Zum Weinberg (☎ 283 550; Hinter dem Rathaus 3; mains €7-17) This lovely Renaissance house, with painted ceiling, stained-glass windows and

uneven walls, serves huge portions of fruity Mecklenburg specialities, including *Rippenbraten* (rolled roast pork stuffed with lemon, apple and plums).

Getting There & Away

Trains travel every hour to/from Rostock (€9.10, 65 minutes) and Schwerin (€6.20, 45 minutes).

DARSS-ZINGST PENINSULA

Nature-lovers and artists will be bowled over by the **Darss-Zingst Peninsula** (Fischland-Darss-Zingst; www.fischland-darss-zingst.de, in German), part of the 805-sq-km Vorpommersche Boddenlandschaft (Western Pomeranian Boddenlandschaft) National Park, which also encompasses the island of Hiddensee (see p733) and the west coast of Rügen (see p732).

The 'Bodden' are lagoons that were once part of the sea here, but have been cut off by shifting landmasses and are now rich with fish-life. The seawards peninsula is raw and bracing, with trees growing sideways away from the constant winds. Further inland you'll find charming 'captains' houses' – reed-thatched houses with colourfully painted doors depicting sunflowers, fish (one of the region's motifs) and other symbols of nature. Also common are *Zeesenboote* (drag-net fishing boats) with striking brown sails.

The area looks a picture, so it's not surprising to learn that it's home to an artists' colony in **Ahrenshoop** (www.ostseebad-ahrenshoop.de), whose **Kunstkaten** (www.kunstkaten.de, in German; Strandweg 1) gallery is in one of the region's most striking reed-thatched houses.

Baltic coastlines – not just in Germany – are the source of almost all the world's amber. As well as the jewellery on sale throughout Mecklenburg-Western Pomerania, you'll find the **Deutsches Bernsteinmuseum** (German Amber Museum; www.deustches-bernsteinmuseum.de, in German; Im Kloster 1-2) in **Ribnitz-Damgarten** (www.ribnitz-damgarten.de).

Prerow (www.ostseebad-prerow.de, in German) is renowned for its seamens' church and lighthouse.

The national park is the biggest resting ground in central Europe for migratory cranes. Some 60,000 birds stop over here every spring and autumn. Contact the park authority, **Nationalparkamt Vorpommersche Boddenlandschaft** (☎ 038234-5020; poststelle@nlp-vbl.de; Im Forst 5, Born, Darss), for further information.

WESTERN POMERANIA

STRALSUND

☎ 03831 / pop 58,770

Once the second most important member of the Hanseatic League, after Lübeck, Unesco-protected Stralsund maintains its elegant medieval profile – despite these days being principally the gateway to the holiday island of Rügen.

Square gables interspersed with Gothic turrets, ornate portals and vaulted arches make it one of the leading examples of *Backsteingotik* (classic red-brick Gothic gabled architecture) in northern Germany.

Add the unusual sight of holidaymakers in shorts and flip-flops wandering along its historic cobbled streets and you have a rare – but thoroughly enjoyable – combination indeed.

Orientation

The Altstadt is effectively on its own island, surrounded by lakes and the sea. Its main hubs are Alter Markt in the north and Neuer Markt in the south; a few blocks south of the latter is the central bus station. The Hauptbahnhof is across the Tribseer Damm causeway, west of the Neuer Markt. The harbour is on the Altstadt's eastern side.

Information

Main post office (Neuer Markt 4; ☼ 9am-6pm Mon-Fri, to noon Sat)

Matrix (☎ 278 80; Wasserstrasse 8-9; per hr €4; ☼ 2pm-midnight) Internet access.

Toffi's Web Café (☎ 309 385; Am Lobshagen 8a; per hr €3; ☼ noon-10pm)

Tourismuszentrale (☎ 246 90; www.stralsund.de; Alter Markt 9; ☼ 9am-7pm Mon-Fri, to 2pm Sat, 10am-2pm Sun May-Sep, 9am-5pm Mon-Fri, 10am-2pm Sat Oct-Apr; 🖳) Tourist information and room bookings.

Sights

ALTER MARKT

Stralsund's symbol, bar none, is its splendid **Rathaus**, the city's retort to Lübeck. The seven copper turrets and six triangular gables of its decorative, red-brick Gothic façade (1370) now grace postcards and marketing brochures far afield. The upper portion of the northern façade, or *Schauwand* (show wall), has openings to prevent strong winds from knocking

it over. Inside, the sky-lit colonnade boasts shiny black pillars on carved and painted bases; on the western side of the building is an ornate portal.

Through the Rathaus' eastern walkway you'll come to the main portal of the other dominant Alter Markt building, the 1270 **Nikolaikirche** (☎ 299 799; Alter Markt; ☼ 10am-5pm Mon-Sat, 11.15am-noon & 2-4pm Sun). Modelled after the Marienkirche in Lübeck and bearing a fleeting resemblance to Notre Dame, it's filled with art treasures. The **main altar** (1708), designed by the baroque master Andreas Schlüter, shows the eye of God flanked by cherubs, capped with a depiction of the Last Supper. Also worth a closer look is the **high altar** (1470), 6.7m wide and 4.2m tall, showing Jesus' entire life. Behind the altar is the **astronomical clock** (1394).

Opposite the Rathaus you'll find the **Wulflamhaus** (Alter Markt 5), a beautiful 15th-century townhouse named after an old mayor. Its turreted step gable imitates the Rathaus façade.

OTHER CHURCHES & CLOISTERS

The Neuer Markt is dominated by the massive 14th-century **Marienkirche** (☎ 298 965; Neuer Markt; ☼ 10am-6pm Mon-Fri, to 5pm Sat & Sun), another superb example of north German red-brick construction. You can climb the steep wooden steps up the tower (€1) for a sweeping view of the town, with its lovely red-tiled roofs, and Rügen Island.

On Schillstrasse, reached via Külpstrasse, is the **Johanniskloster** (☎ 666 488; Schillstrasse 26; adult/concession €2/1.50; ☼ 10am-6pm Wed-Sun May-Oct), a former Franciscan monastery that's now a concert venue. It's famous for its 'smoking attic' (there was no chimney), chapter hall and cloister.

Don't forget to look at the lovely ivy-covered face of the **Heilgeistkirche** (Wasserstrasse).

OCEANOGRAPHIC MUSEUM

Stralsund's **Meeresmuseum** (☎ 265 010; www .meeresmuseum.de; Katharinenberg 14-20; adult/child/ concession/family €6.50/4.50/4.50/17; ☼ 9am-6pm Jun-Sep, 10am-5pm Oct-May) boasts an excellent large natural history section, including a 1000kg skeleton of a finback whale (hanging over your head!).

However, its highlight is the atmospheric aquarium in the basement of this 13th-century convent building. Turn left for recreated North Sea environments and right for

Baltic fish (including huge sturgeon). There's also a tropical section and a 350,000-litre sea-turtle pool, the top of which extends to the café above.

There are English audio-guides available. The museum is planning to extend and turn into a 21st-century **Ozeaneum** (www.ozeaneum.com) by 2008.

Activities

Weisse Flotte (☎ 0180-321 2120; www.weisse-flotte .com; Fährstrasse 16; adult/child €6/4) offers four one-hour harbour cruises a day (from May to October), circling the island of Dänholm, between Stralsund and Rügen.

West of Tribseer Damm, the massive **Hanse-Dom** (☎ 373 30; www.hansedom.de; Grünhufer Bogen

18-20; adult from €9.70; ☺ 8am-midnight) boasts pools, baths, saunas and sports facilities, plus the four-star Dorint Hotel.

Tours

For the deposit of a passport and €4, the tourist office will let you hire an English-language **MP3 audio-guide** tour of the city. Apart from this, it offers a variety of themed tours in German (€3) at 11am every day of the week.

Festivals & Events

A *Seebühne*, or floating stage, is erected in the harbour every year from June to August for opera performances during the **Ostseefest-spiele** (☎ 264 6150; www.ostseefestspiele.de).

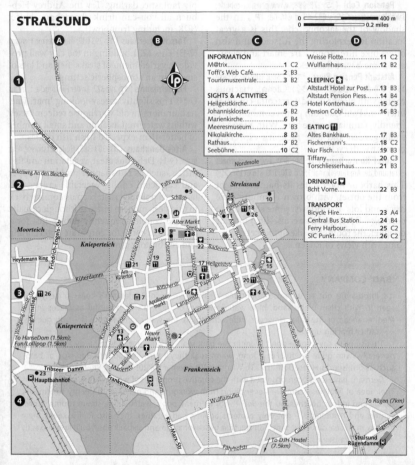

STRALSUND

INFORMATION	
M@trix..........................1 C2	
Toffi's Web Café...............2 B3	
Tourismuszentrale.............3 B2	
SIGHTS & ACTIVITIES	
Heilgeistkirche................4 C3	
Johanniskloster................5 B2	
Marienkirche...................6 B4	
Meeresmuseum..................7 B3	
Nikolaikirche..................8 B2	
Rathaus........................9 B2	
Seebühne.......................10 C2	

Weisse Flotte.................11 C2	
Wulflamhaus...................12 B2	
SLEEPING	
Altstadt Hotel zur Post......13 B3	
Altstadt Pension Piess.......14 B4	
Hotel Kontorhaus.............15 C3	
Pension Cobi.................16 B3	
EATING	
Altes Bankhaus...............17 B3	
Fischermann's................18 C2	
Nur Fisch....................19 B3	
Tiffany......................20 C3	
Torschliesserhaus............21 B3	
DRINKING	
8cht Vorne...................22 B3	
TRANSPORT	
Bicycle Hire.................23 A4	
Central Bus Station..........24 B4	
Ferry Harbour................25 C2	
SIC Punkt....................26 C2	

In the third week of July, Stralsund celebrates repelling an enemy invasion in 1628 with the **Wallensteintage** historic festival.

In early September, some 50 public buildings open their doors all night and welcome visitors with light displays, concerts, performing art, dance and cabaret during the **Lange Nacht des Offenen Denkmals** (Long Night of the Open Monuments).

Sleeping

DJH hostel (☎ 490 289; www.djh-mv.de; Strandstrasse 21, Devin; dm under/over 26yr €17.50/20.50; ✗) Stralsund no longer has a hostel, but you'll find this pleasant option 8km from town in Devin, right on the Strelasund channel with a terrace and views of Rügen. Take bus 3 to Devin.

Pension Cobi (☎ 278 288; www.pension-cobi.de; Jakobiturmstrasse 15; s €32-45, d €46-68; P) In the shadow of the Jakobikirche, this is a great location for exploring the Altstadt, and also offers bike hire. Rooms are smart and clean, and some have balconies.

Altstadt Pension Piess (☎ 303 580; Tribseer Strasse 15; s €50-60, d €55-85; P ✗) Clean, spacious rooms with blonde wood, terracotta-coloured linen and Paul Gauguin prints combine with friendly, familiar service here. With a terrace, small garden and bike rack, it's especially popular with cyclists.

Hotel Kontorhaus (☎ 289 800; www.kontorhaus -stralsund.de; Am Queerkanal 1; s/d €70/100, ste €115; ✗) This harbour hotel states its nautical intent from the outset, with brown Hamburg-style brick and lots of windows, some shaped like portholes. Developed by a cruise-liner interior designer, the rooms feel like upmarket cabins, some with views of Rügen.

Altstadt Hotel zur Post (☎ 200 500; www.altstadthotel -stralsund.de; Tribseer Strasse 22; s €95, d €120-140; P ✗) Right on the Neuer Markt, this place presents all the comforts you would expect of a modern business hotel, right down to TV and radio piped into the bathrooms. Good internet booking deals make it popular with holiday-makers as well.

Eating

Nur Fisch (☎ 306 609; Heilgeiststrasse 92; dishes €2.50-13; ⏱ 10am-6pm Mon-Fri, 11am-2pm Sat) As the name suggests, this simple bistro is only about marine delights, from fish sandwiches to a gourmet platter of sumptuous seafood.

Tiffany (☎ 309 0088; Am Langenwall; buffet €5.50) This very loosely themed breakfast bar is simply fantastic, darling. Try the Audrey Hepburn all-you-can-drink champagne buffet (€28, including fruit bowl).

Torschliesserhaus (☎ 293 032; Am Kütertor 1; mains €7-13) This 1281 building in the city wall provides a varied menu of steaks, fish and lots of snacks in an atmospheric setting.

Fischermann's (☎ 292 322; An der Fährbrücke 3; mains €7-14) This slightly cheesy-looking 'maritime' restaurant in an old warehouse redeems itself with its waterfront location and small number of better-than-expected fresh fish dishes.

Altes Bankhaus (☎ 303 388; Heilgeiststrasse 43a; mains €9-14) Delicious meat, vegetarian and fish dishes, such as red snapper on black pepper and capsicum coulis, vegetable crêpes and lamb in a polenta crust, keep us coming back to this sleek modern bistro. Although casually dressed couples frequently pop in just for a beer, others come for corporate entertaining and celebratory dinners.

'BAD' COMPANY

It's impossible not to eulogise about Mecklenburg-Western Pomerania's coast once you've seen it. With clean white sand, blue water and lots of trees, it's as beautiful as places in the Mediterranean or Australia. However, here's the thing: the water temperature is – you guessed it – rather bracing up here.

That's not to say people don't swim in the cool sea. They do, but they're hardy folk and they generally swim quite briefly. For a long, warm soak they'll turn instead to a *Bad* (spa or bath), such as Stralsund's HanseDom (p723), Wismar's Wonnemar (p720) or Binz' Vitamar (p729).

Germans have long been obsessed with the curative properties of warm waters and hot steam. Their idea of 'wellness' combines everything from workouts and massage to beauty treatments, solaria and indoor beaches. So the *Bad* – with its many pools, water slides, steam rooms, fitness centres and restaurants – not only protects against bad weather, they also feel it keeps them healthy in all seasons. Next time you see that unseasonal tan and sixpack abs, you'll know exactly where they've been...

Drinking & Entertainment

8cht Vorne (☎ 281 888; Badenstrasse 45) A scene stalwart, this place furnishes Stralsund's student population with drink, DJs and dancing every night.

Fun/Lollipop (☎ 399 039; Grünhufer Bogen 11-14) Out by the HanseDom, this is the biggest mainstream club in town.

Getting There & Away

BOAT

See Getting There & Away on p727 for details of services to Rügen Island, and Getting There & Away, p733, for boat services to Hiddensee Island.

CAR & MOTORCYCLE

If coming from the west – Lübeck, Wismar or Rostock – avoid travelling on the slow B105. Instead get on the A20, or take the B110 from Rostock to the B194 (via Bad Sülze) and head north. From points east, you'll use the B96.

TRAIN

Regional trains travel to/from Rostock (€11.70, 1¼ hours), Berlin-Hauptbahnhof (from €32.30, 3½ hours) and Hamburg (from €34.60, 3½ hours) at least every two hours. There are frequent trains to Sassnitz (from €9.10, 50 minutes) and Binz (from €9.10, 50 minutes), on Rügen Island.

Getting Around

Your feet will do just fine in the Altstadt. You can also hire a bicycle from the **train station** (☎ 625 81) or **SIC Punkt** (☎ 280 155; Harbour).

GREIFSWALD

☎ 03834 / pop 54,200

The old university town of Greifswald is an oddity, largely unscathed by WWII thanks to a courageous German colonel who surrendered to Soviet troops (a move usually punishable by execution). Although it's the fourth largest city in the state, its handsome medieval centre makes it principally a tourist town.

The skyline of this former Hanseatic city – as once perfectly captured by local son Caspar David Friedrich – is defined by three churches, the 'Long Nicholas' the 'Fat Mary' and the 'Kleine Jakob'.

However, Greifswald also has a pretty harbour in the charming district of Wieck, reached by a Dutch-style wooden drawbridge,

and its old city walls have been turned into a nice promenade. The town is a convenient gateway for the island of Usedom, too.

Orientation & Information

The Altstadt is northeast of the train station, on the bank of the Ryck River. It's partly encircled by a road, partly by railway tracks. The mostly pedestrianised Lange Strasse bisects the Altstadt from east to west and is quickly reached via Karl-Marx-Platz. Around 4km east is the gull- and mast-filled harbour neighbourhood of Wieck. (Incidentally, if you're a Caspar David Friedrich fan, the ruins of the Eldena cloister portrayed in one of his famous paintings are a few minutes' walk south of Wieck.)

Greifswald Information (☎ 521 380; www.greifswald .de; Markt; ⏰ 9am-6pm Mon-Fri, to noon Sat) is in the Rathaus.

Sights

DOM ST NIKOLAI

The 100m onion-domed tower of the **Dom St Nikolai** (☎ 2627; Domstrasse; ⏰ 10am-4pm Mon-Sat, 11.30am-12.30pm Sun) rises above a row of historic façades, giving the cathedral the nickname 'Long Nicholas'. It has an austere, whitewashed interior with a large and solitary golden cross. You can climb the tower (adult/concession €2/1.50) and, yes, there is a great view from the top.

MARKT & AROUND

The many historical buildings on the Markt hint at Greifswald's stature in the Middle Ages. The **Rathaus**, at the western end, started life as a 14th-century department store with characteristic arcaded walkways. The red-brick **gabled houses** on the eastern side are worthy of inspection; the **Coffee House** (No 11) is gorgeous and a good example of a combined living and storage house owned by Hanseatic merchants.

Walk one block east on Mühlenstrasse to the now complete **Pommersches Landesmuseum** (Pomeranian State Museum; ☎ 831 20; www.pommersches -landesmuseum.de; Theodor-Pyl-Strasse 1-2; adult/concession €4.50/2.50; ⏰ 10am-6pm Tue-Sun Apr-Oct, to 5pm Nov-Mar). Renovated and reopened in 2005, it consists of three historic buildings of a Franciscan monastery, all linked by a 73m-long, glassed-in hall. There's a major gallery of paintings, including half a dozen by Caspar David Friedrich, as well as history and natural history exhibits.

Northeast of the Markt is the 12th-century red-brick **Marienkirche** (☎ 2263; Brüggstrasse; 🕙 10am-5pm Mon-Fri, to noon Sat & Sun), a square three-nave tower trimmed with turrets. It's easy to see why it's teasingly called 'Fat Mary'.

UNIVERSITY AREA

Close to the train station is the university district, with Rubenowplatz at its heart. There's a fanciful neo-Gothic **monument to Heinrich Rubenow**, the university's founder, in the middle of the little park. The university's main building flanks the square's south side. Only the **Aula**, the assembly hall, is worth a closer look. East of Rubenowplatz is the 'Kleine Jakob', the modest **Jakobikirche**.

Sleeping & Eating

ALTSTADT

Hotel Alter Speicher (☎ 777 00; www.alter-speicher.de; Rossmühlenstrasse 25; s/d €70/85; P 🚫) This place occupies a renovated warehouse overlooking the river just outside the centre. It has lovely quarters and a good regional restaurant.

Hotel Galerie (☎ 773 7830; www.hotelgalerie.de; Mühlenstrasse 10; s/d €75/95; P 🚫) Rooms in this sparkling modern hotel across from the state museum are filled with a changing collection of work by contemporary artists.

WIECK

Maritimes Jugenddorf Wieck (☎ 830 2950; www.majuwi.de; Yachtweg 3; dm €27; P 🚫 🖳) Offering super-modern hostel accommodation, this place has nice en suite rooms and a vast range of activities on offer across its 15,000-sq-m complex. Geared towards school and youth groups, it has a café on site.

Schipp In (☎ 840 026; Am Hafen 3; r €36-62) This tiny *pension* acts as a branch of the tourist office and has a public coin laundry and sauna. Breakfast is not included.

Getting There & Away

There are regular train services to Stralsund (€6.20, 25 minutes), Rostock (from €17, 1½ hours) and Berlin-Lichtenberg (from €29, 2½ to three hours).

The B105 and B96 roads from Rostock and Stralsund are notoriously slow; the B96 also continues to Berlin.

Getting Around

It's easy to get around Greifswald's centre on foot, but to reach outlying areas you may want to make use of the bus system. Single/day tickets cost €1.50/3.30. You reach Wieck via a 4km foot/bike path, or bus 6 ends here. If you're driving, head east towards Wolgast; the turn-off is on your left.

USEDOM ISLAND

Usedom lies in the delta of the Oder River about 30km east of Greifswald, and is separated from the Pomeranian mainland by the wide Peene River. The greatest assets of this island, which Germany shares with Poland, are the 42km stretch of beautiful beach and the average 1906 annual hours of sunshine, which makes it the sunniest place in Germany. It earned the nickname *Badewanne Berlins* (Berlin's Bathtub) in the prewar period and was a sought-after holiday spot in GDR days.

Since the *Wende* (fall of communism), Usedom has been somewhat overshadowed by neighbouring Rügen, but as sprucing up continues it's coming into its own. Elegant 1920s villas with wrought-iron balconies grace many traditional resorts, including Zinnowitz and Ückeritz in the western half and Bansin, Heringsdorf and Ahlbeck further east.

Usedom Tourismus (☎ 038372-708 90; www.usedom.de; Bäderstrasse 5, Ückeritz; 🕙 9am-6pm Mon-Fri) books accommodation all over the island; holiday apartments are common here.

Peenemünde

Usedom's only attraction of historical importance is Peenemünde, on the island's western tip. It was here that Wernher von Braun developed the V2 rocket, first launched in October 1942. It flew 90km high and a distance of 200km before plunging into the Baltic and marked the first time in history that a flying object had exited the earth's atmosphere. The research and testing complex was destroyed by the Allies in July 1944, but the Nazis continued their research in Nordhausen in the southern Harz (see Mittelbau Dora, p242).

At the **Historisch-Technisches Informationszentrum** (Historical & Technological Information Centre; ☎ 038371-5050; www.peenemuende.de; adult/concession €5/4; 🕙 9am-6pm Apr-Oct, 10am-4pm Nov-Mar, closed Mon Oct-May) Peenemünde is immodestly billed as 'the birthplace of space travel'.

The harbour is another popular spot for visitors, with plenty of boats and the battered **U461 submarine** (☎ 285 66; www.u-461.de; admission €5.50; 🕙 10am-6pm Apr-Jun & Oct, 9am-9pm Jul-Sep, 10am-4pm Nov-Mar).

Getting There & Away

Züssow is the gateway to Usedom, reached by train from Stralsund (€11, 30 minutes) and Greifswald (€6, 15 minutes); **Usedomer Bäderbahn** (www.ubb-online.com; day card €11) trains continue to Zinnowitz, Peenemünde and other resorts. Buses also connect Wolgast, one stop from Züssow, with the island.

RÜGEN ISLAND

Rügen is much mythologised in the German national imagination. Frequented in the late 19th and early 20th century by the country's good and great, including Bismarck, Thomas Mann and Einstein, its chalk coastline was also immortalised by Romantic artist Caspar David Friedrich in 1818.

Unfortunately, Hitler was also beguiled by Germany's largest island, choosing one of its most beautiful sandy beaches to build a monstrous holiday resort for his loyal troops. Later, GDR governments made Rügen the holiday choice for dedicated comrades, as well as top apparatchik Erich Honecker.

Although it boasts 574km of coast, much of Rügen is covered in leafy vegetation. Driving across the island, you'll pass beneath lush canopies of chestnut, oak, elm and poplar trees. Its surrounding waters are national parks or protected nature reserves.

Many visitors make a beeline for the main resort of Binz and the *Stubbenkammer* area of white chalk cliffs in the Jasmund National Park. However, Rügen has many corners to explore and also features some interesting, historic buildings.

Its resorts' white villas have been refurbished since 1990, as the island has reclaimed its place in tourist itineraries. A couple of flights of architectural fancy are found in the planned town of Putbus (p731) and the Jagdschloss Granitz (p729).

Orientation

Rügen's 1000-sq-km surface divides into several distinct areas. The Mönchgut Peninsula in the southeast is where most of the resorts, such as Sellin and Göhren, lie. The main resort, Binz, sits at the top of this. North of Binz lies the Jasmund National Park, and west is the more remote area of Wittow, with Germany's most northeasterly point, Kap Arkona (Cape Arkona).

The island's official capital is Bergen, but it's of little interest to visitors other than as a transport hub.

Information

Medical Services (☎ 03838-802 30)
Tourismus Rügen (☎ 03838-807 70; www.ruegen .de; Am Markt 4, Bergen) The island's main information office does not book rooms.
Touristik Service Rügen (☎ 038306-6160; Hauptstrasse 18, Altefähr)
Verbund Rügener Zimmervermittlungen (☎ 01805-334 433; www.insel-ruegen.org) Island-wide reservations.

Dangers & Annoyances

In 2005–06, there was an outbreak of H5N1 bird flu in a remote region of Rügen near the Wittow Ferry (Wittower Fähre). It was widely reported in the media but swiftly brought under control. Check out the latest before travelling, but unless the situation changes drastically, there's no need to avoid the island, although you should take sensible precautions and not handle birds or feathers.

Getting There & Away

BOAT

Rügen is a stop for domestic ferries to the mainland and international ferries (Denmark and Sweden). For ferries to Hiddensee, see Getting There & Away on p733.

The Mainland

Weisse Flotte (☎ 0180-321 2120; www.weisse-flotte .com; Fährstrasse 16, Stralsund) operates passenger and car ferries to Rügen.

The passenger ferries leave Stralsund harbour for Altefähr on Rügen's southwestern shore (one-way/return €2.50/3.80, 15 minutes, hourly 9am to 7pm).

Car ferries leave from Stahlbrode, 15km southeast of Stralsund, for Glewitz every 20 minutes, between 6am and 8pm from April to November only (car/passenger €3.80/1.10).

Sweden

Scandlines (☎ 01805-116 688; www.scandlines.de) runs five ferries daily from Sassnitz Mukran, several kilometres south of Sassnitz, to Trelleborg (adult/child €15/7, 50 daily in high season, 3¾ hours). Cars cost from €100 in the high season.

Denmark

Scandlines also runs ferries between Sassnitz and Rønne on Bornholm Island from April to November (Thursday, Saturday and Sunday April to June and September to November; daily in July and August). The trip takes 3¾ hours and costs €21/10 per adult/child in the high season. Cars cost from €115 in the high season.

CAR & MOTORCYCLE

From 2007, there will be two crossings from the mainland to Rügen, which should mean no more – or at least fewer – traffic bottlenecks in the high season. The new Rügenbrücke bridge joins the older Rügendamm (1936) in crossing the Strelasund channel.

Both are reached via Stralsund's Karl Marx Strasse.

TRAIN

IC trains connect Binz to Hamburg (€44.20, four hours) and beyond, all via Stralsund. Local trains run hourly from Stralsund to Binz (€9.10, 1¼ hours) and also to Sassnitz (€9.10, 50 minutes). To get to Putbus, change RE trains in Bergen. Other destinations are served by the historic Rasender Roland train (see Train, opposite).

Getting Around

BICYCLE

Sharing roads with cars cannot always be avoided. Ask at tourist offices for the *Fahrrad*

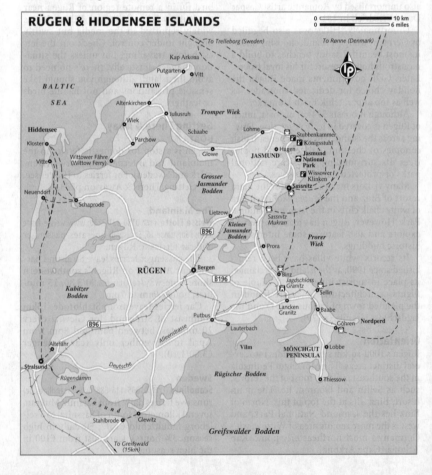

RÜGEN & HIDDENSEE ISLANDS

0 — 10 km
0 — 6 miles

To Trelleborg (Sweden)

To Rønne (Denmark)

BALTIC
SEA

Kap Arkona

Putgarten · Vitt

WITTOW

Altenkirchen

Juliusruh

Wiek

Tromper Wiek

Hiddensee

Parchow

Schaabe

Lohme

Stubbenkammer

Kloster

Glowe

Königsstuhl

Hagen

Vitte

Wittower Fähre
(Wittow Ferry)

JASMUND

Jasmund
National
Park

Wissower
Klinken

Neuendorf

Grosser
Jasmunder
Bodden

Sassnitz

Schaprode

Lietzow

Kleiner
Jasmunder
Bodden

Sassnitz
Mukran

Prorer
Wiek

896

RÜGEN

Prora

Kubitzer
Bodden

Bergen

B196

Binz

Jagdschloss
Granitz

Sellin

Putbus

Lancken
Granitz

Baabe

Göhren

Nordperd

896

Lauterbach

Vilm

MÖNCHGUT
PENINSULA

Lobbe

Altefähr

Deutsche

Stralsund

Rügendamm

Rügischer Bodden

Thiessow

Strelasund

Stahlbrode · Glewitz

Greifswalder Bodden

To Greifswald
(15km)

& *Nahverkehrskarte*: besides being a map, it includes route recommendations and a list of hire and repair shops.

BOAT

Reederei Ostsee-Tour (☎ 038392-3150; www.reederei-ostsee-tour.de) will carry you around the coast from Göhren to Sassnitz, via Binz between April and October. There are five services a day; sample fares include Göhren–Binz for €4.50, and Göhren–Sassnitz for €8. An extra three ferries travel solely between Sassnitz and Binz (€6). Some services are operated by boats sailing around the chalk cliffs of the Jasmund National Park (see p732).

BUS

RPNV Buses (☎ 03838-194 49; www.rpnv.de, in German) link to practically all communities. In summer, there are half-hourly services from Binz to Göhren and Sassnitz, but service to other towns is more sporadic.

Fares are according to distance. Sassnitz–Königsstuhl costs €1.55, for example, Binz–Königsstuhl €4.10, Binz–Göhren €3.60 and Göhren–Bergen €4.60. A day card for the whole network is often a good deal at €9. Local tourist offices usually have timetables and maps.

CAR & MOTORCYCLE

If you don't have much time, a car is the best mode of transport on Rügen Island, although environmental concerns are strong here and driving will be frowned upon in some quarters. The main artery is the B96. Parking meters abound, so carry plenty of change.

TRAIN

The **Rasender Roland** (☎ 038301-801 12; www.rasender-roland.de) steam train shuttles between Putbus and Göhren from 7.45am to 9.30pm daily, stopping in Binz, Jagdschloss Granitz, Sellin and Baabe. Several services a day also go beyond Putbus to Lauterbach Mole. The route is divided into five zones, each costing €1.60 (Putbus–Binz is two zones; Putbus–Göhren or Göhren–Lauterbach Mole five zones). Bikes cost €2.10.

BINZ

☎ 038393 / pop 5600

Rügen's largest and most celebrated seaside resort, 'Ostseebad' Binz is a vision of ornate, white 19th-century villas, white sand and blue water. Its roads are signed in Gothic script and lined with coastal pines and chestnut trees. So even if all the signs of 21st-century capitalism abound, especially along jam-packed Hauptstrasse, you can still feel the pull of history.

The town's renovated *Bäderarchitektur* (spa architecture) – as the villas with their wrought-iron latticework or carved wood balconies are collectively called – is separated from the beach by the long tree-lined Strandpromenade. Once you step down onto the sand, you have glorious views of Prorer Wiek bay and its white chalk cliffs.

Information

Fremdenverkehrsein (☎ 2782; www.gastgeber-binz.de; Paulstrasse 2; 🕑 9am-7pm Mon-Fri, 10am-6pm Sat, 10am-2pm Sun) Room booking.

Kurverwaltung (☎ 148 148; www.ostseebad-binz.de; Heinrich-Heine-Strasse 7; 🕑 9am-6pm Mon-Fri, 10am-6pm Sat & Sun) For general information and lists of hotels.

Tourismusgesellschaft Binz (☎ 134 60; www.binz.de; Zeppelinstrasse 7) Room booking.

Sights & Activities

Binz has a 4km-long north–south beach promenade. At the southern end of the built-up area, you'll find the palatial **Kurhaus**, a lovely-looking historic building that's now a luxury hotel. In front of it is the long pier. Strandpromenade does continue further south from here, but becomes markedly less busy.

At the northern end of the beach is the IFA holiday park and its state-of-the-art **Vitamar pool** (☎ 911 02; Strandpromenade 74; adult per 1/3hr €2.50/5; 🕑 7.30am-8pm), with slides, whirlpool, saunas and waterfalls.

Forgeries of some of the world's most famous paintings, including the *Mona Lisa* and Caspar David Friedrich's Rügen paintings (natch), are on view at the **Fälschermuseum/Galerie Jahreszeiten** (Museum of Art Forgeries; ☎ 131 48; Margaretenstrasse 20; adult/concession €3.50/2.50; 🕑 10am-6pm Tue-Sun). Not only that, if you have a spare €2000 or so, you can buy them as well.

Jagdschloss Granitz (☎ 2263; adult/concession €3/2; 🕑 9am-6pm May-Sep, 9am-4pm Oct, 10am-4pm Tue-Sun Nov-Apr), a hunting palace built in 1723 on top of the 107m-high Tempelberg, was significantly enlarged and altered by Wilhelm Malte I, whose flights of fancy also gave Rügen the grandiose Putbus. Malte added the palace's main attraction, a 38m-high tower.

From Binz, you can catch the motorised Jagdschloss-Express minitrain (adult/child return €7.50/3.50), which handily passes through town, or walk to the Rasender Roland train station. If you're driving, you must leave your vehicle in a parking lot before heading to the palace.

Sleeping

Private rooms (from €15 per person) are available in Binz. There's also a spa tax of €2.10. Prices given in the following reviews are all high-season.

DJH hostel (☎ 325 97; www.jh-binz.de; Strandpromenade 35; dm under/over 26yr €19.90/23.90, s/d from €28/42; (P) (X) (Q)) One of the best-situated hostels in Germany – right on the beach – this place has been refurbished to the tune of several million. The exterior still looks a bit scuffed, but all mod cons are provided in the lounge and dining room, while bunk beds have been creatively painted with a sea-green wash. Book well ahead.

Villa Schwanenbeck (☎ 2013; www.villa-schwanenbeck .de; Margaretenstrasse 18; s €30-60, d €55-60; (P) (X)) Rather old-fashioned but comfortable and spacious, this place has a central location, a well-respected restaurant and reasonable room availability.

Pension Haus Colmsee (☎ 325 56; www.hauscolmsee .de; Strandpromenade 8; d €65-85; (P) (X)) At the leafy, quieter and altogether most pleasant eastern edge of town, this historic villa has relatively modern rooms. Its reasonable prices make it just as popular as the neighbouring Kempinski hotel, so book ahead.

Villa Undine (☎ 7970 6185; www.villa-undine-binz .de, in German; Strandpromenade 30; apt €85-90; (P)) Binz has scores of historic villas, but only four are heritage listed and this apartment is one of them. Its brick-red wooden exterior has A-line roofs and an onion-domed tower, while the rooms inside have been renovated and modernised. Longer stays are necessary in the high season.

Hotel Villa Neander (☎ 5290; www.glasner.de; Hauptstrasse 16; d €85-110; (P)) In the centre of town, the upmarket Neander has lovely, large rooms with nice bathrooms, plus charming staff and owners.

Hotel am Meer & Spa (☎ 440; www.hotel-am-meer .de; Strandpromenade 34; s/d from €150/180; (P) (X) (Q)) Sixty newly renovated and light-filled rooms, some over two floors, are decorated in light and cheerful colours at this hotel, just minutes from the beach. There's also a spa, opened in 2005.

Also recommended:

meerSinn Hotel (☎ 6630; www.meersinn.de; Schillerstrasse 8; s €125-195, d €155-195, ste €290; (P) (X) (Q)) Stylish designer hotel mixing Oriental and ocean-going themes.

Kurhaus Binz (☎ 6650; www.travelcharme.de; Strandpromenade 27; s/d from €135/205; (P) (X) (Q)) Traditional style and luxury, including many restaurants.

Eating

Strandcafé (☎ 323 87; Strandpromenade 29; mains €6-18) This enormous beachfront place is a good catch-all option, with a wide range of offerings from coffee, cake and ice cream to meals.

Poseidon (☎ 337 10; Lottumstrasse 1; mains €8-17) For years one of the most respected fish restaurants in Binz, this lovely historic building with terrace serves fresh catches of the day and even has a menu section that takes you 'round the herring'. If that's not to your tastes, venison is another speciality.

PRORA
☎ 038393

Prora was going to be the largest holiday camp in the world, according to the Nazis. The 5km of uninterrupted, fine white-sand beach just north of Binz still bears testament to this, one of the regime's (unfortunately lesser) follies. Running parallel to the beautiful coast is a wall of six hideous six-storey buildings, each 500m long. Begun in 1936, this was intended as a *Kraft-durch-Freude* (strength through joy) resort for 20,000 people. The outbreak of WWII stopped its completion; after the war, Soviet troops tried to blow it up, but somehow failed miserably.

What to do with the buildings is an ongoing debate. The Museumsmeile (Museum Row) that occupied a portion of the buildings from 1994 was told to quit the location in 2006 by new owners, possibly to make way for a huge hotel, although at the time of writing there were no concrete plans. Check the latest with the tourist office in Binz.

SOUTH RÜGEN
Göhren
☎ 038308 / pop 1400

Göhren is a quiet, somewhat unassuming resort on the Nordperd spit. Non-Germans seldom stay here, and it's less conveniently located than Binz, but it might appeal to those who find Binz too touristy. Göhren claims to have the best resort beach on the island, a contention you wouldn't dismiss out of hand. Its 7km-long stretch of sand is divided into the quieter Südstrand and the more developed Nordstrand. Göhren is served by buses and is on the Rasender Roland steam train route.

The **Kurverwaltung** (☎ 667 90; www.ostseebad-goehren.de; Poststrasse 9; 9am-6pm Mon-Fri, to noon Sat, reduced hours in winter) and **Fremdenverkehrsverein** (☎ 259 40; www.zimmervermittlung-goehren-ostsee.de; Berliner Strasse 8; 9am-6pm Mon-Fri, 10am-6pm Sat & Sun) can both help with information and room bookings.

The mildly diverting **Monchgüter Museen** (☎ 2175; www.moenchguter-museen-ruegen.de; combined ticket €8) combines a collection of four historic sites: the Heimatsmuseum, the Museumshof farm, the Rookhus (an unusual chimneyless house) and the museum ship *Luise*.

SLEEPING & EATING

Regenbogen Resort (☎ 901 20; Nordstrand; adult/tent/car €5/8/4, plus tax €2.10) In the woods behind the dunes, this is the island's largest camping ground (open from April to October). While well equipped, the 1000-plus crowd does detract a little from the idyllic location.

Robinson Jr (☎ 250 97; www.robinson-jr.de; Nordstrand 1; s €45-65, d €55-85; P) Breakfasting on the beachfront terrace, it occurs to you that this former boathouse converted into a 14-room *pension* among the dunes is just right for Göhren's castaway style. However, the restaurant-pub downstairs hosts live bands, which is surely something Robinson (Crusoe) Snr never had to contend with?

Also available:

Waldhotel (☎ 505 00; www.waldhotelgoehren.de; Waldstrasse 7; s €60-80, d €70-100; P) Comfortable villa near the beach.

Hotel Hanseatic Rügen (☎ 515; www.hotel-hanseatic.de; Nordperdstrasse 2; s/d from €115/140; P) Palatial rooms and a panoramic tower café.

Putbus

☎ 038301 / pop 2700

The planned town of Putbus rises up like a sci-fi mirage from the middle of modest farming villages. At its heart lies a gigantic circular plaza, known as the **Circus**, resembling a roulette wheel, with its alternating wedges of green and paving. Around this, 16 large white neoclassical buildings are dotted. Nearby, the town's 75-hectare **English park**, filled with ginkgoes, cypresses, Japanese spruces and other exotic trees, lets you take a botanical journey around the world.

This civic oddity was conceived and realised in the 19th century by an overly ambitious local prince, Wilhelm Malte I of Putbus (1783–1854), and stands today as the last European town to be purpose-built as a royal seat. Priding itself on being Rügen's cultural centre, it has the island's only **theatre** (www.theatre-putbus.de; Markt 13).

Putbus Info (☎ 431; www.putbus.de; Orangerie, Alleestrasse 35; 9am-5pm Mon-Fri, 11am-5pm Sat & Sun Apr-Sep, to 4pm Oct-Mar) provides information and hotel assistance and is in the popular Orangerie gallery, a town highlight.

Rügen-Besucher-Service (☎ 605 13; www.ruegenbesucherservice.de; August-Bebel-Strasse 1) books rooms. That said, most accommodation in Putbus is in holiday apartments, and there are very few hotels. Unless you're coming to the theatre, the town is best seen during a day trip.

Putbus is on the Rasender Roland route (p729); bus 30 also runs here from Bergen.

THE AUTHOR'S CHOICE

Strandhalle (☎ 315 64; Strandpromenade 5; mains €7-17) A local legend and deservedly so, Toni Münsterteicher's Strandhalle promises – and delivers – fine cooking at everyday prices. Lauded by *Feinschmecker* magazine, Michelin and other gourmet heavyweights, its food is simple but delicious. To get yourself acquainted, order the €21 menu for which Münsterteicher is most famous: pear-and-celery soup with red peppercorns, Baltic cod cooked in a potato crust, and the *Scheiterhaufen* (literally 'pyre') dessert of baked and caramelised apple.

Located on the quiet eastern end of Strandpromenade, with sea views, Strandhalle's vaulted-ceiling, wood-lined interior is decked out with an eclectic mix of church statues, fairy lights, chandeliers and dried plant arrangements.

Can't get a table? Sister restaurant **Münsterteicher** (☎ 143 80; Strandpromenade 17-18; mains €7-28) serves Argentine steaks, pasta, fish and sushi.

Lauterbach

☎ 038301

The yacht harbour southeast of Putbus will be of interest to keen sailors, with all kinds of boat hire and a couple of sailing schools. Lauterbach's stand-out feature, however, is its **Swimming Holiday Homes** (Schwimmenden Ferienhäuser; ☎ 8090; www.im-jaich.de; Am Yachthafen; apt 2-4 people €115, 6 people €140), which is made up of new Scandinavian-looking bungalows and two-storey huts that float in the harbour on individual pontoons. The same company also runs one of the sailing schools, and has land-based accommodation.

Lauterbach Mole is the westerly terminus of the Rasender Roland steam train.

JASMUND NATIONAL PARK

The rugged beauty of Jasmund National Park first came to national attention thanks to the romanticised paintings of Caspar David Friedrich in the early 19th century. His favourite spot was the **Stubbenkammer**, an area at the northern edge of the park, where jagged white-chalk cliffs plunge into the jade-coloured sea. Today the area symbolises Rügen; it's a sight most Germans are familiar with through some medium and want to see in reality.

By far the most famous of the Stubbenkammer cliffs is the **Königsstuhl** (King's Chair; admission €1) – at 117m, it's Rügen's highest point. Sadly, enjoyment of the scenery is often marred by everyone else trying to see it too; on busy weekends, up to 10,000 people visit. Fortunately, fewer people make the trek a few hundred metres east to the **Victoria-Sicht** (Victoria View), which provides the best view of the Königsstuhl itself.

The **Nationalpark-Zentrum Königsstuhl** (☎ 038392-661 766; www.koenigsstuhl.com; adult/child €6/3; ☼ 9am-7pm Apr-Oct, 10am-5pm Nov-Mar) has multimedia displays on environmental themes, a 'climbing forest' and a restaurant, Caspar's.

Bus 20 (from Göhren) and 23 (from Bergen) go to the Königsstuhl, passing the train stations at Sassnitz and Binz. For speed tourists, it's sometimes possible to get off the ICE from Hamburg at Binz and step right on to a bus to the Königsstuhl! In summer, each service runs half-hourly between 8am and 4pm, with a few hourly services before and after that.

From April to October, **Reederei Ostsee-Tour** (☎ 038392-3150; www.reederei-ostsee-tour.de) operates several daily trips from Binz (€14.50) and Sassnitz (€11) around the chalk cliffs. The first morning service departs from as far away as Göhren (€16) at 10.15am. The round-trip takes 1¼ hours from Sassnitz and 2¾ hours from Binz, and offers what many believe to be the best views of the cliffs. **Adler Schiffe** (☎ 038378-477 90; www.adler-schiffe.de) offers similar packages.

For the fit, a spectacular way to approach the area is by making the 10km trek from Sassnitz along the coast through the ancient forest of Stubnitz. The trail also takes you past the gorgeous **Wissower Klinken** chalk cliffs, another famous vista painted by Friedrich.

If you're driving, leave your vehicle in the (paid) parking lot in Hagen, then either catch the shuttle bus (€1.30) or walk 2.5km past the legendary Herthasee through the forest.

Panorama-Hotel Lohme (☎ 038302-9221; www.lohme.com; Dorfstrasse 35, Lohme; s €60, d €90-120; P) This hotel, west of the Stubbenkammer, has what may be the island's most romantic restaurant, particularly when the sun sets over Kap Arkona on summer nights. Its *Eintopf* (potato stew served with vinegar and sugar on the side) is renowned.

While most people only pass through Sassnitz, the town has been redeveloping its Altstadt and has a nice fishing harbour. Its **tourist office** (☎ 038392-6490) Bahnhofstrasse 19a; (☼ 9am-6pm Mon-Fri, 10am-6pm Sat, 2-6pm Sun); Strandpromenade 1; ☼ 10am-5pm) can help with information and room bookings.

KAP ARKONA

Rügen ends at the rugged cliffs of **Kap Arkona**, with its famous pair of lighthouses. The older **Schinkel-Leuchtturm** (☎ 038391-121 15; adult/concession €3/2.50), designed by the legendary Karl Friedrich Schinkel, was completed in 1827. It's square, squat and 19.3m high, and inside are exhibits by Rügen artists. From the lookout platform there's a wonderful view over a colourful quilt of rape fields, meadows and white beaches, all set against the dark-blue Baltic Sea. The views are better still from the adjacent 36m-high **Neuer Leuchtturm** (adult/concession €3/2.50), which has been in business since 1902.

A few metres east of the lighthouses is the **Burgwall**, a complex that harbours the remains of the Tempelburg, a Slavic temple and fortress. The castle was taken over by the Danes in 1168, paving the way for the Christianisation of Rügen.

The gateway to Kap Arkona is the village of Putgarten, served by hourly bus 11 from Altenkirchen in central Wittow. (To get to Altenkirchen, you need to travel from Sassnitz or Bergen and change in Wiek.)

From Putgarten, take the gas-powered **Arkona Bahn** (☎ 038391-132 13; www.arkonabahn.de; per person €2) or make the 1.5km journey by foot or bicycle. Driving all the way to the cape is not allowed, for environmental reasons. You must leave your vehicle in Putgarten.

Reederei Ostsee-Tour (☎ 038392-3150; www.reederei-ostsee-tour.de; tour €19.50; Tue-Fri Jun-Sep) operates boat tours around the cape (without landing). The four-hour tours leave from Binz at 1.15pm and Sassnitz at 2pm.

For a slightly different approach to this area, contact **Rügen Safari** (☎ 0173-610 6514; www.ruegen-safari.de, in German), which runs unusual adventure tours here and in Jasmund National Park. You can try a jeep safari, mountain biking or an Indian canoe tour with real tepees!

HIDDENSEE ISLAND

☎ 038300 / pop 1280

If Rügen is exalted, the mention of Hiddensee island makes Germans swoon. 'Dat söte Länneken' (the sweet little land) is a tiny patch off Rügen's western coast, 17km long and 1.8km at its widest point. What makes it so special is its remote, breathtaking landscape. North of the village of Kloster are the heath and meadows of the 'Dornbush' area, with the island's landmark lighthouse (it has another, too) and wind-buckled trees. From the main village of Vitte, dunes wend their way south to Neuendorf. In the 19th and early 20th centuries, Hiddensee bewitched artists like Thomas Mann, Bertolt Brecht and Gerhart Hauptmann, the last of whom is buried here.

Cars are banned on Hiddensee; the best way to get around is by bike. Hire places are everywhere.

The **tourist office** (☎ 642 26; www.seebad-hiddensee.de; Norderende 162, Vitte; 8.30am-5pm Mon-Fri, 10am-noon Sat May-Sep, reduced hours in winter) has another **branch** (9.30am-12.30pm & 1.30-5pm Mon-Fri, 10am-noon Sat May-Sep) at Kloster harbour.

There are no camp sites on Hiddensee. **Private rooms** (high season per person from €10) are available in all three villages.

Cheap dorm-style accommodation is provided in the cabins of the **Hotelschiff Caprivi 93** (☎ 501 62; www.hotelschiff-hiddensee.de; Springe 39, Vitte; s/d from €24/38, plus final cleaning fee €5).

The **Hotel Hitthim** (☎ 6660; www.hitthim.de; Hafenweg, Kloster; s €50-65, d €70-110; P) might have a funny name, but this appealing timbered building is one of Hiddensee's best accommodation options.

Reederei Hiddensee (☎ 0180-321 2150; www.reederei-hiddensee.de) ferries leave Schaprode, on Rügen's western shore, several times daily year-round. Return fares to Neuendorf are €12.70, to Kloster and Vitte €14.80.

The same company offers services from Stralsund up to three times daily between May and September. Return tickets to Neuendorf cost €16.20; to Vitte and Kloster it's €16.70. Check the website for other services.

Directory

CONTENTS

ACCOMMODATION

Germany has all types of places to unpack your suitcase, from hostels, camping grounds and family hotels to chains, business hotels and luxury resorts. Reservations are a good idea, especially if you're travelling in the busy summer season (June to September). Rooms can also be scarce and prices high around major holidays (p746), local festivals and events (mentioned throughout this book and also on p744) and, in business-oriented cities, during trade shows.

This book lists accommodation as budget, midrange and top end. Listings are in ascending order starting with the cheapest property.

Unless noted, rates include VAT and breakfast, which is usually a generous all-you-can-eat buffet.

There are some regional variations, but generally budget recommendations won't put you more than €80 (per double, less in rural areas) out of pocket and will have you checking in at hostels, *pensions* or family hotels where facilities may be shared.

Midrange properties generally offer the best value for money. Expect to pay between €80 and €150 for a clean, comfortable, decent-sized double with at least a modicum of style, a private bathroom, cable TV and direct-dial telephone. A surprising number of midrange properties also have saunas and some basic fitness equipment.

Accommodation at the top end (from €150) offers an international standard of amenities and perhaps a scenic location, special décor or historical ambience. Some may also have pools, saunas, business centres or other up-market facilities. Unless you're going to use these, though, it's rarely worth the extra cost over most midrange hotels.

Properties with designated nonsmoking rooms are on the rise and identified with the nonsmoking icon (⊠) in this book. Air-conditioning is not a standard amenity and is most commonly found in high-end chain hotels. Properties with air-con in at least some of their rooms are denoted with the ❄ icon.

Hotels with on-site parking are listed with the parking icon (Ⓟ). Note that on-site parking is rather rare for city hotels, forcing you either to search for street parking or to steer towards an expensive public garage.

Prices listed in this book do not – and in fact cannot – take into account promotional discounts. City hotels geared to the suit brigade often try to lure leisure travellers with weekend specials. Also check hotel websites (listed throughout this book) for discount rates or packages.

Reservations

An excellent source for last-minute bargains is **Hotel Reservation Service** (HRS; ☎ 0221-207 7600; www.hrs.com), a searchable database of available hotel rooms throughout Germany. Bookings

---

PRACTICALITIES

■ Electrical supply is at 220V AC, 50 Hz.

■ Widely read daily newspapers include the *Süddeutsche Zeitung, Die Welt* and *Der Tagesspiegel* (all quite centrist), as well as the more conservative *Frankfurter Allgemeine Zeitung. Die Zeit* is a high-brow weekly with in-depth reporting.

■ *Der Spiegel* and *Focus* magazines are popular German news weeklies, and *The Economist, Time* and *Newsweek* are sold in train stations and major newsstands.

■ Radio stations are regional with most featuring a mixed format of news, talk and music.

■ Germany uses the metric system (see conversion chart on inside front cover).

■ The GSM 900/1800 system is used for mobile phones (compatible with Europe and Australia, but not the US or Japan).

■ The PAL system (not compatible with NTSC or SECAM) is used for videos.

■ For women's clothing sizes, a German size 36 equals size 6 in the US and size 10 in the UK, then increases in increments of two, making size 38 a US 8 and UK 12.

---

are free and can be made online or via the telephone. Other online booking services are www.venere.com and www.hotel.de.

If you have no advance booking, contact the local tourist office where staff can help you find lodging, sometimes for a small fee. Outside office hours, vacancies may be posted in the window or a display case. Sometimes branches have electronic reservation boards or touch terminals that connect you directly to local establishments.

When making a room reservation directly with a property, always tell your host what time they can expect you and stick to your plan or ring again. Many well-meaning visitors have lost rooms by showing up late.

Kurtaxe

One of the most annoying practices in most German resort and spa towns is the levying of a *Kurtaxe* (resort tax). This is a fee ranging from €0.50 to €3.50 per person per night, which is added to your hotel bill. The money is used to subsidise visitor-oriented events

---

BOOK ACCOMMODATION ONLINE

For more accommodation reviews and recommendations by Lonely Planet authors, check out the online booking service at www.lonelyplanet.com. You'll find the true, insider lowdown on the best places to stay. Reviews are thorough and independent. Best of all, you can book online.

(concerts, lectures, workshops, etc), but you have to pay the tax no matter whether you intend to take advantage of these offerings or not.

Camping

Camping in Germany can be a lot more than just a cheap way to spend the night. The nicest sites have you waking up next to shimmering lakes, below steep mountains or beneath a canopy of trees. Some camping grounds remain open year-round, but generally the season runs from April to October.

Sites are ubiquitous (about 2500 at last count) and well maintained, although they do get jammed in summer. Make reservations as early as possible or show up by midday to snap up any spots that may have been vacated that morning. Having your own wheels is definitely an asset, as many sites are in remote locales that are not, or only poorly, served by public transport.

Facilities vary widely, but even simple sites have toilets and communal washing facilities, including showers, and a shop. The nicest are fully fledged resorts with swimming pools, playgrounds, supermarkets, restaurants and other creature comforts. Some rent out cabins, caravans or rooms.

Camping on public land is not permitted. Pitching a tent on private property requires the consent of the landowner.

Prices depend on facilities and location. There's usually an entire menu of fees with separate charges per person (between €3 and

€6), tent (€2.50 to €8, depending on size) and car (€2 to €4). Additional fees may be levied for hot showers, resort tax, electricity and sewage disposal. Most campsites accept the Camping Card International (see p743), which may shave up to 25% off the final tally.

The ADAC motoring association (see p765) publishes a comprehensive camping guide, *ADAC Camping & Caravaning Führer*, available in bookshops. Other handy sources include **Alan Rogers Camping Guides** (www.alanrogers.com) and **ACSI Eurocampings** (www.eurocampings.de). The latter publish free searchable databases with contact information and short descriptions about a large number of sites throughout Germany. Printed versions are also available through the websites.

Farm Holidays

A holiday on a working farm (*Urlaub auf dem Bauernhof*) is inexpensive and a great opportunity for city slickers to get close to nature in relative comfort. This type of vacation is especially popular with families. Kids get to meet their favourite barnyard animals up close and may even get to help with everyday chores. Accommodation ranges from bare-bones rooms with shared facilities to fully furnished holiday flats. Minimum stays are common. A variety of farm types are on offer, including organic, dairy and equestrian farms as well as wine estates. Places advertising *Landurlaub* (country holiday) no longer actively work their farms. The best establishments are quality controlled by the Deutsche Landwirtschafts-Gesellschaft (DLG; German Agricultural Association). To learn more farm holidays, check www.landtourismus.de. German-speakers can get even more detailed information from www.bauernhofurlaub.com.

Holiday Flats

Renting a furnished flat for a week or longer is a popular form of holiday accommodation in Germany, especially with budget-minded self-caterers, families and small groups. Tourist offices have lists of holiday flats (*Ferienwohnungen* or *Ferien-Appartements*). Some *pensions,* inns, hotels and even farmhouses also rent out apartments. Most owners impose a minimum rental period of three days to a week. Shorter stays may be possible by paying a surcharge.

Hostels

DJH HOSTELS

Here's a piece of trivia that might come in handy at your next cocktail party: the first youth hostel opened in Germany in 1912 on Burg Altena in the Sauerland. Since then the concept has, of course, taken the world by storm.

No matter how remote the region, you'll usually stumble across a DJH hostel. At last count, Germany had 542 hostels that are affiliated with Hostelling International (HI), and run by the Deutsches Jugendherbergswerk (denoted as 'DJH' throughout this book).

DJH hostels are government-subsidised and welcome some 10 million overnight guests every year, more than 90% of whom are Germans. Although they cater primarily for school groups and families, hostels do of course accept single travellers as well. Once places of 'monastic' charm, most properties have recently been modernised and upgraded. Smaller dorms and private rooms for families and couples, often with en suite bathroom, are increasingly common.

Amenities vary widely but the better ones offer internet access, bistros, party rooms and even indoor pools. Almost all can accommodate mobility-impaired travellers. Curfews and daytime lockouts are becoming less common, especially in the cities. Hostels are generally open year-round. Dorms and washrooms are gender-segregated.

Staying at a DJH hostel requires membership with your home country's HI association. Nonmembers can still get a bed by buying an HI card for €15.50 (valid for one year) or individual 'Welcome Stamps' costing €3.10 per night for a maximum of five nights. Both are available at any DJH hostel.

A night in a dorm costs from €12 to €25 and always includes linen and breakfast; optional lunch and supper cost around €5 extra each. In some areas, people over 26 (so-called 'seniors') are charged €3 extra. If hostels are busy, priority is given to people under 26 and to those over 26 travelling with at least one underage child.

About 400 German DJH hostels can now be booked online on the DJH website (www.jugendherberge.de in German). Only 40 can also be booked on the HI website (www.iyhf.org). Alternatively, just contact the hostel directly by phone, fax or email.

INDEPENDENT HOSTELS

Germany was slow in embracing the backpacker hostel concept but in recent years indies have been popping up all over the country. Although they sometimes accept school groups to pad the bottom line, they generally cater for individual travellers, welcome people of all ages and attract a more convivial, international crowd than DJH hostels. They're an excellent budget choice even if you're not a backpacker, as most now offer private rooms with en suite facilities, and even small apartments alongside traditional dorm accommodations.

No two hostels are alike, but typical facilities include communal kitchens, bars, cafés, TV lounges, lockers, internet terminals and laundry. There are no curfews, and staff tend to be savvy, energetic, eager to help and multilingual. Dorms are mixed, although most hostel owners will set up women-only dorms on request. Rates sometimes include bed linen but not breakfast, which can be purchased for €3 to €5.

Most hostels have fewer than 100 beds; the smallest ones can accommodate only 20 or so people. At the other end of the spectrum are megahostels, such as those in the A&O and Meininger minichains, and with several hundred beds.

Approximately 40 German hostels have joined together in an alliance known as the **Backpacker Network** (www.backpackernetwork.de, partly in English), whose website contains full contact information and a link to each of its member. Some hostels can also be booked via this site.

Online booking systems that are not Germany specific include www.gomio.com, www.hostelworld.com, www.hostels.com and www.hostels.net.

Hotels

German hotels range from luxurious international chains to comfortable midrange hotels and small family-run properties. Some are located in elegant estates or ancient castles. Those serving breakfast only are called Hotel Garni. An official classification system exists, based on a scale of one to five stars, but it's voluntary and most hotels choose not to participate. Even so, this being Germany, standards are controlled even in the lower price categories and even the cheapest places are invariably clean, comfortable and well

run. Rooms usually have TV, often with cable or satellite reception, and direct-dial phones are common in all but budget places. Rooms in newer or recently renovated hotels often feature minibars, hairdryers and alarm clocks. Even midrange hotels may have so-called 'wellness' areas with a sauna, spa and fitness equipment.

In most older, privately run hotels, rooms vary dramatically in terms of size, décor and amenities. In the cheapest ones you must share facilities, while others may come with a shower cubicle installed but no private toilet; only the pricier ones have en suite bathrooms. If possible, ask to see several rooms before committing.

Long-Term Rentals

If you're going to stay in any particular German city for a month or longer, you might consider renting a room or a flat through a *Mitwohnzentrale* (flat-sharing agency). These agencies match up visitors with fully furnished vacant flats, houses or rooms in shared houses. Rates vary by agency, city and type of accommodation but, generally speaking, a room in a flat goes for about €200 to €350 per month and a one-bedroom flat ranges from €400 to €900, excluding commission and VAT (19%). The final tally is likely to be less than what you'd pay for a similar standard in a hotel. Even if you're not staying for an entire month, it may still work out cheaper to pay the monthly rent and leave early. Many *Mitwohnzentralen* now also arrange short-term stays, although prices are higher then.

Home Company (www.home-company.de) is a nationwide network of agencies; its website has all the details, also in English. **Apartments Apart** (www.apartmentsapart.com) arranges Europe-wide holiday rentals.

Pensions, Inns & Private Rooms

Essentially B&Bs, these types of lodging are smaller, less formal and inexpensive. You can expect clean rooms but only minimal amenities: maybe a radio, sometimes a TV, but almost never a phone. Facilities are often, but not always, shared. What rooms lack in amenities, they sometimes make up for in charm and authenticity, often augmented by friendly and helpful hosts who take a personal interest in ensuring that you enjoy your stay. Rates always include breakfast.

Throughout the country, *pensions (Pensionen)* are common, while inns (*Gasthof, Gaststätte* or *Gasthaus*) are more prevalent in rural areas. The latter two usually operate their own restaurant serving regional and German food to a local clientele.

Private rooms are most prevalent in resort towns, where empty-nesters and other locals like to pad their income by offering their guest rooms to travellers. People in need of lots of privacy may find these places a bit too intimate. On the other hand, such a stay does allow you a rare glimpse into how local people live.

Tourist offices keep lists of available rooms or you can simply look for signs saying *Zimmer Frei* (rooms available) in houses or shop windows. Rooms start as low as €13 per person and rarely exceed €35. If a landlord is reluctant to rent for a single night, offer to pay a little extra. It's a good idea to say right up front how long you intend to stay. A central source for advance reservations is www.bed-and-breakfast.de.

ACTIVITIES

For outdoor enthusiasts Germany offers the mother lode of possibilities. No matter what kind of activity gets you off that couch, you'll be able to pursue it in this land of lakes and rivers, mountains and forests. Everywhere you go, you'll find outfitters and local operators eager to gear you up.

Cycling

Strap on your helmet! Germany is superb cycling territory, no matter whether you're off on a leisurely spin along the beach, an adrenaline-fuelled mountain exploration or a multiday bike-touring adventure. There are more than 200 long-distance routes alone, which total some 40,000km. Routes are clearly signposted and are typically a combination of lightly travelled back roads, forest roads and paved highways with dedicated bike lanes. Many traverse nature preserves, meander along rivers or venture into steep mountain terrain.

For inspiration and route planning, there's no better free source than www.germany-tourism.de/biking, which details, in English, dozens of routes and provides useful links to local organisations. The website of the **European Cyclists' Federation** (www.ecf.com) has more generalised information.

For day tours, staff at local tourist offices often serve as founts of information. They also sell route maps and can refer you to local bicycle-hire outfits, many of which are listed throughout this book.

The best maps are those published by the national cycling organization **Allgemeiner Deutscher Fahrrad Club** (ADFC; www.adfc.de, in German) and available for about €7 in tourist offices, bookstores and from its website.

ADFC also publishes a useful online directory called **Bett & Bike** (www.bettundbike.de, in German) that lists hundreds of bicycle-friendly hotels, inns and hostels. Bookstores carry the printed version (€11.90).

For an overview of transporting your bike within Germany, see p762.

Hiking & Nordic Walking

Got wanderlust? With lovely scenery throughout, Germany is perfect for exploring on foot, no matter whether you've got your heart set on rambling through romantic river valleys, going peak-bagging in the Alps or simply going for a walk by the lake. Nordic walking, where you strut with poles just like a cross-country skier, has taken Germany by storm in recent years.

The Black Forest, the Harz Mountains, the Bavarian Forest, Saxon Switzerland, the Thuringian Forest and the Sauerland are among the most popular regions to explore on foot. Many of the nicest trails traverse national and nature parks or biosphere reserves.

Trails are usually marked with signs or symbols, sometimes quaintly painted on tree trunks. To find a route matching your fitness level and time frame, talk to the staff at local tourist offices, who will also supply you with maps and tips. Many also offer multiday 'hiking without luggage' packages that include accommodation and luggage transfer between hotels.

The **Deutscher Wanderverband** (German Hiking Federation; ☎ 0561-938 7313; www.dt-wanderverband.de) has an excellent website filled with route descriptions, tips and maps at www.wanderbares-deutschland.de, but, alas, it's in German only.

Mountaineering

'Climb every mountain…' the Mother Superior belted out in the *Sound of Music,* and the Bavarian Alps, the centre of mountaineering in Germany, will give you plenty of opportunity to do just that. You can venture out

TOP FIVE LONG-DISTANCE CYCLING ROUTES

- **Altmühltal Radweg** (190km) This easy to moderate route goes from Rothenburg ob der Tauber to Beilngries, following the Altmühl River through the Altmühltal Nature Park.

- **Bodensee-Königssee Radweg** (414km) Lindau to Berchtesgaden; a moderate route running along the foot of the Alps with magnificent views of the mountains, lakes and forests.

- **Elberadweg** (860km) Follows the Elbe River from Saxon Switzerland to Hamburg through wine country, heath and marshland and past such cities as Dresden, Dessau and Wittenberg. Also see the boxed text, p216.

- **Donauradweg** (434km) Travelling from Neu-Ulm to Passau, this is a delightful, easy to moderate riverside trip along one of Europe's great streams.

- **Romantische Strasse** (359km) Würzburg to Füssen; this easy to moderate route is one of the nicest ways to explore Germany's most famous holiday route, though it can get busy during the summer peak season.

on day treks or plan multiday clambers from hut to hut, as long as you keep in mind that hiking in the Alps is no walk in the park. You need to be in reasonable condition and come equipped with the right shoes, gear and topographic maps. Trails can be narrow, steep and have icy patches, even in summer.

Before heading out, seek local advice on trails, equipment and weather and take all precautions concerning clothing and provisions. And always let someone know where you're going. If you're inexperienced, ask at the tourist offices about local outfitters offering instruction, equipment rental and guided tours. These are usually run by energetic and English-speaking folk with an infectious love for and deep knowledge of the mountains. For potential problems and how to deal with hypothermia, see p772.

The **Deutscher Alpenverein** (DAV; German Alpine Club; ☎ 089-140 030; www.alpenverein.de, in German) is a good resource for information on hiking and mountaineering with local chapters throughout Germany. It also maintains numerous Alpine mountain huts, many of them open to the public, where you can spend the night and get a meal. Local DAV chapters also organise various courses (climbing, mountaineering etc) as well as guided treks, with which you can link up. Staff at local tourist offices should be able to hook you up.

Rock Climbing

Clambering around steep rock faces chiselled and carved by time and the elements is a popular pursuit in various parts of the country. Rock hounds, from beginner to expert,

gravitate towards the Jurassic limestone formations in the Naturpark Altmühltal (p372) in Bavaria and around Saxon Switzerland (Sächsische Schweiz; p180) in Saxony. Wherever you go, there are local outfitters that can set you up with equipment and advice.

Saunas & Spas

Germans love to sweat it out in the sauna, and many public baths (Stadtbäder) have sauna facilities, sometimes with fixed hours for men and women, although most sessions are mixed. Prices average €10 per session. Note that not a stitch of clothing is worn, so leave your modesty in the locker. Bring, or hire, a towel.

Experiencing a regimen of sauna, bath, massage and exercise in a spa resort (Kurort) is also a popular pastime. The local spa centres (Kurzentrum) or spa administrations (Kurverwaltung) can provide price lists for their services. Expect to pay upwards of €30 for a full massage. Sauna and massage combinations are very popular, as are a wide range of beauty and health treatments. Bookings for these can usually be made at short notice.

In spa towns and resort areas you'll also find a growing number of sparkling water parks with several indoor and outdoor pools (often filled with thermal water from local mineral springs), Jacuzzis, surge channels, massage jets and waterfalls, multiple saunas plus a menu of pampering options, including massages. A few hours in such a wellness oasis is especially great on rainy afternoons.

DIRECTORY

Skiing & Snowboarding

Modern lifts, trails from 'Sesame Street' to 'Death Tunnel', breathtaking scenery, cosy mountain huts, steaming mulled wine, hearty dinners by a crackling fire – all these are the hallmarks of a German skiing vacation.

The Bavarian Alps, only an hour's drive south of Munich, offer the best slopes and most reliable snow conditions. The Olympic Games town of Garmisch-Partenkirchen (p346) has world-class facilities and is popular with the international set. Other major resorts are Oberstdorf (p350) in the Allgäu Alps and Berchtesgaden (p353).

There's also plenty of skiing and snowboarding to be done elsewhere in the country, where the mountains may not soar as high but the crowds are smaller, the prices lower, the ambience less frenetic and yet the snow conditions still reliable. Many less-experienced ski hounds and families prefer these more low-key places.

Among Germany's low mountain ranges, the Bavarian Forest (p389) has the most reliable snow levels with plenty of good downhill action on the Grosser Arber mountain. Cross-country skiing is especially wonderful in the Bavarian Forest National Park. In snowy winters, the Black Forest (p430), the Harz (p230), the Thuringian Forest (p270) and the Sauerland (p589) also attract scores of snow fans.

At higher elevations, the season generally runs from late November/early December to March. In many places snowmaking equipment guarantees winter fun in years when nature doesn't play along. All resorts have equipment-hire facilities. Rates for downhill gear start at about €10 per day, with discounts for longer hiring periods. Cross-country equipment costs slightly less. Daily ski-lift passes start around €20.

Water Sports

Germany's coasts, lakes, rivers and canals are all popular playgrounds for water-based pursuits. Canoeing and kayaking are popular in such places as the Spreewald (p156) in Brandenburg, the Naturpark Altmühltal (p372) in Bavaria and the Müritz National Park (p711) in Mecklenburg-Western Pomerania. Sailors should head for the North Sea and Baltic Sea or lakes such as the one in Starnberg (p322) or the Chiemsee (p323) in Bavaria.

BUSINESS HOURS

Official trading hours in Germany allow shops to open until 8pm Monday to Saturday. Actual hours, though, vary widely. In rural areas and city suburbs, shop owners usually close doors at 6pm or 6.30pm Monday to Friday and at 2pm or 4pm on Saturday. Some establishments also observe a two- or three-hour lunch break. Train stations and petrol stations are good for stocking up on basic supplies after hours, although prices will be inflated. Many bakeries open for three hours on Sunday morning and for two hours on Sunday afternoon.

Banking hours are from 8.30am to 4pm Monday to Friday, with suburban and rural branches usually closing for lunch. Most branches stay open until 5.30pm or 6.30pm on Thursday. Post office hours vary widely, but core hours are 8am to 6pm Monday to Friday and to 1pm on Saturday (also see p749).

Travel agencies and other service-oriented businesses are usually open from 9am to 6pm weekdays and till 1pm or 2pm on Saturday. Government offices, on the other hand, close for the weekend as early as 1pm on Friday. Many museums are closed on Monday but stay open late one evening a week.

Restaurant hours vary greatly, but many still close in the afternoon, stop serving food at about 9.30pm and observe a closing day (Ruhetag). This rule generally does not apply in big cities where you'll have no problem packing your tummy all day long and until late in the evening.

Pubs and bars pour libations from around 6pm, unless they serve food, in which case they're also open during the day. Happy hours are practically mandatory, and are usually between 5pm and 10pm. In cities without closing hours, such as Hamburg and Berlin, bars stay open until the wee hours if business is good; otherwise, 1am or 2am are typical closing times. Clubs don't really get going before 11pm or midnight and often keep buzzing until sunrise or later. In places like Berlin there is now a growing number of daytime clubs, so it's quite possible not to go home at all on weekends!

All shops, banks, government departments and post offices are closed on public holidays.

Variations on the above are noted in individual reviews.

CHILDREN

Germany is a great destination for travelling with kids, especially if you keep a light schedule and involve the little ones in the day-to-day trip planning. Lonely Planet's *Travel with Children* offers a wealth of tips and tricks on how to make it child's play. The websites www.travelwithyourkids.com and www.flyingwithkids.com are also good general resources.

Practicalities

Children enjoy lots of discounts for everything from museum admissions to bus fares and hotel stays, although the cut-off age can be anything from six to 18.

At hotels, ask for family rooms with three or four beds. Those that don't have them can provide rollaway beds or cots, usually for a small charge. Some properties (usually chains) allow children below a certain age to stay for free in their parents' room, although this may apply only if no extra bedding is required.

Car-rental firms (p765) rent children's safety seats (which are compulsory) for about €5 per day, but be sure to book them in advance. Airlines usually allow infants (up to two years old) to fly for free, while older children requiring a seat of their own may qualify for reduced fares.

Baby food, infant formulas, soy and cow's milk, disposable nappies (diapers) and the like are widely available in supermarkets and chemists (drugstores). Breastfeeding in public is practised, especially in the cities, although most women are discreet about it. Most tourist offices can lead you to local resources for children's programmes, childcare facilities and English-speaking paediatricians.

Kids are welcome in casual restaurants, where highchairs are standard, but taking them to upmarket ones might raise eyebrows, especially at dinnertime. Also see p84.

Sights & Activities

It's easy to keep the kids entertained no matter where you travel in Germany. The great outdoors, of course, yields endless possibilities. A day spent swimming, bicycling, windsurfing, walking or otherwise engaging in physical activity is sure to send the little ones quickly off to dreamland. Farm holidays (p736) are an excellent way for city kids to get a full immersion in nature. Germany's legend-shrouded

WEATHER YOU LIKE IT OR NOT

Germans have a few indigenous expressions for their weather patterns. A brief cool period that occurs regularly in May is called *die drei Eisheiligen* (the three ice saints). *Schafskälte* (loosely a 'sheep's cold spell') corresponds with shearing time in June. *Altweibersommer* (old maid's summer) is an Indian summer, while mild weather between Christmas and New Year's is called *Weihnachtstauwetter* (Christmas thaw weather).

castles, including the medieval fortresses along the Romantic Rhine (p483), the stately Wartburg (p270) in Thuringia or dreamy Schloss Neuschwanstein (p342) in Bavaria, are sure to fuel the imagination of many a Harry Potter fan.

Theme parks are also perennially popular playgrounds, including Phantasialand (p561) in Brühl, Europa Park (p445) in the Black Forest, and the CentrO Adventure Park (p579) in the Ruhrgebiet. Older kids get a kick out of Hollywood magic made in Germany at Bavaria Filmstadt (p305) in Munich, Filmpark Babelsberg (p151) in Potsdam near Berlin and Movie Park Germany (p580) in the Ruhrgebiet.

Even in the cities, possibilities for keeping kids entertained abound. Take them to parks, playgrounds, swimming pools, zoos or such kid-friendly museums as the Schokoladen Museum (Chocolate Museum, p554) in Cologne, the Spielzeugmuseum (Toy Museum, p358) in Nuremberg or the technology museums in Munich (Deutsches Museum, p304), Speyer (Technik Museum; p475) and Berlin (Deutsches Technikmuseum; p114). Berlin (p116), Münster (p583), Leipzig (p188) and Gelsenkirchen (p580) are among those cities with wonderful zoos.

CLIMATE CHARTS

The German weather is highly capricious: on any given day it can be cold or warm, sunny or rainy, windy or calm – or any combination thereof. Meteorologists blame this lack of stability on colliding maritime and continental air masses, but for you this simply means packing a wardrobe that's as flexible as possible.

The weather tends to be most pleasant in summer, which is rarely suffocatingly hot

DIRECTORY

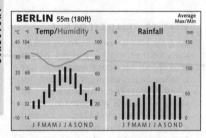

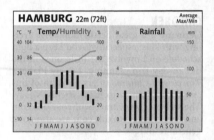

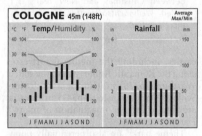

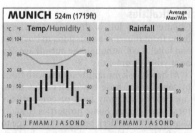

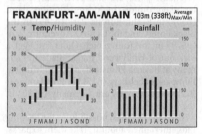

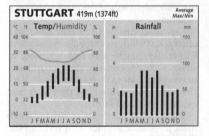

(usually around 28°C), the occasional heat wave notwithstanding. Humidity levels tend to be quite high, making afternoon thunderstorms fairly common. Spring is beautiful but it can be slow to arrive, even if jackets are sometimes stripped off as early as April. Autumn arrives in September and brings the added bonus of bright foliage. Though temperatures can still be quite high, which can keep beer gardens and outdoor cafés open until October. Predictably, December to February is the coldest period, when the mercury can plunge well below 0°C. At the higher elevations, snowfall is possible from November.

For general advice on the best times to travel around the country, see p15.

COURSES

Plenty of courses are offered throughout Germany, including hands-on sessions that don't require fluency in German. Options are literally endless. How about learning rock climbing in Saxon Switzerland, taking a workshop in porcelain painting in Meissen, joining a wine seminar in a Mosel village, getting a tutorial in woodcarving in the Black Forest or taking cooking lessons in Berlin? Tourist offices are usually the best sources for what's on offer locally, although the classifieds in listings magazines and local newspapers may also yield some leads.

If learning German is your aim, you could hire a private tutor or join a language school. Among the most respected are those run by the **Goethe Institut** (www.goethe.de), a government-subsidised nonprofit organisation promoting German language and culture abroad. Programmes cater for all levels of proficiency, usually last a few weeks and are offered in 16 German cities, including Berlin, Dresden and Munich.

Many universities offer summer courses, which are sometimes held in English. The website of the **Deutscher Akademischer Austausch-dienst** (DAAD, German Academic Exchange Service; www.daad.de) has a searchable database of available programmes. For the complete lowdown on study and research at German universities, see www.campus-germany.de.

CUSTOMS

Most articles that you take to Germany for your personal use may be imported free of duty and tax. The following allowances apply to duty-free goods purchased in a non-European Union (EU) country. In addition, you can bring in other products up to a value of €175.

Alcohol 1L of strong liquor or 2L of less than 22% alcohol by volume and 2L of wine (if over age 17)

Coffee & tea 500g of coffee or 200g of coffee extracts and 100g of tea or 40g tea extracts (if over age 15)

Perfume 50g of perfume or scent and 0.25L of eau de toilette

Tobacco 200 cigarettes, 100 cigarillos, 50 cigars or 250g of loose tobacco (if over age 17)

DANGERS & ANNOYANCES

Germany is a very safe country in which to live and travel, with crime rates that are quite low by international standards. Theft and other crimes against travellers occur rarely. Of course, to be on the safe side, you should still take all the usual sensible precautions, such as locking hotel rooms and cars, not leaving valuables unattended, keeping an eye out for pickpockets in crowded places and not taking midnight strolls in city parks. Train stations tend to be magnets for the destitute and drug-dependent who might harass you or make you feel otherwise uncomfortable, especially if you are in the area at night.

Definitely avoid groups of intoxicated football (soccer) hooligans, especially those whose team was on the losing side. These people are erratic, unpredictable and often violent. Many belong to neo-Nazi and skinhead organisations who tend to target especially those they perceive as 'foreign-looking'. Assaults are also possible in a nonfootball setting, of course. Statistics sadly show the eastern states to have higher rates of racially motivated crimes. While we won't go so far as to recommend avoiding these areas altogether if your skin colour is not white, you should exercise extra caution in these states, especially in rural areas. Cities are generally safer, although they too may have so-called 'no-go zones'. Ask at your hotel or phone the local police for advice. If you do find yourself in a threatening situation, try not to provoke these aggressors, get away from the scene as fast as possible and notify the police. Also see the boxed text, p50.

DISCOUNT CARDS

Besides the cards mentioned below, general discounts are widely available for seniors, children, families and the disabled, with no special cards needed. In some cases you may be asked to show ID to prove your age.

Camping Card International

This card is available from your local camping or motoring associations and may net you discounts of up to 25% at German camping grounds. It also includes third-party liability insurance for any accidental damage you may cause. See www.campingcardinternational.com for details.

Student & Youth Cards

If you're a full-time student, the **International Student Identity Card** (ISIC; www.isiccard.com) is your ticket to savings on airline tickets, travel insurance and admission to local attractions. For nonstudents under 26, the **International Youth Travel Card** (IYTC; www.istc.org) or the **Euro<26 Youth Card** (www.euro26.org) grant similar benefits. Both cards are issued by student unions, hostelling organisations and youth-oriented travel agencies such as STA Travel.

Welcome Cards

Many cities offer Welcome Cards, entitling visitors to discounts on museums, sights and tours, plus unlimited trips on local public transportat. Cards are usually available for individuals, families or groups. They can be good value if you plan on taking advantage of most of the benefits and don't qualify for any of the standard discounts.

EMBASSIES & CONSULATES

For German missions around the world, as well as foreign missions in Germany not listed here, check the website of the German **Federal Foreign Office** (www.auswaertiges-amt.de); link to 'English', then 'Addresses'.

German Embassies & Consulates

Germany has diplomatic representation in almost every country in the world. The embassy is generally located in the capital city but consulates, which handle visas and other travel-related services, are usually found in other major cities as well. Contact the German embassy in your country for a referral to the consulate nearest you.

Australia (☎ 02-6270 1911; www.germanembassy.org.au; 119 Empire Circuit, Yarralumla, ACT 2600)

Canada (☎ 613-232 1101; www.ottawadiplo.de; 1 Waverley St, Ottawa, Ont K2P 0T8)

France (☎ 01 53 83 45 00; www.amb-allemagne.fr; 13-15 Ave Franklin Roosevelt, 75008 Paris)

Ireland (☎ 01-269 3011; www.germany.ie; 31 Trimleston Ave, Booterstown, Dublin)

Japan (☎ 03-5791 7700; www.tokyo.diplo.de; 4-5-10, Minami-Azabu, Minato-ku, Tokyo 106-0047)

New Zealand (☎ 04-473 6063; www.wellington.diplo.de; 90-92 Hobson St, Thorndon, Wellington)

Russia (☎ 495-937 9500; www.moskau.diplo.de; Ulitsa Mosfilmovskaya 56, 119285 Moscow)

South Africa (☎ 012-427 8900; www.pretoria.diplo.de; 180 Blackwood St, Arcadia, Pretoria 0083)

Switzerland (☎ 031-359 4111; www.bern.diplo.de; Willadingweg 83, 3006 Bern)

UK (☎ 020-7824 1300; www.london.diplo.de; 23 Belgrave Sq, London SW1X 8PZ)

USA (☎ 202-298 8140; www.germany-info.org; 4645 Reservoir Rd NW, Washington, DC 20007-1998)

Embassies & Consulates in Germany

All countries have their embassies in Berlin but maintain consulates in German cities such as Frankfurt, Munich, Hamburg and Düsseldorf. Call the embassy number listed here to find out which consulate is closest to your location. Most can be reached by phone from 8am or 9am until 5pm or 5.30pm Monday to Friday.

Australia (Map p98; ☎ 030-880 0880; www.australian-embassy.de; Wallstrasse 76-79)

Canada (Map pp100-1; ☎ 030-203 120; www.kanada-info.de; Leipziger Platz 17)

Czech Republic (Map p98; ☎ 030-226 380; www.mzv.cz/berlin; Wilhelmstrasse 44)

France (Map p98; ☎ 030-590 039 000; www.botschaft-frankreich.de; Pariser Platz 5)

Ireland (Map p98; ☎ 030-220 720; www.botschaft-irland.de; Friedrichstrasse 200)

Italy (Map p98; ☎ 030-254 400; www.botschaft-italien.de; Hiroshimastrasse 1)

Japan (Map p98; ☎ 030-210 940; www.botschaft-japan.de; Hiroshimastrasse 6)

Netherlands (Map p98; ☎ 030-209 560; www.dutchembassy.de; Klosterstrasse 50)

New Zealand (Map p98; ☎ 030-206 210; www.nzembassy.com; Friedrichstrasse 60)

Poland (☎ 030-223 130; www.botschaft-polen.de; Lassenstrasse 19-21)

Russia (Map p98; ☎ 030-229 1110; www.russische-botschaft.de; Unter den Linden 63-65)

South Africa (Map p98; ☎ 030-220 730; www.suedafrika.org; Tiergartenstrasse 18)

Spain (Map pp96-7; ☎ 030-254 0070; www.spanischebotschaft.de; Lichtensteinallee 1)

Switzerland (Map p98; ☎ 030-390 4000; www.botschaft-schweiz.de; Otto-von-Bismarck-Allee 4a)

UK (Map p98; ☎ 030-204 570; www.britischebotschaft.de; Wilhelmstrasse 70)

USA (Map p98; ☎ 030-238 5174; www.us-botschaft.de; Neustädtische Kirchstrasse 4-5) The embassy is expected to move to new building on Pariser Platz in 2008.

FESTIVALS & EVENTS

Germany has a packed schedule of festivals and special events. Mentioned here are those celebrated either throughout the nation or in specific regions. For more merriment, see the Festivals & Events sections in the destination chapters.

January & February

Karneval/Fasching (Carnival) The pre-Lent season is celebrated with costumed street partying, parades, satirical shows and general revelry, mostly in cities that are located along the Rhine such as Düsseldorf, Cologne and Mainz, but also in the Black Forest and Munich. See the boxed text, p555.

April

Walpurgisnacht Celebrated on 30 April throughout the Harz, this festival of pagan origin has villages roaring to life; young and old dress up as witches and warlocks and parade through the streets singing and dancing. For more, see the boxed text on p249.

May

Maifest (May Festival) Villagers celebrate the end of winter by chopping down a tree (*Maibaum*), painting, carving and decorating it, and staging a merry revelry with traditional costumes, singing and dancing, usually on the eve of 1 May (*Tanz in den Mai*).

Muttertag (Mother's Day) Mothers are honoured on the second Sunday of May, much to the delight of florists, sweet shops and greeting-card companies.

Nördlinger Pfingstmesse Exhibition of regional traders, with a huge market featuring beer tents, food stalls and entertainment; Nördlingen (p338).

Karneval der Kulturen (www.karneval-berlin.de) Multicultural street and music festival and colourful parade; Berlin (p124).

Internationales Dixieland Festival (www.dixieland .de) Major festival with bands from around the world; Dresden (p174).

Hafengeburtstag (Harbour Birthday; www .hafengeburtstag.de) Five-day festival in the harbour area; Hamburg (p664).

Rhein in Flammen (Rhine in Flames) Huge fireworks festival in five Rhine villages; May to September (p484).

June
Vatertag (Father's Day) Now also known as Männertag (Men's Day), this Ascension Day celebration is an excuse for men to get liquored up with the blessing of the missus.

Erlanger Bergkirchweih (www.der-berg-ruft.de in German) Popular folk and beer festival; Erlangen (p364).

Kieler Woche (Kiel Week; www.kieler-woche.de) Giant festival with yachting regattas and nonstop partying; Kiel (p681).

Wave-Gotik-Treffen (www.wave-gotik-treffen.de) The world's largest Goth gathering; Leipzig (p190).

Christopher Street Day (www.csd-germany.de) Major gay celebration with wild street parades and raucous partying, especially in Berlin, Cologne and Hamburg but also in Dresden, Munich, Stuttgart and Frankfurt.

Mainzer Johannisnacht (www.mainz.de/johan nisnacht) Huge street festival whose highlight is the ceremonial initiation of printers' apprentices; Mainz (p470).

Africa-Festival (www.africafestival.org) Europe's largest festival of Black music; Würzburg (p330).

July & August
Schützenfest (Marksmen's Festivals) Over a million Germans (almost all men, naturally) belong to shooting clubs and show off their skills at these festivals where one of them will be crowned *Schützenkönig* (king of the marksmen); the biggest one takes place in July in Hanover, but Düsseldorf has one of the oldest.

Weinfeste As soon as the grapes have been harvested, the wine festival season starts with wine tastings, folkloric parades, fireworks and the election of local and regional wine queens. The Dürkheimer Wurstmarkt (p479) is one of the biggest and most famous.

Kinderzeche (Children's Festival; www.kinderzeche .de) Ten-day festival with children performing in historical re-enactments, a pageant and the usual merriment; Dinkelsbühl (p336).

Samba Festival (www.samba-festival.de in German) An orgy of song and dance that draws around 90 bands and up to 200,000 visitors; Coburg (p371).

Love Parade (www.loveparade.net) No longer techno only but all types of electronic music at the world's largest rave in mid-July; Berlin (p124).

Richard Wagner Festival (www.bayreuther-festspiele .de in German) Prestigious opera and music festival held throughout August; Bayreuth (p369).

September, October & November
Erntedankfest (Harvest Festival) This harvest festival is celebrated in late September/early October with decorated church altars, processions *(Erntedankzug)* and villagers dressed in folkloric garments.

Oktoberfest (www.oktoberfest.de) Legendary beer-swilling party, enough said. Actually starts in mid-September; Munich (p308).

Frankfurt Book Fair (Frankfurter Buchmesse; www .buchmesse.de) October sees the world's largest book fair, with 1800 exhibitors from 100 countries; Frankfurt (p518).

St Martinstag Celebrated on 10 and 11 November, this festival honours a 4th-century saint known for his humility and generosity with a lantern procession and a re-enactment of the scene where St Martin famously cuts his coat in half to share with a beggar. This is followed by a big feast of stuffed, roasted goose.

December
Nikolaustag On the eve of 5 December, German children put their boots outside the door hoping that St Nick will fill them with sweets and small toys overnight. Ill-behaved children, though, may find only a prickly rod left behind by St Nick's helper, Knecht Ruprecht.

Christmas Markets Mulled wine, spicy gingerbread cookies, shimmering ornaments — these and lots more are typical features of German Christmas markets held from late November until December 24. The Christkindlmarkt (p361) in Nuremberg is especially famous.

Silvester The German New Year's Eve is called Silvester in honour of the 4th-century pope under whom the Romans adopted Christianity as their official religion; there's partying all night long, and the new year is greeted with fireworks launched by thousands of amateur pyromaniacs.

FOOD
Though traditionally a meat-and-potatoes country, the cuisine available in Germany is becoming lighter, healthier and more international. For the full rundown, see p74.

Eating recommendations in this guide match all tastes and travel budgets. Budget eateries include takeaways, cafés, *Imbisse* (snack bars), markets and basic restaurants where you can get a meal (defined as a main course and one drink) for less than €10. At midrange establishments, you usually get tablecloths, full menus, beer and wine lists and a bill that shouldn't exceed €25 per person. Top-end places tend to be full gourmet affairs with expert service, creative and

DIRECTORY

freshly prepared food and matching wine lists. Main courses alone here will cost €20 or more; set three- or four-course menus are usually a better deal.

If our reviews do not mention opening hours, standard hours (11am to 11pm) apply. Note that food service may stop earlier, depending on how busy the place is that night.

Nearly all restaurants in Germany allow smoking, although some have a nonsmoking section. Only some restaurants are air-conditioned.

GAY & LESBIAN TRAVELLERS

Germany is a magnet for gay travellers with the rainbow flag flying especially proudly in Berlin. Some 500,000 gays and lesbians currently make their home in the city, which is helmed by Germany's first openly gay mayor, Klaus Wowereit (affectionately dubbed 'Wowi'). For an overview of the Berlin scene, see the boxed text on p136; for Cologne, flick to p560, for Hamburg to p674. All of these hubs have humming nightlife scenes, magazines, associations and support groups, and major Gay Pride celebrations. Frankfurt (p523), Munich (p318) and other cities have smaller but still vibrant scenes.

Overall, Germans are tolerant of gays (*Schwule*) and lesbians (*Lesben*) although, as elsewhere in the world, cities are more liberal than rural areas, and younger people tend to be more open-minded than older generations. Discrimination is more likely in eastern Germany and in the conservative south where gays and lesbians tend to keep a lower profile.

Germany's gay movement took a huge step forward in 2001 with the passing of the *Lebenspartnerschaftsgesetz* (Life Partnership Act, colloquially known as 'Homo-Ehe' or gay marriage). It gives homosexual couples the right to register their partnership at the registry office and to enjoy many of the same rights, duties and protections as married heterosexual couples. Another victory, and not only for gays, was the passage, in July 2006, of the *Gleichbehandlungsgesetz* (Equal Treatment Law), a far-reaching antidiscrimination initiative. It makes it punishable to discriminate against anyone at work or in private life based on age, gender, sexual orientation, race, ethnic background, religion or world view.

Local gay and lesbian magazines and centres are listed throughout this book. Online sites about all things gay in Germany abound, but most are in German only. Try www.gayscape.com, a search tool with hundreds of links, or go directly to www.justbegay.de or www.gay-web.de. Sites specifically for women are www.lesbians-unlimited.org and www.lesarion.de. Sites specialising in gay travel include www.tomontour.de and www.outtraveler.com (in English). National publications include **Lespress** (www.lespress.de), *L.Mag* for lesbians and **Du & Ich** (www.du-und-ich.net) for young gay men.

HOLIDAYS
Public Holidays

Germany observes eight religious and three secular holidays nationwide. Shops, banks, government offices and post offices are closed on these days. States with predominantly Catholic populations, such as Bavaria and Baden-Württemberg, also celebrate Epiphany (6 January), Corpus Christi (10 days after Pentecost), Assumption Day (15 August) and All Saints' Day (1 November). Reformation Day (31 October) is only observed in eastern Germany.

The following are *gesetzliche Feiertage* (public holidays):

Neujahrstag (New Year's Day) 1 January
Ostern (Easter) March/April – Good Friday, Easter Sunday and Easter Monday
Christi Himmelfahrt (Ascension Day) 40 days after Easter
Maifeiertag/Tag der Arbeit (Labour Day) 1 May
Pfingsten (Whit/Pentecost Sunday & Monday) May/June; 50 days after Easter
Tag der Deutschen Einheit (Day of German Unity) 3 October
Weihnachtstag (Christmas Day) 25 December
2. Weihnachtstag (Boxing Day) 26 December

School Holidays

Each state sets its own school holidays but in general kids get six weeks off in summer and two weeks each around Christmas and Easter and in October. In some states, schools are also closed for a few days in February and around Whitsun/Pentecost.

Traffic is worst at the beginning of school holidays in population-rich states like North Rhine-Westphalia and can become a nightmare if several states let out their schools at the same time.

Germans are big fans of miniholidays built around public holidays, especially those in spring like Ascension Day, Labour Day, Corpus Christi and Whit/Pentecost. Expect heavy crowds on the roads, in the towns, on boats, in beer gardens and everywhere else. Lodging is at a premium at these times as well.

INSURANCE

No matter how long or short your trip, make sure you have adequate travel insurance. If you are a citizen of the EU, the European Health Insurance Card (EHIC) entitles you to reduced-cost or free medical treatment due to illness or accident, although not for emergency repatriation home. Check with your local health authorities on how to obtain an EHIC. In most countries, applications may be filed online. Non-EU citizens should check if a similar reciprocal agreement exists between their country and Germany, or if their policy at home provides worldwide healthcare coverage.

If you need to buy travel health insurance, be sure to get a policy that also covers emergency flights back home. Many healthcare providers expect immediate payment from nonlocals but most do not accept credit cards. Except in emergencies, call around for a doctor willing to accept your insurance. Check your policy for what supporting documentation you need to file a claim and be sure to keep all receipts.

Some policies exclude coverage for 'dangerous activities' like scuba diving, motorcycling, mountaineering, hang-gliding etc. If these activities are on your agenda, be sure to get a policy that includes them. For additional details, see p771.

You should also consider coverage for luggage theft or loss. If you already have a homeowners or renters policy, check what it will cover and only get supplemental insurance to protect against the rest. If you have prepaid a large portion of your vacation, trip cancellation insurance is a worthwhile expense.

For information about what kind of insurance coverage you need while driving in Germany, see p766.

Agencies offering comprehensive travel insurance online include the following:

1 Cover (☎ in Australia 1300-368-344; www.1cover .com.au) Australia-based agency.

Insure.com (☎ in US 800-556-9393; www.insure.com) Compares quotes from 200 US-based insurance companies.

THE LEGAL AGE FOR...

- Drinking alcohol: 14
- Being served alcohol in a pub: 16
- Driving a car: 18
- Sexual consent: 14 (with restrictions)
- Voting in an election: 18

Quoteline Direct (☎ in UK 0870-444 0870; www .quotelinedirect.co.uk) Compares quotes from 30 UK-based insurance companies.

Travelex (☎ in US 800-228-9792; www.travelex -insurance.com)

Travel Guard (☎ in US 800-826-4919; www .travelguard.com)

INTERNET ACCESS

Surfing the Web and checking email is rarely a problem while travelling around Germany. Most public libraries offer access, but downsides may include time limits, reservation requirements and queues. In smaller towns, though, this may be your only choice. Hostels and hotels offering guest PCs with internet access are identified in this book with an internet icon (▣).

Otherwise, internet cafés are plentiful and listed in the Information sections throughout this book; online costs range from €1 to €5 per hour. Unfortunately, these cafés tend to have the longevity of a fruit fly, so please forgive us if our listings are outdated and ask staff at your hotel for a recommendation. Internet access is also often available at telephone call shops near train stations. They're not the nicest places but a good fallback if all else fails.

Laptop users may need adapters for German electrical outlets and telephone sockets, which are widely available in such electronics stores as Saturn and Media Markt. Wireless internet access (wi-fi, or W-LAN in Germany) is becoming fairly prevalent in some midrange and many high-end places. Access is sometimes free; where it's not, charges tend to be steep (eg €25 per day), so read the fine print. Unless you have an ISDN-compatible modem, access may be difficult, if not impossible, in hotels using this now outdated data service, which is especially prevalent in the eastern states and in rural areas. Another, though increasingly rare, obstacle is hardwired (ie wired to the wall) telephones.

DIRECTORY

Some cafés and pubs also offer wi-fi access, sometimes at no charge with a purchase. To locate hot spots, check the directories at www .jiwire.com or www.hotspot-locations.com.

For a full run-down on connectivity issues see www.kropla.com.

LEGAL MATTERS

German police are well trained, fairly 'enlightened' and usually treat tourists with respect. Most can speak some English, though communication problems are likely to be more prevalent in the eastern states, especially in rural areas.

By German law you must carry some form of photographic identification, such as your passport, national identity card or driving licence. Reporting theft to the police is usually a simple, if occasionally time-consuming, matter. Remember that the first thing to do is show some form of identification.

If driving in Germany, you should carry your driving licence and obey road rules carefully (see p766). Penalties for drinking and driving are stiff. The permissible blood-alcohol limit is 0.05%; drivers caught exceeding this amount are subject to stiff fines, a confiscated licence and even jail time.

The sensible thing is to avoid illegal drugs entirely, as penalties can be harsh. Although treated as a minor offence, the possession of even small quantities of cannabis for personal use remains illegal, and getting caught may result in a court appearance. In practice, the courts often waive prosecution if it's a first offence involving only a small amount of cannabis. The definition of 'small', however, is up to the judge, so there are no guarantees. Most other drugs are treated more seriously.

If you are arrested, you have the right to make a phone call and are presumed innocent until proven guilty. If you don't know a lawyer, contact your embassy.

MAPS

Most tourist offices distribute free (but often very basic) maps, but for driving around Germany you'll need a detailed road map or atlas such as those published by Falkplan, Hallwag, RV Verlag or ADAC. Look for them in bookshops, tourist offices, newsagents and petrol stations. **Map 24** (www.map24.de) and **Stadtplandienst** (www.stadtplandienst.de) have downloadable driving directions.

MONEY

The euro has been Germany's official currency since 2002. Euros come in seven notes (five, 10, 20, 50, 100, 200 and 500 euros) and eight coins (one- and two-euro coins and one-, two-, five-, 10-, 20- and 50-cent coins). At the time of writing, the euro was a strong and stable currency, although some minor fluctuations are common. The exchange-rate table on the inside front cover can only offer guidelines. For current rates, check with your bank or online at www.xe.com/ucc or www .oanda.com.

You can exchange money at many banks and post offices as well as foreign-exchange offices. Rates are quite good and service swift and unbureaucratic at Reisebank offices at large train stations; look for branches listed throughout this book. American Express and Thomas Cook/Travelex offices are also reliable stand-bys.

For an overview of the costs you can expect in Germany, see p15.

ATMs

ATMs are ubiquitous and usually the easiest and quickest way to obtain cash from your home bank account. Most are linked to international networks such as Cirrus, Plus, Star and Maestro.

Many ATMs also spit out cash if you use a credit card. This method tends to be more costly because, in addition to a service fee, you'll be charged interest immediately (ie there's no grace period as with purchases).

For exact fees, check with your bank or credit-card company. Always keep the number handy for reporting lost or stolen cards.

Cash

Cash is still king in Germany, so you can't really avoid having at least some notes and coins, say €100 or so, on you at all times. Plan to pay in cash almost everywhere (see the next section for likely exceptions). Banks only exchange foreign paper money and not coins.

Credit Cards

Major credit cards are becoming more widely accepted, but it's best not to assume that you'll be able to use one – enquire first. Some shops may require a minimum purchase, while others may refuse to accept a card even if the credit card company's logo is displayed in their window.

Even so, a piece of plastic is vital in emergencies and also useful for phone or internet bookings. Report lost or stolen cards to the following:

American Express (☎ 01805-840 840)
MasterCard (☎ 0800-819 1040)
Visa (☎ 0800-811 8440)

Tipping

Restaurant bills always include a service charge (Bedienung) but most people add 5% or 10% unless the service was truly abhorrent. At hotels, bellhops get about €1 per bag and it's also nice to leave a few euros for the room cleaners. Tip bartenders about 5% and taxi drivers around 10%.

Travellers Cheques

Once a popular alternative to large wads of cash, travellers cheques are becoming increasingly obsolete in the age of network-linked ATMs. It doesn't help that German businesses generally don't accept them, even if denominated in euros, and that even banks often refuse to cash them or charge exorbitant fees for the service. Currency exchange offices are usually the best places to go. American Express offices cash their own cheques free of charge. Always keep a record of the cheque numbers separate from the cheques themselves.

PHOTOGRAPHY

Germany is a photographer's dream, with its gorgeous countryside, fabulous architecture, quaint villages, exciting cities, lordly

---

TAXES & REFUNDS

Prices for goods and services include a value-added tax (VAT), called Mehrwertsteuer, which is 19% for regular goods and 7% for food and books. If your permanent residence is outside the European Union, you can have a large portion of the VAT refunded, provided you shop at a store displaying the 'Tax-Free for Tourists' sign and obtain a tax-free form for your purchase from the sales clerk. At the airport, show this form, your unused goods and your receipt to a custom official before checking your luggage. The customs official will stamp the form, which you can then take straight to the cash refund office at the airport.

---

cathedrals, lively cafés and picture-perfect castles, palaces and old towns. A good general reference guide is Lonely Planet's Travel Photography by Richard I'Anson.

If photography means only digital to you, you need only go to www.malektips.com for advice on how to keep your pixels poppin' in nearly every situation you can imagine. If you still have a 'traditional' camera with actual film, keep in mind that for general shooting – either prints or slides – 100 ASA film is the most useful and versatile as it gives you good colour and enough speed to capture most situations. If you plan to shoot in dark areas or in brightly lit night scenes without a tripod, switch to 400 ASA. For slides, Fuji Velvia and Kodak E100VS are easy to process and provide good quality. For print film, you can't beat Kodak Gold or Fuji.

Film of any type is inexpensive in Germany, so there's no need to stock up at home. For a roll of 36-exposure standard print film, expect to pay around €1.50 to €3, while quality slide film should cost from €5 to €7. The cost goes down if you buy in multipacks. Big chain electronics stores like Saturn or Media Markt tend to have the best prices for film.

Film can be damaged by excessive heat, so avoid leaving your camera and film in the car (this goes for digital cameras too). Carry spare batteries to avoid disappointment when your camera dies in the middle of nowhere or on a Sunday afternoon. With any new camera, practise before leaving for your trip.

Germans tend to be deferential around photographers and will make a point of not walking in front of your camera, even if you want them to. No-one seems to mind being photographed in the context of an overall scene, but if you want a close-up shot, you should ask first.

POST

Main post offices, which are often near train stations, are usually open from 8am to 6pm Monday to Friday and till 1pm on Saturday. Suburban and rural branches often close at lunchtime and at 5pm or 5.30pm weekdays and noon on Saturday. Our destination chapters list only opening hours deviating from this standard.

Stamps are officially sold at post offices only, though hotel staff and souvenir and postcard shops in tourist resorts may also carry some.

Within Germany and the EU, standard-sized postcards cost €0.45, a 20g letter is €0.55 and a 50g letter is €1. Postcards to North America and Australasia cost €1, a 20g airmail letter is €1.55 and a 50g airmail letter is €2. A surcharge applies to oversized mail. The post office's website (www.deutsche-post.de) has full details.

Letters sent within Germany take one to two days for delivery; those addressed to destinations within Europe or to North America take three to five days and those to Australasia five to seven days.

Sending a parcel up to 2kg within Germany costs €4.10. Surface-mail parcels up to 2kg within Europe are €8.20 and to destinations elsewhere €12.30. Airmail parcels up to 1kg are €10.30/21 within Europe/elsewhere; parcels over 1kg cost €14.30/29.70.

SHOPPING

Germany is a fun place to shop, with an enormous selection of everyday and wonderfully unique items. Much of the shopping is done in pedestrianised shopping zones in the city centres rather than in big shopping malls, which are often relegated to the suburbs. There's really nothing you can't buy in Germany, but even in the age of globalism, there are still some treasures you'll unearth here better than anywhere else.

Regional products include traditional Bavarian outfits, including dirndl dresses, lederhosen and Loden jackets. Beer mugs are the classic souvenir, no matter whether made of glass or stoneware, plain or decorated, with or without pewter lids – the choice is endless.

Germans make excellent clocks, and not only of the cuckoo variety. Precision instruments such as microscopes and binoculars with lenses by Carl Zeiss are also a speciality. Cutlery is first-rate, with WMF, Wüsthof and JA Henckels being leading brands.

Top-quality woodcarvings are widely available in the Alpine regions, the Harz and Saxony. Fans of the fragile can pick up exquisite china made by Meissen, Villeroy & Boch, Rosenthal, KPM or Nymphenburger Porzellanmanufaktur. The glass artisans in the Bavarian Forest make beautiful vases, bowls and ornaments.

Famous toy brands include stuffed animals by Steiff (the inventor of the teddy bear) and collectible Käthe Kruse dolls. At Christmas markets you'll discover wonderful ornaments, classic nutcrackers and other decorations. Sea-sonal treats include Lebkuchen, a spicy gingerbread, and Stollen, a loaf-shaped fruit cake.

German wine is another excellent purchase, especially since some of the best bottles are not available outside the country. If you're into street fashion, head to Berlin, which makes the most *Zeitgeist*-capturing outfits. See the boxed text on p141 for specifics.

Bargaining

Bargaining almost never occurs in Bavaria, except at flea markets. At hotels, you can sometimes get lower rates if business is slow.

SOLO TRAVELLERS

There are no particular problems or difficulties associated with travelling alone in Germany. Germans are generally friendly but rather reserved and not likely to initiate a conversation with strangers. This shouldn't stop you from approaching them, though, since most will quite happily respond and even be extra helpful once they find out you're a traveller. And don't let your lack of German deter you. Young people especially speak at least some English and many are keen to practise it.

Women don't need to be afraid of initiating a conversation, not even with men. Unless you're overtly coquettish, this most likely won't be interpreted as a sexual advance. Issues of safety, though, are slightly different for women than they are for men; see p752 for more specific advice.

For more on the subject, check out the website of the nonprofit **Connecting: Solo Travel Network** (www.cstn.org). It's membership-based but much information is accessible without joining.

TELEPHONE & FAX
Fax

Faxes can be sent from and received at most hotels, photocopy shops and internet cafés.

Mobile Phones

Mobile (cell) phones are called 'handys' and work on the GSM 900/1800 standard, which is compatible with the rest of Europe, Australia and parts of Asia, but not the North American GSM1900 or the totally different system in Japan. Multiband phones that work worldwide are becoming increasingly common.

If you have an unlocked GSM900/1800 or multiband phone, buying a local prepaid, rechargeable SIM card is likely to work out cheaper than using your own network. Cards are available at any telecommunications store (eg T-Online, Vodafone, E-Plus or O2) and give you a local number without signing any contract. All include voice mail, text messaging and free incoming calls. Recharge with scratch cards from news kiosks and general stores.

If your phone doesn't work in Germany, you can buy a GSM prepaid phone, including some airtime, starting at €30 at any telecommunications store.

Note: calls made to a mobile phone are more expensive than those to a stationary number, but incoming calls are free.

Phone Codes

German phone numbers consist of an area code, which always starts with 0, and the local number. Area codes can be up to six digits, local numbers up to nine digits long. If dialling from a landline within the same city, you don't need to dial the area code. If using a mobile, you must dial it.

If calling Germany from abroad, first dial your country's international access code, then 49 (Germany's country code), then the area code (dropping the initial 0) and the local number. Germany's international access code is ☎ 00. If you need to put through a reverse-charge call or 'R'-Gespräch, contact the operator on ☎ 0180-200 1033.

Deutsche Telekom offers fast and reliable live directory assistance, but it's ridiculously expensive. Numbers within Germany (☎ 118 37 for an English-speaking operator) are charged at €1.29 per minute, while numbers outside Germany (☎ 118 34) command a base rate of €0.99 plus €1.19 per minute. If you have online access, you can get the same information for free at www.telefonbuch.de. A much cheaper provider is the fully automated Telix (☎ 118 86), which charges only €0.29 per minute.

Numbers starting with 0800 are toll free, 01801 numbers are charged at 4.6 cents per minute, 01803 at €0.09 and 01805 at €0.12. Calls to numbers starting with 01802 cost a flat €0.06, while those to 01804 numbers cost a flat €0.24. Avoid numbers starting with 0190 or 900, which are charged at exorbitant rates. Direct-dialled calls made from hotel rooms are also usually charged at a premium.

If you have access to a private phone, you can benefit from cheaper rates by using a call-by-call access code (eg 01016 or 010090).

Daily newspapers often list providers that offer the currently cheapest rates, although the most comprehensive source is online at www .billigertelefonieren.de (in German).

Telephone call shops, which tend to cluster around train stations, may also offer competitive calling rates, although they often charge rather steep connection fees. Always make sure you understand the charges involved.

Phonecards

Most public pay phones only work with Deutsche Telekom (DT) phonecards, available in denominations of €5, €10 and €20 from DT stores as well as post offices, newsagents and tourist offices. Occasionally you'll see non-DT pay phones, but these may not necessarily offer better rates.

For long-distance or international calls, prepaid calling cards issued by other companies tend to offer better rates than DT's phonecards. Look for them at newsagents and telephone call shops. Most of these cards also work with payphones but usually at a surcharge – read the fine print on the card itself. Those sold at Reisebank (p748) outlets have some of the most competitive rates.

TIME

Clocks in Germany are set to central European time (GMT/UTC plus one hour). Daylight-saving time comes into effect at 2am on the last Sunday in March and ends on the last Sunday in October. Without taking daylight-saving times into account, when it's noon in Berlin, it's 11am in London, 6am in New York, 3am in San Francisco, 8pm in Tokyo, 9pm in Sydney and 11pm in Auckland. The use of the 24-hour clock (eg 6.30pm is 18.30) is common. Refer to the map on pp814–15 for additional times.

TOURIST INFORMATION
Local Tourist Offices

Just about every community in Germany has a walk-in tourist office where you can pick up information, maps, pamphlets and often book a room, sometimes for a small fee. Contact details are listed throughout this book in the Information section of each town.

Tourist offices in big cities and resort areas usually have English-language brochures. With few exceptions, there's at least one staff member more or less fluent in English and willing to make the effort to help you.

DIRECTORY

Tourist Offices Abroad

The best pre-trip planning source is the **German National Tourist Office** (GNTO; www.germany -tourism.com), whose comprehensive website is available in a dozen or so languages. For specific enquiries, contact the GNTO office in your country. Here's a selection:

Austria (☎ 01-513 2792; www.deutschland-tourismus.de)

Belgium (☎ 02-245 9700; www.duitsland-vakantieland .be, www.vacances-en-allemagne.be)

Canada (☎ 416-968 1685; www.cometogermany.com)

France (☎ 01 40 20 01 88; www.allemagne-tourisme.com)

Italy (☎ 02-8474 4444; www.vacanzeingermania.com)

Japan (☎ 13-3586 0735; www.visit-germany.jp)

Netherlands (☎ 020-697 8066; www.duitsverkeers bureau.nl)

Spain (☎ 91-429 3551; www.alemania-turismo.com)

Switzerland (☎ 01-213 2200; www.deutschland -tourismus.de)

UK (☎ 020-7317 0908; www.germany-tourism.de)

USA (☎ 212-661-7200; www.cometogermany.com)

TRAVELLERS WITH DISABILITIES

Overall, Germany caters well for the needs of the disabled *(Behinderte)*, especially the wheelchair-bound. You'll find access ramps and/or lifts in many public buildings, including train stations, museums, theatres and cinemas, especially in the cities. In historic places, though, cobblestone streets make getting around quite cumbersome.

Newer hotels have special rooms for mobility-impaired guests with extra-wide doors and spacious bathrooms. Nearly all trains are accessible, and local buses and U-Bahns are becoming increasingly so as well. For details, call the local transport organisations listed throughout this book. Seeing-eye dogs are allowed on all forms of public transport.

Some car-rental agencies offer hand-controlled vehicles and vans with wheelchair lifts at no charge, but you m ust reserve them well in advance. In parking lots and garages, look for designated disabled spots marked with a painted wheelchair.

Many local and regional tourist offices have special brochures for people with disabilities, although usually in German.

At the **Deutsche Bahn Mobility Service Centre** (☎ 01805-512 512; www.bahn.de; 🕑 8am-8pm Mon-Fri, 8am-2pm Sat) operators provide train access information and help with route planning. The website has useful information in English (link to 'International Guests').

Other resources:

Access Travel (☎ in UK 01942-888 844; www.access -travel.co.uk) Tour operator specialising in holidays for travellers with disabilities.

Access-Able Travel Source (☎ in US 303-232 2979; www.access-able.com) Operates an excellent website with many links.

All Go Here (www.everybody.co.uk) Directory that provides information on disabled services offered by most major airlines.

E-Bility (☎ in Australia 02-9810 2216; www.e-bility .com) Australia-based destination website with disability-related information, services and products.

Mobility International (☎ in UK 020-7403-5688, in US 541-343-1284; www.miusa.org) Advises disabled travellers on mobility issues and runs an educational exchange programme.

Natko (☎ in Germany 06131-250 410; www.natko.de in German) Central clearing house for inquiries about travelling in Germany as a disabled person.

Society for Accessible Travel & Hospitality (SATH; ☎ in US 212-447-7284; www.sath.org) Lots of useful links and information for disabled travellers.

VISAS

Most EU nationals only need their national identity card or passport to enter, stay and work in Germany. Citizens of Australia, Canada, Israel, Japan, New Zealand, Poland, Switzerland and the US are among those countries that need only a valid passport but no visa if entering Germany as tourists for up to three months within a six-month period. Passports should be valid for at least another four months from the planned date of departure from Germany.

Nationals from most other countries need a so-called Schengen Visa, named for the 1995 Schengen Agreement that abolished passport controls between Austria, Belgium, Denmark, Finland, France, Germany, Iceland, Italy, Greece, Luxembourg, Netherlands, Norway, Portugal, Spain and Sweden. You must apply for the Schengen Visa with the embassy or consulate of the country that is your primary destination. It is valid for stays up to 90 days. Legal residency in any Schengen country makes a visa unnecessary, regardless of your nationality.

Visa applications are usually processed within two to 10 days, but it's always best to start the process as early as possible. For full details, see www.auswaertiges-amt.de and check with a German consulate in your country.

WOMEN TRAVELLERS

Germany is generally a safe place for women to travel, even alone and even in the cities. Of course, this doesn't mean you can let your guard down and trust your life to every stranger. Simply use the same common sense as you would at home.

Getting hassled in the streets happens infrequently and is usually limited to wolf-whistles and unwanted stares. In crowded situations, ie on public transport or at events, groping is rare.

German women are quite outspoken and emancipated. It's normal to split dinner bills, even on dates, or for a woman to pick up a man. Going alone to cafés and restaurants is perfectly acceptable, even at night, although how comfortable you feel doing so depends entirely on you. In bars and nightclubs, solo women are likely to attract some attention, but if you don't want company, most men will respect a firm 'no thank you'. If you feel threatened, protesting loudly will often make the offender slink away with embarrassment – or at least spur other people to come to your defence.

Some recommended online resources for women travellers include **Journeywoman** (www.journeywoman.com) and **Her Own Way** (www.voyage.gc.ca/main/pubs/PDF/her_own_way-en.pdf). While the latter is published by the Canadian government, it still contains lots of good general advice.

Physical attack is very unlikely but, of course, it does happen. If you're assaulted, call the police immediately (☎ 110) or, if you're too traumatised, contact a women's crisis centre. For a complete list, see www.frauennotrufe.de (also in English) or call ☎ 030-3229 9500. Hotlines are not staffed around the clock.

Berlin (☎ 030-216 8888)
Cologne (☎ 0221-562 035)
Frankfurt-am-Main (☎ 069-709 494)
Hamburg (☎ 040-255 566)
Hanover (☎ 0511-332 112)
Leipzig (☎ 0341-391 1199)
Mainz (☎ 06131-221 213)
Munich (☎ 089-763 737)
Nuremberg (☎ 0911-284 400)
Stuttgart (☎ 0711-285 9001)

WORK

Non-EU citizens cannot work legally in Germany without a residence permit (*Aufenthaltserlaubnis*) and a work permit (*Arbeitserlaubnis*). EU citizens don't need a work permit but they must have a residence permit, although obtaining one is a mere formality. Since regulations change from time to time, it's best to contact the German embassy in your country for the latest information.

Because of fairly high unemployment, finding skilled work in Germany can be a full-time job in itself, except in high-demand fields such as information technology. A good place to start is at the local employment offices (*Arbeitsamt*), which maintain job banks of vacancies. The classified sections of the daily papers are another source, as are private placement and temp agencies. The three largest temp agencies are **Randstadt** (☎ 06196-4080; www.randstadt.de), **Adecco** (☎ 01802-900 900; www.adecco.de) and **Persona** (☎ 02351-9500). All have comprehensive websites (in German) that allow you to search for job openings. Computer specialists might want to visit www.computerjobs24.de, a data bank that allows you to search for jobs or list your services at no cost. Obviously, the better your German, the greater your chances.

If you're not in the market for a full-time job but simply need some casual work to pad your travel budget, options include babysitting, cleaning, English tutoring, tour guiding, bar tending, yoga teaching, donating sperm or perhaps nude modelling for art classes. You won't get rich, but neither will you need a high skill level, much training, or fluent German. Start by placing a classified ad in a local newspaper or listings guide. Other places to advertise include noticeboards at universities, photocopy shops and supermarkets.

Au pair work is relatively easy to find and can be done legally even by non-EU citizens. Fluent German is not expected, although you should have some basic language skills. For the full story, get the latest edition of *The Au Pair and Nanny's Guide to Working Abroad* by Susan Griffith and Sharon Legg. The website www.au-pair-agenturen.de has links to numerous agencies in Germany.

Citizens of Australia, New Zealand and Canada between the ages of 18 and 30 may apply for a Working Holiday Visa, entitling them to work for up to 90 days in a 12-month period. Contact your German embassy for details (p743).

Transport

CONTENTS

GETTING THERE & AWAY

ENTERING THE COUNTRY

Entering Germany is usually a very straight-forward procedure. If you're arriving in Germany from any of the 15 Schengen countries, such as the Netherlands or Austria, you no longer have to show your passport or go through customs in Germany, no matter which nationality you are. For a list of Schengen countries as well as an overview of visa requirements, see p752.

Passport

Passports must be valid for at least six months after the end of your trip. Citizens of most Western countries can enter Germany without a visa; other nationals may need a Schengen Visa; see p752 for details.

AIR
Airports

Frankfurt International Airport (FRA; ☎ 01805-372 4636; www.frankfurt-airport.de) is the main gateway for transcontinental flights, although **Düsseldorf** (DUS; ☎ 0211-4210; www.duesseldorf-international .de) and **Munich** (MUC; ☎ 089-975 00; www.munich

-airport.de) also receive their share of overseas air traffic. Berlin has two international airports, **Tegel** (TXL; ☎ 0180-500 0186; www.berlin-airport.de) and **Schönefeld** (SXF; ☎ 0180-500 0186; www.berlin-airport .de). There are also sizeable airports in **Hamburg** (HAM; ☎ 040-507 50; www.ham.airport.de), **Cologne/ Bonn** (CGN; ☎ 02203-404 001; www.airport-cgn.de) and **Stuttgart** (STR; ☎ 01805-948 444; www.stuttgart-airport .com), and smaller ones in such cities as Bremen, Dresden, Erfurt, Hanover, Leipzig, Münster-Osnabrück and Nuremberg.

Some of the budget airlines – Ryanair in particular – keep their fares low by flying to remote airports, which may be little more than recycled military airstrips. The biggest of these is **Frankfurt-Hahn** (HHN; ☎ 06543-509 200; www.hahn-airport.de), which is actually near the Moselle River, about 110km northwest of Frankfurt proper.

For details about individual German airports, including getting to and from information, see the destination chapters.

Airlines

The main airline serving Germany is the national flagship carrier and Star Alliance member **Lufthansa** (LH; ☎ 01805-838 426; www.lufthansa.de), which operates a vast network of domestic and international flights and has one of the world's best safety records. Of the many other national and discount carriers also serving Germany, the main ones are listed here along with their telephone numbers in Germany for reservations, flight changes and information. For contact information in your home country, see the airlines' websites.

Low-budget airlines rule the skies these days with some fares as low as a taxi ride. UK-based Ryanair and easyJet as well as German airlines Air Berlin, Germanwings and HLX offer the most flights to Germany.

NATIONAL CARRIERS
Aeroflot (SU; ☎ 0180-375 5555; www.aeroflot.com)
Air Canada (AC; ☎ 01805-0247 226; www.aircanada.ca)
Air France (AF; ☎ 01805-830 830; www.airfrance.com)
Air Lingus (EI; ☎ 01805-975 900; www.airlingus.com)
Air New Zealand (NZ; ☎ 0800-5494 5494; www.airnz.co.nz)
Alitalia (AZ; ☎ 01805-074 747; www.alitalia.com)
American Airlines (AA; ☎ 0180-324 2324; www.aa.com)
British Airways (BA; ☎ 01805-266 522; www.britishairways.com)
Cathay Pacific Airways (CX; ☎ 069-710 080; www.cathaypacific.com)
Continental Air Lines (CO; ☎ 0180-321 2610; www.continental.com)
Delta Air Lines (DL; ☎ 01803-337 880; www.delta.com)
Iberia (IB; ☎ 01803-000 613; www.iberia.com)
KLM (KL; ☎ 01805-214 201; www.klm.com)
LOT (LO; ☎ 01803-000 336; www.lot.com)
LTU (LT; ☎ 0211-941 8888; www.ltu.de)

Malev Hungarian Airlines (MA; ☎ 069-238 5800; www.malev.hu)
Olympic Airlines (OA; ☎ 069-970 670; www.olympic-airways.com)
Qantas Airways (QF; ☎ 01805-250 620; www.qantas.com.au)
Scandinavian Airlines/SAS (SK; ☎ 01805-117 002; www.scandinavian.net)
Singapore Airlines (SQ; ☎ 069-719 5200; www.singaporeair.com)
South African Airways (SA; ☎ 069-2998 0320; www.flysaa.com)
Swiss (LX; ☎ 01803-000 337; www.swiss.com)
Turkish Airlines (TK; ☎ 089-9759 2710; www.turkishairlines.com)
United Airlines (UA; ☎ 069-5007 0387; www.united.com)
US Airways (US; ☎ 01803-000 609; www.usairways.com)

DISCOUNT CARRIERS
Air Berlin (AB; ☎ 01805-737 800; www.air-berlin.com)
Centralwings (CO; ☎ 0180-454 545; www.centralwings.com) A subsidiary of LOT Polish Airlines.
Cirrus (C9; ☎ 0180-444 4888; www.cirrus-world.de)
easyJet (EZY; ☎ in Germany 0900-1100 161; www.easyjet.com)
Germania Express (ST; ☎ 01805-737 100; www.gexx.com)

CLIMATE CHANGE & TRAVEL
Climate change is a serious threat to the ecosystems that humans rely upon, and air travel is the fastest-growing contributor to the problem. Lonely Planet regards travel, overall, as a global benefit, but believes we all have a responsibility to limit our personal impact on global warming.

Flying & Climate Change
Pretty much every form of motorized travel generates CO2 (the main cause of human-induced climate change) but planes are far and away the worst offenders, not just because of the sheer distances they allow us to travel, but because they release greenhouse gases high into the atmosphere. The statistics are frightening: two people taking a return flight between Europe and the US will contribute as much to climate change as an average household's gas and electricity consumption over a whole year.

Carbon Offset Schemes
Climatecare.org and other websites use 'carbon calculators' that allow travellers to offset the level of greenhouse gases they are responsible for with financial contributions to sustainable travel schemes that reduce global warming – including projects in India, Honduras, Kazakhstan and Uganda.

Lonely Planet, together with Rough Guides and other concerned partners in the travel industry, support the carbon offset scheme run by climatecare.org. Lonely Planet offsets all of its staff and author travel.

For more information check out our website: www.lonelyplanet.com.

TRANSPORT

Germanwings (4U; ☎ 0900-191 9100; www
.germanwings.com)
Hapagfly (HF; ☎ 01805-787 510; www.hapagfly.com)
HLX (X3; ☎ 01805-093 509; www.hlx.com)
Jet2 (LS; ☎ in UK 0871 226 1737; www.jet2.com)
Norwegian Air Shuttle (DY; ☎ in Norway
08152-1815; www.norwegian.no)
OLT (OL; ☎ 01805-658 659; www.olt.de)
Ryanair (FR; ☎ 0900-116 0500; www.ryanair.com)
Snowflake (03; ☎ in Sweden 08-797 4000; www
.flysnowflake.com) A subsidiary of SAS.
Virgin Express (TV; ☎ 01805-133 212;
www.virgin-express.com)

Tickets

Everybody loves a bargain and timing is key
when it comes to snapping up cheap airfares.
You can generally save a bundle by booking early, travelling midweek (Tuesday to
Thursday) or in the off-season (October to
March/April in the case of Germany). Early-
morning or late-night flights may also be
cheaper than those catering for the suit bri-
gades. Some airlines offer lower fares if you
stay over a Saturday.

Your best friend in ferreting out deals is
the internet. Start by checking fares at online
travel agencies such as **Expedia** (www.expedia.com),
Opodo (www.opodo.com) or **Zuji** (www.zuji.com), then
run the same flight request through meta-
search engines such as **SideStep** (www.sidestep
.com), **Kayak** (www.kayak.com), **Mobissimo** (www
.mobissimo.com), **Qixo** (www.qixo.com) or **Farechase**
(www.farechase.com). These so-called aggregators
find the lowest fares by combing the websites
of major airlines, online consolidators, online
travel agencies and low-cost carriers.

To get the skinny on which budget airlines currently serve German airports, consult
www.whichbudget.com or www.skyscanner
.net. For bookings on discount carriers go
to the airline websites directly or try an online agency such as www.openjet.com. Phone
reservations usually incur a ticket surcharge.

If you're North America–based and flexible with regard to the airline and departure
times or dates, you might be able to save a
bundle through **Priceline** (www.priceline.com) and
Hotwire (www.hotwire.com). You name the fare
you're willing to pay, then wait and see if any
airline bites.

Many airlines now guarantee that you'll
find the lowest fare on their own websites,
so check these out as well. A good way to
learn about late-breaking bargain fares is by

signing on to airlines' free weekly email news-
letters. Even the old-fashioned newspaper
can yield deals, especially in times of fare
wars. And don't forget about travel agents,
who can be especially helpful when planning
complex itineraries. STA Travel and Flight
Centre, both with worldwide branches, are
recommended.

Intercontinental RTW Tickets

Coming from Australia or New Zealand,
round-the-world (RTW) tickets may work out
cheaper than regular return fares, especially
if you're planning on visiting other countries
besides Germany. They're of most value for
trips that combine Germany with Asia or
North America.

Official airline RTW tickets are usually
put together by a combination of airlines or
an entire alliance and permit you to fly to a
specified number of stops and/or a maximum
mileage, so long as you don't backtrack. Tickets are usually valid for one year. Some airlines
'black out' a few heavily travelled routes.

For more details and tickets, check out
these websites:
Air Brokers (www.airbrokers.com)
Air Treks (www.airtreks.com)
Circle the Planet (www.circletheplanet.com)
Just Fares (www.justfares.com)

Australia & New Zealand

Many airlines compete for business between
Australia and New Zealand and Europe, with
fares starting at about A$2100/1300 in high/
low season. The dominant carriers are Qantas, British Airways and Singapore Airlines.
Depending on the airline, you'll fly via Asia
or the Middle East, with possible stopovers in
such cities as Singapore or Bahrain, or across
Canada or the US, with possible stopovers in
Honolulu, Los Angeles or Vancouver. Definitely look into a round-the-world (RTW)
ticket, which may work out cheaper than regular return fares. Some recommended agents:

AUSTRALIA

Flight Centre (☎ in Australia 133 133, in New Zealand
0800 243 544; www.flightcentre.com.au, www.flightcentre
.co.nz)
STA Travel (☎ in Australia 1300 733 035, in New
Zealand 0508 782 872; www.statravel.com.au,
www.statravel.co.nz)
Travel.com (www.travel.com.au, www.travel.co.nz)
Zuji (www.zuji.com)

Canada

Lufthansa and Air Canada fly to Frankfurt and Munich from all major Canadian airports, with prices starting at C$1250/850 in high/low season. Some flights may involve a stopover. **Travel Cuts** (☎ 800-667-2887; www.travelcuts .com) is Canada's national student travel agency. For online bookings try www.expedia.ca and www.travelocity.ca.

Continental Europe

Air Berlin, easyJet, Germanwings, HLX and Ryanair are the dominant discount carriers with flights to all major and minor German airports from throughout Europe. Smaller airlines servicing less busy routes from Scandinavia include Snowflake and Norwegian Air Shuttle. From Eastern Europe, Centralwings and Sky Europe are among carriers with flights to Germany. One-way fares to Berlin can be as low as €99 from Madrid or Barcelona, €39 from Milan or €59 from Rome. Check www.whichbudget.com for which airlines fly where.

National carriers such as Air France, Alitalia, Iberia, SAS and, of course, Lufthansa offer numerous flights to all major German airports.

Recommended travel agencies:

Anyway (www.anyway.fr) France
Barceló Viajes (www.barceloviajes.com) Spain
CTS (www.cts.it) Italy
Last Minute (www.fr.lastminute.com) France
Nouvelles Frontières (www.nouvelles-frontieres.fr) France
Opodo (www.opodo.fr) France
Opodo (www.opodo.it) Italy
OTU (www.otu.fr) France

UK & Ireland

About a dozen airlines fly to some 22 destinations in Germany from practically every airport in the UK and Ireland. Lufthansa and British Airways are the main national carriers, but naturally prices are a lot lower on the dominant discount carriers Ryanair, easyJet, Air Berlin and Germanwings. Their extensive route network has made travelling even to smaller, regional destinations such as Dortmund, Nuremberg and Münster very inexpensive. Rock-bottom fares start as low as £20 one way, including airport taxes.

Recommended travel agencies:

Ebookers (☎ 0870 010 7000; www.ebookers.com)
Flight Centre (☎ 0870 890 8099; www.flightcentre.co.uk)
Opodo (www.opodo.co.uk)
Quest Travel (☎ 0870 442 3542; www.questtravel.com)

STA Travel (☎ 0870 160 0599; www.statravel.co.uk)
Trailfinders (www.trailfinders.co.uk)
Travel Bag (☎ 0870 890 1456; www.travelbag.co.uk)

USA

The US–Germany route is busier than ever and competition means that good deals are often available. All major US carriers as well as Lufthansa operate flights from nearly every big US city to Germany. In addition, German carriers LTU and Condor operate seasonal (ie summer) service from select US cities. (Condor flies from Anchorage and Fairbanks, for instance.) Good fares are often available from Asia-based airlines, such as Air India and Singapore Airlines, that stop in the US en route to their final destination.

Most flights land in Frankfurt, but Düsseldorf and Munich are also seeing more incoming traffic and even Hamburg, Cologne and Berlin are now served directly from New York. There's even a direct flight from Atlanta to Stuttgart. But even if you land in Frankfurt – and it's not your final destination – it's a snap to catch a connecting domestic flight or to continue your travels on Germany's ever-efficient train system.

Airfares rise and fall in a cyclical pattern. The lowest fares are available from early November to mid-December and then again from mid-January to Easter, gradually rising in the following months. Peak months are July and August, after which prices start to drop again. Fares start at around US$600/450 return in high/low season from New York, US$850/550 from Chicago and US$1000/700 from Los Angeles.

If you're flexible with your travel dates, flying stand-by may save you a bundle. Fares offered through **Air Hitch** (☎ 877-247-4482, 212-736-0505; www.air-hitch.org) can be as low as US$155 one way from east coast cities and US$240 from the west coast in peak season.

STA Travel (☎ 800-781-4040; www.statravel.com) and **FlightCentre** (☎ 866-967-5351; www.flightcentre.us) are both reliable budget travel agencies offering online bookings and bricks-and-mortar branches throughout the country. To scour the web for cheap fares, try the following:

Cheap Air (www.cheapair.com)
Cheap Tickets (www.cheaptickets.com)
Expedia (www.expedia.com)
Lowest Fare (www.lowestfare.com)
Orbitz (www.orbitz.com)
Travelocity (www.travelocity.com)

TRANSPORT

TRANSPORT

LAND
Border Crossings
Germany is bordered anticlockwise by Denmark, the Netherlands, Belgium, Luxembourg, France, Switzerland, Austria, the Czech Republic and Poland. The Schengen Agreement (p752) abolished passport and customs formalities between Germany and all bordering countries except Poland, the Czech Republic and Switzerland.

Bus
Riding the bus to Germany is slower and less comfortable yet generally cheaper than taking the train. However, fares often can't beat cheap flights offered by the budget airlines. Still, buses have their use if you missed out on those super-low air fares, you're travelling at short notice, or you live in an area poorly served by air or train.

Eurolines (www.eurolines.com) is the umbrella organisation of 32 European coach operators whose route network serves 500 destinations in 30 countries, including most major German cities. Its website has links to each company's site with detailed fare and route information, contact numbers and, in most cases, an online booking system. Children between the ages of four and 12 pay half price and there's a 10% discount for teens, students and seniors. In Germany, Eurolines is represented by **Deutsche Touring** (☎ 069-790 350; www.deutsche-touring.com).

Route	Price	Duration (hr)
Warsaw–Berlin	€45/74	11
Budapest–Frankfurt	€99/156	13-18
Lille–Dresden	€60/107	14-15 hrs
Parma–Munich	€60/107	13
Aarhus–Hanover	€63/115	13

If Germany is part of your European-wide itinerary, a **Eurolines Pass** (www.eurolines-pass.com) may be a ticket to savings. It offers unlimited travel between 40 cities within a 15- or 30-day day period. From mid-June to mid-September, the cost is €329/439 (15/30 days) for those over 26 and €279/359 for travellers over 26. Lower prices apply during the rest of the year; the website has full details. The pass is available online and from travel agents.

Berlin-based **BerlinLinienBus** (☎ 030-861 9331; www.berlinlinienbus.de) is a similar organisation with some 55 national and Europe-wide companies serving 350 destination all over the continent. There is some overlap between services provided by BerlinLinienBus and Eurolines.

A smaller company is **Gulliver's** (☎ 030-311 0211; www.gullivers.de), also based in Berlin. All companies offer discounts for students, and people under 26 and over 60.

BUSABOUT
Backpacker-geared **Busabout** (☎ in UK 020-7950 1661; www.busabout.com) is a hop-on, hop-off service that runs coaches along three interlocking European loops between May and October. Germany is part of the northern loop, which includes stops in Berlin, Dresden, Munich and Stuttgart. Loops can be combined. In Munich, for instance, the northern loop intersects with the southern loop to Italy. Trips on one loop cost £275, on two loops £450 and on three £575.

If you don't like travelling along predetermined routes, you can buy the Flexitrip Pass, which allows you to travel between cities across different loops. It costs £225 for the minimum six stops and £25 for each additional stop.

For other options or to buy a pass, check the website. Passes are also available from such travel agencies as STA Travel and Flight Centre.

In many cities, buses drop off and pick up at centrally located hostels.

Car & Motorcycle
When bringing your car to Germany, all you need is a valid driving licence, your car registration certificate and proof of insurance. Foreign cars must display a nationality sticker unless they have official Euro-plates (number plates that include their country's Euro symbol). You also need to carry a warning (hazard) triangle and first-aid kit.

There are no special requirements for crossing the border into Germany. Under the Schengen Agreement there are no longer any passport controls for cars coming from the Netherlands, Belgium, Luxembourg, Denmark and Austria. Controls do exist, if arriving from Poland, the Czech Republic and Switzerland, but these are a mere formality.

For road rules and other driving-related information see p763.

EUROTUNNEL
Coming from the UK, the fastest way to the continent is aboard the high-speed **Eurotunnel** (☎ in UK 08705-353 535, in Germany 01805-000 248;

www.eurotunnel.com). These shuttle trains whisk cars, motorbikes, bicycles and coaches from Folkestone in England through the Channel Tunnel to Coquelles (near Calais, in France) in about 35 minutes. From there, you can be in Germany in about three hours.

Shuttles run daily around the clock with up to three departures hourly during peak periods. Fares are calculated per vehicle, including passengers, and depend on such factors as time of day, season and length of stay. Expect to pay between £70 and £145 for a standard one-way ticket. The website and travel agents have full details.

For details about bringing your car across the Channel by ferry, see p761.

Hitching & Ride Services

Lonely Planet does not recommend hitching, but travellers intending to hitch shouldn't have too many problems getting to and from Germany via the main autobahns and highways. See p767 for a discussion of the potential risks.

Aside from hitching, the cheapest way to get to, away from or around Germany is as a paying passenger in a private car. In Germany, such rides are arranged by *Mitfahrzentralen* (ride-share agencies) found in many cities (see destination chapters). Most belong to umbrella networks like **ADM** (☎ 194 40; www.mitfahrzentralen.de) or **Citynetz** (☎ 01805-194 444; www.citynetz-mitfahrzentrale.de).

Fares comprise a fee to the agency and a per-kilometre charge to the driver. Expect to pay about €16 (one way) going from Hamburg to Berlin, €33 from Berlin to Amsterdam and €15 from Prague to Berlin.

Another way to find rides is by consulting online bulletin boards such as www.hitchhikers .de, www.mitfahrgelegenheit.de and www .mitfahrzentrale.de (all in German). Prices may be even lower, but you will have to get in touch with the driver yourself.

Train

Long-distance trains connecting major German cities with those in other countries are called EuroCity (EC) trains. Seat reservations are highly recommended, especially during the peak summer season and around major holidays (p746).

For overnight travel on a *Nachtzug* (night train, NZ), you can choose between *Schlafwagen* (sleepers), which are comfortable com-partments for up to three people; *Liegewagen* (couchettes), which sleep four to six people; and *Sitzwagen* (seat carriage), which have roomy reclining seats. If you have a rail pass, you only pay a supplement for either. Women can ask for a berth in a single-sex couchette when booking, but book early. For full details, contact Deutsche Bahn's (DB) **night train specialists** (☎ in Germany 01805-141 514; www.nachtzugreise.de).

EURAIL PASS

Eurailpasses (www.eurail.com) are convenient and good value if you're covering lots of territory in a limited time. They're valid for unlimited travel on national railways (and some private lines) in 18 European countries and also cover many ferries, eg from Finland to Germany, as well as KD Line's river cruises on the Rhine and Moselle. Available only to nonresidents of Europe, they should be bought before leaving your home country, although a limited number of outlets, listed on their website, also sell them in Europe.

The standard Eurailpass provides unlimited 1st-class travel and costs US$605/785 for 15/21 days and US$975/1378/1703 for one/two/three months of travel. If you're under 26, you qualify for the Eurailpass Youth and prices drop to US$394/510/634/896/1108.

A variety of other options, such as group passes and flexi passes, are available as well. Children under age four travel free; those between ages four and 11 pay half price.

In the US, Canada and the UK, an excellent resource for all sorts of rail passes and regular train tickets is **Rail Europe** (www.raileurope .com), a major agency specialising in train travel around Europe. In Australia, passes are sold by Flight Centre (www.flightcentre .com.au); in New Zealand try www.railplus .com.au.

EUROSTAR

Linking the UK with continental Europe, the **Eurostar** (www.eurostar.com) needs only two hours and 20 minutes to travel from London to Brussels, where you can change to regular or other high-speed trains, such as the French Thalys or the ICE (InterCity Express) train, to destinations in Germany.

Eurostar fares depend on such factors as class, time of day and season. Children, rail-pass holders and those aged between 12 and 25 and over 60 qualify for discounts. For the latest fare information, including promotions and special packages, check the website or contact Rail Europe (p759).

INTERRAIL & EURODOMINO PASSES

If you've been a permanent resident of a European country, Russia, Morocco or Turkey for at least six months, you qualify for the InterRail Pass. It divides Europe into eight zones (Germany shares one with Denmark, Austria and Switzerland) and is available for 16 days of travel in one zone (under/over 26 years €195/286), for 22 days of travel in two zones (€275/396) and for one month of travel in all zones (€385/546).

The EuroDomino Pass is good for three to eight days of travel within one of 27 European countries. For anyone aged over 26, the three-day pass costs €269 in 1st class and €189 in 2nd, with extra days costing €30/20. If you're under 26, the fare drops to €139 for three days and €15 for additional days, but only in 2nd class. People over 60 pay €229/159 in 1st/2nd class and €15/25 per each add-on day.

Both passes are sold at travel agents and train stations throughout Europe and online at www.bahn.de.

LAKE

The Romanshorn-Friedrichshafen car ferry provides the quickest way across Lake Constance between Switzerland and Germany. It's operated year-round by **Schweizerische Bodensee-Schiffahrtsgesellschaft** (☎ in Switzerland 071-466 7888; www.sbsag.ch), takes 40 minutes and costs €6.60 per person. Bicycles are €4.20, cars start at €25.50.

SEA

Germany's main ferry ports are Kiel, Lübeck and Travemünde in Schleswig-Holstein, and Rostock and Sassnitz (on Rügen Island) in Mecklenburg-Western Pomerania. All have services to Scandinavia and the Baltic states. Return tickets are often cheaper than two one-way tickets. Prices fluctuate dramatically according to the season, the day and time of departure and, for overnight ferries, cabin amenities. All prices quoted are for one-way fares. Car prices are for a standard passenger vehicle up to 6m in length and include all passengers. Also see the individual port towns' Getting There & Away sections in the destination chapters.

Denmark

GEDSER–ROSTOCK

Scandlines (☎ 01805-116 688; www.scandlines.de) runs year-round ferries every two hours to/from Gedser, about 100km south of Copenhagen. The 1¾-hour trip costs €100 per car in high season. Walk-on passengers pay €10/5 per adult/child. It's €13 for a bike and you.

RØDBY–PUTTGARDEN

Scandlines (☎ 01805-116 688; www.scandlines.de) operates a 45-minute ferry every half-hour for €56 for a regular car. Foot passengers pay €7/4 per adult/child in peak season one way or same-day return. It's €11 if you bring a bicycle.

RØNNE–SASSNITZ

From March to October, **Scandlines** (☎ 01805-116 688; www.scandlines.de) operates daily ferries to/from this town on Bornholm Island. The trip takes 3¾ hours and costs from €81 per car, €21 per person (kids €10) and €27 with bike, all in peak season.

Finland

HELSINKI–TRAVEMÜNDE

Finnlines (☎ in Germany 0451-15070, in Finland 09-251 0200; www.finnlines.de) goes to Travemünde (near Lübeck) daily, year-round. On their new, faster boats the trip has been cut by 12 hours to 26 hours. Berths start at €134 and include food and some drinks. Bikes are €20, cars start at €100.

Latvia

RIGA–LÜBECK

DFDS Lisco (☎ 0431-2097 6420; www.dfdslisco.com) operates this epic 34-hour journey twice weekly with berths starting at €91 and cars costing from €89; bikes are a flat €6.

VENTSPILS–ROSTOCK

Scandlines (☎ 01805-116 688; www.scandlines.de) offers this fairly new service, which costs from €80 per car and €85 per cabin berth in peak season. Bikes are €10. Kids pay half price. Ferries run daily and make the journey in 27 hours.

Lithuania

KLAIPEDA–KIEL

DFDS Lisco (☎ 0431-2097 6420; www.dfdslisco.com) makes daily 22-hour runs on this route. Passengers pay from €87 for a berth in a four-person cabin in peak season. Bikes are a flat €6, cars from €91.

KLAIPEDA–SASSNITZ

DFDS Lisco (☎ 0431-2097 6420; www.dfdslisco.com) also operates ferries on this route twice weekly in either direction. Costs start at €81 per berth in peak season, plus €61 for a regular car and €6 per bike.

Norway
OSLO–KIEL

Color Line (☎ 0431-730 0300; www.colorline.de) makes this 20-hour journey almost daily. The fare, including a berth in the most basic two-bed cabin, is around €200, including car. Children, seniors and students pay half-price on select departures.

Sweden
GOTHENBURG–KIEL

The daily overnight ferry that's run by **Stena Line** (☎ 0431-9099; www.stenaline.com) takes 13½ hours and costs €50 for foot passengers (only €25 for children, students and seniors). Taking your car will cost €165 in peak season, and single berths in four-bed cabins start from €21.

MALMÖ–TRAVEMÜNDE

Skan-Link (☎ in Germany 04502-805 20, in Sweden 040-176 800; www.nordoe-link.com) makes the trip in nine hours. Passenger fees are €25 for adults and €12.50 for children who are aged six to 12. Cars start at €100, while bicycles cost a mere €5.

TRELLEBORG–ROSTOCK

This **Scandlines** (☎ 01805-116 688; www.scandlines.de) service runs up to thrice daily, takes between 5¾ and 6½ hours and in peak season costs €140 per car and all passengers. Foot passengers pay €24 (kids €12) or €25 if you bring a bike.

TT-Line (☎ 040-360 1442; www.ttline.de) makes the same crossing in about 5½ hours. A car with passengers starts at €112. Adult walk-ons pay €30; children, seniors and students cost €15.

TRELLEBORG–SASSNITZ

Scandlines (☎ 01805-116 688; www.scandlines.de) operates a quick ferry to Sweden, popular with day-trippers. There are five departures daily and the trip takes 3¾ hours. Peak season fares are €115 for regular cars, €15/7.50 for adult/child foot passengers and €21 for you and a bike.

TRELLEBORG–TRAVEMÜNDE

TT-Line (☎ 040-360 1442; www.ttline.de) operates up to five ferries daily on this route, which takes seven hours and costs €30 for adult foot passengers and €15 for students, seniors and children. Cars, including all passengers, start at €112. Bicycles are €5.

Russia
ST PETERSBURG–LÜBECK

Finnlines (☎ 0451-150 7443; www.tre.de) operates the 60-hour TransRussiaExpress, via Sassnitz. It is essentially a cargo vessel offering passenger services, not a regular ferry. Fares start at €292 per adult, €146 per child; cars cost from €150.

UK

There are no longer any direct ferry services between Germany and the UK, but you can just as easily go via the Netherlands, Belgium or France and drive or train it from there. Check the ferries' websites for fare details.

TO FRANCE

P&O Ferries (☎ 0870-598 0333; www.poferries.com) Dover–Calais; 75 minutes.
SeaFrance (☎ 0870-443 1653; www.seafrance.com) Dover–Calais; 75 minutes.
Norfolk Lines (☎ 0870-870 1020; www.norfolklines-ferries.com) Dover–Dunkerque; two hours.

TO BELGIUM

P&O Ferries (☎ 0870-598 0333; www.poferries.com) Hull–Zeebrugge; 13½ hours.
Superfast Ferries (☎ 0870-234 2222; www.superfast.com) Rosyth (Edinburgh)–Zeebrugge; 17½ hours.

TO THE NETHERLANDS

P&O Ferries (☎ 0870-598 0333; www.poferries.com) Hull–Rotterdam; 14 hours.
Stena Line (☎ 0870-570 7070; www.stenaline.co.uk) Harwich–Hoek van Holland; 3¾ hours.
DFDS Seaways (☎ 0870-252 0524; www.dfds.co.uk) Newcastle–Amsterdam; 15 hours.

GETTING AROUND

Germans are whizzes at moving people around, and the public transport network is among the best in Europe. The two best ways of getting around the country are by car and by train. Regional bus services fill the gaps in areas not well served by the rail network.

TRANSPORT

AIR

Most large and many smaller German cities have their own airports (also see p754) and numerous carriers operate domestic flights within Germany. Lufthansa, of course, has the most dense route network. Other airlines offering domestic flights include Air Berlin, Cirrus Air and Germanwings.

Unless you're flying from one end of the country to the other, say Berlin to Munich or Hamburg to Munich, planes are only marginally quicker than trains if you factor in the time it takes to get to and from the airports. Even the big carriers often have some very attractive fares, finally making domestic air travel a viable option.

BICYCLE

Bicycling is allowed on all roads and highways but not on the autobahns. Cyclists must follow the same rules of the road as vehicles. Helmets are not compulsory, not even for children.

Hire & Purchase

Most towns and cities have some sort of bicycle-hire station, which is often at or near the train station. Hire costs range from €9 to €25 per day and €35 to €85 per week, depending on the model of bicycle you hire. A minimum deposit of €30 (more for fancier bikes) and/or ID are required. Many agencies are listed in the Getting Around sections of the destination chapters in this book. Some outfits also offer repair service or bicycle storage facilities.

Hotels, especially in resort areas, sometimes keep a stable of bicycles for their guests, often at no charge.

If you plan to spend several weeks or longer in the saddle, buying a second-hand bike may work out cheaper than renting one and easier than bringing your own. You may get a cheap, basic two-wheeler for around €60, although for good reconditioned models you'll probably have to shell out at least €200. The hire stations sometimes sell used bicycles or may be able to steer you to a good place locally. Flea markets are another source as are the classified sections of daily newspapers and listings magazines. Notice boards at universities, hostels or supermarkets may also yield some leads. A useful website for secondhand purchases is www.zweitehand .de, although it's in German only.

Transportation

Bicycles may be taken on most trains but require purchasing a separate ticket *(Fahrradkarte)*. These cost €8 on long-distance trains (IC and EC, reservations required) and €3.50 on regional trains (IRE, RB, RE and S-Bahn; see p768 for train types). Bicycles are not allowed on high-speed ICE trains. If bought in combination with one of the saver tickets, such as Länderticket or the Schönes-Wochenende-Ticket (see p770) the €3.50 fee is good for all trips you take while the ticket is valid. There is no charge at all on some trains. For full details, enquire at a local station or call the **DB Radfahrer-Hotline** (bicycle hotline; ☎ 01805-151 415). Free lines are also listed in DB's complimentary *Bahn & Bike* brochure (in German), as are the almost 50 stations where you can rent bikes. It's also available for downloading from www.bahn.de.

Many regional companies use buses with special bike racks. Bicycles are also allowed on practically all boat and ferry services on Germany's lakes and rivers. See p758 for taking bikes on the Europabus.

For additional information on cycling in Germany, see p738.

BOAT

With two seas and a lake- and river-filled interior, don't be surprised to find yourself in a boat at some point or other. For basic transport, boats are primarily used when travelling to or between the East Frisian Islands in Lower Saxony; the North Frisian Islands in Schleswig-Holstein; Helgoland, which also belongs to Schleswig-Holstein; and the islands of Poel, Rügen and Hiddensee in Mecklenburg-Western Pomerania. Scheduled boat services operate along sections of the Rhine, the Elbe and the Danube. There are also ferry services in areas with no or only a few bridges as well as on major lakes such as the Chiemsee and Lake Starnberg in Bavaria and Lake Constance in Baden-Württemberg.

From around April to October, local operators run scenic river or lake cruises lasting from one hour to a full day. For details, see the individual entries in the destination chapters.

BUS

Basically, wherever there is a train, take it. Buses are generally much slower and less dependable, but in some rural areas they may be your only option for getting around without your own vehicle. This is especially true of the Harz Mountains, sections of the Bavarian Forest and the Alpine foothills. Separate bus companies operate in the different regions, each with their own tariffs and schedules. In this book we only list bus services if they're a viable and sensible option.

The frequency of service varies from 'rarely' to 'constantly'. Commuter-geared routes offer limited or no service in the evenings and at weekends. If you depend on buses to get around, always keep this in mind or risk finding yourself stuck in a remote place on a Saturday night.

In cities, buses generally converge at the central bus station (*Busbahnhof* or *Zentraler Omnibus Bahnhof/ZOB*), which is often close or adjacent to the Hauptbahnhof (central train station). Tickets are sold by the bus companies, which often have offices or kiosks at the bus station, or by the driver on board. Special fare deals, such as day passes, weekly passes or special tourist tickets, are quite common, so make it a habit to ask about them.

Berlin Linien Bus

An umbrella for several German bus operators, **Berlin Linien Bus** (☎ 030-861 9331; www .berlinlinienbus.de) has 30 national bus routes connecting Berlin with all corners of Germany. Destinations include major cities, such as Munich, Düsseldorf and Frankfurt, and holiday regions such as the Harz and the Bavarian Forest. One of the most popular routes is the express bus to Hamburg, which makes the journey from Berlin in 3¼ hours up to eight times daily (€24/39 one-way/return).

Tickets are available online and from travel agencies. Children under four travel for free and discounts are available for older children, students, those over 60 and groups of six or more. Full one-way/return fares include €33/52 for Berlin to Göttingen, €37/55 for Hamburg to Hamelin and €30/50 for Coburg to Leipzig .

Deutsche Touring

A subsidiary of Deutsche Bahn, **Deutsche Touring** (☎ 069-790 350; www.deutsche-touring.com), runs Europabus coach services geared towards individual travellers on three routes within Germany:

Romantische Strasse (Romantic Road) The most popular route operates between Würzburg and Füssen from April to October. There are links to Würzburg from Frankfurt and

to Füssen from Munich. Sample fares: Frankfurt–Munich €99/138 one-way/return; Würzburg–Füssen €59/82; Rothenburg ob der Tauer–Füssen €46/64.

Burgenstrasse (Castle Road) Dozens of castles and palaces line this route from Mannheim to Nuremberg via Heidelberg, Rothenburg ob der Tauer and Ansbach; buses run from May to September. Sample fares: Mannheim–Nuremberg €48/66 one way/return; Rothenburg–Heidelberg €32/45.

Strassbourg-Reutlingen Year-round service from Strassbourg, France to Reutlingen via the Black Forest and such towns as Freudenstadt and Tübingen. Sample fares: Reutlingen–Strassbourg €25.50 each way, Freudenstadt–Strassbourg €13.

There's one coach in either direction daily. You can break the journey as often as you'd like, but plan your stops carefully as you'll have to wait a full day for the next bus to come around (reserve a seat before disembarking). The Romantic Road and the Castle Road both stop in Rothenburg, where you can switch from one line to the other.

Tickets can be purchased by phone or online and are available either for the entire distance or for segments between any of the stops. Eurail and German Rail pass holders get a 60% discount; people under 26 or over 60 qualify for 10% off, while children ages four to 12 pay half-price.

Bicycles may be transported with three days' advance notice. The fee ranges from €3 to €15, depending on the distance travelled.

CAR & MOTORCYCLE

German roads are excellent and motoring around the country can be a lot of fun. The country's pride and joy is its 11,000km of autobahn (motorway, freeway), which is supplemented by an extensive network of *Bundesstrassen* (secondary 'B' roads, highways) and smaller *Landstrassen* (country roads). No tolls are charged on any public roads.

Along each autobahn, you'll find there are elaborate service areas with petrol stations, toilet facilities and restaurants every 40km to 60km; many are open 24 hours. In between are rest stops *(Rastplatz)*, which usually have picnic tables and toilet facilities. Emergency call boxes are spaced about 2km apart. Simply lift the metal flap and follow the (pictorial) instructions.

Seat belts are mandatory for all passengers and there's a €30 fine if you get caught not wearing one. If you're in an accident, not wearing a seatbelt may invalidate your

TRANSPORT

GERMAN AUTOBAHNS

insurance. Children need a child seat if under four years old and a seat cushion if under 12; they may not ride in the front until age 13. Motorcyclists must wear a helmet. The use of hand-held mobile phones while driving is very much *verboten* (forbidden).

Parking in city centres is usually limited to lots and garages charging between €0.50 and €2 per hour. Many cities have electronic parking guidance systems directing you to the nearest garage and indicating the number of available spaces. Street parking usually works on the pay-and-display system and tends to be short-term (one or two hours) only. For long-term and overnight parking, consider leaving your car outside the centre

---

TRAFFIC JAMS

The severity of German traffic jams *(Staus)* seems to be something of a national obsession. Traffic jams are a subject of intense interest to motorists in Germany and are the focus of typical German thoroughness; you can actually get an annual *'Staukalender'* (traffic jam calendar) from motoring organisation ADAC (below).

Some breakfast shows on TV present the worst-afflicted sections every day, and German radio stations broadcast a special tone that interrupts cassette and CD players during traffic reports. Ask the rental agent to disable it unless you want your music peppered with poetic phrases like, *'Die Autobahn von Frankfurt nach Stuttgart ist…'*

Normal *Staus,* however, are nothing when compared with the astounding *Stau aus dem Nichts* (literally, the traffic jam from nowhere). You can be sailing along at 180km/h and suddenly find yourself screeching to a halt and taking the next 8km, 10km or even 30km at a crawl. Most frustrating is that in the vast majority of cases, you'll end up speeding back up again and never see what it was that caused the back-up in the first place. These types of *Staus* are so prevalent that the government actually funded a study of the phenomenon!

---

in a Park & Ride (P+R) lot, which are free or low-cost.

Automobile Associations

Germany's main motoring organisation, the **Allgemeiner Deutscher Automobil-Club** (ADAC; ☎ for roadside assistance 0180-222 2222; www.adac.de) has offices in all major cities and many smaller ones. Its excellent roadside assistance programme is also available to members of its affiliates, including British AA, American AAA and Canadian CAA.

Driving Licence

Drivers need a valid driving licence. International Driving Permits (IDP) are not compulsory but having one may help Germans make sense of your home licence (always carry that one too) and may simplify the car or motorcycle rental process. IDPs are inexpensive, valid for one year and issued by your local automobile association – bring a passport photo and your home licence.

Fuel & Spare Parts

Petrol stations, nearly all of which are self-service, are generally ubiquitous except in sparsely populated rural areas. Petrol is sold in litres. In September 2006, the average cost for mid-grade fuel was around €1.20 per litre.

Finding spare parts should not be a problem, especially in the cities, although availability, of course, depends on the age and model of your car. Be sure to have some sort of roadside emergency assistance plan (above) in case your car breaks down.

Hire

In order to hire your own wheels you'll need to be at least 25 years old, possess a valid driving licence and a major credit card. Some agencies rent to drivers between the ages of 21 and 24 for an additional charge. Those younger or not in possession of a credit card are often out of luck, although some local car-rental outfits may accept cash or a travellers cheque as a deposit. Taking your rental car into an Eastern European country, such as the Czech Republic or Poland, is often a no-no, so check in advance if that's where you're headed.

All major international car-rental companies maintain branches at airports and major train stations, and in towns. Contact the following central reservation numbers for the one nearest you:

Avis (☎ 01805-217 702; www.avis.com)
Budget (☎ 01805-244 388; www.budget.com)
Europcar (☎ 01805-8000; www.europcar.com)
Hertz (☎ 01805-938 814; www.hertz.com)

You could make a booking when calling the reservation agent, although it may be worth checking directly with the local branch for special promotions the agent may not know about. Smaller local agencies sometimes offer better prices, so it's worth checking into that as well.

As always, rates for car rentals vary considerably by model, pick-up date and location, but you should be able to get an economy-size vehicle from about €35 per day, plus insurance and taxes. Expect surcharges for rentals originating at airports and train stations,

TRANSPORT

additional drivers and one-way rentals. Child or infant safety seats may be rented for about €5 per day and should be reserved at the time of booking.

Prebooked and prepaid packages, arranged in your home country, usually work out much cheaper than on-the-spot-rentals. The same is true of fly/drive packages. Check for deals with the online travel agencies, travel agents or car-rental brokers such as the US company **Auto Europe** (☎ in US 888-223-5555, see website for numbers in other countries; www.autoeurope.com) or UK-based **Holiday Autos** (www.holidayautos.co.uk).

Insurance

German law requires that all registered vehicles carry third-party liability insurance. You could get seriously screwed by driving uninsured or underinsured. Germans are very fussy about their cars, and even nudging someone's bumper when jostling out of a tight parking space may well result in you having to pay for an entirely new one.

If you're hiring a vehicle, make sure your contract includes adequate liability insurance at the very minimum. Rental agencies almost never include insurance that covers damage to the vehicle itself, called Collision Damage Waiver (CDW) or Loss Damage Waiver (LDW). It's optional but driving without one is not recommended. Some credit-card companies cover CDW/LDW for a certain period if you charge the entire rental to your card. Always confirm with your card issuer what coverage it provides in Germany.

Road Rules

Driving is on the right-hand side of the road and standard international signs are in use. If you're unfamiliar with these, pick up a pamphlet at your local motoring organisation. Obey the road rules and speed limits carefully. Speed and red-light cameras are common and notices are sent to the car's registration address wherever that may be. If you're renting a car, the police will obtain your home address from the rental agency. There's a long list of finable actions, including using abusive language or gestures and running out of petrol on the autobahn.

The usual speed limits are 50km/h on city streets and 100km/h on highways, unless they

ROAD DISTANCES (KM)

	Bamberg	Berlin	Bonn	Bremen	Cologne	Dresden	Erfurt	Essen	Frankfurt-am-Main	Freiburg	Hamburg	Hanover	Koblenz	Leipzig	Mainz	Munich	Nuremberg	Rostock	Saarbrücken	Stuttgart
Berlin	395																			
Bonn	353	596																		
Bremen	471	376	335																	
Cologne	377	558	28	307																
Dresden	275	187	549	460	565															
Erfurt	147	277	335	332	351	216														
Essen	416	514	105	246	69	547	336													
Frankfurt-am-Main	196	507	177	407	347	451	238	396												
Freiburg	388	778	393	673	419	662	509	488	269											
Hamburg	502	282	476	115	413	453	354	356	482	750										
Hanover	354	273	314	115	288	357	213	243	327	593	150									
Koblenz	300	564	61	392	88	508	295	153	106	332	492	344								
Leipzig	240	160	591	354	472	109	123	438	359	627	354	250	415							
Mainz	226	542	142	437	166	487	273	228	39	261	512	357	80	394						
Munich	225	576	561	696	569	457	371	646	392	332	777	629	473	422	394					
Nuremberg	60	425	412	531	397	304	206	446	216	355	561	417	320	270	246	157				
Rostock	580	226	614	290	587	408	430	532	613	882	175	300	641	357	645	762	609			
Saarbrücken	359	688	215	552	243	633	419	312	182	267	657	503	165	540	146	423	349	792		
Stuttgart	222	613	318	591	345	492	350	410	183	167	650	495	258	457	180	228	182	780	212	
Würzburg	82	475	271	463	294	358	208	339	114	305	504	350	217	320	143	257	102	656	276	141

are otherwise marked. And yes, it's true, there really is no speed limit on autobahns. However, there are many stretches where slower speeds must be observed (eg near towns, road construction), so be sure to keep an eye out for those signs or risk getting ticketed.

The highest permissible blood-alcohol level for drivers is 0.05%, which for most people equates to one glass of wine or two small beers.

Pedestrians at crossings have absolute right of way over all motor vehicles. Always watch out for bicyclists when turning right; they have the right of way. Right turns at a red light are only legal if there's a green arrow pointing to the right.

Drivers unaccustomed to the high speeds on autobahns should be extra careful when passing another vehicle. It takes only seconds for a car in the rear-view mirror to close in at 200km/h. Pass as quickly as possible, then quickly return to the right lane. Try to ignore those annoying drivers who will flash their headlights or tailgate you to make you drive faster and get out of the way. It's an illegal practice anyway, as is passing on the right.

Note that some garages and parking lots close at night and charge an overnight fee.

HITCHING

Hitching (Trampen) is never entirely safe in any country and we don't recommend it. That said, in some rural areas in Germany poorly served by public transport – such as sections of the Alpine foothills and the Bavarian Forest – it is not uncommon to see people thumbing for a ride. If you do decide to hitch, understand that you are taking a small but potentially serious risk. Remember that it's safer to travel in pairs and be sure to let someone know where you are planning to go.

It's illegal to hitchhike on autobahns or their entry/exit ramps. You can save yourself a lot of trouble by arranging a lift through a Mitfahrzentrale (see p759).

LOCAL TRANSPORT

Most towns have efficient, frequent and punctual public transportation systems. Bigger cities, such as Berlin and Munich, have comprehensive transportation networks that integrate buses, trams, and U-Bahn (underground) and S-Bahn (suburban) trains.

Fares may be determined by zones or time travelled, or sometimes both. Multiticket

strips (Streifenkarte) or day passes (Tageskarte) generally offer better value than single-ride tickets. Sometimes tickets must be stamped upon boarding in order to be valid. Fines are levied if you're caught without a valid ticket. For details, see the Getting Around sections in the destination chapters.

Bicycle

From nuns to Lance Armstrong wannabes, Germans love to cycle, be it for errands, commuting, fitness or pleasure. Many cities have dedicated bicycle lanes, which must be used unless obstructed. There's no helmet law, not even for children, although using one is recommended, for obvious reasons. Bicycles must be equipped with a white light in the front, a red one in the back and yellow reflectors on the wheels and pedals. See p762 and p738 for more cycling information.

Bus & Tram

Buses are the most ubiquitous form of public transportation and practically all towns have their own comprehensive network. Buses run at regular intervals, with restricted service in the evenings and at weekends. Some cities operate night buses along the most popular routes to get night owls safely back home.

Occasionally, buses are supplemented by trams, which are usually faster because they travel on their own tracks, largely independent of other traffic. In city centres, they sometimes go underground. Bus and tram drivers normally sell single tickets and day passes only.

S-Bahn

Metropolitan areas such as Berlin and Munich have a system of suburban trains called the S-Bahn. They are faster and cover a wider area than buses or trams but tend to be less frequent. S-Bahn lines are often linked to the national rail network and sometimes interconnect urban centres. Rail passes are generally valid on these services. Specific S-Bahn lines are abbreviated with 'S' followed by the number (eg S1, S7) in the destination chapters.

Taxi

Taxis are expensive and, given the excellent public transport systems, not recommended unless you're in a real hurry. (They can actually be slower than trains or trams if you're

TRANSPORT

A PRIMER ON TRAIN TYPES

Here's a quick lowdown on the alphabet soup of trains operated by Deutsche Bahn (DB).

InterCity Express (ICE) Long-distance, space-age bullet trains that stop at major cities only; special tariffs apply and they're the most comfortable of the trains.

InterCity (IC) & EuroCity (EC) Long-distance trains that are slower than the ICE but still pretty fast; they stop at major cities only. EC trains go to major cities in neighbouring countries.

InterRegio (IRE) Slower medium-distance trains serving cities and linking local with long-distance trains.

Nachtzug (NZ) Night trains with sleeper cars and couchettes.

RegionalBahn (RB) Local trains, mostly in rural areas, with frequent stops, the slowest in the system.

Regional Express (RE) Local trains with limited stops that link rural areas with metropolitan centres and the S-Bahn.

StadtExpress (SE) Local trains primarily connecting cities and geared towards commuters.

S-Bahn Local trains operating within a city and its suburban area.

---

stuck in rush-hour traffic.) In most cities, it's not common to hail a taxi. Instead you either order one by phone or walk over to a taxi rank. The phone numbers of local taxi companies are often listed in the Getting Around sections of the destination chapters.

Taxis are metered and charged at a base rate plus a per-kilometre fee. These are fixed but vary from city to city. Some cabbies charge extra for bulky luggage or night-time rides.

U-Bahn

The fastest and most efficient travel in large German cities is by underground/subway train, known as the U-Bahn. Route maps are posted in all stations and at many stations you'll be able to pick up a printed copy from the stationmaster or ticket office. The frequency of trains usually fluctuates with demand, meaning there are more trains during commuter rush hours than, say, in the middle of the day. Buy tickets from vending machines and validate them before the start of your journey. Specific U-Bahn lines are abbreviated with 'U' followed by the number (eg U1, U7) in the destination chapters.

TRAIN

The German rail system is justifiably known as the most efficient in Europe. With 41,000km of tracks, the network is Europe's most extensive, serving over 7000 cities and towns. A wide range of services and ticket options is available.

Nearly all trains are operated by **Deutsche Bahn** (DB; ☎ reservations & information 118 61, free automated timetable information 0800-150 7090, www.bahn .de), although there are also some private lines

such as the LausitzBahn in Saxony and the Bayerische Oberlandbahn in Bavaria.

The DB website has an entire section in English (click on 'International Guests'), where you'll find detailed information about buying tickets, train types and services, timetables, route maps and lots of other useful pretrip planning nuggets.

Many train stations have a *Reisezentrum* (travel centre) where staff sell tickets and can help you plan an itinerary (ask for an English-speaking clerk). Smaller stations may only have a few ticket windows and the smallest ones aren't staffed at all. In this case, you must buy tickets from vending machines. These are also plentiful at staffed stations and convenient if you don't want to queue at a ticket counter. English instructions are normally provided. Both Reisezentrum agents and machines usually accept major credit cards.

Tickets sold on board (cash only) incur a service fee of €2 to €7 unless the station where you boarded was unstaffed or had a broken vending machine.

For trips over 50km, you can also buy tickets online up to 10 minutes before departure at no surcharge. You'll need a major credit card and a print-out of your ticket to present to the conductor.

Most train stations have coin-operated left-luggage lockers ranging in cost from €0.50 to €3 for each 24-hour period. Larger stations have staffed left-luggage offices (*Gepäckaufbewahrung*), but these are more expensive than lockers. If you leave your suitcase overnight, you're charged for two full days.

See p762 for details on taking your bicycle on the train.

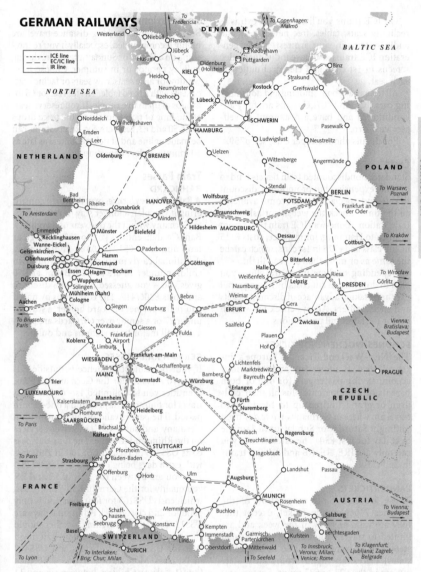

GERMAN RAILWAYS

ICE line
EC/IC line
IR line

Classes

German trains have 1st- and 2nd-class compartments, both of them modern and comfortable. Paying extra for 1st class is usually not worth it, except perhaps on busy travel days (eg Friday, Sunday afternoon and holidays) when 2nd-class cars can get very crowded.

In both 1st and 2nd classes, the seating is either in compartments of up to six people or in open-plan carriages that have panoramic windows. First class generally buys wider seats, a bit more leg-room and – on ICE, IC (InterCity) and EC (EuroCity) trains – drinks and snack service that's brought to you in your seat.

TRANSPORT

On ICE trains you'll enjoy such extras as reclining seats, tables, free newspapers and audio-systems in your armrest. Newer generation ICE trains also have individual video screens in 1st class and electrical outlets at each seat.

All trains have both smoking and nonsmoking cars. ICE and IC/EC trains are fully air-conditioned and have a restaurant or self-service bistro.

For details about sleeper cars, see p759.

Costs

Standard, nondiscounted train tickets tend to be quite expensive, but promotions, discount tickets and special offers become available all the time. Check the website or ask at the train station. A one-way ICE train ticket from Munich to Hamburg, for instance, costs €115 in 2nd class and €175 in 1st class, which can be the same as or more than a cheap flight.

Depending on how much travelling you plan to do, you can cut costs by buying a rail pass or by taking advantage of discount tickets and special offers. Always check www.bahn .de for the latest rail promotions.

SCHÖNES-WOCHENENDE-TICKET

The 'Nice-Weekend-Ticket' is Europe's finest rail deal. It allows you and up to four accompanying passengers (or one or both parents or grandparents plus all their children or grandchildren up to 14 years) to travel anywhere in Germany on *one day* from midnight Saturday or Sunday until 3am the next day for just €30. The catch is that you can only use IRE, RE, RB and S-Bahn trains in 2nd class.

LÄNDERTICKETS

These are essentially a variation of the Schönes-Wochenende-Ticket, except that they are valid any day of the week and are limited to travel within one of the German states (or, in some cases, also in bordering states). Prices vary slightly from state to state but are in the €22 to €27 range. Some states also offer cheaper tickets for solo travellers costing between €17 and €21. Night passes, valid from 7pm until 6am the following day, are available in Berlin-Brandenburg and in Munich. See the destinations for details about specific passes.

Reservations

Seat reservations for long-distance travel are highly recommended, especially if you're travelling on a Friday or Sunday afternoon, during holiday periods or in summer. Choose from window or aisle seats, row seats or facing seats or seats with a fixed table. The fee is €3 or €6 for groups of up to five people. If you reserve seats at the time of ticket purchase, the price drops to €1.50 and €3, respectively. Reservations can be made online and at ticket counters as late as 10 minutes before departure.

Train Passes

BAHNCARD

A **Bahncard** (www.bahn.de) may be worth considering if you plan a longer stay or return trips to Germany within the one year of its validity. BahnCard 25 entitles you to 25% off regular fares and costs €51.50/103 in 2nd/1st class. Additional cards for partners and your own children under 18 are just €5. BahnCard 50 gives you – you guessed it – a 50% discount and costs €206/412. The cost drops by half if you're the partner of a card holder, a student under 27 or a senior over 60. Cards are available at all major train stations and online.

GERMAN RAIL PASSES

If your permanent residence is outside Europe, you qualify for the German Rail Pass. It entitles you to unlimited 1st- or 2nd-class travel for four to 10 days within a one-month period. The pass is valid on all trains within Germany and some KD Line river services on the Rhine and Moselle. The four-day pass costs US$263 in 1st and US$200 in 2nd class with extra days being charged at US$38/25.

If you are between the ages of 12 and 25, you qualify for the German Rail Youth Pass, which costs US$163 for four days and is only good for 2nd class travel. Additional days are US$13. Two adults travelling together should check over the four-day German Rail Twin Pass for US$300 in 2nd class and US$400 in 1st class. More days cost US$38/50 each (2nd/1st class). Children between six and 11 pay half-fare. Children under six travel free.

In the US and Canada, the main agency specialising in selling the German Rail and other passes, as well as regular DB train tickets, is **Rail Europe** (www.raileurope.com). If you live in another country, contact your travel agent.

Health

CONTENTS

BEFORE YOU GO

While Germany has excellent health care, prevention is the key to staying healthy while abroad. A little planning before departure, particularly for pre-existing illnesses, will save trouble later. Bring medications in their original, clearly labelled containers. A signed and dated letter from your physician describing your medical conditions and medications, including generic names, is also a good idea. If carrying syringes or needles, be sure to have a physician's letter documenting their medical necessity. Carry a spare pair of contact lenses and glasses, and take your optical prescription with you.

INSURANCE

If you're an EU citizen, an E111 form, available from health centres or, in the UK, post offices, covers you for most medical care. E111 will not cover you for nonemergencies, or emergency repatriation home. Citizens from other countries should find out if there is a reciprocal arrangement for free medical care between their country and Germany. If you do need health insurance, make sure you get a policy that covers you for the worst possible case, such as an accident requiring an emergency flight home. Find out in advance if your insurance plan will make payments directly to providers or reimburse you later for overseas health expenditures.

RECOMMENDED VACCINATIONS

No jabs are required to travel to Germany. The World Health Organization (WHO), however, recommends that all travellers should be covered for diphtheria, tetanus, measles, mumps, rubella and polio, regardless of their destination.

IN TRANSIT

DEEP VEIN THROMBOSIS (DVT)

Blood clots may form in the legs during plane flights, chiefly because of prolonged immobility. The longer the flight, the greater the risk. The chief symptom of DVT is swelling or pain of the foot, ankle or calf, usually but not always on just one side. When a blood clot travels to the lungs, it may cause chest pain and difficulty breathing. Travellers with any of these symptoms should immediately seek medical attention.

To prevent the development of DVT on long flights you should walk about the cabin, contract the leg muscles while sitting, drink plenty of fluids and avoid alcohol and tobacco.

JET LAG & MOTION SICKNESS

To avoid jet lag (common when crossing more than five time zones) try drinking plenty of nonalchoholic fluids and eating light meals. Upon arrival, get exposure to natural sunlight and readjust your schedule (for meals, sleep etc) as soon as possible.

Antihistamines such as dimenhydrinate (Dramamine) and meclizine (Antivert, Bonine) are usually the first choice for treating motion sickness. A herbal alternative is ginger.

IN GERMANY

AVAILABILITY & COST OF HEALTH CARE

Excellent health care is readily available and for minor self-limiting illnesses pharmacists are able to give you valuable advice and sell over-the-counter medication. They can also advise when more specialised help is required and point you in the right direction.

TRAVELLERS' DIARRHOEA
If you develop diarrhoea, drink plenty of fluids, preferably in the form of an oral rehydration solution such as Dioralyte. If diarrhoea is bloody, persists for more than 72 hours or is accompanied by fever, shaking, chills or severe abdominal pain, seek medical attention.

ENVIRONMENTAL HAZARDS
Heat Illness
Heat exhaustion occurs following excessive fluid loss with inadequate replacement of fluids and salt. Symptoms include headache, dizziness and tiredness. Dehydration is already happening by the time you feel thirsty – aim to drink sufficient water to produce pale, diluted urine. To treat heat exhaustion drink water and/or fruit juice, and cool the body with cold water and fans.

Cold Illness
Hypothermia occurs when the body loses heat faster than it can produce it. As ever,

proper preparation will reduce the risks of getting it. Even on a hot day in the mountains, the weather can change rapidly, so always carry waterproof garments, warm layers and a hat and inform others of your route.

Hypothermia starts with shivering, loss of judgment and clumsiness. Unless rewarming occurs, the sufferer deteriorates into apathy, confusion and coma. Prevent further heat loss by seeking shelter, warm dry clothing, hot sweet drinks and shared bodily warmth.

SEXUAL HEALTH
Emergency contraception is available with a doctor's prescription in Germany. It is most effective if taken within 24 hours after unprotected sex. Condoms are readily available throughout Germany.

TRAVELLING WITH CHILDREN
Make sure the children are up to date with routine vaccinations, and discuss possible travel vaccines well before departure as some vaccines are not suitable for children under aged under one year.

MEDICAL CHECKLIST

All of the following are readily available in Germany. If you are hiking out of town, these items may come in handy.

- antibiotics
- antidiarrheal drugs (eg loperamide)
- acetaminophen (Tylenol) or aspirin
- anti-inflammatory drugs (eg ibuprofen)
- antihistamines (for hay fever and allergic reactions)
- antibacterial ointment (eg Bactroban; for cuts and abrasions)
- steroid cream or cortisone (for poison ivy and other allergic rashes)
- bandages, gauze, gauze rolls
- adhesive or paper tape
- scissors, safety pins, tweezers
- thermometer
- pocketknife
- DEET-containing insect repellent for the skin
- pyrethrin-containing insect spray for clothing, tents and bed nets
- sun block
- oral rehydration salts
- acetazolamide (Diamox; for altitude sickness)

If your child has vomiting or diarrhoea, lost fluid and salts must be replaced. It may be helpful to take rehydration powders with boiled water.

WOMEN'S HEALTH

Emotional stress, exhaustion and travelling through different time zones can all contribute to an upset in a woman's menstrual pattern.

If using oral contraceptives, remember some antibiotics, diarrhoea and vomiting can stop the pill from working. Time zones, gastrointestinal upsets and antibiotics do not affect injectable contraception.

Travelling during pregnancy is usually possible but always consult your doctor before planning your trip. The most risky times for travel are during the first 12 weeks of pregnancy and after 30 weeks.

Language

CONTENTS

German belongs to the Indo-European language group and is spoken by over 100 million people in countries throughout the world, including Austria and part of Switzerland. There are also ethnic-German communities in neighbouring Eastern European countries such as Poland and the Czech Republic, although expulsions after 1945 reduced their number dramatically.

High German used today comes from a regional Saxon dialect. It developed into an official bureaucratic language and was used by Luther in his translation of the Bible, gradually spreading throughout Germany. The impetus Luther gave to the written language through his translations was followed by the establishment of language societies in the 17th century, and later by the 19th-century work of Jakob Grimm, the founder of modern German philology. With his brother, Wilhelm Grimm, he also began work on the first German dictionary.

Regional dialects still thrive throughout Germany, especially in Cologne, rural Bavaria, Swabia and parts of Saxony. The Sorb minority in eastern Germany has its own language. In northern Germany it is common to hear Plattdeutsch and Frisian spoken. Both are distant relatives of English, and the

fact that many German words survive in the English vocabulary today makes things a lot easier for native English speakers.

That's the good news. The bad news is that, unlike English, German has retained clear polite distinctions in gender and case. Though not as difficult as Russian, for instance, which has more cases, German does have its tricky moments. Germans are used to hearing foreigners – and a few notable indigenous sports personalities – make a hash of their grammar, and any attempt to speak the language is always well received.

All German school children learn a second language – usually English – which means most can speak it to a certain degree, and some, very well. You might have problems finding English speakers in eastern Germany, however, where Russian was the main foreign language taught in schools before the *Wende* (change).

The words and phrases included in this language guide should help you through the most common travel situations (see also p86 for food vocabulary). Those with the desire to delve further into the language should get a copy of Lonely Planet's *German Phrasebook*.

GRAMMAR

German grammar can be a nightmare for speakers of other languages. Nouns come in three genders: masculine, feminine and neutral. The corresponding forms of the definite article ('the' in English) are *der, die* and *das*, with the universal plural form, *die*. Nouns and articles will alter according to complex grammatical rules relating to the noun's function within a phrase – known as 'case'. In German there are four cases: nominative, accusative, dative and genitive. We haven't allowed for all possible permutations of case in this language guide – it really is language-course material and simply too complex to cover here. However, bad German is a whole lot better than no German at all, so even if you muddle your cases, you'll find that you'll still be understood – and your efforts will be warmly appreciated regardless.

If you've noticed that written German seems to be full of capital letters, the reason is that German nouns always begin with a capital letter.

PRONUNCIATION

It's not difficult to pronounce German because almost all sounds can be found in English. Follow the pronunciation guide and you'll have no trouble getting your message across.

Vowels

German Example	Pronunciation Guide
hat	**a** (eg the 'u' in 'run')
habe	**aa** (eg 'father')
mein	**ai** (eg 'aisle')
Bär	**air** (eg 'hair', with no 'r' sound)
Boot	**aw** (eg 'saw')
leben	**ay** (eg 'say')
Bett/Männer/kaufen	**e** (eg 'bed')
fliegen	**ee** (eg 'thief')
schön	**eu** (eg 'her', with no 'r' sound)
mit	**i** (eg 'bit')
Koffer	**o** (eg 'pot')
Leute/Häuser	**oy** (eg 'toy')
Schuhe	**oo** (eg 'moon')
Haus	**ow** (eg 'how')
zurück	**ew** ('ee' said with rounded lips)
unter	**u** (eg 'put')

Consonants

The only two tricky consonant sounds in German are **ch** and **r**. All other consonants are pronounced much the same as their English counterparts (except **sch**, which is always as the 'sh' in 'shoe').

The **ch** sound is generally like the 'ch' in *Bach* or Scottish *loch* – like a hiss from the back of the throat. When **ch** occurs after the vowels **e** and **i** it's more like a 'sh' sound, produced with the tongue more forward in the mouth. In this book we've simplified things by using the one symbol **kh** for both sounds.

The **r** sound is different from English, and it isn't rolled like in Italian or Spanish. It's pronounced at the back of the throat, almost like saying a 'g' sound, but with some friction – it's a bit like gargling.

Word Stress

As a general rule, word stress in German mostly falls on the first syllable. To remove any doubt, the stressed syllable is shown in italics in the pronunciation guides for the following words and phrases.

ACCOMMODATION

Where's a ...?
Wo ist ...?   vaw ist ...

bed and breakfast
eine Pension   ai·ne paang·*zyawn*

camping ground
ein Campingplatz   ain *kem*·ping·plats

guesthouse
eine Pension   ai·ne paang·*zyawn*

hotel
ein Hotel   ain ho·*tel*

inn
ein Gasthof   ain *gast*·hawf

room in a private home
ein Privatzimmer   ain pri·*vaat*·tsi·mer

youth hostel
eine Jugendherberge   ai·ne yoo·gent·her·ber·ge

What's the address?
Wie ist die Adresse?
vee ist dee a·*dre*·se

I'd like to book a room, please.
Ich möchte bitte ein Zimmer reservieren.
ikh *meukh*·te *bi*·te ain *tsi*·mer re·zer·*vee*·ren

For (three) nights/weeks.
Für (drei) Nächte/Wochen.
fewr (drai) *nekh*·te/vo·khen

Do you have a ... room?
Haben Sie ein ...?   *haa*·ben zee ain ...

single
Einzelzimmer   *ain*·tsel·tsi·mer

double
Doppelzimmer mit   *do*·pel·tsi·mer mit
einem Doppelbett   ai·nem *do*·pel·bet

twin
Doppelzimmer mit zwei   *do*·pel·tsi·mer mit tsvai
Einzelbetten   *ain*·tsel·be·ten

How much is it per ...?
Wie viel kostet es pro ...?   vee feel *kos*·tet es praw ...

night
Nacht   nakht

person
Person   per·*zawn*

May I see it?
Kann ich es sehen?   kan ikh es *zay*·en

Can I get another room?
Kann ich ein anderes   kan ikh ain *an*·de·res
Zimmer bekommen?   *tsi*·mer be·*ko*·men

LANGUAGE

MAKING A RESERVATION

(for phone and written requests)

To ...	An ...
From ...	Von ...
Date	Datum
I'd like to book ...	Ich möchte ... reservieren.
	(see the list under
	'Accommodation' for
	bed and room options)
in the name of ...	auf den Namen ...
from ... (date) to ...	Vom ... bis zum ...
credit card	Kreditkarte
number	Nummer
expiry date	gültig bis ... (valid until)
Please confirm	Bitte bestätigen Sie
availability and	Verfügbarkeit und Preis.
price.	

It's fine. I'll take it.
Es ist gut, ich nehme es. es ist goot ikh *nay*·me es
I'm leaving now.
Ich reise jetzt ab. ikh *rai*·ze yetst ap

CONVERSATION & ESSENTIALS

You should be aware that German uses polite and informal forms for 'you' (*Sie* and *du* respectively). When addressing people you don't know well you should always use the polite form (though younger people will be less inclined to expect it). In this language guide we use the polite form unless indicated by 'inf' (for 'informal') in brackets.

If you need to ask for assistance from a stranger, remember to always introduce your request with a simple *Entschuldigung* (Excuse me, ...).

Hello.	Guten Tag.	goo·ten taak
(in the south)	Grüss Gott.	grews got
Hi.	Hallo.	ha·lo/ha·law

Good ...	Guten ...	goo·ten ...
day	Tag	taak
morning	Morgen	mor·gen
afternoon	Tag	taak
evening	Abend	aa·bent

Goodbye.
Auf Wiedersehen. owf *vee*·der·zay·en
See you later.
Bis später. bis *shpay*·ter

Bye.
Tschüss./Tschau. chews/chow
How are you?
Wie geht es Ihnen? (pol) vee gayt es *ee*·nen
Wie geht es dir? (inf) vee gayt es deer
Fine. And you?
Danke, gut. *dang*·ke goot
... and you?
Und Ihnen? (pol) unt *ee*·nen
Und dir? (inf) unt deer
What's your name?
Wie ist Ihr Name? (pol) vee ist eer *naa*·me
Wie heisst du? (inf) vee haist doo
My name is ...
Mein Name ist .../ main *naa*·me ist .../
Ich heisse ... ikh *hai*·se ...
Yes.
Ja. yaa
No.
Nein. nain
Please.
Bitte. *bi*·te
Thank you (very much).
Danke./Vielen Dank. *dang*·ke/*fee*·len dangk
You're welcome.
Bitte (sehr). *bi*·te (zair)
Excuse me, ... (before asking for help or directions)
Entschuldigung ... ent·*shul*·di·gung ...
Sorry.
Entschuldigung. ent·*shul*·di·gung

DIRECTIONS

Could you help me, please?
Können Sie mir bitte helfen?
keu·nen zee meer *bi*·te *hel*·fen
Where's (a bank)?
Wo ist (eine Bank).?
vaw ist (*ai*·ne bangk)
I'm looking for (the cathedral).
Ich suche (den Dom).
ikh *zoo*·khe (dayn dawm)
Which way's (a public toilet)?
In welcher Richtung ist eine öffentliche toilette?
in *vel*·kher *rikh*·tung ist (*ai*·ne eu·fent·li·khe to·a·*le*·te)
How can I get there?
Wie kann ich da hinkommen?
vee kan ikh daa *hin*·ko·men
How far is it?
Wie weit ist es?
vee vait ist es
Can you show me (on the map)?
Können Sie es mir (auf der Karte) zeigen?
keu·nen zee es meer (owf dair *kar*·te) *tsai*·gen

EMERGENCIES

Help!
Hilfe!   *hil*·fe
It's an emergency!
Es ist ein Notfall! es ist ain *nawt*·fal
Call the police!
Rufen Sie die Polizei! *roo*·fen zee dee po·li·*tsai*
Call a doctor!
Rufen Sie einen Arzt! *roo*·fen zee *ai*·nen artst
Call an ambulance!
Rufen Sie einen   *roo*·fen zee *ai*·nen
Krankenwagen!   *krang*·ken·vaa·gen
Leave me alone!
Lassen Sie mich in Ruhe! *la*·sen zee mikh in *roo*·e
Go away!
Gehen Sie weg!   *gay*·en zee vek
I'm lost.
Ich habe mich verirrt. ikh *haa*·be mikh fer·*irt*
Where are the toilets?
Wo ist die Toilette? vaw ist dee to·a·*le*·te

left	*links*	lingks
right	*rechts*	rekhts
near	*nahe*	*naa*·e
far away	*weit weg*	vait vek
here	*hier*	heer
there	*dort*	dort
on the corner	*an der Ecke*	an dair *e*·ke
straight ahead	*geradeaus*	ge·raa·de·*ows*
opposite ...	*gegenüber ...*	gay·gen·*ew*·ber ...
next to ...	*neben ...*	*nay*·ben ...
behind ...	*hinter ...*	*hin*·ter ...
in front of ...	*vor ...*	fawr ...
north	*nord*	nord
south	*süd*	zewd
east	*ost*	ost
west	*west*	vest

SIGNS

Polizei	Police
Polizeiwache	Police Station
Eingang	Entrance
Ausgang	Exit
Offen	Open
Geschlossen	Closed
Kein Zutritt	No Entry
Rauchen Verboten	No Smoking
Verboten	Prohibited
Toiletten (WC)	Toilets
Herren	Men
Damen	Women

Turn ...
Biegen Sie ... ab.   *bee*·gen zee ... ap
  left/right
  links/rechts   lingks/rekhts
  at the next corner
  an der nächsten Ecke   an dair *naykhs*·ten *e*·ke
  at the traffic lights
  bei der Ampel   bai dair *am*·pel

HEALTH

Where's the nearest ...?
Wo ist der/die/das nächste ...? (m/f/n)   vaw ist dair/
die/das *naykhs*·te ...
  chemist
  Apotheke (f)   a·po·*tay*·ke
  dentist
  Zahnarzt (m)   *tsaan*·artst
  doctor
  Arzt (m)   artst
  hospital
  Krankenhaus (n)   *krang*·ken·hows

I need a doctor (who speaks English).
Ich brauche einen Arzt (der Englisch spricht).
ikh *brow*·khe *ai*·nen artst (dair *eng*·lish shprikht)
Is there a (night) chemist nearby?
Gibt es in der Nähe eine (Nacht)Apotheke?
gipt es in dair *nay*·e *ai*·ne (nakht·)a·po·*tay*·ke
I'm sick.
Ich bin krank.
ikh bin krangk
It hurts here.
Es tut hier weh.
es toot heer *vay*
I have diarrhoea/fever/headache.
Ich habe Durchfall/Fieber/Kopfschmerzen.
ikh *haa*·be *durkh*·fal/fee·ber/kopf·shmer·tsen
(I think) I'm pregnant.
(Ich glaube) Ich bin schwanger.
(ikh *glow*·be) ikh bin *shvang*·er

I'm allergic to ...
Ich bin allergisch gegen ...   ikh bin a·*lair*·gish *gay*·gen ...
  antibiotics
  Antibiotika   an·ti·bi·*aw*·ti·ka
  aspirin
  Aspirin   as·pi·*reen*
  penicillin
  Penizillin   pe·ni·tsi·*leen*

LANGUAGE DIFFICULTIES

Do you speak English?
Sprechen Sie Englisch?
shpre·khen zee *eng*·lish

LANGUAGE

Does anyone here speak English?
Spricht hier jemand Englisch?
shprikht heer *yay*·mant *eng*·lish
Do you understand (me)?
Verstehen Sie (mich)?
fer·*shtay*·en zee (mikh)
I (don't) understand.
Ich verstehe (nicht).
ikh fer·*shtay*·e (nikht)
How do you say ... in German?
Wie sagt man ... auf Deutsch?
vee zagt man ... owf doytsh

Could you please ...?
Könnten Sie...?   keun·ten zee ...
  speak more slowly
  bitte langsamer sprechen bi·te lang·za·mer shpre·khen
  repeat that
  das bitte wiederholen   das bi·te vee·der·haw·len
  write it down
  das bitte aufschreiben   das bi·te owf·shrai·ben

NUMBERS

1	eins	aints
2	zwei	tsvai
3	drei	drai
4	vier	feer
5	fünf	fewnf
6	sechs	zeks
7	sieben	zee·ben
8	acht	akht
9	neun	noyn
10	zehn	tsayn
11	elf	elf
12	zwölf	zveulf
13	dreizehn	drai·tsayn
14	vierzehn	feer·tsayn
15	fünfzehn	fewnf·tsayn
16	sechzehn	zeks·tsayn
17	siebzehn	zeep·tsayn
18	achtzehn	akh·tsayn
19	neunzehn	noyn·tsayn
20	zwanzig	tsvan·tsikh
21	einundzwanzig	ain·unt·tsvan·tsikh
22	zweiundzwanig	tsvai·unt·tsvan·tsikh
30	dreizig	drai·tsikh
31	einunddreizig	ain·und·drai·tsikh
40	vierzig	feer·tsikh
50	fünfzig	fewnf·tsikh
60	sechzig	zekh·tsikh
70	siebzig	zeep·tsikh
80	achtzig	akh·tsikh
90	neunzig	noyn·tsikh
100	hundert	hun·dert
1000	tausend	tow·sent
2000	zwei tausend	tsvai tow·sent

PAPERWORK

name	Name	naa·me
nationality	Staatsan·gehörigkeit	shtaats·an·ge·heu·rikh·kait
date of birth	Geburtsdatum	ge·burts·daa·tum
place of birth	Geburtsort	ge·burts·ort
sex/gender	Sex	seks
passport	(Reise)Pass	(rai·ze·)paas
visa	Visum	vee·zum

QUESTION WORDS

Who?	Wer?	vair
What?	Was?	vas
Where?	Wo?	vo
When?	Wann?	van
How?	Wie?	vee
Why?	Warum?	va·rum
Which?	Welcher?	vel·kher
How much?	Wie viel?	vee feel
How many?	Wie viele?	vee fee·le

SHOPPING & SERVICES
I'm looking for ...
Ich suche ...
ikh zoo·khe ...
Where's the (nearest) ...?
Wo ist der/die/das (nächste) ...? (m/f/n)
vaw ist dair/dee/das (naykhs·te) ...
Where can I buy ...?
Wo kann ich ... kaufen?
vaw kan ikh ... kow·fen
I'd like to buy ...
Ich möchte ... kaufen.
ikh meukh·te ... kow·fen
How much (is this)?
Wie viel (kostet das)?
vee feel (kos·tet das)
That's too much/expensive.
Das ist zu viel/teuer.
das ist tsoo feel/toy·er
Can you lower the price?
Können Sie mit dem Preis heruntergehen?
keu·nen zee mit dem prais he·run·ter·gay·en
Do you have something cheaper?
Haben Sie etwas Billigeres?
haa·ben zee et·vas bi·li·ge·res
I'm just looking.
Ich schaue mich nur um.
ikh show·e mikh noor um
Can you write down the price?
Können Sie den Preis aufschreiben?
keu·nen zee dayn prais owf·shrai·ben

Do you have any others?
Haben Sie noch andere?
haa·ben zee nokh an·de·re

Can I look at it?
Können Sie ihn/sie/es mir zeigen? (m/f/n)
keu·nen zee een/zee/es meer tsai·gen

more	*mehr*	mair
less	*weniger*	vay·ni·ger
smaller	*kleiner*	klai·ner·tee
bigger	*grosser*	gro·ser

Do you accept ...?
Nehmen Sie ...?   nay·men zee ...
credit cards
Kreditkarten   kre·deet·kar·ten
travellers cheques
Reiseschecks   rai·ze·sheks

I'd like to ...
Ich möchte ...   ikh meukh·te ...
change money (cash)
Geld umtauschen   gelt um·tow·shen
cash a cheque
einen Scheck einlösen   ai·nen shek ain·leu·zen
change some travellers cheques
Reiseschecks einlösen   rai·ze·sheks ain·leu·zen

an ATM	*ein Geldautomat*	ain gelt·ow·to·maat
an exchange	*eine Geldwechsel-*	ai·ne gelt·vek·sel·
office	*stube*	shtoo·be
a bank	*eine Bank*	ai·ne bangk
the ... embassy	*die ... Botschaft*	dee bot·shaft
the market	*der Markt*	dair markt
the police	*die Polizei*	dee po·li·tsai
the post office	*das Postamt*	das post·amt
a public phone	*ein öffentliches*	ain eu·fent·li·khes
	Telefon	te·le·fawn
a public toilet	*eine öffentliche*	ain eu·fent·li·khe
	Toilette	to·a·le·te

Where's the local internet café?
Wo ist hier ein Internet-Café?
vaw ist heer ain in·ter·net·ka·fay

I'd like to ...
Ich möchte ...   ikh meukh·te ...
get internet access
Internetzugang haben   in·ter·net·tsoo·gang haa·ben
check my email
meine E-Mails checken   mai·ne ee·mayls che·ken

What time does it open/close?
Wann macht er/sie/es auf/zu? (m/f/n)
van makht air/zee/es owf/tsoo

I want to buy a phonecard.
Ich möchte eine Telefonkarte kaufen.
ikh meukh·te ai·ne te·le·fawn·kar·te kow·fen

TIME & DATES
What time is it?
Wie spät ist es?   vee shpayt ist es
It's (one) o'clock.
Es ist (ein) Uhr.   es ist (ain) oor
Twenty past one.
Zwanzig nach eins.   tsvan·tsikh naakh ains
Half past one.
Halb zwei. ('half two')   halp tsvai
Quarter to one.
Viertel vor eins.   fir·tel fawr ains
am
morgens/vormittags   mor·gens/fawr·mi·taaks
pm
nachmittags/abends   naakh·mi·taaks/aa·bents

now	*jetzt*	yetst
today	*heute*	hoy·te
tonight	*heute Abend*	hoy·te aa·bent
tomorrow	*morgen*	mor·gen
morning	*Morgen*	mor·gen
afternoon	*Nachmittag*	naakh·mi·taak
evening	*Abend*	aa·bent

Monday	*Montag*	mawn·taak
Tuesday	*Dienstag*	deens·taak
Wednesday	*Mittwoch*	mit·vokh
Thursday	*Donnerstag*	do·ners·taak
Friday	*Freitag*	frai·taak
Saturday	*Samstag*	zams·taak
Sunday	*Sonntag*	zon·taak

January	*Januar*	yan·u·aar
February	*Februar*	fay·bru·aar
March	*März*	merts
April	*April*	a·pril
May	*Mai*	mai
June	*Juni*	yoo·ni
July	*Juli*	yoo·li
August	*August*	ow·gust
September	*September*	zep·tem·ber
October	*Oktober*	ok·taw·ber
November	*November*	no·vem·ber
December	*Dezember*	de·tsem·ber

TRANSPORT
Public Transport
metro
U-Bahn   oo·baan
(metro) station
(U-)Bahnhof   (oo·)baan·hawf

tram
Strassenbahn shtraa·sen·baan
tram stop
Strassenbahnhalte- shtraa·sen·baan·hal·te·
   stelle shte·le
urban railway
S-Bahn es·baan

What time does the ... leave?
Wann fährt ... ab? van fairt ... ap
  boat *das Boot* das bawt
  bus *der Bus* dair bus
  train *der Zug* dair tsook

What time's the ... bus?
Wann fährt der ... Bus? van fairt dair ... bus
  first *erste* ers·te
  last *letzte* lets·te
  next *nächste* naykhs·te

Where's the nearest metro station?
Wo ist der nächste U-Bahnhof?
vaw ist dair naykhs·te oo·baan·hawf
Which (bus) goes to ...?
Welcher Bus fährt nach ...?
vel·kher bus fairt nakh ...

A ... ticket to (Berlin).
Einen ... nach (Berlin). ai·nen ... naakh (ber·leen)
  one-way
  einfache Fahrkarte ain·fa·khe faar·kar·te
  return
  Rückfahrkarte rewk·faar·kar·te
  1st-class
  Fahrkarte erster Klasse faar·kar·te ers·ter kla·se
  2nd-class
  Fahrkarte zweiter Klasse faar·kar·te tsvai·ter kla·se

The ... is cancelled.
... ist gestrichen. ... ist ge·shtri·khen
The ... is delayed.
... hat Verspätung. ... hat fer·shpay·tung
Is this seat free?
Ist dieser Platz frei? ist dee·zer plats frai
Do I need to change trains?
Muss ich umsteigen? mus ikh um·shtai·gen
Are you free? (taxi)
Sind Sie frei? zint zee frai
How much is it to ...?
Was kostet es bis ...? vas kos·tet es bis ...
Please take me to (this address).
Bitte bringen Sie mich bi·te bring·en zee mikh
zu (dieser Adresse). tsoo (dee·zer a·dre·se)

ROAD SIGNS	
Gefahr	Danger
Einfahrt Verboten	No Entry
Einbahnstrasse	One-Way
Einfahrt	Entrance
Ausfahrt	Exit
Ausfahrt Freihalten	Keep Clear
Parkverbot	No Parking
Halteverbot	No Stopping
Mautstelle	Toll
Radweg	Cycle Path
Umleitung	Detour
Überholverbot	No Overtaking

Private Transport
Where can I hire a...?
Wo kann ich ... mieten? vaw kan ikh ... mee·ten
I'd like to hire a/an ...
Ich möchte ... mieten. ikh meukh·te ... mee·ten
  automatic
  ein Fahrzeug mit ain faar·tsoyk mit
   Automatik ow·to·maa·tik
  bicycle
  ein Fahrrad ain faar·raat
  car
  ein Auto ain ow·to
  4WD
  ein Allradfahrzeug ain al·raat·faar·tsoyk
  manual
  ein Fahrzeug mit ain faar·tsoyk mit
   Schaltung shal·tung
  motorbike
  ein Motorrad ain maw·tor·raat

How much is it per ...?
Wie viel kostet es pro ...? vee feel kos·tet es praw ...
  day
  Tag taak
  week
  Woche vo·khe

diesel
Diesel dee·zel
LPG
Autogas ow·to·gaas
petrol (gas)
Benzin ben·tseen

Where's a petrol station?
Wo ist eine Tankstelle?
vaw ist ai·ne tangk·shte·le
Does this road go to ...?
Führt diese Strasse nach ...?
fewrt dee·ze shtraa·se naakh ...

(How long) Can I park here?
(Wie lange) Kann ich hier parken?
(vee *lang*·e) kan ikh heer *par*·ken
Where do I pay?
Wo muss ich bezahlen?
vaw mus ikh be·*tsaa*·len
I need a mechanic.
Ich brauche einen Mechaniker.
ikh *brow*·khe *ai*·nen me·*khaa*·ni·ker
The car has broken down (at ...)
Ich habe (in ...) eine Panne mit meinem Auto.
ikh *haa*·be (in ...) *ai*·ne *pa*·ne mit *mai*·nem *ow*·to
I had an accident.
Ich hatte einen Unfall.
ikh *ha*·te *ai*·nen *un*·fal
The car/motorbike won't start.
Das Auto/Motorrad springt nicht an.
das *ow*·to/*maw*·tor·raat shpringkt nikht an
I have a flat tyre.
Ich habe eine Reifenpanne.
ikh *haa*·be *ai*·ne *rai*·fen·pa·ne
I've run out of petrol.
Ich habe kein Benzin mehr.
ikh *haa*·be kain ben·*tseen* mair

TRAVEL WITH CHILDREN
I need a ...
Ich brauche ...   ikh *brow*·khe ...

Is there a/an ...?
Gibt es ...?   gipt es ...
  baby change room
  einen Wickelraum   *ai*·nen *vi*·kel·rowm
  baby seat
  einen Babysitz   *ai*·nen *bay*·bi·zits
  booster seat
  einen Kindersitz   *ai*·nen *kin*·der·zits
  child-minding service
  einen Babysitter-Service   *ai*·nen *bay*·bi·si·ter·*ser*·vis
  children's menu
  eine Kinderkarte   *ai*·ne *kin*·der·kar·te
  (English-speaking) babysitter
  einen (englisch-   *ai*·nen (*eng*·lish·
    sprachigen) Babysitter   shpra·khi·gen) *bay*·bi·si·ter
  infant formula (milk)
  Trockenmilch für Säuglinge   tro·ken·milkh fewr *soyg*·ling·e
  highchair
  einen Kinderstuhl   *ai*·nen *kin*·der·shtool
  potty
  ein Kindertöpfchen   ain *kin*·der·teupf·khen

Do you mind if I breastfeed here?
Kann ich meinem Kind hier die Brust geben?
kan ikh *mai*·nem kint heer dee brust *gay*·ben
Are children allowed?
Sind Kinder erlaubt?
zint *kin*·der er·*lowpt*

Also available from Lonely Planet:
German Phrasebook

Glossary

(pl) indicates plural

Abfahrt – departure (trains)
Abtei – abbey
ADAC – Allgemeiner Deutscher Automobil Club (German Automobile Association)
Allee – avenue
Altstadt – old town
Ankunft – arrival (trains)
Antiquariat – antiquarian bookshop
Apotheke – pharmacy
Arbeitsamt – employment office
Arbeitserlaubnis – work permit
Ärzte – doctor
Ärztehaus – medical clinic
Ärztlicher Notdienst – emergency medical service
Aufenthaltserlaubnis – residency permit
Auflauf, Aufläufe (pl) – casserole
Ausgang, Ausfahrt – exit
Aussiedler – German settlers who have returned from abroad (it usually refers to post-WWII expulsions), sometimes called *Spätaussiedler*
autobahn – motorway
Autofähre – car ferry
Autonome (pl) – left-wing anarchists
AvD – Automobilclub von Deutschland (Automobile Club of Germany)

Bad – spa, bath
Bahnhof – train station
Bahnsteig – train station platform
Bau – building
Bedienung – service; service charge
Behinderte – disabled
Berg – mountain
Bergbaumuseum – mining museum
Besenwirtschaft – seasonal wine restaurant indicated by a broom above the doorway
Bezirk – district
Bibliothek – library
Bierkeller – cellar pub
Bierstube – traditional beer pub
Bildungsroman – literally 'novel of education'; literary work in which the personal development of a single individual is central
BRD – Bundesrepublik Deutschland or FRG (Federal Republic of Germany); the name for Germany today; before reunification it applied to West Germany; see also *DDR, FRG, GDR*
Brücke – bridge

Brunnen – fountain or well
Bundesland – federal state
Bundesliga – Germany's premier football (soccer) league
Bundesrat – upper house of the German parliament
Bundestag – lower house of the German parliament
Bundesverfassungsgericht – Federal Constitutional Court
Burg – castle
Busbahnhof – bus station

CDU – Christian Democratic Union
Christkindlmarkt – Christmas market; see also *Weihnachtsmarkt*
CSU – Christian Social Union; Bavarian offshoot of CDU

DB – Deutsche Bahn (German national railway)
DDR – Deutsche Demokratische Republik or, in English, GDR (German Democratic Republic); the name for former East Germany; see also *BRD, FRG, GDR*
Denkmal – memorial
Deutsche Reich – German Empire: refers to the period 1871–1918
Dirndl – traditional women's dress (Bavaria only)
DJH – Deutsches Jugendherbergswerk (German youth hostels association)
Dom – cathedral
Dorf – village
DZT – Deutsche Zentrale für Tourismus (German National Tourist Office)

Eingang – entrance
Eintritt – admission
Einwanderungsland – country of immigrants
Eiscafé – ice-cream parlour

Fahrplan – timetable
Fahrrad – bicycle
Fasching – pre-Lenten carnival (term used in southern Germany)
FDP – Free Democratic Party
Ferienwohnung, Ferienwohnungen (pl) – holiday flat or apartment
Fest – festival
FKK – nude bathing area
Flammekuche – Franco-German dish consisting of a thin layer of pastry topped with cream, onion, bacon and sometimes cheese or mushrooms, and cooked in a wood-fired oven. Especially prevalent on menus in the Palatinate and the Black Forest.
Fleets – canals in Hamburg

Flohmarkt – flea market
Flughafen – airport
Föhn – an intense autumn wind in the Agerman Alps and Alpine foothills
Forstweg – forestry track
Franken – 'Franks', Germanic people influential in Europe between the 3rd and 8th centuries
Freikorps – WWI volunteers
Fremdenverkehrsamt/Fremdenverkehrsverein – tourist office
Fremdenzimmer – tourist room
FRG – Federal Republic of Germany; see also *BRD*
Fussball – football, soccer

Garten – garden
Gasse – lane or alley
Gastarbeiter – literally 'guest worker'; labourer from primarily Mediterranean countries who came to Germany in the 1950s and 1960s to fill a labour shortage
Gästehaus – guesthouse
Gaststätte, Gasthaus – informal restaurant, inn
GDR – the German Democratic Republic (the former East Germany); see also *BRD, DDR, FRG*
Gedenkstätte – memorial site
Gemütlichkeit – a particularly convivial, cosy ambience and setting, for instance in a pub, restaurant or living room
Gepäckaufbewahrung – left-luggage office
Gesamtkunstwerk – literally 'total artwork'; integrates painting, sculpture and architecture
Gestapo – Nazi secret police
Glockenspiel – literally 'bell play'; carillon, often on a cathedral or town hall, sounded by mechanised figures depicting religious or historical characters
Gründerzeit – literally 'foundation time'; the period of industrial expansion in Germany following the founding of the German Empire in 1871

Hafen – harbour, port
Halbtrocken – semi-dry (wine)
Hauptbahnhof – central train station
Heide – heath
Heiliges Römisches Reich – Holy Roman Empire, which lasted from the 8th century to 1806; the German lands comprised the bulk of the Empire's territory
Herzog – duke
Heu Hotels – literally 'hay hotels'; cheap forms of accommodation that are usually set in farmhouses and similar to bunk barns in the UK
Hitlerjugend – Hitler Youth organisation
Hochdeutsch – literally 'High German'; standard spoken and written German, developed from a regional Saxon dialect
Hochkultur – literally 'high culture'; meaning 'advanced civilisation'
Hof, Höfe (pl) – courtyard

Höhle – cave
Hotel Garni – hotel without a restaurant where you are only served breakfast

Imbiss – stand-up food stall; see also *Schnellimbiss*
Insel – island

Jugendgästehaus – youth guesthouse of a higher standard than a youth hostel
Jugendherberge – youth hostel
Jugendstil – Art Nouveau
Junker – originally a young, noble landowner of the Middle Ages; later used to refer to reactionary Prussian landowners

Kabarett – cabaret
Kaffee und Kuchen – literally 'coffee and cake'; traditional afternoon coffee break in Germany
Kaiser – emperor; derived from 'Caesar'
Kanal – canal
Kantine – cafeteria, canteen
Kapelle – chapel
Karneval – pre-Lenten festivities (along the Rhine)
Karte – ticket
Kartenvorverkauf – ticket-booking office
Kino – cinema
Kirche – church
Kloster – monastery, convent
Kneipe – pub
Kommunales Kino – art-house cinema
Konditorei – cake shop
König – king
Konsulat – consulate
Konzentrationslager (KZ) – a concentration camp
KPD – German Communist Party
Krankenhaus – hospital
Kreuzgang – cloister
Kristallnacht – literally 'night of broken glass'; attack on Jewish synagogues, cemeteries and businesses by Nazis and their supporters on the night of 9 November 1938, marking the beginning of full-scale persecution of Jews in Germany (also known as *Reichspogromnacht*)
Kunst – art
Kunstlieder – early German 'artistic songs'
Kurfürst – prince-elector
Kurhaus – literally 'spa house', but usually a spa town's central building, used for social gatherings and events and often housing the town's casino
Kurort – spa resort
Kurtaxe – resort tax
Kurverwaltung – spa resort administration
Kurzentrum – spa centre

Land, Länder (pl) – state
Landtag – state parliament

Lederhosen – traditional leather trousers with attached braces (Bavaria only)
Lesbe, Lesben (pl) – lesbian (n)
lesbisch – lesbian (adj)
lieblich – sweet (wine)
Lied – song

Maare – crater lakes in the Eifel Upland area west of the Rhine
Markgraf – margrave; German nobleman ranking above a count
Markt – market; often used instead of *Marktplatz*
Marktplatz – marketplace or square; often abbreviated to *Markt*
Mass – 1L tankard or stein of beer
Meer – sea
Mehrwertsteuer (MwST) – value-added tax
Meistersinger – literally 'master singer'; highest level in medieval troubadour guilds
Mensa – university cafeteria
Milchcafé – milk coffee, *café au lait*
Mitfahrzentrale – ride-sharing agency
Mitwohnzentrale – an accommodation-finding service that is usually for long-term stays; see also *Zimmervermittlung*
Münster – minster or large church, cathedral
Münzwäscherei – coin-operated laundrette

Nord – north
Notdienst – emergency service
NSDAP – National Socialist German Workers' Party

Ossi – nickname for an East German
Ost – east
Ostalgie – a romanticised yearning for the GDR era, derived from 'nostalgia'
Ostler – old term for an *Ossi*
Ostpolitik – former West German chancellor Willy Brandt's foreign policy of 'peaceful coexistence' with the *GDR*

Palast – palace, residential quarters of a castle
Pannenhilfe – roadside breakdown assistance for motorists
Paradies – literally 'paradise'; architectural term for a church vestibule or anteroom
Parkhaus – car park
Parkschein – parking voucher
Parkscheinautomat – vending machine selling parking vouchers
Passage – shopping arcade
Pension, Pensionen (pl) – relatively cheap boarding house
Pfand – deposit for bottles and sometimes glasses (in beer gardens)
Pfarrkirche – parish church

Plattdeutsch – literally 'Low German'; German dialect of northwestern Germany (especially Lower Saxony)
Platz – square
Postamt – post office
Postlagernd – poste restante
Priele – tideways on the Wadden Sea *(Wattenmeer)* on the North Sea coast
Putsch – revolt

Radwandern – bicycle touring
Radweg – bicycle path
Rathaus – town hall
Ratskeller – town hall restaurant
Reich – empire
Reichspogromnacht – see *Kristallnacht*
Reisezentrum – travel centre located in train or bus stations
Reiterhof – riding stable or centre
Rezept – medical prescription
R-Gespräch – reverse-charge call
Ruhetag – literally 'rest day'; closing day at a shop or restaurant
Rundgang – tour, route

Saal, Säle (pl) – hall, room
Sammlung – collection
Säule – column, pillar
S-Bahn – suburban-metropolitan trains; Schnellbahn
Schatzkammer – treasury
Schiff – ship
Schifffahrt – shipping, navigation
Schloss – palace, castle
Schnaps – schnapps
Schnellimbiss – stand-up food stall; see also *Imbiss*
schwul – gay (adj)
Schwuler, Schwule (pl) – gay (n)
SED – Sozialistische Einheitspartei Deutschlands (Socialist Unity Party)
See – lake
Sekt – sparkling wine
Selbstbedienung (SB) – self-service (restaurants, laundrettes etc)
Sesselbahn – chairlift
Soziale Marktwirtschaft – literally 'social market economy'; the German form of a market-driven economy with built-in social protection for employees
Spätaussiedler – see *Aussiedler*
SPD – Sozialdemokratische Partei Deutschlands (Social Democratic Party)
Speisekarte – menu
Sportverein – sports association
SS – Schutzstaffel; organisation within the Nazi party that supplied Hitler's bodyguards, as well as concentration-camp guards and the Waffen-SS troops in WWII
Stadt – city or town

Stadtbad, Stadtbäder (pl) – public pool
Stadtwald – city or town forest
Stasi – *GDR* secret police (from Ministerium für Staatssicherheit, or Ministry of State Security)
Stau – traffic jam
Staudamm, Staumauer – dam
Stausee – reservoir
Stehcafé – stand-up café
Strand – beach
Strasse – street; often abbreviated to Str
Strausswirtschaft – seasonal wine pub indicated by wreath above the doorway
Süd – south
Szene – scene (ie where the action is)

Tageskarte – daily menu or day ticket on public transport
Tal – valley
Teich – pond
Thirty Years' War – pivotal war in Central Europe (1618–48) that began as a German conflict between Catholics and Protestants
Tor – gate
trampen – hitchhiking
Treuhandanstalt – trust established to sell off *GDR* assets after the *Wende*
Trocken – dry (wine)
Trödel – junk
Turm – tower

U-Bahn – underground train system
Übergang – transit or transfer point
Ufer – bank

Verboten – forbidden
Verkehr – traffic

Verkehrsamt/Verkehrsverein – tourist office
Viertel – quarter, district
Volkslieder – folk song

Waffen-SS – the combat wing of the SS
Wald – forest
Waldfrüchte – wild berries
Wäscherei – laundry
Wattenmeer – tidal flats on the North Sea coast
Wechselstube – currency exchange office
Weg – way, path
Weihnachtsmarkt – Christmas market; see also *Christkindlmarkt*
Weingut – wine-growing estate
Weinkeller – wine cellar
Weinprobe – wine tasting
Weinstube – traditional wine bar or tavern
Wende – 'change' of 1989, ie the fall of communism that led to the collapse of the *GDR* and German reunification
Weser Renaissance – ornamental architectural style found around the Weser River
Wessi – nickname for a West German
West – west
Westler – old term for a *Wessi*
Wiese – meadow
Wirtschaftswunder – Germany's post-WWII 'economic miracle'

Zahnradbahn – cog-wheel railway
Zeitung – newspaper
Zimmer frei – room available (for accommodation purposes)
Zimmervermittlung – a room-finding service, primarily for short-term stays; see also *Mitwohnzentrale*
ZOB – Zentraler Omnibusbahnhof (central bus station)

Behind the Scenes

THIS BOOK

The first edition of Germany, back in 1998, was written by Steve Fallon, Anthony Haywood, Andrea Schulte-Peevers and Nick Selby. This 5th edition was written by Jeremy Gray, Anthony Haywood, Sarah Johnstone and Daniel Robinson, under the expert coordination of Andrea Schulte-Peevers. Andrea also coordinated the 4th edition, working with Sarah Johnstone, Etain O'Carroll, Jeanne Oliver, Tom Parkinson and Nicola Williams. The Health chapter was adapted from material written by Dr Caroline Evans. This guidebook was commissioned in Lonely Planet's London office, and produced by the following:

Commissioning Editor Janine Eberle
Coordinating Editors Barbara Delissen, Victoria Harrison
Coordinating Cartographer Corey Hutchison
Coordinating Layout Designer Clara Monitto
Managing Editor Imogen Bannister
Managing Cartographer Mark Griffiths
Assisting Editors Michelle Bennett, Kate Evans, Pat Kinsella, Cahal McGroarty, Jocelyn Harewood, Brooke Clark, Charlotte Harrison
Assisting Cartographers Andrew Smith, Owen Eszeki, Anneka Imkamp, Joshua Geoghegan, Valentina Kremenchutskaya
Assisting Layout Designers Tamsin Wilson, Carlos Solarte, Wibowo Rusli
Cover Designer Pepi Bluck
Project Manager Sarah Sloane
Language Content Coordinator Quentin Frayne

Thanks to Helen Christinis, Sally Darmody, Celia Wood, Laura Jane, Jennifer Garrett

THANKS
ANDREA SCHULTE-PEEVERS

A small army of folks deserves a heartfelt thank you, starting with Judith Bamber for entrusting me with this gig, Janine Eberle who smoothly picked up the baton and patiently answered all my questions, Mark Griffiths for steering me through my mapping issues and the league of editors, cartographers and other LP folks who capably got this book into print. Victoria Larsen in New York deserves a gold medal for being so supportive of this project. On the ground in Germany, a big bear hug goes to Holm Friedrich and Christina Rasch for being perfect landlords and to the entire Schulte family for again being such generous and fun friends and hosts. Thanks also to any number of old and new friends who again made me feel at home in my homeland, including Kerstin, Marco, Jörg, Chris, Holger, Alex, Henrik, Bettina, Torsten, Mark, Sabine, Anne and Erez. Other capable folks who've helped me along the way include Christoph Münch, Wolfgang Gärtner, Gunter Winkler, Matthias Schneider, Matthias Rose, Dr Volker Dudeck, Hiskia Wiesner, Annett Morche, Birgit Freitag, Natasha Kompatzki, Oliver Lücking and Creixell Espilla – great big thanks to all of you. Last but certainly not least, an extra-special nod to David, my husband, soul mate and companion in life and travel for his love, patience, support (and for doing all those dishes).

JEREMY GRAY

The long list of tourist professionals who made my life easier include Hedda Manhard and Robert Leckel of the Munich tourist office. Maxine Ryder

---

THE LONELY PLANET STORY

The story begins with a classic travel adventure: Tony and Maureen Wheeler's 1972 journey across Europe and Asia to Australia. There was no useful information about the overland trail then, so Tony and Maureen published the first Lonely Planet guidebook to meet a growing need.

From a kitchen table, Lonely Planet has grown to become the largest independent travel publisher in the world, with offices in Melbourne (Australia), Oakland (USA) and London (UK). Today Lonely Planet guidebooks cover the globe. There is an ever-growing list of books and information in a variety of media. Some things haven't changed. The main aim is still to make it possible for adventurous travellers to get out there – to explore and better understand the world.

At Lonely Planet we believe travellers can make a positive contribution to the countries they visit – if they respect their host communities and spend their money wisely. Every year 5% of company profit is donated to charities around the world.

and Michael Flossmann were my fun-loving hosts in Munich. My fellow authors – Andrea, Anthony, Daniel and Sarah – were a dream team. Commissioning editors Janine Eberle and Judith Bamber were good enough to entrust me with the gig. A big, never-ending hug to my wife Petra, for enduring me, my absences and the weird schedules that are part and parcel of this job. And a *danke schön* to the Bavarians, a genuine, big-hearted people full of surprises even when the *Föhn* doesn't blow. Germany would be a lot less captivating without them.

ANTHONY HAYWOOD

I'd like to thank the many people who assisted in one way or another during road research and write-up. Very special thanks go to Frau Langer and Frau Wittekind in Rudolstadt, Frau Schröder in Saalfeld, Frau Schmidt in Bad Harzburg, Frau Klein and the folks at Erfurt-Tourismus, and Frau Martin in Marburg (with those geography skills Ludwig Leichhardt would have found his way through in time for dinner). Thanks also to Anke in Frankfurt for valuable insight and the run of the flat, to Sylvia for support, timely advice and ideas; and last but not least to Judith Bamber and Janine Eberle from Lonely Planet.

SARAH JOHNSTONE

Who says Germany's dull? Having covered the country before, I was a little surprised to fall in love with it again in 2006, although I think the FIFA World Cup means a lot of the world unexpectedly did too. Thanks to *all* the people in tourist offices, hostels, hotels and elsewhere who helped me out. Individual mention of Doris Annette Schütz of Lübeck und Travemünde Tourist-Service, Christine Lambrecht, Dr Annette Zehnter, Paul Gronert and Nadine in Dessau, Kathrin in Osnabrück, Eve in Hamburg, Silke in Kiel, Iris and Gerd in Rostock can't be missed.

DANIEL ROBINSON

Special thanks to Emily Silverman for charming Max into letting me use his excellent Freiburg facilities, Gerhard and Ursula Schwarz of Tübingen for their hospitality, Kathrin Ziemens for giving me the grand tour of Heidelberg's Neckarufer and Brigitte Durst of Bingen and Jim Sunthimer of Boppard for lending an enthusiastic hand. In Mannheim 'twas Hannes Greiling of the Jugendforum der Deutsch-Israelischen Gesellschaft who spotted the mouse scurrying across a restaurant that – obviously – didn't make it into the guide. My parents, Bernie and Yetta Robinson, audacious

independent travellers even in retirement, deserve a medal for their patience in Worms and Speyer.

I'd also like to express my appreciation to Commissioning Editor Janine Eberle for her understanding and support during July and August of 2006; Frau Dolkart, Susannah, Hilde, Eva and Bella of Tel Aviv's Goethe Institut for guiding me gently through the quicksand of German grammar; Meital Lior for snapping my blurb photo; and Kristy Zofrea of DriveAway Holidays for arranging the purchase-repurchase Peugeot 206 that served me for 4400 problem-free kilometres.

An old family friend, Eva Linker, grew up in Weimar-era Karlsruhe but escaped just in time. Her spirit, in the form of a happy little girl, danced through my thoughts as I strolled the streets of her hometown.

OUR READERS

Many thanks to the travellers who used the last edition and wrote to us with helpful hints, useful advice and interesting anecdotes:

A Ryan Adserias, Gianantonio & Carla Altissimo, Trevor Angel **B** Mike Bada, Dustin Baer, Leyla Bagloul, Graeme Baker, Richard Baker, William Ballantine, Suzanne Barker, Brian & Shea Barnett, Gregory Becker, Anthony Bevan, Michael Blaxland, Michelle Brazier, Catherine Brinkley, Julian Bryers, Lucinda Butler, Linde

Butterhoff **C** Peter Callaghan, Eric Carlson, Euginia Cervero, Phillip Chamberlin, Peter Chapman, George Chatziargyris, Karen Chen, John Kin Ning Chiu, William Christ, Richard Clatworthy, Matt Colonell, Rita Colonell, Geoffrey Cook, Peter Courtney **D** John Davies, Emilie Davine, Brynmor Davis, Joziene de Wolf, Timothy Douglas, My Le Ducharme **E** Ole Eklöf, Jakob Engblom, Hartmut Evermann **F** Olivia Faul, Kirsty Finlay, Katja Flasche, Jacob Florence **G** Marg Gelilander, Karen Gissel, Jenny Gore, Helen Graham, Marilyn Green, Karen Greenwood **H** Andrew Haggard, Ronald Hakenberg, Jack Hathaway, Adam Hobill, Heather Hofmeister, Mike & Liz Holt, Christiane Holzenbecher, Gail Hull, Nadia Hume, Christopher Hunt, Malcolm Hunt **I** José Manue Infante, Jeremy Irwin **J** Dylan Jackson, Zoe Jackson, Corinna Jhimb-Jäger, Rob Jones, Anne Julh **K** Richard Keirstead, Bianca Kesselring, Michelle Knaeble, Floris Kortie, Shirley Krencichlost **L** Mark Ladd, Benjamin Lee, Chris Lightfoot, Andrew Llera, Marc Lobmann, Ute Loeffelsend, John Longsworth, Christopher Lynn **M** Liz Mackinlay, Angel Marcos, Robert Marquez, JS McLintock, Gabi Mcnicol, Timothy McVitty, AJL Meadowcroft, Martin Meder, Mark Melislande, Jim Meyer, Thomas Mickan, Bil Mihajlovic, Tina Mizgalski, Mark Mocicka, Heather Monell, Seung Hyun Moon, John Morrell, Hendrik Mueller-Ide **N** Rainer Neumann, Carrie Ng **O** Amy Oldham, Elisabeth Olovson **P** Ilona Pabst, Antonio Palagiano, Daniele Palombi, Lance Patford, Carla Peterson, Julie Porter, Ebi Poweigha, Aljaz Prusnik, Urska Prusnik **Q** Lorraine Quirke **R** Donna Rabin, Monika Ratz, Stefanie Reska, Maria Katja Ressel, Thomas Reydon, Anke Riccio, Florian Ritter, Anne & Peter Rolston, Janet Russell **S** Saltuk Saldamli, Niina Sallanen, Katrin Samlik, Seumas Sargent, Hagen Schäfer, Jewell Schamotta, Janet Schofield, Richard Scotton, Vicente Serrano, Linda Shaw, Nicole Sheldon, Lawrence Siddall, Debbie Smith, Fraser Smith, Nick Sowko, David Spooner, Jon Springer, Alistair Staton, Isla Stephenson, Kewin Stoeckigt, Bill & Ann Stoughton, Henk Suer **T** Melanie Taillon, Sven Terlinden, Fab Tomlin, Peter Townsend, Alec Toynton, Frederick Trinder **V** Manuel Valencia, Sara Venturi **W** Margaret Walker, David Weber, Andreas Weeger, Vera Wellner, Stephanie Weng, Liz Wightwick, Christian Winkler **Y** Calina Yee **Z** Hans Zimmerer

ACKNOWLEDGMENTS

Many thanks to the following for the use of their content:

Berlin S+U-Bahn Map ©2006 Berliner Verkehrbetreibe (BVG)

Munich S+U-Bahn Map ©2006 Münchner Verkehrs- und Tarifverbund GmbH (MVV)

.

Index

Index

000 Map pages
000 Photograph pages

INDEX

INDEX

INDEX

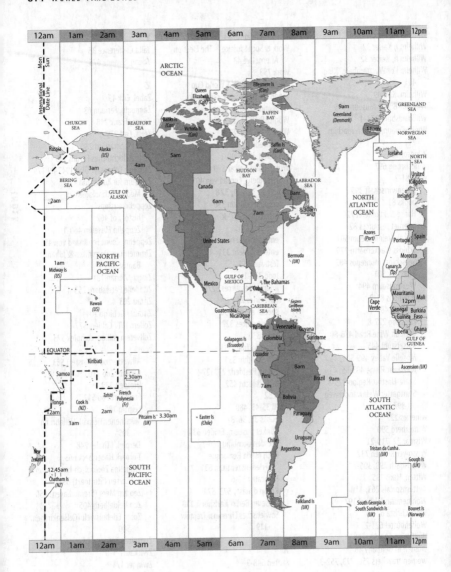

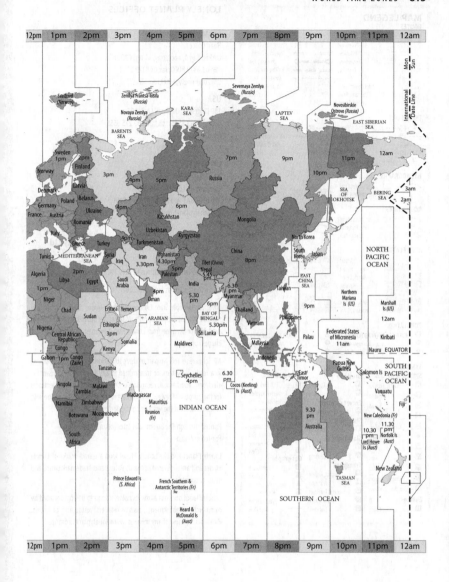

MAP LEGEND
ROUTES

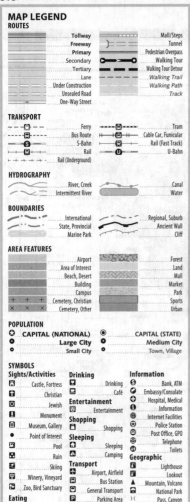

LONELY PLANET OFFICES

Australia
Head Office
Locked Bag 1, Footscray, Victoria 3011
☎ 03 8379 8000, fax 03 8379 8111
talk2us@lonelyplanet.com.au

USA
150 Linden St, Oakland, CA 94607
☎ 510 893 8555, toll free 800 275 8555
fax 510 893 8572
info@lonelyplanet.com

UK
72-82 Rosebery Ave,
Clerkenwell, London EC1R 4RW
☎ 020 7841 9000, fax 020 7841 9001
go@lonelyplanet.co.uk

Published by Lonely Planet Publications Pty Ltd
ABN 36 005 607 983